CPAG's

Child Support

The Legislation

Eleventh edition

2013/2014

Commentary by
Edward Jacobs, *Barrister and Upper Tribunal Judge*

Pub

CPAG promotes action for the prevention and relief of poverty among children and families with children. To achieve this, CPAG aims to raise awareness of the causes, extent, nature and impact of poverty, and strategies for its eradication and prevention; bring about positive policy changes for families with children in poverty; and enable those eligible for income maintenance to have access to their full entitlement. If you are not already supporting us, please consider making a donation, or ask for details of our membership schemes and publications.

Published by Child Poverty Action Group
94 White Lion Street, London N1 9PF
020 7837 7979
staff@cpag.org.uk
www.cpag.org.uk

Child Poverty Action Group is a charity registered in England and Wales (registration number 294841) and in Scotland (registration number SC039339), and is a company limited by guarantee, registered in England (registration number 1993854). VAT number: 690 808117

A CIP record for this book is available from the British Library

ISBN: 978 1 906076 75 7

Content management system by Konnect Soft www.konnectsoft.com
Cover photograph by David Mansell/reportdigital.co.uk
Typeset by David Lewis XML Associates Limited
Printed and bound by CPI Group (UK) Ltd, Croydon, CR0 4YY

Contents

Contents

Part IV: PROCEDURAL RULES

Preface

This book has been a nightmare to produce. Not only do we now have at least three versions of the rules that may apply – it might even be four, depending on how you count – but the commencement provisions have continued to flow and to increase in complexity throughout the production process. I have learnt from my mistake in 2002 and not made any assumption about the latest rules coming into force immediately or even at all. So the commentaries remain under the provisions for the 2003 rules, which I hope will be the most useful place for most users. I have added a commentary for the 2013 rules that identifies the new aspects of the rules and refers the reader to the equivalent provisions in the 2003 rules. Having mentioned the statutory complexity, I have to pay a special tribute to the work of Susan Mitchell who has not only produced the text of the legislation but has managed to make as clear as humanly possible which provisions apply to which schemes from which date.

This book could not have been produced without the support of all those involved at CPAG. Thanks to Nicola Johnston for editing and managing the production of the book. Many thanks to Katherine Dawson for updating the index and to Mike Hatt at David Lewis XML.

A complete child support law online package is also available from CPAG. This includes an online version of this book plus CPAG's *Child Support Handbook*. For more information visit www.cpag.org.uk/onlineservices.

Edward Jacobs
Harp House
83 Farringdon Street
London EC4A 4DH

Table of cases

Table of commissioners' decisions

Table of Upper Tribunal decisions

Abbreviations

the Act	Child Support Act 1991
the 1995 Act	Child Support Act 1995
the 2000 Act	Child Support, Pensions and Social Security 2000
the 2008 Act	Child Maintenance and Other Payments Act 2008
Amendment Regulations	Child Support (Miscellaneous Amendments) Regulations 1993
Amendment Regulations 1995	Child Support and Income Support (Amendment) Regulations 1995
Amendment Regulations 2005	Social Security, Child Support and Tax Credits (Miscellaneous Amendments) Regulations 2005
Amendment (No.2) Regulations 1996	Social Security (Adjudication) and Child Support Amendment (No.2) Regulations 1996
Appeals Regulations	Social Security and Child Support (Decisions and Appeals) Regulations 1999
Appeals Amendment Regulations 2000	Child Support (Decisions and Appeals) (Amendment) Regulations 2000
Appeals Amendment Regulations 2002	Social Security and Child Support (Decisions and Appeals) (Miscellaneous Amendments) Regulations 2002
Arrears, Interest and Adjustment of Maintenance Assessments Regulations	Child Support (Arrears, Interest and Adjustment of Maintenance Assessments) Regulations 1992
Child Benefit Amendment Regulations	Child Benefit, Child Support and Social Security (Miscellaneous Amendments) Regulations 1996
Civil Partnership Consequential Provisions Order	Civil Partnership (Pensions, Social Security and Child Support) (Consequential, etc. Provisions) Order 2005
Collection and Enforcement Regulations	Child Support (Collection and Enforcement) Regulations 1992
Collection and Enforcement and Miscellaneous Amendments Regulations 2000	Child Support (Collection and Enforcement and Miscellaneous Amendments) Regulations 2000
Collection and Enforcement of Other Forms of Maintenance Regulations	Child Support (Collection and Enforcement of Other Forms of Maintenance) Regulations 1992
Commencement No.7 Order 1999	Social Security Act 1998 (Commencement No.7 and Consequential and Transitional Provisions) Order 1999
Commencement No.3 Order 2000	Child Support, Pensions and Social Security Act 2000 (Commencement No.3) Order 2000

Commencement No.5 Order 2000	Child Support, Pensions and Social Security Act 2000 (Commencement No.5) Order 2000
Commencement No. 12 Order 2003	Child Support, Pensions and Social Security Act 2000 (Commencement No. 12) Order 2003
Commissioners Procedure Amendment Regulations 2005	Social Security and Child Support Commissioners (Procedure) (Amendment) Regulations 2005
Departure Regulations	Child Support Departure Direction and Consequential Amendments Regulations 1996
Housing Benefit Consolidation Regulations 2006	Housing Benefit and Council Tax Benefit (Consequential Provisions) Regulations 2006
Information, Evidence and Disclosure Regulations	Child Support Evidence and Regulations 1992
Information, Evidence and Disclosure and Maintenance Arrangements and Jurisdiction Amendment Regulations 2000	Child Support (Information, Evidence and Disclosure and Maintenance Arrangements and Jurisdiction) (Amendment) Regulations 2000
Jobseeker's Amendment Regulations	Social Security and Child Support Jobseeker's Allowance) (Consequential Amendments) Regulations 1996
Jobseeker's Miscellaneous Amendments Regulations	Social Security and Child Support Jobseeker's Allowances) (Miscellaneous Amendments) Regulations 1996
Maintenance Arrangements and Jurisdiction Regulations	Child Support (Maintenance Arrangements and Jurisdiction) Regulations 1992
Maintenance Assessment Procedure Regulations	Child Support (Maintenance Assessment Procedure) Regulations 1992
Maintenance Calculation Procedure Regulations	Child Support (Maintenance Calculation Procedure) Regulations 2000
Maintenance Calculations and Special Cases Regulations	Child Support (Maintenance Calculations and Special Cases) Regulations 2000
Maintenance Assessments and Special Cases Regulations	Child Support (Maintenance Assessments and Special Cases) Regulations 1992
Miscellaneous Amendments Regulations 1994	Child Support (Miscellaneous Amendments and Transitional Provisions) Regulations 1994
Miscellaneous Amendments Regulations 1995	Child Support (Miscellaneous Amendments) Regulations 1995
Miscellaneous Amendments Regulations 1996	Child Support (Miscellaneous Amendments) Regulations 1996
Miscellaneous Amendments Regulations 1998	Child Support (Miscellaneous Amendments) Regulations 1998
Miscellaneous Amendments Regulations 1999	Child Support (Miscellaneous Amendments) Regulations 1999
Miscellaneous Amendments Regulations 2000	Social Security and Child Support (Miscellaneous Amendments) Regulations 2000

Miscellaneous Amendments Regulations 2002	Child Support (Miscellaneous Amendments) Regulations 2002
Miscellaneous Amendments Regulations 2003	Child Support (Miscellaneous Amendments) Regulations 2003
Miscellaneous Amendments Regulations 2004	Child Support (Miscellaneous Amendments) Regulations 2004
Miscellaneous Amendments Regulations 2005	Child Support (Miscellaneous Amendments) Regulations 2005
Miscellaneous Amendments Regulations 2006	Child Support (Miscellaneous Amendments) Regulations 2006
Miscellaneous Amendments (No.2) Regulations 1995	Child Support (Miscellaneous Amendments) (No.2) Regulations 1995
Miscellaneous Amendments (No.3) Regulations 1995	Child Support (Miscellaneous Amendments) (No.3) Regulations 1995
Miscellaneous Amendments (No.2) Regulations 1996	Child Support (Miscellaneous Amendments) (No.2) Regulations 1996
Miscellaneous Amendments (No.2) Regulations 1998	Child Support (Miscellaneous Amendments) (No.2) Regulations 1998
Miscellaneous Amendments (No.2) Regulations 1999	Child Support (Miscellaneous Amendments) (No.2) Regulations 1999
Miscellaneous Amendments (No.2) Regulations 2003	Child Support (Miscellaneous Amendments) (No.2) Regulations 2003
SEC Rules	Tribunal Procedure (First-tier Tribunal) (Social Entitlement Chamber) Rules 2008
SSHD	Secretary of State for the Home Department
SSWP	Secretary of State for Work and Pensions
State Pension Credit Regulations	State Pension Credit (Consequential, Transitional and Miscellaneous Provisions) (No.2) Regulations 2002
Tax Credits Amendments Regulations 1999	Social Security and Child Support (Tax Credits) Consequential Amendments Regulations 1999
Transitional Amendments Regulations 2003	Child Support (Transitional Provision) (Miscellaneous Amendments) Regulations 2003
Transitional Provisions Order	Child Support Act 1991 (Commencement No.3 and Transitional Provisions) Order 1992
Variation Regulations	Child Support (Variations) regulations 2000

Using the book

Those users who are unfamiliar with child support law or who are new to tribunal work may find it helpful to understand how the book is structured so that they can find their way around it. The structure may not always be apparent and may on occasions break down, but understanding it should stand users in good stead.

The book may need to be consulted in one of three ways: to find a known provision or decision; to find a definition of a word or phrase; or to find a provision or decision on a particular topic.

In order to find a known legislative provision or decision by a court or a Commissioner or the Upper Tribunal, consult the tables at the beginning of the book.

In order to find the meaning of a word or phrase in a particular provision, look at the "Definitions" list at the end of the provision in question. This will indicate which words and phrases are defined elsewhere and where the definitions may be found. In the case of regulations, also check the Act for any relevant definitions. If a definition is adopted from another statute, that definition will be reproduced in the General Note.

The most difficult task is to find a provision or decision on a particular topic. The key to doing this successfully is twofold. First think of the concept involved and the context in which it is likely to occur. Then use the statutes and the general notes to home in on the relevant provision or decision. The following example shows how this works in practice.

Suppose that the topic is the significance of the fact that the child is at a boarding school. Begin by identifying the concept involved in the topic or the context in which the topic is likely to occur. The "Overview" section may help with this. In the case of a child at a boarding school, the relevant concept is day to day care of the child. This may lead to the definition of person with care. Another possibility is that it may be identified as an exception, which in child support law is defined as a special case.

Once the concept and the likely context have been identified, use the "Arrangement of Sections" list at the beginning of the relevant statute in order to find the relevant statutory provision. The general note to that provision will refer to any relevant regulations. Relevant decisions will be referred to in the appropriate general note. The general note will contain cross-references to any other significant related provisions. The index of the main work may also be helpful in finding the relevant pages.

Some concepts, such as waiver and estoppel, have no place in the legislative structure.

This process is easier to explain than to apply in practice and a number of possible avenues may have to be explored before the search is successful. Ultimately, however, it should lead to the relevant provision or decision.

Part I

INTRODUCTION

AN OVERVIEW OF THE REFORMS
TO THE CHILD SUPPORT SYSTEM

There are now three sets of child support rules operating. There are still some cases that are governed by the 1993 rules, which were introduced under the Child Support Act 1991. Most cases are still governed by the 2003 rules, which were introduced under the Child Support, Pensions and Social Security Act 2000. The 2013 rules, which have been introduced under the Child Maintenance and Other Payments Act 2008, are currently being brought into force in stages. The book contains the legislation for all three sets of rules. The commentary in the general notes to the legislation is focussed on the 2003 rules, which at this stage are likely to be most used by readers. A full statement of the law can be found in CPAG's *Child Support Handbook*.

The 1993 rules

The child support scheme was introduced in an attempt to remedy the deficiencies in the court child maintenance scheme. In summary, those deficiencies were:

(i)   the amounts of maintenance were usually unrealistically low;
(ii)   there was inconsistency in the amounts between courts;
(iii)   the amount was not automatically uprated and could not be easily varied;
(iv)   enforcement was costly and arrears were often remitted;
(v)   the courts and the parties were willing to place the burden on the social security scheme rather than on the parents.

The child support scheme tried to identify the cost of bringing up a child and then to allocate that cost between the parents according to their incomes. The amount of maintenance was based on a formula assessment that ensured consistency and was regularly uprated. Enforcement was undertaken by the State. Responsibility for maintenance was placed on the parents rather than on the social security scheme.

As well as political opposition from interested parties, there were problems inherent in the scheme itself. The complexity of the scheme led to lengthy delays in making assessments both initially and when changes of circumstances occurred. The scheme contained so many elements that these changes were frequent. The rigidity of the scheme was capable of producing unfairness. Enforcement was sporadic and often ineffective, especially for the self-employed. The problems of enforcement were compounded by the complexity and delays in adjudication, which led to uncertainty in the amount of an absent parent's liability and to arrears for which the absent parent was not to blame.

The opposition to, and defects in, the scheme led to a regular procession of amendments. The most radical was the introduction of the departure direction scheme, which recognised that the formula was too rigid to take account of all matters that properly affected the amount of child support maintenance that should be payable.

The 2003 rules

These reforms were merely another, radical amendment of the scheme. In essence, the reforms were pragmatic. They attempted to create a modified scheme that would be easier to operate, would command wider respect and would be more easily and effectively enforced. Their implementation was delayed by computer problems and the scheme has never been fully extended to cases that originated under the original scheme.

Behind the changes of terminology, the focus shifted to the amount that the non-resident parent could afford to pay rather than on the joint finances of the parents. It sought to address the problem of arrears that built up pending the making of a maintenance calculation by a voluntary payment scheme. This allowed for a payment on account of child support maintenance in advance of the calculation being made and notified that would be set off against arrears that arose pending the making of a calculation.

In order to assist with compliance, the new s14A made it an offence to make a statement or representation knowing it to be false or to provide a document or other information that is known to be false in a material particular. It is also an offence to fail to comply with a request for information, subject to a defence of reasonable excuse. The penalty is a fine.

The 2013 rules

These are more fundamental than those previously made and are a further development of reforms that began under the 2008 legislation. They represent a much reduced version of the 2003 rules, removing much of the discretion that existed in the previous rules and encouraging parties to come to private arrangements for maintenance. The procedural and substantive rules are to be found together in the Child Support Maintenance Calculation Regulations 2012.

CITATION AND PRECEDENT

Apart from the legislation, the decisions of the Upper Tribunal and the former Social Security and Child Support Commissioners constitute the principal source of law that tribunals have to apply. Members and users of tribunals will need to be familiar with how these decisions are cited and applied. This note explains how decisions of the Upper Tribunal and the former Commissioners are cited and reported, together with the binding system of precedent which governs when they must be followed.

Citation of decisions

The more significant decisions of the Upper Tribunal are cited by the name or initials of the parties. Organisations and public authorities are cited by name. Other parties are usually cited by initials in order to preserve anonymity. This is followed by a flag (*CSM* for child support maintenance) and a neutral citation number – eg, *RC, Child Maintenance and Enforcement Commission and WC (CSM)* [2009] UKUT 62 (AAC). A neutral citation number is only allocated to decisions that appear on the Upper Tribunal's website. Decisions continue to be given file numbers, in the same form as that used by the former Child Support Commissioners. The *RC* decision was numbered *CCS 1296/2008*. These numbers have to be used if there is no neutral citation number. For decisions on appeals from tribunals in Scotland, there is an additional S after the initial C. When decisions were reported, they used to be given a new number in this form: *R(CS) 1/98*. The R indicated that the decision was a reported one. The letters in brackets stood for child support. The numbers showed that this was the first child support decision to be reported in 1998. This followed the format for the numbering of reported social security decisions. Those decisions were cited in this form: *R(IS) 4/91*. The R indicated that the decision was a reported one. The letters in brackets indicated the benefit that was involved in the appeal. In this example, IS stood for income support. The numbers showed that this was the fourth income support decision reported in 1991. In 2010, the system has changed. Decisions are reported by name following by a reference in the form: [2010] AACR No 1.

Highlighted decisions

All decisions of general interest or significance are on the Upper Tribunal's website. Those that are considered of particular importance are highlighted by the Upper Tribunal's editorial board, which advises on reporting. This process draws them to the attention of those who visit the website. This system replaced the starring system.

Website

The Upper Tribunal's database of decisions may be accessed through the Justice website at www.justice.gov.uk/guidance/courts-and-tribunals/tribunals/aa/index.htm.

Precedent

Precedent is the name given to the principle which determines which decisions a court or tribunal must follow. The First-tier Tribunal and the Upper Tribunal must follow all binding court decisions. Consent orders which are made without reasons being given and without the court hearing argument are only binding on the parties to them (*R(FC) 1/97*, para 28), although they may be of persuasive value. The reason is that, in English law, an appeal is against the decision rather than the reasons for the decision. The setting aside of the decision of the Upper Tribunal on appeal does not of itself set aside the judge's reasoning. This will only cease to have authoritative value if reasons are given for allowing the appeal which are incompatible with the judge's.

The Court of Appeal has held that judgments given by courts on applications for permission to appeal are not binding and, although they may be persuasive, reference to them is not encouraged (*Clark v University of Lincolnshire and Humberside* [2000] 3 All ER 752 *at 762 per* Lord Woolf MR). This has been confirmed by a Practice Note that prohibits the citation as authority of judgments given on applications that were attended by one party only or were for permission to appeal, unless they purported to establish a new principle or to extend the present law ([2001] 2 All ER 510). For an example of the application of this principle, see *CCS 2567/1998* (paras 14-22) in which the commissioner considered both the accuracy of the remarks made by the Court of Appeal and their scope. The same principles apply to reasons given by the Upper Tribunal when granting or refusing leave to appeal.

The principles governing the relationship within the First-tier Tribunal and between that tribunal and the Upper Tribunal are set out in *R(I) 12/75* and confirmed in *R(U) 4/88* (para 6). They have been affirmed by the Upper Tribunal in *Dorset Healthcare NHS Foundation Trust v MH* [2009] UKUT 4 (AAC) at [37] and *Secretary of State for Defence v AD and MM* [2009] UKUT 10 (AAC) at [132].

1.   A First-tier Tribunal is not bound by the decision of any other First-tier Tribunal.
2.   A First-tier Tribunal is bound by all decisions of the Upper Tribunal. This applies whether the decision is reported or unreported and whether or not it has been highlighted.
3.   If there is a conflict between decisions of the Upper Tribunal, the First-tier Tribunal should give more weight to a reported decision than to an unreported decision. It should follow a decision of a three-judge panel of the Upper Tribunal in preference to that single- or two-judge panel. Any Upper Tribunal is entitled to disregard a decision of a three-judge panel. However, this is not a practice which should be followed by the First-tier Tribunal.
4.   Where it is not possible to choose between decisions on the bases indicated in 3 above, the First-tier Tribunal is entitled to follow the decision which it considers the better. There is no obligation to prefer an earlier decision or a later decision. The only governing factor is the quality of the decision itself.

The child support jurisdiction is separate from the social security and other jurisdictions of the Upper Tribunal. However, the judges are the same and the law is in many respects the same or similar. There will often be a "sufficient practical relationship" between child support and social security provisions such that they should be interpreted uniformly and differences between them may be assumed to have some significance (see the approach of the Tribunal of Commissioners in the Common Appendix to *R(IS) 3/91* and *R(IS) 4/91*, para 9). In practice, therefore, the First-tier Tribunal will regard itself as bound by relevant social security decisions just as it is by child support decisions in accordance with the above rules of precedent. This is of course subject to the important proviso that neither the wording nor the context of a particular provision requires a different interpretation in child support law. Care will therefore always be needed to ensure that decisions are not applied without consideration first being given to whether they are relevant.

So far as the Upper Tribunal is concerned, single- or two- judge panels will generally follow decisions of other single- or two-judge panels, for reasons of comity and to avoid uncertainty and confusion, although they are not bound to do so and should not do so if it would lead to the perpetuation of error (*R(I) 12/75*, para 21). They will also follow a decision of a three-judge panel, unless there are compelling reasons to do otherwise (*R(I) 12/75*, para 21). This has been said to be as a matter of comity rather than law (*CSIS 118/1990*, para 8), although *R(I) 12/75* (para 21) refers to comity only in the context of the practice of what is now a single-judge panel of the Upper Tribunal following decisions of other single-judge panels.

For three-judge panels, precedent applies on the principles followed by the House of Lords and not on the principles followed by the Court of Appeal. The panel will normally follow the decision of an earlier panel (or tribunal of commissioners), but is free to depart from it if it is right to do so. There is no more specific principle. However, panels bear in mind the danger of disturbing retrospectively the settled basis on which decisions have been made and which have passed the scrutiny of Parliament without adverse comment. See *R(U) 3/88* (paras 8 and 17).

The courts paid particular respect to decisions by commissioners as being specialist, expert decision makers. Accordingly, both the Court of Appeal and the House of Lords stated that courts should be slow to depart from a consistent, longstanding line of authority from the commissioners (*R v National Insurance Commissioner ex p Stratton* [1979] 2 All ER 278 at 828 *per* Lord Denning MR, *Presho v Insurance Officer* [1984] 1 All ER 97 at 102, *per* Lord Brandon and *Cockburn v Chief Adjudication Officer and Secretary of State for Social Security v Fairey (aka Holliday) R(A) 2/98*). No doubt, the same approach will be taken to the Upper Tribunal.

Decisions of the First-tier Tribunal are of no precedent value in later cases (*DY v CMEC* [2010] UKUT 19 (AAC); AACR 32, paras 46-52).

Scotland

The jurisdiction of the Upper Tribunal covers the whole of Great Britain. As a matter of practice, it follows decisions of both the Court of Appeal and the Court of Session regardless of where it is sitting and of where the tribunal heard the case under appeal. However, as a matter of strict precedent, decisions of the Court of Appeal are only binding in England and Wales and those of the Court of Session are only binding in Scotland (*Clarke v Frank Staddon Ltd* [2004] EWCA Civ 422).

Scope of the Upper Tribunal's Decisions

Care needs to be taken in deciding the scope of a decision of the Upper Tribunal, as it will only be authority for those propositions of law which it decides. The need for care arises because the Upper Tribunal only has power to set aside a decision on the ground that it involved the making of an error on a point of law. Accordingly, when dealing with the facts found by the First-tier Tribunal, the Upper Tribunal only has power to overturn the tribunal's decision if its findings were outside the scope of those which it was entitled to make. If the evidence was such that a tribunal, properly advised as to the law and acting judicially, might have come to more than one conclusion, the appeal will not be allowed merely because the Upper Tribunal would have reached a different conclusion on the evidence. In such a case it is essential that subsequent tribunals should not read into the acceptance of the tribunal's findings a decision by the Upper Tribunal that the conclusion reached was the only permissible one so that, if the same facts should arise, the same conclusion must be drawn.

Retrospective effect of decisions

In accordance with the general principle of the effect of judicial decisions, the Upper Tribunal is deemed to state the law as it has always been and its decisions have a retrospective effect (*CCS 8189/1995*, para 6). This is subject to s28ZC of the Act.

Northern Ireland

Northern Ireland has its own structure of tribunals and its own commissioners separate from the Upper Tribunal that hears appeals in England, Wales and Scotland. The proper approach of the First-tier Tribunal in Great Britain to a decision of a child support commissioner in Northern Ireland or a court decision in Northern Ireland relating to child support law is set out in *R(SB) 1/90*. If there is no decision from Great Britain, a decision of a child support commissioner in Northern Ireland should be followed, provided that two conditions are met. First, the relevant statutory provision must be identically worded to the provision to be applied in Great Britain. Second, if the decision is a court decision or that of a tribunal of commissioners it must be unanimous. The precedent value of comments that are not necessary to the decision depends on the circumstances in which they are made (*R(IB) 4/04*, para 30). So express guidance given after hearing full argument on the interpretation of a controversial provision should generally be followed (*ibid*).

Northern Ireland has broadly followed Great Britain in the numbering, naming and reporting of decisions. Its neutral citation number is in the form: [2010] NICom 1.

CHILD SUPPORT AND EUROPEAN LAW

European law in this context means the law of the European Community (EC) and the European Convention on Human Rights (ECHR). Each needs to be considered separately, but they are not wholly unconnected as the Court of Justice of the European Community has recognised the European Convention as part of the general principles of law to which it has regard.

1. **EC law – tribunals' powers and duties**

   The law of the EC is part of UK law. The European Communities Act 1972 provides that enforceable Community rights are to be given legal effect in the UK and that in any clash between such a right and national law the former shall prevail.

   A tribunal has power to refer a question to the European Court of Justice. A decision to make a reference is a final decision which is appealable to the Upper Tribunal (*CIS 501/1993*). The First-tier Tribunal should resist any temptation to refer a question to the European Court. Such references are better left to the Upper Tribunal, which has the benefit of better researched arguments and more time to consider the issues. In deciding whether to make a reference, the normal doctrine of precedent does not apply (*Trent Taverns Ltd v Sykes* [1999] *The Times,* March 5, 1999). The Court of Appeal has power to order the withdrawal of a reference (*Royscot Leasing Ltd v Commissioners of Customs and Excise* [1999] *The Times,* November 11, 1998).

   It is an error of law for a tribunal to fail to deal with an issue of European law raised before it (*R(SB) 6/91,* para 5). It should use its inquisitorial function to investigate any issue of European law raised on the facts.

2. **The validity and interpretation of child support law under the ECHR**

   Under the Human Rights Act 1998 most but not all of the Convention has become enforceable in accordance with, and within the limits set by, the Act. However, the use of the terms of the Convention in interpreting legislation and overseeing the exercise of discretions remains available as an alternative to the procedures under the Act and in order to try to alleviate any limitations in those procedures or in the extent of incorporation. Child support law has come before tribunals, the courts and the ECHR. In all cases, the legislation has been held to comply in general terms with the parties' Convention rights, but with the acknowledgement that there might be a violation on the individual facts of a particular case.

3. **The validity of child support law under EC law**

   Challenges to all or part of the child support scheme by reference to EC law have so far been unsuccessful. See *R(CS) 3/96* and *R(CS)* 2/95. There is, perhaps, scope to argue that the scheme, or its application in a particular case, may violate equal treatment provisions or impede a parent's freedom of movement.

4. **Relationship between EC Law and the ECHR**

   The ECHR is part of the general principles of law whose observance the European Court of Justice ensures, but the Court will not give guidance to national courts on the interpretation of the Convention in an area which does not fall within the field of application of European law (*Kremzow v Austria* [1997] ECR I-2629). For an attempt to rely on the ECHR in conjunction with freedom of movement, see *CMEC v NC* [2009] UKUT 106 (AAC); [2010] AACR 1.

Part II

STATUTES

Child Support Act 1991
(1991 c48)

SCHEDULES

The basic principles

The duty to maintain

1.–(1)   For the purposes of this Act, each parent of a qualifying child is responsible for maintaining him.

(2)   For the purposes of this Act, [³a non-resident parent] shall be taken to have met his responsibility to maintain any qualifying child of his by making periodical payments of maintenance with respect to the child of such amount, and at such intervals, as may be determined in accordance with the provisions of this Act.

(3)   Where a [¹maintenance calculation] made under this Act requires the making of periodical payments, it shall be the duty of the [³non-resident parent] with respect to whom the [²calculation] was made to make those payments.

Amendments

1.   Child Support, Pensions and Social Security Act 2000 (2000 c.19) s1(2) (March 3, 2003 for the types of cases in art 3 Child Support, Pensions and Social Security Act 2000 (Commencement No.12) Order 2003 (SI 2003 No.192)). For other types of cases see '1993 rules' below.

2.   Child Support, Pensions and Social Security Act 2000 (2000 c.19) s1(2) (March 3, 2003 for the types of cases in art 3 Child Support, Pensions and Social Security Act 2000 (Commencement No.12) Order 2003 (SI 2003 No.192)). For other types of cases see '1993 rules' below.

3.   Child Support, Pensions and Social Security Act 2000 (2000 c.19) s26 and Sch 3 para 11(2) (March 3, 2003 for the types of cases in art 3 Child Support, Pensions and Social Security Act 2000 (Commencement No.12) Order 2003 (SI 2003 No.192)). For other types of cases see '1993 rules' below.

1993 rules

Ss1(2) and 26 and Sch 3 of the Child Support, Pensions and Social Security Act 2000 (2000 c.19) amend s1 of the Child Support Act 1991 and have been brought into force only for the types of cases in art 3 of the Child Support, Pensions and Social Security Act 2000 (Commencement No.12) Order 2003 (SI 2003 No.192 – see p683). For other types of cases the 1993 rules apply and the original wording is retained – ie, "maintenance assessment" is retained in place of "maintenance calculation", "assessment" is retained in place of "calculation" and "absent parent" is retained in place of "non-resident parent".

Definitions

"maintenance calculation": see s54.
"non-resident parent": see s3(2).
"parent": see s54.
"qualifying child": see s3(1).

General Note

This section sets the framework of parental obligations around which the child support maintenance structure is built. Each parent of a qualifying child is responsible for maintaining that child. If a parent is a non-resident parent, a maintenance calculation may be made. It is the non-resident parent's duty to pay the amounts fixed by that calculation. If payment is made as required, the duty imposed by this section is discharged. The child support maintenance for which the non-resident parent is liable may be nil. If that is the case, the non-resident parent is effectively absolved from paying child support maintenance under this Act for so long as the calculation remains in force.

The obligations imposed by this section only apply for the purposes of this Act. They do not affect the rights and obligations which apply outside the scope of the Act: see Pt II of the Matrimonial Causes Act 1973, Pt I of the Domestic Proceedings and Magistrates' Courts Act 1978, Pt III of the Matrimonial and Family Proceedings Act 1984, Family Law (Scotland) Act 1985, Sch 1 to the Children Act 1989 and ss78(6) and 105 of the Social Security Administration Act 1992. The principal limitations on the scope of the duty are therefore as follows: (i) it does not apply unless one of the parents (as defined by s54) is a non-resident parent as defined by s3(2); (ii) it does not apply unless the child has a home with someone who qualifies as a person with care under s3(3); (iii) it ceases to apply when the child ceases to be a child for the purposes of the Act under s55; (iv) the Act does not affect cases where the court has jurisdiction under s8; (v) finally, the Act does not affect any consensual maintenance arrangements to which the parents may agree, except to the extent that the parties may not contract out of the Act (s9).

For a survey of a non-resident parent's liability to maintain before and apart from this Act, see the judgment of Ward LJ in *R (Kehoe) v SSWP* [2004] 1 FLR 1132.

Welfare of children: the general principle

2.   Where, in any case which falls to be dealt with under this Act, the [²[³Secretary of State]] [¹...] is considering the exercise of any discretionary power conferred by this Act, [² [³the Secretary of State]] shall have regard to the welfare of any child likely to be affected by [²[³the]] decision.

Amendments

1.   Repealed (1.6.99) by Sch 8 Social Security Act 1998 (c.14).
2.   Child Maintenance and Other Payments Act 2008 (2008 c.6) s13 and Sch 3 para 2 (November 1, 2008). Child Maintenance and Other Payments Act 2008 (Commencement No.4 and Transitional Provision) Order 2008 (SI 2008 No.2675) art 3.
3.   Public Bodies (Child Maintenance and Enforcement Commission: Abolition and Transfer of Functions) Order 2012 (SI 2012 No.2007) art 3(2) and Sch para 2 (August 1, 2012).

Definition

"child": see s55.

General Note

This section attaches a general condition to all the discretionary powers given to the Secretary of State by this Act, that the welfare of any child likely to be affected by a decision must be taken into account.

The section applies to the First-tier Tribunal and Upper Tribunal when they are considering on appeal the decision which the Secretary of State should have made, but it does not apply when they are considering the exercise of powers of their own, such as the powers given to the Upper Tribunal by s24. However, in cases to which this section does not apply, the welfare of any children likely to be affected will, on general principles, be a proper consideration in the exercise of any discretion.

The requirement imposed by this section is not a freestanding one authorising the welfare of children to be taken into account at any stage, but rather a qualification on the way in which powers conferred by this Act are to be exercised (*R(CS)* 2/98, para 17). The duty is a continuing one: *R (Joplin) v CMEC* [2010] 2 FLR 1510, para 17.

This section applies only to the exercise of discretionary powers in individual cases, including the enforcement powers under this Act (*Brookes v SSWP and CMEC* [2010] 2 FLR 1038, para 16). As the section only applies to discretionary powers, it is irrelevant whether or not regard has been had to this section in the case where the exercise of a duty is involved, such as under s11 (*R(CS) 4/96*, para 8 and *CCS 14/1994*, para 10). Where, however, the exercise of discretionary power is involved, the tribunal should be satisfied that s2 has been considered and, if in doubt, should require evidence or confirmation to be produced (*CCS 14/1994*, para 9).

The Secretary of State must have regard to the welfare of any child likely to be affected by her/his decisions. It is only necessary that "regard" shall be had to the welfare of the child. This is less stringent than the requirement that the welfare of the child should be the "first" or "paramount" (*R(CS) 4/96*, para 8; *Brookes*, para 13(1)) consideration, which applies in s25(1) Matrimonial Causes Act 1973 and s1(1) Children Act 1989 respectively.

The children whose welfare must be considered are all those who are likely to be affected. Children other than the qualifying children may need to be considered. For example, if the non-resident parent has other children, their welfare must also be taken into account (*Brookes*, para 12). One or both of the parents may also be a child within the meaning of the Act.

The welfare of children covers all the needs relating to their present condition and future development: physical, mental, emotional, educational and social (see especially the so-called "welfare checklist" in s1(3) Children Act 1989, although it has no direct application to this Act). In an appropriate case the views of the child may be taken into account. A specific factor which should be taken into account is the possible prejudical effect of delay on the welfare of a child. So important is this consideration that it is expressly made a general principle for the purpose of the Children Act 1989 by s1(2) of that Act.

In considering children's welfare, the emphasis will often be on the finances necessary and available to allow their needs to be met. These needs are not exclusively dependent upon money, but a minimum is necessary and among the most difficult decisions are likely to be those which involve assessing the impact of the distribution of limited resources on the welfare of the children affected. However, the requirement imposed by this section must be applied so as not to impede the basic objective of the child support legislation that non-resident parents should pay maintenance calculated in accordance with the child support scheme (*R(CS) 4/96*, para 8).

This section does not require the Secretary of State to achieve any particular result. There is no duty to promote a child's welfare, only to take it into account. Nor does the section require the Secretary of State to refrain from making a decision that will impact adversely on a child's welfare. Nor, conversely, does the duty to make maintenance payments always override welfare considerations. See *Brookes* at paras 13(i) and (ii) and 14. As Hughes LJ explained in that case:

"14. ...The correct position is clearly that all the circumstances of each case must be considered. What section 2 requires is that any impact on children's welfare be taken into account as a factor in deciding whether or not to do something discretionary under the Act. Clearly, the greater the likely negative impact on welfare, the greater the case against making the decision. But the welfare considerations must still be balanced against all other relevant considerations. Those will include, but are not limited to: the welfare of other children with different interests, the duty of the paying parent to support his/her children, the general public interest in a parent meeting that duty and the particular interest of the public, qua taxpayer, in that duty being enforced rather than the support of the children being left to fall on the State."

See also *Ishak v Thowfeek* [1968] 1 WLR 1718 at 1725.

The duty under this section may require the Secretary of State to make inquiries about the children who may be affected by a decision. The issue did not arise for decision in *Brookes*, but Hughes LJ commented:

"15. ... On the face of it, the duty to have regard to welfare can only arise in relation to those children of whose existence the Commission knows, or of whom it has been put on notice, and in relation to circumstances of theirs which it knows about or ought to be able to infer from information in its hands. If, however, the information known to the Commission is such as to suggest that there is or may be a child of particular sensitivity or vulnerability, or there is otherwise a particular reason to think that an unusual impact on welfare might be the result of a discretionary decision, then on ordinary principles one would expect a decision maker to make such enquiries as are reasonable. That is to say no more than that anyone charged with making a discretionary decision ought to behave reasonably."

This section only applies to discretionary powers conferred *by* this Act. It does not, therefore, apply to such powers conferred by regulations made under the Act. This is to some extent underlined by the fact that elsewhere it has been felt necessary to make specific provision that the interests (rather than welfare) of a child are to be considered (reg 14(2) Maintenance Calculations and Special Cases Regulations). However, the welfare of any children likely to be affected will always be a factor which those exercising a power are entitled to take into consideration, regardless of whether or not there is specific provision to that effect.

In practice, this section is likely to have little impact on the decisions made. It is, however, important for the authorities to show that regard has been had to the welfare of children affected. A person who wishes to assert that welfare has not been considered may challenge the decision taken by means of judicial review (*R v Secretary of State for Social Security ex p Biggin* [1995] 1 FLR 851). However, Thorpe J in that case considered that welfare appears to have no influence on the quantification of liability and very little on the discretion to enforce an assessment, so that the heading words of the section "seem hollow indeed".

If a tribunal is faced with a question which involves the exercise of a discretion by the Secretary of State, it will need first to identify any children who might be affected by the decision. If the tribunal decides that the welfare of one of those children is not likely to be affected, it should decide why that is so. The tribunal's record of decision should record the children whose interests were considered, its decision and the reasons for it. If the welfare of any child is likely to be affected, the tribunal should decide how it might be affected. Then it will need to weigh the competing interests of all the children affected. Finally, it will have to decide the impact which its conclusions on these matters should have on the exercise of the discretion. These matters should be included in the record of decision.

In any case which directly affects the welfare of a child there is power in exceptional cases to bar disclosure to a party in the case of information which might be damaging to the child (*Re B (A minor) (Disclosure of Evidence)* [1993] 1 FLR 191). Clearly, this can never be relied upon to prevent the disclosure of information to the Secretary of State. It is also doubtful whether the rule would apply in child support law (*R(CS) 3/06*, para 17). According to Balcombe LJ (at 203), it only applies "in any case which is directly concerned with the welfare of a child". And according to Glidewell LJ (at 201), it only operates if "the disclosure of the evidence would be so detrimental to the welfare of the child or children under consideration as to outweigh the normal requirements for a fair trial that all evidence must be disclosed, so that all parties can consider it and if necessary seek to rebut it". This issue would now be dealt with under r14(2) of the Tribunal Procedure (First-tier Tribunal) (Social Entitlement Chamber) Rules 2008 (see p825).

Provisions like this section are inevitable in any legislation affecting children. However, the scope for the exercise of discretion is extremely limited in this Act. Where there is a discretion it may be supplemented by other specified criteria, as for example in s28F(i)(b), although these do not displace the general duty created by this section. It may be that this section states one of the principles underlying the Act as a whole, but beyond that the recitation of the principle seems more to serve a ritual, political significance, than to provide a touch-stone for the practical implementation of the Act.

The Secretary of State is not under a duty of care in negligence when exercising its powers under this section or any other provision of child support law (*Jones v Department of Employment* [1988] 1 All ER 725; *W v Home Office, The Times,* March 14 1997; *R (Rowley) v SSWP* [2007] 2 FLR 945).

Meaning of certain terms used in this Act

3.–(1)   A child is a "qualifying child" if–
(a)   one of his parents is, in relation to him, [⁴a non-resident parent]; or
(b)   both of his parents are, in relation to him, [⁴non-resident parents].
(2)   The parent of any child is [³a non-resident parent], in relation to him, if–
(a)   that parent is not living in the same household with the child; and
(b)   the child has his home with a person who is, in relation to him, a person with care.
(3)   A person is a "person with care", in relation to any child, if he is a person–
(a)   with whom the child has his home;
(b)   who usually provides day to day care for the child (whether exclusively or in conjunction with any other person); and
(c)   who does not fall within a prescribed category of person.
(4)   The Secretary of State shall not, under subsection (3)(c), prescribe as a category–
(a)   parents;
(b)   guardians;
(c)   persons in whose favour residence orders under section 8 of the Children Act 1989 are in force;
(d)   in Scotland, persons having the right of custody of a child.
(5)   For the purposes of this Act there may be more than one person with care in relation to the same qualifying child.
(6)   Periodical payments which are required to be paid in accordance with a [²maintenance calculation] are referred to in this Act as "child support maintenance".
(7)   Expressions are defined in this section only for the purposes of this Act.

Amendments
1.   1989 c.41.
2.   Child Support, Pensions and Social Security Act 2000 (2000 c.19) s1(2) (March 3, 2003 for the types of cases in art 3 Child Support, Pensions and Social Security Act 2000 (Commencement No.12) Order 2003 (SI 2003 No.192)). For other types of cases see '1993 rules' below.
3.   Child Support, Pensions and Social Security Act 2000 (2000 c.19) s26 and Sch 3 para 11(2) (January 31, 2001 for the purposes of ss15(4A), 44(1) and 44(2A) of this Act and March 3, 2003 for the types of cases in art 3 Child Support, Pensions and Social Security Act 2000 (Commencement No.12) Order 2003 (SI 2003 No.192)). For other types of cases see '1993 rules' below.
4.   Child Support, Pensions and Social Security Act 2000 (2000 c.19) s26 and Sch 3 para 11(2) (March 3, 2003 for the types of cases in art 3 Child Support, Pensions and Social Security Act 2000 (Commencement No.12) Order 2003 (SI 2003 No.192)). For other types of cases see '1993 rules' below.

1993 rules
Ss1(2) and 26 and Sch 3 of the Child Support, Pensions and Social Security Act 2000 (2000 c.19) amend s3 of the Child Support Act 1991 and have been brought into force only for the types of cases in art 3 of the Child Support, Pensions and Social Security Act 2000 (Commencement No.12) Order 2003 (SI 2003 No.192 – see p683). For other types of cases the 1993 rules apply and the original wording is retained – ie, "maintenance assessment" is retained in place of "maintenance calculation" and "absent parent" is retained in place of "non-resident parent".

Definitions
"child": see s55.
"maintenance calculation": see s54.
"parent": see s54.
"prescribed": see s54.

General Note

Subsection (1)

To be a qualifying child, a person must satisfy two conditions. First, the person must be a child within the meaning of the Act. The basic definition in s55 is elaborated on by Sch 1 to the Maintenance Calculation Procedure Regulations. Second, one or both of the child's parents must be non-resident as defined in subs (2). In this subsection "qualifying child" means a child who falls within the scheme at large regardless of whether or not there has been an application for a maintenance calculation in respect of the child *(CCS 806/1995,* para 14).

Subsection (2)

If a person is to be a non-resident parent in relation to a child, three conditions must be satisfied. Two relate to the parent and one to the living arrangements of the child. First, the person must be a parent of the child as defined in s54. Second, the person must not live in the same household with the child. Finally, the child's home must be with a person with care as defined in subs (3). It is relevant only that these conditions are satisfied; it is irrelevant that the child is living apart from a parent against that parent's wishes *(CCS 3128/1995,* paras 7-8).

General approach

The Act uses three different expressions: "household", "home" and "living [or residing] with". All three are used in this subsection. It is appropriate to make some general remarks on the proper use of the authorities and the application of the principles which they create to cases involving phrases such as these – ie, cases where the application of the legal principles to the facts of a particular case turns on an individual analysis of the relevant factors of the case and their interrelation, and in which no single factor of itself is conclusive *(Simmons v Pizzey* [1977] 2 All ER 432 at 441-442 *per* Lord Hailsham, and *R(G) 1/79)* and no definitive list of relevant factors is possible *(Crake and Butterworth v Supplementary Benefit Commission* [1982] 1 All ER 498, *per* Woolf J). It will often be possible for different members of a tribunal to attribute different significance to an individual factor and, even when all the factors are considered as a whole, the result will often depend upon the individual member's impression, with the result that different members may quite properly come to different conclusions on the same facts.

These, and similar phrases which have been given the same meaning, occur in a variety of contexts and there are a number of decisions interpreting them. Since there is a broad level of consistency in these phrases across the various contexts, the decisions will be helpful in interpreting these phrases in the context of child support law. Indeed, in *Santos v Santos* [1972] 2 All ER 246, Sachs LJ was able to identify a prima facie meaning of "living apart" (the antithesis, it was said, of "living together") before going on to consider whether it was displaced by the particular statutory context of the Divorce Reform Act 1969. However, it is clear from the nature of the analysis which the courts undertake and the comments which the judges make from time to time (eg, Ormrod LJ, in *Adeoso v Adeoso* [1981] 1 All ER 107) that the context in which they are used may affect the precise scope given to the words and the nature and weight of the factors relevant to their application. In using decisions from other contexts, therefore, it is necessary to take account of the statutory context in which they were made as well as to have due regard to the language and statutory context of child support law.

Usually it will be immediately obvious how the principles apply to the living arrangements of those concerned, because the circumstances will be such that the result will be the same whichever concept is being applied. In such cases failure to reach the correct conclusion will be an error of law *(R v Birmingham Juvenile Court ex pN* [1984] 2 All ER 688, *per* Arnold P). However, the arrangements which can be entered into are subject to infinite variation, and tribunals will on occasion need to determine with precision both the scope of each concept and its application to the individual facts of the particular case. It is particularly likely in such cases that the facts of the case will be open to alternative analyses. If this is so, the decision will be one of fact and degree, and there will be no error of law, provided that (i) the decision is based on the correct legal principles and (ii) it is one that could reasonably be made on the facts of the case *(ibid* and *Simmons v Pizzey,* above at 441-442, *per* Lord Hailsham LC).

Two particular types of case are likely to cause difficulties for tribunals: (i) those where the parties' financial and living arrangements are outside the usual range encountered in everyday experience and (ii) those where those arrangements are in a state of transition.

Applying the law in cases such as this requires the exercise of a number of skills by panel members who sit on tribunals. They must be aware of the manifold variations in living arrangements which exist and analyse them in a way which both reflects the individual circumstances of the case concerned and produces a sensible result within the structure of the legislation. Care will need to be taken in making and recording findings of fact on all relevant matters, as well as in making and explaining the reasons for the tribunal's decision, although it has been said that in cases involving value judgments clear findings on the relevant issues are all that is required by way of reasons *(CIS 87/1993,* para 9). Precedent must be used carefully: decisions must be followed in so far as they lay down general principles, but arguments based on the similarity of facts between two cases will always be misplaced, since minor differences can change the whole complexion of an arrangement. Reasons for decision which are framed by way of comparison with the facts in previous decisions will lead to a successful appeal, since it is not any single factor on its own which is decisive, but rather the combined effect of all relevant factors.

The conflicting decisions by commissioners on consistency in decisions as between the same parties are of relevance in the context of decisions such as those being considered here, where different decisions may properly be reached on the same facts. The issue arises when a tribunal is dealing with an issue which has already been decided in the context of an earlier calculation. In *CM 140/1992* (paras 19-22) and *CM 113/1991*, the same commissioner decided that, if there has been no change in the facts, the tribunal should as a matter of law follow the earlier decision unless to do so would be perverse. The principle in *CM 140/1992* is concerned with the cases which turn on the interpretation of the same facts in successive decisions. It does not apply to cases where the facts in successive decisions are different, since each decision must be made on the facts and in the circumstances then prevailing (*CFC 5/1993*, para 16). This approach to consistency has not found universal favour among the commissioners, however, and in *R(M) 1/96* (para 14) a different commissioner emphasised that each case must be decided on the evidence available without any bias in favour of following any earlier decision made between the same parties. In view of this conflict, tribunals may follow the approach which they prefer. Whatever the correct legal position, there is much to be said for ensuring that, where different decisions may properly be reached on the same facts, parties are treated consistently and are not subjected to differing decisions from time to time, and whatever decision is reached the reasons must be sufficient to explain the reason for it to the parties.

Household

The criteria to be taken into account in deciding which households exist are discussed in the general note to reg 1 of the Maintenance Calculations and Special Cases Regulations (see p576). Although it will usually be obvious which households exist and who lives in which one, difficult cases will arise and attention will need to be paid to the relevant legal criteria. In the context of the definition of absent parent, the financial arrangements will be of central importance. The legal guidance on the factors to be taken into account in deciding whether a person is a member of a household is directed at the activities of adults. Where the circumstances do not provide an obvious answer, the approach to deciding the household in which a child lives should generally be as follows. First, consider the arrangements of the adults concerned and decide which households exist. Then, consider how the child fits into those arrangements by enquiring who bears the immediate financial responsibility for, and who fulfils the usual domestic responsibilities in respect of, that child. Findings of fact must be made on these matters. The relevant household will be the one with which the child has the closest connection. Deciding this will require the exercise of judicial judgment. It will involve identifying the significance of each of the relevant factors and attributing the appropriate weight to each. The reasons for decision should record that this judgment has been exercised and indicate why it was exercised in the way it was. Where a child has a sufficient degree of maturity and financial independence, it may be possible to apply the legal criteria for the existence of a household directly to the child, rather than approach the question in the way suggested here. In all cases, the decision should be based on objective facts, rather than on the perceptions of the persons concerned as to whether they live in the same or separate households, although in marginal cases these perceptions, including (depending on the child's age and maturity) those of the child concerned, may be an important consideration.

The use of the words "lives with", in contrast to the "resides with", points to the emphasis being on the relationship between the parties rather than a connection with the property occupied by the parties (*South Northamptonshire DC v Power* [1987] 3 All ER 831 at 833, per Kerr LJ). The essential attribute of a household is the existence of a domestic establishment (paras 13-18 of the Appendix to *R(IS) 1/99*).

In the context of the Inheritance (Provision for Family and Dependants) Act 1975, the Court of Appeal has held that it is possible for persons to be living in the same household despite the fact that they are living separately at a particular time (*Gully v Dix* [2004] 1 FLR 918). On the other hand, in the context of the Divorce Reform Act 1969, Wrangham J thought that it was not possible for persons to live in the same household without also living with each other (*Mouncer v Mouncer* [1972] 1 All ER 289 at 291). However, as it is the purpose of child support law to require non-resident parents to contribute towards the cost of bringing up their children, it is possible that the position may be different and that there may be cases in which the arrangements within a family are such that one parent is a member of the same household as the child, but does not live in that household *with the child*. In such cases, attention will need to be given both to the question of which households exist and to the separate question of whether a particular member of a household may be described as living in it with the child. One type of case in which this distinction may need to be drawn is where one parent is working for substantial periods away from home (eg, on an oil rig or in another part of the country) while the rest of the family stays in the family home until it is sold. Although the financial arrangements and emotional attachments may be such that the single household survives, the extent of the separation may result in it being inappropriate to regard the absent person as living in that household *with* the child. This analysis may also be appropriate where a relationship is coming to an end and the arrangements are moving in the direction of separate households. Those separate households may not yet have been completely established, but, in view of the steps being taken to separate the lives of the parties, it may nevertheless be appropriate to regard one of them as no longer living *with* the child in the surviving household, especially if responsibility for the child has for all practical purposes been abandoned by that parent. In practice, the evidence may not permit the distinctions suggested in this paragraph to be drawn and the making of the application for a maintenance assessment would be likely to lead to the household ceasing to exist.

It is possible that the child may be living with the non-resident parent, but not in the same household. If, for example, a father still lives in the family home, but has formed a separate household within it, the child may, depending on the circumstances, still be said to be living with both parents. Such circumstances will satisfy the definition in this subsection, since the child does not live in the same household as the father and the child's home is with the mother (albeit it is with the father as well) who can therefore qualify as a person with care. It is also possible for a child to be living under the same roof as a person but to have so little contact with that person that they are not living together (*R(F) 1/71*).

Each person in a household lives with every other member of that household (*Chief Adjudication Officer v Bate* [1996] 1 WLR 814). Living in the same household involves more than a mere transitory presence and involves a settled course of daily living *R(F) 2/81*, para 12; *R(CS)8/99*, paras 14-15). A person will still "reside with" another despite a temporary absence, such as a holiday or a stay in hospital (*Camden London Borough Council v Goldenberg* [1997] FLR 556 at 564, *per* Nourse LJ, quoting Denning LJ in *Middleton v Bull* [1951] 2 TLR 1010 at 1012). In *R(CS)14/98* (para 16), the commissioner declined to draw any distinction between *living* in the same household and *staying* in the same household on the ground that such fine distinctions would be highly contentious and not appropriate for legislation which was designed to produce fairly clear-cut answers by child support officers.

In *CCS14625/1996* (para 17), the commissioner held that household had to be viewed in a realistic way and primarily with reference to the children themselves.

The meaning of "home" and some of the other problems associated with the concept of living or residing with someone are discussed in the general note to subs (3).

Subsection (3)

A number of matters turn on whether or not a person is a person with care – eg, it determines who is entitled to apply for a maintenance assessment under s4, whether s5(1) applies and whether the Secretary of State treated an application for a maintenance calculation as having been made under s6. It is not essential that the person with care should be a parent of the child. Some provisions, however, only apply to a person with care who is also a parent – eg, s6.

If a person is to be a person with care in respect of a child, three conditions must be satisfied. First, the child's home must be with the person. The tribunal's enquiry must concentrate on the nature and extent of the child's association with the person alleged to be the person with care, rather than on the child's association with particular premises. A child could still have a home with a person, although they have no fixed abode. (Compare the definition of "home" in reg 1(2) of the Maintenance Calculations and Special Cases Regulations (see p576), which is concerned with the accommodation.) The financial arrangements are much less important here than when considering the meaning of household. The living and caring arrangements for the child will be an important consideration and in this context an enquiry should always be made as to who has parental responsibility for, or parental rights over, the child, whether, and if so, in whose favour, a residence order under s8 Children Act 1989 has been made in respect of the child, and in whose favour any existing order for custody or care and control of the child was made.

The meaning of "home" was considered in *CCS 1180/1998,* para 10. The commissioner laid down the following propositions.

(i)   A home is a domestic base.

(ii)   In some cases where the location of that base is unclear, an element of perception may be involved.

(iii)   No precise definition of "home" is possible.

(iv)   Where a person has a home is a question of fact.

(v)   The question must be answered by applying ordinary, common sense standards.

(vi)   A person may have a particular home despite lengthy absences from it.

(vii)   A home must be more than an occasional place of convenient resort.

In the case of a child, the perception of the adults who have legal responsibility for the child are central considerations. However, as the emphasis here is on reality of parental responsibility (rather than lawfulness, as in the case when considering habitual residence; see the general note to s44), it will be the wishes of those persons who have actual, as opposed to legal, responsibility for the child that will be the relevant ones. Moreover, the perceptions of the child may deserve consideration, depending on the degree of maturity.

In view of the importance of perception in identifying a child's home, it is possible for a home to be with a particular person despite considerable absences. This is emphasised by reg 12 of the Maintenance Calculations and Special Cases Regulations which makes clear that a child's home may be with a person, although the child lives elsewhere for a substantial part of the year. This regulation provides for the special case where a child is at boarding school or in hospital. It operates only in relation to para (b) of the definition of "person with care" and does not affect para (a). Clearly, therefore, reg 12 envisages that the fact that the child is separated from a person for lengthy periods does not of itself prevent that child's home being with that person. A child's home may be with a person despite the fact that they live in different households – eg, a child and a parent may maintain a separate household within a house which is shared with grandparents who share the care of the child. In such a case, the child does not live in the grandparents' household, but the arrangements may be such that the child's home is with them as well as with the mother.

The Court of Appeal has held that, although unusual, shared or split residence orders, whereby the child lives for part of the time with each parent, may be made under the Children Act 1989 (*A v A (Children) (Shared Residence Order)* [1994] 1 FLR 669). This (which was in any case spelt out in s11(4) of the Act) reverses the attitude of the courts under the old law, where, in *Riley v Riley* [1986] 2 FLR 429, such orders had been disapproved. It may be expected, therefore, that there will be some increase in the making of orders of this type, with consequential implications for all three were living together it was the question of who is the parent with care.

However, even where the more usual form of order is made, giving residence to one parent, and contact to the other, the total period spent by the child in "staying contact" with a parent may be relevant to the question whether there is a special case within the Maintenance Calculations and Special Cases Regulations.

In determining whether a qualifying child lives, resides or has a home with a parent or other person for the purposes of the definitions in this section, it is not necessary for the parent or other person to have a legal interest in the dwelling or for the child to be in a subordinate position in the dwelling (*Chief Adjudication Officer v Bate* [1996] 1 WLR 814). It is possible, therefore, for the qualifying child to be the householder.

In *CCS 5818/1999* (paras 9-10), the child lived with his grandmother, but they both lived with and were supported by his mother during school holidays. The commissioner considered whether the child's home should be determined separately at different periods of the year or an overall view of the whole year should be taken. The commissioner directed a rehearing, but suggested that, as the periods in that case varied from a few weeks to a few months, on the limited evidence available, it seemed appropriate to take an overall view.

The second limb of the definition of a person with care is that the person must provide day to day care for the child. This is not defined by the Act, but is defined by reg 1(2) of the Maintenance Calculations and Special Cases Regulations. It covers persons who on average over the previous 12 months (or such other period as is more representative of the current arrangements for the care of the child) provided care for not less than two nights per week. The need to provide day to day care is modified if (a) the qualifying child is a boarder at a boarding school or an in-patient at a hospital and (b) as a result, the person who would otherwise be providing day to day care is not doing so. These circumstances constitute a special case by virtue of reg 12 of the Maintenance Calculations and Special Cases Regulations. In this case, para (b) of this sub-section is modified so as to apply to the person who would usually be providing day to day care were the child not a boarder or in-patient. If a child is allowed to live with a parent under s23(5) Children Act 1989, there is a special case by virtue of reg 13 of the Maintenance Calculations and Special Cases Regulations and subs 3(b) is modified to apply to that parent rather than to the person who usually provides day to day care.

The definition of day to day care in terms of overnight care can create problems when arrangements for day and night care are separated. A parent who works night shifts, for example, may have overall care of a child, except that the child is looked after by a nanny or sleeps with a neighbour while the parent is at work. In cases like this, the child is still in the parent's care, although that care is exercised through the agency of someone else. The situation becomes more difficult, however, if the person with whom the child spends the night is someone who is not acting on the parent's behalf. The child might, for example, be looked after at night by grandparents, who might wish to set up a claim as persons with care in competition to the parent. In this case, the child's home might be with the parent, but day to day care with the grandparents, with the result that there would be no person with care. The only way to avoid this would be to rely on the fact that the definition of day to day care in terms of overnight care only applies unless the context otherwise requires. Freed from the definition, it would be possible to have regard to the overall pattern of care for a child. However, it is not the case that the context of the legislation requires a different meaning; rather it is that the meaning produces inappropriate results when applied to particular sets of circumstances and those circumstances could arise in relation to any of the provisions in which the words are used. In other words, in order to avoid the inappropriate results, it would be necessary to disregard the definition completely.

In *GR v CMEC (CSM)* [2011] UKUT 101 (AAC), the judge decided that the definition of day to day care did not govern the use of the words in this subsection and that it meant the immediate, short-term and mundane aspects of case considered in *R(CS) 11/02*.

Paragraph (b) expressly caters for the possibility that there may be joint persons with care, that is, that the care for a child may be provided only in conjunction with someone else. It may be difficult to decide in a particular case who is the person with care of a child – eg, both a mother and the maternal grandparents may live with and care for a child. The child's home may be said to be with both mother and grandparents. It will then be necessary to inquire closely into the care arrangements to see who has day to day care of the child. Findings of fact will need to be made on this matter and if there is any dispute, the record of decision of the tribunal must explain why the decision was made. Where the living and caring arrangements do not permit a sensible choice to be made between the persons involved, the appropriate decision will be that there are persons with joint care.

The third condition which must be satisfied if a person is to be a person with care in respect of a child is that the person must not fall within one of the prescribed categories of person who may not be persons with care. These are set out in reg 21 of the Maintenance Calculation Procedure Regulations and cover cases where the person with care is a local authority or a person with whom a child is placed or boarded by a local authority. In line with these exclusions, where a local authority has part-time care of a qualifying child, there is a special case by virtue of reg 9 of the Maintenance Calculations and Special Cases Regulations.

Subsection (5)

There may be more than one person with care in respect of a child. This subsection covers two possibilities. The first is the possibility expressly catered for by subs (3)(b), that there may be persons who jointly have care of a child on a day to day basis. The second possibility is that care is shared between different persons (as opposed to being provided jointly by them) so that each is a person with part-time care. Where there is more than one person with care, only those who have parental responsibility for the child may apply for a maintenance calculation (s5(1)). Where there are applications for maintenance calculations from more than one such person, the one to be proceeded with is determined under reg 4 of, and Sch 2 to, the Maintenance Calculation Procedure Regulations.

A court is entitled to consider the financial consequences of a child support assessment on the "non-resident parent" in determining which parent is to have a residence order in respect of the child, and may conclude that shared residence is appropriate (*Re R (A Minor) (Residence Order: Finance)* [1995] 2 FLR 612).

Subsection (6)

From the point of view of the non-resident parent, payment of child support maintenance is an obligation which must be met. Other debts, such as hire purchase or court fines, do not have priority and are not taken into account when making a maintenance calculation. The parent must renegotiate other financial obligations with the creditors in order to ensure that all obligations may be met, although those cases in which renegotiation is needed may well be those in which it will not be an attractive proposition to lenders. From the point of view of the person with care, child support maintenance is income and may result in this person receiving less benefit than before or ceasing to be entitled to benefit altogether.

In *R(CS) 8/98* (para 24), the commissioner said that it was arguable that the payment of school fees by an absent parent in respect of a qualifying child at a time when the parent with care was treated as providing day to day care should be regarded as a payment of child support maintenance. However, in *CCS37/1997* (paras 25-26), the deputy commissioner, having said that matters for the Secretary of State were better identified as such as then left to the Secretary of State, gave his opinion that, as s8(7) preserved the power of the court to order payments "to meet some or all of the expenses incurred in the provision of the instruction" at an educational establishment, a payment of school fees under a court order would by definition be additional to a payment of child support maintenance and could not be regarded as if it were, in part at least, a payment of child support maintenance.

For the position of child support maintenance in insolvency, see the general note to s33 on p99.

Child support maintenance

4.–(1)   A person who is, in relation to any qualifying child or any qualifying children, either the person with care or the [⁶non-resident parent] may apply to the [¹¹ [¹²Secretary of State]] for a [³maintenance calculation] to be made under this Act with respect to that child, or any of those children.

(2)   Where a [³maintenance calculation] has been made in response to an application under this section the [¹¹[¹²Secretary of State]] may, if the person with care or [⁶non-resident parent] with respect to whom the [⁴calculation] was made applies to [¹¹ [¹²the Secretary of State]] under this subsection, arrange for–

(a)   the collection of the child support maintenance payable in accordance with the [⁴calculation];

(b)   the enforcement of the obligation to pay child support maintenance in accordance with the [⁴calculation].

(3)   Where an application under subsection (2) for the enforcement of the obligation mentioned in subsection (2)(b) authorises the [¹¹[¹²Secretary of State]] to take steps to enforce that obligation whenever [¹¹ [¹²the Secretary of State]] considers it necessary to do so, the [¹¹[¹²Secretary of State]] may act accordingly.

(4)   A person who applies to the [¹¹[¹²Secretary of State]] under this section shall, so far as that person reasonably can, comply with such regulations as may be made by the Secretary of State with a view to the [¹¹[¹²Secretary of State]] [...¹] being provided with the information which is required to enable–

(a)   the [⁶non-resident parent] to be [⁷identified or] traced (where that is necessary);

(b)   the amount of child support maintenance payable by the [⁶non-resident parent] to be assessed; and

(c)   that amount to be recovered from the [⁶non-resident parent].

(5)   Any person who has applied to the [¹¹[¹²Secretary of State]] under this section may at any time request [¹¹[¹²the Secretary of State]] to cease acting under this section.

(6)   It shall be the duty of the [¹¹[¹²Secretary of State]] to comply with any request made under subsection (5) (but subject to any regulations made under subsection (8)).

(7)   The obligation to provide information which is imposed by subsection (4)–

(a)   shall not apply in such circumstances as may be prescribed; and

(b)   may, in such circumstances as may be prescribed, by waived by the [¹¹[¹²Secretary of State]].

(8)   The Secretary of State may by regulations make such incidental, sup-plemental or transitional provision as he thinks appropriate with respect to cases in which he is requested to cease to act under this section.

(9)   [¹⁰...].

[²ʲ(10)   No application may be made at any time under this section with respect to a qualifying child or any qualifying children if–

(a)   there is in force a written maintenance agreement made before 5th April 1993, or a maintenance order [⁵made before a prescribed date], in respect of that child, or those children and the person who is, at that time, the [⁶non-resident parent]; or

[⁵(aa) a maintenance order made on or after the date prescribed for the purposes of paragraph (a) is in force in respect of them, but has been so for less than the period of one year beginning with the date on which it was made; or].

[⁸(ab) a maintenance agreement–

(i)   made on or after the date prescribed for the purposes of paragraph (a); and

(ii)   registered for execution in the Books of Council and Session or the sheriff court books,

is in force in respect of them, but has been so for less than the period of one year beginning with the date on which it was made; [⁹...]]

(b)   [⁹...]]

(11)   [¹⁰...]]

Note

i.   In accordance with s18(6) of the Child Support Act 1995, (c.34), s4(10) is disapplied for maintenance orders under s8(7) or (8).

Amendments

1.   Repealed (1.6.99) by Sch 8 Social Security Act 1998 (c.14).

2.   s4(10) and (11) added (4.9.95) by s18(1) Child Support Act 1995 (c.34).

3.   Child Support, Pensions and Social Security Act 2000 (2000 c.19) s1(2) (March 3, 2003 for the types of cases in art 3 Child Support, Pensions and Social Security Act 2000 (Commencement No.12) Order 2003 (SI 2003 No.192)). For other types of cases see '1993 rules' below.

4.   Child Support, Pensions and Social Security Act 2000 (2000 c.19) s1(2) (March 3, 2003 for the types of cases in art 3 Child Support, Pensions and Social Security Act 2000 (Commencement No.12) Order 2003 (SI 2003 No.192)). For other types of cases see '1993 rules' below.

5.   Child Support, Pensions and Social Security Act 2000 (2000 c.19) s2 (March 3, 2003 for the types of cases in art 3 Child Support, Pensions and Social Security Act 2000 (Commencement No.12) Order 2003 (SI 2003 No.192)). For other types of cases see '1993 rules' below.

6.   Child Support, Pensions and Social Security Act 2000 (2000 c.19) s26 and Sch 3 para 11(2) (March 3, 2003 for the types of cases in art 3 Child Support, Pensions and Social Security Act 2000 (Commencement No.12) Order 2003 (SI 2003 No.192)). For other types of cases see '1993 rules' below.

7.   Child Support, Pensions and Social Security Act 2000 (2000 c.19) s26 and Sch 3 para 11(3) (March 3, 2003 for the types of cases in art 3 Child Support, Pensions and Social Security Act 2000 (Commencement No.12) Order 2003 (SI 2003 No.192)). For other types of cases see '1993 rules' below.

8.   Child Maintenance and Other Payments Act 2008 (2008 c.6) s35(1) (June 6, 2008).

9.   Child Maintenance and Other Payments Act 2008 (2008 c 6) s58 and Sch 8 (July 14, 2008 subject to art 2(4)-(5) Child Maintenance and Other Payments Act 2008 (Commencement) Order 2008 (SI 2008 No.1476 (c.67); October 27, 2008 for all other cases subject to art 4 Child Maintenance and Other Payments Act 2008 (Commencement No.3 and Transitional and Savings Provisions) Order 2008 (SI 2008 No.2548)). This repealed s4(10)(b) and "or" immediately before it, s4(10)(b) read:

"(b)   benefit is being paid to, or in respect of, a parent with care of that child or those children."

10.   Child Maintenance and Other Payments Act 2008 (2008 c.6) s58 and Sch 8 (October 27, 2008 subject to art 4 Child Maintenance and Other Payments Act 2008 (Commencement No.3 and Transitional and Savings Provisions) Order 2008 (SI 2008 No.2548)). This amendment omitted subss 4(9) and (11). Prior to this, these subss read:

"(9)   No application may be made under this section if there is in force with respect to the person with care and [⁶non-resident parent] in question a [³maintenance calculation] made in response to an application [⁷treated as made] under section 6.

(11)   In subsection (10) "benefit" means any benefit which is mentioned in, or prescribed by regulations under, section 6(1)."

11.   Child Maintenance and Other Payments Act 2008 (2008 c.6) s13 and Sch 3 para 3 (November 1, 2008). Child Maintenance and Other Payments Act 2008 (Commencement No.4 and Transitional Provision) Order 2008 (SI 2008 No.2675) art 3.

12.   Public Bodies (Child Maintenance and Enforcement Commission: Abolition and Transfer of Functions) Order 2012 (SI 2012 No.2007) art 3(2) and Sch para 3 (August 1, 2012).

1993 rules

Ss1(2), 2 and 26 and Sch 3 of the Child Support, Pensions and Social Security Act 2000 (2000 c.19) amend s4 of the Child Support Act 1991 and have been brought into force only for the types of cases in art 3 of the Child Support, Pensions and Social Security Act 2000 (Commencement No.12) Order 2003 (SI 2003 No.192 – see p683). For other types of cases the 1993 rules apply and the original wording is retained – ie, "maintenance assessment" is retained in place of "maintenance calculation", "assessment" is retained in place of "calculation" and "absent parent" is retained in place of "non-resident parent". In addition, in subsection 4(4)(a) the words "identified or" are omitted, in subsection 4(9) the words "treated as made" are omitted and in subsection 4(10) the words "made before a prescribed date" and paragraph (aa) are omitted.

Definitions

"child support maintenance": see s3(6).
"maintenance agreement": see s54.
"maintenance calculation": see s54.
"maintenance order": see s54.
"non-resident parent": see s3(2).
"person with care": see s3(3).
"prescribed": see s54.
"qualifying child": see s3(1).

General Note

A child support maintenance calculation is initiated by an application that is actually made or treated as made. It may be initiated by a non-resident parent, a person with care or a child. An application may be made under this section by a non-resident parent or a person with care. In Scotland, an application may also be made under s7 by a child who has attained the age of 12.

Subsection (1)

Any non-resident parent and, subject to s5(1), any person with care may apply for a maintenance assessment in respect of a child. This is subject to subs (9). A non-resident parent may wish to apply in order to fix the extent of responsibility under this Act (see s1(2)).

Subsection (2)

A person with care or a non-resident parent may authorise (subss (2) and (3)) the Secretary of State to arrange for the collection of child support maintenance and the enforcement of the obligation to pay it. The obligation to pay which is referred to in para (b) is the duty created by s1(3). Matters relating to the collection and enforcement of child support maintenance are for the Secretary of State and are dealt with in regs 29 to 41.

Subsection (4)

A person who authorises the Secretary of State to arrange for collection and enforcement under subss (2) and (3) is required to co-operate by providing the information specified in this subsection. The regulations are to be found in the Information Regulations. The duty to co-operate is a qualified one. This subsection provides that it only applies in so far as it is reasonably possible for that person to comply and it is further limited by the conditions set out in the Regulations. Wider duties concerning the provision of information are created under s14(1) which are also contained in Pt 2 of the Regulations. This subsection applies only to the supply of information, whereas s14(1) applies to both information and evidence. For a discussion of the meaning of "information" in this section and for enforcement, see the general note to s14(1) on p39. See also the offence under s14A on p40.

Subsection (5)

This subsection only provides for the Secretary of State to *cease* acting. It does not authorise the cancellation of the maintenance assessment (*CCS 13/1994*, para 6). Accordingly, the assessment remains valid for the period prior to the cessation of action by the Secretary of State. If a tribunal is in doubt whether an application under this section has been received by the Secretary of State, it is an error of law not to clarify this (by adjournment if necessary) if there is evidence to believe that such a request has been made *(ibid,* para 8).

Subsection (8)
No regulations have been made under this subsection, although the circumstances in which the duty to disclose will arise are limited by reg 7(1) of the Information Regulations to cases where either the information or evidence is in the possession of the person concerned or it can reasonably be expected to be acquired by that person.

Subsections (10) and (11)
See the general note to s18 of the 1995 Act on p172. The non-resident parent referred to is the person who was the non-resident parent at the time when the order or agreement was made (*CCS 2567/1998*, para 11, relying on the reasoning of the Court of Appeal in refusing leave to appeal against the decision in *R(CS) 4/96* in *Kirkley v Secretary of State for Social Security and the Child Support Officer,* unreported, December 15, 1995).

Subsection (10)(a)
3 March 2003 is the date prescribed for the purposes of subs (10)(a) by reg 2(a) Child Support (Applications: Prescribed Date) Regulations 2003.

Subsection (10)(aa)
A court order for child maintenance, whether or not made on consent, should use the child support maintenance figure as a starting point in order to discourage an application under this Act as soon as the year has expired (*GW v RW (Financial Provision: Departure from Equality)* [2003] 2 FLR 108). An application for a maintenance calculation that is premature may have continuing effect until it is decided (*YW v CMEC (CSM)* [2011] UKUT 176 (AAC)).

Child support maintenance; supplemental provisions

5.–(1)   Where–

(a)   there is more than one person with care of a qualifying child; and

(b)   one or more, but not all, of them have parental responsibility for [¹ ...] the child;

no application may be made for a [² maintenance calculation] with respect to the child by any of those persons who do not have parental responsibility for [¹ ...] the child.

(2)   Where more than one application for a [² maintenance calculation] is made with respect to the child concerned, only one of them may be proceeded with.

(3)   The Secretary of State may by regulations make provision as to which of two or more applications for a [² maintenance calculation] with respect to the same child is to be proceeded with.

Amendments
1.   Children (Scotland) Act 1995 para 52(3) and Sch 4 (November 1, 1996).
2.   Child Support, Pensions and Social Security Act 2000 (2000 c.19) s1(2) (March 3, 2003 for the types of cases in art 3 Child Support, Pensions and Social Security Act 2000 (Commencement No.12) Order 2003 (SI 2003 No.192)). For other types of cases see '1993 rules' below.

1993 rules
s1(2) of the Child Support, Pensions and Social Security Act 2000 (2000 c.19) amends s5 of the Child Support Act 1991. This has been brought into force only for the types of cases in art 3 of the Child Support, Pensions and Social Security Act 2000 (Commencement No.12) Order 2003 (SI 2003 No.192 – see p683). For other types of cases the 1993 rules apply and the original wording is retained – ie, "maintenance assessment" is retained in place of "maintenance calculation".

Definitions
"maintenance calculation": see s54.
"parental responsibility": see s54.
"person with care": see s3(3).
"prescribed": see s54.
"qualifying child": see s3(1).

General Note
Subsection (1)
If there is more than one person with care, only those with parental responsibility for the qualifying child may apply for a maintenance calculation. However, if there is only one person with care, that person may apply for a calculation regardless of who has parental responsibility.

Subsections (2) and (3)
Only one application for a maintenance calculation in respect of a child may be proceeded with. If more than one is made, the priority between any that cannot be eliminated under subs (1) is determined under the provisions of reg 4 of, and Sch 2 to, the Maintenance Calculation Procedure Regulations. If an attempt is made to make an application for a maintenance calculation at a time when such an application may not be made (as to which see

the general note to s18 of the 1995 Act on p172), that application is ignored and is irrelevant to the question of priority of applications.

[⁴ Applications by those claiming or receiving benefit
6.   [⁶...]]

Amendments

1.   Inserted (7.10.96) by para 20(2) of Sch 2 to Jobseekers Act 1995 (c18).
2.   Social Security Act 1998 (1998 s14) Sch 8 (June 1, 1999).
3.   Tax Credits Act 1999 (1999 c.10) Sch 1 para 17(a) (October 5, 1999).
4.   Child Support, Pensions and Social Security Act 2000 (2000 c.19) s3 (March 3, 2003 for the types of cases in art 4 Child Support, Pensions and Social Security Act 2000 (Commencement No.12) Order 2003 (SI 2003 No.192)).
5.   Child Maintenance and Other Payments Act 2008 (2008 c.6) s13 and Sch 3, para 4 (November 1, 2008). Child Maintenance and Other Payments Act 2008 (Commencement No.4 and Transitional Provision) Order 2008 (SI 2008 No.2675) art 3
6.   Child Maintenance and Other Payments Act 2008 (2008 c.6) s15(a) (July 14, 2008 subject to art 2(4)-(5) Child Maintenance and Other Payments Act 2008 (Commencement) Order 2008 (SI 2008 No.1476 (c.67); October 27, 2008 for all other cases subject to art 4 Child Maintenance and Other Payments Act 2008 (Commencement No.3 and Transitional and Savings Provisions) Order 2008 (SI 2008 No.2548)); June 1, 2009 so far as not already in force, see Child Maintenance and Other Payments Act 2008 (Commencement No.5) Order 2009 (SI 2009 No.1314) art 2(2)(c)).

Right of child in Scotland to apply for assessment

7.–(1)   A qualifying child who has attained the age of 12 years and who is habitually resident in Scotland may apply to the [¹⁰[¹²Secretary of State]] for a [³maintenance calculation] to be made with respect to him if–

(a)   no such application has been made by a person who is, with respect to that child, a person with care of [⁵a non-resident parent]; [⁹...]

[⁶(b)   [⁹,¹¹...]]

(2)   An application made under subsection (1) shall authorise the [¹⁰[¹²Secretary of State]] to make a [³ maintenance calculation] with respect to any other children of the [⁵ non-resident parent] who are qualifying children in the care of the same person as the child making the application.

(3)   Where a [³ maintenance calculation] has been made in response to an application under this section the [¹⁰[¹²Secretary of State]] may, if the person with care, the [⁵ non-resident parent] with respect to whom the [⁴ calculation] was made or the child concerned applies to [¹⁰[¹²the Secretary of State]] under this subsection, arrange for–

(a)   the collection of the child support maintenance payable in accordance with the [⁴ calculation];

(b)   the enforcement of the obligation to pay child support maintenance in accordance with the [⁴ calculation].

(4)   Where an application under subsection (3) for the enforcement of the obligation mentioned in subsection (3)(b) authorises the [¹⁰[¹²Secretary of State]] to take steps to enforce that obligation whenever [¹⁰[¹²the Secretary of State]] considers it necessary to do so, the [¹⁰[¹²Secretary of State]] may act accordingly.

(5)   Where a child has asked the [¹⁰[¹²Secretary of State]] to proceed under this section, the person with care of the child, the [⁵ non-resident parent] and the child concerned shall, so far as they reasonably can, comply with such regulations as may be made by the Secretary of State with a view to the [¹⁰[¹²Secretary of State]] [...¹] being provided with the information which is required to enable–

(a)   the [⁵ non-resident parent] to be traced (where that is necessary);

(b)   the amount of child support maintenance payable by the [⁵non-resident parent] to be [⁴ calculated]; and

(c)   that amount to be recovered from the [⁵non-resident parent].

(6)   The child who has made the application (but not the person having care of him) may at any time request the [¹⁰[¹²Secretary of State]] to cease acting under this section.

(7)   It shall be the duty of the [¹⁰[¹²Secretary of State]] to comply with any request made under subsection (6) (but subject to any regulations made under subsection (9)).

(8)   The obligation to provide information which is imposed by subsection (5)–

(a)   shall not apply in such circumstances as may be prescribed by the Secretary of State; and

(b)   may, in such circumstances as may be so prescribed, be waived by the [¹⁰[¹²Secretary of State]].

(9)   The Secretary of State may by regulations make such incidental, supplemental or transitional provision as he thinks appropriate with respect to cases in which he is requested to cease to act under this section.

[²(10)   No application may be made at any time under this section by a qualifying child if

[⁷ (a)] there is in force a written maintenance agreement made before 5th April 1993, or a maintenance order [⁷ made before a prescribed date], in respect of that child and the person who is, at that time, the [⁵ non-resident parent]] [⁷or

(b)   a maintenance order made on or after the date prescribed for the purposes of paragraph (a) is in force in respect of them, but has been so for less than the period of one year beginning with the date on which it was made.][⁸; or

(c)   a maintenance agreement–

    (i)   made on or after the date prescribed for the purposes of paragraph (a); and

    (ii)   registered for execution in the Books of Council and Session or the sheriff court books,

is in force in respect of them, but has been so for less than the period of one year beginning with the date on which it was made.]

Amendments

1.   Repealed (1.6.99) by Sch 8 Social Security Act 1998 (c.14).

2.   s7(10) added (4.9.95) by Child Support Act 1995 (c.34), s18(2). By virtue of s18(6) Child Support Act 1995 (c.34), s7(10) is disapplied for maintenance orders under s8(7) or (8).

3.   Child Support, Pensions and Social Security Act 2000 (2000 c.19) s1(2) (March 3, 2003 for the types of cases detailed in art 3 Child Support, Pensions and Social Security Act 2000 (Commencement No.12) Order 2003 (SI 2003 No.192)). For other types of cases see '1993 rules' below.

4.   Child Support, Pensions and Social Security Act 2000 (2000 c.19) s1(2) (March 3, 2003 for the types of cases detailed in art 3 Child Support, Pensions and Social Security Act 2000 (Commencement No.12) Order 2003 (SI 2003 No.192)). For other types of cases see '1993 rules' below.

5.   Child Support, Pensions and Social Security Act 2000 (2000 c.19) s26 and Sch 3 para 11(2) (March 3, 2003 for the types of cases in art 3 Child Support, Pensions and Social Security Act 2000 (Commencement No.12) Order 2003 (SI 2003 No.192)). For other types of cases see '1993 rules' below.

6.   Child Support, Pensions and Social Security Act 2000 (2000 c.19) s26 and Sch 3 para 11(4)(a) (March 3, 2003 for the types of cases in art 3 Child Support, Pensions and Social Security Act 2000 (Commencement No.12) Order 2003 (SI 2003 No.192)). For other types of cases see '1993 rules' below.

7.   Child Support, Pensions and Social Security Act 2000 (2000 c.19) s26 and Sch 3 para 11(4)(b) (March 3, 2003 for the types of cases in art 3 Child Support, Pensions and Social Security Act 2000 (Commencement No.12) Order 2003 (SI 2003 No.192)). For other types of cases see '1993 rules' below.

8.   Child Maintenance and Other Payments Act 2008 (2008 c.6) s35 (June 6, 2008).

9.   Child Maintenance and Other Payments Act 2008 (2008 c.6) s58 and Sch 8 (July 14, 2008 subject to art 2(4)-(5) Child Maintenance and Other Payments Act 2008 (Commencement) Order 2008 (SI 2008 No.1476 (c.67)). This repeals s7(1)(b) and the word "or" immediately before it, does not apply in relation to existing cases as defined in art 2(5) of SI 2008 No.1476, and for such cases s7(1)(b) read:

[(b)   no parent has been treated under section 6(3) as having applied for a maintenance calculation with respect to the child.]

10.   Child Maintenance and Other Payments Act 2008 (2008 c.6) Sch 3 para 5 (November 1, 2008). Brought into force by Child Maintenance and Other Payments Act 2008 (Commencement No.4 and Transitional Provision) Order 2008 (SI 2008 No.2675) art 3.

11.   Child Maintenance and Other Payments Act 2008 (2008 c.6) s58 and Sch 8 (June 1, 2009).

12.   Public Bodies (Child Maintenance and Enforcement Commission: Abolition and Transfer of Functions) Order 2012 (SI 2012 No.2007) art 3(2) and Sch para 4 (August 1, 2012).

1993 rules

Ss1(2) and 26 and sch 3 of the Child Support, Pensions and Social Security Act 2000 (2000 c.19) amend s7 of the Child Support Act 1991 and have been brought into force only for the types of cases in art 3 of the Child

Support, Pensions and Social Security Act 2000 (Commencement No.12) Order 2003 (SI 2003 No.192 – see p683). For other types of cases the 1993 rules apply and the original wording is retained – ie, "maintenance assessment" is retained in place of "maintenance calculation", "assessment" is retained in place of "calculation" and "absent parent" is retained in place of "non-resident parent". In addition, if the 1993 rules apply, subsection (1)(b) is as follows:

(b)   the [¹⁰Commission] has not been authorised under section 6 to take action under this Act to recover child support maintenance from the absent parent (other than in a case where he has waived any requirement that he should be so authorised).

and in subsection (10) "(a)" is omitted and the words "made before a prescribed date" and paragraph (b) are not included.

Definitions
"child": see s55.
"child support maintenance": see s3(6).
"maintenance agreement": see s54.
"maintenance calculation": see s54.
"non-resident parent": see s3(2).
"person with care": see s3(3).
"prescribed": see s54.
"qualifying child": see s3(1).

General Note
This section applies only to Scotland (s58(10)) and is a consequence of the different age of legal capacity in Scotland from England and Wales as a result of the limited effect of the Age of Legal Capacity (Scotland) Act 1991. It allows a child who has attained the age of 12 to apply for a maintenance calculation. Two conditions must be satisfied. First, no application must have been made by a non-resident parent or a person with care. Second, the Secretary of State must not have treated an application as made under s6. An application by a child authorises the Sectretary of State to make a calculation in respect of all other qualifying children of the absent parent who are in the care of the person with care of the child who has applied under this section (subs (2)).

After an application has been made the child may request the Secretary of State to cease acting under this section but the parent with care may not do so (subs (6)). If requested by the child the Secretary of State must comply with the request, subject to any regulations made under subs (9).

Except in these respects this section mirrors provisions in ss4 and 6. Reference should be made to the general note to the equivalent provisions in those sections. The regulations referred to are to be found in the Information, Evidence and Disclosure Regulations. No regulations have been made under subss (8) and (9), although the circumstances in which the duty to disclose will arise are limited by reg 2(1) to cases where either the information or evidence is in the possession of the person concerned or it can reasonably be expected to be acquired by that person. Wider duties concerning the provision of information can be acquired by that person. Wider duties concerning the provision of information are created under s14(1) which are also contained in Pt II of the Regulations. This subsection applies only to the supply of information, whereas s14(1) applies to both information and evidence. For a discussion of the meaning of "information" in this section and for enforcement, see the general note to s14(1) on p39. See also the offence under s14A on p40.

Subsection (10)
See the general note to s18 of the 1995 Act on p172.

3 March 2003 is the date prescribed for the purposes of subs (10)(a) by reg 2(b) Child Support (Applications: Prescribed Date) Regulations 2003.

Role of the courts with respect to maintenance for children

8.–(1)   This subsection applies in any case where [⁶ the [¹¹[¹²Secretary of State]] would have jurisdiction to make a [² maintenance calculation] with respect to a qualifying child and [⁴a non-resident parent] of his on an application duly made [⁵ [¹⁰...]] by a person entitled to apply for such [³ a calculation] with respect to that child.

(2)   Subsection (1) applies even though the circumstances of the case are such that [⁶ the [¹¹[¹²Secretary of State]]] would not make [³ a calculation] if it were applied for.

(3)   [⁵ Except as provided in subsection (3A),] in any case where subsection (1) applies, no court shall exercise any power which it would otherwise have to make, vary or revive any maintenance order in relation to the child and [⁴ non-resident parent] concerned.

[⁵ (3A)   Unless a maintenance calculation has been made with respect to the child concerned, subsection (3) does not prevent a court from varying a maintenance order in relation to that child and the non-resident parent concerned–

    (a)   if the maintenance order was made on or after the date prescribed for the purposes of section 4(10)(a) or 7(10)(a); or

    (b)   where the order was made before then, in any case in which section 4(10) or 7(10) prevents the making of an application for a maintenance calculation with respect to or by that child.]

    (4)   Subsection (3) does not prevent a court from revoking a maintenance order.

    (5)   The Lord Chancellor or in relation to Scotland the Lord Advocate may by order provide that, in such circumstances as may be specified by the order, this section shall not prevent a court from exercising any power which it has to make a maintenance order in relation to a child if–

    (a)   a written agreement (whether or not enforceable) provides for the making, or securing, by [⁴a non-resident parent] of the child of periodical payments to or for the benefit of the child; and

    (b)   the maintenance order which the court makes is, in all material respects,

in the same terms as that agreement.

[⁹(5A)   The Lord Chancellor may make an order under subsection (5) only with the concurrence of the Lord Chief Justice.]

    (6)   This section shall not prevent a court from exercising any power which it has to make a maintenance order in relation to a child if–

    (a)   a [²maintenance calculation] is in force with respect to the child;

    [⁵(b)   the non-resident parent's [¹³gross] weekly income exceeds the figure referred to in paragraph 10(3) of Schedule 1 (as it has effect from time to time pursuant to regulations made under paragraph 10A(1)(b)); and]

    (c)   the court is satisfied that the circumstances of the case make it appropriate for the [⁴ non-resident parent] to make or secure the making of periodical payments under a maintenance order in addition to the child support maintenance payable by him in accordance with the [² maintenance calculation].

    (7)   This section shall not prevent a court from exercising any power which it has to make a maintenance order in relation to a child if–

    (a)   the child is, will be or (if the order were to be made) would be receiving instruction at an educational establishment or undergoing training for a trade, profession or vocation (whether or not while in gainful employment);and

    (b)   the order is made solely for the purposes of requiring the person making or securing the making of periodical payments fixed by the order to meet some or all of the expenses incurred in connection with the provision of the instruction or training.

    (8)   This section shall not prevent a court from exercising any power which it has to make a maintenance order in relation to a child if–

    (a)   [¹⁴an allowance under Part 4 of the Welfare Reform Act 2012 (personal independence payment) or] a disability living allowance is paid to or in respect of him; or

    (b)   no such allowance is paid but he is disabled,

and the order is made solely for the purpose of requiring the person making or securing the making of periodical payments fixed by the order to meet some or all of any expenses attributable to the child's disability.

    (9)   For the purposes of subsection (8), a child is disabled if he is blind, deaf or dumb or is substantially and permanently handicapped by illness, injury, mental disorder or congenital deformity or such other disability as may be prescribed.

    (10)   This section shall not prevent a court from exercising any power which it has to make a maintenance order in relation to a child if the order is made against a person with care of the child.

    (11)   In this Act "maintenance order", in relation to any child, means an order which requires the making or securing of periodical payments to or for the benefit of the child and which is made under–

    (a)   Part II of the Matrimonial Causes Act 1973;

    (b)   the Domestic Proceedings and Magistrates' Courts Act 1978;

    (c)   Part III of the Matrimonial and Family Proceedings Act 1984;

(d)   the Family Law (Scotland) Act 1985;
(e)   Schedule 1 to the Children Act 1989; [⁷ ...]
[⁸(ea) Schedule 5, 6 or 7 to the Civil Partnership Act 2004; or]
(f)   any other prescribed enactment.
and includes any order varying or reviving such an order.
   [⁹(12) The Lord Chief Justice may nominate a judicial office holder (as defined in section 109(4) of the Constitutional Reform Act 2005) to exercise his functions under this section.]

Amendments

1.   Inserted (4.9.95) by Child Support Act 1995 (c.34), s18(3).
2.   Child Support, Pensions and Social Security Act 2000 (2000 c.19) s1(2) (March 3, 2003 for the types of cases in art 3 Child Support, Pensions and Social Security Act 2000 (Commencement No.12) Order 2003 (SI 2003 No.192)). For other types of cases, see '1993 rules' below.
3.   Child Support, Pensions and Social Security Act 2000 (2000 c.19) s1(2) (March 3, 2003 for the types of cases in art 3 Child Support, Pensions and Social Security Act 2000 (Commencement No.12) Order 2003 (SI 2003 No.192)). For other types of cases, see '1993 rules' below.
4.   Child Support, Pensions and Social Security Act 2000 (2000 c.19) s26 and Sch 3 para 11(2) (March 3, 2003 for the types of cases in art 3 Child Support, Pensions and Social Security Act 2000 (Commencement No.12) Order 2003 (SI 2003 No.192)). For other types of cases, see '1993 rules' below.
5.   Child Support, Pensions and Social Security Act 2000 (2000 c.19) s26 and Sch 3 para 11(5) (March 3, 2003 for the types of cases in art 3 Child Support, Pensions and Social Security Act 2000 (Commencement No.12) Order 2003 (SI 2003 No.192)). For other types of cases, see '1993 rules' below.
6.   Social Security Act 1998 (1998 c.14) Sch 7 para 22 (June 1, 1999).
7.   Civil Partnership Act 2004 (2004 c.33) s261(4) and Sch 30 (December 5, 2005).
8.   Civil Partnership Act 2004 (2004 c.33) s254 and Sch 24 para 1 (December 5, 2005).
9.   Constitutional Reform Act 2005 (2005 c.4) s15 and Sch 4 para 219 (April 3, 2006).
10.   Child Maintenance and Other Payments Act 2008 (2008 c.6) s58 and Sch 8 (October 27, 2008 subject to art 4 Child Maintenance and Other Payments Act 2008 (Commencement No.3 and Transitional and Savings Provisions) Order 2008 (SI 2008 No.2548)). This omitted "(or treated as made)".
11.   Child Maintenance and Other Payments Act 2008 (2008 c.6) s13 and Sch 3, para 6 (November 1, 2008). Child Maintenance and Other Payments Act 2008 (Commencement No.4 and Transitional Provision) Order 2008 (SI 2008 No.2675) art 3.
12.   Public Bodies (Child Maintenance and Enforcement Commission: Abolition and Transfer of Functions) Order 2012 (SI 2012 No.2007) art 3(2) and Sch para 5 (August 1, 2012).
13.   Child Maintenance and Other Payments Act 2008 (2008 c.6) s57 and Sch 7 para 1(2) (December 10, 2012 for the types of cases falling within art 3 of SI 2012 No.3042, subject to art 5 of that SI – see p767 and July 29, 2013 for the types of cases falling within art 3 of SI 2013 No.1860, subject to art 5 of that SI – see p770). See also art 6 of SI 2012 No,3042 (which had effect up to and including July 28, 2013) and art. 7 of SI 2013 No.1860 for further transitional provisions. For other types of cases see '1993 rules' and '2003 rules' below. Child Maintenance and Other Payments Act 2008 (Commencement No.10 and Transitional Provisions) Order 2012 (SI 2012 No.3042) art 2; Child Maintenance and Other Payments Act 2008 (Commencement No.11 and Transitional Provisions) Order 2013 (SI 2013 No.1860) art 2.
14.   Welfare Reform Act 2012 (2012 c.5) s91 and Sch 9 para 2 (April 8, 2013 in relation to a person whose only or principal residence is, on the date on which that person makes a claim for personal independence payment, located in an area specified in Sch 3 of SI 2013 No.358; June 10, 2013 in relation to all other people); Welfare Reform Act 2012 (Commencement No.8 and Savings and Transitional Provisions) Order 2013 (SI 2013 No.358) art 7 and Welfare Reform Act 2012 (Commencement No.10) Order 2013 (SI 2013 No.1250) art 2.

2003 rules

ss57 and sch 7 of the Child Maintenance and Other Payments Act 2008 (2008 c.6) amends paragraph 8(6)(b) of the Child Support Act 1991 for the types of cases falling within art 3 of SI 2012 No.3042, subject to art 5 of that SI – see p767 and art 3 of of SI 2013 No.1860, subject to art 5 of that SI – see p770. See also art 6 of SI 2012 No.3042 (which had effect up to and including July 28, 2013) and art 7 of SI 2013 No.1860 for further transitional provisions. For other types of cases, this amendment does not apply and the word "net" is retained in place of "gross".

1993 rules

Ss1(2) and 26 and Sch 3 of the Child Support, Pensions and Social Security Act 2000 (2000 c.19) amend s8 of the Child Support Act 1991 and have been brought into force only for the types of cases in art 3 of the Child Support, Pensions and Social Security Act 2000 (Commencement No.12) Order 2003 (SI 2003 No.192 – see p683). For other types of cases the 1993 rules apply and the original wording is retained – ie, "maintenance assessment" is retained in place of "maintenance calculation", "assessment" is retained in place of "calculation" and "absent parent" is retained in place of "non-resident parent". Also, the words "Except as provided in subsection (3A)," are not included in subsection (3), subsection (3A) reads as follows:

[(3A)   In any case in which section 4(10) or 7(10) prevents the making of an application for a maintenance assessment, and–

(a)   no application has been made for a maintenance assessment under section 6, or

(b)   such an application has been made but no maintenance assessment has been made in response to it,

subsection (3) shall have effect with the omission of the word "vary".]

and paragraph (6)(b) reads as follows:

(b)   the amount of the child support maintenance payable in accordance with the assessment was determined by reference to the alternative formula mentioned in paragraph 4(3) of Schedule 1; and

Definitions

"child": see s55.
"child benefit": see s54.
"child support maintenance": see s3(6).
"disability living allowance": see s54.
"maintenance calculation": see s54.
"non-resident parent": see s3(2).
"person with care": see s3(3).
"prescribed": see s54.
"qualifying child": see s3(1).

General Note

Sections 8 to 10 provide for the relationship between maintenance calculation on the one hand and maintenance orders made by the courts and maintenance agreements on the other hand. Section 8 gives the child support scheme priority over the court system if the Secretary of State would have jurisdiction to make a maintenance calculation were an application to be made, regardless of whether or not an application has been made. In such a case the courts may not make, vary or revive a maintenance order, although they may revoke one. This applies even if, despite the child support maintenance calculation, the parents had little or no involvement with the Secretary of State and misled the court on the existence of the calculation (*CCS 2465/2005*).

A startling illustration of the effects of this section is given in *Phillips v Peace* [1996] 2 FLR 230. The father lived in a house valued at £2.6 million and owned three motor cars together worth nearly £200,000. He carried on a share dealing business and, at the time of the child support maintenance assessment, was paid no salary by his (own) company. The child support officer accordingly assessed him as having as nil liability under the Act. The mother sought provision for the child under the remaining jurisdiction of the courts, to award lump sums and property adjustment orders (Sch 1 to the Children Act 1989). Johnson J held that where jurisdiction to make an assessment lay with the Agency, the court should exercise its power to award a lump sum only in order to meet the need of a child in respect of a particular item of capital expenditure. Thus, he would order a sum of £90,000 to be paid so that a home could be purchased for the child and mother to live in, but he could not order a lump sum as a form of capitalised maintenance. If he had been able to do so, he would have ordered an amount based on £90 a week for the next year or so. His lordship commented that this appeared to be a suitable case for a departure direction (now called a variation), but it also seems strange that the child support officer apparently made no attempt to apply the regulations dealing with amounts treated as income (see Pt V of Sch 1 to the Maintenance Assessments and Special Cases, Regulations), still less to extract the minimum amount of support from the father. It is worth comparing the (apparent) powerlessness of the Child Support Agency in this case with the Court of Appeal decision in *Thomas v Thomas* [1995] 2 FLR 668. There, a husband who ran a successful family business and was a Lloyds name, but had cash-flow problems, was ordered to pay a lump sum to his wife in a divorce settlement, even though in effect he would have to be helped to raise it by members of his family. The court considered that, where a husband has liquidity problems but possesses substantial means (a house and pension assets), the onus is on him to satisfy the court that all means of access to funds to make provision for the wife have been found to be impossible. The court was entitled to find that funds would be forthcoming to him. While the courts will be careful not to require a person to sell off a business which provides his livelihood, this case demonstrates that they are able, and willing, to look behind the ostensible picture and to ensure that fair liabilities to the family are met.

An award of child maintenance made under this section will be based on the assumption that a parent with care who has received a substantial share of the parents' assets on divorce will contribute to the support of the child (*GW v RW (Financial Provision: Departure from Equality)* [2003] 2 FLR 108 at para 75). If the award is made in respect of a child who is living abroad, it should be expressed in the currency of the child's residence in order to avoid the risk of currency fluctuation *(ibid,* para 76).

Subsection (3)

Although the court loses its power to make, vary or revive a maintenance order, it retains the power to *enforce* such an order. This, however, will only apply to arrears which accrued prior to the Secretary of State assuming jurisdiction.

Schedule 1 to the Child Maintenance Orders (Backdating) Order 1993 inserts s31(11) into the Matrimonial Causes Act 1973, s20(9A) into the Domestic Proceedings and Magistrates' Courts Act 1978, and Sch 1, para 6(9) into the Children Act 1989 to provide for backdating to the effective date or any later date where an application is made to vary or discharge an order which provided for periodical payments for children without apportioning the payments between them, and a maintenance calculation is made in respect of one or more, but not all of the children. This is to ensure that the non-resident parent is not obliged to continue paying the full amount under the order, in addition to the amount calculated under the maintenance calculation.

The Family Division of the High Court has held that the implementation of the Child Support Act is not an event which fundamentally undermines the assumption upon which a clean break settlement made some years previously between divorcing spouses was based, and thus does not justify the settlement being set aside. In *Crozier v Crozier* [1994] Fam 114, the absent parent had made such a settlement, transferring his interest in the former matrimonial home to the wife at the time of the divorce in 1989. He had been paying £4 a week as a liable relative for his child's maintenance, and faced an increase to around £29 under the formula assessment. Booth J regarded the increase as due to a procedural change and not because of any new power taken by the state. However, in *Mawson v Mawson* [1994] 2 FLR 985, it was held that an appeal in respect of a divorce settlement made in 1993 would be allowed, *inter alia* because it had been predicated upon a maintenance assessment of some £600 a month, which had been reduced by £100 due to regulation changes in 1994. Thorpe J stated that such changes, as distinct from changes in the absent parent's own circumstances, could not have been foreseen by the trial judge, and so should be taken into account in deciding on the appropriate settlement for the wife. It is not easy to discern how it is deemed possible to alter a settlement due to unforeseen changes to the child support formula, as in *Mawson,* but not possible to set aside a settlement due to unforeseen legislation, as in *Crozier.* The cases are distinguishable on the rather narrow point that the passage of time elapsing between the first court order and the attempt to appeal was much less in *Mawson,* and this is a factor which the courts are required to take into account under the leading authority concerning setting-aside, *Barder v Caluori* [1988] AC 20. However, this was not the basis of the courts' reasoning in the two decisions, and the cases would appear to be in conflict at the level of principle. In *Smith v McInerney* [1994] 2 FLR 1077, another decision of Thorpe J, it was held that where a husband had parted with capital in part-commutation of his future obligation to maintain his children under a voluntary separation agreement, he should be provided with an indemnity, by means of a charge on the matrimonial home, in case the wife in future became a benefit recipient and hence probably required to seek a child support calculation under s6 of the Act. Otherwise, the husband would end up being made to pay twice for his children. The case is distinguishable from *Crozier* in so far as it relates to a voluntary agreement rather than a consent order, but once more, it appears to highlight a difference of opinion among the Family Division judges on the principles which should apply to dealing with the relationship between child support and financial relief on divorce.

Subsection (3A)

See the general note to s18 of the 1995 Act on p172.

Subsection (5)

This subsection together with the Child Maintenance (Written Agreements) Order 1993 preserves the courts' power to make consent orders in respect of periodical payments to or for the benefit of a child, even though the Secretary of State has jurisdiction to carry out a calculation.

Subsection (6)

For an example of the operation of this subsection in a complex case involving a consent order, a subsequent maintenance assessment and a later application for additional maintenance, see *H v C* [2009] 2 FLR 1540.

Subsection (7)

A court may make a maintenance order the sole purpose of which is to cover some or all of the payments for a child's instruction or training. The child must be receiving or going to receive some instruction.

A court has made an order to cover school fees even where the maintenance calculation is relatively modest. A district judge has ordered a husband who declared a gross income of £26,000 as a company director and who was required to pay £25 a week child maintenance to pay one-half of the child's school fees of £4,200 a year ([1994] NLJ 702).

An order providing for payment of boarding school fees, notwithstanding that it covers accommodation and maintenance as well as education, since these are paid in connection with the education (*NS v SSWP and PS* [2013] UKUT 0252 (AAC)).

Subsection (8)

A court may make a maintenance order the sole purpose of which is to meet some or all of the expenses attributable to a child's disability provided that either disability living allowance is payable to or in respect of the child or the child is disabled as defined in subs (9).

Subsections (6), (7) and (8)

Maintenance orders covered by these subsections are prescribed for the purposes of s30 by reg 2(a) of the Collection and Enforcement of Other Forms of Maintenance Regulations.

The Child Maintenance Orders (Backdating) Order 1993 adds s29(7) and (8) to the Matrimonial Causes Act 1973, s5(7) and (8) to the Domestic Proceedings and Magistrates' Courts Act 1978 and para 7(7) and (8) to Sch 1 to the Children Act 1989, to provide for where a maintenance calculation ceases to have effect or is cancelled under any provision of the Act, and an application for a periodical payments order in favour of the child is made. If the application for the order is made within six months of the date when the calculation ceased to have effect or, where the calculation was cancelled, the later of either the date it was cancelled or the date from which the cancellation first had effect, the order may begin from the date the calculation ceased to have effect, or the date with effect from which it was cancelled, or any later date. Again, the purpose is to remedy any shortfall in support which might otherwise occur between the ending of the calculation and the making of the order.

Schedule 1 to the Child Maintenance Orders (Backdating) Order 1993 allows maintenance orders to be backdated to the "earliest permitted date" which is the later of either (a) the date six months before the application was made, or (b) the effective date (see the general note to Sch 1 para 11) of a maintenance calculation made under the Child Support Act, (instead of to the date of the application to the court) provided that the application for the maintenance order is made within six months of the date of the calculation. The Order inserts s29(5)(b) into the Matrimonial Causes Act 1973, s5(5)(b) into the Domestic Proceedings and Magistrates' Courts Act 1978 and Sch 1 para 3(5)(b) into the Children Act 1989 to provide that where "top-up maintenance", etc. is awarded by a court, backdating can take place. This will protect the parent with care in the interim period between the making of the calculation (when an earlier order may have been superseded) and the application for the top-up.

Subsection (9)

This definition broadly follows that used in s17(11) Children Act 1989 except that mental disorders must result in the child being substantially and permanently handicapped whereas under the 1989 Act any mental disorder is sufficient regardless of its effect. The extent to which the child must be blind or deaf is not specified. For the purpose of disability living allowance a person has to be 100 per cent blind and 80 per cent deaf: reg 12(2) Social Security (Disability Living Allowance) Regulations 1991. In the context of these provisions the test of blindness and deafness is assessed by reference to the criteria used for the purposes of assessing degrees of disablement for the purposes of disablement benefit *R(DLA)* 3/95). No regulations have been made under this subsection.

Section 1(3) emphasises that a person does not fall within either of the above definitions "by reason only of promiscuity or other immoral conduct, sexual deviancy or dependence on alcohol or drugs".

Subsection (10)

A court may make a maintenance order against a person with care.

Subsection (11)

The other enactments are prescribed for the purposes of this subsection by reg 2 of the Maintenance Arrangements and Jurisdiction Regulations.

For a discussion of the meaning of "maintenance order", see the general note to s18 of the 1995 Act on p172.

Agreement about maintenance

9.–(1)   In this section "maintenance agreement" means any agreement for the making, or for securing the making, of periodical payments by way of maintenance, or in Scotland aliment, to or for the benefit of any child.

(2)   Nothing in this Act shall be taken to prevent any person from entering into a maintenance agreement.

(3)   [¹ Subject to section 4(10)(a) [⁶and (ab)] and section 7(10),] the existence of a maintenance agreement shall not prevent any party to the agreement, or any other person, from applying for a [³maintenance calculation] with respect to any child to or for whose benefit periodical payments are to be made or secured under the agreement.

(4)   Where any agreement contains a provision which purports to restrict the right of any person to apply for a [³maintenance calculation], that provision shall be void.

(5)   Where section 8 would prevent any court from making a maintenance order in relation to a child and [⁴a non-resident parent] of his, no court shall exercise any power that it has to vary any agreement so as–

(a)   to insert a provision requiring that [⁴non-resident parent] to make or secure the making of periodical payments by way of maintenance, or in Scotland aliment, to or for the benefit of that child; or

(b)   to increase the amount payable under such a provision.

[²(6) In any case in which section 4(10) or 7(10) prevents the making of an application for a [³maintenance calculation], [⁷...]

[⁵(a) [⁷...]
(b) [⁷...]]
subsection (5) shall have effect with the omission of paragraph (b).]

Amendments
1. Inserted (4.9.95) in s9(3) by Child Support Act 1995 (c.34), s18(4).
2. Inserted (4.9.95) by Child Support Act 1995 (c.34), s18(4).
3. Child Support, Pensions and Social Security Act 2000 (2000 c.19) s1(2) (March 3, 2003 for the types of cases in art 3 Child Support, Pensions and Social Security Act 2000 (Commencement No.12) Order 2003 (SI 2003 No.192)). For other types of cases, see '1993 rules' below.
4. Child Support, Pensions and Social Security Act 2000 (2000 c.19) s26 and Sch 3 para 11(2) (March 3, 2003 for the types of cases in art 3 Child Support, Pensions and Social Security Act 2000 (Commencement No.12) Order 2003 (SI 2003 No.192)). For other types of cases, see '1993 rules' below.
5. Child Support, Pensions and Social Security Act 2000 (2000 c.19) s26 and Sch 3 para 11(6) (March 3, 2003 for the types of cases in art 3 Child Support, Pensions and Social Security Act 2000 (Commencement No.12) Order 2003 (SI 2003 No.192)). For other types of cases, see '1993 rules' below.
6. Child Maintenance and Other Payments Act 2008 (2008 c.6) s35 (June 6, 2008).
7. Child Maintenance and Other Payments Act 2008 (2008 c.6) s58 and Sch 8 (October 27, 2008 subject to art 4 Child Maintenance and Other Payments Act 2008 (Commencement No.3 and Transitional and Savings Provisions) Order 2008 (SI 2008 No.2548)). Prior to this, these paras read:

"[⁵(a) no parent has been treated under section 6(3) as having applied for a maintenance calculation with respect to the child; or
(b) a parent has been so treated but no maintenance calculation has been made,]"

1993 rules
Ss1(2) and 26 and Sch 3 of the Child Support, Pensions and Social Security Act 2000 (2000 c.19) amend s9 of the Child Support Act 1991 and have been brought into force only for the types of cases in art 3 of the Child Support, Pensions and Social Security Act 2000 (Commencement No.12) Order 2003 (SI 2003 No.192 – see p683). For other types of cases the 1993 rules apply and the original wording is retained ie, "maintenance assessment" is retained in place of "maintenance calculation" and "absent parent" is retained in place of "non-resident parent". Also, paragraphs (6)(a) and (b) read as follows:

(a) no application has been made for a maintenance assessment under section 6, or
(b) such an application has been made but no maintenance assessment has been made in response to it,

Definitions
"child": see s55.
"maintenance assessment": see s54.
"non-resident parent": see s3(2).

General Note
The Act does not prevent the making of a maintenance agreement, whether binding (contractually or otherwise) or not. However, a maintenance agreement cannot affect the operation of the Act. The provisions of such an agreement do not displace the child support scheme, nor can they provide that a person may not apply for a maintenance calculation. A maintenance agreement may still be useful, however. First, it may provide for the payment of a larger amount of maintenance than would be calculated under this Act. The Act does not affect the enforcement of such an arrangement. Second, even if the agreement does not provide for the payment of a larger sum than would be calculated under this Act, the parties may prefer to rely on the methods of enforcement available, in addition to or as a substitute for the mechanisms provided under the Act. Section 8(5) and the Child Maintenance (Written Agreements) Order 1993 allow for provision to be made to permit the incorporation of an agreement into a court order.
Subsection (1)
For a discussion of the meaning of "maintenance agreement", see the general note to s18 of the 1995 Act on p172.
In *CCS 12849/1996* (para 5), the commissioner left open the meaning of "securing the making" of periodical payments.
In *CCS 8328/1995* (para 15), the commissioner held that "for the benefit of any child" was not limited to cases where the child was expressly mentioned in the agreement. The words were not so wide as to cover any payment

to a parent that might ultimately be to the advantage of a child, but there were cases where, without the child being expressly mentioned, the circumstances surrounding the making of the agreement made it abundantly clear that the payments were, at least in part, for the benefit of the child.

Subsection (4)

The effect of this subsection is, in line with the policy decision of Ministers (and with the approach of the private law on maintenance, see, for example, s23(4) Matrimonial Causes Act 1973 and s3 Family Law (Scotland) Act 1985), to prevent clean breaks in respect of children. It refers to agreements in contrast to the other subsections which refer to *maintenance* agreements. It therefore catches all agreements which seek to restrict the right to apply for a maintenance calculation, regardless of whether they are maintenance agreements as defined by subs (1) or not. This prevents the obvious avoidance measure of putting the restriction in a separate agreement, which would not be a maintenance agreement since it would provide for the avoidance of maintenance payments rather than for making or securing them. Agreements which, as part of an overall settlement on breakdown of a marriage or other relationship, make some provision conditional on no application for a maintenance calculation being made may, therefore, be caught by this provision. Whether or not these agreements expressly purport to restrict the right to apply for calculation, such is their clear effect and purpose. However, only the provision itself is void. Other terms in the agreement remain valid, so the other parts of the overall settlement will still be effective. It would appear, relying upon *Smith v McInerney* [1994] 2 FLR 1077, that an agreement incorporating a charge-back arrangement, whereby, for example, the husband transfers his interest in the matrimonial home to the wife, subject to a charge back for the aggregate of any sums payable by him under the Child Support Act, would not be regarded as an attempt to restrict the wife's right to apply under the Act but would simply enable the husband to avoid effectively paying her twice over.

In *CCS 316/1998* (para 23), the commissioner held that an arrangement embodied in a consent order whereby payments of spousal maintenance were to reduce by the amount of any child support maintenance assessment were not void under this subsection, as it merely adjusted the absent parent's overall financial commitments in the light of his liability for child support maintenance. The decision in *Dorney-Kingdom v Dorney-Kingdom* [2000] 2 FLR 855 shows that this is a standard form of order that is accepted as valid by the courts.

The Court of Appeal has held, in *N v N(Consent Order: Variation)* [1993] 2 FLR 868, that a side letter to a maintenance and property settlement embodied in a consent order, whereby the wife agreed not to seek an extension of a fixed term spousal maintenance order, was void under s34 Matrimonial Causes Act 1973 as an attempt to oust the court's jurisdiction. Its suitability in a case where there was a child was also questionable, since it was impossible to anticipate what might have happened by the end of the fixed-term. It was, however, highly relevant to a subsequent variation application, and should have been shown to the district judge who had to approve the original consent order. Query whether the court would regard a similar device, whereby the parent with care agrees in a side letter not to make a child support application, as "highly relevant" to subsequent proceedings between the parents.

Subsections (3), (5) and (6)

See the general note to s18 of the 1995 Act on p172.

Relationship between maintenance assessments and certain court orders and related matters

10.–(1) Where an order of a kind prescribed for the purpose of this subsection is in force with respect to any qualifying child with respect to whom a [¹maintenance calculation] is made, the order–

    (a) shall, so far as it relates to the making or securing of periodical payments, cease to have effect to such extent as may be determined in accordance with regulations made by the Secretary of State; or

    (b) where the regulations so provide, shall, so far as it so relates, have effect subject to such modifications as may be so determined.

(2) Where an agreement of a kind prescribed for the purpose of this subsection is in force with respect to any qualifying child with respect to whom a [¹maintenance calculation] is made, the agreement–

    (a) shall, so far as it relates to the making or securing of periodical payments, be unenforceable to such extent as may be determined in accordance with regulations made by the Secretary of State; or

    (b) where the regulations so provide, shall, so far as it so relates, have effect subject to such modifications as may be so determined.

(3) Any regulations under this section may, in particular, make such provision with respect to–

    (a) any case where any person with respect to whom an order or agreement of a kind prescribed for the purposes of subsection (1) or (2) has effect applies to the prescribed court, before the end of the prescribed period, for the order or agreement to be varied in the light of the [¹maintenance calculation] and of the provisions of this Act;

(b)   the recovery of any arrears under the order or agreement which fell due before the coming into force of the [¹maintenance calculation],

as the Secretary of State considers appropriate and may provide that, in prescribed circumstances, any application to any court which is made with respect to an order of a prescribed kind relating to the making or securing of periodical payments to or for the benefit of a child shall be treated by the court as an application for the order to be revoked.

(4)   The Secretary of State may by regulations make provision for–

(a)   notification to be given by [² the [³[⁴Secretary of State]]] to the prescribed person in any case where [³[⁴the Secretary of State]] considers that the making of a [¹maintenance calculation] has affected, or is likely to affect, any order of a kind prescribed for the purposes of this subsection;

(b)   notification to be given by the prescribed person to the [³[⁴Secretary of State]] in any case where a court makes an order which it considers has affected, or is likely to affect, a [¹ maintenance calculation].

(5)   Rules may be made under section 144 of the Magistrates' Courts Act 1980 (rules of procedure) requiring any person who, in prescribed circumstances, makes an application to a magistrates' court for a maintenance order to furnish the court with a statement in a prescribed form, and signed by [²an officer of the [³[⁴Secretary of State]]], as to whether or not, at the time when the statement is made, there is a [¹maintenance calculation] in force with respect to that person or the child concerned.

In this subsection–

"maintenance order" means an order of a prescribed kind for the making or securing of periodical payments to or for the benefit of a child; and

"prescribed" means prescribed by the rules.

Amendments

1.   Child Support, Pensions and Social Security Act 2000 (2000 c.19) s1(2) (March 3, 2003 for the types of cases detailed in art 3 Child Support, Pensions and Social Security Act 2000 (Commencement No.12) Order 2003 (SI 2003 No.192)). For other types of cases, see '1993 rules' below.

2.   Social Security Act 1998 (1998 c.14) Sch 7 para 23 (June 1, 1999).

3.   Child Maintenance and Other Payments Act 2008 (2008 c.6) s13 and Sch 3 para 7 (November 1, 2008). Child Maintenance and Other Payments Act 2008 (Commencement No.4 and Transitional Provision) Order 2008 (SI 2008 No.2675) art 3.

4.   Public Bodies (Child Maintenance and Enforcement Commission: Abolition and Transfer of Functions) Order 2012 (SI 2012 No.2007) art 3(2) and Sch para 6 (August 1, 2012).

1993 rules

Ss1(2) and 26 and sch 3 of the Child Support, Pensions and Social Security Act 2000 (2000 c.19) amend s10 of the Child Support Act 1991 and have been brought into force only for the types of cases in art 3 of the Child Support, Pensions and Social Security Act 2000 (Commencement No.12) Order 2003 (SI 2003 No.192 – see p683). For other types of cases the 1993 rules apply and the words "maintenance assessment" are retained in place of "maintenance calculation".

Definitions

"child": see s55.

"maintenance calculation": see s54.

"prescribed": see s54.

"qualifying child": see s3(1).

General Note

For the position in Scotland see the Child Support (Amendments to Primary Legislation) (Scotland) Order 1993 and Act of Sederunt (Child Support Act 1991) (Amendment of Ordinary Cause and Summary Cause) Rules 1993.

This section applies to all orders and agreements falling within its terms regardless of the date on which they were made and, in particular, the section is not limited to orders and agreements made after the Act received Royal Assent (*R(CS)* 2/95, para 16).

Subsection (1)

The maintenance orders to which this subsection applies are the same as those which fall within s8(11) and regulations made thereunder (reg 3(1) of the Maintenance Arrangements and Jurisdiction Regulations). These orders cease to have effect in accordance with reg 3(2) to (4). In summary the orders cease to have effect in respect of any children with respect to whom a maintenance calculation has been made as from the effective date of the calculation. For this purpose the effective date is two days after the assessment is made. This is subject to some exceptions. These are: (i) where the order covers children in addition to those in respect of whom the maintenance calculation has been made without specifying separate amounts of maintenance for each child and (ii) where the order was made under s8(7) or (8). In the case of Scotland, when a maintenance order ceases to have effect and the Secretary of State subsequently loses jurisdiction to make a maintenance calculation with respect to a particular child covered by the order, the order revives so far as that child is concerned.

If a maintenance calculation is made while a maintenance order is in force in respect of the same child but is subsequently cancelled as having been made in error, and the maintenance order has ceased to have effect by virtue of reg 3, the order is treated as having continued in force and any payments under the calculation are treated as if they were made under the order (reg 8(1) of the Maintenance Arrangements and Jurisdiction Regulations as amended).

Neither this subsection nor the Maintenance Arrangements and Jurisdiction Regulations expressly provide for the date on which the order must be in force. Normally the relevant date would be the effective date of the maintenance calculation. The wording of reg 3(2) provides that an order ceases to have effect when a maintenance calculation is made, which suggests that the relevant date on which the order must be in force is the date the calculation is made.

If a maintenance order is made while a maintenance calculation is in force in respect of the same child and subsequently revoked as having been made in error, the calculation is treated as not having been cancelled and any payments under the order are treated as if they were made under the calculation (reg 8(2) of the Maintenance Arrangements and Jurisdiction Regulations).

In England and Wales, an order that has ceased to have effect does not revive automatically and cannot be revived. The position is different in Scotland by virtue of reg 3(4) of the Maintenance Arrangements and Jurisdiction Regulations. See *CCS 2567/1998*, paras 23-48.

Subsection (2)

The agreements to which this subsection applies are maintenance agreements as defined by s9(1) (reg 4(1) of the Maintenance Arrangements and Jurisdiction Regulations). The extent of the enforceability of these agreements is covered by reg 4(2) and (3). In summary the agreements become unenforceable in respect of any children with respect to whom a maintenance calculation has been made as from the effective date of the calculation. For the effective date where a court order is or has been in force see reg 3 of those Regulations. This is subject to an exception where the agreement covers children in addition to those in respect of whom the maintenance calculation has been made without specifying separate amounts of maintenance for each child. When a maintenance agreement becomes unenforceable and the Sectretary of State subsequently loses jurisdiction to make a maintenance calculation with respect to a particular child covered by the agreement, the agreement becomes enforceable again so far as that child is concerned.

Subsection (3)(a)

Schedule 1 para 3 to the Child Maintenance Orders (Backdating) Order 1993 inserts s31(12) into the Matrimonial Causes Act 1973 and s20(9B) into the Domestic Proceedings and Magistrates' Courts Act 1978 to permit an order varying or discharging/revoking periodical payments in favour of a spouse to be backdated to the effective date (see the general note to Sch 1 para 11) of a maintenance calculation provided that the application for the maintenance order is made within six months of the date of the calculation. This is intended, *inter alia,* to cater for the situation where a previous order which contained provision for spousal maintenance and child maintenance is partly superseded by a maintenance calculation. The order might have provided a relatively small element for spousal maintenance, and a relatively large portion for child maintenance. A spouse might seek an upward variation of *her* maintenance where the calculation has produced an amount for the child smaller than that contained in the maintenance order, in order to ensure no overall loss of income for the family.

Subsection (4)

Regulation 5 of the Maintenance Arrangements and Jurisdiction Regulations provides for the Secretary of State to give notice of any maintenance calculation which is likely to affect a court order to the persons in respect of whom the maintenance calculation is in force and to the court itself. Regulation 6 provides for the court to give notice to the Secretary of State of any maintenance order which it makes and which is likely to affect a maintenance calculation. The way in which an order or calculation might be "affected" would appear to be that it should cease to have effect, or be cancelled. Where a calculation is made, reg 3 will provide that the order, or part of it, will cease to have effect. A party to the order might seek a variation of the remaining part to take account of the calculation. Where an order is made, this will either be because the Secretary of State no longer has jurisdiction under s44 or because it is an order which may continue to be made by virtue of s8(6) to (8). Where the former is the case, the calculation should be cancelled under s44. See s8 on p28 for further discussion of the provision made to avoid clashes of jurisdiction between the courts and the Secretary of State.

Maintenance calculations

[¹ **Maintenance calculations**

11.–(1)   An application for a maintenance calculation made to the [³[⁴Secretary of State]] shall be dealt with by [³[⁴the Secretary of State]] in accordance with the provision made by or under this Act.

(2)   The [³[⁴Secretary of State]] shall (unless [³[⁴the Secretary of State]] decides not to make a maintenance calculation in response to the application, or makes a decision under section 12) determine the application by making a decision under this section about whether any child support maintenance is payable and, if so, how much.

(3)   [²...]

(4)   [²...]

(5)   [²...]

(6)   The amount of child support maintenance to be fixed by a maintenance calculation shall be determined in accordance with Part I of Schedule 1 unless an application for a variation has been made and agreed.

(7)   If the [³[⁴Secretary of State]] has agreed to a variation, the amount of child support maintenance to be fixed shall be determined on the basis [³ ...][⁴determined] under section 28F(4).

(8)   Part II of Schedule 1 makes further provision with respect to maintenance calculations.]

Amendments

1.   Child Support, Pensions and Social Security Act 2000 (2000 c.19) s1(1) (March 3, 2003 for the types of cases in art 3 Child Support, Pensions and Social Security Act 2000 (Commencement No.12) Order 2003 (SI 2003 No.192)). For other types of cases, see '1993 rules' below.

2.   Child Maintenance and Other Payments Act 2008 (2008 c.6) s58 and Sch 8 (October 27, 2008 subject to art 4 Child Maintenance and Other Payments Act 2008 (Commencement No.3 and Transitional and Savings Provisions) Order 2008 (SI 2008 No.2548)). This omitted subss 11(3) to (5) which read:

"(3)   Where–

(a)   a parent is treated under section 6(3) as having applied for a maintenance calculation; but

(b)   the [³Commission] becomes aware before determining the application that the parent has ceased to fall within section 6(1),

[³the Commission] shall, subject to subsection (4), cease to treat that parent as having applied for a maintenance calculation.

(4)   If it appears to the [³Commission] that subsection (10) of section 4 would not have prevented the parent with care concerned from making an application for a maintenance calculation under that section [³the Commission] shall–

(a)   notify her of the effect of this subsection; and

(b)   if, before the end of the period of one month beginning with the day on which notice was sent to her, she asks [³the Commission] to do so, treat her as having applied not under section 6 but under section 4.

(5)   Where subsection (3) applies but subsection (4) does not, the [³Commission] shall notify–

(a)   the parent with care concerned; and

(b)   the non-resident parent (or alleged non-resident parent), where it appears to [³the Commission] that that person is aware that the parent with care has been treated as having applied for a maintenance calculation."

3.   Child Maintenance and Other Payments Act 2008 (2008 c.6) s13 and Sch 3 para 8 (November 1, 2008) brought into force by Child Maintenance and Other Payments Act 2008 (Commencement No.4 and Transitional Provision) Order 2008 (SI 2008 No.2675) art 3.

4.   Public Bodies (Child Maintenance and Enforcement Commission: Abolition and Transfer of Functions) Order 2012 (SI 2012 No.2007) art 3(2) and Sch para 7 (August 1, 2012).

1993 rules

s1(1) of the Child Support, Pensions and Social Security Act 2000 (2000 c.19) replaces s11 of the Child Support Act 1991 and has been brought into force only for the types of cases in art 3 of the Child Support, Pensions and Social Security Act 2000 (Commencement No.12) Order 2003 (SI 2003 No.192 – see p683). For other types of cases the 1993 rules apply and s11 reads:

Maintenance assessments

11.–(1)   Any application for a maintenance assessment made to the [⁵Commission] shall be [² dealt with by [⁵it]] in accordance with the provision made by or under this Act.

[¹(1A)   [³...]

(1B)   [³,⁴...]

(1C)   [³,⁴...]]

(2)   The amount of child support maintenance to be fixed by any maintenance assessment shall be determined in accordance with the provisions of Part I of Schedule 1.

(3)   Part II of Schedule 1 makes further provision with respect to maintenance assessments.

Amendments

1.   s11(1A)–(1C) inserted (4.9.95) by Child Support Act 1995 (c.34), s19.
2.   Substituted (1.6.99) by Sch 8 to S.S. Act 1998 (c.14).
3.   Child Maintenance and Other Payments Act 2008 (2008 c.6) Sch 7 para 1(34)(a) (July 14, 2008 subject to art 2(4)-(5) Child Maintenance and Other Payments Act 2008 (Commencement) Order 2008 (SI 2008 No.1476 (c.67)). This amendment which repealed s11(1A) to (1C) did not apply in relation to existing cases as defined in art 2(5) of SI 2008 No.1476.
4.   Child Maintenance and Other Payments Act 2008 (2008 c.6) Sch 7 para 1(34)(a) (so far as not already in force: June 1, 2009).
5.   Child Maintenance and Other Payments Act 2008 (2008 c.6) s13 and Sch 3, para 8 (November 1, 2008) brought into force by Child Maintenance and Other Payments Act 2008 (Commencement No.4 and Transitional Provision) Order 2008 (SI 2008 No.2675) art 3.

Definitions

"application for a variation": see s54.
"child support maintenance": see s54.
"maintenance calculation": see s54.
"non-resident parent": see s54.
"parent": see s54.
"parent with care": see s54.

General Note

Decision making by the Secretary of State

The duties and status of the Secretary of State when dealing with applications under the child support legislation must largely be spelt out from the authorities on social security decision makers.

The Secretary of State has a duty to act fairly and to obtain information necessary to deal with an application (*Duggan v Chief Adjudication Officer* reported as an Appendix to *R(SB) 13/89; R(CS)* 2/98, para 20). Adjudication officers had administrative duties only and had no judicial or quasi-judicial function, because there were no competing contentions on which the officer had to adjudicate (*R v Deputy Industrial Injuries Commissioner ex p Moore* [1965] 1 QB 456 at 486, *per* Diplock LJ; *R(SB) 11/89*, para 7). In child support cases, there is likely to be competing contentions and this may lead the Secretary of State to be held to have at least a quasi-judicial function.

The officers acting for the Secretary of State have the same powers to decide on the validity of delegated legislation as tribunals. In *Chief Adjudication Officer v Foster* [1993] 1 All ER 705 the House of Lords said in the context of the social security legislation that an adjudication officer would be expected to refer the question to a tribunal. This course is not available under the child support legislation.

In dealing with application under the child support legislation, the officers acting for the Secretary of State have an independent statutory function and are not bound by an undertaking given by anyone else (*R(SB) 14/88*, paras 20-22), even when the officer is exercising a discretion that could be exercised in accordance with the undertaking (*R(SB) 14/89*, para 12). These principles apply in child support law, as they applied to adjudication officers in social security law (*R(CS) 2/97*).

Some decisions turn on the state of mind of the Secretary of State; they may depend on suspicion or opinion. On appeal, the tribunal may substitute its view for that of the Secretary of State (*R(SB) 5/81*, para 8; *MC v Secretary of State for Defence* [2009] UKUT 173 (AAC), paras 10-16).

Subsection (1)

This imposes a duty on the Secretary of State to deal with an application that has been made. It does not expressly refer to applications that are treated as made under s6, although it is clear from subs (3) that it does apply to them. It only applies to effective applications. If the Secretary of State does not act under s6(3), no application is treated as made and this section does not apply.

For provisions governing applications for a maintenance calculation, see Pt II of the Maintenance Calculation Procedure Regulations.

For the position regarding proceedings for, or implementation and enforcement of, a maintenance calculation pending resolution of a paternity issue, see the general note to Art 4 in either the Child Support Appeals (Jurisdiction of Courts) Order 2002 or the Child Support Appeals (Jurisdiction of Courts) (Scotland) Order 2002, as appropriate.

Subsection (2)

If an application is effective, the Secretary of State must (a) determine the application, (b) decide not to make a maintenance calculation or (c) make a decision under s12. Unless the case falls within (b) or (c), the Secretary of State is under a duty to determine the application. There is no discretion and s2 does not apply (*R(CS) 4/96*, para 8; *R(CS) 2/98*, paras 17-21).

There is no limitation period on the Secretary of State making a maintenance calculation (*R(CS) 10/02*).

Subsection (3)

If the parent with care ceases to fall within s6(1) before the application is determined, s6 ceases to apply and no application is treated as having been made under s6. This applies if a parent with care's claim is refused or if an existing award is terminated. This reverses the effect of *R v Secretary of State for Social Security ex p Harris* unreported, July 1 1998.

However, the parent with care has one month within which to opt under subs (4) below for the application to be treated as if it had been made under s4.

Subsection (4)

The Secretary of State may, at the parent with care's request, treat an application as having been made under s4. However, this is not reflected elsewhere in the Act, which distinguishes between (a) applications made under s4 and (b) applications treated as made under s6. No reference is made to applications treated as made under s4. See the wording of s7(1)(b).

[¹ Default and interim maintenance decisions

12.–(1)   Where the [³[⁴Secretary of State]]–

(a)   is required to make a maintenance calculation; or

(b)   is proposing to make a decision under section 16 or 17,

and it appears to [³ the [⁴Secretary of State]] that [³ [⁴the Secretary of State]] does not have sufficient information to enable [³][⁴such a decision to be made], [³[⁴the Secretary of State]] may make a default maintenance decision.

(2)   Where an application for a variation has been made under section 28A(1) in connection with an application for a maintenance calculation [²...], the [³[⁴Secretary of State]] may make an interim maintenance decision.

(3)   The amount of child support maintenance fixed by an interim maintenance decision shall be determined in accordance with Part I of Schedule 1.

(4)   The Secretary of State may by regulations make provision as to default and interim maintenance decisions.

(5)   The regulations may, in particular, make provision as to–

(a)   the procedure to be followed in making a default or an interim maintenance decision; and

(b)   a default rate of child support maintenance to apply where a default maintenance decision is made.]

Amendments

1.   Child Support, Pensions and Social Security Act 2000 (2000 c.19) s4 (March 3, 2003 for the types of cases detailed in art 3 Child Support, Pensions and Social Security Act 2000 (Commencement No.12) Order 2003 (SI 2003 No.192)). For other types of cases, see '1993 rules' below.

2.   Child Maintenance and Other Payments Act 2008 (2008 c.6) s58 and Sch 8 (October 27, 2008 subject to art 4 Child Maintenance and Other Payments Act 2008 (Commencement No.3 and Transitional and Savings Provisions) Order 2008 (SI 2008 No.2548)). This omitted "(or in connection with such an application which is treated as having been made)" from subs 12(2).

3.   Child Maintenance and Other Payments Act 2008 (2008 c.6) s13 and Sch 3 para 9 (November 1, 2008). Child Maintenance and Other Payments Act 2008 (Commencement No.4 and Transitional Provision) Order 2008 (SI 2008 No.2675) art 3.

4.   Public Bodies (Child Maintenance and Enforcement Commission: Abolition and Transfer of Functions) Order 2012 (SI 2012 No.2007) art 3(2) and Sch para 8 (August 1, 2012).

1993 rules
s4 of the Child Support, Pensions and Social Security Act 2000 (2000 c.19) replaces s12 of the Child Support Act 1991 and have been brought into force only for the types of cases in art 3 of the Child Support, Pensions and Social Security Act 2000 (Commencement No.12) Order 2003 (SI 2003 No.192 – see p683).

Definitions
"application for a variation": see s54.
"child support maintenance": see s54.
"maintenance calculation": see s54.

General Note
Subsection (1)
A default maintenance decision may be made if the Secretary of State has insufficient information to make a maintenance calculation or a revision or supersession decision. The rate is set by reg 7 of the Maintenance Calculation Procedure Regulations.
Subsection (2)
This confers a power, but not a duty, to make an interim maintenance decision (*CCS 1490/2005*, para 20).
        An interim maintenance decision may be made if an application for a variation is made before a decision has been reached on an application for a maintenance calculation. The interim maintenance decision is made pending the determination of the variation application. It may be subject to a regular payments condition under s28C.
        An interim maintenance decision is treated as replaced by the decision under s11 below that is made when the application for a variation has been determined: see s28F(5).

Section 13 was repealed by the Social Security Act 1998 with effect from 1 June 1999.

Information

Information required by the [7[8Secretary of State]]

14.–(1)   The Secretary of State may make regulations requiring any information or evidence needed for the determination of any application [5made [6...]] under this Act, or any question arising in connection with such an application [4[6...], or needed for the making of any decision or in connection with the imposition of any condition or requirement under this Act], or needed in connection with the collection or enforcement of child support or other maintenance under this Act, to be furnished–
(a)   by such persons as may be determined in accordance with regulations made by the Secretary of State; and
(b)   in accordance with the regulations.
[1 (1A)   Regulations under subsection (1) may make provision for notifying any person who is required to furnish any information or evidence under the regulations of the possible consequences of failing to do so.]
        [...2]
(3)   The Secretary of State may by regulations make provision authorising the disclosure by [7 the [8Secretary of State]] [...3], in such circumstances as may be prescribed, of such information held by [3[7 the [8Secretary of State]]] for purposes of this Act as may be prescribed.
(4) The provisions of Schedule 2 (which relate to information which is held for purposes other than those of this Act but which is required by the [7[8Secretary of State]]) shall have effect.

Amendments
1.   Inserted (1.10.95) by Child Support Act 1995 (c.34) Sch 3 para 3(1).
2.   ss(2) and (2A) shall cease to have effect (8.9.98) by Sch 7 para 27(a) of SS Act 1998 (c.47).
3.   SS Act 1998 (c.14) Sch 8 (1.6.99).
4.   Child Support, Pensions and Social Security Act 2000 (2000 c.19) s12 (March 3, 2003 for the types of cases in art 3 Child Support, Pensions and Social Security Act 2000 (Commencement No.12) Order 2003 (SI 2003 No.192), and September 26, 2008 for all other purposes); Child Support, Pensions and Social Security Act 2000 (Commencement No.14) Order 2008 (SI 2008 No.2545) art 2.

5.   Child Support, Pensions and Social Security Act 2000 (2000 c.19) s26 and Sch 3 para 11(7) (March 3, 2003 for the types of cases in art 3 Child Support, Pensions and Social Security Act 2000 (Commencement No.12) Order 2003 (SI 2003 No.192)).

6.   Child Maintenance and Other Payments Act 2008 (2008 c.6) s58 and Sch 8 (October 27, 2008 subject to art 4 Child Maintenance and Other Payments Act 2008 (Commencement No.3 and Transitional and Savings Provisions) Order 2008 (SI 2008 No.2548)). This omitted "or treated as made" and "(or application treated as made)" from subs 14(1).

7.   Child Maintenance and Other Payments Act 2008 (2008 c.6) s13 and Sch 3 para 10 (November 1, 2008); Child Maintenance and Other Payments Act 2008 (Commencement No.4 and Transitional Provision) Order 2008 (SI 2008 No.2675) art 3.

8.   Public Bodies (Child Maintenance and Enforcement Commission: Abolition and Transfer of Functions) Order 2012 (SI 2012 No.2007) art 3(2) and Sch para 9 (August 1, 2012).

Definitions

"benefit Acts": see s54.

"prescribed": s54.

General Note

This section confers the general rule-making powers relating to the information or evidence needed by the Secretary of State. Subsections (1) and (1A) deal with obtaining information. These are in addition to the more specific rule-making powers, such as that in ss4(4), 6(7) and 7(5). They are supplemented by s14A (offences) and s15 (inspectors). Subsection (3) deals with disclosure of information held for the purposes of this Act.

The relevant regulations are the Information Regulations. The Social Security (Claims and Information) Regulations 1999 are also relevant.

There is no definition of "information" or "evidence". The obvious difference is that information is what the Secretary of State needs to know and evidence is the documentary or other proof of it. So, if the Secretary of State needs to know a parent's wages, the amount of those wages is information and the wage slip that proves those wages is the evidence. In practice, the distinction is less clear cut, because the parent's statement of the amount of the wages is by itself evidence of that amount. Moreover, this distinction causes problems if it is carried over into the disclosure provisions in s50. They relate to information and not to evidence. If they do not include the evidence provided as proof, there is no provision authorising disclosure of that evidence to a tribunal.

Subsection (1)

For the application of this subsection to the Crown, see s57(1) on p138.

This subsection contains the general enabling power under which the Secretary of State may obtain the information or evidence necessary for the implementation of the Act. It applies to both information and to evidence, and therefore covers cases where information has been supplied but the evidence is lacking to prove it. The regulations made under this subsection are contained in Pt II of the Information, Evidence and Disclosure Regulations. They create wider duties than those created under ss4(4), 6(7) and 7(5). These subsections each limit the duty to cases where the person can reasonably comply. There is no equivalent to this limitation in this subsection. However, the duty created by reg 2(1) limits the duty to supply information or evidence to cases where the information or evidence is in a person's possession or it is reasonable to expect a person to acquire it. Thus the Act emphasises the reasonableness of compliance with the duty to *supply* whereas the regulation emphasises the reasonableness of *acquiring* the information or evidence. However, it is difficult to see any practical significance in this difference.

Information supplied to the Secretary of State is not subject to absolute privilege and so statements made therein may give rise to an action for libel (*Purdew v Seress-Smith* [1993] IRLR 77).

There is no single provision dealing with enforcement of the obligation to provide information or evidence. However, a variety of means exist by which pressure may be brought to bear to try to ensure that necessary information or evidence is obtained.

(i)   A default maintenance decision may be made under s12 if the officer has insufficient information.

(ii)   A prosecution may be made for an offence under s14A.

(iii) An inspector may be appointed under s15 and that may lead to an offence being committed under s15(9). This may be directed against any person under a duty to supply information.

(iv)   A reduced benefit decision may be made under s46. This will be directed against the parent with care.

(v)   Failure by one person to provide information or evidence may be remedied by obtaining it from another source under the wide powers given in the Information. Evidence and Disclosure Regulations.

(vi)   A person who fails to maintain a person whom he is liable to maintain may commit an offence under s105 of the Social Security Administration Act 1992, but note that the duty to maintain created by s1(1) of the Child Support Act cannot be used as a basis for that offence since it only applies for the purpose of this Act.

(vii) It may also be possible to obtain an order under s106 of the Social Security Administration Act 1992 for the recovery of benefit from a person liable to maintain another who receives income support. Once again the duty created by s1(1) of this Act cannot be used for this purpose.

(viii)   The failure may provide the basis from which an inference may be drawn. This power is not used by the officers who act for the Secretary of State, but it may be used by a tribunal.

Subsection (3)

The regulations made under this subsection are contained in the Information Regulations and the Child Support (Management of Payment and Arrears) Regulations 2009 . The unauthorised disclosure of information may be an offence under s50.

[¹ Information – offences

14A.–(1)   This section applies to–

(a)   persons who are required to comply with regulations under section 4(4) or 7(5); and

(b)   persons specified in regulations under section 14(1)(a).

(2)   Such a person is guilty of an offence if, pursuant to a request for information under or by virtue of those regulations–

(a)   he makes a statement or representation which he knows to be false; or

(b)   he provides, or knowingly causes or knowingly allows to be provided, a document or other information which he knows to be false in a material particular.

(3)   Such a person is guilty of an offence if, following such a request, he fails to comply with it.

[⁴(3A)   In the case of regulations under section 14 which require a person liable to make payments of child support maintenance to notify–

(a)   a change of address, or

(b)   any other change of circumstances,

a person who fails to comply with the requirement is guilty of an offence.]

(4)   It is a defence for a person charged with an offence under subsection (3) [²or (3A)] to prove that he had a reasonable excuse for failing to comply.

(5)   A person guilty of an offence under this section is liable on summary conviction to a fine not exceeding level 3 on the standard scale.]

[³ (6)   In England and Wales, an information relating to an offence under subsection (2) may be tried by a magistrates' court if it is laid within the period of 12 months beginning with the commission of the offence.

(7)   In Scotland, summary proceedings for an offence under subsection (2) may be commenced within the period of 12 months beginning with the commission of the offence.

(8)   Section 136(3) of the Criminal Procedure (Scotland) Act 1995 (c. 46) (date when proceedings deemed to be commenced) applies for the purposes of subsection (7) as it applies for the purposes of that section.]

Amendments

1.   Child Support, Pensions and Social Security Act, 2000 s13 (January 31, 2001).

2.   Child Maintenance and Other Payments Act 2008 (2008 c.6) s36 (September 26, 2008 for making regulations, October 27, 2008 for all other purposes). See s59 Child Maintenance and Other Payments Act 2008 and art 4 Child Maintenance and Other Payments Act 2008 (Commencement No.3 and Transitional and Savings Provisions) Order 2008 (SI 2008 No.2548) for transitional and savings provisions.

3.   Welfare Reform Act 2009 (2009 c.24) s55(3) (January 14, 2010); Welfare Reform Act 2009 (Commencement No.1) Order 2010 (SI 2010 No.45) art 2(3).

4.   Welfare Reform Act 2009 (2009 c.24) s55(1) and (2) (October 8, 2012).

General Note

This section provides for an offence, punishable by a fine, for failing to comply with some, but not all, of the duties to give information to the Secretary of State. This is outside the jurisdiction of the tribunal, although the tribunal may invite the Secretary of State to consider a prosecution and make findings that show a basis for prosecution.

Subsection (1)

This subsection identifies the persons who may be guilty of an offence under this section. Paragraph (a) applies to ss4(4) and 7(5). It does not apply to the equivalent s6(7).

Subsection (2)

This makes it an offence knowingly to make false statements or representations and to provide or knowingly allow or cause to be provided false documents or information. It is not subject to the defence in subs (4), but depending on the terms of the offence, the prosecution has to prove knowledge on the part of the defendant.

Subsection (3)

This makes it an offence to fail to provide information required under s4(4) or 7(5) above. This is subject to the defence under subs (4).

Subsection (4)

This subsection provides a defence to subss (3) and (3A). There is no definition or indication of what may constitute a reasonable excuse. The burden of proof is on the defendant. Self-incrimination and protecting others from criminal charges is not a reasonable excuse for failing to comply. In *CMEC v Forrest* [2010] EWHC 1264 (Admin), the Divisional Court gave three reasons for this conclusion. First, as such a defence was provided by s15(7), its absence in this section was significant (para 14). Second, following *R v Hertfordshire CC ex p Green Environmental Industries Ltd* [2000] 2 AC 412, such a defence applied in any criminal proceedings but not to the requirement to provide the information (para 17). Third, public policy required compliance. Elias LJ explained:

> '18.   ...There is plainly a powerful public interest here in ensuring that fathers pay the appropriate maintenance to their spouse or partner and their children. That is the purpose behind the requirement of this information, to enable the Child Support Agency to ensure that the appropriate sums are provided in accordance with the legislation.'

Powers of inspectors

15.–[²(1)   The [⁵[⁶Secretary of State]] may appoint, on such terms as [⁵[⁶the Secretary of State]] thinks fit, persons to act as inspectors under this section.

(2)   The function of inspectors is to acquire information which the [⁵[⁶Secretary of State]] needs for any of the purposes of this Act.

(3)   Every inspector is to be given a certificate of his appointment.

(4)   An inspector has power, at any reasonable time and either alone or accompanied by such other persons as he thinks fit, to enter any premises which–

(a)   are liable to inspection under this section; and

(b)   are premises to which it is reasonable for him to require entry in order that he may exercise his functions under this section,

and may there make such examination and inquiry as he considers appropriate.

(4A) Premises liable to inspection under this section are those which are not used wholly as a dwelling house and which the inspector has reasonable grounds for suspecting are–

(a)   premises at which a non-resident parent is or has been employed;

(b)   premises at which a non-resident parent carries out, or has carried out, a trade, profession, vocation or business;

(c)   premises at which there is information held by a person ("A") whom the inspector has reasonable grounds for suspecting has information about a non-resident parent acquired in the course of A's own trade, profession, vocation or business.]

(5)   An inspector exercising his powers may question any person aged 18 or over whom he finds on the premises.

(6)   If required to do so by an inspector exercising his powers, [²any such person] shall furnish to the inspector all such information and documents as the inspector may reasonably require.

(7)   No person shall be required under this section to answer any question or to give any evidence tending to incriminate himself or, in the case of a person who is married [⁴or is a civil partner], his or her spouse [⁴or civil partner].

(8)   On applying for admission to any premises in the exercise of his powers, an inspector shall, if so required, produce his certificate.

(9)   If any person–

(a)   intentionally delays or obstructs any inspector exercising his powers; or

(b)   without reasonable excuse, refuses or neglects to answer any question or furnish any information or to produce any document when required to do so under this section,

he shall be guilty of an offence and liable on summary conviction to a fine not exceeding level 3 on the standard scale.

(10) In this section–

"certificate" means a certificate of appointment issued under this section;

"inspector" means an inspector appointed under this section;

"powers" means powers conferred by this section;

[³ ...]

[²(11) In this section, "premises" includes–

(a) moveable structures and vehicles, vessels, aircraft and hovercraft;

(b) installations that are offshore installations for the purposes of the Mineral Workings (Offshore Installations) Act 1971; and

(c) places of all other descriptions whether or not occupied as land or otherwise,

and references in this section to the occupier of premises are to be construed, in relation to premises that are not occupied as land, as references to any person for the time being present at the place in question.]

Amendments

1. Repealed (1.6.99) by Sch 8 to SS Act 1998 (c.14).
2. Child Support, Pensions and Social Security Act 2000 s14 (January 31, 2001).
3. Child Support, Pensions and Social Security Act 2000 Sch 9 Part I (April 2, 2001).
4. Civil Partnership Act 2004 (2004 c.33) s254 and Sch 24 para 2 (December 5, 2005).
5. Child Maintenance and Other Payments Act 2008 (2008 c.6) s13 and Sch 3 para 11 (November 1, 2008); Child Maintenance and Other Payments Act 2008 (Commencement No.4 and Transitional Provision) Order 2008 (SI 2008 No.2675) art 3.
6. Public Bodies (Child Maintenance and Enforcement Commission: Abolition and Transfer of Functions) Order 2012 (SI 2012 No. 2007) art 3(2) and Sch para 10 (August 1, 2012).

General Note

For the application of this section to the Crown, see s57(2) and (3). An inspector appointed under this section may enter Crown premises in order to exercise any powers conferred by this section provided that the Queen is not in residence.

An inspector may only be appointed to acquire "information". However, the confusion noted in the general note to s14 is apparent here also. Subsection (7) grants exemption from the giving of self-incriminating "evidence", while the offence created by subs (9) applies to the failure to produce documents as well as to the failure to give information, so that the documents must be required as evidence rather than for the information they contain.

Subsection (1)

It is inconsistent with the terms of this subsection for a tribunal to direct the Secretary of State to appoint an inspector, although the tribunal could suggest this as a possible way of obtaining the information necessary in order to make a proper assessment (*CCS 13988/1996*, paras 9 and 11).

Subsection (4A)

The limitation to this subsection only applies to premises which are used *solely* as a dwelling-house. Depending on the circumstances it may not apply in cases where the person is running a business from home. Where there is living accommodation which is separate from the work place (eg, a flat over a shop), the inspector will be able to enter the shop but not the flat. However, where a business is run from the study or a kitchen table, the inspector may enter the whole premises.

Subsection (7)

The defence under this subsection only applies if the question is put under this section. It is not available if the question is asked under another section, such as s14 (*CMEC v Forrest* [2010] EWHC 1264 (Admin), para 12).

Reviews and appeals

[¹ Revisions of decisions

[¹**16**.–(1) [²Any decision [⁵to which subsection (1A) applies]] may be revised by the [⁷[⁹Secretary of State]]–

(a) either within the prescribed period or in prescribed cases or circumstances; and

(b) either on an application made for the purpose or on [⁷[⁹the Secretary of State's]] own initiative;

and regulations may prescribe the procedure by which a decision of the [⁷[⁹Secretary of State]] may be so revised.

[⁵(1A) This subsection applies to–

(a) a decision of the [⁷[⁹Secretary of State]] under section 11, 12 or 17;

(b) [⁶...]

(c)   a decision of [⁸ the First-tier Tribunal] on a referral under section 28D(1)(b).

(1B)   Where the [⁷[⁹Secretary of State]] revises a decision under section 12(1)–

(a)   [⁷[⁹the Secretary of State]] may (if appropriate) do so as if [⁷][⁹...] revising a decision under section 11; and

(b)   if [⁷[⁹the Secretary of State]] does that, [⁷[⁹the]] decision as revised is to be treated as one under section 11 instead of section 12(1) (and, in particular, is to be so treated for the purposes of an appeal against it under section 20).]

(2)   In making a decision under subsection (1), the [⁷[⁹Secretary of State]] need not consider any issue that is not raised by the application or, as the case may be, did not cause [⁷[⁹the Secretary of State] t] to act on [⁷[⁹the Secretary of State's]] own initiative.

(3)   Subject to subsections (4) and (5) [⁴ and section 28ZC], a revision under this section shall take effect as from the date on which the original decision took (or was to take) effect.

(4)   Regulations may provide that, in prescribed cases or circumstances, a revision under this section shall take effect as from such other date as may be prescribed.

(5)   Where a decision is revised under this section, for the purpose of any rule as to the time allowed for bringing an appeal, the decision shall be regarded as made on the date on which it is so revised.

(6)   Except in prescribed circumstances, an appeal against [² a decision of the [⁷[⁹Secretary of State]]] shall lapse if the decision is revised under this section before the appeal is determined.]

Amendments

1.   Substituted by Social Security Act 1998, s40 (7.12.98).
2.   Also applies to decisions of Child Support Officer as from 16.11.98 by Social Security Act 1998 (Commencement No.2) Order 1998/2780 reg 3(1).
3.   As from 16.11.98, s16(1) shall omit reference to s17 Child Support Act 1991 as per Social Security Act 1998 (Commencement No.2) Order 1998/2780 reg 3(2).
4.   As from 16.11.98 omit reference to 28ZC as per Social Security Act 1998 (Commencement No.2) Order 1998/ 2780 reg 3(3).
5.   Child Support, Pensions and Social Security Act 2000 (2000 c.19) s8 (March 3, 2003 for the types of cases detailed in art 3 Child Support, Pensions and Social Security Act 2000 (Commencement No.12) Order 2003 (SI 2003 No.192)). For other types of cases, see '1993 rules' below.
6.   Child Maintenance and Other Payments Act 2008 (2008 c.6) s58 and Sch 8 (July 14, 2008).
7.   Child Maintenance and Other Payments Act 2008 (2008 c.6) s13 and Sch 3, para 12 (November 1, 2008); Child Maintenance and Other Payments Act 2008 (Commencement No.4 and Transitional Provision) Order 2008 (SI 2008 No.2675) art 3.
8.   Transfer of Tribunal Functions Order 2008 (SI 2008 No.2833) art 9 and Sch 3 para 78 (November 3, 2008, subject to the transitional provisions in Sch 4 of SI 2008 No.2833).
9.   Public Bodies (Child Maintenance and Enforcement Commission: Abolition and Transfer of Functions) Order 2012 (SI 2012 No.2007) art 3(2) and Sch para 11 (August 1, 2012).

1993 rules

s8 of the Child Support, Pensions and Social Security Act 2000 (2000 c.19) amends s16 of the Child Support Act 1991 and has been brought into force only for the types of cases in art 3 of the Child Support, Pensions and Social Security Act 2000 (Commencement No.12) Order 2003 (SI 2003 No.192 – see p683). For other types of cases the 1993 rules apply and the original wording is retained ie, in subsection (1) "of the Secretary of State under section 11, 12, or 17" is retained in place of "to which subsection (1A) applies" and subsection (1A) and (1B) are not included.

Definition

"prescribed": see s54.

General Note

This deals with the revision of decisions. It is extended by reg 3A(6) of the Appeals Regulations. It is subject to the saving and transitional provisions in art 3 Social Security Act 1998 (Commencement No.2) Order 1998.

Subsection (1)

Regulation 3A of the Appeals Regulations sets out the circumstances in which and the grounds on which a decision may be revised. They depend either on the time within which action is initiated or on the cause of the error. Regulation 4 of those Regulations deals with late applications for a revision. A change of circumstances cannot be dealt with by way of revision; it can only be dealt with under s17: see reg 3A(2).

A decision that has been revised may be further revised (*CIS 3535/2003*, paras 22-24).

A decision refusing to revise is not appealable under s20. The original decision is appealable as revised. See *RB v CMEC and ED* [2009] UKUT 53 (AAC) reported as *R(CS) 5/09*.

Subsection (1A)

This subsection sets out decisions that may be revised. It is not exhaustive.

Regulation 3A(6) of the Appeals Regulations extends it to include decisions under s41A or s47 and to decisions on adjustment for overpayments or voluntary payments.

It is suggested that a decision is made by a tribunal rather than by the Secretary of State even if the tribunal remits the case to the Secretary of State with directions under s20(8): see the general note to that subsection.

In *CSCS 14/2007*, a commissioner held that a decision not to make a maintenance calculation under s11 could not be revised under this section. It is, however, difficult to understand why this was not "a decision of the Secretary of State under section 11" within subpara (a).

Paragraph (a) confers power to revise a decision under s17. That includes both decisions to supersede under that section and decisions not to supersede (*CCS 1282/2010*, para 9).

Subsection (2)

The Secretary of State need not undertake a complete reconsideration of every issue covered by the original decision. This is in line with the general approach to determinations by both the Secretary of State and tribunals.

Subsections (3) and (4)

These subsections deal with the effective date of a revision. Subsection (3) contains the basic rule governing the effective date of a revision. It is the date on which the original decision took effect or was to take effect. Subsection (4) allows for other cases to be dealt with by regulations. Regulation 5A of the Appeals Regulations is made under that authority.

Subsections (5) and (6)

These subsections deal with the impact of a revision on the appeal rights against the original decision and the revision. Time for appealing begins to run again from the date when the revision is made. Generally, an appeal against a decision lapses if it is revised before the appeal is determined. The exceptions are contained in reg 30 of the Appeals Regulations.

[¹ Decisions superseding earlier decisions

17.–(1)   Subject to subsection (2), the following, namely–

(a)   any decision of the [⁷[¹⁰Secretary of State]] under section 11 or 12 or this section, whether as originally made or as revised under section 16;

(b)   any decision of [⁹an appeal tribunal or] [⁸ the First-tier Tribunal] under section 20; [⁵...]

[³(c)   [⁶...]

(d)   any decision of [⁹an appeal tribunal or] [⁸ the First-tier Tribunal] on a referral under section 28D(1)(b);

(e)   any decision of [⁹a Child Support Commissioner or] [⁸ the Upper Tribunal] on an appeal from such a decision as is mentioned in paragraph (b)or (d)]

may be superseded by a decision made by the [⁷[¹⁰Secretary of State]], either on an application made for the purpose or on [⁷[¹⁰the Secretary of State's]] own initiative.

[¹¹(2)   The Secretary of State may by regulations make provision with respect to the exercise of the power under subsection (1).

(3)   Regulations under subsection (2) may, in particular–

(a)   make provision about the cases and circumstances in which the power under subsection (1) is exercisable, including provision restricting the exercise of that power by virtue of change of circumstance;

(b)   make provision with respect to the consideration by the [¹⁰Secretary of State], when acting under subsection (1), of any issue which has not led to [¹⁰the Secretary of State's] so acting;

(c)   make provision with respect to procedure in relation to the exercise of the power under subsection (1).]

[⁴(4)   Subject to subsection (5) and section 28ZC, a decision under this section shall take effect as from the beginning of the maintenance period in which it is made or, where applicable, the beginning of the maintenance period in which the application was made.

(4A)   In subsection (4), a "maintenance period" is (except where a different meaning is prescribed for prescribed cases) a period of seven days, the first one beginning on the effective date of the first decision made by the [⁷[¹⁰Secretary of State]] under section 11 or (if earlier) [⁷[¹⁰the Secretary of State's]] first default or interim maintenance decision (under section 12) in relation to the non-resident parent in question, and each subsequent one beginning on the day after the last day of the previous one.]

[²(5) Regulations may provide that, in prescribed cases or circumstances, a decision under this section shall take effect as from such other date as may be prescribed.]]

[⁹(6)In this section–

"appeal tribunal" means an appeal tribunal constituted under Chapter 1 of Part 1 of the Social Security Act 1998 (the functions of which have been transferred to the First-tier Tribunal);

"Child Support Commissioner" means a person appointed as such under section 22 (the functions of whom have been transferred to the Upper Tribunal).]

Amendments

1. s17 inserted (4.3.99 and 1.6.99) by s41 Social Security Act 1998 (c.14).
2. Inserted (4.3.99) by Social Security Act 1998 Commencement Order (No.5) 1999/528.
3. Child Support, Pensions and Social Security Act 2000 (2000 c.19) s9(2) (March 3, 2003 for the types of cases detailed in art 3 Child Support, Pensions and Social Security Act 2000 (Commencement No.12) Order 2003 (SI 2003 No.192)). For other types of cases, see '1993 rules' below.
4. Child Support, Pensions and Social Security Act 2000 (2000 c.19) s9(3) (March 3, 2003 for the types of cases detailed in art 3 Child Support, Pensions and Social Security Act 2000 (Commencement No.12) Order 2003 (SI 2003 No.192)). For other types of cases, see '1993 rules' below.
5. Child Support, Pensions and Social Security Act 2000 (2000 c.19) s85 and Sch 9, Part I (March 3, 2003 for the types of cases detailed in art 3 Child Support, Pensions and Social Security Act 2000 (Commencement No.12) Order 2003 (SI 2003 No.192)). For other types of cases, see '1993 rules' below.
6. Child Maintenance and Other Payments Act 2008 (2008 c.6) ss56 and 58 and Sch 8 (July 14, 2008); Child Maintenance and Other Payments Act 2008 (Commencement) Order 2008 (SI 2008 No.1476) art 2(2)(c) and (6).
7. Child Maintenance and Other Payments Act 2008 (2008 c.6) s13 and Sch 3 para 13 (November 1, 2008); Child Maintenance and Other Payments Act 2008 (Commencement No.4 and Transitional Provision) Order 2008 (SI 2008 No.2675) art 3.
8. Transfer of Tribunal Functions Order 2008 (SI 2008 No.2833) art 9 and Sch 3 para 79 (November 3, 2008, subject to the transitional provisions contained in Sch 4 of SI 2008 No.2833).
9. Welfare Reform Act 2012 (2012 c.5) s103 and Sch 12 para 2 (March 8, 2012, but in accordance with s103 of the Welfare Reform Act 2012, this amendment has effect as if it had come into force on November 3, 2008).
10. Public Bodies (Child Maintenance and Enforcement Commission: Abolition and Transfer of Functions) Order 2012 (SI 2012 No.2007) art 3(2) and Sch paras 12 and 77 (August 1, 2012).
11. Child Maintenance and Other Payments Act 2008 (2008 c.6) s17 (December 10, 2012 for the types of cases falling within art 3 of SI 2012 No.3042 only, subject to art 5 of that SI – see p767 and July 29, 2013 for the types of cases falling within art 3 of SI 2013 No.1860, subject to art 5 of that SI – see p770). See also art 6 of SI 2012 No.3042 (which had effect up to July 28, 2013) and art 7 of SI 2013 No.1860 for further transitional provisions. For such cases this amendment replaced subsections (2) and (3). For other types of cases see '2003 and 1993 rules', below; Child Maintenance and Other Payments Act 2008 (Commencement No.10 and Transitional Provisions) Order 2012 (SI 2012 No.3042) art 2; Child Maintenance and Other Payments Act 2008 (Commencement No.11 and Transitional Provisions) Order 2013 (SI 2013 No.1860) art 2.

2003 and 1993 rules

s17 of the Child Maintenance and Other Payments Act 2008 (2008 c.6) amends subsections 17(2) and (3) of the Child Support Act 1991 and has been brought into force for the types of cases falling within art 3 of SI 2012 No.3042, subject to art 5 of that SI – see p767 and those falling within art 3 of SI 2013 No.1860, subject to art 5 of that SI – see p770 (for other transitional provisions see art 6 of SI 2012 No.3042, which had effect up to July 28, 2013, and art 7 of SI 2013 No.1860). For other types of cases, this amendment does not apply and those subsections read:

(2)   In making a decision under subsection (1), the [⁷[¹⁰Secretary of State]] need not consider any issue that is not raised by the application or, as the case may be, did not cause [⁷[¹⁰the Secretary of State]] to act on [⁷[¹⁰the Secretary of State's]] own initiative.

[²(3)   Regulations may prescribe the cases and circumstances in which, and the procedure by which, a decision may be made under this section.]

1993 rules

s9 of the Child Support, Pensions and Social Security Act 2000 (2000 c.19) amends s17 of the Child Support Act 1991 and has been brought into force only for the types of cases in art 3 of the Child Support, Pensions and Social Security Act 2000 (Commencement No.12) Order 2003 (SI 2003 No.192 – see p683). For other types of cases the 1993 rules apply and the amendments are not in force. These amendments repealed the word "and" from the end of paragraph (1)(b), replaced paragraph 1(c) with paragraphs (1)(c)-(e) and replaced paragraph (4). If the 1993 rules apply, paragraph (1)(d) and (e) do not apply (the original paragraph (1)(c) has been repealed from July 14, 2008 by s56 and 58 and Sch 8 of the Child Maintenance and Other Payments Act 2008 (2008 c.6)), and paragraph (4) reads:

(4)   Subject to subsection (5) and section 28ZC, a decision under this section shall take effect as from the date on which it is made or, where applicable, the date on which the application was made.

Definition

"prescribed": see s54.

General Note

This section deals with the supersession of decisions. The nature of a supersession was analysed by the Court of Appeal in *Wood v SSWP* [2003] EWCA Civ 53, CA (reported as *R(DLA) 1/03*). In the case of an application, it is permissible for the Secretary of State to give a decision refusing to supersede. That form of decision is appealable. It is the correct form of decision if no change is made either to the decision which is the subject of the application or to its basis (*CIS 3655/2007*, para 22). See further regs 6A, 6B and 7B of the Appeals Regulations.

Subsection (1)

The Secretary of State may act with or without an application. If a supersession is being considered on the Secretary of State's own initiative, the procedure set out in reg 7C of the Appeals Regulations must be followed.

It is suggested that a decision is made by a tribunal rather than by the Secretary of State even if the tribunal remits the case to the Secretary of State with directions under s20(8): see the general note to that subsection.

Subsection (2)

The Secretary of State need not undertake a complete reconsideration of every issue covered by the original decision. This is in line with the general approach to determinations by both the Secretary of State and tribunals.

Subsection (3)

Regulations 6A and 6B of the Appeals Regulations are made under the authority of this provision.

Subsections (4)-(5)

These deal with the effective date of a supersession. Subsection (4) contains the general rules. The general rule for a supersession made on the Secretary of State's own initiative is that it takes effect from the beginning of the maintenance period in which it was made. The general rule for a supersession made on an application is that it takes effect from the beginning of the maintenance period in which the application was made. Subsection (5) allows for other cases to be dealt with by regulations. Regulation 7B of the Appeals Regulations is made under that authority.

Sections 18 and 19 were repealed by s41 Social Security Act 1998 with effect from 1 June 1999.

[¹ Appeals to [³ First-tier Tribunal]

[¹**20.**–(1)   A qualifying person has a right of appeal to [⁴ the First-tier Tribunal] against–

(a)   a decision of the [³[⁵Secretary of State]] under section 11, 12 or 17 (whether as originally made or as revised under section 16);

(b)   a decision of the [³[⁵Secretary of State]] not to make a maintenance calculation under section 11 or not to supersede a decision under section 17;

(c)   [²...]

(d)   the imposition (by virtue of section 41A) of a requirement to make penalty payments, or their amount;

(e)   [²...]

(2)   In subsection (1), "qualifying person" means–

(a)   in relation to paragraphs (a) and (b)–

(i)   the person with care, or non-resident parent, with respect to whom the [³[⁵Secretary of State]] made the decision, or

(ii)   in a case relating to a maintenance calculation which was applied for under section 7, either of those persons or the child concerned;

(b)   [²...]

(c)   in relation to paragraph (d), the parent who has been required to make penalty payments; and

(d)   in relation to paragraph (e), the person required to pay fees.

[⁶(2A)   Regulations may provide that, in such cases or circumstances as may be prescribed, there is a right of appeal against a decision mentioned in subsection (1)(a) or (b) only if the Commission has considered whether to revise the decision under section 16.

(2B)   The regulations may in particular provide that that condition is met only where–

(a)   the consideration by the Commission was on an application,

(b)   the Commission considered issues of a specified description, or

(c)   the consideration by the Commission satisfied any other condition specified in the regulations.]

(3)   A person with a right of appeal under this section shall be given such notice as may be prescribed of–

(a)   that right; and

(b)   the relevant decision, or the imposition of the requirement.

(4)   Regulations may make–

(a)   provision as to the manner in which, and the time within which, appeals are to be brought; [⁴ ...]

(b)   [⁴...]

[⁶(c)   provision that, where in accordance with regulations under subsection (2A) there is no right of appeal against a decision, any purported appeal may be treated as an application for revision under section 16.]

(5)   The regulations may in particular make any provision of a kind mentioned in Schedule 5 to the Social Security Act 1998.

(6)   [²...]

(7)   In deciding an appeal under this section, [⁴ the First-tier Tribunal]–

(a)   need not consider any issue that is not raised by the appeal; and

(b)   shall not take into account any circumstances not obtaining at the time when the [³[⁵Secretary of State]] made the decision or imposed the requirement.

(8)   If an appeal under this section is allowed, the [⁴ First-tier Tribunal] may–

(a)   itself make such decision as it considers appropriate; or

(b)   remit the case to the [³[⁵Secretary of State]], together with such directions (if any) as it considers appropriate.]]

Amendments

1.   Child Support, Pensions and Social Security Act 2000 (2000 c.19) s10 (March 3, 2003 for the types of cases detailed in art 3 Child Support, Pensions and Social Security Act 2000 (Commencement No.12) Order 2003 (SI 2003 No.192)). See '1993 rules' below for s20 as it has effect apart from s10 of The Child Support, Pensions and Social Security Act 2000.

2.   Child Maintenance and Other Payments Act 2008 (2008 c.6) s58 and Sch 8 (July 14, 2008).

3.   Child Maintenance and Other Payments Act 2008 (2008 c.6) s13 and Sch 3, para 14 (November 1, 2008); Child Maintenance and Other Payments Act 2008 (Commencement No.4 and Transitional Provision) Order 2008 (SI 2008 No.2675) art 3.

4.   Transfer of Tribunal Functions Order 2008 (SI 2008 No.2833) art 9 and Sch 3 para 81 (November 3, 2008, subject to the transitional provisions contained in Sch 4 of SI 2008 No.2833).

5.   Public Bodies (Child Maintenance and Enforcement Commission: Abolition and Transfer of Functions) Order 2012 (SI 2012 No.2007) art 3(2) and Sch para 13 (August 1, 2012).

6.   Welfare Reform Act 2012 (2012 c.5) s102 and Sch 11 para 5 (February 25, 2013 for the purpose of making regulations only); Welfare Reform Act 2012 (Commencement No.8 and Savings and Transitional Provisions) Order 2013 (SI 2013 No.358) art 2 and Sch 1.

Note

i.   In accordance with the Child Support Appeals (Jurisdiction of Courts) Order 2002 (SI 2002 No.1915), from March 3, 2003 for the types of cases detailed in art 3 Child Support, Pensions and Social Security Act 2000 (Commencement No.12) Order 2003 (SI 2003 No.192), an appeal under s20 should be made to a court instead of to a tribunal in the circumstances mentioned in art 4 of SI 2003 No.1915.

1993 rules

s10 of The Child Support, Pensions and Social Security Act 2000 (2000 c.19) replaced s20 of The Child Support Act 1991 only for the types of cases in art 3 Child Support, Pensions and Social Security Act 2000 (Commencement No.12) Order 2003 (SI 2003 No.192 – see p683). For other types of cases the 1993 rules apply and s10 of The Child Support, Pensions and Social Security Act 2000, reads:

"Appeals to [³ First-tier Tribunal]

[¹**20.**–(1)   Where an application for a maintenance assessment is refused,
the person who made that application shall have a right of appeal to [³ the First-tier Tribunal] against the refusal.

(2)   Where a maintenance assessment is in force–

(a)   the absent parent or person with care with respect to whom it was made; or

(b)   where the application for the assessment was made under section 7, either of them or the child concerned,

shall have a right of appeal to [³ the First-tier Tribunal] against the amount of the assessment or the date from which the assessment takes effect.

(3)   Where a maintenance assessment is cancelled, or an application for the cancellation of a maintenance assessment is refused–

(a)   the absent parent or person with care with respect to whom the maintenance assessment in question was, or remains, in force; or

(b)   where the application for that assessment was made under section 7, either of them or the child concerned,

shall have a right of appeal to [³ the First-tier Tribunal] against the cancellation or refusal.

[⁴(3A)   Regulations may provide that, in such cases or circumstances as may be prescribed, there is a right of appeal against a decision only if the Commission has considered whether to revise the decision under section 16.

(3B)   The regulations may in particular provide that that condition is met only where–

(a)   the consideration by the Commission was on an application,

(b)   the Commission considered issues of a specified description, or

(c)   the consideration by the Commission satisfied any other condition specified in the regulations.]

[² (4)   A person with a right of appeal under this section shall be given such notice of that right and, in the case of a right conferred by subsection (1) or (3), such notice of the decision as may be prescribed.

(5)   Regulations may make–

(a)   provision as to the manner in which, and the time within which, appeals are to be brought; [³ ...]

(b)   [³ ...]

[⁴(c)   provision that, where in accordance with regulations under subsection (3A) there is no right of appeal against a decision, any purported appeal may be treated as an application for revision under section 16.]

(6)   The regulations may in particular make any provision of a kind mentioned in Schedule 5 to the Social Security Act 1998]

(7)   In deciding an appeal under this section, [³ the First-tier Tribunal]–

(a)   need not consider any issue that is not raised by the appeal; and

(b)   shall not take into account any circumstances not obtaining at the time when the decision or assessment appealed against was made.]

Amendments

1.   *s20 inserted (1.6.99) by s42 of Social Security Act 1998 (c.14)*

2.   *s20(4)-(6) inserted (4.3.99) by s42 Social Security Act 1998 (c.14).*

3.   *Transfer of Tribunal Functions Order 2008 (SI 2008 No.2833) art 9 and Sch 3 para 80 (November 3, 2008, subject to the transitional provisions contained in Sch 4 of SI 2008 No.2833).*

4.   *Welfare Reform Act 2012 (2012 c.5) s102 and Sch 11 para 6 (February 25, 2013 for the purpose of making regulations only); Welfare Reform Act 2012 (Commencement No.8 and Savings and Transitional Provisions) Order 2013 (SI 2013 No.358) art 2 and Sch 1."*

Definitions

"child": see s55.
"maintenance calculation": see s54.
"non-resident parent": see s54.
"parent": see s54.
"person with care": see s54.

General Note

This section is extended by reg 30A of the Appeals Regulations.

All heads of appeal presuppose a decision on a subsisting application or on the Secretary of State's own initiative.

If an application is withdrawn before it is decided, no decision can be given on an appeal, not even a decision to refuse the application. This applies both to the 1993 scheme (*CCS 2910/2001*) and to the 2003 scheme (*CH v CMEC (CSM)* [2010] UKUT 140 (AAC), para 52). It follows that the First-tier Tribunal has no jurisdiction to hear a dispute about whether an application has been withdrawn.

The core duties of the First-tier Tribunal were set out in *R(IS) 3/09:*

> "10.   Tribunals must act within their statutory jurisdiction, because that defines the limits of their power. They must act judicially, because that is their nature. They must decide the issues that arise for resolution, because that is their function. And they must make decisions that are clear, sufficiently complete and capable of being implemented, because the discharge of their duty to decide the issues judicially must be effective."

Jurisdiction

The tribunal must not act outside its jurisdiction. In deciding whether a particular matter goes to the jurisdiction of the tribunal, the test to be applied is that set out in *Garthwaite v Garthwaite* [1964] 2 All ER 233 at 241 *per* Diplock LJ as follows:

> "In its narrow and strict sense, the 'jurisdiction' of a validly constituted court connotes the limits which are imposed on its power to hear and determine issues between persons seeking to avail themselves of its process by reference (i) to the subject-matter of the issue, or (ii) to the persons between whom the issue is joined, or (iii) to the kind of relief sought, or any combination of these factors."

This is in contrast to the wider use of "jurisdiction" to cover:

> "the settled practice of the court as to the way in which it will exercise its power to hear and determine issues, or as to the circumstances in which it will grant a particular kind of relief, including its settled practice to refuse to exercise such powers or to grant such relief in particular circumstances."

The significance of this distinction is that a tribunal created by statute cannot enlarge its jurisdiction in the strict sense, but has power to alter the way in which that jurisdiction is exercised in practice, subject of course to the limits set by legislation and precedent.

The tribunal's jurisdiction in the strict sense is limited to that given by statute.

That jurisdiction cannot be extended by consent of the parties (*R(SB) 15/87*, paras 10-11; *R(SB) 1/95*, paras 13-16; *R v Secretary of State for Social Services ex p CPAG* [1989] 1 All ER 1047 at 1056, *per* Woolf LJ; *Rydqvist v SSWP* [2002] 1 WLR 3343). It follows that a tribunal has no power simply to give effect to a maintenance agreement reached between the parents (*CCS 2083/2004* and *CCS 2483/2004*, paras 8-15). Likewise, it is not possible for a party to limit the tribunal's jurisdiction by seeking to restrict the appeal to certain issues only (*CCS 1992/1997*, para 31). However, under subs 7(a) the appeal tribunal need not consider any issue that is not raised by the appeal.

It is in the strict sense of the word that commissioners held that tribunals have no inherent jurisdiction (*R 2/94 CSC*), para 10; *R(SB) 42/83*, paras 11-13).

There is no special rule of interpretation that allows tribunals to fill an apparent gap in the tribunal's statutory jurisdiction. Any apparent gap may only be filled if it is possible to do so by applying the normal principles of interpretation (*Pendragon plc v Jackson* [1998] ICR 215).

A tribunal has power to determine whether a case falls within its jurisdiction (*R(SB) 29/83*, para 17; *R(SB) 105/89*, para 12; *R v Fulham Rent Tribunal ex p Zerek* [1951] 1 All ER 482). The tribunal must determine whether it has jurisdiction by strict enquiry ("expiscate") (*CI 78/1990*, para 12; *CI 79/1990*, para 15). The duty is to ensure that it has jurisdiction to make its proposed decision, but not to seek out other bases on which it might have jurisdiction (*B v R* [2010] 1 FLR 563 at paras 33 and 37). Once a question of jurisdiction has been raised, the tribunal must enquire and determine the question and cannot accept a concession that the argument was not valid (*CCS 499/1995*, para 7).

The tribunal's enquiry into its jurisdiction may involve determining whether a decision on which its jurisdiction depends was valid. The tribunal has power to determine that a decision extending time to appeal was invalid (*R(SB) 1/95*, para 12). It also has power to determine that the setting aside of a decision was invalid (*CI 78/1990*, para 12) and so ineffective, thereby depriving the present tribunal of jurisdiction to rehear the case (*CS 51/92*). The tribunal may also refuse to accept jurisdiction if an appeal has been wrongly admitted after an absolute time limit (*R(AF) 1/09*).

It may be appropriate to hold a preliminary hearing into jurisdiction to deal with any issue of jurisdiction (*Potts v IRC* [1982] 56 TC 25 at 35, *per* Walton, J). Generally, however, preliminary hearings of questions are not to be encouraged (*CA 126/1989*, para 10; *Sutcliffe v Big C's Marine* [1998] ICR 913). Guidance on when a preliminary issue is appropriate was given in *Steele v Steele, The Times*, June 5, 2001.

Nature of an appeal

An appeal to a tribunal lies on any ground. In other words, the decision under appeal may be challenged on fact or on law. The tribunal undertakes a reconsideration of the issues arising for determination in substitution for the consideration of the Secretary of State. It is not revising or superseding the decision under ss16 or 17. The tribunal does not, therefore, have to identify a ground for revision or supersession in order to allow the decision under appeal to be changed (*CDLA 1392/2001*).

Delegated legislation

Delegated legislation may only be made within the scope of the power conferred by the Act. The scope of the enabling statutory power is relevant both to the interpretation and to the validity of delegated legislation which purports to be made under it. If the language is susceptible to different meanings, one of which is within the scope of the enabling power and one of which is outside it, the provision will (subject to the Human Rights Act 1998) be given the meaning which renders it valid. There are, however, problems with this approach: (i) It may not be easy to identify the relevant enabling power. Regulations may be made under stated sections and "all other powers enabling in that behalf" (see *Vibixa Ltd v Komori UK Ltd* [2006] 4 All ER 294 for the scope of this formula) and the omission of a power to make a particular type of provision from one enabling section does not prevent that power falling within another (perhaps more generally worded) enabling section (*R v Secretary of State for Social Security ex p Rouse, The Times*, February 1 1993); (ii) The power may be worded very broadly – eg, s51(1).

If a provision in delegated legislation cannot be interpreted in a way which renders it valid, it is said to be *ultra vires* and is invalid and unenforceable. A tribunal has power to interpret delegated legislation. They have no power to carry out a judicial review and declare the delegated legislation to be *ultra vires*, but they do have power to decide in the context of a particular appeal that the legislation is of no effect because it is *ultra vires*. This power applies to cases where the legislation is illegal – ie, that it is outside the scope of the enabling power (*Chief Adjudication Officer v Foster* [1993] 1 All ER 705). Tribunals also have power to determine whether delegated legislation is *ultra vires* on the ground of irrationality (*R(CS) 2/95*, paras 8-9), but should only exercise that power if a serious issue arises and it is necessary to rule on the question in order to determine the appeal (*R(IS) 26/95*, para 45). A decision on whether a provision in Regulations is irrational must concentrate on the regulations as laid before Parliament, without reference to any legislative drafting history (*CIS 14141/1996*, para 21). A provision will only be held to be irrational if the argument for this conclusion is compelling, and it will not be compelling merely because it points to unfairness, absurdity or even perversity in the treatment of different parties *(ibid*, para 21). There is no special test of irrationality where the legislation has been subject to Parliamentary scrutiny. The test to apply is the *Wednesbury* test (*O'Connor v Chief Adjudication Officer* [1999] 1 ELR 1200 at *1210, per* Auld LJ). In an appropriate case a provision which has been held to be irrational can be severed so as to preserve the remainder of the Regulations (*CIS 14141/1996*, para 23). Presumably tribunals will also be held to have power to determine the procedural regularity of delegated legislation. In addition to being within the scope of its enabling provision the delegated legislation must not conflict with statutory rights already enacted by other primary legislation (*R v Secretary of State for Social Security ex p Joint Council for the Welfare of Immigrants* [1996] 4 All ER 385 and *R(IS) 7/99*, para 10). However, this will only be so in the most extreme cases, and the effect of the delegated legislation must go beyond mere interference with the statutory rights such that it renders them valueless in practice *(ibid,* para 13).

Form of decision

It is not necessary for the tribunal to make a full outcome decision; it is sufficient if its decision deals with the issues raised by the appeal (*R(IS) 2/08*).

Revision and refusal to revise

A decision to refuse to revise is not appealable, including a refusal to revise consequent upon the rejection of an application for a variation (*RB v CMEC and ED* [2009] UKUT 53 (AAC) reported as *R(CS) 5/09*).

Duty of members

It should be obvious, but history shows that it bears repeating, that it is the duty of members of to apply the law as it is and not as they would wish it to be (*R(U) 7/81*, para 8).

Subsection (1)

This sets out decisions that are appealable to the First-tier Tribunal. Paragraph (c) is qualified by subs (6).

The list in this subsection is not exhaustive of the decisions that are appealable. It is extended by reg 30A of the Appeals Regulations to cover (a) decisions on adjustments to take account of overpayments or voluntary payments and (b) supersession decisions made under s17, including those that are later revised under s16.

A refusal to revise is not an appealable decision. However, the original decision will be appealable, although the appeal may be late. Although time can be extended under reg 32 of the Appeals Regulations, it may be safer to make an appeal at the same time as an application for a revision.

Variation decisions are made under ss11, 16 or 17. As there is no decision separate from the maintenance calculation, a separate right of appeal is not needed.

Subsections (4)–(5)

The relevant Regulations are the Appeals Regulations.

Subsection (7)

A First-tier Tribunal deals with a case on appeal by way of rehearing. The tribunal stands in the same position as the officer who made the decision under appeal. All aspects of the case that the officer could have considered may be considered by the tribunal. This does not mean that every aspect of the case is considered from scratch. The tribunal has power to reconsider any issue, but is only required to consider those that properly arise before it. See the general notes to paras (a) and (b) below. An issue is a point of fact or law that merits inquiry and decision on the information or evidence before the tribunal.

Subsection (7)(a)

Paragraph (a) provides that a tribunal need not consider any issue that is not raised by the appeal. In *R (Starling) v Child Support Commissioners* [2008] EWHC 1319 (Admin) at para 36, Collins J described this as "the most ill drafted and obscure provision in the field of child support". It is possible that his Lordship was not referred to all the possible contenders for that accolade.

An issue is raised by an appeal if it is raised by any of the parties before or at the hearing (*CH 1229/2002*, paras 13-18). A tribunal is entitled to limit itself to issues raised by a competent representative (*Jeleniewicz v SSWP*, reported as part of R(IS) 3/09).

The tribunal retains power to deal with any issue that arose before the Secretary of State. Its decision will not automatically be wrong in law for considering one of these questions. The tribunal's decision may, though, be wrong in law for failing to exercise correctly its power to deal with other issues. The decision must be taken judicially. This means that it must be taken in accordance with the principles of natural justice and the Convention rights of the parties (*CCS 463/2000* para 17; *R (Starling) v Child Support Commissioners* paras 39-43). In Starling, Collins J held that a tribunal was entitled to raise issues if there was a public interest to do so (paras 30-32). He identified the public in interest in the possible payment of benefit to the person with care and the children's welfare (para 32).

The Upper Tribunal only has power to deal with a point that was not dealt with by the First-tier Tribunal in three circumstances. First, if there was an error of law in respect of one of the issues that the tribunal did deal with. That allows the Upper Tribunal to deal with any other issue that was relevant in substituting a decision or in giving directions on remitting to the Secretary of State or for rehearing. Second, if the new point can be classified not as a separate issue, but as an argument on an issue that was dealt with by the tribunal. Third, if the tribunal improperly exercised its discretion to consider other issues under this provision. See *CIS 3846/2001* (para 6). The Upper Tribunal would also have power to deal with any issue that went to the tribunal's jurisdiction.

In *CH 3513/2003*, the commissioner held that it was perverse in the circumstances of the case for the tribunal to take issues of fact that the claimant would surely have raised if they were relevant. He also held that, if the tribunal had been entitled to take the issue, it should have adjourned to allow the other party to produce evidence, as the pre-hearing directions had not been sufficient to alert that party to the need for further evidence.

This provision cannot be used as a device for extending the tribunal's jurisdiction: see the section on *Jurisdiction* at the beginning of this general note.

Subsection (7)(b)

Paragraph (b) provides that a tribunal must not take into account any circumstances not obtaining at the time when the decision under appeal was made. In other words, it limits the tribunal's jurisdiction by excluding changes of circumstances after the date of the decision.

The relevant date is that of the decision under appeal, not the effective date of the decision. The tribunal must consider any change of circumstances between the effective date and the time when the decision was made and take it into account by way of a series of calculations under Sch 1 para 15. See *CCS 2620/2002*.

It is not possible or appropriate to give an abstract definition of what constitutes a circumstance (*CDLA 4734/1999*, para 56).

The tribunal will usually be concerned not merely with the position on the date when a decision was made, but with the position over the period covered by the decision. Any circumstances that have existed during that period must be considered (*CDLA 4734/1999*, para 55).

The provision deals with circumstances, not with evidence of circumstances. It does not prevent a tribunal from taking account of evidence of circumstances obtaining at or before the date of decision even if that evidence was only produced or obtained after that date. The tribunal may also consider evidence of what occurred after the date of the decision if it throws light on what occurred before that date. Evidence of earnings received after the date of the decision, for example, may throw light on whether before that date a relevant change of circumstances had occurred in the party's income to merit a fresh calculation. If a party wants to rely on evidence that was produced after the relevant date, the tribunal must determine whether it can be related to that date before taking it into account. See *R(DLA) 2/01* para 9 and *CDLA 4734/1999* para 58. If there is evidence of a change of circumstances after the date of the decision under appeal, it is good practice to identify the evidence on which the tribunal's decision was based in order to show that it complied with subs (7)(b) (*CDLA 2822/1999*, para 18). Depending on the circumstances, it may be a mistake of law not to make this clear.

The commissioners commented on the relevance of accounts produced after the time of the decision under appeal. In *CCS 1741/2005*, the commissioner decided that accounts produced after the relevant time could not be used for the purpose of para 7 of the Schedule to the Maintenance Calculations and Special Cases Regulations (para 25). This decision was distinguished by a different commissioner in *CCS 1325/2006*. The commissioner there decided that the accounts of a company of which the non-resident parent was a director were admissible despite the fact that they were not in existence at the time of the decision under appeal or the effective date of that decision, because they were evidence of the parent's financial position at the time when the decision under appeal was made (para. 10). The commissioner left open whether *CCS 1741/2005* was correct in relation to the Schedule to the Regulations. In *CCS 1938/2006*, the commissioner decided that the tribunal had been wrong to calculate the absent parent's income by reference to accounts that included a period after the relevant time (paras 8 and 11). In *CCS 1137/2007*, the commissioner who decided *CCS 1741/2005* repeated his view and emphasised that the accounts produced after the date of decision could be used under the provisions that allow other figures to be used if they allow the parent's normal weekly earnings to be determined more accurately. In view of this, it may be that the difference of view between commissioners is not of practical significance.

In *CCS 2885/2005*, the commissioner considered how this provision applied in the case of an anticipated change of circumstances under reg 6A(3)(a)(ii) of the Appeals Regulations. He concluded (para 24): "Presumably, the fact that a change will occur is a circumstance that obtains at the time of the decision."

Other provisions or principles may further limit the circumstances that the tribunal may take into account. In the case of an appeal against a decision that has been revised, the tribunal may not take account of circumstances that occurred after the date of the original decision but before the date of the revision. This is because a change of circumstances after the date of the original decision can only be considered on a supersession. See *R(CS) 1/03*.

Evidence relating to later than the time of the decision may be used to assess the credibility and reliability of evidence (*CSDLA 854/2003*).

Subsection (8)

If a tribunal allows an appeal, it may give its own decision or remit the case to the Secretary of State with directions. In the former case, the decision is clearly made by the tribunal and not by the Secretary of State. In the latter case, it is suggested that the decision is also made by the tribunal, albeit that the actual arithmetical calculations are carried out on behalf of the tribunal by the Secretary of State in accordance with the tribunal's directions. This is relevant to the scope of the Secretary of State's power to revise and supersede decisions under ss16 and 17. It also prevents an appeal against the decision implementing a tribunal's decision that was possible under the original scheme. An appeal to a tribunal under subs (1) above lies only against decisions and impositions of requirements by the Secretary of State. An appeal against a decision now lies only to the Upper Tribunal. See *CCS 2403/1998*, paras 35.1 and 36.

Section 21 was repealed by s42 Social Security Act 1998 with effect from 1 June 1999.

Child Support Commissioners for Northern Ireland

23.–(1) Her Majesty may from time to time appoint a Chief Child Support Commissioner for Northern Ireland and [³other Child Support Commissioners for Northern Ireland].

(2) The Chief Child Support Commissioner for Northern Ireland and the other Child Support Commissioners for Northern Ireland shall be appointed from among persons who are barristers or solicitors of not less than [¹7] years' standing.

(3) Schedule 4 shall have effect with respect to Child Support Commissioners for Northern Ireland [² ...]

(4) Subject to any Order made after the passing of this Act by virtue of subsection (1)(a) of section 3 of the Northern Ireland Constitution Act 1973, the matters to which this subsection applies shall not be transferred matters for the purposes of that Act but shall for the purposes of subsection (2) of that section be treated as specified in Schedule 3 to that Act.

(5) Subsection (4) applies to all matters relating to Child Support Commissioners, including procedure and appeals, other than those specified in paragraph 9 of Schedule 2 to the Northern Ireland Constitution Act 1973.

Amendments

1. Tribunals, Courts and Enforcement Act 2007 (2007 c.15) Sch 10 para 22(3) (July 21, 2008 subject to arts 3 and 4 Tribunals, Courts and Enforcement Act 2007 (Commencement No.5 and Transitional Provisions) Order 2008 (SI 2008 No.1653). For those to whom this amendment does not apply, the amendment replaced "10" with "7" in subs 23(2).

2. Transfer of Tribunal Functions Order 2008 (SI 2008 No.2833) art 9 and Sch 3 para 83 (November 3, 2008, subject to the transitional provisions in Sch 4 of SI 2008 No.2833).

3. Northern Ireland Act 2009 (2009 c.3) s2 and Sch 4 para 22 (April 12, 2010); Northern Ireland Act 2009 (Commencement No.2) Order 2010 (SI 2010 No.812).

[¹ **Retermination of appeals**

23A.–(1)   This section applies where an application is made [³ to the First-tier Tribunal for permission to appeal to the Upper Tribunal from any decision of the First-tier Tribunal under section 20].

(2)   [³ ...]

(3)   If each of the principal parties to the case expresses the view that the decision was erroneous in point of law, [³ the First-tier Tribunal] shall set aside the decision and refer the case for determination by a differently constituted [³ First-tier Tribunal].

(4)   The "principal parties" are–

[² (za) [⁴...]]

(a)   the Secretary of State; and

(b)   those who are qualifying persons for the purposes of section 20(2) in relation to the decision in question.]

Amendments

1.   Child Support, Pensions and Social Security Act 2000 s11 (February 15, 2001).
2.   Child Maintenance and Other Payments Act 2008 (2008 c.6) s13 and Sch 3, para 15 (November 1, 2008); Child Maintenance and Other Payments Act 2008 (Commencement No.4 and Transitional Provision) Order 2008 (SI 2008 No.2675) art 3.
3.   Transfer of Tribunal Functions Order 2008 (SI 2008 No.2833) art 9 and Sch 3 para 84 (November 3, 2008, subject to the transitional provisions in Sch 4 of SI 2008 No.2833).
4.   Public Bodies (Child Maintenance and Enforcement Commission: Abolition and Transfer of Functions) Order 2012 (SI 2012 No.2007) art 3(2) and Sch para 14 (August 1, 2012).

General Note

Subsection (4)(b) is subject to the transitional protection in reg 11 Child Support (Consequential Amendments and Transitional Provisions) Regulations 2001.

Subsection (2) confers a power, but not a duty, to set aside a tribunal's decision for error of law. The power operates regardless of the views of the parties. Subsection (3) imposes a duty to set it aside if the parties agree that the tribunal went wrong in law. Given the antagonism that often exists between the non-resident parent and the person with care, it is unlikely that they will agree on the error that the tribunal is alleged to have made. However, it is only necessary that they agree that the tribunal has made an error.

The decision under either subsection can only be taken by the person who chaired or constituted the appeal tribunal in question: compare the wording of s24(6)(a). The operation of this section is parasitic on an application for leave to appeal to the Upper Tribunal. In other words, it only operates when a valid application has been made. There is no express provision to this effect, but it is the context in which it applies and explains why there is no time limit on its operation; it is subject to the time limits that apply to applications for leave (*CDLA 1685/ 2004*, para 14). If there is no full statement of the tribunal's decision, the section cannot operate (*ibid*, para 14). Nor can the section be operated once the person has granted or refused leave to appeal to the commissioner (*CF 6923/1999*).

CIB 4427/2002 was concerned with a case in which all the parties were agreed that the tribunal had gone wrong in law, but its decision was not set aside by a district chairman. The commissioner said at para 17 that in those circumstances the parties' right to have the decision set aside had to be preserved, even if the commissioner did not agree that the tribunal had gone wrong in law.

In *CIB 2949/2005*, both the claimant and the Secretary of State applied for leave to appeal from the chairman. The claimant's application was refused and she renewed her application to the commissioner. The Secretary of State's application for leave from the chairman was signed on the same day as the claimant's application for leave from the commissioner arrived at the commissioner's office. The commissioner decided that in those circumstances the social security equivalent of s23 could no longer operate, as the commissioner was seised of the case as soon as the application arrived. Thereafter the control of the ultimate disposal of the case was a matter for the commissioner. See paras 13-20.

[¹ **Appeals to Upper Tribunal**]

24.–[²(1)   Each of the following may appeal [¹to the Upper Tribunal under section 11 of the Tribunals, Courts and Enforcement Act 2007 from any decision of the First-tier Tribunal under section 20 of this Act]–

(a)   [³...]

(b)   the Secretary of State, and

(c)   any person who is aggrieved by the decision of an appeal tribunal.]

[¹(2)   Where a question which would otherwise fall to be determined by [³...] the Secretary of State under this Act first arises in the course of an appeal to the Upper

Tribunal, that tribunal may, if it thinks fit, determine the question even though it has not been considered by [³...] the Secretary of State.]

Amendments

1.   Transfer of Tribunal Functions Order 2008 (SI 2008 No.2833) art 9 and Sch 3 para 85 (November 3, 2008, subject to the transitional provisions in Sch 4 of SI 2008 No.2833).
2.   Child Maintenance and Other Payments Act 2008 (2008 c.6) s13 and Sch 3, para 16 (November 1, 2008); Child Maintenance and Other Payments Act 2008 (Commencement No.4 and Transitional Provision) Order 2008 (SI 2008 No.2675) art 3.
3.   Public Bodies (Child Maintenance and Enforcement Commission: Abolition and Transfer of Functions) Order 2012 (SI 2012 No.2007) art 3(2) and Sch para 15 (August 1, 2012).

General Note

Subsection (1)

The Secretary of State may appeal to the Upper Tribunal.

The meaning of "person ... aggrieved" has been considered in various statutory contexts. It is difficult to distill any general principles from those decisions, as so much depends on the context. These words may limit the scope of the right of appeal in two ways. They may limit its personal scope by preventing someone who is not a person with care, a non-resident parent or (in Scotland) a qualifying child from appealing. It is difficult to envisage who else might be included, although it is possible that a grandparent or someone else with a close personal connection to a child might wish to lodge an appeal in the interests of a child. The words may also limit the material scope of the right of appeal by restricting the circumstances in which a person may appeal. The Secretary of State might wish to appeal in the interests of one of the other parties if it thought that the First-tier Tribunal had made an error of law. Its role as decision maker and its other responsibilities under the 2008 Act might give it sufficient interest to be aggrieved. The issue was considered by the commissioner in *R(CS) 15/98*, para 14. The case concerned a reduced benefit direction. The parent had not taken any part in the procedures leading to the making of the direction. Nonetheless, the commissioner treated the parent as personally aggrieved and said that she might also be vicariously aggrieved on behalf of her child. This leaves open the possibility for, say, a grandparent to appeal in the interests of a child. This limitation on the right of appeal has not been used to exclude appeals that raise points of principle without any effect on the outcome. Even if permission has been given, the Upper Tribunal has sufficient other powers to deal expeditiously with those cases.

(i)   It may refuse to hear the appeal on the ground that the issue is of abstract interest only.
(ii)   It may strike out the proceedings under rule 8(3)(c) of the Tribunal Procedure (Upper Tribunal) Rules 2008.
(iii)   It may exercise its discretion under s12(2)(a) of the Tribunals, Courts and Enforcement Act 2007 not to set aside a First-tier Tribunal's decision even if it contained an error of law.

Subsection (2)

This procedural provision gives a discretion to deal with questions which might have been dealt with by an officer but have not been. It saves the need to refer the matter back to an officer for decision. It is, therefore, a convenient provision and is to be interpreted liberally (*R(I) 4/75*, para 12). It is unfortunate that no equivalent power has been conferred on the First-tier Tribunal.

The Upper Tribunal should consider the application of this subsection in two stages. The first issue to decide is whether the question falls within the subsection. If the question does fall within the subsection, the next issue is whether and, if so, in what manner the discretion should be exercised.

The scope of the subsection

The subsection only applies to questions which would otherwise fall to be determined by the Secretary of State. It can be used where there are questions which are relevant to the decision which the Upper Tribunal will have to make, but which have not been dealt with by the Secretary of State. It is, therefore, an appropriate way to correct errors made by the Secretary of State (*R(F) 1/72*). This is subject to the requirement, discussed below, that the question should first arise in the course of the appeal.

This subsection can, therefore, operate in two ways. It can operate to give power to make decisions which there would otherwise have been power to make, provided the matter had come to the Upper Tribunal on appeal.

Only questions first arising in the course of the appeal are covered. This is ambiguous. It could mean that the question must first be identified in the course of the appeal, or it could mean that the question only arises because of the course taken by the appeal. The commissioners gave it the first meaning. It has been held that a question does not arise until there is some doubt on the matter (*R v Westminster (City) Borough Rent Officer ex p Rendall* [1973] 3 All ER 119 at 122, *per* Lord Denning MR).

The question must first arise in the course of *the appeal*. This is wider than "the course of *the hearing"* (*CS 101/1986*, para 5). The question might, therefore, arise at an interlocutory stage or during an adjournment, as well as during the hearing itself.

The question *must first* arise in the course of the appeal and not before. So if the question has arisen and a decision has been given in respect of it, it does not fall within this subsection (*CS 104/1987*, para 2).

In the context of this power "consideration" means fully considered to the point where the Secretary of State is in a position to reach a decision (*CIS 807/1992,* para 6). Consequently a case falls within the subsection if the Secretary of State has embarked upon consideration of a question, but has not fully considered it.

The discretion

The subsection gives a discretion to deal with a case. It must be exercised judicially. The Upper Tribunal will consider (i) the wishes of the parties and (ii) whether a decision on the question is essential to the disposal of the case, but (iii) the paramount consideration will be the requirements of natural justice. It does not override the need for all parties to have a proper chance to prepare for, and to present evidence and argument on, every matter in issue in the appeal. The tribunal will need to consider whether the parties have had an adequate chance to deal with the question. An important factor will be whether there has been notice of the question, either in the written submission of the Secretary of State or in the grounds stated in the notice of appeal or in some other document which has been sent to all the parties (*R(I) 4/75,* para 12). If the parties have not had a proper chance to deal with the question, the tribunal may decide to adjourn to allow time for this.

Alternatively, the tribunal may decide to exercise the discretion against dealing with the question.

The Upper Tribunal is under a duty to consider whether or not to exercise the discretion in respect of any question first arising (*R(IS) 15/93,* para 8). It will, though, seldom be an error of law for a tribunal to decline to deal with a question first arising, although there may be cases in which the question is so clearly tied to the matter being considered that the tribunal is effectively under a duty, given the technical nature of the jurisdiction and the inquisitorial approach, to deal with the question (*CIS 21/1993,* para 13).

Disputes about parentage

26.–(1)   Where a person who is alleged to be a parent of the child with respect to whom an application for a [⁴maintenance calculation] has been made [⁵[⁸...]] ("the alleged parent") denies that he is one of the child's parents, [⁶ the [⁹ [¹³Secretary of State]]] shall not make a [⁴maintenance calculation] on the assumption that the alleged parent is one of the child's parents unless the case falls within one of those set out in subsection (2).

(2)   The Cases are–

[¹CASE A1

Where–

(a)   the child is habitually resident in England and Wales;

(b)   the [⁹[¹³Secretary of State]] is satisfied that the alleged parent was married to the child's mother at some time in the period beginning with the conception and ending with the birth of the child; and

(c)   the child has not been adopted.

CASE A2

Where–

(a)   the child is habitually resident in England and Wales;

(b)   the alleged parent has been registered as father of the child under section 10 or 10A of the Births and Deaths Registration Act 1953, or in any register kept under section 13 (register of births and still-births) or section 44 (Register of Corrections Etc) of the Registration of Births, Deaths and Marriages (Scotland) Act 1965, or under Article 14 or 18(1)(b)(ii) of the Births and Deaths Registration (Northern Ireland) Order 1976; and

(c)   the child has not subsequently been adopted.

CASE A3

Where the result of a scientific test (within the meaning of section 27A) taken by the alleged parent would be relevant to determining the child's parentage, and the alleged parent–

(a)   refuses to take such a test; or

(b)   has submitted to such a test, and it shows that there is no reasonable doubt that the alleged parent is a parent of the child.]

CASE A

Where the alleged parent is a parent of the child in question by virtue of having adopted him.

[¹¹ CASE B

Where the alleged parent is a parent of the child in question by virtue of an order under section 30 of the Human Fertilisation and Embryology Act 1990 or section 54 of the Human Fertilisation and Embryology Acy 2008 (parental orders).]

[[10]CASE B1

Where the [[9]Commission] is satisfied that the alleged parent is a parent of the child in question by virtue of section 27 or 28 of the Human Fertilisation and Embryology Act 1990 or any of sections 33 to 46 of the Human Fertilisation and Embryology Act 2008 (which relate to children resulting from assisted reproduction).]

CASE C

Where–
(a)   either–
  (i)   a declaration that the alleged parent is a parent of the child in question (or a declaration which has that effect) is in force under section [[2]55A or] 56 of the Family Law Act 1986 (declarations of parentage); or
  (ii)   a declarator by a court in Scotland that the alleged parent is a parent of the child in question (or a declarator which has that effect) is in force; and
(b)   the child has not subsequently been adopted.

CASE D [[3] ...]

CASE E

Where–
(a)   the child is habitually resident in Scotland;
(b)   [[6]the [[9][[13]Secretary of State]]] is satisfied that one or other of the presumptions set out in section 5(1) of the Law Reform (Parent and Child) (Scotland) Act 1986 applies; and
(c)   the child has not subsequently been adopted.

CASE F

Where–
(a)   the alleged parent has been found, or adjudged, to be the father of the child in question–
  (i)   in proceedings before any court in England and Wales which are relevant proceedings for the purposes of section 12 of the Civil Evidence Act 1968; or
  (ii)   in affiliation proceedings before any court in the United Kingdom, (whether or not he offered any defence to the allegation of paternity) and that finding or adjudication still subsists; and
(b)   the child has not subsequently been adopted.
(3)   In this section–
"adopted" means adopted within the meaning of Part IV of the Adoption Act 1976 [[7]or Chapter 4 of Part 1 of the Adoption and Children Act 2002] or, in relation to Scotland, Part IV of the Adoption (Scotland) Act 1978 [[12]or Chapter 3 of Part 1 of the Adoption and Children (Scotland) Act 2007 (asp 4)]; and
"affiliation proceedings", in relation to Scotland, means any action of affiliation and aliment.

Amendments

1.   Child Support, Pensions and Social Security Act 2000 s15 (January 31, 2001).
2.   Child Support, Pensions and Social Security Act 2000 Sch 8 para 12 (April 1, 2001).
3.   Child Support, Pensions and Social Security Act 2000 s85(1) and Sch 9, Part IX (April 1, 2001).
4.   Child Support, Pensions and Social Security Act 2000 (2000 c.19) s1(2) (March 3, 2003 for the types of cases detailed in art 3 Child Support, Pensions and Social Security Act 2000 (Commencement No.12) Order 2003 (SI 2003 No.192)). For other types of cases, see '1993 rules' below.
5.   Child Support, Pensions and Social Security Act 2000 (2000 c.19) s26 and Sch 3 para 11(8) (March 3, 2003 for the types of cases detailed in art 3 Child Support, Pensions and Social Security Act 2000 (Commencement No.12) Order 2003 (SI 2003 No.192)).
6.   Social Security Act 1998 (1998 c.14) Sch 7 para 31 (June 1, 1999).
7.   Adoption and Children Act 2002 (2002 c.38) s139(1) and Sch 3 para 81 (December 30, 2005).
8.   Child Maintenance and Other Payments Act 2008 (2008 c.6) s58 and Sch 8 (October 27, 2008 subject to art 4 Child Maintenance and Other Payments Act 2008 (Commencement No.3 and Transitional and Savings Provisions) Order 2008 (SI 2008 No.2548)). This omitted "or treated as made" from subsection 26(1).
9.   Child Maintenance and Other Payments Act 2008 (2008 c.6) s13 and Sch 3, para 18 (November 1, 2008); Child Maintenance and Other Payments Act 2008 (Commencement No.4 and Transitional Provision) Order 2008 (SI 2008 No.2675) art 3.

10. Human Fertilisation and Embryology Act 2008 (c.22) s56 and Sch 6 para 36 (April 6, 2009); Human Fertilisation and Embryology Act 2008 (Commencement No.1 and Transitional Provisions) Order 2009 (SI 2009 No.479) art 6.
11. Human Fertilisation and Embryology Act 2008 (c.22) s56 and Sch 6 para 36 (April 6, 2010); Human Fertilisation and Embryology Act 2008 (Commencement No.3) Order 2010 (SI 2010 No.987) art 2(g).
12. Adoption and Children (Scotland Act) 2007 (2007 asp 4) s120(1) and Sch 2 para 7 (September 28, 2009).
13. Public Bodies (Child Maintenance and Enforcement Commission: Abolition and Transfer of Functions) Order 2012 (SI 2012 No.2007) art 3(2) and Sch para 16 (August 1, 2012).

1993 rules

s1(2) of the Child Support, Pensions and Social Security Act 2000 (2000 c.19) amends s26 of the Child Support Act 1991 and has been brought into force only for the types of cases in art 3 of the Child Support, Pensions and Social Security Act 2000 (Commencement No.12) Order 2003 (SI 2003 No.192 – see p683). For other types of cases the 1993 rules apply and the original wording is retained – ie, "maintenance assessment" is retained in place of "maintenance calculation". Wording inserted into subsection (1) by s26 and Sch 3 para 11(8) of the Child Support, Pensions and Social Security Act 2000 has since been repealed.

Definitions

"child": see s55.
"maintenance calculation": see s54.
"parent": see s54.

General Note

This section allows the Secretary of State and tribunals to make decisions on parentage in specified, clear-cut cases only. More contentious cases are within the jurisdiction of the court which has the appropriate powers to handle them. Section 27 gives the Secretary of State power to apply to a court for a declaration as to parentage. If the ground of appeal is that a person is or is not a parent of a child, the tribunal must decide that it has no jurisdiction as the appeal lies in such a case to the court: see s45 and the general note thereto.

In at least one case a small claims court has awarded compensation to a man who was wrongly approached by the Child Support Agency regarding maintenance for a child *(The Times,* 8 April 1994).

For the position where the issue of parentage is raised for the first time on appeal to a tribunal, see the Child Support Appeals (Jurisdiction of Courts) Order 2002 and the Child Support Appeals (Jurisdiction of Courts) (Scotland) Order 2003, and the general note to art 4 of the former Order.

If an application is made in respect of two children and parentage is disputed in respect of one of them, the application may proceed in respect of the other child without waiting for the dispute to be resolved (*CCS 2626/ 1999*).

Subsection (2) Case F

A person may have been found to be a parent of a child even if parentage was not in issue in the relevant proceedings, but such a finding is only relevant where it is open to the "parent" to make an application to the court for the finding to be set aside *R(CS)* 2/98, para 24). If the finding is set aside, this will not always imply a finding that the person is not a parent of the child, and a reference under s27 below may be necessary in order to determine the issue *(ibid,* para 24). This question was before the Divisional Court on judicial review, leave having been granted by the Court of Appeal (*R v Secretary of State for Social Security ex p West, The Times,* November 26 1998). In granting leave, Henry LJ said that it was arguable that the granting of a parental responsibility order in favour of a father on an application in which paternity was not contested was sufficient to bring the case within Case F. The parties were the same as in *R(CS)* 2/98, but the judicial review was not against the commissioner's decision.

For the meaning of "relevant proceedings" for the purposes of s12, Civil Evidence Act 1968 and the difficulties with the references to the various sections therein, see Halsbury, *Statutes* (4th ed), Vol 17, pp184-185. See also subs (5) of this section.

[¹ Applications for declaration of parentage under Family Law Act 1986

27.–(1)   This section applies where–

(a)   an application for a maintenance calculation has been made [²...], or a maintenance calculation is in force, with respect to a person ("the alleged parent") who denies that he is a parent of a child with respect to whom the application or calculation was made [²...];

(b)   the [³[⁴Secretary of State]] is not satisfied that the case falls within one of those set out in section 26(2); and

(c)   the [³[⁴Secretary of State]] or the person with care makes an application for a declaration under section 55A of the Family Law Act 1986 as to whether or not the alleged parent is one of the child's parents.

(2) Where this section applies–

(a) if it is the person with care who makes the application, she shall be treated as having a sufficient personal interest for the purposes of subsection (3) of that section; and

(b) if it is the [³[⁴Secretary of State]] who makes the application, that subsection shall not apply.

(3) This section does not apply to Scotland.]

Amendments

1.   s27 substituted by Child Support, Pensions and Social Security Act 2000 Sch 8 para 13 (April 1, 2001), replacing s27 previously amended by Child Support Act 1995 s20 on September 4, 1995.

2.   Child Maintenance and Other Payments Act 2008 (2008 c.6) s58 and Sch 8 (October 27, 2008 subject to art 4 Child Maintenance and Other Payments Act 2008 (Commencement No.3 and Transitional and Savings Provisions) Order 2008 (No.2548)). This omitted "(or is treated as having been made)" and "or treated as made".

3.   Child Maintenance and Other Payments Act 2008 (2008 c.6) s13 and Sch 3 para 19 (November 1, 2008); Child Maintenance and Other Payments Act 2008 (Commencement No.4 and Transitional Provision) Order 2008 (SI 2008 No.2675) art 3.

4.   Public Bodies (Child Maintenance and Enforcement Commission: Abolition and Transfer of Functions) Order 2012 (SI 2012 No.2007) art 3(2) and Sch para 17 (August 1, 2012).

Definitions

"child": see s55.

"maintenance calculation": see s54.

"parent": see s54.

"person with care": see s3(3).

General Note

Section 55A of the Family Law Act 1986 was inserted by s83(2) of the 2000 Act. It reads:

"Declarations of parentage

55A.–(1)   Subject to the following provisions of this section, any person may apply to the High Court, a county court or a magistrates' court for a declaration as to whether or not a person named in the application is or was the parent of another person so named.

(2)   A court shall have jurisdiction to entertain an application under subsection (I) above if, and only if, either of the persons named in it for the purposes of that subsection–

(a)   is domiciled in England and Wales on the date of the application, or

(b)   has been habitually resident in England and Wales throughout the period of one year ending with that date, or

(c)   died before that date and either–

(i)   was at death domiciled in England and Wales, or

(ii)   had been habitually resident in England and Wales throughout the period of one year ending with the date of death.

(3)   Except in a case falling within subsection (4) below, the court shall refuse to hear an application under subsection (1) above unless it considers that the applicant has a sufficient personal interest in the determination of the application (but this is subject to section 27 of the Child Support Act 1991).

(4)   The excepted cases are where the declaration sought is as to whether or not–

the applicant is the parent of a named person;

(b)   a named person is the parent of the applicant; or

(c)   a named person is the other parent of a named child of the applicant. (5) Where an application under subsection (1) above is made and

one of the persons named in it for the purposes of that subsection is a child, the court may refuse to hear the application if it considers that the determination of the application would not be in the best interests of the child.

(6)   Where a court refuses to hear an application under subsection (1) above it may order that the applicant may not apply again for the same declaration without leave of the court

(7)   Where a declaration is made by a court on an application under subsection (1) above, the prescribed officer of the court shall notify the Registrar General, in such a manner and within such period as may be prescribed, of the making of that declaration."

The Court of Appeal sent a strong message to courts considering whether to direct blood tests to establish paternity in *Re H (Paternity: Blood Test)* [1996] 2 FLR 65. While it is clear that a party cannot be ordered to provide a sample, a refusal to do so when certainty could be established justifies the inference that the refusal is made to hide the truth. A child has a right, under Art 7 of the UN Convention on the Rights of the Child, to know the truth about her/his identity unless her/his welfare clearly justifies the cover-up. Thus, it is likely that a direction will normally be given and, if there is a failure to comply, the court is entitled to draw the appropriate inference, regardless of whether the refusal comes from the parent with care or the absent parent. This was the approach taken in *F v Child Support Agency, The Times,* April 9 1999. A child was born to a wife, but she alleged that F was the father and not her husband. The normal presumption that the child was her husband's was rebutted by inferences drawn from F's refusal to provide a blood sample and hearsay evidence that a DNA test had shown that the husband was not the child's father. The same approach was taken in *SSWP v Jones* [2004] 1 FLR 282.

[¹ Recovery of fees for scientific tests

  [¹**27A.**–(1)   This section applies in any case where–
- (a)   an application for a [³maintenance calculation] has been made [⁵[⁶...]] or a [³maintenance calculation] is in force;
- (b)   scientific tests have been carried out (otherwise that under a direction or in response to a request) in relation to bodily samples obtained from a person who is alleged to be a parent of a child with respect to whom the application or [⁴calculation] is made [⁵[⁶...]];
- (c)   the results of the tests do not exclude the alleged parent from being one of the child's parents; and
- (d)   one of the conditions set out in subsection (2) is satisfied.
  (2)   The conditions are that–
- (a)   the alleged parent does not deny that he is one of the child's parents;
- (b)   in proceedings under [²section 55A of the Family Law Act 1986], a court has made a declaration that the alleged parent is a parent of the child in question; or
- (c)   in an action under section 7 of the Law Reform (Parent and Child) (Scotland) Act 1986, brought by the [⁷[⁸Secretary of State]] by virtue of section 28, a court has granted a decree of declarator of parentage to the effect that the alleged parent is a parent of the child in question.
  (3)   In any case to which this section applies, any fee paid by the [⁷[⁸Secretary of State]] in connection with scientific tests may be recovered by [⁷[⁸the Secretary of State]] from the alleged parent as a debt due to the Crown.
  (4)   In this section–
"bodily sample" means a sample of bodily fluid or bodily tissue taken for the purpose of scientific tests;
"direction" means a direction given by a court under section 20 of the Family Law Reform Act 1969 (tests to determine paternity);
"request" means a request made by a court under section 70 of the Law Reform (Miscellaneous Provisions) (Scotland) Act 1990 (blood and other samples in civil proceedings); and
"scientific tests" means scientific tests made with the object of ascertaining the inheritable characteristics of bodily fluids or bodily tissue.
  (5)   Any sum recovered by the [⁷[⁸Secretary of State]] under this section shall be paid by [⁷[⁸the Secretary of State]] into the Consolidated Fund.]

Amendments
1.   s27A inserted (4.9.95) by Child Support Act 1995 (c.34), s21.
2.   Child Support, Pensions and Social Security Act, 2000 Sch 8, para. 14 (April 1, 2001).
3.   Child Support, Pensions and Social Security Act 2000 (2000 c.19) s1(2) (March 3, 2003 for the types of cases in art 3 Child Support, Pensions and Social Security Act 2000 (Commencement No.12) Order 2003 (SI 2003 No.192)). For other types of cases, see '1993 rules' below.
4.   Child Support, Pensions and Social Security Act 2000 (2000 c.19) s1(2) (March 3, 2003 for the types of cases in art 3 Child Support, Pensions and Social Security Act 2000 (Commencement No.12) Order 2003 (SI 2003 No.192)). For other types of cases, see '1993 rules' below.

5. Child Support, Pensions and Social Security Act 2000 (2000 c.19) s26 and Sch 3 para 11(9) (March 3, 2003 for the types of cases in art 3 Child Support, Pensions and Social Security Act 2000 (Commencement No.12) Order 2003 (SI 2003 No.192)).

6. Child Maintenance and Other Payments Act 2008 (2008 c.6) s58 and Sch 8 (October 27, 2008 subject to art 4 Child Maintenance and Other Payments Act 2008 (Commencement No.3 and Transitional and Savings Provisions) Order 2008 (SI 2008 No.2548)). This omitted "or treated as made" from para (a) and "or, as the case may be, treated as made" from para (b).

7. Child Maintenance and Other Payments Act 2008 (2008 c.6) s13 and Sch 3 para 20 (November 1, 2008); Child Maintenance and Other Payments Act 2008 (Commencement No. 4 and Transitional Provision) Order 2008 (SI 2008 No.2675) art 3.

8. Public Bodies (Child Maintenance and Enforcement Commission: Abolition and Transfer of Functions) Order 2012 (SI 2012 No.2007) art 3(2) and Sch para 18 (August 1, 2012).

1993 rules

s1(2) of the Child Support, Pensions and Social Security Act 2000 (2000 c.19) amends s27A of the Child Support Act 1991 and have been brought into force only for the types of cases in art 3of the Child Support, Pensions and Social Security Act 2000 (Commencement No.12) Order 2003 (SI 2003 No.192 – see p683). For other types of cases the 1993 rules apply and the original wording is retained – ie, "maintenance assessment" is retained in place of "maintenance calculation" and "assessment" is retained in place of "calculation". Wording inserted into subsection (1)(a) and (b) by s26 and Sch 3 para 11(9) of the Child Support, Pensions and Social Security Act 2000 has since been repealed.

Power of [⁹[¹⁰Secretary of State]] to initiate or defend actions of declarator: Scotland

28.–[¹ (1)   Subsection (1A) applies in any case where–

(a)   an application for a [⁴maintenance calculation] has been made [⁶[⁸...]], or a [⁴maintenance calculation] is in force, with respect to a person ("the alleged parent") who denies that he is a parent of a child with respect to whom the application [⁷was made [⁸...] or the calculation was made]; and

(b)   [²the [⁹[¹⁰Secretary of State]]] is not satisfied that the case falls within one of those set out in section 26(2).

(1A)   In any case where this subsection applies, the [⁹[¹⁰Secretary of State]] may bring an action for declarator of parentage under section 7 of the Law Reform (Parent and Child) (Scotland) Act 1986.]

(2)   The [⁹[¹⁰Secretary of State]] may defend an action for declarator of non-parentage or illegitimacy brought by a person named as the alleged parent in an application for a [⁴maintenance calculation] [³ or in a [⁴maintenance calculation] which is in force].

(3)   This section applies to Scotland only.

Amendments

1. s28(1) and (1A) substituted (4.9.95) for s28(1) by Child Support Act 1995 (c.34), s20(6).

2. Substituted in s28(1)(b) (5.7.99) by Social Security Act 1998 (1998 c.14) Sch 7 para 30.

3. Inserted (4.9.95) in s28(2) by Child Support Act 1995 (c.34), s20(7).

4. Child Support, Pensions and Social Security Act 2000 (2000 c.19) s1(2) (March 3, 2003 for the types of cases in art 3 Child Support, Pensions and Social Security Act 2000 (Commencement No.12) Order 2003 (SI 2003 No.192). For other types of cases, see '1993 rules' below .

5. Child Support, Pensions and Social Security Act 2000 (2000 c.19) s1(2) (March 3, 2003 for the types of cases in art 3 Child Support, Pensions and Social Security Act 2000 (Commencement No.12) Order 2003 (SI 2003 No.192)). For other types of cases, see '1993 rules' below. "

6. Child Support, Pensions and Social Security Act 2000 (2000 c.19) s26 and Sch 3 para 11(10)(a) (March 3, 2003 for the types of cases in art 3 Child Support, Pensions and Social Security Act 2000 (Commencement No.12) Order 2003 (SI 2003 No.192)).

7. Child Support, Pensions and Social Security Act 2000 (2000 c.19) s26 and Sch 3 para 11(10)(b) (March 3, 2003 for the types of cases in art 3 Child Support, Pensions and Social Security Act 2000 (Commencement No.12) Order 2003 (SI 2003 No.192)). For other types of cases, see '1993 rules' below.

8. Child Maintenance and Other Payments Act 2008 (2008 c.6) s58 and Sch 8 (October 27, 2008 subject to art 4 Child Maintenance and Other Payments Act 2008 (Commencement No.3 and Transitional and Savings Provisions) Order 2008 (SI 2008 No.2548)). This omitted the words "or treated as made".

9. Child Maintenance and Other Payments Act 2008 (2008 c.6) s13 and Sch 3 para 21 (November 1, 2008); Child Maintenance and Other Payments Act 2008 (Commencement No.4 and Transitional Provision) Order 2008 (SI 2008 No.2675) art 3.

10.   Public Bodies (Child Maintenance and Enforcement Commission: Abolition and Transfer of Functions) Order 2012 (SI 2012 No.2007) art 3(2) and Sch para 19 (August 1, 2012).

1993 rules
ss1(2) and 26 and Sch 3 para 11(10)(b) of the Child Support, Pensions and Social Security Act 2000 (2000 c.19) amend this section of the Child Support Act 1991 and have been brought into force only for the types of cases in art 3 of the Child Support, Pensions and Social Security Act 2000 (Commencement No.12) Order 2003 (SI 2003 No.192 – see p683). For other types of cases the 1993 rules apply and the original wording is retained ie, "maintenance assessment" is retained in place of "maintenance calculation", "assessment" is retained in place of "calculation" and in (1)(a) the words "assessment was made" is retained in place of "was made [⁸...] or the calculation was made". Another amendment made to subsection (1)(a) by s26 and Sch 3 para 11(10)(a) of the Child Support, Pensions and Social Security Act 2000 has subsequently been repealed.

[¹ Decisions and appeals dependent on other cases

Decisions involving issues that arise on appeal in other cases

[¹**28ZA.**–(1)   This section applies where–
(a)   a decision by the [⁶[⁸Secretary of State]] falls to be made under section 11, 12, 16 or 17 [³[⁵...]]; and
[⁴ (b) an appeal is pending against a decision given in relation to a different matter by [⁷ the Upper Tribunal] or a court.]
(2)   If the [⁶[⁸Secretary of State]] considers it possible that the result of the appeal will be such that, if it were already determined, it would affect the decision in some way–
(a)   [⁶[⁸the Secretary of State]] need not, except in such cases or circumstances as may be prescribed, make the decision while the appeal is pending;
[² (b) [⁶[⁸the Secretary of State]] may, in such cases or circumstances as may be prescribed, make the decision on such basis as may be prescribed.]
(3)   Where the [⁶[⁸Secretary of State]] acts in accordance with subsection (2)(b), following the determination of the appeal [⁶[⁸the Secretary of State]] shall if appropriate revise [⁶[⁸the]] decision (under section 16) in accordance with that determination.
(4)   For the purposes of this section, an appeal against a decision is pending if–
(a)   an appeal against the decision has been brought but not determined;
(b)   an application for leave to appeal against the decision has been made but not determined; or
[² (c) in such circumstances as may be prescribed, an appeal against the decision has not been brought (or, as the case may be, an application for leave to appeal against the decision has not been made) but the time for doing so has not yet expired.]
(5)   In paragraphs (a), (b), and (c) of subsection (4), any reference to an appeal, or an application for leave to appeal, against a decision includes a reference to–
(a)   an application for, or for leave to apply for, judicial review of the decision under section 31 of the Supreme Court Act 1981; or
(b)   an application to the supervisory jurisdiction of the Court of Session in respect of the decision.]

Amendments
1.   ss28ZA & 28ZB inserted (1.6.99) by s43 of the Social Security Act 1998 (c.14).
2.   ss28ZA(2)(b) and (4)(c) inserted (4.3.99) by Social Security Act 1998 (c.14) s43
3.   Child Support, Pensions and Social Security Act 2000 (2000 c.19) s26 and Sch 3 para 11(11)(a) (March 3, 2003 for the types of cases in art 3 Child Support, Pensions and Social Security Act 2000 (Commencement No.12) Order 2003 (SI 2003 No.192)). For other types of cases, see '1993 rules' below.
4.   Child Support, Pensions and Social Security Act 2000 (2000 c.19) s26 and Sch 3 para 11(11)(b) (March 3, 2003 for the types of cases in art 3 Child Support, Pensions and Social Security Act 2000 (Commencement No.12) Order 2003 (SI 2003 No.192)). For other types of cases, see '1993 rules' below.
5.   Child Maintenance and Other Payments Act 2008 (2008 c.6) s58 and Sch 8 (July 14, 2008).
6.   Child Maintenance and Other Payments Act 2008 (2008 c.6) s13 and Sch 3 para 22 (November 1, 2008); Child Maintenance and Other Payments Act 2008 (Commencement No.4 and Transitional Provision) Order 2008 (SI 2008 No.2675) art 3.
7.   Transfer of Tribunal Functions Order 2008 (SI 2008 No.2833) art 9 and Sch 3 para 87 (November 3, 2008, subject to the transitional provisions in Sch 4 of SI 2008 No.2833).

8.	Public Bodies (Child Maintenance and Enforcement Commission: Abolition and Transfer of Functions) Order 2012 (SI 2012 No.2007) art 3(2) and Sch para 20 (August 1, 2012).

1993 rules

s26 and sch 3 para 11(11) of the Child Support, Pensions and Social Security Act 2000 (2000 c.19) amend this section of the Child Support Act 1991 and have been brought into force only for the types of cases in art 3 of the Child Support, Pensions and Social Security Act 2000 (Commencement No.12) Order 2003 (SI 2003 No.192 – see p683). For other types of cases the 1993 rules apply and the original wording is retained – ie, "in relation to a maintenance assessment" is retained in place of "or with respect to a reduced benefit decision under section 46" in subsection (1)(a), and subsection (1)(b) is as follows:

(b)	an appeal is pending against a decision given in relation to a different maintenance assessment by [⁷the Upper Tribunal] or a court.

[¹ **Appeals involving issues that arise on appeal in other cases**
	28ZB.–(1)	This section applies where–
[²(a)	an appeal ("appeal A") in relation to a decision or the imposition of a requirement falling within section 20(1) is made to [⁵ the First-tier Tribunal, or from the First-tier Tribunal to the Upper Tribunal];]
(b)	an appeal ("appeal B") is pending against a decision given in a different case by [⁵ the Upper Tribunal] or a court.
	(2)	If the [⁴[⁶Secretary of State]] considers it possible that the result of appeal B will be such that, if it were already determined, it would affect the determination of appeal A, [⁴ the [⁶Secretary of State]] may serve notice requiring the [⁵ First-tier Tribunal or Upper Tribunal]–
(a)	not to be determine appeal A but to refer it to [⁴ the [⁶Secretary of State]]; or
(b)	to deal with the appeal in accordance with subsection (4).
	(3)	Where appeal A is referred to the [⁴[⁶Secretary of State]] under subsection (2)(a), following the determination of appeal B and in accordance with that determination, [⁴ the [⁶Secretary of State]] shall if appropriate–
(a)	in a case where appeal A has not been determined by the [⁵ First-tier Tribunal], revise (under section 16) [⁴[⁶the]] decision which gave rise to that appeal; or
(b)	in a case where appeal A has been determined by the [⁵ First-tier Tribunal], make a decision (under section 17) superseding the tribunal's decision.
	(4)	Where appeal A is to be dealt with in accordance with this section, the [⁵ First-tier Tribunal or Upper Tribunal] shall either–
(a)	stay appeal A until appeal B is determined; or
(b)	if the [⁵ First-tier Tribunal or Upper Tribunal] considers it to be in the interests of the appellant to do so, determine appeal A as if–
	(i)	appeal B had already been determined; and
	(ii)	the issues arising on appeal B had been decided in the way that was most unfavourable to the appellant.
In this subsection "the appellant" means the person who appealed or, as the case may be, first appealed against the decision [³or the imposition of the requirement] mentioned in subsection (1)(a).
	(5)	Where the [⁵ First-tier Tribunal or Upper Tribunal] acts in accordance with subsection (4)(b), following the determination of appeal B the [⁴[⁶Secretary of State]] shall, if appropriate, make a decision (under section 17) superseding the decision of the [⁵ First-tier Tribunal or Upper Tribunal] in accordance with that determination.
	(6)	For the purposes of this section, an appeal against a decision is pending if–
(a)	an appeal against the decision has been brought but not determined;
(b)	an application for leave to appeal against the decision has been made but not determined; or
[¹ (c)	in such circumstances as may be prescribed , an appeal against the decision has not been brought (or, as the case may be, an application for leave to appeal against the decision has not been made) but the time for doing so has not yet expired.]
	(7)	In this section–

(a) the reference in subsection (1)(a) to an appeal to [⁵ the Upper Tribunal] includes a reference to an application for leave to appeal to [⁵ the Upper Tribunal]; and

(b) any reference in paragraph (a), (b) or (c) of subsection (6) to an appeal, or to an application for leave to appeal, against a decision includes a reference to–

   (i) an application for, or for leave to apply for, judicial review of the decision under section 31 of the Supreme Court Act 1981; or

   (ii) an application to the supervisory jurisdiction of the Court of Session in respect of the decision.

(8) Regulations may make provision supplementing that made by this section.]

Amendments

1. s28ZB(6)(c) inserted (4.3.99) by Social Security Act 1998 (c.14) s43.

2. Child Support, Pensions and Social Security Act 2000 (2000 c.19) s26 and Sch 3 para 11(12)(a) (March 3, 2003 for the types of cases in art 3 Child Support, Pensions and Social Security Act 2000 (Commencement No.12) Order 2003 (SI 2003 No.192)). For other types of cases, see '1993 rules' below.

3. Child Support, Pensions and Social Security Act 2000 (2000 c.19) s26 and Sch 3 para 11(12)(b) (March 3, 2003 for the types of cases in art 3 Child Support, Pensions and Social Security Act 2000 (Commencement No.12) Order 2003 (SI 2003 No.192)). For other types of cases, see '1993 rules' below.

4. Child Maintenance and Other Payments Act 2008 (2008 c.6) s13 and Sch 3 para 23 (November 1, 2008); Child Maintenance and Other Payments Act 2008 (Commencement No.4 and Transitional Provision) Order 2008 (SI 2008 No.2675) art 3.

5. Transfer of Tribunal Functions Order 2008 (SI 2008 No.2833) art 9 and Sch 3 para 88 (November 3, 2008, subject to the transitional provisions in Sch 4 of SI 2008 No.2833).

6. Public Bodies (Child Maintenance and Enforcement Commission: Abolition and Transfer of Functions) Order 2012 (SI 2012 No.2007) art 3(2) and Sch para 21 (August 1, 2012).

1993 rules

s26 and sch 3 para 11(12) of the Child Support, Pensions and Social Security Act 2000 (2000 c.19) amend this section of the Child Support Act 1991 and have been brought into force only for the types of cases in art 3 of the Child Support, Pensions and Social Security Act 2000 (Commencement No.12) Order 2003 (SI 2003 No.192 – see p683). For other types of cases the 1993 rules apply and the original wording is retained – ie, "or assessment" is retained in place of "or the imposition of the requirement" in subsection (4) and subsection (1)(a) is as follows:

(a) an appeal ("appeal A") in relation to a decision falling within section 20(1) or (3), or an assessment falling within section 20(2), is made to [⁵the First-tier Tribunal, or from the First-tier Tribunal to the Upper Tribunal]; and

[¹ Cases of error

Restrictions on liability in certain cases of error

[¹**28ZC.**–(1) Subject to subsection (2), this section applies where–

(a) the effect of the determination, whenever made, of an appeal to [⁸ the Upper Tribunal] or the court ("the relevant determination") is that the adjudicating authority's decision out of which the appeal arose was erroneous in point of law; and

(b) after the date of the relevant determination a decision falls to be made by the [⁷[¹⁰Secretary of State]] in accordance with that determination (or would, apart from this section, fall to be so made)–

   (i) with respect to an application for a [²maintenance calculation] (made after the commencement date) [⁴[⁶...]];

   (ii) as to whether to revise, under section 16, [⁴any decision (made after the commencement date) referred to in section 16(1A)]; or

   (iii) on an application under section 17 (made after the commencement date) for [⁴any decision (made after the commencement date) referred to in section 17(1).]

(2) This section does not apply where the decision of the [⁷[¹⁰Secretary of State]] mentioned in subsection (1)(b)–

(a) is one which, but for section 28ZA(2)(a), would have been made before the date of the relevant determination; or

(b)   is one made in pursuance of section 28ZB(3) or (5).

(3)   In so far as the decision relates to a person's liability [⁵[⁶...]] in respect of a period before the date of the relevant determination, it shall be made as if the adjudicating authority's decision had been found by the [⁸ Upper Tribunal] or court not to have been erroneous in point of law.

(4)   Subsection (1)(a) shall be read as including a case where–

(a)   the effect of the relevant determination is that part or all of a purported regulation or order is invalid; and

(b)   the error of law made by the adjudicating authority was to act on the basis that the purported regulation or order (or the part held to be invalid) was valid.

(5)   It is immaterial for the purposes of subsection (1)–

(a)   where such a decision as is mentioned in paragraph (b)(i) falls to be made; or

(b)   where such a decision as is mentioned in paragraph (b)(ii) or (iii) falls to be made on an application under section 16 or (as the case may be) section 17,

whether the application was made before or after the date of the relevant determination.

(6)   In this section–

"adjudicating authority" means the [⁷[¹⁰Secretary of State]], or a child support officer [⁵or, in the case of a decision made on a referral under section 28D(1)(b), [⁸ the First-tier Tribunal]];

"the commencement date" means the date of coming into force of section 44 of the Social Security Act 1998; and

"the court" means the High Court, the Court of Appeal, the Court of Session, the High Court or Court of Appeal in Northern Ireland, the [⁹Supreme Court] or the Court of Justice of the European Community.

(7)   The date of the relevant determination shall, in prescribed cases, be determined for the purposes of this section in accordance with any regulations made for that purpose.

(8)   Regulations made under section (7) may include provision–

(a)   for a determination of a higher court to be treated as if it had been made on the date of a determination of a lower court or [⁸ the Upper Tribunal]; or

(b)   for a determination of a lower court or a [⁸ the Upper Tribunal] to be treated as if it had been made on the date of a determination of a higher court.]

Amendments

1.   s28ZC inserted (1.6.99) by Social Security Act 1998 (c14) s44.
2.   Child Support, Pensions and Social Security Act 2000 (2000 c.19) s1(2) (March 3, 2003 for the types of cases in art 3 Child Support, Pensions and Social Security Act 2000 (Commencement No.12) Order 2003 (SI 2003 No.192)). For other types of cases, see '1993 rules' below.
3.   Child Support, Pensions and Social Security Act 2000 (2000 c.19) s1(2) (March 3, 2003 for the types of cases in art 3 Child Support, Pensions and Social Security Act 2000 (Commencement No.12) Order 2003 (SI 2003 No.192)). For other types of cases, see '1993 rules' below.
4.   Child Support, Pensions and Social Security Act 2000 (2000 c.19) s26 and Sch 3 para 11(13)(a) – (c) (March 3, 2003 for the types of cases in art 3 Child Support, Pensions and Social Security Act 2000 (Commencement No.12) Order 2003 (SI 2003 No.192)). For other types of cases, see '1993 rules' below.
5.   Child Support, Pensions and Social Security Act 2000 (2000 c.19) s26 and Sch 3 para 11(13)(d) and (e) (March 3, 2003 for the types of cases in art 3 Child Support, Pensions and Social Security Act 2000 (Commencement No.12) Order 2003 (SI 2003 No.192)). For other types of cases, see '1993 rules' below.
6.   Child Maintenance and Other Payments Act 2008 (2008 c.6) s58 and Sch 8 (July 14, 2008).
7.   Child Maintenance and Other Payments Act 2008 (2008 c.6) s13 and Sch 3 para 24 (November 1, 2008); Child Maintenance and Other Payments Act 2008 (Commencement No.4 and Transitional Provision) Order 2008 (SI 2008 No.2675) art 3.
8.   Transfer of Tribunal Functions Order 2008 (SI 2008 No.2833) art 9 and Sch 3 para 89 (November 3, 2008, subject to the transitional provisions in Sch 4 of SI 2008 No.2833).
9.   Constitutional Reform Act 2005 (2005 c.4) s40 and Sch 9 para 54 (October 1, 2009).
10.   Public Bodies (Child Maintenance and Enforcement Commission: Abolition and Transfer of Functions) Order 2012 (SI 2012 No.2007) art 3(2) and Sch para 22 (August 1, 2012).

1993 rules

s26 and sch 3 para 11(13) of the Child Support, Pensions and Social Security Act 2000 (2000 c.19) amend this section of the Child Support Act 1991 and have been brought into force only for the types of cases in art 3 of the Child Support, Pensions and Social Security Act 2000 (Commencement No.12) Order 2003 (SI 2003 No.192 –

see p683). For other types of cases the 1993 rules apply and the original wording is retained – ie, "maintenance assessment" is retained in place of "maintenance calculation", "assessment" is retained in place of "calculation". Also,

– in subsection (1) in paragraph (b)(ii) the words "a decision (made after the commencement date) with respect to such an assessment" are retained in place of "any decision (made after the commencement date) referred to in section 16(1A)", and in paragraph (b)(iii) the words "a decision with respect to such an assessment to be superseded" are retained in place of "any decision (made after the commencement date) referred to in section 17(1)"

– in subsection (6) the following words are not inserted in the definition of "adjudicating authority" "or, in the case of a decision made on a referral under section 28D(1)(b), [⁸ the First-tier Tribunal]".

Words inserted into subsections (1)(b)(i) and (3) by sch 3 para 11(13)(a) and (d) of the Child Support, Pensions and Social Security Act 2000 have subsequently been repealed.

[¹ Correction of errors and setting aside of decisions

[¹28ZD.–(1)   Regulations may make provision with respect to–

(a)   the correction of accidental errors in any decision [² of the Secretary of State] or record of a decision [² of the Secretary of State] given under this Act; [²...]

(b)   [² ...]

(2)   Nothing in subsection (1) shall be construed as derogating from any power to correct errors [² ...] which is exercisable apart from regulations made virtue of that subsection.]

Amendments

1.   Inserted (4.3.99) by Social Security Act 1998 (c.14) s44.
2.   Transfer of Tribunal Functions Order 2008 (SI 2008 No.2833) art 9 and Sch 3 para 90 (November 3, 2008, subject to the transitional provisions in Sch 4 of SI 2008 No. 2833).

[¹ Variations

[¹Application for variation of usual rules for calculating maintenance

[¹28A.–(1)   Where an application for a maintenance calculation is made under section 4 or 7 [²...] the person with care or the non-resident parent or (in the case of an application under section 7) either of them or the child concerned may apply to the [³[⁴Secretary of State]] for the rules by which the calculation is made to be varied in accordance with this Act.

(2)   Such an application is referred to in this Act as an "application for a variation".

(3)   An application for a variation may be made at any time before the [³[⁴Secretary of State]] has reached a decision (under section 11 or 12(1)) on the application for a maintenance calculation [²...].

(4)   A person who applies for a variation–

(a)   need not make the application in writing unless the [³[⁴Secretary of State]] directs in any case that he must; and

(b)   must say upon what grounds the application is made.

(5)   In other respects an application for a variation is to be made in such manner as may be prescribed.

(6)   Schedule 4A has effect in relation to applications for a variation.]]

Amendments

1.   Child Support, Pensions and Social Security Act 2000 (2000 c.19) s5 (March 3, 2003 for the types of cases detailed in art 3 Child Support, Pensions and Social Security Act 2000 (Commencement No.12) Order 2003 (SI 2003 No.192)). For other types of cases, see '1993 rules' below.
2.   Child Maintenance and Other Payments Act 2008 (2008 c.6) s58 and Sch 8 (October 27, 2008 subject to art 4 Child Maintenance and Other Payments Act 2008 (Commencement No.3 and Transitional and Savings Provisions) Order 2008 (SI 2008 No.2548)). This omitted ", or treated as made under section 6," from subsection 28A(1), and "(or the application treated as having been made under section 6)" from subsection 28A(3).
3.   Child Maintenance and Other Payments Act 2008 (2008 c.6) s13 and Sch 3, para 25 (November 1, 2008); Child Maintenance and Other Payments Act 2008 (Commencement No.4 and Transitional Provision) Order 2008 (SI 2008 No.2675) art 3.

4. Public Bodies (Child Maintenance and Enforcement Commission: Abolition and Transfer of Functions) Order 2012 (SI 2012 No.2007) art 3(2) and Sch para 23 (August 1, 2012).

Note

i. If an application for a variation is made under section 28G, s28A is modified in accordance with Child Support (Variations) (Modification of Statutory Provisions) Regulations 2000 (SI 2000 No.3173) reg 3 (January 31, 2001). See p526.

1993 rules

s5 of the Child Support, Pensions and Social Security Act 2000 (2000 c.19) replaces s28A of the Child Support Act 1991. This has been brought into force only for the types of cases in art 3 of the Child Support, Pensions and Social Security Act 2000 (Commencement No.12) Order 2003 (SI 2003 No.192 – see p683). For other types of cases the 1993 rules apply and s28A and the heading above it read:

[¹ *Departure from usual rules for determining maintenance assessments*
Application for a departure direction
28A.–(1)   Where a maintenance assessment ("the current assessment") is in force–
(a) the person with care, or absent parent, with respect to whom it was made, or
(b) where the application for the current assessment was made under section 7, either of those persons or the child concerned, may apply to the [³Commission] for a direction under section 28(F) (a "departure direction").

(2)   An application for a departure direction shall state in writing the grounds on which it is made and shall, in particular, state whether it is based on–
(a) the effect of the current assessment; or
(b) a material change in the circumstances of the case since the current assessment was made.

(3)   In other respects, an application for a departure direction shall be made in such manner as may be prescribed.

[²(4)   An application may be made under this section even though an application has been made under section 16(1) or 17(1) with respect to the current assessment.]

(5)   If the Secretary of State considers it appropriate to do so, he may by regulations provide for the question whether a change of circumstances is material to be determined in accordance with the regulations.

(6)   Schedule 4A has effect in relation to departure directions.

Amendments

1. ss28A-28H inserted by ss1-8 of Child Support Act 1995 (c.34).
2. Social Security Act 1998 (1998 c.14) Sch 7 para 34 (June 1, 1999).
3. Child Maintenance and Other Payments Act 2008 (2008 c.6) s13 and Sch 3 para 25 (November 1, 2008); Child Maintenance and Other Payments Act 2008 (Commencement No.4 and Transitional Provision) Order 2008 (SI 2008 No.2675) art 3.

Definitions

"application for a variation": see s54.
"child": see s55.
"maintenance calculation": see s54.
"non-resident parent": see s54.
"person with care": see s54.
"prescribed": see s54.

General Note

The variation scheme reaches the parts that Sch 1 to the Act cannot reach (*CCS 8/2000*, para 6). The statutory provisions are supplemented by the Variation Regulations.

By agreeing to a variation, the Secretary of State is permitted to alter the maintenance calculation. This can only be done on a small number of restrictively defined grounds. The scope of the scheme is not discretionary. There is a discretionary element in the scheme, but it only applies to qualify the application of the defined grounds. Some of the grounds for a variation relate to matters covered by Sch 1; others relate to matters outside that Schedule.

Uniquely in the child support scheme, the Secretary of State may either determine an application for a variation or refer it to a tribunal (s28D(1)).

Subsection (1)

This is the main statutory authority under which a variation may be agreed by the Secretary of State. The application may be made before a decision is made on an application for a maintenance calculation (subs (3)) or when a maintenance calculation is in force (s28G(1)). If an application is made under s28 G(1), this section applies as modified by reg 3 Child Support (Variations) (Modification of Statutory Provisions) Regulations 2000.

There is no limit on the form in which an application may be made for a variation. The Secretary of State may accept a letter of appeal to a tribunal against a calculation decision as an application for a variation (*CCS 1838/ 2005,* para 15; *R(CS) 2/06,* paras 24-29). The Secretary of State's duty is to apply the most appropriate procedure to the information provided. There is no duty to go further and investigate to see if a case for a variation can be found. The duty to investigate only arises if there are contradictions of material fact which have to be resolved before a decision can be made. See *DB, CMEC and KB* [2010] UKUT (AAC) 356 (AAC) paras 16-17.

Subsection (3)

This subsection allows an application for a variation to be made before the application for a maintenance calculation has been determined. Section 28G provides for an application for a variation when a maintenance calculation is in force.

If an application is made under this subsection, an interim maintenance decision may be made under s12(2) above, which in turn may be subject to a regular payments condition under s28C below.

The effective date under this subsection is fixed by reg 22 of the Variation Regulations.

Subsection (4)(b)

The Secretary of State may treat an application made on one ground as if it were made on a different ground: see reg 9(8) of the Variation Regulations.

Subsection (5)

Regulations 4 and 5 of the Variation Regulations have been made under this enabling power.

[¹ Preliminary consideration of applications

[¹**28B.**–(1) Where an application for a variation has been duly made to the [²[³Secretary of State]], [²[³the Secretary of State]] may give it a preliminary consideration.

(2) [³The Secretary of State may on completing such a] preliminary consideration, reject the application (and proceed to make [² [³a]] decision on the application for a maintenance calculation without any variation) if it appears to [² the [³Secretary of State]]–

(a) that there are no grounds on which [²][³a variation could be agreed to];

(b) that [²[³the Secretary of State]] has insufficient information to make a decision on the application for the maintenance calculation under section 11 (apart from any information needed in relation to the application for a variation), and therefore that [²[³the Secretary of State's]] decision would be made under section 12(1); or

(c) that other prescribed circumstances apply.]]

Amendments

1. Child Support, Pensions and Social Security Act 2000 (2000 c.19) s5 (March 3, 2003 for the types of cases in art 3 Child Support, Pensions and Social Security Act 2000 (Commencement No.12) Order 2003 (SI 2003 No.192)). For other types of cases, see '1993 rules' below.

2. Child Maintenance and Other Payments Act 2008 (2008 c.6) s13 and Sch 3, para 26 (November 1, 2008); Child Maintenance and Other Payments Act 2008 (Commencement No.4 and Transitional Provision) Order 2008 (SI 2008 No.2675) art 3.

3. Public Bodies (Child Maintenance and Enforcement Commission: Abolition and Transfer of Functions) Order 2012 (SI 2012 No.2007) art 3(2) and Sch para 24 (August 1, 2012).

Note

i. If an application for a variation is made under s28G, s28B is modified in accordance with Child Support (Variations) (Modification of Statutory Provisions) Regulations 2000 (SI 2000 No.3173) reg 4 (January 31, 2001). See p526.

1993 rules

s5 of the Child Support, Pensions and Social Security Act 2000 (2000 c.19) replaces s28B of the Child Support Act 1991. This has been brought into force only for the types of cases in art 3 of the Child Support, Pensions and Social Security Act 2000 (Commencement No.12) Order 2003 (SI 2003 No.192 – see p683). For other types of cases the 1993 rules apply and s28B reads:

Preliminary consideration of applications

28B.–(1)   Where an application for a departure direction has been duly made to the [³Commission], [³it] may give the application a preliminary consideration.

(2)   Where the [³Commission] does so [³it] may, on completing the preliminary consideration, reject the application if it appears to him–

(a)   that there are no grounds on which a departure direction could be given in response to the application; or

(b)   that the difference between the current amount and the revised amount is less than an amount to be calculated in accordance with regulations made by the Secretary of State for the purposes of this subsection and section 28F(4).

(3)   In subsection (2)–

"the current amount" means the amount of the child support maintenance fixed by the current assessment; and "the revised amount" means the amount of child support maintenance which, but for subsection (2)(b) would be fixed if a fresh maintenance assessment were to be made as a result of a departure direction allowing the departure applied for.

[¹...]

[² (6)   Where a decision as to a maintenance assessment is revised or superseded under section 16 or 17, the [³Commission]–

(a)   shall notify the applicant and such other persons as may be prescribed that the decision has been revised or superseded; and

(b)   may direct that the application is to lapse unless, before the end of such period as may be prescribed, the applicant notifies the [³Commission] that he wishes it to stand.]"

Amendments

1.   ss(4) and (5) repealed (1.6.99) by Sch 8 to Social Security Act 1998 (c.14).

2.   s28B(6) substituted (4.3.99) by Social Security Act 1998, Commencement Order (No.5) 1999/ 528.

3.   Child Maintenance and Other Payments Act 2008 (2008 c.6) s13 and Sch 3 para 26 (November 1, 2008); Child Maintenance and Other Payments Act 2008 (Commencement No.4 and Transitional Provision) Order 2008 (SI 2008 No.2675) art 3.

Definitions

"application for a variation": see s54.

"maintenance calculation": see s54.

"prescribed": see s54.

General Note

This section confers a power not a duty (*CCS 1838/2005*, para 17). It will usually be appropriate and have to be used if the procedure in reg 9 of the Variation Regulations is to be used. However, it may not be appropriate if the application is going to be referred to a tribunal *(ibid)*.

When appropriate, this procedure allows the Secretary of State to dispose of an application without detailed consideration, if it becomes clear that it cannot succeed. None of the conditions set out in this section or in regulations made under it involve discretionary considerations. Rejection at this preliminary stage will only be appropriate in clear cases, which should be apparent with little more than a cursory consideration. It is for this reason that reg 9 of the Variation Regulations does not apply until there has been a preliminary consideration (*CCS 1838/2005*, para 16).

If an application is made under s28G(1), this section applies as modified by reg 4 Child Support (Variations) (Modification of Statutory Provisions) Regulations 2000.

If the Secretary of State rejects an application under this section but a tribunal decides that this was wrong, the tribunal has power to determine the application (*R(CS) 2/06*, paras 33-42).

Subsection (2)(c)

Regulation 6 of the Variation Regulations has been made under this enabling power.

[¹ Imposition of regular payment condition

[¹28C.–(1)   Where–

(a)   an application for a variation is made by the non-resident parent; and

(b)   the [²[³Secretary of State]] makes an interim maintenance decision,

the [²[³Secretary of State]] may also, if [²[³the Secretary of State]] has completed [² [³a]] preliminary consideration (under section 28B) of the application for a variation and has not rejected it under that section, impose on the non-resident parent one of the conditions mentioned in subsection (2) (a "regular payments condition").

(2) The conditions are that–

(a) the non-resident parent must make the payments of child support maintenance specified in the interim maintenance decision;

(b) the non-resident parent must make such lesser payments of child support maintenance as may be determined in accordance with regulations made by the Secretary of State.

(3) Where the [²[³Secretary of State]] imposes a regular payments condition, [²[³the Secretary of State]] shall give written notice of the imposition of the condition and of the effect of failure to comply with it to–

(a) the non-resident parent;

(b) all the persons with care concerned; and

(c) if the application for the maintenance calculation was made under section 7, the child who made the application.

(4) A regular payments condition shall cease to have effect–

(a) when the [²[³Secretary of State]] has made a decision on the application for a maintenance calculation under section 11 (whether [²[³the Secretary of State]] agrees to a variation or not);

(b) on the withdrawal of the application for a variation.

(5) Where a non-resident parent has failed to comply with a regular payments condition, the [²[³ Secretary of State]] may in prescribed circumstances refuse to consider the application for a variation, and instead reach [² [³a]] decision under section 11 as if no such application had been made.

(6) The question whether a non-resident parent has failed to comply with a regular payments condition is to be determined by the [²[³Secretary of State]].

(7) Where the [²[³Secretary of State]] determines that a non-resident parent has failed to comply with a regular payments condition [²[³the Secretary of State]] shall give written notice of [³the] determination to–

(a) that parent;

(b) all the persons with care concerned; and

(c) if the application for the maintenance calculation was made under section 7, the child who made the application.]]

Amendments

1. Child Support, Pensions and Social Security Act 2000 (2000 c.19) s5 (March 3, 2003 for the types of cases in art 3 Child Support, Pensions and Social Security Act 2000 (Commencement No.12) Order 2003 (SI 2003 No.192)). For other types of cases, see '1993 rules' below.

2. Child Maintenance and Other Payments Act 2008 (2008 c.6) s13 and Sch 3, para 27 (November 1, 2008); Child Maintenance and Other Payments Act 2008 (Commencement No.4 and Transitional Provision) Order 2008 (SI 2008 No.2675) art 3.

3. Public Bodies (Child Maintenance and Enforcement Commission: Abolition and Transfer of Functions) Order 2012 (SI 2012 No.2007) art 3(2) and Sch para 25 (August 1, 2012).

Note

i. If an application for a variation is made under s28G, s28C is modified in accordance with Child Support (Variations) (Modification of Statutory Provisions) Regulations 2000 (SI 2000 No.3173) reg 5 (January 31, 2001). See p526.

1993 rules

s5 of the Child Support, Pensions and Social Security Act 2000 (2000 c.19) replaces s28C of the Child Support Act 1991. This has been brought into force only for the types of cases in art 3 of the Child Support, Pensions and Social Security Act 2000 (Commencement No.12) Order 2003 (SI 2003 No.192 – see p683). For other types of cases the 1993 rules apply and s28C and the heading above it read:

Imposition of a regular payments condition

28C.–(1) Where an application for a departure direction is made by an absent parent, the [²Commission] may impose on him one of the conditions mentioned in subsection (2) ("a regular payments condition").

(2)   The conditions are that–

(a)   the applicant must make the payments of child support maintenance fixed by the current assessment;

(b)   the applicant must make such reduced payments of child support maintenance as may be determined in accordance with regulations made by the Secretary of State.

(3)   Where the [²Commission] imposes a regular payments condition, [²it] shall give written notice to the absent parent and person with care concerned of the imposition of the condition and of the effect of failure to comply with it.

(4)   A regular payments condition shall cease to have effect on the failure or determination of the application.

(5)   For the purposes of subsection (4), an application for a departure direction fails if–

(a)   it lapses or is withdrawn; or

(b)   the [²Commission] rejects it on completing a preliminary consideration under section 28B.

(6)   Where an absent parent has failed to comply with a regular payments condition–

(a)   the [²Commission] may refuse to consider the application; and

(b)   in prescribed circumstances the application shall lapse.

(7)   The question whether an absent parent has failed to comply with a regular payments condition shall be determined by the [²Commission].

(8)   Where the [²Commission] determines that an absent parent has failed to comply with a regular payments condition [²it] shall give that parent, and the person with care concerned, written notice of [²its] decision.

Definitions

"application for a variation": see s54.

"child": see s55.

"child support maintenance": see s54.

"interim maintenance decision"; see s54.

"maintenance calculation": see s54.

"non-resident parent": see s54.

"person with care": see s54.

"prescribed": see s54.

General Note

If an application is made under s28G(1), this section applies as modified by reg 5 Child Support (Variations) (Modification of Statutory Provisions) Regulations 2000.

Paragraph (1)

This section is discretionary and subject to s2. It only applies if the Secretary of State (a) has made an interim maintenance decision, (b) has given the application a preliminary consideration under s28B above and (c) has not rejected the application under that consideration.

If the section applies, the Secretary of State is authorised to impose a condition on the non-resident parent to maintain regular payment of child support maintenance. This prevents a non-resident parent from using an outstanding application for a variation as an excuse for not making payments of child support maintenance. This is balanced by the power to fix a lower amount than that set by the interim maintenance decision (subs (2)(b)). Notice of the imposition of a regular payments condition must be given under subs (3) to the parties to the application.

Subsection (2)

Regulation 31(1) of the Variation Regulations has been made under the enabling power in para (b).

Subsection (4)

A regular payments condition can last no longer than the application in respect of which it was made. So, this subsection provides that it ceases to have effect when the application is determined or withdrawn. Withdrawal is authorised by reg 5(1) of the Variation Regulations.

If the Secretary of State refuses to consider the application further under subss (5)-(7), the regular payments condition does not cease to have effect. It only ceases to have effect once the Secretary of State has reached a decision under s11.

Subsection (5)

The consequence of failing to comply with a regular payments condition is that the Secretary of State may refuse to consider the application and reach a decision undder s11 above as if the application had not been made. Notice of this determination must be given under subs (7).

The application does not cease to have effect as soon as the Secretary of State refuses to consider it further: see the general note to subs (4). That leaves open the possibility that the non-resident parent might try to remedy the breach by complying with the condition and paying any arrears that have built up. There is no provision for the Secretary of State to consider the application again if that happens, but neither is there anything to prohibit it. In practice, it is likely that there would not be the time for the non-resident parent to repent before the Secretary of State had made a decision under s11. Although it is not expressly stated, the application must at that point be no longer capable of being considered.

Regulation 31(2) and (3) of the Variation Regulations have been made under the enabling power in this subsection. Regulation 31(3) contains the prescribed circumstances in which the Secretary of State may refuse to consider the application further.

Subsection (7)

Notice of the refusal to consider the application further must be given to the parties to the application. Reasons do not have to be given; they will be apparent from the circumstances.

[¹ Determination of applications

[¹**28D**.–[²(1)   Where an application for a variation has not failed, the [⁴[⁵Secretary of State]] shall, in accordance with the relevant provisions of, or made under, this Act–

(a)   either agree or not to a variation, and make a decision under section 11 or 12(1); or

(b)   refer the application to [³ the First-tier Tribunal] for the tribunal to determine what variation, if any, is to be made.]

(2)   For the purposes of subsection (1), [²an application for a variation] has failed if–

(a)   it has [²…] been withdrawn; or

(b)   the [⁴[⁵Secretary of State]] has rejected it on completing a preliminary consideration under section 28B [²; or

(c)   the [⁴[⁵Secretary of State]] has refused to consider it under section 28C(5)] .

[⁸(2A)   Subsection (2B) applies if–

(a)   the application for a variation is made by the person with care or (in the case of an application for a maintenance calculation under section 7) the person with care or the child concerned, and

(b)   it appears to the [⁶Secretary of State] that consideration of further information or evidence may affect [⁶the] decision under subsection (1)(a) whether or not to agree to a variation.

(2B)   Before making the decision under subsection (1)(a) the [⁶Secretary of State] must–

(a)   consider any such further information or evidence that is available to [⁶the Secretary of State], and

(b)   where necessary, take such steps as the [⁶Secretary of State] considers appropriate to obtain any such further information or evidence.]

(3)   In dealing with [²an application for a variation] which has been referred to it under subsection (1)(b), [¹[³ the First-tier Tribunal]] shall have the same powers, and be subject to the same duties[⁸, apart from the duty under subsection (2B)], as would the [⁴][⁵Secretary of State in] dealing with the application.

Amendments

1.   Social Security Act 1998 (1998 c.14) Sch 7 para 36 (June 1, 1999).

2.   Child Support, Pensions and Social Security Act 2000 (2000 c.19) ss5(3) and 85 and Sch 9 Part I (March 3, 2003 for the types of cases in art 3 Child Support, Pensions and Social Security Act 2000 (Commencement No.12) Order 2003 (SI 2003 No.192)). For other types of cases, see '1993 rules' below.

3.   Transfer of Tribunal Functions Order 2008 (SI 2008 No.2833) art 9 and Sch 3 para 91 (November 3, 2008, subject to the transitional provisions in Sch 4 of SI 2008 No.2833).

4.   Child Maintenance and Other Payments Act 2008 (2008 c.6) s13 and Sch 3, para 28 (November 1, 2008); Child Maintenance and Other Payments Act 2008 (Commencement No.4 and Transitional Provision) Order 2008 (SI 2008 No.2675) art 3.

5.   Public Bodies (Child Maintenance and Enforcement Commission: Abolition and Transfer of Functions) Order 2012 (SI 2012 No.2007) art 3(2) and Sch para 26 (August 1, 2012).

6.   Public Bodies (Child Maintenance and Enforcement Commission: Abolition and Transfer of Functions) Order 2012 (SI 2012 No.2007) art 3(2) and Sch para 78 (August 1, 2012).

7.   Public Bodies (Child Maintenance and Enforcement Commission: Abolition and Transfer of Functions) Order 2012 (SI 2012 No.2007) art 3(3) (August 1, 2012).

8.　Child Maintenance and Other Payments Act 2008 (2008 c.6) ss18 and 56(2) (December 10, 2012 for the types of cases falling within art 3 of SI 2012 No.3042, subject to art 5 of that SI – see p767 and July 29, 2013 for the types of cases falling within art 3 of SI 2013 No.1860, subject to art 5 of that SI – see p770). See also art 6 of SI 2012 No.3042 (which had effect up to and including July 28, 2013) and art 7 of SI 2013 No.1860 for further transitional provisions. For other types of cases see '2003 and 1993 rules' below; Child Maintenance and Other Payments Act 2008 (Commencement No.10 and Transitional Provisions) Order 2012 (SI 2012 No.3042) art 2; Child Maintenance and Other Payments Act 2008 (Commencement No.11 and Transitional Provisions) Order 2013 (SI 2013 No.1860) art 2; Child Maintenance and Other Payments Act 2008 (Commencement) Order 2008 (SI 2008 No.1476) art 2(6).

Note

i.　If an application for a variation is made under s28G, s28D is modified in accordance with Child Support (Variations) (Modification of Statutory Provisions) Regulations 2000 (SI 2000 No.3173) reg 6 (January 31, 2001). See p527.

2003 and 1993 rules

s18 of the Child Maintenance and Other Payments Act 2008 (2008 c.6) inserts subsections (2A) and (2B) and, in subsection (3), inserts the words ", apart from the duty under subsection (2B)" into s28D of the Child Support Act 1991 and has been brought into force for the types of cases falling within art 3 of SI 2012 No.3042 subject to art 5 of that SI – see p767 and July 29, 2013 for the types of cases falling within art 3 of SI 2013 No.1860, subject to art 5 of that SI – see p770). See also art 6 of SI 2012 No.3042 (which had effect up to and including July 28, 2013) and art 7 of SI 2013 No.1860 for further transitional provisions. For other types of cases, these insertions do not apply.

1993 rules

ss5 and 85 and Sch 9 of the Child Support, Pensions and Social Security Act 2000 (2000 c.19) amend s28D of the Child Support Act 1991. These amendments have been brought into force only for the types of cases in art 3 of the Child Support, Pensions and Social Security Act 2000 (Commencement No.12) Order 2003 (SI 2003 No.192 – see p683). For other types of cases the 1993 rules apply. If the 1993 rules apply, s28D(1) reads:

28D.–(1) Where an application for a departure direction has not failed, the [⁴[⁷Secretary of State]] shall–

(a)　determine the application in accordance with the relevant provisions of, or made under, this Act; or

(b)　refer the application to [¹[³the First-tier Tribunal]] for the tribunal to determine it in accordance with those provisions.

In subsections (2) and (3) the words "an application for a departure direction" are retained in place of "an application for a variation".

In subsection (2) the words "lapsed or" in paragraph (a) are not omitted and paragraph (c) and the "or" preceding it are omitted.

Definitions

"application for a variation": see s54.

"appeal tribunal": see s54.

General Note

If an application is made under s28G(1), this section applies as modified by reg 6 Child Support (Variations) (Modification of Statutory Provisions) Regulations 2000.

Subsection (1)

The Secretary of State must determine the application or refer it to a tribunal. This is a unique power in the child support scheme. It is used in the more complex and controversial disputes.

A referral under para (b) is a referral of the application. The application may be amended by notice in writing under reg 5 of the Variation Regulations, although see the general note to subs (3) below. This allows the addition of a new head to the application before the case is decided by the tribunal. Even if the additional head is contained in a letter addressed to the tribunal, that will be sufficient notice to the Secretary of State which is a party to the proceedings before the tribunal. So, the tribunal has jurisdiction to deal with the additional head, provided that the principles of natural justice and the Convention rights of the parties are observed. See *R(CS) 3/01*, para 50.

If the applicant withdraws an application that has been referred to a tribunal, the referral continues in existence until it is withdrawn by the Secretary of State (*Milton v SSWP* reported as *R(CS) 1/07*, refusing permission to appeal against the decision of the commissioner in *CCS 1031/2005*). This produces that result that, until the Secretary of State acts, the tribunal has jurisdiction to decide an application that no longer exists. It is possible that it could refuse to do so on the ground that the issue has become academic.

In *CCS 1495/2005,* the Secretary of State argued that a tribunal deciding a reference had power to decide whether a ground for a variation existed, but did not have power to decide what the variation should be. The commissioner rejected this argument (paras 19-34).

A tribunal may, if it considers it appropriate, consider a referral at the same time as an appeal under s20 above against an interim maintenance decision: see Sch 4A para 5(3).

Subsection (2)

If the application is rejected on preliminary consideration, it no longer exists and cannot be referred to a tribunal. The proper course for a disappointed applicant is to appeal against the decision rejecting the application (*CCS 1838/2005,* para 18). This paragraph is not an authority that a preliminary consideration is necessary before an application may be referred *(ibid,* para 19).

Subsection (3)

On a referral the tribunal has the same powers and duties as the Secretary of State. This *may* allow the appeal tribunal to receive notice of the amendment or withdrawal of an application under reg 5 of the Variation Regulations.

[¹ Matters to be taken into account

[²**28E.**–(1)   In determining [³whether to agree to a variation] the [⁴[⁵Secretary of State]] shall have regard both to the general principles set out in subsection (2) and to such other considerations as may be prescribed.

(2)   The general principles are that–

(a)   parents should be responsible for maintaining their children whenever they can afford to do so;

(b)   where a parent has more than one child, his obligation to maintain any one of them should be no less of an obligation than his obligation to maintain any other of them.

(3)   In determining [³whether to agree to a variation], the [⁴[⁵Secretary of State]] shall take into account any representations made to [⁴[⁵the Secretary of State]]–

(a)   by the person with care or [²non-resident parent] concerned; or

(b)   where the application for the current [¹calculation] was made under section 7, by either of them or the child concerned.

(4)   In determining [³whether to agree to a variation], no account shall be taken of the fact that–

(a)   any part of the income of the person with care concerned is, or would be if [³the [⁴[⁵Secretary of State]] agreed to a variation], derived from any benefit; or

(b)   some or all of any child support maintenance might be taken into account in any manner in relation to any entitlement to benefit.

(5)   In this section "benefit" has such meaning as maybe prescribed.]

Amendments

1.   Child Support, Pensions and Social Security Act 2000 (2000 c.19) s1(2) (March 3, 2003 for the types of cases in art 3 Child Support, Pensions and Social Security Act 2000 (Commencement No.12) Order 2003 (SI 2003 No.192)). For other types of cases, see '1993 rules' below.

2.   Child Support, Pensions and Social Security Act 2000 (2000 c.19) s26 and Sch 3 para 11(2) (March 3, 2003 for the types of cases in art 3 Child Support, Pensions and Social Security Act 2000 (Commencement No.12) Order 2003 (SI 2003 No.192)). For other types of cases, see '1993 rules' below.

3.   Child Support, Pensions and Social Security Act 2000 (2000 c.19) s5(4) (March 3, 2003 for the types of cases in art 3 Child Support, Pensions and Social Security Act 2000 (Commencement No.12) Order 2003 (SI 2003 No.192)). For other types of cases, see '1993 rules' below.

4.   Child Maintenance and Other Payments Act 2008 (2008 c.6) s13 and Sch 3, para 29 (November 1, 2008); Child Maintenance and Other Payments Act 2008 (Commencement No.4 and Transitional Provision) Order 2008 (SI 2008 No.2675) art 3.

5.   Public Bodies (Child Maintenance and Enforcement Commission: Abolition and Transfer of Functions) Order 2012 (SI 2012 No.2007) art 3(2) and Sch para 27 (August 1, 2012).

Note

i.   If an application for a variation is made under s28G, s28E is modified in accordance with Child Support (Variations) (Modification of Statutory Provisions) Regulations 2000 (SI 2000 No.3173) reg 6 (January 31, 2001). See p527.

1993 rules

ss 1(2), 5 and 26 and Sch 3 of the Child Support, Pensions and Social Security Act 2000 (2000 c.19) amend s28E of the Child Support Act 1991. These amendments have been brought into force only for the types of cases in art 3 of the Child Support, Pensions and Social Security Act 2000 (Commencement No.12) Order 2003 (SI 2003 No.192 -see p683). For other types of cases the 1993 rules apply. If the 1993 rules apply:

–   the word "assessment" is retained in place of "calculation" and the words "absent parent" are retained in place of "non-resident parent";
–   in subsections (1), (3) and (4), the words "any application for a departure direction" are retained in place of "whether to agree to a variation";
–   in subsection (4)(a) the words "a departure direction were made" are retained in place of "the Secretary of State agreed to a variation".

Definitions

"application for a variation": see s54.
"benefit": see reg 32 of the Variation Regulations.
"child": see s55.
"child support maintenance": see s54.
"non-resident parent": see s54.
"parent": see s54.
"person with care": see s54.
"prescribed": see s54.

General Note

If an application is made under s28G(1), this section applies as modified by reg 6 Child Support (Variations) (Modification of Statutory Provisions) Regulations 2000.

Subsections (1)-(4)

The principles set out in these subsections control the determining of an application for a variation. They, therefore, operate at the stage of applying the law to the facts of the case and are not relevant in interpreting the legislation, although the interpretation must be made in the context of the general scheme of the child support legislation of which these principles are part. They are not free-standing, but infuse all relevant stages of the determination. They are, therefore, relevant to the just and equitable test and to any judgment-based element of any of the heads under which a variation may be agreed.

The general principles in subs (2) apply only to parents as defined by s54 below and to children as defined by s55 below. Expenses relating to other children may, however, constitute a special expense under reg 11 of the Variation Regulations. Also there is a wider requirement, in s28F(2)(a) below, when considering the just and equitable condition, to have regard to the welfare of any child likely to be affected by a direction.

The requirement under subs (3) to take into account representations is complemented by reg 21(2)(g) of the Variation Regulations which excludes representations other than by relevant persons from being taken into account in the application of the just and equitable test.

Subsection (4)

Tribunals will need to be careful to distinguish between para (a) of this subsection and reg 21(1)(a)(i) of the Variation Regulations.

Subsection (5)

The prescribed benefits are contained in reg 32 of the Variation Regulations (see p646).

[¹ Agreement to a variation

[¹**28F**.–(1)   The [³[⁴Secretary of State]] may agree to a variation if–

(a)   [³[⁴the Secretary of State]] is satisfied that the case is one which falls within one or more of the cases set out in Part I of Schedule 4B or in regulations made under that Part; and

(b)   it is [³[⁴the Secretary of State's]] opinion that, in all the circumstances of the case, it would be just and equitable to agree to a variation.

(2)   In considering whether it would be just and equitable in any case to agree to a variation, the [³[⁴Secretary of State]]–

(a)   must have regard, in particular, to the welfare of any child likely to be affected if [³[⁴the Secretary of State]] did agree to a variation; and

(b)   must, or as the case may be must not, take any prescribed factors into account, or must take them into account (or not) in prescribed circumstances.

(3)   The [³[⁴Secretary of State]] shall not agree to a variation (and shall proceed to make [⁴a] decision on the application for a maintenance calculation without any variation) if [⁴...] satisfied that–

(a)   [³[⁴the Secretary of State]] has insufficient information to make a decision on the application for the maintenance calculation under section 11, and therefore that [³ [⁴the]] decision would be made under section 12(1); or

(b) other prescribed circumstances apply.

(4) Where the [³[⁴Secretary of State]] agrees to a variation, [³[⁴the Secretary of State]] shall–

(a) determine the basis on which the amount of child support maintenance is to be calculated in response to the application for a maintenance calculation [²...]; and

(b) make a decision under section 11 on that basis.

(5) If the [³[⁴Secretary of State]] has made an interim maintenance decision, it is to be treated as having been replaced by [³[⁴the Secretary of State's]] decision under section 11, and except in prescribed circumstances any appeal connected with it (under section 20) shall lapse.

(6) In determining whether or not to agree to a variation, the [³[⁴Secretary of State]] shall comply with regulations made under Part II of Schedule 4B.]]

Amendments

1. Child Support, Pensions and Social Security Act 2000 (2000 c.19) s5(5) (March 3, 2003 for the types of cases in art 3 Child Support, Pensions and Social Security Act 2000 (Commencement No.12) Order 2003 (SI 2003 No.192)). For other types of cases, see '1993 rules' below.

2. Child Maintenance and Other Payments Act 2008 (2008 c.6) s58 and Sch 8 (October 27, 2008 subject to art 4 Child Maintenance and Other Payments Act 2008 (Commencement No.3 and Transitional and Savings Provisions) Order 2008 (SI 2008 No.2548)). This omitted "(including an application treated as having been made)".

3. Child Maintenance and Other Payments Act 2008 (2008 c.6) s13 and Sch 3 para 30 (November 1, 2008); Child Maintenance and Other Payments Act 2008 (Commencement No.4 and Transitional Provision) Order 2008 (SI 2008 No.2675) art 3.

4. Public Bodies (Child Maintenance and Enforcement Commission: Abolition and Transfer of Functions) Order 2012 (SI 2012 No.2007) art 3(2) and Sch para 28 (August 1, 2012).

Note

i. If an application for a variation is made under s28G, s28F is modified in accordance with Child Support (Variations) (Modification of Statutory Provisions) Regulations 2000 (SI 2000 No.3173) reg 7 (January 31, 2001). See p527.

1993 rules

s5 of the Child Support, Pensions and Social Security Act 2000 (2000 c.19) replaces s28F of the Child Support Act 1991. This has been brought into force only for the types of cases in art 3 of the Child Support, Pensions and Social Security Act 2000 (Commencement No.12) Order 2003 (SI 2003 No.192 – see p683). For other types of cases the 1993 rules apply and s28F reads:

Departure directions

28F.–(1) The [²Commission] may give a departure direction if–

(a) [²it] is satisfied that the case is one which falls within one or more of the cases set out in Part I of Schedule 4B or in regulations made under that Part; and

(b) it is [²its] opinion that, in all the circumstances of the case, it would be just and equitable to give a departure direction.

(2) In considering whether it would be just and equitable in any case to give a departure direction, the [²Commission] shall have regard, in particular, to–

(a) the financial circumstances of the absent parent concerned;

(b) the financial circumstances of the person with care concerned; and

(c) the welfare of any child likely to be affected by the direction.

(3) The Secretary of State may by regulations make provision–

(a) for factors which are to be taken into account in determining whether it would be just and equitable to give a departure direction in any case;

(b) for factors which are not to be taken into account in determining such action.

(4) The [²Commission] shall not give a departure direction if [²it] is satisfied that the difference between the current amount and the revised amount is less than an amount to be calculated in accordance with regulations made by the Secretary of State for the purposes of this subsection and section 28B(2).

(5)　In subsection (4)–

"the current amount" means the amount of the child support maintenance fixed by the current assessment, and "the revised amount" means the amount of child support maintenance which would be fixed if a fresh maintenance assessment were to be made as a result of the departure direction which the [²Commission] would give in response to the application but for subsection (4).

(6)　A departure direction shall–

(a)　require ['the making of] one or more fresh maintenance assessments; and

(b)　specify the basis on which the amount of child support maintenance is to be fixed by any assessment made in consequence of the direction.

(7)　In giving a departure direction, the [²Commission] shall comply with the provisions of regulations made under Part II of Schedule 4B.

(8)　Before the end of such period as may be prescribed, the [²Commission] shall notify the applicant for a departure direction, and such other persons as may be prescribed–

(a)　of [²its] decision in relation to the application, and

(b)　of the reasons for [²its] decision.

Amendments

1.　Social Security Act 1998 (1998 c.14) Sch 7 para 37 (June 1, 1999).

2.　Child Maintenance and Other Payments Act 2008 (2008 c.6) s13 and Sch 3 para 30 (November 1, 2008); Child Maintenance and Other Payments Act 2008 (Commencement No.4 and Transitional Provision) Order 2008 (SI 2008 No.2675) art 3.

Definitions

"child": see s55.

"child support maintenance": see s54.

"interim maintenance decision": see s54.

"maintenance calculation": see s54.

"prescribed": see s54.

General Note

If an application is made under s28G(1), this section applies as modified by reg 7 Child Support (Variations) (Modification of Statutory Provisions) Regulations 2000.

Subsection (1)(a)

The cases are set out in regs 10-14 and 18-20 of the Variation Regulations.

Subsection (1)(b)

This paragraph imposes a general requirement that applies to all cases: it must be just and equitable to agree to a variation. It is supplemented by subs (2). There can be no definitive list of considerations which must be taken into account (*Crake and Butterworth v Supplementary Benefit Commission* [1982] 1 All ER 498 at *502, per Woolf J)*. Still less is it possible to give definitive guidance on the weight to be given to any particular consideration. This provision allows a tribunal "a broad discretion to ensure justice and equity" having regard to all relevant circumstances as a whole (*CCS 114/2005*, para 38).

The just and equitable requirement does not allow the amount of maintenance that would otherwise be fixed under the Variation Regulations to be increased (*R(CS) 5/06*, para 14). However, it is discretionary and the amount may be reduced under the authority of subs(4)(a) below (*RC v CMEC and WC* [2009] UKUT 62 (AAC), para 37).

CCS 3543/1998 decided that the just and equitable requirement was not separate from the individual issues of judgment and discretion that were to be found in the Departure Regulations governing the grounds on which a variation may be agreed and the effect of a variation on a maintenance calculation. Rather it was a general discretion that included those issues. In *CCS 1131/2005*, a different commissioner disagreed. If *CCS 2018/2005* is correct the decision in *CCS 3543/1998* only applies to the departure direction scheme, not to the variation scheme.

Although the duty under this paragraph is expressed as a requirement that it be just and equitable to agree to a variation, in practice this must refer to the effect that the particular variation being considered would have under the Variation Regulations.

The phrase "just and equitable" is used in a number of statutory contexts and there are many authorities dealing with its interpretation in those contexts. It is, however, the nature of the test that no general principles emerge from them beyond the comments of Salmon LJ in *Hanning v Maitland (No.2)* [1970] 1 All ER 812 at 819:

"I do not think that the words 'just and equitable' ... are used in the Act as terms of art [ie, as having a definite and fixed legal meaning]. Nor are they capable of precise definition. The words should be interpreted broadly to mean just what they say."

The Secretary of State and a tribunal must reach a positive conclusion that it would be just and equitable to agree to a variation. In *R(CS) 3/01,* the tribunal recorded that it did not have information on important and relevant matters, but that there was no reason to suspect that the giving of the direction would not be just and equitable. The commissioner held that this was not sufficient (para 43). He also held that the tribunal had been wrong to apply a burden of proof, as the balance of probabilities had no application to the exercise of judgment involved (para 44). He left open whether the burden might apply to the finding of facts on which the judgment was based *(ibid).*

The fact that a parent has paid school fees is not a factor that can be taken into account udner the just and equitable requirement in view of the express legislative between the responsibility of the courts and the Secretary of State (*DB, CMEC and KB* [2010] UKUT (AAC) 356 (AAC), paras 33-34).

The effect of satisfying a case for a variation is specified in the Variation Regulations in absolute terms. The Regulations make no allowance for a partial implementation of a variation, for example, by allowing only part of the special expenses incurred by a non-resident parent. That appears to have the effect that a variation must be agreed to in full or not at all. A commissioner held that the just and equitable requirement is not as blunt an instrument as that and that it can be used to override the apparently absolute terms of the Regulations (*CCS 3151/1999,* para 23). The case before the commissioner concerned the amended departure direction scheme under which partial effect was expressly permitted. However, he was commenting on the effect of the original scheme, under which the effect of a departure direction was stated in absolute terms similar to the present Variation Regulations.

The application of the just and equitable requirement involves an exercise of judgment. This affects the approach to the adequacy of reasons given by tribunals. The reasons must be sufficient to show that the tribunal approached the exercise in the correct way and that its application was not perverse. It is not necessary for the reasons to include comment on every consideration on which there was evidence. It is sufficient for tribunals to deal with those considerations that were particularly significant in the circumstances of the case. See *CCS 3543/1998,* paras 32 and 36.

Subsection (2)(a)

This duty to have regard to the welfare of any child likely to be affected by a variation is in similar terms to s2 of the Act. There are two possible reasons why it has been included. The first reason is for emphasis. The second reason is that the tests like the just and equitable requirement may not be a discretionary power for the purposes of s2 (*George Mitchell (Ghesterhall) Ltd v Finney Lock Seeds Ltd* [1983] 2 All ER 737 at 743 *per* Lord Bridge).

The one difference between this provision and s2 is that this refers to a child likely to be affected if a *variation* is given whereas s2 refers to a child likely to be affected by a *decision.* This may have the effect of excluding from this provision how a child would be affected if a variation were not given. In practice though, this is unlikely to be significant, because the provision does not exclude the broad power given by subs (1)(b), under which that could be taken into account.

Subsection (2)(b)

Regulation 21 of the Variation Regulations has been made under this enabling power.

Subsection (3)

Regulation 30 of the Variation Regulations contains the prescribed circumstances.

Subsection (5)

This deals with the possibility that an interim maintenance decision was made pending the determination of the application for a variation. If a variation is agreed to, a decision is made under s11 of the Act. That decision replaces the interim maintenance decision. If an appeal was made against the interim maintenance decision, it lapses when the s11 decision is made. However, a new right of appeal arises against the s11 decision. No disadvantage arises, because the effective date of the s11 decision will be the same as for the interim maintenance decision.

[¹ Variations: revision and supersession]

[²**28G**.–(1)   An application for a variation may also be made when a maintenance calculation is in force.]

[¹(2)   The Secretary of State may by regulations provide for–

(a)   sections 16, 17 and 20; and

(b)   sections 28A to 28F and Schedules 4A and 4B,

to apply with prescribed modifications in relation to such applications.]

[²(3)   The Secretary of State may by regulations provide that, in prescribed cases (or except in prescribed cases), a decision under section 17 made otherwise than pursuant to an application for a variation may be made on the basis of a variation agreed to for the purposes of an earlier decision without a new application for a variation having to be made.]

Amendments

1.   Child Support, Pensions and Social Security Act, 2000 s7 (for the purpose of the exercise of the power to make regulations, November 10, 2000; for all other purposes, January 1, 2001); Child Support, Pensions and Social Security Act 2000 (Commencement No. 3) Order 2000 (SI 2000 No.2994) art 2 and Sch.

2.   Child Support, Pensions and Social Security Act 2000 (2000 c.19) s7 (for the purpose of the exercise of powers to make regulations and Acts of Sederunt, November 10, 2000; for all other purposes, March 3, 2003 for the types of cases in art 3 Child Support, Pensions and Social Security Act 2000 (Commencement No.12) Order 2003 (SI 2003 No.192)).

1993 rules

s7 of the Child Support, Pensions and Social Security Act 2000 (2000 c.19) substitutes s28G of the Child Support Act 1991. The substituted subsections 28G(1) and (3) were brought into force for the purpose of the exercise of powers to make regulations and Acts of Sederunt on November 10, 2000. For all other purposes they have been brought into force only for the types of cases in art 3 of the Child Support, Pensions and Social Security Act 2000 (Commencement No.12) Order 2003 (SI 2003 No.192 – see p683). For other types of cases subsections 28G(1) and (3), shown above, do not apply.

Definitions

"application for a variation": see s54.
"maintenance calculation": see s54.
"prescribed": see s54.

General Note

Subsection (1)

Section 28A(3) allows an application for a variation to be made before the Secretary of State has reached a decision on an application for a maintenance calculation. This subsection allows an application for a variation to be made when a maintenance calculation is in force. The application takes effect as an application for a revision of the maintenance calculation decision under s16 above (see reg 3A(1)(a)(ii) of the Appeals Regulations) or for a supersession under s17 (see reg 6A(4) of the Appeals Regulations).

Subsection (2)(b)

The provisions covered by this paragraph are drafted to apply to applications for a variation made under s28A(3) above before a decision on an application for a maintenance calculation has been made. The Child Support (Variations) (Modification of Statutory Provisions) Regulations 2000 have been made under the enabling power in this paragraph to modify those provisions so that they apply to applications under subs (1) of this section.

Subsection (3)

Regulation 7 of the Variation Regulations has been made under this enabling power.

    Sections 28H and 28I were repealed by para 11(14) of Sch 3 and by Sch 9 to the 2000 Act. Article 3 of, and the Schedule to, the Commencement No.12 Order 2003 provided that they ceased to have effect from 3 March 2003 for the purposes of the cases there specified.

[¹ Voluntary payments

28J.–(1)   This section applies where–

(a)   a person has applied for a maintenance calculation under section 4(1) or 7(1) [²...];

(b)   the [³[⁴Secretary of State]] has neither made a decision under section 11 or 12 on the application, nor decided not to make a maintenance calculation; and

(c)   the non-resident parent makes a voluntary payment.

(2)   A "voluntary payment" is a payment–

(a)   on account of child support maintenance which the non-resident parent expects to become liable to pay following the determination of the application (whether or not the amount of the payment is based on any estimate of his potential liability which the [³[⁴Secretary of State]] has agreed to give); and

(b)   made before the maintenance calculation has been notified to the non-resident parent or (as the case may be) before the [³[⁴Secretary of State]] has notified the non-resident parent that [³[⁴the Secretary of State]] has decided not to make a maintenance calculation.

(3)   In such circumstances and to such extent as may be prescribed–

(a)   the voluntary payment may be set off against arrears of child support maintenance which accrued by virtue of the maintenance calculation taking effect on a date earlier than that on which it was notified to the non-resident parent;

(b)   the amount payable under a maintenance calculation may be adjusted to take account of the voluntary payment.

(4)   A voluntary payment shall be made to the [³[⁴Secretary of State]] unless [³[⁴the Secretary of State]] agrees, on such conditions as [³[⁴the Secretary of State]] may specify, that it may be made to the person with care, or to or through another person.

(5)   The [³Commission] may by regulations make provision as to voluntary payments, and the regulations may in particular–

(a)   prescribe what payments or descriptions of payment are, or are not, to count as "voluntary payments";

(b)   prescribe the extent to which and circumstances in which a payment, or a payment of a prescribed description, counts.]

Amendments

1.   Child Support, Pensions and Social Security Act 2000 (2000 c.19) s20 (March 3, 2003 for the types of cases in art 5 Child Support, Pensions and Social Security Act 2000 (Commencement No.12) Order 2003 (SI 2003 No.192)). For other types of cases, see '1993 rules' below.

2.   Child Maintenance and Other Payments Act 2008 (2008 c.6) s58 and Sch 8 (October 27, 2008 subject to art 4 of Child Maintenance and Other Payments Act 2008 (Commencement No.3 and Transitional and Savings Provisions) Order 2008 (SI 2008 No.2548)). This omitted ", or is treated as having applied for one by virtue of section 6".

3.   Child Maintenance and Other Payments Act 2008 (2008 c.6) s13 and Sch 3 para 31 (November 1, 2008); Child Maintenance and Other Payments Act 2008 (Commencement No.4 and Transitional Provision) Order 2008 (SI 2008 No.2675) art 3.

4.   Public Bodies (Child Maintenance and Enforcement Commission: Abolition and Transfer of Functions) Order 2012 (SI 2012 No.2007) art 3(2) and Sch para 29 (August 1, 2012).

1993 rules

s20 of the Child Support, Pensions and Social Security Act 2000 (2000 c.19) inserts s28J of the Child Support Act 1991. This has been brought into force only for the types of cases in art 5 of the Child Support, Pensions and Social Security Act 2000 (Commencement No.12) Order 2003 (SI 2003 No.192 – see p685). For other types of cases s28J does not apply.

Definitions

"child support maintenance": see s54.
"maintenance calculation": see s54.
"non-resident parent": see s54.
"prescribed": see s54.
"voluntary payment": see s54.

General Note

This section makes provision to ameliorate the problems for non-resident parents that arise when arrears build up while their maintenance liability is being calculated. It provides a method that protects the non-resident parent without loss to the person with care. It avoids the need to meet the cost of delay from public funds, as under s27(7)(b) of the 2000 Act.

Only arrears that arise on the initial application for a maintenance calculation are covered. Arrears that arise from a delay in dealing with revisions and supersessions are not.

The impact of the arrears is lessened by the non-resident parent making voluntary payments pending the Secretary of State's decision on the application. Those payments are then offset against arrears of child support maintenance. If the amount of the voluntary payments exceed the arrears, they are dealt with under s41B(1A) and (7) below as overpaid child support maintenance.

The payment of school fees could be taken in to account as a voluntary payment (*DB, CMEC and KB* [2010] UKUT (AAC) 356 (AAC), para 33).

The Child Support (Voluntary Payments) Regulations 2000 supplement the provisions of this section. They prescribe the acceptable methods of payment (reg 3 (a)), the matters to which the payments may be attributed (reg 3(b)) and the evidence that is acceptable as proof of payment (reg 4). The scheme is limited to payments made after the effective date of the maintenance calculation that was made or would have been made had the Secretary of State decided not to make one. The payments may be made to the person with care or to someone else, like an electricity supplier.

Subsection (3)

The Child Support (Management of Payment and Arrears) Regulations 2009 are made in part under this subsection.

Collection and enforcement

General Note

According to the Court of Appeal in *Department of Social Security v Butler* [1995] 1 WLR 1528, the child support legislation provides a complete code for the collection of payments due under maintenance assessments and the enforcement of liability orders made. The duty to pay a maintenance assessment is not expressed as a civil debt and cannot be directly enforced by action in any civil court or by any means other than as provided in the Act. Consequently, the Secretary of State is not entitled to be granted a *Mareva* injunction to prevent a liable person from disposing of assets before a liability order can be obtained. However, once a liability order has been made under s33, the country court has jurisdiction to grant a *Mareva* injunction under reg 3(3)(a) and (c) County Court Remedies Regulations 1991.

Section 2 of the Act may apply to discretionary decisions on enforcement. As Hughes LJ explained in *Brookes v SSWP and CMEC* [2010] EWCA Civ 420:

"16.   ...Some discretionary decisions related to potential enforcement may not of themselves have any potential for impact on children, whether supported children or those in the payer's present household. An example will ordinarily be a decision to seek a liability order under s33, which of itself accomplishes no enforcement but only establishes the sum owing and opens a gateway to particular kinds of possible subsequent enforcement. It might be possible to postulate an unusual situation in which a child was so vulnerable that even the possible knowledge that a parent would have to attend court could have a dramatic adverse effect, but absent such a circumstance, the seeking of a liability order must be followed by other discretionary enforcement decisions before there can be any question of impact on welfare. However, the decision under s35 to seek distraint via bailiffs is capable of having some impact on the welfare of both supported children, if any recovered sum may benefit them, and children in the payer's present household since chattels may be removed from that household. Similarly, a decision to seek committal of the non-payer by the magistrates could have an impact on both groups of children. That section 2 is applicable to both kinds of decision has not been in question before us."

A decision to take discretionary enforcement action has a limited duration. It lasts for a reasonable time to allow it to be put into effect, but after that time it must be remade before it can be acted on. In *Brookes* (para 38), the Court of Appeal decided that an enforcement decision would have lapsed after two years. This does not mean that an enforcement decision is effective for two years; only that it is not effective thereafter.

The effect of a non-resident parent's personal insolvency was considered in *CMEC v Beesley and Whyman* [2010] EWCA Civ 1344. The non-resident parent agreed with his other creditors to pay 27 pence in the pound over five years. The bulk of his debts were arrears of child support maintenance. The Court of Appeal accepted the argument for the CMEC that it was not a creditor for the purposes of an individual voluntary arrangement (IVA) and so was not bound by the arrangement.

Collection of child support maintenance

29.–(1)   The [⁵ [⁷Secretary of State]] may arrange for the collection of any child support maintenance payable in accordance with a [¹maintenance calculation] where–

(a)   [⁴...]

(b)   an application has been made to the [⁵[⁷Secretary of State]] under section 4(2) or 7(3) for [⁵[⁷the Secretary of State]] to arrange for its collection.

(2)   Where a [¹maintenance calculation] is made under this Act, payments of child support maintenance under the [²calculation] shall be made in accordance with regulations made by the Secretary of State.

(3)   The regulations may, in particular, make provision–

(a)   for payments of child support maintenance to be made–

(i)   to the person caring for the child or children in question;

(ii)   to, or through, the [⁵[⁷Secretary of State]]; or

(iii)   to, or through, such other person as the [⁵[⁷Secretary of State]] may, from time to time, specify;

(b)   as to the method by which payments of child support maintenance are to be made;

[⁶(c)   for determining, on the basis of prescribed assumptions, the total amount of the payments of child support maintenance payable in a reference period (including provision for adjustments to such an amount);

(ca)   requiring payments of child support maintenance to be made–

(i)   by reference to such an amount and a reference period; and

(ii)   at prescribed intervals falling in a reference period;]

(d)   as to the method and timing of the transmission of payments which are made, to or through the [⁵[⁷Secretary of State]] or any other person, in accord-ance with the regulations;

(e)   empowering the [⁵[⁷Secretary of State]] to direct any person liable to make payments in accordance with the [²calculation]–

    (i)   to make them by standing order or by any other method which requires one person to give his authority for payments to be made from an account of his to an account of another's on specific dates during the period for which the authority is in force and without the need for any further authority from him;

    (ii)   to open an account from which payments under the [²calculation] may be made in accordance with the method of payment which that person is obliged to adopt;

(f)   providing for the making of representations with respect to matters with which the regulations are concerned.

[⁶(3A) In subsection (3)(c) and (ca) "a reference period" means–

(a)   a period of 52 weeks beginning with a prescribed date; or

(b)   in prescribed circumstances, a prescribed period.]

[³(4)   If the regulations include provision for payment by means of deduction in accordance with an order under section 31, they must make provision–

(a)   for that method of payment not to be used in any case where there is good reason not to use it; and

(b)   for the person against whom the order under section 31 would be made to have a right of appeal to a magistrates' court (or, in Scotland, to the sheriff) against a decision that the exclusion required by paragraph (a) does not apply.]

(5)   On an appeal under regulations made under subsection (4)(b) the court or (as the case may be) the sheriff shall not question the maintenance calculation by reference to which the order under section 31 would be made.

(6)   Regulations under subsection (4)(b) may include–

(a)   provision with respect to the period within which a right of appeal under the regulations may be exercised;

(b)   provision with respect to the powers of a magistrates' court (or, in Scotland, of the sheriff) in relation to an appeal under the regulations.

(7)   If the regulations include provision for payment by means of deduction in accordance with an order under section 31, they may make provision–

(a)   prescribing matters which are, or are not, to be taken into account in determining whether there is good reason not to use that method of payment;

(b)   prescribing circumstances in which good reason not to use that method of payment is, or is not, to be regarded as existing.]

Amendments

1.   Child Support, Pensions and Social Security Act 2000 (2000 c.19) s1(2) (March 3, 2003 for the types of caases in art 3 Child Support, Pensions and Social Security Act 2000 (Commencement No.12) Order 2003 (SI 2003 No.192)). For other types of cases, see '1993 rules' below.

2.   Child Support, Pensions and Social Security Act 2000 (2000 c.19) s1(2) (March 3, 2003 for the types of cases in art 3 Child Support, Pensions and Social Security Act 2000 (Commencement No.12) Order 2003 (SI 2003 No.192)). For other types of cases, see '1993 rules' below.

3.   Child Maintenance and Other Payments Act 2008 (2008 c.6) s20 (September 26, 2008 for making regulations, October 27, 2008 for all other purposes). See s59 Child Maintenance and Other Payments Act 2008 and art 4 Child Maintenance and Other Payments Act 2008 (Commencement No.3 and Transitional and Savings Provisions) Order 2008 (SI 2008 No.2548) for transitional and savings provisions.

4.   Child Maintenance and Other Payments Act 2008 (2008 c.6) s58 and Sch 8 (October 27, 2008 subject to art 4 Child Maintenance and Other Payments Act 2008 (Commencement No.3 and Transitional and Savings Provisions) Order 2008 (SI 2008 No.2548)). This omitted para (a) from subs 29(1), para (a) read:

    "(a)   the [²calculation] is made by virtue of section 6; or"

5.   Child Maintenance and Other Payments Act 2008 (2008 c.6) s13 and Sch 3, para 32 (November 1, 2008); Child Maintenance and Other Payments Act 2008 (Commencement No.4 and Transitional Provision) Order 2008 (SI 2008 No.2675) art 3.

6.   Welfare Reform Act 2009 (2009 c.24) s54 (October 8, 2012).
7.   Public Bodies (Child Maintenance and Enforcement Commission: Abolition and Transfer of Functions) Order 2012 (SI 2012 No.2007) art 3(2) and Sch para 30 (August 1, 2012).

1993 rules

s1(2) of the Child Support, Pensions and Social Security Act 2000 (2000 c.19) amends this section of the Child Support Act 1991 and has been brought into force only for the types of cases in art 3 of the Child Support, Pensions and Social Security Act 2000 (Commencement No.12) Order 2003 (SI 2003 No.192 – see p683). For other types of cases the 1993 rules apply and the original wording is retained – ie, "maintenance assessment" is retained in place of "maintenance calculation" and "assessment" is retained in place of "calculation".

Definitions

"child": see s3(6).
"child support maintenance": see s3(6).
"maintenance": calculation see s54.

General Note

Subsection (1)

The Secretary of State may arrange for the collection of child support maintenance in two different cases. First, if the parent with care has been treated as applying for a maintenance calculation under s6 above, recovery is automatic under s6(3)(b) and no further application is necessary. Second, where an application for child support maintenance has been made under s4(1) or 7(1), an application to the Secretary of State may be made under s4(2) or 7(3). It is possible for parties to have sought a maintenance calculation under these sections, but to make their own private arrangements for collection of the child support maintenance so assessed. In such a case, either party may subsequently apply to use the collection service at a later date.

   If collection of child support maintenance is arranged under this section in respect of a qualifying child whose parent with care is a spouse or former spouse to whom periodical payments under a maintenance order are payable, that order is prescribed for the purposes of s30 by reg 2(b) Collection and Enforcement of Other Forms of Maintenance Regulations.

Subsection (2)

This subsection applies to payment of child support maintenance generally and not just to cases where collection is being arranged by the Secretary of State under subs (1). The regulations are contained in Pt II of the Collection and Enforcement Regulations. They deal with the person to whom payment should be made (reg 2), the method, interval and method of transmission of payment and representations about these matters (regs 3 to 6), and notice to the liable person concerning payment (reg 7).

Subsection (3)

Payments may be required to be made by the "liable person" (see reg 2(2) and s31 of the Act): (i) direct to the person caring for the child or children in question, or, where an application was made by a child under s7, to that child; (ii) to or through the Secretary of State; or (iii) to or through such other person as is specified by the Secretary of State. The liable person and the person entitled to receive the payments will be provided with an opportunity to make representations as to the method of payment, and these will be taken into account when determining how the maintenance is to be paid. The aim is to arrange the most secure approach to payment.

   The method of payment will vary according to the particular circumstances in the case. Payment direct by the liable person to the person caring for the child or children may be required to be made by standing order or equivalent, such as direct debit, cheque or postal order, or cash. Although para (e)(ii) provides for the Regulations to give the Secretary of State the power to direct the liable person to open an account from which payments can be made, reg 3(2) more realistically empowers the Secretary of State to direct the liable person to take all reasonable steps to open an account. There may be situations where a bank or similar institution is not prepared to take a liable person on as a customer, in which case one of the other methods will have to be specified. These provisions may be compared with those under the Maintenance Enforcement Act 1991, where courts are given similar powers to collect maintenance. Under s1(6) of that Act, the court must first give the debtor an opportunity to open an account, and may, if satisfied that the debtor has failed, without reasonable excuse, to do so, then order him or her to comply. Under s29 and the regulations, the Secretary of State may require the liable person to take reasonable steps to comply without first offering an opportunity to him or her to do so voluntarily.

   The date and intervals of payment will be specified by the Secretary of State, and timed to coincide with the liable person's receipt of salary or wages, with due allowance made for clearance of cheques, etc. Where the payments are made to or through the Secretary of State rather than to the person caring for the child or children, payments may be made to the recipient at different times or intervals from when they are received by the Secretary of State, but only where the Secretary of State is satisfied that it would otherwise cause undue hardship to either the person liable to make the payments or to the person entitled to receive them. For example, the liable person may make payments monthly, but the person caring for the child or children may be paid by the Secretary of State fortnightly.

A notice will be sent to the liable person under reg 7 as to the requirements about payment, as soon as is reasonably practicable after the making of the maintenance assessment and after any change in the requirements referred to in any previous such notice.

Collection and enforcement of other forms of maintenance

30.–(1)   Where the [⁵[⁶Secretary of State]] is arranging for the collection of any payments under section 29 or subsection (2), [⁵[⁶the Secretary of State]] may also arrange for the collection of any periodical payments, or secured periodical payments, of a prescribed kind which are payable to or for the benefit of any person who falls within a prescribed category.

[¹[³(2)   The [⁵[⁶Secretary of State]] may, except in prescribed cases, arrange for the collection of any periodical payments, or secured periodical payments, of a prescribed kind which are payable for the benefit of a child even though [⁵[⁶the Secretary of State]] is not arranging for the collection of child support maintenance with respect to that child.]]

(3)   Where–

(a)   the [⁵[⁶Secretary of State]] is arranging, under this Act, for the collection of different payments ("the payments") from the same [² non-resident parent];

(b)   an amount is collected by the [⁵[⁶Secretary of State]] from the [² non-resident parent] which is less than the total amount due in respect of the payments; and

(c)   the [²non-resident parent] has not stipulated how that amount is to be allocated by the [⁵[⁶Secretary of State]] as between the payments,

the [⁵[⁶Secretary of State]] may allocate that amount as [⁵[⁶the Secretary of State]] sees fit.

(4)   In relation to England and Wales, the Secretary of State may by regulations make provision for sections 29 and 31 to 40 to apply, with such modifications (if any) as he considers necessary or expedient, for the purpose of [⁶enabling the Secretary of State to enforce any obligation to pay any amount for the collection of which the Secretary of State is authorised under this section to make arrangements].

(5)   In relation to Scotland, the Secretary of State may by regulations make provision for the purpose of [⁶enabling the Secretary of State to enforce any obligation to pay any amount for the collection of which the Secretary of State is authorised under this section to make arrangements]–

(a)   empowering [⁵ the [⁶Secretary of State]] to bring any proceedings or take any other steps (other than diligence against earnings) which could have been brought or taken by or on behalf of the person to whom the periodical payments are payable;

(b)   applying sections 29, 31 and 32 with such modifications (if any) as he considers necessary or expedient.

Amendments

1.   s30(2) is prosp.

2.   Child Support, Pensions and Social Security Act 2000 (2000 c.19) s26 and Sch 3, para 11(2) (March 3, 2003 for the types of cases in art 3 Child Support, Pensions and Social Security Act 2000 (Commencement No.12) Order 2003 (SI 2003 No.192)). For other types of cases, see '1993 rules' below.

3.   Child Support, Pensions and Social Security Act 2000 (2000 c.19) s26 and Sch 3 para 11(15) (March 3, 2003).

4.   Child Maintenance and Other Payments Act 2008 (2008 c.6) Sch 7 para 1(7) (June 1, 2009).

5.   Child Maintenance and Other Payments Act 2008 (2008 c.6) s13 and Sch 3 para 33 (November 1, 2008); Child Maintenance and Other Payments Act 2008 (Commencement No.4 and Transitional Provision) Order 2008 (SI 2008 No.2675) art 3.

6.   Public Bodies (Child Maintenance and Enforcement Commission: Abolition and Transfer of Functions) Order 2012 (SI 2012 No.2007) art 3(2) and Sch para 30 (August 1, 2012).

1993 rules

s26 and Sch 3 of the Child Support, Pensions and Social Security Act 2000 (2000 c.19) amends this section of the Child Support Act 1991 and has been brought into force only for the types of cases in art 3 of the Child Support, Pensions and Social Security Act 2000 (Commencement No.12) Order 2003 (SI 2003 No.192 – see p683). For other types of cases the 1993 rules apply and the original wording is retained – ie, "absent parent" is retained in place of "non-resident parent".

Definitions
"child": see s55.
"child support maintenance": see s3(6).
"non-resident parent": see s54.
"prescribed": see s54.

General Note
The payments and categories of persons covered by this section are prescribed by reg 2 Collection and Enforcement of Other Forms of Maintenance Regulations. In the case of England and Wales, reg 3 applies the provisions of subs 29(2) and (3) and 31 to 40 to payments covered by this section. In the case of Scotland, reg 4 provides that the Secretary of State may bring any proceedings or take any other steps other than diligence against earnings which could have been taken by or on behalf of the person to whom the payments are payable, and applies the provisions of subs 29(2) and (3), 31 and 32 to those payments.

This section empowers the Secretary of State to collect periodical payments ordered by a court, when arranging for the collection of child support maintenance under the Act. Periodical payments are not defined, but the Regulations (see below) provide that secured periodical payments are included. The periodical payments may be to or for the benefit of the person with care who is a spouse or former spouse, and not just for children.

Magistrates may order that payments of other forms of maintenance be made through the Agency's collection system where that is already being used in respect of a maintenance assessment (Child Support Act 1991 (Consequential Amendments) Order 1994).

Arrangements for the collection of other forms of maintenance are provided for by the Collection and Enforcement of Other Forms of Maintenance Regulations. These prescribe the following periodical payments and persons as covered by s30(1).

(i)   Payments under a maintenance order (note, not a maintenance agreement) made in relation to a child in accordance with s8(6) (top-up maintenance); s8(7) (maintenance to cover the costs of education or training); or s8(8) (periodical payments to meet expenses attributable to disability).

(ii)   Periodical payments under a maintenance order (not a maintenance agreement in England and Wales, but, in Scotland, registered minutes of agreement are included) payable to or for the benefit of a spouse or former spouse, who is the person with care of a child who is a qualifying child in respect of whom a child maintenance assessment is in force for which collection has been arranged under s29.

(iii)   Periodical payments under a maintenance order (not an agreement) payable to or for the benefit of a former child of the family of the person against whom the order is made, and who has his home with the person with care.

A child of the family is defined for England and Wales by s52(1) Matrimonial Causes Act 1973, as amended by Sch 12, para 33 to the Children Act 1989, as:

"in relation to the parties to a marriage ...

(a)   a child of both of those parties; and

(b)   any other child, not being a child who is placed with those parties as foster parents by a local authority or voluntary organisation, who has been treated by both of those parties as a child of their family."

Whether a child has been treated as a child of the family is a question of fact judged objectively (*Teeling v Teeling* [1984] FLR 808). The fact that the husband mistakenly believes the child is his does not prevent the child being a child of the family, if the husband treats the child as such (*W (RJ) v W (SJ)* [1972] Fam 152).

The aim of this third category is to provide a collection mechanism for all the children having their home with the person with care, and to avoid the situation where only one or some children are benefiting from the collection service because they are the subjects of a maintenance assessment, while another or others are dependent upon the court machinery for enforcement.

Subsection (2)
This provides that periodical payments for the benefit of a child may be collected even though the Secretary of State is not collecting child support maintenance with respect to that child. This subsection has not been brought into force.

Subsection (3)
This provision gives the Secretary of State a discretion to apportion payments between different families to whom the non-resident parent is liable, as he sees fit. If the non-resident parent has stipulated how an amount is to be allocated, this would appear to be binding, but it is arguable that it would not be permitted where the non-resident parent chose to give priority to children whose carer is not a parent in receipt of benefit under s6, or to a former spouse rather than the children.

Subsection (4)
The aim of the section is to enable the Secretary of State to use the same methods of collection and enforcement regardless of the origin of the payments. Hence, reg 3 of the Regulations provides that, in relation to England and Wales, subss 29(2) and (3) and 31 to 40 of the Act and any regulations made under those sections, apply for the

purpose of enabling the Secretary of State to enforce any obligation to pay the prescribed forms of maintenance, as modified to provide that references to child support maintenance shall be read as references to periodical payments and references to maintenance assessments as maintenance orders.

Subsection (5)

Regulation 4 of the Regulations provides that, in relation to Scotland, the Secretary of State may bring any proceedings and take any other steps (other than diligence against earnings) which could have been brought or taken by or on behalf of the person to whom the periodical payments are payable. Sections 29(2) and (3), 31 and 32 of the Act and any regulations made under those sections, apply as modified to read as if referring to periodical payments and maintenance orders.

These Regulations do not apply to any periodical payments which fall due before the date specified by notice in writing to the non-resident parent that the Secretary of State is arranging for payments to be collected, and that date shall not be earlier than the date the notice is given (reg 5).

Deduction from earnings orders

31.–(1)   This section applies where any person ("the liable person") is liable to make payments of child support maintenance.

(2)   The [³[⁴Secretary of State]] may make an order ("a deduction from earnings order") against the liable person to secure the payment of any amount due under the [¹maintenance calculation] in question.

(3)   A deduction from earnings order may be made so as to secure the payment of–

(a)   arrears of child support maintenance payable under the [²calculation];

(b)   amounts of child support maintenance which will become due under the [²calculation]; or

(c)   both such arrears and such future amounts.

(4)   A deduction from earnings order–

(a)   shall be expressed to be directed at a person ("the employer") who has the liable person in his employment; and

(b)   shall have effect from such date as may be specified in the order.

(5)   A deduction from earnings order shall operate as an instruction to the employer to–

(a)   make deductions from the liable person's earnings; and

(b)   pay the amounts deducted to the [³[⁴Secretary of State]].

(6)   The [³[⁴Secretary of State]] shall serve a copy of any deduction from earnings order [⁴made] under this section on–

(a)   the person who appears to the [³[⁴Secretary of State]] to have the liable person in question in his employment; and

(b)   the liable person.

(7)   Where–

(a)   the deduction from earnings order has been made; and

(b)   a copy of the order has been served on the liable person's employer,

it shall be the duty of that employer to comply with the order; but he shall not be under any liability for non-compliance before the end of the period of 7 days beginning with the date on which the copy was served on him.

(8)   In this section and in section 32 "earnings" has such meaning as may be prescribed.

Amendments

1.   Child Support, Pensions and Social Security Act 2000 (2000 c.19) s1(2) (March 3, 2003 for the types of cases in art 3 Child Support, Pensions and Social Security Act 2000 (Commencement No.12) Order 2003 (SI 2003 No.192)). For other types of cases, see '1993 rules' below.

2.   Child Support, Pensions and Social Security Act 2000 (2000 c.19) s1(2) (March 3, 2003 for the types of cases in art 3 Child Support, Pensions and Social Security Act 2000 (Commencement No.12) Order 2003 (SI 2003 No.192)). For other types of cases, see '1993 rules' below.

3.   Child Maintenance and Other Payments Act 2008 (2008 c.6) s13 and Sch 3, para 34 (November 1, 2008); Child Maintenance and Other Payments Act 2008 (Commencement No.4 and Transitional Provision) Order 2008 (SI 2008 No. 2675) art 3.

4.   Public Bodies (Child Maintenance and Enforcement Commission: Abolition and Transfer of Functions) Order 2012 (SI 2012 No.2007) art 3(2) and Sch para 32 (August 1, 2012).

1993 rules

s1(2) of the Child Support, Pensions and Social Security Act 2000 (2000 c.19) amends this section of the Child Support Act 1991 and has been brought into force only for the types of cases in art 3 of the Child Support, Pensions and Social Security Act 2000 (Commencement No.12) Order 2003 (SI 2003 No.192 – see p683). For other types of cases the 1993 rules apply and the original wording is retained – ie, "maintenance assessment" is retained in place of "maintenance calculation" and "assessment" is retained in place of "calculation".

Definitions

"child support maintenance": see s3(6).
"maintenance calculation": see s54.
"non-resident parent": see s54.
"prescribed": see s54.

General Note

The enforcement of a liability to pay child support maintenance is a matter for the Secretary of State and not for the person with care. In securing the enforcement of a liability to pay, the Secretary of State must first consider whether or not a deduction from earnings order under this section is appropriate. If it is appropriate, one must be made and further action can only be taken if it proves ineffective (s33(1)(b)(ii)). If it is inappropriate, any default in payment of child support maintenance allows the Secretary of State to proceed to the next step, which is to apply for a liability order from a magistrates' court or sheriff under s33. This opens the way for steps to be taken to recover the maintenance. In England and Wales, these steps are distress and sale, garnishee proceedings and a charging order (ss35 and 36). If these steps are unsuccessful, a warrant for commitment to prison may be issued under s40. In Scotland, the relevant steps are arrestment and action of forthcoming or sale (s38).

A deduction from earnings order operates as an instruction to the liable person's employer to deduct amounts from her/his earnings and pay these to the Secretary of State. It is similar to attachment of earnings in England and Wales (earnings arrestment in Scotland). As with attachment of earnings orders, as amended by the Maintenance Enforcement Act 1991 ss1(4)(b) and 2(3)(d), an order can be made before the liable person has fallen into arrears. Nonetheless, such an order is intended to be used only when other methods have failed or appear likely to fail. The Secretary of State will first have tried to deal with arrears by means of agreement with the liable person or by trying a new method of payment (see s41 below). A deduction from earnings order is also commonly made when an interim maintenance assessment is imposed. The limitations of the deduction from earnings order are that it can only be used where the liable person is employed and that it is not appropriate if the person changes jobs frequently. The fact that a person's earnings fluctuate is not a bar to the making of a deduction of earnings order (*R v York Magistrates' Court ex p Grimes, The Times*, June 27, 1997). Regulations providing for the detailed arrangements are made under s32.

Previous overpayments of child support maintenance are only relevant to the issue whether a non-resident parent is in arrears if they were expressly made to cover future liability (*R v Secretary of State for Social Security ex p Newmarch Singh* [2000] 2 FLR 664).

Where a deduction from earnings order is made in Great Britain and the liable person works for an employer in Northern Ireland, or vice versa, the deduction from earnings order will have effect in the territory in which the liable person is working, as if made under the provision for that territory. Any appeal in connection with the order shall be made under the provision for the territory in which the liable person is resident (Sch 1 paras 10 and 12 Child Support (Northern Ireland Reciprocal Arrangements) Regulations 1993).

For arrangements concerning deductions from the pay of servicemen and merchant seamen, see the Child Support Act 1991 (Consequential Amendments) Order 1993.

Subsection (1)

The "liable person" will be the non-resident parent.

Subsection (2)

A deduction from earnings order is made by the Secretary of State. This should make it possible for one to be made more quickly and easily than an attachment of earnings or earnings arrestment order, which has to be made by a court. Giving a public authority, rather than a court, the power to make such an order is not new. It also exists in relation to collection of council tax. A deduction from earnings order may be made against someone in the employment of the Crown, but in such a case the operation of s32(8) is modified (s57(4)).

Subsection (8)

"Earnings" is defined in reg 8 of the Collection and Enforcement Regulations (see p376).

Regulations about deduction from earnings orders

32.–(1)   The Secretary of State may by regulations make provision with respect to deduction from earnings orders.

(2)   The regulations may, in particular, make provision–

(a)   as to the circumstances in which one person is to be treated as employed by another;

(b) requiring any deduction from earnings under an order to be made in the prescribed manner;

[²(bb) for the amount or amounts which are to be deducted from the liable person's earnings not to exceed a prescribed proportion of his earnings (as determined by the employer);]

(c) requiring an order to specify the amount or amounts to which the order relates and the amount or amounts which are to be deducted from the liable person's earnings in order to meet his liabilities under the [¹maintenance calculation] in question;

(d) requiring the intervals between deductions to be made under an order to be specified in the order;

(e) as to the payment of sums deducted under an order to the [³[⁵Secretary of State]];

(f) allowing the person who deducts and pays any amount under an order to deduct from the liable person's earnings a prescribed sum towards his administrative costs;

(g) with respect to the notification to be given to the liable person of amounts deducted, and amounts paid, under the order;

(h) requiring any person on whom a copy of an order is served to notify the [³[⁵Secretary of State]] in the prescribed manner and within a prescribed period if he does not have the liable person in his employment or if the liable person ceases to be in his employment;

(i) as to the operation of an order where the liable person is in the employment of the Crown;

(j) for the variation of orders;

(k) similar to that made by section 31(7), in relation to any variation of an order;

(l) for an order to lapse when the employer concerned ceases to have the liable person in his employment;

(m) as to the revival of an order in such circumstances as may be prescribed;

(n) allowing or requiring an order to be discharged;

(o) as to the giving of notice by the [³[⁵Secretary of State]] to the employer concerned that an order has lapsed or has ceased to have effect.

(3) The regulations may include provision that while a deduction from earnings order is in force–

(a) the liable person shall from time to time notify the [³[⁵Secretary of State]], in the prescribed manner and within a prescribed period, of each occasion on which he leaves any employment or becomes employed, or re-employed, and shall include in such a notification a statement of his earnings and expected earnings from the employment concerned and of such other matters as may be prescribed;

(b) any person who becomes the liable person's employer and knows that the order is in force shall notify the [³[⁵Secretary of State]], in the prescribed manner and within a prescribed period, that he is the liable person's employer, and shall include in such a notification a statement of the liable person's earnings and expected earnings from the employment concerned and of such other matters as may be prescribed.

(4) The regulations may include provision with respect to the priority as between a deduction from earnings order and–

(a) any other deduction from earnings order;

(b) any order under any other enactment relating to England and Wales which provides for deductions from the liable person's earnings;

(c) any diligence against earnings.

(5) The regulations may include a provision that a liable person may appeal to a magistrates' court (or in Scotland to the sheriff) if he is aggrieved by the making of a deduction from earnings order against him, or by the terms of any such order, or there is a dispute as to whether payments constitute earnings or as to any other prescribed matter relating to the order.

(6)　On an appeal under subsection (5) the court or (as the case may be) the sheriff shall not question the [¹maintenance calculation] by reference to which the deduction from earnings order was made.

(7)　Regulations made by virtue of subsection (5) may include provision as to the powers of a magistrates' court, or in Scotland of the sheriff, in relation to an appeal (which may include[⁴ –

(a)　provision with respect to the period within which a right of appeal under these regulations may be exercised;

(b)]　provision as to the quashing of a deduction from earnings order or the variation of the terms of such an order).

(8)　If any person fails to comply with the requirements of a deduction from earnings order, or with any regulation under this section which is designated for the purposes of this subsection, he shall be guilty of an offence.

(9)　In subsection (8) "designated" means designated by the regulations.

(10)　It shall be a defence for a person charged with an offence under subsection (8) to prove that he took all reasonable steps to comply with the requirements in question.

(11)　Any person guilty of an offence under subsection (8) shall be liable on summary conviction to a fine not exceeding level two on the standard scale.

Amendments

1.　Child Support, Pensions and Social Security Act 2000 (2000 c.19) s1(2) (March 3, 2003 for the types of cases in art 3 Child Support, Pensions and Social Security Act 2000 (Commencement No.12) Order 2003 (SI 2003 No.192)). For other types of cases, see '1993 rules' below.

2.　Child Support, Pensions and Social Security Act 2000 (2000 c.19) s26 and Sch 3 para 11(16) (March 3, 2003 for the types of cases in art 3 Child Support, Pensions and Social Security Act 2000 (Commencement No.12) Order 2003 (SI 2003 No.192), and in as far as it is not already in force September 26, 2008 for making regulations and October 27, 2008, for all other purposes).

3.　Child Maintenance and Other Payments Act 2008 (2008 c.6) s13 and Sch 3, para 35 (November 1, 2008); Child Maintenance and Other Payments Act 2008 (Commencement No.4 and Transitional Provision) Order 2008 (SI.2008 No.2675) art 3.

4.　Child Maintenance and Other Payments Act 2008 (2008 c.6) Sch 7 para 1(9) (June 1, 2009).

5.　Public Bodies (Child Maintenance and Enforcement Commission: Abolition and Transfer of Functions) Order 2012 (SI 2012 No.2007) art 3(2) and Sch para 33 (August 1, 2012).

1993 rules

s1(2) of the Child Support, Pensions and Social Security Act 2000 (2000 c.19) amends this section of the Child Support Act 1991 and has been brought into force only for the types of cases in art 3 of the Child Support, Pensions and Social Security Act 2000 (Commencement No.12) Order 2003 (SI 2003 No.192 – see p683). For other types of cases the 1993 rules apply and the original wording is retained – ie, "maintenance assessment" is retained in place of "maintenance calculation".

Definitions

"earnings": see s31(8).
"liable person": see s31(1).
"maintenance calculation": see s54.
"prescribed": see s54.

General Note

The regulations made under this section are contained in Pt III of the Collection and Enforcement Regulations.

They apply, as modified, to other forms of maintenance prescribed for the purposes of s30 by the Collection and Enforcement of Other Forms of Maintenance Regulations. The scheme set out is based closely on that which applies to the Attachment of Earnings Act 1971. However, the time limits for compliance by the liable person and the employer are more restrictive in relation to deduction from earnings orders (a seven-day requirement is used, compared with 10 days or a "specified period" in the Attachment of Earnings Act 1971). Whereas a court has power to order the debtor to attend to give employment details, the Secretary of State has no such power, although see below for powers to require these details to be supplied.

Subsection (2)

Regulation 8(2) provides that a relationship of employer and employee is treated as subsisting where one person, as principal and not as servant or agent, pays to the other any sum defined as earnings. Earnings are defined in paras (3) and (4) of this regulation. They are any sums payable by way of wages or salary (including fees, bonus, commission, overtime pay or other emoluments); sums payable by way of pension (including an annuity in respect of past service); and statutory sick pay. They do not include sums payable by any public department of the Government of Northern Ireland or a territory outside the UK; pay or allowances to members of Her Majesty's forces; pension, allowances or benefit payable under any enactment relating to social security; pension or allowances payable in respect of disablement or disability; guaranteed minimum pension within the meaning of the Social Security Pensions Act 1975. Regulation 9 provides that a deduction from earnings order shall specify certain items of information, including the name and address of the liable person, the normal deduction rate, protected earnings rate, and address to which the deducted amounts must be sent. Regulation 11 specifies various protected earnings rates where there is an interim maintenance assessment, dependent upon the amount of information which has been given by the absent parent.

As with the Attachment of Earnings Act 1971, a deduction from earnings order is made up of a normal deduction rate and a protected earnings rate. The former specifies the amount to be deducted from earnings by the employer at each pay-day: the latter specifies that the liable person's earnings must not fall below his or her exempt income, as calculated for the current maintenance assessment. The employer may pay the amounts deducted to the Secretary of State by cheque, automated credit transfer, or other method specified by the Secretary of State.

In order to enable the Secretary of State to direct a deduction from earnings order to the employer, reg 15 requires the liable person, within seven days of being given written notice, to provide details of her/his employer's name and address, the amount of earnings, place and nature of work and any works or pay number. If the liable person leaves employment or becomes employed or reemployed, he or she must notify the Secretary of State in writing within seven days. Regulations 2(2) and 3 of the Information, Evidence and Disclosure Regulations also make provision for the liable person and/or a current or recent employer to provide information to enable the Secretary of State to discover the liable person's gross earnings and deductions from those earnings.

Regulation 23 provides for the case where the liable person is in the employment of the Crown.

In *Secretary of State for Social Security v Shotton and Others* [1996] 2 FLR 241, the High Court ruled that magistrates hearing an appeal against a deduction from earnings order may not question the validity of the assessment in respect of which the order is made. The absent parent's remedy is to seek a review of the assessment.

Subsection (7)

Regulation 22 provides that a liable person may appeal against a deduction from earnings order to a magistrates' court in England and Wales, or the sheriff in Scotland, having jurisdiction in the area in which he or she resides. The grounds for such an appeal are: (a) that the order is defective; or (b) that the payments in question do not constitute earnings. A "defective" order is one, according to reg 8(1) (as amended by the Amendment Regulations 1995, codifying *R v Secretary of State for Social Security ex p Biggin* [1995] 1 FLR 851), which does not comply with the requirements of regs 9 to 11, the failure having made it impracticable for the employer to comply with his obligations under the Act and Regulations. An appeal under reg 22 may not be used to argue that the Secretary of State has failed to consider the welfare of a child before making the deduction from earnings order. While considerable weight should be given to welfare before making the order, challenge on this ground must be by way of judicial review (*R v Secretary of State for Social Security ex p Biggin,* above). If justices declare a deduction from earnings order defective, they have no power to order the Secretary of State to repay money paid under the order (*Secretary of State for Social Security v Shotton and Others*).

Subsection (8)

The requirements for which failure to comply (in the absence of a defence under subs (10)) will amount to an offence are: (i) the requirements on the liable person to supply details of her/his employment under reg 15; (ii) the requirements on the employer to notify the Secretary of State when the liable person is not, or has ceased to be in her/his employment, or when a person in relation to whom a deduction from earnings order is in force is one of her/his employees, under reg 16; (iii) the requirement on the employer to comply with any variation of a deduction from earnings order under reg 19.

If a deduction from an earnings order is made under s31 against someone in the employment of the Crown, this section only applies to failures to comply with regulations made under this section (s57(4)).

[¹ Orders for regular deductions from accounts

32A.–(1)   If in relation to any person it appears to the [²Secretary of State]–

(a)   that the person has failed to pay an amount of child support maintenance; and

(b)   that the person holds an account with a deposit-taker;

[²the Secretary of State] may make an order against that person to secure the payment of any amount due under the maintenance calculation in question by means of regular deductions from the account.

(2)   An order under this section may be made so as to secure the payment of–

(a)   arrears of child support maintenance payable under the calculation;

(b)   amounts of child support maintenance which will become payable under the calculation; or

(c)   both such arrears and such future amounts.

(3)   An order under this section may be made in respect of amounts due under a maintenance calculation which is the subject of an appeal only if it appears to the [²Secretary of State]–

(a)   that liability for the amounts would not be affected were the appeal to succeed; or

(b)   where paragraph (a) does not apply, that the making of an order under this section in respect of the amounts would nonetheless be fair in all the circumstances.

(4)   An order under this section–

(a)   may not be made in respect of an account of a prescribed description; and

(b)   may be made in respect of a joint account which is held by the person against whom the order is made and one or more other persons, and which is not of a description prescribed under paragraph (a), if (but only if) regulations made by the Secretary of State so provide.

(5)   An order under this section–

(a)   shall specify the account in respect of which it is made;

(b)   shall be expressed to be directed at the deposit-taker with which the account is held; and

(c)   shall have effect from such date as may be specified in the order.

(6)   An order under this section shall operate as an instruction to the deposit-taker at which it is directed to–

(a)   make deductions from the amount (if any) standing to the credit of the account specified in the order; and

(b)   pay the amount deducted to the [²Secretary of State].

(7)   The [²Secretary of State] shall serve a copy of any order made under this section on–

(a)   the deposit-taker at which it is directed;

(b)   the person against whom it is made; and

(c)   if the order is made in respect of a joint account, the other account-holders.

(8)   Where–

(a)   an order under this section has been made; and

(b)   a copy of the order has been served on the deposit-taker at which it is directed,

it shall be the duty of that deposit-taker to comply with the order; but the deposit-taker shall not be under any liability for non-compliance before the end of the period of 7 days beginning with the day on which the copy was served on the deposit-taker.

(9)   Where regulations have been made under section 29(3)(a), a person liable to pay an amount of child support maintenance is to be taken for the purposes of this section to have failed to pay an amount of child support maintenance unless it is paid to or through the person specified in, or by virtue of, the regulations for the case in question.]

Amendments

1.   Child Maintenance and Other Payments Act 2008 (2008 c.6) s22 (June 1, 2009 for making regulations, August 3, 2009 for all other purposes). See Child Maintenance and Other Payments Act 2008 (Commencement No.5) Order 2009 (SI 2009 No.1314) art 2.

2.   Public Bodies (Child Maintenance and Enforcement Commission: Abolition and Transfer of Functions) Order 2012 (SI 2012 No.2007) art 3(2) and Sch para 34 (August 1, 2012).

[¹ Orders under section 32A: joint accounts

32B.–(1)   Before making an order under section 32A in respect of a joint account the [²Secretary of State] shall offer each of the account-holders an opportunity to make representations about–

(a)   the proposal to make the order; and

(b)   the amounts to be deducted under the order, if it is made.

(2)   The amounts to be deducted from a joint account under such an order shall not exceed the amounts that appear to the [²Secretary of State] to be fair in all the circumstances.

(3)   In determining those amounts the [²Secretary of State] shall have particular regard to–

(a) any representations made in accordance with subsection (1)(b);
(b) the amount contributed to the account by each of the account-holders; and
(c) such other matters as may be prescribed.]

Amendments

1. Child Maintenance and Other Payments Act 2008 (2008 c.6) s22 (June 1, 2009 for making regulations, August 3, 2009 for all other purposes). See Child Maintenance and Other Payments Act 2008 (Commencement No.5) Order 2009 (SI 2009 No.1314) art 2.

2. Public Bodies (Child Maintenance and Enforcement Commission: Abolition and Transfer of Functions) Order 2012 (SI 2012 No.2007) art 3(2) and Sch para 35 (August 1, 2012).

[¹ Regulations about orders under section 32A

32C.–(1)   The Secretary of State may by regulations make provision with respect to orders under section 32A.

(2)   Regulations under subsection (1) may, in particular, make provision–

(a) requiring an order to specify the amount or amounts in respect of which it is made;

(b) requiring an order to specify the amounts which are to be deducted under it in order to meet liabilities under the maintenance calculation in question;

(c) requiring an order to specify the dates on which deductions are to be made under it;

(d) for the rate of deduction under an order not to exceed such rate as may be specified in, or determined in accordance with, the regulations;

(e) as to circumstances in which amounts standing to the credit of an account are to be disregarded for the purposes of section 32A;

(f) as to the payment of sums deducted under an order to the [²Secretary of State];

(g) allowing the deposit-taker at which an order is directed to deduct from the amount standing to the credit of the account specified in the order a prescribed amount towards its administrative costs before making any deduction required by section 32A(6)(a);

(h) with respect to notifications to be given to the person against whom an order is made (and, in the case of an order made in respect of a joint account, to the other account-holders) of amounts deducted, and amounts paid, under the order;

(i) requiring the deposit-taker at which an order is directed to notify the [²Secretary of State] in the prescribed manner and within a prescribed period–
   (i) if the account specified in the order does not exist at the time at which the order is served on the deposit-taker;
   (ii) of any other accounts held with the deposit-taker at that time by the person against whom the order is made;

(j) requiring the deposit-taker at which an order is directed to notify the [²Secretary of State] in the prescribed manner and within a prescribed period if, after the time at which the order is served on the deposit-taker–
   (i) the account specified in the order is closed;
   (ii) a new account of any description is opened with the deposit-taker by the person against whom the order is made;

(k) as to circumstances in which the deposit-taker at which an order is directed, the person against whom the order is made and (in the case of an order made in respect of a joint account) the other account-holders may apply to the [²Secretary of State] for [²the Secretary of State] to review the order and as to such a review;

(l) for the variation of orders;

(m) similar to that made by section 32A(8), in relation to any variation of an order;

(n) for an order to lapse in such circumstances as may be prescribed;

(o) as to the revival of an order in such circumstances as may be prescribed;

(p) allowing or requiring an order to be discharged;

(q) as to the giving of notice by the [²Secretary of State] to the deposit-taker that an order has lapsed or ceased to have effect.

(3)   The Secretary of State may by regulations make provision with respect to priority as between an order under section 32A and–

(a) any other order under that section;

(b) any order under any other enactment relating to England and Wales which provides for deductions from the same account;

(c) any diligence done in Scotland against the same account.

(4) The Secretary of State shall by regulations make provision for any person affected to have a right to appeal to a court–

(a) against the making of an order under section 32A;

(b) against any decision made by the [²Secretary of State] on an application under regulations made under subsection (2)(k).

(5) On an appeal under regulations made under subsection (4)(a), the court shall not question the maintenance calculation by reference to which the order was made.

(6) Regulations under subsection (4) may include–

(a) provision with respect to the period within which a right of appeal under the regulations may be exercised;

(b) provision with respect to the powers of the court to which the appeal under the regulations lies.]

Amendments

1. Child Maintenance and Other Payments Act 2008 (2008 c.6) s22 (June 1, 2009 for making regulations, August 3, 2009 for all other purposes). See Child Maintenance and Other Payments Act 2008 (Commencement No. 5) Order 2009 (SI 2009 No.1314) art 2.

2. Public Bodies (Child Maintenance and Enforcement Commission: Abolition and Transfer of Functions) Order 2012 (SI 2012 No.2007) art 3(2) and Sch para 36 (August 1, 2012).

[¹ Orders under section 32A: offences

32D.–(1) A person who fails to comply with the requirements of–

(a) an order under section 32A, or

(b) any regulation under section 32C which is designated by the regulations for the purposes of this paragraph,

commits an offence.

(2) It shall be a defence for a person charged with an offence under subsection (1) to prove that the person took all reasonable steps to comply with the requirements in question.

(3) A person guilty of an offence under subsection (1) shall be liable on summary conviction to a fine not exceeding level two on the standard scale.]

Amendment

1. Child Maintenance and Other Payments Act 2008 (2008 c.6) s22 (June 1, 2009 for making regulations, August 3, 2009 for all other purposes). See Child Maintenance and Other Payments Act 2008 (Commencement No.5) Order 2009 (SI 2009 No.1314) art 2.

[¹ Lump sum deductions: interim orders

32E.–(1) The [²Secretary of State] may make an order under this section if it appears to the [²Secretary of State] that a person (referred to in this section and sections 32F to 32J as "the liable person") has failed to pay an amount of child support maintenance and–

(a) an amount stands to the credit of an account held by the liable person with a deposit-taker; or

(b) an amount not within paragraph (a) that is of a prescribed description is due or accruing to the liable person from another person (referred to in this section and sections 32F to 32J as the "third party").

(2) An order under this section–

(a) may not be made by virtue of subsection (1)(a) in respect of an account of a prescribed description; and

(b) may be made by virtue of subsection (1)(a) in respect of a joint account which is held by the liable person and one or more other persons, and which is not of a description prescribed under paragraph (a) of this subsection, if (but only if) regulations made by the Secretary of State so provide.

(3)   The Secretary of State may by regulations make provision as to conditions that are to be disregarded in determining whether an amount is due or accruing to the liable person for the purposes of subsection (1)(b).

(4)   An order under this section–

(a)   shall be expressed to be directed at the deposit-taker or third party in question;

(b)   if made by virtue of subsection (1)(a), shall specify the account in respect of which it is made; and

(c)   shall specify the amount of arrears of child support maintenance in respect of which the [²Secretary of State] proposes to make an order under section 32F.

(5)   An order under this section may specify an amount of arrears due under a maintenance calculation which is the subject of an appeal only if it appears to the [²Secretary of State]–

(a)   that liability for the amount would not be affected were the appeal to succeed; or

(b)   where paragraph (a) does not apply, that the making of an order under section 32F in respect of the amount would nonetheless be fair in all the circumstances.

(6)   The [²Secretary of State] shall serve a copy of any order made under this section on–

(a)   the deposit-taker or third party at which it is directed;

(b)   the liable person; and

(c)   if the order is made in respect of a joint account, the other account-holders.

(7)   An order under this section shall come into force at the time at which it is served on the deposit-taker or third party at which it is directed.

(8)   An order under this section shall cease to be in force at the earliest of the following–

(a)   the time at which the prescribed period ends;

(b)   the time at which the order under this section lapses or is discharged; and

(c)   the time at which an order under section 32F made in pursuance of the proposal specified in the order under this section is served on the deposit-taker or third party at which that order is directed.

(9)   Where regulations have been made under section 29(3)(a), a person liable to pay an amount of child support maintenance is to be taken for the purposes of this section to have failed to pay the amount unless it is paid to or through the person specified in, or by virtue of, the regulations for the case in question.]

Amendments

1.   Child Maintenance and Other Payments Act 2008 (2008 c.6) s23 (June 1, 2009 for making regulations, August 3, 2009 for all other purposes). See Child Maintenance and Other Payments Act 2008 (Commencement No.5) Order 2009 (SI 2009 No.1314) art 2(b).

2.   Public Bodies (Child Maintenance and Enforcement Commission: Abolition and Transfer of Functions) Order 2012 (SI 2012 No.2007) art 3(2) and Sch para 37 (August 1, 2012).

[¹ Lump sum deductions: final orders

32F.–(1)   The [²Secretary of State] may make an order under this section in pursuance of a proposal specified in an order under section 32E if–

(a)   the order in which the proposal was specified ("the interim order") is in force;

(b)   the period prescribed for the making of representations to the [²Secretary of State] in respect of the proposal specified in the interim order has expired; and

(c)   the [²Secretary of State] has considered any representations made to [²the Secretary of State] during that period.

(2)   An order under this section–

(a)   shall be expressed to be directed at the deposit-taker or third party at which the interim order was directed;

(b)   if the interim order was made by virtue of section 32E(1)(a), shall specify the account specified in the interim order; and

(c)   shall specify the amount of arrears of child support maintenance in respect of which it is made.

(3)   The amount so specified–

(a)   shall not exceed the amount of arrears specified in the interim order which remain unpaid at the time at which the order under this section is made; and

(b)   if the order is made in respect of a joint account, shall not exceed the amount that appears to the Commission to be fair in all the circumstances.

(4)   In determining the amount to be specified in an order made in respect of a joint account the [²Secretary of State] shall have particular regard–

(a)   to the amount contributed to the account by each of the account-holders; and

(b)   to such other matters as may be prescribed.

(5)   An order under this section may specify an amount of arrears due under a maintenance calculation which is the subject of an appeal only if it appears to the [²Secretary of State]–

(a)   that liability for the amount would not be affected were the appeal to succeed; or

(b)   where paragraph (a) does not apply, that the making of an order under this section in respect of the amount would nonetheless be fair in all the circumstances.

(6)   The [²Secretary of State] shall serve a copy of any order made under this section on–

(a)   the deposit-taker or third party at which it is directed;

(b)   the liable person; and

(c)   if the order is made in respect of a joint account, the other account-holders.]

Amendments

1.   Child Maintenance and Other Payments Act 2008 (2008 c.6) s23 (June 1, 2009 for making regulations, August 3, 2009 for all other purposes). See Child Maintenance and Other Payments Act 2008 (Commencement No.5) Order 2009 (SI 2009 No.1314) art 2(b).

2.   Public Bodies (Child Maintenance and Enforcement Commission: Abolition and Transfer of Functions) Order 2012 (SI 2012 No.2007) art 3(2) and Sch para 38 (August 1, 2012).

[¹ Orders under sections 32E and 32F: freezing of accounts etc.

32G.–(1)   During the relevant period, an order under section 32E or 32F which specifies an account held with a deposit-taker shall operate as an instruction to the deposit-taker not to do anything that would reduce the amount standing to the credit of the account below the amount specified in the order (or, if already below that amount, that would further reduce it).

(2)   During the relevant period, any other order under section 32E or 32F shall operate as an instruction to the third party at which it is directed not to do anything that would reduce the amount due to the liable person below the amount specified in the order (or, if already below that amount, that would further reduce it).

(3)   Subsections (1) and (2) have effect subject to regulations made under section 32I(1).

(4)   In this section "the relevant period", in relation to an order under section 32E, means the period during which the order is in force.

(5)   In this section and section 32H "the relevant period", in relation to an order under section 32F, means the period which–

(a)   begins with the service of the order on the deposit-taker or third party at which it is directed; and

(b)   (subject to subsection (6)) ends with the end of the period during which an appeal can be brought against the order by virtue of regulations under section 32J(5).

(6)   If an appeal is brought by virtue of the regulations, the relevant period ends at the time at which–

(a)   proceedings on the appeal (including any proceedings on a further appeal) have been concluded; and

(b)   any period during which a further appeal may ordinarily be brought has ended.

(7)   References in this section and sections 32H and 32J to the amount due to the liable person are to be read as references to the total of any amounts within section 32E(1)(b) that are due or accruing to the liable person from the third party in question.]

Amendment

1.   Child Maintenance and Other Payments Act 2008 (2008 c.6) s23 (June 1, 2009 for making regulations, August 3, 2009 for all other purposes). See Child Maintenance and Other Payments Act 2008 (Commencement No.5) Order 2009 (SI 2009 No.1314) art 2(b).

[¹ Orders under section 32F: deductions and payments

32H.–(1)   Once the relevant period has ended, an order under section 32F which specifies an account held with a deposit-taker shall operate as an instruction to the deposit-taker–

    (a)   if the amount standing to the credit of the account is less than the remaining amount, to pay to the [²Secretary of State] the amount standing to the credit of the account; and

    (b)   otherwise, to deduct from the account and pay to the [²Secretary of State] the remaining amount.

    (2)   If an amount of arrears specified in the order remains unpaid after any payment required by subsection (1) has been made, the order shall operate until the relevant time as an instruction to the deposit-taker–

    (a)   to pay to the [²Secretary of State] any amount (not exceeding the remaining amount) standing to the credit of the account specified in the order; and

    (b)   not to do anything else that would reduce the amount standing to the credit of the account.

    (3)   Once the relevant period has ended, any other order under section 32F shall operate as an instruction to the third party at which it is directed–

    (a)   if the amount due to the liable person is less than the remaining amount, to pay to the [²Secretary of State] the amount due to the liable person; and

    (b)   otherwise, to deduct from the amount due to the liable person and pay to the [²Secretary of State] the remaining amount.

    (4)   If an amount of arrears specified in the order remains unpaid after any payment required by subsection (3) has been made, the order shall operate until the relevant time as an instruction to the third party–

    (a)   to pay to the [²Secretary of State] any amount (not exceeding the remaining amount) due to the liable person; and

    (b)   not to do anything else that would reduce any amount due to the liable person.

    (5)   This section has effect subject to regulations made under sections 32I(1) and 32J(2)(c).

    (6)   In this section–

"the relevant time" means the earliest of the following–

    (a)   the time at which the remaining amount is paid;

    (b)   the time at which the order lapses or is discharged; and

    (c)   the time at which a prescribed event occurs or prescribed circumstances arise;

"the remaining amount", in relation to any time, means the amount of arrears specified in the order under section 32F which remains unpaid at that time.]

Amendments

1.   Child Maintenance and Other Payments Act 2008 (2008 c.6) s23 (June 1, 2009 for making regulations, August 3, 2009 for all other purposes). See Child Maintenance and Other Payments Act 2008 (Commencement No.5) Order 2009 (SI 2009 No.1314) art 2(b).

2.   Public Bodies (Child Maintenance and Enforcement Commission: Abolition and Transfer of Functions) Order 2012 (SI 2012 No.2007) art 3(2) and Sch para 39 (August 1, 2012).

[¹ Power to disapply sections 32G(1) and (2) and 32H(2)(b) and (4)(b)

32I.–(1)   The Secretary of State may by regulations make provision as to circumstances in which things that would otherwise be in breach of sections 32G(1) and (2) and 32H(2)(b) and (4)(b) may be done.

    (2)   Regulations under subsection (1) may require the [²Secretary of State's] consent to be obtained in prescribed circumstances.

    (3)   Regulations under subsection (1) which require the [²Secretary of State's] consent to be obtained may provide for an application for that consent to be made–

(a)   by the deposit-taker or third party at which the order under section 32E or 32F is directed;

(b)   by the liable person; and

(c)   if the order is made in respect of a joint account, by any of the other account-holders.

(4)   If regulations under subsection (1) require the [²Secretary of State's] consent to be obtained, the Secretary of State shall by regulations provide for a person of a prescribed description to have a right of appeal to a court against the withholding of that consent.

(5)   Regulations under subsection (4) may include–

(a)   provision with respect to the period within which a right of appeal under the regulations may be exercised;

(b)   provision with respect to the powers of the court to which the appeal under the regulations lies.]

Amendments

1.   Child Maintenance and Other Payments Act 2008 (2008 c.6) s23 (June 1, 2009 for making regulations, August 3, 2009 for all other purposes). See Child Maintenance and Other Payments Act 2008 (Commencement No.5) Order 2009 (SI 2009 No.1314) art 2(b).

2.   Public Bodies (Child Maintenance and Enforcement Commission: Abolition and Transfer of Functions) Order 2012 (SI 2012 No.2007) art 3(2) and Sch para 40 (August 1, 2012).

[¹ Regulations about orders under section 32E or 32F

32J.–(1)   The Secretary of State may by regulations make provision with respect to orders under section 32E or 32F.

(2)   The regulations may, in particular, make provision–

(a)   as to circumstances in which amounts standing to the credit of an account are to be disregarded for the purposes of sections 32E, 32G and 32H;

(b)   as to the payment to the [²Secretary of State] of sums deducted under an order under section 32F;

(c)   allowing a deposit-taker or third party at which an order under section 32F is directed to deduct from the amount standing to the credit of the account specified in the order, or due to the liable person, a prescribed amount towards its administrative costs before making any payment to the [²Secretary of State] required by section 32H;

(d)   with respect to notifications to be given to the liable person (and, in the case of an order made in respect of a joint account, to the other account-holders) as to amounts deducted, and amounts paid, under an order under section 32F;

(e)   requiring a deposit-taker or third party at which an order under section 32E or 32F is directed to supply information of a prescribed description to the [²Secretary of State], or to notify the [²Secretary of State] if a prescribed event occurs or prescribed circumstances arise;

(f)   for the variation of an order under section 32E or 32F;

(g)   for an order under section 32E or 32F to lapse in such circumstances as may be prescribed;

(h)   as to the revival of an order under section 32E or 32F in such circumstances as may be prescribed;

(i)   allowing or requiring an order under section 32E or 32F to be discharged.

(3)   Where regulations under subsection (1) make provision for the variation of an order under section 32E or 32F, the power to vary the order shall not be exercised so as to increase the amount of arrears of child support maintenance specified in the order.

(4)   The Secretary of State may by regulations make provision with respect to priority as between an order under section 32F and–

(a)   any other order under that section;

(b)   any order under any other enactment relating to England and Wales which provides for payments to be made from amounts to which the order under section 32F relates;

(c)   any diligence done in Scotland against amounts to which the order under section 32F relates.

(5)　The Secretary of State shall by regulations make provision for any person affected by an order under section 32F to have a right to appeal to a court against the making of the order.

(6)　On an appeal under regulations under subsection (5), the court shall not question the maintenance calculation by reference to which the order under section 32F was made.

(7)　Regulations under subsection (5) may include–

(a)　provision with respect to the period within which a right of appeal under the regulations may be exercised;

(b)　provision with respect to the powers of the court to which the appeal under the regulations lies.]

Amendments

1.　Child Maintenance and Other Payments Act 2008 (2008 c.6) s23 (June 1, 2009 for making regulations, August 3, 2009 for all other purposes). See Child Maintenance and Other Payments Act 2008 (Commencement No.5) Order 2009 (SI 2009 No.1314) art 2(b).

2.　Public Bodies (Child Maintenance and Enforcement Commission: Abolition and Transfer of Functions) Order 2012 (SI 2012 No.2007) art 3(2) and Sch para 41 (August 1, 2012).

[¹ Lump sum deduction orders: offences

32K.–(1)　A person who fails to comply with the requirements of–

(a)　an order under section 32E or 32F; or

(b)　any regulation under section 32J which is designated by the regulations for the purposes of this paragraph,

commits an offence.

(2)　It shall be a defence for a person charged with an offence under subsection (1) to prove that the person took all reasonable steps to comply with the requirements in question.

(3)　A person guilty of an offence under subsection (1) shall be liable on summary conviction to a fine not exceeding level two on the standard scale.

Amendment

1.　Child Maintenance and Other Payments Act 2008 (2008 c.6) s23 (June 1, 2009 for making regulations, August 3, 2009 for all other purposes). See Child Maintenance and Other Payments Act 2008 (Commencement No.5) Order 2009 (SI 2009 No.1314) art 2(b).

[¹ Orders preventing avoidance

32L.–(1)　The [²Secretary of State] may apply to the court, on the grounds that a person–

(a)　has failed to pay an amount of child support maintenance, and

(b)　with the intention of avoiding payment of child support maintenance, is about to make a disposition or to transfer out of the jurisdiction or otherwise deal with any property,

for an order restraining or, in Scotland, interdicting the person from doing so.

(2)　The [²Secretary of State] may apply to the court, on the grounds that a person–

(a)　has failed to pay an amount of child support maintenance, and

(b)　with the intention of avoiding payment of child support maintenance, has at any time made a reviewable disposition,

for an order setting aside or, in Scotland, reducing the disposition.

(3)　If the court is satisfied of the grounds mentioned in subsection (1) or (2) it may make an order under that subsection.

(4)　Where the court makes an order under subsection (1) or (2) it may make such consequential provision by order or directions as it thinks fit for giving effect to the order (including provision requiring the making of any payments or the disposal of any property).

(5)　Any disposition is a reviewable disposition for the purposes of subsection (2), unless it was made for valuable or, in Scotland, adequate consideration (other than marriage) to a person who, at the time of the disposition, acted in relation to it in good faith and without notice of an intention to avoid payment of child support maintenance.

(6)   Subsection (7) applies where an application is made under this section with respect to–

(a)   a disposition or other dealing with property which is about to take place, or

(b)   a disposition which took place after the making of the application on which the maintenance calculation concerned was made.

(7)   If the court is satisfied–

(a)   in a case falling within subsection (1), that the disposition or other dealing would (apart from this section) have the consequence of making ineffective a step that has been or may be taken to recover the amount outstanding, or

(b)   in a case falling within subsection (2), that the disposition has had that consequence,

it is to be presumed, unless the contrary is shown, that the person who disposed of or is about to dispose of or deal with the property did so or, as the case may be, is about to do so, with the intention of avoiding payment of child support maintenance.

(8)   In this section "disposition" does not include any provision contained in a will or codicil but, with that exception, includes any conveyance, assurance or gift of property of any description, whether made by an instrument or otherwise.

(9)   This section does not apply to a disposition made before the coming into force of section 24 of the Child Maintenance and Other Payments Act 2008.

(10)   In this section "the court" means–

(a)   in relation to England and Wales, the High Court;

(b)   in relation to Scotland, the Court of Session or the sheriff.

(11)   An order under this section interdicting a person–

(a)   is effective for such period (including an indefinite period) as the order may specify;

(b)   may, on application to the court, be varied or recalled.]

Amendments

1.   Child Maintenance and Other Payments Act 2008 (2008 c.6) s24 (April 6, 2010).

2.   Public Bodies (Child Maintenance and Enforcement Commission: Abolition and Transfer of Functions) Order 2012 (SI 2012 No.2007) art 3(2) and Sch para 42 (August 1, 2012).

Liability orders

33.–(1)   This section applies where–

(a)   the person who is liable to make payments of child support maintenance ("the liable person") fails to make one or more of those payments; and

(b)   it appears to the [⁵[⁶Secretary of State]] that–

(i)   it is inappropriate to make a deduction from earnings order against him (because, for example, he is not employed); or

(ii)   although such an order has been made against him, it has proved ineffective as a means of securing that payments are made in accordance with the [³maintenance calculation] in question.

(2)   The [⁵[⁶Secretary of State]] may apply to a magistrates' court or, in Scotland, to the sheriff for an order ("the liability order") against the liable person.

(3)   Where the [⁵[⁶Secretary of State]] applies for a liability order, the magistrates' court or (as the case may be) sheriff shall make the order if satisfied that the payments in question have become payable by the liable person and have not been paid.

(4)   On an application under subsection (2), the court or (as the case may be) the sheriff shall not question the [³maintenance calculation] under which the payments of child support maintenance fell to be made.

[¹ (5)   If the [⁵[⁶Secretary of State]] designates a liability order for the purposes of this subsection it shall be treated as a judgment entered in a county court for the purposes of [⁴section 98 of the Courts Act 2003 (register of judgments and orders etc)].]

[²(6)   Where regulations have been made under section 29(3)(a)–

(a)   the liable person fails to make a payment (for the purposes of subsection (1)(a) of this section); and

(b)   a payment is not paid (for the purposes of subsection (3)),
unless the payment is made to, or through, the person specified in or by virtue of those
regulations for the case of the liable person in question.]

Amendments
1.   s33(5) inserted (4.9.95) by Child Support Act (c.34) Sch 3 para 10.
2.   Child Support, Pensions and Social Security Act, 2000 s26 and Sch 3 para 11(17) (January 1, 2001).
3.   Child Support, Pensions and Social Security Act 2000 (2000 c.19) s1(2) (March 3, 2003 for the types of
      cases in art 3 Child Support, Pensions and Social Security Act 2000 (Commencement No.12) Order 2003
      (SI 2003 No.192)). For other types of cases, see '1993 rules' below.
4.   Courts Act 2003 (Consequential Amendment) Order 2006 (SI 2006 No.1001) art 2 (April 6, 2006).
5.   Child Maintenance and Other Payments Act 2008 (2008 c.6) s13 and Sch 3 para 36 (November 1, 2008);
      Child Maintenance and Other Payments Act 2008 (Commencement No.4 and Transitional Provision)
      Order 2008 (SI 2008 No.2675) art 3.
6.   Public Bodies (Child Maintenance and Enforcement Commission: Abolition and Transfer of Functions)
      Order 2012 (SI 2012 No.2007) art 3(2) and Sch para 43 (August 1, 2012).

1993 rules
s1(2) of the Child Support, Pensions and Social Security Act 2000 (2000 c.19) amends this section of the Child
Support Act 1991 and has been brought into force only for the types of cases in art 3 of the Child Support,
Pensions and Social Security Act 2000 (Commencement No.12) Order 2003 (SI 2003 No.192 – see p683). For
other types of cases the 1993 rules apply and the original wording is retained – ie, "maintenance assessment" is
retained in place of "maintenance calculation".

Definitions
"child support maintenance": see s3(6).
"maintenance calculation": see s54.

General Note
Where payments have not been made or made regularly, the Secretary of State may decide to seek a liability
order from the Magistrates' Court, in England and Wales, or the sheriff in Scotland. In determining whether to do
so, the Secretary of State must have regard to the welfare of any child likely to be affected (s2). Unlike a deduction
from an earnings order, a liability order can only be made when payments have fallen into arrears, and it is
therefore to be seen as a method of enforcement rather than collection. The liability order does not of itself
operate to enforce the maintenance assessment, but enables the Secretary of State to use other enforcement
measures to do so. It operates in the same way as liability orders used to enforce council tax. The enforcement
measures are contained in the following sections. There is provision for enforcement of liability orders throughout
the UK in s39. Not all the mechanisms available to courts to enforce their orders have been included for the
benefit of the Secretary of State. There is no provision for oral examination of the liable person as governed by r7
of the Family Proceedings Rules 1991, which enables rigorous cross-examination of a respondent to take place
as a means of discovering exactly what his income, assets and liabilities are, on pain of being in contempt of
court. Nor can a judgment summons be sought, which enables the court to examine the respondent on oath as
to his means, and to make such order as it considers appropriate as to the payment of arrears. The judgment
summons has become popular as a means of enforcing financial orders made on divorce (see *Woodley v
Woodley (No.2)* [1994] 1 WLR 1167), but presumably it has been omitted from the Secretary of State's possible
armoury because control vests with the court, not the applicant for the summons. The possibility of instituting
bankruptcy proceedings has also been omitted, no doubt because this would not be appropriate to seeking to
ensure that the liable person pays, and continues to pay his or her maintenance assessment. Access to the High
Court for enforcement is also not available, perhaps because of the cost. Orders made in family proceedings
(including lump sums – *Woodley v Woodley (No.2)*), and maintenance assessments made under the Child
Support Act are not provable as debts against a bankrupt. It is not unknown for a maintenance debtor to petition
for his own bankruptcy (as was indeed the case in *Woodley* above) to avoid liability to the creditor, and hence the
availability of liability orders may be crucial to the enforcement of the child support obligation.

An appeal against a liability order lies by way of case stated to a magistrates' court under the Magistrates'
Courts Act 1980. The time allowed for this appeal cannot be extended. However, judicial review is available if
that time has expired and there has been an obvious miscarriage of justice. If necessary, the time for applying for
judicial review will be extended. See *Giltinane v Child Support Agency, The Times,* April 7, 2006.

Where an application is to be made for a liability order against a liable person who is resident in Northern
Ireland, it shall be made under the provision for that territory, even though the liability arose, or the maintenance
assessment was made, under the provisions for Great Britain, and vice versa. Any appeal in connection with the
liability order, or action as a consequence of the order, shall be made under the provision for the territory in which
the liable person is resident (Sch 1 paras 11 and 12 Child Support (Northern Ireland Reciprocal Arrangements)
Regulations 1993).

Subsection (1)

This subsection sets out the criteria which must be satisfied before the Secretary of State can seek a liability order. The liable person must have failed to make one or more payments of child support maintenance, and it must appear that a deduction from earnings order is inappropriate or has proved ineffective. A deduction from earnings order will be inappropriate where the liable person is unemployed, and unlikely to be appropriate where s/he is self-employed. It might also be inappropriate where it would prove embarrassing to the liable person for her/his employer to discover that child support maintenance had been assessed.

The Information Regulations contain powers to allow the Secretary of State to discover the liable person's gross earnings and the deductions from those earnings, which will inform the decision whether to apply for a liability order.

In *CMEC v Smith* in the Sherrifdom of Tayside, Central and Fife at Kirkcaldy (reference B92/09), the Sheriff held that it was not permissible to inquire whether it was appropriate to make a deduction from earnings order under subs(1)(b)(i). He applied *Farley v Child Support Agency* [2006] 1 WLR 1817 as authority for the proposition that the court had to grant the liability order sought 'without investigating [the Secretary of State's] deliberative procedures.' *Farley* decided that the court could not question the underlying maintenance calculation. *Smith* extends that reasoning. Although subs(1) sets out conditions that must be satisfied before an order can be made, it is sufficient if it appears to the Secretary of State that a deduction from earnings order is inappropriate. As the Sheriff noted, the court was not acting in an appellate capacity under s33.

Subsection (2)

The application for a liability order is made by way of complaint to the magistrates' court having jurisdiction in the area in which the liable person resides (reg 28(1) of the Collection and Enforcement Regulations). The application may not be instituted more than six years after the day on which the payment in question became due. For Scotland, see Act of Sederunt (Child Support Rules) 1993.

Subsection (3)

The only questions for the magistrates' court or sheriff are whether the payments have become payable by the liable person and have not been paid. It may not question the amount of arrears (*Secretary of State for Social Security v Shotton and Others* [1996] 2 FLR 241). The court may not, for example, question the desirability of the Secretary of State choosing to seek a liability order in the light of the welfare of any child likely to be affected, or the appropriateness of the enforcement mechanisms which result from obtaining the liability order. A liable person wishing to challenge the Secretary of State's decision to seek the order must go by way of judicial review. Nor do the magistrates have jurisdiction to question whether the parent was liable to pay child support maintenance (*Farley v Child Support Agency* [2006] 1 WLR 1817). They do, though, have power to consider whether the person before them is the non-resident parent concerned and payments have been made that can count towards the parent's obligations under the calculation (*Child Support Agency v Learad and Buddles* [2009] 1 FLR 31 paras 14 and 17).

Subsection (4)

The magistrates' court or sheriff may not question the maintenance calculation. This is in line with the exclusive jurisdiction of the Secretary of State and tribunals over calculations. If the maintenance calculation is to be challenged, the liable person would have to utilise the usual procedures for review.

Subsection (5)

Entry on the register of judgments may affect a person's credit rating and may prove a useful incentive to the liable person to pay up. Liability orders have been designated by the Register of County Court Judgements (Amendment) Regulations 1996.

Subsection 6

This subsection does not apply if the liable person has paid the child support to the person specified but by a different method from that specified (*Bird v SSWP* [2009] 2 FLR 660).

Regulations about liability orders

34.–(1) The Secretary of State may make regulations in relation to England and Wales–

(a)   prescribing the procedure to be followed in dealing with an application by the [²[³Secretary of State]] for a liability order;

(b)   prescribing the form and contents of a liability order; and

(c)   providing that where a magistrates' court has made a liability order, the person against whom it is made shall, during such time as the amount in respect of which the order was made remains wholly or partly unpaid, be under a duty to supply relevant information to the [²[³Secretary of State]].

[¹ (2)   In subsection (1) "relevant information" means any information of a prescribed description which is in the possession of the liable person and which the [²[³Secretary of State]] has asked him to supply.]

Amendments
1.   s34(2) is prosp.
2.   Child Maintenance and Other Payments Act 2008 (2008 c.6) s13 and Sch 3 para 37 (November 1, 2008); Child Maintenance and Other Payments Act 2008 (Commencement No.4 and Transitional Provision) Order 2008 (SI 2008 No.2675) art 3.
3.   Public Bodies (Child Maintenance and Enforcement Commission: Abolition and Transfer of Functions) Order 2012 (SI 2012 No.2007) art 3(2) and Sch para 44 (August 1, 2012).

Definitions
"liability order"; see s33(2).
"prescribed"; see s54.

General Note
This section provides for regulations concerning England and Wales. Section 37 below covers Scotland. The relevant regulations are contained in Pt IV of, and Sch 1 to, the Collection and Enforcement Regulations. They apply, as modified, to other forms of maintenance prescribed for the purposes of s30 by the Collection and Enforcement of Other Forms of Maintenance Regulations.

Subsection (1)
Part IV of the Regulations provides for the Secretary of State to give the liable person at least seven days' notice of intention to apply for a liability order. The notice must set out the amount of child support maintenance which is claimed to be owing and not paid, and the amount of any interest on arrears payable (see s41 on p109). The application may not be made more than six years after the day on which payment of the amount in question became due (see s41 on p109 for comparison with the courts' approach to payments in arrears). Schedule 1 to the Regulations sets out the form prescribed for the liability order. Regulation 29 provides for the enforcement of liability orders made in different parts of the UK.

Subsection (2)
This subsection has not been brought into force.

Enforcement of liability orders by distress

35.–(1)   Where a liability order has been made against a person ("the liable person"), the [¹[²Secretary of State]] may levy the appropriate amount by distress and sale of the liable person's goods.

(2)   In subsection (1), "the appropriate amount" means the aggregate of–

(a)   the amount in respect of which the order was made, to the extent that it remains unpaid; and

(b)   an amount, determined in such manner as may be prescribed, in respect of the charges connected with the distress.

(3)   The [¹[²Secretary of State]] may, in exercising [¹[²the]] powers under subsection (1) against the liable person's goods, seize–

(a)   any of the liable person's goods except–

    (i)   such tools, books, vehicles and other items of equipment as are necessary to him for use personally by him in his employment, business or vocation;

    (ii)   such clothing, bedding, furniture, household equipment and provisions as are necessary for satisfying his basic domestic needs; and

(b)   any money, banknotes, bills of exchange, promissory notes, bonds, specialities or securities for money belonging to the liable person.

(4)   For the purposes of subsection (3), the liable person's domestic needs shall be taken to include those of any member of his family with whom he resides.

(5)   No person levying a distress under this section shall be taken to be a trespasser–

(a)   on that account; or

(b)   from the beginning, on account of any subsequent irregularity in levying the distress.

(6)   A person sustaining special damage by reason of any irregularity in levying a distress under this section may recover full satisfaction for the damage (and no more) by proceedings in trespass or otherwise.

(7)   The Secretary of State may make regulations supplementing the provisions of this section.

(8)   The regulations may, in particular–

(a)   provide that a distress under this section may be levied anywhere in England and Wales;

(b) provide that such a distress shall not be deemed unlawful on account of any defect or want of form in the liability order;

(c) provide for an appeal to a magistrates' court by any person aggrieved by the levying of, or an attempt to levy, a distress under this section;

(d) make provision as to the powers of the court on an appeal (which may include provision as to the discharge of goods distrained or the payment of compensation in respect of goods distrained and sold).

Amendments

1. Child Maintenance and Other Payments Act 2008 (2008 c.6) s13 and Sch 3 para 38 (November 1, 2008); Child Maintenance and Other Payments Act 2008 (Commencement No.4 and Transitional Provision) Order 2008 (SI 2008 No.2675) art 3.

2. Public Bodies (Child Maintenance and Enforcement Commission: Abolition and Transfer of Functions) Order 2012 (SI 2012 No.2007) art 3(2) and Sch para 45 (August 1, 2012).

Definitions

"liability order": see s33(2).

"prescribed": see s54.

General Note

This section does not extend to Scotland (s58(9)).

Where the Secretary of State decides to levy distress as the appropriate means of enforcement, the liability order will operate to authorise the Secretary of State to levy distress within the terms of this section and of regs 30 to 32 of the Collection and Enforcement Regulations.

It may be reasonable for the Secretary of State to decide on enforcing immediate payment and the use of a bailiff to do so is not necessarily contrary to s2 of the Act. The Court of Appeal rejected arguments to the contrary in *Brookes v SSWP and CMEC* [2010] EWCA Civ 420, paras 24 and 28.

Subsection (1)

By reg 30, the person levying distress on behalf of the Secretary of State must carry written authorisation, which must be shown to the liable person if requested. Copies of regs 30 and 31 of, and Sch 2 to, the regulations, a memorandum setting out the appropriate amount (see below), a memorandum setting out details of any arrangement entered into regarding the taking into possession of goods distrained and a notice setting out the liable person's rights of appeal under reg 31 must be handed to the liable person or left at the premises where the distress is levied.

Subsection (2)

The amount to be raised by distress and sale is the amount of child support maintenance unpaid, which may include interest on the arrears (see s41 on p109). The provisions dealing with charges in relation to distress are reg 32 of, and Sch 2 to, the Collection and Enforcement Regulations.

Subsection (3)

Under subs (3) (b) cash belonging to the liable person may not be seized, contrary to the position under r54(2) of the Magistrates' Courts Rules 1981.

Subsection (7)

The regulations are contained in Pt IV of the Collection and Enforcement Regulations.

Subsection (8)

Regulation 31(1) provides that a person aggrieved by the levy of, or attempt to levy, distress may appeal by way of complaint to the magistrates' court having jurisdiction in the area in which that person resides. The right is not limited to the liable person; it would appear that a member of that person's family, or a person disputing ownership of the goods seized, could appeal. However, the only ground for allowing the appeal is that the levy or attempted levy was irregular (reg 31(3) and (4) Collection and Enforcement Regulations). The matrimonial courts have tended to use the threat of issuing a warrant for distress as an inducement to the debtor to pay up, and that approach is open to the Secretary of State as well. However, once the Secretary of State has decided to levy distress, the magistrates will not be able, as they could under their matrimonial powers, to postpone the process.

Enforcement in county courts

36.–(1) Where a liability order has been made against a person, the amount in respect of which the order was made, to the extent that it remains unpaid, shall [²] be recoverable by means of [¹ a third party debt order] or a charging order, as if it were payable under a county court order.

[² (2)]

Amendments

1. Child Maintenance and Other Payments Act 2008 (2008 c.6) Sch 7 para 1(10) (June 1, 2009).

2. Child Maintenance and Other Payments Act 2008 (2008 c.6) Sch 8 (June 1, 2009).

Definition
"liability order": see s33(2).

General Note
The section gives jurisdiction only to the county courts, not the High Court. Garnishee proceedings are used to obtain arrears from the liable person, by diverting money owed to him or her by a third party or held by a third party on behalf of the liable person. The usual example will be where the liable person has a bank account with a credit balance, which is a debt owed to that person by the bank. The effect of a garnishee order is to require the third party to pay the money to the creditor. The procedures governing the making of garnishee orders are contained in the County Court Rules 1981, Ord 30.

Charging orders secure payment of arrears from funds or property belonging to the liable person. They are governed by the Charging Orders Act 1979 and the County Court Rules 1981, Ord.31. Section 1(1) of that Act defines a charging order as one "imposing on any such property of the debtor as may be specified in the order a charge for securing the payment of any money due or to become due under the judgment or order." By s2, a charge may be imposed only on a beneficial interest held by the debtor in land, securities consisting of government stock, stock of any body (other than a building society) incorporated within England and Wales, stock of any body incorporated outside England and Wales, but registered in England and Wales, or funds in court. The charge may be imposed, for example, upon a matrimonial home which is jointly owned by the debtor and a new spouse or partner, in respect of the debtor's beneficial interest in that home. The charging order may be enforced by an application for an order for sale. Difficulties may arise in deciding whether a charging order should take priority over the interest of the new spouse or partner. In *Harman v Glencross* [1986] 2 FLR 241, the Court of Appeal held that the court must consider the position of the creditor and strike a balance between his normal expectation that an order enforcing a money judgment lawfully obtained would be made, and the hardship to the wife and children that such an order would entail, but the voice of the creditor will usually prevail unless there are exceptional circumstances (*Lloyds Bank plc v Byrne and Byrne* [1993] 1 FLR 369). A *Mesher* order, whereby sale of the property is postponed until the children have grown up, may be appropriate (*Austin-Pell v Austin-Pell and Midland Bank* [1989] 2 FLR 497). However, in *Harman v Glencross* the court noted that the creditor was an individual rather than a "faceless corporation" (*per* Balcombe LJ, at p251). Section 1(5) of the Charging Orders Act requires the court to consider all the circumstances of the case in deciding whether to make the order; the Court considered that the competing interests of the spouse and the creditor should be weighed. Since the spouse is likely to suffer more hardship than the Secretary of State, it is arguable that a charging order might be refused where such hardship could be demonstrated.

Regulations about liability orders: Scotland

37.–(1)   Section 34(1) does not apply to Scotland.

[¹ (2)   In Scotland, the Secretary of State may make regulations providing that where the sheriff has made a liability order, the person against whom it is made shall, during such time as the amount in respect of which the order was made remains wholly or partly unpaid, be under a duty to supply relevant information to the [²[³Secretary of State]].

(3)   In this section "relevant information" has the same meaning as in section 34(2).]

Amendments
1.   s37(2) and (3) is prosp.
2.   Child Maintenance and Other Payments Act 2008 (2008 c.6) s13 and Sch 3, para 39 (November 1, 2008); Child Maintenance and Other Payments Act 2008 (Commencement No.4 and Transitional Provision) Order 2008 (SI 2008 No.2675) art 3.
3.   Public Bodies (Child Maintenance and Enforcement Commission: Abolition and Transfer of Functions) Order 2012 (SI 2012 No.2007) art 3(2) and Sch para 46 (August 1, 2012).

Definition
"liability order": see s33(2).

General Note
Subsection (2) and (3)
These subsections have not been brought into force.

Enforcement of liability orders by diligence: Scotland

38.–(1)   In Scotland, where a liability order has been made against a person, the order shall be warrant anywhere in Scotland–

(a)   for the [³[⁴Secretary of State]] to charge the person to pay the appropriate amount and to recover that amount by [¹an attachment] and, in connection therewith, for the opening of shut and lockfast places;

(b)　　for an arrestment (other than an arrestment of the person's earnings in the hands of his employers) and action of furthcoming or sale,

[² (c)　for an inhibition.]

(2)　　In subsection (1) the "appropriate amount" means the amount in respect of which the order was made, to the extent that it remains unpaid.

Amendments

1.　　Debt Arrangement and Attachment (Scotland) Act 2002 (2002 asp 17) s61 and Sch 3 para 20 (December 30, 2002).

2.　　Bankruptcy and Diligence etc. (Scotland) Act 2007 (asp 3) Sch 5 para 18(a)(ii) (April 22, 2009, for all purposes except substituting the reference to an action of adjudication). This amendment substituted sub-paragraph 38(1)(c) for the words "and shall be apt to found a Bill of Inhibition or an action of adjudication at the instance of the Secretary of State." Where the old wording applies, the reference to the Secretary of State has effect as a reference to the Commission in accorance with the Child Maintenance and Other Payments Act 2008 (2008 c.6) Sch 3 para 40(c) (November 1, 2008).

3.　　Child Maintenance and Other Payments Act 2008 (2008 c.6) Sch 3 para 40(a) (November 1, 2008). Child Maintenance and Other Payments Act 2008 (Commencement No.4 and Transitional Provision) Order 2008 (SI 2008 No.2675) art 2.

4.　　Public Bodies (Child Maintenance and Enforcement Commission: Abolition and Transfer of Functions) Order 2012 (SI 2012 No.2007) art 3(2) and Sch para 47 (August 1, 2012).

Definition

"liability order": see s33(2).

Liability orders: enforcement throughout United Kingdom

39.–(1)　　The Secretary of State may by regulations provide for–

(a)　　any liability order made by a court in England and Wales; or

(b)　　any corresponding order made by a court in Northern Ireland,

to be enforced in Scotland as if it had been made by the sheriff.

(2)　　The power conferred on the Court of Session by section 32 of the Sheriff Courts (Scotland) Act 1971 (power of Court of Session to regulate civil procedure in the sheriff court) shall extend to making provision for the registration in the sheriff court for enforcement of any such order as is referred to in subsection (1).

(3)　　The Secretary of State may by regulations make provision for, or in connec-tion with, the enforcement in England and Wales of–

(a)　　any liability order made by the sheriff in Scotland; or

(b)　　any corresponding order made by a court in Northern Ireland,

as if it had been made by a magistrates' court in England and Wales.

(4)　　Regulations under subsection (3) may, in particular, make provision for the registration of any such order as is referred to in that subsection in connection with its enforcement in England and Wales.

Definition

"liability order": see s33(2).

General Note

This section provides for the enforcement of liability orders throughout the UK.

It obviates the need for the Secretary of State to seek fresh orders should the liable person move to another part of the UK. For the position concerning orders made, or to be enforced, in Northern Ireland, see Sch 1 para 12 Child Support (Northern Ireland Reciprocal Arrangements) Regulations 1993 (provisions for the territory in which the liable person is resident to govern the action to be taken).

Subsection (1)

The provisions dealing with enforcement in Scotland are regs 26 and 29(2) of the Collection and Enforcement Regulations.

Subsection (3)

The provision dealing with enforcement in England and Wales is reg 29(3) and (4) of the Collection and Enforcement Regulations.

Subsections (3) and (4)

Before a liability order made in Scotland or Northern Ireland can be enforced in England and Wales it must be registered in accordance with the provisions of Pt II of the Maintenance Orders Act 1950. Regulation 29(4) provides that a Scottish liability order shall be treated as if it were a decree for payment of aliment within s26(2)(b) of that Act, and that a liability order made in Northern Ireland shall be treated as if it were an order for alimony, maintenance or other payments within s16(2)(c). Section 17 of the 1950 Act sets out the procedure for registration. It requires the application for registration to be made to the court which made the original order, which then sends a certified copy of the order to the appropriate court in England and Wales, which will be the magistrates' court for the area in which the liable person appears to be. The order will then be enforced as if it had been made by a magistrates' court in England and Wales.

[¹ Commitment to prison and disqualification from driving

39A.–(1)   Where the [²[³Secretary of State]] has sought–

(a)   in England and Wales to levy an amount by distress under this Act; or

(b)   to recover an amount by virtue of section 36 or 38,

and that amount, or any portion of it, remains unpaid [²[³the Secretary of State]] may apply to the court under this section.

(2)   An application under this section is for whichever the court considers appropriate in all the circumstances of–

(a)   the issue of a warrant committing the liable person to prison; or

(b)   an order for him to be disqualified from holding or obtaining a driving licence.

(3)   On any such application the court shall (in the presence of the liable person) inquire as to–

(a)   whether he needs a driving licence to earn his living;

(b)   his means; and

(c)   whether there has been wilful refusal or culpable neglect on his part.

(4)   The [²[³Secretary of State]] may make representations to the court as to whether [²[³the Secretary of State]] thinks it more appropriate to commit the liable person to prison or to disqualify him from holding or obtaining a driving licence; and the liable person may reply to those representations.

(5)   In this section and section 40B, "driving licence" means a licence to drive a motor vehicle granted under Part III of the Road Traffic Act 1988.

(6)   In this section "the court" means–

(a)   in England and Wales, a magistrates' court;

(b)   in Scotland, the sheriff.]

Amendments

1.   Child Support, Pensions and Social Security Act, 2000 s16 (April 2, 2001).

2.   Child Maintenance and Other Payments Act 2008 (2008 c.6) s13 and Sch 3 para 41 (November 1, 2008); Child Maintenance and Other Payments Act 2008 (Commencement No.4 and Transitional Provision) Order 2008 (SI 2008 No.2675) art 3.

3.   Public Bodies (Child Maintenance and Enforcement Commission: Abolition and Transfer of Functions) Order 2012 (SI 2012 No.2007) art 3(2) and Sch para 48 (August 1, 2012).

General Note

Regulation 35 of the Collection and Enforcement Regulations is relevant to this section.

This section was considered by the Court of Appeal in *CMEC v Mitchell and Clements* [2010] EWCA Civ 333. The Secretary of State was attempting to recover arrears of child support maintenance for the period from 1996 to 2001. It applied for an order disqualifying the non-resident parent from driving. The magistrates made the order for 12 months, suspended on condition that he pays £5 a week towards the arrears. This decision was reversed on appeal by the circuit judge, who decided that the proceedings were barred under s9 Limitation Act 1980. The Court of Appeal allowed the appeal, deciding that the proceedings were not statute barred as they were not an 'action to recover any sum recoverable by virtue of any enactment'. They were not a money claim, but an application for a committal order or a disqualification order, even if they might indirectly lead to the recovery of money. Aikens LJ noted (paras 41 and 53) that the court's powers were discretionary. He left open (para 53) whether an application brought under this section more than six years after the date of the liability order might be an abuse of process.

In *CMEC v Gibbons and Karoonian* [2012] EWCA Civ 1379, *The Times,* December 27, 2012, the Court of Appeal decided that this section was penal in nature and had to be interpreted strictly. No order for committal should be made until there had been a genuine attempt to enforce payment through normal court procedures for the recovery of a debt. An order disqualifying from driving should be considered before seeking a committal.

Commitment to prison

40.–(1)   [¹ ...]

(2)   [¹ ...]

(3)   If, but only if, the court is of the opinion that there has been wilful refusal or culpable neglect on the part of the liable person it may–

(a)   issue a warrant of commitment against him; or

(b)   fix a term of imprisonment and postpone the issue of the warrant until such time and on such conditions (if any) as it thinks just.

(4)   Any such warrant–

(a)   shall be made in respect of an amount equal to the aggregate of–

   (i)   the amount mentioned in section 35(1) or so much of it as remains outstanding; and

   (ii)   an amount (determined in accordance with regulations made by the Secretary of State) in respect of the costs of commitment; and

(b)   shall state that amount.

(5)   No warrant may be issued under this section against a person who is under the age of 18.

(6)   A warrant issued under this section shall order the liable person–

(a)   to be imprisoned for a specified period; but

(b)   to be released (unless he is in custody for some other reason) on payment of the amount stated in the warrant.

(7)   The maximum period of imprisonment which may be imposed by virtue of subsection (6) shall be calculated in accordance with Schedule 4 to the Magistrates' Courts Act 1980 (maximum periods of imprisonment in default of payment) but shall not exceed six weeks.

(8)   The Secretary of State may by regulations make provision for the period of imprisonment specified in any warrant issued under this section to be reduced where there is part payment of the amount in respect of which the warrant was issued.

(9)   A warrant issued under this section may be directed to such person or persons as the court issuing it thinks fit.

(10)   Section 80 of the Magistrates' Courts Act 1980 (application of money found on defaulter) shall apply in relation to a warrant issued under this section against a liable person as it applies in relation to the enforcement of a sum mentioned in subsection (1) of that section.

(11)   The Secretary of State may be regulations make provision–

(a)   as to the form of any warrant issued under this section;

(b)   allowing an application under this section to be renewed where no warrant is issued or term of imprisonment is fixed;

(c)   that a statement in writing to the effect that wages of any amount have been paid to the liable person during any period, purporting to be signed by or on behalf of his employer, shall be evidence of the facts stated;

(d)   that, for the purposes of enabling an inquiry to be made as to the liable person's conduct and means, a justice of the peace may issue a summons to him to appear before a magistrates' court and (if he does not obey) may issue a warrant for his arrest;

(e)   that for the purpose of enabling such an inquiry, a justice of the peace may issue a warrant for the liable person's arrest without issuing a summons;

(f)   as to the execution of a warrant for arrest.

[[2](12)   This section does not apply to Scotland.]

Amendments

1.   Child Support, Pensions and Social Security Act, 2000 s16 and Sch 9 Part I (April 2, 2001).

2.   Child Support, Pensions and Social Security Act, 2000 s17 (April 2, 2001).

Definitions

"liability order": see s33(2).

"liable person": see s33(1)(a).

General Note

The ultimate sanction for the Secretary of State will be to seek to have the liable person committed to prison for non-payment. Apart from council tax, the only civil debt for which imprisonment remains a sanction is maintenance.

The sanction is intended for those who will not, rather than those who cannot, pay. It has been said that such a sanction is:

> "a power of extreme severity. Indeed, it might be argued that the existence of such a power in a society which long ago closed the Marshalsea prison and abandoned imprisonment as a remedy for the enforcement of debts, is anomalous. Certainly, Parliament has made it plain that the power is to be exercised sparingly and only as a last resort." (Waite J, in *R v Luton Magistrates' Court ex p Sullivan* [1992] 2 FLR 196 at 201.)

Subsections (1) to (11) do not apply to Scotland (subs (12)); subss (13) and (14) provide that the Civil Imprisonment (Scotland) Act 1882 applies to commitment in Scotland for non-payment of child support maintenance.

The court has a discretion whether to commit, or suspend commitment of, the liable person to prison, and must take account of her/his means. It, therefore, has an opportunity to reassess the financial assumptions about the non-resident parent upon which the Secretary of State has worked in arriving at the maintenance assessment. No doubt, if the court considered that a warrant of commitment should not be made, the Secretary of State would consider reviewing his assessment.

Subsection (3)

It is common to postpone issue of the warrant on condition that the liable person makes regular payments of maintenance as they fall due and pays towards clearing the arrears. A liable person who breaches the condition may be committed to prison in her/his absence, provided that notice of the hearing was given (*R v Northampton Magistrates' Court Ex p Newell* [1992] RA 283). The warrant must be in the form specified in Sch 3 to the Collection and Enforcement Regulations.

Subsection (4)

Regulation 34(2) provides that the amount in respect of costs shall be such amount as in the view of the court is equal to the costs reasonably incurred by the Secretary of State in respect of the costs of commitment.

Subsection (7)

Schedule 4 to the Magistrates' Courts Act 1980 provides a sliding scale relating the length of imprisonment to the amount of arrears.

Subsection (8)

The provision dealing with part-payment is reg 34(5) and (6) of the Collection and Enforcement Regulations.

Subsection (11)

The provisions dealing with these matters are regs 33 and 34 of, and Sch 3 to, the Collection and Enforcement Regulations.

[¹ Commitment to prison: Scotland

40A.–(1)　If, but only if, the sheriff is satisfied that there has been wilful refusal or culpable neglect on the part of the liable person he may–

(a)　issue a warrant for his committal to prison; or

(b)　fix a term of imprisonment and postpone the issue of the warrant until such time and on such conditions (if any) as he thinks just.

(2)　A warrant under this section–

(a)　shall be made in respect of an amount equal to the aggregate of–

(i)　the appropriate amount under section 38; and

(ii)　an amount (determined in accordance with regulations made by the Secretary of State) in respect of the expenses of commitment; and

(b)　shall state that amount.

(3)　No warrant may be issued under this section against a person who is under the age of 18.

(4)　A warrant issued under this section shall order the liable person–

(a)　to be imprisoned for a specified period; but

(b)　to be released (unless he is in custody for some other reason) on payment of the amount stated in the warrant.

(5)　The maximum period of imprisonment which may be imposed by virtue of subsection (4) is six weeks.

(6)　The Secretary of State may by regulations make provision for the period of imprisonment specified in any warrant issued under this section to be reduced where there is part payment of the amount in respect of which the warrant was issued.

(7)　A warrant issued under this section may be directed to such person as the sheriff thinks fit.

(8)　The power of the Court of Session by Act of Sederunt to regulate the procedure and practice in civil proceedings in the sheriff court shall include power to make provision–

(a) as to the form of any warrant issued under this section;
(b) allowing an application under this section to be renewed where no warrant is issued or term of imprisonment is fixed;
(c) that a statement in writing to the effect that wages of any amount have been paid to the liable person during any period, purporting to be signed by or on behalf of his employer, shall be sufficient evidence of the facts stated;
(d) that, for the purposes of enabling an inquiry to be made as to the liable person's conduct and means, the sheriff may issue a citation to him to appear before the sheriff and (if he does not obey) may issue a warrant for his arrest;
(e) that for the purpose of enabling such an inquiry, the sheriff may issue a warrant for the liable person's arrest without issuing a citation;
(f) as to the execution of a warrant of arrest.]

Amendment

1.   Child Support, Pensions and Social Security Act, 2000 s17 (April 2, 2001).

General Note

The Child Support (Civil Imprisonment) (Scotland) Regulations 2001 are made under the authority of this section.

[¹ Disqualification from driving: further provisions

40B.–(1)   If, but only if, the court is of the opinion that there has been wilful refusal or culpable neglect on the part of the liable person, it may–
(a) order him to be disqualified, for such period specified in the order but not exceeding two years as it thinks fit, from holding or obtaining a driving licence (a "disqualification order"); or
(b) make a disqualification order but suspend its operation until such time and on such conditions (if any) as it thinks just.
(2)   The court may not take action under both section 40 and this section.
(3)   A disqualification order must state the amount in respect of which it is made, which is to be the aggregate of–
(a) the amount mentioned in section 35(1), or so much of it as remains outstanding; and
(b) an amount (determined in accordance with regulations made by the Secretary of State) in respect of the costs of the application under section 39A.
(4)   A court which makes a disqualification order shall require the person to whom it relates to produce any driving licence held by him, and its counterpart (within the meaning of section 108(1) of the Road Traffic Act 1988).
(5)   On an application by the [²[³Secretary of State]] or the liable person, the court–
(a) may make an order substituting a shorter period of disqualification, or make an order revoking the disqualification order, if part of the amount referred to in subsection (3) (the "amount due") is paid to any person authorised to receive it; and
(b) must make an order revoking the disqualification order if all of the amount due is so paid.
(6)   The [²[³Secretary of State]] may make representations to the court as to the amount which should be paid before it would be appropriate to make an order revoking the disqualification order under subsection (5)(a), and the person liable may reply to those representations.
(7)   The [²[³Secretary of State]] may make a further application under section 39A if the amount due has not been paid in full when the period of disqualification specified in the disqualification order expires.
(8)   Where a court–
(a) makes a disqualification order;
(b) makes an order under subsection (5); or
(c) allows an appeal against a disqualification order,
it shall send notice of that fact to the [²[³Secretary of State]]; and the notice shall contain such particulars and be sent in such manner and to such address as the [²[³Secretary of State]] may determine.

(9)   Where a court makes a disqualification order, it shall also send the driving licence and its counterpart, on their being produced to the court, to the [²[³Secretary of State]] at such address as [²[³the Secretary of State]] may determine.

(10)   Section 80 of the Magistrates' Courts Act 1980 (application of money found on defaulter) shall apply in relation to a disqualification order under this section in relation to a liable person as it applies in relation to the enforcement of a sum mentioned in subsection (1) of that section.

(11)   The Secretary of State may by regulations make provision in relation to disqualification orders corresponding to the provision he may make under section 40(11).

(12)   In the application to Scotland of this section–

(a)   in subsection (2) for "section 40" substitute "section 40A";

(b)   in subsection (3) for paragraph (a) substitute-

"(a)   the appropriate amount under section 38;";

(c)   subsection (10) is omitted; and

(d)   for subsection (11) substitute–

"(11) The power of the Court of Session by Act of Sederunt to regulate the procedure and practice in civil proceedings in the sheriff court shall include power to make, in relation to disqualification orders, provision corresponding to that which may be made by virtue of section 40A(8)."]

Amendments

1.   Child Support, Pensions and Social Security Act, 2000 s16 (April 2, 2001).

2.   Child Maintenance and Other Payments Act 2008 (2008 c.6) s13 and Sch 3, para 42 (November 1, 2008); Child Maintenance and Other Payments Act 2008 (Commencement No.4 and Transitional Provision) Order 2008 (SI 2008 No.2675) art 3.

3.   Public Bodies (Child Maintenance and Enforcement Commission: Abolition and Transfer of Functions) Order 2012 (SI 2012 No.2007) art 3(2) and Sch para 49 (August 1, 2012).

General Note

This is one of the provisions designed to ensure compliance with the child support scheme. It supplements s39A, which allows the Secretary of State to apply for the non-resident parent to be disqualified from holding or obtaining a driving licence. It may be used as a punishment or as a threat. An order under this section could be counter-productive, if it resulted in a non-resident parent being unable to get to work or to pursue work as, for example, a taxi driver: see s39A(3)(a). The threat of disqualification may be more potent in those circumstances than actual disqualification. Even that will not be effective, if a recalcitrant non-resident parent calls the authorities' bluff and suffers a loss of livelihood rather than pay the child support maintenance.

Regulation 35 of the Collection and Enforcement Regulations is relevant to this section.

Arrears of child support maintenance

41.–(1)   This section applies where–

(a)   the [⁷[⁹Secretary of State]] is authorised under section 4 [⁶...] or 7 to recover child support maintenance payable by [⁴ a non-resident parent] in accordance with a [² maintenance calculation]; and

(b)   the [⁴ non-resident parent] has failed to make one or more payments of child support maintenance due from him in accordance with that [²calculation].

[¹ (2)   Where the [⁷[⁹Secretary of State]] recovers any such arrears [⁷[⁹the Secretary of State]] may, in such circumstances as may be prescribed and to such extent as may be prescribed, retain them if [⁷[⁹the Secretary of State]] is satisfied that the amount of any benefit paid to or in respect of the person with care of the child or children in question would have been less had the [⁴ non-resident parent] made the payment or payments of child support maintenance in question.

(2A)   In determining for the purposes of subsection (2) whether the amount of any benefit paid would have been less at any time than the amount which was paid at that time, in a case where the [² maintenance calculation] had effect from a date earlier than that on which it was made, the [² calculation] shall be taken to have been in force at that time.]

(3)   [³...]

(4)   [³...]

(5)   [³...]

(6)   Any sums retained by the [7[9Secretary of State]] by virtue of this section shall be paid by [7[9the Secretary of State]] into the Consolidated Fund.

Amendments

1.   s41(2) and (2A) substituted (1.10.95) for s41(2) by Child Support Act 1995(c34) Sch para 11.
2.   Child Support, Pensions and Social Security Act 2000 (2000 c.19) s1(2) (March 3, 2003 for the types of cases in art 3 Child Support, Pensions and Social Security Act 2000 (Commencement No.12) Order 2003 (SI 2003 No.192)). For other types of cases, see '1993 rules' below.
3.   Child Support, Pensions and Social Security Act 2000 (2000 c.19) ss18(1) and 85 and Sch 9 Part I (March 3, 2003 for the types of cases in art 3 Child Support, Pensions and Social Security Act 2000 (Commencement No.12) Order 2003 (SI 2003 No.192)). For those types of cases s41(3)–(5) ceased to have effect, for other types of cases, see '1993 rules' below.
4.   Child Support, Pensions and Social Security Act 2000 (2000 c.19) s26 and Sch 3 para 11(2) (March 3, 2003 for the types of cases in art 3 Child Support, Pensions and Social Security Act 2000 (Commencement No.12) Order 2003 (SI 2003 No.192)). For other types of cases, see '1993 rules' below.
5.   Child Maintenance and Other Payments Act 2008 (2008 c.6) Sch 7 para 1(34)(a) (July 14, 2008 subject to art 2(4)-(5) Child Maintenance and Other Payments Act 2008 (Commencement) Order 2008 (SI 2008 No.1476 (c.67)). This amendment, which repealed s41(4)(c) and (d), does not apply to existing cases as defined in art 2(5) of SI 2008 No.1476.
6.   Child Maintenance and Other Payments Act 2008 (2008 c.6) s58 and Sch 8 (October 27, 2008 subject to art 4 Child Maintenance and Other Payments Act 2008 (Commencement No.3 and Transitional and Savings Provisions) Order 2008 (SI 2008 No.2548)).
7.   Child Maintenance and Other Payments Act 2008 (2008 c.6) s13 and Sch 3 para 43 (November 1, 2008); Child Maintenance and Other Payments Act 2008 (Commencement No.4 and Transitional Provision) Order 2008 (SI 2008 No.2675) art 3.
8.   Child Maintenance and Other Payments Act 2008 (2008 c.6) Sch 7 para 1(34)(a) (so far as not already in force: June 1, 2009).
9.   Public Bodies (Child Maintenance and Enforcement Commission: Abolition and Transfer of Functions) Order 2012 (SI 2012 No.2007) art 3(2) and Sch para 50 (August 1, 2012).

1993 rules

Ss1(2), 18(1) and 26 and schs 3 and 9 of the Child Support, Pensions and Social Security Act 2000 (2000 c.19) amend this section of the Child Support Act 1991 and have been brought into force only for the types of cases in art 3 of the Child Support, Pensions and Social Security Act 2000 (Commencement No.12) Order 2003 (SI 2003 No.192 – see p683). For other types of cases the 1993 rules apply. If the 1993 rules apply, "maintenance assessment" is retained in place of "maintenance calculation", "assessment" is retained in place of "calculation", "absent parent" is retained in place of "non-resident parent" and subsections 41(3) – (5), reproduced below, have effect.

(3)   In such circumstances as may be prescribed, the absent parent shall be liable to make such payments of interest with respect to the arrears of child support maintenance as may be prescribed.

(4)   The Secretary of State may by regulations make provision–

(a)   as to the rate of interest payable by virtue of subsection (3);

(b)   as to the time at which, and person to whom, any such interest shall be payable;

(c)   [5,8...]

(d)   [5,8...]

(5)   The provisions of this Act with respect to–

(a)   the collection of child support maintenance;

(b)   the enforcement of any obligation to pay child support maintenance,

shall apply equally to interest payable by virtue of this section.

Definitions

"child": see s55.

"child support maintenance": see s3(6).

"maintenance calculation": see s54.

"non-resident parent": see s54.

"person with care": see s3(3).

"prescribed": see s54.

General Note

This section applies when the non-resident parent has failed to pay child support maintenance. It deals with recovery of arrears. In addition, the non-resident parent may be subject to a penalty payment under s41A below, as well as to other enforcement and punitive provisions in ss31 to 40B above. It relieves the person with care of the need to enforce payment of arrears by the non-resident parent and of the time and cost involved in doing so. Instead, the state accepts that responsibility.

If the Secretary of State is considering taking action to enforce a collection arrangement under s29 of the Act, an arrears notice must be served under reg 2 of the Arrears, Interest and Adjustment of Maintenance Assessments Regulations.

If there are arrears, the Secretary of State has a discretion whether to attribute any payment that is made towards the satisfaction of those arrears or towards the discharge of the current liability for child support maintenance: reg 2 of the Arrears, Interest and Adjustment of Maintenance Assessments Regulations. An overpayment of child support maintenance may also be applied to reduce arrears owing under a previous maintenance calculation: reg 8(1) Child Support (Management of Payments and Arrears) Regulations 2009.

Subsection (2)

Regulation 8 of the Arrears, Interest and Adjustment of Maintenance Assessments Regulations provides that where the person with care is paid income support or an income-based jobseeker's allowance, the Secretary of State may retain the amount of arrears equal to the difference between the amount of that benefit actually paid to that person, and the amount which would have been paid if the arrears had not accrued.

This prevents the person with care benefiting at the expense of the social security system from late payment by the non-resident parent.

[¹ **Penalty payments**

41A.–(1) The Secretary of State may by regulations make provision for the payment to [² the [³Secretary of State]] by non-resident parents who are in arrears with payments of child support maintenance of penalty payments determined in accordance with the regulations.

(2) The amount of a penalty payment in respect of any week may not exceed 25 percent of the amount of child support maintenance payable for that week, but otherwise is to be determined by the [²[³Secretary of State]].

(3) The liability of a non-resident parent to make a penalty payment does not affect his liability to pay the arrears of child support maintenance concerned.

(4) Regulations under subsection (1) may, in particular, make provision–

(a) as to the time at which a penalty payment is to be payable;

(b) for the [²[³Secretary of State]] to waive a penalty payment, or part of it.

(5) The provisions of this Act with respect to–

(a) the collection of child support maintenance;

(b) the enforcement of an obligation to pay child support maintenance,

apply equally (with any necessary modifications) to penalty payments payable by virtue of regulations under this section.

(6) The [²[³Secretary of State]] shall pay penalty payments received by [²[³the Secretary of State]] into the Consolidated Fund.]

Amendments

1. Child Support, Pensions and Social Security Act 2000 (2000 c.19) s18(2) (March 3, 2003 for the types of cases in art 3 Child Support, Pensions and Social Security Act 2000 (Commencement No.12) Order 2003 (SI 2003 No.192)).

2. Child Maintenance and Other Payments Act 2008 (2008 c.6) s13 and Sch 3, para 44 (November 1, 2008); Child Maintenance and Other Payments Act 2008 (Commencement No.4 and Transitional Provision) Order 2008 (SI 2008 No.2675) art 3.

3. Public Bodies (Child Maintenance and Enforcement Commission: Abolition and Transfer of Functions) Order 2012 (SI 2012 No.2007) art 3(2) and Sch para 51 (August 1, 2012).

1993 rules

s18(2) of the Child Support, Pensions and Social Security Act 2000 (2000 c.19) inserts s41A of the Child Support Act 1991. This has been brought into force only for the types of cases in art 3 of the Child Support, Pensions and Social Security Act 2000 (Commencement No.12) Order 2003 (SI 2003 No.192 – see p683). For other types of cases s41A does not apply.

Definitions

"child support maintenance": see s54.

"non-resident parent": see s54.

General Note

This is an enforcement measure. It allows the Secretary of State to impose a penalty payment on the non-resident parent whose payments are in arrears. It may be up to 25 per cent of the weekly child support maintenance payable. It is in addition to liability for the arrears (subs (2)). The penalty does not benefit the person with care, as it has to be paid into the Consolidated Fund (subs (6)).

Regulation 7A of the Collection and Enforcement Regulations is made under the authority of this section.

[¹ Repayment of overpaid child support maintenance

[¹**41B.**–(1) This section applies where it appears to the [⁶[⁷Secretary of State]] that [³ a non-resident parent] has made a payment by way of child support maintenance which amounts to an overpayment by him of that maintenance and that–

(a) it would not be possible for the [³ non-resident parent] to recover the amount of the overpayment by way of an adjustment of the amount payable under a [² maintenance calculation]; or

(b) it would be inappropriate to rely on an adjustment of the amount payable under a [² maintenance calculation] as the means of enabling the [³ non-resident parent] to recover the amount of the overpayment.

[⁴ (1A)   This section also applies where the non-resident parent has made a voluntary payment and it appears to the [⁶[⁷Secretary of State]]–

(a) that he is not liable to pay child support maintenance; or

(b) that he is liable, but some or all of the payment amounts to an overpayment,

and, in a case falling within paragraph (b), it also appears to [⁶[⁷the Secretary of State]] that subsection (1)(a) or (b) applies.]

(2)   The [⁶[⁷Secretary of State]] may make such payment to the [³ non-resident parent] by way of reimbursement, or partial reimbursement, of the overpayment as the [⁶[⁷Secretary of State]] considers appropriate.

(3)   Where the [⁶[⁷Secretary of State]] has made a payment under this section [⁶[⁷the Secretary of State]] may, in such circumstances as may be prescribed, require the relevant person to pay to [⁶[⁷the Secretary of State]] the whole, or a specified proportion, of the amount of that payment.

(4)   Any such requirement shall be imposed by giving the relevant person a written demand for the amount which the [⁶[⁷Secretary of State]] wishes to recover from him.

(5)   Any sum which a person is required to pay to the [⁶[⁷Secretary of State]] under this section shall be recoverable from him by the [⁶[⁷Secretary of State]] as a debt due to the Crown.

(6)   The Secretary of State may by regulations make provision in relation to any case in which–

(a) one or more overpayments of child support maintenance are being reimbursed to the [⁶[⁷Secretary of State]] by the relevant person; and

(b) child support maintenance has continued to be payable by the [³non-resident parent] concerned to the person with care concerned, or again becomes so payable.

[⁵ (7)   For the purposes of this section–

(a) a payment made by a person under a maintenance calculation which was not validly made; and

(b) a voluntary payment made in the circumstances set out in subsection (1A)(a),

shall be treated as an overpayment of child support maintenance made by a non-resident parent.]

(8)   In this section "relevant person", in relation to an overpayment, means the person with care to whom the overpayment was made.

(9)   Any sum recovered by the [⁶[⁷Secretary of State]] under this section shall be paid by [⁶[⁷the Secretary of State]] into the Consolidated Fund.]

Amendments

1.   s41B inserted (4.9.95 for subss (1), (2) and (7), 1.10.95 for subss (3)-(6), (8) and (9) by Child Support Act 1995 (c.34), s23.

2. Child Support, Pensions and Social Security Act 2000 (2000 c.19) s1(2) (March 3, 2003 for the types of cases in art 3 Child Support, Pensions and Social Security Act 2000 (Commencement No.12) Order 2003 (SI 2003 No.192)). For other types of cases see the '1993 rules', below.

3. Child Support, Pensions and Social Security Act 2000 (2000 c.19) s26 and Sch 3 para 11(2) (March 3, 2003 for the types of cases in art 3 Child Support, Pensions and Social Security Act 2000 (Commencement No.12) Order 2003 (SI 2003 No.192). For other types of cases see the '1993 rules', below.

4. Child Support, Pensions and Social Security Act 2000 (2000 c.19) s20(3) (March 3, 2003 for the types of cases in art 5 Child Support, Pensions and Social Security Act 2000 (Commencement No.12) Order 2003 (SI 2003 No.192). For other types of cases see the '1993 rules', below.

5. Child Support, Pensions and Social Security Act 2000 (2000 c.19) s20(4) (March 3, 2003 for the types of cases in art 5 Child Support, Pensions and Social Security Act 2000 (Commencement No.12) Order 2003 (SI 2003 No.192)). For other types of cases see the '1993 rules', below.

6. Child Maintenance and Other Payments Act 2008 (2008 c.6) s13 and Sch 3 para 45 (November 1, 2008); Child Maintenance and Other Payments Act 2008 (Commencement No.4 and Transitional Provision) Order 2008 (SI 2008 No.2675) art 3.

7. Public Bodies (Child Maintenance and Enforcement Commission: Abolition and Transfer of Functions) Order 2012 (SI 2012 No.2007) art 3(2) and Sch para 52 (August 1, 2012).

1993 rules
s1(2) and 26 and sch 3 of the Child Support, Pensions and Social Security Act 2000 (2000 c.19) amend this section of the Child Support Act 1991 and have been brought into force only for the types of cases in art 3 of the Child Support, Pensions and Social Security Act 2000 (Commencement No.12) Order 2003 (SI 2003 No.192 – see p683). For other types of cases the 1993 rules apply and the original wording is retained – ie, "maintenance assessment" is retained in place of "maintenance calculation" and "absent parent" is retained in place of "non-resident parent".

s20(3) and (4) of the Child Support, Pensions and Social Security Act 2000 inserts subsection 41B(1A) and and substitutes subsection 41B(7). It has been brought into force only for the types of cases in art 5 of SI 2003 No.192 (see p685). For other types of cases, subsection (1A) does not apply and subsection (7) reads:

(7)   For the purposes of this section any payments made by a person under a maintenance assessment which was not validly made shall be treated as overpayments of child support maintenance made by an absent parent.

Definitions
"child support maintenance": see s54.
"non-resident parent": see s54.
"person with care": see s54.

General Note
This section deals with overpayments by the non-resident parent. The Secretary of State may apply the overpayment first to reduce arrears under previous maintenance calculations and then to adjust the amount payable under the current calculation. See reg 8 Child Support (Management of Payments and Arrears) Regulations 2009. The Secretary of State may in turn recover the amount from the person who benefited from it: see regs 10A and 10B Arrears, Interest and Adjustment of Maintenance Assessments Regulations.

Subsection (6)
Where the circumstances set out in this subsection apply, the Secretary of State may retain, out of the child support maintenance collected from the non-resident parent in respect of a maintenance application made under ss4 or 7, such sums as are required from the person with care to offset his reimbursement of the non-resident parent for an overpayment (reg 10A(2) of the Arrears, Interest and Adjustment of Maintenance Assessments Regulations).

[¹ Power to treat liability as satisfied

41C.–(1)   The Secretary of State may by regulations–

(a)   make provision enabling the [²Secretary of State] in prescribed circumstances to set off liabilities to pay child support maintenance to which this section applies;

(b)   make provision enabling the [²Secretary of State] in prescribed circumstances to set off against a person's liability to pay child support maintenance to which this section applies a payment made by the person which is of a prescribed description.

(2)   Liability to pay child support maintenance shall be treated as satisfied to the extent that it is the subject of setting off under regulations under subsection (1).

(3)   In subsection (1), the references to child support maintenance to which this section applies are to child support maintenance for the collection of which the [²Secretary of State] is authorised to make arrangements.]

Amendments
1.   Child Maintenance and Other Payments Act 2008 (2008 c.6) s31 (November 26, 2009 for making regulations; January 25, 2010 for all other purposes).
2.   Public Bodies (Child Maintenance and Enforcement Commission: Abolition and Transfer of Functions) Order 2012 (SI 2012 No.2007) art 3(2) and Sch para 53 (August 1, 2012).

Definition
"Commission": see s54.

General Note
Part 2 of the Child Support (Management of Payments and Arrears) Regulations 2009 are made under this section.

[²Power to accept part payment of arrears in full and final satisfaction

41D.–(1)   The [¹Secretary of State] may, in relation to any arrears of child support maintenance, accept payment of part in satisfaction of liability for the whole.

(2)   The Secretary of State must by regulations make provision with respect to the exercise of the power under subsection (1).

(3)   The regulations must provide that unless one of the conditions in subsection (4) is satisfied the [¹Secretary of State] may not exercise the power under subsection (1) without the appropriate consent.

(4)   The conditions are–

(a)   that the [¹Secretary of State] would be entitled to retain the whole of the arrears under section 41(2) if [¹Secretary of State] recovered them;

(b)   that the [¹Secretary of State] would be entitled to retain part of the arrears under section 41(2) if [¹Secretary of State] recovered them, and the part of the arrears that the [¹Secretary of State] would not be entitled to retain is equal to or less than the payment accepted under subsection (1).

(5)   Unless the maintenance calculation was made under section 7, the appropriate consent is the written consent of the person with care with respect to whom the maintenance calculation was made.

(6)   If the maintenance calculation was made under section 7, the appropriate consent is–

(a)   the written consent of the child who made the application under section 7(1), and

(b)   if subsection (7) applies, the written consent of the person with care of that child.

(7)   This subsection applies if–

(a)   the maintenance calculation was made under section 7(2), or

(b)   the Secretary of State has made arrangements under section 7(3) on the application of the person with care.]

Amendments
1.   Public Bodies (Child Maintenance and Enforcement Commission: Abolition and Transfer of Functions) Order 2012 (SI 2012 No.2007) art 3(2) and Sch para 84 (August 1, 2012).
2.   Child Maintenance and Other Payments Act 2008 (2008 c. 6) s32 (for the purpose of making regulations, October 8, 2012; for all other purposes December 10, 2012); Child Maintenance and Other Payments Act 2008 (Commencement No.9) and the Welfare Reform Act 2009 (Commencement No.9) Order 2012 (SI 2012 No.2523) art 2(2)(d); Child Maintenance and Other Payments Act 2008 (Commencement No.10 and Transitional Provisions) Order 2012 (SI 2012 No.3042) art 4.

[²Power to write off arrears

41E.–(1)   The [¹Secretary of State] may extinguish liability in respect of arrears of child support maintenance if it appears to [¹the Secretary of State]–

(a) that the circumstances of the case are of a description specified in regulations made by the Secretary of State, and

(b) that it would be unfair or otherwise inappropriate to enforce liability in respect of the arrears.

(2) The Secretary of State may by regulations make provision with respect to the exercise of the power under subsection (1).]

Amendments

1. Public Bodies (Child Maintenance and Enforcement Commission: Abolition and Transfer of Functions) Order 2012 (SI 2012 No.2007) art 3(2) and Sch para 85 (August 1, 2012).

2. Child Maintenance and Other Payments Act 2008 (2008 c.6) s33 (for the purpose of making regulations, October 8, 2012; for all other purposes, December 10, 2012); Child Maintenance and Other Payments Act 2008 (Commencement No.9) and the Welfare Reform Act 2009 (Commencement No.9) Order 2012 (SI 2012 No.2523) art 2(2)(d) and Child Maintenance and Other Payments Act 2008 (Commencement No.10 and Transitional Provisions) Order 2012 (SI 2012 No.3042) art 4.

Special cases

Special cases

42.–(1) The Secretary of State may by regulations provide that in prescribed circumstances a case is to be treated as a special case for the purposes of this Act.

(2) Those regulations may, for example, provide for the following to be special cases–

(a) each parent of a child is ['a non-resident parent] in relation to the child;

(b) there is more than one person who is a person with care in relation to the same child;

(c) there is more than one qualifying child in relation to the same ['non-resident parent] but the person who is the person with care in relation to one of those children is not the person who is the person with care in relation to all of them;

(d) a person is ['a non-resident parent] in relation to more than one child and the other parent of each of those children is not the same person;

(e) the person with care has care of more than one qualifying child and there is more than one ['non-resident parent] in relation to those children;

(f) a qualifying child has his home in two or more separate households;

[²(g) the same persons are the parents of two or more children and each parent is–

(i) a non-resident parent in relation to one or more of the children, and

(ii) a person with care in relation to one or more of the children.]

(3) The Secretary of State may by regulations make provision with respect to special cases.

(4) Regulations made under subsection (3) may, in particular–

(a) modify any provision made by or under this Act, in its application to any special case or any special case falling within a prescribed category;

(b) make new provision for any such case; or

(c) provide for any prescribed provision made by or under this Act not to apply to any such case.

Amendments

1. Child Support, Pensions and Social Security Act 2000 (2000 c.19) s26 and Sch 3 para 11(2) (March 3, 2003 for the types of cases in art 3 Child Support, Pensions and Social Security Act 2000 (Commencement No.12) Order 2003 (SI 2003 No.192)). For other types of cases see the '1993 rules', below.

2. Child Maintenance and Other Payments Act 2008 (2008 c.6) s37 (October 8, 2012).

1993 rules

s26 and Sch 3 of the Child Support, Pensions and Social Security Act 2000 (2000 c.19) amend this section of the Child Support Act 1991 and have been brought into force only for the types of cases in art 3 of the Child Support, Pensions and Social Security Act 2000 (Commencement No.12) Order 2003 (SI 2003 No.192 – see p683). For other types of cases the 1993 rules apply and the original wording is retained – ie, "absent parent" is retained in place of "non-resident parent".

Definitions
"child": see s55.
"non-resident parent" see s54.
"parent": see s54.
"person with care": see s3(3).
"prescribed": see s54.
"qualifying child": see s3(1).

General Note
Subsection (1)
The basic structure of the Act presupposes the typical case of a child who has two parents, one of whom has left the household. However, there are a number of ways in which reality may vary from this model. These are represented by the special cases which adjust the provisions of the Act to cater for these variations. The regulations made under this section are contained in Pt III of the Maintenance Calculations and Special Cases Regulations.
Subsection (3)
The regulations made under this section are contained in Pt III of the Maintenance Calculations and Special Cases Regulations.
Subsection (4)
Where a statute permits regulations which modify its provisions, that modification must be expressed; it cannot be inferred or implied from the content of the regulation (*R(CS)14/98*, para 10). However, the regulation will be validly made if the modification is on its proper interpretation expressly made, even if it is not clearly so *(ibid,* para 10).

This subsection is to be interpreted fairly widely, but it cannot be used to subvert the whole purpose of the Act or make provision beyond the scope of its long title. Moreover it must be read as a consistent whole such that other provisions may limit the scope of this subsection. See *R(CS)14/98*, para 11.

[¹ **Recovery of child support maintenance by deduction from benefit**
43.–(1)   This section applies where–
(a)   a non-resident parent is liable to pay a flat rate of child support maintenance (or would be so liable but for a variation having been agreed to), and that rate applies (or would have applied) because he falls within paragraph 4(1)(b) or (c) or 4(2) of Schedule 1; and
(b)   such conditions as may be prescribed for the purposes of this section are satisfied.
(2)   The power of the Secretary of State to make regulations under section 5 of the Social Security Administration Act 1992 by virtue of subsection (1)(p) (deductions from benefits) may be exercised in relation to cases to which this section applies with a view to securing that payments in respect of child support maintenance are made or that arrears of child support maintenance are recovered.
(3)   For the purposes of this section, the benefits to which section 5 of the 1992 Act applies are to be taken as including war disablement pensions and war widows' pensions (within the meaning of section 150 of the Social Security Contributions and Benefits Act 1992 (interpretation)).]

Amendment
1.   Child Support, Pensions and Social Security Act 2000 (2000 c.19) s21 (March 3, 2003 for the types of cases in art 3 Child Support, Pensions and Social Security Act 2000 (Commencement No.12) Order 2003 (SI 2003 No.192)).

1993 rules
s21 of the Child Support, Pensions and Social Security Act 2000 (2000 c.19) substitutes s43 of The Child Support Act 1991 with the version shown above. This has been brought into force only for the types of cases in art 3 of the Child Support, Pensions and Social Security Act 2000 (Commencement No.12) Order 2003 (SI 2003 No.192 – see p683). For other types of cases the 1993 rules apply and the earlier version of s43 is retained.

Definitions
"child support maintenance": see s54.
"non-resident parent": see s54.

General Note

Subsection (2)

This subsection is only worded as an enabling provision. The legal basis for liability to make payments in place of child support maintenance is provided by s1 above which imposes an obligation on both parents to maintain their children which is to be met by a non-resident parent by making periodical payments of maintenance *(not necessarily child support maintenance)*. See *CCS 16904/1996*, para 21. The liability may be imposed directly and not only by deduction from benefits for a prospective period *(R(CS) 5/05)*.

Schedule 9, paras 2, 7A and 8 to the Social Security (Claims and Payments) Regulations 1987 (as amended) set out how deductions from benefit are to be made to third parties, including child support recipients, and the order of priorities in which various deductions are to be taken.

[¹ **Recovery of arrears from deceased's estate**

43A.–(1)   The Secretary of State may by regulations make provision for the recovery from the estate of a deceased person of arrears of child support maintenance for which the deceased person was liable immediately before death.

(2)   Regulations under subsection (1) may, in particular–

(a)   make provision for arrears of child support maintenance for which a deceased person was so liable to be a debt payable by the deceased's executor or administrator out of the deceased's estate to the [²Secretary of State];

(b)   make provision for establishing the amount of any such arrears;

(c)   make provision about procedure in relation to claims under the regulations.

(3)   Regulations under subsection (1) may include provision for proceedings (whether by appeal or otherwise) to be instituted, continued or withdrawn by the deceased's executor or administrator.]

Amendments

1.   Child Maintenance and Other Payments Act 2008 (2008 c.6) s38 (November 26, 2009).

2.   Public Bodies (Child Maintenance and Enforcement Commission: Abolition and Transfer of Functions) Order 2012 (SI 2012 No.2007) art 3(2) and Sch para 54 (August 1, 2012).

Definition

"Commission": see s54.

General Note

Part 4 of the Child Support (Management of Payments and Arrears) Regulations 2009 are made in part under this section.

Jurisdiction

Jurisdiction

44.–(1)   [⁴ The [⁶[⁸Secretary of State]]] shall have jurisdiction to make a [²maintenance calculation] with respect to a person who is–

(a)   a person with care;

(b)   [²a non-resident parent]; or

(c)   a qualifying child,

only if that person is habitually resident in the United Kingdom[¹, except in the case of a non-resident parent who falls within subsection (2A).].

(2)   Where the person with care is not an individual, subsection (1) shall have effect as if paragraph (a) were omitted.

[¹(2A)   A non-resident parent falls within this subsection if he is not habitually resident in the United Kingdom, but is-

(a)   employed in the civil service of the Crown, including Her Majesty's Diplomatic Service and Her Majesty's Overseas Civil Service;

(b)   a member of the naval, military or air forces of the Crown, including any person employed by an association established for the purposes of Part XI of the Reserve Forces Act 1996;

(c)   employed by a company of a prescribed description [⁵ registered under the Companies Act 2006]; or

(d)   employed by a body of a prescribed description.]

(3)   [³...]

[⁷ (4)   The [⁸Secretary of State] does not have jurisdiction under this section if the exercise of jurisdiction would be contrary to the jurisdictional requirements of the Maintenance Regulation.

(5)   In subsection (4) "the Maintenance Regulation" means Council Regulation (EC) No 4/2009 including as applied in relation to Denmark by virtue of the Agreement made on 19th October 2005 between the European Community and the Kingdom of Denmark.]

Amendments

1.   Child Support, Pensions and Social Security Act 2000 s22 (January 31, 2001).
2.   Child Support, Pensions and Social Security Act 2000 (2000 c.19) ss1(2) and 26 and Sch 3 para 11(2) (March 3, 2003 for the types of cases in art 3 Child Support, Pensions and Social Security Act 2000 (Commencement No.12) Order 2003 (SI 2003 No.192)). For other types of cases, see the '1993 rules' below.
3.   Child Support, Pensions and Social Security Act 2000 (2000 c.19) s22(4) and 85 and Sch 9 (March 3, 2003 for the types of cases in art 3 Child Support, Pensions and Social Security Act 2000 (Commencement No.12) Order 2003 (SI 2003 No.192)). For other types of cases, see the '1993 rules' below.
4.   Social Security Act 1998 (1998 c.14) Sch 7 para 41 (June 1, 1999).
5.   Companies Act 2006 (Consequential Amendments, Transitional Provisions and Savings) Order 2009 (SI 2009 No.1941) Sch 1 para 123 (October 1, 2009).
6.   Child Maintenance and Other Payments Act 2008 (2008 c.6) s13 and Sch 3 para 46 (November 1, 2008); Child Maintenance and Other Payments Act 2008 (Commencement No.4 and Transitional Provision) Order 2008 (SI 2008 No.2675) art 3.
7.   Civil Jurisdiction and Judgments (Maintenance) Regulations 2011 (SI 2011 No.1484) reg 9 and Sch 7 para 13 (June 18, 2011).
8.   Public Bodies (Child Maintenance and Enforcement Commission: Abolition and Transfer of Functions) Order 2012 (SI 2012 No.2007) art 3(2) and Sch para 55 (August 1, 2012).

1993 rules

Ss1(2), 22(4), 26 and 85 and Schs 3 and 9 of the Child Support, Pensions and Social Security Act 2000 (2000 c.19) amend this section of the Child Support Act 1991 and have been brought into force only for the types of cases in art 3 of the Child Support, Pensions and Social Security Act 2000 (Commencement No.12) Order 2003 (SI 2003 No.192 – see p683). For other types of cases the 1993 rules apply. If the 1993 rules apply, "maintenance assessment" is retained in place of "maintenance calculation", "absent parent" is retained in place of "non-resident parent" and subsection 44(3), reproduced below, has effect.

(3)   The Secretary of State may by regulations make provision for the cancellation of any maintenance assessment where–

(a)   the person with care, absent parent or qualifying child with respect to whom it was made ceases to be habitually resident in the United Kingdom;

(b)   in a case falling within subsection (2), the absent parent, or qualifying child with respect to whom it was made ceases to be habitually resident in the United Kingdom; or

(c)   in such circumstances as may be prescribed, a maintenance order of a prescribed kind is made with respect to any qualifying child with respect to whom the maintenance assessment was made.

Definitions

"maintenance calculation": see s54.
"non-resident parent": see s54.
"person with care": see s3(3).
"prescribed": see s54.
"qualifying child": see s3(1).

General Note

Subsection (1)

Jurisdiction depends on all the relevant parties being habitually resident in the UK. This is subject to subs (2A).

The preponderance of authority is that there is no discernible difference between habitual residence and ordinary residence (*V v B* [1991] 1 FLR 266; *Kapur v Kapur* [1984] FLR 928; *I v I* [2001] 1 FLR 913 confirmed in *Ikimi v Ikimi* [2001] 2 FLR 1288; *Mark v Mark* [2005] 3 All ER 912 at para 33), although the expression may have different meanings in different statutes depending on their context and purpose *(Mark, para 15)*. The authorities are used interchangeably in this note. Also, there is authority that a person may be habitually resident in more than one jurisdiction at the same time *(Ikimi v Ikimi; Armstrong v Armstrong* [2003] 2 FLR 375). *Cv FC (Brussels II: Freestanding application for parental responsibility)* [2004] 1 FLR 317 is an extreme example in which the court decided that the parents had retained their habitual residence in England, despite being absent for more than two years and possibly having obtained habitual residence in Hong Kong.

In order to apply the authorities, it is convenient to consider habitual residence in four categories. Regardless of category, the issue is one of fact *(Re M (Abduction:Habitual Residence)* [1996] 1 FLR 887; *Cameron v Cameron* [1996] SLT 306 at 313F).

The first category is actual habitual residence. Most of the general note to this subsection is concerned with actual habitual residence. The leading authority is the decision of the House of Lords in *Shah v Barnet London Borough Council* [1983] 1 All ER 226, especially Lord Scarman at 234-236. In order to have actual habitual residence, two conditions must be satisfied. One is that the person must be resident in the UK. That requires the person to have established a home here. It is not sufficient to intend to do that. See *CIS 15927/1996*, para 6-9. The other condition is that the person must have been resident for an appreciable period. In *CSCS 8/2001*, para 16, the commissioner relied on a Scottish authority for the proposition that a person could not be habitually resident in two jurisdictions at the same time. However, in *LA v SSWP and TVI* unreported on March 25, 2004, the Inner House of the Court of Session set aside the commissioner's decision that the tribunal had gone wrong in law. Outside of Scotland, dual habitual residence may be possible, albeit unlikely on the facts.

The second category is retained habitual residence. Habitual residence is retained if the person leaves the UK in circumstances that do not bring habitual residence to an end. In law, this is not a separate category. It is, however, convenient to label it in order to help identify the proper starting point if the issue of a person's habitual residence arises. It is often assumed that a person who has left the UK has thereby ceased to be habitually resident. The inquiry then centres on the circumstances of the person's return and when and whether habitual residence was again established. That is the wrong starting point. The person may never have ceased to be habitually resident. The proper starting point is not the person's return, but the person's departure.

The third category is resumed habitual residence. This was recognised by the House of Lords in *Nessa v Chief Adjudication Officer* [1999] 4 All ER 677. It arises when someone who was habitually resident in the UK returns after ceasing to be habitually resident here. This differs from actual habitual residence in that resumed habitual residence may be established more quickly, perhaps immediately. This category was analysed in detail in the joined cases of *CIS 1304/1997* and *CJSA 5394/1998*. These were his conclusions. The only difference between actual and resumed habitual residence is that the appreciable period of residence is reduced or removed in the latter. Habitual residence is not automatically resumed on return. The key consideration in establishing actual habitual residence is the character of a person's residence. That may be coloured by three factors: (a) the circumstances in which the person ceased to be habitually resident; (b) the links retained with the UK while absent; and (c) the circumstances of the return.

The fourth category is deemed habitual residence. This arises under subs (2A). See the general note to that provision on p123.

Decisions made on a person's residence (and on other matters) by officers acting in other capacities than under the child support legislation are persuasive but not conclusive *(R (ota Nahar) v Social Security Commissioners* [2002] 1 FLR 670).

From *Shah* and other authorities the following propositions emerge.

(i)   The words are not a term of art and are to be given their ordinary and natural meaning unless it can be shown that the statutory framework or the legal context in which the words are used requires a different meaning *(Shah)*. In *CCS 7207/1995* (para 6), the commissioner emphasised the importance of the context in which habitual residence has to be considered. The same commissioner set out his view in *R(CS) 5/96* (para 9):

> "the purpose underlying the child support legislation is the social need to require absent parents to maintain, or contribute to the maintenance of, their children. In determining as question of fact whether in the above context a person has ceased to be habitually resident in this country, it appears to me that the emphasis should be put on factors directed to establishing the nature and degree of his past and continuing connection with this country and his intentions as to the future, albeit the original reason for his move abroad, and the nature of any work being undertaken there are also material. It is not enough merely to look at the length and continuity of the actual residence abroad."

(ii)   The normal meaning of habitual residence is "a man's abode in a particular place or country which he has adopted voluntarily and for settled purposes as part of the regular order of his life for the time being, whether of short or long duration" *(Shah)*, including on a trial basis *(Re A (Abduction: Habitual Residence: Consent)* [2006] 2 FLR 1 at para 53(i)). Residence is therefore something different from presence *(CA 35/92*, paras 5 and 14). Accordingly, a person may be habitually resident within the jurisdiction while working abroad. Residence must also be distinguished from the English concept of domicile *(R(U) 8/88*, Appendix 1, para 6).

(iii)   Lawfulness of residence may be relevant in two ways. It may be an implied requirement in the statute that a person's presence must be lawful *(Mark,* para 31). The cases cited by Lord Scarman in *Shah* are an example; they were both immigration cases. Lawfulness may also be relevant as evidence that residence is habitual. For example, a person who is evading a deportation order may find it difficult to show habitual residence *(Mark,* para 36).

(iv)   For the most part the definition concentrates on observable facts, but there will seldom be direct evidence of a person's intention. The proper approach to dealing with conflicts of affidavit evidence on intention was explained by the Court of Appeal in *Re F (A Minor) (Child Abduction)* [1992] 1 FLR 548. In the context of summary proceedings for the return of a child to a country in which it was alleged that he had been habitually resident before being abducted, the court held that where there is irreconcilable affidavit evidence and no oral testimony available, the judge should look to see if there is independent extraneous evidence in support of one side, although that evidence would have to be compelling before it could be preferred to the sworn testimony of a deponent. Usually, however, the person's intention will have to be inferred from all the circumstances of the case, in which case the primary facts will have to be included in the findings of fact and the drawing of the inference explained in the tribunal's reasons for decision.

(v)   The person's intention will be relevant in two respects. First, the residence must be voluntary. Involuntary residence such as a result, for example, of kidnapping or imprisonment would negative the will to be there *(Shah)*. However, this may not be a universal requirement. In *Re MacKenzie* [1940] 4 All ER 310 a lady came on a visit to this country which she intended to be temporary. She became insane while here and spent the next 54 years in an asylum. Morton J, discussed *IRC v Lysaght* [1928] AC 234, (one of the decisions relied on by the House of Lords in *Shah),* but distinguished it, holding that it did not decide that involuntary residence had to be wholly disregarded for ascertaining a person's habitual residence. In view of the very great degree of continuity in the case he held that the lady was habitually resident in this country despite her lack of choice. Where someone is looking after an adult who lacks the capacity to form an intention, the residence and wishes of the former will be relevant to the habitual residence of the latter: see the discussion of the habitual residence of children in (xi) below.

(vi)   The second way in which intention is relevant is that there must be a settled purpose. There need be no intention to remain permanently or even indefinitely. Residence for a short period or conditional on future events may be sufficient to establish habitual residence *(Re P-J (Abduction: Habitual residence: Consent)* [2009] 2 FLR 1051, para 26(4)). In *CA 35/92*, for example, a lady was held to be ordinarily resident in Malta when she went there for health reasons with the intention of returning within 18 months. All that is required is that there should be sufficient continuity that can properly be described as settled. Education can be a sufficient purpose *(Kapur v Kapur),* as would health *(CA 35/92)*. Residence for a short period or conditional on future events may be sufficient to establish habitual residence *(Re P-J (Abduction: Habitual residence: Consent)* [2009] 2 FLR 1051, para 26(4)).

(vii)   Lack of evidence of the actual places within a jurisdiction where a person has stayed is not fatal to a decision that a person has been habitually resident there, although it is a factor to be taken into account *(Re Brauch Ex p Britannic Securities and Investments Ltd* [1978] 1 All ER 1004).

(viii)   In order to acquire habitual residence it is necessary to show not only a settled purpose but also that the person has spent an appreciable period of time in the jurisdiction *(Re J (a minor) (Abduction: Custody Rights)* [1990] 2 AC 562). What constitutes a sufficient period is a decision to be reached in the light of the circumstances of the individual case. Ultimately, however, it is the quality rather than the duration of the residence that is important *(Cruse v Chittum* [1974] 2 All ER 940). This suggests that in appropriate circumstances habitual residence could be acquired in a single day. However, it is unclear how quickly habitual residence can be acquired. The proposition attributed to *Re J* above appears inconsistent with *Lewis v Lewis* [1956] 1 All ER 375, in which it was held that the boarding of ship to resume a former home in this country would be sufficient to establish habitual residence here. This case is a clear authority for the proposition that habitual residence can be acquired in a single day if the person concerned has had an habitual residence in one place, moved to another, and then abandoned that other place to return to the former home. However, the authority on which this decision was based, *Macrae v Macrae* [1949] 2 All ER 34, is suspect in suggesting, contrary to the view of the House of Lords in *Re J,* that habitual residence may be acquired as easily as it is lost. The fact of resumption of a former home may be sufficient to distinguish *Re J*, although it must be admitted that the case of *R v Lancashire County Council ex p Huddleston* [1986] 2 All ER 941, which is discussed below, is inconsistent with this argument. Moreover, in *Re M(Minors) (Residence Order: Jurisdiction)* [1993] 1 FLR 495 a mother with parental responsibility for children allowed them to go to live in Scotland (a separate jurisdiction) and then decided on their returning to stay with her for a holiday that they should remain with her in England. Balcombe LJ, thought that the children did not thereby immediately become habitually resident in England, whereas Hoffmann LJ thought they did. However, since the issue was not essential to the court's decision, these views are *obiter*. *Lewis* has been distinguished by the Court of Appeal on the ground that it applies where a period of ordinary (or habitual) residence has to be shown in order to establish jurisdiction *(Nessa v Chief Adjudication Officer* [1998] 2 All ER 728 at *882-3, per* Sir Christopher Staughton).

It appears to be accepted in the caselaw on the meaning of habitual residence for the purposes of the Child Abduction and Custody Act 1985 that habitual residence probably *cannot* be acquired in a single day. In *Re F (A Minor) (Child Abduction)* [1992] 1 FLR 548 one month was accepted as sufficient. In *Re*

B (Minors) (Abduction) (No.2) [1993] 1 FLR 993 where parents went from England to live in the mother's home town in Germany "to provide a base for reconciliation and for planning a fresh start", it was held that after seven months' stay the habitual residence of the children was in Germany. Waite J, at p995 said: "Although habitual residence can be lost in a single day, for example upon departure from the initial abode with no intention of returning, the assumption of habitual residence requires an appreciable period of time and a settled intention .... Logic would suggest that provided the purpose was settled, the period of habitation need not be long." In *A v A (Child Abduction) (Habitual Residence)* [1993] 2 FLR 225, habitual residence had been acquired after eight months.

(ix)   Since habitual residence depends upon there being a settled purpose, a person will cease to be habitually resident once such a settled purpose ceases to exist. Habitual residence can therefore be lost in a single day *(Re J)*. It is not necessary for the person to form a settled intention not to return *(Re R (Abduction: Habitual Residence)* [2004] 1 FLR 216 at para 41). Since it may not be so easily acquired, it is possible that a person may have no place of habitual residence: see *CSCS 8/2001,* para 16 and the discussion in (viii) above. A person who has been habitually resident in the UK has the evidential burden of proving that that habitual residence has ceased *(CSCS 8/2001,* para 16).

(x)   Absences from a place are not sufficient to lose habitual residence if they are purely temporary *(Shah* and *Lewis)*. It will be necessary for the tribunal to establish the number and duration of any absences, as well as the reasons for them, in order to decide whether on balance they are sufficient to displace a person's habitual residence. However, lengthy absences will result in loss of habitual residence even if there is an intention ultimately to return. In *Huddleston* a family had left England for Hong Kong when their daughter was five-years-old, intending ultimately to return. However, they remained abroad for 13 years as a result of the father's employment which required him to be exclusively abroad. When the daughter returned, it was held that she was not ordinarily resident in the UK.

(xi)   Usually the habitual residence of children will be determined by that of the persons with whom they live lawfully *(Re J)*. If parents are habitually resident in different countries when a child is born, the habitual residence of the child will depend on the particular circumstances *(Re G (Abduction: Withdrawal of Proceedings, Acquiescence and Habitual Residence)* [2008] 2 FLR 351, para 100). In that case the mother was habitually resident in England and the father, who was habitually resident in Canada, had agreed that the child should be in the mother's care pending an agreement on moving to Canada. The court held that the child was habitually resident in England. If both parents have parental responsibility for a child, one of the parents cannot unilaterally change the child's habitual residence *(ReN (Abduction: Habitual Residence)* [2000] 2 FLR 899). If parents want to sever a child's habitual residence from their own (eg, by sending the child to live with relatives abroad), they must have a settled intention that the child will not return, except for visits, and will live in a different jurisdiction from them for the long-term, although not necessarily permanently *(Re V (Jurisdiction: Habitual Residence)* [2001] 1 FLR 253). If the child lives with only one parent by agreement, it will be that parent's residence which is significant. However, this will not be the case if the child has been abducted, unless the dispossessed parent has acquiesced. Acquiescence is the informed consent by a person to something which would otherwise amount to an infringement of that person's rights. Where the person has not expressly acquiesced, acquiescence may be inferred. The approach to be taken in deciding whether or not to infer that a person has acquiesced was explained by Balcombe LJ, in *Re A (Minors) (Abduction: Acquiescence)* [1992] 2 FLR 14 at 22:

"acquiescence can be inferred from inactivity and silence on the part of the parent from whose custody, joint or single, the child has been wrongfully removed. In such a case ... the court would have to look at all the circumstances of the case, and in particular, the reasons for the inactivity on the part of the wronged parent and the length of the period over which the inactivity persisted, in order to decide whether it was legitimate to infer acquiescence on his or her part."

A parent does not need to have knowledge of her/his specific legal rights over a child to be held to have acquiesced in the child's wrongful retention abroad. The issue is whether the parent conducted her/ himself in a way which would be inconsistent with her/him later seeking a summary order for the child's return. It is enough that the parent knows that the child has been retained in another jurisdiction against her/his wishes and s/he is capable of seeking legal advice as to what proceedings be might take, but does nothing to bring about the child's return *(Re AZ (A Minor) (Abduction: Acquiescence)* [1993] 1 FLR 682).

An Australian father who, on being told by the mother that she was going to take their child to England for a holiday, said to her "Go for six months, 12 months, I do not care" had not acquiesced in the child's wrongful retention. On the other hand, his failure to take any effective steps to recover the child for the next 10 months did amount to such acquiescence *(W v W (Child Abduction: Acquiescence)* [1993] 2 FLR 211).

Acquiescence is primarily to be established by inference drawn from an objective survey of the acts and omissions of the parent, but it is permissible to inquire into the state of the parent's knowledge of her/his rights, and it may be necessary to examine private motives and other influences affecting the parent's conduct. Hence, where a parent does not take action to recover her/his child because of erroneous legal advice, s/he may be able to rebut the inference of acquiescence otherwise arising from his inactivity (*Re S (Minors) (Abduction: Custody Rights)* [1994] 1 FLR 819).

It has been said that implied acquiescence will occur certainly after six months and in appropriate cases after as little as three months (*Re P* (G E) *(An Infant)* [1964] 3 All ER 977 at 982, *per* Lord Denning MR), although the authority is an old one and the proposition may be stated too starkly. In some cases children will be of sufficient age and maturity to form a settled purpose separate from that of the persons with whom they live. This of itself will not affect the children's habitual residence, unless the circumstances permit a separate habitual residence to exist. This might occur, for example, where a child is at a school or college abroad during term-time and returns home only for the vacations. In cases where children are of an age likely to be capable of forming their own settled purpose, an inquiry and findings of fact will be necessary as to their maturity to decide on such a purpose and on their freedom to act on it.

The important factor in the case of children is with whom they lawfully reside. In deciding this, any existing order for custody or care and control will be an important consideration as in *Re P (G E) (An Infant)*. As cases in which the concept of custody is still relevant become fewer, as a result of the Children Act 1989, the emphasis will be on who has parental responsibility and on the effect of any residence order made under s8 of that Act. In *Re M(Minors) (Residence Order: Jurisdiction)* [1993] 1 FLR 495, for example, a decision by an unmarried mother, who lived in England and who had sole parental responsibility for children who were then living with their grandparents in Scotland, that they should henceforth live with her, was sufficient to end their habitual residence in Scotland.

The child's habitual residence remains unchanged until a court order which would have the effect of ending that habitual residence takes effect. In *Re O(A Minor) (Abduction: Habitual Residence)* [1993] 2 FLR 594, an American court order had given custody of a child to the mother, whose habitual residence was the UK. A later American order that custody be transferred to the father, habitually resident in Nevada, the order to take effect at a later date, did not end the child's habitual residence being that of the mother *until* that later date. (Her removal of the child from Nevada in the interim was therefore not a wrongful removal within the terms of child abduction law, as the child was still habitually resident in the UK.)

Re M(Minors) (Residence Order: Jurisdiction) shows that it is not necessarily the place where the parent who has habitual residence (or custody) lives that matters, but the place where the parent allows the children to live; so the children's habitual residence was initially in Scotland until permission to live there was withdrawn by the mother. Where both parents have equal parental responsibility (ie, they are married to each other, or the father has obtained parental responsibility under the Children Act 1989) and both are habitually resident in one country, there is a strong burden imposed upon anyone seeking to argue that the child's habitual residence is different. The parents may agree to change the child's habitual residence, but sending the child to a boarding school abroad would not suffice. One parent cannot unilaterally change the child's habitual residence without the other's agreement (*Re A (A Minor) (Wardship: Jurisdiction)* [1995] 1 FLR 767). In the context of the Child Abduction and Custody Act 1985 it has been held that whether consent to the removal of a child from one jurisdiction to another is valid depends upon the circumstances of the particular case, but that it is unlikely that consent which has been obtained by means of a calculated and deliberate fraud will be considered valid (*Re B (A Minor) (Child Abduction: Consent)* [1994] 2 FLR 249).

A temporary absence for the purpose of formal education does not affect a child's habitual residence (*P v P* [2007] 2 FLR 439).

It is impossible to lay down rigid rules as to the habitual residence of children. This is shown by *Wand B v H (Child Abduction: Surrogacy)* [2002] 1 FLR 1008 especially at para 25, in which Hedley J decided that twin children were not habitually resident anywhere. The case concerned a surrogacy agreement between a husband and wife who lived in California and a surrogate mother. The twins were conceived of the husband's sperm and an anonymous donor's egg, and born to a surrogate mother. The surrogate mother gave birth in England and refused to honour the surrogacy agreement. Hedley J found that although the husband had the right of custody under Californian law, the children were not habitually resident in California, where they had never been. He also found that although the children were physically present in this country and the surrogate mother was habitually resident here, they were not habitually resident here either, because the surrogate had no biological connection with them. There are comments in the judgment of Charles J in *B v H (Habitual Residence: Wardship)* [2002] 1 FLR 388, which appear to suggest that children will always have the same habitual residence as their parents at birth, regardless of where in the world they happen to be born. Hedley J disagreed with that proposition (para 23).

(xii) Whether or not habitual residence has been established is a question of fact to be decided in all the circumstances of the case (*Shah* and *Re J*). The tribunal will therefore need to make findings of fact on all of the factors considered above that are relevant to the appeal and to indicate in the reasons for decision that the correct test has been applied. It will be dangerous and an error of law to make decisions based on the similarity of the facts to those in other reported decisions, since each case depends on its own combination of facts. Commissioners' decisions do, however, provide some indication of the range of factors which a tribunal might wish to investigate in deciding on habitual residence (see the factors taken into account in *R(U) 8/88* and the decisions cited therein).

(xiii) Although a person may retain habitual residence here despite being physically absent (as in *R(CS) 5/96*), there comes a time when absence outweighs all other considerations (as in *CCS 7207/1995*, paras 9-10 where a tour of duty abroad for 20 years with only two and a half spent in this country was held to be incompatible with habitual residence here).

Where one of the parties is habitually resident abroad, the courts may still have powers to make maintenance and property orders for a child. Such powers are broad. In *A v A (A Minor) (Financial Provision)* [1994] 1 FLR 657, for example, a wealthy father was required to pay as follows in respect of one particular child: a house was settled on trust for the child until she ceased education (including tertiary education); while the child remained under the control of the mother, the mother was to have the right to occupy the house rent-free in order to provide a home for the child; the father was to pay the child's school fees, extras, and secured periodical payments of £20,000 a year for her maintenance (it being immaterial that some of this money would actually be spent on the mother's other children, of whom he was not the father). (Of course, even had the father been habitually resident in the UK, the circumstances suggest that the court would certainly have made a top-up order under s8(6) and property adjustment orders under Sch 1 to the Children Act 1989.)

(xiv) Fraud or mistake may prevent habitual residence being acquired or retained, although the person may nonetheless become habitually resident. Everything depends on the facts of the case (*Re Z (Abduction)* [2009] 2 FLR 298, para 13).

For a discussion of the possible conflict between this section and European Community law, see the section on Child Support and European Law on p5.

In *CH v CMEC (CSM)* [2010] UKUT 140 (AAC), the judge dealt with the possibility that a non-resident parent might avoid the child support scheme by moving abroad:

"84. ...In such cases, as the Commission has no jurisdiction, the courts may still have jurisdiction to make a child maintenance order. I also acknowledge that cross-border enforcement of such a civil order in practice under the Maintenance Orders (Reciprocal Enforcement) Act 1972 may not be easy. However, the Official Solicitor has a special unit devoted to the Reciprocal Enforcement of Maintenance Orders (see further www.officialsolicitor.gov.uk/os/remo.htm)."

Subsection (2A)

This subsection operates effectively to deem a non-resident parent habitually resident in the UK if the person's employment relationship with the UK falls into one of the specified categories. Regulation 7A of the Maintenance Arrangements and Jurisdiction Regulations is made under the authority of this subsection. Regulation 7A(1) is made under para (c) and reg 7A(2) is made under para (d).

Jurisdiction of courts in certain proceedings under this Act

45.–(1) The Lord Chancellor or, in relation to Scotland, the Lord Advocate may by order make such provision as he considers necessary to secure that appeals, or such class of appeals as may be specified in the order–

(a) shall be made to a court instead of being made to [¹[³ the First-tier Tribunal]]; or

(b) shall be so made in such circumstances as may be so specified.

(2) In subsection (1), "court" means–

(a) in relation to England and Wales and subject to any provision made under Schedule 11 to the Children Act 1989 (jurisdiction of courts with respect to certain proceedings relating to children) the High Court, a county court or a magistrates' court; and

(b) in relation to Scotland, the Court of Session or the sheriff.

(3) Schedule 11 to the Act of 1989 shall be amended in accordance with subsections (4) and (5).

(4) The following sub-paragraph shall be inserted in paragraph 1, after sub-paragraph (2)–

"(2A) Sub-paragraphs (1) and (2) shall also apply in relation to proceedings–

(a) under section 27 of the Child Support Act 1991 (reference to court for declaration of parentage); or

(b) which are to be dealt with in accordance with an order made under section 45 of that Act (jurisdiction of courts in certain proceedings under that Act)."

(5) In paragraphs 1(3) and 2(3), the following shall be inserted after "Act 1976"–

"(bb) section 20 (appeals) or 27 (reference to court for declaration of parentage) of the Child Support Act 1991;".

(6)   [³ ...]

(7)   Any order under subsection (1) [³ ...] may make–

(a)   such modifications of any provision of this Act or of any other enactment; and

(b)   such transitional provision,

as the Minister making the order considers appropriate in consequence of any provision made by the order.

[²(8)   The functions of the Lord Chancellor under this section may be exercised only after consultation with the Lord Chief Justice.

(9)   The Lord Chief Justice may nominate a judicial office holder (as defined in section 109(4) of the Constitutional Reform Act 2005) to exercise his functions under this section.]

Amendments

1.   Social Security Act 1998 (1998 c.14) Sch 7 para 42 (June 1, 1999).
2.   Constitutional Reform Act 2005 (2005 c.4) s15 and Sch 4 para 220 (April 3, 2006).
3.   Transfer of Tribunal Functions Order 2008 (SI 2008 No.2833) art 9 and Sch 3 para 92 (November 3, 2008, subject to the transitional provisions in Sch 4 of SI 2008 No. 2833).

General Note

The Child Support Appeals (Jurisdiction of Courts) Order 2002 and the Child Support Appeals (Jurisdiction of Courts) (Scotland) Order 2003 provides that appeals under s20 are to go to a court rather than to a tribunal where the question involved is whether a particular person is a parent of the child. This will enable the court to direct scientific tests to determine parentage by virtue of powers available under ss20-25 of the Family Law Reform Act 1969 as amended.

Schedule 2 Child Maintenance Orders (Backdating) Order 1993 amends s65(1) Magistrates' Courts Act 1980 to provide that appeals under s20, or references for a declaration of parentage, brought to the magistrates by virtue of s27, are family proceedings.

Subsections (3) to (5)

The Children (Allocation of Proceedings) (Amendment) Order 1993 provides that child support cases heard by courts in accordance with ss20, 27 and 45 are commenced in the magistrates' courts and may be transferred to another magistrates' court or up to the county court or High Court in line with the same criteria as apply in the Children (Allocation of Proceedings) Order 1991. The Family Proceedings Courts (Child Support Act 1991) Rules 1993 apply to parentage questions heard by the magistrates' court.

The High Court (Distribution of Business) Order 1993 provides that any proceedings under the Child Support Act which are heard in the High Court are to be assigned to the Family Division.

The Family Proceedings Rules 1991 (as amended) cater for where a child support case has been transferred up from the magistrates' court. Rules 3.21 and 3.22 provide that r4.6 shall apply to an application under s27 of the Child Support Act for a declaration of parentage, and to an appeal under s20. The rules allow the court to give such directions as it thinks proper with regard to the conduct of the proceedings. In particular, the court may direct that the proceedings shall proceed as if they had been commenced by originating summons or originating application and that any document served or other thing done while the proceedings were pending in another court, including a magistrates' court, shall be treated for such purposes as may be specified in the direction as if provided for by the rules of court applicable in the court to which the proceedings have been transferred.

An application under s27 (but not an appeal under s20) may be heard and determined by a district judge (r3.21(4)).

The Children (Admissibility of Hearsay Evidence) Order 1993 extends to civil proceedings under the Child Support Act in the magistrates' courts the power to admit evidence notwithstanding that it is hearsay.

Miscellaneous and supplemental

[⁷ Reduced benefit decisions

46.   [⁹...]

Amendments

1.   Inserted (1.10.95) in s46(5) by Child Support Act 1995 (c.34), Sch 3 para 12.
2.   Substituted (4.3.99) by SS Act 1998 Commencement Order (No.5) 1999/528.
3.   Repealed (1.6.99) by Sch 8 to SS Act 1998 (c.14).
4.   Inserted (7.10.96) in s46 (11) by para 20(4) of Sch 2 to Jobseekers Act 1995 (c.18).
5.   Tax Credits Act 1999 (1999 c.10) Sch 6 (October 5, 1999).
6.   Social Security Act 1998 (1998 c.14) Sch 7 para 43 (June 1, 1999).

7.   Child Support, Pensions and Social Security Act 2000 (2000 c.19) s19 (March 3, 2003 for the types of cases in art 4 Child Support, Pensions and Social Security Act 2000 (Commencement No.12) Order 2003 (SI 2003 No.192)). This amendment substituted s.46 for those types of cases. For other types of cases, the previous form of s46 applied (see below).

8.   Child Maintenance and Other Payments Act 2008 (2008 c.6) s13 and Sch 3 para 47 (November 1, 2008); Child Maintenance and Other Payments Act 2008 (Commencement No. 4 and Transitional Provision) Order 2008 (SI 2008 No.2675) art 3.

9.   Child Maintenance and Other Payments Act 2008 (2008 c 6) s15(b) (July 14, 2008). Child Maintenance and Other Payments Act 2008 (Commencement) Order 2008 (SI 2008 No.1476) art 2(2).

General Note

This section, and the regulations made under it, provided for the consequences of a person with care's failure to co-operate under s6. The relevant Regulations are contained in Pt IV of the Maintenance Calculation Procedure Regulations.

Subsection (2)

The period is prescribed by reg 9 of the Maintenance Calculation Procedure Regulations.

Subsection (3)

No reduced benefit decision may be made, if there are reasonable grounds to believe that there would be a risk of the parent or any child living with the parent suffering harm or undue distress. The risk need not be substantial and the tribunal must not concern itself with whether harm or undue distress would actually happen, but there must be a realistic possibility of it occurring (*CCS 1037/1995*, para 9). The child who suffers harm or distress need not be the child of the non-resident parent. If more than one child might be affected, the possible impact on each must be considered separately *(ibid,* para 11). The emphasis is on the suffering of harm or distress. How it comes about is not relevant. Consequently, it will be sufficient if the person with care suffers undue distress as a result of believing, however unreasonably, that the giving of the authorisation might lead to violence on the part of the absent parent (*CCS588/1998*, paras 7 and 9). The harm which may be suffered may be physical or mental. It can come from any source; it need not be inflicted by the person who is or may be the non-resident parent (*R(CS) 8/02*, para 13). Any physical harm will suffice as will any mental effect which amounts to harm. However, if the mental effect does not amount to harm, it must be undue. Whether or not distress is undue is a matter of fact to be decided in the circumstances of each case, but if a child is likely to be distressed at never seeing a father again, it would be difficult to say that the distress would not be undue *(ibid,* para 10). This test is narrower than, but additional to *(ibid,* para 13), that which applies under s2 where the "welfare" of a child has to be taken into account. In applying s2 in the context of a reduced benefit decision, the issue is whether there is some exceptional or special factor, such as concerning the age or state of health of the child or parent with care, which would suggest that the welfare of a child would be adversely affected *(ibid,* para 13).

In *SSWP v Roach* [2006] (reported as *R(CS) 4/07*), the Court dealt with the meaning of "undue" and whether it was tested objectively or subjectively:

"41. ... I add the observation of Peter Gibson J in *Tote Bookmakers Ltd v Development & Property Holding Co Ltd* [1985] Ch 261 at 269 when, in the context of section 27 of the Arbitration Act 1950, he defmed undue hardship as 'hardship ... not warranted by the circumstances'.

I do not accept that the question of undue distress should be approached on a purely subjective basis: if it was, the word 'undue' would have no real meaning. In my view, in order to judge whether a particular claimant has shown reasonable grounds for believing that there would be a risk of undue distress (that is to say, a realistic possibility of undue distress) to her or a child, an objective judgement must be made as to whether the foreseeable distress is unjustified or unreasonable in the context of the personal, subjective, characteristics of the claimant or child. Irrationality or paranoia are factors to be taken into account as providing the context against which the extent of the distress is to be assessed but are not determinative."

The bar to a reduced benefit decision only applies, if the risk of harm or distress would arise as a result of complying. If the risk would exist regardless of compliance and is not increased thereby, the bar does not apply and a direction may still be given, although these matters may not easily be susceptible to proof. Any consequence of non-compliance must be disregarded. Accordingly, it is not permissible to take into account the consequences of the reduction in benefit as a result of the making of the decision (*CSC8/1994*, para 6).

Statements made in the course of conciliation which indicate that the maker is likely to cause serious harm to the well-being of a child are admissible (*Re D (Minors) (Conciliation: Disclosure of Information)* [1993] 1 FLR 932).

Subsection (5)

There is a discretion, even if reasonable grounds do not exist under subs (3). The provisions of subss (3), (4) and (5) do not displace the duty in s2. The welfare of any children affected must still be considered, if the terms of subs (3) are not satisfied.

The circumstances in which an officer may not make a reduced benefit direction are prescribed by reg 10 of the Maintenance Calculation Procedure Regulations.

Subsection (6)

The period is specified in reg 9A of the Maintenance Calculation Procedure Regulations.

[¹ **Finality of decisions**

[¹**46A.**–(1) Subject to the provisions of this Act [³ and to any provision made by or under Chapter 2 of Part 1 of the Tribunals, Courts and Enforcement Act 2007], any decision of [⁴ [⁵...]] the Secretary of State or [³ the First-tier Tribunal] made in accordance with the foregoing provisions of this Act shall be final.]

[² (2) If and to the extent that regulations so provide, any finding of fact or other determination embodied in or necessary to such a decision, or on which such a decision is based, shall be conclusive for the purposes of–

(a) further such decisions;

(b) decisions made in accordance with sections 8 to 16 of the Social Security Act 1998, or with regulations under section 11 of that Act; and

(c) decisions made under the Vaccine Damage Payments Act 1979.

Amendments

1.   s46A(1) inserted (1.6.99) by Sch 7 para 44 Social Security Act 1998 (c.14).
2.   s46A(2) inserted (4.3.99) by Social Security Act 1998 (1998 c.14) Sch 7 para 44.
3.   Transfer of Tribunal Functions Order 2008 (SI 2008 No.2833) art 9 and Sch 3 para 93 (November 3, 2008, subject to the transitional provisions in Sch 4 of SI 2008 No.2833).
4.   Child Maintenance and Other Payments Act 2008 (2008 c.6) s13 and Sch 3 para 48 (November 1, 2008); Child Maintenance and Other Payments Act 2008 (Commencement No.4 and Transitional Provision) Order 2008 (SI 2008 No.2675) art 3.
5.   Public Bodies (Child Maintenance and Enforcement Commission: Abolition and Transfer of Functions) Order 2012 (SI 2012 No.2007) art 3(2) and Sch para 56 (August 1, 2012).

General Note

See also Sch 4 para 6(2) and s17 Social Security Act 1998.

This section displaces the principle of *res judicata*, which provides for the finality of decisions by prohibiting an issue that has once been decided from being raised again between the same parties (*CIS 3655/2007*, paras 14-16).

The fact that a decision is final does not prevent it being subject to judicial review (*R v Medical Appeal Tribunal ex p Gilmore* [1957] 1 QB 574).

A finding of fact in one decision is not conclusive for the purpose of later decisions, even if the decisions are related to each other. Subsection (2) does not provide for this. However, it follows from basic principle. Also, subs (2) presupposes that findings of fact are not conclusive for later decisions. Otherwise, regulations to provide for that effect would be unnecessary. See *CIS 1330/02*, para 19.

[¹ **Matters arising as respects decisions**

[¹**46B.**–(1) Regulations may make provision as respects matters arising pending–

(a) any decision of the [³[⁵Secretary of State]] under section 11, 12 or 17;

(b) any decision of [⁴ the First-tier Tribunal] under section 20; or

(c) any decision of [⁴ the Upper Tribunal in relation to a decision of the First-tier Tribunal under this Act].

(2) Regulations may also make provision as respects matters arising out of the revision under section 16, or on appeal, of any such decision as is mentioned in subsection (1).

(3)   [²...]]

Amendments

1.   Inserted (4.3.99) by Social Security Act 1998 (1998 c.14) Sch 7 para 44.
2.   Child Support, Pensions and Social Security Act 2000 (2000 c.19) s85 and Sch 9 Part I (March 3, 2003 for the types of cases detailed in art 3 Child Support, Pensions and Social Security Act 2000 (Commencement No.12) Order 2003 (SI 2003 No.192)). For other types of cases, see the '1993 rules' below.
3.   Child Maintenance and Other Payments Act 2008 (2008 c.6) s13 and Sch 3 para 49 (November 1, 2008); Child Maintenance and Other Payments Act 2008 (Commencement No.4 and Transitional Provision) Order 2008 (SI 2008 No.2675) art 3.
4.   Transfer of Tribunal Functions Order 2008 (SI 2008 No.2833) art 9 and Sch 3 para 94 (November 3, 2008, subject to the transitional provisions in Sch 4 of SI 2008 No.2833).
5.   Public Bodies (Child Maintenance and Enforcement Commission: Abolition and Transfer of Functions) Order 2012 (SI 2012 No.2007) art 3(2) and Sch para 57 (August 1, 2012).

1993 rules
s85 and Sch 9 of the Child Support, Pensions and Social Security Act 2000 (2000 c.19) amend this section of the Child Support Act 1991 and have been brought into force only for the types of cases in art 3 of the Child Support, Pensions and Social Security Act 2000 (Commencement No.12) Order 2003 (SI 2003 No.192 – see p683). For other types of cases the 1993 rules apply. If the 1993 rules apply, subsection 46(3), reproduced below, is not repealed.

(3) Any reference in this section to section 16, 17 or 20 includes a reference to that section as extended by Schedule 4C.

Fees

General Note
The regulations made under this section (the Child Support Fees Regulations 1992) have been revoked by the Act.

Right of audience
48.–(1) Any [¹ officer of the [²[³Secretary of State]] who is authorised] by the [²[³Secretary of State]] for the purposes of this section shall have, in relation to any proceedings under this Act before a magistrates' court, a right of audience and the right to conduct litigation.

(2) In this section "right of audience" and "right to conduct litigation" have the same meaning as in section 119 of the Courts and Legal Services Act 1990.

Amendments
1. Words Substituted (4.9.95) in s48(1) by Child Support Act 1995 (c.34), Sch 3 para 14.
2. Child Maintenance and Other Payments Act 2008 (2008 c.6) s13 and Sch 3 para 50 (November 1, 2008); Child Maintenance and Other Payments Act 2008 (Commencement No.4 and Transitional Provision) Order 2008 (SI 2008 No.2675) art 3.
3. Public Bodies (Child Maintenance and Enforcement Commission: Abolition and Transfer of Functions) Order 2012 (SI 2012 No.2007) art 3(2) and Sch para 58 (August 1, 2012).

General Note
This section does not extend to Scotland (s58(9)).

Section 119(1) Courts and Legal Services Act 1990 defines "right of audience" as meaning the right to exercise any of the functions of appearing before and addressing a court including the calling and examining of witnesses, and "right to conduct litigation" as meaning the right to exercise all or any of the functions of issuing a writ or otherwise commencing proceedings before any court and to perform any ancillary functions in relation to proceedings (such as entering appearances to actions).

Right of audience: Scotland
49. In relation to any proceedings before the sheriff under any provision of this Act, the power conferred on the Court of Session by section 32 of the Sheriff Courts (Scotland) Act 1971 (power of Court of Session to regulate civil procedure in sheriff court) shall extend to the making of rules permitting a party to such proceedings, in such circumstances as may be specified in the rules, to be represented by a person who is neither an advocate nor a solicitor.

General Note
This section applies to Scotland only: s58(10).

Unauthorised disclosure of information
50.–(1) Any person who is, or has been, employed in employment to which [⁵this subsection] applies is guilty of an offence if, without lawful authority, he discloses any information which–

(a) was acquired by him in the course of that employment; and

(b) relates to a particular person.

[⁵(1A) Subsection (1) applies to employment as–

[⁶(za) any member of staff appointed under section 40(1) of the Tribunals, Courts and Enforcement Act 2007 in connection with the carrying out of any functions in relation to appeals from decisions made under this Act;]

(a)   any clerk to, or other officer of, an appeal tribunal [⁶constituted under Chapter 1 of Part 1 of the Social Security Act 1998];

(b)   any member of the staff of [⁶any such] appeal tribunal;

(c)   a civil servant in connection with the carrying out of any functions under this Act;

(d)   [⁷...]

(e)   any person who provides, or is employed in the provision of, services to the [⁷Secretary of State],

and to employment of any other kind which is prescribed for the purposes of this subsection.

(1B) Any person who is, or has been, employed in employment to which this subsection applies is guilty of an offence if, without lawful authority, he discloses any information which–

(a)   was acquired by him in the course of that employment;

(b)   is information which is, or is derived from, information acquired or held for the purposes of this Act; and

(c)   relates to a particular person.

(1C) Subsection (1B) applies to any employment which–

(a)   is not employment to which subsection (1) applies, and

(b)   is of a kind prescribed for the purposes of this subsection.]

(2)   It is not an offence under this section–

(a)   to disclose information in the form of a summary or collection of information so framed as not to enable information relating to any particular person to be ascertained from it; or

(b)   to disclose information which has previously been disclosed to the public with lawful authority.

(3)   It is a defense for a person charged with an offence under this section to prove that at the time of the alleged offence–

(a)   he believed that he was making the disclosure in question with lawful authority and had no reasonable cause to believe otherwise; or

(b)   he believed that the information in question had previously been disclosed to the public with lawful authority and had no reasonable cause to believe otherwise.

(4)   A person guilty of an offence under this section shall be liable–

(a)   on conviction on indictment, to imprisonment for a term not exceeding two years or a fine or both; or

(b)   on summary conviction, to imprisonment for a term not exceeding six months or a fine not exceeding the statutory maximum or both.

(5)   [⁴...]

(6)   For the purposes of this section a disclosure is to be regarded as made with lawful authority if, and only if, it is made–

(a)   by a civil servant in accordance with his official duty; or

(b)   by any other person either–

(i)   for the purposes of the function in the exercise of which he holds the information and without contravening any restriction duly imposed by the responsible person; or

(ii)   to, or in accordance with an authorisation duly given by, the responsible person;

(c)   in accordance with any enactment or order of a court;

(d)   for the purpose of instituting, or otherwise for the purposes of, any proceedings before a court or before any tribunal or other body or person mentioned in this Act; or

(e)   with the consent of the appropriate person.

(7)   "The responsible person" means–

(a)   the Lord Chancellor;

(b)   the Secretary of State;

[⁵(ba) [⁷...]]

[⁷(c) any person authorised for the purposes of this subsection by the Lord Chancellor [⁷or the Secretary of State];]

(d) any other prescribed person, or person falling within a prescribed category.

(8) "The appropriate person" means the person to whom the information in question relates, except that if the affairs of that person are being dealt with–

(a) under a power of attorney; [³or]

(b) [³...]

(c) by a Scottish mental health custodian, that is to say [²a guardian or other person entitled to act on behalf of the person under the Adults with Incapacity (Scotland) Act 2000 (asp 4)]; [³...]

(d) [³...]

the appropriate person is the attorney, [³or custodian] (as the case may be) or, in a case falling within paragraph (a), the person to whom the information relates.

[³(9) Where the person to whom the information relates lacks capacity (within the meaning of the Mental Capacity Act 2005) to consent to its disclosure, the appropriate person is–

(a) a donee of an enduring power of attorney or lasting power of attorney (within the meaning of that Act), or

(b) a deputy appointed for him, or any other person authorised, by the Court of Protection,

with power in that respect.]

Amendments

1. Social Security Act 1998 (1998 c.14) Sch 7 para 45 (June 1, 1999).
2. **Scotland:** Adults with Incapacity (Scotland) Act 2000 (2000 asp 4) s88 and Sch 5 para 22 (April 2, 2001 and April 1, 2002 – see Adults with Incapacity (Scotland) Act 2000 (Commencement No.1) Order 2001 (SSI 2001 No.81) for relevant commencement date).
   England and Wales: Adults with Incapacity (Scotland) Act 2000 (Consequential Modifications) (England, Wales and Northern Ireland) Order 2005 (SI 2005 No.1790) art 2 (June 30, 2005).
3. Mental Capacity Act 2005 (2005 c.9) s67(1) and (2) Sch 6 para 36 and Sch 7 (October 1, 2007).
4. Child Maintenance and Other Payments Act 2008 (2008 c.6) s58 and Sch 8 (November 1, 2008).
5. Child Maintenance and Other Payments Act 2008 (2008 c.6) s57(1) and Sch 7 para 1(19)-(21) (November 1, 2008).
6. Transfer of Tribunal Functions Order 2008 (SI 2008 No.2833) art 9 and Sch 3 para 95 (November 3, 2008, subject to the transitional provisions in Sch 4 of SI 2008 No. 2833).
7. Public Bodies (Child Maintenance and Enforcement Commission: Abolition and Transfer of Functions) Order 2012 (SI 2012 No.2007) art 3(2) and Sch para 59 (August 1, 2012).

Definition

"prescribed": see s54.

General Note

Subsections (1A) and (1C)

Regulation 14(1) and (2) of the Information Regulations is made under these subsections. The other kinds of employment prescribed for the purposes of these subsections are contained in reg 14 of the Information Regulations (see p701).

Subsection (6)

A court has no power under this section to give leave to, or direct the Secretary of State to disclose information to enable a child (or person with care) to trace the non-resident parent with a view to bringing proceedings for a s8 order under the Children Act 1989 (*Re C (A Minor) (Child Support Agency: Disclosure)* [1995] 1 FLR 201).

Subsection (6)(a)

The "official duty" of an officer may go beyond what is specified in the legislation. It includes the requirements of natural justice, so that matters may be notified to a party which are not expressly covered by the Maintenance Calculation Procedure Regulations (*Huxley v Child Support Officer and Huxley* [2000] 1 FLR 898 at 906 *per* Hale LJ).

Subsection (6)(d)

See also the Data Protection Act 1998 on p212, which exempts from its provisions disclosure under an enactment or in relation to legal proceedings.

[¹ **Use of computers**

50A.   Any decision falling to be made under or by virtue of this Act by the [²Secretary of State] may be made, not only by a person authorised to exercise the [²Secretary of State's] decision-making function, but also by a computer for whose operation such a person is responsible.]

Amendments

1.　Child Maintenance and Other Payments Act 2008 (2008 c.6) s13 and Sch 3 para 51 (November 1, 2008); Child Maintenance and Other Payments Act 2008 (Commencement No.4 and Transitional Provision) Order 2008 (SI 2008 No.2675) art 3.

2.　Public Bodies (Child Maintenance and Enforcement Commission: Abolition and Transfer of Functions) Order 2012 (SI 2012 No.2007) art 3(2) and Sch para 60 (August 1, 2012).

Supplementary powers to make regulations

51.–(1)   The Secretary of State may by regulations make such incidental, supplemental and transitional provision as he considers appropriate in connection with any provision made by or under this Act.

(2)　The regulations may, in particular, make provision–

(a)　as to the procedure to be followed with respect to–

　(i)　the making of applications for [³maintenance calculation]s;

　[⁴(ii)　the making of decisions under section 11;

　(iii)　the making of decisions under section 16 or 17;]

[⁵(b)　extending the categories of case to which section 16, 17 or 20 applies;]

(c)　as to the date on which an application for a [³maintenance calculation] is to be treated as having been made;

(d)　for attributing payments made under [³maintenance calculations] to the payment of arrears;

(e)　for the adjustment, for the purpose of taking account of the retrospective effect of a [³maintenance calculation], of amounts payable under the assessment;

(f)　for the adjustment, for the purpose of taking account of over-payments or under-payments of child support maintenance, of amounts payable under a [³maintenance calculation];

(g)　as to the evidence which is to be required in connection with such matters as may be prescribed;

(h)　as to the circumstances in which any official record or certificate is to be conclusive (or in Scotland, sufficient) evidence;

(i)　with respect to the giving of notices or other documents;

(j)　for the rounding up or down of any amounts calculated, estimated or otherwise arrived at in applying any provision made by or under this Act.

(3)　No power to make regulations conferred by any other provision of this Act shall be taken to limit the powers given to the Secretary of State by this section.

Amendments

1.　Substituted (16.11.98) by Social Security Act 1998 Sch 7 para 46(a).

2.　Substituted (4.3.99) by Social Security Act 1998 (1998 c.14) Sch 7 para 46(b).

3.　Child Support, Pensions and Social Security Act 2000 (2000 c.19) s1(2) (March 3, 2003 for the types of cases in art 3 Child Support, Pensions and Social Security Act 2000 (Commencement No.12) Order 2003 (SI 2003 No.192)). For other types of cases see the '1993 rules', below.

4.　Child Support, Pensions and Social Security Act 2000 (2000 c.19) s26 and Sch 3 para 11(19)(a) (March 3, 2003 for the types of cases in art 3 Child Support, Pensions and Social Security Act 2000 (Commencement No.12) Order 2003 (SI 2003 No.192)). For other types of cases see the '1993 rules', below.

5.　Child Support, Pensions and Social Security Act 2000 (2000 c.19) s26 and Sch 3 para 11(19)(b) (March 3, 2003 for the types of cases in art 3 Child Support, Pensions and Social Security Act 2000 (Commencement No.12) Order 2003 (SI 2003 No.192)). For other types of cases see the '1993 rules', below.

1993 rules

Ss1(2) and 26 and Sch 3 of the Child Support, Pensions and Social Security Act 2000 (2000 c.19) amend this section of the Child Support Act 1991 and have been brought into force only for the types of cases in art 3 of the

Child Support, Pensions and Social Security Act 2000 (Commencement No.12) Order 2003 (SI 2003 No.192 – see p683). For other types of cases the 1993 rules apply. If the 1993 rules apply, "maintenance assessment" is retained in place of "maintenance calculation", subsections 51(2)(a)(ii) and (iii) are not substituted and read:

(ii)   the making, cancellation or refusal to make [³maintenance calculations] [¹ (iii) the making of decisions under section 16 or 17];

and subsection 51(2)(b) is not substituted and reads:

(b)   extending the categories of case to which [² Schedule 4C] applies;

In accordance with the Social Security Act 1998 (Commencement No.2) Order 1998 (SI 1998 No.2780) art 3(5), in respect of reviews under s16 which commenced on or before 8 December 1996 the following version of subsection 51(2)(a)(iii) continues to apply:

(iii)   reviews under sections 16 to 19;

Definitions

"child support maintenance": see s3(6).
"maintenance calculation": see s54.
"prescribed": see s54.

General Note

Subsection (1)

Words such as "incidental" and "supplemental" tend to be interpreted narrowly.

Power to make "supplementary" provision has been held to mean power "to fill in details or machinery for which the. .. Act itself does not provide-supplementary in the sense that it is required to implement what was in the ... Act" (*Daymond v South West Water Authority* [1976] 1 All ER 39 at 53, *per* Viscount Dilhorne, followed in *R v Customs and Excise Commissioners ex p Hedges and Bulter Ltd* [1986] 2 All ER 164 at 171, *per* Mustill LJ). The terms of subs (3) will not be sufficient to displace this approach.

Subsection (2) removes any doubt over the scope of this section in so far as the matters there specified are concerned.

Subsection (2)

The Child Support (Management of Payment and Arrears) Regulations 2009 are made in part under paras (d), (e) and (f).

Subsection (2)(a)(iii)

The amendment to this provision is subject to the saving and transitional provisions in art 3(5) Social Security Act 1998 (Commencement No.2) Order 1998.

Subsection (2)(f)

The regulations dealing with the adjustment of the amount payable under a maintenance assessment are contained in the Arrears, Interest and Adjustment of Maintenance Assessments Regulations.

[¹Pilot schemes

51A.–(1)   Any regulations made under this Act may be made so as to have effect for a specified period not exceeding 24 months.

(2)   Regulations which, by virtue of subsection (1), are to have effect for a limited period are referred to in this section as a "pilot scheme".

(3)   A pilot scheme may provide that its provisions are to apply only in relation to–

(a)   one or more specified areas or localities;

(b)   one or more specified classes of person;

(c)   persons selected by reference to prescribed criteria, or on a sampling basis.

(4)   A pilot scheme may make consequential or transitional provision with respect to the cessation of the scheme on the expiry of the specified period.

(5)   A pilot scheme may be replaced by a further pilot scheme making the same or similar provision.]

[²(6)   This section does not apply to regulations under–

(a)   subsection (2A) of section 20 as substituted by section 10 of the Child Support, Pensions and Social Security Act 2000;

(b)   subsection (3A) of section 20 as it has effect apart from section 10 of the Child Support, Pensions and Social Security Act 2000.]

Amendments

1.   Child Maintenance and Other Payments Act 2008 (2008 c.6) s41 (October 8, 2012).

2.   Welfare Reform Act 2012 (2012 c. 5) s102 and Sch 11 para 7 (February 25, 2013 for the purpose of making regulations only); Welfare Reform Act 2012 (Commencement No.8 and Savings and Transitional Provisions) Order 2013 (SI 2013 No.358) art 2 and Sch 1.

Regulations and orders

52.–(1)   Any power conferred on [³...] the Lord Advocate or the Secretary of State by this Act to make regulations or orders (other than a deduction from earnings order) shall be exercisable by statutory instrument.

[²(2)   No statutory instrument containing (whether alone or with other provisions) regulations made under–

(a)   section [⁴...] 12(4) (so far as the regulations make provision for the default rate of child support maintenance mentioned in section 12(5)(b)), [⁸20(2A), 20(3A)] 28C(2)(b), 28F(2)(b), 30(5A), [⁵ 32A to 32C, 32E to 32J,] 41(2), 41A, 41B(6), [⁶41E(1)(a),] 43(1), 44(2A)(d) [⁴...] or 47;

(b)   paragraph 3(2) or 10A(1) of Part I of Schedule 1; or

(c)   Schedule 4B,

or an order made under section 45(1) or (6), shall be made unless a draft of the instrument has been laid before Parliament and approved by a resolution of each House of Parliament.

[⁶(2A)   No statutory instrument containing (whether alone or with other provisions)–

(a)   the first regulations under section 17(2) to make provision of the kind mentioned in section 17(3)(a) or (b),

(b)   the first regulations under section 39F, 39M(4), 39P, 39Q, 41D(2), 41E(2) or 49A,

(c)   the first regulations under paragraph 5A(6)(b) of Schedule 1,

(d)   the first regulations under paragraph 9(1)(ba) of Schedule 1 to make provision of the kind mentioned in sub-paragraph (2) of that paragraph, or

(e)   the first regulations under paragraph 10(1) of Schedule 1 to make provision of the kind mentioned in sub-paragraph (2)(a) or (b) of that paragraph,

shall be made unless a draft of the instrument has been laid before Parliament and approved by a resolution of each House of Parliament.]

[⁷(2B) No statutory instrument containing (whether alone or with other provisions) regulations which by virtue of section 51A are to have effect for a limited period shall be made unless a draft of the instrument has been laid before Parliament and approved by a resolution of each House of Parliament.]

(2A)   No statutory instr

ument containing (whether alone or with other provisions) the first set of regulations made under paragraph 10(1) of Part I of Schedule 1 as substituted by section 1(3) of the Child Support, Pensions and Social Security Act 2000 shall be made unless a draft of the instrument has been laid before Parliament and approved by a resolution of each House of Parliament.]

(3)   Any other statutory instrument made under this Act (except an order made under section 58(2)) shall be subject to annulment in pursuance of a resolution of either House of Parliament.

(4)   Any power of a kind mentioned in subsection (1) may be exercised–

(a)   in relation to all cases to which it extends, in relation to those cases but subject to specified exceptions or in relation to any specified cases or classes of case;

(b)   so as to make, as respects the cases in relation to which it is exercised–

    (i)   the full provision to which it extends or any lesser provision (whether by way of exception or otherwise);

    (ii)   the same provision for all cases, different provision for different cases or classes of case or different provision as respects the same case or class of case but for different purposes of this Act;

    (iii) provision which is either unconditional or is subject to any specified condition;

(c)   so to provide for a person to exercise a discretion in dealing with any matter.

Amendemnts

1.   Inserted (4.9.95) by Child Support Act 1995 (c.34), Sch 3 para 15.

2.   Child Support, Pensions and Social Security Act 2000 (2000 c.19) s25 (March 3, 2003 for the types of cases in art 3 Child Support, Pensions and Social Security Act 2000 (Commencement No.12) Order 2003 (SI 2003 No.192)). For other types of cases see the '1993 rules', below.

3.   Constitutional Reform Act 2005 (2005 c.4) s146 and Sch 18 Part 2 (April 3, 2006).

4.   Child Maintenance and Other Payments Act 2008 (2008 c.6) s58 and Sch 8 (October 27, 2008 subject to art 4 Child Maintenance and Other Payments Act 2008 (Commencement No.3 and Transitional and Savings Provisions) Order 2008 (SI 2008 No.2548)).

5.   Child Maintenance and Other Payments Act 2008 (2008 c.6) Sch 7 para 1(22)(a) (June 1, 2009 for making regulations, August 3, 2009 for all other purposes). See Child Maintenance and Other Payments Act 2008 (Commencement No.5) Order 2009 (SI 2009 No.1314) art 2(b).

6.   Child Maintenance and Other Payments Act 2008 (2008 c.6) s57 and Sch 7 para 1(22)(b) and (23) (June 27, 2012).

7.   Child Maintenance and Other Payments Act 2008 (2008 c.6) s57 and Sch 7 para 1(24) (October 8, 2012).

1993 rules

s25 of the Child Support, Pensions and Social Security Act 2000 (2000 c.19) amends this section of the Child Support Act 1991 and has been brought into force only for the types of cases in art 3 of the Child Support, Pensions and Social Security Act 2000 (Commencement No.12) Order 2003 (SI 2003 No.192 – see p683). For other types of cases the 1993 rules apply. If the 1993 rules apply, subsection 52(2) reads:

(2)   No statutory instrument containing (whether alone or with other provisions) regulations made under section 4(7), 5(3), 6(1), (9) or (10), 7(8), 12(2), [[1] 28C(2)(b), 28F(3), 30(5A)], 41(2), (3) or (4) [[1] 41A, 41B(6)], 42, 43(1), 46 or 47 or under Part I of Schedule 1 [[1] or under Schedule 4B], or an order made under section 45(1) or (6), shall be made unless a draft of the instrument has been laid before Parliament and approved by a resolution of each House of Parliament.

and subsection 52(2A) does not apply.

Financial provisions
53.   Any expenses of the Lord Chancellor or the Secretary of State under this Act shall be payable out of money provided by Parliament.

Interpretation
54.–(1)   In this Act–

''[[7] non-resident parent]'', has the meaning given in section 3(2);

[[1] ...]

[[14] [[17] ...]]

[[2] "application for a [[8] variation]" means an application under section 28A [[8] or 28G];]

[[12] ...]

"benefits Acts" means the [[4] Social Security Contributions and Benefits Act 1992 and the Social Security Administration Act 1992];

[[1] ...]

[[19] "charging order" has the same meaning as in section 1 of the Charging Orders Act 1979;]

"child benefit" has the same meaning as in Child Benefit Act 1975;

[[1] ....]

"child support maintenance" has the meaning given in section 3(6);

[[19] [[20] ...]]

[[1] ...]

[[12] ...]

"deduction from earnings order" has the meaning given in section 31(2);

[[9] "default maintenance decision" has the meaning given in section 12;]

[[12] ...]

[[19] "deposit-taker" means a person who, in the course of a business, may lawfully accept deposits in the United Kingdom;]

"disability living allowance" has the same meaning as in the [[3] benefit Acts];

[[13] ...]

[[16] ...]

"income support" has the same meaning as in the benefit Acts;

[[4] "income-based jobseeker's allowance" has the same meaning as in the Jobseekers Act 1995;]

[[15] "income-related employment and support allowance" means an income-related allowance under Part 1 of the Welfare Reform Act 2007 (employment and support allowance);]

"interim maintenance [[10]decision]" has the meaning given in section 12;

"liability order" has the meaning given in section 33(2);

"maintenance agreement" has the meaning given in section 9(1);

[[11] "maintenance calculation" means a calculation of maintenance made under this Act and, except in prescribed circumstances, includes a default maintenance decision and an interim maintenance decision;]

"maintenance order" has the meaning given in section 8(11);

[[12]...]

"parent", in relation to any child, means any person who is in law the mother or father of the child;

"parent with care" means a person who is, in relation to a child, both a parent and a person with care.

"parental responsibility" has the same meaning as in the Children Act 1989;

"parental rights" has the same meaning as in the Law Reform (Parent and Child) (Scotland) Act 1986;

"person with care" has the meaning given in section 3(3);

"prescribed" means prescribed by regulations made by the Secretary of State;

"qualifying child" has the meaning given in section 3(1);

[[9] "voluntary payment" has the meaning given in section 28J.]

[[18] (2)   The definition of "deposit-taker" in subsection (1) is to be read with–

(a)   section 22 of the Financial Services and Markets Act 2000;

(b)   any relevant order under that section; and

(c)   Schedule 2 to that Act.]

Amendments

1.   Repealed (1.6.99) by Sch 8 to Social Security Act 1998 (c.14).

2.   Inserted (4.9.95) by Child Support Act 1995 (c.34), Sch 3 para 16.

3.   Substituted (1.7.92) by Social Security (Consequential Provisions) Act 1992 (c.6), Sch 2 para 114.

4.   Inserted (7.10.96) by para 20(6) of Sch 2 to Jobseekers Act 1995 (c.18).

5.   Child Support, Pensions and Social Security Act 2000 (2000 c.19) s1(2) (March 3, 2003 for the cases detailed in art 3 Child Support, Pensions and Social Security Act 2000 (Commencement No.12) Order 2003 (SI 2003 No.192)). For other types of cases, see the '1993 rules' below.

6.   Child Support, Pensions and Social Security Act 2000 (2000 c.19) s1(2) (March 3, 2003 for the types of cases in art 3 Child Support, Pensions and Social Security Act 2000 (Commencement No.12) Order 2003 (SI 2003 No.192)). For other types of cases, see the '1993 rules' below..

7.   Child Support, Pensions and Social Security Act 2000 (2000 c.19) s26 and Sch 3 para 11(2) (March 3, 2003 for the types of cases in art 3 Child Support, Pensions and Social Security Act 2000 (Commencement No.12) Order 2003 (SI 2003 No.192)). For other types of cases, see the '1993 rules' below.

8.   Child Support, Pensions and Social Security Act 2000 (2000 c.19) s26 and Sch 3 para 11(20)(a) (March 3, 2003 for the types of cases in art 3 Child Support, Pensions and Social Security Act 2000 (Commencement No.12) Order 2003 (SI 2003 No.192)). For other types of cases, see the '1993 rules' below. .

9.   Child Support, Pensions and Social Security Act 2000 (2000 c.19) s26 and Sch 3 para 11(20)(b) and (f) (March 3, 2003 for the types of cases in art 3 Child Support, Pensions and Social Security Act 2000 (Commencement No.12) Order 2003 (SI 2003 No.192)). For other types of cases, see the '1993 rules' below.

10.   Child Support, Pensions and Social Security Act 2000 (2000 c.19) s26 and Sch 3 para. 11(20)(c) (March 3, 2003 for the types of cases in art 3 Child Support, Pensions and Social Security Act 2000 (Commencement No.12) Order 2003 (SI 2003 No.192)). For other types of cases, see the '1993 rules' below.

11.   Child Support, Pensions and Social Security Act 2000 (2000 c.19) s26 and Sch 3 para 11(20)(d) (March 3, 2003 for the types of cases in art 3 Child Support, Pensions and Social Security Act 2000 (Commencement No.12) Order 2003 (SI 2003 No.192)). For other types of cases, see the '1993 rules' below.

12. Child Support, Pensions and Social Security Act 2000 (2000 c.19) ss26 and 85 and Schs 3 para 11(20)(e) and 9, Part I (March 3, 2003 for the types of cases in art 3 Child Support, Pensions and Social Security Act 2000 (Commencement No.12) Order 2003 (SI 2003 No.192)). For other types of cases, see the '1993 rules' below.
13. Tax Credits Act 2002 (2002 c.21) s60 and Sch 6 (April 6, 2003).
14. Social Security Act 1998 (1998 c.14) Sch 7 para 47(a) (June 1, 1999).
15. Welfare Reform Act 2007 (2007 c.5) s28 and Sch 3 para 7(7) (October 27, 2008).
16. Tribunals, Courts and Enforcement Act 2007 (2007 c.15) s.146 and sch 23, part 2 (November 3, 2008). Brought into force by the Tribunals, Courts and Enforcement Act 2007 (Commencement No.6 and Transitional Provisions) Order 2008 (SI 2008 No.2696) art 5.
17. Transfer of Tribunal Functions Order 2008 (SI 2008 No.2833) art 9 and Sch 3 para 96 (November 3, 2008, subject to the transitional provisions in Sch 4 of SI 2008 No.2833).
18. Child Maintenance and Other Payments Act 2008 (2008 c.6) Sch 7 para 1(26) (June 1, 2009).
19. Child Maintenance and Other Payments Act 2008 (2008 c.6) Sch 7 para 1(25)(a) (June 1, 2009).
20. Public Bodies (Child Maintenance and Enforcement Commission: Abolition and Transfer of Functions) Order 2012 (SI 2012 No.2007) art 3(2) and Sch para 61 (August 1, 2012).

1993 rules

Ss1(2) and 26 and sch 3 of the Child Support, Pensions and Social Security Act 2000 (2000 c.19) amend this section of the Child Support Act 1991 and have been brought into force only for the types of cases in art 3 of the Child Support, Pensions and Social Security Act 2000 (Commencement No.12) Order 2003 (SI 2003 No.192 – see p683). For other types of cases the 1993 rules apply. If the the 1993 rules apply:

−   "maintenance assessment" is retained in place of "maintenance calculation", "assessment" is retained in place of "calculation" and "absent parent" is retained in place of "non-resident parent";
−   in the definition of "application for a departure direction", "departure direction" ' is retained in place of "variation" and "or 28G" is not inserted;
−   the definitions of "default maintenance decision" and "voluntary payment" are not inserted;
−   in the definition of "interim maintenance assessment", the word "assessment" is retained in place of "decision ";
−   the following definition of "maintenance assessment" is retained in place of the definition of "maintenance calculation"

"maintenance assessment" means an assessment of maintenance made under this Act and, except in prescribed circumstances, includes an interim maintenance assessment;

−   the following definitions are not omitted:

"assessable income" has the meaning given in paragraph 5 of Schedule 1;
[² "current assessment", in relation to an application for a departure direction, means (subject to any regulations made under paragraph 10 of Schedule 4A) the maintenance assessment with respect to which the application is made;]
[² "departure direction" has the meaning given in section 28A;]
"maintenance requirement" means the amount calculated in accordance with paragraph 1 of Schedule 1;.

General Note

Although the definitions contained in this section are not prefaced by words such as "unless the contrary appears", they are subject to this qualification (*Meux v Jacobs* (1875) LR 7 HL 481 at 493, *per* Lord Selborne and *Robinson v Local Board of Barton-Eccles, Winton and Morton* (1883) 8 App Cas 798 at 801, *per* Lord Selborne LC).

By virtue of s11 Interpretation Act 1978 expressions used in this Act bear, unless the contrary intention appears, the same meaning in delegated legislation made under this Act.

In interpreting the child support legislation it is permissible in order to resolve an ambiguity to have regard to reports of committees presented to Parliament in order to help to identify the mischief which the legislation was intended to remedy (*Black Clawson International Ltd v Papierwerke Waldhof-Aschaffenburg A G* [1975] 1 All ER 810).

It is also permissible to have regard to parliamentary material as part of the objective circumstances to which the statutory language relates and in the context of which it must be interpreted (*R (Westminster City Council) v National Asylum Support Service* [2002] 4 All ER 654 *per* Lord Steyn at para 5). The material may also be used as a direct indication of the meaning of a provision provided that three conditions are satisfied: (i) the legislation is ambiguous or obscure or its apparent interpretation would lead to absurdity: (ii) the material relied on consists of statements of a minister or promoter of the legislation, supplemented as necessary to understand the statements and their effect; and (iii) the statements are clear (*Pepper v Hart* [1993] 1 All ER 47 at 69, *per* Lord Browne-Wilkinson. The material that may be considered includes the explanatory notes to a statute (*R (Westminster City Council) v National Asylum Support Service per* Lord Steyn at para 5). However, where it is sought to interpret legislation consistently with provisions of European or international law, it is of particular importance that the true purpose of the legislation should be identified and reference to a wider range of material is permissible (*Three Rivers DC v Bank of England (No.2)* [1996] 2 All ER 363). Citation of Hansard should take the form of reference to specific passages that satisfy the above conditions and it is not appropriate merely to produce a list of references to debates without referring specifically to particular passages *R(G) 1/98*, para 13). It is only in exceptional circumstances that a reference to Hansard will be relevant in identifying the scope of an enabling power (*R v Secretary of State for the Environment, Transport and the Regions ex p Spath Holme Ltd* [2001] 1 All ER 195).

If words have been left out of a statutory instrument by mistake, it can be rectified on interpretation by reference to the explanatory notes to the instrument and to the Secretary of State's letter authorising the making of the instrument (*Confederation of Passenger Transport UK v Humber Bridge Board* [2004] QB 310).

The general approach to interpretation of the child support legislation should be practical and purposive, rather than detached and literal, so as to produce a coherent structure devoid so far as possible of inconsistencies and arbitrary distinctions (*CCS 12/1994*, paras 22-34). It is proper to bear in mind that the legislation "does seem designed to produce fairly clear-cut answers to most cases so that a relatively junior child support officer is able to apply the law" (*R(CS)14/98*, para 16), although there are a number of decisions which cannot readily be reconciled with this approach. However, Arden LJ argued that greater use should be made of secondary legislation in *Campbell v SSWP* [2005] EWCA Civ 989.

In interpreting this Act, it is not proper to consider the contents of regulations made under it (*CCS 12806/1996*, para 13). In interpreting the legislation, little of value is to be found in consulting any forms used by the Secretary of State *(ibid,* para 17). The general scheme of the legislation should be initially determined as it originally existed, although it is legitimate to check that construction against subsequent amendments so that it may be reconsidered if those amendments are not consonant with it *(ibid,* para 25).

Regulations must be made under the authority of an enabling provision. Sometimes enabling provisions are compulsory. Usually, they are not. If an enabling provision is not compulsory, there is no duty to implement it and the regulations cannot be interpreted as if it were (*CCS 2348/2000*, paras 8-10). In principle, the enabling provision under the authority of which a regulation is made sets the limit to what the regulation may provide. However, their value as guidance is reduced if there are a variety of enabling powers and no compelling reasons to maintain a strict separation between them (*Banks v Chief Adjudication Officer* [2001] 4 All ER 62 at 74 *per* Lord Hope).

"child benefit"
By virtue of s17(2)(a) Interpretation Act 1978 reference to the Child Benefit Act 1975 is to be construed as a reference to the Social Security Contributions and Benefits Act 1992.

"disability living allowance"
By virtue of s17(2)(a) Interpretation Act 1978 reference to the Social Security Act 1975 is to be construed as a reference to the Social Security Contributions and Benefits Act 1992.

"maintenance agreement"
See the general notes to s9(1) above and s18 of the 1995 Act.

"parent"
A parent is someone who is in law the mother or father of a child. The person may be a natural or adoptive parent. Step-parents, foster parents and persons who treat a child as their own are not within the definition, although they may become so if they adopt the child (*R(CS) 6/03*, paras 8-10). Likewise grandparents and other relatives are not within the definition unless they adopt the child (*CCS 3128/1995*, para 8). Having parental responsibility or a residence order does not make a person a parent (*CCS 736/2002*).

A person may not become a parent by virtue of estoppel (*Re M(Child Support Act: Parentage)* [1997] 2 FLR 90 at 93-94, *per* Bracewell J).

"parental responsibility"
This is defined by s3 Children Act 1989 as all the rights, duties, powers, responsibility and authority which by law a parent of a child has in relation to the child and the child's property including those of a guardian of the child's estate.

[²**Meaning of "child"**

55.–(1)   In this Act, "child" means (subject to subsection (2)) a person who–

(a)   has not attained the age of 16, or

(b)   has not attained the age of 20 and satisfies such conditions as may be prescribed.

(2)   A person who is or has been party to a marriage or civil partnership is not a child for the purposes of this Act.

(3)   For the purposes of subsection (2), "marriage" and "civil partnership" include a void marriage and a void civil partnership respectively.]

Amendments

1.   Civil Partnership Act 2004 (2004 c.33) s254 and Sch 24 para 3 (December 5, 2005).

2.   Child Maintenance and Other Payments Act 2008 (2008 c.6) s42 (for the purpose of making regulations, October 8, 2012; for all other purposes, December 10, 2012; Child Maintenance and Other Payments Act 2008 (Commencement No.9) and the Welfare Reform Act 2009 (Commencement No.9) Order 2012 (SI 2012 No.2523) art 2(2)(e) and Child Maintenance and Other Payments Act 2008 (Commencement No.10 and Transitional Provisions) Order 2012 (SI 2012 No.3042) art 4.

Definition

"prescribed": see s54.

General Note

This section must be read in conjunction with Sch 1 to the Maintenance Calculation Procedure Regulations. References to paragraphs in this note are to paragraphs in that Schedule.

This section provides for the meaning of "child". There were many commissioners' decisions on provisions similar to those used here, but as the wording of those provisions has varied considerably from time to time great care is required in applying those decisions to the present wording.

The following rules apply to determine whether a person is a child for the purposes of this Act.

Marriage and civil partnership

A person who has been through a ceremony of marriage or civil partnership is not a child, even if the marriage or partnership was void (s55(2)and(3)).

Aged under 16

A person who is under the age of 16 is a child, even if the person is not in education (s55(1)(a)). A person attains an age on the beginning of the relevant anniversary of the date of their birth (s9(1) Family Law Reform Act 1969 and s6(1) Age of Legal Capacity (Scotland) Act 1991).

Aged 16 to 19 inclusive

Persons between the age of 16 and 19 inclusive will be a child in two circumstances (s55(1)(b)). Those circumstances are: (i) the person is in full-time education (para 1(2)); or (ii) child benefit is payable in respect of the person (para 1(3)).

In education

In order to be a child, the person must be (a) receiving full-time education, (b) which is not advanced education, (c) by attendance (d) at either an educational establishment recognised by the Secretary of State as comparable to a university, college or school or (e) elsewhere if the education is recognised by the Secretary of State. (paras 1(2) and 6). This note relies in part on decisions on the commissioners on similar provisions in the social security legislation. They are relevant, provided that the wording is comparable and due regard is paid to the diferent context (*CCS 1181/2005*, para 9). The person must be receiving full-time education. This may be established in two ways. The first way is to bring the case within para 3. This paragraph does not provide an exhaustive definition of full-time education, but deems a person to be in full-time education if certain facts are established (*CCS 1181/2005*, paras 7-8). These are that the person (a) attends (b) a course of education (c) at a recognised educational establishment and (d) that the hours spent on receiving instruction or tuition, undertaking supervised study, examination or practical work or taking part in any exercise, experiment or project for which provision is made in the curriculum of the course, exceed 12 per week. The time spent on meal breaks and unsupervised study is disregarded. Study is supervised if the person is in the presence or close proximity of a teacher or tutor who may preserve order, enhance diligence and give appropriate assistance (*R(F) 1/93*, para 13). Attendance requires physical presence, so following a correspondence course will not satisfy this definition (*R(F) 2/95*, para 5). In view of requirement (c), this way of proving full-time education is of no use to someone who is not in a recognised educational establishment. A tribunal will need to make findings of fact on all these matters. In the case of (c) the relevant facts will be the name of the establishment attended and whether or not the Secretary of State has recognised it as an educational establishment (s55(3)). The relevant Secretary of State is the Secretary of State for Work and Pensions, not the Secretary of State for Education (*R(F) 2/95*, para 6).

The second way is to prove as a matter of fact in all the circumstances of the case that the person is undergoing full-time education (*R(F) 2/85*, paras 13 and 17(2)). These words are to be given their natural and ordinary meaning (*R(F) 4/62*, para 5). In that case a course which involved attendance for 13 hours and 45 minutes a week did not constitute "full-time instruction". Attendance solely for the purpose of taking examinations was not sufficient in *R(F) 2/85*, since the person had left school and returned solely to sit for examinations. This must be distinguished from the normal case of someone who continues at school but whose time is free before and between examinations for revision. In such a case it is within the usual meaning of the words in this context to say that the person is receiving fulltime education.

The education must not be advanced education. This is defined by para 2. Put shortly, advanced education means education above A-level standard.

Finally, either the educational establishment attended or the education itself must be recognised by the Secretary of State. Where a person who has reached 16 is receiving education which is not provided at a recognised educational establishment, it can only be recognised by the Secretary of State if the person was receiving such education immediately before reaching 16 (para 7). This provision differs from the similar provision in s142(2) Social Security Contributions and Benefits Act 1992. As the legislation does not specify any particular Secretary of State, s5 of, and Sch 1 to, the Interpretation Act 1978 apply so that it suffices if the education has been recognised by any of Her Majesty's Principal Secretaries of State (*CCS 2865/2001*, para 9(e)). The approval of a child's education by an officer of the local education authority is not the approval of a Secretary of State (*CF v CMEC (CSM)* UKUT 39 (AAC), paras 45-50).

Certain interruptions are ignored for the purpose of this head and these are set out in para 4. A period of up to six months of any interruption is ignored to the extent to which it is attributable to a reasonable cause. School holidays (provided the person intends to return to education afterwards), illness and delays associated with moving house or school are obvious examples of delays with reasonable causes. The six-month period may be extended where the interruption or its continuance is attributable to the illness or disability of mind or body of the person concerned. The extension may be for such period as is reasonable in the circumstances. The illness or disability need not have been the original cause of the interruption; it is sufficient if it merely prolongs an interruption. The tribunal will need to find facts as to the duration of the interruption and the reasons for it. The reasons for decision will need to record that the tribunal gave its mind to the question of the reasonableness of the cause and, where appropriate, the extension of the six-month period.

However, any interruption for whatever cause is not ignored in two cases (para 4(2)). The first case is where the interruption is, or is likely to be, immediately followed by a period during which youth training with an allowance is provided. The second case is where it is, or is likely to be, immediately followed by a period during which the person receives education by virtue of the person's employment or office.

Child benefit is payable

This effectively aligns the scope of the child support legislation with the scope of child benefit.

The form of language regularly causes problems. It is only necessary that child benefit is payable, not that it is in payment. This focuses attention on whether the conditions of entitlement are satisfied rather than on whether an award has been made. However, there may be an issue whether child benefit in payment is properly payable to the recipient. See *JF v SSWP and DB (CSM)* [2013] UKUT 0209 (AAC).

Corresponding provision for and co-ordination with Northern Ireland

56.–(1)   An Order in Council made under paragraph 1(1)(b) of Schedule 1 to the Northern Ireland Act 1974 which contains a statement that it is made only for purposes corresponding to those of the provisions of this Act, other than provisions which relate to the appointment of Child Support Commissioners for Northern Ireland–

(a)   shall not be subject to sub-paragraphs (4) and (5) of paragraph 1 of that Schedule (affirmative resolution of both Houses of Parliament); but

(b)   shall be subject to annulment in pursuance of a resolution of either House of Parliament.

(2)   The Secretary of State may make arrangements with the Department of Health and Social Services for Northern Ireland with a view to securing, to the extent allowed for in the arrangements, that–

(a)   the provision made by or under this Act ("the provision made for Great Britain"); and

(b)   the provision made by or under any corresponding enactment having effect with respect to Northern Ireland ("the provision made for Northern Ireland"),

provide for a single system within the United Kingdom.

(3)   The Secretary of State may make regulations for giving effect to any such arrangements.

(4)   The regulations may, in particular–

(a)   adapt legislation (including subordinate legislation) for the time being in force in Great Britain so as to secure its reciprocal operation with the provision made for Northern Ireland; and

(b)   make provision to secure that acts, omissions and events which have any effect for the purposes of the provision made for Northern Ireland have a corresponding effect for the purposes of the provision made for Great Britain.

Application to Crown

57.–(1)   The power of the Secretary of State to make regulations under section 14 requiring prescribed persons to furnish information may be exercised so as to require information to be furnished by persons employed in the service of the Crown or otherwise in the discharge of Crown functions.

(2)   In such circumstances, and subject to such conditions, as may be prescribed, an inspector appointed under section 15 may enter any Crown premises for the purpose of exercising any powers conferred on him by that section.

(3)   Where such an inspector duly enters any Crown premises for those purposes, section 15 shall apply in relation to persons employed in the service of the Crown or otherwise in the discharge of Crown functions as it applies in relation to other persons.

(4)   Where a liable person is in the employment of the Crown, a deduction from earnings order may be made under section 31 in relation to that person; but in such a case subsection (8) of section 32 shall apply only in relation to the failure of that person to comply with any requirement imposed on him by regulations made under section 32.

Definitions

"deduction from earnings order": see s31(2).
"liable person": see s31(1)(a).
"prescribed": see s54.

General Note

Subsection (1)

This subsection refers generally to s14. However, since it relates to the Secretary of State's powers to "require" disclosure it only applies to s14(1) and not to s14(3) which allows him to "authorise" disclosure. For a discussion of the meaning of "information" in this section, see the commentary to s14(1). Regulation 4(2)(h) and (3) of the Information Regulations is made under this subsection.

Subsection 2

Regulation 11 of the Information Regulations is made under this subsection.

Short title, commencement and extent, etc.

58.–(1)   This Act may be cited as the Child Support Act 1991.

(2)   Section 56(1) and subsections (1) to (11) and (14) of this section shall come into force on the passing of this Act but otherwise this Act shall come into force on such date as may be appointed by order made by the Lord Chancellor, the Secretary of State or Lord Advocate, or by any of them acting jointly.

(3)   Different dates may be appointed for different provisions of this Act and for different purposes (including, in particular, for different cases or categories of case).

(4)   An order under subsection (2) may make such supplemental, incidental or transitional provision as appears to the person making the order to be necessary or expedient in connection with the provisions brought into force by the order, including such adaptations or modifications of–

(a)   the provisions so brought into force;

(b)   any provisions of this Act then in force; or

(c)   any provision of any other enactment,

as appear to him to be necessary or expedient.

(5)   Different provision may be made by virtue of subsection (4) with respect to different periods.

(6)   Any provision made by virtue of subsection (4) may, in particular, include provision for–

(a)   the enforcement of a [²maintenance calculation] (including the collection of sums payable under the [³calculation]) as if the [³calculation] were a court order of a prescribed kind;

(b)   the registration of [²maintenance calculations] with the appropriate court in connection with any provision of a kind mentioned in paragraph (a);

(c)   the variation, on application made to a court, of the provisions of a [²maintenance calculation] relating to the method of making payments fixed by the [³calculation] or the intervals at with such payments are to be made;

(d)   a [²maintenance calculation], or an order of a prescribed kind relating to one or more children, to be deemed, in prescribed circumstances, to have been validly made for all purposes or for such purpose as may be prescribed.

In paragraph (c) "court" includes a single justice.

(7)   The Lord Chancellor, the Secretary of State of the Lord Advocate may by order make such amendments or repeals in, or such modifications of, such enact-ments as may be specified in the order, as appear to him to be necessary or expedient in consequence of any provision made by or under this Act (including any provision made by virtue of subsection (4)).

(8)   This Act shall, in its application to the Isles of Scilly, have effect subject to such exceptions, adaptations and modifications as the Secretary of State may by order prescribe.

(9)   Sections 27, 35[⁴, 40] and 48 and paragraph 7 of Schedule 5 do not extend to Scotland.

(10)   Sections 7, 28[⁴, 40A] and 49 extend only to Scotland.

(11)   With the exception of sections 23 and 56(1), subsections (1) to (3) of this section and Schedules 2 and 4, and (in so far as it amends any enactment extending to Northern Ireland) Schedule 5, this Act does not extend to Northern Ireland.

[¹ (12)   Until Schedule 1 to the Disability Living Allowance and Disability Working Allowance Act 1991 comes into force, paragraph 1(1) of Schedule 3 shall have effect with the omission of the words "and disability appeal tribunals" and the insertion, after "social security appeal tribunals", of the word "and".]

(13)   The consequential amendments set out in Schedule 5 shall have effect.

(14)   In Schedule 1 to the Children Act 1989 (financial provision for children), paragraph 2(6)(b) (which is spent) is hereby repealed..

Amendments

1.   s58(12) has not been commenced. ·

2.   Child Support, Pensions and Social Security Act 2000 (2000 c.19) s1(2) (March 3, 2003 for the types of cases in art 3 Child Support, Pensions and Social Security Act 2000 (Commencement No.12) Order 2003 (SI 2003 No.192)). For other types of cases see the '1993 rules', below.

3.   Child Support, Pensions and Social Security Act 2000 (2000 c.19) s1(2) (March 3, 2003 for the types of cases in art 3 Child Support, Pensions and Social Security Act 2000 (Commencement No.12) Order 2003 (SI 2003 No.192)). For other types of cases see the '1993 rules', below.

4.   Child Support, Pensions and Social Security Act 2000 (2000 c.19) s26 and Sch 3 para 11(21) (March 3, 2003 for the types of cases in art 3 Child Support, Pensions and Social Security Act 2000 (Commencement No.12) Order 2003 (SI 2003 No.192)). For other types of cases see the '1993 rules', below.

1993 rules

Ss1(2) and 26 and sch 3 of the Child Support, Pensions and Social Security Act 2000 (2000 c.19) amend this section of the Child Support Act 1991 and have been brought into force only for the types of cases in art 3 of the Child Support, Pensions and Social Security Act 2000 (Commencement No.12) Order 2003 (SI 2003 No.192 – see p683). For other types of cases the '1993 rules' apply. If the 1993 rules apply, "maintenance assessment" is retained in place of "maintenance calculation", "assessment" is retained in place of "calculation", "40" is not inserted after "35" in subsection (9) and "40A" is not inserted after "28" in subsection (10).

Definitions

"child": see s55.
"maintenance calculation": see s54.
"prescribed": see s54.

General Note

Subsection (12)

It has not been necessary to bring this subsection into force.

SCHEDULE 1

[¹PART I

CALCULATION OF WEEKLY AMOUNT OF CHILD SUPPORT MAINTENANCE

General rule

1.–(1)   [⁷Subject to paragraph 5A,] the weekly rate of child support maintenance is the basic rate unless a reduced rate, a flat rate or the nil rate applies.

(2)   Unless the nil rate applies, the amount payable weekly to a person with care is–

(a)   the applicable rate, if paragraph 6 does not apply; or

(b)   if paragraph 6 does apply, that rate as apportioned between the persons with care in accordance with paragraph 6,

as adjusted, in either case, by applying the rules about shared care in paragraph 7 or 8.

Basic rate

[⁷2. (1)   Subject to sub-paragraph (2), the basic rate is the following percentage of the non-resident parent's gross weekly income–

12% where the non-resident parent has one qualifying child;

16% where the non-resident parent has two qualifying children;

19% where the non-resident parent has three or more qualifying children.

(2)   If the gross weekly income of the non-resident parent exceeds £800, the basic rate is the aggregate of the amount found by applying–

9% where the non-resident parent has one qualifying child;

12% where the non-resident parent has two qualifying children;

15% where the non-resident parent has three or more qualifying children.

(3)   If the non-resident parent also has one or more relevant other children, gross weekly income shall be treated for the purposes of sub-paragraphs (1) and (2) as reduced by the following percentage–

[¹⁰11%] where the non-resident parent has one relevant other child;

10 14%] where the non-resident parent has two relevant other children;

[¹⁰16%] where the non-resident parent has three or more relevant other children.]

Reduced rate

3.–(1)   A reduced rate is payable if–

(a)   neither a flat rate nor the nil rate applies; and

(b)   the non-resident parent's [⁶ gross] weekly income is less than £200 but more than £100.

(2)   The reduced rate payable shall be prescribed in, or determined in accordance with, regulations.

(3)   The regulations may not prescribe, or result in, a rate of less than £5.

Flat rate

4.–(1)   Except in a case falling within sub-paragraph (2), a flat rate of £5 is payable if the nil rate does not apply and–

(a)   the non-resident parent's [⁶ gross] weekly income is £100 or less; or

(b)   he receives any benefit, pension or allowance prescribed for the purposes of this paragraph of this sub-paragraph; or

(c)   he or his partner (if any) receives any benefit prescribed for the purposes of this paragraph of this sub-paragraph.

(2)   A flat rate of a prescribed amount is payable if the nil rate does not apply and–

(a)   the non-resident parent has a partner who is also a non-resident parent;

(b)   the partner is a person with respect to whom a maintenance calculation is in force; and

(c)   the non-resident parent or his partner receives any benefit prescribed under sub-paragraph (1)(c).

(3)   The benefits, pensions and allowances which may be prescribed for the purposes of sub-paragraph (1)(b) include ones paid to the non-resident parent under the law of a place outside the United Kingdom.

Nil rate

5.   The rate payable is nil if the non-resident parent–

(a)   is of a prescribed description; or

(b)   has a [⁶ gross] weekly income of below £5.

[⁶Non-resident parent party to other maintenance arrangement

5A.–(1)   This paragraph applies where–

(a)   the non-resident parent is a party to a qualifying maintenance arrangement with respect to a child of his who is not a qualifying child, and

(b)   the weekly rate of child support maintenance apart from this paragraph would be the basic rate or a reduced rate or calculated following agreement to a variation where the rate would otherwise be a flat rate or the nil rate.

(2)   The weekly rate of child support maintenance is the greater of [¹¹£5] and the amount found as follows.

(3)   First, calculate the amount which would be payable if the non-resident parent's qualifying children also included every child with respect to whom the non-resident parent is a party to a qualifying maintenance arrangement.

(4)   Second, divide the amount so calculated by the number of children taken into account for the purposes of the calculation.

(5)   Third, multiply the amount so found by the number of children who, for purposes other than the calculation under sub-paragraph (3), are qualifying children of the non-resident parent.

(6)   For the purposes of this paragraph, the non-resident parent is a party to a qualifying maintenance arrangement with respect to a child if the non-resident parent is–

(a)   liable to pay maintenance or aliment for the child under a maintenance order, or

(b)   a party to an agreement of a prescribed description which provides for the non-resident parent to make payments for the benefit of the child,
and the child is habitually resident in the United Kingdom.]

Apportionment
6.–(1)   If the non-resident parent has more than one qualifying child and in relation to them there is more than one person with care, the amount of child support maintenance payable is (subject to paragraph 7 or 8) to be determined by apportioning the rate between the persons with care.

(2)   The rate of maintenance liability is to be divided by the number of qualifying children, and shared among the persons with care according to the number of qualifying children in relation to whom each is a person with care.

Shared care – basic and reduced rate
7.–[8(1)   This paragraph applies where the rate of child support maintenance payable is the basic rate or a reduced rate or is determined under paragraph 5A.]

(2)   [7 If the care of a qualifying child is, or is to be, shared] between the non-resident parent and the person with care, so that the non-resident parent from time to time has care of the child overnight, the amount of child support maintenance which he would otherwise have been liable to pay the person with care, as calculated in accordance with the preceding paragraphs of this Part of this Schedule, is to be decreased in accordance with this paragraph.

(3)   First, there is to be a decrease according to the number of such nights which the [3 [4Secretary of State]] determines there to have been, or expects there to be, or both during a prescribed twelve-month period.

(4)   The amount of that decrease for one child is set out in the following Table–

Number of nights	*Fraction to subtract*
52 to 103	One-seventh
104 to 155	Two-sevenths
156 to 174	Three-sevenths
175 or more	One-half

(5)   If the person with care is caring for more than one qualifying child of the non-resident parent, the applicable decrease is the sum of the appropriate fractions in the Table divided by the number of such qualifying children.

(6)   If the applicable fraction is one-half in relation to any qualifying child in the care of the person with care, the total amount payable to the person with care is then to be further decreased by £7 for each such child.

(7)   If the application of the preceding provisions of this paragraph would decrease the weekly amount of child support maintenance (or the aggregate of all such amounts) payable by the non-resident parent to the person with care (or all of them) to less than £5, he is instead liable to pay child support maintenance at the rate of £5 a week, apportioned (if appropriate) in accordance with paragraph 6.

Shared care-flat rate
8.–(1)   This paragraph applies only if–
(a)   the rate of child support maintenance payable is a flat rate; and
(b)   that rate applies because the non-resident parent falls within paragraph 4(1)(b) or (c) or 4(2).
(2)   [9If the care of a qualifying child is, or is to be, shared] as mentioned in paragraph 7(2) for at least 52 nights during a prescribed 12-month period, the amount of child support maintenance payable by the non-resident parent to the person with care of that child is nil.

Regulations about shared care
9. [6(1)]   The Secretary of State may by regulations provide–
[6(za) for how it is to be determined whether the care of a qualifying child is to be shared as mentioned in paragraph 7(2);]
(a)   for which nights are to count for the purposes of shared care under paragraphs 7 and 8, [9...];
(b)   for what counts, or does not count, as "care" for those purposes;
[6(ba) for how it is to be determined how many nights count for those purposes;] and
(c)   for paragraph 7(3) or 8(2) to have effect, in prescribed circumstances, as if the period mentioned there were other than 12 months, and in such circumstances for the Table in paragraph 7(4) (or that Table as modified pursuant to regulations made under paragraph 10A(2)(a)), or the period mentioned in paragraph 8(2), to have effect with prescribed adjustments.
[6(2)   Regulations under sub-paragraph (1)(ba) may include provision enabling the [4Secretary of State] to proceed for a prescribed period on the basis of a prescribed assumption.]

[6 Gross] weekly income
10.–(1)   For the purposes of this Schedule, [6 gross] weekly income is to be determined in such manner as is provided for in regulations.
[6(2)   The regulations may, in particular–

(a)   provide for determination in prescribed circumstances by reference to income of a prescribed description in a prescribed past period;

(b)   provide for the [⁴Secretary of State] to estimate any income or make an assumption as to any fact where, in [⁴Secretary of State's] view, the information at [⁴Secretary of State's] disposal is unreliable or insufficient, or relates to an atypical period in the life of the non-resident parent.]

(3)   Any amount of [⁶ gross] weekly income (calculated as above) over [⁷ £3,000] is to be ignored for the purposes of this Schedule.

Regulations about rates, figures, etc.

10A.–(1)   The Secretary of State may by regulations provide that–

(a)   paragraph 2 is to have effect as if different percentages were substituted for those set out there;

(b)   paragraph [⁵2(2),] 3(1) or (3), 4(1), 5, [⁵5A(2),] 7(7) or 10(3) is to have effect as if different amounts were substituted for those set out there.

(2)   The Secretary of State may by regulations provide that–

(a)   the Table in paragraph 7(4) is to have effect as if different numbers of nights were set out in the first column and different fractions were substituted for those set out in the second column;

(b)   paragraph 7(6) is to have effect as if a different amount were substituted for that mentioned there, or as if the amount were an aggregate amount and not an amount for each qualifying child, or both.

Regulations about income

10B.   The Secretary of State may by regulations provide that, in such circumstances and to such extent as may be prescribed–

(a)   where the [³[⁴Secretary of State]] is satisfied that a person has intentionally deprived himself of a source of income with a view to reducing the amount of his [⁶ gross] weekly income, his [⁶ gross] weekly income shall be taken to include income from that source of an amount estimated by the [³[⁴Secretary of State]];

(b)   a person is to be treated as possessing income which he does not possess;

(c)   income which a person does possess is to be disregarded.

References to various terms

10C.–(1)   References in this Part of this Schedule to "qualifying children" are to those qualifying children with respect to whom the maintenance calculation falls to be made [⁵or with respect to whom a maintenance calculation in respect of the non-resident parent has effect].

(2)   References in this Part of this Schedule to "relevant other children" are to–

(a)   children other than qualifying children in respect of whom the non-resident parent or his partner receives child benefit under Part IX of the Social Security Contributions and Benefits Act 1992; and

(b)   such other description of children as may be prescribed.

(3)   In this Part of this Schedule, a person "receives" a benefit, pension, or allowance for any week if it is paid or due to be paid to him in respect of that week.

(4)   In this Part of this Schedule, a person's "partner" is–

(a)   if they are a couple, the other member of that couple;

(b)   if the person is a husband or wife by virtue of a marriage entered into under a law which permits polygamy, another party to the marriage who is of the opposite sex and is a member of the same household.

[²(5)   In sub-paragraph (4)(a), "couple" means–

(a)   a man and a woman who are married to each other and are members of the same household,

(b)   a man and a woman who are not married to each other but are living together as husband and wife,

(c)   two people of the same sex who are civil partners of each other and are members of the same household, or

(d)   two people of the same sex who are not civil partners of each other but are living together as if they were civil partners.

(6)   For the purposes of this paragraph, two people of the same sex are to be regarded as living together as if they were civil partners if, but only if, they would be regarded as living together as husband and wife were they instead two people of the opposite sex.]]

Amendments

1.   Child Support, Pensions and Social Security Act 2000 (2000 c.19) s1(3) and Sch 1 (March 3, 2003 for the types of cases in art 3 Child Support, Pensions and Social Security Act 2000 (Commencement No.12) Order 2003 (No.192) – see p683). For other types of cases see '1993 rules' below. This amendment replaced Part I of Sch 1.

2.   Civil Partnership Act 2004 (2004 c.33) s254 and Sch 24 para 6 (December 5, 2005).

3.   Child Maintenance and Other Payments Act 2008 (2008 c.6) s13 and Sch 3, para 52 (November 1, 2008); Child Maintenance and Other Payments Act 2008 (Commencement No.4 and Transitional Provision) Order 2008 (SI 2008 No.2675) art 3.

4.   Public Bodies (Child Maintenance and Enforcement Commission: Abolition and Transfer of Functions) Order 2012 (SI 2012 No.2007) art 3(2) and Sch para 62(2) and 95 (August 1, 2012).

5. Child Maintenance and Other Payments Act 2008 (2008 c.6) s57 and Sch 7 para 1(30) and (31) (October 8, 2012).
6. Child Maintenance and Other Payments Act 2008 (2008 c.6) s16 and Sch 4 paras 2, 5(2) and 7 – 9 (December 10, 2012 for the types of cases falling within art 3 of SI 2012 No.3042 only, subject to art 5 of that SI – see p767 and July 29, 2013 for the types of cases falling within art 3 of SI 2013 No.1860, subject to art 5 of that SI – see p770). See also art 6 of SI 2012 No.3042 (which had effect up to and including July 28, 2013) and art 7 of SI 2013 No.1860 for further transitional provisions. For other types of cases see '2003 rules' and '1993 rules' below. Child Maintenance and Other Payments Act 2008 (Commencement No.10 and Transitional Provisions) Order 2012 (SI 2012 No.3042) art 2 and Child Maintenance and Other Payments Act 2008 (Commencement No.11 and Transitional Provisions) Order 2013 (SI 2013 No.1860) art 2. These amendments were also brought into force for the purpose only of making regulations on October 8, 2012 by the Child Maintenance and Other Payments Act 2008 (Commencement No.9) and the Welfare Reform Act 2009 (Commencement No.9) Order 2012 (SI 2012 No.2523) art 2(2)(b).
7. Child Maintenance and Other Payments Act 2008 (2008 c.6) s16 and Sch 4 paras 3, 5(1), 6 and 10 (December 10, 2012 for the types of cases falling within art 3 of SI 2012 No.3042 only, subject to art 5 of that SI – see p767 and July 29, 2013 for the types of cases falling within art 3 of SI 2013 No.1860, subject to art 5 of that SI – see p770). See also art 6 of SI 2012 No.3042 (which had effect up to and including July 28, 2013) and art 7 of SI 2013 No.1860 for further transitional provisions. Child Maintenance and Other Payments Act 2008 (Commencement No.10 and Transitional Provisions) Order 2012 (SI 2012 No.3042) art 2 and Child Maintenance and Other Payments Act 2008 (Commencement No.11 and Transitional Provisions) Order 2013 (SI 2013 No.1860) art 2. For other types of cases see '2003 rules' and '1993 rules' below.
8. Child Maintenance and Other Payments Act 2008 (2008 c.6) s57 and Sch 7 para 1(29) (December 10, 2012 for the types of cases falling within art 3 of SI 2012 No.3042, subject to art 5 of that SI – see p767 and July 29, 2013 for the types of cases falling within art 3 of SI 2013 No.1860, subject to art 5 of that SI – see p770). See also art 6 of SI 2012 No.3042 (which had effect up to and including July 28, 2013) and art 7 of SI 2013 No.1860 for further transitional provisions. Child Maintenance and Other Payments Act 2008 (Commencement No.10 and Transitional Provisions) Order 2012 (SI 2012 No.3042) art 2; Child Maintenance and Other Payments Act 2008 (Commencement No.11 and Transitional Provisions) Order 2013 (SI 2013 No.1860) art 2. For other types of cases see '2003 rules' and '1993 rules' below.
9. Child Maintenance and Other Payments Act 2008 (2008 c.6) s58 and Sch 8 (December 10, 2012 for the types of cases falling within art 3 of SI 2012 No. 3042 only, subject to art 5 of that SI - see p767and July 29, 2013 for the types of cases falling within art 3 of SI 2013 No.1860, subject to art 5 of that SI – see p770). See also art 6 of SI 2012 No.3042 (which had effect up to and including July 28, 2013) and art 7 of SI 2013 No.1860 for further transitional provisions. Child Maintenance and Other Payments Act 2008 (Commencement No.10 and Transitional Provisions) Order 2012 (SI 2012 No.3042) art 2; Child Maintenance and Other Payments Act 2008 (Commencement No.11 and Transitional Provisions) Order 2013 (SI 2013 No.1860) art 2. For other types of cases see '2003 rules' and '1993 rules' below.
10. Child Support Maintenance (Changes to Basic Rate Calculation and Minimum Amount of Liability) Regulations 2012 (SI 2012 No.2678) reg 2 (comes into force in relation to a particular case immediately after the day on which paragraph 3 of Schedule 4 to the Child Maintenance and Other Payments Act 2008 comes into force in relation to that type of case). Paragraph 3 of Schedule 4 to the Child Maintenance and Other Payments Act 2008 came into force for the types of cases falling within art 3 of SI 2012 No.3042 on December 10, 2012 – see pp243 and 767 and for the types of cases falling within art 3 of SI 2013 No.1860 on July 29, 2013 – see p770. For other types of cases see the '2003 rules' and '1993 rules' below.
11. Child Support Maintenance (Changes to Basic Rate Calculation and Minimum Amount of Liability) Regulations 2012 (SI 2012 No.2678) reg 3 (comes into force in relation to a particular case immediately after the day on which paragraph 5 of Schedule 4 to the Child Maintenance and Other Payments Act 2008 comes into force in relation to that type of case). Paragraph 5 of Schedule 4 to the Child Maintenance and Other Payments Act 2008 came into force for the types of cases falling within art 3 of SI 2012 No.3042 on December 10, 2012 – see pp243 and 767 and for the types of cases falling within art 3 of SI 2013 No.1860 on July 29, 2013 – see p770.

2003 rules

Certain amendments to Part I of Schedule 1 made by the Child Maintenance and Other Payments Act 2008 (2008 c.6) are in force only for the types of cases falling within art 3 of the Child Maintenance and Other Payments Act 2008 (Commencement No.10 and Transitional Provisions) Order 2012 (SI 2012 No.3042) and art 3 of the Child Maintenance and Other Payments Act 2008 (Commencement No.11 and Transitional Provisions) Order 2013 (SI 2013 No.1860). For other types of cases, unless the 1993 rules apply, the following wording differs from that reproduced above.

- The word 'gross' in each place it occurs should be read as 'net'.
- In subparagraph 1(1) the words 'Subject to paragraph 5A', are omitted.
- Paragraph 2 is as follows:

"**2.**–(1) The basic rate is the following percentage of the non-resident parent's net weekly income–
15% where he has one qualifying child;
20% where he has two qualifying children;
25% where he has three or more qualifying children.
 (2) If the non-resident parent also has one or more relevant other children, the appropriate percentage referred to in sub-paragraph (1) is to be applied instead to his net weekly income less-
15% where he has one relevant other child;
20% where he has two relevant other children;
25% where he has three or more relevant other children."

- Paragraph 5A is omitted.
- Subparagraph 7(1) is as follows:

"**7.**–(1) This paragraph applies only if the rate of child support maintenance payable is the basic rate or a reduced rate."

- In subparagraphs 7(2) and 8(2) the words "If the care of a qualifying child is, or is to be, shared" should be read as "If the care of a qualifying child is shared"
- In paragraph 9, subparagraphs (1)(za), (ba) and (2) are omitted, "(1)" is removed from the start of the paragraph, and the following wording is inserted in subparagraph 9(a) after "paragraphs 7 and 8,":

"or for how it is to be determined whether a night counts"

- Subparagaph 10(2) is as follows:

"(2) The regulations may, in particular, provide for the [³[⁴Secretary of State]] to estimate any income or make an assumption as to any fact where, in [³[⁴the Secretary of State's]] view, the information at [³[⁴the Secretary of State's]] disposal is unreliable, insufficient, or relates to an atypical period in the life of the non-resident parent."

- In subparagraph 10(3) replace "£3,000" with "£2,000".

1993 rules

s1(3) and Sch 1 of the Child Support, Pensions and Social Security Act 2000 (2000 c.19) substituted Part I of schedule 1 of the Child Support Act 1991. This substitution has been brought into force only for the types of cases in art 3 of the Child Support, Pensions and Social Security Act 2000 (Commencement No.12) Order 2003 (SI 2003 No.192 – see p683). For other types of cases (except those covered by art 3 of SI 2012 No.3042 or art 3 of SI 2013 No.1860) the '1993 rules' apply and the earlier version of Part 1 of Schedule 1, reproduced below, is retained:

PART I
CALCULATION OF CHILD SUPPORT MAINTENANCE
The maintenance requirement

 ***1.**–(1) In this Schedule "the maintenance requirement" means the amount, calculated in accordance with the formula set out in sub-paragraph (2), which is to be taken as the minimum amount necessary for the maintenance of the qualifying child or, where there is more than one qualifying child, all of them.*
 (2) The formula is–

$$MR = AG - CB$$

where–
MR is the amount of the maintenance requirement;
AG is the aggregate of the amounts to be taken into account under sub-paragraph (3); and
CB is the amount payable by way of child benefit (or which would be so payable if the person with care of the qualifying child were an individual) or, where there is more than one qualifying child, the aggregate of the amounts so payable with respect to each of them.
 (3) The amounts to be taken into account for the purpose of calculating AG are–
 (a) such amount or amounts (if any), with respect to each qualifying child, as may be prescribed;
 (b) such amount or amounts (if any), with respect to the person with care of the qualifying child or qualifying children, as may be prescribed; and
 (c) such further amount or amounts (if any) as may be prescribed.
 (4) For the purposes of calculating CB it shall be assumed that child benefit is payable with respect to any qualifying child at the basic rate.
 (5) In sub-paragraph (4) "basic rate" has the meaning for the time being pre-scribed.

___

The general rule
 ***2.**–(1) In order to determine the amount of any maintenance assessment, first calculate–*

$$(A + C) \times P$$

where–
A is the absent parent's assessable income;

C is the assessable income of the other parent, where that parent is the person with care, and otherwise has such value (if any) as may be prescribed; and

P is such number greater than zero but less than 1 as may be prescribed.

(2)   Where the result of the calculation made under sub-paragraph (1) is an amount which is equal to, or less than, the amount of the maintenance requirement for the qualifying child or qualifying children, the amount of maintenance payable by the absent parent for that child or those children shall be an amount equal to–

$$A \times P$$

where A and P have the same values as in the calculation made under sub-paragraph (1)

(3)   Where the result of the calculation made under sub-paragraph (1) is an amount which exceeds the amount of the maintenance requirement for the qualifying child or qualifying children, the amount of maintenance payable by the absent parent for that child or those children shall consist of–

(a)   a basic element calculated in accordance with the provisions of paragraph 3; and

(b)   an additional element calculated in accordance with the provisions of paragraph 4.

The basic element

3.–(1)   The basic element shall be calculated by applying the formula–

$$BE = A \times G \times P$$

where–

BE is the amount of the basic element;

A and P have the same values as in the calculation made under paragraph 2(1); and

G has the value determined under sub-paragraph (2).

(2)   The value of G shall be determined by applying the formula–

$$G = \frac{MR}{(A + C) \times P}$$

where–

MR is the amount of the maintenance requirement for the qualifying child or qualifying children; and

A, C and P have the same values as in the calculation made under paragraph 2(1).

The additional element

4.–(1)   Subject to sub-paragraph (2), the additional element shall be calculated by applying the formula–

$$AE = (1 - G) \times A \times R$$

where–

AE is the amount of the additional element;

A has the same value as in the calculation made under paragraph 2(1);

G has the value determined under paragraph 3(2); and

R is such number greater than zero but less than 1 as may be prescribed.

(2)   Where applying the alternative formula set out in sub-paragraph (3) would result in a lower amount for the additional element, that formula shall be applied in place of the formula set out in sub-paragraph (1).

(3)   The alternative formula is–

$$AE = 2 \times Q \times \left\{ \frac{A}{A + C} \right\}$$

where–

A and C have the same values as in the calculation made under paragraph 2(1);

Z is such number as may be prescribed; and

Q is the aggregate of–

(a)   any amount taken into account by virtue of paragraph 1(3)(a) in calculat-ing the maintenance requirement; and

(b)   any amount which is both taken into account by virtue of paragraph 1(3)(c) in making that calculation and is an amount prescribed for the purposes of this paragraph.

Assessable income

5.–(1)   The assessable income of an absent parent shall be calculated by applying the formula–

$$A = N - E$$

where–

A is the amount of that parent's assessable income;

N is the amount of that parent's net income, calculated or estimated in accordance with regulations made by the Secretary of State for the purposes of this sub-paragraph; and

E is the amount of that parent's exempt income, calculated or estimated in accordance with regulations made by the Secretary of State for those purposes.

(2)   The assessable income of a parent who is a person with care of the qualifying child or children shall be calculated by applying the formula–

$$C = M - F$$

where–

C is the amount of that parent's assessable income;

M is the amount of that parent's net income, calculated or estimated in accordance with regulations made by the Secretary of State for the purposes of this sub-paragraph; and

F is the amount of that parent's exempt income, calculated or estimated in accordance with regulations made by the Secretary of State for those purposes.

(3)   Where the preceding provisions of this paragraph would otherwise result in a person's assessable income being taken to be a negative amount his assessable income shall be taken to be nil.

(4)   Where [⁵universal credit (in such circumstances as may be prescribed),] income support [¹, an income-based jobseeker's allowance][⁴, an income-related employment and support allowance] or any other benefit of a prescribed kind is paid to or in respect of a parent who is an absent parent or a person with care that parent shall, for the purpose of this Schedule, be taken to have no assessable income.

Protected income

6.–(1)   This paragraph applies where–

(a)   one or more maintenance assessments have been made with respect to an absent parent; and

(b)   payment by him of the amount, or the aggregate of the amounts, so assessed would otherwise reduce his disposable income below his protected income level.

(2)   The amount of the assessment, or (as the case may be) of each assessment, shall be adjusted in accordance with such provisions as may be prescribed with a view to securing so far as is reasonably practicable that payment by the absent parent of the amount, or (as the case may be) aggregate of the amounts, so assessed will not reduce his disposable income below his protected income level.

(3)   Regulations made under sub-paragraph (2) shall secure that, where the prescribed minimum amount fixed by regulations made under paragraph 7 applies, no maintenance assessment is adjusted so as to provide for the amount payable by an absent parent in accordance with that assessment to be less than that amount.

(4)   The amount which is to be taken for the purposes of this paragraph as an absent parent's disposable income shall be calculated, or estimated, in accordance with regulations made by the Secretary of State.

(5)   Regulations made under sub-paragraph (4) may, in particular, provide that, in such circumstances and to such extent as may be prescribed–

(a)   income of any child who is living in the same household with the absent parent; and

[³(b)   where the absent parent–

(i)   is living together in the same household with another adult of the opposite sex (regardless of whether or not they are married),

(ii)   is living together in the same household with another adult of the same sex who is his civil partner, or

(iii)   is living together in the same household with another adult of the same sex as if they were civil partners,

income of that other adult,]

is to be treated as the absent parent's income for the purposes of calculating his disposable income.

[³(5A)   For the purposes of this paragraph, two adults of the same sex are to be regarded as living together in the same household as if they were civil partners if, but only if, they would be regarded as living together as husband and wife were they instead two adults of the opposite sex.]

(6)   In this paragraph the "protected income level" of a particular absent parent means an amount of income calculated, by reference to the circumstances of that parent, in accordance with regulations made by the Secretary of State.

The minimum amount of child support maintenance

7.–(1)   The Secretary of State may prescribe a minimum amount for the purpose of this paragraph.

(2)   Where the amount of child support maintenance which would be fixed by a maintenance assessment but for this paragraph is nil, or less than the prescribed minimum amount, the amount to be fixed by the assessment shall be the prescribed minimum amount.

(3)   In any case to which section 43 applies, and in such other cases (if any) as may be prescribed, sub-paragraph (2) shall not apply.

Housing costs

8.   Where regulations under this Schedule require [²the Secretary of State] to take account of the housing costs of any person in calculating, or estimating, his assessable income or disposable income, those regulations may make provision–

(a)   as to the costs which are to be treated as housing costs for the purpose of the regulations;

(b)   for the apportionment of housing costs; and

(c)   for the amount of housing costs to be taken into account for prescribed purposes not to exceed such amount (if any) as may be prescribed by, or determined in accordance with, the regulations.

Regulations about income and capital

9.   The Secretary of State may by regulations provide that, in such circumstances and to such extent as may be prescribed–

(a)   income of a child shall be treated as income of a parent of his;

(b)   where [²the Secretary of State] is satisfied that a person has intentionally deprived himself of a source of income with a view to reducing the amount of his assessable income, his net income shall be taken to include income from that source of an amount estimated by [²the Secretary of State];

(c)   a person is to be treated as possessing capital or income which he does not possess;

(d)   capital or income which a person does possess is to be disregarded;

(e)   income is to be treated as capital;

(f)   capital is to be treated as income.

References to qualifying children

10.   References in this Part of this Schedule to "qualifying children" are to those qualifying children with respect to whom the maintenance assessment falls to be made."

Amendments

1.   *Jobseekers Act 1995 (1995 c.18) Sch 2, para 20(7) (October 7, 1996); Jobseekers Act 1995 (Commencement No.4) Order 1996 (SI 1996 No. 2208) art 2(b).*

2.   *Social Security Act 1998 (1998 c.14) Sch 7 para 48(1) amd (2) (June 1, 1999); Social Security Act 1998 (Commencement No.7 and Consequential and Transitional Provisions) Order 1999 (SI 1999 No.1510) art 2.*

3.   *Civil Partnership Act 2004 (2004 c.33) s254 and Sch 24 paras 4 and 5 (December 5, 2005); Civil Partnership Act 2004 (Commencement No.2) Order 2005 (SI 2005 No.3175) art 2 and sch 1.*

4.   *Welfare Reform Act 2007 (2007 c.5.) s28 and Sch 3 para 7(8) (October 27, 2008); Welfare Reform Act 2007 (Commencement No.6 and Consequential Provisions) Order 2008 (SI 2008 No.787) art 2(4).*

5.   *Welfare Reform Act 2012 (2012 c.5) s31 and Sch 2, para 2 (February 25, 2013 for the purpose of making regulations only; April 29, 2013 for all other purposes); Welfare Reform Act 2012 (Commencement No.8 and Savings and Transitional Provisions) Order 2013 (SI 2013 No.358) art 2 and Sch 1; Welfare Reform Act 2012 (Commencement No. 9 and Transitional and Transitory Provisions and Commencement No.8 and Savings and Transitional Provisions (Amendment)) Order 2013 (SI 2013 No.983) art 3(1)(b).*

PART II
GENERAL PROVISIONS ABOUT [³ MAINTENANCE CALCULATIONS]

Effective date of [⁴calculation]

11.–(1)   A [³maintenance calculation] shall take effect on such date as may be determined in accordance with regulations made by the Secretary of State.

(2)   That date may be earlier than the date on which the [⁴calculation] is made.

Form of [⁴calculation]

12.   Every [³maintenance calculation] shall be made in such form and contain such information as the [⁸ [¹¹Secretary of State]] may direct.

Assessments where amount of child support is nil

13.   [⁵...]

Consolidated applications and [⁴calculations]

[⁹**14.**   The Secretary of State may by regulations provide–

(a)   for two or more applications for maintenance calculations to be treated, in prescribed circumstances, as a single application; and

(b)   for the replacement, in prescribed circumstances, of a maintenance calculation made on the application of one person by a later maintenance calculation made on the application of that or any other person.]

Separate [⁴calculations] for different periods

15.   Where [² the [⁸[¹¹Secretary of State]]] is satisfied that the circumstances of a case require different amounts of child support maintenance to be assessed in respect of different periods, [⁸[¹¹the Secretary of State]] may make separate [³maintenance calculations] each expressed to have effect in relation to a different specified period.

Termination of [⁴ calculations]

16.–(1)   A [³ maintenance calculation] shall cease to have effect–

(a)   on the death of the [⁶ non-resident parent], or of the person with care, with respect to whom it was made;

(b)   on there no longer being any qualifying child with respect to whom it would have effect;

(c)   on the [⁶ non-resident parent] with respect to whom it was made ceasing to be a parent of–

(i)   the qualifying child with respect to whom it was made; or

(ii)   where it was made with respect to more than one qualifying child, all of the qualifying children with respect to whom it was made;

(d)   [5...]
(e)   [5...]
(2)   [5...]
(3)   [5,7,10...]
(4)   [5...]
[1(4A)   [5...]]
(5)   [5...]
(6)   [5...]
(7)   [5...]
(8)   [5...]
(9)   [5...]

(10)   *A person with care with respect to whom a [3maintenance calculation] is in force shall provide the [8[11Secretary of State]] with such information, in such circumstances, as may be prescribed, with a view to assisting the [8[11Secretary of State]] [2...] in determining whether the [4calculation] has ceased to have effect, [5...].*

(11)   *The Secretary of State may by regulations make such supplemental, incidental or transitional provision as he thinks necessary or expedient in consequence of the provisions of this paragraph.*

Amendments

1.   Child Support Act 1995 (1995 c.34) Inserted (22.1.96) by s14(2) and (3) Child Support Act 1995 (c.34).
2.   Social Security Act 1998 (1998 c.14) Sch 7 para 48(3) – (5) and Sch 8 (June 1, 1999).
3.   Child Support, Pensions and Social Security Act 2000 (2000 c.19) s1(2) (March 3, 2003 for the types of cases in art 3 Child Support, Pensions and Social Security Act 2000 (Commencement No.12) Order 2003 (SI 2003 No.192 – see p683). For other types of cases see '1993 rules' below.
4.   Child Support, Pensions and Social Security Act 2000 (2000 c.19) s1(2) (March 3, 2003 for the types of cases in art 3 Child Support, Pensions and Social Security Act 2000 (Commencement No.12) Order 2003 (SI 2003 No.192 – see p683). For other types of cases see '1993 rules' below.
5.   Child Support, Pensions and Social Security Act 2000 (2000 c.19) s26 and Sch 3 para 11(22)(a) – (c) (March 3, 2003 for the types of cases in art 3 Child Support, Pensions and Social Security Act 2000 (Commencement No.12) Order 2003 (SI 2003 No.192 – see p683). For other types of cases see '1993 rules' below.
6.   Child Support, Pensions and Social Security Act 2000 (2000 c.19) s26 and Sch 3 para 11(2) (March 3, 2003 for the types of cases in art 3 Child Support, Pensions and Social Security Act 2000 (Commencement No.12) Order 2003 (SI 2003 No.192 – see p683). For other types of cases see '1993 rules' below.
7.   Child Maintenance and Other Payments Act 2008 (2008 c.6) Sch 7 para 1(34)(b) (July 14, 2008 subject to art 2(4)-(5) Child Maintenance and Other Payments Act 2008 (Commencement) Order 2008 (SI 2008 No.1476 (c.67)). This amendment, which repealed para 16(3) and (4A)(b), did not apply in relation to existing cases as defined in art 2(5) of SI 2008 No.1476.
8.   The Child Maintenance and Other Payments Act 2008 (2008 c.6) s13 and Sch 3, para 52(5) – (7) (November 1, 2008); Child Maintenance and Other Payments Act 2008 (Commencement No.4 and Transitional Provision) Order 2008 (SI 2008 No.2675) art 3.
9.   Child Maintenance and Other Payments Act 2008 (2008 c.6) Sch 7 para 1(32) (June 1, 2009); Child Maintenance and Other Payments Act 2008 (Commencement No.5) Order 2009 (SI 2009 No.1314) art 2(2).
10.   Child Maintenance and Other Payments Act 2008 (2008 c.6) Sch 7 para 1(34)(b) (in so far as not already in force: June 1, 2009; Child Maintenance and Other Payments Act 2008 (Commencement No.5) Order 2009 (SI 2009 No.1314) art 2(2).
11.   Public Bodies (Child Maintenance and Enforcement Commission: Abolition and Transfer of Functions) Order 2012 (SI 2012 No.2007) art 3(2) and Sch para 62(3) (August 1, 2012).

1993 rules
Part II of schedule 1:
Amendments to Part II of schedule 1 to the Child Support Act 1991 contained in ss1(2) and 26, and Sch 3 para 11 of the Child Support, Pensions and Social Security Act 2000 (2000 c.19) have been brought into force (from March 3, 2003) only for the types of cases in art 3 of The Child Support, Pensions and Social Security Act 2000 (Commencement No.12) Order 2003 (SI 2003 No.192 – see p683). The amended version of Part II is shown above. For other types of cases the '1993 rules' apply. If the 1993 rules apply, in each case they occur the words "maintenance calculation" should be read as "maintenance assessment", "calculation" should be read as "assessment" and "non-resident parent" should be read as "absent parent". Also, paragraphs 13, 16(1)(d) and (e), and 16(2)–(9), reproduced below, should not be omitted. In subparagraphs 16(10) the words ", or should be cancelled" should be included at the end of the subparagraph. If the 1993 rules apply, paragraph 13 is as follows:

"Assessments where amount of child support is nil
        13.   [2The [8[11Secretary of State]]] shall not decline to make a maintenance assessment only on the ground that the amount of the assessment is nil."

paragraphs 16(1)(d) and (e) are as follows:

(d)   *where the absent parent and the person with care with respect to whom it was made have been living together for a continuous period of six months;*

(e)   *where a new maintenance assessment is made with respect to any qualifying child with respect to whom the assessment in question was in force immediately before the making of the new assessment."*

and paragraphs 16 (2) – (9) are as follows:

"(2)   A maintenance assessment made in response to an application under section 4 or 7 shall be cancelled by [² the Secretary of State] if the person on whose application the assessment was made asks him to do so.

(3)   [⁷,¹⁰...]

(4)   Where [² the Secretary of State] is satisfied that the person with care with respect to whom a maintenance assessment was made has ceased to be a person with care in relation to the qualifying child, or any of the qualifying children, with respect to whom the assessment was made, he may cancel the assessment with effect from the date on which, in his opinion, the change of circumstances took place.

[¹(4A)   A maintenance assessment may be cancelled by [² the Secretary of State] if he is [² proposing to make a decision under section 16 or 17] and it appears to him–

(a)   that the person with care with respect to whom the maintenance assessment in question was made has failed to provide him with sufficient information to enable him to [² make the decision]; and

(b)   [⁷,¹⁰...]]

(5)   Where–

(a)   at any time a maintenance assessment is in force but [²the Secretary of State] would no longer have jurisdiction to make it if it were to be applied for at that time; and

(b)   the assessment has not been cancelled, or has not ceased to have effect, under or by virtue of any other provision made by or under this Act,

it shall be taken to have continuing effect unless cancelled by [² the Secretary of State] in accordance with such prescribed provision (including provision as to the effective date of cancellation) as the Secretary of State considers it appropriate to make.

(6)   Where both the absent parent and the person with care with respect to whom a maintenance assessment was made request [² the Secretary of State] to cancel the assessment, he may do so if he is satisfied that they are living together.

(7)   Any cancellation of a maintenance assessment under sub-paragraph [¹ (4A),] (5) or (6) shall have effect from such date as may be determined by [² the Secretary of State].

(8)   Where [² the Secretary of State] cancels a maintenance assessment, he shall immediately notify the absent parent and person with care, so far as that is reasonably practicable.

(9)   Any notice under sub-paragraph (8) shall specify the date with effect from which the cancellation took effect."

Definitions

"child": see s55.

"child benefit": see s54.

"income support": see s54.

"maintenance calculation": see s54.

"non-resident parent": see s3(2).

"parent": see s54.

"person with care": see s3(3).

"prescribed": see s54.

"qualifying child": s3(1).

General Note

Paragraph 1

This paragraph makes three provisions.

First, it sets the basic rate as the relevant rate unless the conditions for one of the other rates is satisfied (subpara (1)). All the rates are defined and fixed by reference to the circumstances of the non-resident parent's present family. The circumstances of the person with care's present family are irrelevant.

Second, it provides that, except if the nil rate applies, the weekly amount payable is the applicable amount (subpara (2)).

Third, it determines the order in which that rate is reduced to take account of apportionment (between persons with care to which the non-resident parent is liable) and adjustment (for shared care). The rate is first apportioned and then adjusted (subpara (2)).

Although the paragraph refers to the amount *payable,* it may not be the amount that the non-resident parent actually has to pay. That amount may be greater, to take account of arrears, or less, to take account of an overpayment.

The wording of subpara (1) makes clear that only one of the four rates is payable.

It is not possible for a non-resident parent to be liable at more than one rate. This may appear to create unfairness. For example, a non-resident parent who is in receipt of a prescribed benefit and therefore liable at the flat rate under para 4(1)(b), may have substantial income that would otherwise give rise to liability at the basic rate. The unfairness in this situation is to some extent remedied by the possibility of a variation under reg 19(1) of the Variation Regulations. However, this is not entirely satisfactory, because: (i) the person with care may not know of the other income; (ii) a further application is necessary; and (iii) there are discretionary elements in the variation scheme that are not present in a calculation under this Schedule.

Paragraph 2

It is not necessary to define the basic rate, because it is the one that applies if no other rate is applicable. So, this paragraph only needs to specify the percentage of the non-resident parent's net weekly income that is payable as the basic rate. The percentage varies according to the number of qualifying children (subpara (1)) and the number of other relevant children, as defined by para 10C(2) below (subpara (2)).

Net weekly income is determined under para 10. It is capped at £2,000 by para 10(3). "Qualifying children" is defined in para 10C(I) and "relevant other children" in para 10C(2).

Paragraph 3

This paragraph sets the conditions for, and determines the amount of, the reduced rate. It is defined by two criteria. The first is negative: neither a flat rate nor the nil rate must apply. The second is positive: the non-resident parent's weekly net income must be over £100 but under £200.

The amount of the reduced rate is fixed by regulations (subpara (2)). Regulation 3 of the Maintenance Calculations and Special Cases Regulations is made under the authority of this provision.

The reduced rate payable must be at least £5 (subpara (3)). This ensures that the reduced rate payable is never less than the flat rate of £5 (see para 4(1) below).

Paragraph 4

This paragraph sets the conditions for, and determines the amount of, the flat rate. There are two flat rates. They only apply if the nil rate does not.

Subparagraph (1) provides for a flat rate of £5. This is payable if one of three conditions is satisfied. The first is that the non-resident parent's net weekly income is £100 or less (subpara (1)(a)). The second is that the non-resident parent is receiving a prescribed benefit, pension or allowance (subpara (1)(b)), including non-UK ones (subpara (3)). Regulation 4(1) of the Maintenance Calculations and Special Cases Regulations is made under the authority of this provision. The third is that the non-resident parent or that parent's partner receives a prescribed benefit (subpara (1)(c)). Regulation 4(2) of the Maintenance Calculations and Special Cases Regulations is made under the authority of this provision.

Subparagraph (2) provides for a flat rate of a prescribed amount. The amount is prescribed by reg 4(3) of the Maintenance Calculations and Special Cases Regulations. This is payable if three conditions are satisfied. The first is that the non-resident parent has a partner who is also a non-resident parent (subpara (2)(a)). The second is that a maintenance calculation is in force in respect of the partner (subpara (2)(b)). The third is that the non-resident parent or the partner receives a benefit prescribed for subpara (1)(c) (subpara (c)).

"Receives" is defined in para 10C(3) below and "partner" in para 10C(4) and (5).

Paragraph 5

This paragraph sets the conditions for the nil rate. It applies if one of two conditions is satisfied. The first is that the non-resident parent is of a prescribed description (subpara (a)). Regulation 5 of the Maintenance Calculations and Special Cases Regulations is made under the authority of this provision. The second is that the non-resident parent's net weekly income is less than £5 (subpara (b)).

Paragraph 6

This paragraph deals with the possibility that a non-resident parent is liable to pay child support maintenance to different persons with care for different qualifying children. The child support maintenance payable by the non-resident parent is apportioned between the persons with care according to the number of children.

This paragraph is supplemented by reg 6 of the Maintenance Calculations and Special Cases Regulations.

"Qualifying children" is defined in para 10C(1).

Paragraph 7

This paragraph and para 8 deal with the possibility that the non-resident parent may sometimes have overnight care of the qualifying child. This is called shared care. Shared care is a concept that is separate from, but is linked to, day to day care under the Maintenance Calculations and Special Cases Regulations. Shared care is only relevant to the basic, reduced and flat rates. It is irrelevant to the nil rate, which obviously cannot be further reduced.

Care is shared if the non-resident parent from time to time has care of a qualifying child overnight. Two conditions must be satisfied: see reg 7(1)(a) and (b) of the Maintenance Calculations and Special Cases Regulations. First, the non-resident parent must have care of the child overnight. Care of a child means looking after that child: see reg 7(2) of those Regulations. Second, the child must stay at the same address as the non-resident parent. So, a non-resident parent whose child comes to stay and is looked after by a grandparent does not have care of the child.

The calculation of the number of nights is governed by reg 7(3)-(6) of the Maintenance Calculations and Special Cases Regulations.

The legislation refers to overnight care. This is in distinction to day to day care that is used elsewhere. In practice, there is likely to be no difference between the application of these two concepts. But there is a difference in the nuance of the language. Although day to day care is defined in terms of nights (see reg 1(2) of the Maintenance Calculations and Special Cases Regulations), it carries connotations of care from day to day, emphasising continuity over time appropriate to someone who is a principal carer and, therefore, a person with care under s3(3)(b) of the Act. Overnight care, on the other hand, has connotations of occasional stays away from home. This may convey an accurate picture of some cases of shared care, like those where a child stays with a non-resident parent for one or two nights a week. But it can convey a misleading impression in cases in which the shared care is calculated by averaging over a period if, for example, a non-resident parent has a child for a period of time over a school holiday.

The effect of having shared care varies according to the rate of child support maintenance payable. This paragraph deals with shared care if the non-resident parent is paying the basic rate or a reduced rate. For these rates, the amount of child support maintenance payable by the non-resident parent is reduced. The reduction is determined by the number of nights for which the non-resident parent has the child overnight. Paragraph 8 deals with the flat rate.

The effect on a non-resident parent's liability for child support maintenance, and in particular on the shared care arrangements, is not relevant in deciding a child's contact (*Re B (A Child)* [2006] EWCA Civ 1574).

"Qualifying child" is defined in para 10C(1).

Paragraph 8

This paragraph and para 7 deal with shared care. See the general note to reg 7. This paragraph deals with shared care if the non-resident parent is paying the flat rate. If that rate would otherwise apply, the amount payable is nil.

Paragraph 10

Net weekly income is calculated under the Schedule to the Maintenance Calculations and Special Cases Regulations. It is capped at £2,000 under subpara (3).

Paragraph 10C(2)(b)

Regulations 1(3) and 10 of the Maintenance Calculations and Special Cases Regulations are made under the authority of this provision.

Paragraph 10C(4) and (5)

These definitions reflect those in reg 1(2) Maintenance Calculations and Special Cases Regulations.

Paragraph 15

This paragraph complements and extends reg 2(4) of the Maintenance Calculation and Special Cases Regulations. That provision applies to changes of circumstances that occur before the effective date. This paragraph is not so limited. It applies to changes of circumstances between the effective date and the date of decision and to future changes that can be anticipated. This bypasses the need to apply the revision and supersession rules (*MB v CMEC* [2009] UKUT 29 (AAC)). The result is a series of calculations that are separate but given as a parcel and part of a single process. This paragraph also allows retrospective calculations to bridge a gap when a calculation is not permissible (eg, if the care of the child was temporarily transferred to the other parent), thereby avoiding the need for a new application (*R(CS) 8/08*).

In contrast to reg 2(4) this paragraph is worded permissively, but it has been held that its operation is mandatory, not discretionary (*CCS 2657/1998*, para 9).

The effective date of maintenance calculations made under this paragraph is governed by reg 25(5) of the Maintenance Calculation Procedure Regulations.

Paragraph 16

Where a person with care believes that an assessment has ceased to have effect or should be cancelled, that person is under a duty to notify the Secretary of State of this belief and the reasons for it, and to provide the Secretary of State with such information as s/he reasonably requires to allow a determination to be made as to whether the assessment has ceased to have effect or should be cancelled (reg 6 of the Information, Evidence and Disclosure Regulations).

If the non-resident parent returns to live with the person with care and the qualifying child, the child ceases to be a qualifying child under s3(1) as there is no longer a non-resident parent. The case then falls within subpara (1)(b). See *R(CS) 8/99*, para 16. The commissioner considered the suggestion (set out in the 1997 edition) that in this subparagraph "qualifying child" concentrated on the person's status as a child, but rejected it on the ground that it was not appropriate in the context of the Act as a whole (paras 17-18). The commissioner recognised that the effect of his decision was to leave little or no scope for the (now repealed) subpara (1)(d) (para 16). It was to avoid rendering this provision redundant that it was suggested that "qualifying child" must bear a different meaning in subpara (1)(b).

In *Brough v Law and the CMEC* [2012] AACR 25, the Court of Appeal decided that this provision contemplated a reconciliation that was permanent and not short-term.

This paragraph does not apply retrospectively to cover a period during which separate decisions are appropriate in respect of different periods. Rather, para 15 above should be used to ensure the appropriate outcome (*R(CS) 8/08*).

Paragraph 16(1)(b) and (d)
The authorities on these provisions were reviewed in *SL v CMEC* [2009] UKUT 270 (AAC); [2010] AACR. The judge disagreed with *R(CS) 8/99* and decided (at para 32): 'the correct analysis is that paragraph 16(1)(b) is indeed about there no longer being a qualifying "child", rather than being about the particular child no longer "qualifying".' This decision was approved by the Court of Appeal in *Brough v Law and the CMEC* [2012] AACR 25.

Paragraph 16(10)
Regulation 10 of the Information Regulations is made under this subparagraph.

General Note on Schedule 1 of the original scheme
Overview of Part I
Part I of this Schedule contains the core provisions which deal with the calculation of maintenance assessments. It must be read in conjunction with the Maintenance Assessments and Special Cases Regulations. The calculations which must be made are expressed as formulae; this makes it easy to state the calculation which must be made, but not necessarily easy to understand why the calculation is relevant or what its effect will be. It is helpful to have an overview of the structure and terminology in order better to understand the details. The following paragraphs provide this overview.

There are broadly two types of calculation which have to be made in order to calculate a maintenance assessment. One is based on the actual financial circumstances of the person concerned. The other is based on figures from income support law (supplemented sometimes by an element based on the party's actual financial circumstances). These figures are used for the purpose of the calculation only. It is not necessary that any party should be in receipt of, or entitled to, income support. As the income support figures increase each year in the annual uprating of benefits, so the figures used for child support purposes increase, although they are only be fed into an existing maintenance assessment when it is reviewed.

Child support law is concerned with the financial responsibility of parents for their children (s1). In this context "parent" means the parent in law (s54) and covers natural parents, parents by virtue of adoption and parents by virtue of the operation of the Human Fertility and Embryology Act 1990.

Accordingly, child support law has no relevance where (a) a child has no parents, or (b) the child is living in a single household which includes both parents or the only parent.

In all other cases child support law provides that each parent is responsible for maintaining a child (s1). Parents who are looking after their children must meet all or part of the costs from their income, including benefit income. Parents who are absent must usually pay child support maintenance to the person with care of the child, whether or not that person is also a parent of the child.

The law does not identify the actual cost of maintaining a child. (There is a *maintenance requirement* which may approach the minimum cost, but it is too simple to see that as the actual cost of bringing up a child. See below.) Rather it concentrates on how much an absent parent is required to pay towards maintaining a child.

The extent to which each parent is expected to meet the cost of maintaining a child depends on that parent's available income. "Available income" is not a term that is used in the child support legislation. It is used here to capture the essence of a series of complex calculations which have to be made, but whose overall purpose is to identify the pot of money from which an absent parent is expected to contribute towards a child's maintenance. Where the other parent is also involved in the calculation, the size of the pot will be fixed by taking into account the other parent's available income.

Where both parents are involved in maintaining their child, the respective levels of their income are relevant in fixing the amount of child support maintenance to be paid by the absent parent However, where the person with care is not a parent of the child and the child support calculation only concerns one parent, only that person's available income is taken into account.

The first stage of a maintenance assessment is to calculate the *maintenance requirement*. This is based on income support allowances and premiums minus child benefit payments. It varies according to the following factors:
(a) the number of children concerned;
(b) their ages;
(c) whether the person with care has a partner; *and*
(d) the rate of child benefit payable in respect of each child.

In essence the maintenance requirement consists of the additional amount of income support which would be paid to the person with care on account of the presence of the child in that person's household plus an allowance to reflect the care provided by that person. However, it does not represent even the minimum cost of maintaining a child, as it excludes the additional housing costs attributable to the child's presence in the household as well as the services which are provided free to a person with care who is in receipt of income support.

The maintenance requirement fulfils two functions. First, it provides a yardstick by reference to which the level of child support maintenance is set. Second, given that one of the policies underlying the child support scheme is that parents rather than the State should bear the cost of bringing up their children, it sets as a target the amount of income support attributable to the child's presence and therefore to be recouped from the absent parent.

The second stage of a maintenance assessment is to determine the available income of the absent parent, and also of the person with care if that person is also a parent of the child. This involves a number of separate steps.

(a)   First, the parent's income has to be determined. This consists mostly of the parent's actual income, such as earnings, interest on savings, dividends from shares and so on. However, some income is attributed to the parent and some income is disregarded.

(b)   From this is deducted key work-related costs, such as income tax, national insurance, half of any pension contributions and essential expenses.

(c)   The result is the parent's *net income*. In simple terms this is the money in the parent's pocket.

(d)   The next step is to make allowance for the key living expenses such as food, clothing and housing. This is called the parent's *exempt income*. It is based in part on income support allowances and premiums and in part on the parent's actual expenses, particularly housing (capped if excessive). Allowances are also made in respect of travel to work costs and to compensate for a clean break settlement. Some of the income support premiums are reduced if the parent has a child who lives as part of the household for only part of the week. Some are also reduced if the parent has a partner and a child, and the partner's income exceeds a threshold.

(e)   The exempt income is deducted from the net income to produce the *assessable income*.

The result of the maintenance assessment so far has been to identify the amount of child support maintenance that is prima facie payable. However, this amount may be reduced in order to preserve a minimum level of income available to the absent parent's household. This is the *protected income* calculation. It looks at the effect of the prima facie child support maintenance figure not just on the absent parent's net income, but on the combined net incomes of the absent parent and that parent's current partner (if any). This (combined) total is called the *disposable income*. Part of this income is ring fenced. This ring fence is known as the *protected income level*. If the result of paying the prima facie figure would be to reduce the household's disposable income below this level, the child support maintenance payable is capped to prevent this occurring. The protected income level is a minimum of 70 per cent of the absent parent's net income. It will be more if the alternative calculation produces a higher figure. The alternative calculation is in some respects very similar to that for exempt income. It is based in part on income support allowances and premiums and in part on the actual expenses, particularly housing costs (an allowance is made if the housing costs are treated as nil) and council tax. Allowance is also made in respect of travel to work costs. Some of the income support premiums are reduced if the parent has a child who lives as part of the household for only part of the week. There is included a flat rate amount and an additional percentage of the household's income in excess of the remainder of the calculation, the latter being an incentive to increase the household's income by ensuring that any increase in low income families is not lost pound for pound by an increase in the amount of child support maintenance payable. It is important to distinguish between the exempt income and the income disregarded in determining the net income. The former is a figure largely derived from income support figures, while the latter is actual income from specified sources. They must not be confused, as the net income figure (which excludes disregarded income but not exempt income) is used for another purpose (see below).

Now that the assessable income of the parents has been calculated, it is possible to move to the third stage and calculate the prima facie amount of child support maintenance payable. As a minimum, the parents are expected to put up to one half of their assessable incomes towards meeting the maintenance requirement for their child (para 2). They contribute in proportion to their respective incomes. If their joint assessable incomes exceed the maintenance requirement, a greater contribution to the cost of the child's upbringing is expected. If this is the case, any maintenance payable by an absent parent will be made up of two elements, a *basic element* and an *additional element*. The basic element is a percentage of half of the absent parent's assessable income (para 3). It will either be equal to the maintenance requirement or, if the person with care is a parent who has income as well as the absent parent, it will be the same percentage of the maintenance requirement as the absent parent's income represents of the parents' joint incomes. The additional element reflects the fact that there are extra resources for the parents to devote to the child. It is a percentage of one-quarter of the absent parent's assessable income (or less if there are fewer than three children) and is subject to a ceiling (para 4).

The figure produced by these formulae is not necessarily the amount of child support maintenance that will be paid. The Schedule contains two longs tops which provide a measure of protection for the child and the absent parent. The protection for the child is found in para 7, which provides that in most cases there is a minimum amount of child support maintenance which must be paid, regardless both of the results of the calculations in the third step and of the respective incomes of the absent parent and the person with care. This is known as the *prescribed minimum amount* and is fixed at a percentage of an income support figure. The protection for the absent parent is found in para 6 which provides that as far as possible the amount of child support maintenance payable should not reduce the parent's *disposable income* below the *protected income level*. The calculation of disposable income takes account of the income of the absent parent and of any partner as well as of any children living with them. It is calculated in very much the same way as the net income (hence the importance of distinguishing between disregarded income and exempt income). The protected income level is fixed by reference to income support figures supplemented by some elements of the family's actual financial circumstances. If there is a conflict between these two protections, the protection for the child has priority and the prescribed minimum amount is payable, even if the result is to reduce the absent parent's disposable income below the protected income level.

Although child support maintenance only determines the maintenance payable for the child, its receipt may increase the person with care's family income above the income support applicable amount. If this is the case, the person with care may have only the child support maintenance on which to support the whole family. When the loss of the fringe benefits associated with income support is also taken into account, the result of a child support maintenance assessment may be to reduce the carer family's income, although in the case of a s6 application the burden on the public purse will have been removed.

Special cases

Where the case is a special case within Pt III of the Maintenance Assessments and Special Cases Regulations, the provisions of this Schedule may be modified. Modifications which are relevant to a particular paragraph of this Schedule are noted either in the general note to that paragraph or in the general note to the relevant regulation thereunder. The modifications which are of general application are as follows.

Where both parents of a qualifying child are absent parents and an application is made in relation to them both, separate assessments must be made in respect of each (reg 19(2) (a) of the Maintenance Assessments and Special Cases Regulations).

Where one parent is an absent parent and the other is *treated as* an absent parent under reg 20 of the Maintenance Assessments and Special Cases Regulations, references in this Schedule to a parent who is a person with care should be read as references to the person who is treated as an absent parent under reg 20 (reg 21).

Where two or more persons who do not live in the same household each provide day to day care for the same qualifying child and none of those persons is a parent who is treated as an absent parent under reg 20 of the Maintenance Assessments and Special Cases Regulations, the case is a special one by virtue of reg 24 of those Regulations. The person whose application is being dealt with is entitled to receive the whole of the child support maintenance payable, subject to the Secretary of State's right to apportion the payment in proportion to the provision of care (reg 24(2)). As this is a decision which relates to payment rather than calculation, it is not a matter for a decision maker. Consequently, no appeal lies to a tribunal.

Where a local authority and a person each provide day to day care for a qualifying child, the case is a special case by virtue of reg 25 of the Maintenance Assessments and Special Cases Regulations. If this case applies, the child support maintenance is calculated in accordance with this Schedule. It is then divided by seven in order to find a daily amount. The daily amount is paid for each night in respect of which the person other than the local authority provides day to day care. Maintenance is not payable in respect of any night for which the local authority provides day to day care. See reg 25(2). Special provision is made for the case where more than one child is included in an assessment (reg 25(3)).

Paragraph 1

This paragraph provides for the calculation of the maintenance requirement for a qualifying child. The maintenance requirement is not necessarily the amount of maintenance which will become payable. That figure may be either more or less than the requirement. The significance of the maintenance requirement is that it provides a figure which is the minimum desirable maintenance payment, although it will not always be attained. For the significance of the maintenance requirement in other calculations see para 2(2) and (3). It is also used to fix the amount of a Category A interim maintenance assessment (see the original s12 of the Act and the regulations made thereunder).

The maintenance requirement is the total of certain amounts derived from income support law (AG in the formula) less the amount of child benefit in respect of the child (CB in the formula).

The words "person with care" in para 1(3)(b) include a parent of the qualifying child *(R(CS)* 2/95, para 17).

AG is prescribed by reg 3 of the Maintenance Assessments and Special Cases Regulations. It is the total of the following amounts fixed by reference to the Income Support Schedule. The appropriate amounts are those applicable on the effective date (reg 3(2)).

(a)   The personal allowance for a child of the age of each qualifying child. The age is that of the child on the effective date.

(b)   If the child is aged less than 16 all or part of the personal allowance for a single claimant aged not less than 25. The age of the child is determined at the effective date. Although the personal allowance is that of an adult aged not less than 25, the age of the person with care is irrelevant and will apply even if that person is aged less than 25.

(c)   The family premium.

(d)   If the person with care has no partner, the amount appropriate to a lone parent. This does not apply if both parents are absent parents and the person with care is a body of persons corporate or unincorporate (reg 19 of the Maintenance Assessments and Special Cases Regulations).

The amounts under (b), (c), and (d) need to be modified if the case is a special case by virtue of reg 23 of the Maintenance Assessments and Special Cases Regulations. See the general note to reg 3.

CB is prescribed by reg 4 of the Maintenance Assessments and Special Cases Regulations. It is the rate of child benefit applicable to the child in question at the effective date.

Paragraph 2

The first step in applying this paragraph is to decide whose assessable incomes are to be taken into account for the purpose of this paragraph. If the person with care is not a parent of the child, only the assessable income of the absent parent is taken into account under this paragraph. This is the effect of reg 5(a) of the Maintenance Assessments and Special Cases Regulations. If the person with care is a parent of the child, the joint assessable incomes of the absent parent and the person with care are taken into account. There is a special case if both parents are absent parents. In this case if the application has been made in respect of both absent parents, the joint assessable incomes of both parents are considered (reg 19(2)(b) of the Maintenance Assessments and Special Cases Regulations). However, if there is information about the income of one parent but not about the other's, the maintenance assessment in relation to the first parent is calculated on the basis that the income of the other parent is nil and a fresh assessment is made when the information about the other parent's income becomes available (reg 19(3) and (4)). These special provisions do not apply if the application for a maintenance assessment has been made in respect of only one parent. In this case that parent's assessable income is the only relevant income for the purposes of this paragraph.

The second step is to determine the assessable income of each relevant parent under para 5 of this Schedule. This income is usually applied directly in the formula. However, in two special cases only a proportion is fed into the formula. Since this may be relevant to the calculation under both this and some subsequent paragraphs, the third step is to decide if either of these special cases applies and if so, its effect. The first special case arises where two or more applications for maintenance assessments have been made in respect of the same person who is, or who is treated as, an absent parent but those applications relate to different children (reg 22 of the Maintenance Assessments and Special Cases Regulations). In this case the proportion of the absent parent's assessable income that is taken into account is determined by the formula in reg 22(2). The amount treated as the absent parent's assessable income for this purpose is the same proportion of the total of the absent parent's assessable income and all allowances for qualifying transfers as the maintenance requirement for the application being considered represents of the total of the maintenance requirements for all the applications in question less the value of the qualifying transfer in respect of the assessment in question. The second special case is where the person with care is the person with care of two or more qualifying children and there are different persons who are, or who are treated as, absent parents in relation to at least two of those children (reg 23(4)). In this case, if the person with care is the parent of any of the children, the proportion of the parent with care's assessable income which is taken into account is determined by the formula in reg 22(2). In other words, the amount of assessable income taken into account in this case is the same proportion as the maintenance requirement for the application being considered represents of the total of the maintenance requirements for all the applications made by the person with care.

The amount of the assessable income which is taken into account for the purposes of this paragraph may therefore be 100 per cent or, if one of the special cases applies, less. In either case it will be referred to as "the relevant income." The relevant incomes fixed under this paragraph will also be used in paras 3 and 4.

When the relevant incomes to be used in the formula have been assessed, the fourth step is to multiply those incomes by P. P is prescribed by reg 5(b) of the Maintenance Assessments and Special Cases Regulations. It is 0.5. Thus the result of the calculation will be half of the total of the relevant incomes.

The fifth step is to compare this figure with the maintenance requirement fixed under para 1. If it is equal to or less than the maintenance requirement, the maintenance payable by the absent parent for that child is half of the absent parent's relevant income (para 2(2)). The effect is that the maintenance payable is half of the absent parent's relevant income regardless of the person with care's relevant income. It is the person with care who must bear the consequences of the shortfall. This is all subject to paras 6 and 7 (see below).

If the figure produced by the formula is more than the maintenance requirement, it is necessary to make further calculations in order to decide the maintenance payable. The amount payable will consist of two elements: a basic element and an additional element (para 2(3)). The calculation of the basic element is governed by para 3 and the calculation of the additional element is governed by para 4. The essence of these calculations is that half of the absent parent's relevant income is used in calculating the basic element, up to a quarter is used in calculating the additional element and the remainder is not used at all.

Paragraph 3

This paragraph provides for the fixing of the basic element of maintenance which is payable. It only applies if the calculation under para 2(1) results in a figure which is higher than the maintenance requirement. The relevant formula is set out in para 3(1). At first sight the formula may appear complicated. However its effect is simple. If the person with care is either not a parent of the child or is a parent but has no relevant income, the basic element is equal to the maintenance requirement. In any other case the basic element is the same percentage of the maintenance requirement as the absent parent's relevant income represents of the joint relevant incomes of the parents. It is only in this latter case that it is necessary to work through the formula.

The formula starts with the absent parent's relevant income. It then takes half (ie, the value of P) of this and further reduces it by the value of G. The formula for calculating G is in para 3(2). It is found by dividing the result of the calculation made under para 2(1) (half of the relevant incomes) into the maintenance requirement fixed under para 1 The figure produced when the formula has been applied is equal to that proportion of the maintenance requirement which is equivalent to the absent parent's share of the joint relevant incomes. The effect is that as the absent parent's relevant income rises in relation to the parent with care's relevant income, so the percentage represented by G goes up and the higher the amount of the maintenance requirement which is payable as the basic element. The proportion of the maintenance requirement which the parent with care is expected to bear correspondingly reduces.

With the maintenance requirement covered, the calculation goes on to fix an additional amount. This reflects the fact that the absent parent alone or in conjunction with the parent with care can afford to contribute more than the maintenance requirement towards the child's maintenance.

Paragraph 4

This paragraph provides for two different formulae which may be used for setting the additional element of maintenance which is payable. They only apply if the calculation under para 2(1) results in a figure which is higher than the maintenance requirement. The so-called "alternative formula" in para 4(3) sets the ceiling on the amount of additional element which an absent parent will be expected to pay. The other formula, which is set out in para 4(1), will be used if it produces a lower figure than the alternative formula (para 4(2)).

Subparagraph 4(1)

The formula in para 4(1) fixes a percentage of the absent parent's relevant income

It starts with the absent parent's relevant income. It then takes a percentage (ie, the value of R set by reg 6(1) of the Maintenance Assessments and Special Cases Regulations) of this and further reduces it. The proportion of the absent parent's relevant income which is, subject to the overall ceiling, to form the additional element is found by deducting the figure for G (which was fixed under para 3(2)) from 1.

Subparagraph 4(3)

The alternative formula sets the maximum amount of additional element which will be payable. The formula for the additional element which is used in para 4(1) fixes the additional element as a percentage of the absent parent's relevant income. However, the alternative formula in para 4(3) sets the ceiling on the amount of additional element by reference to figures from income support law, although relevant incomes do have a part to play.

The alternative formula is fixed as follows. Start with the relevant income support personal allowance figures for the children. They were used in the calculation of the maintenance requirement under para 1. Then add to these an amount equal to the income support family premium for *each* child (reg 6(2) (b) of the Maintenance Assessments and Special Cases Regulations). The total is Q. Next multiply this by Z which is 1.5 (reg 6(2)(a) of the Maintenance Assessments and Special Cases Regulations). The final step is only necessary if the person with care is a parent of the child and has relevant income. This step fixes a proportion of the Q X Z calculation. This proportion is equal to the percentage which the absent parent's relevant income presents of the total relevant incomes. It is found by dividing the latter into the former.

Assuming that no special case applies, the overall effect of this calculation is as follows: if the person with care is the other parent of the child, the higher the absent parent's relevant income in relation to the parent with care's relevant income, the higher the percentage of the Q X Z calculation that is taken into account and therefore the higher the maximum amount of additional element payable. If the person with care is not the other parent of the child, the ceiling on the additional amount is simply Q multiplied by 1.5.

Paragraph 5

This paragraph is extended by reg 10A of the Maintenance Assessment and Special Cases Regulations by adding working tax credit to the benefits payment of which results in a parent with care or, to the limited extent allowed by reg 10A(2), an absent parent being treated as having no assessable income.

The assessable income of the absent parent and of any parent with care is determined by reference to regs 7 to 10 of, and Schs 1, 2, 3A and 3B to, the Maintenance Assessments and Special Cases Regulations.

The Court of Appeal decided that the reference in subpara (4) to payment of benefit means actual, not lawful, payment *(Secretary of State for Social Security v Harmon, Carter and Cocks* [1998] 2 FLR 598). A Tribunal of Commissioners was appointed to consider whether this decision is still good law, but the issue was not decided because it was discovered at the last moment that the case involved contribution-based jobseeker's allowance and not income-based jobseeker's allowance *(CCS 2725/2004)*. The issue remains to be determined in an appropriate case. The Court of Appeal for Northern Ireland confirmed *Harmon* in *Department for Social Development v MacGeagh* [2005] NICA 28(1).

Paragraph 6

"Maintenance assessment" refers to any stage of the calculation undertaken with respect of the remaining provisions of para 6 *(Secretary of State for Social Security v Harmon, Carter and Cocks* reported as *R(IS) 1/ 00 per* Hale LJ).

The absent parent's protected income level must be calculated in accordance with reg 11 of the Maintenance Assessments and Special Cases Regulations. It is the total of the following amounts fixed by reference to the Income Support Schedule. The appropriate amounts are those applicable on the effective date (reg 11(5)). The effective date is determined under para 11. In summary the amounts to be added together are as follows. Any income support premiums are only taken into account if the conditions of entitlement would be satisfied.

(i)   Appropriate income support premium for the absent parent according to whether or not there is a partner.

(ii)   Housing costs.

(iii)   The income support lone parent rate of the family premium but only if the conditions are satisfied.

(iv)   The income support disability premium.

(v)   The income support severe disability premium and/or the carer premium.

(vi)   The income support family premium,

(vii)   The relevant income support personal allowances for each child who is a member of the absent parent's family and the disabled child premium for each relevant child.

(viii) Any other income support premium, the conditions for which would be satisfied by the absent parent or his family if that parent were a claimant.

(ix)   Fees payable for living in accommodation provided under the National Assistance Act 1948 or the National Health Service Act 1977 or in a nursing or residential care home.

(x)   Council tax less any council tax benefit.

(xi)   £30.00.

(xii)   Travelling costs.

(xiii) If the total of the income of the absent parent, of any partner of the absent parent and of any child who is a member of the absent parent's family exceeds the total of (i) to (xi) 15 per cent of the excess. For this purpose the income of the absent parent and of any partner is calculated as follows: Take their net income as calculated under reg 7. Add to this the basic rate of child benefit and any maintenance payable in respect of any member of the family. Then deduct any maintenance payments by the absent parent or the partner under a maintenance order where a maintenance assessment could not be made.

Where there are two or more applications for a maintenance assessment in respect of the same person who is, or who is treated as, an absent parent but those applications relate to different qualifying children, the case is a special case by virtue of reg 22 of the Maintenance Assessments and Special Cases Regulations. In this case if the total of the assessments made would reduce the disposable income of that absent parent below the protected income level, the total is reduced by the minimum necessary to prevent this occurring. However, the total must not be reduced below the minimum amount of child support maintenance under para 7. The individual assessments are reduced in the same proportion as they bear to each other (see reg 22(3)).

If there is a person who is treated as an absent parent under reg 20 of the Maintenance Assessments and Special Cases Regulations, the provisions of this paragraph are only applied after the application of the effect of the formula in reg 20(4) has been calculated (reg 20(6)).

Paragraph 7

Minimum amount

In most cases an absent parent will be required to pay a minimum amount of child support maintenance even if the maintenance assessment as calculated under this Schedule would otherwise be lower. The minimum amount is fixed by reg 13 of the Maintenance Assessments and Special Cases Regulations. It is 10 per cent of the income support allowance for a single claimant aged not less than 25. If the figure is not a multiple of 5, it is rounded up to the next higher multiple of 5 pence.

Nil assessment

In some cases the minimum amount does not apply and the child support maintenance is fixed at nil. This is the position in those cases which are special cases by virtue of reg 26 of the Maintenance Assessments and Special Cases Regulations. In order to come within that regulation, the circumstances must be such that the minimum amount fixed under this paragraph would otherwise be payable and one of certain additional factors applies. These factors are in summary:

(i)   the absent parent's income includes one or more of the items listed in Schedule 4 to the Maintenance Assessments and Special Cases Regulations;

(ii)   the absent parent is a member of a family of which at least one member is a child or young person;

(iii)   the absent parent is a child;

(iv)   the absent parent is a prisoner;

(v)   the absent parent's net income is less than the minimum amount of child support maintenance.

Payments in place of child support maintenance

In some cases no child support maintenance is payable, but payments in place of child support maintenance may be deducted from the parent's benefit. This is governed by s43 and reg 28 of, and Sch 5 to, the Maintenance Assessments and Special Cases Regulations. Such payments may have to be made if the following conditions are satisfied in respect of the absent parent:

(i)   the absent parent is taken to have no assessable income by virtue of income support or an income-based jobseeker's allowance being paid to or in respect of that parent;

(ii)   the absent parent is aged 18 or over;

(iii)   the absent parent is not a member of a family containing a child or young person;

(iv)   the absent parent does not have day-to-day care of *any* child;

(v)   the absent parent is not in receipt of any listed income relating to disability.

Special provision

Where there are two or more applications for a maintenance assessment in respect of the same person who is, or who is treated as, an absent parent but those applications relate to different qualifying children, the case is a special case by virtue of reg 22 of the Maintenance Assessments and Special Cases Regulations. In this case the minimum amount of child support maintenance is payable and is apportioned between the individual assessments in the same ratio as the maintenance requirements bear to each other (reg 22(4)).

If there is a person who is treated as an absent parent under reg 20 of the Maintenance Assessments and Special Cases Regulations, the provisions of this paragraph are only applied after the application of the effect of the formula in reg 20(4) has been calculated (reg 20(6)). There is no apportionment of the minimum amount. There is no provision expressly permitting such an apportionment. Moreover, the wording of para 7(2) requires a knowledge of the assessment that would otherwise be made apart from the minimum payment provision, thereby making it clear that the minimum payment provision operates at the end of the calculation after any apportionment has been made.

Paragraph 11

There are some cases in respect of which no provision is made for fixing the effective date.

(i)   There is no general provision for the fixing of the effective date of an assessment made under para 15 of this Schedule, whether on a review under the original s18(10) or otherwise. The provisions relating to changes of circumstances taken into account on reviews under the original s17 or s19 do not apply. There are three possible approaches:

    (a) One approach is to fix the effective date as the day on which the relevant change occurred.

    (b) Another approach is to fix the effective date as the first day of the maintenance period in which the change occurred. This approach is more consistent with the express provisions in the Maintenance Assessment Procedure Regulations.

    (c) The third possibility is to fix the effective date as the first day of the maintenance period following that in which the change occurred. This is in line with reg 9(2) of the Maintenance Assessment Procedure Regulations and reg 32(1)(b) of the Departure Regulations which fixes this date in respect of changes occurring before the date of the current assessment while taking approach (b) in respect of changes after that date.

Either of these last two approaches could be justified under the purposive approach to interpretation of the child support legislation advocated by the commissioner in *CCS 12/1994*. The general approach to follow is that suggested under (b) above *(CCS 1992/1997*, para 59). However, any such general approach must be taken as subject to the following qualifications:

    (a) The legislation may specify a day as the effective date, as in reg 63(5) of the Amendment Regulations 1995.

    (b) The legislation may provide that the effective date may not be before a specified day, as in reg 30A(3) of the Maintenance Assessment Procedure Regulations.

    (c) Where the change of circumstances results from a change in the legislation, it can be argued that it is not permissible to fix an effective date before the commencement date of the legislation as this would be to make the legislation retrospective contrary to express provision.

    (d) Where the legislation specifies that the facts are to be determined on the effective date, it is by definition impossible to fix an earlier date when the facts were different. For example, Sch 1 para 6(3) to the Maintenance Assessments and Special Cases Regulations provides that amount of any benefit payment taken into account shall be that payable on the effective date. Any fresh assessment which involves a change in the amount of a benefit payment cannot, therefore, predate the change. Likewise reg 16 of those Regulations provides that the housing costs shall be those payable at the effective, so that date cannot pre-date the change.

Qualification such as these will apply to any general rule on the fixing of the effective date, so their existence is not an argument against having a general rule or against any particular version of a general rule.

(ii)   There is also no provision permitting the fixing of an effective date later than that which would otherwise be applicable if jurisdiction to make an assessment did not exist until a later date. This may arise, for example, because a parent is still living in the same household as the other parent and the qualifying child at the time of the application and of the issue of the Maintenance Enquiry Form, only leaving at a later date. If the tribunal allows the appeal on this basis, it cannot substitute a later effective date for the assessment. It must hold that the Secretary of State did not have jurisdiction to make the assessment. No assessment is then permissible until a fresh application has been made. These circumstances arose in *CCS14625/1996*, para 10. The child support officer made an assessment on the basis that the father was at all relevant times an absent parent. The commissioner decided that he had only become an absent parent at a later date. The commissioner discharged the assessment that should not have been made, but directed the child support officer to calculate an assessment in respect of the father from the time when he became an absent parent, the effective date being fixed on the basis that the child support officer was making *a fresh* assessment under s18. The commissioner did not examine the arguments for and against treating the assessment to be made as a fresh one. The result achieved has the benefit of avoiding the need for a fresh application for an assessment. *If* this is the solution to this apparent deficiency in the effective date provisions, the decision highlights an anomaly in its operation which can be seen by changing the facts. If the child support officer had correctly declined initially to make an assessment on the basis that the father was not an absent father, the approach taken in this case would not allow an assessment to be made from the date when the parent became an absent parent. In this case a fresh application would have to be made.

(iii)   If the Maintenance Enquiry Form is returned promptly and the assessment is made soon after its receipt, the date of the assessment may be before the effective date determined under reg 30(2)(a)(i) of the Maintenance Assessment Procedure Regulations. If a change of circumstances occurs between the date of the assessment and the effective date, it must be dealt with under an original s17 review. An application for a s17 review can only be made where a maintenance assessment is in force (see the wording of s17(1)). The words "in force" are not defined. If the assessment does not come into force until the effective date, no problem arises since any application made before that date can be treated as made as soon as the assessment comes into force and the effective date of any change will be the first day of the maintenance period in which the application was made (reg 31(3) of the Maintenance Assessment Procedure Regulations), which will be the same as the effective date. However, if an assessment is in force as soon as it is made, any application under s17 which is made before the effective date will not be in a maintenance period and there is no provision under which an effective date for the change may be fixed.

Departure Directions

The effective date of decisions relating to departure directions are governed by Pt VII of the Departure Regulations and, in the case of transitional cases, by regs 48 and 49 of those Regulations.

Paragraph 15

The use of this provision is mandatory and not discretionary *(CCS 2657/1998,* para 9).

At the time an assessment is made it may be certain that changes (eg, a new job, a pay rise, a change in mortgage interest rate, a change in benefit rates) will shortly occur. These may be taken into account under this paragraph. When relying on this provision the decision maker makes a series of separate assessments and not a single stepped assessment (see the wording of the original s19(6) and of reg 8C(4) of the Maintenance Assessment Procedure Regulations as well as the wording of this paragraph).

As by definition the period of at least one of the assessments will have expired before the application for an original s18 review has been made, that assessment will no longer be in force and it does not fall within the wording of s18(2).

However, the scope of that subsection is extended by reg 29 of the Maintenance Assessment Procedure Regulations to cover such cases. If the case does not fall within reg 29, there can be no appeal in respect of that assessment. The original s18(6A) cannot be used to overcome this because it only applies when a review is being conducted. The original s19(1)(c) can be used, but unless this gives rise to an assessment in force an appeal is only possible if reg 29 applies.

A periodical review can be undertaken only in respect of the last assessment in the series which is still in effect and the effective date of that periodical review must be fixed by reference to the effective date of that last assessment and not by reference to the first assessment of the series.

The minimum change provisions which normally constrain reviews on the basis of a change of circumstance do not usually apply to assessments made under Sch 1 para 15. They are expressed to apply to reviews under s17 (regs 20-22 of the Maintenance Assessment Procedure Regulations). They also apply to s19 reviews which are conducted as if an application for a s17 review had been made (reg 23 of those Regulations). They only apply to s18 (and s19) reviews where the review is of the refusal of an application for a s17 review (regs 27 and 28 of those Regulations).

If the series of assessments was made under s18, it is possible to appeal all or only some of them. Usually, the person making the appeal will not be aware of this and will simply appeal the officer's "decision", in which case the appeal will be against all the assessments, but the letter of appeal may be so worded as to identify only one of the series of assessments. If there is an appeal against a series of assessments, the tribunal must (subject to s20(2A)) find an error in every assessment during which a change of circumstances occurred and may not open one assessment in the series on the basis of an error in another of the assessments in the series. The task may be made easier by the possibility that an error in one of the assessments will have a knock-on effect on later assessments in the series, although an error in later assessment can never affect earlier ones in the series.

As to the effective date of an assessment made under this paragraph, see the general note to Sch 1, para 11.

Paragraph 16

Although subpara (1) is worded as having automatic effect, heads (a) to (d) are given effect to by a termination decision under reg 52 of the Maintenance Assessment Procedure Regulations.

If a decision maker acting under the original s18 or a tribunal on appeal makes a fresh assessment, the assessment under review does not cease to have effect nor is it cancelled under this paragraph *(CCS 3/1993,* para 4). However, where a tribunal decides that a maintenance assessment should never have been made, it should direct that the assessment be cancelled despite the lack of any express power to do so *(CCS 7062/1995,* paras 11 and 12). In *CCS 14625/1996* para 1, the commissioner used the word "discharged" rather than "cancelled".

Where a person with care believes that an assessment has ceased to have effect or should be cancelled, that person is under a duty to notify the Secretary of State of this belief and the reasons for it, and to provide the Secretary of State with such information as he reasonably requires to allow a determination to be made as to whether the assessment has ceased to have effect or should be cancelled (reg 6 of the Information, Evidence and Disclosure Regulations).

If the absent parent returns to live with the person with care and the qualifying child, the child ceases to be a qualifying child under s3(1) as there is no longer an absent parent. The case then falls within subpara (1)(b). See *R(CS) 8/99*, para 16. The commissioner considered the suggestion (set out in the 1997 edition) that in this subparagraph "qualifying child" concentrated on the person's status as a child, but rejected it on the ground that it was not appropriate in the context of the Act as a whole (paras 17-18). The commissioner recognised that the effect of his decision was to leave little or no scope for subpara (1)(d) (para 16). It was to avoid rendering this provision redundant that it was suggested that "qualifying child" must bear a different meaning in subpara (1)(b).

The date from which cancellation under subpara (3) takes effect is determined under reg 32 of the Maintenance Assessment Procedure Regulations. Cancellation of assessments when an absent parent, person with care or qualifying child ceases to be habitually resident in the jurisdiction is covered by reg 32A of those Regulations and reg 7 of the Maintenance Arrangements and Jurisdiction Regulations. The date of cancellation varies according to the relevant provision. Cancellation under subparas (2) and (3) takes effect on the day of receipt of the application or such later date as the decision maker determines, whereas cancellation under subpara (4) takes effect on the date of the relevant change, as does cancellation where a person ceases to be habitually resident in the jurisdiction. This reflects the difference that in the former case the Agency's involvement is dependent upon the continuing consent of the applicant for a maintenance assessment and cancellation is not appropriate until that consent is withdrawn, which occurs on the making of the request, while in the latter cases the child support authorities no longer have jurisdiction and the cancellation is merely recognising this fact.

SCHEDULE 2
Provision of Information to Secretary of State

[⁷...]

Amendments

1. Para 1(2) repealed (1.6.99) by Sch 8 Social Security Act 1998 (c.14).
2. Para 1A inserted (11.11.99) by s80 Welfare Reform & Pensions Act 1999.
3. Para 2 shall cease to have effect (8.9.98) by Sch 7 para 49 SS Act 1998 (c.14).
4. Child Support, Pensions and Social Security Act 2000 (2000 c.19) s1(2) (March 3, 2003 for the types of cases in art 3 Child Support, Pensions and Social Security Act 2000 (Commencement No.12) Order 2003 (SI 2003 No.192)). This substituted "calculation" for "assessment".
5. Child Support, Pensions and Social Security Act 2000 (2000 c.19) s26 and Sch 3 para 11(2) (March 3, 2003 for the types of cases in art 3 Child Support, Pensions and Social Security Act 2000 (Commencement No.12) Order 2003 (SI 2003 No.192)). This substituted "non-resident parent" for "absent parent".
6. Commissioners for Revenue and Customs Act 2005 (2005 c.11) s50 and Sch 4 para 42 (April 18, 2005).
7. Child Maintenance and Other Payments Act 2008 (2008 c.6) ss57(1) and 58 and Sch 7 para 1(33) and Sch 8 (November 1, 2008).

Definition

"non-resident parent": see s3(2).

SCHEDULE 3

[...¹]

Amendment

1. Sch 3 repealed (1.6.99) by Sch 8 Social Security Act 1998 (c.14).

SCHEDULE 4
Child Support Commissioners [⁴ for Northern Ireland]

Tenure of office

1.–(1)   Every Child Support Commissioner [⁴ for Northern Ireland] shall vacate his office [¹ on the date on which he reaches the age of 70; but this sub-paragraph is subject to section 26(4) to (6) of the Judicial Pensions and Retirement Act 1993 (power to authorise continuance in office up to the age of 75)].

(2)   [²...]
(3)   [⁴ ...]
[³(3A)   [⁴ ...]
(3B)   [⁴ ...]]

Amendments

1. Substituted (31.3.95) by Judicial Pensions and retirement Act 1993 (c.8), Sch 6 para 23(2)(a).
2. Repealed (31.3.95) by Judicial and Pensions and Retirement Act 1993 (c.8), Sch 6 para 23(2)(b) and Sch 9.
3. Constitutional Reform Act 2005 (2005 c.4) s15 and Sch 4 para 221 (April 3, 2006).
4. Transfer of Tribunal Functions Order 2008 (SI 2008 No.2833) art 9 and Sch 3 para 97 (November 3, 2008, subject to the transitional provisions in Sch 4 of SI 2008 No.2833).

Commissioners' remuneration and their pensions

2.–(1)   The Lord Chancellor may pay, or make such payments towards the provision of such remuneration, [² ...] allowances or gratuities to or in respect of persons appointed as Child Support Commissioners [² for Northern Ireland] as, with the consent of the Treasury, he may determine.

(2)   The Lord Chancellor shall pay to a Child Support Commissioner [² for Northern Ireland] such expenses incurred in connection with his work as such a Commissioner as may be determined by the Treasury.

[¹ (3)   Sub-paragraph (1), so far as relating to pensions, allowances or gratuities, shall not have effect in relation to any person to whom Part I of the Judicial Pensions and Retirement Act 1993 applies, except to the extent provided by or under that Act.]

Amendments
1.   Inserted (31.3.95) by Judicial Pensions and Retirement Act 1993 (c.8), Sch 8 para 21(2).
2.   Transfer of Tribunal Functions Order 2008 (SI 2008 No.2833) art 9 and Sch 3 para 97 (November 3, 2008, subject to the transitional provisions in Sch 4 of SI 2008 No.2833).

[¹ Expenses of other persons
2A.–[³ ...]]

Amendments
1.   Para 2A inserted (18.12.95) by Child Support Act 1995 (c.34), Sch 3 para 18(1).
2.   Social Security Act 1998 (1998 c.14) Sch 7 para 51 (June 1, 1999).
·3.   Transfer of Tribunal Functions Order 2008 (SI 2008 No.2833) art 9 and Sch 3 para 97 (November 3, 2008, subject to the transitional provisions in Sch 4 of SI 2008 No. 2833).

Commissioners barred from legal practice

[¹**3.**   A Child Support Commissioner for Northern Ireland, so long as he holds office as such, shall not practise as a barrister or act for any renumeration to himself as arbitrator or reference or be directly or indirectly concerned in any matters as a conveyancer, notary public or solicitor.]

Amendment
1.   Transfer of Tribunal Functions Order 2008 (SI 2008 No.2833) art 9 and Sch 3 para 97 (November 3, 2008, subject to the transitional provisions in Sch 4 of SI 2008 No.2833).

Deputy child support commissioners

4.–[⁵(1) The Northern Ireland Judicial Appointments Commission may appoint persons to act as Child Support Commissioners for Northern Ireland (but to be known as deputy Child Support Commissioners for Northern Ireland) in order to facilitate the disposal of the business of Child Support Commissioners for Northern Ireland.

(2)   A deputy Child Support Commissioner for Northern Ireland shall be appointed–

(a)   from among persons who are barristers or solicitors of not less than the number of years' standing specified in section 23(2), and

(b)   subject to sub-paragraph (2A), for such period or on such occasions as the Commission determines with the agreement of the justice department (within the meaning of the Justice (Northern Ireland) Act 2002).]

[¹ (2A)   No appointment of a person to be a deputy Child Support Commissioner [³ for Northern Ireland] shall be such as to extend beyond the date on which he reaches the age of 70; but this sub-paragraph is subject to section 26(4) to (6) of the Judicial Pensions and Retirement Act 1993 (power to authorise continuance in office up to the age of 75).]

[³ (3)   Paragraph 2 applies to deputy Child Support Commissioners for Northern Ireland, but paragraph 3 does not apply to them.]

Amendments
1.   Inserted (31.3.95) by Judicial Pensions and Retirement Act 1993 (c.8), Sch 6 para. 23(3).
2.   Tribunals, Courts and Enforcement Act 2007 (2007 c.15) Sch 10 para 22(4) (July 21, 2008 subject to arts 3 and 4 of Tribunals, Courts and Enforcement Act 2007 (Commencement No.5 and Transitional Provisions) Order 2008 (SI 2008 No.1653). For those to whom this does not apply, the amendment substituted "satisfy the judicial-appointment eligibility condition on a 7-year basis" for "have a 10 year general qualification" and "7" for "10" in subpara 4(2)(a).
3.   Transfer of Tribunal Functions Order 2008 (SI 2008 No.2833) art 9 and Sch 3 para 97 (November 3, 2008, subject to the transitional provisions in Sch 4 of SI 2008 No.2833).
4.   Transfer of Tribunal Functions (Lands Tribunal and Miscellaneous Amendments) Order 2009 (SI 2009 No.1307) art 5 and Sch 1 para 226 (June 1, 2009). This amendment does not have effect at any time after the commencement of para 23 of Sch 4 to the Northern Ireland Act 2009 (2009 c.3).
5.   Northern Ireland Act 2009 (2009 c.3) s2 and Sch 4 para 23 (April 12, 2010); Northern Ireland Act 2009 (Commencement No.2) Order 2010 (SI 2010 No.812).

[¹ Determination of questions by other officers
4A.　[² ...]]

Amendments
1.　Para 4A inserted (18.12.95) by s17(1) Child Support Act 1995 (c.34).
2.　Transfer of Tribunal Functions Order 2008 (SI 2008 No.2833) art 9 and Sch 3 para 97 (November 3, 2008, subject to the transitional provisions in Sch 4 of SI 2008 No.2833).

Tribunals of commissioners
5.　[² ...]]

Amendments
1.　Social Security Act 1998 (1998 c.14) Sch 7 para 52(1)-(3) (June 1, 1999).
2.　Transfer of Tribunal Functions Order 2008 (SI 2008 No.2833) art 9 and Sch 3 para 97 (November 3, 2008, subject to the transitional provisions in Sch 4 of SI 2008 No.2833).

Finality of decisions
6.　[² ...]

Amendments
1.　s6(2) substituted (4.3.99) by Social Security Act 1999 (1998 c.14) Sch 7 para 52(4).
2.　Transfer of Tribunal Functions Order 2008 (SI 2008 No.2833) art 9 and Sch 3 para 97 (November 3, 2008, subject to the transitional provisions in Sch 4 of SI 2008 No.2833).

Consultation with Lord Advocate
7.　[³...]

Amendments
1.　Substituted (31.3.95) by Judicial Pensions and Retirement Act 1993 (c.8), Sch 6 para 23(4).
2.　Substituted (18.12.95) by s17(2) of Child Support Act 1995 (c.34).
3.　Transfer of Tribunal Functions Order 2008 (SI 2008 No.2833) art 9 and Sch 3 para 97 (November 3, 2008, subject to the transitional provisions in Sch 4 of SI 2008 No.2833).

Northern Ireland
8. [⁵ ...]

Amendments
1.　Para 8(bb) inserted (18.12.95) by Child Support Act 1995 (c.34), Sch 3 para 18(2).
2.　Substituted (18.12.95) in para 8(e) by s17(3) of Child Support Act 1995 (c.34).
3.　Constitutional Reform Act 2005 (2005 c.4) s15 and Sch 4 para 221 (April 3, 2006).
4.　Tribunals, Courts and Enforcement Act 2007 (2007 c.15) Sch 10 para 22(5) (July 21, 2008 subject to arts 3 and 4 Tribunals, Courts and Enforcement Act 2007 (Commencement No.5 and Transitional Provisions) Order 2008 (SI 2008 No.1653). For those to whom this does not apply, the amendment substituted "7" for "10" in sub-paragraph 8(d)(i).
5.　Transfer of Tribunal Functions Order 2008 (SI 2008 No.2833) art 9 and Sch 3 para 97 (November 3, 2008, subject to the transitional provisions in Sch 4 of SI 2008 No. 2833).

Definition
"general qualification": see s54.

General Note
A person who is on the solicitors' roll but who does not hold a practising certificate is entitled to hold office as a Commissioner (see the reasons given by the Chief Commissioner for refusing leave in *CIS 1344/2004*).

[¹SCHEDULE 4A
APPLICATIONS FOR A VARIATION

Interpretation
1.　In this Schedule, "regulations" means regulations made by the Secretary of State.

Applications for a variation
2.　Regulations may make provision–
(a)　as to the procedure to be followed in considering an application for a variation;

(b)   [⁴ ...]

Completion of preliminary consideration
3.   Regulations may provide for determining when the preliminary consideration of an application for a variation is to be taken to have been completed.

Information
4.   If any information which is required (by regulations under this Act) to be furnished to the [³[⁵Secretary of State]] in connection with an application for a variation has not been furnished within such period as may be prescribed, the [³[⁵Secretary of State]] may nevertheless proceed to consider the application.

Joint consideration of applications for a variation and appeals
5.–[¹ (1)   Regulations may provide for two or more applications for a variation with respect to the same application for a maintenance calculation to be considered together.]
(2)   [² ...]
(3) [⁴ ...]]

Amendments
1.   Child Support, Pensions and Social Security Act 2000 (2000 c.19) s6 and Sch 2 (March 3, 2003 for the types of cases in art 3 Child Support, Pensions and Social Security Act 2000 (Commencement No.12) Order 2003 (SI 2003 No.192)). For other types of cases see the '1993 rules', below.
2.   Child Maintenance and Other Payments Act 2008 (2008 c.6) s58 and Sch 8 (October 27, 2008 subject to art 4 Child Maintenance and Other Payments Act 2008 (Commencement No.3 and Transitional and Savings Provisions) Order 2008 (SI 2008 No.2548)). This omitted para 5(2). Paragraph 5(2) read:

(2)   In sub-paragraph (1), the reference to an application for a maintenance calculation includes an application treated as having been made under section 6.

3.   Child Maintenance and Other Payments Act 2008 (2008 c.6) s13 and Sch 3 para 53 (November 1, 2008); Child Maintenance and Other Payments Act 2008 (Commencement No.4 and Transitional Provision) Order 2008 (SI 2008 No.2675) art 3.
4.   Transfer of Tribunal Functions Order 2008 (SI 2008 No.2833) art 9 and Sch 3 para 99 (November 3, 2008, subject to the transitional provisions in Sch 4 of SI 2008 No.2833).
5.   Public Bodies (Child Maintenance and Enforcement Commission: Abolition and Transfer of Functions) Order 2012 (SI 2012 No.2007) art 3(2) and Sch para 63 (August 1, 2012).

Note
i.   If an application for a variation is made under s28G, para 5(1) of Sch 4A is modified in accordance with Child Support (Variations) (Modification of Statutory Provisions) Regulations 2000 (SI 2000 No.3173) reg 8 (January 31, 2001).

1993 rules
s6 and Sch 2 of the Child Support, Pensions and Social Security Act 2000 (2000 c.19) substitutes sch 4A of the Child Support Act 1991 with the version shown above. This substitution has been brought into force only for the types of cases in art 3 of the Child Support, Pensions and Social Security Act 2000 (Commencement No.12) Order 2003 (SI 2003 No.192 – see p683). For other types of cases the '1993 rules' apply and the earlier version of Sch 4A, reproduced below, is retained.

[¹ SCHEDULE 4A
Departure directions

Interpretation
1.   In this Schedule–
"departure application" means an application for a departure direction;
"regulations" means regulations made by the Secretary of State;
[...²]

Amendments
1.   Schs 4A and 4B inserted by Schs 1 and 2 respectively to Child Support Act 1995 (c.34).
2.   Repealed (1.6.99) by Sch 8 to Social Security Act 1998 (c.14).

Applications for departure directions

2. Regulations may make provision–

(a)   as to the procedure to be followed in considering a departure application;

(b)   [² ...]

(c)   for the giving of a direction by the Secretary of State as to the order in which, in a particular case, [¹a decision on a departure application and a decision under section 16 or 17 are to be made];

(d)   for the reconsideration of a departure application in a case where further information becomes available to the Secretary of State after the application has been determined.

Amendments

1.   Social Security Act 1998 (1998 c.14) Sch 7 para 53(2) (June 1, 1999).

2.   Transfer of Tribunal Functions Order 2008 (SI 2008 No.2833) art 9 and Sch 3 para 98 (November 3, 2008, subject to the transitional provisions contained in Sch 4 of SI 2008 No.2833).

Completion of preliminary consideration

3. Regulations may provide for determining when the preliminary consideration of a departure application is to be taken to have been completed.

Information

4.–(1)   Regulations may make provision for the use for any purpose of this Act of–

(a)   information acquired by the [²Commission] in connection with an application for, or the making of, a departure direction;

(b)   information acquired by [...¹] the [²Commission] in connection with an application for, or the making of, a maintenance assessment.

(2)   If any information which is required (by regulations under this Act) to be furnished to the [²Commission] in connection with a departure application has not been furnished within such period as may be prescribed, the [²Commission] may nevertheless proceed to determine the application.

Amendments

1.   Words repealed (1.6.99) by Sch 8 Social Security Act 1998 (c.14).

2.   Child Maintenance and Other Payments Act 2008 (2008 c.6) s13 and Sch 3 para 53 (November 1, 2008); Child Maintenance and Other Payments Act 2008 (Commencement No.4 and Transitional Provision) Order 2008 (SI 2008 No.2675) art 3.

Anticipation of change of circumstances

5.–(1)   A departure direction may be given so as to provide that if the circumstances of the case change in such manner as may be specified in the direction a fresh maintenance assessment is to be made.

(2)   Where any such provision is made, the departure direction may provide for the basis on which the amount of child support maintenance is to be fixed by the fresh maintenance assessment to differ from the basis on which the amount of child support maintenance was fixed by an earlier maintenance assessment made as a result of the direction.

Reviews and departure directions

6.   [¹ ...]

Amendment

1.   Para 6 repealed (1.6.99) by Sch 8 Social Secuity Act 1998 (c.14).

Subsequent departure directions

7.–(1)   Regulations may make provision with respect to any departure application made with respect to a maintenance assessment which was made as a result of a departure direction.

(2)   The regulations may, in particular, provide for the application to be considered by reference to the maintenance assessment which would have been made had the departure direction not been given.

Joint consideration of departure applications and appeals

8.–(1)   Regulations may provide for two or more departure applications with respect to the same current assessment to be considered together.

(2)   [² ...]

Amendments

1.   Substituted (4.3.99) by Social Security Act 1998 (1998 c.14) Sch7 para 53(5).

2.   Transfer of Tribunal Functions Order 2008 (SI 2008 No.2833) art 9 and Sch 3 para 98 (November 3, 2008, subject to the transitional provisions in Sch 4 of SI 2008 No.2833).

[¹Appeal tribunals]
   9.   [²...]

Amendments
1.   Social Security Act 1998 (1998 c.14) Sch 7 para 53(6) (June 1, 1999).
2.   Transfer of Tribunal Functions Order 2008 (SI 2008 No.2833) art 9 and Sch 3 para 98 (November 3, 2008, subject to the transitional provisions in sch 4 of SI 2008 No.2833).

Current assessments which are replaced by fresh assessments
   10.   Regulations may make provision as to the circumstances in which prescribed references in this Act to a current assessment are to have effect as if they were references to any later maintenance assessment made with respect to the same persons as the current assessment.

Definitions
"appeal tribunal": see s54.
"application for a variation": see s54
"maintenance calculation": see s54.

General Note
If an application is made under s28G(1), this Schedule applies as modified by reg 8(1) Child Support (Variations) (Modification of Statutory Provisions) Regulations 2000.

[¹ SCHEDULE 4B
PART I
THE CASES

General
   1.–(1)   The cases in which a variation may be agreed are those set out in this Part of this Schedule or in regulations made under this Part.
   (2)   In this Schedule "applicant" means the person whose application for a variation is being considered.

Special expenses
   [²**2.**–(1)   A variation applied for by a non-resident parent may be agreed with respect to his special expenses.
   (2)   In this paragraph "special expenses" means the whole, or any amount above a prescribed amount, or any prescribed part, of expenses which fall within a prescribed description of expenses.
   (3)   In prescribing descriptions of expenses for the purposes of this paragraph, the Secretary of State may, in particular, make provision with respect to–
   (a)   costs incurred by a non-resident parent in maintaining contact with the child, or with any of the children, with respect to whom the application for a maintenance calculation has been made [²...];
   (b)   costs attributable to a long-term illness or disability of a relevant other child (within the meaning of paragraph 10C(2) of Schedule 1);
   (c)   debts of a prescribed description incurred, before the non-resident parent became a non-resident parent in relation to a child with respect to whom the maintenance calculation has been applied for [²...]–
      (i)   for the joint benefit of both parents;
      (ii)   for the benefit of any such child; or
      (iii)   for the benefit of any other child falling within a prescribed category;
   (d)   boarding school fees for a child in relation to whom the application for a maintenance calculation has been made [²...];
   (e)   the cost to the non-resident parent of making payments in relation to a mortgage on the home he and the person with care shared, if he no longer has an interest in it, and she and a child in relation to whom the application for a maintenance calculation has been made [²...] still live there.
   (4)   For the purposes of sub-paragraph (3)(b)–
   (a)   "disability" and "illness" have such meaning as may be prescribed; and
   (b)   the question whether an illness or disability is long-term shall be determined in accordance with regulations made by the Secretary of State.
   (5)   For the purposes of sub-paragraph (3)(d), the Secretary of State may prescribe–
   (a)   the meaning of "boarding school fees"; and
   (b)   components of such fees (whether or not itemised as such) which are, or are not, to be taken into account,
and may provide for estimating any such component.

Property or capital transfers
   3.–(1)   A variation may be agreed in the circumstances set out in sub-paragraph (2) if before 5th April 1993–

(a)   a court order of a prescribed kind was in force with respect to the non-resident parent and either the person with care with respect to the application for the maintenance calculation or the child, or any of the children, with respect to whom that application was made; or

(b)   an agreement of a prescribed kind between the non-resident parent and any of those persons was in force.

(2)   The circumstances are that in consequence of one or more transfers of property of a prescribed kind and exceeding (singly or in aggregate) a prescribed minimum value–

(a)   the amount payable by the non-resident parent by way of maintenance was less than would have been the case had that transfer or those transfers not been made; or

(b)   no amount was payable by the non-resident parent by way of maintenance.

(3)   For the purposes of sub-paragraph (2), "maintenance" means periodical payments of maintenance made (otherwise than under this Act) with respect to the child, or any of the children, with respect to whom the application for a maintenance calculation has been made.]

Additional cases

4.–(1)   The Secretary of State may by regulations prescribe other cases in which a variation may be agreed.

(2)   Regulations under this paragraph may, for example, make provision with respect to cases where–

(a)   the non-resident parent has assets which exceed a prescribed value;

(b)   a person's lifestyle is inconsistent with his income for the purposes of a calculation made under Part I of Schedule 1;

(c)   a person has income which is not taken into account in such a calculation;

(d)   a person has unreasonably reduced the income which is taken into account in such a calculation.

PART II
REGULATORY CONTROLS

5.–(1)   The Secretary of State may by regulations make provision with respect to the variations from the usual rules for calculating maintenance which may be allowed when a variation is agreed.

(2)   No variations may be made other than those which are permitted by the regulations.

(3)   Regulations under this paragraph may, in particular, make provision for a variation to result in–

(a)   a person's being treated as having more, or less, income than would be taken into account without the variation in a calculation under Part I of Schedule 1;

(b)   a person's being treated as liable to pay a higher, or a lower, amount of child support maintenance than would result without the variation from a calculation under that Part.

(4)   Regulations may provide for the amount of any special expenses to be taken into account in a case falling within paragraph 2, for the purposes of a variation, not to exceed such amount as may be prescribed or as may be determined in accordance with the regulations.

(5)   Any regulations under this paragraph may in particular make different provision with respect to different levels of income.

6.   The Secretary of State may by regulations provide for the application, in connection with child support maintenance payable following a variation, of paragraph 7(2) to (7) of Schedule 1 (subject to any prescribed modifications).]

Amendments

1.   Child Support, Pensions and Social Security Act 2000 (2000 c.19) s6 and Sch 2 (March 3, 2003 for the types of cases in art 3 Child Support, Pensions and Social Security Act 2000 (Commencement No.12) Order 2003 (SI 2003 No.192)). For other types of cases see the '1993 rules', below.

2.   Child Maintenance and Other Payments Act 2008 (2008 c.6) s58 and Sch 8 (October 27, 2008 subject to art 4 Child Maintenance and Other Payments Act 2008 (Commencement No.3 and Transitional and Savings Provisions) Order 2008 (SI 2008 No.2548)). This omitted "(or treated as made)" from paras 2(3)(a), (d) and (e) and "(or treated as having been applied for)" from para 2(3)(c).

Note

i.   If an application for a variation is made under s28G, paras 2 and 3 of Sch 4B are modified in accordance with Child Support (Variations) (Modification of Statutory Provisions) Regulations 2000 (SI 2000 No.3173) reg 8 (January 31, 2001).

1993 rules

s6 and Sch 2 of the Child Support, Pensions and Social Security Act 2000 (2000 c.19) substitutes Sch 4B of The Child Support Act 1991 with the version shown above. This substitution has been brought into force only for the types of cases in art 3 of the Child Support, Pensions and Social Security Act 2000 (Commencement No.12) Order 2003 (SI 2003 No.192 – see p683). For other types of cases the '1993 rules' apply and the earlier version of Sch 4B, reproduced below, is retained.

SCHEDULE 4B
Departure directions: the cases and controls
PART I
THE CASES

General
1.–(1)   The cases in which a departure direction may be given are those set out in this Part of this Schedule or in regulations made under this Part.

(2)   In this Schedule "applicant" means the person whose application for a departure direction is being considered.

Special expenses
2.–(1)   A departure direction may be given with respect to special expenses of the applicant which were not, and could not have been, taken into account in determining the current assessment in accordance with the provisions of, or made under, Part I of Schedule 1.

(2)   In this paragraph "special expenses" means the whole, or any prescribed part, of expenses which fall within a prescribed description of expenses.

(3)   In prescribing descriptions of expenses for the purposes of this paragraph, the Secretary of State may, in particular, make provision with respect to–
(a)   costs incurred in travelling to work;
(b)   costs incurred by an absent parent in maintaining contact with the child, or with any of the children, with respect to whom he is liable to pay child support maintenance under the current assessment;
(c)   costs attributable to a long-term illness or disability of the applicant or of a dependant of the applicant;
(d)   debts incurred, before the absent parent became an absent parent in relation to a child with respect to whom the current assessment was made–
    (i)   for the joint benefit of both parents;
    (ii)   for the benefit of any child with respect to whom the current assessment was made; or
    (iii)   for the benefit of any other child falling within a prescribed category;
(e)   pre-1993 financial commitments from which it is impossible for the parent concerned to withdraw or from which it would be unreasonable to expect that parent to have to withdraw;
(f)   costs incurred by a parent in supporting a child who is not his child but who is part of his family.
(4)   For the purposes of sub-paragraph (3)(c)–
(a)   the question whether one person is a dependent of another shall be determined in accordance with regulations made by the Secretary of State;
(b)   disability" and "illness" have such meaning as may be prescribed; and
(c)   the question whether an illness or disability is long-term shall be determined in accordance with regulations made by the Secretary of State.

(5)   For the purposes of sub-paragraph (3)(e), "pre-1993 financial commitments" means financial commitments of a prescribed kind entered into before 5th April 1993 in any case where-
(a)   a court order of a prescribed kind was in force with respect to the absent parent and the person with care concerned at the time when they were entered into; or
(b)   an agreement between them of a prescribed kind was in force at that time.
(6)   For the purposes of sub-paragraph (3)(fJ, a child who is not the child of a particular person is a part of that person's family in such circumstances as may be prescribed.

Property or capital transfers
3.–(1)   A departure direction may be given if–
(a)   before 5th April 1993–
    (i)   a court order of a prescribed kind was in force with respect to the absent parent and either the person with care with respect to whom the current assessment was made or the child, or any of the children, with respect to whom that assessment was made; or
    (ii)   an agreement of a prescribed kind between the absent parent and any of those persons was in force;
(b)   in consequence of one or more transfers of property of a prescribed kind
    (i)   the amount payable by the absent parent by way of maintenance was less than would have been the case had that transfer or those transfers not been made; or
    (ii)   no amount was payable by the absent parent by way of maintenance; and
(c)   the effect of that transfer, or those transfers, is not properly reflected in the current assessment;
(2)   For the purposes of sub-paragraph (1)(b), "maintenance" means periodical payments of maintenance made (otherwise than under this Act) with respect to the child, or any of the children, with respect to whom the current assessment was made.

(3)   For the purposes of sub-paragraph (1)(c), the question whether the effect of one or more transfers of property is properly reflected in the current assessment shall be determined in accordance with regulations made by the Secretary of State.

4.–(1)   A departure direction may be given if–

(a)   before 5th April 1993–

    (i)   a court order of a prescribed kind was in force with respect to the absent parent and either the person with care with respect to whom the current assessment was made or the child, or any of the children, with respect to whom that assessment was made, or

    (ii)   an agreement of a prescribed kind between the absent parent and any of those persons was in force;

(b)   in pursuance of the court order or agreement, the absent parent has made one or more transfers of property of a prescribed kind;

(c)   the amount payable by the absent parent by way of maintenance was not reduced as a result of that transfer or those transfers;

(d)   the amount payable by the absent parent by way of child support maintenance under the current assessment has been reduced as a result of that transfer or those transfers, in accordance with provisions of or made under this Act; and

(e)   it is nevertheless inappropriate, having regard to the purposes for which the transfer or transfers was or were made, for that reduction to have been made.

(2)   For the purposes of sub-paragraph (1)(c), "maintenance" means periodical payments of maintenance made (otherwise than under this Act) with respect to the child, or any of the children, with respect to whom the current assessment was made.

Additional cases

5.–(1)   The Secretary of State may by regulations prescribe other cases in which a departure direction may be given.

(2)   Regulations under this paragraph may, for example, make provision with respect to cases where–

(a)   assets which do not produce income are capable of producing income;

(b)   a person's life-style is inconsistent with the level of his income;

(c)   housing costs are unreasonably high;

(d)   housing costs are in part attributable to housing persons whose circumstances are such as to justify disregarding a part of those costs;

(e)   travel costs are unreasonably high; or

(f)   travel costs should be disregarded.

PART II
REGULATORY CONTROLS

6.–(1)   The Secretary of State may by regulations make provision with respect to the directions which may be given in a departure direction.

(2)   No directions may be given other than those which are permitted by the regulations.

(3)   Regulations under this paragraph may, in particular, make provision for a departure direction to require–

(a)   the substitution, for any formula set out in Part I of Schedule 1, of such other formula as may be prescribed;

(b)   any prescribed amount by reference to which any calculation is to be made in fixing the amount of child support maintenance to be increased or reduced in accordance with the regulations;

(c)   the substitution, for any provision in accordance with which any such calculation is to be made, of such other provision as may be prescribed.

(4)   Regulations may limit the extent to which the amount of the child support maintenance fixed by a maintenance assessment made as a result of a departure direction may differ from the amount of the child support maintenance which would be fixed by a maintenance assessment made otherwise than as a result of the direction.

(5)   Regulations may provide for the amount of any special expenses to be taken into account in a case falling within paragraph 2, for the purposes of a departure direction, not to exceed such amount as may be prescribed or as may be determined in accordance with the regulations.

(6)   No departure direction may be given so as to have the effect of denying to an absent parent the protection of paragraph 6 of Schedule 1.

(7)   Sub-paragraph (6) does not prevent the modification of the provisions of, or made under, paragraph 6 of Schedule 1 to the extent permitted by regulations under this paragraph.

(8)   Any regulations under this paragraph may make different provision with respect to different levels of income.

Definitions

"child": see s55.
"child support maintenance": see s54.
"maintenance calculation": see s54.
"non-resident parent": see s54.
"parent": see s54.
"person with care": see s54.
"prescribed": see s54.

General Note

If an application is made under s28G(1), this Schedule applies as modified by reg 8(2)-(5) Child Support (Variations) (Modification of Statutory Provisions) Regulations 2000.

Paragraph 2

These grounds are prescribed in regs 10–14 to of the Variation Regulations.

Paragraph 3

In essence, this paragraph allows for a variation to reflect the effect of property transfers made under a court order or written agreement that was made before the child support scheme came into force and had the consequence that the amount of maintenance payable for the qualifying child was less than it would otherwise have been. The effect of satisfying the conditions in this paragraph is governed by reg 17 of the Variation Regulations.

Subparagraph (1)

The kinds of court orders and agreements are prescribed by reg 16(1) of the Variation Regulations.

Subparagraph (2)

The kind of transfer of property is prescribed by reg 16(2)-(3) of the Variation Regulations and the minimum value is prescribed by reg 16(4) of those Regulations.

On the strict wording of subpara (2), the transfer need not have been made under the court order or agreement, although that will usually have been the case (*R(CS) 4/00*, para 18). In the rare case where it was not so made, there must still have been a link between the transfer and the amount of maintenance. Evidence will be needed to show the link – eg, in the recitals.

It may be difficult to show that maintenance was reduced in consequence of the transfer, especially in view of the variation in practice between courts and the evidentiary problems of producing evidence often many years after the event. The issue is the effect of a transfer in the circumstances of a particular case. In practice, it will have to be determined on the probabilities having regard to the state of the law and common practice at the time.

In *R(CS) 4/00*, the commissioner dealt with a case in which the transfer of property and the maintenance in respect of the children were dealt with by court orders.

(i)   ***Admissible evidence and considerations (paras 19-23).*** The commissioner held that the following were admissible. First, the terms of the court order must be considered, although it was unlikely that the effect of a transfer of property on maintenance payments would be spelt out. Second, any contemporaneous documents relevant to the making of the court order must be considered. (a) Correspondence between the parties or their legal advisers was relevant, although this had to be treated with caution, as it would be partisan and represent negotiating positions or posturing. (b) The documents filed in the court or created by a party's advisers for their own use were relevant and likely to be less partisan, but could not be treated as an entirely reliable basis for determining the effect of a transfer. (c) The best information would come from the terms of any judgment that was given to explain why the judge made the order. This is only likely to be available in the form of a note of the judgment taken by counsel or a solicitor. Third, the legal context in which the court order was made for (a) the transfer of the property and (b) the maintenance of the children must be considered. This includes (i) the range of orders that may be made, including an order for the capitalised payment of maintenance and (ii) the factors to which a judge must have regard when making particular orders. Specifically relevant to maintenance orders for children is ss25(1), (2) and (3) of the Matrimonial Causes Act 1973. Fourth, oral evidence given to the tribunal or the Commissioner by the parties must be considered, although this evidence was likely to be oflimited value, as it might be partisan and reflect a party's misunderstanding or later rationalisation of what happened and why.

(ii)   ***The causal link (paras 23, 26 and 27).*** Except in the case of capitalised maintenance payment, there will not be a direct link between a transfer of capital or property and the amount of maintenance payable in respect of children. The causal link must be established in terms of the factors that a judge must take into account when making an order for maintenance. The link will be an indirect one. For example, a father who transfers his share in the family home to a mother will have a smaller deposit for a suitable home for himself than if some of the capital had been released to him. This will lead to higher mortgage payments, which will reduce the amount available for the payment of maintenance.

(iii)   ***The proximity of the link (paras 30 and 38).*** The transfer and the maintenance order need not be contemporaneous in order to establish a causal link. A maintenance order may be affected by a transfer that has not taken place, provided that it was in contemplation of the court when the maintenance order was made. Likewise, a maintenance order may be affected by a transfer that occurred some time before; the passage of time is not alone sufficient to break the causal link.

Subparagraph (3)

This subparagraph does not define "maintenance". Instead, it limits its scope to maintenance that is provided by way of periodical payments and to a child with respect to whom an application for a maintenance calculation has been made.

A periodical payment is essential. The transfer of one parent's interest in the former family home to the other parent in order to provide a stable base for the upbringing and education of the couple's children does not constitute maintenance within this defmition (*R(CS) 4/00*, para 16).

Maintenance is defined in reg 17(4) of the Variation Regulations as "the normal day-to-day living expenses of the qualifying child". This overcomes the apparent flaw in subpara (3) which refers not to the qualifying child but to any child with respect to whom an application is made.

Paragraph 4

These grounds are prescribed in regs 18-20 to of the Variation Regulations (see p630).

Paragraph 5: Subparagraph (1)

The Variation Regulations contain the cases.

Subparagraph (2)

The cases listed in the Variation Regulations are exhaustive of the variations that the Secretary of State may agree to. There is no residual power to agree to others. This is surely obvious and, anyway, repeats para 1(1). Schedule 4C was repealed by s85 of, and Sch 9 to, the 2000 Act. Article 3 of, and the Schedule to, the Commencement No.12 Order 2003 provided that it ceased to have effect from 3 March 2003 for the purposes of the cases there specified.

Child Support Act 1995
(1995 c34)

Miscellaneous

Deferral of right to apply for maintenance assessment

18.–(1)-(4)   *[Omitted]*

(5)   [¹...]

(6)   Neither section 4(10) nor section 7(10) of the 1991 Act shall apply in relation to a maintenance order made in the circumstances mentioned in sub- section (7) or (8) of section 8 of the 1991 Act.

(7)   The Secretary of State may by regulations make provision for section 4(10), or section 7(10), of the 1991 Act not to apply in relation to such other cases as may be prescribed.

(8)   Part I of the Schedule to the Child Support Act 1991 (Commencement No.3 and Transitional Provisions) Order 1992 (phased take-on of certain cases) is hereby revoked.

(9)   At any time before 7th April 1997, neither section 8(3), nor section 9(5)(b), of t he 1991 Act shall apply in relation to any case which fell within paragraph 5(2) of the Schedule to the 1992 order (pending cases during the transitional period set by that order).

Amendment

1.   Child Support, Pensions and Social Security Act 2000 (2000 c19) ss26 and 85 and Schs 3 para 13(2) and 9 Part I, (March 3, 2003 for the types of cases detailed in art 3 Child Support, Pensions and Social Security Act 2000 (Commencement No.12) Order 2003 (SI 2003 No.192) see p683) . For other types of cases see the '1993 rules' below.

Commencement

September 4, 1995.

1993 rules

Ss26 and 85 and Schs 3 and 9 of the Child Support, Pensions and Social Security Act 2000 (2000 c.19) amend this section of the Child Support Act 1995 and have been brought into force only for the types of cases in art 3 of the Child Support, Pensions and Social Security Act 2000 (Commencement No.12) Order 2003 (SI 2003 No.192 – see p683). For other types of cases the 1993 rules apply and subsection 18(5) still has effect. It reads:

(5)   The Secretary of State may by order repeal any of the provisions of this section.

Definition

"the 1991 Act": see s27(1).

General Note

This section must be read in conjunction with ss4(10) and (11), 7(10), 8(3A), 9(3) and (6) and 11(1A)-(1C) of the Act and reg 9 of the Maintenance Arrangements and Jurisdiction Regulations.

Subsection (8) of this section revokes Pt I of the Schedule to the Transitional Provisions Order which dealt with the phased take on of cases into the child support scheme, but re-enacts most of those provisions, although omitting the phasing element. The equivalent provisions are as follows.

Applications under s4 of the Act

A non-resident parent or a person with care may apply for a maintenance calculation under s4 of the Act except where either of the following two cases applies.

1. There is in force (see p175 for the meaning of "in force" in this context) in respect of every child covered by the application one of the following.

(a) A written maintenance agreement made before 5 April 1993 (when the child support scheme came into force) (s4(10)(a) – see below for a discussion of written maintenance agreement).

(b) A maintenance order (s4(10)(a) and (aa)), either made before a prescribed date or on or after that date but in force for less than one year, except:

    (i) one dealing with educational needs or disability (subs (6) of this section – the existence of such orders is not incompatible with a child support maintenance assessment as they have always been preserved for the courts' jurisdiction under s8(7) and (8) of the Act); *or*

    (ii) one made after 22 January 1996, where the court has decided that it either has no power to vary the maintenance order or that it has no power to enforce it (reg 9 of the Maintenance Arrangements and Jurisdiction Regulations – this prevents parties being excluded from both the courts and the child support scheme).

    Accordingly, when these limitations are taken into account alongside the limitations on the powers of the parties and the courts under ss8 and 9, the overall effect is in essence that private client applications may not be made where there were in force at the inception of the child support maintenance scheme maintenance arrangements under a written agreement or court order.

2. The person with care is a parent of the child and a benefit which would trigger the operation of s6 of the Act is in payment to or in respect of that parent (s4(10)(b) and (11)). This ensures that the operation of s4 and s6 is mutually exclusive.

Applications under s7 of the Act

In Scotland a qualifying child may apply for a maintenance calculation under s7 of the Act unless there is in force (see p175 for the meaning of "in force" in this context) in respect of that child either:

(a) a written maintenance agreement made before 5 April 1993 (when the child support scheme came into force) (s7(10) – see below for a discussion of written maintenance agreement); *or*

(b) a maintenance order (ss7(10)(a) and (b)), either made before a prescribed date or on or after that date but in force for less than one year, except:

    (i) one dealing with educational needs or disability (subs (6) of this section); *or*

    (ii) one made after 22 January 1996, where the court has decided that it either has no power to vary the maintenance order or that it has no power to enforce it (reg 9 of the Maintenance Arrangements and Jurisdiction Regulations).

See above under *Applications under s4 of the Act* for the overall effect of these provisions and the reasons for the exceptions.

Unsuccessful applications under s6 of the Act

If an application for a maintenance calculation under s6 of the Act fails because the relevant benefit has been disallowed or withdrawn, the Secretary of State must invite the parent to apply for a maintenance calculation under s4 if it appears that s4(10) would not prevent the application (s11(1A)-(1C) of the Act). The definition of "benefit" for the purposes of s4(10) and s6 is the same. Consequently, if a benefit claim is withdrawn or disallowed, it is only the existence of a maintenance agreement or order made before 5 April 1993 that can in the normal case prevent a parent with care having the option of switching from s6 to s4 (*CCS 12806/1996*, para 21).

Powers of the courts and the parties

1. The courts retain jurisdiction to make maintenance orders in the following cases. Some are expressly reserved to the courts under the child support legislation. These are where the maintenance order:

(a) is the same as a written maintenance agreement (s8(5) of the Act and the Child Maintenance (Written Agreements) Order 1993). In *V v V (Child Maintenance)* [2001] 2 FLR 799, Wilson J explained how the courts use this provision as a way of avoiding the child support scheme. The approach is certainly outside the spirit of the legislation and, as his Lordship admitted, sometimes even outside the letter as well;

(b) tops-up a child support maintenance assessment (s8(6));

(c) deals with educational needs (s8(7));

(d) deals with needs arising from disability (s8(8));

(e) is against a person with care of the child (s8(10)).

    Other cases arise because they fall outside the basic definitions which set the limits to the child support scheme. These are where:

(f) the child falls outside the definition of child for the purposes of the legislation (s55 and Sch 1 to the Maintenance Calculation Procedure Regulations);

(g) there is no one who is both the natural or adoptive parent of the child (s54 definition of "parent") and an absent parent in relation to the child (ss3(1) and (2));

(h) all the parties are not habitually resident in the UK (s44).

2. In other cases, where the Secretary of State would have jurisdiction to make a maintenance calculation, even if one would not be made, the position is as follows in 3-7.

    Courts have no power to make or revive a maintenance order (s8(3)).

    They have power to vary an existing order, if either:

(a) a maintenance calculation has not been made; *and*

(i)   the order was made on or after the prescribed date (s8(3) and (3A) (a)); *or*

(ii)   the order was made before the prescribed date and s4(10) or 7(10) prevents an application for a maintenance calculation being made (s8(3) and (3A)(b)); *or*

(b)   there is at any time before 7 April 1997, pending before a court an application made before 5 April 1993, to make a maintenance order (subs (9) of this section).

5.   The child support legislation does not prevent parties making a maintenance agreement (s9(3)).

6.   If the agreement was a written maintenance agreement and was made before 5 April 1993, it prevents an application under s4 and s7 if it falls within s4(10)(a) and s7(10), respectively (s9(3)).

7.   Otherwise the existence of a maintenance agreement does not prevent an application being made for a maintenance assessment (s9(3)).

8.   Where the courts have no power to make a maintenance order by virtue of s8 of the Act (as to which see 1, 2 and 3 above), the position is as follows in 9-12.

9.   The courts may not vary a maintenance agreement so as to insert a provision requiring the making or securing of periodical payments (s9(5)(a)).

10.   They have power to vary an agreement so as to increase the amount of periodical payments, if either:

(a)   the following two conditions are satisfied:

(i)   no application can be made under s4 or s7 because of subs (10) of each of those sections; *and*

(ii)   no maintenance calculation has been made under s6 even if there is an outstanding application under that section (s9(5)(b) and (6)); *or*

(b)   there is at any time before 7 April 1997, pending before a court an application made before 5 April 1993, to vary a maintenance agreement (subs (9) of this section).

11.   When dealing with an application to vary the amount of maintenance payable, the court should take into account the amount which would be payable under a maintenance assessment, although this is not decisive (*E v C (Child Maintenance)* [1996] 1 FLR 472).

12.   The child support legislation makes no express provision in relation to the powers of the courts in any other area than periodical payments of maintenance for children. However, the courts have taken the child support scheme into account in making decisions in other areas. See *Phillips v Peace* [1996] 2 FLR 230 (lump sum payments and property adjustment orders for children) and *Re R (A Minor) (Residence Order: Finance)* [1995] 2 FLR 612 (residence).

Maintenance

There is no statutory definition of maintenance in the child support or any other legislation, except perhaps reg 17(4) of the Variation Regulations (see p629). It covers recurring payments of an income nature to meet the costs of daily living, but daily living is not to be interpreted literally and restrictively (*A v A (Maintenance Pending Suit: Provision for Legal Fees)* [2001] 1 FLR 377). It includes payments to provide for education, including private education (*Secretary of State for Social Security v Foster,* reported as *R(CS) 1/01*).

Written maintenance agreement

For jurisdiction to decide whether a written maintenance agreement exists, see the discussion of *R(CS) 1/96,* paras 11-13, and *R(CS) 3/97* in the general note to reg 3 to the Maintenance Calculation Procedure Regulations on p652.

It is essential that there should be an "agreement". It is not sufficient that there has been an offer, even an offer in writing, to make an agreement (*CCS 11052/1995,* para 7). No agreement arises unless and until the offer is accepted. An agreement may be reached between the parties or through representatives. However, if solicitors are negotiating, it is necessary to distinguish between an agreement on terms that the clients might incorporate into an agreement and a final agreement on those terms (*CCS 1305/2000,* para 13).

The agreement must be a "maintenance agreement". Section 54 of the Act defines this phrase as having the meaning given in s9(1) of that Act. This will apply to regulations made under the statute unless the context otherwise requires (see the general note to s54). There was no definition of this phrase in Pt I of the Schedule to the Transitional Provisions Order (see the 1995 edition of this book) most of which has been re-enacted above. Accordingly, on general principles, the phrase had the same meaning as in the Act, unless the context otherwise required (see again the general note to s54). The whole of this reasoning, and in particular the definition in s54, was unfortunately overlooked by the commissioner in *CCS 12849/1996* (para 5) when dealing with para 2 of the Schedule to the Order, which has been re-enacted as s4(10) of the Act.

Payments by a parent under the social security liable relative provisions are not made under a maintenance agreement, even if the parent agrees to make them (*CCS 13475/1995,* para 13).

The maintenance agreement must be a "written maintenance agreement". In *CCS 15849/1996* (paras 9-13), the commissioner drew attention to the difference between a written maintenance agreement and a maintenance agreement that was merely *evidenced* in writing. A maintenance agreement made in writing was a written maintenance agreement, but one merely evidenced in writing was not. The commissioner's decision contains a helpful analysis of the types of evidence that are often produced to show that there was a written maintenance agreement. The commissioner declined to follow *CCS 12767/1996* (para 10), in which another commissioner had treated an agreement that was evidenced in writing as a written maintenance agreement. That commissioner had relied on wording in para 7(1)(a)(iii) of Pt II of the Schedule to the Transitional Provisions Order, but this was distinguishable on the ground that Pt II of the Schedule dealt with the phasing in of maintenance assessments and it was appropriate for a less strict test to be applied to that stage than to the question whether an application for a maintenance assessment could be made at all. The reasoning in *CCS 15849/1996* is preferable as it is consistent with the interpretation that has been given to "written agreement" (in different contexts) by the courts (*Ahmed v Government of the Kingdom of Saudi Arabia* [1996] 2 All ER 248 at 254-55, *per* Peter Gibson LJ and *CCS 5354/1997*, para 6).

On general principles, an agreement may be formed in the course of discussions relating to a possible consent order and may be written by reason of being contained in the correspondence. If a written agreement is reached, it is irrelevant that one party later seeks to resile from it (*Soulsbury v Soulsbury* [2008] 1 FLR 90, disapproving *Xydhias v Xydhias* [1999] 1 FLR 683), unless of course it is mutually rescinded. It is also irrelevant that it is not for some reason incorporated into a consent order, unless this step was a condition of the agreement coming into, or remaining, in force. An agreement may be concluded in correspondence even though the correspondence is labelled "without prejudice". See *CCS 12767/1996*. The same principles apply if the maintenance agreed for the child is nominal (*CCS12849/1996*, para 6). Once the agreement has been incorporated into a consent order, the order thereafter subsumes and supersedes the agreement (*de Lasala v de Lasala* [1979] 2 All ER 1146 at 1155, *per* Lord Diplock and *AMS v the Child Support Officer and* LM [1998] 1 FLR 955 at *962, per* Simon Brown LJ).

An agreement may also be formed, and be written, by being given as an undertaking to a court (*CCS 8328/1995*, para 18). The commissioner did not discuss whether an agreement that is incorporated into an undertaking is superseded as it would be if it were incorporated into a consent order. For a discussion of when an undertaking may be part of a maintenance order, see the following section of this note.

The agreement must be one which is an enforceable legal agreement (*CCS 12797/1996*, para 15). Accordingly an arrangement which is made and carried out without any legal obligation is not an agreement *(ibid)*.

In the context of child support law an agreement between the non-resident parent and the qualifying child does not fall within the meaning of "maintenance agreement" (*R(CS) 7/98*, paras 20-21).

Maintenance order

A consensual arrangement relating to financial payments following a divorce may consist in part of a court order by consent and in part of one or more undertakings by one of the parties to pay specified sums of money. Usually these undertakings will relate to matters which the court has no jurisdiction to order (*Jenkins v Livesey* [1985] 1 All ER 106 at 118-119, *per* Lord Brandon). The question arises of whether such undertakings are part of the order.

In the general law, an undertaking which is referred to in an order does not thereby become part of the order (*Re Hudson* [1966] 1 All ER 110). Support for this proposition is also to be found in *Thwaite v Thwaite* [1981] 2 All ER 789. That case involved an undertaking which was referred to in a court order and performance of which was a condition precedent to the operation of the order. Despite the close connection between the undertaking and the order, the Court of Appeal treated the undertaking as merely the basis of the bargain on which the consent order was based *(ibid* at 795(iii)). For some purposes, an undertaking may be equivalent to an order (eg, *Gandolfo v Gandolfo* [1980] 1 All ER 833 and *Symmons v Symmons* [1993] 1 FLR 317), but this does not turn the undertaking into an order.

This approach has been followed in the child support legislation. "Order" bears its literal meaning and does not include an undertaking that is recited to order the performance of which is perhaps conditional upon compliance with the undertaking (*CCS 8328/1995*, para 13 and *R(CS) 6/99*, para 22). It is, however, appropriate in the case of a consent order to interpret the undertakings and the orders of the court as a single whole, because the settlement was negotiated as a package (*CCS 316/1998,* para 19).

Whether payments are for the benefit of the child is determined by the proper interpretation of the court order. Usually the language of the order will be decisive on the question. Exceptionally a payment may be for the benefit of the child, although the order is not so worded. When this is so, it is because this is the proper interpretation of the order. The effect of the payment or the use to which it is put or was intended to be put is irrelevant. See *CCS 316/1998* (para 27), qualifying *CCS 8328/1995* (para 15).

In Scotland, a commissioner held that an extract of a minute of agreement registered in the Books of Council and Session is an order (*R(CS) 3/99*), but this has been doubted by Temporary Judge Coutts in *Woodhouse v Wright Johnston & Mackenzie,* 2004 SLT 911.

In force

In *CCS 4049/2007*, a commissioner decided that a court order remains in force until it is determined by further order, under its terms or by operation of law. In *R(CS) 4/96*, another commissioner had decided that an order was only in force for so long as it was of practical effect between the parties. The commissioner in *CCS 4049/2007* held that that case was wrongly decided. Permission to the Court of Appeal against that decision had been refused, but on grounds that differed from those given by the commissioner.

In *CCS 12849/1996* (para 7), the commissioner held, reluctantly, that an agreement to pay a nominal sum had a bearing on the financial relationship of the parties and so remained "in force". It is not clear from the decision whether the nominal sum of one pence per child per year was being paid.

Section 24 (compensation payments) was repealed by para 13(3) of Sch 3 to the 2000 Act. Article 3 of, and the Schedule to, the Commencement No.12 Order 2003 provided that it ceased to have effect from 3 March 2003 for the purposes of the cases there specified.

Supplemental

Regulations and orders

26.–(1)   Any power under this Act to make regulations or orders shall be exercisable by statutory instrument.

(2)   Any such power may be exercised to make different provision for different cases, including different provision for different areas.

(3)   Any such power includes power–

(a)   to make such incidental, supplemental, consequential or transitional provision as appears to the Secretary of State to be expedient; and

(b)   to provide for a person to exercise a discretion in dealing with any matter.

(4)   Subsection (5) applies to–

(a)   the first regulations made under section 10;

(b)   any order made under section 18(5);

(c)   [¹...]

(5)   No regulations or order to which this subsection applies shall be made unless a draft of the statutory instrument containing the regulations or order has been laid before Parliament and approved by a resolution of each House.

(6)   Any other statutory instrument made under this Act, other than one made under section 30(4), shall be subject to annulment in pursuance of a resolution of either House of Parliament.

Amendment

1.   Child Support, Pensions and Social Security Act 2000 (2000 c.19) s85 and Sch 9, Part I, (March 3, 2003 for the types of cases detailed in art 3 Child Support, Pensions and Social Security Act 2000 (Commencement No.12) Order 2003 (SI 2003 No.192) – see p683). For other types of cases, see the '1993 rules' below.

Commencement

Except subs (4)(a) and (c) September 4,1995
Subsection (4)(c) October 1, 1995
Otherwise October 14, 1996

1993 rules

Ss26 and 85 and schs 3 and 9 of the Child Support, Pensions and Social Security Act 2000 (2000 c.19) amend this section of the Child Support Act 1995 and have been brought into force only for the types of cases in art 3 of the Child Support, Pensions and Social Security Act 2000 (Commencement No.12) Order 2003 (SI 2003 No.192 – see p683). For other types of cases the 1993 rules apply and section 26(4)(c) still has effect. It reads:

(c)   the first regulations made under section 24.

Interpretation

27.–(1)   In this Act "the 1991 Act" means the Child Support Act 1991.

(2)   Expressions in this Act which are used in the 1991 Act have the same meaning in this Act as they have in that Act.

Commencement

September 4, 1995.

Financial provisions

28.   There shall be paid out of money provided by Parliament–

(a)   any expenditure incurred by the Secretary of State under or by virtue of this Act;

(b)   any increase attributable to this Act in the sums payable out of money so provided under or by virtue of any other enactment.

Commencement

September 4,1995.

Short title, commencement, extent etc.

30.–(1)   This Act may be cited as the Child Support Act 1995.

(2)   This Act and the 1991 Act may be cited together as the Child Support Acts 1991 and 1995.

(3)   Section 29 and this section (apart from subsection (5)) come into force on the passing of this Act.

(4)   The other provisions of this Act come into force on such day as the Secretary of State may by order appoint and different days may be appointed for different purposes.

(5)   Schedule 3 makes minor and consequential amendments.

(6)   This Act, except for–

(a)   sections 17, 27 and 29,

(b)   this section, and

(c)   paragraphs 1, 18, 19 and 20 of Schedule 3,

does not extend to Northern Ireland.

Social Security Act 1998

(1998 c14)

PART I
DECISIONS AND APPEALS
Chapter I
General
Decisions

Use of information

3.–(1) Subsection (2) below applies to information relating to [²any of the matters specified in subsection (1A) below] which is held–

(a) by the Secretary of State or the Northern Ireland Department; or

(b) by a person providing services to the Secretary of State or the Northern Ireland Department in connection with the provision of those services.

[²(1A) The matters are–

(a) social security [⁴ ...] or war pensions;

[⁴(aa) child support in Northern Ireland;]

(b) employment or training;

(c) private pensions policy;

(d) retirement planning.]

(2) Information to which this subsection applies–

(a) may be used for the purposes of, or for any purposes connected with, the exercise of functions in relation to [²any of the matters specified in subsection (1A) above]; and

(b) may be supplied to, or to a person providing services to, the Secretary of State or the Northern Ireland Department for use for those purposes.

(3) [¹...]

(4) In this section "the Northern Ireland Department" means the Department of Health and Social Services for Northern Ireland [¹or the Department for Employment and Learning in Northern Ireland].

[²(5) In this section–

"private pensions policy" means policy relating to

[³(a)] occupational pension schemes or personal pension schemes (within the meaning given by section 1 of the Pension Schemes Act 1993); [³or

(b) occupational pension schemes or private pension schemes within the meaning of Part 1 of the Pensions Act 2008, if they do not fall within paragraph (a);]

"retirement planning" means promoting financial planning for retirement.]

Amendments

1. Employment Act 2002 ss50, 54, Sch 6 paras 1 and 4 and Sch 8 Part (1) (September 9, 2002).
2. Pensions Act 2004 (c.35) s236 and Sch 10 para 1 (November 18, 2004).
3. Pensions Act 2008 (c.30) s63(5) and (6) (January 26, 2009).
4. Child Maintenance and Other Payments Act 2008 (Commencement No.7) Order 2009 (SI 2009 No.697) art 2(b) and para 3 Sch 7 of the 2008 Act (April 6, 2010).

Commencement

September 8, 1998.

Definition

"the Administration Act": see s84.

Chapter II
Social Security Decisions and Appeals
Procedure etc.

Finality of decisions

17.–(1) Subject to the provisions of this Chapter [¹and to any provision made by or under Chapter 2 of Part 1 of the Tribunals, Courts and Enforcement Act 2007], any decision made in accordance with the foregoing provisions of this Chapter shall be final; and subject to the provisions of any regulations under section 11 above, any decision made in accordance with those regulations shall be final.

(2) If and to the extent that regulations so provide, any finding of fact or other determination embodied in or necessary to such a decision, or on which such a decision is based, shall be conclusive for the purposes of–

    (a) further such decisions;

    (b) decisions made under the Child Support Act; and

    (c) decisions made under the Vaccine Damage Payments Act.]

Amendment

    1.   Transfer of Tribunal Functions Order 2008 (SI 2008 No.2833) art 9 and Sch 3 para 155 (November 3, 2008, subject to the transitional provisions in Sch 4 of SI 2008 No.2833).

Commencement

    March 1999 to allow regulations to be made.

Definition

    "the Child Support Act": see s84.

General Note

    This section applies to the Child Support Act 1991, but not to the Child Support Act 1995. See also s46A of the Act on p126.

PART IV

Miscellaneous and Supplemental

Regulations and orders

79.–(1) [³Subject to subsection (2A) below,] regulations under this Act shall be made by the [¹ Secretary of State].

(2) [³...]

[²(2A) Subsection (1) has effect subject to any provision providing for regulations to be made by the Treasury or the Commissioners of Inland Revenue.]

(3) Powers under this Act to make regulations or orders are exercisable by statutory instrument.

(4) Any power conferred by this Act to make regulations or orders may be exercised–

    (a) either in relation to all cases to which the power extends, or in relation to those cases subject to specified exceptions, or in relation to any specified cases or classes of case;

    (b) so as to make, as respects the cases in relation to which it is exercised–

        (i) the full provision to which the power extends or any less provision (whether by way of exception or otherwise);

        (ii) the same provision for all cases in relation to which the power is exercised, or different provision for different cases or different classes of case or different provision as respects the same case or class of case for different purposes of this Act;

        (iii) any such provision either unconditionally or subject to any specified condition; and where such a power is expressed to be exercisable for alternative purposes it may be exercised in relation to the same case for any or all of those purposes.

(5) Powers to make regulations for the purposes of any one provision of this Act are without prejudice to powers to make regulations for the purposes of any other provision.

(6) Without prejudice to any specific provision in this Act, a power conferred by this Act to make regulations includes power to make thereby such incidental, supplementary, consequential or transitional provision as appears to the authority making the regulations to be expedient for the purposes of those regulations.

[⁴(6A)   The provision referred to in subsection (6) includes, in a case where regulations under this Act require or authorise the use of electronic communications, provision referred to in section 8(4) and (5) and 9(5) of the Electronic Communications Act 2000.

(6B)   For the purposes of subsection (6A), references in section 8(4) and (5) and 9(5) of the Electronic Communications Act 2000 to an order under section 8 of that Act are to be read as references to regulations under this Act; and references to anything authorised by such an order are to be read as references to anything required or authorised by such regulations.]

(7)   Without prejudice to any specific provisions in this Act, a power conferred by any provision of this Act to make regulations includes power to provide for a person to exercise a discretion in dealing with any matter.

(8)   [*Omitted*]

(9)   [³...]

Amendments

1.   In relation to tax credits the reference to the Secretary of State is to be construed as a reference to the Treasury or the Commissioners of Inland Revenue, as the case may be, with effect from October 5, 1999 (Tax Crdits Act 1999, s2(4) and Sch 2 para 20(g)).

2.   Tax Credits Act 2002 (2002 c.21) s51 and Sch 4 para 13 (February 26, 2003, April 1, 2003 and April 7, 2003 – see art 2 of the Tax Credits Act 2002 (Commencement No.2) Order 2003, SI 2003 No.392, for relevant commencement date).

3.   Transfer of Tribunal Functions Order 2008 (SI 2008 No.2833) art 9 and Sch 3 para 168 (November 3, 2008, subject to the transitional provisions in Sch 4 of SI 2008 No.2833). In respect of certain appeals under the Health and Social Care (Community Health and Standards) Act 2003 (2003 c.43), this amendment does not extend to Scotland, see arts 1(5) and 3(3) of SI 2008 No.2833 for details.

4.   Welfare Reform Act 2012 (2012 c.5) s104(2) (February 25, 2013); Welfare Reform Act 2012 (Commencement No.8 and Savings and Transitional Provisions) Order 2013 (SI 2013 No.358) art 2 and Sch 2 para 38.

Commencement

May 21, 1998.

General Note

Subsection (6)

For a discussion of "incidental" and "supplementary", see the general note to s51(1) on p131.

Interpretation – general

84.   In this Act–

"the Administration Act" means the Social Security Administration Act 1992;

"the Child Support Act" means the Child Support Act 1991;

"the Contributions and Benefits Act" means the Social Security Contributions and Benefits Act 1992;

"the Jobseekers Act" means the Jobseekers Act 1995;

"the Vaccine Damage Payments Act" means the Vaccine Damage Payments Act 1979;

"prescribe" means prescribe by regulations.

Commencement

May 21, 1998.

Short title, commencement and extent

87.–(1)   This Act may be cited as the Social Security Act 1998.

(2)   This Act, except–

(a)   sections 66, 69, 72 and 77 to 85, this section and Schedule 6 to this Act; and

(b)   subsection (1) of section 50 so far as relating to a sum which is chargeable to tax by virtue of section 313 of the Income and Corporation Taxes Act 1988, and subsections (2) to (4) of that section,

shall come into force on such day as may be appointed by order made by the Secretary of State; and different days may be appointed for different provisions and for different purposes.

(3)   An order under subsection (2) above may make such savings, or such transitional or consequential provision, as the Secretary of State considers necessary or expedient–

(a)   in preparation for or in connection with the coming into force of any provision of this Act; or

(b)   in connection with the operation of any enactment repealed or amended by a provision of this Act during any period when the repeal or amendment is not wholly in force.

(4)   This Act, except–

(a)   section 2 so far as relating to war pensions;

(b)   sections 3, 15, 45 to 47, 59, 78 and 85 and this section; and

(c)   section 86 and Schedules 7 and 8 so far as relating to enactments which extend to Northern Ireland,

does not extend to Northern Ireland.

(5)   The following provisions of this Act extend to the Isle of Man, namely–

(a)   in section 4, subsections (1)(c) and (2)(c);

(b)   sections 6 and 7 and Schedule 1 so far as relating to appeals under the Vaccine Damage Payments Act;

(c)   sections 45 to 47 and this section;

(d)   paragraphs 5 to 10 of Schedule 7 and section 86(1) so far as relating to those paragraphs; and

(e)   section 86(2) and Schedule 8 so far as relating to the Vaccine Damage Payments Act.

Commencement

May 21, 1998.

Human Rights Act 1998
(1998 c42)

General Note

Inappropriate reference to a Convention right on appeal to the Upper Tribunal is not encouraged (*CDLA 2259/2000*, para 11).

The Act originally conferred functions on the Lord Chancellor. These were transferred to the Secretary of State (for Constitutional Affairs) by the Secretary of State for Constitutional Affairs Order 2003. They have now been conferred again on the Lord Chancellor, by the Transfer of Functions (Lord Chancellor and Secretary of State) Order 2005. This allows them to be exercised by the holder of either office.

Introduction

The Convention Rights

1.–(1)   In this Act "the Convention rights" means the rights and fundamental freedoms set out in–

(a)   Articles 2 to 12 and 14 of the Convention,

(b)   Articles 1 to 3 of the First Protocol, and

(c)   [³Article 1 of the Thirteenth Protocol]

as read with Articles 16 to 18 of the Convention.

(2)   Those Articles are to have effect for the purposes of this Act subject to any designated derogation or reservation (as to which see sections 14 and 15).

(3)   The Articles are set out in Schedule 1.

(4)   The [¹[²Secretary of State]] may by order make such amendments to this Act as he considers appropriate to reflect the effect, in relation to the United Kingdom, of a protocol.

(5)   In subsection (4) "protocol" means a protocol to the Convention–

(a)   which the United Kingdom has ratified; or

(b)   which the United Kingdom has signed with a view to ratification.

(6)   No amendment may be made by an order under subsection (4) so as to come into force before the protocol concerned is in force in relation to the United Kingdom.

Commencement

October 2, 2000: The Human Rights Act 1998 (Commencement No.2) Order 2000 (SI 2000 No.1851).

Amendments

1.   Transfer of Functions (Miscellaneous) Order 2001 (SI 2001 No.3500) art 8 and Sch 2 para 7 (November 26, 2001).

2.   Secretary of State for Constitutional Affairs Order 2003 (SI 2003 No.1887) art 9 and Sch 2 para 10(1) (August 19, 2003).

3.   Human Rights Act 1998 (Amendment) Order 2004 (SI 2004 No.1574) art 2(1) (June 22, 2004).

Definitions

"amend": see s21(1).

"the Convention": see s21(1).

"the First Protocol": see s21(1).

"the Thirteenth Protocol": see s21(1).

General Note

This section incorporates parts of the Convention and its Protocols into domestic law, designating them "Convention rights". Those rights also retain their existence under the Convention itself and it may be that resort will be had directly to them in the ways developed before this Act came into force, rather than to Convention rights based on them, in order to avoid or alleviate problems with the procedures under this Act.

The other parts of the Convention and its protocols are not incorporated as Convention rights and cannot be relied on (*CCS 6373/1999*, para 8). However, they may still be relevant. (i) They may be relevant to the interpretation of Convention rights. (ii) They may be taken into account in the variety of ways that the courts previously used, despite the apparently limiting effect of the decision of the House of Lords in *Brind v SSHD* [1991] 1 All ER 720, to make use of the Convention. (iii) They may be taken into account when applying European law which recognises them as part of the general principles of law to which it has regard, although the European Court of Justice will not give interpretative guidance on whether national legislation complies with the Convention unless the legislation falls within the field of application of European law (*Kremzow v Republik Osterreich, The Times*, August 11, 1997).

Interpretation of Convention rights

2.–(1)   A court or tribunal determining a question which has arisen in connection with a Convention right must take into account any–

(a)   judgment, decision, declaration or advisory opinion of the European Court of Human Rights,

(b)   opinion of the Commission given in a report adopted under Article 31 of the Convention,

(c)   decision of the Commission in connection with Article 26 or 27(2) of the Convention, or

(d)   decision of the Committee of Ministers taken under Article 46 of the Convention,
whenever made or given, so far as, in the opinion of the court or tribunal, it is relevant to the proceedings in which that question has arisen.

(2)   Evidence of any judgment, decision, declaration or opinion of which account may have to be taken under this section is to be given in proceedings before any court or tribunal in such manner as may be provided by rules.

(3)   In this section "rules" means rules of court or, in the case of proceedings before a tribunal, rules made for the purposes of this section–

(a)   by [1...] [2the Lord Chancellor or] the Secretary of State, in relation to any proceedings outside Scotland;

(b)   by the Secretary of State, in relation to proceedings in Scotland; or

(c)   by a Northern Ireland department, in relation to proceedings before a tribunal in Northern Ireland–

    (i)   which deals with transferred matters; and

    (ii)   for which no rules made under paragraph (a) are in force.

Commencement

October 2, 2000: The Human Rights Act 1998 (Commencement No.2) Order 2000 (SI 2000 No.1851).

Amendments

1.   Secretary of State for Constitutional Affairs Order 2003 (SI 2003 No.1887) art 9 and Sch 2 para 10(2) (August 19, 2003).

2.   Transfer of Functions (Lord Chancellor and Secretary of State) Order 2005 (SI 2005 No.3429) art 8 and Sch para 3 (January 12, 2006).

Definitions

"the Commission": see s21(1).

"the Convention": see s.21(1).

"the Convention rights": see s1(1).

"transferred matters": s21(1).

"tribunal": see s21(1).

General Note

The materials listed must be taken into account. They are not necessarily decisive (*Gough v Chief Constable of the Derbyshire Constabulary* [2001] 4 All ER 289 *per* Laws LJ at para 32) and they do not have the status of Convention rights. This reflects the fact that the Court does not regard itself as bound by its previous decisions, which in turns reflects the fact that the Convention is interpreted in a dynamic way to keep up to date with changing conditions.

As the materials must be taken into account in determining a question which has arisen in connection with a Convention right, they are relevant both to the interpretation and to the application of those rights.

In *CH 4574/2003,* the commissioner considered how the duty under this section could be reconciled with the doctrine of precedent (paras 30-37). He decided that generally the doctrine of precedent applied. The duty under this section was relevant (a) as the starting point for consideration when an issue first arose in domestic law or (b) when changed conditions and developing Strasbourg jurisprudence justified distinguishing domestic authority. This anticipated the reasoning of the House of Lords in *Kay v London Borough of Lambeth* [2006] UKHL 10. The House decided that the normal doctrine of precedent for domestic decisions applied unaffected by any developments in the Strasbourg jurisprudence. The proper course in the event of a conflict between domestic and European authorities was for the case to progress on appeal to the appropriate level where the conflict could be resolved. This was subject to a limited exception for extreme cases, the only example of which involved a case decided before the Human Rights Act 1998 was passed and whose policy basis was undermined by that Act.

Legislation

Interpretation of legislation

3.–(1)   So far as it is possible to do so, primary legislation and subordinate legislation must be read and given effect in a way which is compatible with the Convention rights.

(2)   This section–

(a) applies to primary legislation and subordinate legislation whenever enacted;
(b) does not affect the validity, continuing operation or enforcement of any incompatible primary legislation; and
(c) does not affect the validity, continuing operation or enforcement of any incompatible subordinate legislation if (disregarding any possibility of revocation) primary legislation prevents removal of the incompatibility.

Commencement
October 2, 2000: The Human Rights Act 1998 (Commencement No.2) Order 2000 (SI 2000 No.1851).

Definitions
"the Convention rights": see s1(1).
"primary legislation": see s21(1).
"subordinate legislation": see s21(1).

General Note
Subsection (1)
The Convention rights are not merely to be applied directly by courts and tribunals. They have to be taken into account both when interpreting ("read") and when applying ("given effect") domestic legislation in order to ensure as far as possible that the legislation operates compatibly with those rights.

The limits within which it will be "possible" to interpret and apply legislation which on its wording is incompatible with a Convention right will have to be set by the courts. In theory the present limit is set by the decision of the House of Lords in *Brind v SSHD* [1991] 1 All ER 720, which is authority that the Convention can only be taken into account if the domestic legislation is ambiguous. However, there are numerous examples of courts at all levels applying a less restrictive approach, showing that there are possibilities beyond ambiguity.

The courts have discussed the approach that must be taken under this section.

The best guidance was given by the Court of Appeal in *Poplar Housing and Regeneration Community Association Ltd v Donoghue* [2001] 4 All ER 604. The court has no power to modify the meaning of a provision more than is necessary to ensure compatibility. Its function is one of interpretation. It is not given power to legislate. The more radical the modification of the meaning that is involved, the more likely it is that the court would be legislating rather than interpreting.

The proper approach was also considered by the commissioner in *CI 4421/2000,* paras 16-24. The commissioner made the following points. First, in the absence of clear guidance from the courts, the only authoritative guide is the terms of this subsection. Second, the essential starting point was to identify the provision that had to be interpreted. The more closely that provision was connected with the violation of the Convention right, the greater the justification for stretching its meaning. Third, this subsection required a broad approach to be taken to the interpretation of the provision. However, fourth, that did not authorise the commissioner to disregard completely the context in which the provision appeared.

It is permissible to refer to *Hansard* only as a source of background information on a statutory provision, such as the mischief it was intended to remedy and the impact it was likely to have (*Wilson v First County Trust Ltd* [2003] 4 All ER 97).

The proportionality of a statutory provision as a response to a legitimate aim is determined at the time when the issue arises, not when the legislation was enacted or came into force (*Wilson v First County Trust Ltd*).

In *CCS 1153/2003*, the commissioner relied on the "unless the context otherwise requires" qualification in the definition section to disapply a definition, thereby removing its discriminatory effect. On appeal, the Court of Appeal disapproved of this approach (*M v SSWP* [2005] 1 FLR 498). Sedley LJ said that this Act provided a filter not a context (para 84). The House of Lords reversed the decision of the Court of Appeal, but did not deal with this issue ([2006] UKHL 11).

Subsection (2)
This subsection makes three provisions.
Paragraph (a)
This paragraph provides that subs (1) operates retrospectively on legislation enacted before this Act came into force.
Paragraph (b)
This paragraph provides that if primary legislation cannot be interpreted or applied compatibly with Convention rights, it nevertheless remains valid, continues to operate and must be applied. This may lead either to a case being taken to the European Court of Human Rights or to a declaration of incompatibility under s4.
Paragraph (c)
This paragraph deals with incompatible subordinate legislation. It provides that subordinate legislation remains valid, continues to operate and must be applied if the enabling legislation prevents the removal of the incompatibility. It is not clear what is meant by primary legislation preventing removal. If subordinate legislation is declared *ultra vires*, it ceases to have effect. Any incompatibility with a Convention right is thereby removed by

force of law and not under the primary legislation. If a tribunal or Commissioner has power to decide that subordinate legislation is not authorised by primary legislation, despite its clear wording, because it is incompatible with a Convention right, this paragraph would be redundant. Perhaps this paragraph prevents this approach being taken and *ultra vires* on this basis is confined to the nominated courts under s4(4). Otherwise, this paragraph and s4(4) would be redundant.

Declaration of incompatability

4.–(1) Subsection (2) applies in any proceedings in which a court determines whether a provision of primary legislation is compatible with a Convention right.

(2) If the court is satisfied that the provision is incompatible with a Convention right, it may make a declaration of that incompatibility.

(3) Subsection (4) applies in any proceedings in which a court determines whether a provision of subordinate legislation, made in the exercise of a power conferred by primary legislation, is compatible with a Convention right.

(4) If the court is satisfied–

(a) that the provision is incompatible with a Convention right, and

(b) that (disregarding any possibility of revocation) the primary legislation concerned prevents removal of the incompatibility,

it may make a declaration of that incompatibility.

(5) In this section "court" means–

[²(a) the Supreme Court;]

(b) the Judicial Committee of the Privy Council;

(c) the [³Court Martial Appeal Court];

(d) in Scotland, the High Court of Justiciary sitting otherwise than as a trial court or the Court of Session;

(e) in England and Wales or Northern Ireland, the High Court or the Court of Appeal;

[¹(f) the Court of Protection, in any matter being dealt with by the President of the Family Division, the [⁴Chancellor of the High Court] or a puisne judge of the High Court.]

(6) A declaration under this section ("a declaration of incompatibility")–

(a) does not affect the validity, continuing operation or enforcement of the provision in respect of which it is given; and

(b) is not binding on the parties to the proceedings in which it is made.

Amendments

1.   Mental Capacity Act 2005 (2005 c.9) s67(1) and Sch 6 para 43 (October 1, 2007).

2.   Constitutional Reform Act 2005 (2005 c 4) s40 and Sch 9 para 66 (October 1, 2009).

3.   Armed Forces Act 2006 (2006 c.52) s378 and Sch 16 para 156 (March 28, 2009 for the purposes outlined in art 3 Armed Forces Act 2006 (Commencement No.4) Order 2009 (SI 2009 No.812); October 31, 2009 for all other purposes). For the date that the Armed Forces Act 2006 is due to expire, see the Armed Forces Act (Continuation) Order 2012 (SI 2012 No.1750) art 2.

4.   Crime and Courts Act 2013 (2013 c.22) s21 and Sch 14 para 5(5) (October 1, 2013); Crime and Courts Act 2013 (Commencement No.4) Order 2013 (SI 2013 No.2200) art 3.

Commencement

October 2, 2000: The Human Rights Act 1998 (Commencement No.2) Order 2000 (SI 2000 No.1851).

Definitions

"the Convention rights": see s1(1).

"primary legislation": see s21(1).

"subordinate legislation": see s21(1).

General Note

This section provides the procedure by which a court may deal with primary or subordinate legislation that cannot be interpreted or applied compatibly with Convention rights. If a court declares legislation to be incompatible with a Convention right, remedial action may be taken under s10 and Sch 2.

Tribunals do not have power to make a declaration under this section.

Subsection (2)
The court has a power, but not a duty, to make a declaration (*Poplar Housing and Regeneration Community Association Ltd v Donoghue* [2001] 4 All ER 604).
Subsection (4)
See the general note to s3(2)(c) on p185.

Right of Crown to intervene

5.–(1)   Where a court is considering whether to make a declaration of incompatibility, the Crown is entitled to notice in accordance with rules of court.

(2)   In any case to which subsection (1) applies–

(a)   a Minister of the Crown (or a person nominated by him),

(b)   a member of the Scottish Executive,

(c)   a Northern Ireland Minister,

(d)   a Northern Ireland department,

is entitled, on giving notice in accordance with rules of court, to be joined as a party to the proceedings.

(3)   Notice under subsection (2) may be given at any time during the proceedings.

(4)   A person who has been made a party to criminal proceedings (other than in Scotland) as the result of a notice under subsection (2) may, with leave, appeal to the [¹Supreme Court]against any declaration of incompatibility made in the proceedings.

(5)   In subsection (4)–

"criminal proceedings" includes all proceedings before the [²Court Martial Appeal Court]; and

"leave" means leave granted by the court making the declaration of incompatibility or by the [¹Supreme Court].

Commencement
October 2, 2000: The Human Rights Act 1998 (Commencement No.2) Order 2000 (SI 2000 No.1851).

Amendments
1.   Constitutional Reform Act 2005 (2005 c.4) s40 and Sch 9 para 66(3) (October 1, 2009).
2.   Armed Forces Act 2006 (2006 c.52) s378 and Sch 16 para 157 (March 28, 2009 for the purposes outlined in art 3 Armed Forces Act 2006 (Commencement No.4) Order 2009 (SI 2009 No.812); October 31, 2009 for all other purposes). For the date that the Armed Forces Act 2006 is due to expire, see the Armed Forces Act (Continuation) Order 2012 (SI 2012 No.1750) art 2.

Definitions
"declaration of incompatibility": see s21(1).
"Minister of the Crown": see s21(1).
"Northern Ireland Minister": see s21(1).

Public authorities

Acts of public authorities

6.–(1)   It is unlawful for a public authority to act in a way which is incompatible with a Convention right.

(2)   Subsection (1) does not apply to an act if–

(a)   as the result of one or more provisions of primary legislation, the authority could not have acted differently; or

(b)   in the case of one or more provisions of, or made under, primary legislation which cannot be read or given effect in a way which is compatible with the Convention rights, the authority was acting so as to give effect to or enforce those provisions.

(3)   In this section "public authority" includes–

(a)   a court or tribunal, and

(b)   any person certain of whose functions are functions of a public nature,

but does not include either House of Parliament or a person exercising functions in connection with proceedings in Parliament.

(4)   [¹...]

(5)   In relation to a particular act, a person is not a public authority by virtue only of subsection (3)(b) if the nature of the act is private.

(6)   "An act" includes a failure to act but does not include a failure to–

(a)   introduce in, or lay before, Parliament a proposal for legislation; or

(b)   make any primary legislation or remedial order.

Commencement

October 2, 2000: The Human Rights Act 1998 (Commencement No.2) Order 2000 (SI 2000 No.1851).

Amendment

1.   Constitutional Reform Act 2005 (2005 c.4) s40 and Sch 9 para 66(4) (October 1, 2009).

Definitions

"the Convention rights": see s1(1).

"primary legislation": see s21(1).

"remedial order": see s21(1).

"tribunal": see s21(1).

General Note

The tribunals and the commissioners in both their administrative and judicial capacities are public authorities under this section. An act by a public authority is unlawful if it is avoidably incompatible with a Convention right. For what is unavoidable, see subs (2). Proceedings against the public authority in respect of the unlawful act and compensation are governed by ss7 and 9, subject in the case of judicial acts to s9.

Proceedings

7.–(1)   A person who claims that a public authority has acted (or proposes to act) in a way which is made unlawful by section 6(1) may–

(a)   bring proceedings against the authority under this Act in the appropriate court or tribunal, or

(b)   rely on the Convention right or rights concerned in any legal proceedings,

but only if he is (or would be) a victim of the unlawful act.

(2)   In subsection (1)(a) "appropriate court or tribunal" means such court or tribunal as may be determined in accordance with rules; and proceedings against an authority include a counterclaim or similar proceeding.

(3)   If the proceedings are brought on an application for judicial review, the applicant is to be taken to have a sufficient interest in relation to the unlawful act only if he is, or would be, a victim of that act.

(4)   If the proceedings are made by way of a petition for judicial review in Scotland, the applicant shall be taken to have title and interest to sue in relation to the unlawful act only if he is, or would be, a victim of that act.

(5)   Proceedings under subsection (1)(a) must be brought before the end of–

(a)   the period of one year beginning with the date on which the act complained of took place; or

(b)   such longer period as the court or tribunal considers equitable having regard to all the circumstances,

but that is subject to any rule imposing a stricter time limit in relation to the procedure in question.

(6)   In subsection (1)(b) "legal proceedings" includes–

(a)   proceedings brought by or at the instigation of a public authority; and

(b)   an appeal against the decision of a court or tribunal.

(7)   For the purposes of this section, a person is a victim of an unlawful act only if he would be a victim for the purposes of Article 34 of the Convention if proceedings were brought in the European Court of Human Rights in respect of that act.

(8)   Nothing in this Act creates a criminal offence.

(9)   In this section "rules" means–

(a)   in relation to proceedings before a court or tribunal outside Scotland, rules made by [¹...] [²the Lord Chancellor or] the Secretary of State for the purposes of this section or rules of court,

(b)   in relation to proceedings before a court or tribunal in Scotland, rules made by the Secretary of State for those purposes,

(c)   in relation to proceedings before a tribunal in Northern Ireland–

    (i)   which deals with transferred matters; and

    (ii)   for which no rules made under paragraph (a) are in force,

    rules made by a Northern Ireland department for those purposes,

and includes provision made by order under section 1 of the Courts and Legal Services Act 1990.

(10)   In making rules, regard must be had to section 9.

(11)   The Minister who has power to make rules in relation to a particular tribunal may, to the extent he considers it necessary to ensure that the tribunal can provide an appropriate remedy in relation to an act (or proposed act) of a public authority which is (or would be) unlawful as a result of section 6(1), by order add to–

(a)   the relief or remedies which the tribunal may grant; or

(b)   the grounds on which it may grant any of them.

(12)   An order made under subsection (11) may contain such incidental, supplemental, consequential or transitional provision as the Minister making it considers appropriate.

(13)   "The Minister" includes the Northern Ireland department concerned.

Commencement

October 2, 2000: The Human Rights Act 1998 (Commencement No.2) Order 2000 (SI 2000 No.1851).

Amendments

1.   Secretary of State for Constitutional Affairs Order 2003 (SI 2003 No.1887) art 9 and Sch 2 para 10(2) (August 19, 2003).

2.   Transfer of Functions (Lord Chancellor and Secretary of State) Order 2005 (SI 2005 No.3429) art 8 and Sch para 3 (January 12, 2006).

Definitions

"the Convention": see s21(1).

"the Convention rights": see s1(1).

"transferred matters": see s21(1).

"tribunal": see s21(1).

Judicial remedies

8.–(1)   In relation to any act (or proposed act) of a public authority which the court finds is (or would be) unlawful, it may grant such relief or remedy, or make such order, within its powers as it considers just and appropriate.

(2)   But damages may be awarded only by a court which has power to award damages, or to order the payment of compensation, in civil proceedings.

(3)   No award of damages is to be made unless, taking account of all the circumstances of the case, including–

(a)   any other relief or remedy granted, or order made, in relation to the act in question (by that or any other court), and

(b)   the consequences of any decision (of that or any other court) in respect of that act,

the court is satisfied that the award is necessary to afford just satisfaction to the person in whose favour it is made.

(4)   In determining–

(a)   whether to award damages, or

(b)   the amount of an award,

the court must take into account the principles applied by the European Court of Human Rights in relation to the award of compensation under Article 41 of the Convention.

(5)   A public authority against which damages are awarded is to be treated–

(a)   in Scotland, for the purposes of section 3 of the Law Reform (Miscellaneous Provisions) (Scotland) Act 1940 as if the award were made in an action of damages in which the authority has been found liable in respect of loss or damage to the person to whom the award is made;

(b) for the purposes of the Civil Liability (Contribution) Act 1978 as liable in respect of damage suffered by the person to whom the award is made.

(6) In this section–

"court" includes a tribunal;

"damages" means damages for an unlawful act of a public authority; and

"unlawful" means unlawful under section 6(1).

Commencement

October 2, 2000: The Human Rights Act 1998 (Commencement No.2) Order 2000 (SI 2000 No.1851).

Definitions

"the Convention": see s21(1).

"tribunal": see s21(1).

Judicial acts

9.–(1) Proceedings under section 7(1)(a) in respect of a judicial act may be brought only–

(a) by exercising a right of appeal;

(b) on an application (in Scotland a petition) for judicial review; or

(c) in such other forum as may be prescribed by rules.

(2) That does not affect any rule of law which prevents a court from being the subject of judicial review.

(3) In proceedings under this Act in respect of a judicial act done in good faith, damages may not be awarded otherwise than to compensate a person to the extent required by Article 5(5) of the Convention.

(4) An award of damages permitted by subsection (3) is to be made against the Crown; but no award may be made unless the appropriate person, if not a party to the proceedings, is joined.

(5) In this section–

"appropriate person" means the Minister responsible for the court concerned, or a person or government department nominated by him;

"court" includes a tribunal;

"judge" includes a member of a tribunal, a justice of the peace [[1](or, in Northern Ireland, a lay magistrate)] and a clerk or other officer entitled to exercise the jurisdiction of a court;

"judicial act" means a judicial act of a court and includes an act done on the instructions, or on behalf, of a judge; and

"rules" has the same meaning as in section 7(9).

Commencement

October 2, 2000: The Human Rights Act 1998 (Commencement No.2) Order 2000 (SI 2000 No.1851).

Amendment

1. Justice (Northern Ireland) Act 2002 (2002 c.26) s10 and Sch 4 para 39 (April 1, 2005).

Definitions

"the Convention": see s21(1).

"tribunal": see s21(1).

General Note

This section qualifies ss7 and 8 in the case of judicial acts.

Subsection (1)

This subsection limits the way in which proceedings in respect of an unlawful judicial act may be brought to an appeal or an application for judicial review.

Subsection (3)

Compensation will be awarded in respect of an unlawful judicial act in two cases: (i) if the act was not done in good faith; (ii) under Art 5(5). As Art 5(5) cannot apply in child support cases, compensation can only be awarded if the judicial act was not done in good faith.

There will be no point in arguing that a judicial act of a tribunal was done in bad faith, because the tribunal has no power to award damages or order the payment of compensation and, therefore by virtue of s8(2), has no power to award compensation for the unlawful judicial act.

Remedial action

Power to take remedial action

10.–(1)   This section applies if–

(a)   a provision of legislation has been declared under section 4 to be incompatible with a Convention right and, if an appeal lies–

(i)   all persons who may appeal have stated in writing that they do not intend to do so;

(ii)   the time for bringing an appeal has expired and no appeal has been brought within that time; or

(iii)   an appeal brought within that time has been determined or abandoned; or

(b)   it appears to a Minister of the Crown or Her Majesty in Council that, having regard to a finding of the European Court of Human Rights made after the coming into force of this section in proceedings against the United Kingdom, a provision of legislation is incompatible with an obligation of the United Kingdom arising from the Convention.

(2)   If a Minister of the Crown considers that there are compelling reasons for proceeding under this section, he may by order make such amendments to the legislation as he considers necessary to remove the incompatibility.

(3)   If, in the case of subordinate legislation, a Minister of the Crown considers–

(a)   that it is necessary to amend the primary legislation under which the subordinate legislation in question was made, in order to enable the incompatibility to be removed, and

(b)   that there are compelling reasons for proceeding under this section,

he may by order make such amendments to the primary legislation as he considers necessary.

(4)   This section also applies where the provision in question is in subordinate legislation and has been quashed, or declared invalid, by reason of incompatibility with a Convention right and the Minister proposes to proceed under paragraph 2(b) of Schedule 2.

(5)   If the legislation is an Order in Council, the power conferred by subsection (2) or (3) is exercisable by Her Majesty in Council.

(6)   In this section "legislation" does not include a Measure of the Church Assembly or of the General Synod of the Church of England.

(7)   Schedule 2 makes further provision about remedial orders.

Commencement

October 2, 2000: The Human Rights Act 1998 (Commencement No.2) Order 2000 (SI 2000 No.1851).

Definitions

"amend": see s21(1).
"the Convention": see s21(1).
"the Convention rights": see s1(1).
"Minister of the Crown": see s21(1).
"primary legislation": see s21(1).
"remedial order": see s21(1).
"subordinate legislation": see s21(1).

Other rights and proceedings

Safeguard for existing human rights

11.   A person's reliance on a Convention right does not restrict–

(a)   any other right or freedom conferred on him by or under any law having effect in any part of the United Kingdom; or

(b)   his right to make any claim or bring any proceedings which he could make or bring apart from sections 7 to 9.

Commencement

October 2, 2000: The Human Rights Act 1998 (Commencement No.2) Order 2000 (SI 2000 No.1851).

Definition

"the Convention rights": see s1(1).

General Note

This section ensures that Convention rights provide a minimum legal guarantee.

They do not affect any greater legal protection than may exist. Although the side note refers to safeguarding *human* rights, the section itself is not limited and applies to all rights and freedoms. It will not be necessary to determine whether other rights or freedoms are properly classified as "human rights".

Freedom of expression

12.–(1)   This section applies if a court is considering whether to grant any relief which, if granted, might affect the exercise of the Convention right to freedom of expression.

(2)   If the person against whom the application for relief is made ("the respondent") is neither present nor represented, no such relief is to be granted unless the court is satisfied–

(a)   that the applicant has taken all practicable steps to notify the respondent; or

(b)   that there are compelling reasons why the respondent should not be notified.

(3)   No such relief is to be granted so as to restrain publication before trial unless the court is satisfied that the applicant is likely to establish that publication should not be allowed.

(4)   The court must have particular regard to the importance of the Convention right to freedom of expression and, where the proceedings relate to material which the respondent claims, or which appears to the court, to be journalistic, literary or artistic material (or to conduct connected with such material), to–

(a)   the extent to which–

(i)   the material has, or is about to, become available to the public; or

(ii)   it is, or would be, in the public interest for the material to be published;

(b)   any relevant privacy code.

(5)   In this section–

"court" includes a tribunal; and

"relief" includes any remedy or order (other than in criminal proceedings).

Commencemnt

October 2, 2000: The Human Rights Act 1998 (Commencement No.2) Order 2000 (SI 2000 No.1851).

Definitions

"the Convention rights": see s1(1).

"tribunal": see s21(1).

Freedom of thought, conscience and religion

13.–(1)   If a court's determination of any question arising under this Act might affect the exercise by a religious organisation (itself or its members collectively) of the Convention right to freedom of thought, conscience and religion, it must have particular regard to the importance of that right.

(2)   In this section "court" includes a tribunal.

Commencement

October 2, 2000: The Human Rights Act 1998 (Commencement No.2) Order 2000 (SI 2000 No.1851).

Definitions

"the Convention rights": see s1(1).

"tribunal": see s21(1).

Derogations and reservations

Derogations
14.–(1)   In this Act "designated derogation" means–

(a)   [¹ ...

(b)]   any derogation by the United Kingdom from an Article of the Convention, or of any protocol to the Convention, which is designated for the purposes of this Act in an order made by the [²[³Secretary of State]].

(2)   [¹ ...]

(3)   If a designated derogation is amended or replaced it ceases to be a designated derogation.

(4)   But subsection (3) does not prevent the [²[³Secretary of State]] from exercising his power under subsection (1)[¹ ...] to make a fresh designation order in respect of the Article concerned.

(5)   The [²[³Secretary of State]] must by order make such amendments to Schedule 3 as he considers appropriate to reflect–

(a)   any designation order; or

(b)   the effect of subsection (3).

(6)   A designation order may be made in anticipation of the making by the United Kingdom of a proposed derogation.

Commencement

October 2, 2000: The Human Rights Act 1998 (Commencement No.2) Order 2000 (SI 2000 No.1851).

Amendments

1.   The Human Rights Act (Amendment) Order 2001 (SI 2001 No.1216) art 2 (April 1 2001).

2.   Transfer of Functions (Miscellaneous) Order 2001 (SI 2001 No.3500) art 8 and Sch 2 para 7 (November 26, 2001).

3.   Secretary of State for Constitutional Affairs Order 2003 (SI 2003 No.1887) art 9 and Sch 2 para 10(1) (August 19, 2003).

Definitions

"amend": see s21(1).
"the Convention": see s21(1).

Reservations
15.–(1)   In this Act "designated reservation" means–

(a)   the United Kingdom's reservation to Article 2 of the First Protocol to the Convention; and

(b)   any other reservation by the United Kingdom to an Article of the Convention, or of any protocol to the Convention, which is designated for the purposes of this Act in an order made by the [¹[²Secretary of State]].

(2)   The text of the reservation referred to in subsection (1)(a) is set out in Part II of Schedule 3.

(3)   If a designated reservation is withdrawn wholly or in part it ceases to be a designated reservation.

(4)   But subsection (3) does not prevent the [¹[²Secretary of State]] from exercising his power under subsection (1)(b) to make a fresh designation order in respect of the Article concerned.

(5)   The [¹[²Secretary of State]] must by order make such amendments to this Act as he considers appropriate to reflect–

(a)   any designation order; or

(b)   the effect of subsection (3).

Commencement

October 2, 2000: The Human Rights Act 1998 (Commencement No.2) Order 2000 (SI 2000 No.1851).

Amendments

1.   Transfer of Functions (Miscellaneous) Order 2001 (SI 2001 No.3500) art 8 and Sch 2 para 7 (November 26, 2001).

2.   Secretary of State for Constitutional Affairs Order 2003 (SI 2003 No.1887) art 9 and Sch 2 para 10(1) (August 19, 2003).

Definitions
"amend": see s21(1).
"the Convention": see s21(1).
"the First Protocol": see s21(1).

Period for which designated derogations have effect

16.–(1)   If it has not already been withdrawn by the United Kingdom, a designated derogation ceases to have effect for the purposes of this Act–

[¹ ...] at the end of the period of five years beginning with the date on which the order designating it was made.

(2)   At any time before the period–

(a)   fixed by subsection (1)[¹ ...], or

(b)   extended by an order under this subsection,

comes to an end, the [²[³Secretary of State]] may by order extend it by a further period of five years.

(3)   An order under section 14(1) [¹ ...] ceases to have effect at the end of the period for consideration, unless a resolution has been passed by each House approving the order.

(4)   Subsection (3) does not affect–

(a)   anything done in reliance on the order; or

(b)   the power to make a fresh order under section 14(1)[¹ ...].

(5)   In subsection (3) "period for consideration" means the period of forty days beginning with the day on which the order was made.

(6)   In calculating the period for consideration, no account is to be taken of any time during which–

(a)   Parliament is dissolved or prorogued; or

(b)   both Houses are adjourned for more than four days.

(7)   If a designated derogation is withdrawn by the United Kingdom, the [²[³Secretary of State]] must by order make such amendments to this Act as he considers are required to reflect that withdrawal.

Commencement
October 2, 2000: The Human Rights Act 1998 (Commencement No.2) Order 2000 (SI 2000 No.1851).

Amendments
1.   The Human Rights Act (Amendment) Order 2001 (SI 2001 No.1216) art 3 (April 1, 2001).
2.   Transfer of Functions (Miscellaneous) Order 2001 (SI 2001 No.3500) art 8 and Sch 2 para 7 (November 26, 2001).
3.   Secretary of State for Constitutional Affairs Order 2003 (SI 2003 No.1887) art 9 and Sch 2 para 10(1) (August 19, 2003).

Definition
"amend": see s21(1).

Periodic review of designated reservations

17.–(1)   The appropriate Minister must review the designated reservation referred to in section 15(1)(a)–

(a)   before the end of the period of five years beginning with the date on which section 1(2) came into force; and

(b)   if that designation is still in force, before the end of the period of five years beginning with the date on which the last report relating to it was laid under subsection (3).

(2)   The appropriate Minister must review each of the other designated reservations (if any)–

(a)   before the end of the period of five years beginning with the date on which the order designating the reservation first came into force; and

(b)   if the designation is still in force, before the end of the period of five years beginning with the date on which the last report relating to it was laid under subsection (3).

(3)   The Minister conducting a review under this section must prepare a report on the result of the review and lay a copy of it before each House of Parliament.

Commencement

October 2, 2000: The Human Rights Act 1998 (Commencement No.2) Order 2000 (SI 2000 No.1851).

Definition

"the appropriate Minister": see s21(1).

Judges of the European Court of Human Rights

Appointment to European Court of Human Rights
18.–(1)   In this section "judicial office" means the office of–
(a)   Lord Justice of Appeal, Justice of the High Court or Circuit judge, in England and Wales;
(b)   judge of the Court of Session or sheriff, in Scotland;
(c)   Lord Justice of Appeal, judge of the High Court or county court judge, in Northern Ireland.

(2)   The holder of a judicial office may become a judge of the European Court of Human Rights ("the Court") without being required to relinquish his office.

(3)   But he is not required to perform the duties of his judicial office while he is a judge of the Court.

(4)   In respect of any period during which he is a judge of the Court–
(a)   a Lord Justice of Appeal or Justice of the High Court is not to count as a judge of the relevant court for the purposes of section 2(1) or 4(1) of the [²Senior Courts Act 1981] (maximum number of judges) nor as a judge of the [²Senior Courts] for the purposes of section 12(1) to (6) of that Act (salaries etc.);
(b)   a judge of the Court of Session is not to count as a judge of that court for the purposes of section 1(1) of the Court of Session Act 1988 (maximum number of judges) or of section 9(1)(c) of the Administration of Justice Act 1973 ("the 1973 Act") (salaries etc.);
(c)   a Lord Justice of Appeal or judge of the High Court in Northern Ireland is not to count as a judge of the relevant court for the purposes of section 2(1) or 3(1) of the Judicature (Northern Ireland) Act 1978 (maximum number of judges) nor as a judge of the [²Court of Judicature] of Northern Ireland for the purposes of section 9(1)(d) of the 1973 Act (salaries etc.);
(d)   a Circuit judge is not to count as such for the purposes of section 18 of the Courts Act 1971 (salaries etc.);
(e)   a sheriff is not to count as such for the purposes of section 14 of the Sheriff Courts (Scotland) Act 1907 (salaries etc.);
(f)   a county court judge of Northern Ireland is not to count as such for the purposes of section 106 of the County Courts Act Northern Ireland) 1959 (salaries etc.).

(5)   If a sheriff principal is appointed a judge of the Court, section 11(1) of the Sheriff Courts (Scotland) Act 1971 (temporary appointment of sheriff principal) applies, while he holds that appointment, as if his office is vacant.

(6)   Schedule 4 makes provision about judicial pensions in relation to the holder of a judicial office who serves as a judge of the Court.

(7)   The Lord Chancellor or the Secretary of State may by order make such transitional provision (including, in particular, provision for a temporary increase in the maximum number of judges) as he considers appropriate in relation to any holder of a judicial office who has completed his service as a judge of the Court.

[¹(7A)   The following paragraphs apply to the making of an order under subsection (7) in relation to any holder of a judicial office listed in subsection (1)(a)–
(a)   before deciding what transitional provision it is appropriate to make, the person making the order must consult the Lord Chief Justice of England and Wales;

(b) before making the order, that person must consult the Lord Chief Justice of England and Wales.

(7B) The following paragraphs apply to the making of an order under subsection (7) in relation to any holder of a judicial office listed in subsection (1)(c)–

(a) before deciding what transitional provision it is appropriate to make, the person making the order must consult the Lord Chief Justice of Northern Ireland;

(b) before making the order, that person must consult the Lord Chief Justice of Northern Ireland.

(7C) The Lord Chief Justice of England and Wales may nominate a judicial office holder (within the meaning of section 109(4) of the Constitutional Reform Act 2005) to exercise his functions under this section.

(7D) The Lord Chief Justice of Northern Ireland may nominate any of the following to exercise his functions under this section–

(a) the holder of one of the offices listed in Schedule 1 to the Justice (Northern Ireland) Act 2002;

(b) a Lord Justice of Appeal (as defined in section 88 of that Act).]

Amendments

1. Constitutional Reform Act 2005 (2005 c.4) s15 and Sch 4 para 278 (April 3, 2006).
2. Constitutional Reform Act 2005 (2005 c.4) s59 and Sch 11 paras 1, 4 and 6 (October 1, 2009).

Parliamentary procedure

Statements of compatibility

19.–(1) A Minister of the Crown in charge of a Bill in either House of Parliament must, before Second Reading of the Bill–

(a) make a statement to the effect that in his view the provisions of the Bill are compatible with the Convention rights ("a statement of compatibility"); or

(b) make a statement to the effect that although he is unable to make a statement of compatibility the government nevertheless wishes the House to proceed with the Bill.

(2) The statement must be in writing and be published in such manner as the Minister making it considers appropriate.

Commencement

Section 19 entered into force on November 24, 1998: (SI 1998 No.2882).

Definitions

"the Convention rights": see s1(1).
"Minister of the Crown": see s21(1).

Supplemental

Orders, etc. under this Act

20.–(1) Any power of a Minister of the Crown to make an order under this Act is exercisable by statutory instrument.

(2) The power of [¹...] [²the Lord Chancellor or] the Secretary of State to make rules (other than rules of court) under section 2(3) or 7(9) is exercisable by statutory instrument.

(3) Any statutory instrument made under section 14, 15 or 16(7) must be laid before Parliament.

(4) No order may be made by [¹...] [²the Lord Chancellor or] the Secretary of State under section 1(4), 7(11) or 16(2) unless a draft of the order has been laid before, and approved by, each House of Parliament.

(5) Any statutory instrument made under section 18(7) or Schedule 4, or to which subsection (2) applies, shall be subject to annulment in pursuance of a resolution of either House of Parliament.

(6) The power of a Northern Ireland department to make–

(a) rules under section 2(3)(c) or 7(9)(c), or

(b)   an order under section 7(11),

is exercisable by statutory rule for the purposes of the Statutory Rules (Northern Ireland) Order 1979.

(7)   Any rules made under section 2(3)(c) or 7(9)(c) shall be subject to negative resolution; and section 41(6) of the Interpretation Act Northern Ireland) 1954 (meaning of "subject to negative resolution") shall apply as if the power to make the rules were conferred by an Act of the Northern Ireland Assembly.

(8)   No order may be made by a Northern Ireland department under section 7(11) unless a draft of the order has been laid before, and approved by, the Northern Ireland Assembly.

Amendments

1.   Secretary of State for Constitutional Affairs Order 2003 (SI 2003 No.1887) art 9 and Sch 2 para 10(2) (August 19, 2003).

2.   Transfer of Functions (Lord Chancellor and Secretary of State) Order 2005 (SI 2005 No.3429) art 8 and Sch para 3 (January 12, 2006).

Definition

"Minister of the Crown": see s21(1).

Interpretation, etc.

21.–(1)   In this Act–

"amend" includes repeal and apply (with or without modifications);

"the appropriate Minister" means the Minister of the Crown having charge of the appropriate authorised government department (within the meaning of the Crown Proceedings Act 1947);

"the Commission" means the European Commission of Human Rights;

"the Convention" means the Convention for the Protection of Human Rights and Fundamental Freedoms, agreed by the Council of Europe at Rome on 4th November 1950 as it has effect for the time being in relation to the United Kingdom;

"declaration of incompatibility" means a declaration under section 4;

"Minister of the Crown" has the same meaning as in the Ministers of the Crown Act 1975;

"Northern Ireland Minister" includes the First Minister and the deputy First Minister in Northern Ireland;

"primary legislation" means any–

(a)   public general Act;

(b)   local and personal Act;

(c)   private Act;

(d)   Measure of the Church Assembly;

(e)   Measure of the General Synod of the Church of England;

(f)   Order in Council–

(i)   made in exercise of Her Majesty's Royal Prerogative;

(ii)   made under section 38(1)(a) of the Northern Ireland Constitution Act 1973 or the corresponding provision of the Northern Ireland Act 1998; or

(iii)   amending an Act of a kind mentioned in paragraph (a), (b) or (c);

and includes an order or other instrument made under primary legislation (otherwise than by the [²Welsh Ministers, the First Minister for Wales, the Counsel General to the Welsh Assembly Government,] a member of the Scottish Executive, a Northern Ireland Minister or a Northern Ireland department) to the extent to which it operates to bring one or more provisions of that legislation into force or amends any primary legislation;

"the First Protocol" means the protocol to the Convention agreed at Paris on 20th March 1952;

[¹...]

"the Eleventh Protocol" means the protocol to the Convention (restructuring the control machinery established by the Convention) agreed at Strasbourg on 11th May 1994;

[¹"the Thirteenth Protocol" means the protocol to the Convention (concerning the abolition of the death penalty in all circumstances) agreed at Vilnius on 3rd May 2002;]

"remedial order" means an order under section 10;

"subordinate legislation" means any–

(a) Order in Council other than one–
   (i) made in exercise of Her Majesty's Royal Prerogative;
   (ii) made under section 38(1)(a) of the Northern Ireland Constitution Act 1973 or the corresponding provision of the Northern Ireland Act 1998; or
   (iii) amending an Act of a kind mentioned in the definition of primary legislation;

(b) Act of the Scottish Parliament;

[²(ba) Measure of the National Assembly for Wales;

(bb) Act of the National Assembly for Wales;]

(c) Act of the Parliament of Northern Ireland;

(d) Measure of the Assembly established under section 1 of the Northern Ireland Assembly Act 1973;

(e) Act of the Northern Ireland Assembly;

(f) order, rules, regulations, scheme, warrant, byelaw or other instrument made under primary legislation (except to the extent to which it operates to bring one or more provisions of that legislation into force or amends any primary legislation);

(g) order, rules, regulations, scheme, warrant, byelaw or other instrument made under legislation mentioned in paragraph (b), (c), (d) or (e) or made under an Order in Council applying only to Northern Ireland;

(h) order, rules, regulations, scheme, warrant, byelaw or other instrument made by a member of the Scottish Executive [², Welsh Ministers, the First Minister for Wales, the Counsel General to the Welsh Assembly Government,] a Northern Ireland Minister or a Northern Ireland department in exercise of prerogative or other executive functions of Her Majesty which are exercisable by such a person on behalf of Her Majesty;

"transferred matters" has the same meaning as in the Northern Ireland Act 1998; and

"tribunal" means any tribunal in which legal proceedings may be brought.

(2) The references in paragraphs (b) and (c) of section 2(1) to Articles are to Articles of the Convention as they had effect immediately before the coming into force of the Eleventh Protocol.

(3) The reference in paragraph (d) of section 2(1) to Article 46 includes a reference to Articles 32 and 54 of the Convention as they had effect immediately before the coming into force of the Eleventh Protocol.

(4) The references in section 2(1) to a report or decision of the Commission or a decision of the Committee of Ministers include references to a report or decision made as provided by paragraphs 3, 4 and 6 of Article 5 of the Eleventh Protocol (transitional provisions).

(5) [³...]

Commencement

s21(5) entered into force on November 9, 1998. The remainder of the section entered into force on October 2, 2000: The Human Rights Act 1998 (Commencement No.2) Order 2000 (SI 2000 No.1851).

Amendments

1. Human Rights Act 1998 (Amendment) Order 2004 (SI 2004 No.1574) art 2(2) (June 22, 2004).
2. Government of Wales Act 2006 (2006 c.32) s160 and Sch 10 para 56 (May 3, 2007, subject to s164(4) and (5) Government of Wales Act 2006).
3. Armed Forces Act 2006 (2006 c.52) s378 and Sch 17 (March 28, 2009 for the purposes outlined in art 3 Armed Forces Act 2006 (Commencement No.4) Order 2009 (SI 2009 No 812); October 31, 2009 for all

other purposes). For the date that the Armed Forces Act 2006 is due to expire, see the Armed Forces Act (Continuation) Order 2012 (SI 2012 No.1750) art 2.

General Note
Subsection (1)
"the appropriate Minister" is given a narrower definition for the purposes of Sch 4 by para 4 to that Schedule.

Short title, commencement, application and extent

22.–(1)   This Act may be cited as the Human Rights Act 1998.

(2)   Sections 18, 20 and 21(5) and this section come into force on the passing of this Act.

(3)   The other provisions of this Act come into force on such day as the Secretary of State may by order appoint; and different days may be appointed for different purposes.

(4)   Paragraph (b) of subsection (1) of section 7 applies to proceedings brought by or at the instigation of a public authority whenever the act in question took place; but otherwise that subsection does not apply to an act taking place before the coming into force of that section.

(5)   This Act binds the Crown.

(6)   This Act extends to Northern Ireland.

(7)   [¹...]

Commencement
This section entered into force on 9 November 1998.

Amendment
1.   Armed Forces Act 2006 (2006 c.52) s378 and Sch 17 (March 28, 2009 for the purposes outlined in art 3 Armed Forces Act 2006 (Commencement No.4) Order 2009 (SI 2009 No.812); October 31, 2009 for all other purposes). For the date that the Armed Forces Act 2006 is due to expire, see the Armed Forces Act (Continuation) Order 2012 (SI 2012 No.1750) art 2.

General Note
Subsection (4)
This subsection contains a comprehensive code for the application of the Act to decisions taken before it came into force. This limitation cannot be bypassed by relying on the duties in ss3 and 6. See *R v Lambert* [2001] 3 All ER 577 and *Pearce v Governing Body of Mayfield School* [2001] EWCA Civ 1347. This reflects the views of the Commissioners in *CG 2356/2000* and *CIS 1077/1999*. It has been reaffirmed by the House of Lords in *R v Kansal (No.2)* [2002] 1 All ER 257 and *Wilson v First County Trust Ltd* [2003] 4 All ER 97 especially at para 92.

SCHEDULE 1

General Note
There is probably no limit to the inventive ways in which a party in a child support case may try to identify a breach of the Convention. In *Logan v United Kingdom* (1996) 22 EHRR CD 178, for example, one of the arguments used by the applicant absent parent was that the financial burden of the child support maintenance assessment interfered with his freedom of religion under Art 9. For this reason, the whole of the Convention as incorporated in British law is set out. However, most challenges are likely to be made under Arts 6 (fair hearing), 8 (family life) and 14 (discrimination). The commentary covers the general approach to the Convention and Arts 6(1) and 14. It is less easy to make useful general statements about the scope of Art 8 in the child support context.
Interpretation and application
The Convention is an international treaty. It must be interpreted as a treaty in accordance with the Vienna Convention on the Law of Treaties 1969, especially Arts 31-33 (*Golder v United Kingdom* (1975) 1 EHRR 524).

There are two texts: English and French. As there is no provision for one or the other to take precedence, each is equally authoritative: Art 33 of the Vienna Convention. Only the English text is reproduced in the Act. Section 2 does not specify the French text as something to be taken into account. However, it must be taken into account when interpreting the English text in order to give a meaning that best reconciles the different language consistently with the object and purpose of the Convention: *Wemhoff v Federal Republic of Germany* (1968) 1 EHRR 55.

Each provision must be interpreted in the context of the Convention and its Protocols as a whole. This means that account must be taken of those provisions that are not incorporated by this Act.

Sometimes the scope of a concept is determined by reference to the domestic law of the State concerned. On these occasions, the classification by the State will determine whether a case falls within the scope of a

Convention right. However, States do not always have this freedom. Sometimes the scope of a concept is determined autonomously under the Convention. On these occasions, the classification by the State will not automatically prevent a case from falling within the scope of a Convention right. A classification in domestic law that brings a case within the scope of a concept that has an autonomous meaning under the Convention is likely to be accepted, but a classification that takes a case outside the scope of a concept will not: *Engel v The Netherlands (No.1)* (1976) 1 EHRR 647.

Closely linked to the autonomous meaning of some concepts is the margin of appreciation that is allowed in the interpretation and application of some aspects of some Convention rights. The margin of appreciation applies in two ways. First, it applies to restrict the scope of a right when there is a divergence of views in the States who are parties to the Convention: *Handyside v United Kingdom* (1976) 1 EHRR 737. The greater the divergence of view, the wider the margin of appreciation: *X, Y and Z v United Kingdom* (1997) 24 EHRR 143. Second, the margin of appreciation applies when there are different ways in which a state may give effect to a right: *Airey v Ireland* (1979) 2 EHRR 305. Whichever way the margin of appreciation is used, it is only a margin and the courts police the boundary of the margin to ensure that it is not exceeded: *Stubbings v United Kingdom* (1996) 23 EHRR 213.

The courts and the commissioners referred in their decisions to a margin of appreciation. Sometimes they refer to a margin or degree of deference instead. This alternative formulation has not found universal favour, as it is thought to convey the wrong relationship between the Parliament and the judiciary. However, it is useful in distinguishing the way that the margin operates supranationally in Strasbourg and nationally in the domestic courts. Whatever the language used, the concept as used in domestic law is not based on a recognition that different Member States have different laws on a point. Nevertheless, a margin of appreciation is applied domestically (*Ofulue v Bossert, The Times,* February 11 2008) and these expressions are useful in indicating the scope of freedom for action that is accorded under this Act to the legislature and executive. The extent of that freedom will vary according to the circumstances. It will be at its greatest in laws that deal with social and economic policy and at its least in laws which are of constitutional importance. See *R (Carson) v SSWP* [2003] 3 All ER 577 *per* Laws LJ at para 73. This freedom exists only for the purpose of justification that may be permitted within a Convention right; it does not apply to the scope of a Convention right (*ibid.* at para 62). The extent to which the courts will show respect or deference also varies according to the nature of the issue. In *Huang v Secretary of State for the Home Department* [2005] 3 All ER 435, the Court of Appeal decided that it applies to judgments on the formation of reasons the courts are not in a position to arrive at an autonomous decision, but not to decisions on the application of the policy.

The margin of appreciation includes in appropriate cases an appropriate period of time in which to bring domestic law into compliance with the Convention rights (*R (Hooper) v SSWP* [2003] 3 All ER 673 at para 78). This was also the approach taken by the House of Lords in *Mv SSWP,* reported as *R(CS) 4/06.*

A purposive approach is taken to interpretation in order to ensure that the aim of the Convention is realised and its object is achieved (*Wemhoff,* above). This involves interpreting the Convention in a way that renders the rights practical and effective rather than theoretical or illusory: *Artico v Italy* (1980) 2 EHRR 7. It also means that the Convention is interpreted dynamically in order to reflect changing present day conditions: *Tyrer v United Kingdom* (1978) 2 EHRR 1.

As the Convention is interpreted dynamically, the European Court of Human Rights does not regard its case law as binding. However, it follows its previous decisions unless there are cogent reasons for doing otherwise: *Cossey v United Kingdom* (1990) 13 EHRR 622. It does not draw a distinction between those parts of its judgments that were essential to the decision in a particular case and those that were not. The highest British courts should take the same approach, although the doctrine or precedent will probably continue to apply.

Only live issues have to be considered. This prevents an issue being raised in the abstract. This is achieved in two ways. First, only someone who is a victim may rely on a Convention right. Second, the law is not concerned with theoretical or illusory violations of Convention rights where the victim had not in practice suffered as a consequence: *R(M) v Commissioner of Police for the Metropolis, The Times,* August 1, 2001.

RIGHTS AND FREEDOMS
PART I
THE CONVENTION
RIGHTS AND FREEDOMS

Article 2 – right to life

1.   Everyone's right to life shall be protected by law. No one shall be deprived of his life intentionally save in the execution of a sentence of a court following his conviction of a crime for which this penalty is provided by law.

2.   Deprivation of life shall not be regarded as inflicted in contravention of this Article when it results from the use of force which is no more than absolutely necessary:
(a)   in defence of any person from unlawful violence;
(b)   in order to effect a lawful arrest or to prevent the escape of a person lawfully detained;
(c)   in action lawfully taken for the purpose of quelling a riot or insurrection.

Article 3 – prohibition of torture
No one shall be subjected to torture or to inhuman or degrading treatment or punishment.

Article 4 – prohibition of slavery and forced labour
1. No one shall be held in slavery or servitude.
2. No one shall be required to perform forced or compulsory labour.
3. For the purpose of this Article the term "forced or compulsory labour" shall not include:
(a) any work required to be done in the ordinary course of detention imposed according to the provisions of Article 5 of this Convention or during conditional release from such detention;
(b) any service of a military character or, in case of conscientious objectors in countries where they are recognised, service exacted instead of compulsory military service;
(c) any service exacted in case of an emergency or calamity threatening the life or well-being of the community;
(d) any work or service which forms part of normal civic obligations.

Article 5 – right to liberty and security
1. Everyone has the right to liberty and security of person. No one shall be deprived of his liberty save in the following cases and in accordance with a procedure prescribed by law:
(a) the lawful detention of a person after conviction by a competent court;
(b) the lawful arrest or detention of a person for non-compliance with the lawful order of a court or in order to secure the fulfilment of any obligation prescribed by law;
(c) the lawful arrest or detention of a person effected for the purpose of bringing him before the competent legal authority on reasonable suspicion of having committed an offence or when it is reasonably considered necessary to prevent his committing an offence or fleeing after having done so;
(d) the detention of a minor by lawful order for the purpose of educational supervision or his lawful detention for the purpose of bringing him before the competent legal authority;
(e) the lawful detention of persons for the prevention of the spreading of infectious diseases, of persons of unsound mind, alcoholics or drug addicts or vagrants;
(f) the lawful arrest or detention of a person to prevent his effecting an unauthorised entry into the country or of a person against whom action is being taken with a view to deportation or extradition.
2. Everyone who is arrested shall be informed promptly, in a language which he understands, of the reasons for his arrest and of any charge against him.
3. Everyone arrested or detained in accordance with the provisions of paragraph 1(c) of this Article shall be brought promptly before a judge or other officer authorised by law to exercise judicial power and shall be entitled to trial within a reasonable time or to release pending trial. Release may be conditioned by guarantees to appear for trial.
4. Everyone who is deprived of his liberty by arrest or detention shall be entitled to take proceedings by which the lawfulness of his detention shall be decided speedily by a court and his release ordered if the detention is not lawful.
5. Everyone who has been the victim of arrest or detention in contravention of the provisions of this Article shall have an enforceable right to compensation.

Article 6 – right to a fair trial
1. In the determination of his civil rights and obligations or of any criminal charge against him, everyone is entitled to a fair and public hearing within a reasonable time by an independent and impartial tribunal established by law. Judgment shall be pronounced publicly but the press and public may be excluded from all or part of the trial in the interest of morals, public order or national security in a democratic society, where the interests of juveniles or the protection of the private life of the parties so require, or to the extent strictly necessary in the opinion of the court in special circumstances where publicity would prejudice the interests of justice.
2. Everyone charged with a criminal offence shall be presumed innocent until proved guilty according to law.
3. Everyone charged with a criminal offence has the following minimum rights:
(a) to be informed promptly, in a language which he understands and in detail, of the nature and cause of the accusation against him;
(b) to have adequate time and facilities for the preparation of his defence;
(c) to defend himself in person or through legal assistance of his own choosing or, if he has not sufficient means to pay for legal assistance, to be given it free when the interests of justice so require;
(d) to examine or have examined witnesses against him and to obtain the attendance and examination of witnesses on his behalf under the same conditions as witnesses against him;
(e) to have the free assistance of an interpreter if he cannot understand or speak the language used in court.

General Note

This Article is not retrospective in its operation (*Law v Society of Lloyd's, The Times,* January 23 2004).

The Article was considered by the Commission in *Logan v United Kingdom* (1996) 22 EHRR CD 178. The absent parent complained of a violation of Art 6 on the ground that the child support maintenance formula made no allowance for the costs of access to his children. He did not dispute that the formula had been correctly applied. The Commission decided that the complaint should be rejected as manifestly ill-founded because either there was no dispute as to the application of the domestic law (as opposed to a dispute about what that law should be) or there was dispute of a genuine or serious nature. This conclusion is not an authority that Art 6 has no application to the resolution of disputes about the application of the formula in an individual case. The Judicial Studies Board Seminar Paper on *Family Law and the Human Rights Act 1998* cites this case as authority that child support assessments are public rights rather than civil rights (para 9.1). The Commission's reasoning does not support that proposition.

The right given by this Article contains similar wording to s11(1)(d) of the Canadian Charter of Rights and Freedoms, which guarantees as a Legal Right that:

"Any person charged with an offence has the right (d) to be presumed innocent until proven guilty according to law in a fair and public hearing by an independent and impartial tribunal".

Decisions interpreting and applying the final words of this right are admissible in interpreting and applying Convention rights, subject to giving the appropriate weight to the Strasbourg jurisprudence under s2(1) of the Act: *Starrs and Chambers v Procurator Fiscal, Linlithgow* [2000] HRLR 191. No doubt the same approach will be taken with other comparable human rights provisions.

This right is a fundamental principle within a democratic society: *Sutter v Switzerland* (1984) 6 EHRR 272. As such it must be interpreted liberally. However, the right is not absolute and may be subject to limitation, provided that the limitations are not such that the very essence of the right is impaired: *Hall and Co v Simons* [2000] 2 FLR 545 at 612.

Compliance with this right must be judged by reference to the adjudication system as a whole. If a decision of a body does not comply with this right, there will be no breach of the Convention if that body is under the control of a judicial body that does satisfy the right: *Albert and Le Compte v Belgium* (1983) 5 EHRR 533; *Bryan v United Kingdom* (1995) 21 EHRR 342. The higher body must undertake a rehearing or a careful review of the case on its merits: in *Re Medicaments and Related Classes of Goods (No.4), The Times,* August 7 2001. It is not essential that the higher body rehears the evidence of witnesses: *Preiss v General Dental Council* [2001] 1 WLR 1926. In particular, a violation by the appeal tribunal may be remedied by proceedings before the Upper Tribunal. As a violation of Art 6(1) would be a mistake of law requiring the Upper Tribunal to set aside a tribunal's decision, the tribunal would be able to refer the case for rehearing before another tribunal that would comply with Art 6(1) or, if this is not possible, consider the case on its merits and give a decision without referring the case to another tribunal.

This Convention right does not give a right to any particular tribunal; only a right to *a* tribunal hearing: *OT Africa Line Ltd v Fayad Hijazy, The Times,* November 28 2000.

Determination

A determination presupposes a dispute. This is emphasised by the word "contestation" in the French text. This underlines that the Article does not give a person a right to have an issue determined in the abstract. There must be an arguable case that a right exists under domestic law: *Lithgow v United Kingdom* (1986) 8 EHRR 329. There must a dispute about the right that is genuine and serious: *Benthem v Netherlands* (1985) 8 EHRR 1. The need for a genuine and serious dispute may mean that there is no violation of Art 6(1) in the striking out of misconceived appeals under reg 46 of the Appeals Regulations.

There will certainly be a dispute on an appeal to a tribunal. There may be some doubt about a referral to a tribunal of an application for a variation. The reason for the doubt lies in the reasoning of the European Court of Human Rights in *Feldbrugge v Netherlands* (1986) 8 EHRR 425, in which, at para 25, the Court referred to the dispute as arising only after the initial decision on entitlement to a sickness benefit. As the determination of a referral is a first determination, it may be that no dispute has arisen at that stage. However, the Court's reasoning may not apply. In the case of a social security benefit, the initial determination is by an officer whose concern is merely to ensure that the law is correctly applied. No dispute arises until a decision has been made. In the case of an application for a departure direction, in contrast, there will be disagreement between the non-resident parent and the person with care from the outset.

Article 6(1) is concerned with the determination of disputes. It is concerned with the way in which a dispute is handled. It is not concerned with the merits of the decision reached, provided that the procedure followed was fair. In other words, Art 6(1) must not be used as a further level of appeal. This is known as the *quatrieme instance* doctrine. See *Locabail (United Kingdom) Ltd v Waldorf Investment Corporation (No.4), The Times,* May 25 2000.

Also, Art 6(1) is not concerned with the content of the rights which are in dispute. Any challenge to the content of rights must be made under other articles. So, it is not possible to use this Article to challenge either (i) the terms of the child support legislation (*Powell and Rayner v United Kingdom* (1990) 12 EHRR 355) or (ii) its interpretation by commissioners and the courts (*X and Y v Netherlands* (1985) 8 EHRR 235).

If there is a dispute about civil rights, the party has a right to go before a tribunal. That right is not expressed in Art 6(1), but it is inherent: *Golder v United Kingdom* (1975) 1 EHRR 524. The right to access must, of course, be effective, but the means by which it is achieved is within the margin of appreciation: *Airey v Ireland* (1979) 2 EHRR 305. It may be achieved by legal aid or by other means, like simplified procedures *(ibid)*. The inquisitorial approach contributes to the access to the tribunal. However, in the most complex of cases, it may be arguable that financial assistance is essential: *Granger v United Kingdom* (1990) 12 EHRR 469, but it has been held that the restriction of legal aid is not a violation of this Convention right: *Procurator Fiscal, Fort William v McLean, The Times,* August 11 2000.

The right of access may be subject to limitations provided that they pursue a legitimate objective, are proportionate to that objective and do not destroy the essence of the right: *Stubbings v United Kingdom* (1996) 23 EHRR 213 and *Ashingdane v UK* (1985) 7 EHRR 528.

The time limit for appealing to a tribunal is one month and it can only be extended on stringent conditions. It is possible for this type of restriction to be in violation of Art 6(1).

Some aspects of the child support legislation can only be challenged by judicial review. The European Court of Human Rights has left open whether judicial review satisfies Art 6(1): *Air Canada v UK* (1995) 20 EHRR 150. However, it has been held that judicial review would be sufficient to cure any lack of independence in the fact-finding tribunal: *R (Hussain) v Asylum Support Adjudicator, The Times,* November 15 2001. It is very likely that judicial review will be sufficient to do this if, regardless of appearances, there is no reason of substance to question the objective integrity of the decision maker (*R (Beeson) v Dorset CC, The Times,* December 18 2002; *Begum v Tower Hamlets LBC* [2003] 1 All ER 731).

The right of access is to a tribunal that complies with this Article. There is no right to a further appeal. However, the existence of a right of appeal to a body that complies with Art 6(1) may be sufficient to remedy a deficiency in the lower body. If there is a right of further appeal, it must not be discriminatory (*Belgian Linguistic Case (No.2)* (1968) 1 EHRR 252 at para 9).

Civil rights and obligations

Article 6(1) is concerned with private rights and not with public rights. Private rights have an autonomous Convention meaning: *Konig v Federal Republic of Germany* (1978) 2 EHRR 170. The classification depends on the substantive content and effects of the right under domestic law and not on the legal classification of the right in domestic law *(ibid)*. The question to ask is: is the outcome of the determination decisive for private rights and obligations? (*Stran Greek Refineries and Stratis Andreadis v Greece* (1994) 19 EHRR 293).

It is suggested that child support rights and obligations, in so far as they come before tribunals, are civil for the purposes of Art 6(1). There is an issue whether some other aspects of the scheme are criminal. This is determined by reference to (a) form of procedure involved, (b) whether an offence is created by the legislation and (c) whether the action taken by the court is in the form of a punishment: *R (McCann) v Crown Court at Manchester* [2001] 4 All ER 264.

Fair hearing

A margin of appreciation applies in the procedures adopted to ensure a fair hearing: *Dombo Beheer v Netherlands* (1993) 18 EHRR 213.

The margin of appreciation operates in respect of evidence, which is primarily a matter for the domestic court, provided that the proceedings as a whole are fair. This applies both to the admissibility of evidence (*Schenk v Switzerland* (1988) 13 EHRR 242) and to its evaluation (*Ludi v Switzerland* (1992) 15 EHRR 173).

Equality of arms is an essential requirement for a fair hearing, although there is a margin of appreciation in how it is achieved: *Dombo Beheer v Netherlands* (1993) 18 EHRR 213. This means that a party must have a reasonable opportunity to present a case, including evidence, under conditions that do not put that party at a disadvantage as against the other parties *(ibid)*. It is the responsibility of the tribunal to ensure that the parties see, and have the chance to comment on, all evidence available to the tribunal (*H.A.L. v Finland* (Application No.38267/97) decided on 27 January 2004). Equality of arms is largely guaranteed by natural justice and the inquisitorial approach, if properly applied. There is, though, scope for a violation of this requirement. For example, submissions put to the First-tier Tribunal by the Secretary of State merely refer to, rather than quote, the relevant law, leaving the parties to find it for themselves (*CCS 3517/2000*, para 10.2).

Article 6 is concerned with the fairness of the hearing and not with extra-judicial activities: *R v Hertfordshire County Council ex p Green* [2000] 1 All ER 773. This means, for example, that it is not concerned with the way in which evidence is obtained, although it is concerned with the use of evidence at the hearing *(ibid)*.

The use of double translation from one language into another via a third language is not in principle a breach of Art 6: *West London Youth Court ex p N* [2000] 1 All ER 823. However, a party is entitled to a professional service from an interpreter at a hearing and, if the service appears to be below that standard, the matter should be investigated by the tribunal (*CDLA 2748/2002*, para 13).

Fairness also requires that reasons be given for a decision. The standard to be attained varies according to the circumstances of the case. Reasons are needed to show that an issue has been considered and how it was determined: *Ruiz Torija v Spain* (1994) Series A No.303-A. The reasons must indicate with sufficient clarity the grounds on which the decision was based in order to allow a party usefully to exercise the rights of appeal: *Hadjianastassiou v Greece* (1992) 16 EHRR 219. Important issues must be covered: *Hiro Balani v Spain* (1994) 19 EHRR 565. However, it is not necessary to deal with every point. In particular, there is no need to deal with a point that is not raised timeously: *Vander Hurk v Netherlands* (1994) 18 EHRR 481. In considering reasons for detention under Art 5(3), the European Court of Human Rights has appeared unimpressed by reasons that are in identical or stereotyped form: *Mansur v Turkey* [1995] Series A No.319-B. These principles are broadly in line with the approach that was taken by the commissioners.

Striking out a case for contempt is likely to be a breach of Art 6(1), unless the act which constituted the breach led to a real risk that a fair hearing could not happen: *Arrow Nominees Inc v Blackledge, The Times,* December 8 1999. The reasoning does not appear from the short newspaper report, but it is unlikely to cover striking out for want of prosecution.

The Privy Council has held (but not in the context of a Convention right) that in an extreme case the incompetence of a representative can result in unfairness and deprive the representative's client of due process: *Boodram v State of Trinidad and Tobago, The Times,* May 15 2001.

The Court of Appeal has held, albeit in a committal case, that the failure to give a party a reasonable opportunity to obtain legal funding may involve a breach of the party's right to a fair hearing (*Berry Trade Ltd v Moussavi* [2002] 1 WLR 1910).

In *CCS 1018/02,* it was argued that there was an unfairness because the parent was an unrepresented and uninformed layman who was trying to negotiate the complex child support adjudication system. The parent was trying to challenge a decision of a child support appeal tribunal, which had given a departure direction against him. He tried to challenge it by way of appeal to a commissioner and then to the Court of Appeal. He also applied for a revision of the tribunal's decision by the Secretary of State. The application for a revision was outside the maximum time allowed. His unfairness argument was presented in order to show that the relevant provision should be interpreted so that time would run not from the date of the decision of the tribunal, but from the date of the decision of the Court of Appeal. The commissioner rejected the argument, making three points. First, the child support adjudication procedures are complex, but it is not necessary to understand them in order to operate them, because any attempt to challenge a decision is inter-substance and not its form. Second, the application for a revision was formally a separate proceeding from the proceedings before the tribunal, but in reality it was but another attempt by the parent to challenge the tribunal's decision. His argument had to be evaluated and applied in that context. Third, it was not appropriate to extend the time allowed for making an application, as this would not promote certainty or finality. The non-resident parent's application for leave to appeal was dismissed by the Court of Appeal (*Denson v SSWP* reported as *R(CS) 4/04*). The court decided that the time limits on an appeal against a decision by the Secretary of State were compatible with the Convention right to a fair hearing. They did not impair his access to a tribunal. The non-resident parent had one month to appeal, subject to an extension for cause up to a maximum of 13 months. That was a legitimate and proportionate response to the need for certainty and finality in litigation.

The Secretary of State's power to enforce or not to enforce the non-resident parent's liability is not within the scope of this article (by the House of Lords in *R (Kehoe) v SSWP* [2006] 1 AC 42 and the European Court on Human Rights in *Kehoe v United Kingdom* [2008] 1 FLR 1014).

The fairness of a hearing must be determined in the context of the evidence, not in the abstract (*Coles v Barracks, The Times,* August 7 2006 *per* Mummery LJ) and in relation to the proceedings as a whole, not just one part of it *(ibid, per* Wall LJ).

Public hearing

A private hearing is the normal practice in court cases involving children. This practice is consistent with the Convention (*Re PB (Hearings in open court)* [1996] 2 FLR 765 at *768, per* Butler-Sloss LJ and *Band P v UK* [2001] 2 FLR 261). Article 6(1) expressly allows the public and the press to be excluded if the interests of juveniles or the private lives of the parties require it. A direction by a chairman in a child support case that the hearing be in private would not be a violation of this right.

Also, the right may be waived: *Hakansson v Sweden* (1990) 13 EHRR 1. This is likely to be the wish of most parties in a child support case.

It has been held to be a contravention of this right to refuse an oral hearing if issues of fact may arise. However, if only an issue of law arises and no issue of fact is involved, an oral hearing is not required by this right. Also, if the whole of the system is considered, there is a right to an oral hearing. There was a violation of this right in *Fischer v Austria* (1995) Series A No.312, but in that case there was no right to a hearing at all at any level.

There may be a conflict between the right to have evidence given at a public hearing and the Convention right under Art 8 in respect of the content of that evidence. If this arises, the rights have to balanced. One solution is to hear the evidence that would breach Art 8 in private (*XXX v YYY and ZZZ,* unreported, decided by the Employment Appeal Tribunal on April 9 2003).

Within reasonable time

There is no set time within which a case must be heard. The time that is reasonable depends on the individual circumstances of the case, including matters like the complexity of the legal and factual issues and the conduct of the parties. It has been held that particular diligence is required in social security cases: *Deumeland v Germany* (1986) 8 EHRR 448. No doubt the same approach applies to child support.

Only delays for which the State is responsible will be a violation of this right. So, it is necessary to show a causal link between the delay and something that is within the control of the State. It is not sufficient simply to prove that one of the parties has brought about a delay. However, the State must provide tribunals with the necessary powers and resources to prevent delays that can be anticipated and with the powers and resources to minimise unforeseeable delays when they occur: See *Zimmerman and Steiner v Switzerland* (1983) 6 EHRR 17 and *Buchholz v Federal Republic of Germany* (1981) 3 EHRR 597. The necessary powers exist, but resources are not always sufficient.

It is only appropriate to stay proceedings for delay if it has become impossible for there to be a fair hearing. Otherwise, the proceedings should continue and another, appropriate remedy be found for the delay. See *Attorney General's Reference (No.2 of 2001)* [2004] 1 All ER 1049.

The commissioners discussed when proceedings begin for the purposes of this provision (*R(IS) 1/04* and *R(IS) 2/04*). However, the value of this is debatable, because the Upper Tribunal has no jurisdiction to give a remedy if there has been unreasonable delay. The House of Lords has decided that time begins at the earliest time when the likelihood of proceedings becomes known (*Attorney General's Reference (No.2 of 2001)*).

A person with care may be concerned about the delay in the enforcement of a child support maintenance assessment. However, that is not within the jurisdiction of tribunals.

Independent and impartial tribunal

There is no doubt that tribunals have the necessary judicial function to be a tribunal under this right: *Benthem v Netherlands* (1985) 8 EHRR 1.

Although independence and impartiality are closely linked, each has a distinct role to play in ensuring a fair hearing.

Independence is concerned with the institutional relationship between the tribunal and (a) the executive and (b) the parties: *Campbell and Fell v United Kingdom* (1984) 7 EHRR 165.

The decision maker who acts on behalf of the Secretary of State is not independent, even though in practice the officer may be impartial (*Begum v Tower Hamlets LBC* [2003] 1 All ER 731). This can be remedied by an appeal to the First-tier Tribunal, which lies on both fact and law, if the tribunal is itself independent (*R (Beeson) v Dorset CC, The Times,* December 18 2002). It may even be remedied if the tribunal does not have full fact-finding powers, provided that the decision maker was impartial *(Begum).*

However, these authorities only apply if the appeal tribunal is itself independent. If it is not, the lack of independence of the decision maker and the tribunal can only be remedied by the availability of an appeal to the Upper Tribunal or by judicial review.

Impartiality is concerned with the attitude, actual and perceived, of the judge to the parties and the issues.

Partiality may be subjective or objective. There is subjective partiality if the judge is actually prejudiced or biased. There is objective partiality if there is a legitimate doubt in this respect. See *Findlay v United Kingdom* (1997) 24 EHRR 221. Subjective partiality is covered by natural justice. So is objective partiality (*Porter v Magill* [2002] 1 All ER 465 *per* Lord Hope at paras 99-103, foreshadowed by Lord Browne-Wilkinson in *R v Bow Street Metropolitan Stipendiary Magistrate ex p Pinochet (No.2)* [1999] 1 All ER 577 at 589).

Impartiality is presumed: *Le Compte, Um Leuven and D Meyere v Belgium* (1981) 6 EHRR 583.

It is permissible for judges to comment, critically or otherwise, on the law and its development, but the nature of a criticism or the language in which it is expressed may create a legitimate apprehension that they would not be able to apply the law impartially: *Hoekstra v H MAdvocate, The Times,* April 14 2000.

This Convention right may be waived. Waiver signifies a voluntary, informed and unequivocal election not to claim a right or raise an objection. It may be express or tacit. See *Millar v Dickson (Procurator Fiscal, Elgin)* [2002] 3 All ER 1041.

Established by law

The First-tier Tribunal and Upper Tribunal both satisfy this requirement.

Judgment pronounced publicly

The European Court of Human Rights has not required that every decision must be read in public. The degree of publicity depends on the circumstances of the case, especially the special features of the proceedings involved, judged by reference to the object and purpose of Art 6(1). It is sufficient in cases involving children and which do not establish an issue of general principle for the decision to be available to those who had a legitimate interest in the outcome of the case: *Band P v UK* [2001] 2 FLR 261.

All decisions by the Upper Tribunal are publicly available. Decisions by the First-tier Tribunals have been described as public documents (*CSDLA 5/1995,* para 11). This is questionable. Certainly, they are not available to the public.

Article 7 – no punishment without law

1.   No one shall be held guilty of any criminal offence on account of any act or omission which did not constitute a criminal offence under national or international law at the time when it was committed. Nor shall a heavier penalty be imposed than the one that was applicable at the time the criminal offence was committed.

2.   This Article shall not prejudice the trial and punishment of any person for any act or omission which, at the time when it was committed, was criminal according to the general principles of law recognised by civilised nations.

Article 8 – right to respect for private and family life

1.   Everyone has the right to respect for his private and family life, his home and his correspondence.

2.   There shall be no interference by a public authority with the exercise of this right except such as is in accordance with the law and is necessary in a democratic society in the interests of national security, public safety or the economic well-being of the country, for the prevention of disorder or crime, for the protection of health or morals, or for the protection of the rights and freedoms of others.

General Note

Paragraph (1)

The right to a home is limited to issues of the right to privacy rather than a right to accommodation (*Harrow LBC v Qazi* [2003] 4 All ER 461 at paras 70, 89 and 120; *R(Erskine) v London Borough of Lambeth and the Office of the Deputy Prime Minster* [2003] EWHC 2479 (Admin)).

The Strasbourg authorities, the commissioners and the courts have concluded that there is nothing in the general nature of the child support scheme or its application that renders it incompatible with this Article, although there is still scope for argument that there has been a violation on the facts of a particular case.

In *Logan v United Kingdom* (1996) 22 EHRR CD 178, the absent parent complained of a violation of Art 8 on the ground that the amount of child support maintenance for which he was liable left him insufficient money to enable him to maintain reasonable contact with his children. The Commission decided that the complaint should be rejected as manifestly ill-founded, because the child support legislation did not by its very nature affect family life and, looking at the absent parent's income and expenses including the costs of access, he had not shown that the effect of the operation of the legislation in his case was of such a nature or degree as to disclose a lack of respect for family life. This conclusion leaves open the possibility that a breach of this Article may be shown on the facts of another case.

The child support scheme, including the variation scheme, is not in violation of this Article, because it is necessary to the economic well-being of the country and for the protection of the rights and freedoms of qualifying children (*CCS 6373/1999*, para 13). The courts have taken the same view, holding that neither the legislation nor the administration and enforcement (short of imprisonment) of the scheme is in violation (*R (Denson) v Child Support Officer* [2002] 1 FLR 938 at para 22 and *Brookes v SSWP and CMEC* [2010] EWCA Civ 420 at para 39).

In *Denson*, Munby J held that the making of a liability order, as a lever for compliance or as a gateway to further action, did not affect a person's private life under this paragraph (paras 38-45). The possibility was left open that this Article might be engaged if, for reasons known to the Child Support Agency, the person concerned was particularly vulnerable (para 44).

Cranston J summarised the position under this article in *Treharne v SSWP* [2009] 1 FLR 853, where children had sued the Child Support Agency in respect of its failure to enforce maintenance assessments in respect of them:

"32.   Art 8 cannot be extended to found any claim for damages for the failure of the CSA properly to pursue the maintenance assessments which it had made against the claimants' father. A comprehensive statutory scheme has been put in place. There is the possibility of judicial review. On the claimants' own case the scheme is European Convention compliant. There is no scope for contending that because of maladministration in an individual case Art 8 rights have been infringed. There is no basis on which the claimants can show an interference with their family and private life as those are conceptualised in the European Convention jurisprudence."

If this article is engaged, any enforcement decision must be proportionate. Hughes LJ explained what this entailed in *Brookes*:

"41.   The test of proportionality is not identical to the question whether an action in *Wednesbury* unreasonable, albeit that in many cases both tests may on the facts yield the same answer. Whereas the *Wednesbury* test involves asking whether the decision was within the range of those reasonably or rationally available to the decision maker, where proportionality is in question, the court must apply anxious scrutiny to ensure that the decision maker has struck the balance fairly between the conflicting interests of the claimant's right to respect for family life on the one hand and the public or competing interests within Article 8(2) on the other. In doing so, however, the court does not simply substitute its own decision. Its function is supervisory. It recognises and allows to the public body's decision maker a discretionary area of judgment. It will often be appropriate to adopt the two-stage process of asking first whether the intended objective can be achieved by means less interfering with the Article 8 right and second whether, if not, yet still the effect is excessive or disproportionate. For those various propositions see amongst other cases *R (Daly) v SSHD* [2001] 2 AC 532 and *Samaroo v SSHD* [2001] EWCA Civ 1139."

The Court of Appeal decided that, in the circumstances of the case, it was neither disproportionate nor excessive to ask magistrates to use their powers if the non-resident parent's conduct justified it (para 42).

Paragraph (2)

The requirement that the interference must be in accordance with the law (the principle of legality) involves three elements: it must have a basis in domestic law; it must be sufficiently accessible to those affected by it and sufficiently precise for them to understand it and foresee the consequences of violating it; and it must not be applied in a way that is arbitrary, such as if its exercise was in bad faith or not proportionate (*R v Shayler* [2002] 2 All ER 477 at paras 55-56).

Necessity also involves three elements: whether the objective justifies interfering with the right; whether the means chosen are rational, fair and not arbitrary; and whether the means impair the right as minimally as is reasonably possible (*R v Shayler* at paras 57 and 61).

So, proportionality is both an aspect of the third element of the principle of legality and an aspect of the third element of necessity. It requires, in both contexts, a consideration of the procedural safeguards to ensure that a decision is not made arbitrarily (*Denson* at paras 55(iv) and 56).

In *Denson*, Munby J held that, even if this Article was engaged by the making of a liability order, the interference with the para (1) right was justified and proportionate (para 46). The key issue was whether the order had been made arbitrarily (para 58). And in *R (Qazi) v Secretary of State*, reported as *R(CS) 5/04*, Charles J held that any infringement with this article by the departure direction scheme (now replaced by the variation scheme) was a proportionate response to a pressing social need (para 45).

Article 9 – freedom of thought, conscience and religion
1.   Everyone has the right to freedom of thought, conscience and religion; this right includes freedom to change his religion or belief and freedom, either alone or in community with others and in public or private, to manifest his religion or belief, in worship, teaching, practice and observance.
2.   Freedom to manifest one's religion or beliefs shall be subject only to such limitations as are prescribed by law and are necessary in a democratic society in the interests of public safety, for the protection of public order, health or morals, or for the protection of the rights and freedoms of others.

Article 10 – freedom of expression
1.   Everyone has the right to freedom of expression. This right shall include freedom to hold opinions and to receive and impart information and ideas without interference by public authority and regardless of frontiers. This Article shall not prevent States from requiring the licensing of broadcasting, television or cinema enterprises.
2.   The exercise of these freedoms, since it carries with it duties and responsibilities, may be subject to such formalities, conditions, restrictions or penalties as are prescribed by law and are necessary in a democratic society, in the interests of national security, territorial integrity or public safety, for the prevention of disorder or crime, for the protection of health or morals, for the protection of the reputation or rights of others, for preventing the disclosure of information received in confidence, or for maintaining the authority and impartiality of the judiciary.

Article 11 – freedom of assembly and association
1.   Everyone has the right to freedom of peaceful assembly and to freedom of association with others, including the right to form and to join trade unions for the protection of his interests.
2.   No restrictions shall be placed on the exercise of these rights other than such as are prescribed by law and are necessary in a democratic society in the interests of national security or public safety, for the prevention of disorder or crime, for the protection of health or morals or for the protection of the rights and freedoms of others. This Article shall not prevent the imposition of lawful restrictions on the exercise of these rights by members of the armed forces, of the police or of the administration of the State.

Article 12 – right to marry
Men and women of marriageable age have the right to marry and to found a family, according to the national laws governing the exercise of this right.

Article 14 – prohibition of discrimination
The enjoyment of the rights and freedoms set forth in this Convention shall be secured without discrimination on any ground such as sex, race, colour, language, religion, political or other opinion, national or social origin, association with a national minority, property, birth or other status.

General Note
The right conferred by this Article has no independent existence. Its function is to safeguard the other rights. Those other rights may be violated alone or in conjunction with this Article. If there is a violation of another right, it is not necessary to consider this right, unless the clear inequality of treatment in the enjoyment of the other right is a fundamental aspect of the case. See *Airey v Ireland* (1979) 2 EHRR 305. Although the other right in respect of which there is discrimination need not have been violated alone, the facts must fall within the ambit of that right: *Rasmussen v Denmark* (1984) 7 EHRR 371.

Discrimination means treating differently, without an objective and reasonable justification, persons who are in relevantly similar situations: *Fredin v Sweden* (1991) 13 EHRR 142. The difference of treatment may be on any ground. At one time, it was necessary for the difference in treatment to be based on a personal characteristic or status (*R (Barber) v SSWP* [2002] 2 FLR 1181 at paras 28-34). However, that line of Strasbourg authority is now out of date (*R (Hooper) v SSWP* [2003] 3 All ER 673 at para 91).

Discrimination may take the form of treating persons in analogous circumstances differently or of failing to treat differently persons whose circumstances are significantly different (*Thlimmenos v Greece* (2001) 31 EHRR 411 at para 44).

The European Court has defined "other status" as requiring a personal characteristic (*Kjeldsen, Busk and Pedersen v Denmark* (1976) 1 EHRR 711 at para 56). Possessing or not possessing something like accommodation is not a personal characteristic (*R(RJM) v SSWP* [2006] EWHC 1761 (Admin), para 29). But having a family relationship and obligations may be (*Francis v SSWP* [2006] 1 All ER 748 at para 27).

The former approach of considering the application of this article in a series of questions was disapproved by the House of Lords in *R (Carson and Reynolds) v SSWP* [2005] 4 All ER 545 in favour of considering more simply whether the difference in treatment can stand scrutiny.

In *Barber* (para 39), the judge doubted whether indirect discrimination was relevant under this article. However, in *CH 5125/2002* (paras 36-55), the commissioner expressed the view that any form of discrimination was relevant under this article, although this part of his reasoning was not essential to his decision. The Court of Appeal dismissed the appeal against the commissioner's decision without dealing with this issue (*R(H) 8/04*).

A margin of appreciation applies, especially where there is a wide divergence of approaches between States: *Rasmussen v Denmark* (1984) 7 EHRR 371.

The reason for discrimination put forward by a State is not decisive. The reason must be examined to see if it is objective and reasonable. Differences can be justified on utilitarian grounds (*RJM*, para 33). If there is a legitimate justification for discrimination, the means employed must be proportionate to the aim pursued: *Hoffmann v Austria* (1993) 17 EHRR 293.

As the Convention must be interpreted dynamically, the justification must be valid in current conditions.

In *CCS 1153/2003*, the commissioner decided that the distinction in the former protected income provisions between gay and straight couples discriminated against the former. The Court of Appeal dismissed an appeal against this decision (*Mv SSWP* [2005] 1 FLR 498), but on further appeal the House of Lords decided that the provision was not discriminatory within Art 14 (*R(CS) 4/06*). However, the European Court of Human Rights decided that there had been discrimination (*JM v United Kingdom* [2011] 1 FLR 491). In *TD v SSWP* [2013] UKUT 282 (AAC), the Upper Tribunal decided that it had to follow the decision of the House of Lords rather than that of the European Court. The parents in that case had equally shared care of their child. As the mother was receiving child benefit, the father was treated as the non-resident parent. The judge decided that this was not discriminatory.

However, the European Court of Human Rights decided that the legislation was discriminatory (*JM v United Kingdom* Application No.37060/06, decided on 28 September 2010).

In *CCS 1077/2006*, the commissioner rejected a very general argument by an absent parent that the failure to bring the reformed scheme into force generally for existing cases was discriminatory. The absent parent's solicitor failed to comply with the commissioner's direction to identify the Convention rights on which he relied and to state his case. The commissioner assumed that the case was within the ambit of the Convention right to respect for family life, but decided that there was no discrimination. The absent parent's argument was self-interest dressed up as discrimination. If correct, it would lead to an unbreakable circle of discrimination. If the reformed scheme had been brought into force for this case, the parent with care could have used the absent parent's argument to show that she was now being discriminated against. And in turn he could have used the argument to show that he was then suffering discrimination. The only way in which this circle of argument could be avoided would be to bring the reformed scheme into force for all cases at the same time. That would have been a recipe for administrative chaos. The commissioner decided that there was nothing in the Human Rights Act 1998 to prevent a phased introduction. It was sensible for administrative convenience and to test the new scheme on a limited number of cases. These considerations provided an objective and reasonable justification for the difference in treatment.

There can be no discrimination on the basis of nationality on account of differences in English and Scottish law, because there is no such thing as Scottish nationality (*CG 1259/2002*, para 7).

Article 16 – restrictions on political activity of aliens

Nothing in Articles 10, 11 and 14 shall be regarded as preventing the High Contracting Parties from imposing restrictions on the political activity of aliens.

Article 17 – prohibition of abuse of rights

Nothing in this Convention may be interpreted as implying for any State, group or person any right to engage in any activity or perform any act aimed at the destruction of any of the rights and freedoms set forth herein or at their limitation to a greater extent than is provided for in the Convention.

Article 18 – limitation on use of restrictions on rights

The restrictions permitted under this Convention to the said rights and freedoms shall not be applied for any purpose other than those for which they have been prescribed.

PART II
THE FIRST PROTOCOL

Article 1 – protection of property

Every natural or legal person is entitled to the peaceful enjoyment of his possessions. No one shall be deprived of his possessions except in the public interest and subject to the conditions provided for by law and by the general principles of international law.

The preceding provisions shall not, however, in any way impair the right of a State to enforce such laws as it deems necessary to control the use of property in accordance with the general interest or to secure the payment of taxes or other contributions or penalties.

General Note

Possession has an autonomous meaning in the Convention (*R (Carson) v SSWP* [2003] 3 All ER 577 *per* Laws LJ at para 45).

This Convention right is not exclusively concerned with the expropriation of private property for public purposes. Payments of child support maintenance are "contributions" within the meaning of the second paragraph (*JM v United Kingdom* Application No.37060/06, decided on 28 September 2010).

The making of a liability order, as a step towards possible enforcement measures, does not engage this Article (*R (Denson) v Child Support Officer* [2002] 1 FLR 938 at para 59). And in *R (Qazi) v Secretary of State*, reported as *R(CS) 5/04*, Charles J held that any infringement with this article by the departure direction scheme (now replaced by the variation scheme) was a proportionate response to a pressing social need (para 45).

Article 2 – right to education

No person shall be denied the right to education. In the exercise of any functions which it assumes in relation to education and to teaching, the State shall respect the right of parents to ensure such education and teaching in conformity with their own religious and philosophical convictions.

Article 3 – right to free elections

The High Contracting Parties undertake to hold free elections at reasonable intervals by secret ballot, under conditions which will ensure the free expression of the opinion of the people in the choice of the legislature.

[¹*PART 3*
ARTICLE 1 OF THE THIRTEENTH PROTOCOL

Abolition of the death penalty

The death penalty shall be abolished. No one shall be condemned to such penalty or executed.]

Amendment

1. Human Rights Act 1998 (Amendment) Order 2004 (SI 2004 No.1574) art 2(3) (June 22, 2004).

SCHEDULE 2

REMEDIAL ORDERS
Orders

1.–(1) A remedial order may–
(a) contain such incidental, supplemental, consequential or transitional provision as the person making it considers appropriate;
(b) be made so as to have effect from a date earlier than that on which it is made;
(c) make provision for the delegation of specific functions;
(d) make different provision for different cases.
(2) The power conferred by sub-paragraph (1)(a) includes–
(a) power to amend primary legislation (including primary legislation other than that which contains the incompatible provision); and
(b) power to amend or revoke subordinate legislation (including subordinate legislation other than that which contains the incompatible provision).
(3) A remedial order may be made so as to have the same extent as the legislation which it affects.
(4) No person is to be guilty of an offence solely as a result of the retrospective effect of a remedial order.

Procedure

2. No remedial order may be made unless–
(a) a draft of the order has been approved by a resolution of each House of Parliament made after the end of the period of 60 days beginning with the day on which the draft was laid; or
(b) it is declared in the order that it appears to the person making it that, because of the urgency of the matter, it is necessary to make the order without a draft being so approved.

Orders laid in draft

3.–(1) No draft may be laid under paragraph 2(a) unless–
(a) the person proposing to make the order has laid before Parliament a document which contains a draft of the proposed order and the required information; and

(b)   the period of 60 days, beginning with the day on which the document required by this sub-paragraph was laid, has ended.

(2)   If representations have been made during that period, the draft laid under paragraph 2(a) must be accompanied by a statement containing–

(a)   a summary of the representations; and

(b)   if, as a result of the representations, the proposed order has been changed, details of the changes.

Urgent cases

4.–(1)   If a remedial order ("the original order") is made without being approved in draft, the person making it must lay it before Parliament, accompanied by the required information, after it is made.

(2)   If representations have been made during the period of 60 days beginning with the day on which the original order was made, the person making it must (after the end of that period) lay before Parliament a statement containing–

(a)   a summary of the representations; and

(b)   if, as a result of the representations, he considers it appropriate to make changes to the original order, details of the changes.

(3)   If sub-paragraph (2)(b) applies, the person making the statement must–

(a)   make a further remedial order replacing the original order; and

(b)   lay the replacement order before Parliament.

(4)   If, at the end of the period of 120 days beginning with the day on which the original order was made, a resolution has not been passed by each House approving the original or replacement order, the order ceases to have effect (but without that affecting anything previously done under either order or the power to make a fresh remedial order).

Definitions

5.   In this Schedule–

"representations" means representations about a remedial order (or proposed remedial order) made to the person making (or proposing to make) it and includes any relevant Parliamentary report or resolution; and

"required information" means–

(a)   an explanation of the incompatibility which the order (or proposed order) seeks to remove, including particulars of the relevant declaration, finding or order; and

(b)   a statement of the reasons for proceeding under section 10 and for making an order in those terms.

Calculating periods

6.   In calculating any period for the purposes of this Schedule, no account is to be taken of any time during which–

(a)   Parliament is dissolved or prorogued; or

(b)   both Houses are adjourned for more than four days.

[¹**7.**–(1)   This paragraph applies in relation to–

(a)   any remedial order made, and any draft of such an order proposed to be made–

    (i)   by the Scottish Ministers; or

    (ii)   within devolved competence (within the meaning of the Scotland Act 1998) by Her Majesty in Council; and

(b)   any document or statement to be laid in connection with such an order (or proposed order).

(2)   This Schedule has effect in relation to any such order (or proposed order), document or statement subject to the following modifications.

(3)   Any reference to Parliament, each House of Parliament or both Houses of Parliament shall be construed as a reference to the Scottish Parliament.

(4)   Paragraph 6 does not apply and instead, in calculating any period for the purposes of this Schedule, no account is to be taken of any time during which the Scottish Parliament is dissolved or is in recess for more than four days.]

Amendment

1.   Scotland Act 1998 (Consequential Modifications) Order 2000 (SI 2000 No.2040) art 2 and Sch para 21 (July 27, 2000, subject to saving provision in art 3 of SI 2000 No.2040).

Definitions

"amend": see s21(1).

"primary legislation": see s21(1).

"remedial order": see s21(1).

"subordinate legislation": see s21(1)

SCHEDULE 3

PART I

[¹ ...][²[³...]]

PART II
Reservation

At the time of signing the present (First) Protocol, I declare that, in view of certain provisions of the Education Acts in the United Kingdom, the principle affirmed in the second sentence of Article 2 is accepted by the United Kingdom only so far as it is compatible with the provision of efficient instruction and training, and the avoidance of unreasonable public expenditure.

Dated 20 March 1952

Made by the United Kingdom Permanent Representative to the Council of Europe.

Amendments

1.   The Human Rights Act (Amendment) Order 2001 (SI 2001 No.1216) Art 3 (April 1 2001).
2.   The Human Rights Act 1998 (Amendment No.2) Order 2001 (SI 2001 No.4032) reg 2 and sch. (December 20, 2001).
3.   The Human Rights Act 1998 (Amendment) Order 2005 (SI 2005 No.1071) reg 2 (April 8, 2005).

SCHEDULE 4
Duty to make orders about pensions

1.–(1)   The appropriate Minister must by order make provision with respect to pensions payable to or in respect of any holder of a judicial office who serves as an ECHR judge.

(2)   A pensions order must include such provision as the Minister making it considers is necessary to secure that–

(a)   an ECHR judge who was, immediately before his appointment as an ECHR judge, a member of a judicial pension scheme is entitled to remain as a member of that scheme;

(b)   the terms on which he remains a member of the scheme are those which would have been applicable had he not been appointed as an ECHR judge; and

(c)   entitlement to benefits payable in accordance with the scheme continues to be determined as if, while serving as an ECHR judge, his salary was that which would (but for section 18(4)) have been payable to him in respect of his continuing service as the holder of his judicial office.

Contributions

2.   A pensions order may, in particular, make provision–

(a)   for any contributions which are payable by a person who remains a member of a scheme as a result of the order, and which would otherwise be payable by deduction from his salary, to be made otherwise than by deduction from his salary as an ECHR judge; and

(b)   for such contributions to be collected in such manner as may be determined by the administrators of the scheme.

Amendments of other enactments

3.   A pensions order may amend any provision of, or made under, a pensions Act in such manner and to such extent as the Minister making the order considers necessary or expedient to ensure the proper administration of any scheme to which it relates.

Definitions

4.   In this Schedule–

"appropriate Minister" means–

(a)   in relation to any judicial office whose jurisdiction is exercisable exclusively in relation to Scotland, the Secretary of State; and

(b)   otherwise, the Lord Chancellor;

"ECHR judge" means the holder of a judicial office who is serving as a judge of the Court;

"judicial pension scheme" means a scheme established by and in accordance with a pensions Act;

"pensions Act" means–

(a)   the County Courts Act Northern Ireland) 1959;

(b)   the Sheriffs' Pensions (Scotland) Act 1961;

(c)   the Judicial Pensions Act 1981; or

(d)   the Judicial Pensions and Retirement Act 1993; and

"pensions order" means an order made under paragraph 1.

Data Protection Act 1998
(1998 c29)

Disclosures required by law or made in connection with legal proceedings, etc.

35.–(1)   Personal data are exempt from the non-disclosure provisions where the disclosure is required by or under any enactment, by any rule of law or by order of a court.

(2)   Personal data are exempt from the non-disclosure provisions where the disclosure is necessary–

(a)   for the purposes of, or in connection with, any legal proceedings (including prospective legal proceedings), or

(b)   for the purpose of obtaining legal advice,

or is otherwise necessary for the purpose of establishing, exercising or defending legal rights.

General Note

If a tribunal directs disclosure, s35(1) applies and the Act cannot be relied on to justify non-disclosure (*R (Davies) v Commissioners Office* [2008] 1 FLR 1651 at paras 11 and 14).

Supplementary definitions

70.   (1) In this Act, unless the context otherwise requires–

"enactment" includes an enactment passed after this Act [[1]and any enactment comprised in, or in any instrument made under, an Act of the Scottish Parliament];

Amendment

1.   Scotland Act 1998 (Consequential Modifications) (No.2) Order 1999 (SI 1999 No.1820) art 4 and Sch 2 para 133 (July 1, 1999).

Gender Recognition Act 2004
(2004 c7)

Parenthood

12. The fact that a person's gender has become the acquired gender under this Act does not affect the status of the person as the father or mother of a child.

Child Maintenance and Other Payments Act 2008

(2008 c6)

PART 4
LUMP SUM PAYMENTS: MESOTHELIOMA ETC.

PART 5
GENERAL

PART 1
THE CHILD MAINTENANCE AND ENFORCEMENT COMMISSION

The Child Maintenance and Enforcement Commission
1.–[¹...]

Amendment

  1.   Public Bodies (Child Maintenance and Enforcement Commission: Abolition and Transfer of Functions) Order 2012 (SI 2012 No.2007) art 3(2) and Sch para 71 (August 1, 2012).

Objectives of the Commission
2.–[¹...]

Amendment

  1.   Public Bodies (Child Maintenance and Enforcement Commission: Abolition and Transfer of Functions) Order 2012 (SI 2012 No.2007) art 3(2) and Sch para 71 (August 1, 2012).

Functions of the Commission: general
3.–[¹...]

Amendment

  1.   Public Bodies (Child Maintenance and Enforcement Commission: Abolition and Transfer of Functions) Order 2012 (SI 2012 No.2007) art 3(2) and Sch para 71 (August 1, 2012).

Promotion of child maintenance
4. [¹...]

Amendment

1.   Public Bodies (Child Maintenance and Enforcement Commission: Abolition and Transfer of Functions) Order 2012 (SI 2012 No.2007) art 3(2) and Sch para 71 (August 1, 2012).

Provision of information and guidance
5.–[¹...]

Amendment

1.   Public Bodies (Child Maintenance and Enforcement Commission: Abolition and Transfer of Functions) Order 2012 (SI 2012 No.2007) art 3(2) and Sch para 71 (August 1, 2012).

Fees
6.–(1)   The Secretary of State may by regulations make provision about the charging of fees by the [²Secretary of State] in connection with the exercise of its functions.

(2)   Regulations under subsection (1) may, in particular, make provision–

(a)   about when a fee may be charged;

(b)   about the amount which may be charged;

(c)   for the supply of information needed for the purpose of determining the amount which may be charged;

(d)   about who is liable to pay any fee charged;

(e)   about when any fee charged is payable;

(f)   about the recovery of fees charged;

(g)   about waiver, reduction or repayment of fees.

(3)   The power conferred by subsection (1) includes power to make provision for the charging of fees which are not related to costs.

(4)   The Secretary of State may by regulations provide that the provisions of the Child Support Act 1991 (c. 48) with respect to–

(a)   the collection of child support maintenance,

(b)   the enforcement of any obligation to pay child support maintenance,

shall apply equally (with any necessary modifications) to fees payable by virtue of regulations under subsection (1).

(5)   The Secretary of State may by regulations make provision for a person affected by a decision of the [²Secretary of State] under regulations under subsection (1) to have a right of appeal against the decision to [¹ the First-tier Tribunal].

(6)   Subsections (3) to (5), (7) and (8) of section 20 of the Child Support Act 1991 (appeals to [¹ First-tier Tribunal]) apply to appeals under regulations under subsection (5) as they apply to appeals under that section.

(7)   The [²Secretary of State] shall pay into the Consolidated Fund any amount which [²the Secretary of State] receives in respect of fees charged by [²the Secretary of State] under regulations under this section.

Commencement

Child Maintenance and Other Payments Act 2008 (Commencement No.2) Order (SI 2008 No.2033 (C.97)) art 2 (July 24, 2008).

Amendments

1.   Transfer of Tribunal Functions Order 2008 (SI 2008 No.2833) art 9 and Sch 3 para 225 (November 3, 2008 subject to the transitional provisions in Sch 4 of SI 2008 No.2833).

2.   Public Bodies (Child Maintenance and Enforcement Commission: Abolition and Transfer of Functions) Order 2012 (SI 2012 No.2007) art 3(2) and Sch para 72 (August 1, 2012).

General Note

No regulations have been made under this section.

Agency arrangements and provision of services
7.–[¹...]

Amendment

    1.   Public Bodies (Child Maintenance and Enforcement Commission: Abolition and Transfer of Functions) Order 2012 (SI 2012 No.2007) art 3(2) and Sch para 73 (August 1, 2012).

Contracting out

    8.–(1)   Any function of the [¹Secretary of State relating to child support] may be exercised by, or by employees of, such person (if any) as the [¹Secretary of State] may authorise for the purpose.

    (2)   An authorisation given by virtue of subsection (1) may authorise the exercise of the function concerned–

    (a)   either wholly or to such extent as may be specified in the authorisation,

    (b)   either generally or in such cases or areas as may be so specified, and

    (c)   either unconditionally or subject to the fulfilment of such conditions as may be so specified.

    (3)   An authorisation given by virtue of subsection (1)–

    (a)   may specify its duration,

    (b)   may be revoked at any time by the [¹Secretary of State], and

    (c)   shall not prevent the [¹Secretary of State] or any other person from exercising the function to which the authorisation relates.

    (4)   Where a person is authorised to exercise any function by virtue of subsection (1), anything done or omitted to be done by or in relation to that person (or an employee of that person) in, or in connection with, the exercise or purported exercise of the function shall be treated for all purposes as done or omitted to be done by or in relation to the [¹Secretary of State].

    (5)   Subsection (4) shall not apply–

    (a)   for the purposes of so much of any contract made between the authorised person and the [¹Secretary of State] as relates to the exercise of the function, or

    (b)   for the purposes of any criminal proceedings brought in respect of anything done or omitted to be done by the authorised person (or an employee of that person).

    (6)   Where–

    (a)   a person is authorised to exercise any function by virtue of subsection (1), and

    (b)   the authorisation is revoked at a time when a relevant contract is subsisting,

the authorised person shall be entitled to treat the relevant contract as repudiated by the [¹Secretary of State] (and not as frustrated by reason of the revocation).

    (7)   In subsection (6), the reference to a relevant contract is to so much of any contract made between the authorised person and the [¹Secretary of State] as relates to the exercise of the function.

Commencement

    Child Maintenance and Other Payments Act 2008 (Commencement No.2) Order 2008 (SI 2008 No.2033 (C.97)) art 2 (July 24, 2008).

Amendment

    1.   Public Bodies (Child Maintenance and Enforcement Commission: Abolition and Transfer of Functions) Order 2012 (SI 2012 No.2007) art 3(2) and Sch para 74 (August 1, 2012).

Annual report to Secretary of State

    9.–[¹...]

Amendment

    1.   Public Bodies (Child Maintenance and Enforcement Commission: Abolition and Transfer of Functions) Order 2012 (SI 2012 No.2007) art 3(2) and Sch para 75 (August 1, 2012).

Directions and guidance

    10.–[¹...]

Amendment

1. Public Bodies (Child Maintenance and Enforcement Commission: Abolition and Transfer of Functions) Order 2012 (SI 2012 No.2007) art 3(2) and Sch para 75 (August 1, 2012).

Review of the status of the Commission
11.–[¹...]

Amendment

1. Public Bodies (Child Maintenance and Enforcement Commission: Abolition and Transfer of Functions) Order 2012 (SI 2012 No.2007) art 3(2) and Sch para 75 (August 1, 2012).

Supplementary provisions
12.–[¹...]

Amendment

1. Public Bodies (Child Maintenance and Enforcement Commission: Abolition and Transfer of Functions) Order 2012 (SI 2012 No.2007) art 3(2) and Sch para 75 (August 1, 2012).

PART 2
TRANSFER OF CHILD SUPPORT FUNCTIONS ETC. TO THE COMMISSION

Transfer of child support functions
13.–[¹...]

Amendment

1. Public Bodies (Child Maintenance and Enforcement Commission: Abolition and Transfer of Functions) Order 2012 (SI 2012 No.2007) art 3(2) and Sch para 76 (August 1, 2012).

Transfer of property, rights and liabilities
14.–[¹...]

Amendment

1. Public Bodies (Child Maintenance and Enforcement Commission: Abolition and Transfer of Functions) Order 2012 (SI 2012 No.2007) art 3(2) and Sch para 76 (August 1, 2012).

PART 3
CHILD SUPPORT ETC.
Removal of compulsion for benefit claimants

Repeal of sections 6 and 46
15. The following provisions of the Child Support Act 1991 (c. 48) cease to have effect–

(a) section 6 (under which the claim of benefit by or in respect of a parent with care, or the payment of benefit to or in respect of such a person, triggers an application by her or him for child support maintenance), and

(b) section 46 (which enables the Secretary of State in certain circumstances to reduce the benefit of a person in relation to whom section 6 triggers the making of an application for child support maintenance).

Commencemnt

s15(b): Child Maintenance and Other Payments Act 2008 (Commencement) Order 2008 (SI 2008 No.1476 (C.67)) art 2(2) (June 10, 2008).

s15(a): Child Maintenance and Other Payments Act 2008 (Commencement) Order 2008 (SI 2008 No.1476 (C.67)) art 2(3) (July 14, 2008 subject to the saving provision in art 2(4)-(5) of SI 2008 No.1476).

Maintenance calculations

Changes to the calculation of maintenance
16. Schedule 4 (which makes various changes to the provisions about the calculation of maintenance) has effect.

Commencement
So far as this section relates to paragraphs 2, 5(2) and 7 to 9 of Schedule 4 of this Act, this section was brought into force for the purpose only of making regulations by the Child Maintenance and Other Payments Act 2008 (Commencement No.9) and the Welfare Reform Act 2009 (Commencement No.9) Order 2012 (SI 2012 No.2523) art 2(2)(a) and (b) (October 8, 2012).

So far as this section relates to paragraphs 2, 3 and 5 to 10 of Schedule 4 it has been brought into force for the purposes for certain types of cases by the Child Maintenance and Other Payments Act 2008 (Commencement No.10 and Transitional Provisions) Order 2012 (SI 2012 No.3042) art 2 (December 10, 2012, for the purposes of the types of cases falling within article 3 of SI 2012 No.3042 – see p767) and the Child Maintenance and Other Payments Act 2008 (Commencement No.11 and Transitional Provisions) Order 2013 (SI 2013 No.1860) art 2 (July 29, 2013 for the purposes of the types of cases falling within article 3 of SI 2013 No.1860 – see p770).

General Note
Not yet fully in force.

Power to regulate supersession

17. In section 17 of the Child Support Act 1991 (c. 48) (decisions superseding earlier decisions), for subsections (2) and (3) substitute–

"(2)   The Secretary of State may by regulations make provision with respect to the exercise of the power under subsection (1).

(3)   Regulations under subsection (2) may, in particular–

(a)   make provision about the cases and circumstances in which the power under subsection (1) is exercisable, including provision restricting the exercise of that power by virtue of change of circumstance;

(b)   make provision with respect to the consideration by the [¹Secretary of State], when acting under subsection (1), of any issue which has not led to [¹the Secretary of State's] so acting;

(c)   make provision with respect to procedure in relation to the exercise of the power under subsection (1)."

Commencement
In force for the purpose of making regulations: Child Maintenance and Other Payments Act 2008 (Commencement No.9) and the Welfare Reform Act 2009 (Commencement No.9) Order 2012 (SI 2012 No.2523) art 2(2)(c) (October 8, 2012).

In force for the purpose of the types of cases falling within art 3 of SI 2012 No.3042 (see p767): Child Maintenance and Other Payments Act 2008 (Commencement No.10 and Transitional Provisions) Order 2012 (SI 2012 No.3042) art 2 (December 10, 2012) and for the purpose of the types of cases falling within article 3 of SI 2013 No.1860 (see p770): Child Maintenance and Other Payments Act 2008 (Commencement No.11 and Transitional Provisions) Order 2013 (SI 2013 No.1860) art 2 (July 29, 2013).

Amendment
1.   Public Bodies (Child Maintenance and Enforcement Commission: Abolition and Transfer of Functions) Order 2012 (SI 2012 No.2007) art 3(2) and Sch para 77 (August 1, 2012).

Determination of applications for a variation

18.–(1)   Section 28D of the Child Support Act 1991 is amended as follows.

(2)   After subsection (2) insert–

"(2A) Subsection (2B) applies if–

(a)   the application for a variation is made by the person with care or (in the case of an application for a maintenance calculation under section 7) the person with care or the child concerned, and

(b)   it appears to the [¹Secretary of State] that consideration of further information or evidence may affect [¹the] decision under subsection (1)(a) whether or not to agree to a variation.

(2B)   Before making the decision under subsection (1)(a) the [¹Secretary of State] must–

(a)   consider any such further information or evidence that is available to [¹the Secretary of State], and

(b)   where necessary, take such steps as the [¹Secretary of State] considers appropriate to obtain any such further information or evidence."

(3)   In subsection (3), after "duties" insert ", apart from the duty under subsection (2B)".

Commencement
In force for the purpose of the types of cases falling within art 3 of SI 2012 No.3042 (see p767): Child Maintenance and Other Payments Act 2008 (Commencement No.10 and Transitional Provisions) Order 2012 (SI 2012 No.3042) art 2 (December 10, 2012) and for the purpose of the types of cases falling within article 3 of SI 2013 No. 1860 (see p770): Child Maintenance and Other Payments Act 2008 (Commencement No.11 and Transitional Provisions) Order 2013 (SI 2013 No.1860) art 2 (July 29, 2013).

Amendment
1.   Public Bodies (Child Maintenance and Enforcement Commission: Abolition and Transfer of Functions) Order 2012 (SI 2012 No.2007) art 3(2) and Sch para 78 (August 1, 2012).

Transfer of cases to new rules
19.   Schedule 5 (which makes provision for, and in connection with, enabling the Commission to require existing cases to transfer to the new maintenance calculation rules or to leave the statutory scheme, so far as future accrual of liability is concerned) has effect.

General Note
Not yet in force.

Collection and enforcement

Use of deduction from earnings orders as basic method of payment
20.   [...]

General Note
Section 20 inserted subss 29(4)-(7) into the 1991 Act (see p81).

Deduction from earnings orders: the liable person's earnings
21.   In section 31 of the Child Support Act 1991 (deduction from earnings orders), for subsection (8) substitute–

"(8)   In this section and section 32 "earnings" means (subject to such exceptions as may be prescribed) any sums payable to a person which fall within one or more of the following paragraphs–

(a)   sums payable by way of wages or salary (including any fees, bonus, commission, overtime pay or other emoluments payable in addition to wages or salary or payable under a contract of service);

(b)   periodical payments by way of pension (including an annuity payable for the purpose of providing a pension), whether or not in respect of past services;

(c)   periodical payments by way of compensation for the loss, abolition or relinquishment, or diminution in the emoluments, of any office or employment;

(d)   sums payable by way of statutory sick pay.

(9)   For the purposes of this section and section 32 any person who (as a principal and not as a servant or agent) pays to the liable person any earnings is to be treated as having the liable person in his employment; and the following are to be read accordingly–

(a)   in this section and section 32, references to the liable person's employer; and

(b)   in section 32(3), "employment", "employed" and "reemployed"."

General Note
Not yet in force.

Orders for regular deductions from accounts
22.   [...]

General Note
Section 22 inserted ss32A, 32B, 32C and 32D into the 1991 Act from 1 June 2009 for making regulations and 3 August 2009 for all other purposes (see pp89, 90, 91 and 92).

Lump sum deduction orders
23. [...]

General Note

Sections 32E to 32K inserted into the 1991 Act (see p92).

Orders preventing avoidance
24. [...]

General Note

Section 32L inserted into the 1991 Act (see p97).

Administrative liability orders
25. After section 32L of the Child Support Act 1991 (c. 48) (inserted by section 24 of this Act) insert–

"32M   Liability orders
(1)   If it appears to the [¹Secretary of State] that a person has failed to pay an amount of child support maintenance, [¹the Secretary of State] may make an order against the person in respect of that amount.

(2)   An order under subsection (1) (a "liability order") may be made in respect of an amount due under a maintenance calculation which is the subject of an appeal only if it appears to the [¹Secretary of State]–

(a)   that liability for the amount would not be affected were the appeal to succeed, or

(b)   where paragraph (a) does not apply, that the making of a liability order in respect of the amount would nonetheless be fair in all the circumstances.

(3)   A liability order shall not come into force before–

(a)   the end of the period during which an appeal can be brought under section 20 against the making of the order, and

(b)   if an appeal is brought under section 20, the time at which proceedings on the appeal (including any proceedings on a further appeal) have been concluded and any period during which a further appeal may ordinarily be brought has ended.

(4)   Where regulations have been made under section 29(3)(a), a person liable to pay an amount of child support maintenance is to be taken for the purposes of this section to have failed to pay the amount, unless it is paid to or through the person specified in, or by virtue of, the regulations for the case in question.

32N   Regulations about liability orders
(1)   The Secretary of State may by regulations make provision with respect to liability orders.

(2)   Regulations under subsection (1) may, in particular–

(a)   make provision about the form and content of a liability order;

(b)   make provision for a liability order not to come into force if, before it does so, the whole of the amount in respect of which it is made is paid;

(c)   make provision for the discharge of a liability order;

(d)   make provision for the revival of a liability order in prescribed circumstances."

Amendment

1.   Public Bodies (Child Maintenance and Enforcement Commission: Abolition and Transfer of Functions) Order 2012 (SI 2012 No.2007) art 3(2) and Sch para 79 (August 1, 2012).

General Note

Not yet in force.

Enforcement in county courts
26. In section 36 of the Child Support Act 1991 (enforcement in county courts), in subsection (1) (under which the amount in respect of which a liability order is made is

recoverable by a third party debt order or charging order as if it were payable under a county court order, but only if a county court so orders), the words '', if a county court so orders," are omitted.

General Note
Not yet in force.

Disqualification for holding or obtaining travel authorisation
　　27.　Before section 40 of the Child Support Act 1991 (c. 48) insert–

"39B　Disqualification for holding or obtaining travel authorisation
　　(1)　The ['Secretary of State] may apply to the court for an order under this section against a person where–
　　(a)　['the Secretary of State] has sought to recover an amount from the person by means of taking enforcement action by virtue of section 35 or 38, or by means of a third party debt order or a charging order by virtue of section 36;
　　(b)　the whole or any part of the amount remains unpaid; and
　　(c)　the ['Secretary of State] is of the opinion that there has been wilful refusal or culpable neglect on the part of the person.
　　(2)　For the purposes of subsection (1)(a), the ['Secretary of State] is to be taken to have sought to recover an amount by means of a charging order if an interim charging order has been made, whether or not any further steps have been taken to recover the amount.
　　(3)　A person against whom an order under this section is made is disqualified for holding or obtaining a travel authorisation while the order has effect.
　　(4)　On an application under subsection (1) for an order against a person the court shall (in the presence of that person) inquire as to–
　　(a)　whether the person needs a travel authorisation to earn a living;
　　(b)　the person's means;
　　(c)　whether there has been wilful refusal or culpable neglect on the part of the person.
　　(5)　If, but only if, the court is of the opinion that there has been wilful refusal or culpable neglect on the part of the person, it may make an order under this section.
　　(6)　The court may not take action under both this section and section 40.
　　(7)　On an application under subsection (1) the court shall not question–
　　(a)　the liability order by reference to which the ['Secretary of State] acted as mentioned in paragraph (a) of that subsection; or
　　(b)　the maintenance calculation by reference to which that liability order was made.
　　(8)　An order under this section shall specify the amount in respect of which it is made, which shall be the aggregate of–
　　(a)　the amount sought to be recovered as mentioned in subsection (1)(a), or so much of it as remains unpaid; and
　　(b)　an amount (determined in accordance with regulations made by the Secretary of State) in respect of the costs of the application under this section.
　　(9)　A court which makes an order under this section shall require the person to whom it relates to produce any travel authorisation that the person holds.
　　(10)　The court shall send to the prescribed person any travel authorisation produced to the court under subsection (9).
　　(11)　Where a court–
　　(a)　makes an order under this section, or
　　(b)　allows an appeal against such an order,
it shall send notice of that fact to the ['Secretary of State]; and the notice shall contain such particulars and be sent in such manner and to such address as the ['Secretary of State] may determine.
　　(12)　In this section "travel authorisation" means–
　　(a)　a United Kingdom passport (within the meaning of the Immigration Act 1971);
　　(b)　an ID card issued under the Identity Cards Act 2006 that records that the person to whom it has been issued is a British citizen.

(13)   In this section (except for the purposes of subsection (11)(b)) and in sections 39C to 39E, "court" means–
(a)   in relation to England and Wales, a magistrates' court;
(b)   in relation to Scotland, the sheriff.

39C   Period for which orders under section 39B are to have effect

(1)   Disqualification by an order under section 39B shall be for such period not exceeding two years as the court may specify in the order.
(2)   On making an order under section 39B, the court may include in the order provision suspending the running of the period for which the order is to have effect until such day and on such conditions (if any) as the court thinks just.
(3)   After making such an order the court may by order suspend the running of the period for which it has effect until such day and on such conditions (if any) as the court thinks just.
(4)   The powers conferred by subsections (2) and (3) may be exercised by the court only–
(a)   if the person against whom the order under section 39B is made agrees to pay the amount specified in the order; or
(b)   if the court is satisfied that the suspension in question is justified by exceptional circumstances.
(5)   The [¹Secretary of State] may make a further application under section 39B if the amount specified in an order under that section has not been paid in full by the end of the period for which the order has effect.

39D   Power to order search

(1)   On making an order under section 39B the court may order the person against whom the order is made to be searched.
(2)   Any money found on such a search shall, unless the court otherwise directs, be applied towards payment of the amount specified under section 39B(8); and the balance (if any) shall be returned to the person searched.
(3)   The court shall not allow the application under subsection (2) of money found on a search under subsection (1) if it is satisfied that the money does not belong to the person searched.

39E   Variation and revocation of orders following payment

(1)   If part of the amount specified in an order under section 39B is paid to any person authorised to receive it, the court may, on an application made by the [¹Secretary of State] or the person against whom the order is made, by order–
(a)   reduce the period for which the order under section 39B is to have effect; or
(b)   revoke the order under section 39B.
(2)   If the whole of the amount specified in an order under section 39B is paid to any person authorised to receive it, the court shall, on an application made by the [¹Secretary of State] or the person against whom the order is made, by order revoke the order under section 39B.
(3)   The [¹Secretary of State] may make representations to the court as to the amount which should be paid before it would be appropriate to make an order under subsection (1) revoking an order under section 39B, and the person against whom the order was made may reply to those representations.
(4)   The court may exercise the powers conferred on it by subsection (1) or (2) without the need for an application where money found on a search under section 39D(1) is applied towards payment of the amount specified in the order under section 39B.
(5)   Where a court makes an order under this section, it shall send notice of that fact to the [¹Secretary of State]; and the notice shall contain such particulars and be sent in such manner and to such address as the [¹Secretary of State] may determine.

39F   Power to make supplementary provision

(1)   The Secretary of State may by regulations–

(a)   make provision in relation to orders under section 39B corresponding to the provision that may be made under section 40(11);

(b)   make provision for sections 39C to 39E to have effect with prescribed modifications in cases where a person against whom an order under section 39B has effect is outside the United Kingdom.

39G   Application of sections 39B and 39F to Scotland

(1)   In their application to Scotland, sections 39B and 39F have effect with the following modifications.

(2)   In section 39B(6) for "section 40" substitute "section 40A".

(3)   For section 39F substitute–

"39F   Power to make supplementary provision

In relation to orders under section 39B–

(a)   the Secretary of State may by regulations make provision–

(i)   for sections 39C to 39E to have effect with prescribed modifications in cases where a person against whom such an order has effect is outside the United Kingdom;

(ii)   that a statement in writing to the effect that wages of any amount have been paid to a person during any period, purporting to be signed by or on behalf of the person's employer, shall be sufficient evidence of the facts stated; and

(b)   the power of the Court of Session by Act of Sederunt to regulate the procedure and practice in civil proceedings in the sheriff court shall include power to make provision corresponding to that which may be made by virtue of section 40A(8).''

Amendment

1.   Public Bodies (Child Maintenance and Enforcement Commission: Abolition and Transfer of Functions) Order 2012 (SI 2012 No.2007) art 3(2) and Sch para 80 (August 1, 2012).

General Note

Not yet in force.

Curfew orders

28.   After section 39G of the Child Support Act 1991 (c. 48) (inserted by section 27 of this Act) insert–

"39H   Applications for curfew orders

(1)   The ['Secretary of State] may apply to the court for an order requiring a person to remain, for periods specified in the order, at a place so specified (a "curfew order") where–

(a)   ['the Secretary of State] has sought to recover an amount from the person by means of taking enforcement action by virtue of section 35 or 38, or by means of a third party debt order or a charging order by virtue of section 36;

(b)   the whole or any part of the amount remains unpaid; and

(c)   the ['Secretary of State] is of the opinion that there has been wilful refusal or culpable neglect on the part of the person.

(2)   For the purposes of subsection (1)(a), the ['Secretary of State] is to be taken to have sought to recover an amount by means of a charging order if an interim charging order has been made, whether or not any further steps have been taken to recover the amount.

(3)   On an application for a curfew order the court shall (in the presence of the person from whom the ['Secretary of State] has sought to recover the amount) inquire as to–

(a)   the person's means; and

(b)   whether there has been wilful refusal or culpable neglect on the part of the person.

(4)   On an application for a curfew order the court shall not question–

(a) the liability order by reference to which the [¹Secretary of State] acted as mentioned in subsection (1)(a); or

(b) the maintenance calculation by reference to which that liability order was made.

(5) If, but only if, the court is of the opinion that there has been wilful refusal or culpable neglect on the part of the person from whom the [¹Secretary of State] has sought to recover the amount, it may make a curfew order against the person.

(6) The court may not make a curfew order against a person who is under the age of 18.

(7) In this section and sections 39I to 39O "the court" means–

(a) in England and Wales, a magistrates' court;

(b) in Scotland, the sheriff.

39I Curfew orders: duration etc.

(1) The periods and places specified as mentioned in section 39H(1) may include different periods and different places for different days, but shall not include periods which amount to less than 2 hours or more than 12 hours in any one day.

(2) A curfew order shall specify the period for which the requirements imposed by the order shall have effect.

(3) The period so specified–

(a) shall not exceed 6 months; and

(b) shall begin to run with the day on which the order is made unless the order provides (subject to such conditions, if any, as may be specified in the order) for it to begin to run with a later day.

(4) The court shall (so far as practicable) ensure that any requirement imposed by a curfew order is such as to avoid–

(a) any conflict with the religious beliefs of the person against whom the order is made; and

(b) any interference with the times (if any) at which that person normally works or attends any educational establishment.

(5) On making a curfew order–

(a) a magistrates' court may not specify in the order any place outside England and Wales; and

(b) the sheriff may not specify in the order any place outside Scotland.

39J Recovery of costs relating to curfew orders

(1) On making a curfew order the court shall also make an order requiring the person against whom the curfew order is made to pay an amount (determined in accordance with regulations made by the Secretary of State) specified in the order in respect of–

(a) the costs of the application for the curfew order; and

(b) the costs of monitoring compliance with the requirements imposed by the curfew order.

(2) The provisions of this Act with respect to–

(a) the collection of child support maintenance; and

(b) the enforcement of an obligation to pay child support maintenance,

apply equally (with any necessary modifications) to amounts which a person is required to pay by an order under this section.

39K Curfew orders: the amount due

(1) A curfew order shall specify the amount in respect of which it is made, which shall be the aggregate of–

(a) the amount sought to be recovered as mentioned in section 39H(1)(a), or so much of it as remains unpaid; and

(b) the amount which the person against whom the curfew order is made is required to pay by the order under section 39J.

(2) If part of the amount in respect of which a curfew order was made is paid to any person authorised to receive it, the court may, on an application by the [¹Secretary of State] or the person against whom the curfew order was made, by order–

(a)   *reduce the period for which the requirements imposed by the curfew order have effect;*

(b)   *provide for that period to begin to run with a day later than that with which it would otherwise have begun to run;*

(c)   *suspend the running of that period, or provide for any existing such suspension to be extended, until a day specified in the order; or*

(d)   *revoke the curfew order.*

(3)   *An order under subsection (2)(b) or (c) may include provision for its effect to be subject to specified conditions.*

(4)   *On the hearing of an application made under subsection (2) the [¹Secretary of State] may make representations to the court as to which of the powers conferred by that subsection it would be appropriate for the court to exercise, and the person against whom the curfew order was made may reply to those representations.*

(5)   *If the whole of the amount in respect of which a curfew order was made is paid to any person authorised to receive it, the court shall, on an application by the [¹Secretary of State] or the person against whom the order was made, by order revoke the curfew order.*

(6)   *The [¹Secretary of State] may make a further application under section 39H if the amount in respect of which a curfew order was made has not been paid in full when the requirements imposed by the order cease to have effect.*

39L   *Power to order search*

(1)   *On making a curfew order, the court may order the person against whom the order is made to be searched.*

(2)   *Any money found on such a search shall, unless the court otherwise directs, be applied towards payment of the amount in respect of which the curfew order is made; and the balance (if any) shall be returned to the person searched.*

(3)   *The court shall not allow the application under subsection (2) of money found on a search under this section if it is satisfied that the money does not belong to the person searched.*

(4)   *The court may exercise the powers conferred on it by section 39K(2) and (5) without the need for an application where money found on a search under this section is applied towards payment of the amount in respect of which a curfew order is made.*

39M   *Monitoring of curfew orders*

(1)   *A curfew order shall–*

(a)   *provide for a person's compliance with the requirements imposed by the order to be monitored; and*

(b)   *make a person specified in the order responsible for that monitoring.*

(2)   *The court may not make a curfew order unless–*

(a)   *it has been notified by the [¹Secretary of State] that arrangements for monitoring compliance with the requirements imposed by such orders are available in the area in which the place proposed to be specified in the order is situated and the notice has not been withdrawn;*

(b)   *it is satisfied that the necessary provision can be made under those arrangements; and*

(c)   *it has the consent of any person (other than the person against whom the order is to be made) whose co-operation is necessary to secure the monitoring of compliance with the requirements imposed by the order.*

(3)   *If a curfew order cannot be made because of the absence of any consent required by subsection (2)(c), the court may treat the application for the order as an application under section 40 (or, in the case of an application made to the sheriff, as an application under section 40A).*

(4)   *The Secretary of State may by regulations make provision as to–*

(a)   *the cases or circumstances in which the person responsible for monitoring a person's compliance with the requirements imposed by a curfew order may*

> allow that person to be absent from the place specified in the curfew order during a period so specified; and
>
> (b) the requirements which may be imposed in connection with such an absence.

39N Breaches of curfew orders

(1) The person responsible for monitoring a person's compliance with the requirements imposed by a curfew order, or the [¹Secretary of State], may apply to the court where it appears that the person subject to the requirements in question has failed to comply with–

(a) any of those requirements; or

(b) any requirements imposed by virtue of section 39M(4).

(2) On any such application the court shall (in the presence of the person subject to the requirements in question) inquire as to whether the person has failed without reasonable excuse to comply with any of those requirements.

(3) If the court is of the opinion that the person has failed without reasonable excuse to comply with any of those requirements, it may–

(a) issue a warrant of commitment against that person; or

(b) by order provide for the requirements imposed by the curfew order to have effect for a specified further period.

(4) A warrant issued under subsection (3)(a) shall order the person against whom it is issued–

(a) to be imprisoned for a period specified in the warrant; but

(b) to be released (unless in custody for some other reason) on payment of the amount in respect of which the curfew order in question was made.

(5) A warrant issued under subsection (3)(a) may be directed to such person or persons as the court issuing it thinks fit.

(6) The power conferred by subsection (3)(b) may not be exercised so as to provide for the requirements imposed by the curfew order to have effect for a period exceeding 6 months after the making of the order under that subsection.

(7) Where, following the issue of a warrant under subsection (3)(a), part of the amount specified in the curfew order is paid to any person authorised to receive it, the court may, on an application by the [¹Secretary of State] or the person against whom the warrant was issued–

(a) reduce the period specified in the warrant; or

(b) order the release of the person against whom the warrant was issued.

(8) On the hearing of an application made under subsection (7) the [¹Secretary of State] may make representations to the court as to which of the powers conferred by that subsection it would be appropriate for the court to exercise, and the person against whom the warrant was issued may reply to those representations.

39O Effect of custody on curfew orders and power to make curfew orders

(1) The court may not make a curfew order against a person at any time when the person is in custody for any reason.

(2) The running of the period during which the requirements imposed by a curfew order have effect shall be suspended for the whole of any day during any part of which the person against whom the order is made is in custody for any reason.

(3) If the period during which the requirements imposed by a curfew order have effect would have begun to run but for its being suspended by virtue of this section, that period shall instead begin to run with the first day when its running is no longer suspended.

39P Power to make supplementary provision about curfew orders: England and Wales

(1) The Secretary of State may by regulations make provision for England and Wales with respect to curfew orders.

(2) The regulations may, in particular, make provision–

(a) as to the form and content of a curfew order;

(b)   allowing an application for a curfew order to be renewed where no curfew order is made;

(c)   that a statement in writing to the effect that wages of any amount have been paid during any period to a person, purporting to be signed by or on behalf of that person's employer, shall be evidence of the facts stated;

(d)   that a justice of the peace may issue a summons to a person to appear before a magistrates' court and (if that person does not appear) may issue a warrant for that person's arrest;

(e)   that, for the purpose of securing a person's presence before a magistrates' court, a justice of the peace may issue a warrant for that person's arrest without issuing a summons;

(f)   as to the execution of a warrant for arrest;

(g)   for the amendment or revocation of requirements imposed by a curfew order, on an application made to a magistrates' court by the [¹Secretary of State] or the person against whom the order was made;

(h)   similar to that made by sections 39J, 39L and 39M(2) and (3), in relation to any amendment of a curfew order;

(i)   as to the exercise by a magistrates' court of the powers conferred by sections 39K(2) and (3) and 39N(7).

(3)   Regulations under subsection (2)(g) may confer power on a magistrates' court to substitute for the place or places specified in the order a place or places in Scotland.

(4)   Where a magistrates' court exercises such a power, the functions of the magistrates' court in relation to the order as so amended shall be exercisable instead by the sheriff.

39Q   Power to make supplementary provision about curfew orders: Scotland

(1)   The Secretary of State may by regulations make provision for Scotland with respect to curfew orders.

(2)   The regulations may, in particular, make provision–

(a)   as to the content of a curfew order;

(b)   that a statement in writing to the effect that wages of any amount have been paid during any period to a person, purporting to be signed by or on behalf of that person's employer, shall be sufficient evidence of the facts stated;

(c)   for the amendment or revocation of requirements imposed by a curfew order, on an application made to the sheriff by the [¹Secretary of State] or the person against whom the order was made;

(d)   similar to that made by sections 39J, 39L and 39M(2) and (3), in relation to any amendment of a curfew order;

(e)   as to the exercise by the sheriff of the powers conferred by sections 39K(2) and (3) and 39N(7).

(3)   Regulations under subsection (2)(c) may confer power on the sheriff to substitute for the place or places specified in the order a place or places in England and Wales.

(4)   Where the sheriff exercises such a power, the functions of the sheriff in relation to the order as so amended shall be exercisable instead by a magistrates' court.

(5)   The power of the Court of Session by Act of Sederunt to regulate the procedure and practice in civil proceedings in the sheriff court shall include power to make provision–

(a)   as to the form of a curfew order;

(b)   allowing an application for a curfew order to be renewed where no curfew order is made;

(c)   that the sheriff may issue a citation to a person to appear before the sheriff and (if the person does not appear) may issue a warrant for the person's arrest;

(d)   that, for the purpose of securing a person's presence before the sheriff, the sheriff may issue a warrant for the person's arrest without issuing a citation;

(e)   as to the execution of a warrant of arrest."

Amendment

1.　　Public Bodies (Child Maintenance and Enforcement Commission: Abolition and Transfer of Functions) Order 2012 (SI 2012 No.2007) art 3(2) and Sch para 81 (August 1, 2012).

General Note

Not yet in force.

Commitment to prison

29.–*(1)　In section 40 of the Child Support Act 1991 (c. 48) (commitment to prison), before subsection (3) insert–*

"*(2A)　The [¹Secretary of State] may apply to a magistrates' court for the issue of a warrant committing a person to prison where–*

(a)　[¹*the Secretary of State] has sought to recover an amount from the person by means of taking enforcement action by virtue of section 35 or 38, or by means of a third party debt order or a charging order by virtue of section 36;*

(b)　*the whole or any part of the amount remains unpaid; and*

(c)　*the [¹Secretary of State] is of the opinion that there has been wilful refusal or culpable neglect on the part of the person from whom [¹the Secretary of State] has sought to recover the amount ("the liable person").*

(2B)　For the purposes of subsection (2A)(a), the [¹Secretary of State] is to be taken to have sought to recover an amount by means of a charging order if an interim charging order has been made, whether or not any further steps have been taken to recover the amount.

(2C)　On an application under subsection (2A) the court shall (in the presence of the liable person) inquire as to–

(a)　*the liable person's means; and*

(b)　*whether there has been wilful refusal or culpable neglect on the part of the liable person.*

(2D)　On an application under subsection (2A) the court shall not question–

(a)　*the liability order by reference to which the [¹Secretary of State] acted as mentioned in paragraph (a) of that subsection; or*

(b)　*the maintenance calculation by reference to which that liability order was made.*"

(2)　For subsection (10) of that section, substitute–

"*(10)　On acting as mentioned in subsection (3), the court may order the liable person to be searched.*

(10A)　Any money found on such a search shall, unless the court otherwise directs, be applied towards payment of the relevant amount; and the balance (if any) shall be returned to the person searched.

(10B)　The reference in subsection (10A) to the relevant amount is–

(a)　*where the order under subsection (10) is made by virtue of the court acting under subsection (3)(a), to the amount mentioned in subsection (4)(a);*

(b)　*where the order under subsection (10) is made by virtue of the court acting under subsection (3)(b), to the amount mentioned in subsection (4)(a)(i).*

(10C)　The court shall not allow the application under subsection (10A) of money found on a search under subsection (10) if it is satisfied that the money does not belong to the person searched."

(3)　In section 40A of that Act (commitment to prison: Scotland), before subsection (1) insert–

"*(A1)　The [¹Secretary of State] may apply to the sheriff for the issue of a warrant committing a person to prison where–*

(a)　[¹*the Secretary of State] has sought to recover an amount from the person by means of taking enforcement action by virtue of section 35 or 38, or by means of a third party debt order or a charging order by virtue of section 36;*

(b)　*the whole or any part of the amount remains unpaid; and*

(c)　*the [¹Secretary of State] is of the opinion that there has been wilful refusal or culpable neglect on the part of the person from whom [¹the Secretary of State] has sought to recover the amount ("the liable person").*

(A2)   For the purposes of subsection (A1)(a), the[¹Secretary of State] is to be taken to have sought to recover an amount by means of a charging order if an interim charging order has been made, whether or not any further steps have been taken to recover the amount.

(A3)   On an application under subsection (A1), the sheriff shall (in the presence of the liable person) inquire into–

(a)   the liable person's means; and

(b)   whether there has been wilful refusal or culpable neglect on the part of the liable person.

(A4)   On an application under subsection (A1), the sheriff shall not question–

(a)   the liability order by reference to which the [¹Secretary of State] acted as mentioned in paragraph (a) of that subsection; or

(b)   the maintenance calculation by reference to which that liability order was made."

(4)   After subsection (7) of that section, insert–

"(7A)   On acting as mentioned in subsection (1), the sheriff may order the liable person to be searched.

(7B)   Any money found on such a search shall, unless the sheriff otherwise directs, be applied towards payment of the relevant amount; and the balance (if any) shall be returned to the person searched.

(7C)   The reference in subsection (7B) to the relevant amount is–

(a)   where the order under subsection (7A) is made by virtue of the court acting under subsection (1)(a), to the amount mentioned in subsection (2)(a);

(b)   where the order under subsection (7A) is made by virtue of the court acting under subsection (1)(b), to the amount mentioned in subsection (2)(a)(i).

(7D)   The sheriff shall not allow the application under subsection (7B) of money found on a search under subsection (7A) if the sheriff is satisfied that the money does not belong to the person searched."

Amendment

1.   Public Bodies (Child Maintenance and Enforcement Commission: Abolition and Transfer of Functions) Order 2012 (SI 2012 No.2007) art 3(2) and Sch para 82 (August 1, 2012).

General Note

Not yet in force.

Disqualification for driving

30.–(1)   In section 40B of the Child Support Act 1991 (c. 48) (disqualification from driving), for the heading and subsection (1) substitute–

"40B   Disqualification for holding or obtaining driving licence

(A1)   The [¹Secretary of State] may apply to the court for an order disqualifying a person for holding or obtaining a driving licence where–

(a)   [¹the Secretary of State] has sought to recover an amount from the person by means of taking enforcement action by virtue of section 35 or 38, or by means of a third party debt order or a charging order by virtue of section 36;

(b)   the whole or any part of the amount remains unpaid; and

(c)   the [¹Secretary of State] is of the opinion that there has been wilful refusal or culpable neglect on the part of the person from whom [¹the Secretary of State] has sought to recover the amount ("the liable person").

(A2)   Disqualification by an order under subsection (A1)(a "disqualification order") shall be for such period not exceeding two years as the court may specify in the order.

(A3)   For the purposes of subsection (A1)(a), the[¹Secretary of State] is to be taken to have sought to recover an amount by means of a charging order if an interim charging order has been made, whether or not any further steps have been taken to recover the amount.

(A4)   On an application under subsection (A1) the court shall (in the presence of the liable person) inquire as to–

(a) whether the liable person needs a driving licence to earn a living;

(b) the liable person's means; and

(c) whether there has been wilful refusal or culpable neglect on the part of the liable person.

(A5) On an application under subsection (A1) the court shall not question–

(a) the liability order by reference to which the [¹Secretary of State] acted as mentioned in paragraph (a) of that subsection; or

(b) the maintenance calculation by reference to which that liability order was made.

(1) If, but only if, the court is of the opinion that there has been wilful refusal or culpable neglect on the part of the liable person, it may–

(a) make a disqualification order against the liable person; or

(b) make such an order but suspend its operation until such time and on such conditions (if any) as it thinks just."

(2) For subsection (10) of that section, substitute–

"(10) On making a disqualification order, the court may order the liable person to be searched.

(10A) Any money found on such a search shall, unless the court otherwise directs, be applied towards payment of the amount due; and the balance (if any) shall be returned to the person searched.

(10B) The court shall not allow the application under subsection (10A) of money found on a search under subsection (10) if it is satisfied that the money does not belong to the person searched.

(10C) The court may exercise the powers conferred on it by subsection (5) without the need for an application where money found on a search under subsection (10) is applied towards payment of the amount due."

Amendment

1. Public Bodies (Child Maintenance and Enforcement Commission: Abolition and Transfer of Functions) Order 2012 (SI 2012 No.2007) art 3(2) and Sch para 83 (August 1, 2012).

General Note

Not yet in force.

Debt management powers

Power to treat liability as satisfied
31. [...]

General Note

Section 31 inserted s41C into the 1991 Act (see p113).

Power to accept part payment of arrears in full and final satisfaction
32. [...]

Commencement

In force only for the purpose of making regulations: Child Maintenance and Other Payments Act 2008 (Commencement No.9) and the Welfare Reform Act 2009 (Commencement No.9) Order 2012 (SI 2012 No.2523) art 2(2)(d) (October 8, 2012).

In force for all other purposes: Child Maintenance and Other Payments Act 2008 (Commencement No. 10 and Transitional Provisions) Order 2012 (SI 2012 No. 3042) art 4 (December 10, 2012).

Amendment

1. Public Bodies (Child Maintenance and Enforcement Commission: Abolition and Transfer of Functions) Order 2012 (SI 2012 No.2007) art 3(2) and Sch para 84 (August 1, 2012).

General Note

s32 inserted s41D into the Child Support Act 1991 (see p114).

Power to write off arrears
33.   [...]

Commencement

In force only for the purpose of making regulations: Child Maintenance and Other Payments Act 2008 (Commencement No.9) and the Welfare Reform Act 2009 (Commencement No.9) Order 2012 (SI 2012 No.2523) art 2(2)(d) (October 8, 2012).

In force for all other purposes: Child Maintenance and Other Payments Act 2008 (Commencement No.10 and Transitional Provisions) Order 2012 (SI 2012 No. 3042) art 4 (December 10, 2012).

Amendment

1.   Public Bodies (Child Maintenance and Enforcement Commission: Abolition and Transfer of Functions) Order 2012 (SI 2012 No.2007) art 3(2) and Sch para 85 (August 1, 2012).

General Note

s33 inserted s41E into the Child Support Act 1991 (see p114).

Transfer of arrears
34.   *After section 49 of the Child Support Act 1991 insert–*

"49A   Transfer of arrears
(1)   The Secretary of State may by regulations make provision enabling the [¹Secretary of State] in prescribed circumstances to enter into arrangements ("transfer arrangements") under which liability in respect of arrears of child support maintenance becomes debt due to the person with whom the arrangements are entered into ("the transferee").

(2)   Liability which is the subject of transfer arrangements–

(a)   ceases to be liability in relation to which the [¹Secretary of State's] functions with respect to collection and enforcement are exercisable, and

(b)   becomes debt in which only the transferee has an interest.

(3)   Regulations under subsection (1) must provide that unless one of the conditions in subsection (4) is satisfied the [¹Secretary of State] may not enter into transfer arrangements in relation to arrears of child support maintenance without the appropriate consent.

(4)   The conditions are–

(a)   that the [¹Secretary of State] would be entitled to retain the whole of the arrears under section 41(2) if [¹the Secretary of State] recovered them;

(b)   that the [¹Secretary of State] would be entitled to retain part of the arrears under section 41(2) if [¹the Secretary of State] recovered them, and the part of the arrears that the [¹Secretary of State] would not be entitled to retain is equal to or less than the transfer payment.

(5)   In subsection (4)(b), "transfer payment" means–

(a)   the payment that the [¹Secretary of State] would receive from the transferee on the arrangements taking effect, and

(b)   such other payments under the transfer arrangements as may be prescribed.

(6)   Unless the maintenance calculation was made under section 7, the appropriate consent is the written consent of the person with care with respect to whom the maintenance calculation was made.

(7)   If the maintenance calculation was made under section 7, the appropriate consent is–

(a)   the written consent of the child who made the application under section 7(1), and

(b)   if subsection (8) applies, the written consent of the person with care of that child.

(8)   This subsection applies if–

(a)   the maintenance calculation was made under section 7(2), or

(b)   the Secretary of State has made arrangements under section 7(3) on the application of the person with care.

(9)   *Regulations under subsection (1) may, in particular–*

(a)   *specify when arrears of child support maintenance may be the subject of transfer arrangements;*

(b)   *specify the descriptions of person with whom transfer arrangements may be entered into;*

(c)   *specify terms and conditions which transfer arrangements must include;*

(d)   *provide that a payment made to the [¹Secretary of State] under transfer arrangements may be treated for prescribed purposes as if it were a payment of child support maintenance.*

(10)   *Regulations under subsection (1) may include–*

(a)   *provision with respect to the recovery of debt to which a person is entitled by virtue of transfer arrangements;*

(b)   *provision enabling the [¹Secretary of State] in prescribed circumstances to prevent a person entitled to debt by virtue of transfer arrangements from taking steps to recover it;*

(c)   *provision enabling the [¹Secretary of State] to supply information of a prescribed description to a person entitled to debt by virtue of transfer arrangements for the purpose of enabling the debt to be recovered."*

Amendment

1.   Public Bodies (Child Maintenance and Enforcement Commission: Abolition and Transfer of Functions) Order 2012 (SI 2012 No.2007) art 3(2) and Sch para 86 (August 1, 2012).

General Note

Not yet in force.

Miscellaneous

Registered maintenance agreements: Scotland
35. [...]

General Note

Section 35 inserted text into subss 4(10), 7(10) and 9(3) of the 1991 Act (see pp20, 24 and 30).

Offence of failing to notify change of address
36. [...]

General Note

Section 35 inserted subs (3A) into s14A of the 1991 Act (see p40).

Additional special case
37. [...]

Commencement

Child Maintenance and Other Payments Act 2008 (Commencement No.9) and the Welfare Reform Act 2009 (Commencement No.9) Order 2012 (SI 2012 No.2523) art 2 (October 8, 2012).

General Note

Section 37 inserted subs (2)(g) into s42 of the 1991 Act (see p115).

Recovery of arrears from deceased's estate
38. [...]

General Note

Section 38 inserted s43A into the 1991 Act.

Disclosure of information relating to family proceedings
39.–*(1)   After section 49A of the Child Support Act 1991 (inserted by section 34 of this Act), insert–*

    *"**49B   Disclosure of information relating to family proceedings***

(1)   Where this section applies, a disclosure of information relating to family proceedings made to the [¹Secretary of State for the purposes of the Secretary of State's functions relating to child support], or to a person providing services to the [¹Secretary of State for those purposes], by a party to the proceedings is not (if it would otherwise be) a contempt of court or punishable as a contempt of court.

(2)   This section applies if–

(a)   the party is a person with care or non-resident parent in relation to a child,

(b)   child support maintenance is payable, or an application for a maintenance calculation has been made, in respect of the child, and

(c)   the party reasonably considers that the information is relevant to the exercise of the [¹Secretary of State's] functions relating to child support in relation to the child.

(3)   This section also applies if–

(a)   an application for a maintenance calculation has been made under section 7(1) by the party, or child support maintenance is payable in accordance with a maintenance calculation made on an application made under section 7(1) by the party, and

(b)   the party reasonably considers that the information is relevant to the exercise of the [¹Secretary of State's] functions relating to child support in relation to the party.

(4)   A disclosure by a party's representative is to be treated for the purposes of this section as a disclosure by the party, if the representative is instructed by the party to make the disclosure.

(5)   In this section, "representative" means

(a)   in England and Wales–

(i)   a barrister or a solicitor, solicitor's employee or other authorised litigator (as defined in the Courts and Legal Services Act 1990) who has been instructed to act for a party in relation to the proceedings,

(ii)   a non-professional person who gives lay advice on behalf of an organisation in the lay advice sector, or

(iii)   any person permitted by the court to sit beside an unrepresented litigant in court to assist that litigant by prompting, taking notes and giving advice to the litigant;

(b)   in Scotland, a legal representative.

(6)   This section does not apply if the court dealing with the proceedings so directs.

49C   Meaning of "family proceedings"

(1)   In section 49B, "family proceedings" means any of the following proceedings commenced on or after the day on which that section comes into force–

(a)   proceedings for ancillary relief (within the meaning of subsection (2));

(b)   proceedings under section 17 of the Married Women's Property Act 1882 (questions between husband and wife as to property);

(c)   proceedings under any of the following provisions of the 1973 Act–

(i)   section 27 (financial provision in cases of neglect to maintain);

(ii)   section 35 (alteration of maintenance agreements);

(d)   proceedings under Part 1 of the Domestic Proceedings and Magistrates' Courts Act 1978 (powers of court to make orders for financial provision);

(e)   proceedings relating to orders for financial provision within the meaning of section 8 of the Family Law (Scotland) Act 1985;

(f)   proceedings relating to an action for aliment within the meaning of section 2 of that Act;

(g)   proceedings under Part 3 of the Matrimonial and Family Proceedings Act 1984 (financial relief in England and Wales after overseas divorce etc.);

(h)   proceedings under Schedule 1 to the Children Act 1989 (financial provision for children);

(i)   proceedings under sections 33 to 40 of the Family Law Act 1996 (occupation orders);

(j)   proceedings under any of the following provisions of the 2004 Act–
 (i)   section 66 (disputes between civil partners about property);
 (ii)   paragraph 41 of Schedule 5 (orders where failure to maintain);
 (iii)   paragraph 69 of Schedule 5 (alteration of maintenance agreements by the court);
 (iv)   Schedule 6 (financial relief in magistrates' courts etc.);
 (v)   Schedule 7 (financial relief in England and Wales after overseas dissolution etc. of a civil partnership).

(2)   In subsection (1), "ancillary relief" means any of the following–

(a)   an order under section 37(2)(b) or (c) of the 1973 Act or paragraph 74(3) or (4) of Schedule 5 to the 2004 Act (avoidance of disposition orders);

(b)   any of the orders mentioned in section 21(1) of the 1973 Act (except an order under section 27(6) of that Act) or any of the orders mentioned in paragraph 2(1) of Schedule 5 to the 2004 Act (financial provision orders) made under Part 1 of that Schedule;

(c)   an order under section 22 of the 1973 Act (orders for maintenance pending suit);

(d)   an order under paragraph 38 of Schedule 5 to the 2004 Act (orders for maintenance pending outcome of proceedings);

(e)   any of the orders mentioned in section 21(2) of the 1973 Act or any of the orders mentioned in paragraph 7(1) of Schedule 5 to the 2004 Act (property adjustment orders);

(f)   an order under section 31 of the 1973 Act or an order under Part 11 of Schedule 5 to the 2004 Act (variation orders);

(g)   an order under section 24B of the 1973 Act or an order under paragraph 15 of Schedule 5 to the 2004 Act (pension sharing orders).

(3)   The Secretary of State may by order amend this section so as to provide that "family proceedings" in section 49B includes proceedings of a description specified in the order, other than proceedings commenced before the day on which the order comes into force.

(4)   An order under subsection (3) may be made only with the consent of the Lord Chancellor.

(5)   In this section–
"the 1973 Act" means the Matrimonial Causes Act 1973;
"the 2004 Act" means the Civil Partnership Act 2004."

Amendment

 1. Public Bodies (Child Maintenance and Enforcement Commission: Abolition and Transfer of Functions) Order 2012 (SI 2012 No.2007) art 3(2) and Sch para 87 (August 1, 2012).

General Note

 Not yet in force.

Disclosure of information to credit reference agencies

40. After section 49C of the Child Support Act 1991 (c. 48) (inserted by section 39 of this Act) insert–

"49D   Disclosure of information to credit reference agencies

(1)   Subject to subsection (3), the [¹Secretary of State] may supply qualifying information to a credit reference agency for use for the purpose of furnishing information relevant to the financial standing of individuals.

(2)   The reference in subsection (1) to qualifying information is to information which–

(a)   is held by the [¹Secretary of State] for the purposes of this Act,

(b)   relates to a person who is liable to pay child support maintenance, and

(c)   is of a prescribed description.

(3)   Information may not be supplied under subsection (1) without the consent of the person to whom it relates, unless a liability order against that person is in force.

(4)   No provision may be made under section 14(3) authorising the supply of information by the [¹Secretary of State] to credit reference agencies.

(5)   In this section, "credit reference agency" has the same meaning as in the Consumer Credit Act 1974. "

Amendment
1.   Public Bodies (Child Maintenance and Enforcement Commission: Abolition and Transfer of Functions) Order 2012 (SI 2012 No.2007) art 3(2) and Sch para 88 (August 1, 2012).

General Note
Not yet in force.

Pilot schemes
41.   [...]

Commencement
Child Maintenance and Other Payments Act 2008 (Commencement No.9) and the Welfare Reform Act 2009 (Commencement No.9) Order 2012 (SI 2012 No.2523) art 2 (October 8, 2012).

General Note
Section 41 inserted s51A into the 1991 Act (see p131).

Meaning of "child"
42.   [...]

Commencement
In force only for the purpose of making regulations: Child Maintenance and Other Payments Act 2008 (Commencement No.9) and the Welfare Reform Act 2009 (Commencement No.9) Order 2012 (SI 2012 No.2523) art 2(2)(e) (October 8, 2012).
In force for all other purposes: Child Maintenance and Other Payments Act 2008 (Commencement No.10 and Transitional Provisions) Order 2012 (SI 2012 No.3042) art 4 (December 10, 2012)

General Note
s42 substituted s55 of the Child Support Act 1991 (see p136).

Extinction of liability in respect of interest and fees
43.   Any outstanding liability in respect of the following is extinguished–
(a)   interest under the Child Support (Arrears, Interest and Adjustment of Maintenance Assessments) Regulations 1992 (S.I. 1992/1816);
(b)   fees under the Child Support Fees Regulations 1992 (S.I. 1992/3094)

Commencement
Child Maintenance and Other Payments Act 2008 (Commencement No.2) Order 2008 (SI 2008 No.2033) art 2(2) (August 5, 2008).

Use of information
44.   [¹...]

Commencement
Child Maintenance and Other Payments Act 2008 (Commencement No.4 and Transitional Provision) Order 2008 (SI 2008 No.2675 (C.116)) art 3 (November 1, 2008).

Amendment
1.   Public Bodies (Child Maintenance and Enforcement Commission: Abolition and Transfer of Functions) Order 2012 (SI 2012 No.2007) art 3(2) and Sch para 89 (August 1, 2012).

Liable relative provisions: exclusion of parental duty to maintain
45.–(1)   In section 105 of the Social Security Administration Act 1992 (c. 5) (failure to maintain), for subsection (3) substitute–

"(3) Subject to subsection (4), for the purposes of this Part, a person shall be liable to maintain another person if that other person is–

(a) his or her spouse or civil partner, or

(b) a person whom he or she would be liable to maintain if sections 78(6)(c) and (9) had effect for the purposes of this Part."

(2) In that section, in subsection (4), for the words from "a person" to the end, substitute "subsection (3)(b) shall not apply".

Commencement

Child Maintenance and Other Payments Act 2008 (Commencement) Order 2008 (SI 2008 No.1476 (c.67)) art 2(2) (July 14, 2008).

PART 4
LUMP SUM PAYMENTS: MESOTHELIOMA ETC.

46.–54. Omitted.

PART 5
GENERAL

Regulations and orders: general

55.–(1) This section has effect in relation to regulations under this Act, except Part 4.

(2) Power to make regulations is exercisable by statutory instrument.

(3) Power to make regulations includes power to make incidental, supplementary, consequential or transitional provision or savings.

(4) Power to make regulations may be exercised–

(a) in relation to all cases to which it extends, in relation to those cases but subject to specified exceptions or in relation to any specified cases or classes of case;

(b) so as to make, as respects the cases in relation to which it is exercised–

  (i) the full provision to which it extends or any lesser provision (whether by way of exception or otherwise);

  (ii) the same provision for all cases, different provision for different cases or classes of case or different provision as respects the same case or class of case but for different purposes of this Act;

  (iii) provision which is either unconditional or is subject to any specified condition;

(c) so as to provide for a person to exercise a discretion in dealing with any matter.

(5) A statutory instrument containing–

(a) regulations under section 6(1) or (4), [¹or]

(b) the first regulations under paragraphs 2(1), 3(1), 5(1) or (2), 6(1) or (3) or 7 of Schedule 5, [¹...]

(c) [¹...]

shall not be made unless a draft of the statutory instrument containing the regulations or order has been laid before, and approved by a resolution of, each House of Parliament.

(6) A statutory instrument that–

(a) contains regulations, and

(b) is not subject to a requirement that a draft of the instrument be laid before, and approved by a resolution of, each House of Parliament,

shall be subject to annulment in pursuance of a resolution of either House of Parliament.

Commencement

Child Maintenance and Other Payments Act 2008 (2008 c.6) s62(1) (June 5, 2008).

Amendment

1. Public Bodies (Child Maintenance and Enforcement Commission: Abolition and Transfer of Functions) Order 2012 (SI 2012 No.2007) art 3(2) and Sch para 90 (August 1, 2012).

General interpretation

56.–(1)   [¹...]

(2)   Where–

(a)   this Act amends or repeals an enactment contained in the Child Support Act 1991 (c. 48) which has been amended by the Child Support, Pensions and Social Security Act 2000 (c. 19), and

(b)   the amendment by the 2000 Act has been brought into force for limited purposes only,

the reference to the enactment shall, unless the contrary intention appears, be read as a reference to the enactment as it has effect apart from the 2000 Act, as well as to the enactment as amended by that Act.

Commencement

Child Maintenance and Other Payments Act 2008 (Commencement) Order 2008 (SI 2008 No.1476 (C.67)) art 2(6) (June 10, 2008).

Amendment

1.   Public Bodies (Child Maintenance and Enforcement Commission: Abolition and Transfer of Functions) Order 2012 (SI 2012 No.2007) art 3(2) and Sch para 91 (August 1, 2012).

Minor and consequential amendments

57.–(1)   Schedule 7 (which makes minor and consequential amendments) has effect.

(2)   The Secretary of State may by regulations make provision consequential on this Act amending, repealing or revoking any provision of–

(a)   an Act passed on or before the last day of the Session in which this Act is passed, or

(b)   an instrument made under an Act before the passing of this Act.

Commencement

s57(2): Child Maintenance and Other Payments Act 2008 (Commencement) Order 2008 (SI 2008 No.1476 (C.67)) art 2(6) (June 10, 2008).

s57(1): Child Maintenance and Other Payments Act 2008 (Commencement No.4 and Transitional Provision) Order 2009 (SI 2008 No.2675 (C.116)) art 3(e) (in so far as it relates to certain paragraphs of Sch 7, November 1, 2008).

s57(1): Child Maintenance and Other Payments Act 2008 (Commencement No.5) Order 2009 (SI 2009 No.1314 (C.72)) art 2(a) (in so far as it relates to certain paragraphs of Sch 7, June 1, 2009).

s57(1): Child Maintenance and Other Payments Act 2008 (Commencement No.9) and the Welfare Reform Act 2009 (Commencement No.9) Order 2012 (SI 2012 No.2523) art 2 (in so far as it relates to paragraph 1(24), (30) and (31) of Sch 7, October 8, 2012).

s57(1) in so far as it relates to paragraph 1(2) and (29) of Sch 7, in force for the purpose of the types of cases falling within art 3 of SI 2012 No.3042 (see p767): Child Maintenance and Other Payments Act 2008 (Commencement No.10 and Transitional Provisions) Order 2012 (SI 2012 No.3042) art 2 (December 10, 2012) and for the purpose of the types of cases falling within article 3 of SI 2013 No.1860 (see p770): Child Maintenance and Other Payments Act 2008 (Commencement No.11 and Transitional Provisions) Order 2013 (SI 2013 No.1860) art 2 (July 29, 2013).

Repeals

58.   The enactments specified in Schedule 8 are repealed to the extent specified.

Commencement

Child Maintenance and Other Payments Act 2008 (Commencement No.4 and Transitional Provision) Order 2008 (C.116) art 3 (in so far as this section relates to certain entries in Sch 8, November 1, 2008).

In so far as it relates to the entry in Sch 8 relating to Sch 1 to the Child Support Act 1991 this section is in force for the purpose of making regulations: Child Maintenance and Other Payments Act 2008 (Commencement No.9) and the Welfare Reform Act 2009 (Commencement No.9) Order 2012 (SI 2012 No.2523) art 2(2)(f) and (g) (October 8, 2012); and is in force for other purposes for the types of cases falling within art 3 of SI 2012 No.3042 (see p767): Child Maintenance and Other Payments Act 2008 (Commencement No.10 and Transitional Provisions) Order 2012 (SI 2012 No.3042) art 2 (December 10, 2012) and for the types of cases falling within article 3 of SI 2013 No.1860 (see p770): Child Maintenance and Other Payments Act 2008 (Commencement No.11 and Transitional Provisions) Order 2013 (SI 2013 No.1860) art 2 (July 29, 2013).

Transition

59.–(1)   [¹...]

(2)   The Secretary of State may by regulations make provision for the Child Support Act 1991, as amended by Schedule 3, to have effect, until the coming into force of section 15, with such modifications as the Secretary of State considers necessary in consequence of the retention of functions under section 46 of that Act.

(3)   The Secretary of State may, in relation to section 6 or 46 of the Child Support Act 1991, by regulations make provision for the section to have effect with such modifications as the Secretary of State considers expedient in anticipation of the coming into force of section 15.

(4)   Sections 20(5A), 32A, 32E, 32F, 32J, 32L, 32M, 41C to 41E, 43A, 49A, 49B and 49D of the Child Support Act 1991 shall have effect as if "child support maintenance" included periodical payments required to be paid in accordance with a maintenance assessment under the Act.

(5)   Sections 20(7A), 32A, 32C, 32E, 32F, 32J, 32L, 32M, 39B, 39H, 40, 40A, 40B and 49B of the Child Support Act 1991 shall have effect as if "maintenance calculation" included a maintenance assessment under the Act.

(6)   Sections 35, 36, 38, 39B, 39H, 39K, 40, 40B and 49D of the Child Support Act 1991 shall have effect as if orders made under section 33 of that Act had been made under section 32M of that Act.

(7)   An order may be made under section 32M of the Child Support Act 1991 in respect of an amount even though the time within which an application could have been instituted under section 33 of that Act for an order in respect of that amount has expired.

(8)   The Secretary of State may by regulations make in connection with the coming into force of any provision of this Act such transitional provision or savings as the Secretary of State considers necessary or expedient.

Commencement

s59(8): Child Maintenance and Other Payments Act 2008 (2008 c.6) s62(1) (June 5, 2008).
Remainder of s59: Child Maintenance and Other Payments Act 2008 (Commencement) Order 2008 (SI 2008 No.1476 (C.67)) art 2(6) (June 10, 2008).

Amendment

1.   Public Bodies (Child Maintenance and Enforcement Commission: Abolition and Transfer of Functions) Order 2012 (SI 2012 No.2007) art 3(2) and Sch para 92 (August 1, 2012).

Financial provisions

60.–(1)   There shall be paid out of money provided by Parliament–

(a)   any expenditure incurred by the Secretary of State or a government department in consequence of this Act, and

(b)   any increase attributable to this Act in the sums payable out of money so provided under any other enactment.

[ⁱ(2)   *There shall be authorised the extinguishing in consequence of this Act of liabilities owed to the Crown under the Child Support Act 1991.*]

Commencement

s60(1): Child Maintenance and Other Payments Act 2008 (Commencement) Order 2008 (SI 2008 No.1476 (C.67)) art 2(6) (June 10, 2008).

Note

i.   Not yet in force.

Extent

61.–(1)   Subject to the following provisions, this Act extends to England and Wales and Scotland only.

(2)   The following provisions also extend to Northern Ireland–

(a)   this section and sections 55, 57(2), 62 and 63;

    (b)   [¹...]
    (3)   Any amendment or repeal made by this Act has the same extent as the enactment to which it relates.

Commencement

Child Maintenance and Other Payments Act 2008 (2008 c.6) s62(1) (June 5, 2008).

Amendment

1.   Public Bodies (Child Maintenance and Enforcement Commission: Abolition and Transfer of Functions) Order 2012 (SI 2012 No. 2007) art 3(2) and sch, para 93 (August 1, 2012).

Commencement

62.–(1) This section and sections 55, 59(8), 61 and 63 shall come into force on the day on which this Act is passed.
    (2)   Section 35 shall come into force on the day after the day on which this Act is passed.
    (3)   The remaining provisions of this Act shall come into force on such day as the Secretary of State may by order made by statutory instrument appoint, and different days may be so appointed for different purposes.
    (4)   An order under subsection (3) may include such transitional provision or savings as the Secretary of State considers necessary or expedient in connection with bringing any provision of this Act into force.
    (5)   An order under subsection (3) appointing the day on which section 39 is to come into force in England and Wales may be made only with the consent of the Lord Chancellor.

Citation

63.   This Act may be cited as the Child Maintenance and Other Payments Act 2008.

Commencement

Child Maintenance and Other Payments Act 2008 (2008 c.6) s62(1) (June 5, 2008).

SCHEDULE 1
THE COMMISSION
SECTION 1

[¹...]

Amendment

1.   Public Bodies (Child Maintenance and Enforcement Commission: Abolition and Transfer of Functions) Order 2012 (SI 2012 No.2007) art 3(2) and Sch para 71 (August 1, 2012).

Commencement

Child Maintenance and Other Payments Act 2008 (Commencement) Order 2008 (SI 2008 No.1476 (c.67)) art 2(1) (June 10, 2008, except in relation to para 1(c), for the purpose only of conferring power to appoint the members of the Commission.
For all other purposes: Child Maintenance and Other Payments Act 2008 (Commencement No.2) Order 2008 (SI 2008 No.2033 (c.97)) art 2 (July 24, 2008).

SCHEDULE 2
TRANSFER OF FUNCTIONS UNDER SUBORDINATE LEGISLATION

[¹...]

Commencement

Child Maintenance and Other Payments Act 2008 (Commencement No.4 and Transitional Provision) Order 2008 (SI 2008 No.2675) art 3 (November 1, 2008).

Amendment

1.   Public Bodies (Child Maintenance and Enforcement Commission: Abolition and Transfer of Functions) Order 2012 (SI 2012 No.2007) art 3(2) and Sch para 76 (August 1, 2012).

SCHEDULE 3
TRANSFER OF CHILD SUPPORT FUNCTIONS

PART 1
CONSEQUENTIAL AMENDMENTS

Child Support Act 1991 (c.48)

General Note

Paras 1-54 omitted. The amendments they make have been consolidated into the 1991 Act. The amendments mainly subsititute "Secretary of State" for "Commission".

PART 2
TRANSITIONAL PROVISION AND SAVINGS

55.–[¹...]

Commencement

Except in relation to para 40(b) of Sch 3: Child Maintenance and Other Payments Act 2008 (Commencement No.4 and Transitional Provision) Order 2008 (SI 2008 No.2675) art 3 (November 1, 2008).

Amendment

1. Public Bodies (Child Maintenance and Enforcement Commission: Abolition and Transfer of Functions) Order 2012 (SI 2012 No.2007) art 3(2) and Sch para 94 (August 1, 2012).

SCHEDULE 4
CHANGES TO THE CALCULATION OF MAINTENANCE

Section 16

Introductory

1.   Part 1 of Schedule 1 to the Child Support Act 1991 (c. 48) (calculation of weekly amount of child support maintenance) is amended as follows.

Calculation by reference to gross weekly income

2.   In Part 1 (under which the weekly amount of child support maintenance payable is calculated by reference to the non-resident parent's net weekly income), for "net", in each place where it occurs, substitute "gross".

Change to basic rate

3.   For paragraph 2 (basic rate) substitute–

"2 (1)   Subject to sub-paragraph (2), the basic rate is the following percentage of the non-resident parent's gross weekly income–

12% where the non-resident parent has one qualifying child;

16% where the non-resident parent has two qualifying children;

19% where the non-resident parent has three or more qualifying children.

(2)   If the gross weekly income of the non-resident parent exceeds £800, the basic rate is the aggregate of the amount found by applying sub-paragraph (1) in relation to the first £800 of that income and the following percentage of the remainder–

9% where the non-resident parent has one qualifying child;

12% where the non-resident parent has two qualifying children;

15% where the non-resident parent has three or more qualifying children.

(3)   If the non-resident parent also has one or more relevant other children, gross weekly income shall be treated for the purposes of sub-paragraphs (1) and (2) as reduced by the following percentage–

12% where the non-resident parent has one relevant other child;

16% where the non-resident parent has two relevant other children;

19% where the non-resident parent has three or more relevant other children."

Increase in flat rate and minimum amounts of liability

4.   *In the following provisions, for "£5" substitute "£7"–*

(a)　　paragraph 3(3) (minimum amount of liability in the case of reduced rate);
(b)　　paragraph 4(1) (amount of flat rate of liability);
(c)　　paragraph 7(7) (minimum amount of liability in the case of basic and reduced rates where reduction because of shared care applies).

Applicable rate where non-resident parent party to other maintenance arrangement

5.–(1)　In paragraph 1(1) (under which the weekly rate of child support maintenance is the basic rate unless a reduced rate, a flat rate or a nil rate applies), at the beginning insert "Subject to paragraph 5A,".

(2)　　After paragraph 5 insert–

"Non-resident parent party to other maintenance arrangement

5A.–(1)　This paragraph applies where–
(a)　　the non-resident parent is a party to a qualifying maintenance arrangement with respect to a child of his who is not a qualifying child, and
(b)　　the weekly rate of child support maintenance apart from this paragraph would be the basic rate or a reduced rate or calculated following agreement to a variation where the rate would otherwise be a flat rate or the nil rate.

(2)　　The weekly rate of child support maintenance is the greater of £7 and the amount found as follows.

(3)　　First, calculate the amount which would be payable if the non-resident parent's qualifying children also included every child with respect to whom the non-resident parent is a party to a qualifying maintenance arrangement.

(4)　　Second, divide the amount so calculated by the number of children taken into account for the purposes of the calculation.

(5)　　Third, multiply the amount so found by the number of children who, for purposes other than the calculation under sub-paragraph (3), are qualifying children of the non-resident parent.

(6)　　For the purposes of this paragraph, the non-resident parent is a party to a qualifying maintenance arrangement with respect to a child if the non-resident parent is–
(a)　　liable to pay maintenance or aliment for the child under a maintenance order, or
(b)　　a party to an agreement of a prescribed description which provides for the non-resident parent to make payments for the benefit of the child,
and the child is habitually resident in the United Kingdom."

Shared care

6.　　In paragraph 7(2) (circumstances in which decrease for shared care applies in cases where child support maintenance is payable at the basic rate or a reduced rate), for "If the care of a qualifying child is shared" substitute "If the care of a qualifying child is, or is to be, shared".

7.　　In paragraph 8(2) (circumstances in which decrease for shared care applies in cases where child support maintenance payable at a flat rate), for "If the care of a qualifying child is shared" substitute "If the care of a qualifying child is, or is to be, shared".

8.–(1)　In paragraph 9 (regulations about shared care), the existing provision becomes sub-paragraph (1).

(2)　　In that sub-paragraph, before paragraph (a) insert–
"(za)　for how it is to be determined whether the care of a qualifying child is to be shared as mentioned in paragraph 7(2);".

(3)　　In that sub-paragraph, after paragraph (b) insert–
"(ba)　for how it is to be determined how many nights count for those purposes;".

(4)　　After that sub-paragraph insert–
"(2)　Regulations under sub-paragraph (1)(ba) may include provision enabling the [¹Secretary of State] to proceed for a prescribed period on the basis of a prescribed assumption."

Amendment

1.　　Public Bodies (Child Maintenance and Enforcement Commission: Abolition and Transfer of Functions) Order 2012 (SI 2012 No.2007) art 3(2) and Sch para 95 (August 1, 2012).

Weekly income

9.　　In paragraph 10 (which confers power to make regulations about the manner in which weekly income is to be determined), for sub-paragraph (2) substitute–
"(2)　The regulations may, in particular–
(a)　　provide for determination in prescribed circumstances by reference to income of a prescribed description in a prescribed past period;
(b)　　provide for the [¹Secretary of State] to estimate any income or make an assumption as to any fact where, in [¹Secretary of State's] view, the information at [¹Secretary of State's] disposal is unreliable or insufficient, or relates to an atypical period in the life of the non-resident parent."

Amendment

1.　　Public Bodies (Child Maintenance and Enforcement Commission: Abolition and Transfer of Functions) Order 2012 (SI 2012 No.2007) art 3(2) and Sch para 95 (August 1, 2012).

10. In paragraph 10(3) (under which weekly income over £2,000 is to be ignored for the purposes of Schedule 1), for "£2,000" substitute "£3,000".

Commencement
Paragraphs 2, 5(2),7, 8 and 9 in force for the purpose of making regulations: Child Maintenance and Other Payments Act 2008 (Commencement No.9) and the Welfare Reform Act 2009 (Commencement No.9) Order 2012 (SI 2012 No.2523) art 2(2)(a) and (b) (October 8, 2012).

Paragraphs 2, 3 and 5-10 for the purpose of the types of cases falling within art 3 of SI 2012 No.3042 (see p767): Child Maintenance and Other Payments Act 2008 (Commencement No.10 and Transitional Provisions) Order 2012 (SI 2012 No.3042) art 2 (December 10, 2012) and for the purpose of the types of cases falling within article 3 of SI 2013 No.1860 – see p770): Child Maintenance and Other Payments Act 2008 (Commencement No.11 and Transitional Provisions) Order 2013 (SI 2013 No.1860) art 2 (July 29, 2013).

General Note
Not yet fully in force.

SCHEDULE 5
MAINTENANCE CALCULATIONS: TRANSFER OF CASES TO NEW RULES

Power to require a decision about whether to stay in the statutory scheme
1.–(1) The [¹Secretary of State] may require the interested parties in relation to an existing case to choose whether or not to stay in the statutory scheme, so far as future accrual of liability is concerned.
(2) The reference in sub-paragraph (1) to an existing case is to any of the following–
(a) a maintenance assessment,
(b) an application for a maintenance assessment,
(c) a maintenance calculation made under existing rules, and
(d) an application for a maintenance calculation which will fall to be made under existing rules.
(3) For the purposes of this paragraph, a maintenance calculation is made (or will fall to be made) under existing rules if the amount of the periodical payments required to be paid in accordance with it is (or will be) determined otherwise than in accordance with Part 1 of Schedule 1 to the Child Support Act 1991 (c. 48) as amended by this Act.

Amendment
1.   Public Bodies (Child Maintenance and Enforcement Commission: Abolition and Transfer of Functions) Order 2012 (SI 2012 No.2007) art 3(2) and Sch para 96 (August 1, 2012).

2.–(1) The Secretary of State may by regulations make provision about the exercise of the power under paragraph 1(1).
(2) Regulations under sub-paragraph (1) may, in particular–
(a) make provision about timing in relation to exercise of the power;
(b) make provision for exercise of the power in stages;
(c) specify principles for determining the order in which particular cases are to be dealt with under the power;
(d) make provision about procedure in relation to exercise of the power;
(e) make provision for exercise of the power in accordance with a scheme prepared by the [¹Secretary of State] [¹...].

Amendment
1.   Public Bodies (Child Maintenance and Enforcement Commission: Abolition and Transfer of Functions) Order 2012 (SI 2012 No.2007) art 3(2) and Sch para 96 (August 1, 2012).

3.–(1) The Secretary of State shall by regulations make such provision as he thinks fit about exercise of the right to make a choice required under paragraph 1(1).
(2) Regulations under sub-paragraph (1) shall, in particular–
(a) make provision about the time within which the choice must be made;
(b) make provision for a choice to stay in the statutory scheme to be made by means of an application to the [¹Secretary of State] for a maintenance calculation;
(c) make provision about the form and content of any application required by provision under paragraph (b).

Amendment
1.   Public Bodies (Child Maintenance and Enforcement Commission: Abolition and Transfer of Functions) Order 2012 (SI 2012 No.2007) art 3(2) and Sch para 96 (August 1, 2012).

4. If, in a particular case, any of the interested parties chooses not to stay in the statutory scheme, that person's choice shall be disregarded if any of the other interested parties chooses to stay in the statutory scheme.

Effect on accrual of liability of exercise of power under paragraph 1

5.–(1) Where the power under paragraph 1(1) is exercised in relation to a maintenance assessment or maintenance calculation, liability under the assessment or calculation shall cease to accrue with effect from such date as may be determined in accordance with regulations made by the Secretary of State.

(2) Where the power under paragraph 1(1) is exercised in relation to an application for a maintenance assessment or maintenance calculation, liability under any assessment or calculation made in response to the application shall accrue only in respect of the period ending with such date as may be determined in accordance with regulations made by the Secretary of State.

Additional powers

6.–(1) The Secretary of State may by regulations make such provision as appears to the Secretary of State to be necessary or expedient for the purposes of, or in connection with, giving effect to a decision not to leave the statutory scheme.

(2) Regulations under sub-paragraph (1) may, in particular–

(a) make provision about procedure in relation to determination of an application made in pursuance of regulations under paragraph 3;

(b) make provision about the application of the Child Support Act 1991 (c. 48) in relation to a maintenance calculation made in response to such an application;

(c) prescribe circumstances in which liability under such a maintenance calculation is to be subject to a prescribed adjustment.

(3) The Secretary of State may by regulations make provision enabling the [¹Secretary of State] to treat an application of the kind mentioned in paragraph 1(2)(b) or (d) as withdrawn if none of the interested parties chooses to stay in the statutory scheme.

Amendment

1. Public Bodies (Child Maintenance and Enforcement Commission: Abolition and Transfer of Functions) Order 2012 (SI 2012 No.2007) art 3(2) and Sch para 96 (August 1, 2012).

Interpretation

7. In this Schedule–

"interested parties" has such meaning as may be prescribed;

"maintenance assessment" means an assessment of maintenance made under the Child Support Act 1991;

"maintenance calculation" means a calculation of maintenance made under that Act;

"prescribed" means prescribed by regulations made by the Secretary of State;

"statutory scheme" means the scheme for child support maintenance under that Act.

SCHEDULE 6
USE OF INFORMATION

Section 44

[¹...]

Commencement

Child Maintenance and Other Payments Act 2008 (Commencement No.4 and Transitional Provision) Order 2008 (SI 2008 No.2675) art 3 (November 1, 2008).

Amendment

1. Public Bodies (Child Maintenance and Enforcement Commission: Abolition and Transfer of Functions) Order 2012 (SI 2012 No.2007) art 3(2) and Sch para 89 (August 1, 2012).

SCHEDULE 7
MINOR AND CONSEQUENTIAL AMENDMENTS

Section 57

Child Support Act 1991 (c. 48)

1.–*(1) The Child Support Act 1991 is amended as follows.*

(2) [In force for some cases and consolidated into the 1991 Act – see p25]

(3) In section 20 (appeals to appeal tribunals), in subsection (1), after paragraph (b) insert–

"(ba) a decision of the [⁴Secretary of State]

to make a liability order under section 32M;".

(4)   In subsection (2) of that section, after paragraph (a) insert–

"(aa)   in relation to paragraph (ba), the person against whom the order is made;".

(5)   After subsection (5) of that section insert–

"(5A)   An appeal lies by virtue of subsection (1)(ba) only on the following grounds–

(a)   that the person has not failed to pay an amount of child support maintenance;

(b)   that the amount in respect of which the liability order is made exceeds the amount of child support maintenance which the person has failed to pay."

(6)   After subsection (7) of that section insert–

"(7A)   In deciding an appeal against a decision of the [⁴Secretary of State] to make a liability order, [¹the First-tier Tribunal] shall not question the maintenance calculation by reference to which the liability order was made."

(7)   In section 30 (collection and enforcement of other forms of maintenance), in subsections (4) and (5) for "which he is authorised to collect under this section" substitute "for the collection of which he is authorised under this section to make arrangements".

(8)   In section 32(2)(i) (regulations about deduction from earnings orders), for "the liable person is in the employment" substitute "any earnings are paid to the liable person by or on behalf".

(9)   In section 32(7) (regulations about appeals), after "include" insert ''–

(a)   provision with respect to the period within which a right of appeal under the regulations may be exercised;

(b)   ''.

(10)   In section 36(1) (enforcement in county courts), for "garnishee proceedings" substitute "a third party debt order".

(11)   For section 39 substitute–

"39 Enforcement in Great Britain of Northern Ireland liability orders

The Secretary of State may by regulations make provision for the enforcement in England and Wales and Scotland of any order made in Northern Ireland under provision corresponding to section 32M or the repealed section 33."

(12)   In section 40 (commitment to prison), in subsection (4)(a)(i) of that section, for "mentioned in section 35(1)" substitute "sought to be recovered as mentioned in subsection (2A)(a)".

(13)   In section 40A (commitment to prison: Scotland)–

(a)   in subsection (1), for "satisfied" substitute "of the opinion";

(b)   for subsection (2)(a)(i) substitute–

"(i)   the amount sought to be recovered as mentioned in subsection (A1)(a), or so much of it as remains outstanding;".

(14)   In that section, in subsection (6), the words from "for" to the end become paragraph (a), and after that paragraph insert–

"(b)   that a statement in writing to the effect that wages of any amount have been paid to the liable person during any period, purporting to be signed by or on behalf of the liable person's employer, shall be sufficient evidence of the facts stated."

(15)   In section 40B (disqualification for driving), in subsection (3)–

(a)   in paragraph (a), for "mentioned in section 35(1)" substitute "sought to be recovered as mentioned in subsection (A1)(a)";

(b)   in paragraph (b), for "section 39A" substitute "this section".

(16)   In subsection (7) of that section, for "section 39A" substitute "this section".

(17)   In subsection (12) of that section (modifications for Scotland), for the subsection (11) substituted by paragraph (d) substitute–

"(11) In relation to disqualification orders–

(a)   the Secretary of State may by regulations make provision that a statement in writing to the effect that wages of any amount have been paid to the liable person during any period, purporting to be signed by or on behalf of the liable person's employer, shall be sufficient evidence of the facts stated; and

(b)   the power of the Court of Session by Act of Sederunt to regulate the procedure and practice in civil proceedings in the sheriff court shall include power to make provision corresponding to that which may be made by virtue of section 40A(8)."

(18)   At the end of that section, insert–

"(13)   In this section–

"court" (except for the purposes of subsection (8)(c)) means–

(a)   in England and Wales, a magistrates' court;

(b)   in Scotland, the sheriff;

"driving licence" means a licence to drive a motor vehicle granted under Part 3 of the Road Traffic Act 1988."

(19)-(21)   [In force and consolidated into the 1991 Act – see p127]

(22)   In section 52 (regulations and orders), in subsection (2)(a) (regulations subject to affirmative resolution procedure)–

(a)   after "30(5A)," insert "32A to 32C, 32E to 32J,";

(b)   [In force and consolidated into the 1991 Act – see p132]

(23)-(24)   [In force and consolidated into the 1991 Act – see p132]

(25)   In section 54 (interpretation), the existing provision becomes subsection (1), and in that subsection–

(a)   at the appropriate places insert–

"charging order" has the same meaning as in section 1 of the Charging Orders Act 1979;";

"Commission" means the Child Maintenance and Enforcement Commission;";

"curfew order" has the meaning given in section 39H(1);";

"deposit-taker" means a person who, in the course of a business, may lawfully accept deposits in the United Kingdom;";

(b)   in the definition of "liability order", for "section 33(2)" substitute "section 32M(2)".

(26)   In that section, after subsection (1) insert–

"(2)   The definition of "deposit-taker" in subsection (1) is to be read with–

(a)   section 22 of the Financial Services and Markets Act 2000;

(b)   any relevant order under that section; and

(c)   Schedule 2 to that Act."

(27)   In section 57(4) (application to Crown), for "a liable person is in the employment" substitute "any sums which are defined as earnings for the purposes of sections 31 and 32 are paid to a liable person by or on behalf".

(28)   In Schedule 1 (maintenance calculations), in paragraph 5(b) (weekly rate of child support maintenance to be nil if the non-resident parent has a weekly income below £5), for "£5" substitute "£7".

(29)   [In force for some cases and consolidated into the 1991 Act – see p142]

(30) – (31)   [In force and consolidated into the 1991 Act – see p143]

(32)   In that Schedule, for paragraph 14 substitute–

"14   The Secretary of State may by regulations provide–

(a)   for two or more applications for maintenance calculations to be treated, in prescribed circumstances, as a single application; and

(b)   for the replacement, in prescribed circumstances, of a maintenance calculation made on the application of one person by a later maintenance calculation made on the application of that or any other person."

(33)-(34)   [In force and consolidated into the 1991 Act.]

Social Security Act 1998 (c. 14)

3.–(1)   The Social Security Act 1998 is amended as follows.

(2)   In section 3 (use of information held by the Secretary of State or the Northern Ireland Department which relates to certain matters), in subsection (1A) (which lists the matters concerned)–

(a)   in paragraph (a), the words ", child support" are omitted;

(b)   after that paragraph insert–

"(aa)   child support in Northern Ireland;".

(3)   [²...]

Commencement

Para 1(34): Child Maintenance and Other Payments Act 2008 (Commencement) Order 2008 (SI 2008 No.1476 (C.67)) art 2(3) (July 14, 2008).

Para 2(1) and (2): Child Maintenance and Other Payments Act 2008 (Commencement No.3 and Transitional and Savings Provisions) Order 2008 (SI 2008 No.2548) art 3 (October 27, 2008).

Para 1(19), (20), (21) and (33): Child Maintenance and Other Payments Act 2008 (Commencement No.4 and Transitional Provision) Order 2008 (SI 2008 No.2675) art 3 (November 1, 2008).

Para 1(7): Child Maintenance and Other Payments Act 2008 (Commencement No.5) Order 2009 (SI 2009 No.1314 (C.72)) art 2(b) (June 1, 2009).

Para 3: Child Maintenance and Other Payments Act 2008 (Commencement No.7) Order 2010 (SI 2010 No.697 (C.44)) art 2 (April 6, 2010).

Para 1(22)(b) and (23): Child Maintenance and Other Payments Act 2008 (Commencement No.8) Order 2012 (SI 2012 No. 1649) art 2 (June 27, 2012).

Para 1(24), (30) and (31): Child Maintenance and Other Payments Act 2008 (Commencement No.9) and the Welfare Reform Act 2009 (Commencement No.9) Order 2012 (SI 2012 No.2523) art 2 (October 8, 2012).

Para 1(2) and (29) in force for the purpose of the types of cases falling within art 3 of SI 2012 No.3042 (see p767): Child Maintenance and Other Payments Act 2008 (Commencement No.10 and Transitional Provisions) Order 2012 (SI 2012 No.3042) art 2 (December 10, 2012) and for the purpose of the types of cases falling within article 3 of SI 2013 No.1860 (see p770): Child Maintenance and Other Payments Act 2008 (Commencement No.11 and Transitional Provisions) Order 2013 (SI 2013 No.1860) art 2 (July 29, 2013).

Amendments

1.   Transfer of Tribunal Functions Order 2008 (SI 2008 No.2833) art 9 and Sch 3 para 81 (November 3, 2008 subject to the transitional provisions in Sch 4 of SI 2008 No.2833).

2.   Welfare Reform Act 2012 (2012 c.5) s147 and Sch 14 Part 14 (May 8, 2012).

3.   Welfare Reform Act 2012 (2012 c.5) s147 and Sch 14 Part 13 (May 8, 2012).

4.   Public Bodies (Child Maintenance and Enforcement Commission: Abolition and Transfer of Functions) Order 2012 (SI 2012 No.2007) art 3(2) and Sch para 97 (August 1, 2012).

General Note

At the time of writing, only paras 1(7), (19)-(21), (22)(b), (23)-(24), (30)-(31), (33) and (34), and 3 were in force. The remainder of this Schedule was not yet in force.

SCHEDULE 8
REPEALS

Section 58

Short title and chapter	Extent of repeal
Debtors (Scotland) Act 1987 (c. 18)	Section 1(5)(cc).
Child Support Act 1991 (c. 48)	In section 4–

Short title and chapter
Debtors (Scotland) Act 1987 (c. 18)
Child Support Act 1991 (c. 48)

Extent of repeal
Section 1(5)(cc).
In section 4–
(a) subsections (9) and (11);
(b) in subsection (10), paragraph (b) and the word "or" immediately before it.
Section 6.
In section 7(1), paragraph (b) and the word "or" immediately before it.
In section 8(1), the words "(or treated as made)".
In section 9(6), paragraphs (a) and (b) and the word "and" immediately preceding them.
Section 11(3) to (5).
In section 12(2), the words from "(or" to "made)".
In section 14(1), the words "or treated as made" and "(or application treated as made)".
Sections 16(1A)(b), 17(1)(c) and 20(1)(c), (2)(b) and (6).
Section 20(1)(e).
In section 26(1), the words "or treated as made".
In section 27(1)(a), the words "(or is treated as having been made)" and "or treated as made".
In section 27A(1)—
(a) in paragraph (a), the words "or treated as made";
(b) in paragraph (b), the words "or, as the case may be, treated as made".
In section 28(1)(a), the words "or treated as made", in both places.
In section 28ZA(1)(a), the words from "or with" to "section 46".
In section 28ZC–
(a) in subsection (1)(b)(i), the words from "or one" to "benefit";
(b) in subsection (3), the words "or the reduction of a person's benefit".
In section 28A–
(a) in subsection (1), the words '', or treated as made under section 6,'';
(b) in subsection (3), the words from "(or" to "section 6)".
In section 28F(4)(a), the words from "(including" to "made)".
In section 28J(1)(a), the words from '', or is" to "section 6".
In section 29(1), paragraph (a) and the word "or" at the end of it.
Section 32(2)(a).
Sections 33 and 34.
In section 36—
(a) in subsection (1), the words '', if a county court so orders,'';
(b) subsection (2).
Sections 37, 39A, 40A(8)(c) and 40B(12)(b) and (c).
In section 41(1)(a), the word '', 6".
Sections 46, 47 and 50(5).
In section 52(2), the words ''6(1)," and '', 46".
In Schedule 1, in paragraph 9(1)(a), the words from "or" to the end.
Schedule 2.
In Schedule 4A, paragraph 5(2).
In Schedule 4B, in paragraph 2(3)–
(a) in paragraphs (a), (d) and (e), the words "(or treated as made)";

	(b) in paragraph (c), the words "(or treated as having been applied for)".
	In Schedule 5, paragraph 8(2).
	Social Security Administration Act 1992 (c. 5)Sections 106(7) and 107.
	In section 122(3), the word "or" at the end of paragraph (b).
Child Support Act 1995 (c. 34)	In Schedule 3, paragraphs 9 and 10.Welfare Reform and Pensions Act 1999 (c. 30)
	Section 80.
Child Support, Pensions and Social Security Act 2000 (c. 19)	Sections 3, 16(1), 19 and 28.
	In Schedule 3, paragraph 11(3)(b), (4)(a), (5)(a), (6), (8), (9), (10)(a), (11)(a), (13)(a) and (d), (17) and (22)(b).
Employment Act 2002 (c. 22)	In Schedule 6, paragraphs 11(a) and 13(a).
Civil Partnership Act 2004 (c. 33)	In Schedule 24, paragraph 3.
Welfare Reform Act 2007 (c. 5)	In Schedule 3, paragraph 7(2) to (5).
Tribunals, Courts and Enforcement Act 2007 (c. 15)	In Schedule 13, paragraphs 96 and 97.

Commencement

Partially commenced by Child Maintenance and Other Payments Act 2008 (Commencement) Order 2008 (SI 2008 No.1476 (c.67)) arts 2(1), (2) and (3) (June 10, 2008 and July 14, 2008), Child Maintenance and Other Payments Act 2008 (Commencement No.3 and Transitional and Savings Provisions) Order 2008 (SI 2008 No.2548) art 3 (October 27, 2008 subject to art 4 of SI 2008 No.2548), Child Maintenance and Other Payments Act 2008 (Commencement No.4 and Transitional Provision) Order 2008 (SI 2008 No.2675) art 3 (November 1, 2008), Child Maintenance and Other Payments Act 2008 (Commencement No.9) and the Welfare Reform Act 2009 (Commencement No.9) Order 2012 (SI 2012 No.2523) art 2(2)(f) and (g) (October 8, 2012, for the purpose only of making regulations), Child Maintenance and Other Payments Act 2008 (Commencement No.10 and Transitional Provisions) Order 2012 (SI 2012 No.3042) art 2 (December 10, 2012, for the types of cases falling within art 3 of SI 2012 No.3042 only – see p767) and Child Maintenance and Other Payments Act 2008 (Commencement No.11 and Transitional Provisions) Order 2013 (SI 2013 No.1860) art 2 (July 29, 2013, but in respect of the entry relating to Schedule 1 of the Child Support Act 1991, only for the types of cases falling within article 3 of SI 2013 No.1860 – see p767).

General Note

At the time of the most recent updating not all of this Schedule was in force. See the Child Maintenance and Other Payments Act 2008 (Commencement) Order 2008 (SI 2008 No.1476 (c.67)) arts 2(1), (2) and (3), the Child Maintenance and Other Payments Act 2008 (Commencement No.3 and Transitional and Savings Provisions) Order 2008 (SI 2008 No.2548) arts 3 and 4, the Child Maintenance and Other Payments Act 2008 (Commencement No.4 and Transitional Provision) Order 2008 (SI 2008 No.2675) art 3, the Child Maintenance and Other Payments Act 2008 (Commencement No.9) and the Welfare Reform Act 2009 (Commencement No.9) Order 2012 (SI 2012 No.2523) art 2(2)(f) and (g), the Child Maintenance and Other Payments Act 2008 (Commencement No.10 and Transitional Provisions) Order 2012 (SI 2012 No.3042) art 2 and the Child Maintenance and Other Payments Act 2008 (Commencement No. 11 and Transitional Provisions) Order 2013 (SI 2013 No.1860) art 2 for details.

Part III

REGULATIONS

The Child Support (Maintenance Assessment Procedure) Regulations 1992
(SI 1992 No.1813)

General Note on the Regulations

The Child Support (Maintenance Assessment Procedure) Regulations 1992 have been revoked for certain cases only by:

(1) the Child Support (Maintenance Calculation Procedure) Regulations 2000 (SI 2001 No.157) reg 30 (this revocation comes into force in relation to a particular case on the date on which the amendments to ss5, 6, 12, 46, 51, 54 and 55 of the Child Support Act 1991 made by the Child Support, Pensions and Social Security Act, 2000 come into force in relation to that type of case, which is March 3, 2003 for the types of cases detailed in arts 3 and 4 Child Support, Pensions and Social Security Act 2000 (Commencement No.12) Order 2003 (SI 2003 No.192), see p683). See reg 30 of SI 2001 No.157, on p663, for savings provisions;

(2) the Child Support (Meaning of Child and New Calculation Rules) (Consequential and Miscellaneous Amendment) Regulations 2012 (SI 2012 No. 2785) reg 10 (this revocation comes into force in relation to a particular case on the day on which paragraph 2 of Schedule 4 to the Child Maintenance and Other Payments Act 2008 (see p243) comes into force in relation to that type of case – which is December 10, 2012, only in relation to the types of cases falling within art 3 of SI 2012 No. 3042 (see p767).

For other types of cases the '1993 rules', which include the Child Support (Maintenance Assessment Procedure) Regulations 1992, continue to apply. The Child Support (Maintenance Assessment Procedure) Regulations 1992 are therefore reproduced below.

PART I
GENERAL

Citation, commencement and interpretation

1.–(1) These Regulations may be cited as the Child Support (Maintenance Assessment Procedure) Regulations 1992 and shall come into force on 5th April 1993.(2)   In these Regulations, unless the context otherwise requires–

"the Act" means the Child Support Act 1991;

"applicable amount" [4, except in regulation 40ZA,] is to be construed in accordance with Part IV of the Income Support Regulations:

"applicable amounts Schedule" means Schedule 2 to the Income Support Regulations;

"award period" means a period in respect of which an award of family credit or disability working allowance is made;

"balance of the reduction period" means, in relation to a direction that is or has been in force, the portion of the period specified in a direction in respect of which no reduction of relevant benefit has been made;

"benefit week", in relation to income support, has the same meaning as in the Income Support Regulations, [⁴in relation to jobseeker's allowance has the same meaning as in the Jobseeker's Allowance Regulations,] [¹²in relation to employment and support allowance has the same meaning as in the Employment and Support Allowance Regulations 2008,] and, in relation to family credit and disability working allowance, is to be construed in accordance with the Social Security (Claims and Payments) Regulations 1987;

[⁸*"designated authority"* has the meaning it has in regulation 2(1) of the Social Security (Work-focused Interviews) Regulations 2000;]

[¹³ ...]

[⁷*"disability working allowance"* means an award of disability working allowance under section 129 of the Social Security Contributions and Benefits Act 1992 which was awarded with effect from a date falling before 5th October 1999.]

"day to day care" has the same meaning as in the Maintenance Assessments and Special Cases Regulations;

"effective application" means any application that complies with the provisions of regulation 2;

"effective date" means the date on which a maintenance assessment takes effect for the purposes of the Act;

[¹¹*"family"* has the same meaning as in the Maintenance Assessments and Special Cases Regulations;]

[⁷*"family credit"* means an award of family credit under section 128 of the Social Security Contributions and Benefits Act 1992 which was awarded with effect from a date falling before 5th October 1999.]

[¹²*"income-related employment and support allowance"* means an income-related allowance under Part 1 of the Welfare Reform Act 2007;]

"Income Support Regulations" means Income Support (General) Regulations 1987;

"Information, Evidence and Disclosure Regulations" means the Child Support (Information, Evidence and Disclosure) Regulations 1992;

[⁴*"the Jobseeker's Allowance Regulations"* means the Jobseeker's Allowance Regulations 1996;]

[¹*"Maintenance Arrangements and Jurisdiction Regulations"* means the Child Support (Maintenance Arrangements and Jurisdiction) Regulations 1992;]

"Maintenance Assessments and Special Cases Regulations" means the Child Support (Maintenance Assessments and Special Cases) Regulations 1992

"maintenance period" has the meaning prescribed in regulation 33;

"obligation imposed by section 6 of the Act" is to be construed in accordance with section 46(1) of the Act;

[⁸*"official error"* means an error made by-

(a) an officer of the Department of Social Security acting as such which no person outside that Department caused or to which no person outside that Department materially contributed;

[⁹(b) a person employed by a designated authority acting on behalf of the authority, which no person outside that authority caused or to which no person outside that authority materially contributed,

but excludes any error of law which is only shown to have been an error by virtue of a subsequent decision of [¹⁴ the Upper Tribunal] or the court;]

"parent with care" means a person who, in respect of the same child or children, is both a parent and a person with care;

"the parent concerned" means the parent with respect to whom a direction is given;

[¹¹*"partner"* has the same meaning as in the Maintenance Assessments and Special Cases Regulations;]

"protected income level" has the same meaning as in paragraph 6(6) of Schedule 1 to the Act;

"relevant benefit" means income support, [⁴income-based jobseeker's allowance,] [¹²income-related employment and support allowance] [⁷or an award of family

   credit or disability working allowance which was awarded with effect from a date falling before 5th October 1999;]

"relevant person" means–

 (a) *a person with care;*

 (b) *an absent parent;*

 (c) *a parent who is treated as an absent parent under regulation 20 of the Maintenance Assessments and Special Cases Regulations;*

 (d) *where the application for an assessment is made by a child under section 7 of the Act, that child, in respect of whom a maintenance assessment has been applied for or is or has been in force [*[15]*;*

   "universal credit" means universal credit under Part 1 of the Welfare Reform Act 2012].

 (3) [*[13]...]*

 (4) *The provisions of Schedule 1 shall have effect to supplement the meaning of "child" in section 55 of the Act.*

 (5) *The provisions of these Regulations shall have general application to cases prescribed in regulations 19 to 26 of the Maintenance Assessments and Special Cases Regulations as cases to be treated as special cases for the purposes of the Act, and the terms "absent parent" and "person with care" shall be construed accordingly.*

 (6) *Except where express provision is made to the contrary, where, by any provision of the Act or of these Regulations–*

 (a) *any document is given or sent to the Secretary of State, that document shall, subject to paragraph (7), be treated as having been so given or sent on the day it is received by the Secretary of State; and*

 (b) *any document is given or sent to any [*[5]*other] person, that document shall, if sent by post to that person's last known or notified address, and subject to paragraph (8), be treated as having been given or sent on the second day after the day of posting, excluding any Sunday or any day which is a bank holiday in England, Wales, Scotland or Northern Ireland under the Banking and Financial Dealings Act 1971.*

 (7) *Except where the provisions of regulation [*[6]*9(1) or 18(4)] apply, the Secretary of State may treat a document given or sent to him as given or sent on such day, earlier than the day it was received by him, as he may determine, if he is satisfied that there was unavoidable delay in his receiving the document in question.*

 (8) *Where, by any provision of the Act or of these Regulations, and in relation to a particular application, notice or notification–*

 (a) *more than one document is required to be given or sent to a person, and more than one such document is sent by post to that person but not all the documents are posted on the same day; or*

 (b) *documents are required to be given or sent to more than one person, and not all such documents are posted on the same day,*

all those documents shall be treated as having been posted on the later or, as the case may be, the latest day of posting.

 (9) *In these Regulations, unless the context otherwise requires, a reference–*

 (a) *to a numbered Part is to the Part of these Regulations bearing that number;*

 (b) *to a numbered Schedule is to the Schedule to these Regulations bearing that number;*

 (c) *to a numbered regulation is to the regulation in these Regulations bearing that number;*

 (d) *in a regulation or Schedule to a numbered paragraph is to the paragraph in that regulation or Schedule bearing that number;*

 (e) *in a paragraph to a lettered or numbered sub-paragraph is to the sub-paragraph in that paragraph bearing that letter or number.*

Amendments

 1. *Child Support (Miscellaneous Amendments) Regulations 1995 (SI 1995 No.123) reg 4 (February 16,1995).*

2. Child Support (Misc Amendments) (No.2) Regulations 1995 (SI 1995 No.3261) reg 15 (January 22, 1996).

3. Child Support (Misc Amendments) (No.2) Regulations 1995 (SI 1995 No.3261) reg 15 (January 22, 1996).

4. Social Security and Child Support (Jobseeker's Allowance) (Consequential Amendments) Regulations 1996 (SI 1996 No.1345) reg 5(2) (October 7, 1996).

5. Child Support (Misc Amendments) (No.2) Regulations 1996 (SI 1996 No.3196) reg 5 (January 13, 1997).

6. Child Support (Misc Amendments) (No.2) Regulations 1999 (SI 1999 No.1047) reg 2(b) (June 1, 1999).

7. Social Security and Child Support (Tax Credits) Consequential Amendments Regulations 1999 (SI 1999 No.2566) reg 5 (October 5, 1999)

8. Social Security (Work-focused Interviews) Regulations 2000 (SI 2000 No.897) reg 16(5) and sch 6 para 8 (April 3, 2000)

9. Social Security (Work-focused Interviews) Regulations 2000 (SI 2000 No.1596) reg 6 (June 19, 2000).

10. Child Support (Miscellaneous Amendments) (No.2) Regulations 2003 (SI 2003 No.2779) reg 3(2) (November 5, 2003). However, see Child Support (Miscellaneous Amendments) (No.2) Regulations 2003 (SI 2003 No.2779) reg 9 for savings provisions. For those covered by the savings provisions, prior to these amendments reg 1(3)(a) and (b) read:

"(a) after that direction has been given, relevant benefit ceases to be payable, or becomes payable at one of the rates indicated in regulation 40(3) [⁴or, as the case may be, regulation 40ZA(4)]; [²...]

(b) at the time that the direction is given, relevant benefit is payable at one of the rates indicated in regulation 40(3) [⁴or, as the case may be, regulation 40ZA(4)], [³or]"

11. Child Support (Misc Amendments) Regulations 2005 (SI 2005 No.785) reg 3(2) (March 16, 2005).

12. Employment and Support Allowance (Consequential Provisions) (No.2) Regulations 2008 (SI 2008 No.1554) reg 57(2) and (3) (October 27, 2008).

13. Child Support (Consequential Provisions) Regulations 2008 (SI 2008 No.2543) reg 2(2) (October 27, 2008).

14. Tribunals, Courts and Enforcement Act 2007 (Transitional and Consequential Provisions) Order 2008 (SI 2008 No.2683) Sch 1 para 57 (November 3, 2008).

15. Universal Credit (Consequential, Supplementary, Incidental and Miscellaneous Provisions) Regulations 2013 (SI 2013 No. 630) reg 40(2) (April 29, 2013).

PART II
APPLICATIONS FOR A MAINTENANCE ASSESSMENT

Applications under section 4 [¹...] or 7 of the Act

2.–(1)   Any person who applies for a maintenance assessment under section 4 or 7 of the Act shall do so on a form (a "maintenance application form") provided by the Secretary of State.

(2)   Maintenance application forms provided by the Secretary of State [¹...] under paragraph (1) shall be supplies without charge by such persons as the Secretary of State appoints or authorises for that purpose.

(3)   A completed maintenance application form shall be given or sent to the Secretary of State.

(4)   Subject to paragraph (5), an application for a maintenance assessment under the Act shall be an effective application if it is made on a maintenance application form and that form has been completed in accordance with the Secretary of State's instructions.

(5)   Where an application is not effective under the provisions of paragraph (4), the Secretary of State may–

(a)   give or send the maintenance application form to the person who made the application, together, if he thinks appropriate, with a fresh maintenance application form, and request that the application be re-submitted so as to comply with the provisions of that paragraph; or

(b)   request the person who made the application to provide such additional information or evidence as the Secretary of State specifies, *and if a completed application form or, as the case may be, the additional information or evidence requested is received by the Secretary of State within 14 days of the date of his request, he shall treat the application as made on the date on which the earlier or earliest application would have been treated as made had it been effective under the provisions of paragraph (4).*

(6) Subject to paragraph (7), a person who has made an effective application may amend his application by notice in writing to the Secretary of State at any time before a maintenance assessment is made.

(7) No amendment under paragraph (6) shall relate to any change of circumstances arising after the effective date of a maintenance assessment resulting from an effective application.

Amendment

1. *Child Support (Consequential Provisions) Regulations 2008 (SI 2008 No.2543) reg 2(3) (October 27, 2008).*

Applications on the termination of a maintenance assessment

3.–(1) Where a maintenance assessment has been in force with respect to a person with care and a qualifying child and that person is replaced by another person with care, an application for a maintenance assessment with respect to that person with care and that qualifying child may for the purposes of regulation 30(2)(b)(ii) and subject to paragraph (3) be treated as having been received on a date earlier than that on which it was received.

(2) Where a maintenance assessment has been made either in response to an application by a child under section 7 of the Act and either–

(a) [¹the Secretary of State] cancels that assessment following a request from that child; or

(b) that child ceases to be a child for the purposes of the Act,

any application for a maintenance assessment with respect to any other children who were qualifying children with respect to the earlier maintenance assessment may for the purposes of regulation 30(2)(b)(ii) and subject to paragraph (3) be treated as having been received on a date earlier than that on which it was received.

(3) No application for a maintenance assessment shall be treated as having been received under paragraph (1) or (2) on a date–

(a) more than 8 weeks earlier than the date on which the application was received; or

(b) on or before the first day of the maintenance period in which the earlier maintenance assessment ceased to have effect.

Amendment

1. *Child Support (Misc Amendments) (No.2) Regulations 1999 (SI 1999 No.1047) reg 3 (June 1, 1999).*

Multiple applications

4.–(1) The provisions of Schedule 2 shall apply in cases where there is more than one application for a maintenance assessment.

(2) The provisions of paragraphs 1, 2 and 3 of Schedule 2 relating to the treatment of two or more applications as a single application shall apply where no request is received for the Secretary of State to cease acting in relation to all but one of the applications.

(3) Where, under the provisions of paragraph 1, 2 or 3 of Schedule 2, two or more applications are to be treated as a single application, that application shall be treated as an application for a maintenance assessment to be made with respect to all of the qualifying children mentioned in the applications, and the effective date of that assessment shall be determined by reference to the earlier or earliest application.

Notice to other persons of an application for a maintenance assessment

5.–*(1)   [¹Subject to paragraph (2A), where] an effective application for a maintenance assessment has been made the Secretary of State shall as soon as is reasonably practicable give notice in writing of that application to the relevant persons other than the applicant.*

(2)   The Secretary of State shall[¹, subject to paragraph (2A),] given or sent to any person to whom notice has been given under paragraph (1) a form (a "maintenance enquiry form") and a written request that the form be completed and returned to him for the purpose of enabling the application for the maintenance assessment to be proceeded with.

[²(2A)   The provisions of paragraphs (1) and (2) shall not apply where the Secretary of State is satisfied that an application for a maintenance assessment can be dealt with in the absence of a completed and returned maintenance enquiry form.]

(3)   Where the person to whom notice is being given under paragraph (1) is an absent parent, that notice shall specify the effective date of the maintenance assessment if one is to be made, and set out in general terms the provisions relating to interim maintenance assessments.

Amendments

1.   *Child Support (Miscellaneous Amendments) Regulations 1993 (SI 1993 No.913) reg 2 (April 5, 1993).*
2.   *Child Support (Miscellaneous Amendments) Regulations 1993 (SI 1993 No.913) reg 3 (April 5, 1993).*

Response to notification of an application for a maintenance assessment

6.–*(1)   Any person who has received a maintenance enquiry form given or sent under regulation 5(2) shall complete that form in accordance with the Secretary of State's instructions and return it to the Secretary of State within 14 days of its having been given or sent.*

(2)   Subject to paragraph (3), a person who has returned a completed maintenance enquiry form may amend the information he has provided on that form at any time before a maintenance assessment is made by notifying the Secretary of State in writing of the amendments.

(3)   No amendment under paragraph (2) shall relate to any change of circumstances arising after the effective date of any maintenance assessment made in response to the application in relation to which the maintenance enquiry form was given or sent.

Death of a qualifying child

7.–*(1)   Where [¹the Secretary of State] is informed of the death of a qualifying child with respect to whom an application for a maintenance assessment has been made, he shall–*

(a)   *proceed with the application as if it had not been made with respect to that child if he has not yet made an assessment;*

(b)   *treat any assessment already made by him as not having been made if the relevant persons have not been notified of it and proceed with the application as if it had not been made with respect to that child.*

(2)   Where all of the qualifying children with respect to whom an application for a maintenance assessment has been made have died, and either the assessment has not been made or the relevant persons have not been notified of it, [¹the Secretary of State] shall treat the application as not having been made.

Amendment

1.   *Child Support (Miscellaneous Amendments) (No.2) Regulations 1999 (SI 1999 No.1047) reg 4 (June 1, 1999).*

PART III
INTERIM MAINTENANCE ASSESSMENTS

[¹Categories of interim maintenance assessment

8.–*(1)   Where [²the Secretary of State] serves notice under section 12(4) of the Act of his intention to make an interim maintenance assessment, he shall not make that* interim assessment before the end of a period of 14 days, commencing with the date that notice was given or sent.

(2)   There shall be four categories of interim maintenance assessment, Category A, Category B, Category C, and Category D interim maintenance assessments.

(3)   An interim maintenance assessment made by [²the Secretary of State] shall be–

(a)   a Category A interim maintenance assessment, where any information, other than information referred to in sub-paragraph (b), that is required by him to enable him to make an assessment in accordance with the provisions of Part I of Schedule 1 to the Act has not been provided by that absent parent, and that parent has that information in his possession or can reasonably be expected to acquire it.

(b)   a Category B interim maintenance assessment, where the information that is required by him as to the income of the partner or other member of the family of the absent parent or parent with care for the purposes of the calculation of the income of that partner or other member of the family under regulation 9(2), 10, 11(2) or 12(1) of the Maintenance Assessment and Special Cases Regulations–

    (i)   has not been provided by that partner or other member of the family, and that partner or other member of the family has that information in his possession or can reasonably be expected to acquire it; or

    (ii)   has been provided by that partner or other member of the family to the absent parent or parent with care, but the absent parent or parent with care has not provided it to the Secretary of State; [²...]

(c)   a Category C interim maintenance assessment where–

    (i)   the absent partner is a self-employed earner as defined in regulation 1(2) of the Maintenance Assessments and Special Cases Regulations; and

    (ii)   the absent parent is currently unable to provide, but has indicated that he expects within a reasonable time to be able to provide, information to enable [²the Secretary of State] to determine the earnings of that absent parent in accordance with paragraphs 3 to 5 of Schedule 1 to the Maintenance Assessments and Special Cases Regulations; and

    (iii)   no maintenance order as defined in section 8(11) of the Act or written maintenance agreement as defined in section 9(1) of the Act is in force with respect to children in respect of whom the Category C interim maintenance assessment would be made; or

(d)   a Category D interim maintenance assessment where it appears to [²the Secretary of State], on the basis of information available to him as to the income of the absent parent, that the amount of any maintenance assessment made in accordance with Part I of Schedule 1 to the Act applicable to that absent parent may be higher than the amount of a Category A interim maintenance assessment in force in respect of him.

(e)   [³...]]

Amendments

1.   *Child Support (Misc Amendments) (No.2) Regulations 1995 (SI 1995 No.3261) reg 16 (January 22, 1996).*

2.   *Child Support (Misc Amendments) (No.2) Regulations 1999 (SI 1999 No.1047) reg 5 (June 1, 1999).*

3.   *Child Support (Misc Amendments) Regulations 2005 (SI 2005 No.785) reg 3(3) (March 16, 2005).*

[¹*Amount of an interim maintenance assessment*

8A.–(1)   The amount of child support maintenance fixed by a Category A interim maintenance assessment shall be 1.5 multiplied by the amount of the maintenance requirement in respect of the qualifying child or qualifying children concerned calculated in accordance with the provisions of paragraph 1 of Schedule 1 to the Act, and paragraphs 2 to 9 of that Schedule shall not apply to Category A interim maintenance assessments.

(2)   Subject to paragraph (5), the amount of child support maintenance fixed by a Category B interim maintenance assessment shall be determined in accordance with paragraphs (3) and (4).

(3)   Where [³the Secretary of State] is unable to determine the exempt income–

(a)   of an absent parent under regulation 9 of the Maintenance Assessments and Special Cases Regulations because he is unable to determine whether regulation 9(2) of those Regulations applies;

(b)   of a parent with care under regulation 10 of those Regulations because he is unable to determine whether regulation 9(2) of those Regulations, as modified by and applied by regulation 10 of those Regulations applies,
the amount of the Category B interim maintenance assessment shall be the maintenance assessment calculated in accordance with Part I of Schedule 1 to the Act on the assumption that–

(i)   in a case falling within sub-paragraph (a), regulation 9(2) of those Regulations does apply;

(ii)   in a case falling within sub-paragraph (b), regulation 9(2) of those Regulations as modified by and applied by regulation 10 of those Regulations does apply.

[²(4)   Where [³the Secretary of State] is unable to ascertain the income of other members of the family of an absent parent so that the disposable income of that absent parent can be calculated in accordance with regulation 12(1)(a) of the Maintenance Assessments and Special Cases Regulations, the amount of the Category B interim maintenance assessment shall be the maintenance assessment calculated in accordance with Part I of Schedule 1 to the Act on the assumption that the provisions of paragraph 6 of that Schedule do not apply to the absent parent.]

(5)   Where the application of the provisions of paragraph (3) or (4) would result in the amount of a Category B interim maintenance assessment being more than 30 per centum of the net income of the absent parent as calculated in accordance with regulation 7 of the Maintenance Assessments and Special Cases Regulations, those provisions shall not apply to that absent parent and instead, the amount of that Category B interim maintenance assessment shall be 30 per centum of this net income as so calculated and where that calculation results in a fraction of a penny, that fraction shall be disregarded.

(6)   The amount of the child support maintenance fixed by a Category C interim maintenance assessment shall be £30.00 but [³the Secretary of State] may set a lower amount, including a nil amount, if he thinks it reasonable to do so in all the circumstances of the case.

(7)   Paragraph 6 of Schedule 1 to the Act shall not apply to Category C interim maintenance assessments.

(8)   [³The Secretary of State] shall notify the person with care where he is considering setting a lower amount for a Category C interim maintenance assessment in accordance with paragraph (6) and shall take into account any relevant representations made by that person with care in deciding the amount of that Category C interim maintenance assessment.

(9)   The amount of child support maintenance fixed by a Category D interim maintenance assessment shall be calculated or estimated by applying to the absent partner's income, in so far as [³the Secretary of State] is able to determine it at the time of the making of that Category D interim maintenance assessment, the provisions of Part I of Schedule 1 to the Act and regulations made under it, subject to the modification that–

(a)   paragraphs 6 and 8 of that Schedule shall not apply;

(b)   only paragraphs (1)(a) and (5) of regulation 9 of the Maintenance Assessments and Special Cases Regulations shall apply; and

(c)   heads (b) and (c) of sub-paragraphs (3) of paragraph 1 of Schedule 1 to the Maintenance Assessments and Special Cases Regulations shall not apply.

(10)   Where the absent parent referred to in paragraph (9) is an employed earner as defined in regulation 1 of the Maintenance Assessments and Special Cases Regulations and the child support officer is unable to calculate the net income of that absent parent,

his net income shall be estimated under the provisions of paragraph (2A)(a) and (b) of that regulation.]

Amendments

1.　　Child Support (Misc Amendments) (No.2) Regulations 1995 (SI 1995 No.3261) reg 16 (January 22, 1996).
2.　　Child Support (Misc Amendments) Regulations 1998 (SI 1998 No.58) reg 35 (January 19, 1998).
3.　　Child Support (Misc Amendments) (No.2) Regulations 1999 (SI 1999 No.1047) reg 6 (June 1, 1999).

[¹**8B**　　[²...]]

Amendments

1.　　Child Support (Misc Amendments) (No.2) Regulations 1995 (SI 1995 No.3261) reg 16 (January 22, 1996)
2.　　Child Support (Misc Amendments) (No.2) Regulations 1999 (SI 1999 No.1047) reg 7 (June 1, 1999).

[¹*Effective date of an interim maintenance assessment*

8C.–(1)　Except where regulation 3(5) of the Maintenance Arrangements and Jurisdiction Regulations (effective date of maintenance assessment where court order in force), regulation [²...] 33(7) or paragraph (2) applies, the effective date of an interim maintenance assessment shall be–

(a)　*in respect of a Category A interim maintenance assessment, subject to [²...] sub-paragraph (d), such date, being not earlier than the first and not later than the seventh day following the date upon which that interim maintenance assessment was made, as falls on the same day of the week as the date determined in accordance with regulation 30(2)(a)(ii) or (b)(ii) as the case may be;*

(b)　*in respect of a Category B interim maintenance assessment made after 22nd January 1996, subject to sub-paragraph (d) [²...], the date specified in regulation 30(2)(a)(ii) or (b)(ii) as the case may be;*

(c)　*in respect of a Category C interim maintenance assessment, subject to sub-paragraph (d) [²...], the date set out in sub-paragraph (a);*

(d)　*in respect of a Category A, Category B or Category C interim maintenance assessment, where the application of the provisions of sub-paragraph (a), (b) or (c) would otherwise set an effective date for an interim maintenance assessment earlier than the end of a period of eight weeks from the date upon which–*

(i)　*the maintenance enquiry form referred to in regulation 30(2)(a)(i) was given or sent to an absent parent; or*

(ii)　*the application made by an absent parent referred to in regulation 30(2)(b)(i) was received by the Secretary of State,*

in circumstances where that absent parent has complied with the provisions of regulation 30(2)(a)(i) or (b)(i) or paragraph (2A) of that regulation applies, the date determined in accordance with regulation 30(2)(a)(i) or (b)(i).

(2)　[²The effective date of an interim maintenance assessment made under 12(1)(b) of the Act shall, subject to regulation 33(7)], be such date, not earlier than the first and not later than the seventh day following the date upon which that interim maintenance assessment was made, as falls on the same day of the week as the effective date of the maintenance assessment calculated in accordance with Part I of Schedule 1 to the Act which [²the Secretary of State is proposing to supersede with a decision under section 17 of the Act].

(3)　In cases where the effective date of an interim maintenance assessment is determined under paragraph (1), [²...], where a maintenance assessment, except a maintenance assessment falling within regulation 8D(7), is made after an interim maintenance assessment has been in force, child support maintenance calculated in

accordance with Part I of Schedule 1 to the Act shall be payable in respect of the period preceding that during which the interim maintenance assessment was in force.

(4)   The child support maintenance payable under the provisions of paragraph (3) shall be payable in respect of the period between the effective date of the assessment (or, where separate assessments are made for different periods under paragraph 15 of Schedule 1 to the Act, the effective date of the assessment in respect of the earliest such period) and the effective date of the interim maintenance assessment.]

Amendments

1.   *Child Support (Misc Amendments) (No.2) Regulations 1995 (SI 1995 No.3261) reg 16 (January 22, 1996.*

2.   *Child Support (Misc Amendments) (No.2) Regulations 1999 (SI 1999 No.1047) reg 8 (June 1, 1999).*

[¹*Miscellaneous provisions in relation to interim maintenance assessments*

8D.–(1)   Subject to paragraph (2), where a maintenance assessment calculated in accordance with Part I of Schedule 1 to the Act is made following an interim maintenance assessment, the amount of child support maintenance payable in respect of the period after 18th April 1995, during which that interim maintenance assessment was in force shall be that fixed by the maintenance assessment.

[³*(1A)   The reference in paragraph (1) to a maintenance assessment calculated in accordance with Part I of Schedule 1 to the Act shall include a maintenance assessment falling within regulation 30A(2)*].

(2)   Paragraph (1) shall not apply where a maintenance assessment calculated in accordance with Part I of Schedule 1 to the Act falls within paragraph (7).

(3)   [⁴...]

(4)   The provisions of regulations [⁴32 and 33(5)] shall not apply to a Category A or Category D interim maintenance assessment.

(5)   Subject to paragraph (6) [⁴...], an interim maintenance assessment shall cease to have effect on the first day of the maintenance period during which the Secretary of State receives the information which enables [⁴the Secretary of State] to make the maintenance assessment or assessments in relation to the same absent parent, person with care, and qualifying child or qualifying children, calculated in accordance with Part I of Schedule 1 to the Act.

(6)   Subject to regulation 9(15), where a child support officer has insufficient information or evidence to enable him to make a maintenance assessment calculated in accordance with Part I of Schedule 1 to the Act for the whole of the period beginning with the effective date applicable to a particular case, an interim maintenance assessment made in that case shall cease to have effect–

(a)   on 18th April 1995 where by that date the Secretary of State has received the information or evidence set out in paragraph (7); or

(b)   on the first day of the maintenance period after 18th April 1995 in which the Secretary of State has received that information or evidence.

(7)   The information or evidence referred to in paragraph (6) is information or evidence enabling [⁴the Secretary of State] to make a maintenance assessment calculated in accordance with Part I of Schedule 1 to the Act, for a period beginning after the effective date applicable to that case, in respect of the absent parent, parent with care and qualifying child or qualifying children in respect of whom the interim maintenance assessment referred to in paragraph (6) was made.

[²(8)   Where the information or evidence referred to in paragraph (6)(a) or (b) is that there has been an award of income support[⁶, an income-related employment and support allowance][⁵, state pension credit] or an income-based jobseeker's allowance, the Secretary of State shall be treated as having received that information or evidence on the first day in respect of which income support[⁶, an income-related employment and support allowance][⁵, state pension credit] or an income-based jobseeker's allowance was payable under that award.]

Amendments
1.	Child Support (Misc Amendments) (No.2) Regulations 1995 (SI 1995 No.3261) reg 16 (January 22, 1996).
2.	Child Support (Misc Amendments) (No.2) Regulations 1996 (SI 1996 No.3196) reg 6 (January 13, 1997).
3.	Child Support (Misc Amendments) Regulations 1998 (SI 1998 No.58) reg 36 (January 19, 1998).
4.	Child Support (Misc Amendments) (No.2) Regulations 1999 (SI 1999 No.1047) reg 9 (June 1, 1999).
5.	Child Support (Misc Amendments) (No.2) Regulations 2003 (SI 2003 No.2779) reg 3(3) (November 5, 2003).
6.	Employment and Support Allowance (Consequential Provisions) (No.2) Regulations 2008 (SI 2008 No.1554) reg 57(4) (October 27, 2008).

[¹Interim maintenance assessments which follow other interim maintenance assessments

9.–*(1)	Where an interim maintenance assessment is being revised on the ground specified in regulation 17(1)(b) and the Secretary of State is satisfied–*

*(a)	that another Category A, Category B or Category D maintenance assessment should be made, and*

*(b)	that there has been unavoidable delay for part of the period during which the assessment which is being revised was in force,*

the effective date of that other–

*(i)	Category A or Category D interim maintenance assessment shall be the first day of the maintenance period following the date upon which, in the opinion of the Secretary of State, the delay became avoidable;*

*(ii)	Category B interim maintenance assessment shall be the date set out in regulation 8C(1)(b).*

*(2)	Where an interim maintenance assessment is revised on either of the grounds set out in regulation 17(4) or (5), payments made under that interim maintenance assessment before the revision shall be treated as payments made under the Category B interim maintenance assessment which replaces it.*

*(3)	Subject to paragraphs (5) and (6), where the Secretary of State makes a Category B interim maintenance assessment following the revision of an interim maintenance assessment in accordance with regulation 17(4), the effective date of that Category B interim maintenance assessment shall be the date determined in accordance with regulation 8C(1)(b).*

*(4)	Where the Secretary of State makes a fresh interim maintenance assessment following the supersession of an interim maintenance assessment in accordance with regulation 20(7), the effective date of that fresh interim maintenance assessment shall be the date from which that supersession took effect.*

*(5)	Where the Secretary of State cancels upon a revision an interim maintenance assessment in accordance with regulation 17(4) which caused a court order to cease to have effect in accordance with regulation 3(6) of the Maintenance Arrangements and Jurisdiction Regulations, the effective date of the Category B interim maintenance assessment referred to in regulation 17(4) shall be the date on which that revision took effect.*

*(6)	Where the revision of an interim maintenance assessment in accordance with regulation 17(5) caused a court order to cease to have effect in accordance with regulation 3(6) of the Maintenance Arrangements and Jurisdiction Regulations, the effective date of the Category B interim maintenance assessment referred to in regulation 17(4) shall be the date on which that revision took effect.]*

Amendment
1.	Child Support (Misc Amendments) (No.2) Regulations 1999 (SI 1999 No.1047) reg 10 (June 1, 1999).

PART IV
NOTIFICATIONS FOLLOWING CERTAIN DECISIONS BY CHILD SUPPORT
OFFICERS

Notification of a new or a fresh maintenance assessment

10.–[⁵*(1)   A person with a right of appeal to [⁶ the First-tier Tribunal] under–*
(a)   section 20 of the Act; and
(b)   section 20 of the Act as extended by paragraph 3(1)(b) of Schedule 4C to the Act,
shall be given notice of that right and of the decision to which that right relates.]
(1A)–(1C)   [⁵…]
(2)   [¹Subject to [²paragraphs (2A) and (2B)], a notification under paragraph(1)] [⁵*of a new or fresh maintenance assessment made under section 11, 16 or 17] shall set out, in relation to the maintenance assessment in question–*
(a)   the maintenance requirements;
(b)   the effective date of assessment;
[³(c)   the net and assessable income of the absent parent and, where relevant, the amount determined under regulation 9(1)(b) of the Maintenance Assessments and Special Cases Regulations (housing costs);]
[³(cc)   where relevant, the absent parent's protected income level and the amount of the maintenance assessment before the adjustment in respect of protected income specified in paragraph 6(2) of Schedule 1 to the Act was carried out;]
[³(d)   the net and assessable income of the parent with care, and, where relevant, an amount in relation to housing costs determined in the manner specified in regulation 10 of the Maintenance Assessments and Special Cases Regulations (calculation of exempt income of parent with care);]
(e)   details as to the minimum amount of child support maintenance payable by virtue of regulations made under paragraph 7 of Schedule 1 to the Act; and
(f)   details as to apportionment where a case is to be treated as a special case for the purposes of the Act under section 42 of the Act;
*(g)*ⁱ
[³(h)   any amount determined in accordance with Schedule 3A or 3B to the Maintenance Assessments and Special Cases Regulations (qualifying transfer of property and travel costs).]
[⁴(i)   where the notification under paragraph (1)(a) [⁵…] follows the giving, or cancellation of a departure direction, the amounts calculated in accordance with Part I of Schedule 1 to the Act, or in accordance with regulation 8A, which have been changed as a result of the giving or cancellation of that departure direction.]
[¹(2A)   Where a new Category A [²Category C or Category D] interim maintenance assessment is made, or a fresh Category A [²Category C or Category D] interim maintenance assessment is made following , [⁵a revision of a maintenance assessment under section 16 of the Act or a supersession of a maintenance assessment under section 17 of the Act] a notification under paragraph (1) shall set out, in relation to that interim maintenance assessment, the maintenance requirement and the effective date.]
[⁴(2AA)   Where a fresh Category D interim maintenance assessment is made following the giving or cancellation of a departure direction, a notification under paragraph (1) shall set out in relation to that interim maintenance assessment the amounts calculated in accordance with regulation 8A which have changed as a result of the giving or cancellation of that departure direction.]
[²(2B)   A notification under paragraph (1) in relation to a Category B interim maintenance assessment shall set out in relation to it–
[⁴(a)   the matters listed in sub-paragraphs (a), (b) and (d) to (f) of paragraph (2);
(b)   where known, the absent parent's assessable income; and
(c)   where the Category B interim maintenance assessment is made following the giving or cancellation of a departure direction, the amounts calculated in

accordance with regulation 8A which have changed as a result of the giving or cancellation of that departure direction.]]

(3)   Except where a person gives written permission to the Secretary of State that the information, in relation to him, mentioned in sub-paragraphs (a) and (b) below may be conveyed to other persons, any document given or sent under the provisions of paragraph (1) or (2) shall not contain–

(a)   the address of any person other than the recipient of the document in question (other than the address of the office [⁵of the officer concerned who is exercising functions of the Secretary of State under the Act]) or any other information the use of which could reasonable be expected to lead to any such person being located;

(b)   any other information the use of which could reasonably be expected to lead to any person, other than a qualifying child or a relevant person, being identified.

[⁵(4)   Where a decision as to a maintenance assessment is made under section 11, 12, 16 or 17 of the Act, a notification under paragraph (1) shall include information as to the provisions of sections 16 and 17 of the Act.]

[⁷(5)   Paragraphs (2) to (4) of this regulation apply in the case of a decision in respect of which there is no right of appeal as the result of regulation 17A (consideration of revision before appeal) as they apply in the case of a decision which may be appealed under section 20 of the Act (as it has effect apart from section 10 of the Child Support, Pensions and Social Security Act 200).]

Amendments

1.   *The Child Support (Misc Amendments) Regulations 1995 (SI 1995 No.123) reg 6 (February 16, 1995).*

2.   *Child Support and Income Support (Amendment) Regulations 1995 (SI 1995 No.1045) reg 30 (April 18, 1995).*

3.   *Child Support (Misc Amendments) (No.2) Regulations 1995 (SI 1995 No.3261) reg 18 (January 22, 1996).*

4.   *Child Support Departure Direction and Consequential Amendments Regulations 1996 (SI 1996 No.2907) reg 67(3) – (5) (December 2, 1996).*

5.   *Child Support (Misc Amendments) (No.2) Regulations 1999 (SI 1999 No.1047) reg 11 (June 1, 1999).*

6.   *Tribunals, Courts and Enforcement Act 2007 (Transitional and Consequential Provisions) Order 2008 (SI 2008 No.2683) Sch 1 para 58 (November 3, 2008).*

7.   *Social Security, Child Support, Vaccine Damage and Other Payments (Decisions and Appeals) (Amendment) Regulations 2013 (SI 2013 No.2380) reg 3(2) (October 28, 2013).*

Note

i.   *Where the provisions of Part II of the Schedule to Child Support Act 1991 (Commencement No.3 and Transitional Provisions) Order 1992 (SI 1992 No.2644) apply, sub-para (g)) is to be included in para (2), see para 10 of that Schedule.*

[¹Notification of increase or reduction in the amount of a maintenance assessment

10A.–*(1)   Where, in a case falling within paragraph (2B) of regulation 22 of the Maintenance Assessments and Special Cases Regulations (multiple applications relating to an absent parent), [²the Secretary of State] has increased or reduced one or more of the other maintenance assessments referred to in that paragraph following the making of the fresh assessment referred to in sub-paragraph (c) of that paragraph, he shall, so far as that is reasonably practicable, immediately notify the relevant persons in respect of whom each maintenance assessment so increased or reduced was made of–*

(a)   the making of that fresh assessment;

(b)   the amount of the increase or reduction in that maintenance assessment; and

(c)   the date on which that increase or reduction shall take effect,

and the notification shall include information as to the provisions of [²sections 16 and 17] of the Act.

(2)   Except where a person gives written permission to the Secretary of State that the information in relation to him mentioned in sub-paragraphs (a) and (b) below may be conveyed to other persons, any document given or sent under the provisions of paragraph (1) shall not contain–

(a) the address of any person other than the recipient of the document in question (other than the address of the office [²of the officer concerned who is exercising functions of the Secretary of State under the Act]) or any other information the use of which could reasonably be expected to lead to any such person being located;

(b) any other information the use of which could reasonably be expected to lead to any person, other than a qualifying child or a relevant person, being identified.]

Amendments

1.   *Child Support (Misc Amendments) Regulations 1998 (SI 1998 No.58) reg 38 (January 19, 1998).*

2.   *Child Support (Misc Amendments) (No.2) Regulations 1999 (SI 1999 No.1047) reg 12 (June 1, 1999).*

Regs 11 to 15A *are revoked by Child Support (Miscellaneous Amendments) (No.2) Regulations 1999 (SI 1999 No.1047) reg 13 (June 1, 1999).*

Notification when an applicant under section 7 of the Act ceases to be a child

16.   Where a maintenance assessment has been made in response to an application by a child under section 7 of the Act and that child ceases to be a child for the purposes of the Act, [²the Secretary of State] shall immediately notify, so far as that is reasonably practicable–

(a) the other qualifying children [¹who have attained the age of 12 years] and the absent parent with respect to whom that maintenance assessment was made; and

(b) the person with care.

Amendments

1.   *Child Support (Misc Amendments) Regulations 1993 (SI 1993 No.913) reg 6 (April 5, 1993).*

2.   *Child Support (Misc Amendments) (No.2) Regulations 1999 (SI 1999 No.1047) reg 14 (June 1, 1999).*

[¹Notfication that an appeal has lapsed

16A.   Where an appeal lapses in accordance with section 16(6) of the Act, the Secretary of State shall, so far as is reasonably practicable, notify the relevant persons that that appeal has lapsed.]

Amendment

1.   *Child Support (Misc Amendments) (No.2) Regulations 1999 (SI 1999 No.1047) reg 15 (June 1, 1999).*

[¹PART V
REVISIONS AND SUPERSESSIONS

Revision of decisions

17.–*(1)*   Subject to paragraphs (6) and (8), any decision may be revised by the Secretary of State–

(a) if the Secretary of State receives an application for the revision of a decision under section 16 of the Act within one month of the date of notification of the decision or within such longer time as may be allowed by regulation 18;

(b) if–

(i)   the Secretary of State notifies a person, who applied for a decision to be revised within the period specified in sub-paragraph (a), that the application is unsuccessful because the Secretary of State is not in possession of all of the information or evidence needed to make a decision; and

(ii) that person reapplies for a decision to be revised within one month of the notification described in head (i) above, or such longer period as the Secretary of State is satisfied is reasonable in the circumstances of the case, and provides in that application sufficient evidence or information to enable a decision to be made;

(c) if the decision arose from an official error;

(d)   *if the Secretary of State is satisfied that the original decision was erroneous due to a misrepresentation of, or failure to disclose, a material fact and that the decision was more advantageous to the person who misrepresented or failed to disclose that fact than it would otherwise have been but for that error; [³...]*

(e)   *if the Secretary of State commences action leading to the revision of a decision within one month of the date of notification of the decision; [³or*

(f)   *if an appeal is made under section 20 of the Act against a decision within the time prescribed in [⁶by The Tribunal Procedure Rules, but the appeal has not been determined.]*

(2)   *A decision may be revised by the Secretary of State in consequence of a departure direction where that departure direction takes effect on the effective date.*

(3)   *Subject to regulation 20(6) a decision of the Secretary of State under section 12 of the Act may be revised where–*

(a)   *the Secretary of State receives information which enables him to make a maintenance assessment calculated in accordance with Part I of Schedule 1 to the Act for the whole of the period beginning with the effective date applicable to a particular case; or*

(b)   *the Secretary of State is satisfied that there was unavoidable delay by the absent parent in–*

    (i)   *completing and returning a maintenance enquiry form under the provisions of regulation 6(1);*

    (ii)   *providing information or evidence that is required by him for the determination of an application for a maintenance assessment; or*

    (iii)   *providing information or evidence that is required by him to enable him to revise a decision under section 16 of the Act or supersede a decision under section 17 of the Act.*

(4)   *Where an interim maintenance assessment is in force which is not a Category B interim maintenance assessment and the Secretary of State is satisfied that it would be appropriate to make a Category B interim maintenance assessment, he may revise the interim maintenance assessment which is in force.*

(5)   *Where the Secretary of State revises an interim maintenance assessment in accordance with paragraph (4) and that interim maintenance assessment was made immediately following a previous interim maintenance assessment, he may also revise that previous interim maintenance assessment.*

[⁵(6)   Paragraph (1) shall not apply in respect of a material change of circumstances which–

(a)   *occurred since the date on which the decision was made; or*

(b)   *is expected, according to information or evidence which the Commission has, to occur.]*

(7)   *In paragraphs (1), (2) and (6) and regulation 18(3) "decision" means a decision of the Secretary of State under section 11 or 12 of the Act and any supersession of such a decision.*

(8)   *Paragraph (1) shall apply in relation to–*

(a)   *any decision of the Secretary of State with respect to [⁴...] a person's liability under section 43 of the Act; and*

(b)   *the supersession of any such decision under section 17 as extended by paragraph 2 of Schedule 4C to the Act,*

as it applies in relation to any decision of the Secretary of State under sections 11, 12 or 17 of the Act.]

Amendments

1.   *Child Support (Misc Amendments) (No.2) Regulations 1999 (SI 1999 No.1047) reg 16 (June 1, 1999).*

2.   *Social Security and Child Support (Misc Amendments) Regulations 2000 (SI 2000 No.1596) reg 7 (June 19, 2000).*

3.   *Child Support (Misc Amendments) Regulations 2004 (SI 2004 No.2415) reg 4 (September 16, 2004).*

4.   *Child Support (Consequential Provisions) Regulations 2008 (SI 2008 No.2543) reg 2(4) (October 27, 2008).*

5.   *Child Support (Misc Amendments) Regulations 2011 (SI 2011 No.1464) reg 3(2) (July 4, 2011).*

6.   *Social Security, Child Support, Vaccine Damage and Other Payments (Decisions and Appeals) (Amendment) Regulations 2013 (SI 2013 No.2380) reg 3(4) (October 28 2013, subject to the transitional and savings provisions in reg 8 of SI 2013 No.2380). For those covered by the transitional and savings provisions read:*

in regulation 31 of the Social Security and Child Support (Decisions and Appeals) Regulations 1999, or in a case to which regulation 32 of those Regulations applies within the time prescribed in that regulation.

[¹ **Consideration of revision before appeal**

    17A.–*(1)*   This regulation applies in a case where–
    (a)   the Secretary of State gives a person written notice of a decision; and
    (b)   that notice includes a statement to the effect that there is a right of appeal to the First-tier Tribunal against the decision only if the Secretary of State has considered an application for a revision of the decision.
    (2)   In a case to which this regulation applies, a person has a right of appeal under section 20 of the Act against the decision only if the Secretary of State has considered on an application whether to revise the decision under section 16 of the Act.
    (3)   The notice referred to in paragraph (1) must inform the person of the time limit specified in regulation 17(1) for making an application for a revision.
    (4)   Where, as the result of paragraph (2), there is no right of appeal against a decision, the Secretary of State may treat any purported appeal as an application for a revision under section 16 of the Act.
    (5)   In this regulation, "decision" means a decision mentioned in section 20 of the Act (as it has effect apart from section 10 of the Child Support, Pensions and Social Security Act 2000).]

Amendment

1.   *Social Security, Child Support, Vaccine Damage and Other Payments (Decisions and Appeals) (Amendment) Regulations 2013 (SI 2013 No.2380) reg 3 (October 28, 2013).*

[¹**Late applications for a revision**

    18.–*(1)*   The period of one month specified in regulation 17(1)(a) may be extended where the requirements specified in the following provisions of this regulation are met.
    (2)   An application for an extension of time shall be made by a relevant person or a person acting on his behalf.
    (3)   An application for an extension of time under this regulation shall–
    (a)   be made within 13 months of the date on which notification of the decision which it is sought to have revised was given or sent; and
    (b)   contain particulars of the grounds on which the extension of time is sought and shall contain sufficient details of the decision which it is sought to have revised to enable that decision to be identified.
    (4)   The application for an extension of time shall not be granted unless the person making the application or any person acting for him satisfies the Secretary of State that–
    (a)   it is reasonable to grant that application;
    (b)   the application for a decision to be revised has merit [³except in a case to which regulation 17A applies]; and
    (c)   special circumstances are relevant to the application for an extension of time,
and as a result of those special circumstances, it was not practicable for the application for a decision to be revised to be made within one month of the date of notification of the decision which it is sought to have revised.
    (5)   In determining whether it is reasonable to grant an application for an extension of time, the Secretary of State shall have regard to the principle that the greater the time that has elapsed between the expiration of the period of one month described in regulation 17(1)(a) from the date of notification of the decision which it is sought to have revised and the making of the application for an extension of time, the more compelling should be the special circumstances on which the application is based.

(6)   *In determining whether it is reasonable to grant the application for an extension of time [³except in a case to which regulation 17A applies], no account shall be taken of the following–*

(a)   *that the person making the application for an extension of time or any person acting for him was unaware of or misunderstood the law applicable to his case (including ignorance or misunderstanding of the time limits imposed by these Regulations); or*

(b)   *that [² the Upper Tribunal] or a court has taken a different view of the law from that previously understood and applied.*

(7)   *An application under this regulation for an extension of time which has been refused may not be renewed.]*

Amendments

1.   *Child Support (Misc Amendments) (No.2) Regulations 1999 (SI 1999 No.1047) reg 16 (June 1, 1999).*

2.   *Tribunals, Courts and Enforcement Act 2007 (Transitional and Consequential Provisions) Order 2008 (SI 2008 No.2683) Sch 1 para 59 (November 3, 2008).*

3.   *Social Security, Child Support, Vaccine Damage and Other payments (Decisions and Appeals) (Amendment) Regulations 2013 (SI 2013 No.2380) reg 3(5) (October 28, 2013).*

[¹Date from which revised decision takes effect

19.   *Where the date from which a decision took effect is found to be erroneous on a revision under section 16 of the Act, the revision shall take effect from the date on which the revised decision would have taken effect had the error not been made.]*

Amendment

1.   *Child Support (Misc Amendments) (No.2) Regulations 1999 (SI 1999 No.1047) reg 16 (June 1, 1999).*

[¹Supersession of decisions

20.–(1)   *Subject to paragraphs (9) and (10), for the purposes of section 17 of the Act, the cases and circumstances in which a decision ("a superseding decision") may be made under that section are set out in paragraphs (2) to (7).*

(2)   *A decision may be superseded by a decision made by the Secretary of State acting on his own initiative–*

(a)   *where he is satisfied that the decision is one in respect of which there has been a material change of circumstances since the decision was made;*

(b)   *where he is satisfied that the decision was made in ignorance of, or was based upon a mistake as to, some material fact; or*

(c)   *in consequence of a departure direction or of a revision or supersession of a decision with respect to a departure direction.*

(3)   *Except where paragraph (8) applies, [⁴but subject to regulation 23(22)] a decision may be superseded by a decision made by the Secretary of State where–*

(a)   *an application is made on the basis that–*

(i)   *there has been a change of circumstances [²since the date from which the decision had effect]; or*

(ii)   *it is expected that a change of circumstances will occur; and*

(b)   *the Secretary of State is satisfied that the change of circumstances is or would be material.*

[⁷ (3A)   For the purposes of paragraph 2 of Schedule 4C to the Act(7), the circumstances in which a decision may be superseded under paragraph (2) or (3) include where the material change of circumstances causes the maintenance assessment to cease by virtue of paragraph 16(1) of Schedule 1 to the Act or where the Commission no longer has jurisdiction by virtue of section 44 of the Act (jurisdiction).]

(4)   *A decision may be superseded by a decision made by the Secretary of State where–*

(a)   *an application is made on the basis that the decision was made in ignorance of, or was based upon a mistake as to, a fact; and*

(b)   *the Secretary of State is satisfied that the fact is or would be material.*

[³(4A)   A decision may be superseded by a decision made by the Secretary of State–

(a)   where an application is made on the basis that; or

(b)   acting on his own initiative where,

the decision to be superseded is a decision of [⁶[⁸an appeal tribunal, the First-tier Tribunal, the Upper Tribunal or of a Child Support Commissioner]] that was made in accordance with section 28ZB(4)(b) of the Act, in a case where section 28ZB(5) of the Act applies.]

(5)   A decision, other than a decision given on appeal, may be superseded by a decision made by the Secretary of State–

(a)   acting on his own initiative where he is satisfied that the decision was erroneous in point of law; or

(b)   where an application is made on the basis that the decision was erroneous in point of law.

(6)   An interim maintenance assessment may be superseded by a decision made by the Secretary of State where he receives information which enables him to make a maintenance assessment calculated in accordance with Part I of Schedule 1 to the Act for a period beginning after the effective date of that interim maintenance assessment.

(7)   Subject to paragraphs (4) and (5) of regulation 17, where the Secretary of State is satisfied that it would be appropriate to make an interim maintenance assessment the category of which is different from that of the interim maintenance assessment which is in force, he may make a decision which supersedes the interim maintenance assessment which is in force.

(8)   This paragraph applies–

(a)   where any paragraph of regulation 21 applies; and

(b)   in the case of a Category A or Category D interim maintenance assessment.

(9)   The cases and circumstances in which a decision may be superseded shall not include any case or circumstance in which a decision may be revised.

(10)   Paragraphs (2) to (6) shall apply neither in respect of–

(a)   a decision to refuse an application for a maintenance assessment; nor

(b)   a decision to cancel a maintenance assessment.

(11)   For the purposes of section 17 of the Act as extended by paragraph 2 of Schedule 4C to the Act, paragraphs (2) to (5) shall apply in relation to–

(a)   a decision with respect to [⁵...] a person's liability under section 43 of the Act; and

(b)   any decision of the Secretary of State under section 17 of the Act as extended by paragraph 2 of Schedule 4C to the Act, whether as originally made or as revised under section 16 of the Act as extended by paragraph 1 of Schedule 4C to the Act, as they apply in relation to any decision as to a maintenance assessment save that paragraph (8) shall not apply in respect of such a decision.]

Amendments

1.   Child Support (Misc Amendments) (No.2) Regulations 1999 (SI 1999 No.1047) reg 16 (June 1, 1999).

2.   Social Security and Child Support (Miscellaneous Amendments) Regulations 2000 (SI 2000 No.1596) reg 8 (June 19, 2000).

3.   Social Security and Child Support (Miscellaneous Amendments) Regulations 2003 (SI 2003 No.1050) reg 5(1) (May 5, 2003).

4.   Child Support (Misc Amendments) Regulations 2005 (SI 2005 No.785) reg 3(4) (March 16, 2005).

5.   Child Support (Consequential Provisions) Regulations 2008 (SI 2008 No.2543) reg 2(5) (October 27, 2008).

6.   Tribunals, Courts and Enforcement Act 2007 (Transitional and Consequential Provisions) Order 2008 (SI 2008 No.2683) Sch 1 para 60 (November 3, 2008).

7.   Child Support (Miscellaneous Amendments) (No.2) Regulations 2009 (SI 2009 No.2909) reg 3(2) (December 4, 2009).

8.   Social Security and Child Support (Supersession of Appeal Decisions) Regulations 2012 (SI 2012 No.1267) reg 2(2) (June 4, 2012, but has effect as if it had come into force on November 3, 2008).

[¹**Circumstances in which a decision may not be superseded**

21.–(1)   A decision of the Secretary of State shall not be superseded in any of the circumstances specified in the following paragraphs of this regulation.

(2)   Except where paragraph (3) or (4) applies and subject to paragraph (5) and regulation 22, this paragraph applies where the difference between–

(a)   the amount of child support maintenance ("the amount") fixed in accordance with the original decision; and

(b)   the amount which would be fixed in accordance with a superseding decision,

is less than £10.00 per week.

(3)   Subject to paragraph (5), this paragraph applies where the circumstances of the absent parent are such that the provisions of paragraph 6 of Schedule 1 to the Act would apply and either–

(a)   the amount fixed in accordance with the original decision is less than the amount that would be fixed in accordance with a superseding decision and the difference between the two amounts is less than £5.00 per week; or

(b)   the amount fixed in accordance with the original decision is more than the amount that would be fixed in accordance with the superseding decision and the difference between the two amounts is less than £1.00 per week.

(4)   Subject to paragraph (5), this paragraph applies where–

(a)   the children, in respect of whom child support maintenance would be fixed in accordance with a superseding decision, are not the same children for whom child support maintenance was fixed in accordance with the original decision; and

(b)   the difference between–

(i)   the amount of child support maintenance ("the amount") fixed in accordance with the original decision; and

(ii)   the amount which would be fixed in accordance with a superseding decision,

is less than £1.00 per week.

(5)   This regulation shall not apply where–

(a)   the absent parent is, by virtue of paragraph 5(4) of Schedule 1 to the Act, to be taken for the purposes of that Schedule to have no assessable income;

(b)   the case falls within paragraph 7(2) of Schedule 1 to the Act; [²...]

(c)   it appears to the Secretary of State that the case no longer falls within paragraph 5(4) of Schedule 1 to the Act[²; or

(d)   a decision is superseded and in relation to that superseding decision a maintenance assessment is made to which paragraph 15 of Schedule 1 to the Act applies.]

(6)   In this regulation–

"original decision" means the decision which would be superseded but for the application of this regulation; and

"superseding decision" means a decision which would supersede the original decision but for the application of this regulation.]

Amendments

1.   *Child Support (Misc Amendments) (No.2) Regulations 1999 (SI 1999 No.1047) reg 16 (June 1, 1999).*

2.   *Child Support (Misc Amendments) Regulations 2011 (SI 2011 No.1464) reg 3(3) (July 4, 2011).*

[¹Special cases and circumstances for which regulation 21 is modified

22.   Where an application is made for a supersession on the basis of a change of circumstances which is relevant to more than one maintenance assessment, regulation 21 shall apply with the following modifications–

(a)   before the word "amount" in each place it occurs there shall be inserted the word "aggregate"; and

(b)   for the word "decision" in each place it occurs there shall be substituted the word "decisions".]

Amendment

1.   *Child Support (Misc Amendments) (No.2) Regulations 1999 (SI 1999 No.1047) reg 16 (June 1, 1999).*

[¹Date from which a decision is superseded
23.–*(1)   Except in a case to which paragraph (2) [¹¹or(25)] applies, where notice is given under regulation 24 in the period which begins 28 days before an application for a supersession is made and ends 28 days after that application is made, the superseding decision of which notice was given under regulation 24 shall take effect as from the first day of the maintenance period in which that application was made.*

[⁸(2) Where a superseding decision is made in a case to which regulation 20(2)(a) applies and–
(a)   *the absent parent begins or ceases to receive a benefit mentioned in Schedule 4 to the Maintenance Assessments and Special Cases Regulations (case where child support maintenance is not to be payable); or*
(b)   *the absent parent or person with care begins or ceases to be a person who receives a benefit referred to in paragraph 5(4) of Schedule 1 to the Act (assessable income),*
the decision takes effect from the first day of the maintenance period in which the change occurred.]

(3)   [¹¹Subject to paragraph (25),] where a superseding decision is made in a case to which either paragraph (2)(b) or (5)(a) of regulation 20 applies, the decision shall take effect as from the first day of the maintenance period in which the decision was made.

(4)   [²Subject to [¹¹paragraphs (19) and (25)], where a superseding decision is made] in a case to which regulation 20(3)(a)(i), (4) or (5)(b) applies, the decision shall take effect as from the first day of the maintenance period in which the application for a supersession was made.

(5)   [¹¹Subject to paragraph (25),] where a superseding decision is made in a case to which regulation 20(3)(a)(ii) applies, the decision shall take effect as from the first day of the maintenance period in which the change of circumstances is due to occur.

(6)   Subject to paragraphs (1), (3) and (14), in a case to which regulation 24 applies, a superseding decision shall take effect as from the first day of the maintenance period in which falls the date which is 28 days after the date on which the Secretary of State gave notice to the relevant persons under that regulation.

(7)   For the purposes of paragraph (6), where the relevant persons are notified on different dates, the period of 28 days shall be counted from the date of the latest notification.

(8)   For the purposes of paragraphs (6) and (7)–
(a)   *notification includes oral and written notification;*
(b)   *where a person is notified in more than one way, the date on which he is notified is the date on which he was first given notification; and*
(c)   *the date of written notification is the date on which it was handed or sent to the person.*

(9)   Regulation 1(6) shall not apply in a case to which paragraph (8)(c) applies.

(10)   [¹¹Subject to paragraph (25),] where–
(a)   *a decision made by [⁶[¹⁰ an appeal tribunal or the First-tier Tribunal under section 20 of the Act or the Upper Tribunal or a Child Support Commissioner]] is superseded on the ground that it was erroneous due to a misrepresentation of, or that there was a failure to disclose, a material fact; and*
(b)   *the Secretary of State is satisfied that the decision was more advantageous to the person who misrepresented or failed to disclose that fact than it would otherwise have been but for that error,*
the superseding decision shall take effect as from the date the decision of the [⁶[¹⁰ an appeal tribunal, the First-tier Tribunal, the Upper Tribunal or the Child Support Commissioner]] took, or was to take effect.

(11)   Any decision given under section 17 of the Act in consequence of a determination which is a relevant determination for the purposes of section 28ZC of the Act (restrictions on liability in certain cases of error) shall take effect as from the date of the relevant determination.

(12) [¹¹Subject to paragraph (25),] where the Secretary of State supersedes a decision in accordance with regulation 20(6), the superseding decision shall take effect as from the first day of the maintenance period in which the Secretary of State has received the information referred to in that paragraph.

(13) [¹¹Subject to paragraph (25),] where the Secretary of State supersedes a decision in accordance with regulation 20(7), the superseding decision shall take effect as from the first day of the maintenance period in which the Secretary of State became satisfied that it would be appropriate to make an interim maintenance assessment the category of which is different from that of the maintenance assessment which is in force.

(14)   Where a decision is superseded in consequence of a departure direction or a revision or supersession of a decision with respect to a departure direction–

(a)   paragraph (6) above shall not apply; and

(b)   the superseding decision shall take effect as from the date on which the departure direction or, as the case may be, the revision or supersession, took effect.

(15)–(18)   [⁵...]

[⁸[⁹(19)   Where a superseding decision is made in a case to which regulation 20(2)(a) or (3) applies and the material circumstance is–

(a)   a qualifying child dies or ceases to be a qualifying child;

(b)   a relevant child dies or ceases to be a relevant child; or

(c)   a child who is a member of the family of the absent parent for the purposes of regulation 11(1)(g) of the Child Support (Maintenance Assessments and Special Cases) Regulations 1992, dies or ceases to be a member of the family of the absent parent for those purposes,

the decision shall take effect as from the first day of the maintenance period in which the change occurred.]]

[³(20)   [¹¹Subject to paragraph (25),] where a superseding decision is made in a case to which regulation 20(4A) applies that decision shall take effect from the first day of the maintenance period following the date on which the [⁶[¹⁰ the decision of the appeal tribunal, the First-tier Tribunal, the Upper Tribunal or the Child Support Commissioner]...] would have taken effect had it been decided in accordance with the determination of the [⁶ Upper Tribunal] [¹⁰or the Child Support Commissioner] or the court in the appeal referred to in section 28ZB(1)(b) of the Act.]]

[⁴(21)   Where a superseding decision is made in a case to which regulation 20(2)(a) or (3) applies, and the relevant circumstance is that a person has ceased to be a person with care in relation to a qualifying child in respect of whom the maintenance assessment was made, the decision shall take effect from the first day of the maintenance period in which that person ceased to be that person with care in relation to that qualifying child.

[⁷ (21A)   Where a superseding decision is made in a case to which regulation 20(3A) applies and the material circumstance is–

(a)   a qualifying child dies or ceases to be a qualifying child;

(b)   the person with care ceases to be a person with care in relation to a qualifying child; or

(c)   the person with care, the absent parent or a qualifying child ceases to be habitually resident in the United Kingdom,

the decision takes effect from the first day of the maintenance period in which the change occurred.]

[⁸(21B)   Where–

(a)   a superseding decision is made in a case to which regulation 20(3) applies; and

(b)   in relation to that decision, a maintenance assessment is made to which paragraph 15 of Schedule 1 to the Act applies,

the effective date of the assessment or assessments is the first day of the maintenance period in which the change of circumstances to which the assessment relates occurred or is expected to occur and where it occurred before the date of the application for the supersession and was notified after that date, the first day of the maintenance period in which that application was made.]

(22)   Regulation 21 shall not apply where a superseding decision is made under regulation 20(3) in the circumstances set out in paragraph (19) or (21).]

[⁸*(23)   The reference in paragraph (2) to when an absent parent begins or ceases to receive a benefit is to the day on which entitlement to the benefit commences or ends, as the case may be.*

(24)   In paragraph (19), "relevant child" has the same meaning as in regulation 1(2) of the Maintenance Assessments and Special Cases Regulations.]

[¹¹*(25)   Where a superseding decision is made under regulation 20(2) or (3) with respect to the circumstance that a parent with care or an absent parent–*

   (a)   has been awarded universal credit on the basis that they have no earned income;

   (b)   was awarded universal credit on that basis and their award has been revised or superseded on the basis of their having, at the time the award was made or after that time, earned income; or

   (c)   was awarded universal credit on the basis that they had earned income and their award has been revised or superseded on the basis of their not having, at the time the award was made or after that time, earned income,

the decision takes effect from the first day of the maintenance period in which the award of universal credit, or the revision or supersession of such an award, as the case may be, took effect or is due to take effect.

(26)   For the purposes of paragraph (25), "earned income" has the meaning given in regulation 52 of the Universal Credit Regulations 2013.]

Amendments

1.   *Child Support (Misc Amendments) (No.2) Regulations 1999 (SI 1999 No.1047) reg 16 (June 1, 1999).*

2.   *Social Security and Child Support (Miscellaneous Amendments) Regulations 2000 (SI 2000 No.1596) reg 9 (June 19, 2000).*

3.   *Social Security and Child Support (Miscellaneous Amendments) Regulations 2003 (SI 2003 No.1050) reg 5(2) (May 5, 2003).*

4.   *Child Support (Misc Amendments) Regulations 2005 (SI 2005 No.785) reg 3(5) (March 16, 2005).*

5.   *Child Support (Consequential Provisions) Regulations 2008 (SI 2008 No.2543) reg 2(6) (October 27, 2008).*

6.   *Tribunals, Courts and Enforcement Act 2007 (Transitional and Consequential Provisions) Order 2008 (SI 2008 No.2683) Sch 1 para 61 (November 3, 2008).*

7.   *Child Support (Miscellaneous Amendments) (No.2) Regulations 2009 (SI 2009 No.2909) reg 3(3) (December 4, 2009).*

8.   *Child Support (Miscellaneous Amendments) Regulations 2011 (SI 2011 No.1464) reg 3(4) (July 4, 2011).*

9.   *Child Support (Miscellaneous Amendments) Regulations 2012 (SI 2012 No.712) reg 4 (April 30, 2012).*

10.   *Social Security and Child Support (Supersession of Appeal Decisions) Regulations 2012 (SI 2012 No.1267) reg 2(3) (June 4, 2012, but has effect as if it had come into force on November 3, 2008).*

11.   *Universal Credit (Consequential, Supplementary, Incidental and Miscellaneous Provisions) Regulations 2013 (SI 2013 No.630) reg 40(3) (April 29, 2013).*

[¹**Procedure where the Secretary of State proposes to supersede a decision on his own initiative**

24.   *Where the Secretary of State on his own initiative proposes to make a decision superseding a decision other than in consequence of a decision with respect to a departure direction or a revision or supersession of such a decision he shall notify the relevant persons who could be materially affected by the decision of that intention.]*

Amendment

1.   *Child Support (Misc Amendments) (No.2) Regulations 1999 (SI 1999 No.1047) reg 16 (June 1, 1999).*

PART VIII
COMMENCEMENT AND TERMINATION OF MAINTENANCE ASSESSMENTS AND MAINTENANCE PERIODS

Effective dates of new maintenance assessments

30.–*(1)   Subject to [³regulation 8C (effective dates of interim maintenance assessments), 30A (effective dates in particular cases), 33(7) (maintenance periods)] [¹and to regulation 3(5)[², (7) and (8)] of the Maintenance Arrangements and Jurisdiction Regulations (maintenance assessments where court order in force)], the effective date of* *a new maintenance assessment following an application under section 4 [⁵...] or 7 of the Act shall be the date determined in accordance with paragraphs (2) to (4).*

[²(2)   Where no maintenance assessment made in accordance with Part I of Schedule 1 to the Act is in force with respect to the person with care and absent parent, the effective date of a new assessment shall be–

(a)   *in a case where the application for a maintenance assessment is made by a person with care or by a child under section 7 of the Act–*

(i)   *eight weeks from the date on which a maintenance enquiry form has been given or sent to an absent parent, where such date is on or after 18th April 1995 and where within four weeks of the date that form was given or sent, it has been returned by the absent parent to the Secretary of State and it contains his name, address and written confirmation that he is the parent of the child or children in respect of whom the application for a maintenance assessment was made;*

(ii)   *in all other circumstances, the date a maintenance enquiry form is given or sent to an absent parent;*

(b)   *in a case where the application for a maintenance assessment is made by an absent parent–*

(i)   *eight weeks from the date on which an application made by an absent parent was received by the Secretary of State, where such date is on or after 18th April 1995 and where, on, or within four weeks of, the date of receipt of that maintenance application, the absent parent has provided his name, address and written confirmation that he is the parent of the child or children in respect of whom the application was made;*

(ii)   *in all other circumstances, the date an effective maintenance application form is received by the Secretary of State.]*

[³(c)   in a case where the application for a maintenance assessment is an application in relation to which the provisions of regulation 3 have been applied, the date an effective maintenance application form is received by the Secretary of State.]

[²(2A)   Where [⁴the Secretary of State] is satisfied that there was unavoidable delay by the absent parent in providing the information listed in sub-paragraphs (a)(i) or (b)(i) of paragraph (2) within the time specified in those sub-paragraphs, he may apply the provisions of those sub-paragraphs for the purpose of setting the effective date of a maintenance assessment even though that information was not provided within the time specified in those sub-paragraphs.]

(3)   The provisions of regulation 1(6)(b) shall not apply to paragraph (2)(a).

(4)   Where [⁴the Secretary of State] is satisfied that an absent parent has deliberately avoided receipt of a maintenance enquiry form, he may determine the date on which the form would have been given or sent but for such avoidance, and that date shall be the relevant date for the purposes of paragraph (2)(a).

Amendments

1.   *Child Support (Misc Amendments) Regulations 1995 (SI 1995 No.123) reg 7 (February 16,1995).*

2.   *Child Support and Income Support (Amendment) Regulations 1995 (SI 1995 No.1045) reg 36(2)–(4) (April 18, 1995).*

3.   *Child Support (Misc Amendments) (No.2) Regulations 1995 (SI 1995 No.3261) reg 32(2) (January 22, 1996).*

4.   *Child Support (Misc Amendments) (No.2) Regulations 1999 (SI 1999 No.1047) reg 17 (June 1, 1999).*

5.   *Child Support (Consequential Provisions) Regulations 2008 (SI 2008 No.2543) reg 2(7) (October 27, 2008).*

[¹Effective dates of new maintenance assessments in particular cases

30A.–*(1)   Subject to regulation 33(7), where a new maintenance assessment is made in accordance with Part I of Schedule 1 to the Act following an interim maintenance assessment which has ceased to have effect in the circumstances set out in regulation 8D(6), the effective date of that maintenance assessment shall be the date upon which that interim maintenance assessment ceased to have effect in accordance with that regulation.*

[²*(2)   Where [⁴the Secretary of State] receives the information or evidence to enable him to make a maintenance assessment, calculated in accordance with the provisions of Part I of Schedule 1 to the Act, for the period from the date set by regulation 3(7) of the Maintenance Arrangements and Jurisdiction Regulations or regulation 30(2)(a) or (b), as the case may be, to the effective date of the maintenance assessment referred to in paragraph (1), the maintenance assessment first referred to in this paragraph shall, subject to regulation 33(7), have effect for that period.]*

[²*(3)   The effective date of a new maintenance assessment made in respect of a person with care and an absent parent shall, where the circumstances set out in paragraph (4) apply, be the first day of the first maintenance period after the [³Secretary of State] has received the information or evidence referred to in paragraph (4)(c) or 13th January 1997, whichever is the later.*

(4)   The circumstances referred to in paragraph (3) are where–

(a)   paragraphs (1) and (2) do not apply to that person with care and that absent parent;

(b)   no maintenance assessment made in accordance with the provisions of Part I of Schedule 1 to the Act is in force in relation to that person with care and that absent parent; and

(c)   on or after 13th January 1997, [⁴the Secretary of State] has sufficient information or evidence to enable him to make a new maintenance assessment, calculated in accordance with the provisions of Part I of Schedule 1 to the Act, in relation to that person with care and that absent parent but in respect only of a period beginning after the effective date applicable in their case by virtue of regulation 30(2).

(5)   Where the information or evidence referred to in paragraph (3) is that there has been an award of income support[⁵, state pension credit] [⁶, an income-based jobseeker's allowance or an income-related employment and support allowance], the Secretary of State shall be treated as having received the information or evidence which enables [⁴him] to make the assessment referred to in that paragraph on the first day in respect of which income support[⁵, state pension credit] [⁶, an income-based jobseeker's allowance or an income-related employment and support allowance], was payable under that award.

(6)   Where, in a case falling within paragraph (3), [⁴the Secretary of State] receives the information or evidence to enable him to make a maintenance assessment calculated in accordance with the provisions of Part I of Schedule 1 to the Act, for the period from the effective date applicable to that case under regulation 30(2)(a) or (b), as the case may be, to the effective date of the assessment referred to in paragraph (3), the maintenance assessment first referred to in this paragraph shall have effect for that period.

(7)   Paragraphs (3) to (6) shall not apply where a case falls within regulation 33(7), or regulation 3 of the Maintenance Arrangements and Jurisdiction Regulations (relationship between maintenance assessments and certain court orders).]

[⁷ *(8)   Subject to paragraph (9), section 16 of the Child Support Act shall apply in relation to any decision of the Secretary of State not to make a maintenance calculation, as it applies in relation to any decision of the Secretary of State under sections 11, 12 or 17 of that Act, or the determination of an appeal tribunal on a referral under section 28D(1)(b) of that Act.*

(9)   Paragraph (8) shall not apply to any decision not to make a maintenance calculation where the Secretary of State makes a decision under section 12 of the Child Support Act.]

Amendments

1.   *Child Support (Misc Amendments) (No.2) Regulations 1995 (SI 1995 No.3261) reg 33 (January 22, 1996).*

2.   *Child Support (Misc Amendments) (No.2) Regulations 1996 (SI 1996 No.3196) reg 8(2) and (3) (January 13, 1997).*

3.   *Child Support (Misc Amendments) Regulations 1998 (SI 1998 No.58) reg 40 (January 19, 1998).*

4.   *Child Support (Misc Amendments) (No.2) Regulations 1999 (SI 1999 No.1047) reg 18 (June 1, 1999).*

5. *Child Support (Misc Amendments) (No.2) Regulations 2003 (SI 2003 No.2779) reg 3(3) (November 5, 2003).*
6. *Employment and Support Allowance (Consequential Provisions) (No.2) Regulations 2008 (SI 2008 No.1554) reg 57(5) (October 27, 2008).*
7. *Child Support (Misc Amendments) No.2) Regulations 2008 (SI 2008 No.2544) reg 4 (October 27, 2008).*

Regs 31to 31C *are revoked by Child Support (Miscellaneous Amendments) (No.2) Regulations 1999 (SI 1999 No.1047) reg 19 from 1 June 1999.*

Cancellation of a maintenance assessment

32. *Where [¹the Secretary of State] cancels a maintenance assessment under paragraph 16(2) [²...] of Schedule 1 to the Act, the assessment shall cease to have effect from the date of receipt of the request for the cancellation of the assessment or from such later date as [¹he] may determine.*

Amendments

1. *Child Support (Misc Amendments) (No.2) Regulations 1999 (SI 1999 No.1047) reg 20 (June 1, 1999).*
2. *Child Support (Consequential Provisions) Regulations 2008 (SI 2008 No.2543) reg 2(8) (October 27, 2008).*

[¹Cancellation of maintenance assessments made under section 7 of the Act where the child is no longer habitually resident in Scotland

32A.–(1) *Where a maintenance assessment made in response to an application by a child under section 7 of the Act is in force and that child ceases to be habitually resident in Scotland, [²the Secretary of State] shall cancel that assessment.*

(2) *In any case where paragraph(1) applies, the assessment shall cease to have effect from the date that the [²the Secretary of State] determines is the date on which the child concerned ceased to be habitually resident in Scotland.]*

Amendments

1. *Child Support (Misc Amendments) Regulations 1993 (SI 1993 No.913) reg 12 (April 5, 1993).*
2. *Child Support (Misc Amendments) (No.2) Regulations 1999 (SI 1999 No.1047) reg 21 (June 1, 1999).*

[¹Notification of intention to cancel a maintenance assessment under paragraph 16(4A) of Schedule 1 to the Act

32B.–(1) *[²The Secretary of State] shall, if it is reasonably practicable to do so, give written notice to the relevant persons of his intention to cancel a maintenance assessment under paragraph 16(4A) of Schedule 1 to the Act.*

(2) *Where a notice under paragraph (1) has been given, [²the Secretary of State] shall not cancel that maintenance assessment before the end of a period of 14 days commencing with the date that notice was given or sent.]*

Amendments

1. *Child Support (Misc Amendments) (No.2) Regulations 1995 (SI 1995 No.3261) reg 35 and Child Support (Misc Amendments) (No.3) Regulations 1995 (SI 1995 No.3265) reg 2 (January 22, 1996).*
2. *Child Support (Misc Amendments) (No.2) Regulations 1999 (SI 1999 No.1047) reg 22 (June 1, 1999).*

Maintenance periods

33.–(1) *The child support maintenance payable under a maintenance assessment shall be calculated at a weekly rate and be in respect of successive maintenance periods, each such period being a period of 7 days.*

(2) *Subject to paragraph (6), the first maintenance period shall commence on the effective date of the first maintenance assessment, and each succeeding maintenance period shall commence on the day immediately following the last day of the preceding maintenance period.*

(3) *The maintenance periods in relation to a fresh maintenance assessment [³made upon the supersession of a decision under section 17 of the Act] shall coincide with the maintenance periods in relation to the earlier assessment, had it continued in force, and the first maintenance period in relation to a fresh assessment shall commence on the day following the last day of the last maintenance period in relation to the earlier assessment.*

(4)   The amount of child support maintenance payable in respect of a maintenance period which includes the effective date of a fresh maintenance assessment shall be the amount of maintenance payable under that fresh assessment.

(5)   The amount of child support maintenance payable in respect of a maintenance period during the course of which a cancelled maintenance assessment ceases to have effect shall be the amount of maintenance payable under that assessment.

[²(6)   Where a case is to be treated as a special case for the purposes of the Act by virtue of regulation 22 of the Maintenance Assessments and Special Cases Regulations (multiple applications relating to an absent parent) and an application is made by a person with care in relation to an absent parent where–

   (a)   there is already a maintenance assessment in force in relation to that absent parent and a different person with care; or

   (b)   sub-paragraph (a) does not apply, but before a maintenance assessment is made in relation to that application, a maintenance assessment is made in relation to that absent parent and a different person with care,

the maintenance periods in relation to an assessment made in response to that application shall coincide with the maintenance periods in relation to the earlier maintenance assessment, except where regulation 3(7) of the Maintenance Arrangements and Jurisdiction Regulations or paragraph (8) applies, and the first such period shall, subject to paragraph (9), commence not later than 7 days after the date of notification to the relevant persons of the later maintenance assessment.]

[¹(7)   Subject to regulation 3(7) of the Maintenance Arrangements and Jurisdiction Regulations and to paragraph (8), the effective date of a maintenance assessment made in response to an application falling within paragraph (6) shall be the date upon which the first maintenance period in relation to that application commences in accordance with that paragraph.

(8)   The first maintenance period in relation to a maintenance assessment which is made in response to an application falling within paragraph (6) and which immediately follows an interim maintenance assessment shall commence on the effective date of that interim maintenance assessment or 22nd January 1996 whichever is the later, and the effective date of that maintenance assessment shall be the date upon which that first maintenance period commences.]

[²(9)   Where the case is one to which, if paragraphs (6) and (7) did not apply, regulation 30(2)(a)(i) or (b)(i) would apply, and the first maintenance period would, under the provisions of paragraph (6), commence during the 8 week period referred to in sub-paragraph (a) or (b) of that regulation, the first maintenance period shall commence not later than 7 days after the expiry of that period of 8 weeks.]

Amendments

   1.   *Child Support (Misc Amendments) (No.2) Regulations 1995 (SI 1995 No.3261) reg 36(2) and (3) (January 22, 1996).*

   2.   *Child Support (Misc Amendments) Regulations 1996 (SI 1996 No.1945) regs 12 and 25 (August 5, 1996). See reg 25 of SI 1996 No.1945 for transitional provisions.*

   3.   *Child Support (Misc Amendments) (No.2) Regulations 1999 (SI 1999 No.1047) reg 23 (June 1, 1999).*

PART IX
REDUCED BENEFIT DIRECTIONS

Prescription of disability working allowance for the purposes of section 6 of the Act
   34.   [¹...]

Amendment

   1.   *Child Support (Consequential Provisions) Regulations 2008 (SI 2008 No.2543) reg 2(9) (October 27, 2008).*

[² Periods for compliance with obligations imposed by section 6 of the Act
   35.   [³...]]

Amendments

1. *Child Support (Misc Amendments) Regulations 1996 (SI 1996 No.1945), reg 13 (October 7, 1996).*
2. *Child Support (Misc Amendments) (No.2) Regulations 1999 (SI 1999 No.1047), reg 24 (June 1, 1999).*
3. *Child Support (Consequential Provisions) Regulations 2008 (SI 2008 No.2543) reg 2(9) (October 27, 2008).*

[¹Circumstances in which a reduced benefit direction shall not be given
35A.   [⁵...]]

Amendments

1. *Child Support (Miscellaneous Amendments) (No.2) Regulations 1995 (SI 1995 No.3261), reg 37 (January 22, 1996).*
2. *Social Security and Child Support (Jobseeker's Allowance) (Consequential Amendments) Regulations 1996 (SI 1996 No.1345), reg 5(5) (October 7, 1996).*
3. *Child Support (Miscellaneous Amendments) (No.2) Regulations 1999 (SI 1999 No.1047), reg 25 (June 1, 1999).*
4. *Child Support (Miscellaneous Amendments) Regulations 2003 (SI 2003 No.328) reg 5 (April 6, 2003).*
5. *Child Support (Consequential Provisions) Regulations 2008 (SI 2008 No.2543) reg 2(9) (October 27, 2008).*

Amount of and period of reduction of relevant benefit under a reduced benefit direction
36.   [⁵...]

Amendments

1. *Child Support and Income Support (Amendment) Regulations 1995 (SI 1995 No.1045), reg 38 (April 18, 1995).*
2. *Social Security and Child Support (Jobseeker's Allowance) (Consequential Amendments) Regulations 1996 (SI 1996 No.1345), reg 5(6) (October 7, 1996).*
3. *Child Support (Miscellaneous Amendments) Regulations 1996 (SI 1996 No.1945), reg 14 (October 7, 1996).*
4. *Child Support (Miscellaneous Amendments) (No.2) Regulations 1999 (SI 1999 No.1047), reg 26 (November 29, 1999).*
5. *Child Support (Consequential Provisions) Regulations 2008 (SI 2008 No.2543) reg 2(9) (October 27, 2008).*

Modification of reduction under a reduced benefit direction to preserve minimum entitlement to relevant benefit
37.   [³...]

Amendments

1. *Social Security and Child Support (Jobseeker's Allowance) (Consequential Amendments) Regulations 1996 (SI 1996 No.1345), reg 5(7) (October 7, 1996).*
2. *Social Security and Child Support (Jobseeker's Allowance) (Miscellaneous Amendments) Regulations 1996 (SI 1996 No.2538), reg 6(2) (October 28, 1996).*
3. *Child Support (Consequential Provisions) Regulations 2008 (SI 2008 No.2543) reg 2(9) (October 27, 2008).*

Suspension of a reduced benefit direction when relevant benefit ceases to be payable
38.   [⁴...]

Amendments

1. *Social Security and Child Support (Jobseeker's Allowance) (Consequential Amendments) Regulations 1996 (SI 1996 No.1345), reg 5(8) (October 7, 1996).*
2. *Child Support (Miscellaneous Amendments) Regulations 1996 (SI 1996 No.1945), reg 15 (October 7, 1996).*
3. *Child Support (Miscellaneous Amendments) (No.2) Regulations 1999 (SI 1999 No.1047), reg 27 (June 1, 1999).*
4. *Child Support (Consequential Provisions) Regulations 2008 (SI 2008 No.2543) reg 2(9) (October 27, 2008).*

Reduced benefit direction where family credit or disability working allowance is payable and income support becomes payable
39.　　*[³...]*

Amendments

1.　　*Social Security and Child Support (Jobseeker's Allowance) (Consequential Amendments) Regulations 1996 (SI 1996 No.1345), reg 5(9) (October 7, 1996).*
2.　　*Child Support (Miscellaneous Amendments) Regulations 1996 (SI 1996 No.1945), reg 16 (October 7, 1996).*
3.　　*Child Support (Consequential Provisions) Regulations 2008 (SI 2008 No.2543) reg 2(9) (October 27, 2008).*

Suspension of a reduced benefit direction [³(income support)]
40.　　*[⁴...]*

Amendments

1.　　*Child Support (Miscellaneous Amendments) Regulations 1993 (SI 1993 No.913), reg 13 (April 5, 1993).*
2.　　*Child Support and Income Support (Amendment) Regulations 1995 (SI 1995 No.1045), reg 39 (April 18, 1995).*
3.　　*Child Support (Miscellaneous Amendments) (No.2) Regulations 2003 (SI 2003 No.2779) reg 3(4) (November 5, 2003). However, see Child Support (Miscellaneous Amendments) (No.2) Regulations 2003 (SI 2003 No.2779) reg 9 for savings provisions.*
4.　　*Child Support (Consequential Provisions) Regulations 2008 (SI 2008 No.2543) reg 2(9) (October 27, 2008).*

[¹Suspension of a reduced benefit direction [²(income-based jobseeker's allowance)]
40ZA.　　[³...]]

Amendments

1.　　*Social Security and Child Support (Jobseeker's Allowance) (Consequential Amendments) Regulations 1996 (SI 1996 No.1345), reg 5(10) (October 7, 1996).*
2.　　*Child Support (Miscellaneous Amendments) (No.2) Regulations 2003 (SI 2003 No.2779) reg 3(5) (November 5, 2003). However, see Child Support (Miscellaneous Amendments) (No.2) Regulations 2003 (SI 2003 No.2779) reg 9 for savings provisions.*
3.　　*Child Support (Consequential Provisions) Regulations 2008 (SI 2008 No.2543) reg 2(9) (October 27, 2008).*

[¹Suspension of a reduced benefit direction where certain deductions are being made from income support
40A.　　[². . .]]

Amendments

1.　　*Child Support (Miscellaneous Amendments) (No.2) Regulations 1995 (SI 1995 No.3261), reg 38 (January 22, 1996).*
2.　　*Child Support (Miscellaneous Amendments) (No.2) Regulations 1996 (SI 1996 No.3196), reg 9 (January 13, 1997).*

[¹Termination of reduced benefit direction
41.　　[²...]]

Amendments

1.　　*Child Support (Miscellaneous Amendments) (No.2) Regulations 1999 (SI 1999 No.1047) reg 28 (June 1, 1999).*
2.　　*Child Support (Consequential Provisions) Regulations 2008 (SI 2008 No.2543) reg 2(9) (October 27, 2008).*

Review of a reduced benefit direction
42.　　[¹...]

Amendment

1.　　*Child Support (Miscellaneous Amendments) (No.2) Regulations 1999 (SI 1999 No.1047) reg 28 (June 1, 1999).*

Termination of a reduced benefit direction where a maintenance assessment is made following an application by a child under section 7 of the Act
　　43.　[¹ ...]

Amendment
　　1.　*Child Support (Miscellaneous Amendments) (No.2) Regulations 1999 (SI 1999 No.1047) reg 28 (June 1, 1999).*

Termination of a reduced benefit direction where a maintenance assessment is made following an application by an absent parent under section 4 of the Act
　　44.　[¹ ...]

Amendment
　　1.　*Child Support (Miscellaneous Amendments) (No.2) Regulations 1999 (SI 1999 No.1047) reg 28 (June 1, 1999).*

Date from which a reduced benefit direction ceases to be in force following a termination under regulation 43 or 44
　　45.　[¹...]

Amendment
　　1.　*Child Support (Miscellaneous Amendments) (No.2) Regulations 1999 (SI 1999 No.1047) reg 28 (June 1, 1999).*

Cancellation of a reduced benefit direction in cases of error
　　46.　[¹...]

Amendment
　　1.　*Child Support (Miscellaneous Amendments) (No.2) Regulations 1999 (SI 1999 No.1047) reg 28 (June 1, 1999).*

Reduced benefit directions where there is an additional qualifying
　　47.　[⁴...]

Amendments
　　1.　*Social Security and Child Support (Jobseeker's Allowance) (Consequential Amendments) Regulations 1996 (SI 1996 No.1345), reg 5(11) (October 7, 1996).*
　　2.　*Child Support (Miscellaneous Amendments) Regulations 1996 (SI 1996 No.1945), reg 17 (October 7, 1996).*
　　3.　*Child Support (Miscellaneous Amendments) (No.2) Regulations 1999 (SI 1999 No. 1047) reg 29 (June 1, 1999).*
　　4.　*Child Support (Consequential Provisions) Regulations 2008 (SI 2008 No.2543) reg 2(9) (October 27, 2008).*

Suspension and termination of a reduced benefit direction where the sole qualifying child ceases to be a child or where the parent concerned ceases to be a person with care
　　48. [¹...]

Amendment
　　1.　*Child Support (Consequential Provisions) Regulations 2008 (SI 2008 No.2543) reg 2(9) (October 27, 2008).*

[¹*Notice of termination of a reduced benefit direction*
　　49.　[²...]]

Amendments
　　1.　*Child Support (Miscellaneous Amendments) (No.2) Regulations 1999 (SI 1999 No.1047) reg 30 (June 1, 1999).*

2.   *Child Support (Consequential Provisions) Regulations 2008 (SI 2008 No.2543) reg 2(9) (October 27, 2008).*

[¹ Notice of termination of suspension of a reduced benefit direction
   49A.   [². . .]]

Amendments
   1.   *Child Support (Miscellaneous Amendments) (No.2) Regulations 1995 (SI 1995 No.3261), reg 39 (January 22, 1996).*
   2.   *Child Support (Miscellaneous Amendments) (No.2) Regulations 1996 (SI 1996 No.3196), reg 9 (January 13, 1997).*

Rounding provisions
   50.   [¹...]

Amendment
   1.   *Child Support (Consequential Provisions) Regulations 2008 (SI 2008 No.2543) reg 2(9) (October 27, 2008).*

PART X
MISCELLANEOUS PROVISIONS

Persons who are not persons with care
   51.–(1)   *For the purposes of the Act the following categories of person shall not be persons with care–*
   (a)   a local authority;
   (b)   a person with whom a child who is looked after by a local authority is placed by that authority under the provisions of the Children Act 1989 [¹except where that person is a parent of such a child and the local authority allow the child to live with that parent under section 23(5) of that Act];
   (c)   in Scotland, a person with whom a child is boarded out by a local authority under the provisions of section 21 of the Social Work (Scotland) Act 1968.
   (2)   In paragraph (1) above–
"local authority" means, in relation to England and Wales, the council of a county, a metropolitan district, a London Borough or the Common Council of the City of London and, in relation to Scotland, a regional council or an islands council;
"a child who is looked after by a local authority" has the same meaning as in section 22 of the Children Act 1989.

Amendment
   1.   *Child Support (Miscellaneous Amendments) Regulations 1993 (SI 1993 No.913), reg 15 (April 5, 1993).*

   52.   [¹...]

Amendment
   1.   *Child Support (Miscellaneous Amendments) (No.2) Regulations 1999 (SI 1999 No.1047) reg 31 (June 1, 1999).*

Authorisation of representative
   53.–(1)   *A person may authorise a representative, whether or not legally qualified, to receive notices and other documents on his behalf and to act on his behalf in relation to the making of applications and the supply of information under any provision of the Act or these Regulations.*
   (2)   Where a person has authorised a representative for the purposes of paragraph (1) who is not legally qualified, he shall confirm that authorisation in writing to the Secretary of State.

   Regs 54 – 57 *revoked by Child Support (Miscellaneous Amendments) (No.2) Regulations 1999 (SI 1999 No.1047) reg 31 (June 1, 1999).*

SCHEDULE 1
Regulation 1(4)
MEANING OF "CHILD" FOR THE PURPOSES OF THE ACT

[⁸Conditions prescribed for the purposes of section 55(1)]

⁶

[⁷1.–(1) A person satisfies such conditions as may be prescribed for the purposes of section 55(1) of the Act if that person satisfies any of the conditions in sub-paragraphs (2) and (3).
(2) The person is receiving full-time education (which is not advanced education)–
(a) by attendance at a recognised educational establishment; or
(b) elsewhere, if the education is recognised by the Secretary of State.
(3) The person is a person in respect of whom child benefit is payable.]

Period for which a person is to be treated as continuing to fall within section 55(1) of the Act
1A.   [⁷...]]

Meaning of "advanced education" for the purposes of section 55 of the Act
[⁶2.   For the purposes of [⁷this Schedule] "advanced education" means education for the purposes of–
(a) a course in preparation for a degree, a diploma of higher education [⁷, a higher national certificate], a higher national diploma or a teaching qualification; or
(b) any other course which is of a standard above ordinary national diploma, a national diploma or national certificate of Edexcel, a general certificate of education (advanced level) or Scottish national qualifications at higher or advanced higher level.]

Circumstances in which education is to be treated as full-time education
3.   For the purposes of [⁷this Schedule] education shall be treated as being full-time if it is received by a person attending a course of education at a recognized educational establishment and the time spent receiving instruction or tuition, undertaking supervised study, examination of practical work or taking part in any exercise, experiment or project for which provision is made in the curriculum of the course, exceeds 12 hours per week, so however that in calculating the time spent in pursuit of the course, no account shall be taken of time occupied by meal breaks or spent on unsupervised study, whether undertaken on or off the premises of the educational establishment.

Interruption of full-time education
4.–(1)   Subject to sub-paragraph (2), in determining whether a person falls within [⁷paragraph 1(2)] no account shall be taken of a period (whether beginning before or after the person concerned attains age 16) of up to 6 months of any interruption to the extent to which it is accepted that the interruption is attributable to a cause which is reasonable in the particular circumstances of the case; and where the interruption or its continuance is attributable to the illness or disability of mind or body of the person concerned, the period of 6 months may be extended for such further period as [⁴the Secretary of State] considers reasonable in the particular circumstances of the case.
[⁶ (2)   The provisions of sub-paragraph (1) do not apply to any period of interruption of a person's full-time education which is followed immediately by a period during which child benefit ceases to be payable in respect of that person.]
5. [⁶...]

Interpretation
[⁶[⁶6.   In this Schedule, "recognised educational establishment" means an establishment recognised by the Secretary of State for the purposes of this Schedule as being, or as comparable to, a university, college or school.]]
[⁷   Education otherwise than at a recognised educational establishment
7.   For the purposes of paragraph 1(2), the Secretary of State may recognise education provided for a person otherwise than at a recognised educational establishment only if satisfied that education was being so provided for that person immediately before that person attained the age of 16.]
[⁸   Person in respect of whom child benefit is payable
8.   For the purposes of paragraphs 1(3) and 4(2), a person in respect of whom child benefit is payable includes a person in respect of whom an election has been made under section 13A(1) of the Social Security Administration Act 1992 (election not to receive child benefit) for payments of child benefit not to be made.]

Amendments
1. *Child Support (Miscellaneous Amendments) Regulations 1993 (SI 1993 No.913) reg 17 (April 5, 1993).*
2. *Child Support (Miscellaneous Amendments) Regulations 1996 (SI 1996 No.1945) reg 5(12) (October 7, 1996).*
3. *Child Support (Miscellaneous Amendments) Regulations 1999 (SI 1999 No.977) reg 5 (April 6, 1999).*

4. *Child Support (Miscellaneous Amendments) (No.2) Regulations 1999 (SI 1999 No.1047) reg 32 (June 1, 1999).*

5. *Child Support (Miscellaneous Amendments) Regulations 2009 (SI 2009 No.396) reg 2 (April 6, 2009).*

6. *Child Support (Miscellaneous Amendments) (No.2) Regulations 2009 (SI 2009 No.2909) reg 3(4) (November 10, 2009).*

7. *Child Support (Meaning of Child and New Calculation Rules) (Consequential and Miscellaneous Amendment) Regulations 2012 (SI 2012 No.2785) reg 2 (December 10, 2012).*

8. *Child Support (Miscellaneous Amendments) Regulations 2013 (SI 2013 No.1517) reg 2(2) (September 30, 2013).*

SCHEDULE 2
Regulation 4
MULTIPLE APPLICATIONS

No maintenance assessment in force: more than one application for a maintenance assessment by the same person under section 4 [⁵...] of the Act

1.–(1)   Where a person makes an effective application for a maintenance assessment under section 4 [⁵...] of the Act and, before that assessment is made, makes a subsequent effective application under that section with respect to the same absent parent or person with care, as the case may be, those applications shall be treated as a single application.

(2)   [⁵...]

No maintenance assessment in force: more than one application by a child under section 7 of the Act

2.   Where a child makes an effective application for a maintenance assessment under section 7 of the Act and, before that assessment is made, makes a subsequent effective application under that section with respect to the same person with care and absent parent, both applications shall be treated as a single application for a maintenance assessment.

No maintenance assessment in force: applications by different persons for a maintenance assessment

3.–(1)   Where the Secretary of State receives more than one effective application for a maintenance assessment with respect to the same person with care and absent parent, he shall [³if no maintenance assessment has been made in relation to any of the applications] determine which application he shall proceed with in accordance with sub-paragraphs (2) to (11).

(2)   Where there is an application by a person with care under section 4 [⁶...] of the Act and an application by an absent parent under section 4 of the Act, [³the Secretary of State] shall proceed with the application of the person with care.

(3)   Where there is an application for a maintenance assessment by a qualifying child under section 7 of the Act and a subsequent application is made with respect to that child by a person who is, with respect to that child, a person with care or an absent parent, [³the Secretary of State] shall proceed with the application of that person with care or absent parent, as the case may be.

(4)   Where, in a case falling within sub-paragraph (3), there is more than one subsequent application, [³the Secretary of State] shall apply the provisions of sub-paragraph (2), (8), (9) or (11), as is appropriate in the circumstances of the case, to determine which application he shall proceed with.

(5)   Where there is an application for a maintenance assessment by more than one qualifying child under section 7 of the Act in relation to the same person with care and absent parent, [³the Secretary of State] shall proceed with the application of the elder or, as the case may be, eldest of the qualifying children.

(6)   Where a case is to be treated as a special case for the purposes of the Act under regulation 19 of the Maintenance Assessments and Special Cases Regulations (both parents are absent) and an effective application is received from each absent parent, [³the Secretary of State] shall proceed with both applications, treating them as a single application for a maintenance assessment.

(7)   Where, under the provisions of regulation 20 of the Maintenance Assessments and Special Cases Regulations (persons treated as absent parents), two persons are to be treated as absent parents and an effective application is received from each such person, [³the Secretary of State] shall proceed with both applications, treating them as a single application for a maintenance assessment.

(8)   [⁶...]

(9)   Where–

(a)   more than one person with care makes an application for a maintenance assessment under section 4 of the Act in respect of the same qualifying child or qualifying children (whether or not any of those applications is also in respect of other qualifying children);

(b)   each such person has parental responsibility for (or, in Scotland, parental rights over) that child or children; and

(c)   under the provisions of regulation 20 of the Maintenance Assessments and Special Cases Regulations one of those persons is to be treated as an absent parent,

[³the Secretary of State] shall proceed with the application of the person who does not fall to be treated as an absent parent under the provisions of regulation 20 of those Regulations.

(10)   Where, in a case falling within sub-paragraph (9), there is more than one person who does not fall to be treated as an absent parent under the provisions of regulation 20 of those Regulations, [³the Secretary of State] shall apply the provisions of paragraph (11) to determine which application he shall proceed with.

(11)   Where–

(a)   more than one person with care makes an application for a maintenance assessment under section 4 of the Act in respect of the same qualifying child or qualifying children (whether or not any of those applications is also in respect of other qualifying children); and

(b)   either–

(i)   none of those persons has parental responsibility for (or, in Scotland,parental rights over) that child or children; or

(ii)   the case falls within sub-paragraph (9)(b) but the child support officer has not been able to determine which application he is to proceed with under the provisions of sub-paragraph (9),

[³the Secretary of State] shall proceed with the application of the principal provider of day to day care, as determined in accordance with sub-paragraph (12).

(12)   Where–

(a)   the applications are in respect of one qualifying child, the application of that person with care with whom the child spends the greater or, as the case may be, the greatest proportion of his time;

(b)   the applications are in respect of more than one qualifying child, the application of that person with care with whom the children spend the greater or, as the case may be, the greatest proportion of their time, taking account of the time each qualifying child spends with each of the persons with care in question;

(c)   [³the Secretary of State] cannot determine which application he is to proceed with under paragraph (a) or (b), and child benefit is paid in respect of the qualifying child or qualifying children to one but not any other of the applicants, the application of the applicant to whom child benefit is paid;

(d)   [³the Secretary of State] cannot determine which application he is to proceed with under paragraph (a), (b) or (c), the application of that applicant who in the opinion of the child support officer is the principal provider or day to day care for the child or children in question.

(13)   Subject to sub-paragraph (14), where, in any case falling within sub-paragraphs (2) to (11), the applications are not in respect of identical qualifying children, the application that [³the Secretary of State] is to proceed with as determined by those paragraphs shall be treated as an application with respect to all of the qualifying children with respect to whom the applications were made.

(14)   Where [³the Secretary of State] is satisfied that the same person with care does not provide the principal day to day care for all of the qualifying children with respect to whom an assessment would but for the provisions of this paragraph by made under sub-paragraph (13), he shall make separate assessments in relation to each person with care providing such principal day to day care.

[⁸(15)   For the purposes of sub-paragraph (12)(c), where a person has made an election under section 13A(1) of the Social Security Administration Act 1992 (election not to receive child benefit) for payments of child benefit not to be made in respect of a child, that person is to be treated as the person to whom child benefit is being paid in respect of that child.]

Maintenance assessment in force: subsequent application for a maintenance assessment with respect to the same persons

4.   Where a maintenance assessment is in force and a subsequent application is made under the same section of the Act for an assessment with respect to the same person with care, absent parent, and qualifying child or qualifying children as those with respect to whom the assessment in force has been made, that application shall not be proceeded with [4…]

Maintenance assessment in force: subsequent application for a maintenance assessment under section 6 of the Act

5.   [⁷…]

Maintenance assessment in force: subsequent application for a maintenance assessment in respect of additional children

6.– [²(1)   Where there is in force a maintenance assessment made in response to an application under section 4 of the Act by an absent parent or person with care and that assessment is not in respect of all of the absent parent's children who are in the care of the person with care with respect to whom that assessment was made–

(a)   if that absent parent or that person with care makes an application under section 4 of the Act with respect to the children in respect of whom the assessment currently in force was made and the additional child or one or more of the additional children in the care of that person with care who are children of that absent parent, an assessment made in response to that application shall replace the assessment currently in force;

(b)   if that absent parent or that person with care makes an application under section 4 of the Act in respect of an additional qualifying child or additional qualifying children of that absent parent in the care of that person with care, that application shall be treated as an application for a

> *maintenance assessment in respect of all the qualifying children concerned and the assessment made shall replace the assessment currently in force.]*

(2)   *[²...]*

(3)   *Where a maintenance assessment made in response to an application by a child under section 7 of the Act is in force and the person with care [² or the absent parent] of that child makes an application for a maintenance assessment under section 4 of the Act in respect of [¹ one or more [²children of that absent parent who are in the care of that person with care], that application shall be treated as an application for maintenance assessment with respect to all the [²children of that absent parent who are in the care of that person with care], and] that assessment shall replace the assessment currently in force.*

Amendments

1.   Child Support (Miscellaneous Amendments) Regulations 1993 (SI 1993 No.913) reg 18 (April 5, 1993).
2.   Child Support (Miscellaneous Amendments) Regulations 1998 (SI 1998 No.58) reg 41(2) and (3) (January 19, 1998).
3.   Child Support (Miscellaneous Amendments) (No.2) Regulations 1999 (SI 1999 No.1047) reg 33(a) (June 1, 1999).
4.   Child Support (Miscellaneous Amendments) (No.2) Regulations 1999 (SI 1999 No.1047) reg 33(b) (June 1, 1999).
5.   Child Support (Consequential Provisions) Regulations 2008 (SI 2008 No.2543) reg 2(10) (October 27, 2008).
6.   Child Support (Consequential Provisions) Regulations 2008 (SI 2008 No.2543) reg 2(11) (October 27, 2008).
7.   Child Support (Consequential Provisions) Regulations 2008 (SI 2008 No.2543) reg 2(12) (October 27, 2008).
8.   Child Support (Miscellaneous Amendments) Regulations 2013 (SI 2013 No.1517) reg 2(3) (September 30, 2013).

The Child Support (Maintenance Assessments and Special Cases) Regulations 1992
(1992 No.1815)

General Note

The Child Support (Maintenance Assessments and Special Cases) Regulations 1992 have been revoked, for particular cases only, by:

(1)   the Child Support (Maintenance Calculations and Special Cases) Regulations 2000 (SI 2001 No.155) reg 15 (this revocation came into force in relation to a particular case on the date on which the amendments to Part I of Schedule 1 of the Child Support Act 1991 made by the Child Support, Pensions and Social Security Act, 2000 came into force in relation to that type of case – which is 3 March 2000 for the types of cases detailed in art 3 Child Support, Pensions and Social Security Act 2000 (Commencement No.12) Order 2003 (SI 2003 No.192), see p683). See reg 15 of SI 2001 No.155, on p591, for savings provisions.

(2)   the Child Support (Meaning of Child and New Calculation Rules) (Consequential and Miscellaneous Amendment) Regulations 2012 (SI 2012 No.2785) reg 10 (this revocation comes into force in relation to a particular case on the day on which paragraph 2 of Schedule 4 to the Child Maintenance and Other Payments Act 2008 (see p243) comes into force in relation to that type of case – which is December 10, 2012, only in relation to the types of cases falling within art 3 of SI 2012 No. 3042 (see p767).

For other types of cases the '1993 rules', which include the Child Support (Maintenance Assessments and Special Cases) Regulations 1992, continue to apply. The Child Support (Maintenance Assessments and Special Cases) Regulations 1992 are therefore reproduced below.

PART I
GENERAL

Citation, commencement and interpretation

1.–(1) These Regulations may be cited as the Child Support (Maintenance Assessments and Special Cases) Regulations 1992 and shall come into force on 5th April 1993.

(2) In these Regulations unless the context otherwise requires–

"the Act" means the Child Support Act 1991;

[15*"care home"* has the meaning assigned to it by section 3 of the Care Standards Act 2000;

[24*"care home service"* has the meaning assigned to it by paragraph 2 of schedule 12 to the Public Services Reform (Scotland) Act 2010;]]

[5*"Child Benefit Rates Regulations"* means the Child Benefit and Social Security (Fixing and Adjustment of Rates) Regulations 1996;]

[14*"child tax credit"* means a child tax credit under section 8 of the Tax Credits Act 2002;]

"claimant" means a claimant for income support;

[25*"clinical commissioning group"* means a body established under section 14D of the National Health Service Act 2006;][27*"contribution-based jobseeker's allowance"* means an allowance under the Jobseekers Act as amended by the provisions of Part 1 of Schedule 14 to the Welfare Reform Act 2012 that remove references to an income-based allowance, and a contribution-based allowance under the Jobseekers Act as that Act has effect apart from those provisions;] *"Contributions and Benefits Act"* means the Social Security Contributions and Benefits Act 1992;

[8*"Contributions and Benefits (Northern Ireland) Act"* means the Social Security Contributions and Benefits (Northern Ireland) Act 1992;]

[26...]

[1[16*"couple"* means–

    (a)   a man and woman who are married to each other and are members of the same household;

    (b)   a man and woman who are not married to each other but are living together as husband and wife;

    (c)   two people of the same sex who are civil partners of each other and are members of the same household; or

    (d)   two people of the same sex who are not civil partners of each other but are living together as if they were civil partners,

and for the purposes of paragraph (d), two people of the same sex are to be regarded as living together as if they were civil partners if, but only if, they would be regarded as living together as husband and wife were they instead two people of the opposite sex;]]
"course of advanced education" means–

(a) *a full-time course leading to a postgraduate degree or comparable qualification, a first degree or comparable qualification, a Diploma of Higher Education, a higher national diploma, a higher national diploma or higher national certificate of the Business and [¹Technology] Education Council or the Scottish Vocation Education Council or a teaching qualification; or*

(b) *any other full-time course which is a course of a standard above that of an ordinary national diploma, a national diploma or national certificate of the Business and [¹Technology] Education Council or the Scottish Vocational Education Council, the advanced level of the General Certificate of Education, Scottish certificate of education (higher level) or a Scottish certificate of sixth year studies;*

"covenant income" means the gross income payable to a student under a Deed of Covenant by a parent;
"day" includes any part of a day;
[²"day to day care" means–

(a) *care of not less than 104 nights in total during the 12 month period ending with the relevant week; or*

(b) *where, in the opinion of the [¹²Secretary of State, a period other than 12 months] is more representative of the current arrangements for the care of the child in question, care during that period of not less in total than the number of nights which bears the same ratio to 104 nights as that period bears to 12 months,*

and for the purpose of this definition–

(i) *where a child is a boarder at a boarding school, or is an in-patient in a hospital, the person who, but for those circumstances, would otherwise provide day to day care of the child shall be treated as providing day to day care during the periods in question;*

[³(ii) *in relation to an application for child support maintenance, "relevant week" shall have the meaning ascribed to it in head (ii) of sub-paragraph (a) of the definition of "relevant week" in this paragraph;]*

[¹²(iii) *in a case where notification is given under regulation 24 of the Maintenance Assessment Procedure Regulations to the relevant persons on different dates, "relevant week" means the period of seven days immediately preceding the date of the latest notification;]]*

[⁹....]
[¹³[¹⁴...]]
"earnings" has the meaning signed to it by paragraph [¹⁰1, 2A or 3], as the case may be, of Schedule 1;
[⁶"earnings top-up" means the allowance paid by the Secretary of State under the rules specified in the Earnings Top-up Scheme;
"The Earnings Top-up Scheme" means the Earnings Top-up Scheme 1996;]
"effective date" means the date on which a maintenance assessment takes effect for the purposes of the Act;
"eligible housing costs" shall be construed in accordance with Schedule 3;
"employed earner" has the same meaning as in section 2(1)(a) of the Contributions and Benefits Act; [⁹except that it shall include a person gainfully employed in Northern Ireland];
[⁶"family" means–

(a) *[¹⁶a couple] (including the members of a polygamous marriage);*

(b) *[¹⁶a couple] (including the members of a polygamous marriage) and any child or children living with them for whom at least one member of that couple has day to day care;*

(c) *where a person who is not a member of [¹⁶a couple] has day to day care of a child or children, that person and any such child or children;*

and for the purposes of this definition a person shall not be treated as having day to day care of a child who is a member of that person's household where the child in question is being looked after by a local authority within the meaning of section 22 of the Children Act 1989 or, in Scotland, where the child is boarded out with that person by a local authority under the provisions of section 21 of the Social Work (Scotland) Act 1968;]
[[8][*[14]...]]*

"grant" means any kind of educational grant or award and includes any scholarship, exhibition, allowance or bursary but does not include a payment made under section 100 of the Education Act 1944 or section 73 of the Education (Scotland) Act 1980;

"grant contribution" means any amount which a Minister of the Crown or an education authority treats as properly payable by another person when assessing the amount of a student's grant and by which that amount is, as a consequence, reduced;

"home" means–
    (a)   the dwelling in which a person and any family of his normally live; or
    (b)   if he or they normally live in more than one home, the principal home of that person and any family of his,

and for the purpose of determining the principal home in which a person normally lives no regard shall be had to residence in [[15]a care home or an independent hospital or to the provision of a care home service or an independent health care service] during a period which does not exceed 52 weeks or, where it appears to the [[12]Secretary of State] that the person will return to his principal home after that period has expired, such longer period as [the Secretary of State] considers reasonable to allow for the return of that person to that home;

"housing benefit" has the same meaning as in section 130 of the Contributions and Benefits Act;

[[18]*"Housing Benefit Regulations"* means the Housing Benefit Regulations 2006;]

[[18]*"Housing Benefit (State Pension Credit) Regulations"* means the Housing Benefit (Persons who have attained the qualifying age for state pension credit) Regulations 2006;]

"Income Support Regulations" means the Income Support (General) Regulations 1987;

[[15][[24]*"independent health care service"* has the meaning assigned to it by section 10F(1)(a) and (b) of the National Health Service (Scotland) Act 1978;]

[[23]*"independent hospital"*–
    (a)   in England, means a hospital as defined by section 275 of the National Health Service Act 2006 that is not a health service hospital as defined by that section; and
    (b)   in Wales, has the meaning assigned to it by section 2 of the Care Standards Act 2000;]]

[[20]*"Independent Living Fund (2006)"* means the Trust of that name established by a deed dated 10th April 2006 and made between the Secretary of State for Work and Pensions of the one part and Margaret Rosemary Cooper, Michael Beresford Boyall and Marie Theresa Martin of the other part;]

[[1]*"Independent Living (1993) Fund"* means the charitable trust of that name established by a deed made between the Secretary of State for Social Security of the one part and Robin Glover Wendt and John Fletcher Shepherd of the other part;

"Independent Living (Extension) Fund" means the charitable trust of that name established by a deed made between the Secretary of State for Social Security of the one part and Robin Glover Wendt and John Fletcher Shepherd of the other part;]

[[4]*"the Jobseekers Act"* means the Jobseekers Act 1995;]

"Maintenance Assessment Procedure Regulations" means the Child Support (Maintenance Assessment Procedure) Regulations 1992;

[[16]...]

"non-dependant" means a person who is non-dependant for the purposes of either–
    (a)   regulation 3 of the Income Support Regulations; or

[¹⁸(b) *regulation 3 of the Housing Benefit Regulations or, as the case may be, regulation 3 of the Housing Benefit (State Pension Credit) Regulations;*]

or who would be a non-dependant for those purposes if another member of the household in which he is living were entitled to income support or housing benefit as the case may be;

[¹⁵...]

"occupational pension scheme" has the same meaning as in [⁹section 1 of the Pension Schemes Act 1993];

"ordinary clothing or footwear" means clothing or footwear for normal daily use, but does not include school uniforms, or clothing or footwear used solely for sporting activities;

"parent with care" means a person who, in respect of the same child or children, is both a parent and a person with care;

"partner" means–

    (a)   *in relation to a member of [¹⁶a couple] who are living together, the other member of that couple;*

    (b)   *in relation to a member of a polygamous marriage, any other member of that marriage with whom he lives;*

"patient" means a person (other than a person who is serving a sentence of imprisonment or detention in a young offender institution within the meaning of the Criminal Justice Act 1982 as amended by the Criminal Justice Act 1988 who is regarded as receiving free in-patient treatment within the meaning of the Social Security (Hospital In-Patients) Regulations 1975;

[²²*"pensionable age" has the meaning given by the rules in paragraph 1 of Schedule 4 to the Pensions Act 1995;*]

"person" does not include a local authority;

"personal pension scheme" has the same meaning as in [⁸section 1 of the Pension Schemes Act 1993] and, in the case of as a self-employed earner, includes a scheme approved by the Inland Revenue under Chapter IV of Part XIV of the Income and Corporation Taxes Act 1988;

"polygamous marriage" means any marriage during the subsistence of which a party to it is married to more than one person and in respect of which any ceremony of marriage took place under the law of a country which at the time of that ceremony permitted polygamy;

[¹⁹[²⁵...]]

"prisoner" means a person who is detained in custody pending trial or sentence upon conviction or under a sentence imposed by a court other than a person whose detention is under the Mental Health Act 1983 or the [¹⁷Part 5, 6 or 7 or section 136 of the Mental Health (Care and Treatment) (Scotland) Act 2003 or section 52D or 52M of the Criminal Procedure (Scotland) Act 1995];

[⁸*"profit related pay" means any payment by an employer calculated by reference to actual or anticipated profits;*]

[²²*"qualifying age for state pension credit" means–*

    (a)   *in the case of a woman, pensionable age; or*

    (b)   *in the case of a man, the age which is pensionable age in the case of a woman born on the same day as the man;*]

[²*"qualifying transfer" has the meaning assigned to it in Schedule 3A;*]

"relevant child" means a child of an absent parent or a parent with care who is a member of the same family as that parent;

"relevant Schedule" means Schedule 2 to the Income Support Regulations (income support applicable amounts);

[¹²*"relevant week" means–*

    (a)   *in relation to an application for child support maintenance–*

        (i)   *in the case of the applicant, the period of seven days immediately preceding the date on which the appropriate maintenance assessment application form (being an effective application within the meaning of regulation 2(4) of the Maintenance Assessment Procedure Regulations) is submitted to the Secretary of State;*

(ii)   *in the case of a person to whom a maintenance assessment enquiry form is given or sent as the result of such an application, the period of seven days immediately preceding the date on which that form is given or sent to him or, as the case may be, the date on which it is treated as having been given or sent to him under regulation 1(6)(b) of the Maintenance Assessment Procedure Regulations;*

(b)   *where a decision ("the original decision") is to be–*

(i)   *revised under section 16 of the Act; or*

(ii)   *superseded by a decision under section 17 of the Act on the basis that the original decision was made in ignorance of, or was based upon a mistake as to some material fact or was erroneous in point of law,*

the period of seven days which was the relevant week for the purposes of the original decision;

(c)   *where a decision ("the original decision") is to be superseded by a decision under section 17 of the Act–*

(i)   *on an application made for the purpose on the basis that a material change of circumstances has occurred since the original decision was made, the period of seven days immediately preceding the date on which that application was made;*

(ii)   *subject to paragraph (b), in a case where a relevant person is given notice under regulation 24 of the Maintenance Assessment Procedure Regulations, the period of seven days immediately preceding the date of that notification;*

except that where, under paragraph 15 of Schedule 1 to the Act, the Secretary of State makes separate maintenance assessments in respect of different periods in a particular case, because he is aware of one or more changes of circumstances which occurred after the date which is applicable to that case under paragraph (a), (b) or (c) the relevant week for the purposes of each separate assessment made to take account of each such change of circumstances, shall be the period of seven days immediately preceding the date on which notification was given to the Secretary of State of the change of circumstances relevant to that separate maintenance assessment;]

[15…]

"retirement annuity contract" means an annuity contract for the time being approved by the Board of Inland Revenue as having for its main object the provision of a life annuity in old age or the provision of an annuity for a partner or dependant and in respect of which relief from income tax may be given on any premium;

"self-employed earner" has the same meaning as in section 2(1)(b) of the Contributions and Benefits Act [9except that it shall include a person gainfully employed in Northern Ireland otherwise than in employed earner's employment (whether or not he is also employed in such employment)];

[15*"state pension credit" means the social security benefit of that name payable under the State Pension Credit Act 2002;]*

"student" means a person, other than person in receipt of a training allowance, who is aged less than 19 and attending a full-time course of advanced education or who is aged 19 or over and attending a full-time course of study at an educational establishment; and for the purposes of this definition–

(a)   *a person who has started on such a course shall be treated as attending it throughout any period of term or vacation within it, until the last day of the course or such earlier date as he abandons it or is dismissed from it;*

(b)   *a person on a sandwich course (within the meaning of paragraph 1(1) of Schedule 5 to the [2Education (Mandatory Awards) (No. 2) Regulations 1993] shall be treated as attending a full-time course of advanced education or, as the case may be, of study;*

"*student loan*" *means a loan which is made to a student pursuant to arrangements made under section 1 of the Education (Student Loans) Act 1990;*

[¹...]

"*training allowance*" *has the same meaning as in regulation 2 of the Income Support Regulations;*

[²⁷*"universal credit" means universal credit under Part 1 of the Welfare Reform Act 2012;*]

[¹⁶...]

"*weekly council tax*" *means the annual amount of the council tax in question payable in respect of the year in which the effective date falls, divided by 52;*

[²¹*"the Welfare Reform Act" means the Welfare Reform Act 2007;*]

[¹¹*"work-based training for young people or, in Scotland, Skillseekers training"] means–*

    (a)   *arrangements made under section 2 of the Employment and Training Act 1973 or section 2 of the Enterprise and new towns (Scotland) Act 1990; or*

    (b)   *arrangements made by the Secretary of State for persons enlisted in Her Majesty's forces for any special term of service specified in regulations made under section 2 of the Armed Forces Act 1966 (power of Defence Council to make regulation as to engagement of persons in regular forces);*

for purposes which include the training of persons who, at the beginning of their training, are under the age of 18.

[¹⁴*"working tax credit" means a working tax credit under section 10 of the Tax Credits Act 2002;*]

"*year*" *means a period of 52 weeks;*

[¹(2A)   *Where any provision of these Regulations requires the income of a person to be estimated and that or any other provision of these Regulations requires that the amount of such estimated income is to be taken into account for any purposes after deducting from it a sum in respect of income tax or of primary Class 1 contributions under the Contributions and Benefits Act [⁸or, as the case may be, the Contributions and Benefits (Northern Ireland) Act;] or of contributions paid by that person towards an occupational or personal pension scheme, then [²subject to sub-paragraph (e)]–*

    (a)   *the amount to be deducted in respect of income tax shall be calculated by applying to that income the rates of income tax applicable at the [⁸relevant week] less only the personal relief to which that person is entitled under Chapter I of Part VII of the Income and Corporation Taxes Act 1988 (personal relief); but if the period in respect of which that income is to be estimated is less than a year, the amount of the personal relief deductible under this sub-paragraph shall be calculated on a pro rata basis; [⁹and the amount of income to which each tax rate applies shall be determined on the basis that the ratio of that amount to the full amount of the income to which each tax rate applies is the same as the ratio of the proportionate part of that personal relief to the full personal relief]*

    (b)   *the amount to be deducted in respect of Class 1 contributions under the Contributions and Benefits Act [⁸or, as the case may be, the Contributions and Benefits (Northern Ireland) Act;] shall be calculated by applying to that income the appropriate primary percentage applicable in the relevant week; and*

    (c)   *the amount to be deducted in respect of contributions paid by that person towards an occupational [²...] pension scheme shall be one-half of the sums so [²paid; and]*

    [²(d)   *the amount to be deducted in respect of contributions towards a personal pension scheme shall be one half of the contributions paid by that person or, where that scheme is intended partly to provide a capital sum to discharge a mortgage secured on that person's home, 37.5 per centum of those contributions;*

    (e)   *in relation to any bonus or commission which may be included in that person's income–*

        (i)   *the amount to be deducted in respect of income tax shall be calculated by applying to the gross amount of that bonus or commission the rate or rates of income tax applicable in the relevant week;*

(ii)   the amount to be deducted in respect of primary class 1 contributions under the Contributions and Benefits Act [⁸or, as the case may be, the Contributions and Benefits (Northern Ireland) Act;] [⁸...] shall be calculated by applying to the gross amount of that bonus or commission the appropriate main primary percentage applicable in the relevant week [³but no deduction shall be made in respect of the portion (if any) of the bonus or commission which, if added to estimated income, would cause such income to exceed the upper earnings limit for Class 1 contributions as provided for in section 5(1)(b) of the Contributions and Benefits Act] [⁸or, as the case may be, the Contributions and Benefits (Northern Ireland) Act;] and

(iii)   the amount to be deducted in respect of contributions paid by that person in respect of the gross amount of that bonus or commission towards an occupational pension scheme shall be one half of any sum so paid.]

[²⁸(2B)   For the purposes of these Regulations, where a person has made an election under section 13A(1) of the Social Security Administration Act 1992 (election not to receive child benefit) for payments of child benefit not to be made–

(a)   that person is to be treated as being in receipt of child benefit; and

(b)   the amount of child benefit that would be otherwise paid in respect of the relevant child is to be treated as being in payment.]

(3)   In these Regulations, unless the context otherwise requires, a reference–

(a)   to a numbered Part is to the Part of these Regulations bearing that number;

(b)   to a numbered Schedule is to the Schedule to these Regulations bearing that number;

(c)   to a numbered regulation it to the regulation in these Regulations bearing that number;

(d)   in a regulation or Schedule to a numbered paragraph it to the paragraph in that regulation or Schedule bearing that number;

(e)   in a paragraph to a lettered or numbered sub-paragraph is to the sub-paragraph in that paragraph bearing that letter or number.

(4)   [⁷These Regulations are subject to the provisions of Parts VIII and IX of the Departure Direction and Consequential Amendments Regulations and] the regulations in Part II and the provisions of the Schedules to these Regulations are subject to the regulations relating to special cases in Part III.

Amendments

1. Child Support (Miscellaneous Amendments) Regulations 1993 (SI 1993 No.913) reg 19(2) and (3) (April 5, 1993).
2. Child Support and Income Support (Amendment) Regulations 1995 (SI 1995 No.1045) reg 41(2) and (3) (April 18, 1995).
3. Child Support (Miscellaneous Amendments) (No.2) Regulations 1995 (SI 1995 No.3261) reg 40(2) and (3) (January 22, 1996).
4. Social Security and Child Support (Jobseeker's Allowance) (Consequential Amendments) Regulations 1996 (SI 1996 No.1345), reg 6(2) (October 7, 1996).
5. Child Benefit, Child Support and Social Security (Miscellaneous Amendments) Regulations 1996 (SI 1996 No.1803) reg 7 (April 7, 1997).
6. Child Support (Miscellaneous Amendments) Regulations 1996 (SI 1996 No.1945) reg 18(2) and (3) (October 7, 1996).
7. Child Support Departure Direction and Consequential Amendments Regulations 1996 (SI 1996 No.2907) reg 68(3) (December 2, 1996).
8. Child Support (Miscellaneous Amendments) (No. 2) Regulations 1996 (SI 1996 No.3196), reg 10(2) and (3) (January 13, 1997).
9. Child Support (Miscellaneous Amendments) Regulations 1998 (SI 1998 No.58) regs 30 and 42 (January 19, 1998).
10. Child Support (Miscellaneous Amendments) Regulations 1999 (SI 1999 No.977) reg 6(2)(a) (October 4, 1999).
11. Child Support (Miscellaneous Amendments) Regulations 1999 (SI 1999 No.977) reg 6(2)(b) (April 6, 1999).
12. Social Security Act 1998 (Commencement No. 7 and Consequential and Transitional Provisions) Order 1999 (SI 1999 No.1510) art 14(1)(a) – (c) (June 1, 1999).

13. Social Security and Child Support (Tax Credits) Consequential Amendments Regulations 1999 (SI 1999 No.2566) Part III, Sch 2 (October 5, 1999).

14. Child Support (Miscellaneous Amendments) Regulations 2003 (SI 2003 No.328) reg 6(2) (April 6, 2003).

15. Child Support (Miscellaneous Amendments) (No.2) Regulations 2003 (SI 2003 No.2779) reg 4(2) (November 5, 2003).

16. Civil Partnership (Pensions, Social Security and Child Support) (Consequential, etc. Provisions) Order 2005 (SI 2005 No.2877) art 2(4) and Sch 4, para 2(2) (December 5, 2005).

17. Mental Health (Care and Treatment) (Scotland) Act 2003 (Consequential Provisions) Order 2005 (SI 2005 No.2078) arts 1(9) and (10) and 15 and Sch 2 para 15 (October 5, 2005); and Mental Health (Care and Treatment) (Scotland) Act 2003 (Modification of Subordinate Legislation) Order 2005 (SSI 2005 No.445) art 2 and Sch para 18 (October 5, 2008).

18. Housing Benefit and Council Tax Benefit (Consequential Provisions) Regulations 2006 (SI 2006 No.217) reg 5 and Sch 2 para 4(2) (March 6, 2006).

19. National Health Service Reform and Health Care Professions Act 2002 (Supplementary, Consequential etc. Provisions) Regulations 2002 (SI 2002 No.2469) reg 11 and Sch 8 (October 1, 2002).

20. Independent Living Fund (2006) Order 2007 (SI 2007 No.2538) reg 3(2) (October 1, 2007).

21. Employment and Support Allowance (Consequential Provisions) (No.2) Regulations 2008 (SI 2008 No.1554) reg 58(2) (October 27, 2008).

22. Child Support (Miscellaneous and Consequential Amendments) Regulations 2009 (SI 2009 No.736) reg 3(2) (April 6, 2009).

23. Health and Social Care Act 2008 (Miscellaneous Consequential Amendments) Order 2010 (SI 2010 No.1881) reg 7 (October 1, 2010).

24. Public Services Reform (Scotland) Act 2010 (Consequential Modifications of Enactments) Order 2011 (SI 2011 No.2581) art 2 and Sch 2 para 18 (October 28, 2011).

25. National Treatment Agency (Abolition) and the Health and Social Care Act 2012 (Consequential, Transitional and Saving Provisions) Order 2013 (SI 2013 No.235) art 11 and Sch 2 para 20(2) (April 1, 2013).

26. Council Tax Benefit Abolition (Consequential Provision) Regulations 2013 (SI 2013 No.458) reg 3 and Sch 1 (April 1, 2013).

27. Universal Credit (Consequential, Supplementary, Incidental and Miscellaneous Provisions) Regulations 2013 (SI 2013 No.630) reg 41(2) (April 29, 2013).

28. Child Support (Miscellaneous Amendments) Regulations 2013 (SI 2013 No.1517) reg 3 (September 30, 2013).

PART II
CALCULATION OR ESTIMATION OF CHILD SUPPORT MAINTENANCE

Calculation or estimation of amounts

2.–(1) Where any amount [³is to be considered in connection with any calculation made under these Regulations], it shall be calculated or estimated as a weekly amount and, except where the context otherwise requires, any reference to such an amount shall be construed accordingly.

(2) Subject to [¹regulations 11(6) and (7) and 13(2) and [²regulation 8A(5)] of the Maintenance Assessment Procedure Regulations], where any calculation made under [¹the Act or] these Regulations results in a fraction of a penny that fraction shall be treated as a penny if it is either one half or exceeds one half, otherwise it shall be disregarded.

(3) [⁴The Secretary of State] shall calculate the amounts to be taken into account for the purposes of these Regulations by reference, as the case may be, to the dates, weeks, months or other periods specified herein provided that if he becomes aware of a material change of circumstances occurring after such date, week, month or other period but before the effective date, he shall take that change of circumstances into account.

Amendments

1. Child Support and Income Support (Amendment) Regulations 1995 (SI 1995 No.1045) reg 42 (April 18, 1995).

2. Child Support (Miscellaneous Amendments) (No 3) Regulations 1995 (SI 1995 No.3265) reg 3 (January 22, 1996).

3. Child Support (Miscellaneous Amendments) Regulations 1998 (SI 1998 No.58) reg 43 (January 19, 1998).

4.   Social Security Act 1998 (Commencement No.7 and Consequential and Transitional Provisions) Order
       1999 (SI 1999 No.1510) art 15 (June 1, 1999).

___

Calculation of AG

3.–(1)   *The amounts to be taken into account for the purposes of calculating AG in
the formula set out in paragraph 1(2) of Schedule 1 to the Act are–*

(a)   *with respect to each qualifying child, an amount equal to the amount specified
        in column (2) of paragraph 2 of the relevant Schedule for a person of the same
        age (income support personal allowance for child or young person);*

[¹(b)   *with respect to a person with care of one or more qualifying children-*

    (i)   *where one or more of those children is aged less than 11, an amount equal
        to the amount specified in column (2) of paragraph 1(1)(e) of the relevant
        Schedule (income support personal allowance for a single claimant aged
        not less than 25);*

    (ii)   *where no one of those children are aged less than 11 but one or more of
        them is aged less than 14, an amount equal to 75 per centum of the amount
        specified in head (i) above; and*

    (iii)   *where no one of those children are aged less than 14 but one or more of
        them is aged less than 16, an amount equal to 50 per centum of the amount
        specified in head (i) above;]*

[³(c)   *an amount equal to the amount specified in paragraph 3(1)(b) of the relevant
        Schedule.]*

(d)   [²...]

(2)   *The amounts referred to in paragraph (1) shall be the amounts applicable at the
effective date.*

Amendments

1.   Child Support (Miscellaneous Amendments and Transitional Provisions) Regulations 1994 (SI 1994
       No.227) reg 4(2) (February 7, 1994).
2.   Child Benefit, Child Support and Social Security (Miscellaneous Amendments) Regulations 1996 (SI
       1996 No.1803) reg 8(b) (April 7, 1997).
3.   Child Support (Miscellaneous Amendments) Regulations 1998 (SI 1998 No.58) reg 44 (April 6, 1998).

___

Basic rate of child benefit

4.   *For the purposes of paragraph 1(4) of Schedule 1 to the Act "basic rate" means
the rate of child benefit which is specified in [¹regulation 2(1)(a)(i) or 2(1)(b) of the
Child Benefit Rates Regulations (weekly rate for only, elder or eldest child and for other
children)] applicable to the child in question at the effective date.*

Amendment

1.   Child Benefit, Child Support and Social Security (Miscellaneous Amendments) Regulations 1996 (SI
       1996 No.1803) reg 9 (April 7, 1997).

Definitions

"the Act": see reg 1(2).
"Child Benefit Rates Regulations": see reg 1(2).
"effective date": see reg1(2).

___

The general rule

5.   *For the purposes of paragraph 2(1) of Schedule 1 to the Act–*

(a)   *the value of C, otherwise than in a case where the other parent is the person
        with care, is nil; and*

(b)   *the value of P is 0.5.*

Definition

"the Act": see reg 1(2).

___

The additional element

6.–[¹(1)   *For the purposes of the formula in paragraph 4(1) of Schedule 1 to the Act,
the value of R is–*

(a) *where the maintenance assessment in question relates to one qualifying child, 0.15;*

(b) *where the maintenance assessment in question relates to two qualifying children, 0.20; and*

(c) *where the maintenance assessment in question relates to three or more qualifying children, 0.25.]*

(2) *For the purposes of the alternative formula in paragraph 4(3) of Schedule 1 to the act–*

(a) *the value of Z is [²1.5];*

(b) *the amount for the purposes of paragraph (b) of the definition of Q is the same as the amount specified in [³regulation 3(1)(c)] (income support family premium) in respect of each qualifying child.*

Amendments

1. *Child Support (Miscellaneous Amendments and Transitional Provisions) Regulations 1994 (SI 1994 No.227) reg 4(3) (February 7, 1994).*

2. *Child Support and Income Support (Amendment) Regulations 1995 (SI 1995 No.1045) reg 43 (April 18, 1995).*

3. *Child Support (Miscellaneous Amendments) Regulations 1998 (SI 1998 No.58) reg 45 (April 6, 1998).*

Definitions

"the Act": see reg 1(2).

Net income: calculation or estimation of N

7.–(1) Subject to the following provisions of this regulation, for the purposes of the formula in paragraph 5(1) of Schedule 1 to the act, the amount of N (net income of absent parent) shall be the aggregate of the following amounts–

(a) *the amount, determined in accordance with part I of schedule 1, of any earnings of the absent parent;*

(b) *the amount, determined in accordance with part II of Schedule 1, of any benefit payments under the Contributions and Benefits Act [¹[⁴, the Jobseekers Act or the Welfare Reform Act]] paid to or in respect of the absent parent;*

(c) *the amount, determined in accordance with Part III of Schedule 1, of any other income of the absent parent;*

(d) *the amount, determined in accordance with Part III of Schedule 1, of any income of a relevant child which is treated as the income of the absent parent;*

(e) *any amount, determined in accordance with Part V of Schedule 1, which is treated as the income of the absent parent.*

(2) *Any amounts referred to in Schedule 2 shall be disregarded.*

(3) *Where an absent parent's income consists–*

(a) *only of [²work-based training for young people or, in Scotland, Skillseekers training] allowance; or*

(b) *in the case of a student, only of grant, an amount paid in respect of grant contribution or student loan or any combination thereof; or*

(c) *only of prisoner's pay,*

then for the purposes of determining N such income shall be disregarded.

(4) *Where a parent and any other person are beneficially entitled to any income but the shares of their respective entitlements are not ascertainable the [³Secretary of State] shall estimate their respective entitlements having regard to such information as is available but where sufficient information on which to base an estimate is not available the parent and that other person shall be treated as entitled to that income in equal shares.*

(5) *Where any income normally received at regular intervals has not been received it shall, if it is due to be paid and there are reasonable grounds for believing it will be received, be treated as if it has been received.*

Amendments

1. *Social Security and Child Support (Jobseeker's Allowance) (Consequential Amendments) Regulations 1996 (SI 1996 No.1345), reg 6(6) and 7(a) (October 7, 1996).*

2.   *Child Support (Miscellaneous Amendments) Regulations 1999 (SI 1999 No.977) reg 6(3) (April 6, 1999).*
3.   *Social Security Act 1998 (Commencement No.7 and Consequential and Transitional Provisions) Order 1999 (SI 1999 No.1510) art 16 (June 1, 1999).*
4.   *Employment and Support Allowance (Consequential Provisions) (No.2) Regulations 2008 (SI 2008 No.1554) reg 58(3) (October 27, 2008).*

Definitions
"the Act": see reg 1(2).
"Contributions and Benefits Act": see reg 1(2).
"earnings": see reg 1(2).
"effective date": see reg 1(2).
"grant": see reg 1(2).
"grant contribution": see reg 1(2).
"the Jobseekers Act": see reg 1(2).
"person": see reg 1(2).
"prisoner": see reg 1(2).
"student": see reg 1(2).
"student loan": see reg 1(2).
"training allowance": see reg 1(2).

Net income; calculation or estimation of M

8.   *For the purposes of paragraph 5(2) of Schedule 1 to the Act, the amount of M (net income of the parent with care) shall be calculated in the same way as N is calculated under regulation 7 but as if references to the absent parent were references to the parent with care.*

Definitions
"the Act": see reg 1(2).
"parent with care": see reg 1(2).

Exempt income; calculation or estimation of E

9.–*(1)   For the purposes of paragraph 5(1) of Schedule 1 to the Act, the amount of E (exempt income of absent parent) shall, subject to paragraphs (3) and (4), be the aggregate of the following amounts–*
(a)   an amount equal to the amount specified in column (2) of paragraph 1(1)(e) of the relevant Schedule (income personal allowance for a single claimant aged not less than 25);
(b)   an amount in respect of housing costs determined in accordance with regulations 14 to [⁵16 and] 18;
[²(bb)   where applicable, an amount in respect of a qualifying transfer of property determined in accordance with schedule 3A;]
(c)   [⁷...]
(d)   where, if the parent were a claimant [¹²who had not attained the qualifying age for state pension credit], the conditions in paragraph 11 of the relevant Schedule (income support disability premium) would be satisfied in respect of him, an amount equal to the amount specified in column (2) of paragraph 15(4)(a) of that Schedule (income support disability premium);
(e)   where–
   (i)   if the parent were a claimant, the conditions in paragraph 13 of the relevant Schedule (income support severe disability premium) would be satisfied, an amount equal to the amount specified in column (2) of paragraph 15(5(a) of that Schedule (except that no such amount shall be taken into account in the case of an absent parent in respect of whom [¹⁰a carer's allowance] under section 70 of the Contributions and Benefits Act is payable to some other person);
   (ii)   if the parent were a claimant, the conditions in paragraph 14ZA of the relevant Schedule (income support a carer premium) would be satisfied in respect of him, an amount equal to the amount specified in column (2) of paragraph 15(7) of that Schedule;

[8(iii) *if the parent were a claimant, the conditions in paragraph 13A of the relevant Schedule (income support enhanced disability premium) would be satisfied in respect of him, an amount equal to the amount specified in paragraph 15(8)(b) of that Schedule;]*

(f) *where, if the parent were a claimant, the conditions in paragraph 3 of the relevant Schedule (income support family premium) would be satisfied in respect of a relevant child of that parent [7…], the amount specified in [4sub-paragraph (b) of] that paragraph or, where those conditions would be satisfied only by virtue of the case being one to which paragraph (2) applies, half that amount;*

(g) *in respect of each relevant child–*

    (i) *an amount equal to the amount of the personal allowance for that child, specified in column (2) of paragraph 2 of the relevant Schedule (income support personal allowance) or, where paragraph (2) applies, half that amount;*

    (ii) *if the conditions set out in paragraph 14(b) and (c) of the relevant Schedule (income support disabled child premium) are satisfied in respect of that child, an amount equal to the amount specified in column (2) of paragraph 15(6) of the relevant Schedule or, where paragraph (2) applies, half that amount;*

    [9(iii) *if the conditions set out in paragraph 13A of the relevant Schedule (income support enhanced disability premium) are satisfied in respect of that child, an amount equal to the amount specified in paragraph 15(8)(a) of that Schedule or, where paragraph (2) applies, half that amount;]*

[11(h) *where the absent parent or his partner is resident in a care home or an independent hospital or is being provided with a care home service or an independent health care service, the amount of fees paid in respect of that home, hospital or service, as the case may be, but where it has been determined that the absent parent in question or his partner is entitled to housing benefit in respect of fees for that home, hospital or service, as the case may be, the net amount of such fees after deduction of housing benefit;]*

[2(i) *where applicable, an amount in respect of travelling costs determined in accordance with schedule 3B.]*

(2) *This paragraph applies where–*

(a) *the absent parent has a partner;*

(b) *the absent parent and the partner are parents of the same relevant child; and*

(c) *the income of the partner, calculated under regulation 7(1) [1(but excluding the amount mentioned in sub-paragraph (d) of that regulation)] as if that partner were an absent parent to whom that regulation applied, exceeds the aggregate of–*

    (i) *the amount specified in column 2 of paragraph 1(1)(e) of the relevant Schedule (income support personal allowance for a single claimant aged not less than 25);*

    (ii) *half the amount of the personal allowance for that child specified in column (2) of paragraph 2 of the relevant Schedule (income support personal allowance);*

    (iii) *half the amount of any income support disabled child premium specified in column (2) of paragraph 15(6) of that Schedule in respect of that child; [2and]*

    (iv) *half the amount of any income support family premium specified in paragraph [43 [7(1)](b) of the relevant Schedule] except where such premium is payable irrespective of that child; [2…].*

    [6(v) *where a departure direction has been given on the grounds that a case falls within regulations 27 of the Departure Direction and Consequential Amendments Regulation (partner's contribution to housing costs), the amount of the housing costs which corresponds to the percentage of the housing costs mentioned in regulation 40(7) of those Regulation.]*

(3)   Where an absent parent does not have day to day care of any relevant child for 7 nights each week but does have day to day care of one or more such children for fewer than 7 nights each week, [⁴any amount] to be taken into account under sub-paragraphs (1)(c) [⁴or (f)] shall be reduced so that they bear the same proportion to the amount referred to in those sub-paragraphs as the average number of nights each week in respect of which such care is provided has to 7.

(4)   Where an absent parent has day to day care of a relevant child for fewer than 7 nights each week, any amounts to be taken into account under sub-paragraph (1)(g) in respect of such child shall be reduced so that they bear the same proportion to the amounts referred to in that sub-paragraph as the average number of nights each week in respect of which such care is provided has to 7.

(5)   The amounts referred to in paragraph (1) are the amounts applicable at the effective date.

Amendments

1.   *Child Support (Miscellaneous Amendments) Regulations 1993 (SI 1993 No 913), reg 20 (April 5, 1993).*
2.   *Child Support and Income Support (Amendment) Regulations 1995 (SI 1995 No.1045) reg 44(2) and (3) (April 18, 1995).*
3.   *Child Support (Miscellaneous Amendments) (No.2) Regulations 1995 (SI 1995 No.3261) reg 42 (January 22, 1996).*
4.   *Child Benefit, Child Support and Social Security (Miscellaneous Amendments) Regulations 1996 (SI 1996 No.1803) reg 11(2)-(4) (April 7, 1997).*
5.   *Child Support (Miscellaneous Amendments) Regulations 1996 (SI 1996 No.1945) reg 19 (October 7, 1996).*
6.   *Child Support Departure Direction and Consequential Amendments Regulations 1996 (SI 1996 No.2907) reg 68(4) (December 2, 1996).*
7.   *Child Support (Miscellaneous Amendments) Regulations 1998 (SI 1998 No.58) reg 47(2) and (3) (April 6, 1998).*
8.   *Child Support (Miscellaneous Amendments) Regulations 2002 (SI 2002 No.1204) reg 5(a) (April 30, 2002).*
9.   *Child Support (Miscellaneous Amendments) Regulations 2002 (SI 2002 No.1204) reg 9(1)(g) (April 30, 2002).*
10. *Child Support (Miscellaneous Amendments) Regulations 2003 (SI 2003 No.328) reg 4(2) (April 1, 2003).*
11. *Child Support (Miscellaneous Amendments) (No.2) Regulations 2003 (SI 2003 No.2779) reg 4(3) (November 5, 2003).*
12. *Child Support (Miscellaneous and Consequential Amendments) Regulations 2009 (SI 2009 No.736) reg 3(3) (April 6, 2009).*

Definitions

"the Act": see reg 1(2).
"care home": see reg 1(2).
"care home service": see reg 1(2).
"claimant": see reg 1(2).
"Contributions and Benefits Act": see reg 1(2).
"day to day care": see reg 1(2).
"Departure Direction and Consequential Amendments Regulations": see reg 1(2).
"effective date": see reg 1(2).
"housing benefit": see reg 1(2).
"Income Support Regulations": see reg 1(2).
"independent health care service": see reg 1(2).
"independent hospital": see reg 1(2).
"partner": see reg 1(2).
"relevant child": see reg 1(2).
"relevant Schedule": see reg 1(2).

Exempt income: calculation or estimation of F

10.   *For the purposes of paragraph 5(2) of Schedule 1 to the Act, the amount of F (exempt income of parent with care) shall be calculated in the same way as E is calculated under regulation 9 but as if references to the absent parent were references to the parent with care [¹except that–*

(a)   *sub-paragraph (bb) of paragraph (1) of that regulation shall not apply unless at the time of the making of the qualifying transfer the parent with care would have been the absent parent had the Child Support Act 1991 been in force at the date of the making of the transfer; and*

(b)   *paragraph (3) and (4) of that regulation shall apply only where the parent with care shares the day to day care of the child mentioned in those paragraphs with one or more other persons.]*

Amendment

1.   Child Support and Income Support (Amendment) Regulations 1995 (SI 1995 No.1045) reg 45 (April 18, 1995).

Definitions

"the Act": see reg 1(2).
"day to day care": see reg 1(2).
"parent with care": see reg 1(2).

[¹*Assessment income:* [³ [⁴*working tax credit]] paid to or in respect of a parent with care or an absent parent]*

10A.–*(1)   Subject to paragraph (2), where [³[⁴working tax credit]] is paid to or in respect of a parent with care or an absent parent, that parent shall, for the purposes of Schedule 1 to the Act, be taken to have no assessable income.*

(2)   *Paragraph (1) shall apply to an absent parent only if–*

(a)   *he is also a parent with care; and*

(b)   *either–*

    (i)   *a maintenance assessment in respect of a child in relation to whom he is a parent with care is in force; or*

    (ii)   *the [²Secretary of State] is considering an application for such an assessment to be made.]*

Amendments

1.   Child Support (Miscellaneous Amendments) (No.2) Regulations 1996 (SI 1996 No.3196) reg 11 (January 13, 1997).

2.   Social Security Act 1998 (Commencement No.7 and Consequential and Transitional Provisions) Order 1999 (SI 1999 No.1510) art 16 (June 1, 1999).

3.   Social Security and Child Support (Tax Credits) Consequential Amendments Regulations 1999 (SI 1999 No.2566) Parts I and II, Sch 2 (October 5, 1999).

4.   Child Support (Miscellaneous Amendments) Regulations 2003 (SI 2003 No.328) reg 6(4) (April 6, 2003).

Definitions

"the Act": see reg 1(2).
"working credit": see reg 1(2).

[¹*Assessable income: state pension credit paid to or in respect of a parent with care or an absent parent*

10B.   *Where state pension credit is paid to or in respect of a parent with care or an absent parent, that parent shall, for the purposes of Schedule 1 to the Act, be taken to have no assessable income.]*

Amendment

1.   Child Support (Miscellaneous Amendments) (No.2) Regulations 2003 (SI 2003 No. 2779) reg 4(4) (November 5, 2003).

Definition

"state pension credit": see reg 1(2).

[¹*Assessable income: universal credit paid to or in respect of the parent concerned*

10C.–*(1)   The circumstances prescribed for the purpose of the reference to universal credit in sub-paragraph (4) of paragraph 5 of Schedule 1 to the Child Support Act 1991 (as that paragraph has effect apart from section 1 of the Child Support, Pensions and*

Social Security Act 2000) are where the universal credit that is paid to or in respect of the parent concerned is calculated on the basis that the parent has no earned income.

(2) In paragraph (1), "earned income" has the meaning given in regulation 52 of the Universal Credit Regulations 2013.]

Amendment

1. Universal Credit (Consequential, Supplementary, Incidental and Miscellaneous Provisions) Regulations 2013 (SI 2013 No.630) reg 41(3) (April 29, 2013).

Protected income

11.–*(1) For the purposes of paragraph 6 of Schedule 1 to the Act the protected income level of an absent parent shall, [²subject to paragraphs (3), (4)[⁶, (6) and (6A),]] be the aggregate of the following amounts–*

(a) *where–*

    (i) *the absent parent does not have a partner, an amount equal to the amount specified in column (2) of paragraph 1(1)(e) of the relevant Schedule (income support personal allowance for a single claimant aged not less than 25 years);*

    (ii) *the absent parent has a partner, an amount equal to the amount specified in column (2) of paragraph 1(3)(c) of the relevant Schedule (income support personal allowance for a couple where both members are aged not less than 18 years);*

    (iii) *the absent parent is a member of a polygamous marriage, an amount in respect of himself and one of his partners, equal to the amount specified in sub-paragraph (ii) and, in respect of each of his other partners, an amount equal to the difference between the amount specified in sub-paragraph (ii) and sub-paragraph (i);*

(b) *an amount in respect of housing costs determined in accordance with regulations 14,15, 16 and 18, or, in a case where the absent parent is a non-dependant member of a household who is treated as having no housing costs by [⁴regulation 15(4)], the non-dependant amount which would be calculated in respect of him under [²paragraphs (1), (2) and (9) of [¹¹regulation 74 of the Housing Benefit Regulations or, as the case may be, regulation 55 of the Housing Benefit (State Pension Credit) Regulations] (non-dependant deductions) if he were a non-dependant in respect of whom a calculation were to be made under those paragraphs (disregarding any other provision of that regulation)];*

(c) *[⁸…]*

(d) *where, if the parent were a claimant, the conditions in paragraph 11 of the relevant Schedule (income support disability premium) would be satisfied, an amount equal to the amount specified in column (2) of the paragraph 15(4) of that Schedule (income support disability premium);*

(e) *where, if the parent were a claimant, the conditions in paragraph 13 or 14ZA of the relevant Schedule (income support severe disability and carer premiums) would be satisfied in respect of either or both premiums, an amount equal to the amount or amounts specified in column (2) of paragraph 15(5) or, as the case may be, (7) of that Schedule in respect of that or those premiums (income support premiums);*

(f) *where, if the parent were a claimant, the conditions in paragraph 3 of the relevant Schedule (income support family premium) would be satisfied, the amount specified in [⁵sub-paragraph (b) of] that paragraph;*

(g) *in respect of each child who is a member of the family of the absent parent–*

    (i) *an amount equal to the amount of the personal allowance for that child, specified in column (2) of paragraph 2 of the relevant Schedule (income support personal allowance);*

    (ii) *if the conditions set out in paragraphs 14(b) and (c) of the relevant Schedule (income support disabled child premium) are satisfied in respect of that child, an amount equal to the amounts specified in column (2) of paragraph 15(6) of the relevant Schedule;*

(h)   where, if the parent where a claimant, the conditions specified in Part III of the relevant Schedule would be satisfied by the absent parent in question or any member of his family in relation to any premium not otherwise included in this regulation, an amount equal to the amount specified in Part IV of that Schedule (income support premiums) in respect of that premium;

[¹⁰(i)   where the absent parent or his partner is resident in a care home or an independent hospital or is being provided with a care home service or an independent health care service, the amount of fees paid in respect of that home, hospital or service, as the case may be, but where it has been determined that the absent parent in question or his partner is entitled to housing benefit in respect of fees for that home, hospital or service, as the case may be, the net amount of such fees after deduction of housing benefit;]

[²(j)   where–
    (i)   the absent parent is, or that absent parent and any partner of his are, the only person or persons resident in, and liable to pay council tax in respect of, the home for which housing costs are included under sub-paragraph (b), the amount of weekly council tax for which he is liable in respect of that home [¹²...];
    (ii)   where other persons are resident with the absent parent in, and liable to pay council tax in respect of, the home for which housing costs are included under sub-paragraph (b), an amount representing the share of the weekly council tax in respect of that home applicable to the absent parent, determined by dividing the total amount of council tax due in that week by the number of persons liable to pay it [¹²...], provided that if the absent parent is required to pay and pays more than that share because of default by one or more of those other persons, the amount for the purposes of this regulation shall be the amount of weekly council tax the absent parent pays [¹²...];]

(k)   an amount of [¹£30.00];
[²(kk) an amount in respect of travelling costs determined in accordance with Schedule 3B;]
(l)   where the income of–
    (i)   the absent parent in question;
    (ii)   any partner of his; and
    (iii)   any child or children for whom an amount is included under sub-paragraph (g)(i);
    exceeds the sum of the amounts to which reference is made in sub-paragraphs [²(a) to (kk)], [¹15 per centum] of the excess.

(2)   For the purposes of sub-paragraph(1) of paragraph (1) "income" shall be calculated–
(a)   in respect of the absent parent in question or any partner of his, in the same manner as N (net income of absent parent) is calculated under regulation 7 except–
    (i)   there shall be taken into account the basic rate of any child benefit and any maintenance which in either case is in payment in respect of any member of the family of the absent parent;
    (ii)   there shall be deducted the amount of any maintenance under a maintenance order which the absent parent or his partner is paying in respect of a child in circumstances where an application for a maintenance assessment could not be made in accordance with the Act in respect of that child; [³...]
    [³(iii) to the extent that it falls under sub-paragraph (b), the income of any child in that family shall not be treated as the income of the parent or his partner and Part IV of Schedule 1 shall not apply; [⁴...]]
    [⁴(iv) paragraph 27 of Schedule 2 shall apply as though the reference to paragraph 3(2) and (4) of Schedule 3 were omitted;

(v)   there shall be deducted the amount of any maintenance which is being paid in respect of a child by the absent parent or his partner under an order requiring such payment made by a court outside Great Britain; and]

[⁹(vi) there shall be taken into account any child tax credit which is payable to the absent parent or his partner; and]

(b)   in respect of any child in that family, as being the total of [³that child's relevant income(within the meaning of paragraph 23 of Schedule 1), there being disregarded any maintenance in payment to or in respect of him,] but only to the extent that such income does not exceed the amount included under sub-paragraph (g) and paragraph (1) (income support personal allowance for a child and income support disabled child premium) reduced, as the case may be, under paragraph (4).

(3)   Where an absent parent does not have day to day care of any child (whether or not a relevant child) for 7 nights each week but does have day to day care of one or more such children for fewer than 7 nights each week [⁵any amount], to be taken into account under [⁸sub-paragraph (f)] of paragraph (1) [⁵…] income support family premium) shall be reduced so that they bear the same proportion to the amounts referred to in those sub-paragraphs as the average number of nights each week in respect of which such care is provided has to 7.

(4)   Where an absent parent has day to day care of a child (whether or not a relevant child) for fewer than 7 nights each week any amounts in relation to that child to be taken into account under sub-paragraph (g) of paragraphs (1) (income support personal allowance for child and income support disabled child premium) shall be reduced so that they bear the same proportion to the amounts referred to in that sub-paragraph as the average number of nights in respect of which such care is provided has to 7.

(5)   The amounts referred to in paragraph (1) shall be the amounts applicable at the effective date.

[³(6)   If the application of the above provisions of this regulation would result in the protected income level of an absent parent being less than 70 per centum of his net income, as calculated in accordance with regulation 7, those provisions shall not apply in his case and instead his protected income level shall be 70 per centum of his net income as so calculated.

[⁷(6A)   In a case to which paragraph (6) does not apply, if the application of paragraphs (1) to (5) and of regulation 12(1)(a) would result in the amount of child support maintenance payable being greater than 30 per centum of the absent parent's net income calculated in accordance with regulation 7, paragraphs (1) to (5) shall not apply in his case and instead his protected income level shall be 70 per centum of his net income as so calculated.]

(7)   Where any calculation under paragraph (6) [⁷or (6A)] results in a fraction of a penny, that fraction shall be treated as a penny.]

Amendments

1.   *Child Support (Miscellaneous Amendments and Transitional Provisions) Regulations 1994 (SI 1994 No.227) reg 4(4) and (5) (February 7, 1994).*

2.   *Child Support and Income Support (Amendment) Regulations 1995 (SI 1995 No.1045) reg 46(2) (April 18, 1995).*

3.   *Child Support and Income Support (Amendment) Regulations 1995 (S.I. 1995 No.1045) reg.46(3)-(6) (April 18, 1995).*

4.   *Child Support (Miscellaneous Amendments) (No.2) Regulations 1995 (SI 1995 No.3261) reg 43(2) – (5) (January 22, 1996).*

5.   *Child Benefit, Child Support and Social Security (Miscellaneous Amendments) Regulations 1996 (SI 1996 No.1803) reg 12(2) and (3) (April 7, 1997).*

6.   *Child Support (Miscellaneous Amendments) Regulations 1996 (SI 1996 No.1945) reg 20(2) (October 7, 1996).*

7.   *Child Support (Miscellaneous Amendments) Regulations 1996 (SI 1996 No.1945) reg 20(3) and (4) (August 5, 1996).*

8.   *Child Support (Miscellaneous Amendments) Regulations 1998 (SI 1998 No.58) reg 49(2) and (3) (April 6, 1998).*

9.   *Child Support (Miscellaneous Amendments) Regulations 2003 (SI 2003 No.328) reg 6(5) (April 6, 2003).*
10.   *Child Support (Miscellaneous Amendments) (No.2) Regulations 2003 (SI 2003 No.2779) reg 4(5) (November 5, 2003).*
11.   *Housing Benefit and Council Tax Benefit (Consequential Provisions) Regulations 2006 (SI 2006 No.217) reg 5 and Sch 2 para 4(3) (March 6, 2006).*
12.   *Council Tax Benefit Abolition (Consequential Provision) Regulations 2013 (SI 2013 No.458) reg 3 and Sch 1 (April 1, 2013).*

Definitions
"the Act": see reg 1(2).
"care home": see reg 1(2).
"care home service": see reg 1(2).
"child tax credit": se reg 1(2).
"claimant": see reg 1(2).
"council tax benefit": see reg 1(2).
"couple": see reg 1(2).
"effective date": see reg 1(2).
"family": see reg 1(2).
"Housing Benefit Regulations": see reg 1(2).
"Housing Benefit (State Pension Credit) Regulations": see reg 1(2).
"Income Support Regulations": see reg 1(2).
"independent health care service": see reg 1(2).
"independent hospital": see reg 1(2).
"non-dependant": see reg 1(2).
"partner": see reg 1(2).
"polygamous marriage": see reg 1(2).
"relevant Schedule": see reg 1(2).

General Note
In reg 11(2)(a)(i), maintenance does not include child support maintenance (*R(CS) 4/02*).

Disposable income

12.–[¹*(1)   For the purpose of paragraph 6(4) of Schedule 1 to the Act (protected incomr), the disposable income of an absent parent shall be–*
    (a)   except in a case to which regulation 11(6) [²or (6A)] applies, the aggregate of his income and any income of any member of his family calculated in like manner as under regulation 11(2); [³...]
    (b)   [³subject to sub-paragraph (c),] in a case to which regulation 11(6) [²or (6A)] applies, his net income as calculated in accordance with regulation 7 [³and]]
    [³(c)   in a case to which regulation 11(6) applies and the absent parent is paying maintenance under an order of a kind mentioned in regulation 11(2)(a)(ii) or (v), his net income as calculated in accordance with regulation 7 less the amount of maintenance he is paying under that order.]
    (2)   Subject to paragraph (3), where a maintenance assessment has been made with respect to the absent parent and payment of the amount of that assessment would reduce his disposable income below his protected income level the amount of the assessment shall be reduced by the minimum amount necessary to prevent his disposable income being reduced below his protected income level.
    (3)   Where the prescribed minimum amount fixed by regulations under paragraph 7 of Schedule 1 to the Act is applicable (such amount being specified in regulation 13) the amount payable under the assessment shall not be reduced to less than the prescribed minimum amount.

Amendments
1.   *Child Support and Income Support (Amendment) Regulations 1995 (SI 1995 No.1045) reg 47 (April 18, 1995).*
2.   *Child Support (Miscellaneous Amendments) Regulations 1996 (SI 1996 No.1945) reg 21 (August 5, 1996).*
3.   *Child Support (Miscellaneous Amendments) (No.2) Regulations 1996 (SI 1996 No.3196) reg 12(2)-(4) (January 13, 1997).*

Definitions
 "the Act": see reg 1(2).
 "family": see reg 1(2).

The minimum amount

13.–*(1)   Subject to regulation 26, for the purposes of paragraph 7(1) of Schedule 1 to the Act the minimum amount shall be [¹2 multiplied by] 5 per centum of the amount specified in paragraph 1(1)(e) of the relevant Schedule (income support personal allowance for a single claimant aged not less than 25).*

(2)   Where the [¹5 per centum amount] calculated under paragraph (1) results in a sum other than a multiple of 5 pence, it shall be treated as the sum which is the next higher multiple of 5 pence.

Amendment
 1.   Child Support (Maintenance Assessments and Special Cases) and Social Security (Claims and Payments) Amendment Regulations 1996 (SI 1996 No.481) reg 2 (April 8, 1996).

Definition
 "the Act": see reg 1(2).

Eligible housing costs

14.   *Schedule 3 shall have effect for the purpose of determining the costs which are eligible to be taken into account as housing costs for the purposes of these Regulations.*

General Note
 There is an allowance for an amount in respect of housing costs in both assessable income and protected income (regs 9(1)(b), 10 and 11(1)(b)). This figure will not necessarily be the same for each type of income, nor will it necessarily be the same as the parent's actual housing costs. In this note that amount is referred to as the allowable housing costs. The tribunal should approach the question of allowable housing costs in the following stages.
 First, identify the parent's home, as defined in reg 1(2). The only allowable housing costs are those in respect of that home (reg 15(1)).
 Second, identify the housing costs in respect of that home. The costs must be determined at the effective date (reg 16). The approach to this stage depends upon whether the parent has been determined by the local authority to be entitled to housing benefit. If so, the parent's housing costs are the weekly rent for the purposes of that benefit less the housing benefit and the non-dependant deductions discussed below (reg 15(2)). If the parent has not been determined to be entitled to housing benefit, the calculation is more complicated.
 (i)   Begin by determining the types of eligible housing costs incurred in respect of the parent's home from those listed in Sch 3, paras 1, 2 and (for assessable income purposes only) 3 (regs 14 and 15(1)).
 (ii)   Then decide whether the general conditions of entitlement for those costs to be taken into account have been met (Sch 3, para 4).
 (iii)   If so, make the following deductions: where those costs are shared with someone other than a member of the parent's family, the share of those costs applicable to the other person (reg 15(3)); apportionment for non-residential accommodation covered by the payments under (i) above (Sch 3, para 5); deductions for ineligible service charges, fuel charges and water and allied environmental services (Sch 3, para 6). The result is the parent's housing costs.
 Third, if the parent has housing costs, the tribunal must determine to whom those costs are paid. If the parent is a non-dependant member of a household and pays housing costs only to another member or members of that household, the parent is treated as having no housing costs (reg 15(10)). This only applies for the purposes of calculating assessable income (regs 9(1)(b) and 10) and does not apply for the purposes of the protected income calculation in respect of which a notional allowance is made for housing costs (reg 11(1)(b)).
 Fourth, if the parent has housing costs, these must be converted to a weekly figure under reg 16.
 Fifth, the tribunal should determine whether the costs exceed the ceiling imposed by reg 18. If they do, no costs are allowed over the ceiling. The result is the allowable housing costs.

Amount of housing costs

15.–*(1)   Subject to the provisions of this regulation and regulations [¹16 and 18] a parent's housing costs shall be the aggregate of the eligible housing costs payable in respect of his home.*

(2)   Where a local authority has determined that a parent is entitled to housing benefit, the amount of his housing costs shall, subject to paragraphs (4) to (9), be the

weekly amount treated as rent under [⁴regulations 12 and 80 of the Housing Benefit Regulations or, as the case may be, regulations 12 and 61 of the Housing Benefit (State Pension Credit) Regulations] (rent and calculation of weekly amounts) less the amount of housing benefit.

(3) Where a parent has eligible housing costs and another person who is not a member of his family is also liable to make payments in respect of the home, the amount of the parent's housing costs shall be his share of those costs [³but where that other person does not make payments in circumstances where head (a) of paragraph 4(2) of Schedule 3 applies, the eligible housing costs of that parent shall include the housing costs for which, because of that failure to pay, that parent is treated as responsible under that head.]

(4)–(9) [¹...]

[¹[²(4) A parent shall be treated as having no housing costs where he is a non dependant member of a household and is not responsible for meeting housing costs except to another member, or other members, of that household.]

Amendments

1. Child Support and Income Support (Amendment) Regulations 1995 (SI 1995 No.1045) reg 48(2)-(4) (April 18, 1995).
2. Child Support (Miscellaneous Amendments) (No. 2) Regulations 1995 (SI 1995 No.3261) reg 44 (January 22, 1996).
3. Child Support (Miscellaneous Amendments) Regulations 1998 (SI 1998 No.58) reg 50 (January 19, 1998).
4. Housing Benefit and Council Tax Benefit (Consequential Provisions) Regulations 2006 (SI 2006 No.217) reg 5 and Sch 2 para 4(4) (March 6, 2006).

Definitions

"eligible housing costs": see reg 1(2).
"family": see reg 1(2).
"home": see reg 1(2).
"housing benefit": see reg 1(2).
"Housing Benefit Regulations": see reg 1(2).
"Housing Benefit (State Pension Credit) Regulations": see reg 1(2).
"non-dependant": see reg 1(2).

General Note

Paragraph (3)

As a result of this provision only half of the housing costs is to be taken into account as an eligible housing cost where the parent whose home the property is is not solely liable for those costs (*CSCS 8/1995*, para 15 and *CCS 8189/1995*). In the latter decision the commissioner refers throughout to reg 50 of these Regulations. There is no such regulation and the words quoted by the commissioner are those of this paragraph.

If the parent occupying the home has to pay the whole of the costs, the case falls within Sch 3 para 4(2)(a) (*CCS 13698/1996*, para 7).

[¹Weekly amount of housing costs

16.–(1) [²Where housing costs are payable by a parent]–

(a) on a weekly basis, the amount of such housing costs shall subject to paragraph (2), be the weekly rate payable at the effective date;

(b) on a monthly basis, the amount of such housing costs shall subject to paragraph (2), be the monthly rate payable at the effective date, multiplied by 12 and divided by 52;

(c) by way of rent payable to a housing association, as defined in section 1(1) of the Housing Associations Act 1985 which is registered in accordance with section 5 of that Act, or to a local authority, on a free week basis, that is to say the basis that he pays an amount by way of rent for a given number of weeks in a 52 week period, with a lesser number of weeks in which there is no liability to pay ("free weeks"), the amount of such housing costs shall be [²the amount payable]–

    (i) in the relevant week if it is not a free week; or

    (ii) in the last week before the relevant week which is not a free week, if the relevant week is a free week;

(d)   on any other basis, the amount of such housing costs shall, subject to paragraph (2), be the rate payable at the effective date, multiplied by the number of payment periods, or the nearest whole number of payment periods (any fraction of one half being rounded up), falling within a period of 365 days and divided by 52.

(2)   Where housing costs consist of payments or a repayment mortgage and the absent parent or parent with care has not provided information or evidence as to the rate of repayment of the capital secured and the interest payable on that mortgage at the effective date and that absent parent or parent with care has provided a statement from the lender, in respect of a period ending not more than 12 months prior to the first day of the relevant week, for the purposes of the calculation of exempt income under regulation 9 and protected income under regulation 11–

(a)   if the amount of capital repaid for the period covered by that statement is shown on it, the rate of repayment of capital owing under that mortgage shall be calculated by reference to that amount; and

(b)   if the amount of capital owing and the interest rate applicable at the end of the period covered by that statement are shown on it, the interest payable on that mortgage shall be calculated by references to that amount and that interest rate.]

Amendments

1.   Child Support (Miscellaneous Amendments) Regulations 1996 (SI 1996 No.1945) reg 22 (August 5, 1996).

2.   Child Support (Miscellaneous Amendments) Regulations 1998 (SI 1998 No.58) reg 51(a) and (b) (January 19, 1998).

17.   [¹…]

Amendment

1.   Child Support and Income Support (Amendment) Regulations 1995 (SI 1995 No.1045) reg 50 (April 18, 1995).

Definitions

"effective date": see reg 1(2).
"relevant week": see reg 1(2).

General Note

Although this regulation provides that the housing costs shall be those payable at the effective date, some of the provisions which determine the effective date have the effect that the effective date may pre-date the change in the housing costs. For example, a change in housing costs which occurs on the second day of a maintenance period and which is notified to the officer on the following day will result in a fresh assessment of which the effective date is the first day of the maintenance period (reg 31(3) of the Maintenance Assessment Procedure Regulations).

Regulation 17 was revoked by reg 50 of the Amendment Regulations 1995 from 18 April 1995.

Excessive housing costs

18.–(1)   Subject to paragraph (2), the amount of the housing costs of an absent parent which are to be taken into account–

(a)   under regulation 9(1)(b) shall not exceed the greater of £80.00 or half the amount of N as calculated or estimated under regulation 7;

(b)   under regulation 11(1)(b) shall not exceed the greater of £80.00 or half of the amount calculated in accordance with regulation 11(2).

(2)   The restriction imposed by paragraph (1) shall not apply where–

(a)   the absent parent in question–

(i)   has been awarded housing benefit (or is awaiting the outcome of a claim to that benefit);

(ii)   has the day to day care of any child; or

(iii) is a person to whom a disability premium under paragraph 11 of the relevant Schedule applies in respect of himself or his partner or would so apply if he were entitled to income support and [²had not attained the qualifying age for state pension credit];

   (b)   *the absent parent in question, following divorce from [¹dissolution of a civil partnership with,] or the breakdown of his relationship with, his former partner, remains in the home he occupied with his former partner;*

   (c)   *the absent parent in question has paid the housing costs under the mortgage, charge or agreement in question for a period in excess of 52 weeks before the date of the first application for child support maintenance in relation to a qualifying child of his and there has been no increase in those costs other than an increase in the interest payable under the mortgage or charge or, as the case may be, in the amount payable under the agreement under which the home is held;*

   (d)   *the housing costs in respect of the home in question would not exceed the amount set out in paragraph (1) but for an increase in the interest payable under a mortgage or charge secured on that home or, as the case may be, in the amount payable under any agreement under which it is held; or*

   (e)   *the absent parent is responsible for making payments in respect of housing costs which are higher than they would be otherwise by virtue of the unavailability of his share of the equity of the property formerly occupied with his partner and which remains occupied by that former partner.*

Amendments

1.   *Civil Partnership (Pensions, Social Security and Child Support) (Consequential, etc Provisions) Order 2005 (SI 2005 No.2877) art 2(4) and Sch 4 para 2(3) (December 5, 2005).*

2.   *Child Support (Miscellaneous and Consequential Amendments) Regulations 2009 (SI 2009 No.736) reg 3(4) (April 6, 2009).*

Definitions

"day to day care": see reg 1(2).
"home": see reg 1(2).
"housing benefit": see reg 1(2).
"partner": see reg 1(2).
"relevant Schedule": see reg 1(2).

General Note

Subparagraph (2)(b)
The partner referred to need not be the person with care of the qualifying child (*CCS 12769/1996*, para 11).

PART III
SPECIAL CASES
Special cases

Both parents are absent

   19.–*(1)   Subject to regulation 27, where the circumstances of a case are that each parent of a qualifying child is an absent parent in relation to that child (neither being a person who is treated as an absent parent by regulation 20(2) that case shall be treated as a special case for the purposes of the Act.*

   (2)   For the purposes of this case–

   (a)   *where the application is made in relation to both absent parents, separate assessments shall be made under Schedule 1 to the Act in respect of each so as to determine the amount of child support maintenance payable by each absent parent;*

   (b)   *subject to paragraph (3), where the application is made in relation to both absent parents, the value of C in each case shall be the assessable income of the other absent parent and where the application is made in relation to only one the value of C in the case of the other shall be nil;*

   (c)   *[²...]*

   [¹(d) *where the application is made in relation to one absent parent only, the amount of the maintenance requirement applicable in that case shall be one-half of the amount determined in accordance with paragraph 1(2) of Schedule 1 to the Act or, where regulation 23 applies (person caring for children of more than one absent parent), of the amount determined in accordance with paragraphs (2) to (3) of that regulation.]*

(3)　Where, for the purposes of paragraph (2)(b), information regarding the income of the other absent parent has not been submitted to the Secretary of State [⁴...] within the period specified in regulation 6(1) of the Maintenance Assessment Procedure Regulations then until such information is acquired the value of C shall be nil.

(4)　When the information referred to in paragraph (3) is acquired the [⁴Secretary of State] shall make a fresh assessment which shall have effect from the effective date in relation to that other absent [³parent or, from the effective date as determined by paragraph (2) of regulation 30 of the Maintenance Assessment Procedure Regulations, whichever is the later.]

Amendments

1.　*Child Support (Miscellaneous Amendments) Regulations 1996 (SI 1996 No.1945) reg 23 and 25(5) (October 7, 1996).*
2.　*Child Support (Miscellaneous Amendments) Regulations 1998 (SI 1998 No.58) reg 52 (April 6, 1998).*
3.　*Child Support (Miscellaneous Amendments) Regulations 1999 (SI 1999 No.977) reg 6(4) (April 6, 1999).*
4.　*Social Security Act 1998 (Commencement No.7 and Consequential and Transitional Provisions) Order 1999 (SI 1999 No.1510) art 17 (June 1, 1999).*

Definitions

"the Act": see reg 1(2).
"effective date": see reg 1(2).
"Maintenance Assessment Procedure Regulations": see reg 1(2).
"person": see reg 1(2).

Persons treated as absent parents

20.–(1)　*Where the circumstances of a case are that–*
(a)　*two or more persons who do not live in the same household each provide day to day care for the same qualifying child; and*
(b)　*at least one of those persons is a parent of that child,*
that case shall be treated as a special case for the purposes of the Act.

(2)　*For the purposes of this case a parent who provides day to day care for a child of his in the following circumstances is to be treated as an absent parent for the purposes of the Act and these Regulations–*
(a)　*a parent who provides such care to a lesser extent that the other parent, person or persons who provide such care for the child in question;*
(b)　*where the persons mentioned in paragraph (1)(a) include both parents and the circumstances are such that care is provided to the same extent by both but each provides care to a greater or equal extent than any other person who provides such care for that child–*
　　(i)　*the parent who is not in receipt of child benefit for the child in question; vor*
　　(ii)　*if neither parent is in receipt of child benefit for that child, the parent who, in the opinion of the [¹Secretary of State], will not be the principal provider of day to day care for that child.*

(3)　*Subject to paragraphs (5) and (6), where a parent is treated as an absent parent under paragraph (2) child support maintenance shall be payable by that parent in respect of the child in question and the amount of the child support maintenance so payable shall be calculated in accordance with the formula set out in paragraph (4).*

(4)　*The formula for the purposes of paragraph (3) is–*

$$T = X - (X + Y) \times \left\{ \frac{J}{7 \times L} \right\}$$

where–
T is the amount of child support maintenance payable;
X is the amount of child support maintenance which would be payable by the parent who is treated as an absent parent, assessed under Schedule 1 to the Act as if paragraphs

6 and 7 of that Schedule did not apply, and, where the other parent is an absent parent, as if the value of C was the assessable income of the other parent;
 Y is–
 (i) *the amount of child support maintenance assessed under Schedule 1 to the Act payable by the other parent if he is an absent parent or which would be payable if he were an absent parent, and for the purposes of such calculation the value of C shall be the assessable income of the parent treated as an absent parent under paragraph(2); or,*
 (ii) *if there is no such other parent, shall be nil;*
 J is the total of the weekly average number of nights for which day to day care is provided by the person who is treated as the absent parent in respect of each child included in the maintenance assessment and shall be calculated to 2 decimal places;
 L is the number of children who are included in the maintenance assessment in question.
 (5) *Where the value of T calculated under the provisions of paragraph (4) is less than zero, no child support maintenance shall be payable.*
 (6) *The liability to pay any amount calculated under paragraph (4) shall be subject to the provision made for protected income and minimum payments under paragraphs 6 and 7 of Schedule 1 to the Act.*

Amendment
 1. *Social Security Act 1998 (Commencement No.7 and Consequential and Transitional Provisions) Order 1999 (SI 1999 No.1510) art 16 (June 1, 1999).*

Definitions
 "the Act": see reg 1(2).
 "day to day care": see reg 1(2).
 "person": see reg 1(2).

One parent is absent and the other is treated as absent

 21.–(1) *Where the circumstances of a case are that one parent is an absent parent and the other parent is treated as an absent parent by regulation 20(2), that case shall be treated as a special case for the purposes of the Act.*
 (2) *For the purpose of assessing the child support maintenance payable by an absent parent where this case applies, each reference in Schedule 1 to the Act to a parent who is a person with care shall be treated as a reference to a person who is treated as an absent parent by regulation 20(2).*

Definition
 "the Act": see reg 1(2).

Multiple applications relating to an absent parent

 22.–(1) *Where an application for a maintenance assessment has been made in respect of an absent parent and–*
 (a) *at least one other application for a maintenance assessment has been made in relation to the same absent parent (or a person who is treated as an absent parent by regulation 20(2) but to different children; or*
 (b) *at least one maintenance assessment is in force in relation to the same absent parent or a person who is treated as an absent parent by regulation 20(2) but to different children,*
that case shall be treated as a special case for the purposes of the Act].
 [²(2) *For the purposes of assessing the amount of child support maintenance payable in respect of each application where [³paragraph (1)(a)] applies [³or in respect of the application made in circumstances where paragraph (1)(b) applies] for references to the assessable income of an absent parent in the Act and in these Regulations[⁴,and subject to paragraph (2ZA),] there shall be substituted references to the amount calculated by the formula–*

$$(A + T) \times \left(\frac{B}{D}\right) - CS$$

where–

A is the absent parent's assessable income;

T is the sum of the amounts allowable in the calculation or estimation of his exempt income by virtue of Schedule 3A;

B is the maintenance requirement calculated in respect of the application in question;

D is the sum of the maintenance requirements as calculated for the purposes of each assessment relating to the absent parent in question; and

CS is the amount (if any) allowable by virtue of Schedule 3A in calculating or estimating the absent parent's exempt income in respect of a relevant qualifying transfer of property in respect of the assessment in question.]

[⁴(2ZA)   Where a case falls within regulation 39(1)(a) of the Departure Direction and Consequential Amendment Regulations, for the purposes of assessing the amount of child support maintenance payable in respect of an application for child support maintenance before a departure direction in respect of the maintenance assessment in question is given, for references to the assessable income of an absent parent in the Act and in these Regulations there shall be substituted references to the amount calculated by the formula–

$$(A + B) \times \frac{B}{D}$$

where A,T,B and D have the same meanings as in paragraph (2).]

[³(2A)   Where paragraph (1)(b) applies, and a maintenance assessment has been made in respect of the application referred to in paragraph (1), each maintenance assessment in force at the time of that assessment shall be reduced using the formula for calculation of assessable income set out in paragraph (2) and each reduction shall take effect on the date specified in regulation 33(7) of the Maintenance Assessment Procedure Regulations.]

[⁵(2B)   Where–

(a)   a case is treated as a special case for the purposes of the Act by virtue of paragraph (1);

(b)   more than one maintenance assessment is in force in respect of the absent parent; and

[⁶(c)   any of those assessments falls to be replaced by a fresh assessment to be made by virtue of a revision under section 16 of the Act or a decision under section 17 of the Act superseding an earlier decision,]

the formula set out in paragraph (2) or, as the case may be, paragraph (2ZA) shall be applied to calculate or estimate the amount of child support maintenance payable under that fresh assessment.

(2C)   Where a maintenance assessment falls within sub-paragraph (b) of paragraph (2B) but [⁶not within] sub-paragraph (c) of that paragraph, the formula set out in paragraph (2) or, as the case may be, paragraph (2ZA) shall be applied to determine whether that maintenance assessment should be increased or reduced as a result of the making of a fresh assessment under sub-paragraph (c) and any increase or reduction shall take effect from the effective date of that fresh assessment.]

(3)   Where more than one maintenance assessment has been made with respect to the absent parent and payment by him of the aggregate of the amounts of those assessments would reduce his disposable income below his protected income level, the aggregate amount of those assessments shall be reduced (each being reduced by reference to the same proportion as those assessments bear to each other) by the minimum amount necessary to prevent his disposable income being reduced below his protected income level provided that the aggregate amount payable under those assessments shall not be reduced to less than the minimum amount prescribed in regulation 13(1).

[¹(4)   Where the aggregate of the child support maintenance payable by the absent parent is less than the minimum amount prescribed in regulation 13(1), the child support maintenance payable shall be–

(a)   that prescribed minimum amount apportioned between the two or more applications in the same ratio as the maintenance requirements in question bear to each other; or

(b)   where, because of the application of regulation 2(2), such an apportionment produces an aggregate amount which is different from that prescribed minimum amount, that different amount.]

(5)   Payment of each of the maintenance assessments calculated under this regulation shall satisfy the liability of the absent parent (or a person treated as such) to pay child support maintenance.

Amendments

1.   *Child Support (Miscellaneous Amendments) Regulations 1993 (SI 1993 No.913) reg 23 (April 5, 1993).*

2.   *Child Support and Income Support (Amendment) Regulations 1995 (SI 1995 No.1045) reg 51 (April 18, 1995).*

3.   *Child Support (Miscellaneous Amendments) (No.2) Regulations 1995 (SI 1995 No.3261) reg 45(2)-(4) (January 22, 1996).*

4.   *Child Support Departure Direction and Consequential Amendments Regulations 1996 (SI 1996 No.2907) reg 68(5) (December 2, 1996).*

5.   *Child Support (Miscellaneous Amendments) Regulations 1998 (SI 1998 No 58) reg 53 (January 19, 1998).*

6.   *Social Security Act 1998 (Commencement No.7 and Consequential and Transitional Provisions) Order 1999 (SI 1999 No.1510) art 18 (June 1, 1999).*

Definitions

"the Act": see reg 1(2).
"Departure Direction and Consequential Amendments Regulations": see reg 1(2).
"Maintenance Assessment Procedure Regulations": see reg 1(2).
"qualifying transfer": see reg 1(2).

Person caring for children of more than one absent parent

23.–(1)   Where the circumstances of a case are that–

(a)   a person is a person with care in relation to two or more qualifying children; and

(b)   in relation to at least two of those children there are different persons who are absent parents or persons treated as absent parents by regulation 20(2);

that case shall be treated as a special case for the purposes of the Act.

(2)   [¹Subject to paragraph (2A)] in calculating the maintenance requirements for the purposes of this case, for any amount which (but for this paragraph) would have been included under regulation 3(1)(b), [²or (c)] (amounts included in the calculation of AG) there shall be substituted an amount calculated by dividing the amount which would have been so included by the relevant number.

[¹(2A)   In applying the provisions of paragraph (2) to the amount which is to be included in the maintenance requirements under regulation 3(1)(b)–

(a)   first take the amount specified in head (i) of regulation 3(1)(b) and divide it by the relevant number;

(b)   then apply the provisions of regulation 3(1)(b) as if the references to the amount specified in column (2) of paragraph 1(1)(e) of the relevant Schedule were references to the amount which is the product of the calculation required by head (a)above, and as if, in relation to an absent parent, the only qualifying children to be included in the assessment were those qualifying children in relation to whom he is the absent parent.]

(3)   [¹In paragraph (2) and (2A)] "the relevant number" means the number equal to the total number of persons who, in relation to those children, are either absent parents or persons treated as absent parents by regulation 20(2) except that where in respect of the same child both parents are persons who are either absent parents or persons who are treated as absent parents under that regulation, they shall count as one person.

(4)   Where the circumstances of a case fall within this regulation and the person with care is the parent of any of the children, for C in paragraph 2(1) of Schedule 1 to the Act (the assessable income of that person) there shall be substituted the amount which

would be calculated under regulation 22(2) if the references therein to an absent parent were references to a parent with care.

Amendments
1.   Child Support (Miscellaneous Amendments and Transitional Provisions) Regulations 1994 (SI 1994 No.227) reg 4(6) and (7) (February 7, 1994).
2.   Child Benefit, Child Support and Social Security (Miscellaneous Amendments) Regulations 1996 (SI 1996 No.1803) reg 14 (April 7, 1996).

Definitions
"the Act": see reg 1(2).
"person": see reg 1(2).

Persons with part-time care-not including a person treated as an absent parent

24.–*(1)   Where the circumstances of a case are that–*
(a)   *two or more persons who do not live in the same household each provide day to day care for the same qualifying child; and*
(b)   *those persons do not include any parent who is treated as an absent parent of that child by regulation 20(2).*
that case shall be treated as a special case of the purposes of the Act.
(2)   *For the purposes of this case–*
(a)   *the person whose application for a maintenance assessment is being proceeded with shall, subject to paragraph (b), be entitled or receive all of the child support maintenance payable under the Act in respect of the child in question;*
(b)   *on request being made to the Secretary of State by–*
(i)   *that person; or*
(ii)   *any other person who is providing day to day care for that child and who intends to continue to provide that care,*
the Secretary of State may make arrangements of the payment of any child support maintenance payable under the Act to the persons who provide such care in the same ratio as that in which it appears to the Secretary of State, that each is to provide such care for the child in question;
(c)   *before making an arrangement under sub-paragraph (b), the Secretary of State shall consider all of the circumstances of the case and in particular the interest of the child, the present arrangements for the day to day care of the child in question and any representations or proposals made by the persons who provide such care of that child.*

Definitions
"the Act": see reg 1(2).
"day to day care": see reg 1(2).
"person": see reg 1(2).

Care provided in part by a local authority

25.–*(1)   Where the circumstances of a case are that a local authority and a person each provide day to day care for the same qualifying child, that case shall be treated as a special case for the purposes of the Act.*
(2)   *[¹Subject to paragraph (3), in a case where this regulation applies]–*
(a)   *child support maintenance shall be calculated in respect of that child as if this regulation did not apply;*
(b)   *the amount so calculated shall be divided by 7 so as to produce a daily amount;*
(c)   *in respect of each night for which day to day care for that child is provided by a person other than the local authority, the daily amount relating to that period shall be payable by the absent parent (or, as the case may be, by the person treated as an absent parent under regulation 20(2);*
(d)   *child support maintenance shall not be payable in respect of any night for which the local authority provides day to day care for that qualifying child.*

[¹(3) *In a case where more than one qualifying child is included in a child support maintenance assessment application and where this regulation applies to at least one of those children, child support maintenance shall be calculated by applying the formula–*

$$S \times \left(\frac{A}{7 \times B} \right)$$

where–
S is the total amount of child support maintenance in respect of all qualifying children included in that maintenance assessment application, calculated as if this regulation did not apply;
A is the aggregate of the number of nights of day to day care for all qualifying children included in that maintenance assessment application provided in each week by a person other than the local authority;
B is the number of qualifying children in respect of whom the maintenance assessment application has been made.]

Amendment

1. Child Support and Income Support (Amendment) Regulations 1995 (SI 1995 No.1045) reg 52(2) and (3) (April 18, 1995).

Definitions

"the Act": see reg 1(2).
"day to day care": see reg 1(2).
"person": see reg 1(2).

Cases where child support maintenance is not to be payable

26.–*(1)* *Where the circumstances of a case are that–*
(a) *but for this regulation the minimum amount prescribed in regulation 13(1) would apply; and*
(b) *any of the following conditions are satisfied–*
  (i) *the income of the absent parent includes one or more of the payments or awards specified in Schedule 4 or would include such a payment but for a provision preventing the receipt of that payment by reason of it overlapping with some other benefit payment or would, in the case of the payments referred to in paragraph (a)(i) or (iv) of that Schedule, include such a payment if the relevant contribution conditions for entailment had been satisfied;*
  (ii) *an amount to which regulation [²11(1)(f)] applies (protected income; income support family premium) is taken into account in calculating or estimating [¹under paragraphs (1) to (5) of regulation 11,] the protected income of the absent parent;*
  (iii) *the absent parent is a child within the meaning of section 55 of the Act;*
  (iv) *the absent parent is a prisoner; or*
  (v) *the absent parent is a person in respect of whom N (as calculated or estimated under regulation 7(1) is less than the minimum amount prescribed by regulation 13(1),*
  the case shall be treated as a special case for the purposes of the Act.
(2) *For the purposes of this case–*
(a) *the requirement in paragraph 7(2) of Schedule 1 to the Act (minimum amount of child support maintenance fixed by an assessment to be the prescribed minimum amount) shall not apply;*
(b) *the amount of the child support maintenance to be fixed by the assessment shall be nil.*

Amendments

1. Child Support and Income Support (Amendment) Regulations 1995 (SI 1995 No.1045) reg 53 (April 18, 1995).
2. Child Support (Miscellaneous Amendments) Regulations 1998 (SI 1998 No.58) reg 54 (April 6, 1998).

Definitions
"the Act": see reg 1(2).
"person": see reg 1(2).
"prisoner": see reg 1(2).

Child who is a boarder or an in-patient

27.–(1)   Where the circumstances of a case are that–
(a)   a qualifying child is a boarder at a boarding school or is an in-patient in a hospital; and
(b)   by reason of those circumstances, the person who would otherwise provide day to day care is not doing so,
that case shall be treated as a special case of the purposes of the Act.

(2)   For the purposes of this case, section 3(3)(b) of the Act shall be modified so [¹that] for the reference to the person who usually provides day to day care for the child there shall be substituted a reference to the person who would usually be providing such care for that child but for the circumstances specified in paragraph (1).

Amendment
1.   *Child Support (Miscellaneous Amendments) Regulations 1993 (SI 1993 No.913) reg 24 (April 5, 1993).*

Definitions
"the Act": see reg 1(2).
"day to day care": see reg 1(2).
"person": see reg 1(2).

[¹Child who is allowed to live with his parent under section 23(5) of the Children Act 1989

27A.–(1)   Where the circumstances of a case are that a qualifying child who is in the care of a local authority in England and Wales is allowed by the authority to live with a parent of his under section 23(5) of the Children Act 1989, that case shall be treated as a special case for the purposes of the Act.

(2)   For the purposes of this case, section 3(3)(b) of the Act shall be modified so that for the reference to the person who usually provides day to day care for the child there shall be substituted a reference to the parent of a child whom the local authority allow the child to live with under section 23(5) the Children Act 1989.]

Amendment
1.   *Child Support (Miscellaneous Amendments) Regulations 1993 (SI 1993 No.913) reg 25 (April 5, 1993).*

Definitions
"the Act": see reg 1(2).
"day to day care": see reg 1(2).

Amount payable where absent parent is in receipt of income support or other prescribed benefit

28.–(1)   Where the condition specified in section 43(1)(a) of the Act is satisfied in relation to an absent parent (assessable income to be nil where income support [³, income-based jobseeker's allowance] [⁵, income-related employment and support allowance under Part 1 of the Welfare Reform Act,] or other prescribed benefit is paid), the prescribed conditions for the purposes of section 43(1)(b) of the Act are that–
(a)   the absent parent is aged 18 or over;
(b)   he does not satisfy the conditions in paragraph [⁴³(1)(a) or (b)] of the relevant Schedule (income support family premium) [¹and does not have day to day care of any child (whether or not a relevant child)]; and
(c)   [¹his income does not include] one or more of the payments or awards specified in Schedule 4 (other than by reason of a provision preventing receipt of overlapping benefits or by reason of a failure to satisfy the relevant contribution conditions).

(2)　For the purposes of section 43(2)(a) of the Act, the prescribed amount shall be equal to the minimum amount prescribed in regulation 13(1) for the purposes of paragraph 7(1) of Schedule 1 to the Act.

[¹[²(3)　Subject to paragraph (4), where–

(a)　an absent parent is liable under section 43 of the Act and this regulation to make payments in place of payments of child support maintenance with respect to two or more qualifying children in relation to whom there is more than one parent with care; or

(b)　that absent parent and his partner (within the meaning of regulation 2(1) of the Social Security (Claims and Payments) Regulations 1987) are both liable to make such payments,

the prescribed amount mentioned in paragraph (2) shall be apportioned between the persons with care in the same ratio as the maintenance requirements of the qualifying child or children in relation to each of those persons with care bear to each other.]

(4)　If, in making the apportionment required by paragraph (3), the effect of the application of regulation 2(2) would be such that the aggregate amount payable would be different from the amount prescribed in paragraph (2) the Secretary of State shall adjust the apportionment so as to eliminate that difference; and that adjustment shall be varied from time to time so as to secure that, taking one week with another and so far as is practicable, each person with care receives the amount which she would have received if no adjustment had been made under this paragraph.

(5)　The provisions of Schedule 5 shall have effect in relation to cases to which section 43 of the Act and this regulation apply.]

Amendments

1.　*Child Support (Miscellaneous Amendments) Regulations 1993 (SI 1993 No.913) reg 26 (April 5, 1993).*

2.　*Child Support (Maintenance Assessment and Special Cases) Amendment Regulations 1993 (SI 1993 No.925) reg 2(2) (April 26, 1993).*

3.　*Social Security and Child Support (Jobseeker's Allowance) (Consequential Amendments) Regulations 1996 (SI 1996 No.1345) reg 6(3) (October 7, 1996).*

4.　*Child Support (Miscellaneous Amendments) Regulations 1998 (SI 1998 No.58) reg 55 (April 6, 1998).*

5.　*Employment and Support Allowance (Consequential Provisions) (No.2) Regulations 2008 (SI 2008 No.1554) reg 58(4) (October 27, 2008).*

Definitions

"the Act": see reg 1(2).

"day to day care": see reg 1(2).

"relevant Schedule": see reg 1(2).

SCHEDULE 1
CALCULATION OF N AND M

PART I
EARNINGS
Chapter 1
Earnings of an employed earner

1.–(1)　*Subject to sub-paragraphs (2) and (3), "earnings" means in the case of employment as an employed earner, any remuneration or profit derived from that employment and includes–*

(a)　*any bonus, commission, [²payment in respect of overtime], royalty or fee;*

[⁶(aa)　*any profit-related pay, whether paid in anticipation of, or following, the calculation of profits;]*

(b)　*any holiday pay except any payable more than 4 weeks after termination of the employment;*

(c)　*any payment by way of a retainer;*

[⁵(d)　*any payments made by the parent's employer in respect of any expenses not wholly, exclusively and necessarily incurred in the performance of the duties of the employment, including any payment made by the parent's employer in respect of–*

(i)　*travelling expenses incurred by that parent between his home and place of employment; and*

(ii)　*expenses incurred by that parent under arrangements made of the care of a member of his family owing to that parent's absence from home;]*

(e)　*any award of compensation made under section 68(2) or 71(2)(a) of the Employment Protection (Consolidation) Act 1978 (remedies and compensation for unfair dismissal);*

(f)   any such sum as is referred to in section 112 of the Contributions and Benefits Act (certain sums to be earnings for social security purposes);

(g)   any statutory sick pay under Part I of the Social Security and Housing Benefits Act 1982 or statutory maternity pay under Part V of the Social Security Act 1986;

[¹³(gg)   any statutory paternity pay under Part 12ZA of the Contributions and Benefits Act or any statutory adoption pay under Part 12ZB of that Act;]

(h)   any payment in lieu of notice and any compensation in respect of the absence or inadequacy of any such notice but only insofar as such payment or compensation represents loss of income;

(i)   any payment relating to a period of less than a year which is made in respect of the performance of duties as–
        (i)   an auxiliary coastguard in respect of cost rescue activities;
        (ii)   [¹⁷...]
        [¹⁶(iia) a part-time fire-fighter employed by a fire and rescue authority;]
        [¹⁷(iib) a part-time fire-fighter employed by [²³ the Scottish Fire and Rescue Service;]]
        (iii)   a person engaged part-time in the manning or launching of a life-boat;
        (iv)   a member of any territorial or reserve force prescribed in part I of Schedule 3 to the Social Security (Contributions) Regulations 1979;

(j)   any payment made by a local authority to a member of that authority in respect of the performance of his duties as a member, to her than any expenses wholly, exclusively and necessarily incurred in the performance of those duties.

(2)   Earnings shall not include–

(a)   any payment in respect of expenses wholly, exclusively and necessarily incurred in the performance of the duties of the employment [⁷except any such payment which is made in respect of housing costs and those housing costs are included in the calculation of the exempt or protected income of the absent parent under regulation 9(1)(b) or, as the case may be, regulation 11(1)(b);]

(b)   any occupational pension;

(c)   any payment where–
        (i)   the employment in respect of which it was made has ceased; and
        (ii)   a period of the same length as the period by reference to which it was calculated has expired since that cessation but prior to the effective date;

(d)   any advance of earnings or any loan made by an employer to an employee;

(e)   any amount received from an employer during a period when the employee has withdrawn his services by reason of a trade dispute;

(f)   any payment in kind;

(g)   where, in any week or other period which falls within the period by reference to which earnings are calculated earnings are received both in respect of a previous employment and in respect of a subsequent employment, the earnings in respect of the previous employment.

[⁶(h)   any tax-exempt allowance made by an employer to an employee [⁷except any such allowance which is made in respect of housing costs and those housing costs are included in the calculation of the exempt or protected income of the absent parent under regulation 9(1) or, as the case may be, regulation 11(1)(b)].]

(3)   The earnings to be taken into account for the purposes of calculating N and M shall be gross earnings less–

(a)   any amount deducted from those earnings by way of–
        (i)   income tax;
        (ii)   primary Class I contributions under the Contributions and Benefits Act [²or under the Social Security Contributions and Benefits (Northern Ireland) Act 1992]; and

(b)   one half of any sums paid by the parent towards an occupational [²...] pension scheme.

[²(c)   one half of any sums paid by the parent towards a personal pension scheme, or, where that scheme is intended partly to provide a capital sum to discharge a mortgage secured upon the parent's home, 37.5 per centum of any such sums.]

2.–[²(1)   Subject to sub-paragraphs [⁶(1A)] to (4), the amount of the earnings to be taken into account for the purpose of calculating N and M shall be calculated or estimated by reference to the average earnings at the relevant week having regard to such evidence as is available in relation to that person's earnings during such period as appears appropriate to the [¹⁰Secretary of State] beginning not earlier than eight weeks before the relevant week and ending not later than the date of the assessment and for the purpose of that calculation or estimate he may consider evidence of that person's cumulative earnings during the period beginning with the start of the year of assessment (within the meaning of section 832 of the Income and Corporation Taxes Act 8 in which the relevant week falls and ending with a date no later than the date of the assessment.]

[⁶(1A)   Subject to sub-paragraph (4), where a person has claimed, or has been paid, [¹¹ [¹²working tax credit or child tax credit]] on any day during the period beginning not earlier than eight weeks before the relevant week and ending not later than the date on which the assessment is made, the [¹⁰Secretary of State] may have regard to the amount of earnings taken into account in determining entitlement to those benefits in order to calculate or estimate the amount of earnings to be taken into account for the purposes of calculating N and M, notwithstanding the fact that entitlement to those benefits may have been determined by reference to earnings attributable to a period other than that specified in sub-paragraph (1).]

[⁶(2)   Where a person's earnings during the period of 52 weeks ending with the relevant week include–

    (a)   *a bonus, commission, or payment of profit-related pay made in anticipation of the calculation profits which is paid separately from or in relation to a longer period than, the other earnings with which it is paid; or*

    (b)   *a payment in respect of profit-related pay made following the calculation of the employer's profits, the amount of that bonus, commission or profit- related payment shall be the determined for the purposes of the calculation of earnings by aggregating any such payments received in that period and dividing by 52.]*

    (3)   *Subject to sub-paragraph (4), the amount of any earnings of a student shall be determined by aggregating the amount received in the year ending with the relevant week and dividing by 52 or, where the person in question has been a student for less than a year, by aggregating the amount received in the period starting with his becoming a student and ending with the relevant week and dividing by the number of complete weeks in that period.*

    [⁶*(3A)   Where a case is one to which regulation 30A(1) or (3) of the Maintenance Assessment Procedure Regulations applies (effective dates of new maintenance assessments in particular cases), the term "relevant week" shall, for the purpose of this paragraph, mean the 7 days immediately proceeding the date on which the information or evidence is received which enables [*¹⁰*the Secretary of State] to make a new maintenance assessment calculation in accordance with the provisions of Part I of Schedule 1 to the Act in respect of that case for a period beginning after the effective date applicable to that case.*

    (4)   *Where a calculation would, but for this sub-paragraph, produce an amount which, in the opinion of the [*¹⁰*Secretary of State], does not accurately reflect the normal amount of the earnings of the person in question, such earnings, or any part of them, shall be calculated by reference to such other period as may, in the particular case, enable the normal weekly earnings of that person to be determined more accurately and for this purpose the [*¹⁰*Secretary of State] shall have regard to–*

    (a)   *the earnings received, or due to be received, from any employment in which the person in question is engaged, has been engaged or is due to be engaged;*

    (b)   *the duration and pattern, or the expected duration and pattern, of any employment of that person.*

Chapter 2
Earnings of a self-employed earner

    [⁸*2A–(1)   Subject to paragraphs [*¹⁹*...], 2C, 4 and 5A, "earnings" in the case of employment as a self-employed earner shall have the meaning given by the following provisions of this paragraph.*

    (2)   *"Earnings" means the [*¹⁹*...] taxable profits from self-employment of that earner [*¹⁹*...], less the following amounts–*

    (a)   *any income tax relating to the taxable profits from the self-employment determined in accordance with sub-paragraph (3);*

    (b)   *any National Insurance Contributions relating to the taxable profits from the self-employment determined in accordance with sub-paragraph (4);*

    (c)   *one half of any premium paid in respect of a retirement annuity contract or a personal pension scheme or, where that scheme is intended partly to provide a capital sum to discharge a mortgage or charge secured upon the self-employed earner's home, 37.5 per centum of the contributions payable.*

    (3)   *For the purposes of sub-paragraph (2)(a) the income tax to be deducted from the [*¹⁹*...] taxable profits shall be determined in accordance with the following provisions–*

    (a)   *subject to head (d), an amount of earnings [*¹⁴*calculated as if it were equivalent to any personal allowance which would be] applicable to the earner by virtue of the provisions of Chapter 1 of Part VII of the Income and Corporation Taxes Act 1988 (personal reliefs) shall be disregarded;*

    (b)   *subject to head (c), an amount equivalent to income tax shall be calculated in relation to the earnings remaining following the application of head(a) (the "remaining earnings");*

    (c)   *the tax rate applicable at the effective date shall be applied to all the remaining earnings,, where necessary increasing or reducing the amount payable to take account of the fact that the earnings relate to a period greater or less than one year;*

    (d)   *the amount to be disregarded by virtue of head (a) shall be calculated by reference to the yearly rate applicable at the effective date, that amount being reduced or increased in the same proportion to that which the period represented by the taxable profits bears to the period of one year.*

    (4)   *For the purposes of sub-paragraph (2)(b) above, the amount to be deducted in respect of National Insurance Contributions shall be the total of–*

    (a)   *the amount of Class 2 contributions (if any) payable under section 11(1) or, as the case may be, (3), of the Contributions and Benefits Act; and*

    (b)   *the amount of Class 4 Contributions (if any) payable under section 15(2) of that Act, at the rates applicable at the effective date.*

    [¹⁹*(5)   For the purposes of this paragraph, "taxable profits" means profits calculated in accordance with Part 2 of the Income Tax (Trading and Other Income) Act 2005.*

    (6)   *A self-employed earner who is a person with care or an absent parent shall provide to the Secretary of State on demand a copy of–*

    (a)   *any tax calculation notice issued to him by Her Majesty's Revenue and Customs; and*

    (b)   *any revised notice issued to him by Her Majesty's Revenue and Customs.]*

    2B.   [¹⁹*...]*

[¹⁹**2C.**   *Where the Secretary of State accepts that it is not reasonably practicable for a self-employed earner to provide any of the information specified in paragraph 2A(6), "earnings" in relation to that earner shall be calculated in accordance with paragraph 3.]]*

3.–*(1)   [⁸Where paragraph 2C applies and subject] to sub-paragraphs (2) and (3) and to paragraph 4, "earnings" in the case of employment as a self-employed earner means the gross receipts of the employment including, where an allowance in the form of periodic payments is paid under section 2 of the Employment and Training Act 1973 or section 2 of the Enterprise and New Towns (Scotland) Act 1990 in respect of the relevant week for the purpose of assisting him in carrying on his business, the total of those payments made during the period by reference to which his earnings are determined under paragraph 5.*

(2)   *Earnings shall not include–*

(a)   *any allowance paid under either of those sections in respect of any part of the period by reference to which his earnings are determined under paragraph 5 if no part of that allowance is paid in respect of the relevant week;*

(b)   *any income consisting of payments received for the provision of board and lodging accommodation unless such payments from the largest element of the recipient's income.*

(3)   *[¹Subject to sub-paragraph (7),] there shall be deducted from the gross receipts referred to in sub-paragraph (1)–*

(a)   *[¹except in a case to which paragraph 4 applies,] any expenses which are reasonably incurred and are wholly and exclusively defrayed for the purposes of the earner's business in the period by reference to which his earnings are determined under paragraph 5(1) or, where paragraph 5(2) applies, any such expenses relevant to the period there mentioned (whether or not defrayed in that period);*

(b)   *[¹except in a case to which paragraph 4 [²or 5(2)applies,] any value added tax paid in the period by reference to which earnings are determined in excess of value added tax received in that period;*

(c)   *any amount in respect of income tax determined in accordance with sub-paragraph (5);*

(d)   *any amount in respect of National Insurance contributions determined in accordance with sub-paragraph (6);*

(e)   *one half of any premium paid in respect of a retirement annuity contract or a personal pension scheme[², or, where that scheme is intended partly to provide a capital sum to discharge a mortgage or charge secured upon the parent's home, 37.5 per centum of the contributions payable].*

(4)   *For the purposes of sub-paragraph (3)(a)–*

(a)   *such expenses include–*

(i)   *repayment of capital on any loan used for the replacement, in the course of business, of equipment or machinery, or the repair of an existing business asset except to the extent that any sum is payable under an insurance policy for its repair;*

(ii)   *any income expended in the repair of an existing business asset except to the extent that any sum is payable under an insurance policy for its repair;*

(iii)   *any payment of interest on a loan taken out for the purposes of the business;*

(b)   *such expenses do not include–*

(i)   *[¹⁹...];*

(ii)   *any capital expenditure;*

(iii)   *[¹⁹...];*

(iv)   *[¹⁹...];*

(v)   *[¹⁹...];*

(vi)   *any expenses incurred in providing business entertainment;*

(vii)   *[¹⁹...].*

[⁶*(5)   For the purposes of sub-paragraph (3)(c), the amount in respect of income tax shall be determined in accordance with the following provisions–*

(a)   *subject to head (c), an amount of chargeable earnings [¹⁴calculated as if it were equivalent to any personal allowance which would be] applicable to the earner by virtue of the provisions of Chapter 1 of Part VII of the Income and Corporate Taxes Act 1988 (Personal Relief) shall be disregarded;*

(b)   *[⁷subject to head (bb),] an amount equivalent to income tax shall be calculated with respect to taxable earnings at the rates applicable at the effective date;*

[⁷*(bb)   where taxable earnings are determined over a period of less or more than one year, the amount of earnings to which each tax rate applies shall be reduced or increased in the same proportion to that which the period represented by the chargeable earnings bears to the period of one year;]*

(c)   *the amount to be disregarded by virtue of head (a) shall be calculated by reference to the yearly rate applicable at the effective date, that amount being reduced or increased in the same proportion to that which the period represented by chargeable earnings bears to the period of one year;*

(d)   *in this sub-paragraph, "taxable earnings" means the chargeable earnings of the earner following the disregard of any applicable personal allowance.]*

(6)   *For the purposes of sub-paragraph (3)(d), the amount to be deducted in respect of National Insurance contributions shall be the total of–*

(a)   *the amount of Class 2 contributions (if any) payable under section 11(1) or, as the case may be, [²(3)] of the Contributions and Benefits Act; and*

(b)   *the amount of Class 4 contributions (if any) payable under section 15(2) of that Act,*

at the rates applicable [¹to the chargeable earnings] at the effective date.

[²(7)   In the case of a self-employed earner whose employment is carried on in partnership or is that of a share fisherman within the meaning of the Social Security (Mariners' Benefits) Regulations 1975, sub-paragraph (3) shall have effect as though it requires–

(a)   a deduction from the earner's estimated or, where appropriate, actual share of the gross receipts of the partnership or fishing boat, of his share of the sums likely to be deducted or, where appropriate, deducted from those gross receipts under heads (a) and (b) of that sub-paragraph; and

(b)   a deduction from the amount so calculated of the sums mentioned in heads (c) to (e) of that sub-paragraph.]

[¹(8)   In sub-paragraphs (5) and (6) "chargeable earnings" means the gross re-receipts of the employment less any deductions mentioned in sub-paragraph (3)(a) and (b).]

4.   In a case where a person is self-employed as a childminder the amount of earnings referable to that employment shall be one-third of the gross receipts.

5.–(1)   Subject to sub-paragraphs [²(2) to (3)]–

(a)   where a person has been a self-employed earner for 52 weeks or more including the relevant week, the amount of his earnings shall be determined by reference to the average of the earnings which he has received in the 52 weeks ending with the relevant week;

(b)   where the person has been a self-employed earner for a period of less than 52 weeks including the relevant week, the amount of his earnings shall be determined by reference to the average of the earnings which he has received during that period.

(2)   [²Subject to sub-paragraph (2A), where] a person who is a self-employed earner provides in respect of the employment a profit and loss account and, where appropriate, a trading account or a balance sheet or both, and the profit and loss accounts in respect of a period at least 6 months but not exceeding 15 months and that period terminates within the [²24 months] immediately preceding the effective date, the amount of his earnings shall be determined by reference to the average of the earnings over the period to which the profit and loss account relates and such earnings shall include receipts relevant to that period (whether or not received in that period).

[²(2A)   Where the [¹⁰Secretary of State] is satisfied that, in relation to the person referred to in sub-paragraph (2) there is more than one profit and loss account, each in respect of different periods, both or all of which satisfy the conditions mentioned in that sub-paragraph, the provisions of that sub-paragraph shall apply only to the account which relates to the latest such period, unless [¹⁰the Secretary of State] is satisfied that the latest such account is not available for reasons beyond the control of that person, in which case he may have regard to any such other account which satisfies the requirements of that sub-paragraph.]

(3)   Where a calculation would, but for this sub-paragraph, produce an amount which, in the opinion of the [¹⁰Secretary of State] , does not accurately reflect the normal amount of the earnings of the person in question, such earnings, or any part of them, shall be calculated by reference to such other period as may, in the particular case, enable the normal weekly earnings of that person to be determined more accurately and for this purpose the [¹⁰Secretary of State] shall have regard to–

(a)   the earnings received, or due to be received, from any employment in which the person in question is engaged, or has been engaged or is due to be engaged;

(b)   the duration and pattern, or the expected duration and pattern, of any employment of that person.

(4)   In sub-paragraph (2)–

(a)   "balance sheet" means a statement of the financial position of the employment disclosing its assets, liabilities and capital at the end of the period in question;

(b)   "profit and loss account" means a financial statement showing net profit or loss of the employment for the period in question; and

(c)   "trading account" means a financial statement showing the revenue from sales, the cost of those sales and the gross profit arising during the period in question.

[⁶(5)   Subject to sub-paragraph (3), where a person has claimed, or has been paid, [¹¹[¹²working tax credit or child tax credit]] on a day during the period beginning not earlier than eight weeks before the relevant week and ending not later than the date on which the assessment is made, the [¹⁰Secretary of State] may have regard to the amount of earnings taken into account in determining entitlement to those benefits in order to calculate or estimate the amount of earnings to be taken into account for the purposes of calculating N and M, notwithstanding the fact that entitlement to those benefits may have been determined by reference to earnings attributable to a period other than that specified in sub-paragraph (1).]

[⁸(6)   This paragraph applies only where the earnings of a self-employed earner have the meaning given by paragraph 3 of this Schedule.

5A.–(1)   Subject to sub-paragraph (2) of this paragraph, the earnings of a self-employed earner may be determined in accordance with the provisions of paragraph 2A only where the [¹⁹...] taxable profits concerned relate to a period of not less than 6, and not more than 15 months, which terminated not more than 24 months prior to the relevant week;

(2)   Where there is more than one week [¹⁹...] taxable profit figure which would satisfy the conditions set out in sub-paragraph (1), the earnings calculation shall be based upon the figure pertaining to the latest such period;

(3)   [¹⁹...]]

[²¹*Chapter 3*
Estimate of earnings where insufficient information available

5B.–*(1)* *Where the [²²Secretary of State] is calculating earnings of an employed earner or a self-employed earner under Part 1 of Schedule 1 and the information available in relation to those earnings is insufficient or unreliable, the [²²Secretary of State] may estimate those earnings and, in doing so, may make any assumptions as to any fact.*

(2) *Where the [²²Secretary of State] is satisfied that the person is engaged in a particular occupation, whether as an employee or a self-employed person, the assumptions referred to in sub-paragraph (1) may include an assumption that the person has the average weekly earnings of a person engaged in that occupation in the United Kingdom or in any part of the United Kingdom.]*

PART II
BENEFIT PAYMENTS

6.–*(1)* *The benefit payments to be taken into account in calculating or estimating N and M shall be determined in accordance with this Part.*

(2) *"Benefit payments" means any benefit payments under the Contributions and Benefits Act [³[²⁰, the Jobseekers Act or the Welfare Reform Act]] except amounts to be disregarded by virtue of Schedule 2.*

(3) *The amount of any benefit payment to be taken into account shall be determined by reference to the rate of that benefit applicable at the effective date.*

7.–*(1)* *Where a benefit payment under the Contributions and Benefits Act includes an adult or child dependency increase–*

(a) *if that benefit is payable to a parent, the income of that parent shall be calculated or estimated as if it did not include that amount;*

(b) *if that benefit is payable to some other person but includes an amount in respect of the parent, the income of the parent shall be calculated or estimated as if it included that amount.*

[³*(1A)* *For the purposes of sub-paragraph (1), an addition to a contribution-based jobseeker's allowance under [⁹regulation 10(4)] of the Jobseekers's Allowance (Transitional Provisions) Regulations [⁹1996] shall be treated as a dependency increase included with a benefit under the Contributions and Benefits Act.]*

(2) [¹²...]

(3) [¹²...]

(4) [¹²...]

(5) [¹²...]

[⁴*(6)* *Where child benefit in respect of a relevant child is in payment at the rate specified in regulation 2(1)(a)(ii) of the Child Benefit Rates Regulations, the difference between that rate and the basic rate applicable to that child, as defined in regulation 4.]*

PART III
OTHER INCOME

8. *The amount of the other income to be taken into account in calculating or estimating N and M shall be the aggregate of the following amounts determined in accordance with this Part.*

9. *Any periodic payment of pension or other benefit under an occupational or personal pension scheme or a retirement annuity contract or other such scheme for the provision of income in retirement.*

[⁹**9A.**–*(1)* *Where a war disablement pension includes an adult or child dependency increase–*

(a) *if that pension, including the dependency increase, is payable to a parent, the income of that parent shall be calculated or estimated as if it did not include that amount;*

(b) *if that pension, including the dependency increase, is payable to some other person but includes an amount in respect of the parent, the income of the parent shall be calculated or estimated as if it included that amount.*

(2) *For the purposes of this paragraph, a "war disablement pension" includes [¹⁸a war widow's pension, a war widower's pension and a surviving civil partner's war pension], a payment made to compensate for non-payment of such a pension, and a pension or payment analogous to such a pension or payment paid by the government of a country outside Great Britain.]*

10. *Any payment received on account of the provision of board and lodging which does not come within Part I of this Schedule.*

11. *Subject to regulation 7(3)(b) and paragraph 12, any payment to a student of–*

(a) *grant;*

(b) *an amount in respect of grant contribution;*

(c) *covenant income except to the extent that it has been taken into account under sub-paragraph (b);*

(d) *a student loan.*

12. *The income of student shall not include any payment–*

(a) *intended to meet tuition fees or examination fees;*

(b) *intended to meet additional expenditure incurred by disabled student in respect of his attendance on a course;*

(c) *intended to meet additional expenditure connected with term time residential study away from the student's educational establishment;*

    (d)   *on account of the student maintaining a home at a place other than that at which he resides during his course;*

    (e)   *intended to meet the cost of books, and equipment (other than special equipment) or, if not so intended, an amount equal to the amount allowed under [¹²regulation 62(2A)(b) of the Income Support (General) Regulations 1987 towards such costs;]*

    (f)   *intended to meet travel expenses incurred as a result of his attendance on the course.*

13.   *Any interest, dividend or other income derived from capital.*

14.   *Any maintenance payments in respect of a parent.*

[⁵14A.–(1)   Subject to sub-paragraph (2), the amount of any earnings top-up paid to or in respect of the absent parent or the parent with care.

    (2)   *Subject to sub-paragraphs (3) and (4), where earnings top-up is payable and the amount which is payable has been calculated by reference to the weekly earnings of either the absent parent and another person or the parent with care and another person–*

    (a)   *if during the period which is used to calculate his earnings under paragraph 2 or, as the case may be, paragraph 5, the normal weekly earnings of that parent exceed those of the other person, the amount payable by way of earnings top-up shall be treated as the income of that parent;*

    (b)   *if during that period, the normal weekly earnings of that parent equal those of the other person, half of the amount payable by way of earnings top-up shall be treated as the income of that parent;*

    (c)   *if during that period, the normal weekly earnings of that parent are less than those of that other person, the amount payable by way of earnings top-up shall both be treated as the income of that parent.*

    (3)   *Where any earnings top-up is in payment and, not later than the effective date, the person, or, if more than one, each of the persons by reference to whose engagement and normal engagement in remunerative work that payment has been calculated is no longer the partner of the person to whom the payment is made, the payment in question shall be treated as the income of the parent in question only where that parent is in receipt of it.*

    (4)   *Where earnings top-up is in payment and, not later that the effective date, either or both of the persons by reference to whose engagement and normal engagement in remunerative work that payment has been calculated has ceased to be employed, half of the amount payable by way of earnings top-up shall be treated as the income of the parent in question.]*

[¹²14B.–(1)   Subject to sub-paragraph (2), payments to a person of working tax credit shall be treated as the income of the parent who has qualified for them by his normal engagement in remunerative work at the rate payable at the effective date.

    (2)   *Where working tax credit is payable and the amount which is payable has been calculated by reference to the earnings of the absent parent and another person–*

    (a)   *if during the period which is used to calculate his earnings under paragraph 2 or, as the case may be, paragraph 5, the normal weekly earnings of that parent exceed those of the other person, the amount payable by way of working tax credit shall be treated as the income of that parent;*

    (b)   *if during that period the normal weekly earnings of that parent equal those of the other person, half of the amount payable by way of working tax credit shall be treated as the income of that parent; and*

    (c)   *if during that period the normal weekly earnings of that parent are less than those of that other person, the amount payable by way of working tax credit shall not be treated as the income of that parent.]*

15.   *Any other payments or other amounts received on a periodical basis which are not otherwise taken into account under Part I, II, IV or V of this Schedule [⁷except payments or other amounts which*

    (a)   *are excluded from the definition of "earnings" by virtue of paragraph 1(2);*

    (b)   *are excluded from the definition of "the relevant income of a child" by virtue of paragraph 23; or*

    (c)   *are the share of housing costs attributed by virtue of paragraph (3) of regulation 15 to any former partner of the partner of the parent of the qualifying child in respect of whom the maintenance assessment is made and are paid to that parent.]*

16.–(1)   *Subject to sub-paragraphs (2) to [¹²(7)] the amount of any income to which this Part applies shall be calculated or estimated–*

    (a)   *where it has been received in respect of the whole of the period of 26 weeks which ends at the end of the relevant week, by dividing such income received in that period by 26;*

    (b)   *where it has been received in respect of part of the period of 26 weeks which ends at the end of the relevant week, by dividing such income received in that period by the number of complete weeks in respect of which such income is received and for this purpose income shall be treated as received in respect of a week if it is received in respect of any day in the week in question.*

    (2)   *The amount of maintenance payments made in respect of a parent–*

    (a)   *where they are payable weekly and have been paid at the same amount in respect of each week in the period of 13 weeks which ends at the end of the relevant week, shall be the amount equal to one of those payments;*

    (b)   *in any other case, shall be the amount calculated by aggregating the total amount of those payments received in the period of 13 weeks which ends at the end of the relevant week and dividing by the number of weeks in that period in respect of which maintenance was due.*

    (3)   *In the case of a student–*

(a)   the amount of any grant and any amount paid in respect of grant contribution shall be calculated by apportioning it equally between the weeks in respect of which it is payable;

(b)   the amount of any covenant income shall be calculated by dividing the amount payable in respect of a year by 52 (or, where such amount is payable in respect of a lesser period, by the number of complete weeks in that period) and, subject to sub-paragraph (4), deducting £5.00;

(c)   the amount of any student loan shall be calculated by apportioning the loan equally between the weeks in respect of which it is payable and, subject to sub-paragraph (4), deducting £10.00.

(4)   For the purposes of sub-paragraph (3)–

(a)   not more than £5.00 shall be deducted under sub-paragraph (3)(b);

(b)   not more than £10.00 in total shall be deducted under sub-paragraphs (3)(b) and (c).

(5)   Where in respect of the period of 52 weeks which ends at the end of the relevant week a person is in receipt of interest, dividend or other income which has been reproduced by his capital, the amount of that income shall be calculated by dividing the aggregate of the income so received by 52.

(6)   Where a calculation would, but for this sub-paragraph, produce an amount which, in the opinion of the [¹⁰Secretary of State], does not accurately reflect the normal amount of the other income of the person in question, such income, or any part of it, shall be calculated by&reference to such other period as may, in the particular case, enable the other income of that person to be determined more accurately and for this purpose the [¹⁰Secretary of State] shall have regard to the nature and pattern of receipt of such income.

[¹²(7)   This paragraph shall not apply to payments of working tax credit referred to in paragraph 14B.]

PART IV
INCOME OF CHILD TREATED AS INCOME OF PARENT

17.   The amount of any income of a child which is to be treated as the income of the parent in calculating or estimating N and M shall be the aggregate of the amounts determined in accordance with this Part.

18.   Where a child has income which falls within the following paragraphs of this Part and that child is a member of the family of his parent (whether that child is a qualifying child in relation to that parent or not), the relevant income of that child shall be treated as that of his parent.

19.   Where child support maintenance is being assessed for the support of only one qualifying child, the relevant income of that child shall be treated as that of the parent with care.

20.   Where child support maintenance is being assessed to support more than one qualifying child, the relevant income of each of those children shall be treated as that of the parent with care to the extent that it does not exceed the aggregate of–

(a)   the amount determined under–

    (i)   regulation 3(1)(a) (calculation of AG) in relation to the child in question; and

    (ii)   the total of any other amounts determined under regulation 3(1)(b) [⁴and c] which are applicable in the case in question divided by the number of children for whom child support maintenance is being calculated,

    less the basic rate of child benefit (within the meaning for regulation 4) for the child in question; and

(b)   [²one-and-a-half times] the total of the amounts calculated under regulation 3(1)(a) (income support personal allowance for child or young person) in respect of that child and regulation [⁷3(1)(c)] (income support family premium).

21.   Where child support maintenance is not being assessed for the support of the child whose income is being calculated or estimated, the relevant income of that child shall be treated as that of this parent to the extent that it does not exceed the amount determined under regulation 9(1)(g).

22.–[³(1)]   Where a benefit under the Contributions and Benefits Act includes an adult or child dependency increase in respect of a relevant child, the relevant income of that child shall be calculated or estimated as if it included that amount.

[³(1A)   For the purposes of sub-paragraph (1), an addition to a contribution-based jobseeker's allowance under [⁹regulation 10(4)] of the Jobseeker's Allowance (Transitional Provisions) Regulation [⁹1996] shall be treated as a dependency increase included with a benefit under the Contributions and Benefits Act.]

[⁹(1B).–(1)   Where a war disablement pension includes a dependency allowance paid in respect of a relevant child, the relevant income of that child shall be calculated or estimated as if it included that amount.

(2)   For the purposes of this paragraph, a "war disablement pension" includes [¹⁸a war widow's pension, a war widower's pension and a surviving civil partner's war pension], a payment made to compensate for non-payment of such a pension, and a pension or payment analogous to such a pension or payment paid by the government to a country outside Great Britain.]

23.   For the purposes of this Part, "the relevant income of a child" does not include–

(a)   any earnings of the child in question;

(b)   payments by an absent parent [⁷to] the child for whose maintenance is being assessed;

(c)   where the class of persons who are capable of benefiting from a discretionary trust include the child in question, payments from that trust except in so far as they are made to provide for food, ordinary clothing and footwear, gas, electricity or fuel charges or housing costs; or

(d)   any interest payable on arrears of child support maintenance for that child;

[²(e)   the first £10 of any other income of that child]

24.   The amount of the income of a child which is treated as the income of the parent shall be determined in the same way as if such income were the income of the parent.

PART V

AMOUNTS TREATED AS THE INCOME OF A PARENT

25.   *The amounts which fall to be treated as income of the parent in calculating or estimating N and M shall include amounts to be determined in accordance with this Part.*

26.   *Where [¹⁰the Secretary of State] is satisfied–*

(a)   *that a person has performed a service either–*

    (i)   *without receiving any remuneration in respect of it; or*

    (ii)   *for remuneration which is less than that normally paid for that service;*

(b)   *that the service in question was for the benefit of–*

    (i)   *another person who is not a member of the same family as the person in question; or*

    (ii)   *a body which is neither a charity nor a voluntary organisation;*

(c)   *that the service in question was performed for a person who, or as the case may be, a body which was able to pay remuneration at the normal rate for the service in question;*

(d)   *that the principal purpose of the person undertaking the service without receiving any or adequate remuneration is to reduce his assessable income for the purposes of the Act; and*

(e)   *that any remuneration foregone would have fallen to be taken into account as earnings,*

    the value of the remuneration foregone shall be estimated by [¹⁰the Secretary of State] and an amount equal to the value so estimated shall be treated as income of the person who performed those services.

27.   *Subject to paragraphs 28 to 30, where the [¹⁰Secretary of State] is satisfied that, otherwise than in the circumstances set out in paragraph 26, a person has intentionally deprived himself of–*

(a)   *any income or capital which would otherwise be a source of income;*

(b)   *any income or capital which it would be reasonable to expect would be secured by him,*

with a view to reducing the amount of his assessable income, his net income shall include the amount estimated by [¹⁰the Secretary of State] as representing the income which that person would have had if he had not deprived himself of or failed to secure that income, or as the case may be, that capital.

28.   *No amount shall be treated as income by virtue of paragraph 27 in relation to–*

[⁴(a)   *if the parent satisfies the conditions for payment of the rate of child benefit specified in regulation 2(1)(a)(ii) of the Child Benefit Rates Regulations, an amount representing the difference between that rate and the basic rate, as defined in regulation 4;]*

(b)   *if the parent is a person to, or in respect of, whom income support is payable, [³a contribution-based jobseeker's allowance];*

(c)   *a payment from a discretionary trust or a trust derived from a payment made in consequence of a personal injury.*

29.   *Where an amount is included in the income of a person under paragraph 27 in respect of income which would become available to him on application, the amount included under that paragraph shall be included from the date on which it could be expected to be acquired.*

30.   *Where [¹⁰the Secretary of State] determines under paragraph 27 that a person has deprived himself of capital which would otherwise be a source of income, the amount of that capital shall be reduced at intervals of 52 weeks, starting with the week which falls 52 weeks after the first week in respect of which income from it is included in the calculation of the assessment in question, by an amount equal to the amount which the [¹⁰Secretary of State] estimates would represent the income from that source in the immediately preceding period of 52 weeks.*

31.   *Where a payment is made on behalf of a parent or a relevant child in respect of food, ordinary clothing or footwear, gas, electricity or fuel charges, housing costs or council tax, an amount equal to the amount which the [¹⁰Secretary of State] estimates represents the value of that payment shall be treated as the income of the parent in question except to the extent that such amount is–*

(a)   *disregarded under paragraph 38 of Schedule 2;*

(b)   *a payment of school fees paid by or on behalf of someone other than the absent parent.*

32.   *Where paragraph 26 applies the amount to be treated as the income of the parent shall be determined as if it were earnings from employment as an employed earner and in a case to which paragraph 27 or 31 applies the amount shall be determined as if it were other income to which Part III of this Schedule applies.*

Amendments

1.   Child Support (Miscellaneous Amendments) Regulations 1993 (SI 1993 No.913) reg 27(1), (3) and (4) (April 5, 1993).

2.   Child Support and Income Support (Amendment) Regulations 1995 (SI 1995 No.1045) reg 54(2)-(11) (April 18, 1995).

3.   Social Security and Child Support (Jobseeker's Allowance) (Consequential Amendments) Regulations 1996 (SI 1996 No.1345) regs 6(4) and (6) and 7(b) (October 7, 1996).

4.   Child Benefit, Child Support and Social Security (Miscellaneous Amendments) Regulations 1996 (SI 1996 No.1803) reg 17(2)-(4) (April 7, 1997).

5.   Child Support (Miscellaneous Amendments) Regulations 1996 (SI 1996 No.1945) reg 24(2)-(4) (October 7, 1996).

6.   *Child Support (Miscellaneous Amendments) (No.2) Regulations 1996 (SI 1996 No.3196) reg 13(2)-(5) (January 13, 1997).*
7.   *Child Support (Miscellaneous Amendments) Regulations 1998 (SI 1998 No.58) reg 56(2)-(6) (January 19, 1998).*
8.   *Child Support (Miscellaneous Amendments) Regulations 1999 (SI 1999 No.977) reg 6(5)(a)-(d) (October 4, 1999).*
9.   *Child Support (Miscellaneous Amendments) Regulations 1999 (SI 1999 No.977) reg 6(5)(e)-(h) (April 6, 1999).*
10.   *Social Security Act 1998 (Commencement No.7 and Consequential and Transitional Provisions) Order 1999 (SI 1999 No.1510) art 19 (a)-(e) (June 1, 1999).*
11.   *Social Security and Child Support (Tax Credits) Consequential Amendments Regulations 1999 (SI 1999 No.2566) Parts I and II, Sch 2 (October 5, 1999).*
12.   *Child Support (Miscellaneous Amendments) Regulations 2003 (SI 2003 No.328) reg 6(6) (April 6, 2003).*
13.   *Child Support (Miscellaneous Amendments) Regulations 2004 (SI 2004 No.2415) reg 5(2) (September 16, 2004).*
14.   *Child Support (Miscellaneous Amendments) Regulations 2005 (SI 2005 No.785) reg 4(2) (March 16, 2005).*
15.   *Child Support (Miscellaneous Amendments) (No.2) Regulations 2003 (SI 2003 No.2779) reg 4(6) (November 5, 2003).*
16.   *Fire and Rescue Services Act 2004 (Consequential Amendments) (England) Order 2004 (SI 2004 No.3168) art 28 (December 30, 2004).*
17.   *Fire (Scotland) Act 2005 (Consequential Provisions and Modifications) Order 2005 (SI 2005 No. 2060) art 3 and Sch Part 2, para 8 (August 2, 2005).*
18.   *Civil Partnership (Pensions, Social Security and Child Support) (Consequential, etc. Provisions) Order 2005 (SI 2005 No.2877) art 2(4) and Sch 4 para 2(4) (December 5, 2005).*
19.   *Child Support (Miscellaneous Amendments) Regulations 2007 (SI 2007 No.1979) reg 4 (August 1, 2007).*
20.   *Employment and Support Allowance (Consequential Provisions) (No.2) Regulations 2008 (SI 2008 No.1554) reg 58(5) (October 27, 2008).*
21.   *Child Support (Miscellaneous Amendments) Regulations 2012 (SI 2012 No.712) reg 5 (April 30, 2012).*
22.   *Public Bodies (Child Maintenance and Enforcement Commission: Abolition and Transfer of Functions) Order 2012 (SI 2012 No.2007) art 3(2) and Sch para 110 (August 1, 2012).*
23.   *Police and Fire Reform (Scotland) Act 2012 (Consequential Provisions and Modifications) Order 2013 (SI 2013 No.602) art 26 and Sch 2 Part 3 para 72 (April 1, 2013).*

Definitions

"the Act": See reg 1(2).
"child tax credit": see reg 1(2).
"Child Benefit Rates Regulations": see reg 1(2).
"Contributions and Benefits Act": see reg 1(2).
"covenant income": see reg 1(2).
"earnings": see reg 1(2).
"earnings top-up": see reg 1(2).
"effective date": see reg 1(2).
"employed earner": see reg 1(2).
"family": see reg 1(2).
"grant": see reg 1(2).
"grant contribution": see reg 1(2).
"Maintenance Assessment Procedure Regulations": see reg 1(2).
"the Jobseekers Act": see reg 1(2).
"occupational pension scheme": see reg 1(2).
"parent with care": see reg 1(2).
"partner": see reg 1(2).
"person": see reg 1(2).
"personal pension scheme": see reg 1(2).
"profit-related pay": see reg 1(2).
"relevant week": see reg 1(2).
"retirement annuity contract": see reg 1(2).
"self-employed earner": see reg 1(2).
"student": see reg 1(2).
"student loan": see reg 1(2).
"working tax credit": see reg 1(2).
"year": see reg 1(2).

General Note

Paragraph 6

The amount of a benefit payment is the amount actually received, not the amount that should have been paid if entitlement had been correctly determined (*CCS 1039/1997*, paras 12-13). Subparagraph (3) identifies the date on which the amount of the payment to be taken into account is determined. If it is later decided that the amount should not have been paid, that cannot alter the fact that at that date that was the amount in payment (*ibid*, para 14).

Paragraph 9

In *R(CS) 2/00*, the commissioner decided that payments of an injury pension paid to a firefighter following an injury on duty come within this paragraph and are not disregarded under Sch 2 para 5. An appeal against this decision was dismissed by the Court of Appeal in *Wakefield v Secretary of State for Social Security* also reported as *R(CS) 2/00*.

Paragraph 14

Tribunals should make adequate findings of fact to indicate whether maintenance is paid as spousal maintenance to the parent with care or maintenance for the qualifying child (*R2/96 (CSC)*, paras 5 and 13). Clearly child support maintenance payments do not fall within this paragraph as they are defined by s1(2) of the Act as being payments with respect to the child rather than the parent.

In *CCS 13698/1996* (paras 11-12) and *CCS 13923/1996* (para 8), it was held that this paragraph did not apply to maintenance paid by the absent parent to the parent with care or vice versa and that a similar qualification was to be implied elsewhere in the Schedule with no distinction being drawn between one parent paying cash to the other and one parent settling a liability of the other. On this view, this paragraph only covers payments of maintenance by a person who is not a parent of the qualifying child. There was unanimity among the commissioners that these two decisions should not be reported.

Paragraph 15

In the case of rental income, the only amounts that may be deducted from the gross rental income are those authorised by Sch 2, especially para 23 (*R(CS) 3/00*, para 23).

It is suggested that this paragraph does not cover child support maintenance payments received by a parent in respect of any child, whether or not a qualifying child. See the general note to Sch 2 para 44 on p334.

Regular payments made by a person other than a parent which are intended and used for the payment of school fees are subject to a trust or equity and are not to be regarded as income of either parent or of the child (*CCS 15/1994*, paras 6-8).

Paragraphs 17-24

These paragraphs provide for income of a child who is living as member of a parent's family to be treated as income of a parent. First it is necessary to identify the child's income. This is done on normal principles. Where benefit is paid (to whom is not specified) which includes an increase in respect of the child, this is counted as the child's income (para 22). Certain items of income are then disregarded under para 23. The overall result is the relevant income of the child. The amount of this income is then determined as provided in para 24. This amount is then attributed by virtue of para 18 to the parent who is identified under paras 19-21, subject to any limits set therein. In the case of the income of a qualifying child, the income is attributed to the parent with care (paras 19-20). This provision is necessary as, where each parent has day to day care of the child, the child will be a member of the family of each.

It is suggested that any income of a child which derives from the parent with care should be disregarded. If it is not the following anomaly can result. Imagine that a parent with care earns a low wage and pays the qualifying child £15 a week pocket money. £10 of that is disregarded under para 23(e). This leaves £5 which is treated as the income of the parent with care. However, if this £5 is so treated, the parent with care will have that sum double counted in the assessable income calculation.

Paragraph 22

The amendments to this paragraph have been appallingly drafted. Original there were no subparagraphs. Then the original paragraph was numbered as subpara (1) and subpara (1A) added. Why was it not numbered (2)? Then the rest was added. The obvious intention was to add subparas (1B) and (2), but that is not how they were numbered in the amending legislation. A superfluous "22" was included for some reason and there seems no reason why subpara (1B) could not be numbered as (2) and subpara (2) as (3). Be that as it may, the legislation as printed is as set out in the amending legislation.

Paragraph 23

All payments by a non-resident parent to the child are disregarded under head (b). Previously all payments "in respect of" the child were disregarded. This would include child support maintenance, which by virtue of s1(2) of the Act is defined as being paid with respect to the child. It would also include any other payments in respect of the child such as those which are covered by para 31. If payments covered by para 31 were not excluded by this head, they would be double counted. If the non-resident parent paid pocket money to a qualifying child, in so far as it was not disregarded under para 23(e), it would be treated as income of the parent with care. Where the person with care was treated as having no assessable income (because the person is not a parent of the child or because the person is in receipt of a relevant benefit under Sch 1 para 5(4) to the Act), the pocket money could not be taken into account under the formula assessment and could only be taken into account in reduction of money owed by the non-resident parent (*R(CS) 9/98*, para 9).

Paragraphs 25-32

These paragraphs only apply to amounts that would not otherwise be treated as income (*CCS 318/1998*, para 26).

Paragraph 26

Tribunals in particular need to pay careful attention to the following points.

(i)   The precise nature of the service needs to be identified. Until this has been done it is impossible to decide the normal rate for the service. Merely identifying a job by a title such as 'shop assistant' will often be insufficient since there will be a range of work and of remuneration associated with such broad descriptions.

(ii)   Evidence will be needed of the normal rate for the services identified. This will need to be examined to ensure that it relates to work of the same description as that performed by the person. Again reliance on job titles may mislead.

(iii)   The paragraph presupposes that the services are such that there is a normal rate for them. This gives rise to a number of problems. The first is that there will often not be a rate for a particular job but a range of payments. Actual payment will depend on a number of factors. The service performed will be one, but others will include the locality where the work is undertaken, the state of the job market at the time, the employee's qualifications and experience, and the ability of the employer to pay. The emphasis in this paragraph is on remuneration that has been foregone and that will require all factors relevant to the level of that remuneration to be considered. Second, it may well be that, quite apart from the matters just considered, there is a range of payments for the work with some employers paying better than others. If the payment falls outside that range there will be no difficulty in applying subpara (a)(ii), although the possible application of subpara (c) will then have to be considered. Otherwise an estimate will have to be made of the payment which the employer in question was likely to make. A third problem is that the services may be unique – eg, a person may be assisting in the running of a business by performing a combination of duties which do not correspond to any single job in the job market. In such a case the tribunal must undertake a more hypothetical exercise and attribute an appropriate income to the work. The alternative approach would be to hold that if there is no equivalent job with which to compare the work in question, the paragraph does not apply and no earnings are attributed to the person in respect of it. This approach cannot be right; it amounts to saying that the more unique and therefore in a sense the more valuable the work to an employer, the less likely it is that earnings will be attributed in respect of it.

(iv)   It is essential to establish that the principal purpose of undertaking the service without appropriate remuneration is to reduce the person's assessable income. This is a subjective test. This was discussed by the commissioner in *CCS 3675/2004*. He emphasised that the issue was the purpose of the parent's actions, not their effect (paras 19 and 23). He decided that the test is whether the parent's principal purpose was to reduce income that would otherwise have been taken into account in determining assessable income (para 24). It is not necessary that the parent's purpose must be directed, principally or even at all, to the child support scheme.

Income which falls within this paragraph is treated as other income to which Part III of this Schedule applies (para 32).

Where a person is paid wholly or partly in kind, the value of the payment in kind is disregarded in deciding whether s/he has been paid less than the amount normally paid for the service provided (*CIS 11482/1995*, paras 11-12). Where there has been a payment partly in kind and partly in cash, it is clear from the wording of this paragraph that only the value of the remuneration foregone is to be attributed to the person concerned. In other words, the value of the cash payment is taken into account as actual earnings and the remuneration forgone is added to it. The wording of this paragraph avoids the contortions of interpretation and application that were found necessary in such circumstances on the wording of the income support provision in *CIS 11482/1995*.

In *CCS 4912/1998*, the commissioner interpreted this paragraph broadly and controversially, producing the same effect as if the veil of incorporation had been lifted from a personal service company. The same result can be achieved more satisfactorily by using a departure direction under reg 24 of the Departure Direction Regulations on the basis of diversion of income or under reg 25 of those Regulations on the basis of lifestyle inconsistent with declared income.

Paragraph 27

This paragraph is the companion to para 26. It deals with disposals of, and failures to obtain, income or income-earning capital whereas para 26 deals with services. Paragraph 27 is unhappily worded. At one point it refers to the intentional deprivation of something a person has never had. The wording used later in the paragraph is better in referring to deprivation or failure to secure.

Subparagraph (a) applies where a person has had income or capital but no longer has it. It only deals with deprivation of income or capital. It is for the person to prove that the income or capital has been disposed of (*R(SB) 38/85*, para 18). If this cannot be proved the person must be taken as still in possession of the income or capital. No question of applying this paragraph then arises and the person will be unable to claim any benefit that might otherwise be derived from para 30. If deprivation is proved, it is necessary to investigate whether it was done intentionally with a view to reducing assessable income. The test is a subjective one, although the reasonableness of a person's action will be a relevant factor in assessing any evidence by that person on the reasons for so acting. Usually the tribunal will have to infer the purpose for the deprivation (see the general note to para 26 on inferences of intention). A person is deprived of capital even if it is replaced by something else (*R(SB) 40/85*, para 8). So a person who spends money on the purchase of an item of equal value is still deprived of that money. However, the fact that something is acquired in exchange will be relevant to the question whether the deprivation was effected with a view to reducing the assessable income. Since there is no discretion in this paragraph, it is only through this reasoning that the expenditure of capital on the purchase of non-income producing assets can escape this paragraph. If an income producing resource is disposed of and replaced by a lower income producing resource, it will be possible to apply this paragraph to the difference.

Subparagraph (b) applies where a person has never had the income or capital in question but has failed to secure it in circumstances in which it would be reasonable to expect that it would be secured. Whether securing the income or capital was to be expected is an objective consideration, but it is still necessary to establish an intention to deprive with a view to reducing assessable income. The application of this paragraph will give rise to difficult decisions for tribunals. Some cases of failure to secure income will be relatively straightforward: the person may have failed to cash a cheque (*CSB 598/1989*, para 11), to claim a benefit (subject to para 28) or to put money in an account bearing as high a rate of interest as possible. In other cases detailed consideration of evidence will be needed before a tribunal can decide whether it was reasonable to expect the income to be secured. For example, a dividend may not have been declared by a company in which a person has an interest. It is obvious that a dividend should have been declared if that person had such control over the company as to be able to determine or influence the dividend provided that it would be appropriate to declare a dividend given the financial position and the plans of the company. Evidence on each of these matters will need to be considered. Yet other cases will present difficult decisions on how far a person can be expected to act in securing income – eg, the chances of a person securing a particular job or type of job. Decisions on failure to secure capital will almost always be difficult. Capital here must mean capital which produces income. A person with sufficient cash may be expected to subscribe to a rights issue, but a tribunal cannot be expected to decide which shares a stock market investor could reasonably be expected to purchase. Moreover, the concern with this paragraph is with income which will be derived from the capital that should have been secured. There will, however, often be a risk attached to capital investment and this will need to be taken into account in deciding whether or not it was reasonable to expect a particular investment to be secured. In practice it is unlikely that a tribunal will be willing to second-guess investment decisions even with the benefit of hindsight except in blatant cases.

In contrast to para 26, it is only necessary to establish that the deprivation or failure to secure was "with a view to" reducing assessable income. It is not necessary to show that this was its principal purpose. It may therefore be possible to catch cases under this paragraph which fail to satisfy the principal purpose test for para 26. The Upper Tribunal undertook a detailed analysis of the meaning of "with a view to" in *AC v CMEC* [2009] UKUT 152 (AAC); [2011] AACR 25. The judge concluded that the dominant purpose test (used in bankruptcy law) did not apply and that the test was whether the parent had the reduction of assessable income as an operative purpose. This approach was approved in *GR v CMEC (CSM)* [2010] UKUT 436 (AAC).

Income attributed under this paragraph is part of the parent's net income and is treated as other income to which Part III of this Schedule applies (para 32). Net income is calculated under regs 7 and 8. It includes income determined in accordance with Part III. It excludes any amount specified in Sch 2 and para 2. It follows that income tax should be deducted from the income attributed (*GR v CMEC (CSM)*). This makes sense, as income tax would be deducted if the income were actually received. See *CCS 185/2005*, para 15.

In *CCS 4912/1998*, the commissioner interpreted this paragraph broadly and controversially, producing the same effect as if the veil of incorporation had been lifted from a personal service company. The same result can be achieved more satisfactorily by using a departure direction under reg 24 of the Departure Direction Regulations on the basis of diversion of income or under reg 25 of those Regulations on the basis of lifestyle inconsistent with declared income.

In *CCS 2678/2007*, the commissioner decided that this paragraph could apply to failures to secure employment or self-employment. Any uncertainty in the availability of work would be relevant to the parent's motivation or purpose.

Paragraph 28(c)

Personal injury in the form of a disease also covers injuries as a result of the disease – eg, an amputation necessary as a result of contracting meningitis and septicaemia (*R(SB) 2/89*, para 15). The key factor is the nature of the injury and not the particular loss for which the income from the trust is compensation. It would therefore cover financial loss as a result of an injury (such as loss of earnings) as much as the loss of amenity or the pain and suffering associated with the injury.

Paragraph 31

This provision only applies where a payment is made on behalf of a parent or child. It does not, therefore, cover cases where an item is bought by one parent as a present for a child or out of a sense of responsibility. It is not sufficient that the payment should be for the benefit of the parent or child. There must be evidence which shows that the purchase was on behalf of the other parent or child. This evidence might take the form of a request that the item be purchased. The most obvious cases where this provision will apply are those where the clear legal responsibility is that of the parent with care (eg, to pay rent or an electricity bill), but payment is made by someone else such as a former partner under a divorce settlement or by a grandparent.

The treatment of payment by one parent of the housing costs in respect of the home occupied by the other but for which both are liable is unclear. According to *CSCS 8/1995* (para 16) and *CCS 8189/1995* (para 9) the amount by which the payment exceeds that person's share of the housing costs falls to be treated as income under this paragraph. However, in *CCS 13698/1996* (paras 11-12) the commissioner decided that payments of maintenance by the absent parent to the parent with care fell outside Sch 1, even though the result is to render the concluding words of head (b) *otiose*. Accordingly, payments by the non-resident parent of the parent with care's share of the housing costs are not to be taken into account as the parent with care's income. On this view the commissioner did not have to decide whether the payments should be treated as for the joint benefit of the parent with care and the child (*ibid*, para 10). *CCS 13923/1996* (para 8) is to the same effect as *CCS 13698/1996* (paras 11-12). There was unanimity among the commissioners that these two decisions should not be reported. On housing costs, see further reg 15(3) and the general note thereto.

This paragraph first lists items of expenditure on which may be attributed to a parent, and then exempts from its scope certain payments. One of these is school fees. As this is an exemption for an item which would otherwise fall within this paragraph, the reference to school fees cannot include tuition fees, which would not fall within any of the items listed earlier. The school fees which are not to be treated as the parent's income must be those related to accommodation and board rather than tuition. The exemption does not apply when the fees are paid by the absent parent, although according to *CCS 13698/1996* (para 12) the reference to the absent parent is *otiose*.

A payment is made "on behalf of" a parent or a child if the person making payment undertakes liability as agent of the parent or child or discharges a liability of the parent or child as their agent (*CCS 1318/1997* para 16 approved in *CCS 318/1998* para 27).

SCHEDULE 2
AMOUNTS TO BE DISREGARDED WHEN CALCULATING OR ESTIMATING N
and M

1.   The amounts referred to in this Schedule are to be disregarded when calculating or estimating N and M (parent's net income).

2.   An amount in respect of income tax applicable to the income in question where not otherwise allowed for under these Regulations.

3.   Where a payment is made in a currency other than sterling, an amount equal to any banking charge or commission payable in converting that payment to sterling.

4.   Any amount payable in a country outside the United Kingdom where there is a prohibition against the transfer to the United Kingdom of that amount.

5.   Any compensation for personal injury and any payments from a trust fund set up for that purpose.

6.   Any advance of earnings or any loan made by an employer to an employee.

7.   Any payment by way of, or reduction or discharge of liability resulting from entitlement to, housing benefit [19...].

[227A.   Any payment of universal credit.]

[208.   Any disability living allowance, personal independence payment, mobility supplement [21, armed forces independence payment under the Armed Forces and Reserve Forces (Compensation Scheme) Order 2011] or any payment intended to compensate for the non-payment of any such allowance, payment or supplement.]

9.   Any payment which is–

(a)   an attendance allowance under section 64 of the Contributions and Benefits Act;

(b)   an increase of disablement pension under section 104 or 105 of that Act (increases where constant attendance needed or for exceptionally severe disablement);

(c)   a payment made under regulations made in exercise of the power conferred by Schedule 8 to that Act (payments for pre- 1948 cases);

(d)   an increase of an allowance payable in respect of constant attendance under that Schedule;

(e)   payable by virtue of articles 14,15,16, 43 or 44 of the Personal Injuries (Civilians) Scheme 1983 (allowances for constant attendance and exceptionally severe disablement and severe disablement occupational allowance) or any analogous payment; or

(f)   a payment based on the need for attendance which is paid as part of a war disablement pension.

10.   Any payment under section 148 of the Contributions and Benefits Act (pensioners' Christmas bonus).

11.   Any social fund payment within the meaning of Part VIII of the Contributions and Benefits Act.

12.   Any payment made by the Secretary of State to compensate for the loss (in whole or in part) of entitlement to housing benefit.

13.   Any payment made by the Secretary of State to compensate for loss of housing benefit supplement under regulation 19 of the Supplementary Benefit (Requirements) Regulations 1983.

14.   Any payment made by the Secretary of State to compensate a person who was entitlement to supplementary benefit in respect of a period ending immediately before 11th April 1988 but who did not become entitlement to income support in respect of a period beginning with that day.

15. Any concessionary payment made to compensate for the non-payment of income support, [¹³ state pension credit] [⁵income-based jobseeker's allowance,] disability living allowance, [²⁰personal independence payment,] [²¹armed forces independence payment under the Armed Forces and Reserve Forces (Compensation Scheme) Order 2011,] or any payment to which paragraph 9 applies.

[¹⁶**15A.** A payment made by the Secretary of State under section 2 of the Employment and Training Act 1973 by way of In-Work Credit, Better Off In-Work Credit or Return to Work Credit.]

16. Any payments of child benefit to the extent that they do not exceed the basic rate of that benefit as defined in regulation 4.

17. Any payment made under regulations 9 to 11 or 13 of the Welfare Food Regulations 1988 (payments made in place of milk tokens or the supply of vitamins).

18. Subject to paragraph 20 and to the extent that it does not exceed £10.00–

(a) war disablement pension or war widow's pension [¹³or war widower's pension] or a payment made to compensate for non-payment of such a pension;

(b) a pension paid by the government of a country outside Great Britain and which either–
    (i) is analogous to a war disablement pension; or
    (ii) is analogous to a war widow's pension [¹³or war widower's pension].

[¹²**18A.** Subject to paragraph 20, and to the extent that it does not exceed £10.00, a payment made in respect of a parent under a scheme mentioned in section 1(2) of the Armed Forces (Pensions and Compensation) Act 2004 (compensation schemes for armed and reserve forces).]

19.–(1) Except where sub-paragraph (2) applies and subject to sub-paragraph (3) and paragraphs 20,38 and 47, [⁴up to £20.00] of any charitable or voluntary payment made, or due to be made, at regular intervals.

(2) Subject to sub-paragraph (3) and paragraphs 38 and 47, any charitable or voluntary payment made or due to be made at regular intervals which is intended and used for an item other than food, ordinary clothing or footwear, gas, electricity or fuel charges, housing costs of any member of the family or the payment of council tax.

(3) Sub-paragraphs (1) and (2) shall not apply to a payment which is made by a person for the maintenance of any member of his family or of his former partner or of his children.

(4) For the purposes of sub-paragraph (1) where a number of charitable or voluntary payments fall to be taken into account they shall be treated as though they were one such payment.

20.–(1) Where, but for this paragraph, more than [⁴£20.00] would be disregarded under paragraphs [¹²18 to 19(1)] in respect of the same week, only [⁴£20.00] in aggregate shall be disregarded and where an amount falls to be deducted from the income of a student under paragraph 16(3)(b) or (c) of Schedule 1, that amount shall count as part of the [⁴£20.00] disregard allowed under this paragraph.

(2) Where any payment which is due to be paid in one week is paid in another week, sub-paragraph (1) and paragraphs [¹²18 to 19(1)] shall have effect as if that payment were received in the week in which it was due.

21. In the case of a person participating in arrangements for training made under section 2 of the Employment and Training Act 1973 or section 2 of the Enterprise and New Towns (Scotland) Act 1990 (functions in relation to training for employment etc.) or attending a course at an employment rehabilitation centre established under section 12 of the 1973 Act–

(a) any travelling expenses reimbursed to the person;
(b) any living away from home allowance under section 2(2)(d) of the 1973 Act or section 2(4)(c) of the 1990 act;
(c) any training premium,
but this paragraph, except in so far as it relates to a payment mentioned in sub-paragraph (a), (b), or (c), does not apply to any part of any allowance under section 22(d) of the 1973 Act or section 2(4)(c) of the 1990 Act.

22. Where a parent occupies a dwelling as his home and that dwelling is also occupied by a person, other than a non-dependant or a person who is provided with board and lodging accommodation, and that person is contractually liable to make payments in respect of his occupation of the dwelling to the parent, the amount or, as the case may be, the amounts specified in [⁹paragraph 19 of Schedule 9 to the Income Support (General) Regulations 1987 which would have applied if he had been in receipt of income support.]

23. Where a parent, who is not a self-employed earner, is in receipt of rent or any other money in respect of the use and occupation of property other than his home, that rent or other payment to the extent of any sums which that parent is liable to pay by way of–

[¹(a) payments which are to be taken into account as eligible housing costs under sub-paragraphs (b), (c), (d) and (t) of paragraph 1 of schedule 3 (eligible housing costs for the purposes of determining exempt income and protected income) and paragraph 3 of that Schedule (exempt income; additional provisions relating to eligible housing costs);]
(b) council tax payable in respect of that property;
(c) water and sewerage charges payable in respect of that property.

24. [²For each week in which a parent provides] board and lodging accommodation in his home otherwise than as a self-employed earner–

(a) £20.00 of any payment for that accommodation made by[², on behalf or in respect of] the person to whom that accommodation is provided; and
(b) where any such payment exceeds £20.00, 50 per centum of the excess.

25. Any payment made to a person in respect of an adopted child who is a member of his family that is made in accordance with any regulations made under section 57A or pursuant to section 57A(6) of the Adoption

Act 1976 (permitted allowances) [¹²or paragraph 3 of Schedule 4 to the Adoption and Children Act 2002] or, as the case may be, [⁸section 51A] of the Adoption (Scotland) Act 1978 (schemes for the payment of allowances to adopters) [¹⁷or in accordance with an adoption allowance scheme made under section 71 of the Adoption and Children (Scotland) Act 2007 (adoption allowances schemes)]–

    (a)   *where the child is not a child in respect of whom child support maintenance is being assessed, to the extent that it exceeds [¹the aggregate of the amounts to be taken into account in the calculation of E under regulation 9(1)(g)], reduced, as the case may be, under regulation 9(4);*

    (b)   *in any other case, to the extent that it does not exceed the amount of the income of a child which is treated as that of his parent by virtue of Part IV [⁷of Schedule 1.]*

    [¹²25A.   Any payment made to a person in accordance with regulations made pursuant to section 14F of the Children Act 1989 (special guardianship support services) in respect of a child who is a member of his family.]

    26.   *Where a local authority makes a payment in respect of the accommodation and maintenance of a child in pursuance of paragraph 15 of Schedule 1 to the Children Act 1989 (local authority contribution to child's maintenance) to the extent that it exceeds the amount referred to in [¹regulation 9(1)(g)] (reduced, as the case may be, under regulation 9(4)).*

    27.   *Any payment received under a policy of insurance taken out to insure against the risk of being unable to maintain repayments on a loan taken out to acquire an interest in, or to meet the cost of repairs or improvements to, the parent's home and used to meet such repayments, to the extent that the payment received under that policy [²exceeds] [³the total of the amount of the payments set out in paragraphs 1(b), 3(2) and (4) of Schedule 3 as modified, where applicable, by regulation 18.]*

    28.   *In the calculation of the income of the parent with care, any maintenance payments made by the absent parent in respect of his qualifying child.*

    29.   *Any payment made by a local authority to a person who is caring for a child under section 23(2)(a) of the Children Act 1989 (provision of accommodation and maintenance by a local authority for children whom the authority is looking after) or, as the case may be, section 21 of the Social Work (Scotland) Act 1968 or by a voluntary organisation under section 59(1)(a) of the Children Act authority under regulation 9 of the Boarding Out and Fostering of Children (Scotland) Regulations 1985 (provision of accommodation and maintenance for children in care).*

    30.   *Any payment made by a health authority[¹⁵, [¹⁸clinical commissioning group]], local authority or voluntary organization [¹⁸or the National Health Service Commissioning Board] in respect of a person who is not normally a member of the household but is temporarily in the care of a member of it.*

    31.   *Any payment made by a local authority under section 17 or 24 of the Children Act 1989 or, as the case may be, section 12, 24 or 26 of the Social Work (Scotland) Act 1968 (local authorities' duty to promote welfare of children and powers to grant financial assistance to persons looked after, or in, or formerly in, their care).*

    32.   *Any resettlement benefit which is paid to the parent by virtue of regulation 3 of the Social Security (Hospital In-Patients) Amendment (No. 2) Regulations 1987 (transitional provisions).*

    33.–(1)   *Any payment or repayment made–*

    (a)   *as respects England and Wales, under regulation 3,5, or 8 of the National Health Service (Travelling Expenses and Remission of Charges) Regulations 1988 (travelling expenses and health service supplies);*

    (b)   *as respects Scotland, under regulation 3, 5 or 8 of the National Health Service (Travelling Expenses and Remission of Charges) (Scotland) Regulation 1988 (travelling expenses and health service supplies).*

    (2)   *Any payment or repayment made by the Secretary of State for Health, the Secretary of State for Scotland or the Secretary of State for Wales which is analogous to a payment or repayment mentioned in sub-paragraph (1).*

    34. *Any payment made (other than a training allowance), whether by the Secretary of State or any other person, under the Disabled Persons Employment Act 1944 or in accordance with arrangements made under section 2 of the Employment and training act 1973 to assist disabled persons to obtain or retain employment despite their disability.*

    35.   *Any contribution to the expenses of maintaining a household which is made by a non-dependant member of that household.*

    36.   *Any sum in respect of a course of study attended by a child payable by virtue of regulations and under section 81 of the Education Act 1944 (assistance by means of scholarship or otherwise), or by virtue of section 2(1) of the Education Act 1962 (awards for courses of further education) or section 49 of the Education (Scotland) Act 1980 (power to assist persons to take advantage of educational facilities).*

    [¹¹36A.   Any sum in respect of financial assistance given, or given under arrangements made, by the Secretary of State (in relation to England) or the National Assembly for Wales (in relation to Wales) under section 14 of the Education Act 2002 (power of Secretary of State and National Assembly for Wales to give financial assistance for purposes related to education), to a child.]

    37.   *Where a person receives income under an annuity purchased with a loan which satisfies the following conditions–*

    (a)   *that loan was made as part of a scheme under which not less than 90 per centum of the proceeds of the loan were applied to the purchase by the person to whom it was made of an annuity ending with*

> his life or with the life of the survivor of two or more persons (in this paragraph referred to as "the annuitants" who include the person to whom the loan was made;

(b)   that the interest on the loan is payable by the person to whom it was made or by one of the annuitants;

(c)   that at the time the loan was made the person to whom it was made or each of the annuitants had attained the age of 65;

(d)   that the loan was secured on a dwelling in Great Britain and the person to whom the loan was made or one of the annuitants owns an estate or interest in that dwelling; and

(e)   that the person to whom the loan was made or one of the annuitants occupies the dwelling on which it was secured as his home at the time the interest is paid, the amount, calculated on a weekly basis equal to–

       (i)   where, or insofar as, section 26 of the Finance Act 1982 (deduction of tax for certain loan interest) applies to the payments of the interest on the loan, the interest which is payable after the deduction of a sum equal to income tax on such payments at the basis rate for the year of assessment in which the payment of interest becomes due;

       (ii)   in any other case the interest which is payable on the loan without deduction of such a sum.

38.   Any payment of the description specified in paragraph 39 of Schedule 9 to the Income Support Regulations (disregard of payments made under certain trusts and disregard of certain other payments) and any income derived from the investment of such payments.

39.   Any payment made to a juror or witness in respect of attendance at court other than compensation for loss of earnings or for loss of a benefit payable under the Contributions and Benefits Act [⁵or the Jobseekers Act].

40.   Any special war widow's payment made under–

(a)   the Naval and Marine Pay and Pensions (Special War Widows Payment) Order 1990 made under section 3 of the Naval and Marine Pay and Pensions Act 1865;

(b)   the Royal Warrant dated 19th February 1990 amending the Schedule to the Army Pensions warrant 1977;

(c)   the Queen's Order dated 26th February 1990 made under section 2 of the Air Force (Constitution) Act 1917;

(d)   the Home Guard War Widows Special Payments Regulations 1990 made under section 151 of the Reserve Forces Act 1980;

(e)   the Orders dated 19th February 1990 amending Orders made on 12th December 1980 concerning the Ulster Defence Regiment made in each case under section 140 of the Reserve Forces Act 1980,

and any analogous payment by the Secretary of State for Defence to any person who is not a person entitled under the provisions mentioned in sub-paragraphs (a) to (e).

41.   Any payment to a person as holder of the Victoria Cross or the George Cross or any analogous payment.

42.   Any payment made either by the Secretary of State for the Home Department or by the Security of State for Scotland under a scheme established to assist relatives and other persons to visit persons in custody.

43.   Any amount by way of a refund of income tax deducted from profits or emoluments chargeable to income tax under Schedule D or Schedule E.

44.   Maintenance payments (whether paid under the Act or otherwise) insofar as they are not treated as income under Part III or IV [⁷of Schedule 1.]

45.   Where following a divorce[¹⁴, dissolution of a civil partnership] or separation–

(a)   capital is divided between the parent and the person who was his partner before the divorce[14, dissolution of the civil partnership] or separation; and

(b)   that capital is intended to be used to acquire a new home for that parent or to acquire furnishing for a home of his,

income derived from the investment of that capital for one year following the date on which that capital became available to the parent.

[¹**46.**   Except in the case of a self-employed earner, payments in kind.]

47.   Any payment made by the Joseph Rowntree Memorial Trust from money provided to it by the Secretary of State for Health for the purpose of maintaining a family fund for the benefit of severely handicapped children.

48.   Any payment of expenses to a person who is–

(a)   engaged by a charitable or voluntary body; or

(b)   a volunteer,

if he otherwise derives no remuneration or profit from the body or person paying those expenses.

[¹**48A.**   Any guardian's allowance under Part III of the Contributions and Benefits Act.

48B.   Any payment in respect of duties mentioned in paragraph 1(1)(i) of Chapter I of Part I of Schedule 1 relating to a period of one year or more.]

[⁶**48C.**   Any payment to a person under section 1 of the Community Care (Direct Payments) Act 1996 or section 12B of the Social Work (Scotland) Act 1968(c) in respect of his securing community care services, as defined in section 46 of the National Health Services and Community Care Act 1990.]

[⁹**48D.**   Any payment of child tax credit.]

[¹⁰[¹³**48E.** *Any payment made by a local authority, or by the National Assembly for Wales, to a person relating to a service which is provided to develop or sustain the capacity of that person to live independently in his accommodation.]]*

[¹³**48F.** *Any supplementary pension under article 29(1A) of the Naval, Military and Air Forces etc. (Disablement and Death) Service Pensions Order 1983 (pensions to [¹⁴widows, widowers and surviving civil partners]) or under article 27(3) of the Personal Injuries (Civilians) Scheme 1983 (pensions to [¹⁴widows, widowers and surviving civil partners]).]*

49. *In this Schedule–*

"concessionary payment" means a payment made under arrangements made by the Secretary of State with the consent of the Treasury which is charged either to the National Insurance Fund or to a Departmental Expenditure Vote to which payments of benefit under the Contributions and Benefits Act [⁵or the Jobseekers Act] are charged;

"health authority" means a health authority established under the National Health Service Act 1977 or the National Health Service (Scotland) Act 1978;

"mobility supplement" has the same meaning as in regulation 2(1) of the Income Support Regulations;

"war disablement pension" and "war widow" have the same meanings as in section 150(2) of the Contributions and Benefits Act.

Amendments

1. Child Support (Miscellaneous Amendments) Regulations 1993 (SI 1993 No.913) regs 28-32 (April 5, 1993).
2. Child Support and Income Support (Amendment) Regulations 1995 (SI 1995 No.1045) reg 55(2)-(4) (April 18, 1995).
3. Child Support (Miscellaneous Amendments) (No.2) Regulations 1995 (SI 1995 No.3261) reg 46 (January 22, 1996).
4. Child Support (Maintenance Assessments and Special Cases) and Social Security (Claims and Payments) Amendment Regulations 1996 (SI 1996 No.481) reg 3 (April 8, 1996, but see reg 4 of SI 1996 No.481 for transitional provisions).
5. Social Security and Child Support (Jobseeker's Allowance) (Consequential Amendments) Regulations 1996 (SI 1996 No.1345) regs 6(5), (6) and (7)(c) (October 7, 1996).
6. Child Support (Miscellaneous Amendments) (No.2) Regulations 1996 (SI 1996 No.3196) reg 14 (January 13, 1997).
7. Child Support (Miscellaneous Amendments) Regulations 1998 (SI 1998 No.58) reg 57 (January 19, 1998).
8. Child Support (Miscellaneous Amendments) Regulations 1999 (SI 1999 No.977) reg 6(6) (April 6, 1999).
9. Child Support (Miscellaneous Amendments) Regulations 2003 (SI 2003 No.328) reg 6(7)(a) and (b) (April 6, 2003).
10. Child Support (Miscellaneous Amendments) Regulations 2003 (SI 2003 No.328) reg 6(7)(c) (April 1, 2003).
11. Child Support (Miscellaneous Amendments) Regulations 2004 (SI 2004 No.2415) reg 5(3) (September 16, 2004).
12. Child Support (Miscellaneous Amendments) Regulations 2005 (SI 2005 No.785) reg 4(3) (March 16, 2005).
13. Child Support (Miscellaneous Amendments) (No.2) Regulations 2003 (SI 2003 No.2779) reg 4(7) (November 5, 2003).
14. Civil Partnership (Pensions, Social Security and Child Support) (Consequential, etc. Provisions) Order 2005 (SI 2005 No.2877) art 2(4) and Sch 4, para 2(5) (December 5, 2005).
15. National Health Service Reform and Health Care Professions Act 2002 (Supplementary, Consequential etc. Provisions) Regulations 2002 (SI 2002 No.2469) reg 9 and Sch 6 (October 1, 2002).
16. Child Support (Miscellaneous and Consequential Amendments) Regulations 2009 (SI 2009 No.736) reg 3(5) (April 6, 2009).
17. Adoption and Children (Scotland) Act 2007 (Consequential Modifications) Order 2011 (SI 2011 No.1740) art 2 and Sch 1 para 15 (July 15, 2011).
18. National Treatment Agency (Abolition) and the Health and Social Care Act 2012 (Consequential, Transitional and Saving Provisions) Order 2013 (SI 2013 No.235) art 11 and Sch 2, para 20(3) (April 1, 2013).
19. Council Tax Benefit Abolition (Consequential Provision) Regulations 2013 (SI 2013 No.458) reg 3 and Sch 1 (April 1, 2013).
20. Personal Independence Payment (Supplementary Provisions and Consequential Amendments) Regulations 2013 (SI 2013 No.388) reg 8 and Sch para 13(2) (April 8, 2013).
21. Armed Forces and Reserve Forces Compensation Scheme (Consequential Provisions: Subordinate Legislation) Order 2013 (SI 2013 No.591) reg 7 and Sch para 7(2) (April 8, 2013).
22. Universal Credit (Consequential, Supplementary, Incidental and Miscellaneous Provisions) Regulations 2013 (SI 2013 No.630) reg 41(4) (April 29, 2013).

Definitions

"child tax credit": see reg 1(2).
"Contributions and Benefits Act": see reg 1(2).
"council tax benefit": see reg 1(2).
"earnings": see reg 1(2).
"family": see reg 1(2).
"home": see reg 1(2).
"housing benefit": see reg 1(2).
"the Jobseekers Act": see reg 1(2).
"non-dependant": see reg 1(2).
"ordinary clothing or footwear": see reg 1(2).
"parent with care": see reg 1(2).
"partner": see reg 1(2).
"person": see reg 1(2).
"self-employed earner": see reg 1(2).
"state pension credit": see reg 1(2).
"student": see reg 1(2).
"training allowance": see reg 1(2).

General Note

Paragraph 5

This paragraph applies to compensation for "personal injury". A personal injury may be physical or mental. In the latter case there must be a recognisable psychiatric illness (*McLoughlin v O'Brian* [1983] 1 AC 410). It may also take the form of a disease (*R(SB) 2/89*, para 11) and will include any injuries sustained as a result of the disease – eg, an amputation following meningitis and septicaemia (*ibid*, para 15).

The compensation must be paid for the personal injury and not merely because of it. Strictly, compensation is not paid for an injury, but for the consequences of the injury (*Baker v Willoughby* [1969] 3 All ER 1528 at 1532, per Lord Reid). This is true not only of a civil claim for damages, but also a claim for disablement benefit under which entitlement depends on the degree of the resulting disablement. The paragraph cannot, therefore, be read literally.

In *R(CS) 2/00* (para 16), the commissioner held that "compensation for personal injury" only covers payment to an injured party by the person who was liable in tort to make reparation for the injury or who accepted such liability. Any other interpretation would render the reference to a trust fund superfluous as cases where a trust fund was set up would be covered by the earlier words of the paragraph. On this reasoning, the paragraph covers all compensation paid on a civil claim for damage, including compensation for the loss of earnings as a result of the injury. It is arguable that, in the context of child support and having regard to the nature of the type of exclusion covered by this Schedule, compensation should not include compensation for loss of future income, as compensation which replaces income that would otherwise have been received is out of step with the character of the contents of the Schedule. On this reasoning, payments of disablement benefit will not count as compensation for the purposes of this paragraph. This also would be out of step with the character of the contents of the Schedule. An appeal against the commissioner's decision was dismissed by the Court of Appeal in *Wakefield v Secretary of State for Social Security*, also reported as *R(CS) 2/00*.

Paragraph 6

This paragraph is in the same terms as Sch 1 para 1(2)(d).

Paragraph 19

Whether a payment is voluntary is judged by looking at the payer and not the payee. Consequently a payment by British Coal to a miner's widow in lieu of concessionary coal is not a voluntary payment (*R v Doncaster BC ex p Boulton* [1992] 25 HLR 195, QBD and *R(IS) 4/94*). It is irrelevant whether or not the payment in question was legally enforceable (*ibid*). Where payments are made under an annuity which was purchased with money given for the purpose, they are not voluntary since they are made under the terms of the annuity which is a form of contract (*CIS 702/1991*, para 15).

Paragraph 23

This paragraph is not comprehensive of the disregards for parents that fall within it. In particular it does not displace the disregard in para 2 (*CCS 185/2005*, para 16). However, it is not possible to apply the reasoning in *Parsons v Hogg* [1985] 2 All ER 897, as this would override the express terms of the provision (*CCS 1992/2008*, para 11).

Paragraph 44

The question arises of whether or not child support maintenance payments received by a parent, whether or not in respect of a qualifying child, are to be disregarded under this paragraph. Maintenance payments in respect of a parent are covered by Sch 1 para 14, but there is no express reference to child support maintenance payments in Pt III or IV of Sch 1. However, Sch 1 para 15 covers any other payments or amounts received on a periodical basis. This wording is wide enough to cover payments of child support maintenance, but the never ending circles of calculations involved in doing so point to these payments not falling within the words of para 15. Take, as an example, the case of a mother with care of a child whose child support maintenance is being calculated on review. The child support maintenance ultimately payable would have to be taken into account before it was fixed, a plain impossibility. There would be even greater complexities if the mother had care of two children by different fathers and received child support maintenance payments in respect of each. The only way to avoid these circles is by interpreting para 15 as not covering payments of child support maintenance.

Paragraph 45

Capital earmarked for the purpose or acquiring a new home falls within this paragraph for as long as it remains earmarked, although the parent could have used it for another purpose (*CCS 4923/1995*, para 5).

Paragraph 49

Concessionary payments are only made to compensate for the effects of defective legislation and do not include ex gratia payments for the loss of statutory entitlement – eg, was a result of maladministration (*CIS 2285/1999*).

SCHEDULE 3
ELIGIBLE HOUSING COSTS

Eligible housing costs for the purposes of determining exempt income and protected income
   1.   *Subject to the following provisions of this Schedule, [⁶the following amounts payable] in respect of the provision of a home shall be eligible to be taken into account as housing costs for the purposes of these Regulations–*
   (a)   *[⁶amounts payable by way of rent;]*
   (b)   *[⁶amounts payable by way of mortgage interest;]*
   (c)   *[⁶amounts payable by way of interest] under a hire purchase agreement to buy a home;*
   (d)   *[⁶amounts payable by way of interest] on loans for repairs and improvements to the home [¹, including interest on a loan for any service charge imposed to meet the cost of such repairs and improvements;]*
   (e)   *[⁶amounts payable] by way of ground rent or in Scotland, payments by way of feu duty;*
   (f)   *[⁶amounts payable] payments under a co-ownership scheme;*
   (g)   *[⁶amounts payable] in respect of, or in consequence of, the use and occupation of the home;.*
   (h)   *where the home is a tent, [⁶amounts payable] payments in respect of the tent and the site on which it stands;*
   (i)   *[⁶amounts payable] in respect of a licence or permission to occupy the home (whether or not board is provided);*
   (j)   *[⁶amounts payable] by way of mesne profits or, in Scotland, violent profits;*
   (k)   *[⁶amounts payable by way of] service charges, the payment of which is a condition on which the right to occupy the home depends;*
   (l)   *[⁶amounts payable] under or relating to a tenancy or licence of a Crown tenant;*
   (m)   *mooring charges payable for a houseboat;*
   (n)   *where the home is a caravan or a mobile home, [⁶amounts payable] in respect of the site on which it stands;*
   (o)   *any contribution payable by a parent resident in an almshouse provided by a housing association which is either a charity of which particulars are entered in the register of charities established under section 4 of the Charities Act 1960 (register of charities) or an exempt charity within the meaning of that Act, which is a contribution towards the cost of maintaining that association's almshouses and essential services in them;*
   (p)   *[⁶amounts payable] under a rental purchase agreement, that is to say an agreement for the purchase of a home under which the whole or part of the purchase price is to be paid in more than one instalment and the completion of the purchase is deferred until the whole or a specified part of the purchase price has been paid;*
   (q)   *where, in Scotland, the home is situated on or pertains to a croft within the meaning of section 3(1) of the Crofters (Scotland) Act 1955, the [⁶amounts payable] in respect of the croft land;*
   (r)   *where the home is provided by an employer (whether under a condition or term in a contract of service or otherwise), [⁶amounts payable] to that employer in respect of the home, including [⁶any amount deductible by the employer]*
   (s)   *[¹...]*
   (t)   *[⁶payments in respect of a loan taken out to pay off another loan but only to the extent that it was incurred in respect of amounts eligible to be taken into account as housing costs by virtue of other provisions of this Schedule.]*

Loans for repairs and improvements to the home
   2.   *[³Subject to paragraph 2A (loans for repairs and improvements in transitional cases), for the purposes of] paragraph 1(d) "repairs and improvements" means major repairs necessary to maintain the fabric of the home and any of the following measures undertaken with a view to improving its fitness for occupation–*
   (a)   *installation of a fixed bath, shower, wash basin or lavatory, and necessary associated plumbing;*
   (b)   *damp proofing measures;*

(c)   provision or improvement of ventilation and natural lighting;
(d)   provision of electric lightening and sockets;
(e)   provision or improvement of drainage facilities;
(f)   improvement of the structural condition of the home;
(g)   improvements to the facilities for the storing, preparation and cooking of food;
(h)   provision of heating, including central heating;
(i)   provision of storage facilities for fuel and refuse;
(j)   improvements to the insulation of the home;
(k)   other improvements which the [⁷Secretary of State] considers reasonable in the circumstances.

[³Loans for repairs and improvements in transitional cases
    2A.   In the case of a loan entered into before the first date upon which a maintenance application or enquiry form is given or sent or treated as given or sent to the relevant person, for the purposes of paragraph 1(d) "repairs and improvements" means repairs and improvements of any description whatsoever.]

Exempt income: additional provisions relating to eligible housing costs
    3.–(1)   The additional provisions made by this paragraph shall have effect only for the purpose of calculating or estimating exempt income.
    (2)   Subject to sub-paragraph(6), where the home of an absent parent or, as the case may be, a parent with care, is subject to a mortgage or charge and that parent [⁶is liable to make periodical payments] to reduce the capital secured by that mortgage or charge of an amount provided for in accordance with the terms thereof, [⁶those amounts payable] shall be eligible to be taken into account as the housing costs of that parent.
    [⁴(2A)   Where an absent parent or as the case may be a parent with care has entered into a loan for repairs or improvements of a kind referred to in paragraph 1(d) and that parent [⁶is liable to make periodical payments] of an amount provided for in accordance with the terms of that loan to reduce the amount of that loan, [⁶those amounts payable shall be eligible to be taken into account as housing costs of that parent.]]
    (3)   Subject to sub-paragraph (6), where the home of an absent parent or, as the case may be, a parent with care, is held under an agreement and [⁶certain amounts payable] under that agreement are included as housing costs by virtue of paragraph 1 of this Schedule, [⁶any other amounts payable] in accordance with that agreement by the parent in order either–
    (a)   to reduce his liability under that agreement; or
    (b)   to acquire the home to which it relates,
shall also be eligible to be taken into account as housing costs.
    (4)   Where a policy of insurance has been obtained and retained for the purpose of discharging a mortgage or charge on the home of the parent in question, the amount of the [⁶premiums payable] under that policy shall be eligible to be taken into account as a housing cost [³including for the avoidance of doubt such a policy of insurance whose purpose is to secure the payment of monies due under the mortgage or charge in the event of the unemployment, sickness or disability of the insured.]
    [⁵(4A)   Where–
    (a)   an absent parent or parent with care has obtained a loan which constitutes an eligible housing cost falling within sub-paragraph (d) or (t) of paragraph 1; and
    (b)   a policy of insurance has been obtained and retained, the purpose of which is solely to secure the payment of monies due under that loan in the event of the unemployment, sickness or disability of the insured person,
the amount of the premiums payable under that policy shall be eligible to be taken into account as a housing cost.]
    [²(5)   Where a policy of insurance has been obtained and retained for the purpose of discharging a mortgage or charge on the home of the parent in question and also for the purpose of accruing profits on the maturity of the policy, there shall be eligible to be taken into account as a housing cost–
    (a)   where the sum secured by the mortgage or charge does not exceed £60,000 the whole of the [⁶premiums payable] under that policy; and
    (b)   where the sum secured by the mortgage or charge exceeds £60,000, the part of the [⁶premiums payable] under that policy which are necessarily incurred for the purpose of discharging the mortgage or charge or, where that part cannot be ascertained, 0.0277 per centum of the amount secured by the mortgage or charge.]
    [³(5A)   Where a plan within the meaning of regulation 4 of the Personal Equity Plans Regulations 1989 has been obtained and retained for the purpose of discharging a mortgage or charge on the home of the parent in question and also for the purpose of accruing profits upon the realisation of the plan, there shall be eligible to be taken into account as a housing cost–
    (a)   where the sum secured by the mortgage or charge does not exceed £60,000, the whole of the premiums payable in respect of the plan; and
    (b)   where the sum secured by the mortgage or charge exceeds £60,000, that part of the premiums payable in respect of the plan which is necessarily incurred for the purpose of discharging the mortgage or charge or, where that part cannot be ascertained, 0.0277 per centum of the amount secured by the mortgage or charge.
    (5B)   Where a personal pension plan [⁵derived from a personal pension scheme] has been obtained and retained for the purpose of discharging a mortgage or charge on the home of the parent in question and also

for the purpose of securing the payment of pension to him, there shall be eligible to be taken into account as a housing cost 25 per centum of the contributions payable in respect of that personal pension plan.]

(6)   For the purposes of sub-paragraphs (2) and (3), housing costs shall not include–

(a)   [³any payments in excess of those required] to be made under or in respect of a mortgage, charge or agreement to which either of those sub-paragraphs related;

(b)   [⁶amounts payable] under any second or subsequent mortgage on the home to the extent that [³they would not be eligible] to be taken into account as housing costs;

(c)   premiums payable in respect of any policy of insurance against loss caused by the destruction of or damage to any building or land.

Conditions relating to eligible housing costs

4.–(1)   Subject to the following provisions of this paragraph the housing costs referred to in this Schedule shall be included as housing costs only where–

(a)   [⁵they are necessarily incurred for the purpose of purchasing, renting or otherwise securing possession of the home for the parent and his family, or for the purpose of carrying out repairs and improvements to that home,]

(b)   the parent or, if he is one of a family, he or a member of his family, is responsible for those costs; and

(c)   the liability to meet those costs is to a person other than a member of the same household.

[⁵(1A)   For the purposes of sub-paragraph (1)(a) "repairs and improvements" shall have the meaning given in paragraph 2 of this Schedule.]

(2)   For the purposes of sub-paragraph (1)(b) a parent shall be treated as responsible for housing costs where–

(a)   because the person liable to meet those costs is not doing so, he has to meet those costs in order to continue to live in the home and either he was formerly the partner of the person liable, or he is some other person whom it is reasonable to treat as liable to meet those costs; or

(b)   he pays a share of those costs in a case where–

(i)   he is living in a household with other persons;

(ii)   those other persons include persons who are not close relatives of his or his partner;

(iii)   a person who is not such a close relative is responsible for those costs under the preceding provisions of this paragraph or has an equivalent responsibility for housing expenditure; and

(iv)   it is reasonable in the circumstances to treat him as sharing that responsibility.

[⁵(3)   Subject to sub-paragraph (4), payments on a loan shall constitute an eligible housing cost only if that loan has been obtained for the purposes specified in sub-paragraph (1)(a).

(4)   Where a loan has been obtained only partly for the purposes specified in sub-paragraph (1)(a), the eligible housing cost shall be limited to that part of the payment attributable to those purposes.]

Accommodation also used for other purposes

5.   Where amounts are payable in respect of accommodation which consists partly of residential accommodation and partly of other accommodation, only such proportion thereof as is attributable to residential accommodation shall be eligible to be taken into account as housing costs.

Ineligible service and fuel charges

6.   Housing costs shall not include–

[⁴[⁹(a)   where the costs are inclusive of ineligible service charges within the meaning of paragraph 1(a)(i) of Schedule 1 to the Housing Benefit Regulations or, as the case may be, paragraph 1(a)(i) of Schedule 1 to the Housing Benefit (State Pension Credit) Regulations (ineligible service charges), the amounts specified as ineligible in paragraph 2 of the appropriate Schedule 1;

(b)   where the costs are inclusive of any of the items mentioned in paragraph 6(2) of Schedule 1 to the Housing Benefit Regulations or, as the case may be, paragraph 6(2) of Schedule 1 to the Housing Benefit (State Pension Credit) Regulations (payment in respect of fuel charges), the deductions prescribed in that paragraph unless the parent provides evidence on which the actual or approximate amount of the service charge for fuel may be estimated, in which case the estimated amount;]

(c)   charges for water, sewerage or allied environmental services and where the amount of such charges is not separately identified, such part of the charges in question as is attributable to those services; [⁴and

(d)   where the costs are inclusive of charges, other than those which are not to be included by virtue of sub-paragraphs (a) to (c), that part of those charges which exceeds the greater of the following amounts–

(i)   the total of the charges other than those which are ineligible service charges within the meaning of paragraph 1 of Schedule 1 to the Housing Benefit Regulations (housing costs);

(ii)   25 per centum of the total amount of eligible housing costs,

and for the purposes of this sub-paragraph, where the amount of those charges is not separately identifiable, that amount shall be such amount as is reasonably attributable to those charges.]

Interpretation

7.   In this schedule except where the context otherwise requires–

"close relative" means a parent, parent-in-law, son, son-in-law, daughter, daughter-in-law, step-parents, step-son, step-daughter, brother, sister, [⁸or if any of the preceding persons is one member of a couple, the other member of that couple];

"co-ownership scheme" means a scheme under which the dwelling is let by a housing association and the tenant, or his personal representative, will, under the terms of the tenancy agreement or of the agreement under which he became a member of the association, be entitled, on his ceasing to be a member and subject to any conditions stated in either agreement, to a sum calculated by reference directly or indirectly to the value of the dwelling;

"housing association" has the meaning assigned to it by section 1(1) of the Housing Association Act 1985.

Amendments

1.   Child Support (Miscellaneous Amendments) Regulations 1993 (SI 1993 No.913) reg 33 (April 5, 1993).
2.   Child Support (Miscellaneous Amendments and Transitional Provisions) Regulations 1994 (SI 1994 No.227) reg 4(8) (February 7, 1994).
3.   Child Support and Income Support (Amendment) Regulations 1995 (SI 1995 No.1045) regs 56(3)-(6), 57 and Sch 1 (April 18, 1995).
4.   Child Support (Miscellaneous Amendments) (No.2) Regulations 1995 (SI 1995 No.3261) reg 47(2) and (3) (January 22, 1996).
5.   Child Support (Miscellaneous Amendments) (No.2) Regulations 1996 (SI 1996 No.3196) reg 15(3) and (4) (January 13, 1997).
6.   Child Support (Miscellaneous Amendments) Regulations 1998 (SI 1998 No.58) regs 58(2) and (3) (January 19, 1998).
7.   Social Security Act 1998 (Commencement No.7 and Consequential and Transitional Provisions) Order 1999 (SI 1999 No.1510) art 20 (June 1, 1999).
8.   Civil Partnership (Pensions, Social Security and Child Support) (Consequential, etc. Provisions) Order 2005 (SI 2005 No.2877) art 2(4) and Sch 4 para 2(6) (December 5, 2005).
9.   Housing Benefit and Council Tax Benefit (Consequential Provisions) Regulations 2006 (SI 2006 No.217) reg 5 and Sch 2 para 4(5) (March 6, 2006).

Definitions

"family": see reg 1(2).
"home": see reg 1(2).
"Housing Benefit Regulations": see reg 1(2).
"Housing Benefit (State Pension Credit) Regulations": see reg 1(2).
"parent with care": see reg 1(2).
"partner": see reg 1(2).
"person": see reg 1(2).
"personal pension scheme": see reg 1(2).

General Note

The provisions dealing with housing costs are mandatory and contain no element of discretion. Accordingly s2 of the Act has no application to them (*CCS 9/1995*, para 8).

Paragraph 1

This paragraph lays down the eligible housing costs for all purposes except the calculation of exempt income where the provisions are supplemented by para 3. Where repayment of a loan or credit is concerned, only interest payments are included and not capital payments. Housing costs are not defined. They bear their normal meaning of costs associated with the provision of housing for an individual or a family (Common Appendix to *R(IS) 3/91* and *R(IS) 4/91*, para 10). This is subject to para 4. The housing costs allowable are those which are reasonably necessary for providing a home or repairs or improvements to it, and do not include other costs which happen to be secured upon it (*CCS 12/1994*, para 35), even if those costs were incurred in order to avoid loss of the home (*ibid*, para 39). They do, however, include loans to a partner to purchase the other partner's former interest in the property from the partner's trustee in bankruptcy (*R(IS) 6/94*). As a result of the Amendment Regulations, payments analogous to those listed are not within the scope of the paragraph.

In *R(CS) 6/98* (para 12), the commissioner declined to express a view on whether the "home" in question was the home at the time in respect of which maintenance is being assessed or the home at the time the expenditure was incurred, although he did say that the former might be the case.

For the significance of the reference to the provision of a home, see the general note to para 4.

The language of "costs" and "payments" makes it clear that housing costs only include actual expenditure and not cases where there is liability but no payment – eg, in a deferred repayment mortgage (*CIS 636/1992*, para 8).

There is no power for decision makers or tribunals to make allowance for voluntary payments by a non-resident parent towards housing costs of the former matrimonial home now occupied by the parent with care and the qualifying child (*CCS 12/95*, para 5; *R(CS) 9/98*, para 8). The giving of credit for such payments is relevant only to recovery of child support maintenance and not to its assessment: see the Child Support (Management of Payments and Arrears) Regulations 2009 on p705.

Subparagraph (b)

It is implicit that the mortgage must be on the parent's home (*NM v CMEC (CSM)* [2010] UKUT 58 (AAC); [2010] AACR 33, para 32).

An Islamic Trust Funding Arrangement to facilitate the acquisition of a home under which the property is conveyed into the name of the parent to be held on trust in unequal shares for that parent and the funding provider with the former required to buy shares from the latter by way of payments which are called mesne profits but calculated by reference to interest rates, is not to be equated with a mortgage under which interest payments are made (*CIS 14483/1996*, para 10). Since the commissioner looked at the legal form of the arrangement rather than its economic substance, it is likely that in child support law the arrangement would fall within subpara (j).

In *R(CS) 3/05*, the commissioner decided that for a current account mortgage the eligible housing costs are limited to the minimum amounts that have to be paid under the terms of the loans. Additional payments that were made in order to reduce the outstanding balance and thereby save interest did not count.

Subparagraph (d)

If this head is to be satisfied there must be a loan. It is not sufficient that a debt (eg, to cover private street works) is deferred and paid in instalments with interest (*R(SB) 3/87*, para 7). It is undecided whether loans taken out in respect of work already undertaken are within this head (*CIS 264/1993*, para 13). Repairs and improvements are defined in paras 2 and 2A.

Tribunals have to consider three matters: (i) the basis upon which the loan was made; (ii) the nature of the works for which the money was borrowed; (iii) the use to which the money was put. In the case of a loan from a commercial lender, its basis is to be found either (a) in a term of the contract of loan requiring that the money be used for a specified purpose or (b) in the representation by the non-resident parent to the lender of the reason why the money was needed. The basis on which the loan was entered into is likely to be stated in general terms that are not sufficiently detailed and precise to show whether the other conditions are satisfied. So, it is necessary to identify the nature of the work for which the money was borrowed in order to check if the conditions in paras 2 or 2A are satisfied. Interest on money which is borrowed for repairs or improvements, but put to other use, is not a payment in respect of the home for the purposes of the opening words of para 1. See *CCS 349/1997*, paras 9-11. The person's motive in carrying out the repairs or improvements is irrelevant (*ibid*, para 12).

Subparagraph (f)

This provision does not apply where possession proceedings have been brought by a lender against the borrower, since in due course the whole of the lender's interest may pass to the borrower, but at no stage will there be joint ownership between lender and borrower (*CIS 392/1994*, para 9).

Subparagraph (g)

The common law meaning of "use and occupation" is a payment for the use and occupation of land which is made where a person has been given permission to occupy the land of another without any binding terms being agreed about payment, and the words "in respect of, or in consequence of" are restrictive (*R v Bristol CC ex p Jacobs* (1999) 32 HLR 841).

The commissioners decided that the extent of the provision is uncertain (*R(CS) 3/96*, para 23). It does not cover capital repayments as they are the subject of special provision in para 3 which would be anomalous and unnecessary if such repayments fell within this subparagraph. The following do not fall within this provision: premiums on contents and property insurance, because they are also covered by para 3 and anomalies would arise if this subparagraph were interpreted so as to cover them (*R(CS) 3/96*, paras 20-23 and R1/94 (CSC)); payments in respect of the purchase of a home (*R(CS) 6/98*, para 12); repayments on a loan to restock a home with items taken by the other partner on separation (*CSC 2/1996*, para 5); water rates (*CSC 3/1996*, para 5); council tax (*R(CS) 11/98*, paras 9-10). Payments in respect of road charges and interest paid on them are charges in respect of a home (*R(SB) 3/87*, para 8).

Subparagraph (j)

The decision in *CIS 14483/1996*, dealing with an Islamic Trust Funding Arrangement, is explained in the general note to subpara (b) above. On the basis of the commissioner's reasoning it is likely that such an arrangement will fall within this subparagraph.

Subparagraph (k)

Service charges are not defined. Their meaning was discussed by the Tribunal of Commissioners whose decision appears in the Common Appendix to *R(IS) 3/91* and *R(IS) 4/91* (paras 11 and 15). The words are to be interpreted liberally and mean charges made for services provided in connection with housing. They must be charges which involve the determination and arrangement of a service, which would otherwise be for the occupier to decide on and arrange, in a manner binding on the occupier and which cannot be withdrawn from at leisure. They must bind all those with the same interest in the property or they must run with the land so as to bind successors in occupancy. Buildings insurance is not a service charge (*Dunne v Department of Health and Social Security*, unreported, Court of Appeal in Northern Ireland, January 22 1992 and *CSIS 4/90*, para 8), but counselling and other support services can be (*R v North Cornwall District Council ex p Singer, The Times*, January 12, 1994). The service charges which are covered are limited by para 6.

A service charge may be fixed, in which case the amount changes only when the rent is changed, or variable, in which case the amount varies as the costs to which the charge relates varies. A service charge may be difficult to identify as the landlord may merely quote a figure for "rent" without specifying any amount as relating, for example, to water rates.

The essence of a service charge is that it consists of an arrangement for determining whether a particular service, such as redecoration, is required and, if so, for providing the service or arranging for it to be provided. The arrangement must not only be binding, but be binding on all those with the same interest in the property. See the Common Appendix to *R(IS) 3/91* and *R(IS) 4/91* (para 15). This draws a clear and logical distinction between charges which are payable as an incident of the owner's estate or interest in the property and those which arise in some other way such as under a personal contract with the tenant or owner (*R(IS) 19/93*, para 12).

Payments required to be made under the terms of a lease for repairs, redecoration, renewal or insurance are service charges and are connected with the provision of adequate accommodation (Common Appendix, para 18, and *R(IS) 4/92*, paras 12-15). Payment of premiums for insurance required under the terms of mortgage is not a service charge since the obligation arises not from the borrower's interest or estate in the property but from the mortgage. In other words, it arises from the financial arrangements for purchase and not out of the ownership of the property itself (*R(IS) 19/93*, para 14). Likewise, insurance premiums effected between an owner-occupier and an insurance company are not a service charge (*CIS 17/1988*, approved in *R(IS) 4/92*, para 15, and *R(IS) 19/93*, para 15), although they are connected with the provision of adequate accommodation (*R(IS) 4/92*, para 15, and *R(IS) 19/93*, para 15). Payments of administration and other charges related to arrears of mortgage payments are not service charges connected to the adequacy of the accommodation (*CIS 392/1994*, para 7).

Paragraph 2

This paragraph defines repairs and improvements for the purposes of para 1(d).

Repair covers both the remedying of defects and steps taken to prevent these, such as the painting of a house to preserve the woodwork (*CSB 420/1985*, paras 11-12). However, where the alleged repair is of the preventive kind, evidence and findings of fact will be needed on whether the work may properly be considered to have been undertaken as a repair or only for cosmetic reasons (*ibid*, para 12). It would, for example, if the painting of a house were being considered, be necessary to inquire into the state of the paint work at the time and whether the change was merely to change the colour. Repairs must be "necessary to maintain the fabric of the home", a strict test.

They must also be "major". Whether a repair is or is not major is a question of fact (*CSB265/1987*, para 10). It is a comparative term whose meaning is bound to be somewhat fluid and imprecise, but it will always be relevant to take into account the cost as well as the nature of and the time taken for the work (*ibid*, paras 10 and 12). Chimney-sweeping cannot be a repair (*ibid*, para 7). Where the home consists of a flat or some other part of the building, repairs to some other part of the building than the flat itself are not repairs to the fabric of the home (*CIS616/1992*, para 16).

The proper approach to improvements was exemplified by the commissioner in *CSCS 3/1996* (para 4) as follows. First facts have to be found as to the previous state of the home so that it can be seen that the work led to an improvement. Then it has to be shown that the improvement was properly undertaken in order to improve the fitness for occupation of the home. The facts, in other words, must show that there was some existing unfitness to be remedied.

Improvements need not be major but they must fall within one of the categories listed and they must be undertaken with a view to improving the fitness of the home for occupation. The reasonableness of the improvements is not a factor except under (k) but this will be a relevant consideration in assessing the credibility of the evidence on this issue. Moreover the work must be undertaken with a view not just to improving the home but to improving its fitness for occupation. The paragraph assumes that there should be a minimum standard of accommodation and allows the cost of bringing the home up to that standard to be taken into account as eligible housing costs. So the test is whether the work is carried out with a view to bringing the home up to a standard above the minimum in a particular respect. This provision is not a licence to install a replacement or additional bathroom or further electric sockets where the current provision is adequate. Care is also needed with self-build homes to ensure that this paragraph is not used to cover the costs of completion rather than of the improvement of a home.

The improvements must be improvements to the home (in other words, to the dwelling – reg 1(2)), although they need not be to the fabric of the home (*CIS 264/1993*, paras 15 and 16).

Subparagraph (a)

Unlike its social security counterpart, this sub-paragraph does not cover sinks.

Subparagraph (k)

The improvements must be made with a view to improving the home's fitness for occupation, which is wider than fitness for habitation and would cover access to the premises (*R(SB) 3/87*, para 10). The improvement must not be viewed from either a subjective or an objective viewpoint, but overall in the broadest possible terms. The tribunal should balance the advantage of the improvement to the person carrying it out against the consequences viewed objectively. An extension to accommodate a large, young family, for example, would be reasonable, despite the fact that it was not reflected in any comparable increase in the value of the property, whereas a similar extension built when most of the family were about to leave home would not be (*CIS 453/1993*, para 8).

Paragraph 2A
"Improvements" bears its ordinary meaning (*CCS 349/1997*, para 10.1).

Paragraph 3
The terms of this paragraph are useful not only in their own right but also for the light they shed on the scope of some of the subparagraphs in paragraph 1. It makes special provision for the purposes of calculating exempt income by extending the eligible housing costs under para 1 to include capital repayments and endowment policy premiums in so far as they cover the capital repayments. Where the policy is designed to produce a profit as well as to cover the capital (eg, in a with profits endowment or a pension mortgage), the part of the premiums necessarily incurred for the purpose of discharging a mortgage or charge should be identifiable by expert evidence. Where this is not possible or the evidence is not available, 0.0277 per cent of the sum secured is used as the eligible housing cost. This figure is sufficient to ensure that the capital would be covered assuming an annual rate of return of 8 per cent over 25 years. Payments of arrears or voluntary additional payments of capital are not covered, nor is the cost of insurance against loss of or damage to the building or land.

This paragraph, like para 1, is limited to costs incurred for the provision of a home or for repairs or improvements to it (*CCS 12/1994*, para 43).

This paragraph is not restricted to policies that are obtained at a time when the mortgage to be secured has already been obtained (*CCS 1321/1997*, para 13).

In *CCS 2750/1995* (para 18), the commissioner held that subpara (4) applied to term assurances while subpara (5) applied to endowment policies. He held that both types of policy, if taken out and retained for the purpose of discharging the loan, were allowable, although the reason for the retention of both policies would require investigation in order to be sure that they were being retained for the specified purpose. With respect to the commissioner, it is doubtful whether his analysis of the relationship of these two subparagraphs is correct. It is suggested that subpara (4) is the general provision which catches any type of assurance or insurance, while subpara (5) provides for a limit on the amount where there is a with-profits element in the arrangement. This does not, however, detract from the need to investigate any apparent over-provision in the finance arrangements. Without expressing a concluded opinion on the point, the commissioner in *CCS 2750/1995* (para 29) said that where only a proportion of a loan is eligible as housing costs, the allowable portion will determine whether the case falls under head (a) or (b).

Subparagraph (2)
This covers an equitable mortgage by deposit of title deeds or certificate (*CCS 9/1995*, para 12). It covers payments which are not fixed at the outset but are subsequently provided for by variation or novation (*ibid*, para 17).

A charge on a co-owner's beneficial interest is a charge under this provision, despite the fact that it is not, and cannot be, registered against the title (*NM v CMEC (CSM)* [2010] UKUT 58 (AAC); [2010] AACR 33, paras 36-37).

Subparagraphs (4) and (5)
There is no need for the policy to be tied to the mortgage or charge as part of an endowment mortgage. An endowment policy taken out for the purpose of discharging early a repayment mortgage (eg, an arrangement used by a person in poor health in order to avoid the high life premiums involved in an endowment mortgage) is within the wording of these paragraphs with the result that both the premiums on the policy and the capital repayments under the mortgage are eligible housing costs for the purpose of exempt income.

The purpose of the policy must be the discharge of the mortgage or charge. It is not sufficient for the purpose to be to reduce the outstanding capital, as it is only when the whole of the balance of the loan is repaid that the mortgage or charge will be discharged.

In the case of a mortgage which is part repayment and part endowment, the endowment element is within these paragraphs as it is intended that the policy will discharge the outstanding balance at the date of maturity.

The amendment to subpara (4) is made "for the avoidance of doubt" which shows that it is retrospective in its effect. However, in its terms it only applies to policies which secure payment of monies due under the mortgage or charge. The words "monies due" are in contrast to "discharging the mortgage or charge" and suggest that the amendment applies to periodical payments only. Policies which provide for repayment of the capital were considered in *R(CS) 10/98*. This case concerned an assessment for a period before the amendment came into force. The policy concerned was one which secured the payment of all or part of the mortgage capital in the event of death or serious illness. The commissioner held, at para 18, that this fell within the subparagraph as it stood at the relevant time. He did not mention the amendment, nor did he consider whether or not it was necessary, as is suggested above, for the policy to provide for the payment of all, rather than merely part, of the sum secured.

Subparagraph (5B)
The words "personal pension plan" are not defined. The words "personal pension scheme" are used elsewhere in these Regulations, so the choice of different wording must be significant. Technically, a personal pension plan could not be made under the pre-1988 legislation. However, it would be anomalous if this subparagraph were interpreted to exclude these earlier arrangements. Accordingly, it is suggested that the words should be interpreted generally and not limited to any technical meaning.

The plan must have been obtained and retained for the purpose of discharging a mortgage or charge. That purpose need not have been an absolute one, as it is the nature of things that a person might well wish to have as large a pension as possible and intend to resort to the plan only if some other source of finance was not available.

Subparagraph (6)(a)

This provision may not cover the type of mortgage considered in *CIS 141/1993* where the mortgagor had the option at each interest rate increase of continuing with the existing level of payments, with the capital being increased and the term of the mortgage extended. In such a case there are never arrears owing under the terms of the mortgage.

Paragraph 4(1)

This subparagraph lays down three conditions all of which must be satisfied in order for the housing costs to be eligible for child support purposes. First, the costs must be necessarily incurred for the purchasing, renting or otherwise securing the possession of the home or carrying out repairs and improvements to it. The requirement of necessity must be interpreted and applied sensibly with appropriate regard to the realities of property acquisition and of the mortgage market (*Pabari v SSWP* [2005] 1 All ER 287). The costs must relate to the parent's own home; costs which are met, for example, in respect of the home of a relative or a divorced spouse are not covered. In *CCS 2750/1995* (para 14), the commissioner held that the former version of this head was concerned solely with limiting eligible housing costs to the home of the parent concerned. Clearly in its present form it has a wider function of additionally emphasising the essential purpose of the expenditure. Second, the parent or a member of the parent's family must be responsible for them. It is clear from para 4(1)(c) and (2) that what matters is legal responsibility rather than a voluntary assumption of payment. However, in two cases persons are treated as responsible for costs which they are not legally liable to meet: see subpara (2). What matters is legal liability and not whether the person liable is paying the costs. It will not be unusual, for example, for spouses or partners to be jointly and severally liable on a mortgage but for the payments to be met by only one of them. Third, the liability must be to someone who is not a member of the same household. This goes some way to prevent collusion between members of a household. It may be possible for parties to arrange their affairs so that there are separate households, and tribunals will need to be astute to distinguish genuine arrangements which do result in separate households, even if those arrangements are made in order to fall within subpara (1), and shams.

In order to amount to an eligible housing cost the payment must be made in respect of the provision of the home under para 1 above and must additionally fall within the terms of head (a) of this subparagraph. The terms used in para 1 and head (a) are narrower than "acquiring an interest in the dwelling" which is the equivalent phrase in income support law. The meaning of "provision of a home" was discussed in *R(CS) 12/98* (paras 9-14). According to that decision it covers the initial acquisition of the person's interest in the home and matters which serve to preserve the home, such as repairs and improvements to it. Whether or not it covers the acquisition of a higher or further interest in the home (eg, the purchase by a lessee of the freehold or the purchase of one joint owner of the other's share) is a matter of degree. For example, in the case of the purchase of the freehold, it will be relevant to consider how long the lease has to run, and in the case of the purchase of a joint owner's interest, it will be relevant to consider how secure the person's occupancy is in view of the possibility of the other owner obtaining an order for sale. This interpretation is reinforced by head (a) which requires that the costs be "necessarily incurred" and uses the phrase "otherwise securing possession of the home" in head (a). However, with respect, it is doubtful whether this interpretation gives sufficient weight to the complexities of the analysis which it requires of the officers who will have to implement it. In this respect it is in contrast to the approach taken in *R(CS)14/98* (para 16) where the commissioner declined to distinguish between living with and staying with, commenting that "it is inconceivable that the Secretary of State intended that such fine distinctions should be drawn when they would, in many cases, be highly contentious. No one could describe this legislation as simple, but it does seem designed to produce fairly clear-cut answers to most cases so that a relatively junior child support officer is able to apply the law."

In *SJ v CMEC (CSM)* [2010] UKUT 355 (AAC), the judge followed *R(CS) 12/98* and decided that the purchase of an ex-partner's interest in his home was undertaken to ensure that he continued in possession of his home.

Where a person is on a low income but has a partner with a higher income which can support the family's relatively high housing costs, the person is treated as responsible for those costs, thereby significantly reducing or even eliminating her/his assessable income, although the costs are met in practice by the partner. This is subject to the possibility of a departure direction.

Paragraph 4(2)

This subparagraph provides for two cases in which persons who are paying housing costs for which they are not liable are treated as if they were responsible for those costs. The first is where the person who is liable is not paying and the parent is making payments in order to continue to live in the home. It must be necessary for the parent to meet the costs in order to continue to live in the home. Failure must therefore put the home at risk. So failure to pay a loan which is not secured on the home will not be sufficient. In practice, even if the loan is secured on the home, eviction for non-payment is a difficult and lengthy process. However, tribunals are likely to regard all cases in which the risk of eviction may arise in the event of non-payment as falling within this head. The typical case covered will be where the parent has been deserted by a former partner who is liable for housing costs but is refusing to pay them. If this is the case then the parent is treated as responsible for the costs. The parent may also be treated as responsible in other cases – eg, if a grandparent was meeting the costs. In these other cases, however, it must be reasonable to treat the parent as liable; no issue of reasonableness arises if the person liable was a former partner. The second case covered is where the parent is sharing housing costs with others who also live in the accommodation of whom at least one who is not a close relative is liable or treated as liable for those costs, provided that it is reasonable to treat the parent as sharing the responsibility for the costs. The wording speaks of others in the plural, but by virtue of s6(c) Interpretation Act 1978 this will include the singular. Findings of fact on each element of each case will be necessary and decisions on reasonableness will need to be justified in the reasons for decision.

Subparagraph (2)(a) will apply where a parent is occupying the former joint home in respect of which there is shared liability for the housing costs, but is having to meet the whole of those costs the former partner's share of those costs is not being paid (*CCS 13698/1996*, para 7).

Paragraph 5

This allows costs to be apportioned in cases where premises are used for a dual purpose. However, it only covers cases where there is separate accommodation which is put to each use, such as where living accommodation is connected to retail premises or where a business is run from a distinct and separate part of accommodation. It does not cover cases where a business is run from a part of a person's home which is also used for other purposes, such as a business run from a desk in the corner of the living room.

Paragraph 6

Paragraph 1(a)(i) of each Schedule renders charges for meals (including the preparation of meals or the provision of unprepared food) ineligible as a service charge. Paragraph 6(2) of each Schedule covers charges for heating, hot water, lighting and cooking.

Paragraph 7

In the definition of "close relative", the "step" and "in-law" relationships include appropriate references to civil partners. See s246 Civil Partnership Act 2004 and Schedule para 48 Civil Partnership Act 2004 (Relationships Arising Through Civil Partnership) Order 2005, in force from 5 December 2005.

[¹*SCHEDULE 3A*
AMOUNT TO BE ALLOWED IN RESPECT OF TRANSFERS OF PROPERTY

Interpretation

1.–(1)   In this Schedule–

"property" means–

(a)   *a legal estate or an equitable interest in land; or*

(b)   *a sum of money which is derived from or represents capital, whether in cash or in the form of a deposit with–*

    (i)   *the Bank of England;*

    (ii)   *an authorised institution or an exempted person with the meaning of the Banking act 1987;*

    (iii)   *a building society incorporated or deemed to be incorporated under the Building Societies Act 1986;*

(c)   *any business asset as defined in sub-paragraph (2) (whether in the form of money or an interest in land or otherwise);*

(d)   *any policy of insurance which has been obtained and retained for the purposes of providing a capital sum to discharge a mortgage or charge secured upon an estate or interest in land which is also the subject of the transfer (in this Schedule referred to as an endowment policy);*

"qualifying transfer" means a transfer of property–

(a)   *which was made in pursuance of a court order made, or a written maintenance agreement executed, before 5th April 1993;*

(b)   *which was made between the absent parent and either the parent with care or a relevant child [³or both whether jointly or otherwise including, in Scotland, in common property];*

(c)   *which was made at a time when the absent parent and the parent with care were living separate and apart;*

[³(d)   *the effect of which is that (subject to any mortgage or charge) the parent with care or relevant child is solely beneficially entitled to the property of which the property transferred forms the whole or part, or the business asset, or the parent with care is beneficially entitled to that property or that asset together with the relevant child or absent parent or both, jointly or otherwise or, in Scotland, in common property, or the relevant child is so entitled together with the absent parent;]*

[³(e)   *which was not made for the purpose only of compensating the parent with care either for the loss of a right to apply for, or receive, periodical payments or a capital sum in respect of herself, or for any reduction in the amount of such payments or sum;]*

"compensating transfer" means a transfer of property which would be a qualifying transfer (disregarding the requirement of paragraph (e) of the definition of

"qualifying transfer") if it were made by the absent parent, but which is made by the parent with care in favour of the absent parent [³or] relevant child [³or both whether jointly or otherwise including, in Scotland, in common property];

"relevant date" means the date of the making of the court order or the execution of the written maintenance agreement in pursuance of which the qualifying transfer was made.

(2)   For the purposes of sub-paragraph (1) "business asset" means an asset, whether in the form of money or an interest in land or otherwise which, prior to the date of transfer was used in the course of a trade or business carried on–

(a)   by the absent parent as a sole trader;

(b)   by the absent parent in partnership, whether with the parent with care or not;

(c)   by a close company within the meaning of sections 414 and 415 of the Income and Corporation Taxes Act 1988 in which the absent parent was a participator at the date of the transfer.

(3)   Where the condition specified in regulation 10(a) is satisfied this Schedule shall apply as if references–

(a)   to the parent with care were references to the absent parent; and

(b)   to the absent parent were references to the parent with care.

Evidence to be produced in connection with the allowances for transfers of property

2.–(1)   Where the absent parent produces to the Secretary of State–

(a)   contemporaneous evidence in writing of the making of a court order or of the execution of a written maintenance agreement, which requires the relevant person to make qualifying transfer of property;

(b)   evidence in writing and whether contemporaneous or not as to–

(i)   the fact of the transfer;

(ii)   the value of the property transferred at the relevant date;

(iii)   the amount of any mortgage or charge outstanding at the relevant date,

an amount in respect of the relevant value of the transfer determined in accordance with the following provisions of this Schedule shall be allowed in calculating or estimating the exempt income of the absent parent.

(2)   Where the evidence specified in sub-paragraph (1) is not produced within a reasonable time after the Secretary of State has been notified of the wish of the absent parent that [⁴the Secretary of State] consider the question, [⁴he] shall determine the question on the basis that the relevant value of the transfer is nil.

Consideration of evidence produced by other parent

[⁴3.–(1)   Where an absent parent has notified the Secretary of State that he wishes him to consider whether an amount should be allowed in respect of the relevant value of a qualifying transfer, the Secretary of State shall–

(a)   give notice to the other parent of that application; and

(b)   have regard in determining the application to any representations made by the other parent which are received within the period specified in sub-paragraph (2).

(2)   The period specified in this sub-paragraph is one month from the date on which the notice referred to in sub-paragraph (1)(a) above was sent or such longer period as the Secretary of State is satisfied is reasonable in the circumstances of the case.]

Computation of qualifying value–business assets and land

4.–(1)   Subject to paragraph 6, where the property [³transferred] by the absent parent is, or includes, an estate or interest in land, or a business asset, the qualifying value of that estate, interest or asset shall be determined in accordance with the formula–[³

$$QV = \frac{(VP - MCP)}{2} - (VAP - MCR) - VCR$$

where–

QV is the qualifying value,

VP is the value at the relevant date of the business asset or the property of which the estate or interest forms the whole or part, and for the purposes of this calculation it is assumed that the estate, interest or asset held on the relevant date by the absent parent or by the absent parent and the parent with care is held by them jointly in equal shares or, in Scotland, in common property; MCP is the amount of any mortgage or charge outstanding immediately prior to the relevant date on the business asset or on the property of which the estate or interest forms the whole or part;

VAP is the value calculated at the relevant date of the business asset or of the property of which the estate or interest forms the whole or part beneficially owned by the absent parent immediately following the transfer (if any);

MCR is, where immediately after the transfer the absent parent is responsible for discharging a mortgage or charge on the business asset or on the property of which the estate or interest forms the whole or part, the amount calculated at the relevant date which is a proportion of any such mortgage or charge outstanding immediately following the transfer, being the same percentage as VAP bears to that property as a whole; and

VCR is the value of any charge in favour of the absent parent on the business asset or on the property of which the estate or interest forms the whole or part, being the amount specified in the court order or written maintenance agreement in relation to the charge, or the amount of a proportion of the value of the business asset or the property on the relevant date specified in the court order or written maintenance agreement.]

(2)   For the purposes of sub-paragraph (1) the value of an estate or interest in land is to be determined upon the basis that the parent with care and any relevant child, if in occupation of the land, would quit on completion of the sale.

Computation of qualifying value – cash, deposits and endowment policies

5. Subject to paragraph 6, where the property which is the subject of the qualifying transfer is, or includes–

(i) a sum of money whether in cash or in the form of a deposit with the Bank of England, an authorised institution or exempted person within the meaning of the Banking Act 1987, or a building society incorporated or deemed to be incorporated under the Building Societies Act 1986, derived from or representing capital; or

(ii) an endowment policy,

the amount of the qualifying value shall be determined by applying the formula–

$$QV = \frac{VT}{2}$$

where–

(a) QV is the qualifying value; and

(b) VT is the amount of cash, the balance of the account or the surrender value of the endowment policy on the relevant date [³and for the purposes of this calculation it is assumed that the cash, balance or policy held on the relevant date by the absent parent and the parent with care is held by them jointly in equal shares or, in Scotland, in common property.]

Transfers wholly in lieu of periodical payments for relevant child

6. Where the evidence produced in relation to a transfer to, or in respect of, a relevant child, shows expressly that the whole of that transfer was made exclusively in lieu of periodical payments in respect of that child–

(a) in a case to which paragraph 4 applies, [³the qualifying value shall be treated as being twice the qualifying value calculated in accordance with that paragraph]; and

(b) in a case to which paragraph 5 applies, the qualifying value shall be [³treated as being twice the qualifying value calculated in accordance with that paragraph.]

Multiple transfers to related persons

7.–(1) Where there has been more than one qualifying transfer from the absent parent–

(a) to the same parent with care;

(b) to or for the benefit of the same relevant child;

(c) to or for the benefit of two or more relevant children with respect to all of whom the same persons are respectively the parent with care and the absent parent;

or any combination thereof, the relevant value by reference to which the allowance is to be calculated in accordance with paragraph 10 shall be the aggregate of the qualifying transfers calculated individually in accordance with the preceding paragraphs of this Schedule, less the value of any compensating transfer or where there has been more than one, the aggregate of the values of the compensating transfers so calculated.

(2) Except as provided by sub-paragraph (1), the values of transfers shall not be aggregated for the purposes of this Schedule.

Computation of the value of compensating transfers

8. [²Subject to paragraph 8A, the value of] a compensating transfer shall be determined in accordance with paragraph 4 to 7 above, but as if any reference in those paragraphs–

(a) to the absent parent were a reference to the parent with care;

(b) to the parent with care were a reference to the absent parent; and

(c) to a qualifying transfer were a reference to a compensating transfer.

[²8A.–(1) This paragraph applies where–

(a) the property which is the subject of a compensating transfer is or includes cash or deposits as defined in paragraph 5(i);

(b) that property was acquired by the parent with care after the relevant date;

(c) the absent parent has no legal interest in that property;

(d) if that property is or includes cash obtained by a mortgage or charge, that mortgage or charge was executed by the parent with care after the relevant date and was of property to the whole of which she is legally entitled; and

(e) the effect of the compensating transfer is that the parent with care or a relevant child is beneficially entitled (subject to any mortgage or charge) to the whole of the absent parent's legal estate in the land which is the subject of the qualifying transfer.]

(2) Where sub-paragraph (1) applies, the qualifying value of the compensating transfer shall be the amount of the cash or deposits transferred pursuant to the court order or written maintenance agreement referred to in head (a) of the definition of "qualifying transfer" in paragraph 1(1).

Computation of relevant value of a qualifying transfer

9. The relevant value of a qualifying transfer shall be calculated by deducting from the qualifying value of the qualifying transfer the qualifying value of any compensating transfer between the same persons as are parties to the qualifying transfer.

Amount to be allowed in respect of a qualifying transfer

10. *For the purposes of regulation 9(1)(bb), the amount to be allowed in the computation of E, or in case where regulation 10(a) applies, F, shall be–*

(a) *where the relevant value calculated in accordance with paragraph 9 is less than £5,000, nil;*

(b) *where the relevant value calculated in accordance with paragraph 9 is at least £5,000, but less than £10,000, £20.00 per week;*

(c) *where the relevant value calculated in accordance with paragraph 9 is at least £10,000, but less than £25,000, £40.00 per week;*

(d) *where the relevant value calculated in accordance with paragraph 9 is not less than £25,000, £60.00 per week.*

11. *this schedule in its application to Scotland shall have effect as if–*

(a) *in paragraph 1 for the words "legal estate or equitable interest in land" [³and in head (e) of paragraph 8A(1), for the words "legal estate in the land''] there were substituted the words "an interest in land within the meaning of section 2(6) of the Conveyancing and Feudal Reform (Scotland) Act 1970";*

(b) *in paragraph 4 the word "estate," and the words "estate or" in each place where they respectively occur were omitted.*

[³(c) *in paragraphs 1, 2, 4 and 8A for the word "mortgage" there were substituted the words "heritable security'']]*

Amendments

1. Child Support and Income Support (Amendment) Regulations 1995 (SI 1995 No.1045) reg 57 and Sch 2 (April 18, 1995).

2. Child Support (Miscellaneous Amendments) (No.2) Regulations 1995 (SI 1995 No.3261) reg 48(1) and (2) (December 18, 1995)

3. Child Support (Miscellaneous Amendments) Regulations 1999 (SI 1999 No.977) reg 6(7) (April 6, 1999).

4. Social Security Act 1998 (Commencement No.7 and Consequential and Transitional Provisions) Order 1999 (SI 1999 No.1510) art 21(a) and (b) (June 1, 1999).

General Note

This Schedule makes provision for clean break settlements under court orders or written agreements made before the coming into force of the child support scheme. It provides for an allowance to be made in the non-resident parent's exempt income calculation based on a sliding scale which is fixed as follows. In the case of settlements expressly made solely in substitution for maintenance payments for a relevant child, the whole of the capital value is taken into account. In other cases, only half the capital value is used. Where the asset is an interest in land or a business asset which is mortgaged or charged, only the difference between the value of the asset and the outstanding principal secured is taken into account. Transfers from a parent with care to the non-resident parent are offset. The relevant value is that at the date of the order or agreement.

Paragraph 1

"property" The scope of the definition of property is limited. It does not include, for example, shares. Nor does it include cases where one party has conferred a benefIt on the other by assuming responsibility for debts, such as mortgage debts.

"qualifying transfer" A qualifying transfer is one made between the non-resident parent and either the parent with care or a child. Accordingly, if the person with care is not a parent of the child (eg, a grandparent or a subsequent partner of one of the parents), the provisions of this Schedule can only apply if the settlement was between the absent parent and the child.

"court order" and **"written maintenance agreement"** See the general note to s18 of the 1995 Act. It is arguable that in this context "written maintenance agreement" is not limited to agreements which fall within s9(1) of the Act, as this would introduce an irrelevant and unnecessary limitation on the agreements that are covered by this Schedule.

In construing an order or agreement it is permissible to have regard to evidence contained in another document, such as a side letter, which is intended to contain terms of the arrangement (*CCS 16518/1996*, para 7). In the case of a consent order, it is appropriate to interpret the undertakings and the orders of the court as a single whole, because the settlement was negotiated as a package (*CCS 316/1998*, para 19).

"executed" This word is ambiguous. It is used in relation to agreements to mean either made or performed. It is suggested that the more natural meaning of the word is the former (*Terrapin International Ltd v Inland Revenue Commissioners* [1976] 2 All ER 461). Moreover, interpreting "executed" to mean the performance rather than the making of a written agreement would produce the anomaly that the relevant date for a transfer under a court order would be the date that order was made, whereas if the transfer were pursuant to a written agreement, the relevant date would be the date of the transfer.

"asset" It is important to identify clearly the asset being transferred.

"expressly for the purpose only of compensating" In deciding whether or not the specified purpose is expressed, the order or agreement is to be read as a whole (*CCS 16518/1996*, para 12(3) and *CCS 316/1998*, para 19).

The following are irrelevant: (i) subjective evidence of intention or motive; (ii) speculation or inference; (iii) calculations of who may have derived some direct or indirect benefit; (iv) any incidental benefit to a child, such as going on living at the family home after the transfer; (v) any mere statement of intention not affecting the actual interest taken or the terms on which the property is held, such as the standard certificate to postpone a legal aid charge, that the house is to be used by the parent with care as a home for herself or her dependants. See *R(CS) 9/99*, para 15. The preservation of even a right to a nominal sum by way of maintenance for the other party prevents the transfer being a qualifying one (*CCS 16518/1996*, paras 9 and 15).

"loss" This includes the partial loss of a right (*CCS 1554/1997*, para 6 and *R(CS) 9/99*, para 22).

"any right to apply" There are conflicting decisions by commissioners on whether the reference to the loss of any right to apply for periodical payments or a capital sum means the loss of all right to apply (*CCS 16518/1996*, para 12(1)) or the loss of a right to apply (*R(CS) 9/99*, para 19). The question was left open in *CCS 1554/1997* (para 6).

An Edinburgh-based commissioner decided that para 1(1)(e) can never be satisfied when the transfer is made in implementation of a court decree (*CSCS 1/1998* and *CSCS 2/1998*). The commissioner left open the position in the case of a written agreement (*ibid*, para 13).

Paragraph 5

It is suggested that "money ... derived from ... capital" includes interest which has accrued to that money by the relevant date, namely, the date of the court order or the execution of the written maintenance agreement. This will catch, for example, interest earned on money which is raised from the sale, during the parties' divorce, of the former matrimonial home, but held on deposit in a bank account pending final resolution of the financial settlement.

[¹SCHEDULE 3B
AMOUNT TO BE ALLOWED IN RESPECT OF TRAVELLING COSTS

Interpretation
    1.   In this Schedule–
"day" means, in relation to a person who attends at a work place for one period of work which commences before midnight of one day and concludes the following day, the first of those days;
"journey" means a single journey, and "pair of journeys" means two journeys in opposing directions, between the same two places;
"relevant employment" means an employed earner's employment in which the relevant person is employed and in the course of which he is required to attend at a work place, and "relevant employer" means the employer of the relevant person in that employment;
"relevant person" means–
    (a)   in the application of the provisions of this Schedule to regulation 9, the absent parent or the parent with care; and
    (b)   in the application of the provisions of this Schedule to regulation 11, the absent parent;
[⁴"straight-line distance" means the straight-line distance measured in kilometres and calculated to 2 decimal places, and, where that distance is not a whole number of kilometres, rounded to the nearest whole number of kilometres, a distance which exceeds a whole number of kilometres by 0.50 of a kilometre being rounded up;]
"travelling costs" means the cost of–
    (a)   purchasing either fuel or a ticket for the purposes of travel;
    (b)   contributing to the costs borne by a person other than a relevant employer in providing transport; or
    (c)   paying another to provide transport,
which are incurred by the relevant person in travelling between the relevant person's home and his work place, and where he has more than one relevant employment between any of his work places in those employment's;
"work place" means the relevant person's normal place of employment in a relevant employment, and "deemed work place" means a place which has been selected by the [³Secretary of State] pursuant either to paragraph 8(2) or 15(2) for the purpose of calculating the amount to be allowed in respect of the relevant person's traveling costs.

Computation of amount allowable in respect of travelling costs
    2.   For the purpose of regulation 9 and regulation 11 an amount in respect of the travelling costs of the relevant person shall be determined in accordance with the following provisions of this Schedule if the relevant person–
    (a)   has travelling costs; and
    (b)   provides the information required to enable the amount of the allowance to be determined.

Computation in cases where there is one relevant employment and one work place in that employment
    3.   Subject to paragraphs 21 to 23, where the relevant person has one relevant employment and is normally required to attend at only one work place in the course of that employment the amount to be allowed in respect of travelling costs shall be determined in accordance with paragraphs 4 to 7 below.
    4.   there shall be calculated or, if that is impracticable, estimated–

(a)   the straight-line distance between the relevant person's home and his work place;
(b)   the number of journeys between the relevant person's home and his work place which he makes during a period comprising a whole number of weeks which appears to the [³Secretary of State] to be representative of his normal pattern of work, there being disregarded any pair of journeys between his work place and his home and where the first journey is from his work place to his home and where the time which elapses between the start of the first journey and the conclusion of the second is not more than two hours.

5.   the results of the calculation or estimate produced by sub-paragraph (a) of paragraph 4 shall be multiplied by the result of the calculation or estimate required by sub-paragraph (b) of that paragraph.

6.   The product of the multiplication required by paragraph 5 shall be divided by the number of weeks in the period.

7.   Where the result of the division required by paragraph 6 is less than or equal [⁴240], the amount to be allowed in respect of the relevant person's travelling costs shall be nil, and where it is greater than [⁴240] the weekly allowance to be made in respect of the relevant person's travelling costs shall be [⁴6 pence] multiplied by the number by which that number exceeds [⁴240].

Computation in cases where there is more than one work place but only one relevant employment

8.–(1) Subject to sub-paragraph (2) and paragraphs 21 to 23 below, where the relevant person has one relevant employment but attends at more than one work place the amount to be allowed in respect of travelling costs for the purposes of regulations 9 and 11 shall be determined in accordance with paragraphs 9 to [⁴14].

(2)   Where it appears that the relevant person works at more than one work place but his pattern of work is not sufficiently regular to enable the calculation of the amount to be allowed in respect of his travelling costs to be made readily, the [³Secretary of State] may–
(a)   select a place which is either one of the relevant person's work places or some other place which is connected with the relevant employment; and
(b)   apply the provisions of paragraphs 4 to 7 above to actuate the amount of the allowance to be made in respect of travelling costs upon the basis that the relevant person makes one journey form his home to the deemed work place and one journey from the deemed work place to his home on each day on which he attends at a work place in connection with relevant employment,
and the provisions of paragraphs 9 to [⁴14] shall not apply.

(3)   For the purposes of sub-paragraph (2)(b) there shall be disregarded any day upon which the relevant person attends at a work place and in order to travel to or from that work place he undertakes a journey in respect of which–
(a)   the travelling costs are borne wholly or in part by the relevant employer; or
(b)   the relevant employer provides transport for any part of the journey for the use of the relevant person,
and where he attends at more than one work place on the same day that day shall be disregarded only if the condition specified in this sub-paragraph is satisfied in respect of all the work places at which he attends on that day.

9.   There shall be calculated, or if that is impracticable, estimated–
(a)   the straight-line distances between the relevant person's home and each work place; and
(b)   the straight-line distances between each of the relevant person's work places, other than those between which the does not ordinarily travel.

10.   Subject to paragraph 11, there shall be calculated for each pair of places referred to in paragraph 9 the number of journeys which the relevant person makes between them during a period comprising a whole number of weeks which appears to the [³Secretary of State] to be representative of the normal working pattern of the relevant person.

11.   For the purposes of the calculation required by paragraph 10 there shall be disregarded–
(a)   any pair of journeys between the same work place and the relevant person's home where the first journey is from his work place to his home and the time which elapses between the start of the first journey and the conclusion of the second is not more than two hours; and
(b)   any journey in respect of which–
(i)   the travelling costs are borne wholly or in part by the relevant employer; or
(ii)   the relevant employer provides transport for any part of the journey for the use of the relevant person.

12.   The result of the calculation of the number of journeys made between each pair of places required by paragraph 10 shall be multiplied by the result of the calculation or estimate of the straight-line distance between them required by paragraph 9.

13.   All the products of the multiplication's required by paragraph 12 shall be added together and the resulting sum divided by the number of weeks in the period.

14.   Where the result of the division required by paragraph 13 is less than or equal to [⁴240], the amount to be allowed in respect of travelling costs shall be nil, and where it is greater than [⁴240], the weekly allowance to be made in respect of the relevant person's traveling costs shall be [⁴6 pence]multiplied by the number by which that number excess [⁴240].

Computation in cases where there is more than one relevant employment

15.–*(1)   Subject to sub-paragraph (2) and paragraphs 21 to 23, where the relevant person has more than one relevant employment the amount to be allowed in respect of travelling costs for the purposes of regulations 9 and 11 shall be determined in accordance with paragraphs 16 to 20.*

(2)   Where it appears that in respect of any of his relevant employment's, whilst the relevant person works at more than one work place, his pattern of work is not sufficiently regular to enable the actuation of the amount to be allowed in respect of his traveling costs to be made readily, the [³Secretary of State]–

(a)   may select a place which is either one of the relevant person's work places in that relevant employment or some other place which is connected with that relevant employment;

(b)   may calculate the weekly average distance travelled in the course of his journeys made in connection with the relevant employment upon the basis that–

(i)   the relevant person makes one journey from his home, or form another work place or deemed work place in another relevant employment, to the deemed work place and one journey from the deemed work place to his home, or to another work place or deemed work place in another relevant employment, on each day on which he attends at a work place in connection with the relevant employment in relation to which the deemed work place has been selected, and

(ii)   the distance he travels between those places is the straight-line distance between them; and

(c)   shall disregard any journeys made between work places in the relevant employment in respect of which a deemed work place has been selected.

(3)   For the purposes of sub-paragraph (2)(b) there shall be disregarded any day upon which the relevant person attends at a work place and in order to travel to or from that work place he undertakes a journey in respect of which–

(a)   the travelling costs are borne wholly or in part by the relevant employer; or

(b)   the relevant employer provides transport for any part of the journey for the use of the relevant person,

and where in the course of the particular relevant employment he attends at more than one work place on the same day, that day shall be disregarded only if the condition specified in this paragraph is satisfied in respect of all the work places at which he attends on that day in the course of that employment.

16.   *there shall be calculated, or if that is impracticable, estimated–*

(a)   the straight-line distances between the relevant person's home and each work place; and

(b)   the straight-line distances between each of the relevant person's work places, except–

(i)   those between which he does not ordinarily travel, and

(ii)   those for which a calculation of the distance from the relevant person's home is not required by virtue of paragraph 15(c).

*[²**17.**   Subject to paragraph 17A, there shall be calculated, or if that is impracticable estimated, for each pair of places referred to in paragraph 16 between which straight-line distances are required to be calculated or estimated, the number of journeys which the relevant person makes between them during a period comprising a whole number of weeks which appears to the [³Secretary of State] to be representative of the normal working pattern of the relevant person.*

17A.   *For the purposes of the calculation required by paragraph 17, there shall be disregarded-*

(a)   any pair of journeys between the same work place and his home where the first journey is from his work place to his home and the time which elapses between the start of the first journey and the conclusion of the second is not more than two hours; and

(b)   any journey in respect of which–

(i)   the travelling costs are borne wholly or in part by the relevant employer; or

(ii)   the relevant employer provides transport for any part of the journey for the use of the relevant person.]

18.   *The result of the calculation or estimate of the number of journeys made between each pair of places required by paragraph 17 shall be multiplied by the result of the calculation or estimate of the straight-line distance between them required by paragraph 16.*

19.   *All the products of the multiplication's required by paragraph 18, shall be added together and the resulting sum divided by the number of weeks in the period.*

20.   *Where the result of the division required by paragraph 19, plus where appropriate the result of the calculation required by paragraph 15 in respect of a relevant employment in which a deemed work place has been selected, is less than or equal to [⁴240] the amount to be allowed in respect of travelling costs shall be nil, and where it is greater than [⁴240], the weekly allowance to be made in respect of the relevant person's travelling costs shall be [⁴6 pence] multiplied by the number by which that number exceeds [⁴240].*

Relevant employments in respect of which no amount is to be allowed

21.–*(1)   No allowance shall be made in respect of travelling costs in respect of journeys between the relevant person's home and his work place or between his work place and his home in a particular relevant employment if the condition set out in paragraph 22 or 23 is satisfied in respect of that employment.*

(2)   The condition mentioned in paragraph 22, or as the case may be 23, is satisfied in relation to a case where the relevant person has more than one work place in a relevant employment only where the employer

provides assistance of the kind mentioned in that paragraph in respect of all of the work places to or from which the relevant person travels in the course of that employment, but those journeys in respect of which that assistance is provided shall be disregarded in computing the total distance traveled by the relevant person in the course of the relevant employment.

22.   *The condition is that the relevant employer provides transport of any description in connection with the employment which is available to the relevant person for any part of the journey between his home and his work place or between his work place and his home.*

23.   *The condition is that the relevant employer bears any part of the travelling costs arising from the relevant person travelling between his home and his work place or between his work place and his home in connection with that employment, and for the purposes of this paragraph he does not bear any part of that cost where he does no more than–*

(a)   *make a payment to the relevant person which would fall to be taken into account in determining the amount of the relevant person's net income;*

(b)   *make a loan to the relevant person;*

(c)   *pay to the relevant person an increased amount of remuneration,*

to enable the relevant person to meet those costs himself.]

Amendments

1.   *Child Support and Income Support (Amendment) Regulations 1995 (SI 1995 No.1045) reg 57 and Sch 2 (April 18, 1995).*

2.   *Child Support (Miscellaneous Amendments) (No.2) Regulations 1995 (SI 1995 No.3261) reg 49 (January 22, 1996).*

3.   *Social Security Act 1998 (Commencement No.7 and Consequential and Transitional Provisions) Order 1999 (SI 1999 No.1510) art 22 (June 1, 1999).*

4.   *Child Support (Miscellaneous Amendments) Regulations 2004 (SI 2004 No.2415) reg 5(4) (September 16, 2004).*

General Note

This Schedule provides for allowance to be made in a parent's exempt income and in an absent parent's protected income in respect of costs of travelling between home and work. To qualify the parent must actually incur travelling costs. No sum is allowed, for example, if the parent walks or cycles to work or is taken by a relative or friend free of charge. If a parent does have travelling costs, an allowance is made. It is calculated or estimated by reference to the straight-line distance between home and work place and is based on the travel in a normal week. Straight-line measurement is the method which, by virtue of s8 Interpretation Act 1978, would be applied unless the contrary intention appears. The express reference to this method of measurement avoids any argument that there was a contrary intention. Return journeys from work to home and back to work (eg, for a meal or between shifts) are ignored if the return home lasts for two hours or less. The existence of physical obstructions, such as mountain ranges and river estuaries, is ignored as is the actual distance by road or rail. Where a parent has more than one employer or more than one work place, the decision maker may deem one of them or some other connected place to be the place of work for the purpose of the calculation or estimate. No travelling costs are allowed if the employer provides transport for all or part of the journey or contributes toward the travelling costs, but no contribution is deemed to occur if the employer's sole contribution towards the costs of travel comprises a payment which would be taken into account in calculating net income, a loan or increased pay.

The calculation of distances is made by a computer program based on postcodes. If this issue arises on appeal, the tribunal will need to be satisfied on appropriate evidence of the following matters.

(i)   The decision maker will have to prove the accuracy of the computer program.

(ii)   The postcodes of the parent's home and place of work will need to be established.

(iii)   It will have to be shown that the correct codes were put into the program, and the output from the program on the basis of that input will have to be shown. The tribunal will also need to bear in mind the following factors which may affect the relevance of the outcome of the program to the case under appeal.

(iv)   The postcode may, especially in a rural location, cover a fairly large area.

(v)   A postcode is only provided for buildings to which mail is delivered. Some employers will have mail delivered to a central location or to a Post Office Box number with the result that a person's particular place of work may not have a postcode and may be some distance away from the building to which the postcode applies.

Finally, the tribunal will need to bear in mind two further factors.

(vi)   There is no basis in the legislation for the calculation of distance by reference to postcodes, so the tribunal may calculate the relevant distance by any means that will produce a sufficiently accurate result.

(vii)   The tribunal will only need to concern itself with arguments over the accuracy of the decision maker's calculation if the degree of error is likely to affect the ultimate decision.

SCHEDULE 4
CASES WHERE CHILD SUPPORT MAINTENANCE IS NOT TO BE PAYABLE

The payments and awards specified for the purposes of regulation 26(1)(b)(i) are–
(a)   *the following payments under the Contribution and Benefits Act–*
    [²(i)   *incapacity benefit under section 30A;*
    (ii)   *long-term incapacity benefit for widows under section 40;*
    (iii)   *long-term incapacity benefit for widowers under section 41;]*
    (iv)   *maternity allowance under section 35;*
    (v)   [² . . .];
    (vi)   *attendance allowance under section 64;*
    (vii)   *severe disablement allowance under section 68;*
    (viii)   [⁴carer's allowance] *under section 70;*
    (ix)   *disability living allowance under section 71;*
    (x)   *disablement benefit under section 103;*
    (xi)   [⁵...]
    (xii)   *statutory sick pay within the meaning of section 151;*
    (xiii)   *statutory maternity pay within the meaning of section 164;*
(b)   *awards in respect of disablement made under (or under provisions analogous to)–*
    (i)   *the War Pensions (Coastguards) Scheme 1944 (S.I. 1944 No. 500);*
    (ii)   *the War Pensions (Naval Auxiliary Personnel) Scheme 1964 (S.I. 1964 No. 1985);*
    (iii)   *the Pensions (Polish Forces) Scheme 1964 (S.I. 1964 No. 2007);*
    (iv)   *the War Pensions (Mercantile Marine) Scheme 1964 (S.I. 1964 No. 2058);*
    (v)   *the Royal Warrant of 21st December 1964 (service in the Home Guard before 1945) (Cmnd. 2563);*
    (vi)   *the Order by Her Majesty of 22nd December 1964 concerning pensions and other grants in respect of disablement or death due to service in the Home Guard after 27th April 1952 (Cmnd. 2564);*
    (vii)   *the Order by Her Majesty (Ulster Defence Regiment) of 4th January 1971 (Cmnd. 4567);*
    (viii)   *the Personal Injuries (Civilians) Scheme 1983 (S.I. 1983 No. 686);*
    (ix)   *the Naval, Military and Air Forces Etc. (Disablement and Death) Service Pensions Order 1983 (S.I. 1983 No. 883);* [⁶...]
    [⁶(x)   *the Armed Forces (Pensions and Compensation) Act 2004;* [⁸...]]
(c)   *payments from* [¹[⁷the Independent Living (1993) Fund, the Independent Living (Extension) Fund or the Independent Living Fund (2006)]] [⁸; [⁹...]
(d)   *personal independence payment in accordance with Part 4 of the Welfare Reform Act 2012]* [⁹; and
(e)   *armed forces independence payment under the Armed Forces and Reserve Forces (Compensation Scheme) Order 2011.]*

Amendments
    1.   *Child Support (Miscellaneous Amendments) Regulations 1993 (SI 1993 No. 913) reg 34 (April 5, 1993).*
    2.   *Child Support and Income Support (Amendment) Regulations 1995 (SI 1995 No.1045) reg 58 (April 13, 1995).*
    3.   *Social Security and Child Support (Tax Credits) Consequential Amendments Regulations 1999 (SI 1999 No.2566) reg 2(2) and Sch 2, Part II (October 5, 1999).*
    4.   *Child Support (Miscellaneous Amendments) Regulations 2003 (SI 2003 No.328) reg 6(8)(a) (April 1, 2003).*
    5.   *Child Support (Miscellaneous Amendments) Regulations 2003 (SI 2003 No.328) reg 6(8)(b) (April 6, 2003).*
    6.   *Child Support (Miscellaneous Amendments) Regulations 2005 (SI 2005 No.785) reg 4(4) (March 16, 2005).*
    7.   *Independent Living Fund (2006) Order 2007 (SI 2007 No.2538) reg 3(3) (October 1, 2007).*
    8.   *Personal Independence Payment (Supplementary Provisions and Consequential Amendments) Regulations 2013 (SI 2013 No.388) reg 8 and Sch para 13(3) (April 8, 2013).*
    9.   *Armed Forces and Reserve Forces Compensation Scheme (Consequential Provisions: Subordinate Legislation) Order 2013 (SI 2013 No.591) reg 7 and Sch para 7(3) (April 8, 2013).*

Definitions
    "Contributions and Benefits Act": see reg 1(2).
    "Independent Living (1993) Fund": see reg 1(2).
    "Independent Living (Extension) Fund": see reg 1(2).

[¹SCHEDULE 5
PROVISIONS APPLYING TO CASES TO WHICH SECTION 43 OF THE ACT AND REGULATION 28 APPLY

[²...]

9. The provisions of paragraphs (1) and (2) of regulation 5 of the Child Support (Collection and Enforcement) Regulations 1992 shall apply to the transmission of payments in place of payments of child support maintenance under section 43 of the Act and regulation 28 as they apply to the transmission of payments of child support maintenance.

Amendments

1.   Child Support (Miscellaneous Amendments) Regulations 1993 (SI 1993 No.913) reg 26(3) (April 5, 1993).
2.   Social Security Act 1998 (Commencement No.7 and Consequential and Transitional Provisions) Order 1999 (SI 1999 No.1510) art 23 (June 1, 1999).

Definition

"the Act": see reg 1(2).

The Child Support (Arrears, Interest and Adjustment of Maintenance Assessments) Regulations 1992
(1992 No.1816)

PART I
General

Citation, commencement and interpretation

    1.–(1)   These Regulations may be cited as the Child Support (Arrears, Interest and Adjustment of Maintenance Assessments) Regulations 1992 and shall come into force on 5th April 1993.

    (2)   In these Regulations, unless the context otherwise requires–

[¹…]

"the Act" means the Child Support Act 1991;

"arrears" means arrears of child support maintenance;

"arrears of child support maintenance" is to be construed in accordance with section 41(1) and (2) of the Act;

"arrears notice" has the meaning prescribed in regulation 2;

[²"Maintenance Calculation Procedure Regulations" means the Child Support (Maintenance Calculation Procedure) Regulations 2000;]

[¹…]
[¹…]
[¹…]

[²"non-resident parent" includes a person treated as such under regulation 8 of the Child Support (Maintenance Calculations and Special Cases) Regulations 2000;]

"parent with care" means a person who, in respect of the same child or children, is both a parent and a person with care;

"relevant person" has the same meaning as in the [²Maintenance Calculation Procedure Regulations].

[³"state pension credit" means the social security benefit of that name payable under the State Pension Credit Act 2002.]

(3)   In these Regulations, unless the context otherwise requires, a reference–

(a)   to a numbered regulation is to the regulation in these Regulations bearing that number;

(b)   in a regulation to a numbered paragraph is to the paragraph in that regulation bearing that number;

(c)   in a paragraph to a lettered or numbered sub-paragraph is to the sub-paragraph in that paragraph bearing that letter or number.

Amendments

1.   Child Support (Collection and Enforcement and Miscellaneous Amendments) Regulations 2000 (SI 2001 No.162) reg 5(2)(a) (comes into force in relation to a particular case on the day on which ss1(2) and (3), 4, 18(1) and (2), and 20(1) of and Sch 3 para 11(2) and (16) Child Support, Pensions and Social Security Act 2000 come into force for the purposes of that type of case – which is March 3, 2003 for the types of cases in arts 3 and 5 of SI 2003 No.192). For other types of cases see the '1993 rules', below. See reg 6 of SI 2001 No.162 for savings provisions detailing when these amendments do not apply.

2.   Child Support (Collection and Enforcement and Miscellaneous Amendments) Regulations 2000 (SI 2001 No.162) reg 5(2)(b)-(d) (comes into force in relation to a particular case on the day on which ss1(2) and (3), 4, 18(1) and (2), and 20(1) of and Sch 3 para 11(2) and (16) Child Support, Pensions and Social Security Act 2000 come into force for the purposes of that type of case – which is March 3, 2003 for the types of cases in arts 3 and 5 of SI 2003 No.192). For other types of cases see the '1993 rules', below. See reg 6 of SI 2001 No.162 for savings provisions detailing when these amendments do not apply.

3.   State Pension Credit (Consequential, Transitional and Miscellaneous Provisions) Regulations 2002 (SI 2002 No.3019) reg 26(2) (October 6, 2003).

1993 rules

Reg 5(2) of the Child Support (Collection and Enforcement and Miscellaneous Amendments) Regulations 2000 (SI 2001 No.162) amends this regulation and has been brought into force only for the types of cases in arts 3 and 5 of the Child Support, Pensions and Social Security Act 2000 (Commencement No.12) Order 2003 (SI 2003 No.192) – see p683, subject to savings provisions in reg 6 of SI 2001 No.162. For other types of cases the '1993 rules' apply. If the 1993 rules apply, the definitions of "Maintenance Calculation Procedure Regulations" and "non-resident parent" are omitted, in the definition of "relevant person" the words "Maintenance Assessment Procedure Regulations" are retained in place of "Maintenance Calculation Procedure Regulations" and the following definitions below are still included in this regulation:

"absent parent" includes a person treated as an absent parent by virtue of regulation 20 of the Maintenance Assessments and Special Cases Regulations;

"due date" has the meaning prescribed in regulation 3;

"Maintenance Assessments and Special cases Regulations" means the Child Support (Maintenance Assessments and Special Cases) Regulations 1992;

"Maintenance Assessment Procedure Regulations" means the Child Support (Maintenance Assessment Procedure) Regulations 1992;

PART II
Arrears of child support maintenance [¹...]

Amendment

1.   Child Support (Collection and Enforcement and Miscellaneous Amendments) Regulations 2000 (SI 2001 No.162) reg 5(3)(a) (comes into force in relation to a particular case on the day on which ss1(2) and (3), 4, 18(1) and (2), and 20(1) of and Schedule 3 para 11(2) and (16) Child Support, Pensions and Social Security Act 2000 come into force for the purposes of that type of case – which is March 3, 2003 for the types of cases detailed in arts 3 and 5 of SI 2003 No.192). See reg 6 of SI 2001 No.162 for savings provisions detailing when this amendment does not apply. For those for whom this does not apply, "and interest on arrears" were omitted by this amendment.

Applicability of provisions as to arrears [1...] and arrears notices
2.–[2...]

Amendments
1. Child Support (Collection and Enforcement and Miscellaneous Amendments) Regulations 2000 (SI 2001 No.162) reg 5(3)(b) comes into force in relation to a particular case on the day on which ss1(2) and (3), 4, 18(1) and (2), and 20(1) of and Sch 3 para 11(2) and (16) Child Support, Pensions and Social Security Act 2000 come into force for the purposes of that type of case – which is March 3, 2003 for the types of cases in arts 3 and 5 of SI 2003 No.192). See reg 6 of SI 2001 No.162 for savings provisions detailing when these amendments do not apply.
2. Child Support (Management of Payments and Arrears) Regulations 2009 (SI 2009 No.3151) reg 14 and Sch (January 25, 2010).

Liability to make payments of interest with respect to arrears
3.–[1,2...]

Amendments
1. Child Support (Collection and Enforcement and Miscellaneous Amendments) Regulations 2000 (SI 2001 No.162) reg 5(3)(e) (comes into force in relation to a particular case on the day on which ss1(2) and (3), 4, 18(1) and (2), and 20(1) of and Sch 3 para 11(2) and (16) Child Support, Pensions and Social Security Act 2000 come into force for the purposes of that type of case – which is March 3, 2003 for the types of cases in arts 3 and 5 of SI 2003 No.192). See reg 6 of SI 2001 No.162 for savings provisions.
2. Child Support (Management of Payments and Arrears) Regulations 2009 (SI 2009 No.3151) reg 14 and Sch (January 25, 2010).

Circumstances in which no liability to pay interest arises
4.–[1,2...]

Amendment
1. Child Support (Collection and Enforcement and Miscellaneous Amendments) Regulations 2000 (SI 2001 No.162) reg 5(3)(e) (comes into force in relation to a particular case on the day on which ss1(2) and (3), 4, 18(1) and (2), and 20(1) of and Sch 3 para 11(2) and (16) Child Support, Pensions and Social Security Act 2000 come into force for the purposes of that type of case – which is March 3, 2003 for the types of cases in arts 3 and 5 of SI 2003 No.192). See reg 6 of SI 2001 No.162 for savings provisions.
2. Child Support (Management of Payments and Arrears) Regulations 2009 (SI 2009 No.3151) reg 14 and Sch (January 25, 2010).

Payment of arrears by agreement
5.–[4...]

Amendments
1. Reg 5(1) and (2) substituted by reg 37 of SI 1993/913 as from 5.4.93.
2. Child Support (Collection and Enforcement and Miscellaneous Amendments) Regulations 2000 (SI 2001 No.162) reg 5(3)(c)(i) (comes into force in relation to a particular case on the day on which ss1(2) and (3), 4, 18(1) and (2), and 20(1) of and Sch 3 para 11(2) and (16) Child Support, Pensions and Social Security Act 2000 come into force for the purposes of that type of case – which is March 3, 2003 for the types of cases in arts 3 and 5 of SI 2003 No.192). See reg 6 of SI 2001 No.162 for savings provisions detailing when these amendments do not apply. For those for whom this does not apply, the amendment substituted "non-resident parent" for "absent parent".
3. Child Support (Collection and Enforcement and Miscellaneous Amendments) Regulations 2000 (SI 2001 No.162) reg 5(3)(c)(ii) (comes into force in relation to a particular case on the day on which ss1(2) and (3), 4, 18(1) and (2), and 20(1) of and Sch 3 para 11(2) and (16) Child Support, Pensions and Social Security Act 2000 come into force for the purposes of that type of case – which is March 3, 2003 for the types of cases in arts 3 and 5 of SI 2003 No.192). See reg 6 of SI 2001 No.162 for savings provisions detailing when these amendments do not apply.
4. Child Support (Management of Payments and Arrears) Regulations 2009 (SI 2009 No.3151) reg 14 and Sch (January 25, 2010).

Rate of interest and calculation of interest
6.–[1,2...]

Amendments

1. Child Support (Collection and Enforcement and Miscellaneous Amendments) Regulations 2000 (SI 2001 No.162) reg 5(3)(e) (comes into force in relation to a particular case on the day on which ss1(2) and (3), 4, 18(1) and (2), and 20(1) of and Sch 3 para 11(2) and (16) to the Child Support, Pensions and Social Security Act 2000 come into force for the purposes of that type of case – which is March 3, 2003 for the types of cases in arts 3 and 5 of SI 2003 No.192). See reg 6 of SI 2001 No.162 for savings provisions.
2. Child Support (Management of Payments and Arrears) Regulations 2009 (SI 2009 No.3151) reg 14 and Sch (January 25, 2010).

Receipt and retention of interest paid
7.–[¹,²…]

Amendments

1. Child Support (Collection and Enforcement and Miscellaneous Amendments) Regulations 2000 (SI 2001 No.162) reg 5(3)(e) (comes into force in relation to a particular case on the day on which ss1(2) and (3), 4, 18(1) and (2), and 20(1) of and Sch 3 parag 11(2) and (16) Child Support, Pensions and Social Security Act 2000 come into force for the purposes of that type of case – which is March 3, 2003 for the types of casesin arts 3 and 5 of SI 2003 No.192). See reg 6 of SI 2001 No.162 for savings provisions.
2. Child Support (Management of Payments and Arrears) Regulations 2009 (SI 2009 No.3151) reg 14 and Sch (January 25, 2010).

[¹Retention of recovered arrears of child support maintenance by the Secretary of State

8.–(1)   This regulation applies where–
(i)   the Secretary of State recovers arrears from an [³non-resident parent] under section 41 of the Act; and
(ii)   income support [²or income-based jobseeker's allowance] is paid to or in respect of the person with care or was paid to or in respect of that person at the date or dates upon which the payment or payments of child support maintenance referred to in paragraph (2) should have been made.

(2)   Where paragraph (1) applies, the Secretary of State may retain such amount of those arrears as is equal to the difference between the amount of income support [²or income-based jobseeker's allowance] that was paid to or in respect of the person with care and the amount of income support [²or income-based jobseeker's allowance] that he is satisfied would have been paid had the [³non-resident parent] paid, by the due dates, the amounts due under the child support [⁴maintenance calculation] in force or to be taken to have been in force by virtue of the provisions of section 41(2A) of the Act.]

Amendments

1. Reg 8 substituted by reg 2 of SI 1995/3261 as from 22.1.96.
2. Words inserted in reg 8 by reg 3(1) and (2)(b) of SI 1996/1345 as from 7.10.96.
3. Child Support (Collection and Enforcement and Miscellaneous Amendments) Regulations 2000 (SI 2001 No.162) reg 5(3)(d)(i) (comes into force in relation to a particular case on the day on which ss1(2) and (3), 4, 18(1) and (2), and 20(1) of and Sch 3 para 11(2) and (16) Child Support, Pensions and Social Security Act 2000 come into force for the purposes of that type of case – which is March 3, 2003 for the types of cases in arts 3 and 5 of SI 2003 No.192). For other types of cases see the '1993 rules', below. See reg 6 of SI 2001 No.162 for savings provisions detailing when these amendments do not apply.
4. Child Support (Collection and Enforcement and Miscellaneous Amendments) Regulations 2000 (SI 2001 No.162) reg 5(3)(d)(ii) (comes into force in relation to a particular case on the day on which ss1(2) and (3), 4, 18(1) and (2), and 20(1) of and Sch 3 para 11(2) and (16) Child Support, Pensions and Social Security Act 2000 come into force for the purposes of that type of case – which is March 3, 2003 for the types of cases detailed in arts 3 and 5 of SI 2003 No.192). For other types of cases see the '1993 rules', below. See reg 6 of SI 2001 No.162 for savings provisions detailing when this amendment does not apply.

1993 rules

Reg 5(3)(d) of the Child Support (Collection and Enforcement and Miscellaneous Amendments) Regulations 2000 (SI 2001 No.162) amends this regulation and has been brought into force only for the types of cases in arts 3 and 5 of the Child Support, Pensions and Social Security Act 2000 (Commencement No.12) Order 2003 (SI 2003 No.192) – see p638, subject to savings provisions in reg 6 of SI 2001 No.162. For other types of cases the

'1993 rules' apply. If the 1993 rules apply, "absent parent" is retained in place of "non-resident parent" and "maintenance assessment" is retained in place of "maintenance calculation".

Definition
"the Act": see reg 1(2).
"arrears": see reg 1(2).
"non-resident parent": see reg.1(2).

PART III
Attribution of payments and adjustment of the amount payable under a maintenance [¹calculation]

Amendment
1. Child Support (Collection and Enforcement and Miscellaneous Amendments) Regulations 2000 (SI 2001 No.162) reg 5(4)(a) (comes into force in relation to a particular case on the day on which ss1(2) and (3), 4, 18(1) and (2), and 20(1) of and Sch 3 para 11(2) and (16) Child Support, Pensions and Social Security Act 2000 come into force for the purposes of that type of case – which is March 3, 2003 for the types of cases in arts 3 and 5 of SI 2003 No.192). For other types of cases the '1993 rules' apply. See reg 6 of SI 2001 No.162 for savings provisions detailing when this amendment does not apply. If the 1993 rules apply, "assessment" is retained in place of "calculation".

Attribution of payments
9.   [²...]

Amendments
1. Child Support (Collection and Enforcement and Miscellaneous Amendments) Regulations 2000 (SI 2001 No.162) reg 5(4) (comes into force in relation to a particular case on the day on which ss1(2) and (3), 4, 18(1) and (2), and 20(1) of and Sch 3 para 11(2) and (16) Child Support, Pensions and Social Security Act 2000 come into force for the purposes of that type of case – which is March 3, 2003 for the types of cases detailed in arts 3 and 5 of SI 2003 No.192). See reg 6 of SI 2001 No.162 for savings provisions detailing when these amendments do not apply. For those for whom these amendments do not apply, the amendments substituted "non-resident parent" for "absent parent", and "calculation" for "assessment".
2. Child Support (Management of Payments and Arrears) Regulations 2009 (SI 2009 No.3151) reg 14 and Sch (January 25, 2010).

[¹ Adjustment of the amount payable under a maintenance [⁵calculation]
10.–[⁸...]]

Amendments
1. Reg 10 substituted by reg 8 of SI 1995/1045 as from 18.4.95 (see also in reg 64(4) ibid).
2. Substituted by art 26(a) of SI 1999/1510 as from 1.6.99.
3. Substituted in subpara (2) by art 26(b) of SI 1999/1510 as from 1.6.99.
4. Child Support (Decisions and Appeals) (Amendment) Regulations 2000 (SI 2000 No.3185) reg 14 (only in force for particular cases, and came into force for those cases on the date when certain provisions of the Child Support, Pensions and Social Security Act 2000 came into force in relation to that type of case). For other types of cases see the '1993 rules' below. See reg 1 of SI 2000 No.3185 and arts 3 and 7 SI 2003 No.192 for the relevant commencement date and see reg 14 of SI 2000/3185 for savings provisions. This amendment revokes regulation 10(2) and (3).
5. Child Support (Collection and Enforcement and Miscellaneous Amendments) Regulations 2000 (SI 2001 No.162) reg 5(4) (comes into force in relation to a particular case on the day on which ss1(2) and (3), 4, 18(1) and (2), and 20(1) of and Sch 3 para 11(2) and (16) Child Support, Pensions and Social Security Act 2000 come into force for the purposes of that type of case – which is March 3, 2003 for the types of cases in arts 3 and 5 of SI 2003 No.192). For other types of cases see the '1993 rules' below. See reg 6 of SI 2001 No.162 for savings provisions detailing when these amendments do not apply.
6. Child Support (Collection and Enforcement and Miscellaneous Amendments) Regulations 2000 (SI 2001 No.162) reg 5(4)(d) (comes into force in relation to a particular case on the day on which ss1(2) and (3), 4, 18(1) and (2), and 20(1) of and Sch 3 para 11(2) and (16) Child Support, Pensions and Social Security Act 2000 come into force for the purposes of that type of case – which is March 3, 2003 for the types of cases in arts 3 and 5 of SI 2003 No.192). For other types of cases see the '1993 rules' below. See reg 6 of SI 2001 No.162 for savings provisions detailing when these amendments do not apply.
7. Child Support (Miscellaneous Amendments) Regulations 2009 (SI 2009 No.396) reg 3 (April 6, 2009).

8. Child Support (Management of Payments and Arrears) Regulations 2009 (SI 2009 No.3151) reg 14 and Sch. (January 25, 2010). This revokes regulation 10 subject to the savings provisions in reg 15 of SI 2009 No.3151. Where before regulation 10 was revoked, an adjustment was made under reg 10(1) in respect of a '1993 scheme case' (as defined by reg 2 of SI 2009 No.3151), regs 10(2) and (3) and 11 to 17 continue to apply for certain purposes – see reg 15 of SI 2009 No.3151 for details. Reg 10(2) and (3) as it applies to such cases is reproduced under the '1993 rules' below. Where, before this regulation was revoked, an adjustment was made under reg 10(1) or (3A) in respect of a case other than a '1993 scheme case' (as defined by reg 2 of SI 2009 No.3151), regulation 30A of the Social Security and Child Support (Decisions and Appeals) Regulations 1999 (SI 1999 No.991) continues to apply to that case for the purposes of making and determining any appeal against the adjustment. For such cases reg 10(1) read:

"10.–(1) Where for any reason, including the retrospective effect of a [⁶...] maintenance [⁵calculation], there has been an overpayment of child support maintenance, [²the Secretary of State] may, for the purpose of taking account of that overpayment–

(a) apply the amount overpaid to reduce any arrears of child support maintenance due under any previous maintenance [⁵calculation] made in respect of the same relevant persons; or

(b) where there is no previous relevant maintenance [⁵calculation] or an overpayment remains after the application of sub-paragraph (a), and subject to paragraph (4), adjust the amount payable under a current maintenance [⁵calculation] by such amount as he considers appropriate in all the circumstances of the case having regard in particular to–

(i) the circumstances of the [⁵non-resident parent] and the person with care;

(ii) the amount of the overpayment in relation to the amount due under the current maintenance [⁵calculation]; and

(iii) the period over which it would be reasonable for the overpayment to be rectified."

and reg 10(3A) read:

[⁶(3A) Where there has been a voluntary payment, the Secretary of State may–

(a) apply the amount of the voluntary payment to reduce any arrears of child support maintenance due under any previous maintenance calculation made in respect of the same relevant persons; or

(b) where there is no previous relevant maintenance calculation or an amount of the voluntary payment remains after the application of sub-paragraph (a), and subject to paragraph (4), adjust the amount payable under a current maintenance calculation by such amount as he considers appropriate in all the circumstances of the case having regard in particular to–

(i) the circumstances of the non-resident parent and the person with care;

(ii) the amount of the voluntary payment in relation to the amount due under the current maintenance calculation; and

(iii) the period over which it would be reasonable for the voluntary payment to be taken into account.]

1993 rules

Reg 14 of the Child Support (Decisions and Appeals) (Amendment) Regulations 2000 (SI 2000 No.3185) revoked regulation 10(2) and (3). Subject to regulation 14 of SI 2000 No.3185, this amendment comes into force in relation to a particular case on the date on which sections 16, 17 and 20 of the Child Support Act 1991, as amended by the Child Support, Pensions and Social Security Act 2000, come into force in relation to that type of case – this was on March 3, 2003 for the types of cases detailed in art 3 of SI 2003 No.192 (see p683). For other types of cases paragraphs (2) and (3) of reg 10 continued to apply.

Reg 5(4) of the Child Support (Collection and Enforcement and Miscellaneous Amendments) Regulations 2000 (SI 2001 No.162) amends regulation 10 but has been brought into force only for the types of cases in arts 3 and 5 of the Child Support, Pensions and Social Security Act 2000 (Commencement No.12) Order 2003 (SI 2003 No.192) – see p683, subject to savings provisions in reg 6 of SI 2001 No.162. For other types of cases the amendments did not apply and:

– in the heading to the regulation "assessment" was retained in place of "calculation";

– in paragraph (1) the words "new or fresh" were retained before the words "maintenance assessment";

– paragraph (3A) was not inserted;

– in paragraph (4) the words "(2) or (3)" were retained in place of "(3A) or regulation 15D of the Social Security and Child Support (Decisions and Appeals) Regulations 1999" and the words "minimum amount prescribed under paragraph 7" were retained in place of "an amount equivalent to a flat rate fixed by paragraph 4(1)".

Regulation 10 was revoked from January 25, 2010 by reg 14 of the Child Support (Management of Payments and Arrears) Regulations 2009 (SI 2009 No.3151) subject to savings provisions in reg 15 of SI 2009 No.3151 (see p715). For '1993 scheme cases' (cases other than those for which provisions of the Child Support, Pensions and Social Security Act 2000 were brought into force by art 3 of SI 2003 No.192), if an adjustment was made under regulation 10(1) before January 25, 2010, paragraphs (2) and (3) of reg 10, as reproduced below, continue to apply for certain purposes. For such cases reg 10(1) read:

[¹ Adjustment of the amount payable under a maintenance assessment

10.–(1) Where for any reason, including the retrospective effect of a new or fresh maintenance assessment, there has been an overpayment of child support maintenance, [²the Secretary of State] may, for the purpose of taking account of that overpayment–

(a) apply the amount overpaid to reduce any arrears of child support maintenance due under any previous maintenance assessment made in respect of the same relevant persons; or

(b) where there is no previous relevant maintenance assessment or an over-payment remains after the application of sub-paragraph (a), and subject to paragraph (4), adjust the amount payable under a current maintenance assessment by such amount as he considers appropriate in all the circum-stances of the case having regard in particular to–

   (i) the circumstances of the absent parent and the person with care;

   (ii) the amount of the overpayment in relation to the amount due under the current maintenance assessment; and

   (iii) the period over which it would be reasonable for the overpayment to be rectified.

and 10(2) and (3) are as follows:

(2) Where [²the Secretary of State] has adjusted the amount payable under a maintenance assessment under the provisions of paragraph (1) and that maintenance assessment is subsequently [3replaced by a fresh maintenance assessment made by virtue of a revision under section 16 of the Act or of a decision under section 17 of the Act superseding an earlier decision] that adjustment shall, subject to paragraph (3),continue to apply to the amount payable under that fresh maintenance assessment unless [²the Secretary of State] is satisfied that such adjustment would not be appropriate in all the circumstances of the case.

(3) Where [²the Secretary of State] is satisfied that the adjustment referred to in paragraph (2) would not be appropriate, he may cancel that adjustment or he may adjust the amount payable under that fresh maintenance assessment as he sees fit, having regard to the matters specified in heads (i) to (iii) of sub-paragraph (b) of paragraph (1).

Definitions
"absent parent": see reg 1(2).
"the Act": see reg 1(2).
"arrears of child support maintenance": see reg 1(2).

General Note
This regulation deals with overpayments of child support maintenance.
Paragraph (1)
Overpayments may be attributed to discharge of arrears under a previous maintenance calculation: see subpara (1)(a). If that does not wipe out the overpayment, the Secretary of State may adjust the amount payable under the current maintenance calculation: see subpara (b). The adjustment is to the amount payable under the calculation. It does not alter the calculation itself.

If a fresh maintenance calculation is made, the adjustment may (a) be continued into the fresh calculation, (b) cease to apply or (c) be itself adjusted: see reg 15D of the Appeals Regulations.

If an adjustment is not possible or appropriate, the Secretary of State may reimburse the non-resident parent under s41B of the Act.

Paragraph (2)
This paragraph has not been amended to reflect the terminology of the amended scheme.
Paragraph (3A)
This makes equivalent provision to para (1) for voluntary payments under s28J of the Act. See the general note to that paragraph.

[¹Reimbursement of a repayment of overpaid child maintenance

10A.–(1)   The Secretary of State may require a relevant person to repay the whole or a part of any payment by way of reimbursement made to an [³non-resident parent] under section 41B(2) of the Act where the overpayment referred to in section 41B(1) of the Act arose–

(a)   in respect of the amount payable under a maintenance [³calculation] calculated in accordance with Part I of Schedule 1 to the Act and where income support[⁴, state pension credit] [²or income-based jobseeker's allowance], [³...] was not in payment to that person at any time during the period in which that overpayment occurred or at the date or dates on which the payment by way of reimbursement was made; or

(b)   [³...]

(2)   In a case falling within section 4 or 7 of the Act, where the circumstances set out in section 41B(6) apply, the Secretary of State may retain out of the child support maintenance collected by him in accordance with section 29 of the Act such sums as cover the amount of any payment by way of reimbursement required by him from the relevant person under section 41B(3) of the Act.]

Amendments
1.   Reg 10A inserted by reg 3 of SI 1995/3261 as from 22.1.96.
2.   Words inserted in reg 10A(1)(a) by reg 3(1) and (2)(c) of SI 1996/1345 as from 7.10.96.
3.   Child Support (Collection and Enforcement and Miscellaneous Amendments) Regulations 2000 (SI 2001 No.162) reg 5(4) (comes into force in relation to a particular case on the day on which ss1(2) and (3), 4, 18(1) and (2), and 20(1) of and Sch 3 para 11(2) and (16) Child Support, Pensions and Social Security Act 2000 come into force for the purposes of that type of case – which is March 3, 2003 for the types of cases in arts 3 and 5 of SI 2003 No.192). For other types of cases see the '1993 rules' below. See reg 6 of SI 2001 No.162 for savings provisions detailing when these amendments do not apply.
4.   State Pension Credit (Consequential, Transitional and Miscellaneous Provisions) Regulations 2002 (SI 2002 No.3019) reg 26(3) (October 6, 2003).

1993 rules
Reg 5(4) of the Child Support (Collection and Enforcement and Miscellaneous Amendments) Regulations 2000 (SI 2001 No.162) amends this regulation and has been brought into force only for the types of cases in arts 3 and 5 of the Child Support, Pensions and Social Security Act 2000 (Commencement No.12) Order 2003 (SI 2003 No.192) – see p683, subject to savings provisions in reg 6 of SI 2001 No.162. For other types of cases the '1993 rules' apply. If the 1993 rules apply:
–   in paragraph (1) "absent parent" is retained in place of "non-resident parent" and "assessment" is retained in place of "calculation";
–   in paragraph (1)(a) the words "family credit or disability working allowance" are retained before "was not in payment";
–   paragraph (1)(b), shown below, is retained:

(b)   in respect of the amount payable under an interim maintenance assessment and that amount has not been varied under regulation 8D(1) of the Maintenance Assessment Procedure Regulations following the making of a maintenance assessment calculated in accordance with Part I of Schedule 1 to the Act.

Definitions
"the Act": see reg 1(2).
"Maintenance Calculation Procedure Regulations": see reg 1(2).
"non-resident parent": see reg 1 (2).
"relevant person": see reg 1(2).

General Note

The Secretary of State has power under s41B of the Act to reimburse the non-resident parent an overpayment of child support maintenance. This regulation provides for the Secretary of State to recover that amount from the person with care who would otherwise benefit from the overpayment.

[¹Repayment of a reimbursement of a voluntary payment

10B.   The Secretary of State may require a relevant person to repay the whole or any part of any payment by way of reimbursement made to a non-resident parent under section 41B(2) of the Act where–

(a)   a voluntary payment was made;

(b)   section 41B(1A) applies; and

income support[², state pension credit] or income-based jobseeker's allowance was not in payment to that person at any time during the period in which the voluntary payment was made or at the date or dates on which the payment by way of reimbursement was made.]

Amendments

1.   Child Support (Collection and Enforcement and Miscellaneous Amendments) Regulations 2000 (SI 2001 No.162) reg 5(4)(f) (comes into force in relation to a particular case on the day on which ss1(2) and (3), 4, 18(1) and (2), and 20(1) of and Sch 3 para 11(2) and (16) Child Support, Pensions and Social Security Act 2000 come into force for the purposes of that type of case – which is March 3, 2003 for the types of cases in arts 3 and 5 of SI 2003 No.192). For other types of cases see the '1993 rules', below. See reg 6 of SI 2001 No.162 for savings provisions detailing when this amendment does not apply.

2.   State Pension Credit (Consequential, Transitional and Miscellaneous Provisions) Regulations 2002 (SI 2002 No.3019) reg 26(3) (October 6, 2003).

1993 rules

Reg 5(4) of the Child Support (Collection and Enforcement and Miscellaneous Amendments) Regulations 2000 (SI 2001 No.162) inserts regulation 10B and has been brought into force only for the types of cases in arts 3 and 5 of the Child Support, Pensions and Social Security Act 2000 (Commencement No.12) Order 2003 (SI 2003 No.192) – see p683, subject to savings provisions in reg 6 of SI 2001 No.162. For other types of cases regulation 10B does not apply.

Definitions

"the Act": see reg 1(2).
"non-resident parent": see reg 1(2).
"relevant person": see reg 1(2).

General Note

This regulation makes equivalent provision to reg 10A. See the general note to that regulation.

Regs 11 to 17 were revoked by reg 14(1) of the Appeals Amendment Regulations 2000 (for in force date see regs 1 and 14 of SI 2000/3185).

PART IV
Miscellaneous

11. [⁴,⁵...]

Amendments

1.   Heading to, and para (1) of, reg 11 substituted by reg 9(2) and (3) SI 1995/1045 as from 18.4.95.

2.   Words substituted in reg 11(2) by art 27(b) of SI1999/1510 as from 1.6.99.

3.   Words substituted in reg 11(1) by art 27(a) of SI 1999/1510 as from 1.6.99.

4.   Child Support (Decisions and Appeals) (Amendment) Regulations 2000 (SI 2000 No.3185) reg 14 (only in force for certain cases, and came into force for those cases on the date when certain provisions of the Child Support, Pensions and Social Security Act 2000 (c.19) came into force in relation to that type of case). See reg 1 of SI 2000 No.3185 (p536) and arts 3 and 7 of SI 2003 No.192 (p683) for the relevant commencement date and see reg 14 of SI 2000/3185 for savings provisions. For other types of cases see '1993 rules', below.

5.   Child Support (Management of Payments and Arrears) Regulations 2009 (SI 2009 No.3151) reg 14 and Sch (January 25, 2010). Where, before January 25, 2010, an adjustment had been made under reg 10(1) in respect of a '1993 scheme case' (as defined by reg 2 of SI 2009 No.3151), reg 11 continues to apply

for certain purposes – see reg 15 of SI 2009 No.3151 for details. Reg 11 as it applies to such cases is reproduced under the '1993 rules' below.

1993 rules

Reg 14(1) of the Child Support (Decisions and Appeals) (Amendment) Regulations 2000 (SI 2000 No.3185) revoked this regulation. Subject to regulation 14(2) of SI 2000 No.3185, this revokation was brought into force in relation to a particular case on the date on which sections 16, 17 and 20 of the Child Support Act 1991, as amended by the Child Support, Pensions and Social Security Act 2000, come into force in relation to that type of case – this was on March 3, 2003 for the types of cases detailed in art 3 of SI 2003 No.192 (see p683). For other types of cases regulation 11 continued to apply. Regulation 11 was further revoked from January 25, 2010 by reg 14 of the Child Support (Management of Payments and Arrears) Regulations 2009 (SI 2009 No.3151) subject to savings provisions in reg 15 of SI 2009 No.3151. In accordance with reg 15(1) of SI 2009 No.3151, regulation 11, as reproduced below, continues to apply for certain purposes only (see p715).

[¹ Notifications following a cancellation or adjustment under the provisions of regulation 10]

11.–[¹(1)   Where [²the Secretary of State] has, under the provisions of regulation 10, cancelled an adjustment in accordance with the provisions of paragraph (3) of that regulation or adjusted the amount payable under a maintenance assessment, he shall immediately notify the relevant persons, so far as is reasonably practicable, of the cancellation or, of the amount and period of the adjustment, and the amount payable during the period of the adjustment.]

(2)   A notification under paragraph (1) shall include information as to the provisions of [³regulations 12 to 15.]

12. [²,³....]

Amendments

1.   Regs 12-15 substituted and regs 16-17 inserted by art 28 of SI 1999/1510 as from 1.6.99.
2.   Child Support (Decisions and Appeals) (Amendment) Regulations 2000 (SI 2000 No.3185) reg 14 (only in force for certain cases, and came into force for those cases on the date when certain provisions of the Child Support, Pensions and Social Security Act 2000 (c.19) came into force in relation to that type of case). See reg 1 of SI 2000 No.3185 and arts 3 and 7 of SI 2003 No.192 for the relevant commencement date and see reg 14 of SI 2000/3185 for savings provisions. For other types of cases see the '1993 rules', below.
3.   Child Support (Management of Payments and Arrears) Regulations 2009 (SI 2009 No.3151) reg 14 and Sch (January 25, 2010). Where, before January 25, 2010, an adjustment had been made under reg 10(1) in respect of a '1993 scheme case' (as defined by reg 2 of SI 2009 No.3151), reg 12 continues to apply for certain purposes – see reg 15 of SI 2009 No.3151 for details. For reg 12 as it applies to such cases see the '1993 rules', below.

1993 rules

Reg 14(1) of the Child Support (Decisions and Appeals) (Amendment) Regulations 2000 (SI 2000 No.3185) revoked this regulation, subject to regulation 14(2) of SI 2000 No.3185. This revokation was brought into force in relation to a particular case on the date on which sections 16, 17 and 20 of the Child Support Act 1991, as amended by the Child Support, Pensions and Social Security Act 2000, come into force in relation to that type of case this was on March 3, 2003 for the types of cases detailed in art 3 of SI 2003 No.192 (see p683). For other types of cases regulation 12 continued to apply. Regulation 12 was further revoked from January 25, 2010 by reg 14 of the Child Support (Management of Payments and Arrears) Regulations 2009 (SI 2009 No.3151) subject to savings provisions in reg 15 of SI 2009 No.3151. In accordance with reg 15(1) of SI 2009 No.3151, regulation 12, as reproduced below, continues to apply for certain purposes only (see p715).

12.   Schedule 4C to the Act is hereby extended so that it applies to any decision with respect to the adjustment of amounts payable under maintenance assessments for the purpose of taking account of overpayments of child support maintenance.

13. [¹,²...]

Amendments

1.   Child Support (Decisions and Appeals) (Amendment) Regulations 2000 (SI 2000 No.3185) reg 14 (only in force for certain cases, and came into force for those cases on the date when certain provisions of the

Child Support, Pensions and Social Security Act 2000 (c.19) came into force in relation to that type of case). See reg 1 of SI 2000 No.3185 and arts 3 and 7 of SI 2003 No.192 for the relevant commencement date and see reg 14 of SI 2000/3185 for savings provisions. For other types of cases see the '1993 rules', below.

2.   Child Support (Management of Payments and Arrears) Regulations 2009 (SI 2009 No.3151) reg 14 and Sch (January 25, 2010). Where, before January 25, 2010, an adjustment had been made under reg 10(1) in respect of a '1993 scheme case' (as defined by reg 2 of SI 2009 No.3151), reg 13 continues to apply for certain purposes – see reg 15 of SI 2009 No.3151 for details. For reg 13 as it applies to such cases see the '1993 rules', below.

1993 rules

Reg 14(1) of the Child Support (Decisions and Appeals) (Amendment) Regulations 2000 (SI 2000 No.3185) revoked this regulation, subject to regulation 14(2) of SI 2000 No.3185. This revocation was brought into force in relation to a particular case on the date on which sections 16, 17 and 20 of the Child Support Act 1991, as amended by the Child Support, Pensions and Social Security Act 2000, came into force in relation to that type of case – this was on March 3, 2003 for the types of cases detailed in art 3 of SI 2003 No.192 (see p683). For other types of cases regulation 13 continued to apply. Regulation 13 was further revoked from January 25, 2010 by reg 14 of the Child Support (Management of Payments and Arrears) Regulations 2009 (SI 2009 No.3151) subject to savings provisions in reg 15 of SI 2009 No.3151. In accordance with reg 15(1) of SI 2009 No.3151, regulation 13, as reproduced below, continues to apply for certain purposes only (see p715).

Revision of decisions

13.–(1)   A decision may be revised by the Secretary of State–

(a)   if the Secretary of State receives an application for the revision of a decision under section 16 of the Act as extended by regulation 12 above within one month of the date of notification of the decision or within such longer time as may be allowed by regulation 14;

(b)   if the decision arose from an official error;

(c)   if the Secretary of State commences action leading to the revision of a decision within one month of the date of notification of the decision; or

(d)   if the Secretary of State is satisfied that the original decision was erroneous due to a misrepresentation of, or failure to disclose, a material fact and that the decision was more advantageous to the person who misrepresented or failed to disclose that fact than it would otherwise have been but for that error.

(2)   In paragraph (1)–

"decision" means a decision of the Secretary of State–

(a)   adjusting the amount payable under a maintenance assessment; or

(b)   cancelling an adjustment of an amount payable under a maintenance assessment, under regulation 10 and a decision superseding such a decision;

"official error" means an error made by an officer of the Department of Social Security acting as such which no person outside that Department caused or to which no person outside that Department materially contributed.

(3)   Paragraph (1) shall not apply in respect of a change of circumstances which occurred since the date as from which the decision had effect.

14. [¹,²...]

Amendments

1.   Child Support (Decisions and Appeals) (Amendment) Regulations 2000 (SI 2000 No.3185) reg 14 (only in force for certain cases, and came into force for those cases on the date when certain provisions of the Child Support, Pensions and Social Security Act 2000 (c.19) came into force in relation to that type of case). For other types of cases see the '1993 rules', below. See reg 1 of SI 2000 No.3185 and arts 3 and 7 of SI 2003 No.192 for the relevant commencement date and see reg 14 of SI 2000/3185 for savings provisions.

2.   Child Support (Management of Payments and Arrears) Regulations 2009 (SI 2009 No.3151) reg 14 and Sch (January 25, 2010). Where, before January 25, 2010, an adjustment had been made under reg 10(1) in respect of a '1993 scheme case' (as defined by reg 2 of SI 2009 No.3151), reg 14 continues to apply for certain purposes – see reg 15 of SI 2009 No.3151 for details. For reg 14 as it applies to such cases see the '1993 rules', below.

1993 rules

Reg 14(1) of the Child Support (Decisions and Appeals) (Amendment) Regulations 2000 (SI 2000 No.3185) revoked this regulation, subject to regulation 14(2) of SI 2000 No.3185. This revocation was brought into force in relation to a particular case on the date on which sections 16, 17 and 20 of the Child Support Act 1991, as amended by the Child Support, Pensions and Social Security Act 2000, came into force in relation to that type of case – this was on March 3, 2003 for the types of cases detailed in art 3 of SI 2003 No.192 (see p683). For other types of cases regulation 14 continued to apply. Regulation 14 was further revoked from January 25, 2010 by reg 14 of the Child Support (Management of Payments and Arrears) Regulations 2009 (SI 2009 No.3151) subject to savings provisions in reg 15 of SI 2009 No.3151. In accordance with reg 15(1) of SI 2009 No.3151, regulation 14, as reproduced below, continues to apply for certain purposes only (see p715).

Late application for revision

14.–(1)   The period of one month specified in regulation 13(1)(a) may be extended where the conditions specified in the following provisions of this regulation are satisfied.

(2)   An application for an extension of time shall be made by a relevant person or a person acting on his behalf.

(3)   An application for an extension of time under this regulation shall–

(a)   be made within 13 months of the date on which notification of the decision which it is sought to have revised was given or sent; and

(b)   contain particulars of the grounds on which the extension of time is sought and shall contain sufficient details of the decision which it is sought to have evised to enable that decision to be identified.

(4)   An application for an extension of time shall not be granted unless the person making the application or any person acting for him satisfies the Secretary of State that–

(a)   it is reasonable to grant the application;

(b)   the application for a revision has merit; and

(c)   special circumstances are relevant to the application for an extension of time and as a result of those special circumstances, it was not practicable for the application for a decision to be revised to be made within one month of the date of notification of the decision which it is sought to have revised.

(5)   In determining whether it is reasonable to grant an application for an extension of time, the Secretary of State shall have regard to the principle that the greater the time that has elapsed between the expiration of one month described in regulation 13(1)(a) from the date of notification of the decision which it is sought to have revised and the making of the application for an extension of time, the more compelling should be the special circumstances on which the application is based.

(6)   In determining whether it is reasonable to grant the application for an extension of time, no account shall be taken of the following–

(a)   that the person making the application for an extension of time or any person acting for him was unaware of or misunderstood the law applicable to his case (including ignorance or misunderstanding of the time limits imposed by these Regulations); or

(b)   that [[1] the Upper Tribunal] or a court has taken a different view of the law from that previously understood and applied.

(7)   An application under this regulation for an extension of time which has been refused may not be renewed.

Amendment

1.   Tribunals, Courts and Enforcement Act 2007 (Transitional and Consequential Provisions) Order 2008 (SI 2008 No.2683) Sch 1 para 62 (November 3, 2008).

15. [[1,2]...]

Amendments

1.   Child Support (Decisions and Appeals) (Amendment) Regulations 2000 (SI 2000 No.3185) reg 14 (only in force for certain cases, and came into force for those cases on the date when certain provisions of the Child Support, Pensions and Social Security Act 2000 (c.19) came into force in relation to that type of case). For other types of cases see the '1993 rules', below. See reg 1 of SI 2000 No.3185 and arts 3 and

7 of SI 2003 No.192 for the relevant commencement date and see reg 14 of SI 2000/3185 for savings provisions.

2. Child Support (Management of Payments and Arrears) Regulations 2009 (SI 2009 No.3151) reg 14 and Sch (January 25, 2010). Where, before January 25, 2010, an adjustment had been made under reg 10(1) in respect of a '1993 scheme case' (as defined by reg 2 of SI 2009 No.3151), reg 15 continues to apply for certain purposes – see reg 15 of SI 2009 No.3151 for details. For reg 15 as it applies to such cases, see the '1993 rules', below.

1993 rules

Reg 14(1) of the Child Support (Decisions and Appeals) (Amendment) Regulations 2000 (SI 2000 No.3185) revoked this regulation, subject to regulation 14(2) of SI 2000 No.3185. This revocation was brought into force in relation to a particular case on the date on which sections 16, 17 and 20 of the Child Support Act 1991, as amended by the Child Support, Pensions and Social Security Act 2000, came into force in relation to that type of case – this was on March 3, 2003 for the types of cases detailed in art 3 of SI 2003 No.192 (see p683). For other types of cases regulation 15 continued to apply. Regulation 15 was further revoked from January 25, 2010 by reg 14 of the Child Support (Management of Payments and Arrears) Regulations 2009 (SI 2009 No.3151) subject to savings provisions in reg 15 of SI 2009 No.3151. In accordance with reg 15(1) of SI 2009 No.3151, regulation 15, as reproduced below, continues to apply for certain purposes only (see p715).

Date from which revised decision takes effect

15. Where the date as from which a decision took effect is found to be erroneous on a revision under section 16 of the Act as extended by regulation 12 above, the revision shall take effect as from the date on which the revised decision would have taken effect had the error not been made.

16. [[1,2]...]

Amendments

1. Child Support (Decisions and Appeals) (Amendment) Regulations 2000 (SI 2000 No.3185) reg 14 (only in force for certain cases, and came into force for those cases on the date when certain provisions of the Child Support, Pensions and Social Security Act 2000 (c.19) came into force in relation to that type of case). For other types of cases see the '1993 rules', below. See reg 1 of SI 2000 No.3185 and arts 3 and 7 of SI 2003 No.192 for the relevant commencement date and see reg 14 of SI 2000/3185 for savings provisions.

2. Child Support (Management of Payments and Arrears) Regulations 2009 (SI 2009 No.3151) reg 14 and Sch (January 25, 2010). Where, before January 25, 2010, an adjustment had been made under reg 10(1) in respect of a '1993 scheme case' (as defined by reg 2 of SI 2009 No.3151), reg 16 continues to apply for certain purposes – see reg 15 of SI 2009 No.3151 for details. For reg 16 as it applies to such cases see the '1993 rules', below.

1993 rules

Reg 14(1) of the Child Support (Decisions and Appeals) (Amendment) Regulations 2000 (SI 2000 No.3185) revoked this regulation, subject to regulation 14(2) of SI 2000 No.3185. This revocation was brought into force in relation to a particular case on the date on which sections 16, 17 and 20 of the Child Support Act 1991, as amended by the Child Support, Pensions and Social Security Act 2000, came into force in relation to that type of case – this was on March 3, 2003 for the types of cases detailed in art 3 of SI 2003 No.192 (see p683). For other types of cases regulation 16 continued to apply. Regulation 16 was further revoked from January 25, 2010 by reg 14 of the Child Support (Management of Payments and Arrears) Regulations 2009 (SI 2009 No.3151) subject to savings provisions in reg 15 of SI 2009 No.3151. In accordance with reg 15(1) of SI 2009 No.3151, regulation 16, as reproduced below, continues to apply for certain purposes only (see p715).

Supersession of decisions

16.–(1) For the purposes of section 17 of the Act as extended by regulation 12 above, the cases and circumstances in which a decision adjusting the amount payable under a maintenance assessment may be superseded by a decision under that section as extended are set out in paragraphs (2) to (4).

(2) A decision may be superseded by a decision made by the Secretary of State acting on his own initiative where he is satisfied that the decision–

 (a) is one in respect of which there has been a material change of circumstances since the decision was made; or

 (b) was made in ignorance of, or was based upon a mistake as to, some material fact.

(3)   A decision may be superseded by a decision made by the Secretary of State where an application is made on the basis that–

(a)   there has been a change of circumstances since the decision was made and the Secretary of State is satisfied that the change of circumstances is or would be material; or

(b)   the decision was made in ignorance of, or was based upon a mistake as to, a fact and the Secretary of State is satisfied that the fact is or would be material.

(4)   A decision, other than a decision given on appeal, may be superseded by a decision made by the Secretary of State–

(a)   acting on his own initiative where he is satisfied that the decision was erroneous in point of law; or

(b)   where an application is made on the basis that the decision was erroneous in point of law.

(5)   The cases and circumstances in which a decision may be superseded under section 17 of the Act as extended by regulation 12 above shall not include any case or circumstance in which a decision may be revised.

17.   [[1,2...]]

Amendments

1.   Child Support (Decisions and Appeals) (Amendment) Regulations 2000 (SI 2000 No.3185) reg 14 (only in force for certain cases, and came into force for those cases on the date when certain provisions of the Child Support, Pensions and Social Security Act 2000 (c.19) came into force in relation to that type of case). For other types of cases see the '1993 rules', below. See reg 1 of SI 2000 No.3185 and arts 3 and 7 of SI 2003 No.192 for the relevant commencement date and see reg 14 of SI 2000/3185 for savings provisions. For those for whom this revocation does not apply, reg 17 is reproduced below.

2.   Child Support (Management of Payments and Arrears) Regulations 2009 (SI 2009 No.3151) reg 14 and Sch (January 25, 2010). Where, before January 25, 2010, an adjustment had been made under reg 10(1) in respect of a '1993 scheme case' (as defined by reg 2 of SI 2009 No.3151), reg 17 continues to apply for certain purposes – see reg 15 of SI 2009 No.3151 for details. For reg 17 as it applies to such cases see the '1993 rules', below.

1993 rules

Reg 14(1) of the Child Support (Decisions and Appeals) (Amendment) Regulations 2000 (SI 2000 No.3185) revoked this regulation, subject to regulation 14(2) of SI 2000 No.3185. This revocation was brought into force in relation to a particular case on the date on which sections 16, 17 and 20 of the Child Support Act 1991, as amended by the Child Support, Pensions and Social Security Act 2000, came into force in relation to that type of case – this was on March 3, 2003 for the types of cases detailed in art 3 of SI 2003 No.192 (see p683). For other types of cases regulation 17 continued to apply. Regulation 17 was further revoked from January 25, 2010 by reg 14 of the Child Support (Management of Payments and Arrears) Regulations 2009 (SI 2009 No.3151) subject to savings provisions in reg 15 of SI 2009 No.3151. In accordance with reg 15(1) of SI 2009 No.3151, regulation 17, as reproduced below, continues to apply for certain purposes only (see p715).

Application of regulations 1(6), 10(3) and 53 of the Maintenance Assessment Procedure Regulations

17.–(1)   The provisions of regulation 10(3) of the Maintenance Assessment Procedure Regulations shall apply to any notification–

(a)   under regulation 11; and

(b)   of a decision under the provisions of regulation 13, 14 or 16.

(2)   Regulations 1(6) and 53 of the Maintenance Assessment Procedure Regulations shall apply to the provisions of these Regulations.

The Child Support (Collection and Enforcement) Regulations 1992
(SI 1992 No.1989)

PART I
General

Citation, commencement and interpretation

1.–(1) These Regulations may be cited as the Child Support (Collection and Enforcement) Regulations 1992 and shall come into force on 5th April 1993.

[¹(2) In these Regulations–
"the Act" means the Child Support Act 1991;
"the 2000 Act" means the Child Support, Pensions and Social Security Act 2000;
"interest" means interest which has become payable under section 41 of the Act before its amendment by the 2000 Act; and
"voluntary payment" means a payment as defined in section 28J of the Act and Regulations made under that section.

(2A)   Except in relation to regulation 8(3)(a) and Schedule 2, in these Regulations "fee" means an assessment fee or a collection fee, which for these purposes have the same meaning as in the Child Support Fees Regulations 1992 prior to their revocation by the Child Support (Collection and Enforcement and Miscellaneous Amendments) Regulations 2000.]

(3)   Where under any provision of the Act or of these Regulations–

(a)   any document or notice is given or sent to the Secretary of State, it shall be treated as having been given or sent on the day it is received by the Secretary of State; and

(b)   any document or notice is given or sent to any other person, it shall, if sent by post to that person's last known or notified address, be treated as having been given or sent on [²the day that it is posted.]

(4)   In these Regulations, unless the context otherwise requires, a reference–

(a)   to a numbered Part is to the Part of these Regulations bearing that number;

(b)   to a numbered regulation is to the regulation in these Regulations bearing that number;

(c)   in a regulation to a numbered or lettered paragraph or sub-paragraph is to the paragraph or sub-paragraph in that regulation bearing that number or letter;

(d)   in a paragraph to a lettered or numbered sub-paragraph is to the sub-paragraph in that paragraph bearing that letter or number;

(e)   to a numbered Schedule is to the Schedule to these Regulations bearing that number.

Amendments

1.   Child Support (Collection and Enforcement and Miscellaneous Amendments) Regulations 2000 (SI 2001 No.162) reg 2(2) (comes into force in relation to a particular case on the day on which ss1(2) and (3), 4, 18(1) and (2), and 20(1) of and Sch 3 para 11(2) and (16) Child Support, Pensions and Social Security Act 2000 come into force for the purposes of that type of case – which is March 3, 2003 for the types of cases in arts 3 and 5 of SI 2003 No.192). For other types of cases see the '1993 rules', below. See reg 6 of 2001 No.162 for savings provisions detailing when these amendments do not apply.

2.   Child Support (Collection and Enforcement and Miscellaneous Amendments) Regulations 2000 (SI 2001 No.162) reg 2(2)(c) (comes into force in relation to a particular case on the day on which ss1(2) and (3), 4, 18(1) and (2), and 20(1) of and Sch 3 para 11(2) and (16) Child Support, Pensions and Social Security Act 2000 come into force for the purposes of that type of case – which is March 3, 2003 for the types of cases in arts 3 and 5 of SI 2003 No.192). For other types of cases see the '1993 rules', below. See reg 6 of SI 2001 No.162 for savings provisions detailing when this amendment does not apply.

1993 rules

Reg 2(2) of the Child Support (Collection and Enforcement and Miscellaneous Amendments) Regulations 2000 (SI 2001 No.162) amends this regulation and has been brought into force only for the types of cases in art 3 and 5 of the Child Support, Pensions and Social Security Act 2000 (Commencement No.12) Order 2003 (SI 2003 No.192) – see p683, subject to savings provisions in reg 6 of SI 2001 No.162. For other types of cases the '1993 rules' apply. If the 1993 rules apply:

–   para (2A) is not inserted;

–   the earlier version of para (2) is retained which reads: "(2) In these Regulations "the Act" means the Child Support Act 1991"; *and*

–   in para (3)(b) the words "the second day after the day of posting, excluding any Sunday or any day which is a bank holiday under the Banking and Financial Dealings Act 1971." are retained in place of "the day that it is posted".

PART II
Collection of child support maintenance

Payment of child support maintenance

2.–(1)   Where a maintenance [¹calculation] has been made under the Act and the case is one to which section 29 of the Act applies, the Secretary of State may specify that payments of child support maintenance shall be made by the liable person–

(a)   to the person caring for the child or children in question or, where an application has been made under section 7 of the Act, to the child who made the application;

(b)   to, or through, the Secretary of State; or
(c)   to, or through, such other person as the Secretary of State may, from time to time, specify.
(2)   In paragraph (1) and in the rest of this Part, "liable person" means a person liable to make payments of child support maintenance.

Amendment

1.   Child Support (Collection and Enforcement and Miscellaneous Amendments) Regulations 2000 (SI 2001 No.162) reg 2(3)(a) (comes into force in relation to a particular case on the day on which ss1(2) and (3), 4, 18(1) and (2), and 20(1) of and Sch 3 para 11(2) and (16) Child Support, Pensions and Social Security Act 2000 come into force for the purposes of that type of case – which is March 3, 2003 for the types of cases in arts 3 and 5 of the SI 2003 No.192). For other types of cases see the '1993 rules', below. See reg 6 of SI 2001 No.162 for savings provisions detailing when this amendment does not apply.

1993 rules

Reg 2(3) of the Child Support (Collection and Enforcement and Miscellaneous Amendments) Regulations 2000 (SI 2001 No.162) amends this regulation and has been brought into force only for the types of cases in art 3 and 5 of the Child Support, Pensions and Social Security Act 2000 (Commencement No.12) Order 2003 (SI 2003 No.192) – see p683, subject to savings provisions in reg 6 of SI 2001 No.162. For other types of cases the '1993 rules' apply and the word "assessment" is retained in place of "calculation".

Definition

"the Act": see reg 1(2).

General Note

This regulation only applies if s29 of the Act applies. It allows the Secretary of State to specify in her/his notice (see reg 7) that payment shall be to the person caring for the child, the child (in the case of Scotland), or to or through the Secretary or State or his nominee. The regulation does not refer to the person with care. Instead it departs from the standard wording of the Act and the regulations made under it by referring to the person caring for the child or children. In practice this could be someone other than the person with care, as there could be persons with part-time care or the care of the child could be temporarily entrusted to someone other than the person with care. The use of different terminology may justify payments being made to someone who is not the person with care, such as a relative looking after a child while the person with care is in hospital (*R(CS)14/98*, para 18).

Method of payment

3.–(1)   Payments of child support maintenance[¹, penalty payments, interest and fees] shall be made by the liable person by whichever of the following methods the Secretary of State specifies as being appropriate in the circumstances–
(a)   by standing order;
(b)   by any other method which requires one person to give his authority for payments to be made from an account of his to an account of another's on specific dates during the period for which the authority is in force and without the need for any further authority from him;
(c)   by an arrangement whereby one person gives his authority for payments to be made from an account of his, or on his behalf, to another person or to an account of that other person;
(d)   by cheque or postal order;
(e)   in cash.
[³(f)   by debit card.]
[⁴(g)   by credit card;
(h)   [⁵...]]
[⁵ (i) by deduction from earnings order.]
[³[⁴(1A)   In paragraph (1)–
(a)   "debit card" means a card, operating as a substitute for a cheque, that can be used to obtain cash or to make a payment at a point of sale whereby the card holder's bank or building society account is debited without deferment of payment;
(b)   "credit card" means a card which is a credit-token within the meaning of section 14(1)(b) of the Consumer Credit Act 1974;

(c)   [⁵...]]]

(2)   The Secretary of State may direct a liable person to take all reasonable steps to open an account from which payments under the maintenance [²calculation] may be made in accordance with the method of payment specified under paragraph (1).

[⁵ (3)   Where the Secretary of State is considering specifying a deduction from earnings order by virtue of paragraph (1)(i), that method of payment is not to be used in any case where there is good reason not to use it.

(4)   For the purposes of paragraph (3) the matters which are to be taken into account in determining whether there is good reason not to use that method of payment are whether the making of a deduction from earnings order is likely to result in the disclosure of the parentage of a child and the impact of that disclosure on–

(a)   the liable person's employment;

(b)   any relationship between the liable person and a third party.

(5)   For the purposes of paragraph (3) the circumstances in which good reason not to use that method of payment is to be regarded as existing are–

(a)   a member of the liable person's or parent with care's family is employed by the same relevant employer as the liable person;

(b)   that family member's employment requires knowledge of the relevant employer's functions in giving effect to the deduction from earnings order; and

(c)   as a consequence of these circumstances the liable person's employment status or family relationships may be adversely affected by the use of a deduction from earnings order as a method of payment.

(6)   For the purposes of paragraph (3) the matters which are not to be taken into account in determining whether there is good reason not to use that method of payment are–

(a)   the liable person's preference for a different method of payment;

(b)   the liable person's preference for a relevant employer not to be informed about that parent's maintenance liability;

(c)   that a third party would become aware of the liable person's maintenance liability,

unless they are relevant to any matter falling within paragraph (4) or circumstance falling within paragraph (5).

(7)   Where the Secretary of State is considering specifying the method of payment set out in paragraph (1)(i) and decides that there is no good reason not to use it, that method is not to be specified until–

(a)   the time within which an appeal against that decision may ordinarily be brought (including any period during which a further appeal may ordinarily be brought) has ended; or

(b)   if an appeal is brought on the grounds set out in regulation 22(3A), the time at which proceedings on the appeal (including any proceedings on a further appeal) have been concluded.

(8)   Nothing in this regulation is to prevent the Secretary of State exercising his powers under section 31 of the Act to make a deduction from earnings order where the Secretary of State considers it is appropriate in the circumstances of the case, unless he has specified a deduction from earnings order as a method of payment by virtue of paragraph (1)(i).

(9)   In this regulation–

"couple" means–

(a)   a man and woman who are married to each other and are members of the same household;

(b)   a man and woman who are not married to each other but are living together as husband and wife;

(c)   two people of the same sex who are civil partners of each other and are members of the same household; or

(d)   two people of the same sex who are not civil partners of each other but are living together as if they were civil partners, and for the purposes of paragraph (d), two people of the same sex are to be regarded as living together as if they were civil partners if, but only if, they would be regarded as living together as husband and wife were they instead two people of the opposite sex;

"family" means partner, parent, parent-in-law, son, son-in-law, daughter, daughter-in-law, step-parent, step-son, step-daughter, brother, sister, grand-parent, grand-child, uncle, aunt, nephew, niece, or if any of the preceding persons is one member of a couple, the other member of that couple;

"partner" means where a person is a member of a couple the other member of that couple; and

"relevant employer" means the employer of a liable person in respect of whom the order under section 31 of the Act would be made but for paragraph (3).]

Amendments

1. Child Support (Collection and Enforcement and Miscellaneous Amendments) Regulations 2000 (SI 2001 No.162) reg 2(3)(b)(i) (comes into force in relation to a particular case on the day on which ss1(2) and (3), 4, 18(1) and (2), and 20(1) of and Sch 3 para 11(2) and (16) Child Support, Pensions and Social Security Act 2000 come into force for the purposes of that type of case – which is March 3, 2003 for the types of cases in arts 3 and 5 of SI 2003 No.192). For other types of cases see the '1993 rules', below. See reg 6 of SI 2001 No.162 for savings provisions detailing when these amendments do not apply. .

2. Child Support (Collection and Enforcement and Miscellaneous Amendments) Regulations 2000 (SI 2001 No.162) reg 2(3)(a) (comes into force in relation to a particular case on the day on which ss1(2) and (3), 4, 18(1) and (2), and 20(1) of and Sch 3 parag 11(2) and (16) Child Support, Pensions and Social Security Act 2000 come into force for the purposes of that type of case – which is March 3, 2003 for the types of cases in arts 3 and 5 of SI 2003 No.192). For other types of cases see the '1993 rules', below. See reg 6 of SI 2001 No.162 for savings provisions detailing when these amendments do not apply.

3. Child Support (Collection and Enforcement and Miscellaneous Amendments) Regulations 2000 (SI 2001 No.162) reg 2(3)(b)(ii) and (c) (subject to the savings provisions in reg 6 of SI 2001 No.162 these amendments are in force from March 3, 2003 for the types of cases in arts 3 and 5 of SI 2003 No.192 and from July 12, 2006 for other cases); Child Support (Miscellaneous Amendments) Regulations 2006 (SI 2006 No.1520) reg 6(2).

4. Child Support (Miscellaneous Amendments) Regulations 2006 (SI 2006 No.1520) reg 3(2) (July 12, 2006).

5. Child Support (Miscellaneous Amendments) (No.2) Regulations 2008 (SI 2008 No.2544) reg 2(2) (October 27, 2008).

1993 rules

Reg 2(3) of the Child Support (Collection and Enforcement and Miscellaneous Amendments) Regulations 2000 (SI 2001 No.162) amends this regulation and has been brought into force only for the types of cases in art 3 and 5 of the Child Support, Pensions and Social Security Act 2000 (Commencement No.12) Order 2003 (SI 2003 No.192) – see p683, subject to savings provisions in reg 6 of SI 2001 No.162. For other types of cases the '1993 rules' apply and

– in paragraph (1) the words ", penalty payments, interest and fees" are not inserted after "child support maintenance";
– paragraphs (1)(f) and (1A) are not inserted; and
– in paragraph (2) the word "assessment" is retained in place of "calculation".

Definitions

"fee": see reg 1(2A).
"interest": see reg 1(2).
"liable person": reg 2(2).
"penalty payment": see reg 7A(5).

General Note

Paragraph (1)

Methods (a) to (c) will be preferred to (d) and (e) since they will operate automatically provided there are sufficient funds in the account.

Paragraph (2)

This is a strange provision. It allows the Secretary of State to direct a person to take all reasonable steps to open a suitable account, but it does not operate until the Secretary of State has specified a method of payment under para (1). However, if the liable person is unable to open a suitable account, the effect of specifying payment from an account will have been to delay the payment of child support maintenance. Perhaps this problem could be avoided by specifying an alternative method until (if at all) an account is opened. It would be better if the power in this paragraph could be employed before payment from an account was specified under para (1), but this is not what the provision says.

[²Payments to be scheduled over reference period

4.–(1) The Secretary of State may, for the purposes of determining the frequency and amount of the payments of child support maintenance required to be made by a liable person–

    (a)   determine the total amount payable for the reference period on the assumption that the weekly rate of child support maintenance will not change over that period; and

    (b)   require that amount to be paid by equal instalments over that period at intervals determined by the Secretary of State.

    (2)   The reference period in relation to the maintenance calculation is, subject to paragraph (3), the period of 52 weeks mentioned in section 29(3A) of the Act beginning with–

    (a)   the initial effective date (where it is the first such period in relation to the maintenance calculation); or

    (b)   the review date.

    (3)   In this regulation "initial effective date" and "review date" have the meanings given by regulations 12 and 19 of the Child Support Maintenance Calculation Regulations 2012 respectively.]

Amendments

1.   Reg 4(2) substituted by reg 12 of SI 1995/1045 as from 18.4.95 (see also reg 64(5) ibid).

2.   Child Support (Meaning of Child and New Calculation Rules) (Consequential and Miscellaneous Amendment) Regulations 2012 (SI 2012 No.2785) reg 4(2) (in force in relation to a particular case on the day on which paragraph 2 of Schedule 4 to the Child Maintenance and Other Payments Act 2008 (see p243) comes into force in relation to that type of case – which is December 10, 2012, only in relation to the types of cases falling within art 3 of SI 2012 No.3042 (see p767)). For other types of cases see '2003 and 1993 rules' below.

2003 and 1993 rules

Regulation 4(2) of The Child Support (Meaning of Child and New Calculation Rules) (Consequential and Miscellaneous Amendment) Regulations 2012 (SI 2012 No. 2785) substituted reg 4 of The Child Support (Collection and Enforcement) Regulations 1992 from December 10, 2012, in relation to the types of cases falling within art 3 of SI 2012 No.3042 only (see p767). For other types of cases regulation 4 reads:

Interval of payment

4.–(1)   The Secretary of State shall specify the day and interval by reference to which payments of child support maintenance are to be made by the liable person and may from time to time vary such day or interval.

    [¹(2)   In specifying the day and interval of payment the Secretary of State shall have regard to the following factors–

    (a)   the circumstances of the person liable to make the payments and in particular the day upon which and the interval at which any income is payable to that person;

    (b)   any preference indicated by that person;

    (c)   any period necessary to enable the clearance of cheques or otherwise necessary to enable the transmission of payments to the person entitled to receive them.

and, subject to those factors, to any other matter which appears to him to be relevant in the particular circumstances of the case.]

Definition

"liable person": reg 2(2).

General Note

The Secretary of State has power to vary the interval under reg 5(4).

Transmission of payments

5.–[³(1)   Payments of child support maintenance made through the Secretary of State or other specified person shall be transmitted to the person entitled to receive them–
(a) by transfer of credit to an account nominated by the person entitled to receive the payments; or .
(b) by means other than by transfer of credit as determined by the Secretary of State, where it appears to the Secretary of State to be necessary to do so in the circumstances of the particular case.]

(2)   [²Subject to paragraph (3), the Secretary of State] shall specify the interval by reference to which the payments referred to in paragraph (1) are to be transmit-ted to the person entitled to receive them.

[²(3)   Except where the Secretary of State is satisfied in the circumstances of the case that it would cause undue hardship to either the person liable to make the payments or the person entitled to receive them, the interval referred to in paragraph (2) shall not differ from the interval referred to in regulation 4.

(4)   Subject to paragraph (3) and regulation 4(2), the interval referred to in paragraph (2) and that referred to in regulation 4 may be varied from time to time by the Secretary of State.]

Amendments
1. Words in reg 5(2) substituted by reg 13(2) of SI 1995/1045 as from 18.4.95.
2. Reg 5(3) and (4) substituted by reg 13(3) of SI 1995/1045 as from 18.4.95 (see also reg 64(5) ibid).
3. Child Support (Miscellaneous Amendments) Regulations 2012 (SI 2012 No.712) reg. 2 (April 30, 2012).

General Note
Paragraph (1)
The Secretary of State has no power to require the person entitled to receive payment to take all reasonable steps to open a bank account. This is in contrast with his power in relation to a liable person under reg 3(2).
Paragraph (3)
This regulation has been changed, presumably to simplify the administration of the collection machinery. The presumption is that the interval between payments will be the same both in respect of the liable person and the recipient. Only where undue hardship would be caused to either of these will the Secretary of State permit the interval to differ. Thus, for example, while it might be more convenient for the recipient to receive payments of child support maintenance weekly, if the liable person is paid monthly and prefers to have his payments collected monthly, the recipient will have to show that she would face undue hardship if she only received the payments monthly.

[¹Voluntary Payments

5A.–(1)   Regulation 5(1) shall apply in relation to voluntary payments as if–
(a)   for the words "Payment of child support maintenance" there were substituted the words "Voluntary payments"; and
(b)   the words "or other specified person" were omitted.

(2)   In determining when the Secretary of State shall transmit a voluntary payment to the person entitled to it, the Secretary of State shall have regard to the factor in regulation 4(2)(c).]

Amendment
1. Child Support (Collection and Enforcement and Miscellaneous Amendments) Regulations 2000 (SI 2001 No.162) reg 2(3)(d) (comes into force in relation to a particular case on the day on which ss1(2) and (3), 4, 18(1) and (2), and 20(1) of and Sch 3 para 11(2) and (16) Child Support, Pensions and Social Security Act 2000 come into force for the purposes of that type of case – which is March 3, 2003 for the types of cases in arts 3 and 5 of SI 2003 No.192). This amendment inserted reg 5A. See reg 6 of SI 2001 No.162 for savings provisions detailing when this regulation does not apply.

1993 rules
Reg 2(3) of the Child Support (Collection and Enforcement and Miscellaneous Amendments) Regulations 2000 (SI 2001 No.162) inserted regulation 5A and has been brought into force only for the types of cases in art 3 and 5 of the Child Support, Pensions and Social Security Act 2000 (Commencement No.12) Order 2003 (SI 2003 No.192) – see p683, subject to savings provisions in reg 6 of SI 2001 No.162. For other types of cases regulation 5A does not apply.

Definition

"voluntary payment": see reg 1(2).

Representations about payment arrangements

6. The Secretary of State shall, insofar as is reasonably practicable, provide the liable person and the person entitled to receive the payments of child support maintenance with an opportunity to make representations with regard to the matters referred to in regulations 2 to 5 and the Secretary of State shall have regard to those representations in exercising his powers under those regulations.

Definition

"liable person": reg 2(2).

General Note

The liable person and the person entitled to receive payment are entitled to an opportunity to make representations on the matters covered by regs 2 to 5, but only in so far as that is reasonably practicable. The person entitled to receive payment under this regulation means the person ultimately entitled to receive payment and not the Secretary of State or his nominee. That this is the meaning of these words is clear from the way in which the same words are used in reg 5(1).

Notice to liable person as to requirements about payment

7.–(1)   [²In the case of child support maintenance,] the Secretary of State shall send the liable person a notice stating–

(a)   the amount of child support maintenance payable;

(b)   to whom it is to be paid;

(c)   the method of payment; and

(d)   the day and interval by reference to which payments are to be made.

[²(e)   the amount of any payment of child support maintenance which is overdue and which remains outstanding.]

[²(1A)   In the case of penalty payments, interest or fees, the Secretary of State shall send the liable person a notice stating–

(a)   the amount of child support maintenance payable;

(b)   the amount of arrears;

(c)   the amount of the penalty payment, interest or fees to be paid, as the case may be;

(d)   the method of payment;

(e)   the day by which payment is to be made; and

(f)   information as to the provisions of sections 16 and 20 of the Act.]

(2)   A notice under paragraph (1) shall be sent to the liable person as soon as is reasonably practicable after–

(a)   the making of a maintenance [¹calculation], and.

(b)   after any change in the requirements referred to in any previous such notice.

[²(3)   A notice under paragraph (1A) shall be sent to the liable person as soon as reasonably practicable after the decision to require a payment of the penalty payment, interest or fees has been made.]

Amendments

1.   Child Support (Collection and Enforcement and Miscellaneous Amendments) Regulations 2000 (SI 2001 No.162) reg 2(3)(a) (comes into force in relation to a particular case on the day on which ss1(2) and (3), 4, 18(1) and (2), and 20(1) of and Sch 3 para 11(2) and (16) Child Support, Pensions and Social Security Act 2000 come into force for the purposes of that type of case – which is March 3, 2003 for the types of cases in arts 3 and 5 of SI 2003 No.192). For other types of cases see the '1993 rules', below. See reg 6 of SI 2001 No.162 for savings provisions detailing when this amendment does not apply.

2.   Child Support (Collection and Enforcement and Miscellaneous Amendments) Regulations 2000 (SI 2001 No.162) reg 2(3)(e) (will come into force in relation to a particular case on the day on which ss1(2) and (3), 4, 18(1) and (2), and 20(1) of and Sch 3 para 11(2) and (16) Child Support, Pensions and Social Security Act 2000 come into force for the purposes of that type of case – which is March 3, 2003 for the types of cases in arts 3 and 5 of SI 2003 No.192). For other types of cases see the '1993 rules', below. See reg 6 of SI 2001 No.162 for savings provisions detailing when these amendments do not apply.

1993 rules

Reg 2(3) of the Child Support (Collection and Enforcement and Miscellaneous Amendments) Regulations 2000 (SI 2001 No.162) amends this regulation and has been brought into force only for the types of cases in art 3 and 5 of the Child Support, Pensions and Social Security Act 2000 (Commencement No.12) Order 2003 (SI 2003 No.192) – see p683, subject to savings provisions in reg 6 of SI 2001 No.162. For other types of cases the '1993 rules' apply and:
–   at the beginning of paragraph (1) the words "In the case of child support maintenance," are not inserted;
–   paragraphs (1)(e), (1A) and (3) are not inserted; and
–   in paragraph (2) the word "assessment" is retained in place of "calculation".

Definitions

"fee": see reg 1(2A).
"interest": see reg 1 (2).
"liable person": see reg 2(2).
"penalty payment": see reg 7A(5).

[¹PART IIA
Collection of penalty payments

Payment of a financial penalty

7A.–(1)　This regulation applies where a maintenance calculation is, or has been, in force, the liable person is in arrears with payments of child support maintenance, and the Secretary of State requires the liable person to pay penalty payments to him.

(2)　For the purposes of regulation 7(1)(e) a payment will be overdue if it is not received by the time that the next payment of child support maintenance is due.

(3)　The Secretary of State may require a penalty payment to be made if the outstanding amount is not received within 7 days of the notification in regulation 7(1)(e) or if the liable person fails to pay all outstanding amounts due on dates and of amounts as agreed between the liable person and the Secretary of State.

(4)　Payments of a penalty payment shall be made within 14 days of the notification referred to in regulation 7(1A).

(5)　In this Part a "liable person" means a person liable to make a penalty payment and in Part II and in this Part "penalty payment" is to be construed in accordance with section 41A of the Act.]

Amendment

1.　Child Support (Collection and Enforcement and Miscellaneous Amendments) Regulations 2000 (SI 2001 No.162) reg 2(4) (will come into force in relation to a particular case on the day on which ss1(2) and (3), 4, 18(1) and (2), and 20(1) of and Sch 3 para 11(2) and (16) Child Support, Pensions and Social Security Act 2000 come into force for the purposes of that type of case – which is March 3, 2003 for the types of cases in arts 3 and 5 of the SI 2003 No.192). For other types of cases see the '1993 rules', below. See reg 6 of SI 2001 No.162 for savings provisions detailing when this amendment does not apply.

1993 rules

Reg 2(4) of the Child Support (Collection and Enforcement and Miscellaneous Amendments) Regulations 2000 (SI 2001 No.162) inserted Part IIA including regulation 7A and has been brought into force only for the types of cases in art 3 and 5 of the Child Support, Pensions and Social Security Act 2000 (Commencement No.12) Order 2003 (SI 2003 No.192) – see p683, subject to savings provisions in reg 6 of SI 2001 No.162. For other types of cases regulation 7A does not apply.

PART III
Deduction from earnings orders

Interpretation of this Part

8.–(1)　For the purposes of this Part–
[¹ "defective" means in relation to a deduction from earnings order that it does not comply with the requirements of regulations 9 to 11 and such failure to comply has made it impracticable for the employer to comply with his obligations under the Act and these Regulations;]

[⁸...]

"earnings" shall be construed in accordance with paragraphs (3) and (4);
[⁸...]
[⁸...]
"normal deduction rate" means the rate specified in a deduction from earnings order
(expressed as a sum of money per [¹²month and the equivalent of that sum for a
1, 2 and 4 week period]) at which deductions are to be made from the liable
person's net earnings;
"pay-day" in relation to a liable person means an occasion on which earnings are paid to
him or the day on which such earnings would normally fall to be paid;
[⁹"protected earnings proportion" means the proportion referred to in regulation 11(2).]
[⁸...]
[⁸...]
[⁸...]
(2)   For the purposes of this Part the relationship of employer and employee shall be
treated as subsisting between two persons if one of them, as a principal and not as a
servant or agent, pays to the other any sum defined as earnings under paragraph (1) and
"employment", "employer" and "employee" shall be construed accordingly.
(3)   Subject to paragraph (4), "earnings" are any sums payable to a person–
(a)   by way of wages or salary (including any fees, bonus, commission, overtime
pay or other emoluments payable in addition to wages or salary or payable under
a contract of service);
(b)   by way of pension (including an annuity in respect of past service, whether or
not rendered to the person paying the annuity, and including periodical payments
by way of compensation for the loss, abolition or relinquishment, or diminution
in the emoluments, of any office or em-ployment);
(c)   by way of statutory sick pay.
(4)   "Earnings" shall not include–
(a)   sums payable by any public department of the Government of Northern Ireland
or of a territory outside the United Kingdom;
(b)   pay or allowances payable to the liable person as a member of Her Majesty's
forces [⁶ other than pay or allowances payable by his employer to him as a
special member of a reserve force (within the meaning of the Reserve Forces
Act 1996)];
(c)   pension, allowances or benefit payable under any enactment relating to social
security;
(d)   pension or allowances payable in respect of disablement or disability;
(e)   guaranteed minimum pension within the meaning of the Social Security Pensions
Act 1975.
[¹⁰(f)   working tax credit payable under section 10 of the Tax Credits Act 2002.]
(5)   "Net earnings" means the residue of earnings after deduction of–
(a)   income tax;
(b)   primary class I contributions under Part I of the Contributions and Benefits Act
1992;
(c)   amounts deductible by way of contributions to a superannuation scheme which
provides for the payment of annuities or [⁷ lump] sums–
(i)   to the employee on his retirement at a specified age or on becoming
incapacitated at some earlier age; or
(ii)   on his death or otherwise, to his personal representative, widow,
[¹¹surviving civil partner,] relatives or dependants.

Amendments
1.   Inserted by reg 14(2) of SI 1995/ 1045 as from 18.4.95.
2.   Substituted by reg 14(3) of SI 1995/1045 as from 18.4.95.
3.   Inserted by reg 14(4) of SI 1995/1045 as from 18.4.95.
4.   Substituted by reg 3 of SI 1996/1945 as from 7.10.96.
5.   Inserted by reg 14(5) of SI 1995/1045 as from 18.4.95
6.   Inserted into head (b) by reg 2(2) of SI 1999/977 as from 6.4.99
7.   Substituted by reg 41 of SI 1993/913 as from 5.4.93.

8.   Child Support (Collection and Enforcement and Miscellaneous Amendments) Regulations 2000 (SI 2001 No.162) reg 2(5) (comes into force in relation to a particular case on the day on which ss1(2) and (3), 4, 18(1) and (2), and 20(1) of and Sch 3 para 11(2) and (16) Child Support, Pensions and Social Security Act 2000 come into force for the purposes of that type of case – which is March 3, 2003 for the types of cases detailed in arts 3 and 5 of SI 2003 No.192, see p683). See reg 6 of SI 2001 No.162 (p676) for savings provisions detailing when these amendments do not apply. For other types of cases, including those covered by the savings provisions, see the '1993 rules' below.

9.   Child Support (Collection and Enforcement and Miscellaneous Amendments) Regulations 2000 (SI 2001 No.162) reg 2(5) (comes into force in relation to a particular case on the day on which ss1(2) and (3), 4, 18(1) and (2), and 20(1) of and Sch 3 para 11(2) and (16) Child Support, Pensions and Social Security Act 2000 come into force for the purposes of that type of case – which is March 3, 2003 for the types of cases in arts 3 and 5 of SI 2003 No.192, see p683). See reg 6 of SI 2001 No.162 (p676) for savings provisions detailing when this amendment does not apply. For other types of cases, including those covered by the savings provisions, see the '1993 rules' below.

10.   Child Support (Miscellaneous Amendments) Regulations 2003 (SI 2003 No.328) reg 2 (April 6, 2003).

11.   Civil Partnership (Pensions, Social Security and Child Support) (Consequential, etc. Provisions) Order 2005 (SI 2005 No.2877) art 2(4) and Sch 4 para 3 (December 5, 2005).

12.   Child Support (Meaning of Child and New Calculation Rules) (Consequential and Miscellaneous Amendment) Regulations 2012 (SI 2012 No.2785) reg 4(3) (in force in relation to a particular case on the day on which paragraph 2 of Schedule 4 to the Child Maintenance and Other Payments Act 2008 (see p243) comes into force in relation to that type of case – which is December 10, 2012, in relation to the types of cases falling within art 3 of SI 2012 No.3042). This amendment is subject to the saving and transitional provisions in reg 11 and 12 of SI 2012 No.2785 (see p764). For other types of cases, including those covered by the savings and transitional provisions, see the '2003 and 1993 rules' below.

2003 and 1993 rules

Regulation 4(3) of The Child Support (Meaning of Child and New Calculation Rules) (Consequential and Miscellaneous Amendment) Regulations 2012 (SI 2012 No.2785) substitutes "month and the equivalent of that sum for a 1, 2 and 4 week period" for "week, month or other period", in the definition of "normal deduction rate" in regulation 8(1) from December 10, 2012, for the types of cases falling within art 3 of SI 2012 No.3042 only (see p767). For other types of cases the original wording is retained.

1993 rules

Regulation 2(5) of The Child Support (Collection and Enforcement and Miscellaneous Amendments) Regulations 2000 (SI 2001 No.162) inserted the definition of "protected earnings proportion" and omitted the following definitions from regulation 8(1) of The Child Support (Collection and Enforcement) Regulations 1992. These amendments came into force on March 3, 2003 for the types of cases detailed in arts 3 and 5 of SI 2003 No.192 – see p683, subject to the savings provisions in reg 6 of SI 2001 No.162 (p676). For other types of cases, including those covered by the savings provisions, the definition of "protected earnings proportion" does not apply, and the following definitions are retained in regulation 8(1):

"disposable income" means the amount determined under [² regulation 12(1)(a)] of the Child Support (Maintenance Assessments and Special Cases) Regulations 1992;

"exempt income" means the amount determined under regulation 9 of the Child Support (Maintenance Assessments and Special Cases) Regulations 1992;

[³ "interim maintenance assessment" means a Category A, Category B, Category C or Category D interim maintenance assessment within the meaning of [⁴ regulation 8(3)] of the Child Support (Maintenance Assessment Procedure) Regulations 1992;

"net earnings" shall be construed in accordance with paragraph (5);

"prescribed minimum amount" means the minimum amount prescribed in regulation 13 of the Child Support (Maintenance Assessments and Special Cases) Regulations 1992;

"protected earnings rate" means the level of earnings specified in a deduction from earnings order (expressed as a sum of money per week, month or other period) below which deductions of child support maintenance shall not be made for the purposes of this Part;

"protected income level" means the level of protected income determined in accordance with [⁵paragraphs (1) to (5) of] regulation 11 of the Child Support (Maintenance Assessments and Special Cases) Regulations 1992.

Deduction from earnings orders

9.   A deduction from earnings order shall specify–
(a)   the name and address of the liable person;
(b)   the name of the employer at whom it is directed;
(c)   where known, the liable person's place of work, the nature of his work and any works or pay number;
[¹ (cc) where known, the liable person's national insurance number;]
[² (d) the normal deduction rate or rates and the date upon which each is to take effect;
(e)   the [³protected earnings proportion];]
(f)   the address to which amounts deducted from earnings are to be sent.

Amendments

1.   Reg 9(cc) inserted by reg 6 of SI 1995/3261 as from 22.1.96.
2.   Reg 9(d) and (e) substituted by reg 15 of SI 1995/1045 as from 18.4.95.
3.   Child Support (Collection and Enforcement and Miscellaneous Amendments) Regulations 2000 (SI 2001 No.162) reg 2(5) (comes into force in relation to a particular case on the day on which ss1(2) and (3), 4, 18(1) and (2), and 20(1) of and Sch 3 para 11(2) and (16) Child Support, Pensions and Social Security Act 2000 come into force for the purposes of that type of case – which is March 3, 2003 for the types of cases in arts 3 and 5 of SI 2003 No.192). See reg 6 of SI 2001 No.162 for savings provisions detailing when this amendment does not apply. For other types of cases, including those covered by the savings provisions, see the '1993 rules' below.

1993 rules

Reg 2(5) of the Child Support (Collection and Enforcement and Miscellaneous Amendments) Regulations 2000 (SI 2001 No.162) amends this regulation and has been brought into force only for the types of cases in art 3 and 5 of the Child Support, Pensions and Social Security Act 2000 (Commencement No.12) Order 2003 (SI 2003 No.192) – see p683, subject to savings provisions in reg 6 of SI 2001 No.162. For other types of cases the '1993 rules' apply and the words "protected earnings rate" are retained in place of "protected earnings proportion" in paragraph (e).

Definitions

"earnings": see reg 8(1), (3) and (4).
"employer": see reg 8(2).
"normal deduction rate": see reg 8(1).
"protected earnings proportion": see reg 8(1).

Normal deduction rate

[⁴**10.**–(1)   The period by reference to which the normal deduction rate is set must be the period by reference to which the liable person is normally paid where that period is a 1, 2 or 4 weekly or monthly period.
(2) The employer must select the normal deduction rate which applies depending on the period by reference to which the liable person's earnings are normally paid.
(3) Where the liable person is paid by reference to a period other than at a 1, 2 or 4 weekly or monthly period, the Secretary of State must discharge the deduction from earnings order in accordance with regulation 20.]

Amendments

1.   Substituted by reg 16(2) of SI 1995/1045 as from 18.4.95.
2.   Amended by reg 16(3)(a) and (b) respectively of SI1995/1045 as from 18.4.95.
3.   Child Support (Collection and Enforcement and Miscellaneous Amendments) Regulations 2000 (SI 2001 No.162) reg 2(5)(c) (comes into force in relation to a particular case on the day on which ss1(2) and (3), 4, 18(1) and (2), and 20(1) of and Sch 3 para 11(2) and (16) Child Support, Pensions and Social Security Act 2000 come into force for the purposes of that type of case – which is March 3, 2003 for the types of cases in arts 3 and 5 of SI 2003 No.192). See reg 6 of SI 2001 No.162 for savings provisions detailing when these amendments do not apply. For other types of cases, including those covered by the savings provisions, see the '1993 rules' below.
4.   Child Support (Meaning of Child and New Calculation Rules) (Consequential and Miscellaneous Amendment) Regulations 2012 (SI 2012 No.2785) reg 4(4) (in force in relation to a particular case on the day on which paragraph 2 of Schedule 4 to the Child Maintenance and Other Payments Act 2008 (see p243) comes into force in relation to that type of case – which is December 10, 2012, in relation to the types of cases falling within art 3 of SI 2012 No.3042 only (see p767). This amendment is subject to the saving and transitional provisions in reg 11 and 12 of SI 2012 No.2785 (see p764). For other types of cases see below.

2003 rules

Regulation 4(4) of The Child Support (Meaning of Child and New Calculation Rules) (Consequential and Miscellaneous Amendment) Regulations 2012 (SI 2012 No.2785) substituted regulation 10 of The Child Support (Collection and Enforcement) Regulations 1992 from December 10, 2012, in relation to the types of cases falling within art 3 of SI 2012 No.3042 only (see p767). For other types of cases, (unless the 1993 rules apply – see below), regulation 10 reads:

10.–(1)   The period by reference to which [¹ a normal deduction rate] is set shall be the period by reference to which the liable person's earnings are normally paid or, if none, such other period as the Secretary of State may specify.

(2)   [³...]

(3)   [³...]

1993 rules

Regulation 2(5)(c) of The Child Support (Collection and Enforcement and Miscellaneous Amendments) Regulations 2000 (SI 2001 No.162) omitted paragraphs (2) and (3) from regulation 10 of The Child Support (Collection and Enforcement) Regulations 1992. This amendment came into force on March 3, 2003 for the types of cases in arts 3 and 5 of SI 2003 No.192 subject to the savings provisions in reg 6 of SI 2001 No.162. The 1993 rules apply to other types of cases, including those covered by the savings provisions in reg 6, (unless the case is one which falls within art 3 of SI 2012 No.3042). If the 1993 rules apply, regulation 10(1) is as shown under the heading '2003 rules' above, and reg 10(2) and (3) are as follows:

"(2)   The Secretary of State, in specifying the normal deduction rate, shall not include any amount in respect of arrears or interest [², in a case where there is a current assessment,] if, [²at the date of making of any current maintenance assessment other than an interim maintenance assessment]–

(a)   the liable person's disposable income was below the level specified in paragraph (3); or

(b)   the deduction of such an amount from the liable person's disposable income would have reduced his disposable income below the level specified in paragraph (3).

(3)   The level referred to in paragraph (2) is the liable person's protected income level less the prescribed minimum amount."

Definitions

"the Act": see reg 1(2).
"normal deduction rate": see reg 8(1).

[⁵[⁸Protected earnings proportion]

11.–(1)   The period by reference to which the protected earnings proportion is set must be the same as the period by reference to which the normal deduction rate is set in accordance with regulation 10(1).

(2) The protected earnings proportion in respect of any period shall be 60% of the liable person's net earnings in respect of that period as calculated at the pay-day of the liable person by the employer.]

Amendments

1.   Inserted in reg 11(2) by reg 17(2) of SI 1995/1045 as from 18.4.95 (see also reg 64(1) ibid).

2.   Inserted by reg 17(3) of SI 1995/ 1045 as from 18.4.95 (see also reg 64(1) ibid).

3.   Inserted in reg 11(3) by reg 4 of SI 1996/1945 as from 5.8.96.

4.   Subpara (4) substituted by art 29 of SI 1999/ 1510 as from 1.6.99.

5.   Child Support (Collection and Enforcement and Miscellaneous Amendments) Regulations 2000 (SI 2001 No.162) reg 2(5)(d) (comes into force in relation to a particular case on the day on which ss1(2) and (3), 4, 18(1) and (2), and 20(1) of and Sch 3 para 11(2) and (16) Child Support, Pensions and Social Security Act 2000 come into force for the purposes of that type of case – which is March 3, 2003 for the types of cases in arts 3 and 5 of SI 2003 No.192). See reg 6 of SI 2001 No.162 for savings provisions. For those for whom these amendments do not apply, see the '1993 rules' below.

6.   Child Support (Miscellaneous Amendments) (No.2) Regulations 2008 (SI 2008 No.2544) reg 2(3) (October 27, 2008).

7. Child Support (Miscellaneous Amendments) Regulations 2006 (SI 2006 No.1520) reg 3(3) (July 12, 2006, unless Sch 3 para 11(16) Child Support, Pensions and Social Security Act 2000 (which inserts subpara 32(2)(bb) into the Child Support Act 1991) has not come into force in relation to a particular case before 12 July 2006, when for the purposes of that case this amendment will come into force on the day on which para 11(16) comes into force for that type of case). Para 11(16) came fully into force on March 3, 2003 for the types of cases in art 3 of SI 2003 No.192, and on October 27, 2008 for all other cases.

8. Child Support (Meaning of Child and New Calculation Rules) (Consequential and Miscellaneous Amendment) Regulations 2012 (SI 2012 No.2785) reg 4(5) (in force in relation to a particular case on the day on which paragraph 2 of Schedule 4 to the Child Maintenance and Other Payments Act 2008 (see p243) comes into force in relation to that type of case – which is December 10, 2012 in relation to the types of cases falling within art 3 of SI 2012 No.3042 (see p767). This amendment is subject to the saving and transitional provisions in reg 11 and 12 of SI 2012 No.2785 (see p764). For other types of cases see the '2003 rules' below.

2003 rules

Regulation 4(5) of The Child Support (Meaning of Child and New Calculation Rules) (Consequential and Miscellaneous Amendment) Regulations 2012 (SI 2012 No.2785) substituted reg 11 of The Child Support (Collection and Enforcement) Regulations 1992 from December 10, 2012, in relation to the types of cases falling within art 3 of SI 2012 No.3042 (see p767), subject to the saving and transitional provisions in reg 11 and 12 of SI 2012 No.2785. For other types of cases, unless the 1993 rules apply, regulation 11 reads:

11.–(1) The period by reference to which the [5protected earnings proportion] is set shall be the same as the period by reference to which the normal deduction rate is set under regulation 10(1).

(2) The amount to be specified as the [5protected earnings proportion] in respect of any period shall [1[5...]] be an amount equal to [560% of the liable person's net earnings] in respect of that period [7as calculated–

(a) at the date of the current maintenance calculation; or

(b) if the deduction from earnings order relates only to arrears of child support maintenance, at the date on which the order is made or varied.]

(3) [5...]

(4) [5...]

1993 rules

Regulation 2(5)(d) of The Child Support (Collection and Enforcement and Miscellaneous Amendments) Regulations 2000 (SI 2001 No.162) amends this regulation and has been brought into force from March 3, 2003 for the types of cases in arts 3 and 5 of SI 2003 No.192 subject to the savings provisions in reg 6 of SI 2001 No.162 (see p676). For other types of cases (unless the case is one which falls within art 3 of SI 2012 No.3042) the '1993 rules' apply. If the 1993 rules apply,

– in the heading and in paragraphs (1) and (2), the words "protected earnings rate" are retained in place of "protected earnings proportion";

– in paragraph (2) the words ", except where [6 paragraph (3), paragraph (4) or paragraph (5)] applies," are included after "in respect of any period" , the words "the liable person's exempt income" are retained in place of "60% of the liable person's net earnings" and the word "assessment" is retained in place of "maintenance calculation";

– paragraphs (3) and (4) are not omitted, and para (5)–(8) are inserted by SI 2008 No.2544, and read as follows:

[2(3) Where an interim maintenance assessment [3, except a Category B interim maintenance assessment,] is in force the protected earnings rate shall be–

(a) where there is some knowledge of the liable person's circumstances, the aggregate of the following amounts at the date of the making of the assessment–

(i) the personal allowance applicable by virtue of paragraph 1(1)(e) of Schedule 2 to the Income Support (General) Regulations 1987 (in this paragraph referred to as "the relevant Schedule") or if he is known to have a partner, that applicable for a couple under para-graph 1(3)(c) of that Schedule;

(ii) the personal allowance applicable by virtue of the relevant Schedule in respect of any child or young person who is known to be living with the relevant person (and where the age of the child or young person is not known it shall be assumed to be less than 11);

(iii) the amount of any premium applicable by virtue of the relevant Schedule which is known to be applicable in the circumstances of the case; and
(iv) £30;

(b) in any other case the personal allowance specified in paragraph 1(1)(e) of the relevant Schedule at the date mentioned in sub-paragraph (a), plus £30.

[⁴(4) Where there is a liability to make parents of child support maintenance but no maintenance assessment is in force–

(a) in a case where the last maintenance assessment was a Category A or Category C interim maintenance assessment, the protected earnings rate shall be the amount which would be produced by the application of the provisions of paragraph (3) if a Category A or Category C interim maintenance assessment were in force;

(b) subject to sub-paragraph (a), in a case where the absent parent provides sufficient evidence to satisfy the Secretary of State that his circumstances have changed since the last occasion on which his exempt income was calculated for the purposes of a decision under the Act, the protected earnings rate shall be the exempt amount as it would be calculated in consequence of that change of circumstances if regulation 9 of the Child Support (Maintenance Assessments and Special Cases) Regulations 1992 applied in his case; and

in any other case, the protected earnings rate shall be the amount of the liable person's exempt income as it was on the last occasion that amount was calculated for the purposes of a decision under the Act.]

[⁶ (5) This paragraph applies where the liable person–

(a) has more than one employer; and

(b) the Secretary of State makes an order under section 31 of the Act ("an order") against that person in respect of more than one employer.

(6) Where paragraph (5) applies, the protected earnings rate for each order is to be divided proportionately between the earnings of the liable person with each employer in accordance with paragraph (7).

(7) The amount to be specified as the protected earnings rate in respect of any period in an order is an amount equal to the percentage of the liable person's exempt income which is the same as the amounts earned with an employer, as a percentage of the total earnings with the employers.

(8) Any reference to an "employer" in paragraphs (6) and (7) is to be construed as a reference to an employer subject to an order made in respect of a liable person.]

Definitions
"normal deduction rate": see reg 8(1).
"protected earnings proportion": see reg 8(1).

Amount to be deducted by employer

12.–(1) Subject to the provisions of this regulation, an employer who has been served with a copy of a deduction from earnings order in respect of a liable person in his employment shall, each pay-day, make a deduction from the net earnings of that liable person of an amount equal to the normal deduction rate.

(2) Where the deduction of the normal deduction rate would reduce the liable person's net earnings below the [²protected earnings proportion] the employer shall deduct only such amount as will leave the liable person with net earnings equal to the [²protected earnings proportion].

(3) Where the liable person receives a payment of earnings at an interval greater or lesser than the interval specified in relation to the normal deduction rate and the [²protected earnings proportion] ("the specified interval") the employer shall, for the purpose of such payments, take as the normal deduction rate and the [²protected earnings proportion] such amounts (to the nearest whole penny) as are in the same proportion to the interval since the last pay-day as the normal deduction rate and the [²protected earnings proportion] bear to the specified interval.

[¹ (3A) Where on any pay-day the liable person receives a payment of earnings covering a period longer than the period by reference to which the normal deduction rate is set, the employer shall, subject to paragraph (2), make a deduction from the net earnings paid to that liable person on that pay-day of an amount which is in the same proportion to the normal deduction rate as that longer period is to the period by reference to which that normal deduction rate is set.]

(4)   Where, on any pay-day, the employer fails to deduct an amount due under the deduction from earnings order or deducts an amount less than the amount of the normal deduction rate the shortfall shall, subject to the operation of paragraph (2), be deducted in addition to the normal deduction rate at the next available pay-day or days.

(5)   [³...]

(6)   Where, on any pay-day, an employer makes a deduction from the earnings of a liable person in accordance with the deduction from earnings order he may also deduct an amount not exceeding £1 in respect of his administrative costs and such deduction for administrative costs may be made notwithstanding that it may reduce the liable person's net earnings below the [²protected earnings proportion].

Amendments

1.   Para (3A) inserted into reg 12 by reg 6 of SI1998/58 as from 19.1.98.
2.   Child Support (Collection and Enforcement and Miscellaneous Amendments) Regulations 2000 (SI 2001 No.162) reg 2(5)(e)(i) (comes into force in relation to a particular case on the day on which ss1(2) and (3), 4, 18(1) and (2), and 20(1) of and Sch 3 para 11(2) and (16) Child Support, Pensions and Social Security Act 2000 come into force for the purposes of that type of case – which is March 3, 2003 for the types of cases in arts 3 and 5 of SI 2003 No.192). For other types of cases, see the '1993 rules' below. See reg 6 of SI 2001 No.162 for savings provisions.
3.   Child Support (Collection and Enforcement and Miscellaneous Amendments) Regulations 2000 (SI 2001 No.162) reg 2(5)(e)(ii) (comes into force in relation to a particular case on the day on which ss1(2) and (3), 4, 18(1) and (2), and 20(1) of and Sch 3 para 11(2) and (16) Child Support, Pensions and Social Security Act 2000 come into force for the purposes of that type of case – which is March 3, 2003 for the types of cases in arts 3 and 5 of SI 2003 No.192). For other types of cases see the '1993 rules' below. See reg 6 of SI 2001 No.162 for savings provisions detailing when this amendment does not apply.

1993 rules

Reg 2(5)(e) of the Child Support (Collection and Enforcement and Miscellaneous Amendments) Regulations 2000 (SI 2001 No.162) amends this regulation. Subject to savings provisions in reg 6 of SI 2001 No.162, this amendment has been brought into force from March 3, 2003 only for the types of cases in art 3 and 5 of the Child Support, Pensions and Social Security Act 2000 (Commencement No.12) Order 2003 (SI 2003 No.192) – see p683. For other types of cases the '1993 rules' apply and the words "protected earnings rate" are retained in place of "protected earnings proportion" in paragraphs (2), (3) and (6) and paragraph (5), below, is retained.

(5)   Where, on any pay-day, the liable person's net earnings are less than his protected earnings rate the amount of the difference shall be carried forward to his next pay-day and treated as part of his protected earnings in respect of that pay-day.

Definitions

"earnings": see reg 8(1), (3) and (4).
"employer": see reg 8(2).
"employment": see reg 8(2).
"net earnings": see reg 8(1).
"normal deduction rate": see reg 8(1).
"pay-day": see reg 8(1).
"protected earnings proportion": see reg 8(1).

Employer to notify liable person of deduction

13.–(1)   An employer making a deduction from earnings for the purposes of this Part shall notify the liable person in writing of the amount of the deduction, including any amount deducted for administrative costs under regulation 12(6).

(2)   Such notification shall be given not later than the pay-day on which the deduction is made or, where that is impracticable, not later than the following pay-day.

Definitions

"employer": see reg 8(2).
"pay-day": see reg 8(1).

Payment by employer to Secretary of State

14.–(1)   Amounts deducted by an employer under a deduction from earnings order (other than any administrative costs deducted under regulation 12(6)) shall be paid to the Secretary of State by the 19th day of the month following the month in which the deduction is made.

(2)   Such payment may be made–

(a)   by cheque;

(b)   by automated credit transfer; or

(c)   by such other method as the Secretary of State may specify.

Definition
"employer": see reg 8(2).

Information to be provided by liable person

[¹**15.**–(1)   A liable person in respect of whom a deduction from earnings order is in force must notify the Secretary of State in writing within 7 days of each occasion on which he leaves employment or becomes employed, or re-employed.

(2)   If a liable person becomes employed or re-employed, such notification must include the following details–

(a)   the name and address of his employer;

(b)   the amount of his earnings and expected earnings; and

(c)   his place of work, nature of his work and any works or pay number.]

Amendment
1.   Child Support (Miscellaneous Amendments) Regulations 2008 (SI 2008 No.536) reg 3 (April 6, 2008).

Definitions
"employer": see reg 8(2).
"employment": see reg 8(2).

General Note
Paragraph 2(a)
The employer's address need not necessarily be the address of the office which is responsible for paying the liable person and therefore for administering the deduction from earnings order.

Duty of employers and others to notify Secretary of State

16.–(1)   Where a deduction from earnings order is served on a person on the assumption that he is the employer of a liable person but the liable person to whom the order relates is not in his employment, the person on whom the order was served shall notify the Secretary of State of that fact in writing, at the address specified in the order, within 10 days of the date of service on him of the order.

(2)   Where an employer is required to operate a deduction from earnings order and the liable person to whom the order relates ceases to be in his employment the employer shall notify the Secretary of State of that fact in writing, at the address specified in the order, within 10 days of the liable person ceasing to be in his employment.

(3)   Where an employer becomes aware that a deduction from earnings order is in force in relation to a person who is an employee of his he shall, within 7 days of the date on which he becomes aware, notify the Secretary of State of that fact in writing at the address specified in the order.

Definitions
"employer": see reg 8(2).
"employment": see reg 8(2).

[¹Requirement to review deduction from earnings orders

17.–(1)   Subject to paragraph (2), the Secretary of State shall review a deduction from earnings order in the following circumstances–

(a)   where there is a change in the amount of the maintenance [²calculation];

(b)   where any arrears[², penalty payment, interest or fees] payable under the order are paid off.

(2)   There shall be no obligation to review a deduction from earnings order under paragraph (1) where the normal deduction rates specified in the order take account of the changes which will arise as a result of the circumstances specified in sub-paragraph (a) or (b) of that paragraph.]

Amendments

1.   Reg 17 substituted by reg 18 of SI 1995/1045 as from 18.4.95.

2.   Child Support (Collection and Enforcement and Miscellaneous Amendments) Regulations 2000 (SI 2001 No.162) reg 2(5)(f) (comes into force in relation to a particular case on the day on which ss1(2) and (3), 4, 18(1) and (2), and 20(1) of and Sch 3 para 11(2) and (16) Child Support, Pensions and Social Security Act 2000 come into force for the purposes of that type of case – which is March 3, 2003 for the types of cases in arts 3 and 5 of SI 2003 No.192). For other types of cases, see the '1993 rules' below. See reg 6 of SI 2001 No.162 for savings provisions detailing when these amendments do not apply.

1993 rules

Reg 2(5)(f) of the Child Support (Collection and Enforcement and Miscellaneous Amendments) Regulations 2000 (SI 2001 No.162) amends regulation 17. Subject to the savings provisions in reg 6 of SI 2001 No.162, this amendment has been brought into force from March 3, 2003 only for the types of cases in art 3 and 5 of the Child Support, Pensions and Social Security Act 2000 (Commencement No.12) Order 2003 (SI 2003 No.192) – see p683. For other types of cases the '1993 rules' apply and:

–   in paragraph (1)(a) the word "assessment" is retained in place of "calculation"; *and*

–   in paragraphs (1)(b) the words "and interest on arrears" are retained in place of ", penalty payment, interest or fees".

Definition

"normal deduction rate": see reg 8(1).

Power to vary deduction from earnings orders

18.–(1)   The Secretary of State may (whether on a review under regulation 17 or otherwise) vary a deduction from earnings order so as to–

(a)   include any amount which may be included in such an order or exclude or decrease any such amount;

(b)   substitute a subsequent employer for the employer at whom the order was previously directed.

(2)   The Secretary of State shall serve a copy of any deduction from earnings order, as varied, on the liable person's employer and on the liable person.

Definition

"employer": see reg 8(2).

Compliance with deduction from earnings order as varied

19.–(1)   Where a deduction from earnings order has been varied and a copy of the order as varied has been served on the liable person's employer it shall, subject to paragraph (2), be the duty of the employer to comply with the order as varied.

(2)   The employer shall not be under any liability for non-compliance with the order, as varied, before the end of the period of 7 days beginning with the date on which a copy of the order, as varied, was served on him.

Definition

"employer": see reg 8(2).

Discharge of deduction from earnings orders

20.–[¹(1)   The Secretary of State may discharge a deduction from earnings order where it appears to him that–

(a)   no further payments are due under it;

(b)   the order is ineffective or some other way of securing that payments are made would be more effective;

(c)   the order is defective;

    (d)   the order fails to comply in a material respect with any procedural provision of the Act or regulations made under it other than provision made in regulation 9, 10 or 11;

    (e)   at the time of the making of the order he did not have, or subsequently ceased to have, jurisdiction to make a deduction from earnings order; [³...]

    (f)   in the case of an order made at a time when there is in force [²a default or interim maintenance decision], it is inappropriate to continue deductions under the order having regard to the compliance or the attempted compliance with the [²maintenance calculation] by the liable person.][³; or

    (g)   the circumstances in regulation 10(3) apply.]

    (2)   The Secretary of State shall give written notice of the discharge of the deduction from earnings order to the liable person and to the liable person's employer.

Amendments

1.   Reg 20(1) substituted by reg 19 of SI 1995/1045 as from 18.4.95.

2.   Child Support (Collection and Enforcement and Miscellaneous Amendments) Regulations 2000 (SI 2001 No.162) reg 2(5)(g) (comes into force in relation to a particular case on the day on which ss1(2) and (3), 4, 18(1) and (2), and 20(1) of and Sch 3 para 11(2) and (16) Child Support, Pensions and Social Security Act 2000 come into force for the purposes of that type of case – which is March 3, 2003 for the types of cases in arts 3 and 5 of SI 2003 No.192). See reg 6 of SI 2001 No.162 for savings provisions detailing when these amendments do not apply. For those for whom these amendments do not apply, see '1993 rules' below.

3.   Child Support (Meaning of Child and New Calculation Rules) (Consequential and Miscellaneous Amendment) Regulations 2012 (SI 2012 No.2785) reg 4(6) (in force in relation to a particular case on the day on which paragraph 2 of Schedule 4 to the Child Maintenance and Other Payments Act 2008 (see p243) comes into force in relation to that type of case – which is December 10, 2012, in relation to the types of cases falling within art 3 of SI 2012 No.3042 only (see p767). This amendment is subject to the saving and transitional provisions in reg 11 and 12 of SI 2012 No.2785 (see p764). For other types of cases see '2003 and 1993 rules' below.

2003 and 1993 rules

Regulation 4(6) of The Child Support (Meaning of Child and New Calculation Rules) (Consequential and Miscellaneous Amendment) Regulations 2012 (SI 2012 No.2785) omitted the word "or" from the end of paragraph 20(1)(e) and inserted paragraph 20(1)(g). These amendments came into force on December 10, 2012, in relation to the types of cases falling within art 3 of SI 2012 No. 3042 only (see p767), subject to the saving and transitional provisions in reg 11 and 12 of SI 2012 No.2785. For other types of cases, including those covered by the saving and transitional provisions, regulation 20 should be read without these amendments.

1993 rules

Regulation 2(5)(g) of The Child Support (Collection and Enforcement and Miscellaneous Amendments) Regulations 2000 (SI 2001 No.162) amends regulation 20(1)(f) of The Child Support (Collection and Enforcement) Regulations 1992. The amendments came into force on March 3, 2003 for the types of cases in arts 3 and 5 of SI 2003 No.192, subject to the savings provisions in reg 6 of SI 2001 No.162. The 1993 rules apply to other types of cases (unless the case is one which falls within art 3 of SI 2012 No.3042), including those covered by the savings provisions in reg 6. If the 1993 rules apply, in paragraph (1)(f)

–   the words "an interim maintenance assessment" are retained in place of "a default or interim maintenance decision"; and

–   the words "maintenance assessment" are retained in place of "maintenance calculation".

Definitions

"the Act": see reg 1(2).

"defective": see reg 8(1).

"employer": see reg 8(2).

General Note

Paragraphs (1)(c) and (d)

"Defective" is defined in reg 8(1) as meaning an order which does not comply with the requirements of regs 9 to 11 resulting in its being impracticable for the employer to comply with his obligations under the Act and regulations. This regulation enables the Secretary of State to discharge such an order. S/he may also discharge the order for any other failure of compliance with the Act or regulations. It is difficult to see why such failures are not deemed to make the order "defective" as such, especially since an appeal to the magistrates under reg 22 may only be made in respect of a "defective" order – ie, one defective within reg 8(1).

Lapse of deduction from earnings orders

21.–(1)   A deduction from earnings order shall lapse (except in relation to any deductions made or to be made in respect of the employment not yet paid to the Secretary of State) where the employer at whom it is directed ceases to have the liable person in his employment.

(2)   The order shall lapse from the pay-day coinciding with, or, if none, the pay-day following, the termination of the employment.

(3)   A deduction from earnings order which has lapsed under this regulation shall nonetheless be treated as remaining in force for the purposes of regulations 15 and 24.

(4)   Where a deduction from earnings order has lapsed under paragraph (1) and the liable person recommences employment (whether with the same or another employer), the order may be revived from such date as may be specified by the Secretary of State.

(5)   Where a deduction from earnings order is revived under paragraph (4), the Secretary of State shall give written notice of that fact to, and serve a copy of the notice on, the liable person and the liable person's employer.

(6)   Where an order is revived under paragraph (4), no amount shall be carried forward under regulation 12(4) [¹...] from a time prior to the revival of the order.

Amendment

  1.   Child Support (Collection and Enforcement and Miscellaneous Amendments) Regulations 2000 (SI 2001 No.162) reg 2(5)(h) (comes into force in relation to a particular case on the day on which ss1(2) and (3), 4, 18(1) and (2), and 20(1) and Sch 3 para 11(2) and (16) of the Child Support, Pensions and Social Security Act 2000 come into force for the purpose of that type of case – which is March 3, 2003 for the types of cases in arts 3 and 5 of SI 2003 No.192). For other types of cases see the '1993 rules', below. See reg 6 of SI 2001 No.162 for savings provisions detailing when this amendment does not apply.

1993 rules

      Regulation 2(5)(h) of The Child Support (Collection and Enforcement and Miscellaneous Amendments) Regulations 2000 (SI 2001 No.162) amends this regulation. This amendment came into force on March 3, 2003 for the types of cases in arts 3 and 5 of SI 2003 No.192, subject to the savings provisions in reg 6 of SI 2001 No.162. The 1993 rules apply to other types of cases (unless the case is one which falls within art 3 of SI 2012 No.3042), including those covered by the savings provisions in reg 6. If the 1993 rules apply, in paragraph (6) the words "or (5)" are retained after "regulation 12(4)".

Definitions

      "employer": see reg 8(2).
      "employment": see reg 8(2).
      "pay-day": see reg 8(1).

Appeals against deduction from earnings orders

22.–(1)   A liable person in respect of whom a deduction from earnings order has been made may appeal to the magistrates' court, or in Scotland the sheriff [¹of the sheriffdom in which he resides].

(2)   [²Subject to paragraph (2A),] any appeal shall–

(a)   be by way of complaint for an order or, in Scotland, by way of application;

(b)   [¹where the liable person is resident in the United Kingdom,] be made within 28 days of the date on which the matter appealed against arose.

[¹(c)   where the liable person is not resident in the United Kingdom, be made within 56 days of the date on which the matter appealed against arose.]

[² (2A)   Any appeal against a decision of the Secretary of State that the exclusion required by regulation 3(3) does not apply is–

(a)   where the liable person is resident in the United Kingdom, to be made within 28 days of the date on which that decision is given or sent to the liable person;

(b)   where the liable person is not resident in the United Kingdom, to be made within 56 days of the date on which that decision is given or sent to the liable person.]

(3)   [²Subject to paragraph (3A),] an appeal may be made only on one or both of the following grounds–

(a)   that the deduction from earnings order is defective;

(b)   that the payments in question do not constitute earnings.

[² (3A)   Where the Secretary of State is considering specifying a deduction from earnings order as a method of payment under regulation 3(1)(i) an appeal may also be made against a decision of the Secretary of State that the exclusion required by regulation 3(3) does not apply.]

(4)   [² Subject to paragraph (5),] where the court or, as the case may be, the sheriff is satisfied that the appeal should be allowed the court, or sheriff, may–

(a)   quash the deduction from earnings order; or

(b)   specify which, if any, of the payments in question do not constitute earnings.

[² (5)   Where an appeal is brought on the grounds set out in paragraph (3A), and the court, or as the case may be, the sheriff, is satisfied that the appeal should be allowed the court or the sheriff is to refer the case to the Secretary of State for him to specify whichever of the methods of payment set out in regulation 3(1) he considers to be appropriate in the circumstances.]

Amendments

1.   Child Support (Miscellaneous Amendments) Regulations 2007 (SI 2007 No.1979) reg 2(2) (August 1, 2007).

2.   Child Support (Miscellaneous Amendments) (No.2) Regulations 2008 (SI 2006 No.2544) reg 2(4) (October 27, 2008).

Definitions

"defective": see reg 8(1).

"earnings": see reg 8(1), (3) and (4).

General Note

Paragraph (2)

The appeal must be made within 28 days of the making of the deduction from earnings order and not from a subsequent date at which point the liability to pay the assessment might have ended, for example, when the qualifying child ceased to be such because he went to live with the liable person (*Secretary of State for Social Security v Shotton and Others* [1996] 2 FLR 241).

Paragraph (3)

Magistrates, in deciding whether an order is defective, are limited to considering the matters referred to in regs 9 to 11 above and may not rule on the validity of the assessment itself *(Shotton,* above).

Paragraph (4)

An alleged failure to consider the welfare of any child affected, under s2 of the Act, is not a ground for allowing an appeal against a deduction from earnings order (*R v Secretary of State for Social Security ex p Biggin* [1995] 1 FLR 851).

A magistrates' court made an order that a deduction of earnings order cease until a decision of a tribunal as to whether the child support officer had incorrectly taken into account monies of the absent parent which did not constitute earnings (*Bailey v Secretary of State* (unreported, Lincoln District Magistrates' Court, October 6 1993). It is open to question whether such an order is within the court's powers, given the terms of subs (4), which seem to give the court only three options: to dismiss the complaint; to quash the deduction from earnings order; or itself to decide and specify which payments do not constitute earnings.

Magistrates have no power to order the repayment of monies paid under a defective deduction from earnings order (*Shotton,* above).

Overpayments of child support may be reimbursed under s41B of the Act, or by reduction of arrears or of payments under the current calculation: see reg 8 Child Support (Management of Payments and Arrears) Regulations 2009 on p709.

Crown employment

23.   Where a liable person is in the employment of the Crown and a deduction from earnings order is made in respect of him then for the purposes of this Part–

(a)   the chief officer for the time being of the Department, office or other body in which the liable person is employed shall be treated as having the liable person in his employment (any transfer of the liable person from one Department, office or body to another being treated as a change of employment); and

(b)   any earnings paid by the Crown or a minister of the Crown, or out of the public revenue of the United Kingdom, shall be treated as paid by that chief officer.

Definitions
"earnings": see reg 8(1), (3) and (4).
"employment": see reg 8(2).

Priority as between orders
24.–(1) [²...]
(2) Where an employer would, but for this paragraph, be obliged to comply with [²a deduction from earnings order] and one or more attachment of earnings orders he shall–
  (a) in the case of an attachment of earnings order which was made either wholly or in part in respect of the payment of a judgment debt or payments under an administration order, deal first with the deduction from earnings order [²...] and thereafter with the attachment of earnings order as if the earnings to which it relates were the residue of the liable person's earnings after the making of deductions to comply with the deduction from earnings order [²...];
  (b) in the case of any other attachment of earnings order, [²he shall–
  (i) deal with the orders according to the respective dates on which they were made, disregarding any later order until an earlier one has been dealt with;
  (ii) deal with any later order as if the earnings to which it relates were the residue of the liable person's earnings after the making of any deduction to comply with any earlier order.]
"Attachment of earnings order" in this paragraph means an order made under the Attachment of Earnings Act 1971 or under regulation 32 of the Community Charge (Administration and Enforcement) Regulations 1989 [¹or under regulation 37 of the Council Tax (Administration and Enforcement) Regulations 1992].
(3) Paragraph (2) does not apply to Scotland.
(4) In Scotland, where an employer would, but for this paragraph, be obliged to comply with [²a deduction from earnings order] and one or more diligences against earnings he shall deal first with the deduction from earnings order [²...] and thereafter with the diligence against earnings as if the earnings to which the diligence relates were the residue of the liable person's earnings after the making of deductions to comply with the deduction from earnings order [²...].

Amendments
1.   Inserted by reg 42 of SI 1993/913 as from 5.4.93.
2.   Child Support (Collection and Enforcement and Miscellaneous Amendments) Regulations 2000 (SI 2001 No.162) reg 2(5)(i) (comes into force in relation to a particular case on the day on which ss1(2) and (3), 4, 18(1) and (2), and 20(1) of and Sch 3 para 11(2) and (16) Child Support, Pensions and Social Security Act 2000 come into force for the purposes of that type of case – which is March 3, 2003 for the types of cases in arts 3 and 5 of SI 2003 No.192). For other types of cases see the '1993 rules', below. See reg 6 of SI 2001 No.162 for savings provisions detailing when these amendments do not apply.

1993 rules
Regulation 2(5)(i) of The Child Support (Collection and Enforcement and Miscellaneous Amendments) Regulations 2000 (SI 2001 No.162) amends this regulation.This amendment came into force on March 3, 2003 for the types of cases in arts 3 and 5 of SI 2003 No.192, subject to the savings provisions in reg 6 of SI 2001 No.162. The 1993 rules apply to other types of cases (unless the case is one which falls within art 3 of SI 2012 No.3042), including those covered by the savings provisions in reg 6. If the 1993 rules apply,
–   paragraph (1), shown below, is retained;
–   in paragraph (2)(b) the words ", deal with the orders according to the respective dates on which they were made in like manner as under paragraph (1)" which came after "in the case of any other attachment of earnings order," are retained in place of the substituted wording shown in the sub-paragraph, above;
–   in paragraphs (2) and (4) the words "one or more deduction from earnings orders", are retained in place of "a deduction from earnings order";
–   in paragraphs (2)(a) and (4) the words "or orders" are not omitted after "the deduction from earnings order" in each place these words occur.

24.–(1) Where an employer would, but for this paragraph, be obliged, on any pay-day, to make deductions under two or more deduction from earnings orders he shall–

    (a)   deal with the orders according to the respective dates on which they were made, disregarding any later order until an earlier one has been dealt with;

    (b)   deal with any later order as if the earnings to which it relates were the residue of the liable person's earnings after the making of any deduction to comply with any earlier order.

Definitions
"earnings": see reg 8(1), (3) and (4).
"employer": see reg 8(2).
"pay-day": see reg 8(1).

Offences

25.   The following regulations are designated for the purposes of section 32(8) of the Act (offences relating to deduction from earnings orders)–

[¹(aa) regulation 14(1);]

[¹(ab)] regulation 15(1) and (2);

    (b)   regulation 16(1), (2) and (3);

    (c)   regulation 19(1).

Amendment
1.   Reg 25 amended by reg 2(3) of SI 1999/977 as from 6.4.99.

[¹ PART 3A

Amendment
1.   Child Support Collection and Enforcement (Deduction Orders) Amendment Regulations 2009 (SI 2009 No.1815) reg 2 (August 3, 2009).

Deduction Orders
CHAPTER 1
Interpretation

[¹Interpretation of this Part

25A.–(1)   In this Part–

"assessable income" means the amount calculated in accordance with paragraph 5 of Schedule 1 to the Act as it applies to a 1993 scheme case and regulations made for the purposes of that paragraph;

[³"current income" has the meaning given in regulation 37 of the Child Support Maintenance Calculation Regulations 2012 (current income – general);]

"deduction period" means the period of a week, a month or other period at which deductions are to be made from the amount (if any) standing to the credit of the account specified in a regular deduction order;

"garnishee order" means an order made in accordance with the provisions of order 30 of the County Court Rules 1981 or order 49 of the Rules of the Supreme Court 1965;

[³"gross weekly income" means income calculated under Chapter 1 of Part 4 of the Child Support Maintenance Calculation Regulations 2012;]

[³...]

"lump sum deduction order" means an order under section 32E(1) or, as the case may be, 32F(1) of the Act;

"regular deduction order" means an order under section 32A(1) of the Act;

"third party debt order" means an order made in accordance with the provisions of Part 72 of the Civil Procedure Rules 1998;

"working day" means any day other than a Saturday, a Sunday, Christmas Day, Good Friday or a day which is a bank holiday within the meaning of the Banking and Financial Dealings Act 1971 in the part of the United Kingdom where a copy of a regular deduction order or a lump sum deduction order is served or a notification sent by the [²Secretary of State] is received.

(2)   Any person against whom an order under section 32A(1) of the Act may be made by the [²Secretary of State] is referred to in this Chapter and Chapters 2 and 4 as "the liable person".

(3)   Where a copy of a regular deduction order or a lump sum deduction order is served by the [²Secretary of State] in accordance with section 32A(7), 32E(6) or 32F(6) of the Act–

(a)   on a deposit-taker–

    (i)   where that copy of the order is sent by electronic communication or fax to the deposit-taker's last notified address for electronic communication or, as the case may be, fax number, it is to be treated as having been served at the end of the first working day after the day it was sent by the [²Secretary of State], or

    (ii)   where that copy of the order is sent by post to the deposit-taker's last notified address, it is to be treated as having been served at the end of the second working day after the day it was posted by the [²Secretary of State]; or

(b)   on a liable person, where that copy of the order is sent by post to that person's last known or notified address, it is to be treated as having been served at the end of the day on which the copy of the order is posted.

(4)   Any notification sent by the [²Secretary of State] in accordance with this Part to a deposit-taker or a liable person is to be treated as having been received at the same time as an order is treated as having been served in accordance with the provisions of paragraph (3).

(5)   Where a copy of a regular deduction order or a lump sum deduction order or any notification has been sent by electronic communication in accordance with paragraph (3)(a)(i) the record held on an official computer system is conclusive (or in Scotland, sufficient) evidence–

(a)   that a copy of that order has been sent; and

(b)   of the content of that order.

(6)   This Part applies to a 1993 scheme case in the same way as it applies to a 2003 scheme case and–

(a)   any references to expressions in the Act (including "maintenance calculation") or to regulations made under the Act are to be read, in relation to a 1993 scheme case, with the necessary modifications; and

(b)   [³...]

(7)   In this regulation–

(a)   "electronic communication" has the meaning given in section 15(1) of the Electronic Communications Act 2000;

(b)   "an official computer system" means a computer system maintained by or on behalf of the [²Secretary of State] for sending an order or any notification;

(c)   "1993 scheme case" means a case in respect of which the provisions of the Child Support, Pensions and Social Security Act 2000 have not been brought into force in accordance with article 3 of the Child Support, Pensions and Social Security Act 2000 (Commencement No. 12) Order 2003; and

(d)   "2003 scheme case" means a case in respect of which those provisions have been brought into force.]

Amendments

  1.   Child Support Collection and Enforcement (Deduction Orders) Amendment Regulations 2009 (SI 2009 No.1815) reg 2 (August 3, 2009).

  2.   Public Bodies (Child Maintenance and Enforcement Commission: Abolition and Transfer of Functions) Order 2012 (SI 2012 No. 2007) art 3(2) and Sch para 111(2) (August 1, 2012).

  3.   Child Support (Miscellaneous Amendments) Regulations 2013 (SI 2013 No.1517) reg 4(2) and (3) (September 30, 2013 for cases to which the new calculation rules apply, as defined in reg 1(5) of SI 2013 No.1517). For other types of cases see the '2003 and 1993 rules' below.

2003 and 1993 rules

Regulation 4 of the Child Support (Miscellaneous Amendments) Regulations 2013 (SI 2013 No.1517) amends this regulation and came into force on September 30, 2013 for cases to which the new calculation rules apply. The new calculation rules, as defined by reg 1(5) of SI 2013 No.1517, apply to cases in which liability to pay child support maintenance is calculated in accordance with Part 1 of Schedule 1 to the Child Support Act 1991 as amended by paragraph 2 of Schedule 4 to the Child Maintenance and Other Payments Act 2008 (see p243). For other types of cases the '2003 and 1993 rules' apply. If the 2003 and 1993 rules apply:

–   the definitions of "current income" and "gross weekly income" are not included in reg 25A;

–   the following definition is retained:

"net weekly income" has the meaning given in the Schedule to the Child Support (Maintenance Calculations and Special Cases) Regulations 2000;

–   paragraph (6)(b) is not omitted and reads:

(b)   any reference in this Part to "net weekly income" is to be read as if it were a reference to "assessable income" where these Regulations apply to a 1993 scheme case

CHAPTER 2
Regular Deduction Orders

[¹Regular deduction orders

25B.–(1)   A regular deduction order must specify–

(a)   the amount of the regular deduction; and

(b)   the dates on which regular deductions (referred to in this Chapter as "deduction dates") are due to be made.

(2)   Where the date on which the regular deduction is due to be made is not a working day, the deduction must be made on the first working day after the date specified in the order.]

Amendment

1.   Child Support Collection and Enforcement (Deduction Orders) Amendment Regulations 2009 (SI 2009 No.1815) reg 2 (August 3, 2009).

[¹Maximum deduction rate

25C.–(1)   The deduction rate under a regular deduction order in respect of any deduction period–

(a)   is not to exceed 40% of the liable person's [²gross] weekly income [³...] as calculated–

    (i)   at the date of the current maintenance calculation, or

    (ii)   where a maintenance calculation has been in force and there are arrears of child support maintenance, at the date of the most recent previous maintenance calculation; or

(b)   where a default maintenance decision has been made, is not to exceed £80 per week.

(2)   In this Chapter "previous maintenance calculation" means a maintenance calculation which is no longer in force.]

Amendments

1.   Child Support Collection and Enforcement (Deduction Orders) Amendment Regulations 2009 (SI 2009 No.1815) reg 2 (August 3, 2009).

2.   Child Support (Meaning of Child and New Calculation Rules) (Consequential and Miscellaneous Amendment) Regulations 2012 (SI 2012 No. 2785) reg 4(7) (in force in relation to a particular case on the day on which paragraph 2 of Schedule 4 to the Child Maintenance and Other Payments Act 2008 (see p243) comes into force in relation to that type of case – which is December 10, 2012, in relation to the types of cases falling within art 3 of SI 2012 No. 3042 (see p767). For other types of cases see '2003 and 1993 rules' below.

3. Child Support (Miscellaneous Amendments) Regulations 2013 (SI 2013 No. 1517) reg 4(4) (September 30, 2013 for cases to which the new calculation rules apply, as defined in reg 1(5) of SI 2013 No. 1517). For other types of cases see the '2003 and 1993 rules' below.

2003 and 1993 rules

Regulation 25C(1)(a) has been amended by:

–   regulation 4(7) of The Child Support (Meaning of Child and New Calculation Rules) (Consequential and Miscellaneous Amendment) Regulations 2012 (SI 2012 No.2785) which substituted the word "gross" for "net" in paragraph (1)(a). This amendment came into force on December 10, 2012, in relation to the types of cases falling within art 3 of SI 2012 No.3042 (see p767). For other types of cases paragraph (1)(a) should be read without this amendment;

–   regulation 4 of the Child Support (Miscellaneous Amendments) Regulations 2013 (SI 2013 No.1517) which omitted the words "in respect of that period" after "weekly income" in paragraph (1)(a). This amendment came into force on September 30, 2013 for cases to which the new calculation rules apply. The new calculation rules, as defined by reg 1(5) of SI 2013 No.1517, apply to cases in which liability to pay child support maintenance is calculated in accordance with Part 1 of Schedule 1 to the Child Support Act 1991 as amended by paragraph 2 of Schedule 4 to the Child Maintenance and Other Payments Act 2008 (see p243). For other types of cases the words "in respect of that period" are retained.

[¹**Minimum amount**

25D.–(1)   A deduction must not be made where the amount standing to the credit of the account specified in the regular deduction order is below the minimum amount on the date a deduction is due to be made.

(2)   The minimum amount (for the purposes of this Chapter) is, where the deduction period is–

(a)   monthly, £40;

(b)   weekly, £10; or

(c)   for any other period, £10 for each whole week in that period plus £1 for each additional day in that period,

plus the amount of administrative costs authorised by regulation 25Z(a) (administrative costs).]

Amendment

1. Child Support Collection and Enforcement (Deduction Orders) Amendment Regulations 2009 (SI 2009 No.1815) reg 2 (August 3, 2009).

[¹**Notification by the deposit-taker to the [²Secretary of State]**

25E.–(1)   A deposit-taker at which a regular deduction order is directed must notify the [²Secretary of State] in writing, within 7 days–

(a)   of a copy of the order or the order as varied being served; or

(b)   of notification being received by the deposit-taker that an order has been revived, of the matters set out in paragraph (2).

(2)   The matters are–

(a)   if the account specified in the order does not exist; and

(b)   where the name of the liable person specified in the order is different to the name in which the account specified in the order is held–

(i)   whether the account was previously held in the name of the liable person specified in the order, and

(ii)   if so, the new name in which the account is held,

only where the liable person named in the order is the same person as the person in whose name the account specified in the order is held.

(3)   A deposit-taker at which a regular deduction order is directed must notify the [²Secretary of State] within 7 days of notification being received that an order has lapsed or has been discharged–

(a)   if the account specified in the order does not exist; and

(b)   where the name of the liable person specified in the order is different to the name in which the account specified in the order is held–

(i)   whether the account was previously held in the name of the liable person specified in the order, and

      (ii)   if so, the new name in which the account is held,
only where the liable person named in the order is the same person as the person in whose name the account specified in the order is held.

(4)   The deposit-taker at which a regular deduction order is directed must notify the [²Secretary of State] within 7 days starting on the date on which a deduction is due to be made–

(a)   if the account specified in the order has been closed;

(b)   if the amount standing to the credit of the account specified in the order is less than the minimum amount; and

(c)   where the name of the liable person specified in the order is different to the name in which the account specified in the order is held–

      (i)   whether the account was previously held in the name of the liable person specified in the order, and

      (ii)   if so, the new name in which the account is held,

only where the liable person named in the order is the same person as the person in whose name the account specified in the order is held.

(5)   The deposit-taker at which a regular deduction order is directed must notify the [²Secretary of State] within 7 days of receipt of a request made by the [²Secretary of State] of the details of any other account held by the liable person with that deposit-taker and the details of that account, including–

(a)   the number and sort code of that account; and

(b)   the type of account.

(6)   The requirements of this regulation apply only in so far as the deposit-taker has the information or can reasonably be expected to acquire it.]

Amendments

1.   Child Support Collection and Enforcement (Deduction Orders) Amendment Regulations 2009 (SI 2009 No.1815) reg 2 (August 3, 2009).

2.   Public Bodies (Child Maintenance and Enforcement Commission: Abolition and Transfer of Functions) Order 2012 (SI 2012 No.2007) art 3(2) and Sch para 111(3) (August 1, 2012).

[¹Notification by the [²Secretary of State] to the deposit-taker

25F.   The [²Secretary of State] must notify the deposit-taker within 7 days of making a decision that a regular deduction order has–

(a)   been varied by virtue of regulation 25I (variation of a regular deduction order);

(b)   lapsed under regulation 25J (lapse of a regular deduction order);

(c)   been revived under regulation 25K (revival of a regular deduction order); or

(d)   ceased to have effect by virtue of regulation 25L (discharge of a regular deduction order).]

Amendments

1.   Child Support Collection and Enforcement (Deduction Orders) Amendment Regulations 2009 (SI 2009 No.1815) reg 2 (August 3, 2009).

2.   Public Bodies (Child Maintenance and Enforcement Commission: Abolition and Transfer of Functions) Order 2012 (SI 2012 No.2007) art 3(2) and Sch para 111(4) (August 1, 2012).

[¹Review of a regular deduction order

25G.–(1)   A deposit-taker at which a regular deduction order is directed or the liable person against whom the order is made may apply to the [²Secretary of State] for a review of the order.

(2)   The circumstances in which an application may be made under paragraph (1) are that–

(a)   the liable person or the deposit-taker satisfies the [²Secretary of State] that some or all of the amount standing to the credit of the account specified in the order is not an amount in which the liable person has a beneficial interest;

(b)   there has been a change in the amount of the maintenance calculation in question;

(c)   any amounts payable under the order have been paid;

(d)   the maximum deduction rate has been calculated in accordance with regulation 25C(1)(a)(ii) (maximum deduction rate) and there has been a change in the liable persons [³[⁴current]] income since the date of the most recent previous maintenance calculation;

(e)   due to an official error, an incorrect amount has been specified in the order; or

(f)   the order does not comply with the requirements of section 32A(5) of the Act or regulation 25B(1) or 25C.

(3)   Following a review of an order under this regulation–

(a)   where the [²Secretary of State] changes the amount to be deducted by the deposit-taker under the order, [²the Secretary of State] may vary the order; or

(b)   where the [²Secretary of State] extinguishes the amount to be deducted by the deposit-taker under the order, [² the Secretary of State] must discharge the order.

(4)   In paragraph (2)(e) "official error" has the same meaning as in regulation 1(3) of the Social Security and Child Support (Decisions and Appeals) Regulations 1999 (interpretation).]

Amendments

1.   Child Support Collection and Enforcement (Deduction Orders) Amendment Regulations 2009 (SI 2009 No.1815) reg 2 (August 3, 2009).

2.   Public Bodies (Child Maintenance and Enforcement Commission: Abolition and Transfer of Functions) Order 2012 (SI 2012 No.2007) art 3(2) and Sch para 111(5) (August 1, 2012).

3.   Child Support (Meaning of Child and New Calculation Rules) (Consequential and Miscellaneous Amendment) Regulations 2012 (SI 2012 No.2785) reg 4(7) (in force in relation to a particular case on the day on which paragraph 2 of Schedule 4 to the Child Maintenance and Other Payments Act 2008 (see p243) comes into force in relation to that type of case – which is December 10, 2012, in relation to the types of cases falling within art 3 of SI 2012 No.3042 (see p767). For other types of cases see '2003 and 1993 rules' below.

4.   Child Support (Miscellaneous Amendments) Regulations 2013 (SI 2013 No.1517) reg 4(5) (September 30, 2013 for cases to which the new calculation rules apply, as defined in reg 1(5) of SI 2013 No.1517). For other types of cases see the '2003 and 1993 rules' below.

2003 and 1993 rules

Regulation 25G(2)(d) has been amended by:

–   regulation 4(7) of The Child Support (Meaning of Child and New Calculation Rules) (Consequential and Miscellaneous Amendment) Regulations 2012 (SI 2012 No.2785) which substituted the word "gross" for "net" in paragraph (2)(d). This amendment came into force on December 10, 2012, in relation to the types of cases falling within art 3 of SI 2012 No.3042 (see p767) but has been subsequently amended by SI 2013 No.1517;

–   regulation 4 of the Child Support (Miscellaneous Amendments) Regulations 2013 (SI 2013 No.1517) which substituted the word "current" for "gross weekly" in paragraph (2)(d). This amendment came into force on September 30, 2013 for cases to which the new calculation rules apply. The new calculation rules, as defined by reg 1(5) of SI 2013 No.1517, apply to cases in which liability to pay child support maintenance is calculated in accordance with Part 1 of Schedule 1 to the Child Support Act 1991 as amended by paragraph 2 of Schedule 4 to the Child Maintenance and Other Payments Act 2008 (see p243).

For other types of cases the words "net weekly" are retained in place of "current" in paragraph (2)(d).

[¹Priority as between orders – regular deduction orders

25H.–(1)   Paragraphs (2) to (5) apply where one or more third party debt orders or garnishee orders provide for deductions to be made from the same account as that specified in a regular deduction order.

(2)   Where–

(a)   one or more third party debt orders or garnishee orders are served on a deposit-taker before or on the day a payment is due to be made under a regular deduction order; and

(b)   the regular deduction order was served on the same deposit-taker before those orders,

the deposit-taker must make that payment except where the deposit-taker has taken action to comply with the obligations under any third party debt order or garnishee order.

(3)   Where a regular deduction order is served after an interim third party debt order or a garnishee order nisi the deposit-taker must take action to comply with any of those orders before making a deduction under the regular deduction order.

(4)   Where paragraph (2) or (3) applies, the deposit-taker must take action to comply with any third party debt orders or garnishee orders before making further deductions under the regular deduction order.

(5)   Where a decision to revive a regular deduction order takes effect on the same day as or any day after a third party debt order or garnishee order has been served, the deposit-taker must take action to comply with any of those orders before making a deduction under the regular deduction order.

(6)   Paragraphs (1) to (5) do not apply to Scotland.

(7)   In Scotland, paragraphs (8) to (10) apply where a deposit-taker receives one or more arrestment schedules ("arrestments") and a regular deduction order which apply to the same account.

(8)   Where–
(a)   one or more arrestments are served on a deposit-taker before or on the day a payment is due to be made under a regular deduction order; and
(b)   the regular deduction order was served on the same deposit-taker before any of those arrestments,
the deposit-taker must make that payment except where the deposit-taker has taken action to comply with the obligations under any of the arrestments.

(9)   Where paragraph (8) applies, the deposit-taker must take action to comply with any of those arrestments before making further deductions under the regular deduction order.

(10)   Where a decision to revive a regular deduction order takes effect on the same day as or any day after any arrestments have been served, the deposit-taker must take action to comply with any of those arrestments before making a deduction under the regular deduction order.]

Amendment
1.   Child Support Collection and Enforcement (Deduction Orders) Amendment Regulations 2009 (SI 2009 No.1815) reg 2 (August 3, 2009).

[¹Variation of a regular deduction order

25I.–(1)   The [²Secretary of State] may vary a regular deduction order by changing the amount to be deducted in the circumstances set out in paragraph (2).

(2)   The circumstances are that–
(a)   the [²Secretary of State] has accepted–
  (i)   that a payment of arrears has been made by the liable person, and
  (ii)   no alternative method of payment of child support maintenance has been arranged;
(b)   a decision has been made under section 11, 12, 16 or 17 of the Act or there has been an appeal against a maintenance calculation;
(c)   the [²Secretary of State] has reviewed the order under regulation 25G (review of a regular deduction order); or
(d)   there has been an appeal under regulation 25AB(1)(a) or (b) (appeals).

(3)   The [²Secretary of State] may from time to time vary the deduction period.

(4)   Where–
(a)   a regular deduction order has been varied under this regulation; and
(b)   a copy of the order as varied has been served on the deposit-taker at which it is directed,
that deposit-taker must comply with the order; but the deposit-taker is not to be under any liability for non-compliance before the end of the period of 7 days beginning on the day on which the copy of the order as varied is served on the deposit-taker.]

Amendments
1.   Child Support Collection and Enforcement (Deduction Orders) Amendment Regulations 2009 (SI 2009 No.1815) reg 2 (August 3, 2009).

2.   Public Bodies (Child Maintenance and Enforcement Commission: Abolition and Transfer of Functions) Order 2012 (SI 2012 No.2007) art 3(2) and Sch para 111(6) (August 1, 2012).

[¹Lapse of a regular deduction order

25J.–(1)   A regular deduction order is to lapse in the circumstances set out in paragraph (2).

(2)   The circumstances are where–

(a)   the [²Secretary of State] has agreed with the liable person an alternative method of payment of the child support maintenance due under the maintenance calculation; or

(b)   there is an insufficient amount standing to the credit of the account specified in the order to enable a deduction to be made on two consecutive deduction dates, unless the [²Secretary of State] has decided that the order is to continue for a greater number of deduction dates,

and the [²Secretary of State] considers it is reasonable in all the circumstances that the order is to lapse.

(3)   A regular deduction order lapses on the day on which the deposit-taker receives notification that the order has lapsed from the [²Secretary of State].

(4)   A regular deduction order which has lapsed under this regulation is to be treated as remaining in force for the purposes of regulations 25E (notification by the deposit-taker to the [²Secretary of State]), 25G (review of a regular deduction order) and 25AB (appeals).]

Amendments

1.   Child Support Collection and Enforcement (Deduction Orders) Amendment Regulations 2009 (SI 2009 No.1815) reg 2 (August 3, 2009).

2.   Public Bodies (Child Maintenance and Enforcement Commission: Abolition and Transfer of Functions) Order 2012 (SI 2012 No.2007) art 3(2) and Sch para 111(7) (August 1, 2012).

[¹Revival of a regular deduction order

25K.–(1)   Where a regular deduction order has lapsed it may be revived by the [²Secretary of State] where–

(a)   the liable person has failed to comply with any agreement reached under regulation 25J(2)(a) (lapse of a regular deduction order); or

(b)   the [²Secretary of State] has reason to believe that following the lapse of an order under regulation 25J(2)(b) there is sufficient amount standing to the credit of the account specified in the order to enable a deduction to be made.

(2)   Where the [²Secretary of State] decides to revive a regular deduction order that decision is to take effect on the day notification that the order has been revived is received by the deposit-taker.]

Amendments

1.   Child Support Collection and Enforcement (Deduction Orders) Amendment Regulations 2009 (SI 2009 No.1815) reg 2 (August 3, 2009).

2.   Public Bodies (Child Maintenance and Enforcement Commission: Abolition and Transfer of Functions) Order 2012 (SI 2012 No.2007) art 3(2) and Sch para 111(8) (August 1, 2012).

[¹Discharge of a regular deduction order

25L.–(1)   A regular deduction order must be discharged by the [²Secretary of State] where–

(a)   the account specified in the order has been closed;

(b)   the maintenance calculation in question is no longer in force and the amount of child support maintenance due under that calculation has been paid in full in accordance with regulation 2 (payment of child support maintenance);

(c)   the liable person has complied with any agreement reached under regulation 25J(2)(a) for such period as the [²Secretary of State] considers appropriate in the circumstances of the case;

(d) the [²Secretary of State] has reviewed the order under regulation 25G and [²the Secretary of State] has extinguished the amount to be deducted by the deposit-taker under the order;

(e) on an appeal under regulation 25AB(1)(a) (appeals) the court has set aside the order;

(f) unless sub-paragraph (g) applies, a regular deduction order has lapsed under regulation 25J(2) and 6 months have passed beginning on the day the lapse took effect;

(g) an appeal is brought by virtue of regulation 25AB(1)(a) or (b), against a regular deduction order which has lapsed under regulation 25J(2) and 1 month has passed beginning on–

    (i) the day proceedings on the appeal (including any further appeal) concluded, or

    (ii) the end of any period during which a further appeal may ordinarily be brought,

    whichever is the later; or

(h) the liable person has died.

(2) A regular deduction order may be discharged where the [²Secretary of State] considers it is appropriate to do so in the circumstances of the case.

(3) Where a regular deduction order is discharged that discharge takes effect immediately after the payment of the last regular deduction prior to discharge.]

Amendments

1. Child Support Collection and Enforcement (Deduction Orders) Amendment Regulations 2009 (SI 2009 No.1815) reg 2 (August 3, 2009).

2. Public Bodies (Child Maintenance and Enforcement Commission: Abolition and Transfer of Functions) Order 2012 (SI 2012 No.2007) art 3(2) and Sch para 111(9) (August 1, 2012).

CHAPTER 3
Lump Sum Deduction Orders

[¹Period in which representations may be made

25M. Where a lump sum deduction order has been made under section 32E(1) of the Act the period for making representations to the [²Secretary of State] in respect of the proposal specified in that order is 14 days beginning on the day a copy of the order was served.]

Amendments

1. Child Support Collection and Enforcement (Deduction Orders) Amendment Regulations 2009 (SI 2009 No.1815) reg 2 (August 3, 2009).

2. Public Bodies (Child Maintenance and Enforcement Commission: Abolition and Transfer of Functions) Order 2012 (SI 2012 No.2007) art 3(2) and Sch para 111(10) (August 1, 2012).

[¹Disapplication of sections 32G(1) and 32H(2)(b) of the Act

25N.–(1) Something that would otherwise be in breach of sections 32G(1) and 32H(2)(b) of the Act may, with the consent of the [²Secretary of State], be done in the following circumstances–

(a) the liable person, the liable person's partner or any relevant other child is suffering hardship in meeting ordinary living expenses;

(b) the liable person is under a written contractual obligation, agreed before the lump sum deduction order was made, to make a payment;

(c) the deposit-taker has a right of set off and satisfies the [²Secretary of State] that an intention to exercise that right was formed within 30 days before the date the lump sum deduction order under section 32E of the Act was served;

(d) the deposit-taker and the liable person have made a written agreement in which the availability of an amount standing to the credit of the account specified in the lump sum deduction order was required as security for that agreement; or

(e)   any other circumstances the [²Secretary of State] considers appropriate in the particular case.

(2)   The liable person or the deposit-taker at which a lump sum deduction order is directed may apply to the [²Secretary of State] for consent.

(3)   When deciding whether to give consent, the [²Secretary of State] must take into account–

(a)   any adverse impact the decision may have on the liable person or any other person; and

(b)   any alternative arrangements which may be made by the liable person or the deposit-taker.

(4)   Where the [²Secretary of State] gives consent it is to take effect on the day on which the deposit-taker receives notification from the [²Secretary of State] to disapply section 32G(1) or 32H(2)(b) of the Act.

(5)   Something that would otherwise be in breach of section 32G(1) and 32H(2)(b) of the Act may be done where–

(a)   the amount standing to the credit of the account specified in the lump sum deduction order is less than the amount specified in that order, except in respect of any amount dealt with in compliance with section 32G(1) of the Act; or

(b)   the deposit-taker has made a payment in accordance with section 32H(1)(a) of the Act.

(6)   Paragraph (5) has effect until the [²Secretary of State] gives notice to the deposit-taker that paragraph (5) has ceased to have effect in a particular case and that notification is to take effect on the day on which the deposit-taker receives notification from the [²Secretary of State].

(7)   In this regulation–

"partner" has the same meaning as in regulation 3(9) (method of payment) and the definition of "couple" in that regulation is to apply accordingly; and

"relevant other child" is to be interpreted in accordance with paragraph 10C(2) of Schedule 1 to the Act and regulations made for the purposes of that paragraph.]

Amendments

1.   Child Support Collection and Enforcement (Deduction Orders) Amendment Regulations 2009 (SI 2009 No.1815) reg 2 (August 3, 2009).

2.   Public Bodies (Child Maintenance and Enforcement Commission: Abolition and Transfer of Functions) Order 2012 (SI 2012 No.2007) art 3(2) and Sch para 111(11) (August 1, 2012).

[¹Information

25O.–(1)   A deposit-taker at which a lump sum deduction order is directed must supply to the [²Secretary of State] in writing, within 7 days–

(a)   of a copy of the order or order as varied being served; or

(b)   of notification being received by the deposit-taker that an order has been revived, the information set out in paragraph (2).

(2)   The information is–

(a)   if the account specified in the order–

    (i)   does not exist,

    (ii)   cannot be traced, or

    (iii)   has been closed;

(b)   whether the amount standing to the credit of the account specified in the order–

    (i)   on the day the order is served, or

    (ii)   where an order is revived, on the day the decision to revive the order takes effect,

    is at least the same or less than the amount specified in the order and where it is less, that amount; and

(c)   where the name of the liable person specified in the order is different to the name in which the account specified in the order is held–

    (i)   whether the account was previously held in the name of the liable person specified in the order, and

      (ii)   if so, the new name in which the account is held,
only where the liable person named in the order is the same person as the person in whose name the account specified in the order is held.

(3)   A deposit-taker at which a lump sum deduction order is directed must notify the [²Secretary of State] within 7 days of notification being received that an order has lapsed or has been discharged–

(a)   if the account specified in the order cannot be traced; or

(b)   where the name of the liable person specified in the order is different to the name in which the account specified in the order is held–

      (i)   whether the account was previously held in the name of the liable person specified in the order, and

      (ii)   if so, the new name in which the account is held,
only where the liable person named in the order is the same person as the person in whose name the account specified in the order is held.

(4)   A deposit-taker at which a lump sum deduction order is directed, must supply to the [²Secretary of State] within 7 days of receipt of a request being made by the [²Secretary of State], the following information–

(a)   whether the liable person holds another account or has opened an account with that deposit-taker or with another deposit-taker and, if so, the details of that account, including–

      (i)   the number and sort code of that account, and

      (ii)   the type of account; and

(b)   whether the amount standing to the credit of the account specified in the order on the day the request is received is at least the same or less than the amount specified in the order or the remaining amount and where it is less, that amount.

(5)   In so far as a deposit-taker at which a lump sum deduction order is directed ("A") has the information, the details of an account held with another deposit-taker ("B") must be supplied to the [²Secretary of State] in accordance with paragraph (4) only if–

(a)   the liable person has–

      (i)   closed the account specified in the order and held with A,

      (ii)   opened an account with B, and

      (iii) transferred the amount standing to the credit of the account held with A to the account held with B;

(b)   either–

      (i)   a lump sum deduction order has lapsed, or

      (ii)   A has notified the [²Secretary of State] in accordance with paragraph (2)(a)(iii), that the account specified in the order has been closed; and

(c)   the [²Secretary of State] has made a request for the information within 1 month of the order lapsing or, as the case may be, notification being received by the [²Secretary of State] that the account has been closed.

(6)   The requirements of paragraphs (1) to (3) and paragraph (4) as it applies to a deposit-taker at which a lump sum deduction order is directed, apply only in so far as the deposit-taker has the information or can reasonably be expected to acquire it.

(7)   In paragraph (4)(b) and regulation 25T(1)(b) and (c) "remaining amount" has the same meaning as in section 32H(6) of the Act.]

Amendments

1.   Child Support Collection and Enforcement (Deduction Orders) Amendment Regulations 2009 (SI 2009 No.1815) reg 2 (August 3, 2009).

2.   Public Bodies (Child Maintenance and Enforcement Commission: Abolition and Transfer of Functions) Order 2012 (SI 2012 No.2007) art 3(2) and Sch para 111(12) (August 1, 2012).

[¹Priority as between orders – lump sum deduction orders

25P.–(1) Where a deposit-taker would, but for this paragraph, be obliged to comply with an order under section 32F of the Act, and one or more interim third party debt orders or garnishee orders nisi, it must take action to comply with the orders according to the order in which they were served on the deposit-taker.

(2)   Paragraph (1) does not apply where an order under section 32E of the Act was served after an interim third party debt order or a garnishee order nisi except where there remains an amount standing to the credit of the account specified in the order under section 32F of the Act after any third party debt orders or garnishee orders have been complied with by the deposit-taker (referred to in this regulation as "an outstanding amount").

(3)   Where there is an outstanding amount section 32G(1) of the Act applies in respect of that amount.

(4)   Where a decision to revive a lump sum deduction order takes effect on the same day as or any day after a third party debt order or garnishee order has been served, the deposit-taker must take action to comply with any of those orders before making a deduction under the lump sum deduction order.

(5)   Paragraphs (1) to (4) do not apply to Scotland.

(6)   In Scotland, where a deposit-taker would, but for this paragraph, be obliged to comply with an order under section 32F of the Act, and one or more arrestment schedules ("arrestments") it must give preference to that order and those arrestments according to the order in which they were served on the deposit-taker.

(7)   Where there remains an amount standing to the credit of the account specified in the order under section 32F of the Act after any arrestments have been complied with by the deposit-taker, section 32G(1) of the Act applies in respect of that amount.

(8)   Where a decision to revive a lump sum deduction order takes effect on the same day as or any day after any arrestments have been served, the deposit-taker must take action to comply with any of those arrestments before making a deduction under the lump sum deduction order.]

Amendment

1.   Child Support Collection and Enforcement (Deduction Orders) Amendment Regulations 2009 (SI 2009 No.1815) reg 2 (August 3, 2009).

[¹**Minimum amount**

25Q.–(1)   A deduction must not be made where the amount standing to the credit of the account specified in the lump sum deduction order is below the minimum amount on the date the deduction is due to be made.

(2)   The minimum amount is £55 plus the amount of administrative costs authorised by regulation 25Z(b) (administrative costs).]

Amendment

1.   Child Support Collection and Enforcement (Deduction Orders) Amendment Regulations 2009 (SI 2009 No.1815) reg 2 (August 3, 2009).

[¹**Variation of a lump sum deduction order**

25R.–(1)   The [²Secretary of State] may, in the circumstances set out in paragraph (2), vary a lump sum deduction order by reducing the amount specified in that order.

(2)   The circumstances are that–

(a)   the [²Secretary of State] accepts the liable person's agreement to make a payment;

(b)   a decision has been made under section 11, 12, 16 or 17 of the Act or there has been an appeal against a maintenance calculation;

(c)   the [²Secretary of State] has consented to the doing of things that would otherwise be in breach of sections 32G(1) and 32H(2)(b) of the Act;

(d)   there has been an appeal made under regulation 25AB(1)(c) or (d) (appeals); or

(e)   representations made in respect of the proposals specified in the order made under section 32E of the Act have been accepted by the [²Secretary of State].

(3)   Where–

(a)   a lump sum deduction order has been varied under this regulation; and

(b)   a copy of the order as varied has been served on the deposit-taker at which it is directed,

that deposit-taker must comply with the order when that order is served.]

Amendments

1.   Child Support Collection and Enforcement (Deduction Orders) Amendment Regulations 2009 (SI 2009 No.1815) reg 2 (August 3, 2009).
2.   Public Bodies (Child Maintenance and Enforcement Commission: Abolition and Transfer of Functions) Order 2012 (SI 2012 No.2007) art 3(2) and Sch para 111(13) (August 1, 2012).

[¹Lapse of a lump sum deduction order

25S.–(1)   A lump sum deduction order is to lapse in the circumstances set out in paragraph (2).

(2)   The circumstances are where–

(a)   the amount in the account specified in the order under section 32E of the Act is nil;

(b)   in consequence of the consent given by the [²Secretary of State] under regulation 25N(1) (disapplication of section 32G(1) and 32H(2)(b) of the Act) the amount in the account specified in the lump sum deduction order is reduced to nil; or

(c)   the [²Secretary of State] has agreed with the liable person an alternative method of payment of the child support maintenance due under the maintenance calculation,

and the [²Secretary of State] considers it is reasonable in all the circumstances that the order is to lapse.

(3)   A lump sum deduction order lapses on the day on which the deposit-taker receives notification that the order has lapsed from the [²Secretary of State].

(4)   A lump sum deduction order which has lapsed under this regulation is to be treated as remaining in force for the purposes of regulations 25M (period in which representations may be made), 25O (information) and 25AB (appeals).]

Amendments

1.   Child Support Collection and Enforcement (Deduction Orders) Amendment Regulations 2009 (SI 2009 No.1815) reg 2 (August 3, 2009).
2.   Public Bodies (Child Maintenance and Enforcement Commission: Abolition and Transfer of Functions) Order 2012 (SI 2012 No.2007) art 3(2) and Sch para 111(14) (August 1, 2012).

[¹Revival of a lump sum deduction order

25T.–(1)   Where a lump sum deduction order has lapsed it may be revived by the [²Secretary of State] where–

(a)   in the case of an order under section 32E of the Act, the amount standing to the credit of the account specified in that order was nil and the [²Secretary of State] is informed in accordance with the requirement in regulation 25O(4)(b) that there is an amount at least the same as or less than the amount specified in the order standing to the credit of the account specified in the order;

(b)   a lump sum deduction order has lapsed under regulation 25S(2)(b) (lapse of a lump sum deduction order) and the [²Secretary of State] is informed in accordance with the requirement in regulation 25O(4)(b) that there is an amount at least the same as or less than the amount specified in the order, or the remaining amount, standing to the credit of the account specified in the order; or

(c)   in the case of an order under section 32F of the Act, there is a remaining amount and the liable person has failed to comply with the agreement referred to in regulation 25S(2)(c).

(2)   Where the [²Secretary of State] decides to revive a lump sum deduction order that decision is to take effect on the day notification that the order has been revived is received by the deposit-taker.]

Amendments

1.   Child Support Collection and Enforcement (Deduction Orders) Amendment Regulations 2009 (SI 2009 No.1815) reg 2 (August 3, 2009).
2.   Public Bodies (Child Maintenance and Enforcement Commission: Abolition and Transfer of Functions) Order 2012 (SI 2012 No.2007) art 3(2) and Sch para 111(15) (August 1, 2012).

[¹Discharge of a lump sum deduction order

25U.–(1)   A lump sum deduction order must be discharged where–
(a)   the account specified in the order has been closed;
(b)   the amount of arrears of child support maintenance specified in the order has been paid in full in accordance with regulation 2 (payment of child support maintenance);
(c)   the liable person has paid the total amount of arrears of child support maintenance specified in the order by an alternative method agreed between the [²Secretary of State] and the liable person;
(d)   the [²Secretary of State] has considered representations made in respect of an order under section 32E of the Act and [²the Secretary of State] has decided not to make an order under section 32F of the Act;
(e)   unless sub-paragraph (f) applies–
    (i)   an order under section 32F of the Act has lapsed under regulation 25S(2) and 6 months have passed beginning on the day on which the deposit-taker received notification that the order had lapsed from the [²Secretary of State], or
    (ii)   regulation 25N(5) applies and 6 months have passed beginning on the day on which payment was made under section 32H(1)(a) of the Act;
(f)   an appeal is brought by virtue of regulation 25AB(1)(d) and 1 month has passed beginning on–
    (i)   the day proceedings on the appeal (including any further appeal) concluded, or
    (ii)   the end of any period during which a further appeal may ordinarily be brought,
  whichever is the later; or
(g)   the liable person has died.
(2)   A lump sum deduction order may be discharged where the [²Secretary of State]< considers it is appropriate to do so in the circumstances of the case.
(3)   A lump sum deduction order is discharged on the day notification that the order has been discharged is received by the deposit-taker.]

Amendments

1.   Child Support Collection and Enforcement (Deduction Orders) Amendment Regulations 2009 (SI 2009 No.1815) reg 2 (August 3, 2009).

2.   Public Bodies (Child Maintenance and Enforcement Commission: Abolition and Transfer of Functions) Order 2012 (SI 2012 No.2007) art 3(2) and Sch para 111(16) (August 1, 2012).

[¹Time at which a lump sum deduction order under section 32E of the Act ceases to be in force

25V.   For the purposes of section 32E(8)(a) of the Act the prescribed period is–
(a)   unless paragraph (b) applies, 6 months beginning on–
    (i)   the day the order under section 32E of the Act was served on the deposit-taker, or
    (ii)   where that order has lapsed under regulation 25S, the day on which the deposit-taker received notification that the order had lapsed from the [²Secretary of State]; or
(b)   where an appeal is brought by virtue of regulation 25AB(1)(c) (appeal against the withholding of consent), 1 month beginning on–
    (i)   the day proceedings on the appeal (including any further appeal) concluded, or
    (ii)   the end of any period during which a further appeal may ordinarily be brought,
  whichever is the later.]

Amendments

1.   Child Support Collection and Enforcement (Deduction Orders) Amendment Regulations 2009 (SI 2009 No.1815) reg 2 (August 3, 2009).

2.   Public Bodies (Child Maintenance and Enforcement Commission: Abolition and Transfer of Functions) Order 2012 (SI 2012 No.2007) art 3(2) and Sch para 111(17) (August 1, 2012).

[¹Meaning of "the relevant time"

25W.   For the purposes of the meaning of "the relevant time" in section 32H(6) of the Act the prescribed circumstances are that–

(a)   unless to paragraph (b) applies, 6 months have passed beginning on the day the order under section 32F of the Act was served on the deposit-taker; or

(b)   where an appeal is brought by virtue of regulation 25AB(1)(d), 1 month has passed beginning on–

    (i)   the day proceedings on the appeal (including any further appeal) concluded, or

    (ii)   the end of any period during which a further appeal may ordinarily be brought,

whichever is the later.]

Amendment

1.   Child Support Collection and Enforcement (Deduction Orders) Amendment Regulations 2009 (SI 2009 No.1815) reg 2 (August 3, 2009).

CHAPTER 4
General Matters for Deduction Orders

[¹Accounts of a prescribed description

25X.–(1)   A regular deduction order or a lump sum deduction order may not be made in respect of an account which–

(a)   the liable person operates solely for the purposes of exercising the function of a trustee or office holder and the account is one in which all the funds are held on behalf of other persons or for the purposes of that office; or

(b)   is used wholly or in part for business purposes.

(2)   For the purposes of paragraph (1)(b), whether an account is used wholly or in part for business purposes is to be decided by the [²Secretary of State].

(3)   Paragraph (1)(b) does not apply where a regular deduction order is made in respect of an account which is used by the liable person as a sole trader.]

Amendments

1.   Child Support Collection and Enforcement (Deduction Orders) Amendment Regulations 2009 (SI 2009 No.1815) reg 2 (August 3, 2009).

2.   Public Bodies (Child Maintenance and Enforcement Commission: Abolition and Transfer of Functions) Order 2012 (SI 2012 No.2007) art 3(2) and Sch para 111(18) (August 1, 2012).

[¹Circumstances in which amounts standing to the credit of an account are to be disregarded

25Y.   The circumstances in which amounts standing to the credit of an account are to be disregarded for the purposes of sections 32A, 32E, 32G and 32H of the Act are where the liable person has no beneficial interest in the amount.]

Amendment

1.   Child Support Collection and Enforcement (Deduction Orders) Amendment Regulations 2009 (SI 2009 No.1815) reg 2 (August 3, 2009).

[¹Administrative costs

25Z.   A deposit-taker at which an order under section 32A or 32F of the Act is directed may deduct from the amount standing to the credit of the account specified in the order an amount towards its administrative costs for each deduction made, not exceeding–

(a)   in the case of a regular deduction order, £10; or

(b)   in the case of a lump sum deduction order under section 32F of the Act, £55, before making any payment to the [²Secretary of State] required by section 32A or, as the case may be, section 32H of the Act.]

Amendments

1.   Child Support Collection and Enforcement (Deduction Orders) Amendment Regulations 2009 (SI 2009 No.1815) reg 2 (August 3, 2009).

2.   Public Bodies (Child Maintenance and Enforcement Commission: Abolition and Transfer of Functions) Order 2012 (SI 2012 No.2007) art 3(2) and Sch para 111(19) (August 1, 2012).

[¹Payment by deposit-taker to the [²Secretary of State]

25AA.–(1)   Amounts deducted by a deposit-taker at which a regular deduction order or a lump sum deduction order under section 32F of the Act is directed must be paid to the [²Secretary of State] within–
(a)   in the case of a regular deduction order, 10 days of the date the regular deduction is due to be made; or
(b)   in the case of a lump sum deduction order under section 32F of the Act, 10 days of the end of the relevant period.
(2)   The payment to the [²Secretary of State] of amounts deducted under that order may be made by–
(a)   cheque;
(b)   automated credit transfer; or
(c)   such other method as the [²Secretary of State] may specify.
(3)   In this regulation "the relevant period" has the same meaning as in section 32G(5) and (6) of the Act.]

Amendments

1.   Child Support Collection and Enforcement (Deduction Orders) Amendment Regulations 2009 (SI 2009 No.1815) reg 2 (August 3, 2009).

2.   Public Bodies (Child Maintenance and Enforcement Commission: Abolition and Transfer of Functions) Order 2012 (SI 2012 No.2007) art 3(2) and Sch para 111(20) (August 1, 2012).

[¹Appeals

25AB.–(1)   A qualifying person has a right of appeal to a county court or in Scotland the sheriff of the sheriffdom in which that person resides, against–
(a)   the making of a regular deduction order;
(b)   any decision made by the [²Secretary of State] on an application made under regulation 25G (review of a regular deduction order);
(c)   the withholding of the consent to be obtained in accordance with regulation 25N (disapplication of sections 32G(1) and 32H(2)(b) of the Act);
(d)   the making of an order under section 32F of the Act.
(2)   In this regulation a "qualifying person" means–
(a)   in relation to paragraph (1)(a) and (b), any person affected by–
(i)   a regular deduction order, or, as the case may be,
(ii)   the decision referred to in paragraph (1)(b);
(b)   in relation to paragraph (1)(c), the persons prescribed in regulation 25N(2); and
(c)   in relation to paragraph (1)(d), any person affected by an order under section 32F of the Act.]

Amendments

1.   Child Support Collection and Enforcement (Deduction Orders) Amendment Regulations 2009 (SI 2009 No.1815) reg 2 (August 3, 2009).

2.   Public Bodies (Child Maintenance and Enforcement Commission: Abolition and Transfer of Functions) Order 2012 (SI 2012 No.2007) art 3(2) and Sch para 111(21) (August 1, 2012).

[¹Offences

25AC.   The following regulations are designated for the purposes of sections 32D(1)(b) and 32K(1)(b) of the Act–

(a) regulation 25E(1) to (5) (notification by the deposit-taker to the [²Secretary of State]);

(b) regulation 25I(4) (variation of a regular deduction order);

(c) regulation 25O(1) to (5) (information);

(d) regulation 25R(3) (variation of a lump sum deduction order); and

(e) regulation 25AA(1) (payment by deposit-taker to the [²Secretary of State]).]

Amendments

1. Child Support Collection and Enforcement (Deduction Orders) Amendment Regulations 2009 (SI 2009 No.1815) reg 2 (August 3, 2009).

2. Public Bodies (Child Maintenance and Enforcement Commission: Abolition and Transfer of Functions) Order 2012 (SI 2012 No.2007) art 3(2) and Sch para 111(22) (August 1, 2012).

[¹ [²Secretary of State] to warn of consequences of failing to comply with an order or to provide information

25AD. Where information is required by virtue of regulation 25E or 25O, the [²Secretary of State] must set out in writing the possible consequences of failure to–

(a) comply with a regular deduction order or lump sum deduction order; and

(b) provide the information required under the regulations designated by regulation 25AC(a) and (b) (offences),

including details of the offences provided for by virtue of sections 32D and 32K of the Act, as the case may be.]

Amendments

1. Child Support Collection and Enforcement (Deduction Orders) Amendment Regulations 2009 (SI 2009 No.1815) reg 2 (August 3, 2009).

2. Public Bodies (Child Maintenance and Enforcement Commission: Abolition and Transfer of Functions) Order 2012 (SI 2012 No.2007) art 3(2) and Sch para 111(23) (August 1, 2012).

PART IV
Liability Orders

Extent of this Part

26. This Part, except [¹regulations 29(2) and 35(5)], does not apply to Scotland.

Amendment

1. Child Support (Miscellaneous Amendments) Regulations 2006 (SI 2006/1520) reg 3(4) (July 12, 2006).

Notice of intention to apply for a liability order

27.–(1) [²Subject to paragraph (1A),] the Secretary of State shall give the liable person at least 7 days notice of his intention to apply for a liability order under section 33(2) of the Act.

[²(1A) Where the liable person is not resident in the United Kingdom, the Secretary of State shall give the liable person at least 28 days notice of his intention to apply for a liability order under section 33(2) of the Act.]

(2) Such notice shall set out the amount of child support maintenance which it is claimed has become payable by the liable person and has not been paid and the amount of any interest[¹, penalty payments or fees which have become payable and have not been paid].

(3) Payment by the liable person of any part of the amounts referred to in paragraph (2) shall not require the giving of a further notice under paragraph (1) prior to the making of the application.

Amendments

1. Child Support (Collection and Enforcement and Miscellaneous Amendments) Regulations 2000 (SI 2001 No.162) reg 2(6)(a) (comes into force in relation to a particular case on the day on which ss1(2) and (3), 4, 18(1) and (2), and 20(1) of and Sch 3 para 11(2) and (16) Child Support, Pensions and Social Security Act 2000 come into force for the purposes of that type of case – which is March 3, 2003 for the types of

cases in arts 3 and 5 of SI 2003 No.192). For other types of cases see the '1993 rules', below. See reg 6 of SI 2001 No.162 for savings provisions detailing when this amendment does not apply.

2.   Child Support (Miscellaneous Amendments) Regulations 2007 (SI 2007/1979) reg 2(3) (August 1, 2007).

1993 rules
Reg 2(6)(a) of the Child Support (Collection and Enforcement and Miscellaneous Amendments) Regulations 2000 (SI 2001 No.162) amends this regulation and has been brought into force only for the types of cases in art 3 and 5 of the Child Support, Pensions and Social Security Act 2000 (Commencement No.12) Order 2003 (SI 2003 No.192) – see p683, subject to savings provisions in reg 6 of SI 2001 No.162. For other types of cases the '1993 rules' apply. If the 1993 rules apply, in paragraph (2) the words "in respect of arrears payable under section 41(3) of the Act" are retained in place of ", penalty payments or fees which have become payable and have not been paid".

Application for a liability order
28.–(1)   An application for a liability order shall be by way of complaint for an order to the magistrates' court [²...].

[¹(2)   Subject to paragraph (2A), there is no period of limitation in relation to an application under paragraph (1).]

[¹(2A)   An application under paragraph (1) may not be instituted in respect of an amount payment of which became due on or before 12th July 2000.]

(3)   A warrant shall not be issued under section 55(2) of the Magistrates' Courts Act 1980 in any proceedings under this regulation.

Amendments
1.   Child Support (Miscellaneous Amendments) Regulations 2006 (SI 2006/1520) reg 3(5) (July 12, 2006).
2.   Child Support (Miscellaneous Amendments) Regulations 2007 (SI 2007/1979) reg 2(4) (August 1, 2007).

General Note
Paragraph (2)
This paragraph does not apply to amounts that became due on or before 12 July 2006. Before that the original paragraph continues to apply. This provided:
    "(2) An application under paragraph (1) may not be instituted more than 6 years after the date on which payment of the amount in question became due."
For the purposes of that provision, payment of child support maintenance does not become due for the purposes of this paragraph until an assessment has been made (*R (Sutherland) v SSWP* [2004] EWHC 800 (Admin), paras 26-31). The six-year period applies to the exclusion of the provisions under the Limitation Act 1980 *(ibid,* para 17).
    It seems that the current text of this paragraph may not have been drawn to the attention of the Court of Appeal in *CMEC v Mitchell and Clements* [2010] EWCA Civ 333. See the comments of Aikens LJ at paras 51-52.

Liability orders
29.–(1)   A liability order shall be made in the form prescribed in Schedule 1.

(2)   A liability order made by a court in England or Wales or any corresponding order made by a court in Northern Ireland may be enforced in Scotland as if it had been made by the sheriff.

(3)   A liability order made by the sheriff in Scotland or any corresponding order made by a court in Northern Ireland may, subject to paragraph (4), be enforced in England and Wales as if it had been made by a magistrates' court in England and Wales.

(4)   A liability order made by the sheriff in Scotland or a corresponding order made by a court in Northern Ireland shall not be enforced in England or Wales unless registered in accordance with the provisions of [¹Part II] of the Maintenance Orders Act 1950 and for this purpose–
    (a)   a liability order made by the sheriff in Scotland shall be treated as if it were a decree to which section 16(2)(b) of that Act applies (decree for payment of aliment);
    (b)   a corresponding order made by a court in Northern Ireland shall be treated as if it were an order to which section 16(2)(c) of that Act applies (order for alimony, maintenance or other payments).

Amendment

1.   Words in reg 29(4) substituted by reg 43 of SI 1993/913 as from 5.4.93.

Enforcement of liability orders by distress

30.–(1)   A distress made pursuant to section 35(1) of the Act may be made anywhere in England and Wales.

(2)   The person levying distress on behalf of the Secretary of State shall carry with him the written authorisation of the Secretary of State, which he shall show to the liable person if so requested, and he shall hand to the liable person or leave at the premises where the distress is levied–

(a)   copies of this regulation, regulation 31 and Schedule 2;

(b)   a memorandum setting out the amount which is the appropriate amount for the purposes of section 35(2) of the Act;

(c)   a memorandum setting out details of any arrangement entered into regarding the taking of possession of the goods distrained; and

(d)   a notice setting out the liable person's rights of appeal under regulation 31 giving the Secretary of State's address for the purposes of any appeal.

(3)   A distress shall not be deemed unlawful on account of any defect or want of form in the liability order.

(4)   If, before any goods are seized, the appropriate amount (including charges arising up to the time of the payment or tender) is paid or tendered to the Secretary of State, the Secretary of State shall accept the amount and the levy shall not be proceeded with.

(5)   Where the Secretary of State has seized goods of the liable person in pursuance of the distress, but before sale of those goods the appropriate amount (including charges arising up to the time of the payment or tender) is paid or tendered to the Secretary of State, the Secretary of State shall accept the amount, the sale shall not be proceeded with and the goods shall be made available for collection by the liable person.

General Note

Paragraph (3)

In *Evans v South Ribble BC* [1992] 2 All ER 695, a case concerning unpaid community charge, a bailiff, finding no one at the debtor's home, put a notice of distress in a sealed envelope through the debtor's door. The Queen's Bench Divisional Court ruled that the bailiff had not effected a lawful distress. Regulation 30(3) provides that a distress shall not be deemed unlawful on account of any defect or want of form in the liability order, but query if it would be regarded as "irregular" and thus open to complaint under reg 31(3).

Appeals in connection with distress

31.–(1)   A person aggrieved by the levy of, or an attempt to levy, a distress may appeal to the magistrates' court [1...].

(2)   The appeal shall be by way of complaint for an order.

(3)   If the court is satisfied that the levy was irregular, it may–

(a)   order the goods distrained to be discharge if they are in the possession of the Secretary of State;

(b)   order an award of compensation in respect of any goods distrained and sold of an amount equal to the amount which, in the opinion of the court, would be awarded by way of special damages in respect of the goods if proceedings under section 35(6) of the Act were brought in trespass or otherwise in connection with the irregularity.

(4)   If the court is satisfied that an attempted levy was irregular, it may by order require the Secretary of State to desist from levying in the manner giving rise to the irregularity.

Amendment

1.   Child Support (Miscellaneous Amendments) Regulations 2007 (SI 2007 No.1979) reg 2(5) (August 1, 2007).

General Note

Paragraph (1)

The County Court may also exercise its interlocutory jurisdiction to restrain the levying of excessive distress, provided that a powerful prima facie case for the distress being unlawful has been made out (*Steel Linings v Bibby and Co (a Firm)* [1993] RA 27).

Paragraph (3)

There appears to be no judicial guidance on the meaning of "irregular" and the term may be contrasted with that used in reg 30(3) "unlawful".

Where justices are faced with complicated factual or legal issues relating to the ownership of goods seized, they need not hear the complaint, but may leave the appellant to seek his remedy in the higher courts under the civil law (*R v Basildon Justices ex p Holding and Barnes plc* [1994] RA 157).

Charges connected with distress

32. Schedule 2 shall have effect for the purpose of determining the amounts in respect of charges in connection with the distress for the purposes of section 35(2)(b) of the Act.

Application for warrant of commitment

33.–(1) For the purposes of enabling an inquiry to be made under section [139A] of the Act as to the liable person's conduct and means, a justice of the peace [²...] may–

(a) issue a summons to him to appear before a magistrates' court and (if he does not obey the summons) issue a warrant for his arrest; or

(b) issue a warrant for his arrest without issuing a summons.

(2) In any proceedings under [¹sections 39A and 40] of the Act, a statement in writing to the effect that wages of any amount have been paid to the liable person during any period, purporting to be signed by or on behalf of his employer, shall be evidence of the facts there stated.

(3) Where an application under section [¹39A] of the Act has been made but no warrant of commitment is issued or term of imprisonment fixed, the application may be renewed on the ground that the circumstances of the liable person have changed.

Amendments

1. Child Support (Collection and Enforcement and Miscellaneous Amendments) Regulations 2000 (SI 2001 No.162) reg 2(6)(b) and Child Support (Miscellaneous Amendments) Regulations 2001(SI 2001 No.1775) reg 2 (May 31, 2001, but see reg 6 of SI 2001 No.162 for savings provisions detailing when this regulation does not apply).

2. Child Support (Miscellaneous Amendments) Regulations 2007 (SI 2007/1979) reg 2(6) (August 1, 2007).

Warrant of commitment

34.–(1) A warrant of commitment shall be in the form specified in Schedule 3, or in a form to the like effect.

(2) The amount to be included in the warrant under section 40(4)(a)(ii) of the Act in respect of costs shall be such amount as in the view of the court is equal to the costs reasonably incurred by the Secretary of State in respect of the costs of commitment.

(3) A warrant issued under section 40 of the Act may be executed anywhere in England and Wales by any person to whom it is directed or by any constable acting within his police area.

(4) A warrant may be executed by a constable notwithstanding that it is not in his possession at the time but such warrant shall, on the demand of the person arrested, be shown to him as soon as possible.

(5) Where, after the issue of a warrant, part-payment of the amount stated in it is made, the period of imprisonment shall be reduced proportionately so that for the period of imprisonment specified in the warrant there shall be substituted a period of imprisonment of such number of days as bears the same proportion to the number of days specified in the warrant as the amount remaining unpaid under the warrant bears to the amount specified in the warrant.

(6) Where the part-payment is of such an amount as would, under paragraph (5), reduce the period of imprisonment to such number of days as have already been served

(or would be so served in the course of the day of payment), the period of imprisonment shall be reduced to the period already served plus one day.

Definition
"the Act": see reg 1(2).

[¹**Disqualification from driving order**

35.–(1)   For the purposes of enabling an enquiry to be made under section 39A of the Act as to the liable person's livelihood, means and conduct, a justice of the peace [²...] may issue a summons to him to appear before a magistrates' court and to produce any driving licence held by him, and, where applicable, its counterpart, and, if he does not appear, may issue a warrant for his arrest.

(2)   In any proceedings under sections 39A and 40B of the Act, a statement in writing to the effect that wages of any amount have been paid to the liable person during any period, purporting to be signed for or on behalf of his employer, shall be evidence of the facts there stated.

(3)   Where an application under section 39A of the Act has been made but no disqualification order is made, the application may be renewed on the ground that the circumstances of the liable person have changed.

(4)   A disqualification order shall be in the form prescribed in Schedule 4.

(5)   The amount to be included in the disqualification order under section 40B(3)(b) of the Act in respect of the costs shall be such amount as in the view of the court is equal to the costs reasonably incurred by the Secretary of State in respect of the costs of the application for the disqualification order.

(6)   An order made under section 40B(4) of the Act may be executed anywhere in England and Wales by any person to whom it is directed or by any constable acting within his police area, if the liable person fails to appear or produce or surrender his driving licence or its counterpart to the court.

(7)   An order may be executed by a constable notwithstanding that it is not in his possession at the time but such order shall, if demanded, be shown to the liable person as soon as reasonably practicable.

(8)   In this regulation "driving licence" means a licence to drive a motor vehicle granted under Part III of the Road Traffic Act 1988.]

Amendments
1.   Child Support (Collection and Enforcement and Miscellaneous Amendments) Regulations 2000 (SI 2001 No.162) reg 2(6)(c) (April 2, 2001, but see reg 6 of SI 2001 No.162 for savings provisions).
2.   Child Support (Miscellaneous Amendments) Regulations 2007 (SI 2007/1979) reg 2(6) (August 1, 2007).

Definition
"the Act": see reg 1(2).

SCHEDULE 1
Regulation 29(1)
Liability order prescribed form

Section 33 of the Child Support Act 1991 and regulation 29(1) of the Child Support (Collection and Enforcement) Regulations
. . . . .Magistrates' Court
Date:
Defendant:
Address:

On the complaint of the Secretary of State for Social Security that the sums specified below are due from the defendant under the Child Support Act 1991 and Part IV of the Child Support (Collection and Enforcement) Regulations 1992 and are outstanding, it is adjudged that the defendant is liable to pay the aggregate amount specified below.
Sum payable and outstanding

– child support maintenance
– interest
– [¹ penalty payments
– fees]
– other periodical payments collected by virtue of section 30 of the Child Support Act 1991

Aggregate amount in respect of which the liability order is made:

Amendment

1. Child Support (Collection and Enforcement and Miscellaneous Amendments) Regulations 2000 (SI 2001 No.162) reg 2(7) (comes into force in relation to a particular case on the day on which ss1(2) and (3), 4, 18(1) and (2), and 20(1) of and Sch 3 para 11(2) and (16) Child Support, Pensions and Social Security Act 2000 come into force for the purposes of that type of case – which is March 3, 2003 for the types of cases in arts 3 and 5 of SI 2003 No.192). For other types of cases see the '1993 rules', below. See reg 6 of SI 2001 No.162 for savings provisions detailing when this amendment does not apply.

1993 rules

Reg 2(7) of the Child Support (Collection and Enforcement and Miscellaneous Amendments) Regulations 2000 (SI 2001 No.162) amends this schedule and has been brought into force only for the types of cases in art 3 and 5 of the Child Support, Pensions and Social Security Act 2000 (Commencement No.12) Order 2003 (SI 2003 No.192) – see p683, subject to savings provisions in reg 6 of SI 2001 No.162. For other types of cases the '1993 rules' apply. If the 1993 rules apply, the words "penalty payments" and "fees" are not inserted.

SCHEDULE 2
Regulation 32
Charges connected with distress

1. The sum in respect of charges connected with the distress which may be aggregated under section 35(2)(b) of the Act shall be set out in the following Table–

(1) *Matter connected with distress*	(2) *Charge*
A For making a visit to premises	Reasonable costs and fees incurred, but distress not exceeding an amount which, when aggregated with charges under this head for any previous visits made with a view to levying distress in relation to an amount in respect of which the liability order concerned was made, is not greater than the relevant amount calculated under paragraph 2(1) with respect to the visit.
B For levying distress:	An amount (if any) which, when aggregated with charges under head A for any visits made with a view to levying distress in relation to an amount in respect of which the liability order concerned was made, is equal to the relevant amount calculated under paragraph 2(1) with respect to the levy.
[¹BB For preparing and sending a letter advising the liable person that the written authorisation of the Secretary of State is with the person levying the distress and requesting the total sum due:	£10.00]
	Reasonable costs and fees incurred.
C For the removal and storage of Reasonable costs and fees incurred.	
D For the possession of goods as described in paragraph 2(3)–	
(i) for close possession(the person in possession on behalf of the Secretary of State to provide his own board):	£4.50 per day.
(ii) for walking possession:	[¹10p per day]
E For appraisement of an item distrained, at the request in writing of the liable person	Reasonable fees and expenses of the broker appraising.
F For other expenses of, and commission on, a sale by auction–	
(i) where the sale is held on the auctioneer's premises:	The auctioneer's commission fee and out-of-pocket expenses (but not exceeding in aggregate 15 per cent. of the sum realised), together with reasonable costs and fees incurred in respect of advertising.

(ii) where the sale is held on the liable person's premises:

The auctioneer's commission fee (but not exceeding 7 per cent. of the sum realised), together with the auctioneer's out-of-pocket expenses and reasonable costs and fees incurred in respect of advertising.

G For other expenses incurred in Reasonable costs and fees incurred in connection with a proposed sale where there is no buyer in relation to it:

Reasonable costs and fees incurred.

2.–(1)   In heads A and B of the Table to paragraph 1, "the relevant amount" with respect to a visit or a levy means–

(a)   where the sum due at the time of the visit or of the levy (as the case may be) does not exceed £100, £12.50;

(b)   where the sum due at the time of the visit or of the levy (as the case may be) exceeds £100, 12 per cent. on the first £100 of the sum due, 4 per cent. on the next £400, 2 per cent. on the next £1,500, 1 per cent. on the next £8,000 and 1/4 per cent. on any additional sum;

and the sum due at any time of these purposes means so much of the amount in respect of which the liability order concerned was made as is outstanding at the time.

(2)   Where a charge has arisen under head B with respect to an amount, no further charge may be aggregated under heads A or B in respect of that amount.

(3)   The Secretary of State takes close or walking possession of goods for the purposes of head D of the Table to paragraph 1 if he takes such possession in pursuance of an agreement which is made at the time that the distress is levied and which (without prejudice to such other terms as may be agreed) is expressed to the effect that, in consideration of the Secretary of State not immediately removing the goods distrained upon from the premises occupied by the liable person and delaying the sale of the goods, the Secretary of State may remove and sell the goods after a later specified date if the liable person has not by then paid the amount distrained for (including charges under this Schedule); and the Secretary of State is in close possession of goods on any day for these purposes if during the greater part of the day a person is left on the premises in physical possession of the goods on behalf of the Secretary of State under such an agreement.

3.–(1)   Where the calculation under this Schedule of a percentage of a sum results in an amount containing a fraction of a pound, that fraction shall be reckoned as a whole pound.

(2)   In the case of dispute as to any charge under this Schedule, the amount of the charge shall be taxed.

(3)   Such a taxation shall be carried out by the district judge of the county court for the district in which the distress is or is intended to be levied, and he may give such directions as to the costs of the taxation as he thinks fit; and any such costs directed to be paid by the liable person to the Secretary of State shall be added to the sum which may be aggregated under section 35(2) of the Act.

(4)   References in the table in paragraph 1 to costs, fees and expenses include references to amounts payable by way of value added tax with respect to the supply of goods or services to which the costs, fees and expenses relate.

Amendment

1.   Child Support (Miscellaneous Amendments and Transitional Provisions) Regulations 1994 (SI 1994 No.227) reg 3(2) (February 7, 1994).

General Note

The amendments to para 1 reflect the importance of correspondence with, as opposed to visits to, a debtor and reduce the fee as high charges are counter productive in achieving the aim of the distress, namely the collection of the debt.

SCHEDULE 3
Regulation 34(1)
Form of warrant of commitment

Section 40 of the Child Support Act 1991 and regulation 34(1) of the Child Support (Collection and Enforcement) Regulations 1992

. . . . .Magistrates' Court

Date:

Liable Person:

Address:

A liability order ("the order") was made against the liable person by the [ ] Magistrates' Court on [ ] under section 33 of the Child Support Act 1991 ("the Act") in respect of an amount of [ ].

The court is satisfied–

(i)   that the Secretary of State sought under section 35 of the Act to levy by distress the amount then outstanding in respect of which the order was made;

[and/or]

that the Secretary of State sought under section 36 of the Act to recover through the [ ] County Court, by means of [garnishee proceedings] [¹…] [a charging order], the amount then outstanding in respect of which the order was made;

(ii)   that such amount, or any portion of it, remains unpaid; and

(iii)   having inquired in the liable person's presence as to his means and as to whether there has been [wilful refusal] [¹...] [culpable neglect] on his part, the court is of the opinion that there has been [wilful refusal] [¹...] [culpable neglect] on his part.

The decision of the court is that the liable person be [committed to prison] [detained] for [ ] unless the aggregate amount mentioned below in respect of which this warrant is made is sooner paid.*

This warrant is made in respect of–

Amount outstanding (including any interest, [¹penalty payments, fees,] costs and charges):
Costs of commitment of the Secretary of State:

Aggregate amount:

And you *[name of person or persons to whom warrant is directed]* are hereby required to take the liable person and convey him to *[name of prison or place of detention]* and there deliver him to the [governor] [officer in charge] thereof; and you, the [governor] [officer in charge], to receive the liable person into your custody and keep him for *[period of imprisonment]* from the date of his arrest under this warrant or until he be sooner discharged in due course of law.

Justice of the Peace
[or by order of the Court Clerk of the Court].

Note: The period of imprisonment will be reduced as provided by regulation 34(5) and (6) of the Child Support (Collection and Enforcement) Regulations 1992 if part-payment is made of the aggregate amount.

Amendment

1.   Child Support (Collection and Enforcement and Miscellaneous Amendments) Regulations 2000 (SI 2001 No.162) reg 2(8) (comes into force in relation to a particular case on the day on which ss1(2) and (3), 4, 18(1) and (2), and 20(1) of and Sch 3 para 11(2) and (16) Child Support, Pensions and Social Security Act 2000 come into force for the purposes of that type of case – which is March 3, 2003 for the types of cases in arts 3 and 5 of SI 2003 No.192). For other types of cases see the '1993 rules', below. See reg 6 of SI 2001 No.162 for savings provisions detailing when these amendments do not apply.

1993 rules

Reg 2(8) of the Child Support (Collection and Enforcement and Miscellaneous Amendments) Regulations 2000 (SI 2001 No.162) amends this schedule and has been brought into force only for the types of cases in art 3 and 5 of the Child Support, Pensions and Social Security Act 2000 (Commencement No.12) Order 2003 (SI 2003 No.192) – see p683, subject to savings provisions in reg 6 of SI 2001 No.162. For other types of cases the '1993 rules' apply. If the 1993 rules apply:

–   the words "penalty payments, fees," are not inserted after "interest";

–   in paragraph (i) after "[garnishee proceedings]" the word "or" is retained; *and*

–   in paragraph (iii) after "[wilful refusal]" wherever it appears, the word "or" is retained.

[¹ SCHEDULE 4
Regulation 35(4)

FORM OF ORDER OF DISQUALIFICATION FROM HOLDING OR OBTAINING A DRIVING LICENCE

Sections 39A and 40B of the Child Support Act 1991 and regulation 35 of the Child Support (Collection and Enforcement) Regulations 1992.

. . . . .Magistrates' Court
Date:
Liable Person:
Address:

A liability order ("the order") was made against the liable person by the [ ] Magistrates' Court on [ ] under section 33 of the Child Support Act 1991 ("the Act") in respect of an amount of [ ].

The court is satisfied–

(i)   that the Secretary of State sought under section 35 of the Act to levy by distress the amount then outstanding in respect of which the order was made;

[and/or]

that the Secretary of State sought under section 36 of the Act to recover through [ ] County Court by means of [garnishee proceedings] [a charging order], the amount then outstanding in respect of which the order was made;

(ii)   that such amount, or any proportion of it, remains unpaid; and

(iii)   having inquired in the liable person's presence as to his means and whether there has been [wilful refusal] [culpable neglect] on his part.

The decision of the court is that the liable person be disqualified from [holding or obtaining] a driving licence from [date] for [period] unless the aggregate amount in respect of which this order is made is sooner paid*

This order is made in respect of–

Amount outstanding (including any interest, fees, penalty payments, costs and charges):

Aggregate amount:

And you [the liable person] shall surrender to the court any driving licence and counterpart held.

Justice of the Peace

[*or* by order of the Court

Clerk of the Court]

* *Note:* The period of disqualification may be reduced as provided by section 40B(5)(a) of the Act if part payment is made of the aggregate amount. The order will be revoked by section 40B(5)(b) of the Act if full payment is made of the aggregate amount.]

Amendment

1.   Child Support (Collection and Enforcement and Miscellaneous Amendments) Regulations 2000 (SI 2001 No.162) reg 2(9) (April 2, 2001 but see reg 6 of SI 2001 No.162 for savings provisions detailing when this schedule does not apply).

The Child Support (Collection and Enforcement of Other Forms of Maintenance) Regulations 1992

(1992 No.2643)

Citation, commencement and interpretation

1.–(1) These Regulations may be cited as the Child Support (Collection and Enforcement of Other Forms of Maintenance) Regulations 1992 and shall come into force on 5th April 1993.

(2) In these Regulations–

"the Act" means the Child Support Act 1991;

"child of the family" has the same meaning as in the Matrimonial Causes Act 1973 or, in Scotland, the Family Law (Scotland) Act 1985; and

"periodical payments" includes secured periodical payments.

General Note

The term "child of the family" is defined by s52(1) Matrimonial Causes Act 1973 as follows:

"child of the family", in relation to the parties to a marriage, means–

(a) a child of both of those parties; and

(b) any other child, not being a child who is placed with those persons as foster parents by a local authority or voluntary organisation, who has been treated by both of those parties as a child of their family."

Periodical payments and categories of person prescribed for the purposes of section 30 of the Act

2. The following periodical payments and categories of persons are prescribed for the purposes of section 30(1) of the Act–

(a) payments under a maintenance order made in relation to a child in accordance with the provisions of section 8(6) (periodical payments in addition to child support maintenance), 8(7) (periodical payments to meet expenses incurred in connection with the provision of instruction or training) or 8(8) of the Act (periodical payments to meet expenses attributable to disability);

(b) any periodical payments under a maintenance order [[1]or, in Scotland, registered minutes of agreement] which are payable to or for the benefit of a spouse[[3], civil partner, former spouse or former civil partner] who is the person with care of a child who is a qualifying child in respect of whom a child support [[2]maintenance calculation] is in force in accordance with which the Secretary of State has arranged for the collection of child support maintenance under section 29 of the Act; and

(c) any periodical payments under a maintenance order payable to or for the benefit of a former child of the family of the person against whom the order is made, that child having his home with the person with care.

Amendments

1. Inserted by reg 44 of SI 1993/913 as from 5.4.93

2. Child Support (Collection and Enforcement and Miscellaneous Amendments) Regulations 2000 (SI 2001 No.162) reg 3(2) (comes into force in relation to a particular case on the day on which ss1(2) and (3), 4, 18(1) and (2), and 20(1) of and Sch 3 para 11(2) and (16) Child Support, Pensions and Social Security Act 2000 come into force for the purposes of that type of case – which is March 3, 2003 for the types of cases in arts 3 and 5 of SI 2003 No.192). For other types of cases see the '1993 rules', below. See reg 6 of SI 2001 No.162 for savings provisions detailing when this amendment does not apply.

3. Civil Partnership (Pensions, Social Security and Child Support) (Consequential, etc Provisions) Order 2005 (SI 2005 No.2877) art 2(4) and Sch 4 para 5 (December 5, 2005).

1993 rules

Reg 3(2) of the Child Support (Collection and Enforcement and Miscellaneous Amendments) Regulations 2000 (SI 2001 No.162) amends this regulation and has been brought into force only for the types of cases in arts 3 and 5 of the Child Support, Pensions and Social Security Act 2000 (Commencement No.12) Order 2003 (SI 2003

No.192) – see p683, subject to savings provisions in reg 6 of SI 2001 No.162. For other types of cases the '1993 rules' apply. If the 1993 rules apply, the words "maintenance assessment" are retained in place of "maintenance calculation".

Definitions

"the Act": see reg 1(2).

"child of the family": see reg 1(2).

"periodical payments": see reg 1.

General Note

From 11 April 1994 magistrates have had the power to order that payments under qualifying maintenance orders be made in accordance with arrangements made by the Secretary of State for their collection under s30 of the Act (Child Support Act 1991 (Consequential Amendments) Order 1994).

Thus, where a maintenance calculation is in force and payments are being collected through the CMEC under it, but other types of periodical payments are still in effect (these will be orders for "top up" maintenance, etc and appear also to include spousal maintenance) the magistrates may (see the Magistrates' Courts Act 1980, s59(1) and (3)(cc)) order that all the monies due are paid through the collection machinery of the Child Support Act.

The power does not extend to the county or High Court, even though it is more likely that those courts would have made top-up maintenance order, etc than the magistrates. To take advantage of the magistrates' power, the creditor under the order must have the order registered in the magistrates' court under the Maintenance Orders Act 1958.

Collection and enforcement – England and Wales

3.　In relation to England and Wales, sections 29(2) and (3) and 31 to [¹40B] of the Act, and any regulations made under those sections, shall apply for the purpose of enabling the Secretary of State to enforce any obligation to pay any amount which he is authorised to collect under section 30 of the Act, with the modification that any reference in those sections or regulations to child support maintenance shall be read as a reference to any of the periodical payments mentioned in regulation 2 above, and any reference to a [¹maintenance calculation] shall be read as a reference to any of the maintenance orders mentioned in that regulation.

Amendment

1.　　Child Support (Collection and Enforcement and Miscellaneous Amendments) Regulations 2000 (SI 2001 No.162) reg 3(2) and (3) (comes into force in relation to a particular case on the day on which ss1(2) and (3), 4, 18(1) and (2), and 20(1) of and Sch 3 para 11(2) and (Child Support, Pensions and Social Security Act 2000 come into force for the purposes of that type of case – which is March 3, 2003 for the types of cases in arts 3 and 5 of SI 2003 No.192). For other types of cases see the '1993 rules', below. See reg 6 of SI 2001 No.162 for savings provisions detailing when these amendments do not apply.

1993 rules

Reg 3(2) and (3) of the Child Support (Collection and Enforcement and Miscellaneous Amendments) Regulations 2000 (SI 2001 No.162) amends this regulation and has been brought into force only for the types of cases in arts 3 and 5 of the Child Support, Pensions and Social Security Act 2000 (Commencement No.12) Order 2003 (SI 2003 No.192) – see p683, subject to savings provisions in reg 6 of SI 2001 No.162. For other types of cases the '1993 rules' apply. If the 1993 rules apply, the words "maintenance assessment" are retained in place of "maintenance calculation" and "40" is retained in place of "40B".

Definitions

"the Act": see reg 1(2).

"periodical payments": see reg 1(2).

Collection and enforcement – Scotland

4.　In relation to Scotland, for the purpose of enforcing any obligation to pay any amount which the Secretary of State is authorised to collect under section 30 of the Act–

(a)　the Secretary of State may bring any proceedings and take any other steps (other than diligence against earnings) which could have been brought or taken by or on behalf of the person to whom the periodical payments are payable; and

(b)　sections 29(2) and (3), 31 and 32 of the Act, and any regulations made under those sections, shall apply, with the modification that any reference in those sections or regulations to child support maintenance shall be read as a reference to any of the periodical payments mentioned in regulation 2 above, and any reference to a [¹maintenance calculation] shall be read as a reference to any of the maintenance orders mentioned in that regulation.

Amendment

1. Child Support (Collection and Enforcement and Miscellaneous Amendments) Regulations 2000 (SI 2001 No.162) reg 3(2) (comes into force in relation to a particular case on the day on which ss1(2) and (3), 4, 18(1) and (2), and 20(1) of and Sch 3 para 11(2) and (16) Child Support, Pensions and Social Security Act 2000 come into force for the purposes of that type of case – which is March 3, 2003 for the types of cases in arts 3 and 5 of SI 2003 No.192). For other types of cases see the '1993 rules', below. See reg 6 of SI 2001 No.162 for savings provisions detailing when this amendment does not apply.

1993 rules

Reg 3(2) of the Child Support (Collection and Enforcement and Miscellaneous Amendments) Regulations 2000 (SI 2001 No.162) amends this regulation and has been brought into force only for the types of cases in arts 3 and 5 of the Child Support, Pensions and Social Security Act 2000 (Commencement No.12) Order 2003 (SI 2003 No.192) – see p683, subject to savings provisions in reg 6 of SI 2001 No.162. For other types of cases the '1993 rules' apply. If the 1993 rules apply, the words "maintenance assessment" are retained in place of "maintenance calculation".

Definitions

"the Act": see reg 1(2).
"periodical payments": see reg 1(2).

Collection and enforcement – supplementary

5. Nothing in Regulations 3 or 4 applies to any periodical payment which falls due before the date specified by the Secretary of State by a notice in writing to the [¹non-resident parent] that he is arranging for those payments to be collected, and that date shall be not earlier than the date the notice is given.

Amendment

1. Child Support (Collection and Enforcement and Miscellaneous Amendments) Regulations 2000 (SI 2001 No.162) reg 3(4) (comes into force in relation to a particular case on the day on which ss1(2) and (3), 4, 18(1) and (2), and 20(1) of and Sch 3 para 11(2) and (16) Child Support, Pensions and Social Security Act 2000 come into force for the purposes of that type of case – which is March 3, 2003 for the types of cases in arts 3 and 5 of SI 2003 No.192). For other types of cases see the '1993 rules', below. See reg 6 of SI 2001 No.162 for savings provisions detailing when this amendment does not apply.

1993 rules

Reg 3(4) of the Child Support (Collection and Enforcement and Miscellaneous Amendments) Regulations 2000 (SI 2001 No.162) amends this regulation and has been brought into force only for the types of cases in arts 3 and 5 of the Child Support, Pensions and Social Security Act 2000 (Commencement No.12) Order 2003 (SI 2003 No.192) – see p683, subject to savings provisions in reg 6 of SI 2001 No.162. For other types of cases the '1993 rules' apply. If the 1993 rules apply, the words "absent parent" are retained in place of "non-resident parent".

General Note

Since the regulations made under s29 of the Act apply to regs 3 and 4 above, the day when the notice is treated as given under reg 5 will be determined under reg 1(2)(b) of the Collection and Enforcement Regulations.

The Child Support (Maintenance Arrangements and Jurisdiction) Regulations 1992

(1992 No.2645)

Citation, commencement and interpretation

1.–(1) These Regulations may be cited as the Child Support (Maintenance Arrangements and Jurisdiction) Regulations 1992 and shall come into force on 5th April 1993.

(2) In these Regulations–

"the Act" means the Child Support Act 1991;

[¹[³[⁴...]]]

[³[⁴...]]

"effective date" means the date on which a maintenance [²calculation] takes effect for the purposes of the Act.

"maintenance order" has the meaning given in section 8(11) of the Act.

(3) In these Regulations, unless the context otherwise requires, a reference–

(a) to a numbered regulation is to the regulation in these Regulations bearing that number;

(b) in a regulation to a numbered paragraph is to the paragraph in that regulation bearing that number;

(c) in a paragraph to a lettered or numbered sub-paragraph is to the sub-paragraph in that paragraph bearing that letter or number.

Amendments

1. Definition of "Maintenance Assessment Procedure Regulations" inserted by reg 25 of SI 1995 No.1045 as from 18.4.95. Reg 2 substituted by reg 26 of SI 1995/1045 as from 18.4.95.

2. Child Support (Information, Evidence and Disclosure and Maintenance Arrangements and Jurisdiction) (Amendment) Regulations 2000 (SI 2001 No.161) reg 2 (come into force in relation to a particular case on the date on which paras 11(19) and (20) of Sch 3 Child Support, Pensions and Social Security Act 2000 come into force for the purpose of that type of case – which is March 3, 2003 for the types of cases in art 3 of SI 2003 No.192, see p683). Transitional provisions mean that in certain circumstances this amendment is treated as not having been made. See reg 10 of SI 2001 No.161 (p674) for details. For those for whom this amendment does not apply, see the '1993 rules' below.

3. Child Support (Information, Evidence and Disclosure and Maintenance Arrangements and Jurisdiction) (Amendment) Regulations 2000 (SI 2001 No.161) reg 3 (will come into force in relation to a particular case on the date on which paras 11(19) and (20) of Sch 3 Child Support, Pensions and Social Security Act 2000 come into force for the purpose of that type of case – which is March 3, 2003 for the types of cases in art 3 of SI 2003 No.192, see p683). Transitional provisions mean that in certain circumstances this amendment is treated as not having been made. See reg 10 of SI 2001 No.161 (p674) for details. For those for whom this does not apply, see the '1993 rules' below.

4. Child Support (Meaning of Child and New Calculation Rules) (Consequential and Miscellaneous Amendment) Regulations 2012 (SI 2012 No. 2785) reg 5(2) (in force in relation to a particular case on the day on which paragraph 2 of Schedule 4 to the Child Maintenance and Other Payments Act 2008 (see p243) comes into force in relation to that type of case – which is December 10, 2012, in relation to the types of cases falling within art 3 of SI 2012 No. 3042 only (see p767). For other types of cases see '2003 rules' below.

2003 rules

Regulation 5(2) of the Child Support (Meaning of Child and New Calculation Rules) (Consequential and Miscellaneous Amendment) Regulations 2012 (SI 2012 No.2785) omitted the definitions of "Maintenance Calculation Procedure Regulations" and "Maintenance Calculations and Special Cases Regulations". This amendment came into force on December 10, 2012, in relation to the types of cases falling within art 3 of SI 2012 No. 3042 (see p767). For other types of cases, unless the 1993 rules apply, the following definitions should be included in regulation 1(2):

[¹[³"Maintenance Calculation Procedure Regulations" means the Child Support (Maintenance Calculation Procedure) Regulations 2000]]

[³"Maintenance Calculations and Special Cases Regulations" means the Child Support (Maintenance Calculations and Special Cases) Regulations 2000;]

1993 rules
Regulations 2 and 3 of the Child Support (Information, Evidence and Disclosure and Maintenance Arrangements and Jurisdiction) (Amendment) Regulations 2000 (SI 2001 No.161) substituted the following definitions for those given under '2003 rules' above, and substituted the word "calculation" for "assessment". These amendments came into force on March 3, 2003 for the types of cases in art 3 of SI 2003 No.192 (see p683) subject to the transitional provisions in reg 10 of SI 2001 No.161 (see p674). The '1993 rules' apply to other types of cases, including those covered by the the transitional provisions in reg 10 SI 2001 No.161, (unless the case is one which falls within art 3 of SI 2012 No 3042). If the 1993 rules apply, the following definitions are included in regulation 1(2), and the word "assessment" should be read for "calculation":

"Maintenance Assessment Procedure Regulations" means the Child Support (Maintenance Assessment Procedure) Regulations 1992;
"Maintenance Assessments and Special Cases Regulations" means the Child Support (Maintenance Assessments and Special Cases) Regulations 1992;

[²Prescription of enactments for the purposes of section 8(11) of the Act
2. The following enactments are prescribed for the purposes of section 8(11)(f) of the Act–[¹
  (a) the Conjugal Rights (Scotland) Amendment Act 1861(d);
  (b) the Court of Session Act 1868(e);
  (c) the Sheriff Courts (Scotland) Act 1907;
  (d) the Guardianship of Infants Act 1925;
  (e) the Illegitimate Children (Scotland) Act 1930;
  (f) the Children and Young Persons (Scotland) Act 1932;
  (g) the Children and Young Persons (Scotland) Act 1937;
  (h) the Custody of Children (Scotland) Act 1939;
  (i) the National Assistance Act 1948;
  (j) the Affiliation Orders Act 1952;
  (k) the Affiliation Proceedings Act 1957;
  (1) the Matrimonial Proceedings (Children) Act 1958;
  (m) the Guardianship of Minors Act 1971;
  (n) the Guardianship Act 1973;
  (o) the Children Act 1975;
  (p) the Supplementary Benefits Act 1976;
  (q) the Social Security Act 1986;
  (r) the Social Security Administration Act 1992.]

Amendment
1.   Reg 2 substituted by reg 26 of SI 1995 No.1045 as from 18.4.95

Definition
    "the Act": see reg 1(2).

Relationship between maintenance [⁷calculations] and certain court orders
3.–[¹ (1)   Orders made under the following enactments are of a kind prescribed for the purposes of section 10(1) of the Act–
  (a) the Conjugal Rights (Scotland) Amendment Act 1861;
  (b) the Court of Session Act 1868;
  (c) the Sheriff Courts (Scotland) Act 1907;
  (d) the Guardianship of Infants Act 1925;
  (e) the Illegitimate Children (Scotland) Act 1930;
  (f) the Children and Young Persons (Scotland) Act 1932;
  (g) the Children and Young Persons (Scotland) Act 1937;
  (h) the Custody of Children (Scotland) Act 1939;
  (i) the National Assistance Act 1948;
  (j) the Affiliation Orders Act 1952;
  (k) the Affiliation Proceedings Act 1957;
  (l) the Matrimonial Proceedings (Children) Act 1958;

    (m)   the Guardianship of Minors Act 1971;
    (n)   the Guardianship Act 1973;
    (o)   Part II of the Matrimonial Causes Act 1973;
    (p)   the Children Act 1975;
    (q)   the Supplementary Benefits Act 1976;
    (r)   the Domestic Proceedings and Magistrates Courts Act 1978;
    (s)   Part III of the Matrimonial and Family Proceedings Act 1984;
    (t)   the Family Law (Scotland) Act 1985;
    (u)   the Social Security Act 1986;
    (v)   Schedule 1 to the Children Act 1989;
    (w)   the Social Security Administration Act 1992]
    [9(x)   Schedule 5, 6 or 7 to the Civil Partnership Act 2004.]

    (2)   Subject to paragraphs (3) and (4), where a maintenance [7calculation] is made with respect to–

    (a)   all of the children with respect to whom an order falling within paragraph (1) is in force; or

    (b)   one or more but not all of the children with respect to whom an order falling within paragraph (1) is in force and where the amount payable under the order to or for the benefit of each child is separately specified,

that order shall, so far as it relates to the making or securing of periodical payments to or for the benefit of the children with respect to whom the maintenance [7calculation] has been made, cease to have effect [8on the effective date of the maintenance calculation.]

    (3)   The provisions of paragraph (2) shall not apply where a maintenance order has been made in accordance with section 8(7) or (8) of the Act.

    (4)   In Scotland, where–

    (a)   an order has ceased to have effect by virtue of the provisions of paragraph (2) to the extent specified in that paragraph; and

    (b)   [2the Secretary of State] no longer has jurisdiction to make a maintenance [7calculation] with respect to a child with respect to whom the order ceased to have effect,

that order shall, so far as it relates to that child, again have effect from the date [2the Secretary of State] no longer has jurisdiction to make a maintenance [7calculation] with respect to that child.

    (5)   [8...]
    (6)   [8...]
    (7)   [8...]
    (8)   [8...]

Amendments

1.   Reg 3(1) substituted by reg 27(2) of SI 1995 No.1045 as from 18.4.95.
2.   3(4) by art 31(1) of SI 1999 No.1510 as from 1.6.99.
3.   Words inserted in reg 3(5) by reg 13 of SI 1995 No.3261 as from 22.1.96.
4.   Reg 3(7) inserted by reg 3 of SI 1995 No.123 as from 16.2.95.
5.   Reg 3(8) added by reg 27(3) of SI 1995 No.1045 as from 18.4.95.
6.   Words inserted in reg 3(8) by reg 13 of SI 1995 No.3261 as from 22.1.96.
7.   Child Support (Information, Evidence and Disclosure and Maintenance Arrangements and Jurisdiction) (Amendment) Regulations 2000 (SI 2001 No.161) reg 2 (comes into force in relation to a particular case on the date on which paras 11(19) and (20) of Sch 3 Child Support, Pensions and Social Security Act 2000 come into force for the purpose of that type of case – which is March 3, 2003 for the types of cases detailed in art 3 of SI 2003 No.192 – see p683). For other types of cases see the '1993 rules', below. Transitional provisions mean that in certain circumstances this amendment is treated as not having been made. See reg 10 of SI 2001 No.161 for details (p674).
8.   Child Support (Information, Evidence and Disclosure and Maintenance Arrangements and Jurisdiction) (Amendment) Regulations 2000 (SI 2001 No.161) reg 8(1) (comes into force in relation to a particular case on the date on which paras 11(19) and (20) of Sch 3 Child Support, Pensions and Social Security Act 2000 come into force for the purpose of that type of case – which is March 3, 2003 for the types of cases detailed in art 3 of SI 2003 No.192 see p683). For other types of cases see the '1993 rules', below. Transitional provisions mean that in certain circumstances these amendments and revocations are treated as not having been made. See reg 10 of SI 2001 No.161 for details (p674).

9.   Civil Partnership (Pensions, Social Security and Child Support) (Consequential, etc. Provisions) Order 2005 (SI 2005 No.2877) art 2(4) and Sch 4 para 4 (December 5, 2005).

1993 rules
Regs 2 and 8(1) of the Child Support (Information, Evidence and Disclosure and Maintenance Arrangements and Jurisdiction) (Amendment) Regulations 2000 (SI 2001 No.161) amend this regulation and have been brought into force only for the types of cases in art 3 of the Child Support, Pensions and Social Security Act 2000 (Commencement No.12) Order 2003 (SI 2003 No.192) – see p683, subject to transitional provisions in reg 10 of SI 2001 No.161. For other types of cases the '1993 rules' apply. If the 1993 rules apply:
–   the word "assessment" is retained in place of "calculation";
–   in paragraph (2) the words "on the effective date of the maintenance calculation." are not inserted; *and*
–   paragraphs (5) -(8), as shown below, are not omitted.

(5)   [³Subject to regulation 33(7) of the Maintenance Assessment Procedure Regulations,] where a maintenance assessment is made with respect to children with respect to whom an order falling within paragraph (1) is in force, the effective date of that assessment shall be two days after the assessment is made.

(6)   Where the provisions of paragraph (2) apply to an order, that part of the order to which those provisions apply shall cease to have effect from the effective date of the maintenance assessment.

[⁴(7)   Where at the time an interim maintenance assessment was made there was in force with respect to children in respect of whom that interim maintenance assessment was made an order falling within paragraph (1), the effective date of a maintenance assessment subsequently made in accordance with Part I of Schedule 1 to the Act in respect of those children shall be the effective date of that interim maintenance assessment as determined under paragraph (5).]

[⁵(8)   [⁶Subject to regulation 33(7) of the Maintenance Assessment Procedure Regulations,] where–

(a)   a maintenance assessment is made in accordance with Part I of Schedule 1 to the Act in respect of children with respect to whom an order falling within paragraph (1) was in force; and

(b)   that order ceases to have effect on or after 18th April 1995, for reasons other than the making of an interim maintenance assessment, but prior to the date on which the maintenance assessment is made and after–

(i)   the date on which a maintenance enquiry form referred to in regulation 5(2) of the Maintenance Assessment Procedure Regulations was given or sent to the absent parent, where the application for a maintenance assessment was made by a person with care or a child under section 7 of the Act; or

(ii)   the date on which a maintenance application which complies with the provisions of regulation 2 of the Maintenance Assessment Procedure Regulations was received by the Secretary of State from an absent parent,

the effective date of that maintenance assessment shall be the day following that on which the court order ceased to have effect.]

Definitions
"the Act": see reg 1(2).
"effective date": see reg 1(2).
"maintenance order": see reg 1(2).

General Note
Non-resident parents become angry (and rightly so) when no steps are taken to terminate payments under a maintenance order once a maintenance calculation has been made. However, this failure does not invalidate the maintenance calculation as there is no obligation to notify the court of the making of a maintenance calculation under reg 10 of the Maintenance Assessment Procedure Regulations, since the court is not a "relevant person" within the definition in reg 1(2) of those Regulations.

Relationship between maintenance [²calculation] and certain agreements

4.–(1)   Maintenance agreements within the meaning of section 9(1) of the Act are agreements of a kind prescribed for the purposes of section 10(2) of the Act.

(2)   Where a maintenance [²calculation] is made with respect to–

(a)   all of the children with respect to whom an agreement falling within paragraph (1) is in force; or

(b)   one or more but not all of the children with respect to whom an agreement falling within paragraph (1) is in force and where the amount payable under the agreement to or for the benefit of each child is separately specified,

that agreement shall, so far as it relates to the making or securing of periodical payments to or for the benefit of the children with respect to whom the maintenance [²calculation] has been made, become unenforceable from the effective date of the [²calculation].

(3)   Where an agreement becomes unenforceable under the provisions of paragraph (2) to the extent specified in that paragraph, it shall remain unenforceable in relation to a particular child until such date as [¹the Secretary of State] no longer has jurisdiction to make a maintenance [²calculation] with respect to that child.

Amendments

1.   Words substituted in reg 4(3) by art 31 of SI 1999 No.1510 as from 1.6.99.

2.   Child Support (Information, Evidence and Disclosure and Maintenance Arrangements and Jurisdiction) (Amendment) Regulations 2000 (SI 2001 No.161) reg 2 (comes into force in relation to a particular case on the date on which paras 11(19) and (20) of Sch 3 Child Support, Pensions and Social Security Act 2000 come into force for the purpose of that type of case – which is March 3, 2003 for the types of cases in art 3 of SI 2003 No.192). For other types of cases see the '1993 rules', below. Transitional provisions mean that in certain circumstances this amendment is treated as not having been made. See reg 10 of SI 2001 No.161 for details.

1993 rules

Reg 2 of the Child Support (Information, Evidence and Disclosure and Maintenance Arrangements and Jurisdiction) (Amendment) Regulations 2000 (SI 2001 No.161) amends this regulation and has been brought into force only for the types of cases in art 3 of the Child Support, Pensions and Social Security Act 2000 (Commencement No.12) Order 2003 (SI 2003 No.192) – see p683, subject to transitional provisions in reg 10 of SI 2001 No.161 (see p674). For other types of cases the '1993 rules' apply. If the 1993 rules apply, the word "assessment" is retained in place of "calculation".

Definition

"the Act": see reg 1(2).

Notifications by [¹the Secretary of State]

5.–(1)   Where [¹the Secretary of State] is aware that an order of a kind prescribed in paragraph (2) is in force and considers that the making of a maintenance [³calculation] has affected, or is likely to affect, that order, he shall notify the persons prescribed in paragraph (3) in respect of whom that maintenance [³calculation] is in force, and the persons prescribed in paragraph (4) holding office in the court where the order in question was made or subsequently registered, of the [³calculation] and its effective date.

(2)   The prescribed orders are those made under an enactment mentioned in regulation 3(1).

(3)   The prescribed persons in respect of whom the maintenance [³calculation] is in force are–

(a)   a person with care;

(b)   an [³non-resident parent];

(c)   a person who is treated as an [³non-resident parent] under [⁴[⁶regulation 50 of the Child Support Maintenance Calculation Regulations 2012]];

(d)   a child who has made an application for a maintenance [³calculation] under section 7 of the Act.

(4)   The prescribed person holding office in the court where the order in question was made or subsequently registered is-

(a)   in England and Wales–

(i)   in relation to the High Court, the senior district judge of the principal registry of the Family Division or, where proceedings were instituted in a district registry, the district judge;

(ii)   in relation to a county court, the proper officer of that court within the meaning of Order 1, Rule 3 of the County Court Rules 1981;

(iii) in relation to a magistrates' court, the [²[⁵designated officer] for] that court;

(b) in Scotland–

(i)   in relation to the Court of Session, the Deputy Principal Clerk of Session;

(ii) in relation to a sheriff court, the sheriff clerk.

Amendments

1.   Words substituted in reg 5 by art 31 of SI 1999 No.1510 as from 1.6.99.

2.   Child Support (Information, Evidence and Disclosure and Maintenance Arrangements and Jurisdiction) (Amendment) Regulations 2000 (SI 2001 No.161) reg 4 (April 1, 2001).

3.   Child Support (Information, Evidence and Disclosure and Maintenance Arrangements and Jurisdiction) (Amendment) Regulations 2000 (SI 2001 No.161) reg 2 (comes into force in relation to a particular case on the date on which paras 11(19) and (20) of Sch 3 Child Support, Pensions and Social Security Act 2000 come into force for the purpose of that type of case – which is March 3, 2003 for the types of cases detailed in art 3 of SI 2003 No.192, see p683). Transitional provisions mean that in certain circumstances this amendment is treated as not having been made. See reg 10 of SI 2001 No.161 (p674) for details. For other types of cases, including those covered by the transitional provisions, see the '1993 rules' below.

4.   Child Support (Information, Evidence and Disclosure and Maintenance Arrangements and Jurisdiction) (Amendment) Regulations 2000 (SI 2001 No.161) reg 3 (comes into force in relation to a particular case on the date on which paras 11(19) and (20) of Sch 3 Child Support, Pensions and Social Security Act 2000 come into force for the purpose of that type of case – which is March 3, 2003 for the types of cases detailed in art 3 of SI 2003 No.192, see p683). Transitional provisions mean that in certain circumstances this amendment is treated as not having been made. See reg 10 of SI 2001 No.161 (p674) for details. For other types of cases, including those covered by the transitional provisions, see the '1993 rules' below.

5.   Courts Act 2003 (Consequential Provisions) (No.2) Order 2005 (SI 2005 No.617) art 2 and Sch para 159 (April 1, 2005).

6.   Child Support (Meaning of Child and New Calculation Rules) (Consequential and Miscellaneous Amendment) Regulations 2012 (SI 2012 No. 2785) reg 5(3) (in force in relation to a particular case on the day on which paragraph 2 of Schedule 4 to the Child Maintenance and Other Payments Act 2008 (see p243) comes into force in relation to that type of case – which is December 10, 2012, in relation to the types of cases falling within art 3 of SI 2012 No. 3042 only (see p767). For other types of cases see '2003 rules' below.

2003 rules

Regulation 5(3) of The Child Support (Meaning of Child and New Calculation Rules) (Consequential and Miscellaneous Amendment) Regulations 2012 (SI 2012 No.2785) substituted "regulation 50 of the Child Support Maintenance Calculation Regulations 2012" for "regulation 8 of the Maintenance Calculations and Special Cases Regulations". This amendment came into force on December 10, 2012, in relation to the types of cases falling within art 3 of SI 2012 No.3042 (see p767). For other types of cases, unless the '1993 rules' apply, the words "regulation 8 of the Maintenance Calculations and Special Cases Regulations" are retained.

1993 rules

Regulations 2 and 3 of The Child Support (Information, Evidence and Disclosure and Maintenance Arrangements and Jurisdiction) (Amendment) Regulations 2000 (SI 2001 No.161) substituted "non-resident parent" for "absent parent", "calculation" for "assessment" and "regulation 8 of the Maintenance Calculations and Special Cases Regulations" for "regulation 20 of the Maintenance Assessments and Special Cases Regulations". These amendments came into force on March 3, 2003 for the types of cases in art 3 of SI 2003 No.192 (see p683) subject to the transitional provisions in reg 10 of SI 2001 No.161 (see p674). The '1993 rules' apply to other types of cases, including those covered by the the transitional provisions in reg 10 SI 2001 No.161, (unless the case is one which falls within art 3 of SI 2012 No.3042). If the 1993 rules apply, the original wording is retained.

Definitions

"effective date": see reg 1(2).

"Maintenance Calculations and Special Cases Regulations": see reg 1(2).

Notification by the court

6.–(1)   Where a court is aware that a maintenance [¹calculation] is in force and makes an order mentioned in regulation 3(1) which it considers has affected, or is likely to affect, that [¹calculation], the person prescribed in paragraph (2) shall notify the Secretary of State to that effect.

(2)   The prescribed person is the person holding the office specified below in the court where the order in question was made or subsequently registered–
(a)   in England and Wales–
        (i)   in relation to the High Court, the senior district judge of the principal registry of the Family Division or, where proceedings were instituted in a district registry, the district judge;
        (ii)   in relation to a county court, the proper officer of that court within the meaning of Order 1, Rule 3 of the County Court Rules 1981;
        (iii)   in relation to a magistrates' court, the [¹[²designated officer] for] that court;
(b)   in Scotland–
        (i)   in relation to the Court of Session, the Deputy Principal Clerk of Session;
        (ii)   in relation to a sheriff court, the sheriff clerk.

Amendments
1.   Child Support (Information, Evidence and Disclosure and Maintenance Arrangements and Jurisdiction) (Amendment) Regulations 2000 (SI 2001 No.161) reg 4 (April 1, 2001).
2.   Courts Act 2003 (Consequential Provisions) (No.2) Order 2005 (SI 2005 No.617) art 2 and Sch para 159 (April 1, 2005).

[Cancellation of a maintenance assessment on grounds of lack of jurisdiction
7.–[¹...]]

Amendment
1.   Omitted by Child Support (Miscellaneous Amendments) (No.2) Regulations 2009 (SI 2009 No.2909) reg 2 (December 4, 2009).

[¹Prescription for the purposes of jurisdiction
7A.–(1)   The companies prescribed for the purposes of section 44(2A)(c) of the Act (non-resident parents not habitually resident in the United Kingdom but employed by prescribed companies) are companies which employ employees to work outside the United Kingdom but make calculations and payment arrangements in relation to the earnings of those employees in the United Kingdom so that a deduction from earnings order may be made under section 31 of the Act in respect of the earnings of any such employee who is a liable person for the purposes of that section.
(2)   The following bodies are prescribed for the purposes of section 44(2A)(d) of the Act (non-resident parents not habitually resident in the United Kingdom but employed by a prescribed body)–
(a)   a National Health Service Trust established by order made under section 5 of the National Health Service and Community Care Act 1990 ("the 1990 Act") or under section 12A of the National Health Service (Scotland) Act 1978 ("the 1978 Act");
[³(aa) an NHS foundation trust within the meaning of section 1(1) of the Health and Social Care (Community Health and Standards) Act 2003;]
[⁵(ab) a clinical commissioning group established under section 14D of the National Health Service Act 2006;
        (ac) the National Health Service Commissioning Board;
        (ad) the National Institute for Health and Care Excellence;
        (ae) the Health and Social Care Information Centre;]
(b)   [⁵...]
(c)   a Health Authority established under section 8 of the National Health Service Act 1977 ("the 1977 Act");
(d)   a Special Health Authority established under section 11 of the 1977 Act;
[²(da) [⁵...]]
(e)   a local authority, and for this purpose "local authority" means, in relation to England, a county council, a district council, a London borough council, the Common Council of the City of London or the Council of the Isles of Scilly and, in relation to Wales, a county council or a county borough council and, in

relation to Scotland, a council constituted under section 2 of the Local Government etc (Scotland) Act 1994;

(f)   a Health and Social Service Trust established by order made under Article 10 of the Health and Personal Social Services (Northern Ireland) Order 1991;

(g)   a Health and Social Services Board established by order made under Article 16 of the Health and Personal Social Services (Northern Ireland) Order 1972 ("the 1972 Order");

(h)   the Central Services Agency established by order made under Article 26 of the 1972 Order;

(i)   a Special Agency established by order made under Article 3 of the Health and Personal Social Services (Special Agencies) (Northern Ireland) Order 1990;

(j)   a Health Board constituted under section 2 of the 1978 Act; and

(k)   a Special Health Board constituted under section 2 of the 1978 Act.]

[⁴(l)   Healthcare Improvement Scotland constituted under section 10A of the 1978 Act.]

Amendments

1.   Child Support (Information, Evidence and Disclosure and Maintenance Arrangements and Jurisdiction) (Amendment) Regulations 2000 (SI 2001 No. 161) reg. 8(3) (January 31, 2001).

2.   National Health Service Reform and Health Care Professions Act 2002 (Supplementary, Consequential etc. Provisions) Regulations 2002 (SI 2002 No.2469) reg 4 and Sch 1 para 60 (October 1, 2002).

3.   Health and Social Care (Community Health and Standards) Act 2003 (Supplementary and Consequential Provision) (NHS Foundation Trusts) Order 2004 (SI 2004 No.696) art 2 and Sch 1 para 13 (April 1, 2004).

4.   Public Services Reform (Scotland) Act 2010 (Consequential Modifications of Enactments) Order 2011 (SI 2011 No.2581) art 2 and Sch 2 para 19 (October 28, 2011).

5.   National Treatment Agency (Abolition) and the Health and Social Care Act 2012 (Consequential, Transitional and Saving Provisions) Order 2013 (SI 2013 No.235) art 11 and Sch 2 para 21 (April 1, 2013).

Definition

"the Act": see reg 1(2).

Maintenance [⁴calculations] and maintenance orders made in error

8.–(1)   Where–

(a)   at the time that a maintenance [⁴calculation] with respect to a qualifying child was made a maintenance order was in force with respect to that child;

[¹(aa) the maintenance order has ceased to have effect by virtue of the provisions of regulation 3;]

(b)   the [⁴non-resident parent] has made payments of child support maintenance due under that [⁴calculation]; and

(c)   [⁴the Secretary of State revises the decision as to the maintenance calculation under section 16 of the Act and decides that no child support maintenance was payable on the ground that the previous decision was made in error,]

the payments of child support maintenance shall be treated as payments under the maintenance order and that order shall be treated as having continued in force.

(2)   Where–

(a)   at the time that a maintenance order with respect to a qualifying child was made a maintenance [⁴calculation] was in force with respect to that child;

[¹(aa) the maintenance [⁴calculation] [⁴...] ceases to have effect;]

(b)   the [⁴non-resident parent] has made payments of maintenance due under that order; and

(c)   the maintenance order is revoked by the court on the grounds that it was made in error,

the payments under the maintenance order shall be treated as payments of child support maintenance and the maintenance [⁴calculation] shall be treated [⁴....] [³as not having ceased to have effect].

Amendments

1.   Reg 8(1)(aa) and 8(2)(aa) inserted by reg 46 of SI 1993 No.913 as from 5.4.93.

2.   Words substituted in reg 8(c) by art 31 of SI 1999 No.1510 as from 1.6.99.
3.   Words in reg 8(2) inserted by reg 46 of SI 1993 No.913 as from 5.4.93.
4.   Child Support (Information, Evidence and Disclosure and Maintenance Arrangements and Jurisdiction) (Amendment) Regulations 2000 (SI 2001 No.161) regs 2 and 9 (come into force in relation to a particular case on the date on which paras 11(19) and (20) of Sch 3 of the Child Support, Pensions and Social Security Act 2000 come into force for the purpose of that type of case – which is March 3, 2003 for the types of cases in art 3 of SI 2003 No.192). For other types of cases see the '1993 rules', below. Transitional provisions mean that in certain circumstances these amendments are treated as not having been made. See reg 10 of SI 2001 No.161 for details (p674).

1993 rules

Regs 2 and 9 of the Child Support (Information, Evidence and Disclosure and Maintenance Arrangements and Jurisdiction) (Amendment) Regulations 2000 (SI 2001 No.161) amend this regulation and have been brought into force only for the types of cases in art 3 of the Child Support, Pensions and Social Security Act 2000 (Commencement No.12) Order 2003 (SI 2003 No.192) – see p683, subject to transitional provisions in reg 10 of SI 2001 No.161. For other types of cases the '1993 rules' apply. If the 1993 rules apply:
–   the word "assessment" is retained in place of "calculation";
–   the words "absent parent" are retained in place of "non-resident parent";
–   paragraph (1)(c) is not substituted and instead reads:

(c)   [²the Secretary of State] cancels that assessment on the grounds that it was made in error,

–   in paragraph (2)(aa) the words "is cancelled or" are retained before "ceases to have effect"; *and*
–   in paragraph (2), the words "as not having been cancelled or, as the case may be," are retained before "as not having ceased to have effect".

Definition

"maintenance order": see reg 1(2).

General Note

Paragraph (1)

This paragraph provides for a court order that was cancelled in error to be treated as having continuing effect. However, where the order has been properly cancelled in accordance with the relevant provisions, there is no power to reinstate it (*CSC 5/1995*, para 7).

[¹Maintenance calculations and maintenance orders – payments

8A.   Where–
(a)   a maintenance calculation has been made with respect to a qualifying child in response to an application made under section 4 or 7 of the Act;
(b)   at the time that maintenance calculation was made a maintenance order was in force with respect to that child;
(c)   the maintenance order has ceased to have effect by virtue of the provisions of regulation 3; and
(d)   the non-resident parent has made payments of maintenance due under that order after the date on which the maintenance calculation took effect [²...],

the payments made under the maintenance order shall be treated as payments of child support maintenance.]

Amendments

1.   Child Support (Miscellaneous Amendments) Regulations 2005 (SI 2005 No.785) reg 2 (comes into force on March 16, 2005 for cases for which March 3, 2003 was the day appointed for the coming into force of s1(2)(a) Child Support, Pensions and Social Security Act 2000; for other cases see '1993 rules' below, only comes into force on the day on which that provision comes into force in relation to that type of case).
2.   Child Support (Meaning of Child and New Calculation Rules) (Consequential and Miscellaneous Amendment) Regulations 2012 (SI 2012 No.2785) reg 5(4) (in force in relation to a particular case on the day on which paragraph 2 of Schedule 4 to the Child Maintenance and Other Payments Act 2008 (see p243) comes into force in relation to that type of case – which is December 10, 2012 in relation to the types of cases falling within art 3 of SI 2012 No.3042 (see p767). For other types of cases see '2003 rules' below.

2003 rules

Regulation 5(4) of The Child Support (Meaning of Child and New Calculation Rules) (Consequential and Miscellaneous Amendment) Regulations 2012 (SI 2012 No.2785) omitted the words "in accordance with regulation 26 of the Maintenance Calculation Procedure Regulations" from the end of regulation 8A(d). This amendment came into force on December 10, 2012, in relation to the types of cases falling within art 3 of SI 2012 No.3042 (see p767). For other types of cases the words are not omitted.

1993 rules

Regs 2 of the Child Support (Miscellaneous Amendments) Regulations 2005 (SI 2005 No.785) inserts regulation 8A and has come into force only for the types of cases for which s1(2)(a) of the Child Support, Pensions and Social Security Act 2000 has been brought into force – see reg 3 of the Child Support, Pensions and Social Security Act 2000 (Commencement No.12) Order 2003 (SI 2003 No.192) (p683). For other types of cases regulation 8A does not apply.

Definitions

"Maintenance Calculation Procedure Regulations": see reg 1(2).
"maintenance order": see reg 1(2).

[¹Cases in which application may be made under section 4 or 7 of the Act

9. The provisions of section 4(10) or 7(10) of the Act shall not apply to prevent an application being made under those sections after 22nd January 1996 where a decision has been made by the relevant court either that it has no power to vary or that it has no power to enforce a maintenance order in a particular case.]

Amendment

1. Reg 9 added by reg 14 of SI 1995 No.3261 as from 22.1.96.

Definitions

"the Act": see reg 1(2).
"maintenance order": see reg 1(2).

General Note

See the general note to s18 of the 1995 Act on p172.

The Child Maintenance (Written Agreements) Order 1993
(1993 No.620 (L.4))

1. This order may be cited as the Child Maintenance (Written Agreements) Order 1993 and shall come into force on 5th April 1993.

2. Section 8 shall not prevent a court from exercising any power which it has to make a maintenance order in relation to a child in any circumstances in which paragraphs (a) and (b) of section 8(5) apply.

General Note

This Order was made only by the Lord Chancellor. It applies to England and Wales. Equivalent provision is made for Scotland by the Child Support (Written Agreements) (Scotland) Order 1997.

The Child Support Appeals (Jurisdiction of Courts) Order 1993
(1993 No.961 (L.12))

General Note

The Child Support Appeals (Jurisdiction of Courts) Order 1993, to the extent that it applies to England and Wales, is revoked for certain cases only by the Child Support Appeals (Jurisdiction of Courts) Order 2002 (SI 2002 No.1915) art 2 (comes into force in relation to a particular type of case from the day on which s10 Child Support, Pensions and Social Security Act 2000 comes into force for the purposes of that type of case).

The Child Support Appeals (Jurisdiction of Courts) Order 1993, to the extent that it applies to Scotland, is revoked by Child Support Appeals (Jurisdiction of Courts) (Scotland) Order 2003 (SI 2003 No.96) art 6 (comes into force in relation to a particular type of case on the date on which s10 Child Support, Pensions and Social Security Act 2000 comes into force for the purposes of that type of case).

Section 10 of the Child Support, Pensions and Social Security Act 2000 came into force on March 3, 2003 for the types of cases detailed in art 3 Child Support, Pensions and Social Security Act 2000 (Commencement No.12) Order 2003 (SI 2003 No.192). For other types of cases the '1993 rules' which include the Child Support Appeals (Jurisdiction of Courts) Order 1993 continue to apply. The Child Support Appeals (Jurisdiction of Courts) Order 1993 is therefore reproduced below.

Title, commencement and interpretation

1.   This Order may be cited as the Child Support Appeals (Jurisdiction of Courts) Order 1993 and shall come into force on 5th April 1993.

2.   In this Order, "the Act" means the Child Support Act 1991.

Parentage appeals to be made to courts

3.   An appeal under section 20 of the Act shall be made to a court instead of to a child support appeal tribunal in the circumstances mentioned in article 4.

General Note

This Article has not been amended to reflect the transfer of decision-making.

---

4.   The circumstances are that—

(a)   the decision against which the appeal is brought was made on the basis that a particular person (whether the applicant or some other person) either was, or was not, a parent of a child in question, and

(b)   the ground of the appeal will be that the decision should not have been made on that basis.

General Note

For a commentary to this article, see art 4 of the Child Support Appeals (Jurisdiction of Courts) Order 2002 on p679.

5.–(1)   For the purposes of article 3 above, an appeal may be made to a court in Scotland if—

(a)   the child in question was born in Scotland; or

(b)   the child, the absent parent or the person with care of the child is domiciled in Scotland on the date when the appeal is made or is habitually resident in Scotland on that date.

(2)   Where an appeal to a court in Scotland is to be made to the sheriff, it shall be to the sheriff of the sheriffdom where—

(a)   the child in question was born; or

(b)   the child, the absent parent or the person with care of the child is habitually resident on the date when the appeal is made.

Modification of section 20(2) to (4) of the Act in relation to appeals to courts

6.   In relation to an appeal which is to be made to a court in accordance with this Order, the reference to the chairman of a child support appeal tribunal in section 20(2) of the Act shall be construed as a reference to the court.

7. In relation to an appeal which has been made to a court in accordance with this Order, the references to the tribunal in section 20(3) and (4) of the Act shall be construed as a reference to the court.

Amendment of the Law Reform (Parent and Child) (Scotland) Act 1986

8. In section 8 (Interpretation) of the Law Reform (Parent and Child) (Scotland) Act 1986 at the end of the definition of "action for declarator" there shall be inserted the words "but does not include an appeal under section 20 (Appeals) of the Child Support Act 1991 made to the court by virtue of an order made under section 45 (jurisdiction of courts in certain proceedings) of that Act.

The Child Support and Income Support (Amendment) Regulations 1995
(SI 1995/1045)

Citation, commencement and interpretation
1.–(1)   These Regulations may be cited as the Child Support and Income Support (Amendment) Regulations 1995.

(2)   This regulation and regulation 58 of these Regulations shall come into force on 13th April 1995 and all other regulations shall come into force on 18th April 1995.

(3)   In these Regulations–

[...]

"the Arrears Regulations" means the Child Support (Arrears, Interest and Adjustment of Maintenance Assessments) Regulations 1992;

[...]

"the Maintenance Assessment Procedure Regulations" means the Child Support (Maintenance Assessment Procedure) Regulations 1992;

[...]

Reviews consequent upon the amendments made by these regulations
63.–(1)   [¹Subject to paragraph (3), a decision with respect to a maintenance assessment in force on 13th April 1995 or 18th April 1995 shall not be superseded by a decision under section 17 of the Act if the difference between the amount of child support maintenance currently in force and the amount that would be fixed if the fresh assessment were to be made as a result of a supersession is–]

(a)   less than £1.00 per week where the amount fixed by the assessment currently in force is more than the amount that would be fixed by the fresh assessment; or

(b)   less than £10.00 per week in all other cases.

(2)   Paragraph (1) applies to the following provisions–

(a)   regulation 28(8);

(b)   regulation 43;

(c)   regulation 44(2);

(d)   regulation 45;

(e)   regulation 46(2)(d) and (e), (4) and (6);

(f)   regulation 47;

(g)   regulation 50;

(h)   regulations 51;

(i)   regulation 54(10) and (11).

(3)   Paragraph (1) shall not apply to a [¹decision under section 17 of the Child Support Act 1991 which falls to be made] in consequence only of the amendments made by regulations 44(2), 45, 46(2)(d) and (e) and 51 unless the person to whom the assessment relates [¹notified] the Secretary of State before 18th July 1995 that he wishes a child support officer to consider whether the assessment in his case should be reviewed; but the Secretary of State may accept a later notification for the purposes of this paragraph if he is satisfied that there is good cause for the delay in giving it.

(4)   [¹...]

(5)   [¹...]

(6)   Where a maintenance assessment is in force on 18th April 1995 and–

(a)   the relevant person notifies the Secretary of State on or after 18th July 1995 that he wishes [¹the question to be considered] of whether an amount should be allowed in the computation of the relevant person's exempt income or protected income in respect of travelling costs or his exempt income in respect of a qualifying transfer of property; and

(b)   the Secretary of State is not satisfied that there was good cause for the delay on the part of the relevant person in giving the notification, the effective date of any assessment made [¹by virtue of a decision under section 17 of the Act superseding an earlier decision] shall be the first day of the maintenance period in which the Secretary of State is so notified.

Amendment

1.   Social Security Act 1998 (Commencement No.7 and Consequential and Transitional Provisions) Order 1999 (SI 1999 No.1510) art 37 (June 1, 1999). Subject to transitional provisions contained in art 48 of SI 1999 No.1510.

Transitional provisions

64.–(1)   Where a maintenance assessment, other than an interim maintenance assessment, is in force on 18th April 1995 [¹and] the amount of child support payable under that assessment would be affected by the provisions of these Regulations, only the provisions mentioned in paragraph (2) and (3) shall apply to that assessment until that assessment is reviewed under Section 16, 17 or 18 of the Act.

(2)   The provisions of these Regulations to which paragraph (1) refers are–

(a)   regulation 34;

(b)   regulation 43;

(c)   regulation 46(6);

(d)   regulation 47;

(e)   regulation 50;

(f)   regulation 54(10) and (11);

(g)   [¹...]

(3)   The provisions of regulations 44(2), 45, 46(2)(d) and (e) and 51 and Schedules 1 and 2 to these Regulations shall not apply in a case where there is a maintenance assessment in force on the 18th April 1995 until [²a relevant person applies for a decision under section 17 of the Child Support Act 1991 superseding an earlier decision on the ground that a qualifying transfer of property has been made or that he has travelling costs.]

(4)   Where on 18th April 1995 in any particular case there is in force a maintenance assessment which is subject to an adjustment made under the provisions of regulation 10 of the Arrears Regulations as in force prior to that date that adjustment shall continue until whichever is the earlier of–

(a)   [²a decision under section 17 of the Child Support Act 1991 superseding a decision with respect to] that assessment on grounds other than the coming into force of these Regulations; or

[²(b)   a decision under regulation 13 or 16 of the Arrears Regulations is made on an application made by a relevant person.]

(5)   Regulations 12 and 13 shall not apply to a case in which there is an existing assessment until the Secretary of State first reviews the period by reference to which payments are to be made after these Regulations come into force.

Amendments

1.   Child Support (Miscellaneous Amendments) (No.2) Regulations 1995 (SI 1995 No.3261) reg 50 (January 22, 1996).

2.   Social Security Act 1998 (Commencement No.7 and Consequential and Transitional Provisions) Order 1999 (SI 1999 No.1510) art 38 (June 1, 1999). Subject to transitional provisions contained in art 48 of SI 1999 No.1510.

The Child Support (Miscellaneous Amendments) (No.2) Regulations 1995

(SI 1995 No.3261)

Citation, commencement and interpretation

1.–(1) These Regulations may be cited as the Child Support (Miscellaneous Amendments) (No. 2) Regulations 1995.

(2) This regulation, regulation 23, regulation 48 and regulation 56 of these Regulations shall come into force on 18th December 1995 and all other regulations shall come into force on 22nd January 1996.

(3) In these Regulations–

"the Arrears Regulations" means the Child Support (Arrears, Interest and Adjustment of Maintenance Assessments) Regulations 1992;

"the Child Support Amendment Regulations" means the Child Support and Income Support (Amendment) Regulations 1995;

"the Collection and Enforcement Regulations" means the Child Support (Collection and Enforcement) Regulations 1992;

"the Information, Evidence and Disclosure Regulations" means the Child Support (Information, Evidence and Disclosure) Regulations 1992

"the Maintenance Arrangements and Jurisdiction Regulations" means the Child Support (Maintenance Arrangements and Jurisdictions) Regulations 1992;

"the Maintenance Assessment Procedure Regulations" means the Child Support (Maintenance Assessment Procedure) Regulations 1992;

"the Maintenance Assessments and Special Cases Regulations" means the Child Support (Maintenance Assessments and Special Cases) Regulations 1992;

"the Miscellaneous Amendments Regulations" means the Child Support (Miscellaneous Amendments and Transitional Provisions) Regulations 1994;

"the Northern Ireland Regulations" means the Child Support (Northern Ireland Reciprocal Arrangements) Regulations 1993.

[¹Supersessions consequent on amendments made by these Regulations

56. Where a fresh assessments is made by virtue of a decision under section 17 of the Child Support Act 1991 superseding an earlier decision in consequence of the coming into force of regulations 48–

(a) the decision under section 17; and

(b) that fresh maintenance assessment,

shall have effect as from the first day of the maintenance period following 18th December 1995.]

Amendment

1. Reg 56 substituted by art 39 of SI 1999 No.1510 as from 1.6.99.

Transitional and consequential provisions

57.–[¹(1) A decision with respect to a maintenance assessment shall not be superseded by a decision under section 17 of the Child Support Act 1991 solely to give effect to the provisions set out in paragraph (2).]

(2) The provisions referred to in paragraph (1) are–

(a) regulation 40(3);

(b) regulation 42;

(c) regulation 43(3);

(d) head (v) of sub-paragraph (a) of paragraph (2) of regulation 11 of the Maintenance Assessments and Special Cases Regulations as inserted by regulation 43(5) of these Regulations;

(e) regulation 46; and

(f) regulation 47.

(3)   [¹Where a decision is made under section 17 of the Child Support Act 1991 superseding an earlier decision] is carried out wholly or partly in consequence of one or more of the provisions set out in [²regulation 40, 42, 43(3) or (5), 46, 47 or 49], and the amount of any fresh assessment made following that review is different from the amount of any fresh assessment that would have been made had those provisions not been in force, the effective date of that fresh assessment shall not be earlier than 22nd January 1996.

[³]

Amendments
1.   Substituted by art 40 of SI 1999 No.1510 as from 1.6.99.
2.   Substituted in by reg 4 of SI 1995 No.3265 as from 22.1.96.
3.   Omitted by art 40 of SI 1999 No.1510 as from 1.6.99.

Definitions
"Maintenance Assessment Procedure Regulations": see reg 1(3).
"Maintenance Assessments and Special Cases Regulations": see reg 1(3).

General Note
Paragraphs (2) and (3)
The provisions specified in these paragraphs amend the Maintenance Assessments and Special Cases Regulations.

The Child Support (Maintenance Assessments and Special Cases) and Social Security (Claims and Payments) Amendment Regulations 1996

(SI 1996 No.481)

Citation, commencement and interpretation

1.–(1) These Regulations may be cited as the Child Support (Maintenance Assessments and Special Cases) and Social Security (Claims and Payments) Amendments Regulations 1996 and shall come into force on 8th April 1996.

(2) In these Regulations–

"the Act" means the Child Support Act 1991;

[...]

Transitional provisions

4. A maintenance assessment in force on 8th April 1996 shall not be reviewed solely to give effect to regulation 3 but, on a review of that assessment under section 16, 17 or 18 of the Act, the provisions of that regulation shall have effect from the effective date of any fresh maintenance assessment made following that review.

General Note

This regulation applies only to amendments made by reg 3 which amends paras 19(1) and 20(1) of Sch 2 to the Maintenance Assessments and Special Cases Regulations (now revoked). It does not apply to amendments made by reg 2 which amends reg 13 of those regulations. It applies only to reviews under ss16, 17 and 18, but not to reviews under s19.

The Child Benefit, Child Support and Social Security (Miscellaneous Amendments) Regulations 1996

(SI 1996 No.1893)

Citation, commencement and interpretation

1.–(1) These Regulations may be cited as the Child Benefit, Child Support and Social Security (Miscellaneous Amendments) Regulations 1996 and shall come into force–

...

(b) for the purposes of regulations 2 to 21 and 37 to 49, on 7th April 1997;

...

General Note

The relevant amendments were made to the Maintenance Assessments and Special Cases Regulations by regs 7-17. Regulation 49 deals with decisions giving effect to the changes and is set out below.

Transitional provision relating to maintenance assessments

[¹**49.**–(1) A decision with respect to a maintenance assessment in force on 7th April 1997 shall not be superseded by a decision under section 17 of the Child Support Act 1991 ("the Act") solely to give effect to these Regulations.

(2) These Regulations shall apply to a fresh maintenance assessment made by virtue of–

(a) a revision under section 16 of the Act of a decision with respect to a maintenance assessment; or

(b) a decision under section 17 of the Act which supersedes a decision with respect to a maintenance assessment, as from the effective date of that revision under section 16 of the Act or, as the case may be, decision under section 17 of the Act.]

Amendment

1.   Article 42 of the Commencement No.7 Order 1999 (June 1, 1999).

The Child Support (Miscellaneous Amendments) Regulations 1996
(SI 1996 No.1945)

Citation, commencement and interpretation

1.–(1) These Regulations may be cited as the Child Support (Miscellaneous Amendments) Regulations 1996.

(2) *[Omitted]*

(3) In these Regulations–

[...]

"the Maintenance Assessment Procedure Regulations" means the Child Support (Maintenance Assessment Procedure) Regulations 1992;

"the Maintenance Assessments and Special Cases Regulations" means the Child Support (Maintenance Assessments and Special Cases) Regulations 1992.

[...]

Transitional provisions

25.–(1) The provisions of regulation 33 of the Maintenance Assessment Procedure Regulations in force prior to 5th August 1996 shall continue to apply to any application made prior to that date.

(2) The provisions of regulation 35 of the Maintenance Assessment Procedure Regulations in force prior to 7th October 1996 shall continue to apply to any case where the failure to comply referred to in paragraph (1) of that regulation arose prior to that date.

(3) The provisions of regulation 36 of the Maintenance Assessment Procedure Regulations in force prior to 7th October 1996 shall [[1]apply with the amendments made by regulation 5(6) of the Social Security and Child Support (Jobseeker's Allowance) (Consequential Amendments) Regulations 1996] to a parent in respect of whom a reduced benefit direction was given prior to that date.

(4) The provisions of regulation 47 of the Maintenance Assessment Procedure Regulations in force prior to 7th October 1996 shall [[2]apply with the amendments made by regulation 5(1 1) of the Social Security and Child Support (Jobseeker's Allowance) (Consequential Amendments) Regulations 1996] to any reduced benefit direction made prior to that date, and in relation to an earlier direction referred to in paragraph (4) of that regulation, which was in force prior to that date, whether or not the further direction referred to in that paragraph was made after that date.

(5) The provisions of regulation 19 of the Maintenance Assessments and Special Cases Regulations in force prior to 7th October 1996 shall continue to apply to any application made prior to that date [[3]and a decision with respect to a maintenance assessment in force on that date shall not be superseded by a decision under section 17 of the Child Support Act 1991 solely to give effect to the provisions of regulation 19 as amended by regulation 23.]

Amendments
1. Words in reg 25(3) substituted by reg 3(2) of SI 1996/2378 as from 7.10.96.
2. Words in reg 25(4) substituted by reg 3(3) of SI 1996/2378 as from 7.10.96.
3. Words in para (5) substituted by art 43 of SI 1999/1510 as from 1.6.99.

Definitions
"the Maintenance Assessment Procedure Regulations": see reg 1(3).
"the Maintenance Assessments and Special Cases Procedure Regulations": see reg 1(3).

The Child Support Departure Direction and Consequential Amendments Regulations 1996
(1996 No.2907)

General Note on the Regulations

These Regulations have been revoked,for particular cases only, by:

(1)   the Child Support (Variations) Regulations 2000 (SI 2001 No.156) reg 33 (this revocation comes into force in relation to a particular case on the date on which s5 Child Support, Pensions and Social Security Act 2000 comes into force in relation to that type of case, which is March 3, 2003 for the cases detailed in art 3 Child Support, Pensions and Social Security Act 2000 (Commencement No.12) Order 2003 (SI 2003 No.192), see p683). See reg 30 of SI 2001 No.156, on p646, for savings provisions.

(2)   the Child Support (Meaning of Child and New Calculation Rules) (Consequential and Miscellaneous Amendment) Regulations 2012 (SI 2012 No.2785) reg 10 (this revocation comes into force in relation to a particular case on the day on which paragraph 2 of Schedule 4 to the Child Maintenance and Other Payments Act 2008 (see p243) comes into force in relation to that type of case – which is December 10, 2012, only in relation to the types of cases falling within art 3 of SI 2012 No.3042 (see p767).

For other types of cases the '1993 rules' which include the Child Support Departure Direction and Consequential Amendments Regulations 1996, continue to apply. The Child Support Departure Direction and Consequential Amendments Regulations 1996 are therefore reproduced below.

PART I
General

Citation, commencement and interpretation

1.–(1)   These Regulations may be cited as the Child Support Departure Direction and Consequential Amendments Regulations 1996 and shall come into force on 2nd December 1996.

(2)   In these Regulations, unless the context otherwise requires–

"the Act" means the Child Support Act 1991;

"the Appeal Regulations" means the Child Support Appeal Tribunals (Procedure) Regulations 1992;

"applicant" has the same meaning as in Schedule 4B to the Act;

"application" means [¹except in regulations 32A to 32G] an application for a departure direction;

"Arrears Regulations" means the Child Support (Arrears, Interest and Adjustment of Maintenance Assessments) Regulations 1992;

[⁷[⁸...]]

"Contributions and Benefits Act" means the Social Security Contributions and Benefits Act 1992;

"Departure Direction Anticipatory Application Regulations" means the Child Support Departure Direction (Anticipatory Application) Regulations 1996;

"departure direction application form" means the form provided by the Secretary of State in accordance with regulation 4(1);

[² [⁴"designated authority" means–
   (a)   the Secretary of State;
   (b)   a person providing services to the Secretary of State;
   (c)   a local authority; or
   (d)   a person providing services to, or authorised to exercise any functions of, any such authority;].]

"effective date" in relation to a departure direction means the date on which that direction takes effect;

[⁵"income-related employment and support allowance" means an income-related allowance under Part 1 of the Welfare Reform Act 2007 (employment and support allowance);]

"Information, Evidence and Disclosure Regulations" means the Child Support (Information, Evidence and Disclosure) Regulations 1992;

"Maintenance Arrangements and Jurisdiction Regulations" means the Child Support (Maintenance Arrangement and Jurisdiction) Regulations 1992;

"Maintenance Assessment Procedure Regulations" means the Child Support (Maintenance Assessment Procedure) Regulations 1992;

"Maintenance Assessments and Special Cases Regulations" means the Child Support (Maintenance Assessments and Special Cases) Regulations 1992;

"maintenance period" has the same meaning as in regulation 33 of the Maintenance Assessment Procedure Regulations;

"non-applicant" means–

(a) where the application has been made by a person with care, the absent parent;

(b) where the application has been made by an absent parent, the person with care;

"official error" means an error made by–

(a) an officer of the Department of Social Security acting as such which no person outside the Department caused or to which no person outside the Department materially contributed;

[³(b) a person employed by a designated authority acting on behalf of the authority, which no person outside that authority caused or to which no person outside that authority materially contributed,

but excludes any error of law which is only shown to have been an error by virtue of a subsequent decision of [⁶ the Upper Tribunal] or the court;]

"partner" has the same meaning as in paragraph (2) of regulation 1 of the Maintenance Assessments and Special Cases Regulation;

"relevant person" means–

(a) an absent parent, or a person who is treated as an absent parent under regulation 20 of the Maintenance Assessments and Special Cases regulations (persons treated as absent parents), whose liability under a maintenance assessment may be effected by any departure direction given following an application;

(b) a person with care, or a child to whom section 7 of the Act applies, where the amount of child support maintenance payable under a maintenance assessment relevant to that person with care or that child may be effected by any departure direction given following an application [⁹;

"relevant universal credit" means, in relation to an absent parent or parent with care, an award of universal credit made to the parent in question, where the award is calculated on the basis that the parent does not have any earned income;

"universal credit" means universal credit under Part 1 of the Welfare Reform Act 2012].

[⁹(2A) For the purposes of the definition of *"relevant universal credit"* in paragraph (2), *"earned income"* has the meaning given in regulation 52 of the Universal Credit Regulations 2013.]

(3) In these Regulations unless the context otherwise requires, a reference–

(a) to the Schedule, is to the Schedule to these Regulations;

(b) to a numbered regulation is to the regulation in these Regulations bearing that number;

(c) in a regulation or the Schedule to a numbered paragraph is to the paragraph in that regulation or the Schedule bearing that number;

(d) in a paragraph to a lettered or numbered sub-paragraph is to the sub-paragraph in that paragraph bearing that letter or number.

Amendments

1. *Child Support (Miscellaneous Amendments) (No.2) Regulations 1999 (SI 1999 No.1047) reg 34(a)-(b) (June 1, 1999).*

2. *Social Security (Work-focused Interviews) Regulations 2000 (SI 2000 No.897) reg 9 (April 3, 2000).*

3. *Social Security and Child Support (Miscellaneous Amendments) Regulations 2000 (SI 2000 No.1596) reg 10 (June 19, 2000).*

4. *Social Security (Jobcentre Plus Interviews) Regulations 2002 (SI 2002 No.1703) Sch 2 para 5 (September 30, 2002).*

5. *Employment and Support Allowance (Consequential Provisions) (No.2) Regulations 2008 (SI 2008 No.1554) reg 60(2) (October 27, 2008).*

6. *Tribunals, Courts and Enforcement Act 2007 (Transitional and Consequential Provisions) Order 2008 (SI 2008 No.2683) Sch 1 para 75 (November 3, 2008).*

7.   *Child Support (Miscellaneous and Consequential Amendments) Regulations 2009 (SI 2009 No.736) reg 2(2) (April 6, 2009).*
8.   *Public Bodies (Child Maintenance and Enforcement Commission: Abolition and Transfer of Functions) Order 2012 (SI 2012 No.2007) art 3(2) and Sch para 112(a) (August 1, 2012).*
9.   *Universal Credit (Consequential, Supplementary, Incidental and Miscellaneous Provisions) Regulations 2013 (SI 2013 No.630) reg 42(2) (April 29, 2013).*

Documents

2.–*(1)   Except where express provision is made to the contrary, where, under any provision of these Regulations–*

(a)   *any document is given or sent to the Secretary of State, that document shall, subject to paragraph (2), be treated as having been so given or sent on the date it is received by the Secretary of State; and*

(b)   *any document is given or sent to any other person, that document shall,*

if sent by post to that person's last known or notified address, and subject to paragraph (3), be treated as having been given or sent on the second day after the day of posting, excluding any Sunday or any day which is a Bank Holiday in England, Wales, Scotland or Northern Ireland under the Banking and Financial Dealings Act 1971.

(2)   The Secretary of State may treat any document given or sent to him as given or sent on such day, earlier than the day it was received by him, as he may determine, if he is satisfied that there was unavoidable delay in his receiving the document in question.

(3)   Where, by any provision of these Regulations, and in relation to a particular application, notice or notification–

(a)   *more than one document is required to be given or sent to a person, and more than one such document is sent by post to that person but not all the documents are posted on the same day;*

(b)   *documents are required to be given or sent to more than one person, and not all such documents are posted on the same day, all those documents shall be treated as having been posted on the later or, as the case may be, the latest day of posting.*

Determination of amounts

3.–*(1)   Where any amount is required to be determined for the purposes of these Regulations, it shall be determined as a weekly amount and, except where the context otherwise requires, any reference to such an amount shall be construed accordingly.*

(2)   Where any calculation made under these Regulations results in a fraction of a penny that fraction shall be treated as a penny if it is either one half or exceeds one half and shall be otherwise disregarded.

PART II
Procedure on an application for a departure direction and preliminary consideration

Application for a departure direction

4.–*(1)   Every application shall be made in writing on a form (a "departure direction application form") provided by the Secretary of State, or in such other manner, being in writing, as the Secretary of State may accept as sufficient in the circumstances of any particular case.*

(2)   Departure direction application forms shall be supplied without charge by such persons as the Secretary of States authorises for that purpose.

(3)   Every application shall be given or sent to the Secretary of State or to such persons as he may authorise for that purpose.

(4)   Where an application is defective at the date when it is received, or has been made in writing but not on the departure direction application form provided by the Secretary of State, the Secretary of State may refer that application to the person who made it or, as the case may be, supply him with a departure direction application form.

(5)   In a case to which paragraph (4) applies, if the departure direction application form is received by the Secretary of State properly completed–

(a) within the specified period he shall treat the application as if it had been duly made in the first instance;

(b) outside the specified period, unless he is satisfied that the delay has been unavoidable, he shall treat the application as a fresh application made on the date upon which the properly completed departure direction application form was received.

(6) An application which is made on a departure direction application form is, for the purposes of paragraph (5), properly completed if completed in accordance with the instructions on the form and defective if not so completed.

(7) In a case to which paragraph (4) applies, the specified period for the purposes of paragraph (5) shall be the period of 14 days commencing with the date upon which, in accordance with paragraph (4), the application is referred to the person who made the defective application or a departure direction application form is given or sent to the person who made a written application but not on a departure direction application form.

(8) For the purposes of paragraph (7), the provisions of regulation 2 shall apply to an application referred to in paragraph (4).

(9) A person applying for a departure direction may authorise a representative, whether or not legally qualified, to receive notices and other documents on his behalf, and act on his behalf in relation to an application.

(10) Where a person has, under paragraph (9), authorised a representative who is not legally qualified, he shall confirm that authorisation in writing, or as otherwise required,to the Secretary of State, unless such authorisation has been approved by the Secretary of State under regulation 53 of the Maintenance Assessment Procedure Regulation (authorisation of representative).

[¹]

Amendment

1.   *Child Support (Miscellaneous Amendments) (No.2) Regulations 1999 (SI 1999 No.1047) reg 35 (June 1, 1999).*

Amendment or withdrawal of application

5.   A person who has made an application may amend or withdraw his application by notice in writing to the Secretary of State at any time prior to a determination being made in relation to that application.

Provision of information

6.–*(1)*   Where an application has been made, the Secretary of State may request further information or evidence from the applicant to enable that application to be determined.

(2)   Any information or evidence requested by the Secretary of State in accordance with paragraph (1) shall be given within [¹one month, or such longer period as the Secretary of State is satisfied is reasonable in the circumstances of the case] of the request for such information or evidence having been given or sent.

(3)   Where the time limit specified in paragraph (2) is not complied with, the Secretary of State may determine that application, in the absence of that information or evidence.

Amendment

1.   *Child Support (Miscellaneous Amendments) (No.2) Regulations 1999 (SI 1999 No.1047) reg 36 (June 1, 1999).*

Rejection of application on completion of a preliminary consideration

7.–*(1)*   The Secretary of State may, on completing a preliminary consideration of an application, reject that application on the ground set out in section 28B (2)(b) of the Act if it appears to him that the difference between the current amount and the revised amount is less than £1.00.

(2)   *Where an application has been rejected in accordance with paragraph (1), the Secretary of State shall, as soon as reasonably practicable, given notice of that rejection to the relevant persons.*

Procedure in relation to the determination of an application

8.–(1)   *Subject to paragraph (4), where an application has not failed within the meaning of section 28D of the Act, the Secretary of State shall [1,unless he is satisfied on the information or evidence available to him that a departure direction is unlikely to be given]*

(a)   *give notice of that application to the relevant persons other than the applicant;*

(b)   *send to them details of the grounds on which the application has been made and any relevant information or evidence the applicant has given, except details, information or evidence falling within paragraph (2);*

(c)   *invite representations in writing from the relevant persons other than the applicant on any matter relating to that application; and*

(d)   *set out the provisions of paragraph (2), (5) and (6) in relation to such representations.*

(2)   *The details, information or evidence referred to in paragraph (1)(b), (6) and (7) are–*

(a)   *medical evidence or medical advice that has not been disclosed to the applicant or a relevant person and which the Secretary of State considers would be harmful to the health of the applicant or that relevant person if disclosed to him;*

(b)   *the address of a relevant person, or of any child in relation to whom the assessment was made in respect of which the application has been made, or any other information which could reasonably be expected to lead to that person or that child being located, where that person has not agreed to disclosure of that address or that information, it is not known to the other party to that assessment and–*

(i)   *the Secretary of State is satisfied that that address or that information is not necessary for the determination of that application; or*

(ii)   *the Secretary of State is satisfied that that address or that information is necessary for the determination of that application and that there would be a risk of harm or undue distress to that person or that child if disclosure were made.*

(3)   *Subject to paragraph (4), the notice referred to in paragraph (1)(a) shall be given as soon as reasonably practicable after–*

(a)   *completion of the preliminary consideration of that application under section 28B of the Act; or*

(b)   *where the Secretary of State has requested information or evidence under regulation 6, receipt of that information or the expiry of the period of 14 days, referred to in regulation 6(2).*

(4)   *The provisions of paragraphs (1) and (3) shall not apply where information or evidence requested in accordance with regulation 6 has not been received by the Secretary of State within the period specified in paragraph (2) of that regulation and the Secretary of State is satisfied on the information or evidence available to him that a departure direction should not be given.*

[2(4A)   *Where the provisions of paragraph (1) have not been complied with because the Secretary of State was satisfied on the information or evidence available to him that a departure direction was unlikely to be given, but on further consideration of the application he is minded to give a departure direction in that case, he shall, before doing so, comply with the provisions of this regulation.]*

(5)   *Where the Secretary of State does not receive written representations from a relevant person within 14 days of the date on which representations were invited under paragraph (1), (6) or (7) he may, in the absence of written representations from that person, proceed to determine the application·*

(6)   *The Secretary of State may, if he considers it reasonable to do so, send to the applicant a copy of any written representations made following an invitation under*

paragraph (1)(c), whether or not they were received within the time specified in paragraph (5) except to the extent that the representations contain information or evidence which falls within paragraph (2), and invite him to submit representations in writing on any matters contained in those representations.

(7) Where any information or evidence requested by the Secretary of State under regulation 6 is received after notification has been given under paragraph (1), the Secretary of State may, if he considers it reasonable to do so and except where that information or evidence falls within paragraph (2), send a copy of such information or evidence to the relevant persons and invite them to submit representations in writing on that information or evidence.

[³]

(9) Where the Secretary of State has determined an application he shall, as soon as is reasonably practicable–

(a) notify the relevant persons of that determination;

(b) where a departure direction has been given, refer the case to a child support officer.

(10) A notification under paragraph (9)(a) shall set out–

(a) the reasons for that determination;

(b) where a departure direction has been given, the basis on which the amount of child support maintenance is to be fixed by any assessment made in consequence of that direction.

[⁴...]

Amendments

1. *Child Support (Miscellaneous Amendments) Regulations 1998 (SI 1998 No.58) reg 7(2) (January 19, 1998).*

2. *Child Support (Miscellaneous Amendments) Regulations 1998 (SI 1998 No.58) reg 7(3) (January 19, 1998).*

3. *Social Security and Child Support (Miscellaneous Amendments) Regulations 2000 (SI 2000 No.1596) reg 11 (June 19, 2000).*

4. *Child Support (Miscellaneous Amendments) (No.2) Regulations 1999 (SI 1999 No.1047) reg 37(d) (June 1, 1999).*

[¹Procedure in relation to determination of an application for a revision or a supersession of a decision with respect to a departure direction

8A.–(1) Subject to the modifications described in paragraph (2), regulation 8 shall apply to any application for a revision or a supersession of a decision with respect to a departure direction as it applies to an application for a departure direction.

(2) The modifications described in this paragraph are–

(a) for paragraph (1) there shall be substituted the following paragraphs–

"(1) Except where paragraph (1A) applies, the Secretary of State shall–

(a) give notice of an application for a revision or a supersession of a decision with respect to a departure direction to the relevant persons other than the applicant;

(b) inform them of the grounds on which the application has been made and any relevant information or evidence the application has given, except details, information or evidence falling within paragraph (2);

(c) invite representations from the relevant persons other than the applicant on any matter relating to that application; and

(d) explain the provisions of paragraph (2), (5) and (6) in relation to such representations.

(1A) This paragraph applies where an application for a revision or a supersession has been made and the Secretary of State is satisfied on the information or evidence available to him that either–

(a) a revision or supersession of a departure direction is unlikely to be made; or

(b) in a case where the applicant was the applicant for the decision which is to be revised or superseded, a ground on which the decision to be revised or superseded was made no longer applies."

(b) paragraphs (3), (4) and (7) shall be omitted;

(c)   in paragraph (4A) for the words from "that a departure direction" to the words "in that case" there shall be substituted the words "that decision revising or superseding a decision with respect to a departure direction was unlikely to be made, but on further consideration of the application he is minded to make such a decision";

(d)   in paragraph (5)–
  (i)   for words "(1), (6) or (7)" there shall be substituted the words "(1) or (6)";
  (ii)   after the word "application" there shall be added the words "for a decision revising or superseding a decision";

(e)   in paragraph (8)–
  (i)   for the words "In deciding whether to give a departure direction" there shall be substituted the words "Before deciding whether or not to make a decision revising or, as the case may be, superseding a decision as to a departure direction in consequence of an application for such a decision"; and
  (ii)   in sub-paragraph (a), for the words "by the application for that direction" there shall be substituted the words "in connection with the application";

(f)   for paragraphs (9) and (10) there shall be substituted the following paragraph–
"(9)   Where the Secretary of State has determined an application made for the purpose of revising or superseding a decision he shall, as soon as is reasonably practicable, notify the relevant persons of–
(a)   that determination;
(b)   the reasons for it; and
(c)   where appropriate, the basis on which the amount of child support maintenance is to be fixed by any fresh assessment made in consequence of that determination.'']

Amendment

1.   *Child Support (Miscellaneous Amendments)(No.2) Regulations 1999 (SI 1999 No.1047) reg 38 (June 1, 1999).*

[¹*Departure directions and persons in receipt of income support[⁵, state pension credit] [⁶, income-related employment and support allowance,] income-based jobseeker's allowance [⁷universal credit] [⁴or working tax credit]*

9.–(1)   The costs referred to in regulation 13 to 18 shall not constitute special expenses where they are or were incurred–

(a)   by an absent parent to or in respect of whom income support[⁵, state pension credit] [⁶, income-related employment and support allowance] [⁷, income-based jobseeker's allowance or relevant universal credit] is or was in payment at the date on which any departure direction given in response to that application would take effect;

(b)   by a person with care to or in respect of whom income support[⁵, state pension credit][⁶, income-related employment and support allowance], income-based jobseeker's allowance [⁴[⁷, working tax credit or relevant universal credit]] is or was in payment at the date on which any departure direction given in response to that application would take effect; or

(c)   by a person with care where, at the date on which any departure direction given in response to that application would take effect, income support[⁵, state pension credit][⁶, income-related employment and support allowance] [⁷, income-based jobseeker's allowance or relevant universal credit] is or was in payment to or in respect of the absent parent of the child or children in relation to whom the maintenance assessment in question is made.

(2)   A transfer shall not constitute a transfer of property for the purposes of paragraph 3(1)(b) or 4(1)(b) of Schedule 4B to the Act, or of regulations 21 and 22, where the application is made–

(a)   by an absent parent to or in respect of whom income support[⁵, state pension credit][⁶, income-related employment and support allowance] [⁷, income-based *jobseeker's allowance or relevant universal credit] is or was in payment at the date on which any departure direction given in response to that application would take effect;*

(b)   *by a person with care and, at the date on which any departure direction given in response to that application would take effect, income support[⁵, state pension credit][⁶, income-related employment and support allowance] [⁷, income-based jobseeker's allowance or relevant universal credit], is or was in payment to or in respect of the absent parent of the child or children in relation to whom the maintenance assessment in question is made.*

(3)   A case shall not constitute a case under regulations 23 to 29 where the application is made–

(a)   *by an absent parent to or in respect of whom income support[⁵, state pension credit][⁶, income-related employment and support allowance] [⁷, income-based jobseeker's allowance or relevant universal credit] is or was in payment at the date on which any departure direction given in response to that application would take effect;*

(b)   *by an absent parent where, at the date on which any departure direction given in response to that application would take effect, income support[⁵, state pension credit][⁶, income-related employment and support allowance], income-based jobseeker's allowance [⁴[⁷, working tax credit or relevant universal credit]] is or was in payment to or in respect of the person with care of the child or children in relation to whom the maintenance assessment in question is made;*

(c)   *by a person with care where, at the date on which any departure direction given in response to that application would take effect, income support[⁵, state pension credit][⁶, income-related employment and support allowance] [⁷, income-based jobseeker's allowance or relevant universal credit] is or was in payment to or in respect of the absent parent of the child or children in relation to whom the maintenance assessment is made.]*

Amendments

1.   *Child Support (Miscellaneous Amendments) Regulations 1998 (SI 1998 No.58) reg 8 (January 19, 1998).*

2.   *Social Security and Child Support (Tax Credits) Consequential Amendments Regulations 1999 (SI 1999 No.2566) Sch 2 parts I & II (October 5, 1999).*

3.   *Social Security and Child Support (Tax Credits) Consequential Amendments Regulations 1999 (SI 1999 No.2566) Sch 2 parts I & II (October 5, 1999).*

4.   *Child Support (Miscellaneous Amendments) Regulations 2003 (SI 2003 No.328) reg 4(2) (April 6, 2003).*

5.   *Child Support (Miscellaneous Amendments) (No.2) Regulations 2003 (SI 2003 No.2779) reg 2 (November 5, 2003).*

6.   *Employment and Support Allowance (Consequential Provisions) (No.2) Regulations 2008 (SI 2008 No.1554) reg 60(3) (October 27, 2008).*

7.   *Universal Credit (Consequential, Supplementary, Incidental and Miscellaneous Provisions) Regulations 2013 (SI 2013 No.630) reg 42(3) (April 29, 2013).*

Departure directions and interim maintenance assessments

10.–*(1)   For the purposes of section 28A(1) of the Act, the term "maintenance assessment" does not include–*

(a)   *a Category A or Category C interim maintenance assessment;*

(b)   *a Category B interim maintenance assessment where the application is made under paragraph 2 of Schedule 4B to the Act in respect of expenses prescribed by regulation 18 and that Category B interim maintenance assessment was made because the application fell within paragraph (3)(b) of regulation 8 of the Maintenance Assessment Procedure Regulations;*

(c)   *a Category D interim maintenance assessment, where the application is made under paragraph 3 or 4 of Schedule 4B to the Act or by an absent parent under paragraph 2 or 5 of that Schedule.*

(2)   For the purposes of this regulation, Category A, Category B, Category C and Category D interim maintenance assessments are defined in regulation 8(3) of the Maintenance Assessment Procedure Regulations (categories of interim maintenance assessment).

11. *[¹...]*

Amendment

1.   *Child Support (Miscellaneous Amendments) (No.2) Regulations 1999 (SI 1999 No.1047) reg 39 (June 1, 1999).*

Meaning of "current assessment" for the purposes of the Act

[¹11A.   Where–
(a)   an application under section 28A of the Act has been made in respect of a current assessment; and
(b)   after the making of that application, a fresh maintenance assessment has been made upon a revision of a decision as to a maintenance assessment under section 16 of the Act,
references to the current assessment in sections 28B(3), 28C(2)(a) and 28F(5) of, and in paragraphs 8 of Schedule 4A and paragraphs 2, 3 and 4 of Schedule 4B to, the Act shall have effect as if they were references to the fresh maintenance assessment.]

Amendment

1.   *Child Support (Miscellaneous Amendments) (No.2) Regulations 1999 (SI 1999 No.1047) reg 40 (June 1, 1999).*

Meaning of "benefit" for the purposes of section 28E of the Act

12.   For the purposes of section 28E of the Act, "benefit" means income support [³, state pension credit], income-based jobseeker's allowance[⁴, income-related employment and support allowance,] [¹[²working tax credit]] [⁵and housing benefit][⁶and relevant universal credit] .

Amendments

1.   *Social Security and Child Support (Tax Credits) Consequential Amendments Regulations 1999 (SI 1999 No.2566) Sch 2 parts I & II (October 5, 1999).*
2.   *Child Support (Miscellaneous Amendments) Regulations 2003 (SI 2003 No.328) reg 4(3) (April 6, 2003).*
3.   *Child Support (Miscellaneous Amendments) (No. 2) Regulations 2003 (SI 2003 No.2779) reg 2 (November 5, 2003).*
4.   *Employment and Support Allowance (Consequential Provisions) (No.2) Regulations 2008 (SI 2008 No.1554) reg 60(4) (October 27, 2008).*
5.   *Council Tax Benefit Abolition (Consequential Provision) Regulations 2013 (SI 2013 No.458) reg 4 and Sch 2 para 4 (April 1, 2013).*
6.   *Universal Credit (Consequential, Supplementary, Incidental and Miscellaneous Provisions) Regulations 2013 (SI 2013 No. 630) reg 42(4) (April 29, 2013).*

PART III
Special expenses

Costs incurred in travelling to work

13.–(1)   Subject to paragraphs (2) and (3), the following costs shall constitute expenses for the purposes of paragraph 2(2) of Schedule 4B to the Act where they are incurred by the applicant for the purposes of travel between his home and his normal place of work–
(a)   the cost of purchasing a ticket for such travel;
(b)   the cost of purchasing fuel, where such travel is by a vehicle which is not carrying fare-paying passengers; or
(c)   in exceptional circumstances, the taxi fare for a journey which must unavoidably be undertaken during hours when no other reasonable mode of travel is available,
and any minor incidental costs, such as tolls or fees for the use of a particular road or bridge incurred in connection with such travel.
(2)   Where the Secretary of State considers any costs referred to in paragraph (1) to be unreasonably high or to have been unreasonably incurred he may substitute such lower amount as he considers reasonable, including a nil amount.

(3)   Costs which can be set off against the income of the applicant under the Income and Corporation Taxes Act 1988 shall not constitute expenses for the purposes of paragraph (1).

Contacts costs

14.–(1)   Where at the time a departure direction is applied for a set pattern has been established as to frequency of contact between the absent parent and a child in respect of whom the current assessment was made, the following costs, based upon that pattern and incurred by the absent parent for the purpose of maintaining contact with that child, shall subject to paragraphs (2) to (6), constitute expenses for the purposes of paragraph 2(2) of Schedule 4B to the Act–

(a)   the costs of purchasing a ticket for travel for the purpose of maintaining that contact;

(b)   the cost of purchasing fuel, where travel is for the purpose of maintaining that contact and is by a vehicle which is not carrying fare-paying passengers; or

(c)   the taxi fare for a journey or part of a journey to maintain that contact where the Secretary of State is satisfied that the disability of the absent parent makes it impracticable to use any other form of transport which might otherwise have been available to him.

and any minor incidental costs, such as toll or fees for the use of a particular road or bridge, incurred in connection with such travel.

(2)   Subject to paragraph (3), where the Secretary of State considers any costs referred to in paragraph (1) to be unreasonably high or to have been unreasonably incurred he may substitute such lower amount as he considers reasonable, including a nil amount.

(3)   Any lower amount substituted by the Secretary of State under paragraph (2) shall not be so low as to make it impossible, in the Secretary of State's opinion, for contact to be maintained at the frequency specified in any court order made in respect of the absent parent and the child mentioned in paragraph (1) where the absent parent is maintaining contact at that frequency.

(4)   Paragraph (1) shall not apply where regulation 20 of the Maintenance Assessments and Special Cases Regulations (persons treated as absent parents) applies to the applicant.

(5)   Where sub-paragraph (c) of paragraph (1) applies and the applicant has, at the date an application is made, received, or at the date is in receipt of, financial assistance from any source to meet, wholly or in part, costs of maintaining contact with the child who is referred to in paragraph (1), which arise wholly from his disability and which are in excess of the costs which would be incurred if that disability did not exist, only the net amount of the costs referred to in that sub-paragraph, after the deduction of the financial assistance, shall constitute special expenses for the purposes of paragraph 2(2) of Schedule 4B to the Act.

(6)   For the purposes of this regulation, a person is disabled if he is blind, deaf or dumb or is substantially or permanently handicapped by illness, injury, mental disorder or congenital deformity.

(7)   Where, at the time a departure direction is applied for, no set pattern has been established as to frequency of contact between the absent parent and a child in respect of whom the current assessment was made, but the Secretary of State is satisfied that that absent parent and the person with care of that child have agreed upon a pattern of contact for the future, the costs mentioned in paragraph (1) and which are based upon that intended pattern of contact shall constitute expenses for the purposes of paragraph 2(2) of Schedule 4B to the Act, and paragraphs (2) to (6) shall apply to that application.

[¹(8)   This regulation shall apply in relation to an application made for the purpose of superseding a decision with respect to a departure direction as though–

(a)   for the words "at the time a departure direction is applied for" in paragraphs (1) and (7) there were substituted the words "at the time an application is made for a decision with respect to a departure direction";

(b)   in paragraph (5), after the words "an application" there were inserted the words "for the supersession of a decision with respect to a departure direction.]

Amendment

1.   *Child Support (Miscellaneous Amendments) (No.2) Regulations 1999 (SI 1999 No.1047) reg 41 (June 1, 1999).*

Illness or disability

15.–(1)   Subject to paragraphs (2) to (4), the costs being met by the applicant in respect of the items listed in sub-paragraphs (a) to (m), which arise from long-term illness or disability of that applicant or a dependant of that applicant and which are in excess of the costs which would be incurred if that illness or disability did not exist shall constitute special expenses for the purposes of paragraph 2(2) of Schedule 4B to the Act–

(a)   personal care and attendance;

(b)   personal communication needs;

(c)   mobility;

(d)   domestic help;

(e)   medical aids where these cannot be provided under the health service;

(f)   heating;

(g)   clothing;

(h)   laundry requirements;

(i)   payments for food essential to comply with a debt recommended by a medical practitioner;

(j)   adaptations required to the applicant's home;

(k)   day care;

(l)   rehabilitation; or

(m)   respite care

(2)   Where the Secretary of State considers any costs referred to in paragraph (1) to be unreasonably high or to have been unreasonably incurred he may substitute such lower amount as he considers reasonable, including a nil amount.

(3)   [¹ Subject to paragraph (4A),] where

(a)   an applicant or his dependant has, at the date an application is made, received,or at that date is in receipt of, financial assistance from any source in respect of his long-term illness or disability or that of his dependant; or

(b)   that applicant or his dependant is adjudged eligible for [⁵a disability benefit] referred to in paragraph (4),

only the net amount of the costs incurred in respect of the items listed in paragraph (1),after the deduction of the financial assistance referred to in sub-paragraph (a) and,where applicable, [⁵the disability benefit] referred to in sub-paragraph (b) shall constitute special expenses for the purposes of paragraph 2(2) of Schedule 4B to the Act.

[⁵(4)   Subject to paragraph (4A), where the Secretary of State considers that a person who has made an application in respect of special expenses falling within paragraph (1) or his dependant may be entitled to a disability benefit–

(a)   if that applicant or his dependant has at the date of that application, or within a period of six weeks beginning with the giving or sending to that person of notification of the possibility of entitlement to a disability benefit, applied for a disability benefit, the application made by that applicant shall not be determined until a decision has been made by the Secretary of State on the eligibility for that disability benefit of that applicant or that dependant;

(b)   if that applicant or his dependant has failed to apply for a disability benefit within the six week period specified in sub-paragraph (a), the Secretary of State shall determine the application for a departure direction made by that applicant on the basis that that applicant has income equivalent to the highest rate prescribed in respect of that disability benefit by or under those sections.]

[⁴[⁵(4A)   Paragraphs (3) and (4) do not apply where the dependant of an applicant is adjudged eligible for a disability benefit and in all the circumstances of the case the Secretary of State considers that the costs being met by the applicant in respect of the items listed in paragraph (1) shall constitute special expenses for the purposes of paragraph 2(2) of Schedule 4B to the Act without the deductions in paragraph (3) being made.]]

(5)   For the purposes of this regulation, a dependant of an applicant shall be–

(a)   where the applicant is an absent parent–

(i)   the partner of that absent parent;

(ii)   any child of whom that absent parent or his partner is a parent and who lives with them; or

(b)   where the applicant is a parent with care–

(i)   the partner of that parent with care;

(ii)   any child of whom that parent with care or her partner is a parent and who lives with them, except any child in respect of whom the absent parent against whom the current assessment is made is the parent.

(6)   For the purposes of this regulation–

(a)   a person is disabled if he is blind, deaf or dumb or is substantially or permanently handicapped by illness, injury, mental disorder or congenital deformity;

(b)   "long-term illness" means an illness from which the applicant or his dependant is suffering at the date of the application and which is likely to last for at least 52 weeks from the date or if likely to be shorter than 52 weeks, for the rest of the life of that applicant or his dependant;

(c)   "the health service" has the same meaning as in section 128 of the National Health Service Act 1977 or in section 108(1) of the National Health Service (Scotland) Act 1978.

[5(d)   "disability benefit" means disability living allowance under section 71 of the Contributions and Benefits Act, personal independence payment under Part 4 of the Welfare Reform Act 2012 [6, armed forces independence payment under the Armed Forces and Reserve Forces (Compensation Scheme) Order 2011] or attendance allowance under section 64 of the Contributions and Benefits Act.]

Amendments

1.   Child Support (Miscellaneous Amendments) Regulations 1998 (SI 1998 No.58) reg 11(2) (January 19, 1998).

2.   Child Support (Miscellaneous Amendments) Regulations 1998 (SI 1998 No.58) reg 11(2) (January 19, 1998).

3.   Child Support (Miscellaneous Amendments) (No. 2) Regulations 1999 (SI 1999 No.1047) reg 42 (June 1, 1999).

4.   Child Support (Miscellaneous Amendments) Regulations 1998 (SI 1998 No.58) reg 11(3) (January 19, 1998).

5.   Personal Independence Payment (Supplementary Provisions and Consequential Amendments) Regulations 2013 (SI 2013 No.388) reg 8 and Sch para 19 (April 8, 2013).

6.   Armed Forces and Reserve Forces Compensation Scheme (Consequential Provisions: Subordinate Legislation) Order 2013 (SI 2013 No.591) reg 7 and Sch para 13 (April 8, 2013).

Debts incurred before the absent parent became an absent parent

16.–(1)   Subject to paragraphs (2) to (4), repayments of debts incurred–

(a)   for the joint benefit of the applicant and non-applicant parent;

(b)   for the benefit of the non-applicant parent where the applicant remains legally liable to repay the whole or part of that debt;

(c)   for the benefit of any person who at the time the debt was incurred–

(i)   was a child;

(ii)   lived with the applicant and non-applicant parent; and

(iii) of whom the applicant or the non-applicant parent is the parent, or both are the parents; or

(d)   for the benefit of any child with respect to whom the current assessment was made,

shall constitute expenses for the purposes of paragraph 2(2) of Schedule 4B to the Act where those debts were incurred before the absent parent became an absent parent in relation to a child with respect to whom the current assessment was made and at a time when the applicant and non-applicant parent were [1a couple] who were living together.

(2)   Paragraph (1) shall not apply to repayment of–

(a)   a debt which would otherwise fall within paragraph (1) where the applicant has retained for his own use and benefit the asset the purchase of which incurred the debt;

(b)   a debt incurred for the purposes of any trade or business;

(c)   a gambling debt;

(d)   a fine imposed on the applicant;

[¹(e)   unpaid legal costs in respect of–

(i)   separation or divorce from the non-applicant parent;

(ii)   separation from the non-applicant parent or the dissolution of a civil partnership that had been formed with the non-applicant parent;]

(f)   amounts due after use of a credit card;

(g)   a debt incurred by the applicant to pay any of the items listed in sub-paragraphs (c) to (f) and (j);

(h)   amounts payable by the applicant under a mortgage or loan taken out on the security of any property except where that mortgage or loan was taken out to facilitate the purchase of, or to pay for repairs or improvements to, any property which is the home of the parent with care and any child in respect of whom the current assessment was made;

(i)   amounts payable by the applicant in respect of a policy of insurance of a kind referred to in paragraph 3(4) or (5) of Schedule 3 to the Maintenance Assessment and Special Cares Regulations (eligible housing costs) except where that policy of insurance was obtained or retained to discharge a mortgage or charge taken out to facilitate the purchase of, or to pay for repairs or improvements to, any property which is the home of the parent with care and any child in respect of whom the current assessment was made;

(j)   a bank overdraft except where the overdraft was, at the time it was taken out, agreed to be for a specified amount repayable over a specified period;

(k)   a loan obtained by the applicant, other than a loan obtained from a qualifying lender or the applicant's current or former employer;

(l)   a debt in respect of which a departure direction has already been given and which has not been repaid during the period for which that direction was in force except where the maintenance assessment in respect of which that direction was given was cancelled or ceased to have effect and, during the period for which that direction was in force, a further maintenance assessment was made in respect of the same applicant, non-applicant and qualifying child with respect to whom the earlier assessment was made; or

(m)   any other debt which the Secretary of State is satisfied it is reasonable to exclude.

(3)   Except where the payment is of an amount which is payable under a mortgage or loan, or in respect of a policy of insurance, which falls within the exception set out in sub-paragraph (h) or (i) of paragraph (2), repayment of a debt shall not constitute expenses for the purposes of paragraph (1) where the secretary of State is satisfied that the applicant has taken responsibility for repayment of that debt, as, or as part of, a financial settlement with the non-applicant parent or by virtue of a court order.

(4)   Where an applicant has incurred a debt partly to repay a debt or debts repayment of which would have fallen within paragraph (1), the repayment of that part of the debt incurred which is referable to the debts repayment of which would have fallen within that paragraph shall constitute expenses for the purposes of paragraph 2(2) of Schedule 4B to the Act.

(5)   For the purposes of this regulation–

(a)   [¹"couple"] has the meaning set out in regulation 1 of the Maintenance Assessments and Special Cases Regulations;

(b)   "non-applicant parent" means–

(i)   where the applicant is the person with care, the absent parent;

  (ii) where the applicant is the absent parent, the partner of that absent parent at the time the debt in respect of which the application is made was entered into;

(c) "qualifying lender" has the meaning given to it in section 376(4) of the Income and Corporation Taxes Act 1988;

(d) "repairs and improvements" means major repairs necessary to maintain the fabric of the home and any of the measures set out in sub-paragraphs (a) to (j) of paragraph 2 of Schedule 3 to the Maintenance Assessments and Special Cases Regulations (eligible housing costs) and other improvements which the Secretary of State considers reasonable in the circumstances where those measures or other improvements are undertaken with the a view to improving fitness for occupation of the home.

Amendment

1. Civil Partnership (Pensions, Social Security and Child Support) (Consequential, etc Provisions) Order 2005 (SI 2005 No.2877) art 2(4) and Sch 4 para 6 (December 5, 2005).

Pre-1993 financial commitments

17.–(1) A financial commitment entered into by an absent parent before 5th April 1993, except any commitment of a kind listed in paragraph (2)(b) to (g) and (j) of regulation 16 or which has been wholly or partly taken into account in the calculation of a maintenance assessment shall constitute expenses for the purposes of paragraph 2(2) of Schedule 4B to the Act where–

(a) there was in force on 5th April 1993 and at the date that commitment was entered into [¹ a maintenance order or a written] maintenance agreement made before 5th April 1993 in respect of that absent parent and every child in respect of whom, before that date, he was, or was found, or adjudged to be,the parent; [²...]

[³ (aa) at least one of the children referred to in sub-paragraph (a) is a child in respect of whom the current assessment was made; and]

(b) the Secretary of State is satisfied that it is impossible for the absent parent to withdraw from that commitment or unreasonable to except him to do so.

(2) [⁴...]

Amendments

1. Child Support (Miscellaneous Amendments) Regulations 1998 (SI 1998 No.58) reg 12(2)(a) (January 19, 1998).

2. Child Support (Miscellaneous Amendments) Regulations 1998 (SI 1998 No.58) reg 12(2)(a) (January 19, 1998).

3. Child Support (Miscellaneous Amendments) Regulations 1998 (SI 1998 No.58) reg 12(2)(b) (January 19, 1998).

4. Child Support (Miscellaneous Amendments) Regulations 1998 (SI 1998 No.58) reg 12(3) (January 19, 1998).

Costs incurred in supporting certain children

18.–(1) The costs incurred by a parent in supporting a child who is not his child but who is part of his family [¹ and who was, at the date on which any departure direction given in response to an application under this regulation would take effect, living in the same household as the parent] (a "relevant child") shall constitute special expenses for the purposes of paragraph 2(2) of Schedule 4B to the Act if the conditions set out in paragraph (2) are satisfied and shall, if those conditions are satisfied, equal the amount specified in paragraph (3).

(2) The conditions referred to in paragraph (1) are–

[²(a) the child became a relevant child prior to 5th April 1993 and has remained a relevant child for the whole of the period from that date to the date on which any departure direction given in response to an application under this regulation would take effect;]

[³(b) subject to paragraph (7)–

   (i)   *the liability of the absent parent of a relevant child to pay maintenance to or for the benefit of that child under a maintenance order, a written maintenance agreement or a maintenance assessment; or*

   (ii)   *any deduction from benefit under section 43 of the Act in place of payment of child support maintenance to or for the benefit of that child, is less than the amount specified in paragraph (4), or there is no such liability or deduction; and]*

  (c)   *the net income of the parent's current partner where the relevant child is the child of that partner, calculated in accordance with paragraph (6) ("the partner's outgoings").*

  (3)   *[⁴Subject to paragraph (7A),] the amount referred to in paragraph (1) constituting special expenses for a case falling within this regulation is the difference between the amount specified in paragraph (4) and, subject to paragraph (7), the liability of the absent parent of a relevant child to pay maintenance of a kind mentioned in paragraph (2)(b)[⁴ ((i) or any deduction from benefit mentioned in paragraph 2(b)(ii)] , and if there is no such liability [⁴or deduction] is the amount specified in paragraph (4).*

  (4)   *[⁵Subject to paragraphs (4A) and (4B),] the amount referred to in paragraphs (2)(b) and (3) is the aggregate of–*

  (a)   *an amount in respect of each relevant child equal to the personal allowance for that child specified in column (2) of paragraph 2 of the relevant Schedule (income support personal allowance);*

  (b)   *if the conditions set out in paragraph 14(b) and (c) [⁶of] that Schedule (income support disabled child premium) are satisfied in respect of a relevant child, an amount equal to the amount specified in column (2) of paragraph 15(6) of that Schedule in respect of each such child [⁶and];*

  [⁷(c) except where the family includes other children of the parent, an amount equal to the income support family premium specified in paragraph 3(1)(b) of that Schedule that would be payable if the parent were a claimant.]

  (d)   *[⁸...]*

[⁹(4A)   Where day to day care of the relevant child is shared between the current partner of the person making an application under this regulation and the other parent of that child, the amounts referred to in paragraph (4) shall be reduced by the proportion of those amounts which is the same as the proportion of the week in respect of which the child is not living in the same household as the applicant.

  (4B)   *Where an application under paragraph (1) is made in respect of more than one relevant child and the family does not include any other children of the parent, the amount applicable under sub-paragraph (c) of paragraph (4) in respect of each relevant child shall be calculated by dividing the amount referred to in that sub-paragraph by the number of relevant children in respect of whom that application is made.]*

  (5)   *For the purposes of paragraph (2)(c), the net income of the parent's partner shall be the aggregate of–*

  (a)   *the income of that partner, calculated in accordance with regulation 7(1) of the Maintenance Assessments and Special Cases Regulations (but excluding the amount mentioned in sub-paragraph (d) of that regulation) as if that partner were an absent parent to whom that regulation applied;*

  (b)   *the child benefit payable in respect of each relevant child; and*

  (c)   *any income, other than earnings, in excess of £10.00 per week in respect of each relevant child.*

  (6)   *For the purposes of paragraph (2)(c), a current partner's outings shall be the aggregate of–*

  (a)   *an amount equal to the amount specified in column (2) of paragraph 1(1)(e) of the relevant Schedule (income support personal allowance for a single claimant aged not less than 25);*

  (b)   *where departure direction has already been given in a case falling within regulation 27 in respect of the housing costs any attributable to the partner, the amount determined in accordance with regulation 40(7) as the housing costs the partner is able to contribute;*

(c)   the amount of any reduction in the parent's exempt income, calculated under paragraph (1) of regulation 9 the Maintenance Assessment and Special Cases Regulations, in consequence of the application of paragraph (2) of that regulation; and

(d)   the amount specified in paragraph (3) [¹⁰ or the aggregate of those amounts where paragraph (7A) applies to that partner.]

(7)   The Secretary of State may, if he is satisfied that is appropriate in the particular circumstances of the case, treat a liability of a kind mentioned in paragraph (2)(b) [¹¹ (i)] as not constituting a liability for the purposes of that paragraph and of paragraph (3).

[¹² (7A)   Where an application is made in respect of relevant children of different parents, a separate calculation shall be made in accordance with paragraphs (3) and (4) in respect of each relevant child or group of relevant children who have the same parents and the amount constituting special expenses referred to in paragraph (1) shall be the aggregate of the amounts calculated in accordance with paragraph (3) in respect of each such relevant child or group of relevant children.]

(8)   For the purposes of this regulation–

[¹³(a) a child who is not the child of a particular person is a part of that person's family where–

(i)   that child is the child of a current partner of that person; or

(ii)   that child is the child of a former partner of that person and lives in the same household as the applicant for every night of each week;]

(b)   "relevant Schedule" means Schedule 2 to the Income Support (General) Regulations 1987;

[¹⁴(c) where a person has made an election under section 13A(1) of the Social Security Administration Act 1992 (election not to receive child benefit) for payments of child benefit not to be made, the amount of child benefit that would be otherwise paid in respect of the relevant child is to be treated as being payable.]

Amendments

1.   *Child Support (Miscellaneous Amendments) Regulations 1998 (SI 1998 No.58) reg 13(2) (January 19, 1998).*

2.   *Child Support (Miscellaneous Amendments) Regulations 1998 (SI 1998 No.58) reg 13(3)(a) (January 19, 1998).*

3.   *Child Support (Miscellaneous Amendments) Regulations 1998 (SI 1998 No.58) reg 13(3)(b) (January 19, 1998).*

4.   *Child Support (Miscellaneous Amendments) Regulations 1998 (SI 1998 No.58) reg 13(4) (January 19, 1998).*

5.   *Child Support (Miscellaneous Amendments) Regulations 1998 (SI 1998 No.58) reg 13(5)(a) and (b) (January 19, 1998).*

6.   *Child Support (Miscellaneous Amendments) Regulations 1998 (SI 1998 No.58) reg 13(5)(b) (January 19, 1998).*

7.   *Child Support (Miscellaneous Amendments) Regulations 1998 (SI 1998 No.58) reg 14 (April 6, 1998).*

8.   *Child Support (Miscellaneous Amendments) Regulations 1998 (SI 1998 No.58) reg 13(5)(d) (January 19, 1998).*

9.   *Child Support (Miscellaneous Amendments) Regulations 1998 (SI 1998 No.58) reg 13(6) (January 19, 1998).*

10.   *Child Support (Miscellaneous Amendments) Regulations 1998 (SI 1998 No.58) reg 13(7) (January 19, 1998).*

11.   *Child Support (Miscellaneous Amendments) Regulations 1998 (SI 1998 No.58) reg 13(8) (January 19, 1998).*

12.   *Child Support (Miscellaneous Amendments) Regulations 1998 (SI 1998 No.58) reg 13(9) (January 19, 1998).*

13.   *Child Support (Miscellaneous Amendments) Regulations 1998 (SI 1998 No.58) reg 13(10) (January 19, 1998).*

14.   *Child Support (Miscellaneous Amendments) Regulations 2013 (SI 2013 No.1517) reg 5 (September 30, 2013).*

Special expenses for a case falling within regulation 13, 14, 16, or 17

19.–*(1)   This regulation applies where the expenses of an application fall within one or more of the descriptions of expenses falling within regulation 13 (travel to work costs),*

14 (contact costs), 16 (debts incurred before the absent parent became an absent parent) or 17 (pre-1993 financial commitments).

(2)   Special expenses for the purposes of paragraph 2(2) of Schedule 4B to the Act in respect of the expenses mentioned in paragraph (1) shall be–

(a)   where the expenses fall within only one description of expenses, those expenses in excess of £15.00;

(b)   where the expenses fall within more than one description of expenses, the aggregate of those expenses in excess of £15.00.

Application for a departure direction in respect of special expenses other than those with respect to which a direction has already been given

20.   Where a departure direction with respect to special expenses falling within one or more of the descriptions of expenses falling within regulation 13, 14, 16 or 17 has already been given and an application with respect to special expenses falling within one or more of those descriptions of expenses is made where none of those expenses are ones with respect to which the earlier direction has been given, the expenses with respect to which any later direction is given shall be the expenses, determined in accordance with regulation 13, 14, 16 or 17, as the case may be, with respect to which the later application is made, and the provisions of regulation 19 shall not apply.

PART IV
Property or capital transfers

Prescriptions of certain terms for the purposes of paragraph 3 and 4 of Schedule 4B to the Act

21.–(1)   For the purposes of paragraph 3(1)(a) and 4(1)(a) of Schedule 4B to the Act–

(a)   a court order means an order made–

(i)   under one or more of the enactments listed in or prescribed under section 8(11) of the Act; and

(ii)   in connection with transfer of property of a kind defined in paragraph (2);

(b)   an agreement means a written agreement made in connection with the transfer of property of a kind defined in paragraph (2).

(2)   Subject to paragraphs (3) to (5), for the purposes of paragraph 3(1)(b) and 4(1)(b) of Schedule 4B to the Act, a transfer of property is a transfer by the absent parent of his beneficial interest in any asset to the person with care, to a child in respect of whom the current assessment was made, or to trustees where the object or one of the objects of the trust is the provision of maintenance.

(3)   Where a transfer of property would not originally have fallen within paragraph (2) but the Secretary of State is satisfied that some or all of the amount of that property transferred was subsequently transferred to the person currently with care of a child in respect of whom the current assessment was made, the transfer of that property to the person currently with care shall count as a transfer of property for the purposes of paragraph 3(1)(b) and 4(1)(b) of Schedule 4B to the Act.

(4)   Where, if the Act had been in force at the time a transfer of property falling within paragraph (2) was made, the person who, at the time the application is made is the person with care would have been the absent parent and the person who, at the time the application is made is the absent parent would have been the person with care, that transfer shall not count as a transfer of property for the purposes of this regulation.

(5)   For, the purposes of paragraph 3(3) of Schedule 4B to the Act, the effect of a transfer of property is properly reflected in the current assessment if–

(a)   the amount of child support maintenance payable under any fresh maintenance assessment which would be made in consequence of a departure direction differs from the amount of child support maintenance payable under that current assessment by less than £1.00; or

(b)   *the transfer referred to in paragraph (2) was for a specified period only and that period ended before the effective date of any departure direction which would otherwise have been given.*

Value of a transfer of property and its equivalent weekly value for a case falling within paragraph 3 of Schedule 4B to the Act

22.–*(1)   Where the conditions specified in paragraph 3(1) of Schedule 4B to the Act are satisfied, the value of a transfer of property for the purposes of that paragraph shall be that part of the transfer made by the absent parent (making allowances for any transfer by the person with care to the absent parent) which the Secretary of State is satisfied is in lieu of [¹ periodical payments of] maintenance.*

(2)   The Secretary of State shall, in determining the value of a transfer of property in accordance with paragraph (1), assume that, unless evidence to the contrary is provided to him–

(a)   *the person with care and the absent parent had equal beneficial interests in the assets in relation to which the court order or agreement was made;*

(b)   *where the person with care was married to the absent parent, one half of the value of the transfer was a transfer for the benefit of the person with care; and*

(c)   *where the person with care has never been married to the absent parent, none of the value of the transfer was a transfer for the benefit of the person with care.*

(3)   The equivalent weekly value of a transfer of property shall be determined in accordance with the provisions of the Schedule.

(4)   For the purposes of regulation 21 and this regulation, the term "maintenance" means the normal day-to-day living expenses of the child with respect to whom the current assessment was made.

Amendments

1.   *Child Support (Miscellaneous Amendments) Regulations 1998 (SI 1998 No.58) reg 15 (January 19, 1998).*

PART V
Additional cases

Assets capable of producing income or higher income

23.–*(1)   Subject to paragraphs (2) and (3), a case shall constitute a case for the purposes of paragraph 5(1) of Schedule 4B to the Act where–*

(a)   *the Secretary of State is satisfied that any asset in which the non- applicant has a beneficial interest, or which he has the ability to control–*

    (i)   *is capable of being utilised to produce income but has not been so utilised;*

    (ii) *has been invested in such a way that the income obtained from it is less than might reasonably be expected;*

    (iii) *is a chose in action which has not been enforced where the Secretary of State is satisfied that such enforcement would be reasonable;*

    (iv) *in Scotland, is monies due or an obligation owed whether immediately payable or otherwise and whether the payment or obligation is secured or not and the Secretary of State is satisfied that requiring payment of the monies or the implementation of the obligation would be reasonable; or*

    (v) *has not been sold where the Secretary of State is satisfied that the sale of the asset would be reasonable;*

(b)   *any asset has been transferred by the non-applicant to trustees and the non-applicant is a beneficiary of the trust so created; or*

(c)   *any asset has become subject to a trust created by legal implication of which the non-application is a beneficiary.*

(2)   Paragraph (1) shall not apply where–

(a)   *the total value of the asset or assets referred to in that paragraph does not exceed £10,000.00 after deductions of the amount owing under any mortgage or charge on that asset; or*

(b) the Secretary of State is satisfied that any asset referred to in that paragraph is being retained by the non-applicant to be used for a purpose which the Secretary of State considers reasonable in all the circumstances of the case[²; or

(c) if the non-applicant were a claimant, paragraph 64 of Schedule 10 to the Income Support (General) Regulations 1987 (treatment of relevant trust payments) would apply to the asset referred to in that paragraph.]

(3) [¹]

(4) For the purpose of this regulation the term "asset" means–

(a) money, whether in cash or on deposit;

(b) a beneficial interest in land and rights in or over land;

(c) shares as defined in section 744 of the Companies Act 1985, stock and unit trusts as defined in section 6 of the Charging Orders Act 1979 gilt edged securities as defined in paragraph 1 of Schedule 2 to the Capital Gains Tax Act 1979, and other similar financial instruments.

(5) For the purposes of paragraph (4) the term "asset" includes any asset falling within that paragraph which is located outside Great Britain.

Amendments

1. Child Support (Miscellaneous Amendments) Regulations 1998 (SI 1998 No.58) reg 16 (January 19, 1998).

2. Child Support (Miscellaneous Amendments) Regulations 2002 (SI 2002 No.1204) reg 3 (April 30, 2002).

Diversion of income

[¹**24.**–(1) A case shall constitute a case for the purposes of paragraph 5(1) of Schedule 4B to the Act where–

(a) the non-applicant ("A") has the ability to control the amount of income that–

(i) A receives, or

(ii) is taken into account as A's assessable income,

including earnings from employment or self-employment and dividends from shares, whether or not the whole of that income is derived from the company or business from which those earnings are derived; and

(b) the [²Secretary of State] is satisfied that A has unreasonably reduced the amount of A's income which would otherwise fall to be taken into account under regulation 7 or 8 of the Maintenance Assessments and Special Cases Regulations by diverting it to other persons or for purposes other than the provision of such income for A.

(2) In this regulation "assessable income" means the amount calculated in accordance with paragraph 5(1) to (3) of Schedule 1 to the Act and regulations made for the purposes of that paragraph.]

Amendments

1. Child Support (Miscellaneous and Consequential Amendments) Regulations 2009 (SI 2009 No.736) reg 2(3) (April 6, 2009).

2. Public Bodies (Child Maintenance and Enforcement Commission: Abolition and Transfer of Functions) Order 2012 (SI 2012 No.2007) art 3(2) and Sch para 112(b) (August 1, 2012).

Life-style inconsistent with declared income

25.–(1) Subject to paragraph (2), a case shall constitute a case for the purposes of paragraph 5(1) of Schedule 4B to the Act where the Secretary of State is satisfied that the current [¹] assessment is based upon a level of income of the non-applicant which is substantially lower than the level of income required to support the overall life-style of that non-applicant.

[²(2) Paragraph (1) shall not apply where the Secretary of State is satisfied that the life-style of the non-applicant is paid for–

(a) out of capital belonging to him; or

(b) by his partner, unless the non-applicant is able to influence or control the amount of income received by that partner.]

(3)   Where the Secretary of State is satisfied in a particular case that the provisions of paragraph (1) would apply but for the provisions of paragraph [³ (2)(b)] , he may, whether or not any application on that ground has been made, consider whether the case falls within regulation 27.

Amendments

1.   *Child Support (Miscellaneous Amendments) Regulations 1998 (SI 1998 No.58) reg 17(2) (January 19, 1998).*

2.   *Child Support (Miscellaneous Amendments) Regulations 1998 (SI 1998 No.58) reg 17(3) (January 19, 1998).*

3.   *Child Support (Miscellaneous Amendments) Regulations 1998 (SI 1998 No.58) reg 17(4) (January 19, 1998).*

Unreasonably high housing costs

26.   A case shall constitute a case as for the purposes of paragraph 5(1) of Schedule 4 to the Act where–

(a)   the housing costs of the non-applicant exceed the limits set out in paragraph (1) of regulation 18 of the Maintenance Assessment and Special Cases Regulations (excessive housing costs);

(b)   the non-applicant falls within paragraph (2) of that regulation or would fall within that paragraph if it applied to parents with care; and

(c)   the Secretary of State is satisfied that the housing costs of the non-applicant are substantially higher than is necessary taking into account any special circumstances applicable to that non-applicant.

Partner's contribution to housing costs

27.   A case shall constitute a case for the purposes of paragraph 5(1) of Schedule 4B to the Act where a partner of the non-applicant occupies the home with him and the Secretary of State considers that it is reasonable for that partner to contribute to the payment of the housing costs of the non-applicant.

Unreasonably high travel costs

28.   A case shall constitute a case for the purposes of paragraph 5(1) of Schedule 4B to the Act where an amount in respect of travel to work costs has been included in the calculation of exempt income of the non-applicant under regulation 9(1) of the Maintenance Assessments and Special Cases Regulations(exempt income; calculation or estimation of E) or, as the case may be, under regulation 10 of those Regulations (exempt income: calculation or estimation of F) applying regulation 9(1)(i), and the Secretary of State is satisfied that, is all the circumstances of the case, that amount is unreasonably high.

Travel costs to be disregarded

29.   A case shall constitute a case for the purposes of paragraph 5(1) of Schedule 4B to the Act where

(a)   an amount in respect of travel to work costs has, in the calculation of a maintenance assessment, been included in the calculation of the exempt income of the non-applicant under regulation 9(1)(i) of the Maintenance Assessment and Special Cases Regulations or, as the case may be, under regulation 10 of those Regulations applying regulation 9(1)(i); and

(b)   the Secretary of State is satisfied that the non-applicant has sufficient income remaining after the deduction of the amount that would be payable under that assessment, had the amount referred to in sub-paragraph (a) not been included in its calculation, for it to be inappropriate for all or part of that amount to be included in the exempt income of the non-applicant.

PART VI

Factors to be taken into account for the purposes of section 28f of the Act

Factors to be taken into account and not to be taken into account in determining whether it would be just and equitable to give a departure direction

30.–(1)   The factors to be taken into account in determining whether it would be just and equitable to give a departure direction in any case shall include–

(a)   *where the application is made on any ground–*

    (i)   *whether, in the opinion of the Secretary of State, the giving of a departure direction would be likely to result in a relevant person ceasing paid employment;*

    (ii)   *if the applicant is the absent parent, the extent, if any, of his liability to pay child maintenance under a court order or other agreement in the period prior to the effective date of the maintenance assessment;*

(b)   *where an application is made on the ground that the case falls within regulations 13 to 20 (special expenses), whether, in the opinion of the Secretary of State–*

    (i)   *the financial arrangements made by the applicant could have been such as to enable the whole or part of the expenses cited to be paid without a departure direction being given;*

    (ii)   *the applicant has at his disposal financial resources which are currently utilised for the payment of expenses other than those arising from essential everyday requirements and which could be used to pay the whole or part of the expenses cited.*

(2)   The following factors are not to be taken into account in determining whether it would be just and equitable to give a departure direction in any case–

(a)   *the fact that the conception of a child in respect of whom the current assessment was made was not planned by one or both of the parents;*

(b)   *whether the parent with care or the absent parent was responsible for the breakdown of the relationship between them;*

(c)   *the fact that the parent with care or the absent parent has formed a new relationship with a person who is not a parent of the child in respect of whom the current assessment was made;*

(d)   *the existence of particular arrangements for contact with the child in respect of whom the current assessment was made, including whether any arrangements made are being adhered to by the parents;*

(e)   *the failure by an absent parent to make payments under a maintenance order, a written maintenance agreements, or a maintenance assessment.*

(f)   *representations made by persons other than the relevant persons.*

PART VII

Effective date and duration of a departure direction

Refusal to give a departure direction under section 28F(4) of the Act

31.   The Secretary of State shall not give a departure direction in accordance with section 28F of the Act if he is satisfied that the difference between the current amount and revised amount is less than £1.00.

Effective date of a departure direction

32.–(1)   Where an application is made on the grounds set out in section 28A(2)(a) of the Act (the effect of the current assessment) and that application is given or sent within [¹one month] of the date of notification of the current assessment (whether or not that assessment has been made following an interim maintenance assessment), a departure direction given in response to that application shall take effect–

(a)   *where it is given on grounds that relate to the whole of the period between the effective date of the current assessment and the date on which that assessment and the date on which that assessment is made, on the effective date of that assessment;*

(b)   *in a case not falling within sub-paragraph (a) on the first day of the maintenance period following the date upon which the circumstances giving rise to that application first arose.*

(2)   *Where an application is made on the grounds set out in set 28A(2)(a) of the Act (the effect of the current assessment) and that application is given or sent later than ['one month] after the date of notification of the current assessment (whether or not that assessment has been made following an interim maintenance assessment)–*

(a)   *subject to sub-paragraph (b), a departure direction given in response to that application shall take effect on the first day of the maintenance period during which that application is received;*

(b)   *where the Secretary of State is satisfied that there was unavoidable delay, he may, for purposes of determining the date on which a departure direction takes effect, treat the application as if it were given or sent within ['one month] of the date of notification of the current assessment.*

(3)   *The provisions of paragraph (1) and (2) are subject to the provisions of [²paragraphs (3A) and (6)] and of regulations 47 to 50.*

[³ *(3A)*   [⁴*Subject to paragraph (3B), where] an application is determined in accordance with regulation 14 and is one to which paragraph (7) of that regulation applies, a departure direction given in response to that application shall take effect–*

(a)   *from the first day of the maintenance period immediately following the date on which the absent parent and the parent with care have agreed the pattern of contact for the future is to commence; or*

(b)   *where no such date has been so agreed, from the first day of the maintenance period immediately following the date upon which the departure direction is given.]*

[⁴*(3B)*   *For the purposes of paragraph (3A), paragraph (8) of regulation 14 shall not apply.]*

(4)   *Subject to paragraph (6), where an application for a departure is made on the grounds set out in section 28A(2)(b) of the Act (a material change in the circumstances of the case since the current assessment was made), any departure direction given shall take effect on the first day of the maintenance period during which the application was received.*

(5)   *An application may be made on the grounds set out in section 28A(2)(b) of the Act only if the material change in the circumstances on which it is based has already occurred.*

(6)   *Where–*

(a)   *an application has been determined in accordance with regulation 15(4)(b);*

(b)   *a subsequent application is made with respect to special expenses falling within regulation 15(1) each of which is an expense in respect of which the earlier application was made; and*

(c)   *the Secretary of State is satisfied that there was a good cause for the applicant or his dependant not applying for disability living allowance or, as the case may be, attendance allowance within the six week period specified in regulation 15(4)(a),*

any departure direction given in response to the later application shall take effect from the date that the earlier direction had effect, or would have had effect if an earlier direction had been given.

[⁵*...]*

Amendments

1.   *Child Support (Miscellaneous Amendments) Regulations 1998 (SI 1998 No.58) reg 18(2) (January 19, 1998).*

2.   *Child Support (Miscellaneous Amendments) (No.2) Regulations 1999 (SI 1999 No.1047) reg 43(a) (June 1, 1999).*

3.   *Child Support (Miscellaneous Amendments) Regulations 1998 (SI 1998 No.58) reg 18(3) (January 19, 1998).*

4.   *Child Support (Miscellaneous Amendments) (No.2) Regulations 1999 (SI 1999 No.1047) reg 43(b)-(c) (June 1, 1999).*

5. *Child Support (Miscellaneous Amendments) (No.2) Regulations 1999 (SI 1999 No.1047) reg 43(d) (June 1, 1999).*

[¹*Revision of decisions*

32A.–*(1) Subject to paragraphs (2) and (3), a decision of the Secretary of State or any decision upon referral under section 28D(1)(b) of [³ the First-tier Tribunal] with respect to a departure direction may be revised by the Secretary of State under section 16 of the Act as extended by paragraph 1 of Schedule 4C to the Act–*

(a) *if the Secretary of State receives an application for the revision of a decision under section 16 of the Act as extended within one month of the date of notification of the decision or within such longer time as may be allowed by regulation 32B;*

(b) *if–*

    (i) *the Secretary of State notifies a person, who applied for a decision to be revised within the period specified in sub-paragraph (a), that the application is unsuccessful because the Secretary of State is not in possession of all of the information or evidence needed to make a decision; and*

    (ii) *that person reapplies for a decision to be revised within one month of the notification described in head (i) above or such longer period as the Secretary of State is satisfied is reasonable in the circumstances of the case, and provides in that application sufficient information or evidence to enable a decision to be made;*

(c) *if the decision arose from an official error;*

(d) *if the Secretary of State is satisfied that the original decision was erroneous due to a misrepresentation of, or failure to disclose, a material fact and that the decision was more advantageous to the person who misrepresented or.. failed to disclose that fact than it would otherwise have been but for that error;*

(e) *where a departure direction takes effect in the circumstances described in regulation 35(3); or*

(f) *if the Secretary of State commences action leading to the revision of a decision within one month of the date of notification of the decision.*

(2) *Paragraph (1) shall apply neither–*

(a) *in respect of a material change of circumstances which–*

    (i) *occurred since [²the date on which the decision was made]; or*

    (ii) *is expected, according to information or evidence which the Secretary of State has, to occur; nor*

(b) *where–*

    (i) *an appeal against the original decision has been brought but not determined; and*

    (ii) *from the point of view of the appellant, a revision, if made, would be less to his advantage than the original decision.]*

Amendments

1. *Child Support (Miscellaneous Amendments) (No.2) Regulations 1999 (SI 1999 No.1047) reg 44 (June 1, 1999).*
2. *Social Security and Child Support (Miscellaneous Amendments) Regulations 2000 (SI 2000 No.1596) reg 12 (June 19, 2000).*
3. *Tribunals, Courts and Enforcement Act 2007 (Transitional and Consequential Provisions) Order 2008 (SI 2008 No.2683) Sch 1 para 76 (November 3, 2008).*

[¹*Late applications for a revision*

32B.–*(1) The period of one month specified in regulation 32A(1)(a) may be extended where the requirements specified in the following provisions of this regulation are met.*

(2) *An application for an extension of time shall be made by a relevant person or a person acting on his behalf.*

(3) *An application for an extension of time under this regulation shall–*

(a) be made within 13 months of the date on which notification of the decision which it is sought to have revised was given or sent; and

(b) contain particulars of the grounds on which the extension of time is sought and shall contain sufficient details of the decision which it is sought to have revised to enable that decision to be identified.

(4) The application for an extension of time shall not be granted unless the person making the application, or any person acting for him, satisfies the Secretary of State that–

(a) it is reasonable to grant that application;

(b) the application for the decision to be revised has merit; and

(c) special circumstances are relevant to the application for an extension of time, and as a result of those special circumstances, it was not practicable for the application for a decision to be revised to be made within one month of the date of notification of the decision which it is sought to have revised.

(5) In determining whether it is reasonable to grant an application for an extension of time, the Secretary of State shall have regard to the principle that the greater the time that has elapsed between the expiration of the period of one month described in regulation 32A(1)(a) from the date of notification of the decision which it is sought to have revised and the making of the application for an extension of time, the more compelling should be the special circumstances on which the application is based.

(6) In determining whether it is reasonable to grant an application for an extension of time, no account shall be taken of the following–

(a) that the person making the application for an extension of time or any person acting for him was unaware of or misunderstood the law applicable to his case (including ignorance or misunderstanding of the time limits imposed by these Regulations);

(b) that [² the Upper Tribunal] or a court has taken a different view of the law from that previously understood and applied.

(7) An application under this regulation for an extension of time which has been refused may not be renewed.]

Amendments

1. Child Support (Miscellaneous Amendments) (No.2) Regulations 1999 (SI 1999 No.1047) reg 44 (June 1, 1999).

2. Tribunals, Courts and Enforcement Act 2007 (Transitional and Consequential Provisions) Order 2008 (SI 2008 No.2683) Sch 1 para 77 (November 3, 2008).

[¹Date from which a revision of a decision takes effect

32C. Where the date from which a decision took effect is found to be erroneous on a revision, the revision shall take effect from the date on which the revised decision would have taken effect had the error not been made.]

Amendment

1. Child Support (Miscellaneous Amendments) (No.2) Regulations 1999 (SI 1999 No.1047) reg 44 (June 1, 1999).

[¹Supersession of decisions

32D.–(1) For the purposes of section 17 of the Act as it applies in relation to decisions with respect to departure directions by virtue of paragraph 2 of Schedule 4C to the Act and subject to paragraphs (6), (9) and (10), the cases and circumstances in which a decision with respect to a departure direction may be made under that section are set out in paragraphs (2) to (5).

(2) A decision may be superseded by a decision made by the Secretary of State acting on his own initiative where he is satisfied that–

(a) there has been a material change of circumstances since the decision was made; or

(b) the decision was made in ignorance of, or was based upon a mistake as to, some material fact.

(3)   A decision may be superseded by a decision made by the Secretary of State where–
(a)   an application is made on the basis that-
   (i)   there has been a change of circumstances since the decision was made; or
   (ii)   it is expected that a change of circumstances will occur; and
(b)   the Secretary of State is satisfied that the change of circumstances is or would be material.
(4)   A decision may be superseded by a decision made by the Secretary of State where–
(a)   an application is made on the basis that the decision was made in ignorance of, or was based upon a mistake as to, a fact; and
(b)   the Secretary of State is satisfied that the fact is or would be material.
(5)   A decision, other than a decision given on appeal, may be superseded by a decision made by the Secretary of State–
(a)   where an application is made on the basis that the decision was erroneous in point of law; or
(b)   acting on his own initiative where he is satisfied that the decision was erroneous in point of law.
(6)   Subject to paragraph (7), paragraphs (2)(a) and (3) shall not apply where, if a decision were to be superseded in accordance with section 17 of the Act, the difference between the current amount and the revised amount would be less than £1.00 per week.
(7)   Paragraph (6) shall not apply where the Secretary of State is satisfied on the information or evidence available to him that a ground on which the decision to be superseded was made no longer applies.
(8)   In paragraph (6) "revised amount" means the amount of child support maintenance which would be fixed if a decision with respect to a maintenance assessment were to be superseded by a decision made by the Secretary of State in accordance with paragraphs (2)(a) and (3) but for the operation of paragraph (6).
(9)   The cases and circumstances in which a decision may be superseded by a decision made by the Secretary of State shall not include any case or circumstance in which a decision may be revised.
(10)   Subject to paragraph (11), paragraphs (2) to (5) shall apply in respect of neither–
(a)   a decision to reject or refuse an application for a departure direction; nor
(b)   a decision to cancel a departure direction.
(11)   Paragraph (10) above shall not apply in a case to which either paragraph (2) or (3) of regulation 35 applies.]

Amendment

1.   *Child Support (Miscellaneous Amendments) (No.2) Regulations 1999 (SI 1999 No.1047) reg 44 (June 1, 1999).*

[³Date from which a superseding decision takes effect

32E.–(1)   This regulation contains exceptions to the provisions of section 17(4) of the Act, as it applies in relation to decisions with respect to departure directions by virtue of paragraph 2 of Schedule 4C to the Act, as to the date from which decisions which supersede earlier decisions are to take effect.
(2)   Subject to paragraphs [¹(3), (5)and (12)], where–
(a)   a decision is made by the Secretary of State which supersedes an earlier decision in consequence of an application having been made under section 17 of the Act as it applies in relation to decisions with respect to departure directions by virtue of paragraph 2 of Schedule 4C to the Act; and
(b)   the date on which the application is made is not the first day in a maintenance period,
the decision shall take effect as from the first day of the maintenance period in which the application is made.

(3) *[¹Subject to paragraph (12), where a decision]* *is superseded by a decision made by the Secretary of State in a case to which regulation 32D(2)(a) applies on the basis of evidence or information which was also the basis of a decision made under section 9 or 10 of the Social Security Act 1998 the superseding decision under section 17 of the Act as extended by paragraph 2 of Schedule 7 to the Act shall take effect as from the first day of the maintenance period in which that evidence or information was first brought to the attention of an officer exercising the functions of the Secretary of State under the Act.*

(4) *Where a decision is superseded by a decision made by the Secretary of State under regulation 32D(3) in consequence of an application made on the basis that a material change of circumstances is expected to occur, the superseding decision shall take effect as from the first day of the maintenance period which immediately succeeds the maintenance period in which the material change of circumstances is expected to occur.*

(5) *Where the Secretary of State makes, on his own initiative, a decision superseding a decision in consequence of evidence or information contained in an unsuccessful application for a revision of that decision, the superseding decision shall take effect as from the first day of the maintenance period in which that application was made.*

(6) *Where—*

(a) *a decision made by [⁵an appeal tribunal or] [⁴ the First-tier Tribunal] under section 20 of the Act as extended by paragraph 3 of Schedule 4C to the Act is superseded on the ground that it was erroneous due to a misrepresentation of, or that there was a failure to disclose, a material fact; and*

(b) *the Secretary of State is satisfied that the decision was more advantageous to the person who misrepresented or failed to disclose that fact than it would otherwise have been but for that error,*

the superseding decision shall take effect as from the date the decision it superseded took, or was to take, effect.

(7) *Any decision given under section 17 of the Act as extended by paragraph 2 of Schedule 4C to the Act in consequence of a decision which is a relevant determination for the purposes of section 28ZC of the Act (restrictions on liability in certain cases of error) shall take effect as from the date of the relevant determination.*

(8) *Where a decision with respect to a departure direction is superseded by a decision under section 17 of the Act as extended by paragraph 2 of Schedule 4C to the Act because the departure direction ceases to have effect in accordance with regulation 35(1), the superseding decision shall have effect as from the date on which the decision that the maintenance assessment is cancelled or ceases to have effect, takes or took effect.*

(9) *Where the superseding decision referred to in paragraph (8) above is itself superseded by a further decision made under section 17 of the Act as extended by paragraph 2 of Schedule 4C to the Act in the circumstances described in regulation 35(2), that further decision shall have effect as from the effective date of the fresh maintenance assessment.*

(10) *Where a decision with respect to a departure direction is superseded by a decision under section 17 of the Act as extended by paragraph 2 of Schedule 4C to the Act because the departure direction is suspended in accordance with regulation 35(4),*

the superseding decision shall have effect as from the effective date of the later interim maintenance assessment or, as the case may be, the interim maintenance assessment which replaces a maintenance assessment.

(11) *Where the superseding decision referred to in paragraph (10) above is itself superseded by a further decision under section 17 as extended because the interim maintenance assessment referred to in regulation 35(4)(c) is followed by a maintenance assessment made in accordance with the provisions of Part I of Schedule 1 to the Act or by an interim maintenance assessment to which regulation 10 does not apply, that further decision shall have effect as from the effective date of the fresh maintenance assessment or, as the case may be, interim maintenance assessment.*

[²(12) *Where a superseding decision is made in a case to which regulation 32D(2)(a) or (3) applies and the material circumstance is the death of a qualifying child or a*

qualifying child ceasing to be a qualifying child, the decision shall take effect as from the first day of the maintenance period in which the change occurred.]]

Amendments

1.   *Social Security and Child Support (Miscellaneous Amendments) Regulations 2000 (SI 2000 No.1596) reg 13(a) and (b) (June 19, 2000).*

2.   *Social Security and Child Support (Miscellaneous Amendments) Regulations 2000 (SI 2000 No.1596) reg 13(c) (June 19, 2000).*

3.   *Child Support (Miscellaneous Amendments) (No.2) Regulations 1999 (SI 1999 No.1047) reg 44 (June 1, 1999).*

4.   *Tribunals, Courts and Enforcement Act 2007 (Transitional and Consequential Provisions) Order 2008 (SI 2008 No.2683) Sch 1 para 78 (November 3, 2008).*

5.   *Social Security and Child Support (Supersession of Appeal Decisions) Regulations 2012 (SI 2012 No.1267) reg 3 (June 4, 2012, but this amendment has effect as if it had come into force on November 3, 2008).*

[¹Cancellation of departure directions

32F.   *The Secretary of State may cancel a departure direction where–*

(a)   *regulation 32A(1) applies and he is satisfied that it was not appropriate to have given it; or*

(b)   *regulation 32D applies and he is satisfied that it is no longer appropriate for it to continue to have effect.]*

Amendment

1.   *Child Support (Miscellaneous Amendments) (No.2) Regulations 1999 (SI 1999 No.1047) reg 44 (June 1, 1999).*

[¹Notification of right of appeal, decision and reasons for decision

32G.–*(1)   The Secretary of State shall notify a person with a right of appeal under the Act against the decision under section 16 or 17 of the Act as those sections apply in relation to decisions with respect to departure directions by virtue of paragraphs 1 and 2 of Schedule 4C to the Act with respect to a departure direction of–*

(a)   *that right;*

(b)   *that decision; and*

(c)   *the reasons for that decision.*

(2)   *A written notice provided under paragraph (1)–*

(a)   *shall also contain sufficient information to enable a relevant person to exercise a right of appeal; and*

(b)   *shall not contain any information which it is not necessary for a person to have in order to understand how the decision was reached.]*

Amendment

1.   *Child Support (Miscellaneous Amendments) (No.2) Regulations 1999 (SI 1999 No.1047) reg 44 (June 1, 1999).*

33.   *[¹...]*

Amendment

1.   *Child Support (Miscellaneous Amendments) (No.2) Regulations 1999 (SI 1999 No.1047) reg 45 (June 1, 1999).*

34.   *[¹...]*

Amendment

1.   *Child Support (Miscellaneous Amendments) (No.2) Regulations 1999 (SI 1999 No.1047) reg 45 (June 1, 1999).*

[¹ Correction of accidental errors in departure directions

34A.–*(1)   Subject to paragraphs (3) and (4), accidental errors in any departure direction made by the Secretary of State or record of such a departure direction may, at any time, be corrected by the Secretary of State and a correction made to, or to the* *record of, that departure direction shall be deemed to be part of that direction or of that record.*

(2)   Where the Secretary of State has made a correction under the provisions of paragraph (1), he shall immediately notify the persons who were notified of the departure direction that has been corrected, so far as that is reasonably practicable.

(3)   In determining whether the time limit specified in [² [³ under Tribunal Procedure Rules]] has been complied with, there shall be disregarded any day falling before the day on which notification was given or sent under paragraph (2).

(4)   The powers to correct errors under this regulation shall not be taken to limit any other powers to correct errors that are exercisable apart from these Regulations.]

Amendments

1.   *Child Support (Miscellaneous Amendments) Regulations 1998 (SI 1998 No.58) reg 19 (January 19, 1998).*

2.   *Child Support (Miscellaneous Amendments) (No.2) Regulations 1999 (SI 1999 No.1047) reg 46 (June 1, 1999).*

3.   *Tribunals, Courts and Enforcement Act 2007 (Transitional and Consequential Provisions) Order 2008 (SI 2008 No.2683) Sch 1 para 79 (November 3, 2008).*

Termination and suspension of departure directions

35.–*(1)   Subject to paragraph (2), (3), and (4), where a departure direction has effect in relation to the amount of child support maintenance fixed by a maintenance assessment which is cancelled or ceases to have effect, that departure direction shall cease to have effect and shall not subsequently take effect.*

(2)   Where [¹the Secretary of State] ceases to have jurisdiction to make a maintenance assessment and subsequently acquires jurisdiction to make a maintenance assessment in respect of the same absent parent, person with care and any child with respect to whom the earlier assessment was made, a departure direction for a case falling within paragraph 3 or 4 of Schedule 4B to the Act shall again take effect [¹].

(3)   Where a departure direction had effect in relation to the amount of child support maintenance fixed by a maintenance assessment which is, under regulation 8(2) of the Maintenance Arrangements and Jurisdiction Regulations (maintenance assessments and maintenance orders made in error), treated as not having been cancelled or not having ceased to have effect, that departure direction shall again take effect [¹] except where there has, since that maintenance assessment was cancelled or ceased to have effect, been a material change of circumstances relevant to that departure direction.

(4)   Where–

(a)   a departure direction is in force in respect of an interim maintenance assessment or a maintenance assessment made in accordance with provisions of Part I of Schedule 1 to the Act;

(b)   that interim maintenance assessment is replaced by another ("the later interim maintenance assessment") or, as the case may be, that maintenance assessment is replaced by an interim maintenance assessment; and

(c)   by virtue of regulation 10 a departure direction would not be given if that interim maintenance assessment or that later interim maintenance assessment had been in force at the time that departure direction was given, that departure direction shall be suspended until that interim maintenance assessment or that later interim maintenance assessment has been cancelled or has ceased to have effect and shall again take effect [¹...]

(5)   For the purposes of paragraph (4), a departure direction which is in force shall include a departure direction which is suspended.

Amendment

1.   *Child Support (Miscellaneous Amendments) (No.2) Regulations 1999 (SI 1999 No.1047) reg 47 (June 1, 1999).*

PART VIII
Maintenance assessment following a departure direction

Effect of a departure direction – general

36.–(1)   *Except where a case falls within regulation 22, 41, 42 or 43, a departure direction shall specify, as the basis on which the amount of child support maintenance is to be fixed by any fresh assessment made in consequence of the direction, that the amount of net income or exempt income of the parent with care or absent parent or the amount of protected income of the absent parent be increased or, as the case may be, decreased in accordance with those provisions of regulations 37, 38 and 40 which are applicable to the particular case.*

(2)   *Where the provisions of paragraph (1) apply to a departure direction, the amount of child support maintenance fixed by a fresh maintenance assessment shall be determined in accordance with the provisions of Part I of Schedule 1 to the Act, but with the substitution of the amounts changed in consequence of the direction for the amounts determined in accordance with those provisions.*

Effect of a departure direction in respect of special expenses – exempt income

37.–(1)   *Subject to paragraph (2), where a departure direction is given in respect of special expenses, the exempt income of the absent parent or, as the case may be, or parent with care shall be increased by [¹ the amount specified in that departure direction being the whole of part of] the amount constituting the special expenses or the aggregate of the special expenses determined in accordance with regulations 13 to 20.*

(2)   *Where a departure direction is given with respect to costs incurred in travelling to work or expenses which include such costs, and a component of exempt income has been determined in accordance with regulation 9(1)(i) of the Maintenance Assessments and Special Cases Regulations or regulation 10 of those Regulations applying regulation 9(1)(i), the increase in exempt income determined in accordance with paragraph (1) shall be reduced by that component of exempt income.*

(3)   *A departure direction with respect to special expenses for a case falling within regulation 16 shall be given only for the repayment period remaining applicable to that debt at the date on which that direction takes effect except–*

(a)   *where in consequence of the applicant's unemployment or incapacity for work, the repayment period of that debt has been extended by agreement with the creditor, a departure direction may be given to cover the additional weeks allowed for repayment; or*

(b)   *where the Secretary of State is satisfied that, as a consequence of the income of the applicant having been substantially reduced the repayment period of that debt has been extended by agreement with the creditor, a departure direction may be given for such repayment period as the Secretary of State considers is reasonable.*

(4)   *Where paragraph (4) of relegation 16 applies, a departure direction may be given in respect only of [² the whole or part of the amount required to repay] that part of the debt incurred which is referable to the debt, repayment of which would have fallen within paragraph (1) of that regulation, based upon the amount, rate of repayment and repayment period agreed in respect of that part at the time it was taken out.*

Amendments
1.   *Child Support (Miscellaneous Amendments) Regulations 1998 (SI 1998 No.58) reg 20(2) (January 19, 1998).*
2.   *Child Support (Miscellaneous Amendments) Regulations 1998 (SI 1998 No.58) reg 20(3) (January 19, 1998).*

Effect of a departure direction in respect of special expenses – protected income

38.–(1)   *Subject to paragraphs (2) and (3), where a departure direction is given with respect to special expenses in response to an absent parent's application, his protected income shall be determined in accordance with paragraph (1) of regulation 11 of the*

Maintenance Assessments and Special Cases Regulations with the modification that the increase of exempt income as determined in accordance with regulation 37 shall be added to the aggregate of the amounts mentioned in sub-paragraphs (a) to (kk) of paragraph (1) of regulation 11 of the Maintenance Assessments and Special Cases Regulations.

(2) Protected income shall not be increased in accordance with paragraph (1) on account of special expenses constituted by costs falling within regulation 18 (costs incurred in supporting certain children).

(3) Where a departure direction is given with respect to costs which include costs incurred in travelling to work, the absent parent's protected income shall be determined in accordance with paragraph (1), but without inclusion of the amount determined in accordance with sub-paragraph (kk) of regulation 11(1) of the Maintenance Assessments and Special Cases Regulations within the aggregate of the amounts mentioned in that regulation.

Effect of a departure direction in respect of a transfer of property

39.–(1) Where a departure direction is given in respect of a transfer of property for a case falling within paragraph 3 of Schedule 4B to the Act–
- *(a) where the exempt income of an absent parent includes a component of exempt income determined in accordance with regulation 9(1)(bb) of the Maintenance Assessments and Special Cases Regulations, the exempt income of the absent parent shall be reduced by that component income determined in accordance with regulations 9(1)(bb) of exempt income;*
- *[¹(b) subject to sub-paragraph (c) and paragraphs (2) and (3), the fresh maintenance assessment made in consequence of the direction shall be the lower of–*
  - *(i) the amount, calculated in accordance with the provisions of paragraphs 1 to 5 and 7 to 10 of Part I of Schedule 1 to the Act, as modified in a case to which it applies by sub-paragraph (a) where the sub-paragraph is applicable to the case in question, reduced by the amount specified in that departure direction being the whole or part of the equivalent weekly value of the property transferred as determined in accordance with regulation 22; or*
  - *(ii) where the provisions of paragraph 6 of Schedule 1 to the Act (protected income) apply, the amount, calculated in accordance with the provisions of Part I of Schedule 1 to the Act, as modified in a case to which it applies by sub-paragraph (a) where that sub-paragraph is applicable to the case in question;]*
- *(c) where the equivalent weekly value is nil, the fresh maintenance assessment made in consequence of the direction shall be the maintenance assessment calculated in accordance with the provisions of Part I of Schedule 1 to the Act as modified by sub-paragraph (a), where that sub-paragraph is applicable to the case in question.*

(2) The amount of child support maintenance fixed by an assessment made in consequence of a direction falling within paragraph (1) shall not be less than the amount prescribed by regulation 13 of the Maintenance Assessments and Special Cases Regulations.

(3) Where there has been a transfer by the applicant of property to trustees as set out in regulation 21(2) and the equivalent weekly value is greater than nil, any monies paid to the parent with care out of that trust fund for maintenance of a child with respect to whom the current assessment was made shall be disregarded in calculating the assessable income of that parent with care in accordance with the provisions of Part I of Schedule 1 to the Act.

(4) A departure direction falling within paragraph (1) shall cease to have effect at the end of the number of years of liability, as defined in paragraph 1 of the Schedule, for the case in question.

(5)   Where a departure direction has ceased to have effect under the provisions of paragraph (4), the exempt income of an absent parent shall be determined as if regulation 9(1)(bb) of the Maintenance Assessment and Special Cases Regulations were omitted.

(6)   Where a departure direction is given in respect of a transfer of property for a case falling within paragraph 4 of Schedule 4B to the Act, the exempt income of the absent parent shall be reduced by the component of exempt income determined in accordance with regulation 9(1)(bb) of the Maintenance Assessment and Special Cases Regulations.

(7)   This regulation is subject to regulation 42.

Amendment

1.   *Child Support (Miscellaneous Amendments) Regulations 1998 (SI 1998 No.58) reg 21 (January 19, 1998).*

Effect of a departure direction in respect of additional cases

40.–(1)   This regulation applies where a departure direction is given for an additional case falling within paragraph 5 of Schedule 4B to the Act.

(2)   In a case falling within paragraph (1)(a) of regulation 23 (assets capable of producing income or higher income), subject to paragraph (4), the net income of the non-applicant shall be increased by [¹ the amount specified in that departure direction, being the whole or part of] an amount calculated by applying interest at the statutory rate prescribed for a judgement debt or, in Scotland, at the statutory rate in respect of interest included in or payable under a decree in the Court of Session at the date on which the departure direction is given to–

(a)   any monies falling within that paragraph;

(b)   the net value of any asset, other than monies, falling within that paragraph, after deduction of the amount owing on any mortgage or charge on that asset,

less any income received in respect of that asset which has been taken into account in the calculation of the current assessment.

(3)   In a case falling within paragraph (1)(b) or (c) of regulation 23, subject to paragraph (4), the net income of the non-applicant shall be increased by [² the amount specified in that departure direction, being the whole or part of] an amount calculated by applying interest at the statutory rate prescribed for a judgment debt or, in Scotland, at the statutory rate in respect of interest included in or payable under a decree in the Court of Session at the date of the application to the value of the asset subject to the trust less any income received from the trust which has been taken into account in the calculation of the current assessment.

(4)   In a case to which regulation 24 (diversion of income) applies, the net income of the non-applicant who is a parent of a child in respect of whom the current assessment is made shall be increased by [²the amount specified in that departure direction being the whole or part of] the amount by which the Secretary of State is satisfied that that parent has reduced his income.

(5)   In a case to which regulation 25 (life-style inconsistent with declared income) applies, the net income of the non-applicant who is a parent of a child in respect of whom the current assessment is made shall be increased by [²the amount specified in that departure direction, being the whole or part of] the difference between the two levels of income referred to in paragraph (1) of that regulation.

(6)   In a case to which regulation 26 applies (unreasonably high housing costs) the amount of housing costs included in exempt income and the amount referred to in regulation 11(1)(b) of the Maintenance Assessments and Special Cases Regulations shall not exceed the amounts set out in regulation 18(1)(a) or (b), as the case may be, of the Maintenance Assessments and Special Cases Regulations (excessive housing costs) and the provisions of regulation 18(2) of those Regulations shall not apply.

(7)   In a case to which regulation 27 applies (partner's contribution to housing costs) that part of the exempt income constituted by the eligible housing costs determined in accordance with regulation 14 of the Maintenance Assessments and Special Cases Regulations (eligible housing costs) shall, subject to paragraph (8) and (9), be reduced

by the percentage of the housing costs which the Secretary of State considers appropriate, taking into account the income of that parent and the income or estimated income of that partner.

(8)   Where paragraph (7) applies, the housing costs determined in accordance with regulation 11(1)(b) of the Maintenance Assessments and Special Cases Regulations (protected income) shall remain unchanged.

(9)   Where a Category B interim maintenance assessment is in force in respect of a non-applicant, the whole of the eligible housing costs may be deducted from the exempt income of that non-applicant.

(10)   In a case to which regulation 28 (unreasonably high travel costs) or regulation 29 (travel costs to be disregarded) applies, for the component of exempt income determined in accordance with regulation 9(1)(i) of the Maintenance Assessments and Special Cases Regulations or in accordance with that regulation as applied by regulation 10 of those Regulations and, in the case of an absent parent, for the amount determined in accordance with regulation 11(1)(kk) of those Regulations, there shall be substituted such amount, including a nil amount, as the Secretary of State considers to be appropriate in all the circumstances of the case.

Amendments

1.   *Child Support (Miscellaneous Amendments) Regulations 1998 (SI 1998 No.58) reg 22 (January 19, 1998).*

2.   *Child Support (Miscellaneous Amendments) Regulations 1998 (SI 1998 No.58) reg 22 (January 19, 1998).*

PART IX
Maintenance assessment following a departure direction: particular cases

---

Child support maintenance payable where effect of a departure direction would be to decrease an absent parent's assessable income but case still fell within paragraph 2(3) of Schedule 1 to the Act

41.–(1)   Subject to regulation 42 and paragraph (8), where the effect of a departure direction would, but for the following provisions of this regulation, be to reduce an absent parent's assessable income and his assessable income following that direction would be such that the case fell within paragraph 2(3) of Schedule 1 to the Act (additional element of maintenance payable), the amount of child support maintenance payable shall be determined in accordance with paragraphs (2) to (5).

(2)   There shall be calculated the amount equal to A x P, where A is equal to the amount that would be the absent parent's assessable income if the departure direction referred to in paragraph (1) had been given and P has the value prescribed in regulation 5 of the Maintenance Assessments and Special Cases Regulations.

[¹(3)   There shall be determined the amount that would be payable under a maintenance assessment made in accordance with the provisions of Part I of Schedule 1 to the Act which would be in force at the date any departure direction referred to in paragraph (1) would take effect if it were to be given.]

[²(4)   The revised amount for the purposes of regulation 7 (rejection of application on completion of a preliminary consideration) and regulation 31 (refusal to give a departure direction under section 28F(4) of the Act) shall be the lowest of the following amounts–

(a)   the amount calculated in accordance with paragraph (2);

(b)   the amount determined in accordance with paragraph (3);

(c)   where the provisions of paragraph 6 of Schedule 1 to the Act (protected income) as modified in a case to which they apply by the provisions of regulation 38 (effect of a departure direction in respect of special expenses–protected income) would apply if a departure direction were given, the amount payable under those provisions,

and the Secretary of State may apply regulation 7 and shall apply regulation 31 in relation to the current amount and the revised amount as so construed.]

(5) [³] *Where the application of the provisions of paragraph (4) results in a departure direction being given, the amount of child support maintenance payable following that direction shall be determined by [⁴the Secretary of State] as being the revised amount as defined in paragraph (4).*

(6) *Where the assessable income of an absent parent changes following [⁴a decision under section 16 of the Act revising a decision as to a maintenance assessment or a decision under section 17 of the Act superseding a decision as to a maintenance assessment], the provisions of paragraphs (2) to (5) shall be applied to–*

(a) *the amount calculated under paragraph (2) which takes account of the change in assessable income: and*

(b) *the amount that would be payable under the maintenance assessment calculated in accordance with the provisions of Part 1 of Schedule 1 to the Act which takes account of that change in assessable income.*

(7) [⁵]

(8) *Where a departure direction given in accordance with the provisions of [⁶paragraphs (1) to (6)] has effect, those provisions shall apply, subject to the modifications set out in paragraph (9), where–*

(a) *the effect of a later direction would, but for the provisions of paragraphs (2) to (5), be to change the absent parent's assessable income and his assessable income following the direction would be such that the case fell within paragraph 2(3) of Schedule 1 to the Act (additional element of maintenance payable); and*

(b) *that assessable income following the later direction would be less than the assessable income would be if it were calculated in accordance with the provisions of Part I of Schedule 1 to the Act by reference to the circumstances at the time the application for the later direction is made.*

(9) *The modifications referred to in paragraph (8) are–*

(a) *in paragraph (2), A would be the absent parent's assessable income following the later direction but for the provisions of paragraphs (3) to (5);*

(b) *the references to regulation 7 in paragraph (4) are omitted.*

Amendments

1. *Child Support (Miscellaneous Amendments) Regulations 1998 (SI 1998 No.58) reg 23(2) (January 19, 1998).*

2. *Child Support (Miscellaneous Amendments) Regulations 1998 (SI 1998 No.58) reg 23(3) (January 19, 1998).*

3. *Child Support (Miscellaneous Amendments) Regulations 1998 (SI 1998 No 58) reg 23(4) (January 19, 1998).*

4. *Child Support (Miscellaneous Amendments) (No.2) Regulations 1999 (SI 1999 No.1047) reg 48 (June 1, 1999).*

5. *Child Support (Miscellaneous Amendments) Regulations 1998 (SI 1998 No.58) reg 23(5) (January 19, 1998).*

6. *Child Support (Miscellaneous Amendments) Regulations 1998 (SI 1998 No.58) reg 23(6) (January 19, 1998).*

Application of regulation 41 where there is a transfer of property falling within paragraph 3 of Schedule 4B to the Act

42.–[¹(1) *Where an absent parent applies for a departure direction on the grounds that the case falls within both paragraph 2 of Schedule 4B to the Act (special expenses) and paragraph 3 of that Schedule (property or capital transfers), regulation 41 shall be applied subject to the modifications set out in paragraphs (1A) to (3).*

(1A) *In paragraph (1) of regulation 41, the reference to a departure direction shall be construed as a reference to any departure direction that would be given if the application had been made solely on the grounds that the case falls within paragraph 2 of Schedule 4B to the Act, and the reference to the absent parent's assessable income shall be construed as a reference to the assessable income calculated in consequence of such a direction.]*

(2) *Where the exempt income of an absent parent includes a component of exempt income determined in accordance with regulation 9(1)(bb) of the Maintenance Assessments and Special Cases Regulations, that amount shall be excluded–*

(a) in calculating the amount A defined in paragraph (2) of regulation 41;

(b) in calculating the maintenance assessment specified in paragraph (3) of regulation 41.

[²(3)   For the purposes of this regulation, the revised amount for the purposes of regulations 7 and 31 shall be–

(a) subject to sub-paragraph(b), the lower of the amounts specified in sub-paragraphs (a) and (b) of paragraph (4) of regulation 41, subject to paragraph (2) of this regulation, less the amount determined in accordance with regulation 22 (value of a transfer of property and its equivalent weekly value for a case falling with paragraph 3 of Schedule 4B to the Act);

(b) where the amount specified in sub-paragraph (c) of paragraph (4) of regulation 41 is lower than the amount determined in accordance with sub-paragraph (a), that amount.]

(4)   Where the application of the provisions of paragraph (3) results in a departure direction being given, the amount of child support maintenance payable following that direction shall be [³ determined by [⁴the Secretary of State] as being] the revised amount as defined in paragraph (3).

Amendments

1.   *Child Support (Miscellaneous Amendments) Regulations 1998 (SI 1998 No.58) reg 24(2) (January 19, 1998).*

2.   *Child Support (Miscellaneous Amendments) Regulations 1998 (SI 1998 No.58) reg 24(3) (January 19, 1998).*

3.   *Child Support (Miscellaneous Amendments) Regulations 1998 (SI 1998 No.58) reg 24(4) (January 19, 1998).*

4.   *Child Support (Miscellaneous Amendments) (No.2) Regulations 1999 (SI 1999 No.1047) reg 49 (June 1, 1999).*

[¹Application of regulation 41 where the case falls within paragraph 2 and paragraph 5 of Schedule 4B to the Act

42A.–(1)   Where an absent parent applies for a departure direction on the grounds that the case falls within both paragraph 5 of Schedule 4B to the Act (additional cases) and paragraph 2 of that Schedule (special expenses), and the conditions set out in paragraph (1) of regulation 41 as satisfied, the amount of child support maintenance payable shall be determined in accordance with paragraphs (2) to (6).

(2)   The application shall in the first instance be treated as an application (an "additional cases application") made solely on the grounds that the case falls within paragraph 5 of Schedule 4B to the Act, and a determination shall be made as to whether a departure direction would be given in response to that application.

(3)   Following the determination mentioned in paragraph (2), the application shall be treated as an application (a "special expenses application") made solely on the grounds that the case falls within paragraph 2 of Schedule 4B to the Act, and the provisions of regulation 41 shall be applied to the special expenses application, subject to the provisions of paragraphs (4) to (6).

(4)   Where no departure direction would be given in response to the additional cases application, the provisions of regulation 41 shall be applied to determine the amount of child support maintenance payable.

(5)   Where a departure direction would be given in response to the additional cases application, the provisions of regulation 41 shall be applied to determine the amount of child support maintenance payable, subject to the modification set out in paragraph (6).

(6)   For paragraph (3) of regulation 41 there shall be substituted the following paragraph "(3)There shall be determined the amount that would be payable under the maintenance assessment made in consequence of the direction that would be given in response to the additional cases application mentioned in paragraph (2) of regulation 42A which would be in force at the date any departure direction referred to in paragraph (1) would take effect if it were to be given.".

(7)   Where–

(a) a departure direction has been given in a case where regulation 41 has been applied and an application is then made on the grounds that the case falls within paragraph 5 of Schedule 4B to the Act; or

(b) a departure direction has been given on the grounds that the case falls within paragraph 5 of Schedule 4B to the Act, an application is then made on the grounds that the case falls within paragraph 2 of that Schedule , and the conditions set out in paragraph (1) of regulation 41 are satisfied,

the case shall be treated as a case which falls within paragraph (1),and the date of the later application treated as the date on which both applications were made.

(8) Where a departure direction is given in accordance with the provisions of paragraph (7), the earlier direction shall cease to have effect from the date the later direction has effect.]

Amendment

1.   *Child Support (Misc Amendments) Regulations 1998 (SI 1998 No.58) reg 25 (January 19, 1998).*

Maintenance assessment following a departure direction for certain cases falling within regulation 22 of the Maintenance Assessments and Special Cases Regulations

43.–*(1)   Where the provisions of regulation 41 or 42 are applicable to a case falling within regulation 22 of the Maintenance Assessments and Special Cases Regulations (a) (multiple applications relating to an absent parent), those provisions shall apply for the purposes of determining the total maintenance payable in consequence of a departure direction.*

(2)   In a case falling within paragraph (1), the amount of child support maintenance payable in respect of each application for child support maintenance following the direction shall be the [¹lowest] of–

(a)   the amount as determined in accordance with paragraph (3) of regulation 41, subject to the modification that regulation 22 of the Maintenance Assessments and Special Cases Regulations is applied in determining the amount that would be payable ("Y");

(b)   the amount calculated by the formula–

$$(A \ x \ P) \ x \ \frac{Y}{Q}$$

where A and P have the same meanings as in regulation 41 (2) and Q is the sum of the amounts calculated in accordance with sub-paragraph (a) for each assessment.

[²(c)   where the provisions of paragraph 6 of Schedule 1 to the Act (protected income) apply, as modified in a case to which they apply by the provisions of regulation 38 (effect of a departure direction in respect of special expenses–protected income) or, as the case may be, regulation 40(6), (8) or (10) (effect of a departure direction in respect of additional cases), the amount calculated as payable under those provisions.]

(3)   Where, in a case falling within regulation 22 of the Maintenance Assessments and Special Cases Regulations, a departure direction has been given in respect of an absent parent in a case falling within paragraph 3 of Schedule 4B to the Act (property or capital transfers), the equivalent weekly value of the transfer of property as calculated in accordance with regulation 22 of these Regulations shall be deducted from the amount of the maintenance assessments in respect of the person with care of child to or in respect of whom the property transfer was made.

Amendments

1.   *Child Support (Misc Amendments) Regulations 1998 (SI 1998 No.58) reg 26(a) (January 19, 1998). This amendment substituted a word in reg 43(2). From 2.12.96 to 18.1.98 this word read "lower".*

2.   *Child Support (Misc Amendments) Regulations 1998 (SI 1998 No.58) reg 26(b) (January 19, 1998).*

Maintenance assessment following a departure direction where there is a phased maintenance assessment

44.–*(1)   Where a departure direction is given in a case falling within relevant enactment, the assessment made in consequence of that direction shall be the assessment* *that fixes the amount of child support maintenance that would be payable but for the provisions of that enactment ("the unadjusted departure amount").*

(2)   Where a departure direction takes effect on the effective date of a maintenance assessment to which the provisions of a relevant enactment become applicable, those provisions shall remain applicable to that case following the departure direction.

(3)   Where a departure direction takes effect on a date later than the date on which the provisions of a relevant enactment become applicable to a maintenance assessment, the amount of child support maintenance payable in consequence of that direction shall be–

(a)   where the unadjusted departure amount is more than the formula amount, the phased amount plus the difference between the unadjusted departure amount and the formula amount;

(b)   where the unadjusted departure amount is more than the phased amount but less than the formula amount, the phased amount;

(c)   where the unadjusted departure amount is less than the phased amount, the unadjusted departure amount.

(4)   Regulation 31 shall have effect for cases falling within paragraphs (1) to (3) as if "current amount" referred to the amount payable under the maintenance assessment that would be in force when the departure direction is given but for the provisions of the relevant enactment and "revised amount" referred to the unadjusted departure amount.

(5)   [¹Where the Secretary of State is satisfied that, were a decision as to a fresh maintenance assessment to be made under section 16 or, as the case may be, section 17 of the Act]; in relation to a case to which the provisions of [²paragraphs (1) and (3)] have been applied, and the amount payable under it [¹the fresh unadjusted departure amount] would be–

(a)   more than the unadjusted departure amount, the amount of child support maintenance payable shall be the amount determined in accordance with paragraph (3), plus the difference between the unadjusted departure amount and [the fresh unadjusted departure amount];

(b)   less than the unadjusted departure amount but more than the phased amount, the amount of child support maintenance payable shall be the phased amount;

(c)   less than the phased amount, the amount of child support maintenance payable shall be [³ the fresh unadjusted departure amount].

(6)   In this regulation–

"the 1992 enactment" means Part II of the Schedule to the Child Support Act 1991 (Commencement No.3 and Transitional Provisions) Order 1992 (modification of maintenance assessment in certain cases);

"the 1994 enactment" means Part III of the Child Support (Miscellaneous Amendments and Transitional Provisions) Regulations 1994 (transitional provisions);

"formula amount" has the same meaning as in the relevant enactment;

"phased amount" means–

(a)   where the 1992 enactment is applicable to the particular case, the modified amount as defined in paragraph 6 of that enactment;

(b)   where the 1994 enactment is applicable to the particular case, the transitional amount as defined in regulation 6(1) of that enactment;

"relevant enactment" means–

(a)   the 1992 enactment where that enactment is applicable to the particular case;

(b)   the 1994 enactment where that enactment is applicable to the particular case.

Amendments

1.   *Child Support (Miscellaneous Amendments) (No.2) Regulations 1999 (SI 1999 No.1047) reg 51 (June 1, 1999).*

2.   *Child Support (Miscellaneous Amendments) Regulations 1998 (SI 1998 No.58) reg 27 (January 19, 1998).*

3.   *Child Support (Miscellaneous Amendments) (No.2) Regulations 1999 (SI 1999 No.1047) reg 50 (June 1, 1999).*

PART X
Miscellaneous

Regular payments condition

45.–*(1)   For the purposes of section 28C(2)(b) of the Act (regular payments condition–reduced payments), reduced payments shall, subject to paragraph (3), be such payments as would be equal to the payments of child support maintenance fixed by the fresh maintenance assessment that would be made if the circumstances of the case were those set out in paragraph (2).*

(2)   The circumstances referred to in paragraph (1) are–

(a)   the Secretary of State is satisfied that the case is one which falls within paragraph 2 of Schedule 4B to the Act (special expenses);

(b)   the Secretary of State is satisfied that the expenses claimed by the absent parent are both being incurred and, for a case falling within regulation 13 (costs incurred in travelling to work), 14 (contact costs) or 15 (illness or disability), are neither unreasonably high nor being unreasonably incurred, and that it is just and equitable to give a departure direction in respect of the whole of those expenses; and

(c)   a departure direction is given in response to the application.

(3)   Where the Secretary of State considers it likely that the expenses incurred by the absent parent are lower than those claimed by him or are not reasonably incurred, he may fix such amount as he considers to be reasonable in all the circumstances of the case.

(4)   Where the absent parent, following written notice under section 28C(8) of the Act, fails within 28 days of that notice to comply with the regular payments condition that was imposed on him, the application shall lapse.

Special case – departure direction having effect from date earlier than effective date of current assessment

46.–*(1)   A case shall be treated as a special case for the purposes of the Act if the conditions specified in paragraph (2) are satisfied.*

(2)   The conditions are–

(a)   liability to pay child support maintenance commenced earlier than the effective date of the maintenance assessment in force ("the current assessment");

(b)   an application is made [²...] in relation to the current assessment which results in a departure direction being given in respect of that assessment [¹or, where regulation 11A (meaning of "current assessment" for the purposes of the Act) applies, in respect of the fresh maintenance assessment referred to in that regulation.]

(c)   the applicant was unable to make an application on a date falling within a period in respect of which an earlier assessment had effect because he had not been notified of that earlier assessment during that period; and

(d)   if the applicant had been able to make such an application and had done so, the Secretary of State is satisfied that a departure direction would have been given in response to that application (3) Where a case falls within paragraph (2), references to the "the current assessment" and "the current amount" in these Regulations shall be construed as including references to an earlier assessment falling within paragraph (2)(c) and to the amount of child support maintenance fixed by it, and these Regulations shall be applied to such an earlier assessment accordingly.

Amendments

1.   *Child Support (Miscellaneous Amendments) Regulations 1998 (SI 1998 No.58) reg 28 (January 19, 1998).*

2.   *Child Support (Consequential Provisions) Regulations 2008 (SI 2008 No.2543) reg 3 (October 27, 2008).*

[¹ *Cases to which regulation 11A applies*

46A.–*(1)   A case where the conditions set out in paragraphs (a) [²and (b)] of regulation 11A (meaning of "current assessment" for the purposes of the Act) are satisfied shall be treated as a special case for the purposes of the Act.*

(2)   Where a case falls within paragraph (1), references to "the current assessment" and "the current amount" in these Regulations shall, subject to paragraph (3), be construed as including reference to the fresh maintenance assessment referred to in regulation 11A.

(3)   Paragraph (2) shall not apply to references to "the current assessment" in regulation 32, with the exception of the reference in paragraph (1)(a) of that regulation, and in regulations 46, 49 and 50.]

Amendments

1.   *Child Support (Miscellaneous Amendments) Regulations 1998 (SI.1998 No.58) reg 29 (January 19, 1998).*
2.   *Child Support (Miscellaneous Amendments) (No.2) Regulations 1999 (SI 1999 No.1047) reg 51 (June 1, 1999).*

PART XI
Transitional provisions

Transitional provisions – application before 2nd December 1996

47.–*(1)   This paragraph applies in any case where an application for a departure direction has been made before 2nd December 1996.*

(2)   Where paragraph (1) applies, the Secretary of State shall request the applicant to inform him in writing before 2nd December 1997–

   (a)   whether he wishes the application to be treated as an application under these Regulations in respect of the maintenance assessment in force on 2nd December 1996; and

   (b)   whether there have been any changes in the circumstances which are relevant for the determination or, as the case may be, redetermination of the application which have occurred since his application and, if so, what those changes are.

(3)   Where the applicant fully complies with the request set out in paragraph (2), and states that he wishes the application to be treated as described in paragraph (2)(a), the Secretary of State shall treat the application as an application under these Regulations which contains the statement mentioned in section 28A(2)(a) of the Act, and paragraphs (4) to (10) and regulation 48 shall apply.

(4)   Where the applicant informs the Secretary of State that there have not been any changes of the kind mentioned in paragraph (2)(b), the Secretary of State shall nevertheless invite representations in writing from the relevant persons other than the applicant.

(5)   Where the applicant informs the Secretary of State that there have been changes in the circumstances of the kind mentioned in paragraph (2)(b), the Secretary of State shall–

   (a)   give notice that he has been informed of such changes to the relevant persons other than the applicant;

   (b)   send to them the information as to such changes which the applicant has given except where the Secretary of State considers that information to be information of the kind falling within paragraph (2) for regulation 8;

   (c)   invite representations in writing from the relevant person other than the applicant as to such changes; and

   (d)   set out the provisions of paragraph (6) in relation to such representations.

(6)   The following provisions shall apply to information provided under paragraph (2)(b) or representations made following an invitation made in accordance with paragraph (4) or (5)(c)–

   (a)   paragraphs (2) [¹to (10)] of regulation 8, subject to the modification set out in paragraph (7);

(b)   in relation to an applicant, regulations 6 and 7.

(7)   The modification of regulation 8 mentioned in paragraph (6)(a) is that for the reference to paragraph (1) or, as the case may be, paragraph (1)(c) of that regulation, there were substituted references to paragraph (5) or, as the case may be, paragraph (5)(c) or this regulation.

(8)   Where the Secretary of State has not determined the application in accordance with the Departure Direction Anticipatory Application Regulations, a determination shall be made in accordance with these Regulations.

(9)   Where the Secretary of State has determined the application in accordance with the Departure Direction Anticipatory Application Regulations, he shall determine whether there have been any changes in–

(a)   the circumstances referred to in paragraph (2)(b);

(b)   the relevant provisions of these Regulations compared with the corresponding provisions of the Departure Direction Anticipatory Application Regulations.

(10)   Where the Secretary of State determines that there have been no changes of the kind referred to in paragraph (9)(a) or (b), and the relevant persons other than the applicant have not made any representations in accordance with paragraph (4), his determination of the application in accordance with the Departure Direction Anticipatory Application Regulations shall take effect.

(11)   Where the Secretary of State determines that there have been changes of the kind referred to in paragraph (9)(a) or (b), or where the relevant person other than the applicant have made representations, he shall make a determination of the application, taking those changes and representations into account, in accordance with these Regulations.

Amendment

1.   *Child Support (Miscellaneous Amendments) (No.2) Regulations 1999 (SI 1999 No.1047) reg 52 (June 1, 1999).*

Effective date of departure direction for a case falling with regulation 47

48.–(1)   Where the determination made by the Secretary of State by application of the provisions of paragraphs (1) to (10) of regulation 47 is to give a departure direction, that direction shall take effect on the first day of the first maintenance period commencing on or after 2nd December 1996.

(2)   Where a case falls within paragraph (1) or regulation 47, and the applicant complies with the request for information mentioned in paragraph (2) of that regulation but not by the date mentioned in that paragraph, his response shall be treated as an application for a departure direction.

Transitional provisions – no application before 2nd December 1996

49.–(1)   Where–

(a)   a maintenance assessment was in force on 2nd December 1996;

(b)   no application has been made before that date by any of the persons with respect to whom that assessment was made; and

(c)   an application is made by one of those persons on the grounds set out in section 28A(2)(a) of the Act (the effect of the current assessment) on or after that date and before 2nd December 1997,

any departure direction given in response to that application shall take effect on the first day of the first maintenance period commencing on or after 2nd December 1996.

Transitional provisions – new maintenance assessment made before 2nd December 1996 whose effective date is on or after 2nd December 1996

50.   Where a new maintenance assessment is made before 2nd December 1996 but the effective date of that assessment is a date on or after 2nd December 1996–

(a)   the provisions of paragraph (1) of regulation 32 shall apply as if for the reference to an application being given or sent within one month of the date of notification being given or sent before 30th December 1996;

(b)   the provisions of paragraph (2) of regulation 32 shall apply as if for the reference to an application being given or sent later than [¹one month] after the date of notification of the current assessment there were substituted a reference to an application being given or sent after 29th December 1996.

Amendment

1.   *Child Support (Miscellaneous Amendments) (No.2) Regulations 1999 (SI 1999 No.1047) reg 53 (June 1, 1999).*

SCHEDULE
Regulation 22
Equivalent weekly value of a transfer of a property

1.–(1)   Subject to paragraphs 3 and 4, the equivalent weekly value of a transfer of property shall be calculated by multiplying the value of a transfer of property determined in accordance with regulation 22(1) and (2) by the relevant factor specified in the Table set out in paragraph 2 ("the Table").

(2)   For the purposes of sub-paragraph (1), the relevant factor is the number in the Table at the intersection of the column for the statutory rate and of the row for the number of years of liability

(3)   In sub-paragraph (2)–

(a)   "the statutory rate" means interest at the statutory rate prescribed for a judgement debt or, in Scotland, the statutory rate in respect of interest included in or payable under a decree in the Court of Session, which in either case applies at the date of the court order or written agreement relating to the transfer of the property;

(b)   "the number of years of liability" means the number of years, beginning on the date of the court order or written agreement relating to the transfer of property and ending on–

(i)   the date specified in that order or agreement as the date on which maintenance for the youngest child in respect of whom that order or agreement was made shall cease; or

(ii)   if no such date is specified, the date on which the youngest child specified in the order or agreement reaches the age of 18,

and where that period includes a fraction of a year, that fraction shall be treated as a full year if it is either one half or exceeds one half of a year, and shall otherwise be disregarded.

2.

The Table referred to in paragraph 1(1) is set out below–

THE TABLE

Number of years of liability	Statutory rate							
	[¹7.0%	8.0%	10.0%	[²11.0%	12.0%	12.5%	14.0%	15.0%
1	.02058	.02077	.02115	.02135	.02154	.02163	.02192	.02212
2	.01064	.01078	.01108	.01123	.01138	.01145	.01168	.01183
3	.00733	.00746	.00773	.00787	.00801	.00808	.00828	.00842
4	.00568	.00581	.00607	.00620	.00633	.00640	.00660	.00674
5	.00469	.00482	.00507	.00520	.00533	.00540	.00560	.00574
6	.00403	.00416	.00442	.00455	.00468	.00474	.00495	.00508
7	.00357	.00369	.00395	.00408	.00421	.00428	.00448	.00462
8	.00322	.00335	.00360	.00374	.00387	.00394	.00415	.00429
9	.00295	.00308	.00334	.00347	.00361	.00368	.00389	.00403
10	.00274	.00287	.00313	.00327	.00340	.00347	.00369	.00383
11	.00256	.00269.	.00296	.00310	.00324	.00331	.00353	.00367
12.	.00242	.00255	.00282	.00296	.00310	.00318	.00340	.00355
13	.00230	.00243	.00271	.00285	.00299	.00307	.00329	.00344
14	.00220	.00233	.00261	.00275	.00290	.00298	.00320	.00336
15	.00211	.00225	.00253	.00267	.00282	.00290	.00313	.00329
16	.00204	.00217	.00246	.00261	.00276	.00283	.00307	.00323
17	.00197	.00211	.00240	.00255	.00270	.00278	.00302	.00318
18	.00191]	.00205	.00234	.00250]	.00265	.00273	.00297	.00314

3. The equivalent weekly value of the property transferred shall be nil if the value of the transfer of the property is less than £5,000.

4. The Secretary of State may determine a lower equivalent weekly value than that determined in accordance with paragraphs 1 and 2 where the amount of child support maintenance that would be payable in consequence of a departure direction specifying that value is lower than the amount of [³the periodical payments of maintenance which were] payable under the court order or written agreement referred to in regulation 21.

5. [⁴...]

Amendments

1.   *Child Support (Miscellaneous Amendments) Regulations 1998 (SI 1998 No.58) reg 31(2)(a) (January 19, 1998).*
2.   *Child Support (Miscellaneous Amendments) Regulations 1998 (SI 1998 No.58) reg 31(2)(b) (January 19, 1998).*
3.   *Child Support (Miscellaneous Amendments) Regulations 1998 (SI 1998 No.58) reg 31(3) (January 19, 1998).*
4.   *Child Support (Miscellaneous Amendments) Regulations 1998 (SI 1998 No.58) reg 31(4) (January 19, 1998).*

The Child Support (Miscellaneous Amendments) (No.2) Regulations 1996

(1996 No.3196)

Citation, commencement and interpretation

1.–(1) These Regulations may be cited as the Child Support (Miscellaneous Amendments) (No. 2) Regulations 1996 and shall come into force on 13th January 1997.

(2) In these Regulations–

"the Act" means the Child Support Act 1991;

[...]

"the Maintenance Assessment Procedure Regulations" means the Child Support (Maintenance Assessment Procedure) Regulations 1992;

[...]

Transitional provision

16.–[[1](1) A decision with respect to a maintenance assessment in force on 13th January 1997 shall not be superseded by a decision under section 17 of the Act solely to give effect to these Regulations.]

(2) Where the amount of child support maintenance fixed by any fresh assessment [[1] ...] is affected by the provisions of these Regulations, the effective date of that assessment shall not be earlier than the first day of the first maintenance period which commences on or after 13th January 1997.

(3) The provisions of regulations 40A and 49A of the Maintenance Assessment Procedure Regulations in force prior to 13th January 1997 shall continue to apply to a reduced benefit direction which at that date is suspended under the provisions of regulation 40A.

Amendment

1.   Words substituted in para (1) and deleted in para (2) by art 44 of SI 1999/1510 as from 1.6.99.

Definitions

"the Act"; see reg 1(2).

"the Maintenance Assessment Procedure Regulations"; see reg 1(2).

The Child Support (Written Agreements) (Scotland) Order 1997
(1997 No.2943 (S.188))

1.   This Order may be cited as the Child Support (Written Agreements) (Scotland) Order 1997 and shall come into force on 2nd January 1998.

2.   Section 8 of the Child Support Act 1991 shall not prevent a court from exercising any power which it has to make a maintenance order in relation to a child in any circumstances in which paragraphs (a) and (b) of section 8(5) apply.

General Note

This Order makes provision for Scotland equivalent to that made for England and Wales by the Child Support (Written Maintenance) Order 1993. It applies to maintenance agreements, whether or not they have been registered for execution in the books of Council and Session.

The Child Support (Miscellaneous Amendments) Regulations 1998
(1998 No.58)

Citation, commencement and interpretation

1.–(1) These Regulations may be cited as the Child Support (Miscellaneous Amendments) Regulations 1998.

(2) Subject to paragraph (3), these regulations shall come into force on the first commencement day.

(3) Regulations 14, 39(3), 44, 45, 47, 49, 52, 54, 55 and paragraph (5) of regulation 56 shall come into force on the second commencement day.

(4) In these Regulations, unless the context otherwise requires–

[...]

"first commencement day" means 19th January 1998;

[...]

"second commencement day" means 6th April 1998.

Transitional provisions

[¹**59.**–(1) A decision with respect to a maintenance assessment in force on the first commencement day shall not be superseded by a decision under section 17 of the Child Support Act 1991 ("the Act") solely to give effect to regulation 42(2)(d), regulation 50 or regulation 56(2).

(2) The regulations specified in paragraph (1) shall apply to a fresh maintenance assessment made by virtue of–

    (a) a revision under section 16 of the Act of a decision with respect to a maintenance assessment; or

    (b) a decision under section 17 of the Act which supersedes a decision with respect to a maintenance assessment,

as from whichever is the later of–

    (i) the date as from which that revision or, as the case may be, supersession takes effect; or

    (ii) the first day of the first maintenance period which begins on or after the first commencement day, as the case may be.

(3) A decision with respect to a maintenance assessment in force on the second commencement day shall not be superseded by a decision under section 17 of the Act solely to give effect to regulations 44, 45, 47, 49, 52, 54, 55 and 56(5).

(4) The regulations specified in paragraph (3) shall apply to a fresh maintenance assessment made by virtue of–

    (a) a revision under section 16 of the Act of a decision with respect to a maintenance assessment; or

    (b) a decision under section 17 of the Act which supersedes a decision with respect to a maintenance assessment,

as from whichever is the later of–

    (i) the date as from which that revision or, as the case may be, supersession takes effect; or

    (ii) the first day of the first maintenance period which begins on or after the second commencement day, as the case may be.]

Amendment

1.   Reg 59 substituted by art 45 of SI 1999/1510 as from 1.6.99.

The Social Security Act 1998 (Commencement No.2) Order 1998
(SI 1998 No.2780 (c.66))

Citation and interpretation

1.–(1)   This Order may be cited as the Social Security Act 1998 (Commencement No.2) Order 1998.

(2)   In this Order, except where the context otherwise requires, references to sections and Schedules are references to sections and Schedules to the Social Security Act 1998.

Savings and transitional provisions

3.–(1)   From and including 16th November 1998 the references in section 16(1) and (6) of the Child Support Act 1991 to a decision of the Secretary of State shall be treated as including references to a decision of the child support officer made on or before the coming into force of section 1 (c).

(2)   From and including 16th November 1998 until the coming into force of section 41, section 16 (1) of the Child Support Act 1991 shall have effect as if the reference to section 17 were omitted.

(3)   From and including 16th November 1998 until the coming into force of section 44, section 16(3) of the Child Support Act 1991 shall have effect as if the reference to section 28ZC were omitted.

(4)   Notwithstanding the commencement of section 40, section 16 of the Child Support Act 1991 shall continue to apply with respect to any maintenance assessment which takes effect of the purposes of that Act on or before 8th December 1996 as though section 40 had not been commenced.

(5)   Notwithstanding the commencement of paragraph 46(a) of Schedule 7, section 51 (2) (a) (iii) of the Child Support Act 1991 shall continue to apply with respect to–

(a)   reviews under section 16 of that Act of maintenance assessments to which paragraph (4) of this article applies; and

(b)   reviews under sections 17 to 19 of that Act as though paragraph 46(a) had not been commenced until such time as section 41 is commenced.

The Child Support (Miscellaneous Amendments) Regulations 1999
(1999 No.977)

Citation, commencement and interpretation

1.–(1) These Regulations may be cited as the Child Support (Miscellaneous Amendments) Regulations 1999.

(2) These Regulations shall come into force on 6th April 1999 with the exception of regulations 4(2), 6(2)(a) and (5)(a)(b)(c) and (d), which shall come into force on 4th October 1999.

(3) In these Regulations–

"the Act" means the Child Support Act 1991;

...

"the first commencement day" means 6th April 1999;

...

"the second commencement day" means 4th October 1999.

[¹Transitional provisions

7.–(1) A decision with respect to a maintenance assessment in force on the first or second commencement day shall not be superseded by a decision under section 17 of the Act solely to give effect to these Regulations.

(2) These Regulations shall apply to a fresh maintenance assessment made by virtue of–

    (a) a revision under section 16 of the Act of a decision with respect to a maintenance assessment; or

    (b) a decision under section 17 of the Act which supersedes a decision with respect to a maintenance assessment,

as from whichever is the later of–

    (i)   the date as from which that revision or, as the case may be, supersession takes effect; or

    (ii) the first day of the maintenance period which begins on or after the first or second commencement day, as the case may be.]

Amendment

1.   Reg 7 substituted by art 47 of SI 1999/1510 as from 1.6.99

The Social Security and Child Support (Decisions and Appeals) Regulations 1999
(SI 1999 No.991)

PART I
General

Citation, commencement [²⁹, application and interpretation]

1.–(1)   These Regulations may be cited as the Social Security and Child Support (Decisions and Appeals) Regulations 1999.

(2)   These Regulations shall come into force–

(a)   in so far as they relate to child support and for the purposes of this regulation and regulation 2 on 1st June 1999;

(b)   in so far as they relate to–

(i)   industrial injuries benefit, guardian's allowance and child benefit; and

(ii)   a decision made under the Pension Schemes Act 1993 by virtue of section 170(2) of that Act;

on 5th July 1999;

(c)   in so far as they relate to retirement pension, widow's benefit, incapacity benefit, severe disablement allowance and maternity allowance, on 6th September 1999;

(d)   in so far as they relate to [³ working families' tax credit and disabled person's tax credit], on 5th October 1999;

(e)   in so far as they relate to attendance allowance, disability living allowance, invalid care allowance, jobseeker's allowance, credits of contributions or earnings, home responsibilities protection and vaccine damage payments, on 18th October 1999; and

(f)   for all remaining purposes, on 29th November 1999.

[²⁹(2A) *Omitted.*]]

[²⁹(2B) *Omitted.*]]

(3) In these Regulations, unless the context otherwise requires–

"the Act" means the Social Security Act 1998;

"the 1997 Act" means the Social Security (Recovery of Benefits) Act 1997;

[¹⁰[²⁸...]]

[⁹"assessed income period" is to be construed in accordance with sections 6 and 9 of the State Pension Credit Act;]

"the Claims and Payments Regulations" means the Social Security (Claims and Payments) Regulations 1987;

"appeal" means an appeal to [²²the First-tier Tribunal];

[² "the board" means the Commissioners of Inland Revenue;]

"claimant" means–

(a)   any person who is a claimant for the purposes of section 191 of the Administration Act [⁹section 35(1) of the Jobseekers Act [¹⁸, section 17(1) of the State Pension Credit Act or section 24(1) of the Welfare Reform Act]] or any other person from whom benefit is alleged to be recoverable; and

(b)   any person subject to a decision of [² an officer of the Board] under the Pension Schemes Act 1993;

[²²...]

[²¹[²⁷...]]

[¹⁸"contributory employment and support allowance" means a contributory allowance under Part 1 of the Welfare Reform Act;]

[¹⁵ "couple" means–

(a)   a man and woman who are married to each other and are members of the same household;

(b)   a man and woman who are not married to each other but are living together as husband and wife;

(c)   two people of the same sex who are civil partners of each other and are members of the same household; or

(d)   two people of the same sex who are not civil partners of each other but are living together as if they were civil partners,

and for the purposes of paragraph (d), two people of the same sex are to be regarded as living together as if they were civil partners if, but only if, they would be regarded as living together as husband and wife were they instead two people of the opposite sex; and]

"the date of notification" means–

(a)   the date that notification of a decision of the Secretary of State [³ or an officer of the Board] is treated as having been given or sent in accordance with regulation 2(b); [²⁵...]

(b)   in the case of a social fund payment arising in accordance with regulations made under section 138(2) of the Contributions and Benefits Act–

    (i)   the date seven days after the date on which the Secretary of State makes his decision to make a payment to a person to meet expenses for heating;

    (ii)   where a person collects the instrument of payment at a post office, the date the instrument is collected;

    (iii)   where an instrument of payment is sent to a post office for collection but is not collected and a replacement instrument is issued, the date on which the replacement instrument is issued; or

    (iv)   where a person questions his failure to be awarded a payment for expenses for heating, the date on which the notification of the Secretary of State's decision given in response to that question is issued; [²⁵; or

(c)   where notification of a decision of the Secretary of State is sent by means of an electronic communication (within the meaning given in section 15(1) of the Electronic Communications Act 2000), the date on which the notification is sent.]

[¹⁷"the Deferral of Retirement Pensions etc. Regulations" means the Social Security (Deferral of Retirement Pensions, Shared Additional Pension and Graduated Retirement Benefit) (Miscellaneous Provisions) Regulations 2005;]

[⁴[⁸"designated authority" means–

(a)   the Secretary of State;

(b)   a person providing services to the Secretary of State;

(c)   a local authority; or

(d)   a person providing services to, or authorised to exercise any functions of, any such authority;]]

[¹⁸"the Employment and Support Allowance Regulations" means the Employment and Support Allowance Regulations 2008;

[²⁴"failure determination" means a determination by the Secretary of State under regulation 61(2) of the Employment and Support Allowance Regulations or regulation 8(2) of the Employment and Support Allowance (Work-Related Activity) Regulations 2011 that a claimant has failed to satisfy a requirement of regulation 54 of the Employment and Support Allowance Regulations (requirement to take part in a work-focused interview) or regulation 3 of the Employment and Support Allowance (Work-Related Activity) Regulations 2011 (requirement to undertake work-related activity).]]

[⁶"family" has the same meaning as in section 137 of the Contributions and Benefits Act;]

[²²...]

[¹⁷"the Graduated Retirement Benefit Regulations" means the Social Security (Graduated Retirement Benefit) Regulations 2005;]

[¹⁸"income-related employment and support allowance" means an income-related allowance under Part 1 of the Welfare Reform Act;]

"the Income Support Regulations" means the Income Support (General) Regulations 1987;

"the Jobseeker's Allowance Regulations" means the Jobseeker's Allowance Regulations 1996;

[¹⁶"a joint-claim couple" has the same meaning as in section 1(4) of the Jobseekers Act 1995;

"a joint-claim jobseeker's allowance" has the same meaning as in section 1(4) of the Jobseekers Act 1995;]

[²²...]

[¹⁸"limited capability for work" has the same meaning as in section 1(4) of the Welfare Reform Act]

[¹⁰[²⁸...]

[²⁸...]]

[⁵[²³...]]

[²²...]

[¹⁴...]

[⁴[⁷ "official error" means an error made by–

    (a)   an officer of the Department for Work and Pensions[²¹[²⁷...]] or the Board acting as such which no person outside the Department[²¹[²⁷...]] or the Inland Revenue caused or to which no person outside the Department[²¹[²⁷...]] or the Inland Revenue materially contributed;

    (b)   a person employed by a designated authority acting on behalf of the authority, which no person outside that authority caused or to which no person outside that authority materially contributed,

but excludes any error of law which is shown to have been an error by virtue of a subsequent decision of [²²the Upper Tribunal] or the court;]]

[¹¹[²²...]]

[²²...]

[²²...]

[²²...]

["partner" means–

    (a)   where a person is a member of [¹⁵a couple], the other member of that couple; or

    (b)   where a person is polygamously married to two or more members of his household, any such member;]

"party to the proceedings" means the Secretary of State [²¹[²⁷...]] and any other person–

    (a)   who is one of the principal parties for the purposes of sections 13 and 14;

    (b)   who has a right of appeal to [²²the First-tier Tribunal] under section 11(2) of the 1997 Act, section 20 of the Child Support Act [¹⁰...] [¹², section 2B(6) of the Administration Act] or section 12(2);

[²²...]

"referral" means a referral of an application for a [¹⁰

variation] to [²²the First-tier Tribunal] under section 28D(1)(b) of the Child Support Act.[²⁶[²⁸...]]

[²⁰"the Lump Sum Payments Regulations" means the Social Security (Recovery of Benefits) (Lump Sum Payments) Regulations 2008;]

[¹⁰ [²⁸...]]

[⁶"relevant credit" means a credit of contributions or earnings resulting from a decision in accordance with regulations made under section 22(5) of the Contributions and Benefits Act;]

[⁹"state pension credit" means the benefit payable under the State Pension Credit Act;

"State Pension Credit Act" means the State Pension Credit Act 2002;

"State Pension Credit Regulations" means the State Pension Credit Regulations 2002];

[³ "tax credit" means working families' tax credit or disabled person's tax credit, construing those terms in accordance with section 1(1) of the Tax Credits Act 1999;]

[¹ "the Transfer Act" means the Social Security Contributions (Transfer of Functions, etc.) Act 1999.]

[¹⁰ [²⁸...]]

[¹⁸"the Welfare Reform Act" means the Welfare Reform Act 2007;]

[⁴[⁸[¹³"work-focused interview" means an interview in which a person is required to take part in accordance with regulations made under section 2A or 2AA of the Administration Act;]]]

[⁸...]]

[² (3A) In these Regulations as they relate to any decision made under the Pension Schemes Act 1993 by virtue of section 170(2) of that Act, any reference to the Secretary of State is to be construed as if it were a reference to an officer of the Board.]

(4)   In these Regulations, unless the context otherwise requires, a reference–

(a)   to a numbered section is to the section of the Act bearing that number;

(b)   to a numbered Part is to the Part of these Regulations bearing that number;

(c)   to a numbered regulation or Schedule is to the regulation in, or Schedule to, these Regulations bearing that number;

(d)   in a regulation or Schedule to a numbered paragraph is to the paragraph in that regulation or Schedule bearing that number;

(e)   in a paragraph to a lettered or numbered sub-paragraph is to the sub-paragraph in that paragraph bearing that letter or number.

Amendments

1.   Social Security and Child Support (Decisions and Appeals) Amendment (No.3) Regulations 1999 (SI 1999 No.1670), reg 2(2) (July 5, 1999).

2.   Social Security Contributions (Transfer of Functions, etc.) Act 1999 (Commencement No.2 and Consequential and Transitional Provisions) Order 1999 (SI 1999 No.1662 (C.47)), art 3(2) (July 5, 1999).

3.   Tax Credits (Decisions and Appeals) (Amendment) Regulations 1999 (SI 1999 No.2570), regs 3 and 4 (October 5, 1999). Note that amendments made by these regulations only haved effect with respect to working families' tax credit or disabled person's tax credit (reg 1(2) of the Amendment Regulations).

4.   Social Security (Work-focused Interviews) Regulations 2000 (SI 2000 No.897), reg 16(5) and Sch 6 para 2 (April 3, 2000).

5.   The Social Security (Breach of Community Order) (Consequential Amendments) Regulations 2001 (SI 2001 No.1711) reg 2(2) (October 15, 2001).

6.   Social Security and Child Support (Miscellaneous Amendments) Regulations 2000 (SI 2000 No.1596) reg 14 (June 19, 2000).

7.   Social Security and Child Support (Decisions and Appeals) (Miscellaneous Amendments) Regulations 2002 (SI 2002 No.1379) reg 2 (May 20, 2002).

8.   Social Security (Jobcentre Plus Interviews) Regulations 2002 (SI 2002 No.1703) Sch 2 para 6 (September 30, 2002).

9.   State Pension Credit (Consequential, Transitional and Miscellaneous Provisions) Regulations 2002 (SI 2002 No.3019) reg 16 (April 7, 2003).

10.   Child Support (Decisions and Appeals) (Amendment) Regulations 2000 (SI 2000 No.3185) reg 2 (comes into force for the types of cases detailed in art 3 of SI 2003 No.192 and those detailed in reg 1(2) of SI 2000 No.3185 on March 3, 2003, subject to the saving provision in art 14(3) of SI 2000 No.3185). For other types of cases see the '1993 rules', below.

11.   Social Security and Child Support (Miscellaneous Amendments) Regulations 2003 (SI 2003 No.1050) reg 3(1) (May 5, 2003).

12.   Social Security (Jobcentre Plus Interviews for Partners) Regulations 2003 (SI 2003 No. 1886) reg 15(2) (April 12, 2004).

13.   Social Security (Working Neighbourhoods) Regulations 2004 (SI 2004 No. 959) reg 24(2) (April 26, 2004).

14.   Social Security, Child Support and Tax Credits (Decisions and Appeals) Amendment Regulations 2004 (SI 2004 No.3368) reg 2(2) (December 21, 2004).

15.   Social Security (Civil Partnership) (Consequential Amendments) Regulations 2005 (SI 2005 No.2878) reg 8(2) (December 5, 2005).

16.   Social Security Amendment (Joint Claims) Regulations 2001 (SI 2001 No.518) reg 4(a) (March 19, 2001).

17.   Social Security (Deferral of Retirement Pensions, Shared Additional Pension and Graduated Retirement Benefit) (Miscellaneous Provisions) Regulations 2005 (SI 2005 No.2677) reg 9(2) (April 6, 2006).

18.   Employment and Support Allowance (Consequential Provisions) (No.2) Regulations 2008 (SI 2008 No. 1554) reg 30 (July 27, 2008).

19.   Child Support (Consequential Provisions) Regulations 2008 (SI 2008 No.2543) reg 4(2) (October 27, 2008).

20.   Social Security (Recovery of Benefits) (Lump Sum Payments) Regulations 2008 (SI 2008 No.1596) reg 3 and Sch 2 para 1(a) (October 1, 2008).

21. Child Support (Consequential Provisions) (No.2) Regulations 2008 (SI 2008 No.2656) reg 4 (November 1, 2008).
22. Tribunals, Courts and Enforcement Act 2007 (Transitional and Consequential Provisions) Order 2008 (SI 2008 No.2683) Sch 1 para 96 (November 3, 2008).
23. Welfare Reform Act 2009 (Section 26) (Consequential Amendments) Regulations 2010 (SI 2010 No.424) art 4(2) (March 22, 2010, except in far as this amendment relates to a person who immediately before March 22, 2010 was subject to a restriction under ss 62 or 63 of the Child Support, Pensions and Social Security Act 2000, when it came into force on the first day of the first benefit week to commence for that person on or after March 22, 2010).
24. Employment and Support Allowance (Work-Related Activity) Regulations 2011 (SI 2011 No.1349) reg 21 (June 1, 2011).
25. Social Security (Electronic Communications) Order 2011 (SI 2011 No.1498) art 5 (June 20, 2011).
26. Child Support (Miscellaneous Amendments) Regulations 2011 (SI 2011 No.1464) reg 2(2) (July 4, 2011).
27. Public Bodies (Child Maintenance and Enforcement Commission: Abolition and Transfer of Functions) Order 2012 (SI 2012 No.2007) art 3(2) and Sch para 113(2) (August 1, 2012).
28. Child Support (Meaning of Child and New Calculation Rules) (Consequential and Miscellaneous Amendment) Regulations 2012 (SI 2012 No.2785) reg 6(2) (in force in relation to a particular case on the day on which paragraph 2 of Schedule 4 to the Child Maintenance and Other Payments Act 2008 (see p243) comes into force in relation to that type of case – which is December 10, 2012 in relation to the types of cases falling within art 3 of SI 2012 No.3042 (see p767)). For other types of cases see the '2003 rules' or the '1993 rules', below.
29. Universal Credit, Personal Independence Payment, Jobseeker's Allowance and Employment and Support Allowance (Decisions and Appeals) Regulations 2013 (SI 2013 No.381) reg 55 (in so far as amendments relate to personal independence payment, April 8, 2013; for all remaining purposes, April 29, 2013, subject to the transitional provisions contained in art 21 of The Welfare Reform Act 2012 (Commencement No.9 and Transitional and Transitory Provisions and Commencement No.8 and Savings and Transitional Provisions (Amendment)) Order 2013 (SI 2013 No.983)).

2003 rules

Regulation 6(2) of the Child Support (Meaning of Child and New Calculation Rules) (Consequential and Miscellaneous Amendment) Regulations 2012 (SI 2012 No.2785) amends this regulation and comes into force on December 10, 2012 in relation to the types of cases falling within art 3 of SI 2012 No.3042 (see p767). For other types of cases, the amendments have not been brought into force and, unless the 1993 rules apply, the following definitions are retained in regulation 1(3):

[[10]"the Arrears, Interest and Adjustment of Maintenance Assessments Regulations" means the Child Support (Arrears, Interest and Adjustment of Maintenance Assessments) Regulations 1992;]

[[10]"the Maintenance Calculation Procedure Regulations" means the Child Support (Maintenance Calculation Procedure) Regulations 2000;

"the Maintenance Calculations and Special Cases Regulations" means the Child Support (Maintenance Calculations and Special Cases) Regulations 2000;]

[[29] "relevant other child" is to be interpreted by reference to paragraph 10C(2) of Schedule 1 to the Child Support Act;]

[[10]except where otherwise provided "relevant person" means–
   (a)   a person with care;
   (b)   a non-resident parent;
   (c)   a parent who is treated as a non-resident parent under regulation 8 of the Maintenance Calculations and Special Cases Regulations;
   (d)   a child, where the application for a maintenance calculation is made by that child under section 7 of the Child Support Act,

in respect of whom a maintenance calculation has been applied for [19...] or is or has been in force;]

[[10] "the Variations Regulations" means the Child Support (Variations) Regulations 2000.]

1993 rules

Reg 2 of the Child Support (Decisions and Appeals) (Amendment) Regulations 2000 (SI 2000 No.3185) amends this regulation and has been brought into force on March 3, 2003 for the types of cases in art 3 of the Child Support, Pensions and Social Security Act 2000 (Commencement No.12) Order 2003 (SI 2003 No.192 – see p683) and in reg 1(2) of SI 2000 No.3185 – see p536, subject to the saving provision in art 14(3) of SI 2000 No.3185. For other types of cases, the '1993 rules' apply. These amendments have since been subject to further amendment by reg 6(2) of the Child Support (Meaning of Child and New Calculation Rules) (Consequential and Miscellaneous Amendment) Regulations 2012 (SI 2012 No.2785) in some instances restoring the text to its earlier form. If the 1993 rules apply, regulation 1 is as it is reproduced in the main text, above, with the following variations:

– the definition of 'relevant other child' shown under '2003 rules' is retained in reg 1(3);
– in paragraph (b) in the definition of "party to the proceedings" the words "as extended by para 3 of Sch 4C to that Act" are retained after "the Child Support Act";
– in the definition of "referral" the words "departure direction" are retained in place of "variation".

General Note
"official error"
In *CCS 2819/2000*, the tribunal had reached a decision on the basis of incorrect information provided by the presenting officer at the hearing. When this was discovered during the proceedings before the commissioner, the Secretary of State revised the decision of the tribunal from its effective date. The commissioner gave a direction that in those circumstances the appeal before him had lapsed. He accepted that the words "the decision arose from an official error" were sufficiently wide to cover the circumstances of the case.

In *CDLA 3440/2003* para 8, the commissioner held that official error refers to mistakes in adjudication decisions or to mistakes that affect those decisions. On that basis, making a computer record of a decision was a purely administrative matter that required no legislative authority so that a mistake in doing so could not have had any impact on the decision that was made. In *R(CS) 3/04*, the commissioner held that official error included mistakes made by officials acting in the former capacity of child support officers. In *CH 943/2003*, the commissioner held that a decision by a decision maker that was reversed by an appeal tribunal was made in official error. The principle in this case has been followed and applied by a different commissioner in a social security case (*CG 4495/2004*). The Secretary of State appealed against that decision to the Court of Appeal. The appeal was allowed by consent with a variation being made to the terms of the commissioner's decision. As that variation was made by consent, it is not binding on anyone other than the parties to it. The commissioner's decision remains an authority in its original form. In *R(H) 2/04*, the commissioner held that it was not an error or mistake for decision makers to rely on the best information currently available and to trust the parties concerned to inform them if it was not correct.

"party to the proceedings"
There is no power for anyone other than the persons specified to be identified as, or made, a party to the proceedings.

The Secretary of State is not personally a party to the proceedings and is not a party in a contentious sense. The duty of the officer who makes a decision is to apply the law. It follows that the duty of the officer who attends an oral hearing as a presenting officer is to assist the tribunal in identifying and analysing the evidence and issues relevant to the decision that the appeal tribunal has to make. This role is more like that of a friend of the court than a true party to litigation (*R v National Industrial Injuries Commissioner ex p Moore* [1965] 1 All ER 81 at 93, *per* Diplock LJ). The officer should, though, be cautious of supporting an appeal so as not to raise false hopes, or cause unfounded fears, in the other parties (*CM 361/1992*, para 11). Also, inappropriate support may induce a party not to present all relevant evidence and argument in the belief that the decision of the appeal tribunal is a foregone conclusion.

Service of notices or documents
2. Where, by any provision of the Act[³, of the Child Support Act] or of these Regulations–

(a) any notice or other document is required to be given or sent [⁴...] to an officer authorised by the Secretary of State [¹ or to an officer of the Board], that notice or document shall be treated as having been so given or sent on the day that it is received [⁴...] by an officer authorised by the Secretary of State [¹ or by an officer of the Board], as the case may be, and

(b) any notice (including notification of a decision of the Secretary of State [² or of an officer of the Board]) or other document is required to be given or sent to any person other than [⁴...] [¹an officer] authorised by the Secretary of State [¹ or an officer of the Board], as the case may be, that notice or document shall, if sent by post to that person's last known address, be treated as having been given or sent on the day that it was posted.

Amendments
1.	Tax Credits (Decisions and Appeals) (Amendment) Regulations 1999 (SI 1999 No.2570), reg 5 (October 5, 1999). Note that amendments made by these regulations only have effect with respect to working families' tax credit or disabled person's tax credit (reg 1(2) of the Amendment Regulations).

2. Tax Credits (Decisions and Appeals) (Amendment) Regulations 2000 (SI 2000 No.127), reg 2 (February 14, 2000). This amendment has effect with respect only to tax credit (reg 1(2) of the Amendment Regulations).
3. Child Support (Decisions and Appeals) (Amendment) Regulations 2000 (SI 2000 No.3185) reg 3 (comes into force for the types of cases detailed in art 3 of SI 2003 No.192 and those detailed in reg 1(2) of SI 2000 No.3185 on March 3, 2003, subject to the saving provision in art 14(3) of SI 2000 No.3185). For other types of cases see the '1993 rules', below.
4. Tribunals, Courts and Enforcement Act 2007 (Transitional and Consequential Provisions) Order 2008 (SI 2008 No.2683) Sch 1 para 97 (November 3, 2008). In relation to certain appeals under Health and Social Care (Community Health and Standards) Act 2003 (2003 c.43) some of these amendments do not extend to Scotland – see SI 2008 No.2683 arts 3 and 4 for details.

1993 rules

Reg 3 of the Child Support (Decisions and Appeals) (Amendment) Regulations 2000 (SI 2000 No.3185) amends this regulation and has been brought into force on March 3, 2003 only for the types of cases in art 3 of the Child Support, Pensions and Social Security Act 2000 (Commencement No.12) Order 2003 (SI 2003 No.192) – see p683 and in reg 1(2) of SI 2000 No.3185 – see p536, subject to the saving provision in art 14(3) of SI 2000 No.3185. For other types of cases the '1993 rules' apply. If the 1993 rules apply the words ", of the Child Support Act" are not inserted after the words "of the Act".

Definitions

"the Act": see reg 1(3).
"clerk to the appeal tribunal": see reg 1(3).

General Note

Head (a)

When is a document received? Usually the answer to this question will be decided by the evidence available. In most cases the only evidence of the date of receipt will be the date stamped on the document, not infrequently in a position which obscures important contents. A party will seldom be in a position to challenge this date. Such a challenge is most likely to be made when the party alleges that the document was delivered by hand on a different day, perhaps late in the afternoon or at a weekend. The usual meaning of receipt involves something coming into someone's hands. This suggests that mere delivery to the building is insufficient. There is authority for the proposition that delivery through a letter box is sufficient to constitute notice on the basis that the presence of the letter box impliedly invites communication by that means (*Holwell Securities Ltd v Hughes* [1974] 1 All ER 161 at 164). However, that decision turned on notice. "Receipt", in contrast, is to be given its natural meaning.

Swainston v Hetton Victory Club Ltd [1983] 1 All ER 1179 dealt with when a complaint could be "presented" to an industrial tribunal. In particular, the issue was whether a complaint could be presented on a day when the tribunal office was closed. The Court of Appeal held that, as the tribunal was not required to take any steps, the complaint could be presented by being put through the letterbox of the tribunal office on a Sunday. Accordingly, it was not necessary to disregard that day as one when the tribunal office was closed. This analysis is in accordance with the Court of Appeal in *Um Aken v Camden London Borough Council* [2003] 1 All ER 552. The case was concerned with when a document was filed. The court distinguished between a unilateral act, in which the recipient does not need to take any action and has a purely passive role, and a transactional act, in which the recipient has to take action and has an active role. It decided that the filing of a document was a unilateral act, so that delivery to the court was all that was required. It is possible that these cases are distinguishable in the interpretation of this provision. Presenting a complaint or filing a document concentrates on the action of the person initiating the communication. This is in contrast to receipt which concentrates on the person to whom the communication is directed.

If the Post Office fails to deliver under-stamped mail in accordance with a bulk surcharging arrangement, it holds the mail as bailee for the addressee, and the mail is treated as being delivered on the day it would have arrived in the ordinary course of post (*CIS 4901/2002*).

Head (b)

In *SSWP v Roach* [2006] EWCA Civ 1746 (reported as *R(CS) 4/07*), Leveson LJ said of this head (para 26) that "this fixes the time form which the prescribed period ... starts to run (thus avoiding the risk of a nullity) and, in my view, this provision also operates to prescribe the circumstances in which the notice is to be treated as served whether or not it had actually been received..." He went on to comment that, in that case, the mother had not been prejudiced by the failure of the notice to arrive. The Court left open (para 27) whether this regulation below was mandatory or directory.

The rule applies regardless of whether or not the notice or document is actually received (*R(SB) 55/83*).

The address to which the notice or document must have been sent is the person's last known address. Usually an address will be known because it will have been notified to the clerk to the tribunal by the person concerned. However, if someone else has suggested that a person who has moved may be living at another address, it will have to be decided whether that person's knowledge and the confidence with which the information was conveyed are such that that address is so certain that it may be said to be the person's last known address.

A document is only sent by post if it is sent by the Royal Mail rather than by courier or through a document exchange system (*CIS 550/1993*, para 6).

PART II
REVISIONS, SUPERSESSIONS AND OTHER MATTERS
SOCIAL SECURITY [¹ AND CHILD SUPPORT]
CHAPTER I
Revisions

Amendment

1.   Reg 3 Appeals Amendment Regulations 2000 (for in force date see regs 1 and 14 of SI 2000/3185).

[¹ Consideration of revision before appeal

3ZA.–(1)   This regulation applies in a case where–

(a)   the Secretary of State gives a person written notice of a decision under section 8 or 10 of the Act (whether as originally made or as revised under section 9 of that Act); and

(b)   that notice includes a statement to the effect that there is a right of appeal in relation to the decision only if the Secretary of State has considered an application for a revision of the decision.

(2)   In a case to which this regulation applies, a person has a right of appeal under section 12(2) of the Act in relation to the decision only if the Secretary of State has considered on an application whether to revise the decision under section 9 of the Act.

(3)   The notice referred to in paragraph (1) must inform the person–

(a)   of the time limit specified in regulation 3(1) or (3) for making an application for a revision; and

(b)   that, where the notice does not include a statement of the reasons for the decision ("written reasons"), he may, within one month of the date of notification of the decision, request that the Secretary of State provide him with written reasons.

(4)   Where written reasons are requested under paragraph (3)(b), the Secretary of State must provide them within 14 days of receipt of the request or as soon as practicable afterwards.

(5)   Where, as the result of paragraph (2), there is no right of appeal against a decision, the Secretary of State may treat any purported appeal as an application for a revision under section 9 of the Act.]

Amendment

1.   Social Security, Child Support, Vaccine Damage and Other Payments (Decisions and Appeals) (Amendment) Regulations 2013 (SI 2013 No.2380) reg 4 (October 28, 2013).

[¹ Revision of child support decisions

3A.–[⁸...]

Amendments

1.   Child Support (Decisions and Appeals) (Amendment) Regulations 2000 (SI 2000 No.3185) reg 5 (comes into force for the types of cases detailed in art 3 of SI 2003 No.192 and those detailed in reg 1(2) of SI 2000 No.3185 on March 3, 2003, subject to the saving provision in art 14(3) of SI 2000 No. 3185). For other types of cases see the '1993 rules' below.

2.   Child Support (Miscellaneous Amendments) Regulations 2002 (SI 2002 No.1204) reg 2(2) (comes into force for the types of cases detailed in art 3 of SI 2003 No.192 on March 3, 2003).

3.   Child Support (Misc Amendments) (No.2) Regulations 2008 (SI 2008 No.2544) reg 3 (October 27, 2008).

4.   Child Support (Consequential Provisions) Regulations 2008 (SI 2008 No.2543) reg 4(3) (October 27, 2008).

5.   Tribunals, Courts and Enforcement Act 2007 (Transitional and Consequential Provisions) Order 2008 (SI 2008 No.2683) Sch 1 para 99 (November 3, 2008).

6.   Child Support (Miscellaneous Amendments) Regulations 2009 (SI 2009 No.396) reg 4(2) (April 6, 2009). These amendments do not apply to '1993 scheme cases' as defined by reg 7(2) of SI 2009 No.396.

7.   Public Bodies (Child Maintenance and Enforcement Commission: Abolition and Transfer of Functions) Order 2012 (SI 2012 No.2007) art 3(2) and Sch para 113(3) (August 1, 2012).

8.	Child Support (Meaning of Child and New Calculation Rules) (Consequential and Miscellaneous Amendment) Regulations 2012 (SI 2012 No.2785) reg 6(3) (in force in relation to a particular case on the day on which Sch 4 para 2 to the Child Maintenance and Other Payments Act 2008 (see p243) comes into force in relation to that type of case – which is December 10, 2012 in relation to the types of cases falling within art 3 of SI 2012 No.3042 (see p767)). For other types of cases see '2003 rules' below.

2003 rules

Regulation 6(3) of the Child Support (Meaning of Child and New Calculation Rules) (Consequential and Misc Amendment) Regulations 2012 (SI 2012 No.2785) omits regulation 3A and comes into force on December 10, 2012 in relation to the types of cases falling within art 3 of SI 2012 No.3042 (see p767). For other types of cases regulation 6(3) of SI 2012 No.2785 is not yet in force and regulation 3A, reproduced below, continues to apply.

[¹Revision of child support decisions

3A.–(1)	Subject to paragraph (2), any decision as defined in paragraph (3) may be revised under section 16 of the Child Support Act by the [⁶[⁷Secretary of State]]–

(a)	if [⁶[⁷the Secretary of State]] receives an application for the revision of a decision either–
>	(i)	under section 16; or
>	(ii)	by way of an application under section 28G,
>	of the Child Support Act, within one month of the date of notification of the decision or within such longer time as may be allowed under regulation 4;

(b)	if–
>	(i)	[⁶[⁷the Secretary of State]] notifies the person who applied for a decision to be revised within the period specified in sub-paragraph (a), that the application is unsuccessful because the [⁶[⁷Secretary of State]] is not in possession of all of the information or evidence needed to make a decision; and
>	(ii)	that person reapplies for the decision to be revised within one month of the notification described in head (i) above, or such longer period as the [⁶[⁷Secretary of State]] is satisfied is reasonable in the circumstances of the case, and provides in that application sufficient information or evidence to enable a decision to be made;

(c)	if [⁶[⁷the Secretary of State]] is satisfied that the decision was erroneous due to a misrepresentation of, or failure to disclose, a material fact and that the decision was more advantageous to the person who misrepresented or failed to disclose that fact than it would have been but for that error;

[²(cc)	if an appeal is made under section 20 of the Child Support Act against a decision within the time prescribed [⁵by Tribunal Procedure Rules] but the appeal has not been determined;]

(d)	[⁶[⁷the Secretary of State]] commences action leading to the revision of the decision within one month of the date of notification of the decision; or

(e)	if the decision arose from an official error[²; or

(f)	if the grounds for revision are that a person with respect to whom a maintenance calculation was made was not, at the time the calculation was made, a parent of a child to whom the calculation relates.]

(2)	Paragraph (1)(a) to (d) shall not apply in respect of a change of circumstances which–

(a)	occurred since the date on which the decision had effect; or

(b)	according to information or evidence which the [⁶[⁷Secretary of State]] has, is expected to occur.

[²(3)	In paragraphs (1), (2) and (5A) and in regulation 4(3) "decision" means a decision of the [⁶[⁷Secretary of State]] under section [⁴11 or 12] of the Child Support Act, or a determination of [⁵the First-tier Tribunal] on a referral under section 28D(1)(b) of that Act, or any supersession of a decision under section 17 of that Act, whether as originally made or as revised under section 16 of that Act.]

(4)	A decision made under section 12(2) of the Child Support Act may be revised at any time before it is replaced by a decision under section 11 of that Act.

(5)   Where the [⁶[⁷Secretary of State]] revises a decision made under section 12(1) of the Child Support Act in accordance with section 16(1B) of that Act, that decision may be revised under section 16 of that Act at any time.

[²(5A)   Where–
(a)   the [⁶[⁷Secretary of State]] makes a decision ("decision A") and there is an appeal;
(b)   there is a further decision in relation to the appellant ("decision B") after the appeal but before the appeal results in a decision by [⁵the First-tier Tribunal] ("decision C"); and
(c)   [⁶[⁷Secretary of State]] would have made decision B differently if [⁷...] aware of decision C at the time [⁷of making] decision B,
decision B may be revised at any time.]

(6)   [⁶...]
(7)   [⁶...]]

[³(8)   Subject to paragraph (9), section 16 of the Child Support Act shall apply in relation to any decision of the [⁶[⁷Secretary of State]] not to make a maintenance calculation, as it applies in relation to any decision of the [⁶[⁷Secretary of State]] under sections 11, 12 or 17 of that Act, or the determination of an appeal tribunal on a referral under section 28D(1)(b) of that Act.

(9)   Paragraph (8) shall not apply to any decision not to make a maintenance calculation where the [⁶[⁷Secretary of State]] makes a decision under section 12 of the Child Support Act.]

1993 rules

Reg 5 of the Child Support (Decisions and Appeals) (Amendment) Regulations 2000 (SI 2000 No.3185) inserted reg 3A and was brought into force on March 3, 2003 for the types of cases detailed in art 3 of SI 2003 No.192 (see p683) and those detailed in reg 1(2) of SI 2000 No.3185 (see p536), subject to the saving provision in art 14(3) of SI 2000 No.3185. For other types of cases, the 1993 rules apply and reg 3A is not inserted.

Definitions

"date of notification": see reg 1(3).
"official error": see reg 1(3).
"referral": see reg 1(3).

General Note

Paragraph (1)

A decision may be revised if an application is made or action is initiated by the Secretary of State within the one-month time limit. That limit may be extended under reg 4. The grounds on which a decision may be revised are not specified. An error of fact or law will justify a revision, but the revision jurisdiction is not so limited. A revision may be based on any ground, except a change of circumstances (see para (2)). This includes a different exercise on the same facts of a discretion relevant to the decision.

Outside the time limit, a revision may only be made if an error arose from one of the specified causes.

The powers to revise and to supersede are mutually exclusive. If revision is possible, the decision must be revised and not superseded: see reg 6A(7). In the case of a supersession on the Secretary of State's own initiative, the relevant date for determining whether a revision or a supersession is permissible is the date when the decision is taken. If it is taken within one month of the decision under consideration, only a revision is permissible. If it is taken outside that period, a supersession is permissible. Action on the Secretary of State's own initiative does not require an application. See *CDLA 3688/2001,* paras 7-16.

The power to revise is additional to the provisions that provide for a maintenance calculation to cease to have effect under Sch 1 para 16 to the Act.

The subparagraphs specify circumstances in which a decision may be revised.

Subparagraphs (a), (b) and (d) contain tight timetables. The circumstances covered by subparas (c) and (e) make it inappropriate for there to be time limits. Separate provision is made for interim maintenance decisions in para (4) and for subsequent revisions of default maintenance decisions in para (5).

On appeal, a tribunal has jurisdiction to substitute a revision for a supersession and a supersession for a revision (*R(IB) 2/04*).

Subparagraph (a)

This is the companion to subpara (d). It is the basic provision under which a decision may be challenged. The application must be made within one month, subject to the possibility of an extension under reg 4.

Subparagraph (b)
This allows a further chance to someone whose application for a revision was rejected because of lack of information or evidence. The person is allowed a period of grace in which to provide the information or evidence. The default period is one month, but this may be extended by the Secretary of State.
Subparagraph (c)
This applies without time limit.
Subparagraph (cc)
This allows a decision to be revised if it is under appeal, provided that the appeal has not been determined. The power may be used by the Secretary of State, but not by the tribunal on the appeal itself *CCS 3054/2009*, para 19).
Subparagraph (d)
This is the companion to subpara (a). It gives a correction power to the Secretary of State provided that action is initiated within one month. The time cannot be extended. If the ecretary of State wishes to alter a decision outside this time limit, it may be done by revision for official error under subpara (e) or by supersession under reg 6A.
Subparagraph (e)
This applies without time limit. It allows the Secretary of State to correct official errors.
Subparagraph (f)
This allows a decision to be revised if it is was made on the incorrect basis that a person in respect of whom the maintenance calculation was made was a parent.
Paragraph (2)
A change of circumstances can only be dealt with by way of supersession under s17 of the Act.
Paragraph (5A)
This allows a decision to be revised in order to give knock-on effect to a decision by a tribunal on an earlier decision into another decision that was made while the appeal was pending. Assume that a calculation is made in which the non-resident parent's income is calculated in a particular way. The non-resident parent appeals against that decision. While the appeal is pending another calculation is made on the same basis. If the tribunal changes the basis of calculation of the non-resident parent's income, that can be given effect in respect of the second calculation by revision under this paragraph.

[¹ Consideration of revision before appeal in relation to certain child support decisions

3B.–(1)   This regulation applies in a case where–
(a)   the Secretary of State gives a person written notice of a decision; and
(b)   that notice includes a statement to the effect that there is a right of appeal against the decision only if the Secretary of State has considered an application for a revision of the decision.
(2)   In a case to which this regulation applies, a person has a right of appeal under section 20 of the Child Support Act 1991 (as substituted by section 10 of the Child Support, Pensions and Social Security Act 2000) against the decision only if the Secretary of State has considered on an application whether to revise the decision under section 16 of that Act.
(3)   The notice referred to in paragraph (1) must inform the person of the time limit specified in regulation 3A(1)(a) for making an application for a revision.
(4)   Where, as the result of paragraph (2), there is no right of appeal against a decision, the Secretary of State may treat any purported appeal as an application for a revision under section 16 of that Act.
(5)   In this regulation "decision" means a decision mentioned in section 20(1)(a) or (b) of the Child Support Act 1991 (as substituted by section 10 of the Child Support, Pensions and Social Security Act 2000).]

Amendment
1.   Social Security, Child Support, Vaccine Damage and Other Payments (Decisions and Appeals) (Amendment) Regulations 2013 (SI 2013 No.2380) reg 4 (October 28, 2013).

Late application for a revision
4.–(1)   The time limit for making an application for a revision specified in regulation 3(1) or (3) [²[⁶...]or 3A(1)(a)] may be extended where the conditions specified in the following provisions of this regulation are satisfied.
(2)   An application for an extension of time shall be made by [²[⁶...]] the claimant or a person acting on his behalf.

(3)   An application shall–

(a)   contain particulars of the grounds on which the extension of time is sought and shall contain sufficient details of the decision which it is sought to have revised to enable that decision to be identified; and

(b)   be made within 13 months of the date of notification of the decision which it is sought to have revised [³, but if the applicant has requested a statement of the reasons in accordance with regulation [⁷regulation 3ZA (3)-(b) or] 28(1)(b) the 13 month period shall be extended by–

    (i)   if the statement is provided within one month of the notification, an additional 14 days; or

    (ii)   if it is provided after the elapse of a period after the one month ends, the length of that period and an additional 14 days.].

(4)   An application for an extension of time shall not be granted unless the applicant satisfies the Secretary of State [⁵, the Commission] [¹ or the Board or an officer of the Board] that–

(a)   it is reasonable to grant the application;

(b)   the application for revision has merit[⁷, except in a case to which regulation 3ZA or 3B applies]; and

(c)   special circumstances are relevant to the application and as a result of those special circumstances it was not practicable for the application to be made within the time limit specified in regulation 3 [²[⁶...]].

(5)   In determining whether it is reasonable to grant an application, the Secretary of State [⁵, the Commission][¹ or the Board or an officer of the Board] shall have regard to the principle that the greater the amount of time that has elapsed between the expiration of the time specified in regulation 3(1) and (3) [²[⁶...]] for applying for a revision and the making of the application for an extension of time, the more compelling should be the special circumstances on which the application is based.

(6)   In determining whether it is reasonable to grant the application for an extension of time [⁷, except in a case to whick regulation 3ZA or 3B applies], no account shall be taken of the following–

(a)   that the applicant or any person acting for him was unaware of or misunderstood the law applicable to his case (including ignorance or misunderstanding of the time limits imposed by these Regulations); or

(b)   [⁴the Upper Tribunal] or a court has taken a different view of the law from that previously understood and applied.

(7)   An application under this regulation for an extension of time which has been refused may not be renewed.

Amendments

1.   Tax Credits (Decisions and Appeals) (Amendment) Regulations 1999 (SI 1999 No.2570), reg 7 (October 5, 1999). Note that amendments made by these regulations only have effect with respect to working families' tax credit or disabled person's tax credit (reg 1(2) of the Amendment Regulations).

2.   Child Support (Decisions and Appeals) (Amendment) Regulations 2000 (SI 2000 No.3185) reg 6 (comes into force for the types of cases detailed in art 3 of SI 2003 No.192 and those detailed in reg 1(2) of SI 2000 No.3185 on March 3, 2003, subject to the saving provision in art 14(3) of SI 2000 No.3185). For other types of cases see the '1993 rules' below.

3.   Social Security, Child Support and Tax Credits (Miscellaneous Amendments) Regulations 2005 (SI 2005 No.337) reg 2(3) (March 18, 2005).

4.   Tribunals, Courts and Enforcement Act 2007 (Transitional and Consequential Provisions) Order 2008 (SI 2008 No.2683) Sch 1 para 100 (November 3, 2008).

5.   Child Support (Miscellaneous Amendments) Regulations 2009 (SI 2009 No.396) reg 4(3) (April 6, 2009). This does not apply to '1993 scheme cases' as defined by reg 7(2) of SI 2009 No.396. For such cases see the '1993 rules' below.

6.   Child Support (Meaning of Child and New Calculation Rules) (Consequential and Miscellaneous Amendment) Regulations 2012 (SI 2012 No.2785) reg 6(4) (in force in relation to a particular case on the day on which parag 2 of Sch 4 to the Child Maintenance and Other Payments Act 2008 (see p243) comes into force in relation to that type of case – which is December 10, 2012 in relation to the types of cases falling within art 3 of SI 2012 No.3042 (see p767)). For other types of cases see the '2003 rules' below.

7.   Social Security, Child Support, Vaccine Damage and Other Payments (Decision and Appeals) (Amendment) Regulations 2013 (SI 2013 No.2380) reg 4 (October 28, 2013).

2003 rules

Regulation 6(4) of the Child Support (Meaning of Child and New Calculation Rules) (Consequential and Miscellaneous Amendment) Regulations 2012 (SI 2012 No.2785) amends this regulation and comes into force on December 10, 2012 in relation to the types of cases falling within art 3 of SI 2012 No.3042 (see p767). For other types of cases the amendments have not been brought into force and:

–   in paragraph (1) the words "or 3A(1)(a)" are not omitted after "3(1) or (3)";
–   in paragraph (2) the words "the relevant person," are not omitted after "shall be made by";
–   in paragraph (4)(c) the words "or 3A" are not omitted from the end of the paragraph;
–   in paragraph (5) the words "and regulation 3A(1)(a)" are not omitted after "regulation 3(1) and (3)".

1993 rules

Reg 6 of the Child Support (Decisions and Appeals) (Amendment) Regulations 2000 (SI 2000 No.3185) amended this regulation and was brought into force on March 3, 2003 for the types of cases detailed in art 3 of SI 2003 No.192 (see p683) and those detailed in reg 1(2) of SI 2000 No.3185 (see p536), subject to the saving provision in art 14(3) of SI 2000 No.3185. For other types of cases, the '1993 rules' apply. These amendments have since been subject to further amendment by reg 6(4) of the Child Support (Meaning of Child and New Calculation Rules) (Consequential and Miscellaneous Amendment) Regulations 2012 (SI 2012 No.2785) restoring the text to its earlier form so that for cases to which the 1993 rules apply, regulation 4 is as it is reproduced above.

Definitions

"the date of notification": see reg 1(3).
"decision": see reg 3A(3).
"relevant person": see reg 1(3).

General Note

This regulation allows the time for an application for a revision under reg 3A(1)(a) to be extended. It does not apply to reg 3A(1)(b), which contains its own power to extend or to reg 3A(1)(d), under which action may be initiated by the Secretary of State.

    If the Secretary of State refuses to extend time under this regulation, the party may seek to appeal. The appeal is against the original decision and will be late. The issue arises whether a tribunal will extend the time for appealing under reg 32. If time is extended, the tribunal has power to consider the application for revision without considering this regulation. If time is not extended, the case does not come before a tribunal. There is no power, and no need, for there to be an appeal against the refusal to extend time under this regulation. See *CTC 3433/2003*.

[¹Date from which a decision revised under section 16 of the Child Support Act takes effect

5A. [⁴...]

Amendments

1.   Child Support (Decisions and Appeals) (Amendment) Regulations 2000 (SI 2000 No.3185) reg 7 (comes into force for the types of cases detailed in art 3 of SI 2003 No.192 and those detailed in reg 1(2) of SI 2000 No.3185 on March 3, 2003, subject to the saving provision in art 14(3) of SI 2000 No.3185). For other types of cases see the '1993 rules', below.

2.   Child Support (Decisions and Appeals) (Amendment) Regulations 2003 (SI 2003 No.129) reg 2 (comes into force for the types of cases detailed in art 3 of SI 2003 No.192 on March 3, 2003).

3.   Child Support (Miscellaneous Amendments) Regulations 2006 (SI 2006 No.1520) reg 4 (July 12, 2006).

4.   Child Support (Meaning of Child and New Calculation Rules) (Consequential and Miscellaneous Amendment) Regulations 2012 (SI 2012 No.2785) reg 6(3) (in force in relation to a particular case on the day on which para 2 of Sch 4 to the Child Maintenance and Other Payments Act 2008 (see p243) comes into force in relation to that type of case – which is December 10, 2012 in relation to the types of cases falling within art 3 of SI 2012 No.3042 (see p767)). For other types of cases see '2003 rules' below.

2003 rules

Regulation 6(3) of the Child Support (Meaning of Child and New Calculation Rules) (Consequential and Miscellaneous Amendment) Regulations 2012 (SI 2012 No.2785) omits reg 5A and comes into force on December 10, 2012 in relation to the types of cases falling within art 3 of SI 2012 No.3042 (see p767). For other types of cases reg 6(3) of SI 2012 No.2785 is not yet in force and reg 5A, reproduced below, continues to apply.

[¹Date from which a decision revised under section 16 of the Child Support Act takes effect

5A.–(1)   Where the date from which a decision took effect is found to be erroneous on a revision under section 16 of the Child Support Act, the revision shall take effect from the date on which the decision revised would have taken effect had the error not been made.

(2)   [³..]]

[²(3)   [³...]]

1993 rules

Reg 7 of the Child Support (Decisions and Appeals) (Amendment) Regulations 2000 (SI 2000 No.3185) inserted reg 5A and was brought into force on March 3, 2003 for the types of cases detailed in art 3 of SI 2003 No.192 and those detailed in reg 1(2) of SI 2000 No.3185, subject to the saving provision in art 14(3) of SI 2000 No.3185. For other types of cases, the 1993 rules apply and reg 5A is not inserted.

General Note

The basic rule on the effective date of a revision is contained in s16(3) of the Act. This regulation provides for the effective date where the effective date in the original decision itself was wrong.

CHAPTER II
Supersessions

[¹[⁴ Supersession of child support decisions
6A. [⁷...]

Amendments

1.   Child Support (Decisions and Appeals) (Amendment) Regulations 2000 (SI 2000 No.3185) reg 8 (comes into force for the types of cases detailed in art 3 of SI 2003 No.192 and those detailed in reg 1(2) of SI 2000 No.3185 on March 3, 2003, subject to the saving provision in art 14(3) of SI 2000 No.3185). For other types of cases see the '1993 rules', below.

2.   Social Security and Child Support (Miscellaneous Amendments) Regulations 2003 (SI 2003 No.1050) reg. 3(4) (see reg 1(1)(b) of SI 2003 No.1050 for relevant commencement dates).

3.   Tribunals, Courts and Enforcement Act 2007 (Transitional and Consequential Provisions) Order 2008 (SI 2008 No.2683) Sch 1 para 102 (November 3, 2008).

4.   Child Support (Miscellaneous Amendments) Regulations 2009 (SI 2009 No.396) reg 4(4) (April 6, 2009). This amendment does not apply to '1993 scheme cases' as defined by reg 7(2) of SI 2009 No.396. This replaced regulation 6A.

5.   Social Security and Child Support (Supersession of Appeal Decisions) Regulations 2012 (SI 2012 No.1267) reg 4(3) (June 4, 2012, but this amendment has effect as if it had come into force on November 3, 2008).

6.   Public Bodies (Child Maintenance and Enforcement Commission: Abolition and Transfer of Functions) Order 2012 (SI 2012 No.2007) art 3(2) and Sch para 113(4) (August 1, 2012).

7.   Child Support (Meaning of Child and New Calculation Rules) (Consequential and Miscellaneous Amendment) Regulations 2012 (SI 2012 No.2785) reg 6(3) (in force in relation to a particular case on the day on which paragraph 2 of Schedule 4 to the Child Maintenance and Other Payments Act 2008 (see p243) comes into force in relation to that type of case – which is December 10, 2012 in relation to the types of cases falling within art 3 of SI 2012 No.3042 (see p767)). For other types of cases see the '2003 rules' below.

2003 rules

Regulation 6(3) of the Child Support (Meaning of Child and New Calculation Rules) (Consequential and Miscellaneous Amendment) Regulations 2012 (SI 2012 No.2785) omits reg 6A and comes into force on December 10, 2012 in relation to the types of cases falling within art 3 of SI 2012 No.3042 (see p767). For other types of cases reg 6(3) of SI 2012 No.2785 is not yet in force and reg 6A, reproduced below, continues to apply.

[¹[⁴ Supersession of child support decisions
6A.–(1)   This regulation and regulation 6B set out the circumstances in which a decision may be made by the [⁶Secretary of State] under section 17 of the Child Support Act (decisions superseding earlier decisions).

(2)   A decision may be superseded by a decision of the [⁶Secretary of State], on an application or acting under [⁶the Secretary of State's] own initiative, where–

(a) there has been a relevant change of circumstances since the decision had effect or it is expected that a relevant change of circumstances will occur;

(b) the decision was made in ignorance of, or was based on a mistake as to, some material fact; or

(c) the decision was wrong in law (unless it was a decision made on appeal).

(3) The circumstances in which a decision may be superseded include where the relevant change of circumstances causes the maintenance calculation to cease by virtue of paragraph 16 of Schedule 1 to the Child Support Act or where the [⁶Secretary of State] no longer has jurisdiction by virtue of section 44 of that Act.

(4) A decision may be superseded by a decision of the [⁶Secretary of State] where the [⁶Secretary of State] receives an application for a variation of the decision under section 28G of the Child Support Act.

(5) A decision may not be superseded in circumstances where it may be revised.

(6) A decision to refuse an application for a maintenance calculation may not be superseded.]]

1993 rules

Reg 8 of the Child Support (Decisions and Appeals) (Amendment) Regulations 2000 (SI 2000 No.3185) inserted reg 6A and was brought into force on March 3, 2003 for the types of cases detailed in art 3 of SI 2003 No.192 (see p683) and those detailed in reg 1(2) of SI 2000 No.3185 (see p536), subject to the saving provision in art 14(3) of SI 2000 No.3185. For other types of cases, the 1993 rules apply and reg 6A is not inserted.

Definition

"voluntary payments": see reg 3A(7).

General Note
Appeal and supersession

It may be sensible for a person who disagrees with a decision both to appeal against the decision and to apply for a supersession. One particular reason for doing this is the effect of s20(7)(b) of the Act. This prevents a tribunal from considering change of circumstances that occur after the time of the decision under appeal. These changes may be taken into account on a supersession. The possibility of concurrent appeals and applications can give rise to problems about their interrelation.

One bundle of problems arose in *CDLA 2050/2002*. The claimant both appealed against a decision and applied for it to be superseded. The application related to a change of circumstances that had occurred after the decision, but before tribunal heard the appeal. The tribunal dismissed the appeal before the application for supersession was decided. This raised two issues. Which decision was the subject of the supersession application when it was decided-the original decision or the decision of the tribunal dismissing the appeal? And if the latter, could the Secretary of State's decision maker take account of the change of circumstances that had occurred before the tribunal made its decision? The commissioner decided that the decision that was the proper subject of the supersession became the tribunal's decision, but that it was permissible to take account of changes of circumstances that has occurred before the tribunal made its decision (para 8). He achieved this result by interpreting "decision" in the equivalent of head (a) in paras (2) and (3) as referring to the last decision before the change of circumstances occurred. This result is more easily justified under the child support legislation than under the social security legislation that the commissioner was interpreting. In that legislation, the provision referred to a change of circumstances "since the decision was made", whereas paras (2)(a) and (3)(a) here refer to a change "since the decision had effect".

Another bundle of problems arose in *R(DLA) 2/04*. The claimant appealed against a decision and the tribunal allowed the appeal in part only. The claimant appealed to the commissioner against the tribunal's decision, who set aside the tribunal's decision and directed a rehearing. The claimant then applied to the Secretary of State for a supersession. This was refused. This raised the issue whether the tribunal's decision could extend beyond the date of the Secretary of State's decision refusing to supersede. The commissioner held that it could. He set out three rules (para 12):

"1. An application for supersession that results in a refusal to supersede the original decision does not terminate the period under consideration on an appeal against the original decision.

2. Live proceedings arising out of an application for supersession based on ignorance of, or mistake as to, a material fact lapse when the decision to be superseded is set aside on appeal (provided that there is no further appeal in respect of the original decision).

3. Live proceedings arising out of an application for supersession based on a change of circumstances do not lapse when the decision to be superseded is set aside on appeal (but the application may have to be treated as an application for supersession of a different decision, or perhaps, as a new claim, depending of the circumstances)."

General

This regulation specifies the circumstances in which a decision may be superseded. Action may be taken on the Secretary of State's own initiative or on application. A decision may be superseded to reflect an actual or anticipated change of circumstances, to correct an error of fact or law, or to give effect to a variation. Some decisions cannot be superseded: see para (8). Other decisions may not be superseded in specified circumstances: see para (7) and reg 6B. If action is taken on the Secretary of State's initiative, the procedure in reg 7C must be followed.

The nature of a supersession was analysed by the Court of Appeal in *Wood v SSWP* [2003] EWCA Civ 53, CA (reported as *R(DLA) 1/03*). The court decided that the cases and circumstances specified in these Regulations were outcome criteria, not threshold criteria. In other words, they are criteria that must be satisfied before a decision can be given on supersession. If after consideration of an application, no change is made to the decision or to the basis of the decision, the proper course is to refuse to supersede rather than to give a supersession in the same terms.

On appeal, a tribunal has jurisdiction to substitute a revision for a supersession and a supersession for a revision (*R(IB) 2/04*). If a supersession is instigated by an application, a tribunal on appeal is not limited to the issues raised by the application, but may also consider issues that were not raised and might be decided adversely to the applicant *(ibid)*.

Paragraph (2)

This allows the Secretary of State to supersede without an application on two grounds: change of circumstances or error of fact. The change of circumstances must have occurred. An anticipated change of circumstances may only be considered on application under para (3).

The change of circumstances must be a change from the circumstances taken into account in making the decision that is subject to the supersession procedure (*CDLA 2115/2003*, para 8).

It is not necessary for a specific change to be identified and recorded; what is required is a decision that involves a process of continuous comparison (*Smith v SSWP* unreported [2003] EWCA Civ 437, para 23).

The tolerance, or minimum change, provisions do not apply to a supersession undertaken on the Secretary of State's own initiative (*CCS 509/2002*).

Section 17 of the Act confers a power to supersede, not a duty. There may be circumstances in which that power can only be properly exercised by a supersession, but not every change of circumstances will justify a supersession. Assume, for example, that the mother is the parent with care of a child. While she is in hospital for a month, the father has care of the child. Strictly, the father was for that period the parent with care. However, it might not be considered appropriate to reflect so temporary a change by a supersession. It might be more appropriate to view matters over a longer time scale.

Paragraph (2)(c)

Neither the Secretary of State nor a tribunal may correct a mistake made in error of law by a previous tribunal. If the decision was not changed on appeal, it stands: *NH v CMEC* [2009] UKUT 183 (AAC).

Paragraph (3)

This allows the Secretary of State to supersede on application to reflect an actual or anticipated change of circumstances. For further discussion, see the general note to para (2).

Paragraph (4)

This allows the Secretary of State to supersede on application to correct an error of fact.

Paragraph (5)

This allows the Secretary of State to supersede, with or without an application, to correct an error of law.

For a detailed discussion of error of law, see the general note to s24(1) of the Act. Difficulties arise in cases involving issues of fact and degree, such as whether two people are living together as husband and wife in the same household or whether a person is habitually resident in the UK. It is the nature of these issues that different decision makers may be entitled to form different judgments on the same facts without being in error of law. The decision of one decision maker will not necessarily be erroneous in law just because a later decision maker would form a different judgment on the same facts. There will only be an error of law if the first decision maker forms a judgment that no officer, properly advised and acting reasonably, was entitled to reach on the facts: *Crake and Butterworth v Supplementary Benefit Commission* [1982] 1 All ER 498 at 501, *per* Woolf J. If the case is one that merely involves a legitimate difference of judgment without any accompanying error of fact, the proper challenge is by an application for a revision.

Paragraph (6)

This allows a supersession to give effect to a variation.

A decision on a variation under s28G of the Act can only be made on supersession under this paragraph, not under any other paragraph such as para (2)(b): *TW v SSWP* [2009] UKUT 91 (AAC).

Paragraph (7)

This gives the revision procedure priority over the supersession procedure in any case or circumstance in which they would otherwise overlap. It is stated in absolute terms and cannot be disregarded under the powers given to the Secretary of State and tribunals to limit their consideration under ss16(2), 17(2) and 20(8)(a) of the Act.

Paragraph (8)
A decision to refuse an application for a maintenance calculation cannot be superseded; it may only be revised under s16 of the Act. This prevents a refusal being revised on the ground of error of material fact unless the application for a revision was made within the time limit or the mistake of fact arose from misrepresentation, failure to disclose or official error.

[¹Circumstances in which a child support decision may not be superseded
6B. [⁹...]

Amendments

1. Child Support (Decisions and Appeals) (Amendment) Regulations 2000 (SI 2000 No.3185) reg 8 (comes into force for the types of cases detailed in art 3 of SI 2003 No.192 and those detailed in reg 1(2) of SI 2000 No.3185 on March 3, 2003, subject to the saving provision in art 14(3) of SI 2000 No.3185). For other types of cases see the '1993 rules', below.

2. Child Support (Miscellaneous Amendments) Regulations 2002 (SI 2002 No.1204) reg 2(3) (comes into force for the types of cases detailed in art 3 of SI 2003 No.192 on March 3, 2003). For other types of cases see the '1993 rules', below.

3. Child Support (Miscellaneous Amendments) Regulations 2004 (SI 2004 No.2415) reg 2(2) (comes into force on September 16, 2004 for cases for which March 3, 2003 was the day appointed for the coming into force of ss1(2), 8 and 9 of, and para 11(2) and (7) of Sch 3 the Child Support, Pensions and Social Security Act 2000; for other cases comes into force on the day on which those provisions come into force in relation to that type of case). This amendment replaced reg 6B(3) and inserted a new para: 6B(5).

4. Tribunals, Courts and Enforcement Act 2007 (Transitional and Consequential Provisions) Order 2008 (SI 2008 No.2683) Sch 1 para 103 (November 3, 2008).

5. Child Support (Miscellaneous Amendments) Regulations 2009 (SI 2009 No.396) reg 4(5) (April 6, 2009). These amendments do not apply to '1993 scheme cases' as defined by reg 7(2) of SI 2009 No.396.

6. Child Support (Miscellaneous Amendments) Regulations 2011 (SI 2011 No.1464) reg 2(3) (July 4, 2011).

7. Social Security and Child Support (Supersession of Appeal Decisions) Regulations 2012 (SI 2012 No.1267) reg 4(4) (June 4, 2012, but this amendment has effect as if it had come into force on November 3, 2008).

8. Public Bodies (Child Maintenance and Enforcement Commission: Abolition and Transfer of Functions) Order 2012 (SI 2012 No.2007) art 3(2) and Sch para 113(5) (August 1, 2012).

9. Child Support (Meaning of Child and New Calculation Rules) (Consequential and Miscellaneous Amendment) Regulations 2012 (SI 2012 No.2785) reg 6(3) (in force in relation to a particular case on the day on which paragraph 2 of Schedule 4 to the Child Maintenance and Other Payments Act 2008 (see p243) comes into force in relation to that type of case – which is December 10, 2012 in relation to the types of cases falling within art 3 of SI 2012 No.3042 (see p767)). For other types of cases see the '2003 rules' below.

2003 rules
Regulation 6(3) of the Child Support (Meaning of Child and New Calculation Rules) (Consequential and Miscellaneous Amendment) Regulations 2012 (SI 2012 No.2785) omits reg 6B and comes into force on December 10, 2012 in relation to the types of cases falling within art 3 of SI 2012 No.3042 (see p767). For other types of cases reg 6(3) of SI 2012 No.2785 is not yet in force and reg 6B, reproduced below, continues to apply.

[¹Circumstances in which a child support decision may not be superseded
6B.–(1)   Except as provided in paragraph (4), and subject to paragraph (3), a decision of the [⁵[⁸Secretary of State]], [⁴[⁷an appeal tribunal, the First-tier Tribunal, the Upper Tribunal or a Child Support Commissioner]], on an application made under regulation [⁵6A(2)(a)], shall not be superseded where the difference between–

(a)   the non-resident parent's net income figure fixed for the purposes of the maintenance calculation in force in accordance with Part I of Schedule 1 to the Child Support Act; and

(b)   the non-resident parent's net income figure which would be fixed in accordance with a superseding decision,

is less than 5% of the figure in sub-paragraph (a).

(2)   In paragraph (1) "superseding decision" means a decision which would supersede the decision subject to the application made under regulation [⁵6A(2)(a)] but for the application of this regulation.

[³(3)   Where the application for a supersession is made on more than one ground, if those grounds which do not relate to the net income of the non-resident parent lead to a superseding decision this regulation shall not apply to the ground relating to the net income of that parent.]

(4) This regulation shall not apply to a decision under regulation [⁵6A(2)(a)] where–

(a) the superseding decision is made in consequence of the determination of an application made under section 28G of the Child Support Act;

(b) the superseding decision affects a variation ground in a decision made under section 11 or 17 of the Child Support Act, whether as originally made or as revised under section 16 of that Act;

(c) the decision being superseded was made under section 12(2) of the Child Support Act, or was a decision under section 17 of that Act superseding an interim maintenance decision, whether as originally made or as revised under section 16 of that Act;

(d) [⁵...] [⁶...]

(e) the superseding decision takes effect from the dates prescribed in regulation [⁵paragraph 4 of Schedule 3D]][⁶; or

(f) a decision is superseded and in relation to that superseding decision a maintenance calculation is made to which paragraph 15 of Schedule 1 to the Child Support Act applies.]

[³(5) Where an application has been made to which paragraph (1) applied ("application A") and a further application ("application B") is made for a supersession on a ground other than one relating to the net income of the non-resident parent, the [⁵[⁸Secretary of State]] may make a superseding decision on the basis that application A was made at the same time as application B.]

1993 rules

Reg 8 of the Child Support (Decisions and Appeals) (Amendment) Regulations 2000 (SI 2000 No.3185) inserted reg 6B and was brought into force on March 3, 2003 for the types of cases detailed in art 3 of SI 2003 No.192 (see p683) and those detailed in reg 1(2) of SI 2000 No.3185 (see p536), subject to the saving provision in art 14(3) of SI 2000 No.3185. For other types of cases, the 1993 rules apply and reg 6B is not inserted.

Definition

"voluntary payments": see reg 3A(7).

General Note

This regulation sets out circumstances in which a child support decision may not be superseded. It has no application to a series of calculations made under para 15 of Sch 1 to the Act (*CCS 1490/2005,* para 25). At least, not when the calculations are initial ones made on an application under the authority of s11 of the Act rather than on supersession under the authority of s17 (*CCS 2068/2006,* para 19).

Paragraphs (1)-(3)

These paragraphs impose a threshold to be satisfied before a decision may be superseded on a ground relating solely to the net income of the non-resident parent. The restriction only applies to supersession on an application under reg 6A(3). It does not apply to any other provision in reg 6A. It is subject to the exceptions in para (4).

[¹[⁸ **Effective date of a supersession decision]**
7B. [⁹...]]]

Amendments

1. Child Support (Decisions and Appeals) (Amendment) Regulations 2000 (SI 2000 No.3185) reg 9 (comes into force for the types of cases detailed in art 3 of SI 2003 No.192 and those detailed in reg 1(2) of SI 2000 No.3185 on March 3, 2003, subject to the saving provision in art 14(3) of SI 2000 No.3185). For other types of cases see the '1993 rules', below.

2. Child Support (Miscellaneous Amendments) Regulations 2002 (SI 2002 No.1204) reg 2(4) (comes into force for the types of cases detailed in art 3 of SI 2003 No.192 on March 3, 2003). For other types of cases see the '1993 rules', below.

3. Child Support (Miscellaneous Amendments) Regulations 2003 (SI 2003 No.328) reg 3 (comes into force for the types of cases detailed in art 3 of SI 2003 No.192 on March 3, 2003). For other types of cases see the '1993 rules', below.

4. Social Security and Child Support (Miscellaneous Amendments) Regulations 2003 (SI 2003 No.1050) reg 3(6) (see reg 1(1)(b) of SI 2003 No.1050 for relevant commencement dates).

5. Employment and Support Allowance (Consequential Provisions) (No.2) Regulations 2008 (2008 No.1554) reg 35 (July 27, 2008).

6. Child Support (Consequential Provisions) Regulations 2008 (SI 2008 No.2543) reg 4(4) (October 27, 2008).

7. Tribunals, Courts and Enforcement Act 2007 (Transitional and Consequential Provisions) Order 2008 (SI 2008 No.2683) Sch 1 para 105 (November 3, 2008).

8. Child Support (Miscellaneous Amendments) Regulations 2009 (SI 2009 No.396) reg 4(6) (April 6, 2009). This amendment does not apply to '1993 scheme cases' as defined by reg 7(2) of SI 2009 No.396. This amendment replaced reg 7B.

9. Child Support (Meaning of Child and New Calculation Rules) (Consequential and Miscellaneous Amendment) Regulations 2012 (SI 2012 No.2785) reg 6(3) (in force in relation to a particular case on the day on which paragraph 2 of Schedule 4 to the Child Maintenance and Other Payments Act 2008 (see p243) comes into force in relation to that type of case – which is December 10, 2012 in relation to the types of cases falling within art 3 of SI 2012 No.3042 (see p767)). For other types of cases see the '2003 rules' below.

2003 rules

Regulation 6(3) of the Child Support (Meaning of Child and New Calculation Rules) (Consequential and Miscellaneous Amendment) Regulations 2012 (SI 2012 No.2785) omits reg 7B and comes into force on December 10, 2012 in relation to the types of cases falling within art 3 of SI 2012 No.3042 (see p767). For other types of cases reg 6(3) of SI 2012 No.2785 is not yet in force and reg 7B, reproduced below, continues to apply.

[¹[⁸ Effective date of a supersession decision]

7B.   Schedule 3D provides for cases and circumstances in which a supersession decision takes effect from a date other than the date specified in section 17(4) of the Child Support Act.]]

1993 rules

Reg 9 of the Child Support (Decisions and Appeals) (Amendment) Regulations 2000 (SI 2000 No.3185) inserted reg 7B and was brought into force on March 3, 2003 for the types of cases detailed in art 3 of SI 2003 No.192 (see p683) and those detailed in reg 1(2) of SI 2000 No.3185 (see p536), subject to the saving provision in art 14(3) of SI 2000 No.3185. For other types of cases, the 1993 rules apply and reg 7B is not inserted.

Definitions

"Maintenance Calculation Procedure Regulations": see reg 1(3).
"Maintenance Calculations and Special Cases Regulations": see reg 1(3).
"relevant person": see reg 1(3).

[¹Procedure where the [²Commission] proposes to supersede a decision under section 17 of the Child Support Act on [²its] own initiative

7C.   [⁴...]]

Amendments

1. Child Support (Decisions and Appeals) (Amendment) Regulations 2000 (SI 2000 No.3185) reg 9 (comes into force for the types of cases detailed in art 3 of SI 2003 No.192 and those detailed in reg 1(2) of SI 2000 No.3185 on March 3, 2003, subject to the saving provision in art 14(3) of SI 2000 No.3185) For other types of cases see the '1993 rules', below.

2. Child Support (Miscellaneous Amendments) Regulations 2009 (SI 2009 No.396) reg 4(7) (April 6, 2009). These amendments do not apply to '1993 scheme cases' as defined by reg 7(2) of SI 2009 No.396.

3. Public Bodies (Child Maintenance and Enforcement Commission: Abolition and Transfer of Functions) Order 2012 (SI 2012 No.2007) art 3(2) and Sch para 113(6) (August 1, 2012).

4. Child Support (Meaning of Child and New Calculation Rules) (Consequential and Miscellaneous Amendment) Regulations 2012 (SI 2012 No.2785) reg 6(3) (in force in relation to a particular case on the day on which paragraph 2 of Schedule 4 to the Child Maintenance and Other Payments Act 2008 (see p243) comes into force in relation to that type of case – which is December 10, 2012 in relation to the types of cases falling within art 3 of SI 2012 No.3042 (see p767)). For other types of cases see the '2003 rules' below.

2003 rules

Regulation 6(3) of the Child Support (Meaning of Child and New Calculation Rules) (Consequential and Miscellaneous Amendment) Regulations 2012 (SI 2012 No.2785) omits reg 7C and comes into force on December 10, 2012 in relation to the types of cases falling within art 3 of SI 2012 No.3042 (see p767). For other types of cases reg 6(3) of SI 2012 No.2785 is not yet in force and reg 7C, reproduced below, continues to apply.

[¹Procedure where the [²Commission] proposes to supersede a decision under section 17 of the Child Support Act on [²its] own initiative

7C. Where the [²[³Secretary of State]] on [²[³the Secretary of State's]] own initiative proposes to make a decision superseding a decision [²[³the Secretary of State]] shall notify the relevant persons who could be materially affected by the decision of that intention.]

1993 rules

Reg 9 of the Child Support (Decisions and Appeals) (Amendment) Regulations 2000 (SI 2000 No.3185) inserted reg 7C and was brought into force on March 3, 2003 for the types of cases detailed in art 3 of SI 2003 No.192 (see p683) and those detailed in reg 1(2) of SI 2000 No.3185 (see p536), subject to the saving provision in art 14(3) of SI 2000 No.3185. For other types of cases, the 1993 rules apply and reg 7C is not inserted.

Defintion

"relevant person": see reg 1(3).

General Note

This ensures that those affected by the Secretary of State's proposed action know of it so that they may make representations. However, failure to give this notice does not invalidate the decision given on supersession (*CCS 162/2006*, paras 41-47).

[¹Provision of information
15A. [⁴...]]

Amendments

1. Child Support (Decisions and Appeals) (Amendment) Regulations 2000 (SI 2000 No.3185) reg 10 (comes into force for the types of cases detailed in art 3 of SI 2003 No.192 and those detailed in reg 1(2) of SI 2000 No.3185 on March 3, 2003, subject to the saving provision in art 14(3) of SI 2000 No.3185). For other types of cases see the '1993 rules', below.
2. Child Support (Miscellaneous Amendments) Regulations 2009 (SI 2009 No.396) reg 4(8) (April 6, 2009). These amendments do not apply to '1993 scheme cases' as defined by reg 7(2) of SI 2009 No.396. For such cases see the '1993 rules', below.
3. Public Bodies (Child Maintenance and Enforcement Commission: Abolition and Transfer of Functions) Order 2012 (SI 2012 No.2007) art 3(2) and Sch para 113(7) (August 1, 2012).
4. Child Support (Meaning of Child and New Calculation Rules) (Consequential and Miscellaneous Amendment) Regulations 2012 (SI 2012 No.2785) reg 6(3) (in force in relation to a particular case on the day on which paragraph 2 of Schedule 4 to the Child Maintenance and Other Payments Act 2008 (see p243) comes into force in relation to that type of case – which is December 10, 2012 in relation to the types of cases falling within art 3 of SI 2012 No.3042 (see p767)). For other types of cases see the '2003 rules' below.

2003 rules

Regulation 6(3) of the Child Support (Meaning of Child and New Calculation Rules) (Consequential and Miscellaneous Amendment) Regulations 2012 (SI 2012 No.2785) omits reg 15A and comes into force on December 10, 2012 in relation to the types of cases falling within art 3 of SI 2012 No.3042 (see p767). For other types of cases reg 6(3) of SI 2012 No.2785 is not yet in force and reg 15A, reproduced below, continues to apply.

[¹Provision of information

15A.–(1) Where the [²[³Secretary of State]] has received an application under section 16 or 17 of the Child Support Act in connection with a previously determined variation which has effect on the maintenance calculation in force, [²[³the Secretary of State]] may request further information or evidence from the applicant to enable a decision on that application to be made and any such information or evidence shall be provided within one month of the date of notification of the request, or such longer period as the [²[³Secretary of State]] is satisfied is reasonable in the circumstances of the case.

(2) Where any information or evidence requested in accordance with paragraph (1) is not provided within the time limit specified in that paragraph, the [²[³Secretary of State]] may, where [²[³the Secretary of State]] is able to do so, proceed to make the decision in the absence of that information or evidence.]

1993 rules

Reg 10 of the Child Support (Decisions and Appeals) (Amendment) Regulations 2000 (SI 2000 No.3185) inserted reg 15A and was brought into force on March 3, 2003 for the types of cases detailed in art 3 of SI 2003 No.192 (see p683) and those detailed in reg 1(2) of SI 2000 No.3185 (see p536), subject to the saving provision in art 14(3) of SI 2000 No.3185. For other types of cases, the 1993 rules apply and reg 15A is not inserted.

General Note

This applies to applications for revision or supersession that relate to a variation. It gives the Secretary of State power to require information or evidence from the applicant. It must be provided within one month, subject to extension by the Secretary of State. If the information or evidence is not provided, the Secretary of State may (if possible) determine the application without it. The Secretary of State may also accept the information or evidence late under reg 15B(7).

[¹Procedure in relation to an application made under section 16 or 17 of the Child Support Act in connection with a previously determined variation
15B. [⁴...]]

Amendments

1. Child Support (Decisions and Appeals) (Amendment) Regulations 2000 (SI 2000 No.3185) reg 10 (comes into force for the types of cases detailed in art 3 of SI 2003 No.192 and those detailed in reg 1(2) of SI 2000 No.3185 on March 3, 2003, subject to the saving provision in art 14(3) of SI 2000 No.3185). For other types of cases see the '1993 rules' below.

2. Child Support (Miscellaneous Amendments) Regulations 2009 (SI 2009 No.396) reg 4(9) (April 6, 2009). These amendments do not apply to '1993 scheme cases' as defined by reg 7(2) of SI 2009 No.396. For such cases see the '1993 rules' below.

3. Public Bodies (Child Maintenance and Enforcement Commission: Abolition and Transfer of Functions) Order 2012 (SI 2012 No.2007) art 3(2) and Sch para 113(8) (August 1, 2012).

4. Child Support (Meaning of Child and New Calculation Rules) (Consequential and Miscellaneous Amendment) Regulations 2012 (SI 2012 No.2785) reg 6(3) (in force in relation to a particular case on the day on which paragraph 2 of Schedule 4 to the Child Maintenance and Other Payments Act 2008 (see p243) comes into force in relation to that type of case – which is December 10, 2012 in relation to the types of cases falling within art 3 of SI 2012 No.3042 (see p767)). For other types of cases see the '2003 rules' below.

2003 rules

Regulation 6(3) of the Child Support (Meaning of Child and New Calculation Rules) (Consequential and Miscellaneous Amendment) Regulations 2012 (SI 2012 No.2785) omits regulation 15B and comes into force on December 10, 2012 in relation to the types of cases falling within art 3 of SI 2012 No.3042 (see p767). For other types of cases regulation 6(3) of SI 2012 No.2785 is not yet in force and regulation 15B, reproduced below, continues to apply.

[¹Procedure in relation to an application made under section 16 or 17 of the Child Support Act in connection with a previously determined variation

15B.–(1) Subject to paragraph (3), where the [²[³Secretary of State]] has received an application under section 16 or 17 of the Child Support Act in connection with a previously determined variation which has effect on the maintenance calculation in force, [²[³the Secretary of State]]–

(a) shall give notice of the application to the relevant persons, other than the applicant, informing them of the grounds on which the application has been made and any relevant information or evidence the applicant has given, except information or evidence falling within paragraph (2);

(b) may invite representations, which need not be in writing but shall be in writing if in any case [²[³the Secretary of State]] so directs, from the relevant persons other than the applicant on any matter relating to that application, to be submitted to the [²[³the Secretary of State]] within 14 days of notification or such longer period as the [²[³Secretary of State]] is satisfied is reasonable in the circumstances of the case; and

(c) shall set out the provisions of paragraphs (2)(b) and (c), (4) and (5) in relation to such representations.

(2) The information or evidence referred to in paragraphs (1)(a), (4)(a) and (7), is–

(a) details of the nature of the long-term illness or disability of the relevant other child which forms the basis of a variation application on the ground in regulation 11 of the Variations Regulations (special expenses – illness or disability of relevant other child) where the applicant requests they should not be disclosed and the [²[³Secretary of State]] is satisfied that disclosure is not necessary in order to be able to determine the application;

(b) medical evidence or medical advice which has not been disclosed to the applicant or a relevant person and which the [²[³Secretary of State]] considers would be harmful to the health of the applicant or that relevant person if disclosed to him;

(c) the address of a relevant person or qualifying child, or any other information which could reasonably be expected to lead to that person or child being located, where the [²[³Secretary of State]] considers that there would be a risk of harm or undue distress to that person or that child or any other children living with that person if the address or information were disclosed.

(3) The [²[³Secretary of State]] need not act in accordance with paragraph (1) if–

(a) [³satisfied on the information or evidence available that a variation of the maintenance calculation in force will not be agreed], but if, on further consideration [²[³the Secretary of State]] is minded to do so [²[³the Secretary of State]] shall, before doing so, comply with the provisions of this regulation; and

(b) were the application to succeed, the decision as revised or superseded would be less advantageous to the applicant than the decision before it was so revised or superseded.

(4) Where the [²[³Secretary of State]] receives representations from the relevant persons [²[³the Secretary of State]]–

(a) may, if [²[³the Secretary of State]] considers it reasonable to do so, send a copy of the representations concerned (excluding material falling within paragraph (2) above) to the applicant and invite any comments [²][³to be provided] within 14 days or such longer period as the [²[³Secretary of State]] is satisfied is reasonable in the circumstances of the case; and

(b) where the [²[³Secretary of State]] acts under sub-paragraph (a), shall not proceed to make a decision in response to the application until [²[³the Secretary of State]] has received such comments or the period referred to in sub-paragraph (a) has expired.

(5) Where the [²[³Secretary of State]] has not received representations from the relevant persons notified in accordance with paragraph (1) within the time limit specified in sub-paragraph (b) of that paragraph, [²[³the Secretary of State]] may proceed to make a decision under section 16 or 17 of the Child Support Act in response to the application, in their absence.

(6) In considering an application for a revision or supersession the [²[³Secretary of State]] shall take into account any representations received at the date upon which [²[³the Secretary of State]] makes a decision under section 16 or 17 of the Child Support Act, from the relevant persons including any representations received in connection with the application in accordance with paragraphs (1)(b), (4)(a) and (7).

(7) Where any information or evidence requested by the [²[³Secretary of State]] under regulation 15A is received after notification has been given under paragraph (1), [²[³the Secretary of State]] may, if [²[³the Secretary of State]] considers it reasonable to do so and except where such information or evidence falls within paragraph (2), send a copy of such information or evidence to the relevant persons and may invite them to submit representations, which need not be in writing unless the [²[³Secretary of State]] so directs in any particular case, on that information or evidence.

(8) Where the [²[³Secretary of State]] is considering making a decision under section 16 or 17 of the Child Support Act in accordance with this regulation, [²[³the Secretary of State]] shall apply the factors to be taken into account for the purposes of section 28F of the Child Support Act set out in regulation 21 of the Variations Regulations (factors to be taken into account and not to be taken into account) as factors to be taken into account and not to be taken into account when considering making a decision under this regulation.

(9)　In this regulation "relevant person" means–

(a)　a non-resident parent, or a person treated as a non-resident parent under regulation 8 of the Maintenance Calculations and Special Cases Regulations (persons treated as non-resident parents), whose liability to pay child support maintenance may be affected by any variation agreed;

(b)　a person with care, or a child to whom section 7 of the Child Support Act applies, where the amount of child support maintenance payable by virtue of a calculation relevant to that person with care or in respect of that child may be affected by any variation agreed.]

1993 rules

Reg 10 of the Child Support (Decisions and Appeals) (Amendment) Regulations 2000 (SI 2000 No.3185) inserted reg 15B and was brought into force on March 3, 2003 for the types of cases detailed in art 3 of SI 2003 No.192 (see p683) and those detailed in reg 1(2) of SI 2000 No.3185 (see p536), subject to the saving provision in art 14(3) of SI 2000 No.3185. For other types of cases, the 1993 rules apply and reg 15B is not inserted.

Definition

"Variations Regulations": see reg 1(3).

General Note

This regulation provides for the procedure to be followed on consideration of revision or supersession of the effect of a variation. It reflects the procedure followed on an application for a variation under reg 9 of the Variation Regulations.

Paragraph (9)

This definition overrides the one in reg 1(3).

[¹Notification of a decision made under section 16 or 17 of the Child Support Act

15C. [⁴...]]

Amendments

1.　Child Support (Decisions and Appeals) (Amendment) Regulations 2000 (SI 2000 No.3185) reg 10 (comes into force for the types of cases detailed in art 3 of SI 2003 No.192 and those detailed in reg 1(2) of SI 2000 No.3185 on March 3, 2003, subject to the saving provision in art 14(3) of SI 2000 No.3185). For other types of cases see the '1993 rules', below.

2.　Child Support (Miscellaneous Amendments) Regulations 2009 (SI 2009 No.396) reg 4(10) (April 6, 2009). These amendments do not apply to '1993 scheme cases' as defined by reg 7(2) of SI 2009 No.396. For such cases see the '1993 rules', below.

3.　Public Bodies (Child Maintenance and Enforcement Commission: Abolition and Transfer of Functions) Order 2012 (SI 2012 No.2007) art 3(2) and Sch para 113(9) (August 1, 2012).

4.　Child Support (Meaning of Child and New Calculation Rules) (Consequential and Miscellaneous Amendment) Regulations 2012 (SI 2012 No.2785) reg 6(3) (in force in relation to a particular case on the day on which paragraph 2 of Schedule 4 to the Child Maintenance and Other Payments Act 2008 (see p243) comes into force in relation to that type of case – which is December 10, 2012 in relation to the types of cases falling within art 3 of SI 2012 No.3042 (see p767)). For other types of cases see the '2003 rules' below.

2003 rules

Regulation 6(3) of the Child Support (Meaning of Child and New Calculation Rules) (Consequential and Miscellaneous Amendment) Regulations 2012 (SI 2012 No.2785) omits regulation 15C and comes into force on December 10, 2012 in relation to the types of cases falling within art 3 of SI 2012 No.3042 (see p767). For other types of cases regulation 6(3) of SI 2012 No.2785 is not yet in force and regulation 15C, reproduced below, continues to apply.

[¹Notification of a decision made under section 16 or 17 of the Child Support Act

15C.–(1)　Subject to paragraphs (2) and (5) to (11), a notification of a decision made following the revision or supersession of a decision made under section 11, 12 or 17 of the Child Support Act, whether as originally made or as revised under section 16 of that Act, shall set out, in relation to the decision in question–

(a)　the effective date of the maintenance calculation;

(b)　where relevant, the non-resident parent's net weekly income;

(c)　the number of qualifying children;

(d)   the number of relevant other children;

(e)   the weekly rate;

(f)   the amounts calculated in accordance with Part I of Schedule 1 to the Child Support Act and, where there has been agreement to a variation or a variation has otherwise been taken into account, the Variations Regulations;

(g)   where the weekly rate is adjusted by apportionment or shared care or both, the amount calculated in accordance with paragraph 6, 7 or 8, as the case may be, of Part I of Schedule 1 to the Child Support Act; and

(h)   where the amount of child support maintenance which the non-resident parent is liable to pay is decreased in accordance with regulation 9 of the Maintenance Calculations and Special Cases Regulations (care provided in part by local authority) or 11 (non-resident parent liable to pay maintenance under a maintenance order) of those Regulations, the adjustment calculated in accordance with that regulation.

(2)   A notification of a revision or supersession of a maintenance calculation made under section 12(1) of the Child Support Act shall set out the effective date of the maintenance calculation, the default rate, the number of qualifying children on which the rate is based and whether any apportionment has been applied under regulation 7 of the Maintenance Calculation Procedure Regulations (default rate) and shall state the nature of the information required to enable a decision under section 11 of that Act to be made by way of section 16 of that Act.

(3)   Except where a person gives written permission to the [²[³Secretary of State]] that the information in relation to him, mentioned in sub-paragraphs (a) and (b), may be conveyed to other persons, any document given or sent under the provisions of paragraph (1) or (2) shall not contain–

(a)   the address of any person other than the recipient of the document in question (other than the address of the office of the officer concerned who is exercising functions of the [²[³Secretary of State]] under the Child Support Act) or any other information the use of which could reasonably be expected to lead to any such person being located;

(b)   any other information the use of which could reasonably be expected to lead to any person, other than a qualifying child or a relevant person, being identified.

(4)   Where a decision as to the revision or supersession of a decision made under section 11, 12 or 17 of the Child Support Act, whether as originally made or as revised under section 16 of that Act, is made under section 16 or 17 of that Act, a notification under paragraph (1) or (2) shall include information as to the provisions of sections 16, 17 and 20 of that Act.

(5)   Where the [²[³Secretary of State]] makes a decision that a maintenance calculation shall cease to have effect–

(a)   [²[³the Secretary of State]] shall immediately notify the non-resident parent and person with care, so far as that is reasonably practicable;

(b)   where a decision has been superseded in a case where a child under section 7 of the Child Support Act ceases to be a child for the purposes of that Act, [²[³the Secretary of State]] shall immediately notify the persons in sub-paragraph (a) and the other qualifying children within the meaning of section 7 of that Act; and

(c)   any notice under sub-paragraphs (a) and (b) shall specify the date with effect from which that decision took effect.

(6)   [²...]

(7)   [²...]

(8)   [²...]

(9)   Paragraphs (1) to (3) shall not apply where the [²[³Secretary of State]] has decided not to supersede a decision under section 17 of the Child Support Act, and [²[³the Secretary of State]] shall, so far as that is reasonably practicable, notify the relevant persons of that decision.

(10)   A notification under paragraphs (6) to (9) shall include information as to the provisions of sections 16, 17 and 20 of the Child Support Act.

(11)   Where paragraph (9) applies, and the [²[³Secretary of State]] decides not to supersede under regulation 6B, [²[³the Secretary of State]] shall notify the relevant person, in relation to the decision in question of–

(a)   the fact that regulation 6B applies to the decision;

(b)   the non-resident parent's net income figure fixed for the purposes of the maintenance calculation in force in accordance with Part I of Schedule 1 to the Child Support Act;

(c)   the non-resident parent's net income figure provided by that parent to the [²[³Secretary of State]] with the application for supersession under regulation 6A(3);

(d)   the decision of the [²[³Secretary of State]] not to supersede; and

(e)   the right to appeal against the decision under section 20 of the Child Support Act.

(12)   Where an appeal lapses in accordance with section 16(6) or 28F(5) of the Child Support Act, the [²[³Secretary of State]] shall, so far as that is reasonably practicable, notify the relevant persons that the appeal has lapsed.]

1993 rules

Reg 10 of the Child Support (Decisions and Appeals) (Amendment) Regulations 2000 (SI 2000 No.3185) inserted reg 15C and was brought into force on March 3, 2003 for the types of cases detailed in art 3 of SI 2003 No.192 (see p683) and those detailed in reg 1(2) of SI 2000 No.3185 (see p536), subject to the saving provision in art 14(3) of SI 2000 No.3185. For other types of cases, the 1993 rules apply and reg 15C is not inserted.

Definitions

"Maintenance Calculation Procedure Regulations": see reg 1(3).
"Maintenance Calculations and Special Cases Regulations": see reg 1(3).
"relevant person": see reg 1(3).

[¹ Procedure in relation to the adjustment of the amount payable under a maintenance calculation

15D.   [²,³...]]

Amendments

1.   Child Support (Decisions and Appeals) (Amendment) Regulations 2000 (SI 2000 No.3185) reg 10 (comes into force for the types of cases detailed in art 3 of The Child Support, Pensions and Social Security Act 2000 (Commencement No.12) Order 2003 (SI 2003 No.192) and those detailed in reg 1(2) of SI 2000 No.3185 on March 3, 2003, subject to the saving provision in art 14(3) of SI 2000 No.3185). For other types of cases see the '1993 rules' below.

2.   Child Support (Miscellaneous Amendments) Regulations 2009 (SI 2009 No.396) reg 4(11) (April 6, 2009). This revocation does not apply to '1993 scheme cases' as defined by reg 7(2) of SI 2009 No.396. For such cases see the '1993 rules' below.

3.   Child Support (Management of Payments and Arrears) Regulations 2009 (SI 2009 No.3151) reg 14 and Sch (January 25, 2010).

1993 rules

Reg 10 of the Child Support (Decisions and Appeals) (Amendment) Regulations 2000 (SI 2000 No.3185) inserted reg 15D and was brought into force on March 3, 2003 for the types of cases detailed in art 3 of SI 2003 No.192 (see p683) and those detailed in reg 1(2) of SI 2000 No.3185 (see p536), subject to the saving provision in art 14(3) of SI 2000 No.3185. For other types of cases, the 1993 rules apply and reg 15D is not inserted.

Definition

"Arrears, Interest and Adjustment of Maintenance Assessments Regulations": see reg 1(3).

General Note

Despite the reference to procedure in the heading to this regulation, it is not concerned with procedure but with substance. It allows for an adjustment to carryover to a decision given on revision or supersession. However, this does not apply if the Secretary of State is satisfied that it would not be appropriate. In that case, the adjustment either ceases or is itself adjusted.

PART III
CHAPTER II
Other Matters

Child support decisions involving issues that arise on appeal in other cases
23. [⁶...]

Amendments

1.   Child Support (Consequential Amendments and Transitional Provisions) Regulations 2001 (SI 2001 No.158) reg 4(2) (March 3, 2003 in relation the types of cases outlined in art 3 of SI 2003 No.192). For other types of cases see the '1993 rules', below.
2.   Child Support (Consequential Amendments and Transitional Provisions) Regulations 2001 (SI 2001 No.158) reg 4(3) (March 3, 2003 in relation the types of cases outlined in art 3 of SI 2003 No.192). For other types of cases see the '1993 rules', below.
3.   Tribunals, Courts and Enforcement Act 2007 (Transitional and Consequential Provisions) Order 2008 (SI 2008 No.2683) Sch 1 para 113 (November 3, 2008).
4.   Child Support (Miscellaneous Amendments) Regulations 2009 (SI 2009 No.396) reg 4(12) (April 6, 2009). These amendments do not apply to '1993 scheme cases' as defined by reg 7(2) of SI 2009 No.396.
5.   Public Bodies (Child Maintenance and Enforcement Commission: Abolition and Transfer of Functions) Order 2012 (SI 2012 No.2007) art 3(2) and Sch para 113(10) (August 1, 2012).
6.   Child Support (Meaning of Child and New Calculation Rules) (Consequential and Miscellaneous Amendment) Regulations 2012 (SI 2012 No.2785) reg 6(3) (in force in relation to a particular case on the day on which paragraph 2 of Schedule 4 to the Child Maintenance and Other Payments Act 2008 (see p243) comes into force in relation to that type of case – which is December 10, 2012 in relation to the types of cases falling within art 3 of SI 2012 No.3042 (see p767)). For other types of cases see the '2003 rules' below.

2003 rules

Regulation 6(3) of the Child Support (Meaning of Child and New Calculation Rules) (Consequential and Miscellaneous Amendment) Regulations 2012 (SI 2012 No.2785) omits reg 23 and comes into force on December 10, 2012 in relation to the types of cases falling within art 3 of SI 2012 No.3042 (see p767). For other types of cases reg 6(3) of SI 2012 No.2785 is not yet in force and reg 23, reproduced below, continues to apply.

23.–(1)   For the purposes of section 28ZA(2)(b) of the Child Support Act (prescribed cases and circumstances in which a decision may be made on a prescribed basis), a case which satisfies either of the conditions in paragraph (2) is a prescribed case.

(2)   The conditions referred to in paragraph (1) are that–

(a)   if a decision were not made on the basis prescribed in paragraph (3), the parent with care would become entitled to income support if a claim were made, or to an increased amount of that benefit;

(b)   the [¹non-resident parent] is an employed earner or a self-employed earner.

(3)   For the purposes of section 28ZA(2)(b) of the Child Support Act, the prescribed basis on which the [⁴[⁵Secretary of State]] may make the decision is as if–

(a)   the appeal in relation to the different maintenance [²calculation], which is referred to in section 28ZA(1)(b) of that Act had already been determined; and

(b)   that appeal had been decided in a way that was the most unfavourable to the applicant for the decision mentioned in section 28ZA(1)(a) of that Act.

(4)   The circumstances prescribed under section 28ZA(4)(c) of the Child Support Act (where an appeal is pending against a decision for the purposes of that section, even though an appeal against the decision has not been brought or, as the case may be, an application for [³permission] to appeal against the decision has not been made but the time for doing so has not expired), are that the [⁴[⁵Secretary of State]]–

(a)   certifies in writing that [⁴[⁵the Secretary of State]] is considering appealing against that decision; and

(b)   [⁴[⁵the Secretary of State]] considers that, if such an appeal were to be determined in a particular way–

(i)   there would be no liability for child support maintenance, or

(ii)   such liability would be less than would be the case were an appeal not made.

(5)   In this regulation–

"['non-resident parent]" and "parent with care" have the same meaning as in section 54 of the Child Support Act;

"employed earner" and "self-employed earner" have the same meaning as in section 2(1) of the Contributions and Benefits Act.

1993 rules

Reg 4 of the Child Support (Consequential Amendments and Transitional Provisions) Regulations 2001 (SI 2001 No.158) amended regulation 23 and was brought into force on March 3, 2003 for the types of cases detailed in art 3 of the Child Support, Pensions and Social Security Act 2000 (Commencement No.12) Order 2003 (SI 2003 No.192 – see p683). For other types of cases, the 1993 rules apply and reg 23 is as shown above, under the '2003 rules', but the words "absent parent" are retained in place of "non-resident parent" and "assessment" is retained in place of "calculation".

Definition

"appeal": see reg 1(3).

Child support appeals involving issues that arise in other cases
24.   [⁴...]

Amendments

1.   Tribunals, Courts and Enforcement Act 2007 (Transitional and Consequential Provisions) Order 2008 (SI 2008 No.2683) Sch 1 para 114 (November 3, 2008).
2.   Child Support (Miscellaneous Amendments) Regulations 2009 (SI 2009 No.396) reg 4(13) (April 6, 2009). These amendments did not have effect in relation to '1993 scheme cases' as defined by reg 7(2) of SI 2009 No.396.
3.   Public Bodies (Child Maintenance and Enforcement Commission: Abolition and Transfer of Functions) Order 2012 (SI 2012 No.2007) art 3(2) and Sch para 113(11) (August 1, 2012).
4.   Child Support (Meaning of Child and New Calculation Rules) (Consequential and Miscellaneous Amendment) Regulations 2012 (SI 2012 No.2785) reg 6(3) (in force in relation to a particular case on the day on which paragraph 2 of Schedule 4 to the Child Maintenance and Other Payments Act 2008 (see p243) comes into force in relation to that type of case – which is December 10, 2012 in relation to the types of cases falling within art 3 of SI 2012 No.3042 (see p767)). For other types of cases see the '2003 and 1993 rules' below.

2003 and 1993 rules

Regulation 6(3) of the Child Support (Meaning of Child and New Calculation Rules) (Consequential and Miscellaneous Amendment) Regulations 2012 (SI 2012 No.2785) omits reg 24 and comes into force on December 10, 2012 in relation to the types of cases falling within art 3 of SI 2012 No.3042 (see p767). For other types of cases reg 6(3) of SI 2012 No.2785 is not yet in force and reg 24, reproduced below, continues to apply.

24.   The circumstances prescribed under section 28ZB(6)(c) of the Child Support Act, where an appeal is pending against a decision in the case described in section 28ZB(1)(b) even though an appeal against the decision has not been brought (or, as the case may be, an application for ['permission] to appeal against the decision has not been made), is where the [²[³Secretary of State]]–

(a)   certifies in writing that [²³the Secretary of State]] is considering appealing against that decision, and

(b)   considers that, if such an appeal were already determined, it would affect the determination of the appeal described in section 28ZB(1)(a).

Definition

"appeal": see reg 1(3).

PART IV
RIGHTS OF APPEAL AND PROCEDURE FOR BRINGING APPEALS
CHAPTER 1
General appeals matters including child support appeals

Appeal against a decision which has been [²[⁷...]] revised
30.–[⁷(1) An appeal against a decision of the Secretary of State or the Board or an officer of the Board shall not lapse where–

(a)   the decision is revised under section 9 before the appeal is determined; and

(b)   the decision as revised is not more advantageous to the appellant than the decision before it was revised.]

(2)   Decisions which are more advantageous for the purposes of this regulation include decisions where–

(a)   any relevant benefit paid to the appellant is greater or is awarded for a longer period in consequence of the decision made under section 9;

(b)   it would have resulted in the amount of relevant benefit in payment being greater but for the operation of any provision of the Administration Act or the Contributions and Benefits Act restricting or suspending the payment of, or disqualifying a claimant from receiving, some or all of the benefit;

(c)   as a result of the decision, a denial or disqualification for the receiving of any relevant benefit, is lifted, wholly or in part;

(d)   it reverses a decision to pay benefit to a third party;

[³(dd) it reverses a decision under section 29(2) that an accident is not an industrial accident;]

(e)   in consequence of the revised decision, benefit paid is not recoverable under section 71, 71A or 74 of the Administration Act or regulations made under any of those sections, or the amount so recoverable is reduced; or

(f)   a financial gain accrued or will accrue to the appellant in consequence of the decision.

[⁷(3)   Where a decision as revised under section 9 is not more advantageous to the appellant than the decision before it was revised, the appeal shall be treated as though it had been brought against the decision as revised.]

(4)   The appellant shall have a period of one month from the date of notification of the decision as [²[⁷...]] revised to make further representations as to the appeal.

(5)   After the expiration of the period specified in paragraph (4), or within that period if the appellant consents in writing, the appeal to the [⁴First-tier Tribunal] shall proceed except where, in the light of the further representations from the appellant, the Secretary of State [⁵[⁶...]][¹ or the Board or an officer of the Board] further revises his [¹, or revise their] decision and that decision is more advantageous to the appellant than the decision before it was [²[⁷...]] revised.

Amendments

1.   Tax Credits (Decisions and Appeals) (Amendment) Regulations 1999 (SI 1999 No.2570), reg 21 (October 5, 1999). Note that amendments made by these Regulations have effect only with respect to working families' tax credit and disabled person's tax credit (reg 1(2) of the Amendment Regulations).

2.   Child Support (Decisions and Appeals) (Amendment) Regulations 2000 (SI 2000 No.3185) reg 11 (comes into force for the types of cases detailed in art 3 of SI 2003 No.192 and those detailed in reg 1(2) of SI 2000 No.3185 on March 3, 2003, subject to the saving provision in art 14(3) of SI 2000 No.3185). For other types of cases see the '1993 rules' below.

3.   Social Security, Child Support and Tax Credits (Miscellaneous Amendments) Regulations 2005 (SI 2005 No.337) reg 2(7) (March 18, 2005).

4.   Tribunals, Courts and Enforcement Act 2007 (Transitional and Consequential Provisions) Order 2008 (SI 2008 No.2683) Sch 1 para 119 (November 3, 2008).

5.   Child Support (Miscellaneous Amendments) Regulations 2009 (SI 2009 No.396) reg 4(14) (April 6, 2009). These amendments did not apply to '1993 scheme cases' as defined by reg 7(2) of SI 2009 No.396.

6.   Public Bodies (Child Maintenance and Enforcement Commission: Abolition and Transfer of Functions) Order 2012 (SI 2012 No.2007) art 3(2) and Sch para 113(12) (August 1, 2012).

7.   Child Support (Meaning of Child and New Calculation Rules) (Consequential and Miscellaneous Amendment) Regulations 2012 (SI 2012 No.2785) reg 6(5) and (6) (in force in relation to a particular case on the day on which paragraph 2 of Schedule 4 to the Child Maintenance and Other Payments Act 2008 (see p243) comes into force in relation to that type of case – which is December 10, 2012 in relation to the types of cases falling within art 3 of SI 2012 No.3042 (see p767)). For other types of cases (except those covered by the '1993 rules') see the '2003 rules' below.

2003 rules

Regulation 6(5) and (6) of the Child Support (Meaning of Child and New Calculation Rules) (Consequential and Miscellaneous Amendment) Regulations 2012 (SI 2012 No.2785) amends this regulation and comes into force

on December 10, 2012 in relation to the types of cases falling within art 3 of SI 2012 No. 3042 (see p767). For other types of cases the amendments have not been brought into force and, unless the 1993 rules apply,
–   in the heading and in paragraphs (4) and (5) the words "replaced or" are retained before "revised"
–   paragraph (1) reads:

(1)   An appeal against a decision of the Secretary of State [⁵ [⁶...]][¹ or the Board or an officer of the Board] shall not lapse where the decision [²is treated as replaced by a decision under section 11 of the Child Support Act by section 28F(5) of that Act, or is revised under section 16 of that Act] or section 9 before the appeal is determined and the decision as [²replaced or] revised is not more advantageous to the appellant than the decision before it was [²replaced or] revised.

–   in paragraph (2) the words "the relevant person," are not omitted after "shall be made by";
–   paragraph (3) reads:

(3)   Where a decision as [²replaced under section 28F(5) of the Child Support Act or revised under section 16 of that Act] or under section 9 is not more advantageous to the appellant than the decision before it was [²replaced or] revised, the appeal shall be treated as though it had been brought against the decision as [²replaced or] revised.

1993 rules

Reg 11 of the Child Support (Decisions and Appeals) (Amendment) Regulations 2000 (SI 2000 No.3185) amended this regulation and was brought into force on March 3, 2003 for the types of cases detailed in art 3 of SI 2003 No.192 (see p683) and those detailed in reg 1(2) of SI 2000 No.3185 (see p536), subject to the saving provision in art 14(3) of SI 2000 No.3185. For other types of cases, the '1993 rules' apply. These amendments have since been subject to further amendment by reg 6(5) and (6) of the Child Support (Meaning of Child and New Calculation Rules) (Consequential and Miscellaneous Amendment) Regulations 2012 (SI 2012 No.2785), in some instances restoring the text to its earlier form. If the 1993 rules apply, regulation 30 is as it is reproduced in the main text above with the following variations:
–   reg 30(1) is as it is shown under the 2003 rules except the words "is revised under section 16 of the Child Support Act" are retained in place of the words "is treated as replaced by a decision under section 11 of the Child Support Act by section 28F(5) of that Act, or is revised under section 16 of that Act" and the words "replaced or" are not included after "against the decision as" and "before it was";
–   reg 30(3) is as it is shown under the 2003 rules except the words "is revised under section 16 of the Child Support Act" are retained in place of the words "replaced under section 28F(5) of the Child Support Act or revised under section 16 of that Act" and the words "replaced or" are not included after "before it was" and "against the decision as".

Definitions

"appeal": see reg 1(3).
"the date of notification": see reg 1(3).

General Note

If an appeal does not survive under this regulation, it lapses under s16(6) of the Act.

[¹Appeals to [²the First-tier Tribunal] in child support cases
30A.   [⁴...]]]

Amendments

1.   Child Support (Decisions and Appeals) (Amendment) Regulations 2000 (SI 2000 No.3185) reg 12 (comes into force for the types of cases detailed in art 3 of SI 2003 No.192 and those detailed in reg 1(2) of SI 2000 No.3185 on March 3, 2003, subject to the saving provision in art 14(3) of SI 2000 No.3185). For other types of cases see the '1993 rules' below.
2.   Tribunals, Courts and Enforcement Act 2007 (Transitional and Consequential Provisions) Order 2008 (SI 2008 No.2683) Sch 1 para 120 (November 3, 2008).
3.   Child Support (Miscellaneous Amendments) Regulations 2009 (SI 2009 No.396) reg 4(15) (April 6, 2009). This amendment does not apply to '1993 scheme cases' as defined by reg 7(2) of SI 2009 No.396. For such cases see the '1993 rules' below.
4.   Child Support (Management of Payments and Arrears) Regulations 2009 (SI 2009 No.3151) reg 14 and sch (January 25, 2010, subject to the savings provisions in reg 15 of SI 2009 No.3151). For those to whom this amendment does not apply reg 30A read:

30A.   Section 20 of the Child Support Act shall apply to any decision [³ of the Commission with respect to the adjustment of amounts payable under a maintenance calculation for the purpose of taking account of overpayments of child support maintenance or voluntary payments.]]

1993 rules
Reg 30A was inserted by reg 12 of the Child Support (Decisions and Appeals) (Amendment) Regulations 2000 (SI 2000 No.3185). This amendment came into force on March 3, 2003 for the types of cases detailed in art 3 of SI 2003 No.192 (see p683) and those detailed in reg 1(2) of SI 2000 No.3185 (see p536), subject to the saving provision in art 14(3) of SI 2000 No.3185. For other types of cases the '1993 rules' apply and reg 30A is not inserted.

Definition
"voluntary payments": see reg 3A(7).

General Note
This regulation extends the scope of s20 of the Act, which governs appeals to the First-tier Tribunal. That tribunal has jurisdiction over decisions relating to adjustments in respect of overpayments and voluntary payments. It is revoked under reg 14 Child Support (Management of Payments and Arrears) Regulations 2009, but subject to the saving in reg 15(2) in respect of certain appeals.

[Time within which an appeal is to be brought
31. [¹...]]

Amendment
1.   Tribunals, Courts and Enforcement Act 2007 (Transitional and Consequential Provisions) Order 2008 (SI 2008 No.2683) Sch 1 para 121 (November 3, 2008).

[¹Late appeals
32. [¹...]

Amendment
1.   Social Security, Child Support, Vaccine Damage and Other Payments (Decisions and Appeals) (Amendment) Regulations 2013 (SI 2013 No.2380) reg 4(10) (October 28, 2013, subject to the transitional and savings provisions in reg 8 of SI 2013 No.2380). For those covered by the transitional and savings provisions reg 32 reads:

32.–[²(1)   Where a dispute arises as to whether an appeal was brought within the time specified under Tribunal Procedure Rules the dispute shall be referred to, and determined by, the First-tier Tribunal.

(2)   The Secretary of State [³...] or the Board, as the case may be, may treat a late appeal as made in time in accordance with Tribunal Procedure Rules if the conditions in paragraphs (4) to (8) are satisfied.]

(3)   [²...]

[¹[²(4)   An appeal may be treated as made in time if the Secretary of State [³...] or the Board, as the case may be, is satisfied that it is in the interests of justice.]]

(5)   For the purposes of paragraph (4) it is not in the interests of justice to [²treat the appeal as made in time unless][¹, the Secretary of State or the Board, as the case may be,] is satisfied that–

(a)   the special circumstances specified in paragraph (6) are relevant [²...]; or

(b)   some other special circumstances exist which are wholly exceptional and relevant [²...],

and as a result of those special circumstances, it was not practicable for the [¹appeal to be made] within the time limit specified in [²Tribunal Procedure Rules].

(6)   For the purposes of paragraph (5)(a), the special circumstances are that–

(a)   the [²appellant] or a [¹partner] or dependant of the [²appellant] has died or suffered serious illness;

(b)   the [²appellant] is not resident in the United Kingdom; or

(c)   normal postal services were disrupted.

(7)   In determining whether it is in the interests of justice to [²treat the appeal as made in time], [¹regard shall be had] to the principle that the greater the amount of time

that has elapsed between the expiration of the time [²limit under Tribunal Procedure Rules and the submission of the notice of appeal, the more compelling should be the special circumstances.]

(8)   In determining whether it is in the interests of justice to [²treat the appeal as made in time], no account shall be taken of the following–

(a)   that the applicant or any person acting for him was unaware of or misunderstood the law applicable to his case (including ignorance or misunderstanding of the time limits imposed by [²Tribunal Procedure Rules]); or

(b)   that [²the Upper Tribunal] or a court has taken a different view of the law from that previously understood and applied.

(9)–(11)   [²...]

Amendments

1.   Social Security and Child Support (Decisions and Appeals) (Miscellaneous Amendments) Regulations 2002 (SI 2002 No.1379) reg 10 (May 20, 2002).
2.   Tribunals, Courts and Enforcement Act 2007 (Transitional and Consequential Provisions) Order 2008 (SI 2008 No.2683) Sch 1 para 122 (November 3, 2008).
3.   Public Bodies (Child Maintenance and Enforcement Commission: Abolition and Transfer of Functions) Order 2012 (SI 2012 No.2007) art 3(2) and Sch para 113(13) (August 1, 2012).

Note

i.   Reg 32 is modified by The Child Support Appeals (Jurisdiction of Courts) Order 2002 (SI 2002 No.1915) for appeals brought under that Order. See art 5 of SI 2002 No.1915 for details of the modifications.

Definitions

"appeal": see reg 1(3).
"legally qualified panel member": see reg 1(3).
"partner": see reg 1(3).
"President": see reg 1(3).

General Note

In the case of parentage appeals in England and Wales, this regulation applies as modified by art 5 Child Support Appeals (Jurisdiction of Courts) Order 2002 and for appeals in Scotland, as modified by art 5 Child Support Appeals (Jurisdiction of Courts) (Scotland) Order 2003.

In refusing permission to appeal in *Curtis v SSWP* [2006] EWCA Civ 1556, the Court of Appeal was sympathetic to the applicant but accepted that the absolute time limit in para (1) applied. Buxton LJ commented (para 28) that such a limit was more understandable in the case of an obligation owed by one citizen to another (like child support) than in cases of an obligation to pay by a public authority.

[¹⁰Notice of Appeal]
33. [¹...]

Amendment

1.   Social Security, Child Support, Vaccine Damage and Other Payments (Decisions and Appeals) (Amendment) Regulations 2013 (SI 2013 No.2380) reg 4(10) (October 28, 2013, subject to the transitional and savings provisions in reg 8 of SI 2013 No.2380). For those covered by the transitional and savings provisions reg 33 reads:

33.–(1)   [¹⁰...]

(2)   [¹⁰A notice of appeal made in accordance with Tribunal Procedure Rules and on a form approved by the Secretary of State [¹¹...] or the Board, as the case may be, or in such other format as the Secretary of State [¹¹...] or the Board, as the case may be, accepts, is to be sent or delivered to the following appropriate office]–

(a)   in the case of an appeal under the 1997 Act against a certificate of recoverable benefits [⁹or, as the case maybe, recoverable lump sum payments], the Compensation Recovery Unit of the [⁷Department for Work and Pensions] at [⁵ Durham House, Washington, Tyne and Wear, NE38 7SF];

(b)   in the case of an appeal against a decision relating to a jobseeker's allowance, an office of the [⁷Department for Work and Pensions the address of which was indicated on the notification of the decision which is subject to appeal];

(c)   in the case of a contributions decision which falls within Part II of Schedule 3 to the Act, any National Insurance Contributions office [¹ of the Board, or any office of the [⁷Department for Work and Pensions]];

[¹ (cc) in the case of a decision made under the Pension Schemes Act 1993 by virtue of section 170(2) of that Act, any National Insurance contributions office of the Board;]

(d)   [¹²...]

[² (dd) in the case of an appeal against a decision relating to working families' tax credit, a Tax Credits Office of the Board;]

[⁴ (ddd) in a case where the decision appealed against was a decision arising from a claim to a designated office, an office of a designated authority;] and

(e)   in any other case, an office of the [⁷Department for Work and Pensions the address of which was indicated on the notification of the decision which is subject to appeal].

[¹⁰(3)   Except where paragraph (4) applies, where a form does not contain the information required under Tribunal Procedure Rules the form may be returned by the Secretary of State [¹¹...] or the Board to the sender for completion in accordance with the Tribunal Procedure Rules.]

(4)   Where the Secretary of State is satisfied [² or the Board are satisfied] that the form, although not completed in accordance with the instructions on it, includes sufficient information to enable the appeal [¹⁰...] to proceed, he [² or they] may treat the form as satisfying the requirements of [¹⁰Tribunal Procedure Rules].

(5)   Where [¹⁰a notice of appeal] is made in writing otherwise than on the approved form ("the letter"), and the letter includes sufficient information to enable the appeal [¹⁰...] to proceed, the Secretary of State [² or the Board] may treat the letter as satisfying the requirements of [¹⁰Tribunal Procedure Rules].

(6)   Where the letter does not include sufficient information to enable the appeal [¹⁰...] to proceed, the Secretary of State [² or the Board] may request further information in writing ("further particulars") from the person who wrote the letter.

[⁷(7)   Where a person to whom a form is returned, or from whom further particulars are requested, duly completes and returns the form or sends the further particulars, if the form or particulars, as the case may be, are received by the Secretary of State or the Board within–

(a)   14 days of the date on which the form was returned to him by the Secretary of State or the Board, the time for making the appeal shall be extended by 14 days from the date on which the form was returned;

(b)   14 days of the date on which the Secretary of State's or the Board's request was made, the time for making the appeal shall be extended by 14 days from the date of the request; or

(c)   such longer period as the Secretary of State or the Board may direct, the time for making the appeal shall be extended by a period equal to that longer period directed by the Secretary of State or the Board.]

(8)   Where a person to whom a form is returned or from whom further particulars are requested does not complete and return the form or send further particulars within the period of time specified in paragraph (7)–

(a)   the Secretary of State [² or the Board] shall forward a copy of the form, or as the case may be, the letter, together with any other relevant documents or evidence to [¹⁰the First-tier Tribunal], and

(b)   the [¹⁰First-tier Tribunal] shall determine whether the form or the letter satisfies the requirement of [¹⁰Tribunal Procedure Rules.]

(9)   Where–

(a)   a form is duly completed and returned or further particulars are sent after the expiry of the period of time allowed in accordance with paragraph (7), and

(b)   no decision has been made under paragraph (8) at the time the form or the further particulars are received by the Secretary of State [² or the Board], that form or further particulars shall also be forwarded to the [¹⁰First-tier Tribunal which] shall take into account any further information or evidence set out in the form or further particulars.

[⁶[⁷(10) The Secretary of State or the Board may discontinue action on an appeal where the [¹⁰notice of] appeal has not been forwarded to the [¹⁰First-tier Tribunal] and the appellant or an authorised representative of the appellant has given written notice that he does not wish the appeal to continue.]]

Amendments

1. Social Security Contributions (Transfer of Functions, etc.) Act 1999 (Commencement No.2 and Consequential and Transitional Provisions) Order 1999 (SI 1999 No.1662), art 3(4) (July 5, 1999).
2. Tax Credits (Decisions and Appeals) (Amendment) Regulations 1999 (SI 1999 No.2570), reg 23 (October 5, 1999). Note that amendments made by these regulations only have effect with respect to working families' tax credit and disabled person's tax credit (reg 1(2) of the Amendment Regulations).
3. Social Security and Child Support (Decisions and Appeals), Vaccine Damage Payments and Jobseeker's Allowance (Amendment) Regulations 1999 (SI 1999 No.2677), reg 9 (October 18, 1999).
4. Social Security (Work-focused Interviews) Regulations 2000 (SI 2000 No.897), reg 16(5) and Sch 6 para 6 (April 3, 2000).
5. Social Security (Recovery of Benefits) (Miscellaneous Amendments) Regulations 2000 (SI 2000 No.3030), reg 4 (December 4, 2000).
6. Social Security and Child Support (Miscellaneous Amendments) Regulations 2000 (SI 2000 No.1596) reg 23 (June 19, 2000).
7. Social Security and Child Support (Decisions and Appeals) (Miscellaneous Amendments) Regulations 2002 (SI 2002 No.1379) reg 11 (May 20, 2002).
8. Child Support (Consequential Amendments and Transitional Provisions) Regulations 2001 (SI 2001 No.158) reg 4(4) (March 3, 2003 in relation the types of cases outlined in art 3 of SI 2003 No.192). For other types of cases see the '1993 rules' below.
9. Social Security (Recovery of Benefits) (Lump Sum Payments) Regulations 2008 (SI 2008 No.1596) reg 3 and Sch 2 para 1(e) (October 1, 2008) as amended by Social Security (Miscellaneous Amendments) (No.3) Regulations 2008 (SI 2008 No.2365) reg 6(6) (October 1, 2008).
10. Tribunals, Courts and Enforcement Act 2007 (Transitional and Consequential Provisions) Order 2008 (SI 2008 No.2683) Sch 1 para 123 (November 3, 2008).
11. Public Bodies (Child Maintenance and Enforcement Commission: Abolition and Transfer of Functions) Order 2012 (SI 2012 No.2007) art 3(2) and Sch para 113(14) (August 1, 2012).
12. Child Support (Meaning of Child and New Calculation Rules) (Consequential and Miscellaneous Amendment) Regulations 2012 (SI 2012 No.2785) reg 6(7) (in force in relation to a particular case on the day on which paragraph 2 of Schedule 4 to the Child Maintenance and Other Payments Act 2008 (see p243) comes into force in relation to that type of case – which is December 10, 2012 in relation to the types of cases falling within art 3 of SI 2012 No.3042 (see p767)). For other types of cases (except those covered by the '1993 rules') see the '2003 rules' below.

2003 rules

Regulation 6(7) of the Child Support (Meaning of Child and New Calculation Rules) (Consequential and Miscellaneous Amendment) Regulations 2012 (SI 2012 No.2785) omits paragraph (2)(d) from this regulation and comes into force on December 10, 2012 in relation to the types of cases falling within art 3 of SI 2012 No.3042 (see p767). For other types of cases the amendment has not been brought into force and paragraph (2)(d), shown below, is retained:

(d) in the case of an appeal under section 20 of the Child Support Act [⁸...], an office of the Child Support Agency;

1993 rules

Reg 4(4) of the Child Support (Consequential Amendments and Transitional Provisions) Regulations 2001 (SI 2001 No.158) amended this regulation and was brought into force on March 3, 2003 for the types of cases detailed in art 3 of SI 2003 No.192 (see p683) For other types of cases, the '1993 rules' apply. If the 1993 rules apply, paragraph (2)(d) shown under the heading '2003 rules' is included in regulation 33 but the words "as extended by paragraph 3 of Schedule 4C to that Act" are retained after "Child Support Act" in that paragraph.

34. [¹...]

Amendment

1. Social Security, Child Support, Vaccine Damage and Other Payments (Decisions and Appeals) (Amendment) Regulations 2013 (SI 2013 No.2380) reg 4(10) (October 28, 2013, subject to the transitional

and savings provisions in reg 8 of SI 2013 No.2380). For those covered by the transitional and savings provisions reg 34 reads:

Death of a party to an appeal

34.–(1) In any proceedings, on the death of a party to those proceedings (other than the Secretary of State [¹ or the Board]), the Secretary of State [¹ or the Board] may appoint such person as he thinks [¹ or they think] fit to proceed with the appeal in the place of such deceased party.

(2) A grant of probate, confirmation or letters of administration to the estate of the deceased party, whenever taken out, shall have no effect on an appointment made under paragraph (1).

(3) Where a person appointed under paragraph (1) has, prior to the date of such appointment, taken any action in relation to the appeal on behalf of the deceased party, the effective date of appointment by the Secretary of State [¹ or the Board] shall be the day immediately prior to the first day on which such action was taken.

Amendment

1. Tax Credits (Decisions and Appeals) (Amendment) Regulations 1999 (SI 1999 No.2570), reg 24 (October 5, 1999). Note that amendments made by these regulations only have effect with respect to working families' tax credit and disabled person's tax credit (reg 1(2) of the Amendment Regulations).

Definition

"party to the proceedings": see reg 1(3).

General Note

In the case of a deceased non-resident parent, reg 12(2) Child Support (Management of Payments and Arrears) Regulations 2009 substitutes a different provision for paras (1) and (2).

SCHEDULE 3
Regulations 1(3) and 35
Qualifications of persons appointed to the panel

[⁴...]

Amendments

1. Social Security and Child Support (Decisions and Appeals) (Miscellaneous Amendments) Regulations 2002 (SI 2002 No.1379) reg 22 (May 20, 2002).
2. Social Security, Child Support and Tax Credits (Miscellaneous Amendments) Regulations 2005 (SI 2005 No.337) reg 2(20) (March 18, 2005).
3. Social Security and Child Support (Decisions and Appeals) (Amendment) Regulations 2008 (SI 2008 No.1957) reg 2 (August 20, 2008).
4. Tribunals, Courts and Enforcement Act 2007 (Transitional and Consequential Provisions) Order 2008 (SI 2008 No.2683) Sch 1 para 128 (November 3, 2008). In relation to certain appeals under Health and Social Care (Community Health and Standards) Act 2003 (2003 c.43) this revocation does not extend to Scotland – see SI 2008 No.2683 arts 3 and 4 for details.

[¹ SCHEDULE 3D
Regulation 7B
EFFECTIVE DATES FOR SUPERSESSION OF CHILD SUPPORT DECISIONS

[⁵...]

Amendments

1. Child Support (Miscellaneous Amendments) Regulations 2009 (SI 2009 No.396) reg 4(16) (April 6, 2009). This amendment, which inserted schedule 3D, does not apply to '1993 scheme cases' as defined by reg 7(2) of SI 2009 No.396. See the '1993 rules' below.
2. Child Support (Miscellaneous Amendments) Regulations 2011 (SI 2011 No.1464) reg 2(4) (July 4, 2011).
3. Social Security and Child Support (Supersession of Appeal Decisions) Regulations 2012 (SI 2012 No.1267) reg 4(6) (June 4, 2012, but has effect as if it had come into force on November 3, 2008).
4. Public Bodies (Child Maintenance and Enforcement Commission: Abolition and Transfer of Functions) Order 2012 (SI 2012 No.2007) art 3(2) and Sch para 113(15) (August 1, 2012).

5.   Child Support (Meaning of Child and New Calculation Rules) (Consequential and Miscellaneous Amendment) Regulations 2012 (SI 2012 No.2785) reg 6(8) (in force in relation to a particular case on the day on which paragraph 2 of Schedule 4 to the Child Maintenance and Other Payments Act 2008 (see p243) comes into force in relation to that type of case – which is December 10, 2012 in relation to the types of cases falling within art 3 of SI 2012 No.3042 (see p767)). For other types of cases (except those covered by the '1993 rules') see the '2003 rules' below.

2003 rules

Regulation 6(8) of the Child Support (Meaning of Child and New Calculation Rules) (Consequential and Miscellaneous Amendment) Regulations 2012 (SI 2012 No.2785) omits Schedule 3D and comes into force on December 10, 2012 in relation to the types of cases falling within art 3 of SI 2012 No.3042 (see p767). For other types of cases (except those covered by the 1993 rules) the amendment has not been brought into force and Schedule 3D shown below, is retained:

[¹SCHEDULE 3D
Regulation 7B
EFFECTIVE DATES FOR SUPERSESSION OF CHILD SUPPORT DECISIONS

1.   This Schedule sets out the exceptions to the general rule in section 17(4) of the Child Support Act (that is the rule that a supersession decision takes effect from the beginning of the maintenance period in which it is made or, where applicable, the beginning of the maintenance period in which an application for a supersession is made).

Expected change

2.   Where the ground for the supersession decision is that a relevant change of circumstances is expected to occur or that a ground for a variation is expected to occur, the decision takes effect from the beginning of the maintenance period in which that change or that ground is expected to occur.

Decision backdated to when the change occurred

3.   Where the ground for the supersession decision is that a relevant change of circumstances of the following kind has occurred, the decision takes effect from the beginning of the maintenance period in which the change occurred–

(a)   a qualifying child dies or ceases to be a qualifying child;

[²(aa)   a relevant other child dies or ceases to be a relevant other child;]

(b)   the person with care ceases to be a person with care in relation to a qualifying child;

(c)   the person with care, the non-resident parent or a qualifying child ceases to be habitually resident in the United Kingdom; [²...]

(d)   paragraph 4(2) of Schedule 1 to the Child Support Act (flat rate for a non-resident parent whose partner is a non-resident parent) begins or ceases to apply[²; or

(e)   the non-resident parent begins or ceases to receive a benefit mentioned in regulation 4(1) of the Maintenance Calculations and Special Cases Regulations (flat rate) or begins or ceases to be a person who receives, or whose partner receives, a benefit referred to in regulation 4(2) of those Regulations.]

[²3A.   In paragraph 3, the reference to the day on which a person begins or ceases to receive a benefit is to the day on which entitlement to the benefit commences or ends, as the case may be.]

Non-resident parent or partner on or off benefit

4.   [²...]

New qualifying child

5.   Paragraphs 6 and 7 apply where the ground for the supersession is that there is a new qualifying child in relation to the non-resident parent.

6.   Where there is a new qualifying child in relation to the same person with care–

(a)   if the application is made by the non-resident parent, the decision takes effect from the beginning of the maintenance period in which the application is made; and

(b)   if the application is made by the person with care the decision takes effect from the beginning of the maintenance period in which notification of the application is given to the non-resident parent.

7.   Where there is a new qualifying child in relation to a different person with care and an application for a maintenance calculation has been made under section 4 or section 7 of the Child Support Act, the decision takes effect from the beginning of the maintenance period in which notification of the calculation is given to the non-resident parent.

Series of changes waiting to be actioned

8. Where a decision is superseded on application and, in relation to that decision, a maintenance calculation is made to which paragraph 15 of Schedule 1 to the Child Support Act applies, the effective date of the calculation or calculations is the beginning of the maintenance period in which the change of circumstances to which the calculation relates occurred or is expected to occur and where it occurred before the date of the application for the supersession and was notified after that date, [²the beginning of the maintenance period in which that application was made].

Own initiative decision

9. Unless paragraph 4 applies, where a decision is superseded in a case where the [⁴Secretary of State] is required to give notice under regulation 7C, the decision takes effect from the first day of the maintenance period which includes the date which is 28 days after the date on which the[⁴Secretary of State] has given notice (oral or written) to the relevant persons under that regulation.

Supersession of tribunal decision made pending outcome of a related appeal

10. Where, in accordance with section 28ZB(5) of the Child Support Act (appeals involving issues that arise on appeal in other cases), the [⁴Secretary of State] makes a decision superseding the decision of the First-tier Tribunal or the Upper Tribunal, the superseding decision takes effect from the beginning of the maintenance period following the date on which the decision of the First-tier Tribunal or, as the case may be, the Upper Tribunal would have taken effect had it been decided in accordance with the determination of the Upper Tribunal or the court in the appeal referred to in section 28ZB(1)(b).

Supersession of tribunal decision made in error due to misrepresentation etc.

11. Where–

(a) a decision made by [³an appeal tribunal, the First-tier Tribunal, the Upper Tribunal or of a Child Support Commissioner] is superseded on the ground that it was erroneous due to misrepresentation of, or that there was a failure to disclose, a material fact; and

(b) the [⁴Secretary of State] is satisfied that the decision was more advantageous to the person who misrepresented or failed to disclose that fact than it would otherwise have been but for that error, the superseding decision takes effect from the date on which the decision of [³an appeal tribunal, the First-tier Tribunal, the Upper Tribunal or a Child Support Commissioner (as the case may be)] took, or was to take, effect.

Supersession of look alike case where law reinterpreted by the Upper Tribunal or a court

12. Any decision made under section 17 of the Child Support Act in consequence of a determination which is a relevant determination for the purposes of section 28ZC (cases of error) of that Act takes effect from the date of the relevant determination.]

1993 rules

Schedule 3D was inserted by reg 4(16) of the Child Support (Miscellaneous Amendments) Regulations 2009 (SI 2009 No.396) but this does not have effect in relation to '1993 scheme cases' as defined by reg 7(2) of SI 2009 No.396. This means that if the provisions of the Child Support, Pensions and Social Security Act 2000 have not been brought into force in relation to a case in accordance with article 3 of the Child Support, Pensions, and Social Security Act 2000 (Commencement No.12) Order 2003 (SI 2003 No.192 – see p683) Schedule 3D does not apply to such a case.

Social Security (Claims and Information) Regulations 1999

(SI 1999 No.3108)

Citation and commencement

1. These Regulations may be cited as the Social Security (Claims and Information) Regulations 1999 and shall come into force on 29th November 1999.

Interpretation

2. In these Regulations–

"the Act" means the Welfare Reform and Pensions Act 1999;

"the Child Support Acts" means the Child Support Act 1991 and the Child Support Act 1995;

[¹...]

[¹...]

"relevant authority" means a person within section 72(2) of the Act.

Amendment

1.   Housing Benefit and Council Tax Benefit (Consequential Provisions) Regulations 2006 (SI 2006 No.217) reg 3 and Sch 1 (March 6, 2006).

War pensions and child support

6.–(1) Where a person resides in the area of an authority to which [¹paragraph 3] refers, he may make a claim for a war pension, or submit an application under the Child Support Acts to any office [²of a relevant authority] displaying the One logo (whether or not that office is situated within the area of the local authority in which the person resides).

(2) Any change of circumstances arising since a claim or application was made in accordance with paragraph (1) may be reported to the office to which that claim or application was made.

(3) The areas to which this paragraph refers are those areas which are within both–

(a) the area of a local authority identified in Part I or II of Schedule 1 to these Regulations, and

(b) a postcode area identified in Part I or II of Schedule 2 to these Regulations.

(4) A person making a claim or application to a participating authority in accordance with paragraph (1) shall comply with any requirements for the time being in force in relation to–

(a) claims for war pensions or applications under the Child Support Acts;

(b) the provision of information and evidence in support of such claims or applications,

as if those requirements also applied to the participating authority.

(5) A participating authority shall forward to the Secretary of State–

(a) any claim for a war pension or application under the Child Support Acts made in accordance with this regulation;

(b) details of changes of circumstances reported to the authority in accordance with this regulation; and

(c) any information or evidence–

(i) given to the authority by the person making a claim or application or reporting the change of circumstances; or

(ii) which is relevant to the claim or application or the change reported and which is held by the authority.

(6) For the purpose of this regulation, a "participating authority" means any authority or person to whom a claim or application may be made or change of circumstances reported in accordance with paragraphs (1) and (2).

Amendments

1.   Social Security (Work-focused Interviews) Regulations 2000 (SI 2000 No.897) reg 17(2) (April 3, 2000).

2. Social Security (Work-focused interviews for Lone Parents) and Miscellaneous Amendments Regulations 2000 (SI 2000 No.1926) reg 10 and Sch 2 para 4(b) (August 14, 2000).

Provision of information

8.–(1) A relevant authority may give information or advice to any person, or to a person acting on his behalf, concerning–

(a) a claim he made, or a decision given on a claim he made, for a social security benefit or a war pension;

(b) an application he made, or a decision given on an application he made, under the Child Support Acts.

(2) For the purpose of giving information or advice in accordance with paragraph (1), a relevant authority may obtain information held by any other relevant authority.

Information

13. . . .

(4) A relevant authority which holds social security information may supply that information to any other relevant authority for the purposes of research, monitoring or evaluation in so far as it relates to any purpose specified in paragraph (5).

(5) The purposes specified in this paragraph are–

(b) any purpose for which regulations 3,4 or 6 of these Regulations, or any regulation inserted by these Regulations, applies;

. . .

Purposes for which information may be used

14.–(1) The purposes for which information supplied in connection with matters referred to in paragraph (2) may be used are for–

(a) the processing of any claim for a social security benefit or a war pension or for an application for a maintenance assessment under the Child Support Act 1991;

(b) the consideration of any application for employment by a person to whom information is supplied in connection with any employment opportunity;

(c) the consideration of the training needs of the person who supplied the information;

(d) any purpose for which a work-focused interview may be conducted;

(e) the prevention, detection, investigation or prosecution of offences relating to social security matters.

[[1](f) assessing the employment or training needs of the person to whom the information relates;

(g) evaluating the effectiveness of training, advice, support and assistance provided;

(h) monitoring the retention of employment.]

(2) The matters referred to in this paragraph are–

(a) work-focused interviews; or

(b) any other provision in or introduced by these Regulations.

Amendment

1. Social Security (Claims and Information) (Amendment) Regulations 2010 (SI 2010 No.508) reg 2(4) (April 6, 2010).

Information supplied

15. Information supplied to a person or authority under these Regulations–

(a) may be used for the purposes of amending or supplementing information held by the person or authority to whom it is supplied; and

(b) if it is so used, may be supplied to another person or authority, and used by him or it for any purpose, to whom or for which that other information could be supplied or used.

SCHEDULE 1

Regulation 4(1)

Local Authorities on which functions are conferred

PART I

Local Authority

ENGLAND:
Aylesbury Vale
Barking and Dagenham
Calderdale
Castle Point
Chelmsford
Chiltern
Epping Forest
Kirklees
Maldon
Mendip
Milton Keynes
North Warwickshire
Nuneaton and Bedworth
Redbridge
Rochford
Rugby
Sedgemoor
South Bucks
Southend-on-Sea
South Somerset
Stratford-on-Avon
Taunton Deane
Waltham Forest
Warwick
West Somerset
Wycombe
WALES:
Monmouthshire
Newport
Torfean
SCOTLAND:
Argyll and Bute
East Renfrewshire
Inverclyde
North Ayrshire
Renfrewshire

PART II

Amber Valley
Ashfield
Babergh
Bassetlaw
Bolsover
East Cambridgeshire
Forest Heath
Halton
Ipswich
Leeds
Mansfield
Mid-Suffolk
North East Derbyshire
Newark and Sherwood
St. Edmunsbury
St. Helens
South Cambridgeshire
Suffolk Coastal
Vale Royal
Warrington
Waveney
Wigan

SCHEDULE 2
Regulation 4(2)
Postcode Areas
PART I

B37, B39, B46, B47, B49, B50, B76 to B79 and B93 to B95
BA3 to BA11, BA16, BA20 to BA22, BA24 and BA26 to BA28
CM0 to CM9
CV3, CV4, CV7 to CV12, CV21 to CV23, CV31 to CV35 and CV36 to CV39
DT9
E4, E10, E11, E17 and E18
EX15 and EX16
G78
GL50 and GL55
GL56
HD1 and HD5 to HD8
HP1, HP4 to HP23 and HP27
HX1 and HX7
IG1 to IG11
KA28 to KA30
LE10
LE17
LU6 and LU7
Part I (cont)
MK1 to MK19, MK43 and MK46
NN6, NN11 and NN13
NP1
NP4
NP5
NP6
NP7
NP9, NP16, NP20, NP25, NP26 and NP44
OL14
OX5 to OX7, OX9 and OX15
OX17
PA1 to PA17 and PA20 to PA27
RM6
RM8
RG9
SL0 to SL4 and SL6 to SL9
SS0 to SS7, SS9, SS11 and SS12
SS17
TA1 to TA24
UB9
WD3
WF12 to WF17
WO11

PART II

BD2 to BD4, BD10, BD11, BD16, BD17 and BD20
CB1 and CB5 to CB10
CM11
CO1, CO6 and CO8 to CO11
DE5, DE55 and DE56
DN22
HG3 and HG5
IP2 to IP20, IP22 to IP24 and IP27 to IP33
LS1 to LS15 (except Bramhope), LS16, LS17, LS19, LS21, LS22, LS27 and LS28
NG14 to NG23 and NG25
NR10, NR14, NR15 and NR31 to NR35
S44, S45 and S80
WA1 to WA8 and WA11 to WA13
WF3, WF6, WF10 and WF11
YO8, YO23 and YO26

The Child Support (Variations) (Modification of Statutory Provisions) Regulations 2000

(SI 2000 No.3173)

General Note

Sections 28A to 28F of, and Schs 4A and 4B to, the Act are drafted on the basis that the application for a variation was made under s28A(3) before a decision was made on an application for a maintenance calculation. An application for a variation can also be made under s28G(1) when a maintenance calculation is in force. These Regulations modify the Act to take account of those applications.

Citation, commencement and interpretation

1.–(1)   These Regulations may be cited as the Child Support (Variations) (Modification of Statutory Provisions) Regulations 2000 and shall come into force on 31st January 2001.

(2)   In these Regulations references to "the Act" are to the Child Support Act 1991 and references to sections are to sections of, and to Schedules are to Schedules to, the Act.

Modification of sections 28A to 28F and Schedules 4A and 4B

2.   Where an application for a variation is made under section 28G, sections 28A to 28F, and Schedules 4A and 4B, shall apply subject to the modifications provided for in these Regulations.

Modification of section 28A

3.–(1)   Section 28A (application for variation of usual rules for calculating maintenance) shall be modified by the substitution in subsection (1)–

(a)   for the words "Where an application for a maintenance calculation is made under section 4 or 7, or treated as made under section 6" by the words "Where a maintenance calculation other than an interim maintenance decision is in force"; and

(b)   for the words "(in the case of an application under" by the words "(where the maintenance calculation was made following an application under".

(2)   Subsection (3) shall be omitted.

Modification of section 28B

4.   Section 28B (preliminary consideration of applications) shall be modified–

(a)   by the substitution in subsection (2) for the words "(and proceed to make his decision on the application for a maintenance calculation without any variation)" by the words "(and proceed to revise or supersede a decision under section 16 or 17 respectively without taking the variation into account, or not revise or supersede a decision under section 16 or 17)"; and

(b)   by the omission of paragraph (b) of subsection (2).

Modification of section 28C

5.–(1)   Section 28C (imposition of regular payments condition) shall be modified in accordance with the following paragraphs of this regulation and references to subsections are to subsections of that section.

(2)   Subsection (1)(b) shall be omitted and in the full-out words "also" shall be omitted.

(3)   In subsection (2), for the words "interim maintenance decision" there shall be substituted the words "maintenance calculation in force".

(4)   In subsections (3)(c) and (7)(c), for the words "application for the maintenance calculation was" there shall be substituted the words "maintenance calculation in force was made in response to an application".

(5)   For subsection (4)(a) there shall be substituted the following–

"(a) when in response to the application for a variation the Secretary of State has revised or superseded a decision under section 16 or 17 respectively (whether he agrees to a variation or not) or not revised or superseded a decision under section 16 or 17;".

(6) In subsection (5), for the words from "reach" to the end there shall be substituted "revise or supersede a decision under section 16 or 17 respectively, or not revise or supersede a decision under section 16 or 17, as if the application had failed".

Modification of sections 28D and 28E

6.–(1) Section 28D (determination of applications) shall be modified by the substitution, in paragraph (a) of subsection (1), for the words "under section 11 or 12(1)" by the words "under section 16 or 17".

(2) Section 28E (matters to be taken into account) shall be modified by the substitution for paragraph (b) of subsection (3) of the following–

"(b) where the maintenance calculation in force was made in response to an application under section 7, by either of them or the child concerned.".

Modification of section 28F

7. Section 28F (agreement to a variation) shall be modified–

(a) by the substitution for subsection (3) of the following–

"(3) The Secretary of State shall not agree to a variation (and shall proceed to revise or supersede a decision under section 16 or 17 respectively without taking the variation into account, or not revise or supersede a decision under section 16 or 17) if he is satisfied that prescribed circumstances apply.";

(b) by the omission in paragraph (a) of subsection (4) of the words after the word "application," where it first appears;

(c) by the substitution for subsection (4)(b) of the following–

"(b) revise or supersede a decision under section 16 or 17 respectively on that basis."; and

(d) by the omission of subsection (5).

Modification of Schedules 4A and 4B

8.–(1) In paragraph 5(1) of Schedule 4A, the words [¹"application for a"] shall be omitted.

(2) In paragraphs 2(3)(a), (d) and (e) of Schedule 4B, for the words "the application for a maintenance calculation has been made (or treated as made)" there shall be substituted the words "there is a maintenance calculation in force".

(3) In paragraph 2(3)(c) of Schedule 4B, for the words "has been applied for (or treated as having been applied for)" there shall be substituted "is in force".

(4) In paragraph 3(1)(a) of Schedule 4B, for the words "the application for the maintenance calculation" there shall be substituted "the maintenance calculation in force" and for the words "that application was made" there shall be substituted "that maintenance calculation is in force".

(5) In paragraph 3(3) of Schedule 4B, for the words "the application for a maintenance calculation" there shall be substituted the words "the maintenance calculation in force".

Amendment

1. Child Support (Miscellaneous Amendments) Regulations 2002 (SI 2002 No.1204) reg 10 (April 30, 2002).

527

The Child Support (Temporary Compensation Payment Scheme) Regulations 2000
(SI 2000 No.3174)

Citation, commencement and interpretation

1.–(1)   These Regulations may be cited as the Child Support (Temporary Compensation Payment Scheme) Regulations 2000 and shall come into force on 31st January 2001.

(2)   In these Regulations, unless the context otherwise requires–

"the 2000 Act" means the Child Support, Pensions and Social Security Act 2000;

"the Child Support Act" means the Child Support Act 1991 before its amendment by the 2000 Act; and

"the Social Security Act" means the Social Security Act 1998.

Application of the Regulations

2.–(1)   For the purposes of section 27(2) of the 2000 Act, section 27 shall have effect as if it were modified so as to apply to cases of arrears of child support maintenance which have become due under a fresh maintenance assessment made in the following circumstances:

(a)   where the Secretary of State has given a departure direction under section 28F of the Child Support Act and–

(i)   the revised amount is higher than the current amount; and

(ii)   the effective date of the fresh maintenance assessment is a date before 1st June 1999; or

(b)   following a review under section 18 of the Child Support Act (reviews of decisions of child support officers) or a review under section 19 of that Act (reviews at instigation of child support officers) (as those provisions had effect before their substitution by section 41 of the Social Security Act),

and the effective date of the assessment is earlier than the date on which the assessment was made; or

(c)   following an appeal to [1 the First-tier Tribunal] under section 20 of the Child Support Act (as it had effect before its substitution by section 42 of the Social Security Act) against a decision of a child support officer.

(2)   In this regulation–

"current amount" means the amount of child support maintenance fixed by the current assessment; and

"revised amount" means the amount of child support maintenance fixed by the fresh maintenance assessment as a result of the departure direction given by the Secretary of State.

Amendment

1.   Tribunals, Courts and Enforcement Act 2007 (Transitional and Consequential Provisions) Order 2008 (SI 2008 No.2683) Sch 1 para 141 (November 3, 2008).

Prescribed date

3.   For the purposes of section 27(1)(a) of the 2000 Act, the prescribed date is 1st April [¹2005].

Amendment

1.   Child Support (Temporary Compensation Payment Scheme) (Modification and Amendment) Regulations 2002 (SI 2002 No.1854) reg 3. (July 17, 2002).

Prescribed circumstances

4.–(1)   In relation to cases of arrears which have become due under a maintenance assessment falling within section 27(1)(a) of the 2000 Act or a fresh maintenance assessment falling within section 27(1)(b) of the 2000 Act or regulation 2(1), the prescribed circumstances for the purposes of section 27(3) of the 2000 Act are that–

(a) more than 6 months of arrears of child support maintenance have become due under the maintenance assessment;

(b) at least 3 months of those arrears are due to unreasonable delay due to an act or omission by the Secretary of State or a child support officer as the case may be;

(c) the Secretary of State is authorised under section 29(1) of the Child Support Act to arrange for the collection of child support maintenance payable in accordance with the maintenance assessment;

(d) the Secretary of State is satisfied that the absent parent is, at the time the agreement is made, making such payments as are required of him in accordance with regulations made under section 29(3)(b) or (c) of the Child Support Act;

(e) where the absent parent is liable to make child support maintenance payments under a different maintenance assessment, there are no existing arrears in relation to any of them at the time the agreement is made, except for those arrears that the Secretary of State is satisfied have arisen through no fault of the absent parent; and

(f) in relation to cases under section 27(1)(b) of the 2000 Act or regulation 2(1), the absent parent has paid any arrears which he has been required to pay in relation to the maintenance assessment, or has done so except in relation to–

    (i) arrears of at least 3 months which are due to unreasonable delay due to an act or omission of the Secretary of State or a child support officer as the case may be; or

    (ii) any other arrears that the Secretary of State is satisfied have arisen through no fault of the absent parent.

(2) In this regulation "agreement" means an agreement under section 27 of the 2000 Act.

Terms of the agreement

5.–(1) For the purposes of section 27(4) of the 2000 Act, the terms which may be specified in the agreement are–

(a) the period of the agreement;

(b) payment of the child support maintenance payable in accordance with the maintenance assessment and, where relevant, the arrears, by whichever of the following methods the Secretary of State specifies as being appropriate in the circumstances–

    (i) by standing order;

    (ii) by any other method which requires one person to give his authority for payments to be made from an account of his to an account of another's on specific dates during the period for which the authority is in force and without the need for further authority from him;

    (iii) by an arrangement whereby one person gives his authority for payments to be made from an account of his, or on his behalf, to another person or to an account of that other person;

    (iv) by cheque or postal order;

    (v) in cash;

    (vi) by debit card;

    (vii) where the Secretary of State has made a deduction from earnings order under section 31 of the Child Support Act–

        (aa) by cheque;

        (bb) by automated credit transfer; or

        (cc) by such other method as the Secretary of State may specify;

(c) the amount of the arrears that the absent parent is required to pay (which shall include at least the last 6 months of the arrears due under the maintenance assessment);

(d) the day and interval by reference to which payments of the arrears are to be made by the absent parent; and

(e) the confirmation by the Secretary of State that he will not, while the agreement is complied with, take action to recover any of the arrears.

(2)   In this regulation "debit card" means a card, operating as a substitute for a cheque, that can be used to obtain cash or to make a payment at a point of sale whereby the card holder's bank or building society account is debited without deferment of payment.

Social Security (Child Maintenance Premium and Miscellaneous Amendments) Regulations 2000
(SI 2000 No.3176)

[¹**Citation and commencement**

1.–(1)   These Regulations may be cited as the Social Security (Child Maintenance Premium and Miscellaneous Amendments) Regulations 2000 and shall come into force–

(a)   in relation to any particular case, on the date on which section 23 of the 2000 Act comes into force in relation to that type of case ("the commencement date");

(b)   in relation to a person who, on or after 16th February 2004–

    (i)   makes a claim for income support or an income-based jobseeker's allowance; and

    (ii)   on or after the date of that claim receives any payment of child maintenance made voluntarily,

    on 16th February 2004; or

(c)   in relation to a person who–

    (i)   on 16th February 2004 is entitled to income support or an income-based jobseeker's allowance; and

    (ii)   on or after 16th February 2004 receives any payment of child maintenance made voluntarily and that payment is the first payment of child maintenance received by that person whilst he is entitled to income support or an income-based jobseeker's allowance,

    on 16th February 2004 if a payment referred to in head (ii) above is received on that day, or on the day on which such a payment is received where it is received after 16th February 2004.

(2)   In this regulation–

"the 1991 Act" means the Child Support Act 1991;

"the 2000 Act" means the Child Support, Pensions and Social Security Act 2000;

"child maintenance" shall have the same meaning as that prescribed for the purposes of section 74A of the Social Security Administration Act 1992;

"an income-based jobseeker's allowance" has the meaning given by section 1(4) of the Jobseekers Act1995;

"payment of child maintenance made voluntarily" means any payment of child maintenance other than such a payment made–

(a)   under a court order;

(b)   under a maintenance assessment made under the 1991 Act prior to its amendment by the 2000 Act or under a maintenance calculation made under the 1991 Act after its amendment by the 2000 Act;

(c)   under an agreement for maintenance;

(d)   in accordance with section 28J of the 1991 Act; or

(e)   by the Secretary of State in lieu of child maintenance, including any payment made by the Secretary of State under section 27 of the 2000 Act.]

Amendment

1.   Social Security (Child Maintenance Premium) Amendment Regulations 2004 (SI 2004 No.98) reg 4(1) (February 16, 2004).

Revocations and transitional provisions

[¹**4.**–(1)   Subject to paragraphs (2) to (8) below–

(a)   regulations 2 to 13 of the Social Security (Child Maintenance Bonus) Regulations 1996 ("the Child Maintenance Bonus Regulations");

(b)   the Child Maintenance Bonus (Northern Ireland Reciprocal Arrangements) Regulations 1997 ("the Reciprocal Arrangements Regulations");

(c) regulation 8 of the Social Security (Miscellaneous Amendments) Regulations 1997; and

(d) regulation 2 of the Social Security (Miscellaneous Amendments) Regulations 1998,

are hereby revoked.

(2) Subject to paragraph (6) below, the Reciprocal Arrangements Regulations and regulations 2 to 13 of the Child Maintenance Bonus Regulations shall continue to have effect as if paragraph (1) above had not been made in relation to a person–

(a) who–

    (i) satisfied the requirements of regulation 10 (claiming a bonus) or, as the case may be, regulation 11(4) (claims: further provisions) of the Child Maintenance Bonus Regulations; and

    (ii) satisfied the work condition in accordance with regulation 3(1)(c) of the Child Maintenance Bonus Regulations (entitlement to a bonus: the work condition),

before the commencement date, but whose claim has not been determined before that date;

(b) to whom regulation 8(1) or (2) of the Child Maintenance Bonus Regulations (retirement) applied before the commencement date but whose entitlement has not been determined before that date;

(c) who–

    (i) satisfied the requirements of regulation 10 or, as the case may be, regulation 11(4) of the Child Maintenance Bonus Regulations; and

    (ii) satisfied the requirements of regulation 8(4) of the Child Maintenance Bonus Regulations,

before the commencement date, but whose claim has not been determined before that date; or

(d) who–

    (i) satisfied the requirements of regulation 3(1)(b) to (f) of the Child Maintenance Bonus Regulations before the commencement date; and

    (ii) satisfies the requirements of regulation 10 (claiming a bonus) or, as the case may be, regulation 11(4) (claims: further provisions) of the Child Maintenance Bonus Regulations on or after the commencement date.

(3) Subject to paragraphs (5) and (6) below, the Reciprocal Arrangements Regulations and regulations 2 to 6 and 9 to 13 of the Child Maintenance Bonus Regulations shall continue to have effect as if paragraph (1) above had not been made in relation to–

(a) a person who–

    (i) satisfied the requirements of regulation 10 of the Child Maintenance Bonus Regulations before the commencement date; and

    (ii) has not satisfied the work condition in accordance with regulation 3(1)(c) of the Child Maintenance Bonus Regulations before that date; or

(b) a person–

    (i) who has not claimed a child maintenance bonus before the commencement date; and

    (ii) to whom the provisions of paragraph (4) below apply on the day immediately before the commencement date.

(4) For the purposes of paragraph (3)(b)(ii) above, the provisions of this paragraph are that–

(a) the person or, where the person has a partner, her partner is entitled to, or is treated as entitled to a qualifying benefit whether it is payable or not;

(b) the person has residing with her a qualifying child;

(c) child maintenance is either–

    (i) paid or payable to the person; or

    (ii) retained by the Secretary of State in accordance with section 74A(3) of the Social Security Administration Act 1992; and

    (d)   the person has not satisfied the work condition in accordance with regulation 3(1)(c) of the Child Maintenance Bonus Regulations.

    (5)   For the purposes of paragraph (3) above, regulation 3 of the Child Maintenance Bonus Regulations shall have effect as if in paragraph (1)–

    (a)   the words "no later than the day immediately before the commencement date" were inserted after–

        (i)   "dies" in sub-paragraph (f)(i); and

        (ii)   "has" where that word first appears in sub-paragraph (f)(ii); and

    (b)   for the words "14 days" in sub-paragraph (f)(iii) there were substituted "one month".

    (6)   For the purposes of paragraphs (2) and (3) above, regulation 4 of the Child Maintenance Bonus Regulations (bonus period) shall have effect as if for paragraph (7) there were substituted the following paragraph–

    "(7)   A bonus period which would, but for this paragraph, have continued shall end–

    (a)   where the applicant or, where the applicant has a partner, her partner, satisfies the work condition and claims a bonus, on the last day of entitlement to a qualifying benefit to which any award made on that claim applies;

    (b)   on the date of death of a person with care of a qualifying child to whom child maintenance is payable; or

    (c)   on the day immediately before the commencement date,

whichever is earlier."

    (7)   Nothing in this regulation shall prevent the Secretary of State from issuing a written statement pursuant to regulation 6(1) of the Child Maintenance Bonus Regulations (Secretary of State to issue estimates) to a person who appears to him to satisfy the requirements of regulation 3 of those Regulations.

    (8)   For the purposes of this regulation "child maintenance" has the meaning given by regulation 1(2) of the Child Maintenance Bonus Regulations (interpretation).]

Amendment

    1.   Social Security (Child Maintenance Premium and Miscellaneous Amendments) Amendment Regulations 2003 (SI 2003 No.231) reg 2 (comes into force in relation to any particular case on the date s23 of the Child Support, Pensions and Social Security Act 2000 (c.19) comes into force in relation to that type of case). See art 6 Child Support, Pensions and Social Security Act 2000 (Commencement No.12) Order 2003 (SI 2003 No.192) as amended by Child Support, Pensions and Social Security Act 2000 (Commencement No.13) Order 2003 (SI 2003 No.346) (see p685) and Child Support, Pensions and Social Security Act 2000 (Commencement No.14) Order 2008 (SI 2008 No.2545) art 4 for the date on which s23 comes into force for particular types of cases.

The Child Support (Voluntary Payments) Regulations 2000
(SI 2000 No.3177)

Citation, commencement and interpretation

1.–(1) These Regulations may be cited as the Child Support (Voluntary Payments) Regulations 2000 and shall come into force on the day on which section 28J of the Act as inserted by the Child Support, Pensions and Social Security Act 2000 comes into force.

(2) In these Regulations–

"the Act" means the Child Support Act 1991;

"debit card" means a card, operating as a substitute for a cheque, that can be used to obtain cash or to make a payment at a point of sale whereby the card holder's bank or building society account is debited without deferment of payment;

[²...]

"the qualifying child's home" means the home in which the qualifying child resides with the person with care [²...]; and

"relevant person" means–

(a) a person with care;

(b) a non-resident parent;

(c) a parent who is treated as a non-resident parent under [²regulation 50 of the Child Support Maintenance Calculation Regulations 2012];

(d) where the application for a maintenance calculation is made by a child under section 7 of the Act, that child,

in respect of whom a maintenance calculation has been applied for, [¹...] or is or has been in force.

Amendments

1. Child Support (Consequential Provisions) Regulations 2008 (SI 2008 No.2543) reg 5 (October 27, 2008).
2. Child Support (Meaning of Child and New Calculation Rules) (Consequential and Miscellaneous Amendment) Regulations 2012 (SI 2012 No.2785) reg 7(2) (in force in relation to a particular case on the day on which paragraph 2 of Schedule 4 to the Child Maintenance and Other Payments Act 2008 (see p243) comes into force in relation to that type of case – which is December 10, 2012, in relation to the types of cases falling within art 3 of SI 2012 No.3042 (see p767). For other types of cases see '2003 rules' below.

2003 rules

Regulation 7(2) of The Child Support (Meaning of Child and New Calculation Rules) (Consequential and Miscellaneous Amendment) Regulations 2012 (SI 2012 No.2785) amends this regulation and came into force on December 10, 2012, in relation to the types of cases falling within art 3 of SI 2012 No.3042 (see p767). For other types of cases the '2003 rules' apply. If the 2003 rules apply:

– the following definition is retained in regulation 4(2):

"the Maintenance Calculations and Special Cases Regulations" means the Child Support (Maintenance Calculations and Special Cases) Regulations 2000";

– from the end of the definition of "the qualifying child's home" the words "and "home" has the meaning given in regulation 1 of the Maintenance Calculations and Special Cases Regulations" are not omitted; and

– in the definition of "relevant person", in paragraph (c), the words "regulation 8 of the Maintenance Calculations and Special Cases Regulations" are retained in place of "regulation 50 of the Child Support Maintenance Calculation Regulations 2012".

Voluntary payment

2.–(1) A payment counts as a voluntary payment if it is–

(a) made in accordance with section 28J(2) and (4) of the Act;

(b) of a type to which regulation 3 applies;

(c) made on or after the effective date of the maintenance calculation made, or which would be made but for the Secretary of State's decision not to make one, [¹...]; and

(d)   a payment in relation to which evidence or verification of a type to which regulation 4 applies is provided, if the Secretary of State so requires.

(2)   Where the Secretary of State is considering whether a payment is a voluntary payment, he may invite representations from a relevant person.

Amendment

1.   Child Support (Meaning of Child and New Calculation Rules) (Consequential and Miscellaneous Amendment) Regulations 2012 (SI 2012 No.2785) reg 7(3) (in force in relation to a particular case on the day on which paragraph 2 of Schedule 4 to the Child Maintenance and Other Payments Act 2008 (see p243) comes into force in relation to that type of case – which is December 10, 2012, in relation to the types of cases falling within art 3 of SI 2012 No.3042 only (see p767). For other types of cases see '2003 rules' below.

2003 rules

Regulation 7(3) of The Child Support (Meaning of Child and New Calculation Rules) (Consequential and Miscellaneous Amendment) Regulations 2012 (SI 2012 No.2785) amends this regulation and has been brought into force on December 10, 2012, in relation to the types of cases falling within art 3 of SI 2012 No.3042 (see p767). For other types of cases the '2003 rules' apply. If the 2003 rules apply, the words "and for this purpose "effective date" means the effective date as determined in accordance with the Child Support (Maintenance Calculation Procedure) Regulations 2000" are retained at the end of regulation 2(1)(c).

Types of payment

3.   This regulation applies to a payment made by the non-resident parent–

(a)   by any of the following methods–

      (i)   in cash;

      (ii)   by standing order;

      (iii)   by any other method which requires one person to give his authority for payments to be made from an account of his to an account of another on specific dates during the period for which the authority is in force and without the need for any further authority from him;

      (iv)   by an arrangement whereby one person gives his authority for payments to be made from an account of his, or on his behalf, to another person or to an account of that other person;

      (v)   by cheque or postal order; or

      (vi)   by debit card, and

(b)   which is, or is in respect of,–

(i)   a payment in lieu of child support maintenance and which is paid to the person with care;

(ii)   a mortgage or loan taken out on the security of the property which is the qualifying child's home where that mortgage or loan was taken out to facilitate the purchase of, or to pay for essential repairs or improvements to, that property;

(iii)   rent on the property which is the qualifying child's home;

(iv)   mains-supplied gas, water or electricity charges at the qualifying child's home;

(v)   council tax payable by the person with care in relation to the qualifying child's home;

(vi)   essential repairs to the heating system in the qualifying child's home; or

(vii)   repairs which are essential to maintain the fabric of the qualifying child's home.

Evidence or verification of payment

4.   This regulation applies to–

(a)   evidence provided by the non-resident parent in the form of–

      (i)   a bank statement;

      (ii)   a duplicate of a cashed cheque;

      (iii)   a receipt from the payee; or

      (iv)   a receipted bill or invoice; or

(b)   verification orally or in writing from the person with care.

The Child Support (Decisions and Appeals) (Amendment) Regulations 2000
(SI 2000 No.3185)

Citation, commencement and interpretation

1.–(1)   These Regulations may be cited as the Child Support (Decisions and Appeals) (Amendment) Regulations 2000 and, subject to paragraph (2), shall come into force in relation to a particular case on the date on which sections 16, 17 and 20 of the Child Support Act 1991 as amended by the Child Support, Pensions and Social Security Act 2000 come into force in relation to that type of case.

(2)   For the purposes of any revision, supersession or appeal in relation to a decision which is made as provided in regulation 3 of the Child Support (Transitional Provisions) Regulations 2000 these Regulations shall come into force on the day on which section 29 of the Child Support, Pensions and Social Security Act 2000 comes fully into force.

(3)   In these Regulations "the principal Regulations" means the Social Security and Child Support (Decisions and Appeals) Regulations 1999.

(4)   In these Regulations any reference to a numbered regulation is to the regulation in the principal Regulations bearing that number and any reference to a numbered Part is to the Part of the principal Regulations bearing that number.

Regs 2–12 omitted

Substitution of regulation 45

13.   For regulation 45 (consideration of more than one appeal under section 20 of the Child Support Act) there shall be substituted the following regulation–

"Procedure following a referral under section 28D(1)(b) of the Child Support Act
45.–*(1)   On a referral under section 28D(1)(b) of the Child Support Act an appeal tribunal may–*
  (a)   consider two or more applications for a variation with respect to the same application for a maintenance calculation together; or
  (b)   consider two or more applications for a variation with respect to the same maintenance calculation together.
(2)   In this regulation "maintenance calculation" means a decision under section 11 or 17 of the Child Support Act, as calculated in accordance with Part I of Schedule 1 to that Act, whether as originally made or as revised under section 16 of that Act.".

Revocation and savings

14.–(1)   Subject to [¹the Child Support (Transitional Provisions) Regulations 2000 and] paragraph (2), regulations 10(2) and (3) and 11 to 17 of the Arrears, Interest and Adjustment of Maintenance Assessments Regulations are hereby revoked.

(2)   Where on the commencement date–
(a)   an appeal has not been decided;
(b)   the time limit for lodging an appeal has not expired;
(c)   the time limit for making an application for the revision of a decision has not expired; or
(d)   an application for a supersession of a decision has not been decided,
the provisions in regulations 10(2) and (3) and 11 to 17 of the Arrears, Interest and Adjustment of Maintenance Assessments Regulations shall continue to apply for the purposes of–
  (i)   the decision of the appeal tribunal referred to in sub-paragraph (a);
  (ii)   the ability to lodge the appeal referred to in sub-paragraph (b) and the decision of the appeal tribunal following the lodging of that appeal;
  (iii)   the ability to apply for the revision referred to in sub-paragraph (c) and the decision whether to revise following any such application; or

(iv)   the decision whether to supersede following the application referred to in sub-paragraph (d).

(3)   Where on or after the commencement date an adjustment falls to be made in relation to a maintenance assessment, these Regulations shall not apply for the purposes of making the adjustment.

(4)   In this regulation–

"commencement date" means, with respect to a particular case, the date on which these Regulations come into force with respect to that type of case;

"former Act" means the Child Support Act before its amendment by the Child Support, Pensions and Social Security Act 2000; and

"maintenance assessment" has the meaning given in the former Act.

Amendment

1.   Child Support (Transitional Provision)(Miscellaneous Amendments) Regulations 2003 (SI 2003 No.347) reg 2(1) and (2) (March 3, 2003).

15.–[¹(Z1)   This regulation is subject to the Child Support (Transitional Provisions) Regulations 2000.]

(1)   Where–

(a)   before the commencement date–

    (i)   an application was made and not determined for a departure direction or a revision or supersession of a decision in respect of a departure direction;

    (ii)   the Secretary of State had initiated but not completed a revision or supersession of a decision in respect of a departure direction; or

    (iii)   any appeal was lodged in respect of a departure direction decision which, on the commencement date, had not been decided; or

(b)   on the commencement date any time limit provided for in Regulations for making an application for a departure direction, or revision or, for making an appeal in respect of a departure direction decision, had not expired,

regulation 13 shall not apply for the purposes of any appeal–

    (aa)   made in consequence of the decision on the application, revision or supersession referred to in paragraph (1)(a)(i);

    (bb)   made in consequence of the revision or supersession referred to in paragraph (1)(a)(ii);

    (cc)   referred to in paragraph (1)(a)(iii); or

    (dd)   made within the time limit referred to in paragraph (1)(b) or made in consequence of a decision made on an application for a departure direction or revision made within the time limit referred to in that paragraph.

(2)   In this regulation "commencement date" has the same meaning as in regulation 14.

Amendment

1.   Child Support (Transitional Provision) (Miscellaneous Amendments) Regulations 2003 (SI 2003 No.347) reg 2(3) and (4) (March 3, 2003).

The Child Support (Transitional Provisions) Regulations 2000
(SI 2000 No.3186)

PART V

Savings

33.   Saving in relation to revision of or appeal against a conversion or subsequent decision

PART I

GENERAL

Citation and commencement

1.   These Regulations may be cited as the Child Support (Transitional Provisions) Regulations 2000 and shall come into force on the day on which section 29 of the 2000 Act comes fully into force.

Interpretation

2.–(1)   In Parts I to III and V except where otherwise stated–

"the Act" means the Child Support Act 1991;

[²"the Arrears, Interest and Adjustment Regulations" means the Child Support (Arrears, Interest and Adjustment of Maintenance Assessments) Regulations 1992;]

"the Assessment Calculation Regulations" means the Child Support (Maintenance Assessments and Special Cases) Regulations 1992;

"the Assessment Procedure Regulations" means the Child Support (Maintenance Assessment Procedure) Regulations 1992;

"the 2000 Act" means the Child Support, Pensions and Social Security Act 2000;

"calculation date" means the date the Secretary of State makes a conversion decision;

"capped amount" means the amount of income for the purposes of Part I of Schedule 1 to the Act where that income is limited by the application of paragraph 10(3) of that Schedule;

"case conversion date" means the effective date for the conversion of the non-resident parent's liability to pay child support maintenance from the rate as determined under the former Act and Regulations made under that Act, as provided for in regulation 15;

"commencement date" means the date on which section 1 of the 2000 Act, which amends section 11 of the Act, comes into force for the purposes of maintenance calculations the effective date of which, were they maintenance assessments, applying the [¹regulation 30 or 33(7) (but not regulation 8C or 30A) of the Assessment Procedure Regulations or regulation 3(5), (7) or (8) of the Maintenance Arrangements and Jurisdiction Regulations], and subject to paragraph (2), would be the same as or later than the date prescribed for the purposes of section 4(10)(a) of the Act;

"conversion calculation" means the calculation made in accordance with regulation 16;

"conversion date" means the date on which section 1 of the 2000 Act, which amends section 11 of the Act, comes into force for all purposes;

"conversion decision" means the decision under regulation 3(1) or (4);

"Decisions and Appeals Regulations" means the Social Security and Child Support (Decisions and Appeals) Regulations 1999;

"departure direction" has the meaning given in section 54 of the former Act;

"Departure Regulations" means the Child Support Departure Direction and Consequential Amendments Regulations 1996;

"first prescribed amount" means the amount stated in or prescribed for the purposes of paragraph 4(1)(b) or (c) of Part I of Schedule 1 to the Act (flat rate for non-resident parent in receipt of benefit, pension or allowance);

"former Act" means the Act prior to its amendment by the 2000 Act;

"former assessment amount" means the amount of child support maintenance payable under a maintenance assessment on the calculation date excluding amounts payable in respect of arrears or reductions for overpayments;

"interim maintenance assessment" has the meaning given in section 54 of the former Act; ·

"Maintenance Arrangements and Jurisdiction Regulations" means the Child Support (Maintenance Arrangements and Jurisdiction) Regulations 1992 [¹...];

"maintenance assessment" has the meaning given in section 54 of the former Act other than an interim maintenance assessment;

"Maintenance Calculations and Special Cases Regulations" means the Child Support (Maintenance Calculations and Special Cases) Regulations 2000;

"maintenance period" has the meaning given in regulation 33 of the Assessment Procedure Regulations and, where in relation to a non-resident parent there is in force on the calculation date more than one maintenance assessment with more than one maintenance period, the first maintenance period to begin on or after the conversion date;

"maximum transitional amount" [³has the meaning given in regulation 25(5), (6) or (7), whichever is applicable;]

"new amount" means the amount of child support maintenance payable [²from the case conversion date];

"partner" means, where there is a couple, the other member of that couple, and "couple" for this purpose has the same meaning as in paragraph 10C(5) of Part I of Schedule 1 to the Act;

"phasing amount" means the amount determined in accordance with regulation 24;

"relevant departure direction" and "relevant property transfer" have the meanings given in regulation 17;

"relevant other children" has the meaning given in paragraph 10C(2) of Part I of Schedule 1 to the Act and Regulations made under that paragraph;

"second prescribed amount" means the amount prescribed for the purposes of paragraph 4(2) of Part I of Schedule 1 to the Act (flat rate for non-resident parent who has a partner and who is in receipt of certain benefits);

"subsequent decision" means–
(a)   any decision under section 16 or 17 of the Act to revise or supersede a conversion decision; or
(b)   any such revision or supersession as decided on appeal,
whether as originally made or as revised under section 16 of the Act or decided on appeal;

"subsequent decision amount" means the amount of child support maintenance liability resulting from a subsequent decision;

"transitional amount" means the amount of child support maintenance payable during the transitional period;

"transitional period" means–
(a)   the period from the case conversion date to the end of the last complete maintenance period which falls immediately prior to the–
(i)   fifth anniversary of the case conversion date; or
(ii)   first anniversary of the case conversion date where regulation 12(1), (2), (4) or (5) or 13 applies; or
(b)   if earlier, the period from the case conversion date up to the date when the amount of child support maintenance payable by the non-resident parent is equal to the new amount or the subsequent decision amount, as the case may be; and

"the Variations Regulations" means the Child Support (Variations) Regulations 2000.

(2)   For the purposes of the definition of "commencement date" in paragraph (1)–
(a)   in the application of the Assessment Procedure Regulations, where no maintenance enquiry form, as defined in those Regulations, is given or sent to the non-resident parent, the Regulations shall be applied as if references in regulation 30 of those Regulations–
(i)   to the date when the maintenance enquiry form was given or sent to the non-resident parent were to the date on which the non-resident parent is first notified by the Secretary of State, orally or in writing, that an application for child support maintenance has been made in respect of which he is named as the non-resident parent; and

    (ii)   to the return by the non-resident parent of the maintenance enquiry form containing his name, address and written confirmation that he is the parent of the child or children in respect of whom the application was made, were to the provision of this information by the non-resident parent; or

    (b)   in the application of the Maintenance Arrangements and Jurisdiction Regulations, where no maintenance enquiry form, as defined in the Assessment Procedure Regulations, is given or sent to the non-resident parent, regulation 3(8) shall apply as if the reference to the date when the maintenance enquiry form was given or sent were to the date on which the non-resident parent is first notified by the Secretary of State, orally or in writing, that an application for child support maintenance has been made in respect of which he is named as the non-resident parent.

    (3)   In these Regulations any reference to a numbered Part is to the Part of these Regulations bearing that number, any reference to a numbered regulation is to the regulation in these Regulations bearing that number and any reference in a regulation to a numbered paragraph is to the paragraph in that regulation bearing that number.

Amendments

    1.   Child Support (Miscellaneous Amendments) Regulations 2003 (SI 2003 No.328) reg 9(2) (February 21, 2003).

    2.   Child Support (Miscellaneous Amendments) Regulations 2004 (SI 2004 No.2415) reg 8(2) (September 16, 2004).

    3.   Child Support (Miscellaneous Amendments) (No.2) Regulations 2003 (SI 2003 No.2779) reg 7(2) (November 5, 2003).

PART II

DECISION MAKING AND APPEALS

Decision and notice of decision

    3.–(1)   Subject to paragraph (2), a decision as to the amount of child support maintenance payable under a maintenance assessment or an interim maintenance assessment made under section 11, 12, 16, 17 or 20 of the former Act may be superseded by the Secretary of State on his own initiative under section 17 of the Act, in relation to–

    (a)   a maintenance assessment (whenever made) which [¹...] is in force on the calculation date;

    (b)   a maintenance assessment made following an application for child support maintenance which is made [⁴...] as provided for in regulation 28(1);

    (c)   an interim maintenance assessment [¹(whenever made)] where there is sufficient information held by the Secretary of State to make a decision in accordance with this paragraph.

    [²(2)   Where the Secretary of State acts in accordance with paragraph (1), the information used for the purposes of that supersession will be-

    (a)   that held by the Secretary of State on the calculation date; or

    (b)   where–

        (i)   regulation 5(b) applies; and

        (ii)   the Secretary of State is unable to make the decision required to be made in accordance with that regulation on the basis of the information referred to in [³sub-paragraph] (a),

that which was used or considered to make the maintenance assessment to be superseded in accordance with regulation 3(1)(a) or (b).]

    (3)   Where a superseding decision referred to in paragraph (1) is made the Secretary of State shall–

    (a)   make a conversion calculation;

    (b)   calculate a new amount; and

    (c)   notify to the non-resident parent and the person with care and, where the maintenance assessment was made in response to an application under section 7 of the former Act, the child, in writing–

        (i)   the new amount;

      (ii)   where appropriate, the transitional amount;

      (iii)   any phasing amount applied in the calculation of the transitional amount;

      (iv)   the length of the transitional period;

      (v)   the date the conversion decision was made;

      (vi)   the effective date of the conversion decision;

      (vii) the non-resident parent's net weekly income;

      (viii) the number of qualifying children;

      (ix)   the number of relevant other children;

      (x)   where there is an adjustment for apportionment or shared care, or both, or under regulation 9 or 11 of the Maintenance Calculations and Special Cases Regulations, the amount calculated in accordance with Part I of Schedule 1 to the Act and those Regulations;

      (xi)   any relevant departure direction or relevant property transfer taken into account in the conversion decision; and

      (xii) any apportionment carried out in accordance with regulation 25(3).

    (4)   Where at the calculation date there is an interim maintenance assessment in force and there is insufficient information held by the Secretary of State to make a maintenance assessment, or a decision in accordance with paragraph (1), the Secretary of State shall–

      (a)   supersede the interim maintenance assessment to make a default maintenance decision; and

      (b)   notify the non-resident parent, the person with care and, where the maintenance assessment was made in response to an application under section 7, the child, in writing, in accordance with regulation 15C(2) of the Decisions and Appeals Regulations.

    (5)   In a case to which paragraph (1)(c) or (4) applies, where after the calculation date information is made available to the Secretary of State to enable him to make a maintenance assessment he may–

      (a)   where the decision was made under paragraph (1)(c), revise the interim maintenance assessment in accordance with the Assessment Procedure Regulations, and supersede the conversion decision in accordance with the Decisions and Appeals Regulations;

      (b)   where the decision was made under paragraph (4), revise the interim maintenance assessment in accordance with the Assessment Procedure Regulations, and revise the default maintenance decision in accordance with the Decisions and Appeals Regulations.

    (6)   A decision referred to in paragraph (1) or (4) shall take effect from the case conversion date.

Amendments

1.   Child Support (Miscellaneous Amendments) Regulations 2003 (SI 2003 No.328) reg 9(3) (February 21, 2003).

2.   Child Support (Miscellaneous Amendments) Regulations 2004 (SI 2004 No.2415) reg 8(3) (September 16, 2004).

3.   Child Support (Miscellaneous Amendments) Regulations 2005 (SI 2005 No.785) reg 7(2) (March 16, 2005).

4.   Child Support (Consequential Provisions) Regulations 2008 (SI 2008 No.2543) reg 6 (October 27, 2008).

Definitions

"the Assessment Procedure Regulations": see reg 2(1).

"calculation date": see reg 2(1).

"commencement date": see regs 2(1) and 2(2).

"conversion calculation": see regs 2(1) and 2(2).

"conversion decision": see regs 2(1) and 2(2).

"Decisions and Appeals Regulations": see regs 2(1) and 2(2).

"former Act": see regs 2(1) and 2(2).

"interim maintenance assessment": see regs 2(1) and 2(2).

"maintenance assessment": see regs 2(1) and 2(2).

"Maintenance Calculations and Special Cases Regulations": see regs 2(1) and 2(2).

"new amount": see regs 2(1) and 2(2). "phasing amount": see regs 2(1) and 2(2).
"relevant departure direction": see regs 2(1) and 2(2).
"relevant other children": see regs 2(1) and 2(2).
"relevant property transfer": see regs 2(1) and 2(2).
"transitional amount": see regs 2(1) and 2(2).
"transitional period": see regs 2(1) and 2(2).

General Note

Paragraph (1) has not been brought into operation and this is not a violation of Arts 8 and 14 of the European Convention on Human Rights (*CSCS 15/2006*).

Revision, supersession and appeal of conversion decisions

4.–(1)   Subject to this Part, where–

(a)   an application is made to the Secretary of State or he acts on his own initiative to revise or supersede a conversion decision; or

(b)   there is an appeal in respect of a conversion decision,

such application, action or appeal shall be decided under the Decisions and Appeals Regulations and except as otherwise provided in paragraph (2), notification shall be given in accordance with regulation 3(3).

(2)   Where the Secretary of State acts in accordance with paragraph (1) he shall notify–

(a)   in relation to regulation 3(3)(c)(i), the subsequent decision amount in place of the new amount; and

(b)   where there has been agreement to a variation or a variation has otherwise been taken into account, the amounts calculated in accordance with the Variations Regulations.

(3)   Where after the calculation date–

(a)   an application is made to the Secretary of State or he acts on his own initiative to revise or supersede a maintenance assessment, an interim maintenance assessment or departure direction; or

(b)   there is an appeal in respect of a maintenance assessment, an interim maintenance assessment or departure direction; and

(c)   such application, action or appeal has been decided in accordance with regulations made under the former Act for the determination of such applications, the Secretary of State may revise or supersede the conversion decision in accordance with the Decisions and Appeals Regulations.

[¹(4)   In their application to a decision referred to in these Regulations, the Decisions and Appeals Regulations shall be modified so as to provide–

(a)   on any revision or supersession of a conversion decision under section 16 or 17 respectively of the Act, that–

(i)   the conversion decision may include a relevant departure direction or relevant property transfer; and

(ii)   the effective date of the revision or supersession shall be as determined under the Decisions and Appeals Regulations or the case conversion date, whichever is the later;

(b)   on any appeal in respect of a conversion decision under section 16 or 17 respectively of the Act, that the time within which the appeal must be brought shall be–

(i)   within the time from the date of notification of the conversion decision against which the appeal is brought, to one month after the case conversion date of that decision; or

(ii)   as determined under the Decisions and Appeals Regulations,

whichever is the later.]

(5)   In this Part, for the purposes of any revision or supersession a conversion decision shall include a subsequent decision.

Amendment

1.   Child Support (Miscellaneous Amendments) Regulations 2002 (SI 2002 No.1204) reg 8(2) (April 30, 2002).

Definitions

"the Act": see reg 2(1).
"calculation date": see reg 2(1).
"case conversion date": see reg 2(1).
"conversion decision": see reg 2(1).
"Decisions and Appeals Regulations": see reg 2(1).
"departure direction": see reg 2(1).
"former Act": see reg 2(1).
"interim maintenance assessment": see reg 2(1).
"maintenance assessment": see reg 2(1).
"new amount": see reg 2(1).
"relevant departure direction": see reg 2(1).
"relevant property transfer": see reg 2(1).
"subsequent decision": see reg 2(1).
"the Variations Regulations": see reg 2(1).

[¹Revision and supersession of an adjustment

4A. Where, on or after the calculation date, an application is made to the Secretary of State or he acts on his own initiative to revise or supersede an adjustment of the amounts payable under a maintenance assessment, he may revise or supersede that adjustment in accordance with the Decisions and Appeals Regulations.]

Amendment

1.   Child Support (Miscellaneous Amendments) Regulations 2004 (SI 2004 No.2415) reg 8(4) (September 16, 2004).

Definitions

"calculation date": see reg 2(1).
"Decisions and Appeals Regulations": see reg 2(1).

Outstanding applications at calculation date

5. Where at the calculation date there is outstanding an application for a maintenance assessment or a departure direction, or under section 16 or 17 of the former Act for the revision or supersession of a maintenance assessment, an interim maintenance assessment or a departure direction, the Secretary of State may–

(a)   where the application has been finally decided in accordance with Regulations made under the former Act for deciding such applications, supersede the maintenance assessment in accordance with regulation 3; or

(b)   where he is unable to make a final decision on the application for–

(i)   a departure direction; or
(ii)   a revision or supersession,

supersede the maintenance assessment or the interim maintenance assessment in accordance with regulation 3.

Definitions

"calculation date": see reg 2(1).
"departure direction": see reg 2(1).
"former Act": see reg 2(1).
"interim maintenance assessment": see reg 2(1).
"maintenance assessment": see reg 2(1).

General Note

See reg 5A, for the way in which this regulation applies.

[¹Outstanding revisions and supersessions at calculation date

5A. Regulation 5 shall apply in the same way to a decision of the Secretary of State acting on his own initiative under section 16 or 17 of the former Act to revise or supersede a maintenance assessment, an interim maintenance assessment or a departure direction as it does to an application made for the same purpose.]

Amendment

1.   Child Support (Miscellaneous Amendments) Regulations 2004 (SI 2004 No. 2415) reg 8(5) (September 16, 2004).

Definitions

"departure direction": see reg 2(1).
"former Act": see reg 2(1).
"interim maintenance assessment": see reg 2(1).
"maintenance assessment": see reg 2(1).

Applications for a departure direction or a variation made after calculation date

6.–(1)   Where an application for a departure direction or a variation is made after notification of the conversion decision the Secretary of State shall–

(a)   where the grounds of the application are subject only to a decision under the Departure Regulations, make a decision under the Departure Regulations;

(b)   where the grounds of the application are subject to a decision or determination, as the case may be, under–

(i)   the Departure Regulations; and

(ii)   the Variations Regulations,

make a decision under the Departure Regulations; or

(c)   where the grounds of the application are subject only to a determination under the Variations Regulations, treat the application as an advance application for a variation.

(2)   Where the Secretary of State has made a decision or a determination in which he agrees to the departure direction or variation applied for as provided under paragraph(1) he shall–

(a)   where the decision is made under paragraph (1)(a), supersede the maintenance assessment in accordance with the Assessment Procedure Regulations and the conversion decision in accordance with the Decisions and Appeals Regulations;

(b)   where the decision is made under paragraph (1)(b), supersede the maintenance assessment in accordance with the Assessment Procedure Regulations and the conversion decision in accordance with the Decisions and Appeals Regulations to give effect to any relevant departure direction, and from the case conversion date any variation, in the decision; or

(c)   where a determination is made under paragraph (1)(c), supersede the conversion decision in accordance with the Decisions and Appeals Regulations.

(3)   Where the Secretary of State does not have the information required to make a decision under paragraph (1) he shall not revise or supersede the conversion decision.

Definitions

"the Assessment Procedure Regulations": see reg 2(1).
"case conversion date": see reg 2(1).
"conversion decision": see reg 2(1).
"Decisions and Appeals Regulations": see reg 2(1).
"departure direction": see reg 2(1).
"Departure Directions": see reg 2(1).
"maintenance assessment": see reg 2(1).
"new amount": see reg 2(1).
"relevant departure direction": see reg 2(1).
"the Variations Regulations": see reg 2(1).

Grounds on which a conversion decision may not be revised, superseded or altered on appeal

7.   A decision of the Secretary of State made under regulation 3 shall not be revised, superseded or altered on appeal on any of the following grounds–

(a)   the use of the information held by the Secretary of State at the calculation date;

(b)   that the Secretary of State took into account a relevant departure direction in the conversion decision;

(c)   the application of the phasing amount in the calculation of the transitional amount;

(d)   the phasing amount applied to the calculation of the transitional amount;

(e)   the length of the transitional period;

(f)   that an existing departure direction has not been taken into account by the Secretary of State in the transitional amount;

(g)   that the Secretary of State took into account a relevant property transfer in the conversion decision, except where the application affects a relevant property transfer which has been included in the conversion decision on the grounds that—

   (i)   where the person with care or, where the maintenance assessment was made in response to an application under section 7 of the former Act, the child applies for the relevant property transfer to be removed, that property transfer when awarded did not reflect the true nature, purpose or value of the property transfer; or

   (ii)   [¹...] the person with care, the non-resident parent or, where the maintenance assessment was made in response to an application under section 7 of the former Act, the child applies for [¹...] a variation in relation to the same transfer.

Amendment

1.   Child Support (Miscellaneous Amendments) (No.2) Regulations 2003 (SI 2003 No.2779) reg 7(3) (November 5, 2003).

Definitions

"calculation date": see reg 2(1).
"conversion decision": see reg 2(1).
"departure direction": see reg 2(1).
"former Act": see reg 2(1).
"maintenance assessment": see reg 2(1).
"phasing amount": see reg 2(1).
"relevant departure direction": see reg 2(1).
"relevant property transfer": see reg 2(1).
"transitional period": see reg 2(1).

General Note

Paragraphs (c) and (d) do not deprive a tribunal of jurisdiction if the Secretary of State has failed to apply the phasing provisions at all. This was conceded by the CMEC in *CCS 393/2009*.

Outstanding appeals at calculation date

8.–(1)   Where there is an appeal outstanding at the calculation date against a maintenance assessment, an interim maintenance assessment or an application for a departure direction under the former Act, the Secretary of State shall supersede the maintenance assessment in accordance with regulation 3 using the information held at that date.

(2)   When the appeal is decided—

(a)   it shall be put into effect in accordance with the tribunal's decision; and

(b)   the conversion decision shall be superseded in accordance with the Decisions and Appeals Regulations in consequence of the implementation of the tribunal decision.

Definitions

"calculation date": see reg 2(1).
"conversion decision": see reg 2(1).
"Decisions and Appeals Regulations": see reg 2(1).
"departure direction": see reg 2(1).
"former Act": see reg 2(1).
"interim maintenance assessment": see reg 2(1).
"maintenance assessment": see reg 2(1).

PART III
AMOUNT PAYABLE FOLLOWING CONVERSION DECISION

Amount of child support maintenance payable

9.–(1)　[²Subject to regulation 9A, where] a decision of the Secretary of State is made as provided in regulation 3(1)(a) or (b), the amount of child support maintenance payable by the non-resident parent shall, on and from the case conversion date, including but not limited to those cases referred to in regulation 14, be the new amount [¹unless–

(a)　regulation 10 applies, in which case it shall be a transitional amount as provided for in regulations 11 and 17 to 28; or

(b)　regulation 12 or 13 applies, in which case it shall be a transitional amount as provided for in those regulations.]

(2)　Where a decision under regulation 3(1)(c) relates to a Category B or C interim maintenance assessment, [¹regulations 10 to 14 and 16 to 28] shall apply as if references to a maintenance assessment included references to such an interim maintenance assessment.

(3)　In this regulation the reference to Category B or C interim maintenance assessments, and in regulation 14 the reference to Category A or D interim maintenance assessments, are to those assessments within the meaning given in regulation 8(3) of the Assessment Procedure Regulations.

Amendments

1.　Child Support (Miscellaneous Amendments) Regulations 2002 (SI 2002 No.1204) reg 8(3) (April 30, 2002).

2.　Child Support (Miscellaneous Amendments) Regulations 2004 (SI 2004 No.2415) reg 8(6) (September 16, 2004).

Definitions

"the Assessment Procedure Regulations": see reg 2(1).

"case conversion date": see reg 2(1).

"interim maintenance assessment": see reg 2(1).

"maintenance assessment": see reg 2(1).

"new amount": see reg 2(1).

"transitional amount": see reg 2(1).

[¹Adjustment of the amount of child support maintenance payable

9A.–(1)　Subject to paragraph (2), where–

(a)　there has been an overpayment of child support maintenance under a maintenance assessment; and

(b)　the amount payable under that maintenance assessment has been adjusted under regulation 10 of the Arrears, Interest and Adjustment Regulations as it applies to a maintenance assessment,

that adjustment shall apply to the new amount or the transitional amount in the conversion decision, as the case may be, if–

(i)　the overpayment remains on the case conversion date; and

(ii)　the Secretary of State considers it appropriate in all the circumstances of the case having regard to the matters set out in regulation 10(1)(b) of the Arrears, Interest and Adjustment Regulations as it applies to a conversion decision.

(2)　Where the conversion decision relates to more than one parent with care, the adjustment of the amount payable under a maintenance assessment which applies to the new amount or the transitional amount, as the case may be, in accordance with paragraph (1) shall only apply in respect of the apportioned amount payable to the parent with care in relation to whom the maintenance assessment subject to the adjustment was made.

(3)　In paragraph (2) the "apportioned amount" shall have the meaning given in regulation 11(4).]

Amendment

1. Child Support (Miscellaneous Amendments) Regulations 2004 (SI 2004 No.2415) reg 8(7) (September 16, 2004).

Definitions

"the Arrears, Interest and Adjustment Regulations": see reg 2(1).
"case conversion date": see reg 2(1).
"conversion decision": see reg 2(1).
"maintenance assessment": see reg 2(1).
"new amount": see reg 2(1).
"transitional amount": see reg 2(1).

[¹Attribution of payments

9B.–(1)   Where–

(a)   there are arrears of child support maintenance under a maintenance assessment; and

(b)   the Secretary of State has attributed any payment of child support maintenance made by an absent parent to child support maintenance due as he thinks fit, in accordance with regulation 9 of the Arrears, Interest and Adjustment Regulations as it applies to a maintenance assessment,

that attribution of payments shall apply to the new amount or the transitional amount in the conversion decision, as the case may be, if–

(i)   the arrears remain on the case conversion date; and

(ii)   the Secretary of State has made that attribution of payments as he thought fit, in accordance with regulation 9 of the Arrears, Interest and Adjustment Regulations as it applies to a conversion decision.]

Amendment

1. Child Support (Miscellaneous Amendments) Regulations 2004 (SI 2004 No.2415) reg 8(7) (September 16, 2004).

Definitions

"the Arrears, Interest and Adjustment Regulations": see reg 2(1).
"case conversion date": see reg 2(1).
"conversion decision": see reg 2(1).
"maintenance assessment": see reg 2(1).
"new amount": see reg 2(1).
"transitional amount": see reg 2(1).

Circumstances in which a transitional amount is payable

10.   This regulation applies where the new amount is a basic or reduced rate[¹, an amount calculated under regulation 22][², an amount calculated under regulation 26 of the Variations Regulations] or, except where regulation 12, 13 or 14 applies, a flat rate of child support maintenance; and

(a)   the former assessment amount is greater than the new amount and when the former assessment amount is decreased by the phasing amount, the resulting figure is greater than the new amount; or

(b)   the former assessment amount is less than the new amount and when the former assessment amount is increased by the phasing amount, the resulting figure is less than the new amount.

Amendments

1. Child Support (Miscellaneous Amendments) Regulations 2002 (SI 2002 No.1204) reg 8(4) (April 30, 2002).

2. Child Support (Miscellaneous Amendments) Regulations 2003 (SI 2003 No.328) reg 9(4) (February 21, 2003).

Definitions

"former assessment amount": see reg 2(1).
"new amount": see reg 2(1).
"phasing amount": see reg 2(1).

Transitional amount – basic, reduced and most flat rate cases

11.–(1)   Subject to [¹paragraphs (2) and (3)] and regulation 25, in cases to which regulation 10 applies the transitional amount is the former assessment amount decreased, where that amount is greater than the new amount, or increased, where the latter amount is the greater, by the phasing amount.

[¹(2)   Subject to paragraph (3), where regulation 10 applies and there is at the calculation date more than one maintenance assessment in relation to the same absent parent, which has the meaning given in the former Act, the amount of child support maintenance payable from the case conversion date in respect of each person with care shall be determined by applying regulation 10 and paragraph (1) as if–

   (a)   the references to the new amount were to the apportioned amount payable in respect of the person with care; and

   (b)   the references to the former assessment amount were to that amount in respect of that person with care.

(3)   Where regulation 10 applies and a conversion decision is made in a circumstance to which regulation 15(3C) applies, the amount of child support maintenance payable from the case conversion date–

   (a)   to a person with care in respect of whom an application for a maintenance calculation has been made [²...] which is of a type referred to in regulation 15(3C)(b), shall be the apportioned amount payable in respect of that person with care; and

   (b)   in respect of any other person with care, shall be determined by applying regulation 10 and paragraph (1) as if the references to the new amount were to the apportioned amount payable in respect of that person with care and the references to the former assessment amount were to that amount in respect of that person with care.

(4)   In this regulation, "apportioned amount" means the amount payable in respect of a person with care calculated as provided in Part I of Schedule 1 to the Act and Regulations made under that Part and, where applicable, regulations 17 to 23 and Part IV of these Regulations.]

Amendments

   1.   Child Support (Miscellaneous Amendments) Regulations 2003 (SI 2003 No.328) reg 9(5) (February 21, 2003).

   2.   Child Support (Consequential Provisions) Regulations 2008 (SI 2008 No.2543) reg 6 (October 27, 2008).

Definitions

   "the Act": see reg 2(1).

   "case conversion date": see reg 2(1).

   "former assessment amount": see reg 2(1).

   "new amount": see reg 2(1).

   "phasing amount": see reg 2(1).

   "transitional amount": see reg 2(1).

Transitional amount in flat rate cases

12.–(1)   Except where the former assessment amount is nil, where the new amount would be the first prescribed amount but is nil owing to the application of paragraph 8 of Part I of Schedule 1 to the Act the amount of child support maintenance payable for the year commencing on the case conversion date shall be a transitional amount equivalent to the second prescribed amount and thereafter shall be the new amount, [¹...].

(2)   Except where the former assessment amount is nil, where the new amount would be the second prescribed amount but is nil owing to the application of paragraph 8 of Part I of Schedule 1 to the Act the amount of child support maintenance payable for the year commencing on the case conversion date shall be a transitional amount equivalent to half the second prescribed amount and thereafter shall be the new amount [¹...].

(3)   Where–

   (a)   a non-resident parent has more than one qualifying child and in relation to them there is more than one person with care; and

(b)   the amount of child support maintenance payable from the case conversion date to one or some of those persons with care, but not all of them, would be nil owing to the application of paragraph 8 of Part I of Schedule 1 to the Act,

the amount of child support maintenance payable by the non-resident parent from the case conversion date shall be the new amount, apportioned [¹among the persons with care, other than any in respect of whom paragraph 8 of Part I of Schedule 1 to the Act applies, in accordance with paragraph 6(2) of that Schedule, unless paragraph (4) or (5) applies.]

(4)   Subject to paragraph (6), where the former assessment amount is less than the new amount by an amount which is more than the second prescribed amount or, where paragraph 4(2) of Part I of Schedule 1 to the Act applies to the non-resident parent, half the second prescribed amount, the amount of child support maintenance payable by the non-resident parent shall be as provided in paragraph (1) where paragraph 4(1)(b) [¹or (c)] of Part I of Schedule 1 to the Act applies, and as provided in paragraph (2) where paragraph 4(2) of that Schedule applies.

(5)   Subject to paragraph (6), where the former assessment amount is greater than the new amount the amount of child support maintenance payable by the non-resident parent shall be the new amount unless the new amount is less than the second prescribed amount or, where paragraph 4(2) of Part I of Schedule 1 to the Act applies to the non-resident parent, half the second prescribed amount, in which case the amount of child support maintenance payable by the non-resident parent shall be as provided in paragraph (1) where paragraph 4(1)(b) [¹or (c)] of Part I of Schedule 1 to the Act applies, and as provided in paragraph (2) where paragraph 4(2) of that Schedule applies.

[¹(6)   Where paragraph (4) or (5) applies, the transitional amount shall be apportioned among the persons with care, other than any in respect of whom the former assessment amount is nil and paragraph 8 of Part I of Schedule 1 to the Act applies, in accordance with paragraph 6(2) of that Schedule.]

(7)   In this regulation "former assessment amount" means, in relation to a non-resident parent in respect of whom there is in force on the calculation date more than one maintenance assessment, the aggregate of the amounts payable under those assessments, and [¹...] includes the amount payable where section 43 of the former Act (contribution to maintenance) applies to the non-resident parent.

Amendment

1.   Child Support (Miscellaneous Amendments) Regulations 2002 (SI 2002 No.1204) reg 8(5) (April 30, 2002).

Definitions

"the Act": see reg 2(1).
"case conversion date": see reg 2(1).
"first prescribed amount": see reg 2(1).
"former assessment amount": see reg 2(1).
"new amount": see reg 2(1).
"second prescribed amount": see reg 2(1).
"transitional amount": see reg 2(1).

Transitional amount – certain flat rate cases

13.–[¹(1)]   Where paragraph 4(2) of Part I of Schedule 1 to the Act applies and the former assessment amount is nil, the amount of child support maintenance payable for the year beginning on the case conversion date shall be a transitional amount equivalent to half the second prescribed amount and thereafter shall not be a transitional amount but shall be the new amount.

[¹(2)   Where paragraph 4(1)(b) or (c) of Part I of Schedule 1 to the Act applies and the former assessment amount is nil, the amount of child support maintenance payable for the year beginning on the case conversion date shall be a transitional amount equivalent to half the first prescribed amount and thereafter shall not be a transitional amount but shall be the new amount.]

Amendment

1.   Child Support (Miscellaneous Amendments) Regulations 2002 (SI 2002 No.1204) reg 8(6) (April 30, 2002).

Definitions

"the Act": see reg 2(1).
"conversion date": see reg 2(1).
"former assessment amount": see reg 2(1).
"new amount": see reg 2(1).
"second prescribed amount": see reg 2(1).
"transitional amount": see reg 2(1).

Certain cases where the new amount is payable

14.   The amount of child support maintenance which the non-resident parent is liable to pay on and from the case conversion date is the new amount where–

(a)   the application for the maintenance assessment referred to in regulation 3(1)(a) is determined after the case conversion date, except in a case to which regulation 28(1) applies;

(b)   the former assessment amount is more than nil, including where section 43 of the former Act (contribution to maintenance) applies to the non-resident parent and the new amount is the first or second prescribed amount;

(c)   the new amount is the nil rate under paragraph 5 of Part I of Schedule 1 to the Act; [¹...]

(d)   the former assessment amount is nil and the new amount is nil owing to the application of paragraph 8 of Part I of Schedule 1 (flat rate plus shared care) to the Act; or

(e)   a decision under regulation 3(1)(c) relates to a Category A or D interim maintenance assessment or a decision is made under regulation 3(4).

Amendment

1.   Child Support (Miscellaneous Amendments) Regulations 2002 (SI 2002 No.1204) reg 8(7) (April 30, 2002).

Definitions

"the Act": see reg 2(1).
"conversion date": see reg 2(1).
"former assessment amount": see reg 2(1).
"new amount": see reg 2(1).
"second prescribed amount": see reg 2(1).
"transitional amount": see reg 2(1).

Case conversion date

15.–(1)   Subject to [²paragraphs (2) to (3G)], the case conversion date is the beginning of the first maintenance period on or after the conversion date.

(2)   Where, on or after the commencement date, there is a maintenance assessment in force and a maintenance calculation is made to which paragraph (3) [²or (3A)] applies, the case conversion date for the maintenance assessment [²is] the beginning of the first maintenance period on or after the effective date of the related maintenance calculation.

[²(3)   This paragraph applies where the maintenance calculation is made with respect to a relevant person who is a relevant person in relation to the maintenance assessment whether or not with respect to a different qualifying child.

(3A)   This paragraph applies where the maintenance calculation is made in relation to a partner ("A") of a person ("B") who is a relevant person in relation to the maintenance assessment and–

(a)   A or B is in receipt of a prescribed benefit; and

[⁴ (b)   A is the non-resident parent in relation to the maintenance calculation and B is the absent parent in relation to the maintenance assessment.]

(3B)   The case conversion date of a conversion decision made where paragraph (3C) applies is the beginning of the first maintenance period on or after the date of notification of the conversion decision.

(3C) This paragraph applies where on or after the commencement date–

(a) there is a maintenance assessment in force;

(b) an application is made [³...] which, but for the maintenance assessment, would result in a maintenance calculation being made with an effective date before the conversion date;

(c) the non-resident parent in relation to the application referred to in sub-paragraph (b) is the absent parent in relation to the maintenance assessment referred to in sub-paragraph (a); and

(d) the person with care in relation to the application referred to in sub-paragraph (b) is a different person to the person with care in relation to the maintenance assessment referred to in sub-paragraph (a).

(3D) The case conversion date of a conversion decision made where paragraph (3E) applies is the beginning of the first maintenance period on or after the date on which the superseding decision referred to in paragraph (3E)(d) takes effect.

(3E) This paragraph applies where on or after the commencement date–

(a) a maintenance assessment is in force in relation to a person ("C") and a maintenance calculation is in force in relation to another person ("D");

(b) C or D is in receipt of a prescribed benefit;

(c) either–

(i) C is the absent parent in relation to the maintenance assessment and D is the non-resident parent in relation to the maintenance calculation; or

(ii) C is the person with care in relation to the maintenance assessment and D is the person with care in relation to the maintenance calculation; and

(d) the decision relating to the prescribed benefit referred to in sub-paragraph (b) is superseded on the ground that C is the partner of D.

(3F) The case conversion date of a conversion decision made where paragraph (3G) applies is the beginning of the first maintenance period on or after the date from which entitlement to the prescribed benefit referred to in paragraph (3G)(c) begins.

(3G) This paragraph applies where on or after the commencement date–

(a) a person ("E") in respect of whom a maintenance assessment is in force is the partner of another person ("F") in respect of whom a maintenance calculation is in force;

(b) either–

(i) E is the absent parent in relation to the maintenance assessment and F is the non-resident parent in relation to the maintenance calculation; or

(ii) E is the person with care in relation to the maintenance assessment and F is the person with care in relation to the maintenance calculation; and

(c) E and F become entitled to a prescribed benefit as partners.]

(4) In [¹this regulation]–

[²"absent parent" has the meaning given in the former Act;]

[¹"maintenance assessment" has the meaning given in section 54 of the former Act;]

"relevant person" means, in relation to a maintenance assessment, the absent parent [²...] or person with care and, in relation to a maintenance calculation, the non-resident parent or person with care; and

"prescribed benefit" means a benefit prescribed for the purposes of paragraph 4(1)(c) of Part I of Schedule 1 to the Act.

Amendments

1. Child Support (Miscellaneous Amendments) Regulations 2002 (SI 2002 No.1204) reg 8(8) (April 30, 2002).

2. Child Support (Miscellaneous Amendments) Regulations 2003 (SI 2003 No.328) reg 9(6) (February 21, 2003).

3. Child Support (Consequential Provisions) Regulations 2008 (SI 2008 No.2543) reg 6 (October 27, 2008).

4. Child Support (Miscellaneous Amendments) (No.2) Regulations 2008 (SI 2008 No.2544) reg 7 (October 27, 2008).

Definitions
"case conversion date": see reg 2(1).
"commencement date": see reg 2(1) and (2).
"conversion decision": see reg 2(1) and (2).
"maintenance assessment": see reg 2(1) and (2).
"maintenance period": see reg 2(1) and (2).

Conversion calculation and conversion decision

16.–(1)   A conversion calculation by the Secretary of State shall be made–

(a)   in accordance with Part I of Schedule 1 to the Act;

[³(b)   taking into account the information used in accordance with regulation 3(2); and]

(c)   taking into account any relevant departure direction or any relevant property transfer as provided in regulations 17 to [¹23A].

(2)   A conversion decision shall be treated for the purposes of any revision, supersession, appeal or application for a variation under sections 16, 17, 20 or 28G of the Act, and Regulations made in connection with such matters, as a decision under section 11 of the Act made with effect from the date of notification of that decision and, where a conversion decision has been made, the case shall for those purposes be treated as if there were a maintenance calculation in force.

[¹(2A)   For the purposes of sections 29 to 41B of the Act and regulations made under or by virtue of those sections, a conversion decision shall be treated on or after the case conversion date as if it were a maintenance calculation.]

[²(2B)   For the purposes of regulation 2 of the Social Security Benefits (Maintenance Payments and Consequential Amendments) Regulations 1996 (interpretation for the purposes of section 74A of the Social Security Administration Act 1992), a conversion decision shall be treated on or after the case conversion date as if it were a maintenance calculation.]

[³(2C)   For the purposes of regulations 9 and 10 of the Arrears, Interest and Adjustment Regulations, a conversion decision shall be treated on or after the case conversion date as if it were a maintenance calculation.]

(3)   A [¹conversion decision] shall become a maintenance calculation when the transitional period ends or, if later, any relevant property transfer taken into account in [¹the conversion calculation] ceases to have effect.

Amendments
1.   Child Support (Miscellaneous Amendments) Regulations 2003 (SI 2003 No.328) reg 9(7) (February 21, 2003).
2.   Child Support (Transitional Provision)(Miscellaneous Amendments) Regulations 2003 (SI 2003 No.347) reg 3 (March 3, 2003).
3.   Child Support (Miscellaneous Amendments) Regulations 2004 (SI 2004 No.2415) reg 8(8) (September 16, 2004).

Definitions
"the Arrears, Interest and Adjustment Regulations": see reg 2(1).
"calculation date": see reg 2(1).
"conversion calculation": see reg 2(1).
"conversion decision": see reg 2(1).
"relevant departure direction": see reg 2(1).
"relevant property transfer": see reg 2(1).
"transitional period": see reg 2(1).

Relevant departure [¹direction] and relevant property transfer

17.–(1)   A relevant departure direction means a departure direction given in relation to the maintenance assessment which is the subject of the conversion decision where that direction was given under the provisions of the former Act and Regulations made under that Act, and where it is one to which one of the following paragraphs of this regulation applies.

(2)   This paragraph applies to a departure direction given on the special expenses grounds in paragraph 2(3)(b) (contact costs) or 2(3)(d) (debts) of Schedule 4B to the former Act where and to the extent that they exceed the threshold amount which is–

(a)   £15 per week where the expenses fall within only one of those paragraphs and, where the expenses fall within both paragraphs, £15 per week in respect of the aggregate of those expenses, where the net weekly income is £200 or more; or

(b)   £10 per week where the expenses fall within only one of those paragraphs and, where the expenses fall within both paragraphs, £10 per week in respect of the aggregate of those expenses, where the net weekly income is below £200,

and for this purpose "net weekly income" means the income which would otherwise be taken into account for the purposes of the conversion decision including any additional income which falls to be taken into account under regulation 20.

(3)   This paragraph applies to a departure direction given on the ground in paragraph 2(3)(c) (illness and disability costs) of Schedule 4B to the former Act where the illness or disability is of a relevant other child.

(4)   This paragraph applies to a departure direction given on the ground in paragraph 3 (property or capital transfer) of Schedule 4B to the former Act.

(5)   Subject to paragraph (6), this paragraph applies to a departure direction given on the additional cases grounds in paragraph 5(1) of Schedule 4B to the former Act and regulation 24 (diversion of income) of the Departure Regulations or paragraph 5(2)(b) of Schedule 4B to the former Act and regulation 25 (life-style inconsistent with declared income) of those Regulations.

[¹(6)   Where, but for the application of a relevant departure direction referred to in paragraph (5), the new amount would be–

(a)   the first prescribed amount owing to the application of paragraph 4(1)(b) of Part I of Schedule 1 to the Act;

(b)   the amount referred to in sub-paragraph (a), but is less than that amount or is nil, owing to the application of paragraph 8 of that Part; or

(c)   the nil rate under paragraph 5(a) of that Part,

paragraph (5) applies where the amount of the additional income exceeds £100.]

(7)   This paragraph applies to a departure direction given on the ground in paragraph 5(2)(a) of Schedule 4B to the former Act (assets capable of producing income) where the value of the assets taken into account is greater than £65,000.

(8)   A relevant property transfer is a transfer which was taken into account in the decision as to the maintenance assessment in respect of which the conversion decision is made owing to the application of Schedule 3A to the Assessment Calculation Regulations.

(9)   Where–

(a)   a relevant departure direction is taken into account for the purposes of a conversion calculation; or

(b)   a subsequent decision is made following the application of a relevant departure direction to a maintenance assessment,

the relevant departure direction shall for the purposes of any subsequent decision, including the subsequent decision in paragraph (b), be a variation as if an application had been made under section 28G of the Act for a variation in relation to the same ground and for the same amount.

[²(10)   Where–

(a)   a relevant property transfer is taken into account for the purposes of a conversion decision;

(b)   an application is made for a variation of a type referred to in paragraph 3 of Schedule 4B to the Act and Part IV of the Variations Regulations (property or capital transfers) which relates to the same property or capital transfer as the relevant property transfer referred to in sub-paragraph (a); and

(c)   the variation is agreed to,

the relevant property transfer shall cease to have effect on the effective date of the subsequent decision which resulted from the application for a variation.]

Amendments

1. Child Support (Miscellaneous Amendments) Regulations 2002 (SI 2002 No.1204) reg 8(9) (April 30, 2002).
2. Child Support (Miscellaneous Amendments) (No.2) Regulations 2003 (SI 2003 No.2779) reg 7(4) (November 5, 2003).

Definitions

"the Act": see reg 2(1).
"conversion calculation": see reg 2(1).
"conversion decision": see reg 2(1).
"departure direction": see reg 2(1).
"first prescribed amount": see reg 2(1).
"former Act": see reg 2(1).
"maintenance assessment": see reg 2(1).
"new amount": see reg 2(1).
"relevant departure direction": see reg 2(1).
"relevant property transfer": see reg 2(1).
"subsequent decision": see reg 2(1).
"the Variations Regulations": see reg 2(1).

Effect on conversion calculation – special expenses

18.–(1)   Subject to paragraph (2) and regulations 22 and 23, where the relevant departure direction is one falling within paragraph (2) or (3) of regulation 17, effect shall be given to the relevant departure direction in the conversion calculation by deducting from the net weekly income of the non-resident parent the weekly amount of that departure direction and for this purpose "net weekly income" has the meaning given in regulation 17(2).

(2)   Where the income which, but for the application of this paragraph, would be taken into account in the conversion decision is the capped amount and the relevant departure direction is one falling within paragraph (2) or (3) of regulation 17 then–

(a)   the weekly amount of the expenses shall first be deducted from the net weekly income of the non-resident parent which, but for the application of the capped amount, would be taken into account in the conversion decision including any additional income to be taken into account as a result of the application of paragraphs (5) or (7) of regulation 17 (additional cases);

(b)   the amount by which the capped amount exceeds the figure calculated under sub-paragraph (a) shall be calculated; and

(c)   effect shall be given to the relevant departure direction in the conversion calculation by deducting from the capped amount the amount calculated under sub-paragraph (b).

Definitions

"capped amount": see reg 2(1).
"conversion calculation": see reg 2(1).
"conversion decision": see reg 2(1).
"relevant departure direction": see reg 2(1).

Effect on conversion calculation – property or capital transfer

19.   Subject to regulation 23, where the relevant departure direction is one falling within paragraph (4) of regulation 17–

(a)   the conversion calculation shall be carried out in accordance with regulation 16(1) and, where there is more than one person with care in relation to the non-resident parent, the amount of child support maintenance resulting shall be apportioned among the persons with care as provided in paragraph 6 of Part I of Schedule 1 to the Act and Regulations made under that Part; and

(b)   the equivalent weekly value of the transfer to which the relevant departure direction relates shall be deducted from the amount of child support maintenance which the non-resident parent would otherwise be liable to pay to the person with care with respect to whom the transfer was made.

Definitions

"the Act": see reg 2(1).
"conversion calculation": see reg 2(1).
"relevant property transfer": see reg 2(1).

Effect on conversion calculation – additional cases

20. Subject to regulations 22 and 23, where the relevant departure direction is one falling within paragraph (5) or (7) of regulation 17 (additional cases), effect shall be given to the relevant departure direction in the conversion calculation by increasing the net weekly income of the non-resident parent which would otherwise be taken into account by the weekly amount of the additional income except that, where the amount of net weekly income calculated in this way would exceed the capped amount, the amount of net weekly income taken into account shall be the capped amount.

Definitions

"capped amount": see reg 2(1).
"conversion calculation": see reg 2(1).
"relevant departure direction": see reg 2(1).
"relevant property transfer": see reg 2(1).

Effect on conversion calculation – relevant property transfer

21.–(1) Subject to paragraph (2) and [¹regulation 23 and 23A], a relevant property transfer shall be given effect by deducting from the net weekly income of the non-resident parent which would otherwise be taken into account the amount in relation to the relevant property transfer and for this purpose "net weekly income" has the meaning given in regulation 17(2) but after deduction in respect of any relevant departure direction falling within paragraph (2) or (3) of regulation 17 (special expenses).

(2) Where the net weekly income of the non-resident parent which is taken into account for the purposes of the conversion calculation is the capped amount, a relevant property transfer shall be given effect by deducting the amount in respect of the transfer from the capped amount.

Amendment

1.   Child Support (Miscellaneous Amendments) Regulations 2002 (SI 2002 No.1204) reg 8(10) (April 30, 2002).

Definitions

"capped amount": see reg 2(1).
"conversion calculation": see reg 2(1).
"relevant departure direction": see reg 2(1).
"relevant property transfer": see reg 2(1).

Effect on conversion calculation – maximum amount payable where relevant departure direction is on additional cases ground

22.–(1) Subject to regulation 23, where this regulation applies [¹the new amount] shall be whichever is the lesser of–

[²(a)   a weekly amount calculated by aggregating the first prescribed amount with the result of applying Part I of Schedule 1 to the Act to the additional income arising under the relevant departure direction; or

(b)   a weekly amount calculated by applying Part I of Schedule 1 to the Act to the aggregate of the additional income arising under the relevant departure direction and the weekly amount of any benefit, pension or allowance received by the non-resident parent which is prescribed for the purposes of paragraph 4(1)(b) of that Schedule.]

(2)   This regulation applies where the relevant departure direction is one to which paragraph (5) or (7) of regulation 17 applies (additional cases) and the non-resident parent's liability calculated as provided in Part I of Schedule 1 to the Act, and Regulations made under that Schedule, would, but for the relevant departure direction be–

(a)   the first prescribed amount;

(b)   the first prescribed amount but is less than that amount or nil, owing to the application of paragraph 8 of Part I of that Schedule; or

(c)   the first prescribed amount but for the application of paragraph 5(a) of that Schedule.

(3)   For the purposes of paragraph (1)–

(a)   "additional income" for the purposes of sub-paragraphs (a) and (b) means such income after the application of a relevant departure direction falling within paragraph (2) or (3) of regulation 17 (special expenses) [²or a relevant property transfer]; and

(b)   "weekly amount" for the purposes of sub-paragraphs (a) and (b) means the aggregate of the amounts referred to in the relevant sub-paragraph–

    (i)   adjusted as provided in regulation 23(3) as if the reference in that regulation to child support maintenance were to the weekly amount; and

    (ii)   after any deduction provided for in regulation 23(4) as if the reference in that regulation to child support maintenance were to the weekly amount [²and

(c)   any benefit, pension or allowance referred to in sub-paragraph (b) shall not include–

    (i)   in the case of industrial injuries benefit under section 94 of the Social Security Contributions and Benefits Act 1992, any increase in that benefit under section 104 (constant attendance) or 105 (exceptionally severe disablement) of that Act;

    (ii)   in the case of a war disablement pension within the meaning in section 150(2) of that Act, any award under the following articles of the Naval, Military and Air Forces etc. (Disablement and Death) Service Pensions Order 1983 ("the Service Pensions Order"): article 14 (constant attendance allowance), 15 (exceptionally severe disablement allowance), 16 (severe disablement occupational allowance) or 26A (mobility supplement) or any analogous allowance payable in conjunction with any other war disablement pension; and

    (iii)   any award under article 18 of the Service Pensions Order (unemployability allowances) which is an additional allowance in respect of a child of the non-resident parent where that child is not living with the non-resident parent.]

Amendments

1.   Child Support (Miscellaneous Amendments) Regulations 2002 (SI 2002 No.1204) reg 8(11) (April 30, 2002).

2.   Child Support (Miscellaneous Amendments) Regulations 2003 (SI 2003 No.328) reg 9(8) (February 21, 2003).

Definitions

"the Act": see reg 2(1).
"conversion decision": see reg 2(1).
"first prescribed amount": see reg 2(1).
"maintenance assessment": see reg 2(1).
"relevant departure direction": see reg 2(1).

Effect of relevant departure direction on conversion calculation – general

23.–(1)   Subject to paragraphs (4) and (5), where more than one relevant departure direction applies regulations 18 to 22 shall apply and the results shall be aggregated as appropriate.

(2)   Paragraph 7(2) to (7) of Schedule 1 to the Act (shared care) shall apply where the rate of child support maintenance is affected by a relevant departure direction [¹...] and paragraph 7(2) of that Schedule shall be read as if after the words "as calculated in accordance with the preceding paragraphs of this Part of this Schedule" there were inserted the words '', the Child Support (Transitional Provisions) Regulations 2000".

(3)   Subject to paragraphs (4) and (5), where the non-resident parent shares the care of a qualifying child within the meaning in Part I of Schedule 1 to the Act, or where the care of such a child is shared in part by a local authority, the amount of child support maintenance the non-resident parent is liable to pay the person with care, calculated to take account of any relevant departure direction, shall be reduced in accordance with the provisions of paragraph 7 of that Part, or regulation 9 of the Maintenance Calculations and Special Cases Regulations, as the case may be.

(4)   Subject to paragraph (5), where a relevant departure direction is one falling within paragraph (4) of regulation 17 (property or capital transfer) the amount of the relevant departure direction shall be deducted from the amount of child support maintenance the non-resident parent would otherwise be liable to pay the person with care in respect of whom the transfer was made after aggregation of the effects of any relevant departure directions as provided in paragraph (1) or deduction for shared care as provided in paragraph (3).

(5)   If the application of regulation 19, or paragraphs (3) or (4), would decrease the weekly amount of child support maintenance (or the aggregate of all such amounts) payable by the non-resident parent to the person with care (or all of them) to less than a figure equivalent to the first prescribed amount, the new amount shall instead be the first prescribed amount and shall be apportioned as provided in paragraph 6 of Part I of Schedule 1 to the Act, and Regulations made under that Part.

Amendment

1.   Child Support (Miscellaneous Amendments) Regulations 2002 (SI 2002 No.1204) reg 8(12) (April 30, 2002).

Definitions

"the Act": see reg 2(1).
"first prescribed amount": see reg 2(1).
"new amount": see reg 2(1).
"relevant departure direction": see reg 2(1).

[1Effect of a relevant property transfer and a relevant departure direction – general

23A.   Where–
(a)   more than one relevant property transfer applies; or
(b)   one or more relevant property transfers and one or more relevant departure directions apply,

regulation 23 shall apply as if references to a relevant departure direction were to a relevant property transfer or to the relevant property transfers and relevant departure directions, as the case may be.]

Amendment

1.   Child Support (Miscellaneous Amendments) Regulations 2002 (SI.2002 No.1204) reg 8(13) (April 30, 2002).

Definitions

"relevant departure direction": see reg 2(1).
"relevant property transfer": see reg 2(1).

Phasing amount

24.–(1)   In this Part "phasing amount" means, for the year beginning on the case conversion date, the relevant figure provided in paragraph (2), and for each subsequent year the phasing amount for the previous year aggregated with the relevant figure.

(2)   The relevant figure is–
(a)   £2.50 where the relevant income is £100 or less;
(b)   £5.00 where the relevant income is more than £100 but less than £400; or
(c)   £10.00 where the relevant income is £400 or more.

(3)   [¹Subject to [²paragraphs (4)[³, (5) and (6)], for] the purposes of paragraph (2), the "relevant income" is the net weekly income of the non-resident parent taken into account in the conversion decision.

[¹(4)   Where the new amount is calculated under regulation 22(1), "relevant income" for the purposes of paragraph (2) is the aggregate of the income calculated under regulation 22(1)(b).]

[²(5)   Where the new amount is calculated under regulation 26(1) of the Variations Regulations, the "relevant income" for the purposes of paragraph (2) is the additional income arising under the variation.]

[³(6)   Where a subsequent decision is made the effective date of which is the case conversion date–
    (a)   the reference in paragraph (3) to the conversion decision shall apply as if it were a reference to the subsequent decision; and
    (b)   the reference in paragraph (5) to the new amount shall apply as if it were a reference to the subsequent decision amount.]

Amendments
    1.   Child Support (Miscellaneous Amendments) Regulations 2002 (SI 2002 No.1204) reg 8(14) (April 30, 2002).
    2.   Child Support (Miscellaneous Amendments) Regulations 2003 (SI 2003 No.328) reg 9(9) (February 21, 2003).
    3.   Child Support (Miscellaneous Amendments) (No.2) Regulations 2003 (SI 2003 No.2779) reg 7(5) (November 5, 2003).

Definitions
    "case conversion date": see reg 2(1).
    "conversion date": see reg 2(1).
    "phasing amount": see reg 2(1).

Maximum transitional amount

25.–(1)   Where a conversion decision is made in a circumstance [¹to which regulation 15(3C)] applies (maintenance assessment and related maintenance calculation), or a subsequent decision is made, the liability of the non-resident parent to pay child support maintenance during the transitional period (excluding any amount payable in respect of arrears of child support maintenance and before reduction for any amount in respect of an overpayment) shall be whichever is the lesser of–
    [¹(a)   the transitional amount payable under this Part added to, where applicable, the transitional amount payable under Part IV; and]
    (b)   the maximum transitional amount.
    (2)   Where–
    (a)   a conversion decision to which paragraph (1) applies, or a subsequent decision, results from an application made [³ ...] for a maintenance calculation in respect of the same non-resident parent but a different qualifying child in relation to whom there is a different person with care (referred to in this regulation as "the new application"); and
    (b)   the amount of child support maintenance payable by the non-resident parent from the case conversion date, or the effective date of the subsequent decision, as the case may be, is the maximum transitional amount,
that amount shall be apportioned as provided in paragraph (3).
    (3)   The apportionment referred to in paragraph (2) shall be carried out as follows–
    (a)   the amount of child support maintenance payable by the non-resident parent to the person with care in relation to the new application shall be calculated as provided in Part I of Schedule 1 to the Act and Regulations made under that Part and where applicable, Part IV of these Regulations, and that amount shall be the amount payable to that person with care;
    [¹(aa) the amount of child support maintenance payable to a person with care in respect of whom there was a maintenance assessment in force immediately before the case conversion date and in respect of whom the amount payable is not calculated

by reference to a phasing amount, shall be an amount calculated as provided in sub-paragraph (a) and, where applicable, regulations 17 to 23;]

(b) [¹the amounts calculated as provided in sub-paragraphs (a) and (aa)] shall be deducted from the maximum transitional amount and the remainder shall be apportioned among the other persons with care so that the proportion which each receives bears the same relation to the proportions which the others receive as those proportions would have borne in relation to each other and the new amount, or the subsequent decision amount, as the case may be, if the maximum transitional amount had not been applied.

(4) Where–

(a) apportionment under paragraph (3)(b) results in a fraction of a penny, that fraction shall be treated as a penny if it is either one half or exceeds one half, otherwise it shall be disregarded; and

(b) the application of paragraph (3)(b) would be such that the aggregate amount payable by a non-resident parent would be different from the aggregate amount payable before any such apportionment, the Secretary of State shall adjust that apportionment so as to eliminate that difference and that adjustment shall be varied from time to time so as to secure that, taking one week with another and so far as is practicable, each person with care receives the amount which she would have received if no adjustment had been made under this paragraph.

[²(5) Subject to paragraphs (6) and (7), "maximum transitional amount" means 30% of the non-resident parent's net weekly income taken into account in the conversion decision, or the subsequent decision, as the case may be.

(6) Where the new amount is calculated under regulation 22(1), "maximum transitional amount" means 30% of the aggregate of the income calculated under regulation 22(1)(b).

(7) Where the new amount or the subsequent decision amount, as the case may be, is calculated under regulation 26(1) of the Variations Regulations "maximum transitional amount" means 30% of the additional income arising under the variation.]

Amendments

1. Child Support (Miscellaneous Amendments) Regulations 2003 (SI 2003 No.328) reg 9(10) (February 21, 2003).
2. Child Support (Miscellaneous Amendments) (No.2) Regulations 2003 (SI 2003 No.2779) reg 7(6) (November 5, 2003).
3. Child Support (Consequential Provisions) Regulations 2008 (SI 2008 No.2543) reg 6 (October 27, 2008).

Definitions

"the Act": see reg 2(1).
"conversion decision": see reg 2(1).
"maintenance assessment": see reg 2(1).
"new amount": see reg 2(1).
"subsequent decision": see reg 2(1).
"subsequent decision amount": see reg 2(1).
"transitional amount": see reg 2(1).
"transitional period": see reg 2(1).
"the Variations Regulations": see reg 2(1).

General Note

The operation of these provisions was described in *CCS 393/2009*:

"9. In this case, there was a maintenance assessment in force (for Kaelee) and an application was made for a maintenance calculation by a different parent with care (Ms H) in respect of the same non-resident parent. That is the sequence of events envisaged by regulation 15(3C).

10. The former maintenance assessment was £113.87. The transitional provisions operate to afford some protection to the amount of the maintenance assessment that was in force when the case was converted under the 2000 Act. It is, therefore, necessary to distinguish between the amount payable to Ms J and Ms H.

11. The amount payable in respect of Mr C's children by Ms H is fixed as if the case had not been converted from the original scheme. Mr C's maintenance calculated on that basis was £82. As he has three qualifying children and Ms H is the parent with care of two of them, the amount payable in respect of

those two children is £54.66: see regulation 25(3)(a). That would leave £27.34 in respect of Kaelee. However, the transitional protection operates for her benefit. It does so for the transitional period of 5 years: see regulation 2(1).

12. In order to identify how much Mr C has to pay to Ms J, it is first necessary to decide whether the transitional amount or the maximum transitional amount is payable. The transitional amount is the amount of the maintenance assessment less the phasing amount. As Mr C's net weekly income is £329.48, the phasing amount is £5 for each year, cumulative year on year: see regulation 24(2)(b). So, the transitional amount is £113.87 – £5 in the first year, £10 in the second, and so on. The maximum transitional amount is 30% of Mr C's net weekly income of £329.48 = £98.84: see regulation 25(5). That is less than the transitional amount.

13. The amount payable to Ms H is, therefore, deducted from the maximum transitional amount: see regulation 25(3)(b). The remainder is payable to Ms J for the transitional period: £98.84 – £54.66 = £44.18. Thereafter, the amount payable to Ms J is her share of the maintenance calculation = £27.34. These figures assume that there is no change in the parties' circumstances."

Subsequent decision effective on case conversion date

26.–(1) Where there is a subsequent decision, the effective date of which is the case conversion date, the amount of child support maintenance payable shall be calculated as if the subsequent decision were a conversion decision.

(2) For the purposes of paragraph (1), regulations 9 to 25 shall apply as if references–
(a) to the calculation date, including in relation to the definition of the former assessment amount, were to–
  (i) where there has been a decision under section 16, 17 or 20 in relation to the maintenance assessment, the effective date of that decision; or
  (ii) where sub-paragraph (i) does not apply–
    (aa) the effective date of the subsequent decision; or
    (bb) if earlier, the date the subsequent decision was made;
(b) to the new amount were to the subsequent decision amount; and
(c) to the conversion decision in regulation 24(3) were to the subsequent decision.

Definitions
"calculation date": see reg 2(1).
"case conversion date": see reg 2(1).
"conversion decision": see reg 2(1).
"former assessment amount": see reg 2(1).
"maintenance assessment": see reg 2(1).
"new amount": see reg 2(1).
"subsequent decision": see reg 2(1).

Subsequent decision with effect in transitional period – amount payable

27.–(1) Subject to paragraph (6), where during the transitional period there is a subsequent decision the effective date of which is after the case conversion date, the amount of child support maintenance payable shall be the subsequent decision amount unless any of the following paragraphs applies, in which case it shall be a transitional amount as provided for in those paragraphs.

(2) Where–
(a) the new amount was greater than the former assessment amount; and
(b) the subsequent decision amount is greater than the new amount,
the amount of child support maintenance payable shall be a transitional amount calculated as the transitional amount payable immediately before the subsequent decision ("the previous transitional amount") increased by the difference between the new amount and the subsequent decision amount and the phasing amounts shall apply to that transitional amount as they would have applied to the previous transitional amount had there been no subsequent decision.

(3) Where–
(a) paragraph (2)(a) applies; and
(b) the subsequent decision amount is equal to or less than the new amount ['and greater than the previous transitional amount,]

the amount of child support maintenance payable shall be the previous transitional amount and the phasing amounts shall apply as they would have applied had there been no subsequent decision.

(4)　Where–

(a)　the new amount was less than the former assessment amount; and

(b)　the subsequent decision amount is less than the new amount,

the amount of child support maintenance payable shall be a transitional amount calculated as the previous transitional amount decreased by the difference between the new amount and the subsequent decision amount and the phasing amounts shall apply to that transitional amount as they would have applied to the previous transitional amount had there been no subsequent decision.

(5)　Where–

(a)　paragraph (4)(a) applies; and

(b)　the subsequent decision amount is equal to or more than the new amount, [and less than the previous transitional amount,]

the amount of child support maintenance payable shall be the previous transitional amount and the phasing amounts shall apply as they would have applied had there been no subsequent decision.

(6)　Paragraphs (2) to (5) shall not apply where the subsequent decision amount is the first or second prescribed amount[¹, would be the first or the second prescribed amount but is less than that amount, or is nil, owing to the application of paragraph 8 of Part I of Schedule 1 to the Act, or is the nil rate.]

[²(7) Where paragraph (1) applies and at the date of the subsequent decision there is more than one person with care in relation to the same non-resident parent–

(a)　the amount payable to a person with care in respect of whom the amount payable is calculated by reference to a phasing amount shall be determined by applying paragraphs (1) to (5) as if references to the new amount, the subsequent decision amount and the transitional amount were to the apportioned part of the amount in question; and

(b)　the amount payable in respect of any other person with care shall be the apportioned part of the subsequent decision amount.

[⁵(7A)　This paragraph applies where–

(a)　paragraph (1) applies and at the date of the subsequent decision there is more than one person with care in relation to the same non-resident parent; and

(b)　as a result of the subsequent decision there is one person with care in relation to that non-resident parent.

(7B)　Where paragraph (7A) applies, the amount payable to a person with care in respect of whom the amount payable is calculated by reference to a phasing amount shall be determined by applying paragraphs (1) to (5) as if references to–

(a)　the new amount and the transitional amount were to the apportioned part of the amount in question which had been payable immediately prior to the subsequent decision to the person with care in respect of whom the subsequent decision is made; and

(b)　the subsequent decision amount were to the full amount payable under the subsequent decision.]

(8)　In paragraph (7) [⁵and (7B)], "apportioned part" means the amount payable in respect of a person with care calculated as provided in Part I of Schedule 1 to the Act and Regulations made under that Part and, where applicable, Parts III and IV of these Regulations.

(9)　[³[⁴Where]] a subsequent decision is made in respect of a decision which is itself a subsequent decision, paragraphs (2) to (5) shall apply as if, except in paragraphs (2)(a) and (4)(a), references to the new amount were to the subsequent decision amount which applied immediately before the most recent subsequent decision.]

[³(10)　[⁴Subject to paragraph (11), where] a subsequent decision ("decision B") is made in respect of a decision which is itself a subsequent decision ("decision A") and–

(a)　decision B has the same effective date as decision A; or

(b)　decision B–

(i)   is a revision or alteration on appeal of decision A; and

(ii)   includes within it a determination that the effective date of decision A was incorrect,

paragraphs (2) to (5) shall apply [⁴as if decision A had not been made.]]

[⁴(11)   In the circumstances set out in paragraph (10), paragraph (9) shall not apply where the decision in place before decision A was made was the decision which took effect from the case conversion date.]

Amendments

1.   Child Support (Miscellaneous Amendments) Regulations 2002 (SI 2002 No.1204) reg 8(15) (April 30, 2002).

2.   Child Support (Miscellaneous Amendments) Regulations 2003 (SI 2003 No.328) reg 9(11) (February 21, 2003).

3.   Child Support (Miscellaneous Amendments) (No.2) Regulations 2003 (SI 2003 No.2779) reg 7(7) (November 5, 2003).

4.   Child Support (Miscellaneous Amendments) Regulations 2004 (SI 2004 No.2415) reg 8(9) (September 16, 2004).

5.   Child Support (Miscellaneous Amendments) Regulations 2005 (SI 2005 No.785) reg 7(3) (March 16, 2005).

Definitions

"case conversion date": see reg 2(1).
"fomer assessment amount": see reg 2(1).
"new amount": see reg 2(1).
"phasing amount": see reg 2(1).
"subsequent decision": see reg 2(1).
"subsequent decision amount": see reg 2(1).
"transitional amount": see reg 2(1).
"transitional period": see reg 2(1).

Linking provisions

28.–(1)   ['Subject to paragraph (2A), where], after the commencement date but before the conversion date, an application for a maintenance calculation is made [³...] and within the relevant period a maintenance assessment was in force in relation to the same qualifying child, non-resident parent and person with care–

(a)   the application shall be treated as an application for a maintenance assessment; and

(b)   any maintenance assessment made in response to the application shall be an assessment to which regulations 9 to 28 apply.

(2)   ['Subject to paragraph (2A), where], after the conversion date, an application for a maintenance calculation is made [³...], and within the relevant period a maintenance assessment ("the previous assessment") had been in force in relation to the same qualifying child, non-resident parent and person with care but had ceased to have effect–

(a)   the amount of child support maintenance payable by the non-resident parent from the effective date of the maintenance calculation made in response to the application shall be calculated in the same way that a conversion calculation would have been made had the previous assessment been in force on the date the calculation is made; and

(b)   the provisions of regulations 9 to 28 shall apply accordingly, including the application where appropriate of transitional amounts, phasing amounts and a transitional period, which for this purpose shall begin on the date which would have been the case conversion date in relation to the previous assessment.

[¹(2A)   Paragraph (1) or (2) shall not apply where, before any application for a maintenance calculation of a type referred to in paragraph (1) or (2) is made [³...], an application for a maintenance calculation is made or treated as made in relation to either the person with care or the non-resident parent (but not both of them) to whom the maintenance assessment referred to in paragraph (1) or (2) related.]

(3)   For the purposes of paragraphs (1) and (2) "the relevant period" means 13 weeks prior to the date that the application for the maintenance calculation is made [³...].

(4)   This paragraph applies where–

(a)   the non-resident parent is liable to pay child support maintenance of a transitional amount and there is, during the transitional period, a subsequent decision (in this regulation referred to as "the first subsequent decision") as a result of which the non-resident parent is liable to pay child support maintenance [¹at–

    (i)   the first or second prescribed amount;

    (ii)   what would be an amount referred to in head (i) but is less than that amount, or is nil, owing to the application of paragraph 8 of Part I of Schedule 1 to the Act; or

    (iii)   the nil rate; and]

(b)   a second subsequent decision is made with an effective date no later than 13 weeks after the effective date of the first subsequent decision the effect of which would be that the non-resident parent would be liable to pay child support maintenance at other than [¹a rate referred to in sub-paragraph (a)].

(5)   [¹Subject to paragraph (5A), where] paragraph (4) applies the amount of child support maintenance the non-resident parent is liable to pay from the effective date of the second subsequent decision shall be a transitional amount or, where applicable, the new amount, calculated by making a subsequent decision and, where appropriate, applying a phasing amount, as if the first subsequent decision had not occurred.

[¹(5A)   Paragraph (5) shall not apply where, before any second subsequent decision is made, an application for a maintenance calculation is made [³...] in relation to either the person with care or the non-resident parent (but not both of them) to whom the first subsequent decision referred to in paragraph (4) related.]

(6)   This paragraph applies where during the transitional period a [²conversion decision] ceases to have effect.

(7)   [¹Subject to paragraph (7A), where] paragraph (6) applies and no later than 13 weeks after the [²conversion decision] ceases to have effect [¹an application for a maintenance calculation] is made, [³...] in relation to the same person with care, non-resident parent and qualifying child, the amount of child support maintenance the non-resident parent is liable to pay from the effective date of the new maintenance calculation shall be a transitional amount or, where applicable, the new amount, calculated by making a subsequent decision in relation to the [²conversion decision] as if it had not ceased to have effect, and applying a phasing amount where appropriate.

[¹(7A)   Paragraph (7) shall not apply where, before an application for a maintenance calculation of a type referred to in that paragraph is made [³...], an application for a maintenance calculation is made [³...] in relation to either the person with care or the non-resident parent (but not both of them) to whom the [²conversion decision] referred to in that paragraph related.]

(8)   [¹Subject to paragraph (9), where]–

[¹(a)   a [²conversion decision] is in force, or pursuant to regulation 16(3) a maintenance calculation is in force, ("the calculation") and the new amount–

    (i)   is the first or second prescribed amount;

    (ii)   would be an amount referred to in head (i), but is less than that amount, or is nil, owing to the application of paragraph 8 of Part I of Schedule 1 to the Act; or

    (iii)   is the nil rate;]

(b)   after the case conversion date a subsequent decision is made;

(c)   but for the application of this regulation the subsequent decision amount would be a basic or reduced rate of child support maintenance; and

(d)   within 13 weeks prior to the effective date of the subsequent decision a maintenance assessment was in force in relation to the same non-resident parent, person with care and qualifying child, under which the amount payable by the non-resident parent ("the previous assessment") was more than the amount prescribed for the purposes of paragraph 7 of Schedule 1 to the former Act;

the subsequent decision amount shall be calculated by making a subsequent decision in relation to the previous assessment as if the assessment were in force, and applying a phasing amount where appropriate.

[¹(9)   Paragraph (8) shall not apply where, before a subsequent decision of a type referred to in paragraph (8)(b) is made, an application for a maintenance calculation is made [³...] in relation to the person with care or the non-resident parent (but not both of them) to whom the calculation relates.]

Amendments

1.   Child Support (Miscellaneous Amendments) Regulations 2002 (SI 2002 No.1204) reg 8(16) (April 30, 2002).
2.   Child Support (Miscellaneous Amendments) Regulations 2003 (SI 2003 No.328) reg 9(12) (February 21, 2003).
3.   Child Support (Consequential Provisions) Regulations 2008 (SI 2008 No.2543) reg 6 (October 27, 2008).

Definitions

"calculation date": see reg 2(1).
"case conversion date": see reg 2(1) and (2).
"conversion calculation": see reg 2(1) and (2).
"conversion date": see reg 2(1) and (2).
"conversion decision": see reg 2(1) and (2).
"first prescribed amount": see reg 2(1) and (2).
"maintenance assessment": see reg 2(1) and (2).
"phasing amount": see reg 2(1) and (2).
"second prescribed amount": see reg 2(1) and (2).
"subsequent decision": see reg 2(1) and (2).
"transitional amount": see reg 2(1) and (2).
"transitional period": see reg 2(1) and (2).

General Note

This provision is being used as a way of transferring cases from the formula assessment scheme to the maintenance calculation scheme. The device works by cancelling the formula assessment and making a new application for a maintenance calculation after the 13 weeks linking period has expired. Sometimes this is advantageous to the person with care; sometimes it is advantageous to the non-resident parent. It is possible for the other person to block this device by making an application for a child support maintenance assessment within the 13-week period. If this is done, the Secretary of State must deal with the application. If this is delayed, the remedy lies in seeking compensation for maladministration. See *R(CS) 1/06*, paras 18-19. In that case the parent with care applied for a maintenance calculation before the non-resident parent's application was dealt with. The commissioner held that the parent with care's application had to be given priority under para 3(2) of Sch 2 to the Maintenance Assessment Procedure Regulations (*ibid*, paras 11-14).

The commissioner did not consider whether the Secretary of State could have deferred the cancellation of the formula assessment under reg 32 Maintenance Assessment Procedure Regulations. However, this could hardly have been used to prevent entirely the exploitation of an opportunity that is provided by this regulation.

The failure to bring the reforms under the 2000 Act completely into force is not a violation of the Convention rights under the Human Rights Act 1998. The authorities are reviewed in the Northern Ireland decision in *An application for judicial review by Feargal Magennis* [2008] NIQB 97.

PART IV
COURT ORDER PHASING

Interpretation

29.–(1)   In this Part–

"the Act" means the Child Support Act 1991;

"calculation amount" means the amount of child support maintenance that would, but for the provisions of this Part, be payable under a maintenance calculation which is in force;

"excess" means the amount by which the calculation amount exceeds the old amount;

"maintenance calculation" has the meaning given in section 54 of the Act the effective date of which is on or after the date prescribed for the purposes of section 4(10)(a) of the Act;

"old amount" means, subject to paragraph (2) below, the aggregate weekly amount which was payable under the orders, agreements or arrangements mentioned in regulation 30;

"subsequent decision" means–

(a) any decision under section 16 or 17 of the Act to revise or supersede a maintenance calculation to which regulation 31(1) applies; or

(b) any such revision or supersession as decided on appeal,

whether as originally made or as revised under section 16 of the Act or decided on appeal;

"subsequent decision amount" means the amount of child support maintenance liability resulting from a subsequent decision;

"transitional amount" means an amount determined in accordance with regulation 31; and

"transitional period" means a period beginning on the effective date of the maintenance calculation and ending 78 weeks after that date or, if earlier, on the date on which regulation 31(3) applies.

(2) In determining the old amount the Secretary of State shall disregard any payments in kind and any payments made to a third party on behalf of or for the benefit of the qualifying child or the person with care.

Cases to which this Part applies

30. This Part applies to cases where–

(a) on 4th April 1993, and at all times thereafter until the date when a maintenance calculation is made under the Act there was in force, in respect of one or more of the qualifying children in respect of whom an application for a maintenance calculation is made [1...] under the Act and the non-resident parent concerned, one or more–

(i) maintenance orders;

(ii) orders under section 151 of the Army Act 1955 (deductions from pay for maintenance of wife or child) or section 151 of the Air Force Act 1955 (deductions from pay for maintenance of wife or child) or arrangements corresponding to such an order and made under Article 1 or 3 of the Naval and Marine Pay and Pensions (Deductions for Maintenance) Order 1959; or

(iii) maintenance agreements (being agreements which are made or evidenced in writing);

(b) either–

(i) the non-resident parent was on the effective date of the maintenance calculation and continues to be a member of a family, as defined in regulation 1 of the Child Support (Maintenance Calculations and Special Cases) Regulations 2000 which includes one or more children; or

(ii) the amount of child support maintenance payable under the maintenance calculation referred to in paragraph (a) is a basic or reduced rate under paragraph 7 of Part I of Schedule 1 to the Act (shared care-basic and reduced rate); and

(c) the calculation amount exceeds the old amount.

Amendment

1. Child Support (Consequential Provisions) Regulations 2008 (SI 2008 No.2543) reg 6 (October 27, 2008).

Definitions

"the Act": see reg 29(1).
"calculation amount": see reg 29(1).
"maintenance amount": see reg 29(1).
"old amount": see reg 29(1).

Amount payable during the transitional period

31.–(1) In a case to which this Part applies, the amount of child support maintenance payable under a maintenance calculation during the transitional period shall, instead of being the calculation amount, be the transitional amount.

(2) The transitional amount is–

(a) during the first 26 weeks of the transitional period, the old amount plus either 25 per cent of the excess or £20.00, whichever is the greater;

(b) during the next 26 weeks of the transitional period, the old amount plus either 50 per cent of the excess or £40.00, whichever is the greater; and

(c) during the last 26 weeks of the transitional period, the old amount plus either 75 per cent of the excess or £60.00, whichever is the greater.

(3) If in any case the application of the provisions of this Part would result in an amount of child support maintenance becoming payable which is greater than the calculation amount, then those provisions shall not apply or, as the case may be, shall cease to apply to that case and the amount of child support maintenance payable in that case shall be the calculation amount.

Definitions
"calculation amount": see reg 29(1).
"excess": see reg 29(1).
"conversion decision": see reg 2(1).
"maintenance calculation": see reg 29(1).
"transitional amount": see reg 29(1).
"transitional period": see reg 29(1).

Revision and supersession

32.–(1) Where the Secretary of State makes a subsequent decision in relation to a maintenance calculation to which regulation 31(1) applies, the amount of child support maintenance payable by the non-resident parent shall be–

(a) where the subsequent decision amount is more than the calculation amount, the transitional amount plus the difference between the calculation amount and the subsequent decision amount;

(b) where the subsequent decision amount is less than the calculation amount but more than the transitional amount, the transitional amount; or

(c) where the subsequent decision amount is less than the calculation amount and less than or equal to the transitional amount, the subsequent decision amount.

(2) Regulation 31(2) shall apply to cases where there has been a subsequent decision as if references to the transitional amount were to the amount resulting from the application of paragraph (1).

Definitions
"calculation amount": see reg 29(1).
"maintenance calculation": see reg 29(1).
"subsequent decision": see reg 29(1).
"subsequent decision": see reg 29(1).
"transitional amount": see reg 29(1).

PART V
SAVINGS

Saving in relation to revision of or appeal against a conversion or subsequent decision

33.–(1) This regulation applies where–

(a) a conversion decision has been made under regulation 3, or a subsequent decision has been made under regulation 4, in each case where regulation [¹15(2), (3B), (3D) or (3F)] applies; and

(b) in relation to the decision referred to in paragraph (a)–

    (i) a revised decision is made under regulation 3A(1)(e) of the Decisions and Appeals Regulations; or

    (ii) an appeal tribunal makes a decision that the conversion decision or subsequent decision was made in error,

on the ground that regulation [¹15(2), (3B), (3D) or (3F) as the case may be] did not apply.

(2)   The provisions of the former Act and Regulations made under that Act prior to any amendments or revocations made pursuant to or in consequence of the 2000 Act shall apply, until the effective date of a further conversion decision in relation to the maintenance assessment, for the purposes of that maintenance assessment as if the decision referred to in paragraph (1)(a) had not been made, subject to any revision, supersession or appeal having effect between the dates of the decisions in paragraph 1(a) and (b) which would have affected the maintenance assessment during that period but for the decision referred to paragraph 1(a).

Amendment

1.   Child Support (Miscellaneous Amendments) Regulations 2003 (SI 2003 No.328) reg 9(13) (February 21, 2003).

Definitions

"the 2000 Act": see reg 2(1).
"conversion decision": see reg 2(1).
"conversion decision": see reg 2(1).
"Decisions and Appeals Regulations": see reg 2(1).
"former Act": see reg 2(1).
"maintenance assessment": see reg 2(1).
"subsequent decision": see reg 2(1).

The Child Support (Maintenance Calculations and Special Cases) Regulations 2000
(SI 2001 No.155)

General Note on the Regulations

The Child Support (Maintenance Calculations and Special Cases) Regulations 2000 have been revoked for certain cases only by the Child Support (Meaning of Child and New Calculation Rules) (Consequential and Miscellaneous Amendment) Regulations 2012 (SI 2012 No.2785) reg 10 (this revocation comes into force in relation to a particular case on the day on which paragraph 2 of Schedule 4 to the Child Maintenance and Other Payments Act 2008 (see p243) comes into force in relation to that type of case – which is December 10, 2012, in relation to the types of cases falling within art 3 of SI 2012 No.3042 (see p767).

For other types of cases the '2003 rules', which include the Child Support (Maintenance Calculations and Special Cases) Regulations 2000, continue to apply. The Child Support (Maintenance Calculations and Special Cases) Regulations 2000 are therefore reproduced below.

PART I

General

Citation, commencement and interpretation

1.–(1)   These Regulations may be cited as the Child Support (Maintenance Calculations and Special Cases) Regulations 2000.

(2)   In these Regulations, unless the context otherwise requires–

"the Act" means the Child Support Act 1991;

[³"care home" has the meaning assigned to it by section 3 of the Care Standards Act 2000;

"care home service" has the meaning assigned to it by [⁹paragraph 2 of schedule 12 to the Public Services Reform (Scotland) Act 2010];]

[¹"child tax credit" means a child tax credit under section 8 of the Tax Credits Act 2002;]

[¹¹"contribution-based jobseeker's allowance" means an allowance under the Jobseekers Act as amended by the provisions of Part 1 of Schedule 14 to the Welfare Reform Act 2012 that remove references to an income-based allowance, and a contribution-based allowance under the Jobseekers Act as that Act has effect apart from those provisions;]

"Contributions and Benefits Act" means the Social Security Contributions and Benefits Act 1992;

"Contributions and Benefits (Northern Ireland) Act" means the Social Security Contributions and Benefits (Northern Ireland) Act 1992;

[¹¹"contributory employment and support allowance" means an allowance under Part 1 of the Welfare Reform Act as amended by the provisions of Schedule 3, and Part 1 of Schedule 14, to the Welfare Reform Act 2012 that remove references to an income-related allowance, and a contributory allowance under Part 1 of the Welfare Reform Act as that Part has effect apart from those provisions;]

[⁴"couple" means–
  (a)   a man and woman who are married to each other and are members of the same household;
  (b)   a man and woman who are not married to each other but are living together as husband and wife;
  (c)   two people of the same sex who are civil partners of each other and are members of the same household; or
  (d)   two people of the same sex who are not civil partners of each other but are living together as if they were civil partners,

and for the purposes of sub-paragraph (d), two people of the same sex are to be regarded as living together as if they were civil partners if, but only if, they would be regarded as living together as husband and wife were they instead two people of the opposite sex;]

"course of advanced education" means–
  (a)   a full-time course leading to a postgraduate degree or comparable qualification, a first degree or comparable qualification, a Diploma of Higher Education, a higher national diploma, a higher national diploma or higher national certificate of the Business and Technology Education Council or the Scottish Qualifications Authority or a teaching qualification; or
  (b)   any other full-time course which is a course of a standard above that of an ordinary national diploma, a national diploma or national certificate of the Business and Technology Education Council or the Scottish Qualifications Authority, the advanced level of the General Certificate of Education, a Scottish certificate of education (higher level), a Scottish certificate of sixth year studies or a Scottish National Qualification at Higher Level;

"day" includes any part of a day;

"day to day care" means–
  (a)   care of not less than 104 nights in total during the 12 month period ending with the relevant week; or
  (b)   where, in the opinion of the Secretary of State, a period other than 12 months is more representative of the current arrangements for the care of the child in question, care during that period of not less in total than the number of nights which bears the same ratio to 104 nights as that period bears to 12 months, and for the purpose of this definition–
       (i)   where a child is a boarder at a boarding school or is a patient in a hospital or other circumstances apply, such as where the child stays with a person who is not a parent of the child, and which the Secretary of State regards as temporary, the person who, but for those circumstances, would otherwise provide day to day care of the child shall be treated as providing day to day care during the periods in question; and

(ii)   "relevant week" shall have the meaning ascribed to it in the definition in this paragraph, except that in a case where notification is given under regulation 7C of the Decisions and Appeals Regulations to the relevant persons on different dates, "relevant week" means the period of 7 days immediately preceding the date of the latest notification;

"Decisions and Appeals Regulations" means the Social Security and Child Support (Decisions and Appeals) Regulations 1999;

[¹...]

"effective date" means the date on which a maintenance calculation takes effect for the purposes of the Act;

"employed earner" has the same meaning as in section 2(1)(a) of the Contributions and Benefits Act except that it shall include–

(a)   a person gainfully employed in Northern Ireland; [¹⁰...]

(b)   a person to whom section 44(2A) of the Act applies; [¹⁰and

a person gainfully employed outside the United Kingdom if the person's income from that employment is chargeable to tax under the Income Tax (Earnings and Pensions) Act 2003 or would be were it not for any double taxation arrangements under Part 2 of the Taxation (International and Other Provisions) Act 2010.]

"family" means–

(a)   a couple (including the members of a polygamous marriage) and any member of the same household for whom one or more of them is responsible and who is a child; or

(b)   a person who is not a member of a couple and a member of the same household for whom that person is responsible and who is a child;

"home" means–

(a)   the dwelling in which a person and any family of his normally live; or

(b)   if he or they normally live in more than one home, the principal home of that person and any family of his, and for the purpose of determining the principal home in which a person normally lives no regard shall be had to residence in a [³a care home or an independent hospital or the provision of a care home service or an independent health care service] during a period which does not exceed 52 weeks or, where it appears to the Secretary of State that the person will return to his principal home after that period has expired, such longer period as the Secretary of State considers reasonable to allow for the return of that person to that home;

"Income Support Regulations" means the Income Support (General) Regulations 1987;

[³[⁹"independent health care service" has the meaning assigned to it by section 10F(1)(a) and (b) of the National Health Service (Scotland) Act 1978;]

[⁸"independent hospital"–

(a)   in England, means a hospital as defined by section 275 of the National Health Service Act 2006 that is not a health service hospital as defined by that section; and

(b)   in Wales, has the meaning assigned to it by section 2 of the Care Standards Act 2000;]]

"the Jobseekers Act" means the Jobseekers Act 1995;

"Maintenance Calculation Procedure Regulations" means the Child Support (Maintenance Calculation Procedure) Regulations 2000;

"net weekly income" has the meaning given in the Schedule to these Regulations;

[³...]

"occupational pension scheme" means such a scheme within the meaning in section 1 of the Pension Schemes Act 1993 and which is approved for the purposes of Part XIV of the Income and Corporation Taxes Act 1988 [³or is a statutory scheme to which section 594 of that Act applies];

"partner" means–

(a)   in relation to a member of a couple, the other member of that couple;

(b)   in relation to a member of a polygamous marriage, any other member of that marriage with whom he lives;

"patient" means a person (other than a person who is serving a sentence of imprisonment or detention in a young offender institution within the meaning of the Criminal Justice Act 1982 or the Prisons (Scotland) Act 1989 who is regarded as receiving free in-patient treatment within the meaning of the Social Security (Hospital In-Patients) Regulations 1975;

"person" does not include a local authority;

"personal pension scheme" means such a scheme within the meaning in section 1 of the Pension Schemes Act 1993 and which is approved for the purposes of Part XIV of the Income and Corporation Taxes Act 1988;

"polygamous marriage" means any marriage during the subsistence of which a party to it is married to more than one person and in respect of which any ceremony of marriage took place under the law of a country which at the time of that ceremony permitted polygamy;

"prisoner" means a person who is detained in custody pending trial or sentence upon conviction or under a sentence imposed by a court other than a person whose detention is under the Mental Health Act 1983 or [⁵Part 5, 6 or 7 or section 136 of the Mental Health (Care and Treatment) (Scotland) 2003 Act or section 52D or 52M of the Criminal Procedure (Scotland) Act 1995];

"relevant week" means–

(a) in relation to an application for child support maintenance–

  (i) where the application is made by a non-resident parent, the period of 7 days immediately before the application is made; and

  (ii) in any other case, the period of 7 days immediately before the date of notification to the non-resident parent and for this purpose "the date of notification to the non-resident parent" means the date on which the non-resident parent is first given notice by the Secretary of State under the Maintenance Calculation Procedure Regulations that an application for a maintenance calculation has been made [⁷...] in relation to which the non-resident parent is named as the parent of the child to whom the application relates;

(b) where a decision ("the original decision") is to be–

  (i) revised under section 16 of the Act; or

  (ii) superseded by a decision under section 17 of the Act on the grounds that the original decision was made in ignorance of, or was based upon a mistake as to, some material fact or was erroneous in point of law, the period of 7 days which was the relevant week for the purposes of the original decision;

(c) where a decision ("the original decision") is to be superseded under section 17 of the Act–

  (i) on an application made for the purpose on the basis that a material change of circumstances has occurred since the original decision was made, the period of 7 days immediately preceding the date on which that application was made;

  (ii) subject to sub-paragraph (b), in a case where a relevant person is given notice under regulation 7C of the Decisions and Appeals Regulations, the period of 7 days immediately preceding the date of that notification, except that where, under paragraph 15 of Schedule 1 to the Act, the Secretary of State makes separate maintenance calculations in respect of different periods in a particular case, because he is aware of one or more changes of circumstances which occurred after the date which is applicable to that case, the relevant week for the purposes of each separate maintenance calculation made to take account of each such change of circumstances shall be the period of 7 days immediately before the date on which notification was given to the Secretary of State of the change of circumstances relevant to that separate maintenance calculation;

[³...]

"retirement annuity contract" means an annuity contract for the time being approved by the Board of Inland Revenue as having for its main object the provision of a life annuity in old age or the provision of an annuity for a partner or dependant and in respect of which relief from income tax may be given on any premium;

[¹⁰"self-employed earner" has the same meaning as in section 2(1)(b) of the Contributions and Benefits Act except that it includes a person gainfully employed otherwise than in employed earner's employment (whether or not he is also employed in such employment)–(a) in Northern Ireland; or

(b) outside the United Kingdom if the person's income from that gainful employment is chargeable to tax under the Income Tax (Trading and Other Income) Act 2005 or would be were it not for any double taxation arrangements made under Part 2 of the Taxation (International and Other Provisions) Act 2010.]

[²"state pension credit" means the social security benefit of that name payable under the State Pension Credit Act 2002]

"student" means a person, other than a person in receipt of a training allowance, who is aged less than 19 and attending a full-time course of advanced education or who is aged 19 or over and attending a full-time course of study at an educational establishment; and for the purposes of this definition–

(a) a person who has started on such a course shall be treated as attending it throughout any period of term or vacation within it, until the last day of the course or such earlier date as he abandons it or is dismissed from it;

(b) a person on a sandwich course (within the meaning of paragraph 1(1) of Schedule 5 to the Education (Mandatory Awards) (No. 2) Regulations 1993) shall be treated as attending a full-time course of advanced education or, as the case may be, of study;

[³"training allowance" means a payment under section 2 of the Employment and Training Act 1973 ("the 1973 Act"), or section 2 of the Enterprise and New Towns (Scotland) Act 1990 ("the 1990 Act"), which is paid–

(a) to a person for his maintenance; and

(b) in respect of a period during which that person–

(i)   is undergoing training pursuant to arrangements made under section 2 of the 1973 Act or section 2 of the 1990 Act; and

(ii) has no net weekly income of a type referred to in Part II or Part III of the Schedule;]

[³"war widow's pension" means any pension or allowance payable for a widow which is–

(a) granted in respect of a death due to service or war injury and payable by virtue of the Air Force (Constitution) Act 1917, the Personal Injuries (Emergency Provisions) Act 1939, the Pensions (Navy, Army, Air Force and Mercantile Marine) Act 1939, the Polish Resettlement Act 1947 or Part VII or section 151 of the Reserve Forces Act 1980;

(b) payable under so much of any Order in Council, Royal Warrant, order or scheme as relates to death due to service in the armed forces of the Crown, wartime service in the merchant navy or war injuries;

(c) payable in respect of death due to peacetime service in the armed forces of the Crown before 3rd September 1939, and payable at rates, and subject to conditions, similar to those of a pension within sub-paragraph (b); or

(d) payable under the law of a country other than the United Kingdom and of a character substantially similar to a pension within sub-paragraph (a), (b) or (c),

and "war widower's pension" [⁴and "surviving civil partner's war pension"] shall be construed accordingly;]

[⁶"the Welfare Reform Act" means the Welfare Reform Act 2007;]

"work-based training for young people or, in Scotland, Skillseekers training" means–

(a) arrangements made under section 2 of the Employment and Training Act 1973 or section 2 of the Enterprise and New Towns (Scotland) Act 1990; or

(b) arrangements made by the Secretary of State for persons enlisted in Her Majesty's forces for any special term of service specified in regulations made under section 2 of the Armed Forces Act 1966 (power of Defence Council to make regulations as to engagement of persons in regular forces), for purposes which include the training of persons who, at the beginning of their training, are under the age of 18;

[¹"working tax credit" means a working tax credit under section 10 of the Tax Credits Act 2002;]

"year" means a period of 52 weeks.

[¹²(3) For the purposes of paragraph 10C(2)(b) of Schedule 1 to the Act (which provides for other descriptions of relevant other children to be prescribed) "relevant other child" includes a child, other than a qualifying child, in respect of whom the non-resident parent or the non-resident parent's partner–

(a) would receive child benefit under Part IX of the Contributions and Benefits Act, but in respect of whom they do not do so, solely because the conditions set out in section 146 of that Act (persons outside Great Britain) are not met; or

(b) has made an election under section 13A(1) of the Social Security Administration Act 1992 (election not to receive child benefit) for payments of child benefit not to be made.]

(4) Subject to paragraph (5), these Regulations shall come into force in relation to a particular case on the day on which Part I of Schedule 1 to the 1991 Act as amended by the Child Support, Pensions and Social Security Act 2000 comes into force in relation to that type of case.

(5) Paragraphs (1) and (2) of regulation 4 and, for the purposes of those provisions, this regulation shall come into force on 31st January 2001.

Amendments

1. Child Support (Miscellaneous Amendments) Regulations 2003 (SI 2003 No.328) reg 8(2) (April 6, 2003).
2. State Pension Credit (Consequential, Transitional and Miscellaneous Provisions) Regulations 2002 (SI 2002 No.3019) reg 27(2) (October 6, 2003).
3. Child Support (Miscellaneous Amendments) (No.2) Regulations 2003 (SI 2003 No.2779) reg 6(2) (November 5, 2003).
4. Civil Partnership (Pensions, Social Security and Child Support) (Consequential, etc. Provisions) Order 2005 (SI 2005 No.2877) art 2(4) and Sch 4 para 7(2) (December 5, 2005).
5. Mental Health (Care and Treatment) (Scotland) Act 2003 (Consequential Provisions) Order 2005 (SI 2005 No.2078) arts 1(9) and (10) and 15 and Sch 2 para 21 (October 5, 2005); and Mental Health (Care and Treatment) (Scotland) Act 2003 (Modification of Subordinate Legislation) Order 2005 (SSI 2005 No.445) art 2 and Sch para 30 (October 5, 2005).
6. Employment and Support Allowance (Consequential Provisions) (No.2) Regulations 2008 (SI 2008 No.1554) reg 61(2) (October 27, 2008).
7. Child Support (Consequential Provisions) Regulations 2008 (SI 2008 No.2543) reg 7(2) (October 27, 2008).
8. Health and Social Care Act 2008 (Miscellaneous Consequential Amendments) Order 2010 (SI 2010 No.1881) reg 11 (October 1, 2010).
9. Public Services Reform (Scotland) Act 2010 (Consequential Modifications of Enactments) Order 2011 (SI 2011 No.2581) art 2 and Sch 2 para 30 (October 28, 2011).
10. Child Support (Miscellaneous Amendments) Regulations 2012 (SI 2012 No.712) reg 6(2) and (3) (April 30, 2012).
11. Universal Credit (Consequential, Supplementary, Incidental and Miscellaneous Provisions) Regulations 2013 (SI 2013 No.630) reg 43(2) (April 29, 2013).
12. Child Support (Miscellaneous Amendments) Regulations 2013 (SI 2013 No.1517) reg 6(2) (September 30, 2013).

General Note

"unless the context otherwise requires"

These words are not to be equated with "unless the circumstances otherwise require" (*CCS 499/1995*, para 15).

"day to day care"

This definition is concerned with care given and not with arrangements for such care which has not in fact occurred (*CSCS 6/1995*, paras 10-11; *CCS 3795/1998*).

The provision of care that is relevant to this definition is the direct provision of care and not indirect provision by, for example, the placement by a local authority of a child in a boarding school and the payment of the child's fees there (*CCS 1324/1997*, para 11).

A minor fluctuation in day to day care will not constitute a change of circumstances to justify a fresh calculation (*CCS 11588/1995*, para 15). The legislation contemplates that the matter should be looked at over a period of one year rather than some shorter period (*ibid*, para 15).

For the problems produced by the concentration in this definition on overnight care see the general note to s3(3) of the Act.

The tribunal's findings of fact in relation to day to day care must specify the number of nights spent by each qualifying child with the absent parent (*CSC 7/1994*, para 9). The care that is relevant is care which is provided during the night. It is not necessary that the person should provide 24-hour care (*CCS 499/1995*, para 11). In determining day to day care it is not permissible to disregard any period before the child support scheme came into force (*CCS 6/1994*, para 5). It is not an error of law to fail to consider whether an alternative period should be considered if there was no reason on the evidence to do so (*ibid*, para 6). However, the written or oral evidence before the tribunal will not necessarily be given with the legal definition of day to day care in mind. The tribunal must take an inquisitorial approach to the hearing and this involves ensuring that it probes the evidence in order to determine whether there is any basis for such a consideration, unless it is clear from the evidence given or the circumstances of the case that no such possibility exists. The chairman's record of evidence and proceedings or the statement of the tribunal's reasons should make it clear that this was done. See *CCS 1992/1997*, para 56.

When a child is a boarder a hypothetical decision has to be made as to where the child would have lived if not in school. It is proper to take a broad brush approach to this decision taking into account the pattern of contact when the child is not in school, although the practicalities which may influence that pattern (such as where each parent lives in relation to the school) must be considered (*R(CS) 8/98*, para 21). Which parent pays the school fees is irrelevant to the issue of day to day care (*ibid*, para 19). A local authority does not provide day to day merely by placing a child at a boarding school and paying the fees (*CCS 1324/1997*, para 11).

In *C v SSWP and B* [2003] 1 FLR 829, the Court of Appeal considered the relevance of residence orders to the issue of where a child would be if not at boarding school. The Court held that a residence order was relevant (but not determinative) on the assumption that the parties would be expected to comply with its terms. However, the fact that the father had been refused a shared residence order was not relevant. More important were the arrangements for contact made or approved by the court.

In making provision for boarders, the definition itself refers to "day to day care".

This does not mean that, in order to apply this part of the definition, it is necessary to apply the earlier part of the definition separately to the periods when the child is at boarding school. The second part of the definition applies "for the purposes of" the earlier part. The reference to "day to day care" in the latter part of the definition as means that in determining the number of nights that a child is under the care of a particular person, the child is considered to be under the care of the person who would have care of the child for that night if the child were not a boarder. See *CCS37/1997*, para 32.

"employed earner"

Section 2(1)(a) Social Security (Contributions and Benefits) Act 1992 provides that "employed earner' means a person who is gainfully employed in Great Britain either under a contract of service, or in an office (including elective office) with emoluments chargeable to income tax under Schedule E". Section 122(1) provides that a contract of service "means any contract of service or apprenticeship whether written or oral and whether express or implied", and that "employed' has a corresponding meaning" to "employment" which "includes any trade, business, profession, office or vocation".

In order for there to be a contract of service the contract must require the person to perform the obligations under the contract personally. If the obligations can be carried out by someone other than the contracting party, the contract is one of services. See *Express and Echo Publications Ltd v Tanton* [1999] ICR 693.

A person whose services are provided to a third party through an employment bureau may have an implied contract of employment with the third party (*Brook Street Bureau (UK) Ltd v Dacas, The Times,* March 19 2004).

A majority shareholder in a company may be employed by the company. For a discussion of some of the relevant factors when this possibility is in issue, see *CTC 4080/2002*, paras 12-14.

In deciding in a borderline case whether a particular relationship is one of employment or self-employment, the courts will take account of the label which the parties give to an arrangement. However, the parties cannot change the proper classification of an arrangement which clearly falls into one category by calling it the other (*McManus v Griffiths, The Times,* August 5 1997).

It is perhaps unlikely that a minister of religion would be involved in an assessment of child support maintenance. Should this arise, however, ministers, including curates, do not operate under a contract of service, but are office-holders (*Diocese of Southwark v Coker* [1998] ICR 140). Accordingly they fall within this definition.

A person is gainfully employed if the employment generates income, even if the expenses necessarily incurred exceed the income generated (*Vandyke v Minister of Pensions and National Insurance* [1954] 2 All ER 723) and regardless of whether or not that income has a contractual basis (*Benjamin v Minister of Pensions and National Insurance* [1960] 2 All ER 851). It may be that a person is gainfully employed if working with the hope, intention and desire of ultimate, but not immediate, gain (*ibid* at 855-856, *per* Salmon J).

It is possible for a person to have earnings both as an employed earner and as a self-employed earner (*CIS 14409/1996*, para 13). Where the question arises whether earnings from particular activities are discrete employed earner's earnings or merely part of the person's general pool of self-employed earnings, the issue is to be decided by asking whether or not there was a contract of service in respect of the activities which generated them (*ibid*, paras 25-32). The fact that Class 1 National Insurance contributions have been deducted from particular earnings is not decisive of this issue (*ibid*, para 22).

"home"

The test of which home is a person's principal home is an objective one in the sense that the person's own view is not decisive. The issue is not determined solely by reference to the number of days or nights on which the person is present at the home. As the issue is which home was the principal home as at the date the housing cost calculation is being made, some long-term considerations (such as the fact that a party's job requires occupancy of a particular home at the relevant time, but it is sensible to maintain another home for future use) may be excluded. See *R(CS) 2/96*, para 12.

If the non-resident parent moves to live together with the person with care while retaining another home to return to if the reconciliation is unsuccessful, the issue arises of which is the non-resident parent's principal home during the reconciliation. In considering the interpretation of this definition and its application to such a case, it is relevant to consider para 16(1)(d) of Sch 1 to the Act, which provides that the assessment does not cease to have effect until the parties have lived together for a continuous period of six months. This suggests that child support law should be interpreted and applied so as not to hamper attempts at reconciliation, and the removal from the assessment of housing costs on the "retained" home of the absent parent could prove a powerful disincentive. This result may be unavoidable (eg, where the non-resident parent does not retain another home), but where the facts permit it, it is suggested that short-term reconciliation should not affect a person's principal home.

"partner"

A person's partner is defined as the other member of a couple or another member of a polygamous marriage who is living with the person. A couple may be married or unmarried. Each is defined in reg 1(2). In the case of a married couple they must be of the opposite sex and be members of the same household. In the case of an unmarried couple they must be of the opposite sex and be living together as husband and wife. There is no reference to the need for an unmarried couple to be living in the same household. There may be exceptional cases in which a couple are not members of the same household, and there will be many cases in which a couple live together in the same household but not as husband and wife. Tribunals should, therefore, be alert to the possibility of an unusual case arising.

There is no single model of what constitutes a household or of what amounts to living together as husband and wife. There are nowadays a great variety of arrangements. Some allow couples a great deal of individual freedom within a relationship, while others which exist between unattached individuals are very similar to those which are often associated with couples. The proper approach to cases such as this is discussed in the general note to s3 of the Act.

Household

A household is an abstract concept (*Santos v Santos* [1972] 2 All ER 246 at 255, *per* Sachs LJ). It can survive changes of membership, as *R v Birmingham Juvenile Court ex pN* [1984] 2 All ER 688 shows. The legal test concentrates on the arrangements of the persons concerned rather than the accommodation (*R v Birmingham Juvenile Court ex p N* above at 691, *per* Arnold P). It is not possible to be a member of more than one household at a time (*R(SB) 8/85*).

Whether or not a couple are living in the same household is determined by an analysis of the objective facts of their living arrangements. Findings of fact are needed on the following.

(i)   The nature of the accommodation.

(ii)   The living arrangements within it, including the distribution of domestic duties and the way they spend their leisure time.

(iii)   The financial arrangements between the parties.

(iv)   It will also frequently be useful to investigate how and why the couple came to make the living arrangements which they did. The fact that an arrangement was entered into as a result of a shortage of funds, or in an emergency or in order to secure accommodation, for example, may point towards the couple operating separate households within shared accommodation. On the other hand shift work may explain arrangements which at first sight suggest that the two people are living separate lives.

(v)   The relationship between the couple will also be relevant. If a couple have a close relationship but keep their financial arrangements separate, their relationship may point nonetheless to there being a single household.

Particular care is needed in applying the criteria to arrangements which are just beginning or which are coming to an end (see the comments of Woolf J, in *Crake and Butterworth v Supplementary Benefit Commission* [1982] 1 All ER 498 at 502). A couple may be unwilling to mingle their lives inextricably at first. Alternatively, a developing relationship against a constant background of living arrangements may indicate that a single household has gradually been formed. At the other end of a relationship, it may prove difficult to separate lives which have been shared for a number of years, perhaps decades. In such cases small, perhaps unilateral, alterations in a couple's arrangements will indicate that separate households have been established. Although a household is an abstract concept and the legal test is not primarily concerned with the accommodation, there are limits to the possibilities of establishing separate households in cramped accommodation and in *Adeoso v Adeoso* [1981] 1 All ER 107 at 110 Ormrod LJ, said that it was not possible to form separate households in a two room flat.

Absences from the shared accommodation do not necessarily indicate that a couple are no longer living together (*Re M (An Infant)* [1964] 2 All ER 1017 at 1024, per Buckley J, and *Santos* above at 251-253, *per* Sachs

LJ, and *R(SB) 30/83*), nor do they indicate that there is no longer a single household. It is necessary to consider the frequency and duration of the separations as well as the reasons for them.

More than mere presence in the same place is necessary to constitute a household. There must be some collectivity, some communality and some organisation. There must also be a domestic establishment. Therefore, persons living in some form of institution such as a nursing home cannot be in the same household (*CIS 671/1992*, para 4 and *CIS 81/1993*, para 5).

A person may be a member of a household while on bail (*R(IS) 17/93*).

Living as husband and wife

Financial arrangements within marriage are very varied, and equal if not greater variation is to be expected among unmarried couples. It has already been said, but bears emphasising, that tribunals must be alert both to the range of possible arrangements and to the need to investigate the reason for the arrangements. Arrangements which have an arms' length or even commercial appearance may have an explanation. Neuberger J held that, in view of this diversity, the question to ask is whether, in the opinion of a reasonable person with normal perceptions, it could be said that the two people were living together as husband and wife, but in answering that question it was impossible to ignore the multifarious nature of marital relationships (*Re Watson (Deceased)* [1999] 1 FLR 878).

The fact that a couple are living in the same household is an important, perhaps essential, finding before they can be held to be living as husband and wife. However, of itself this is not sufficient to justify such a conclusion. It is necessary to investigate how and why they share a common household (*Crake and Butterworth v Supplementary Benefit Commission* [1982] 1 All ER 498 at 502, *per* Woolf J). A number of matters have come to be considered as relevant factors in determining whether a couple are living as husband and wife, and the tribunal should investigate each.

The essence of the decision for the tribunal is to identify the parties' general relationship and the matters considered below are only relevant in so far as they throw light on that general relationship (*CIS 87/1993*, para 11). This involves taking into account the less tangible emotional aspects as well as the more concrete observable facts of the parties' relationship (*CIS 17028/1996*, para 26). The mixture of factors that together give character to a relationship were listed in *Fitzpatrick v Sterling Housing Association* [1998] Ch 304 at 318 and 338 and [2001] 1 AC 27 at 38: mutual love, faithfulness, public acknowledgement, sexual relations, shared surname, children, endurance, stability, interdependence and devotion. However, not all of these features need be present and it must be remembered that a couple may be living as husband and wife even though their relationship is unsatisfactory and unhappy. The stage of development of the relationship must be relevant when assessing the significance of a particular feature (*CIS 17028/1996*, para 27).

Stability during the course of a relationship is an important indicator. Instability while not decisive against the couple living as husband and wife, would be an indicator in this direction. However, stability need not and does not by itself show that a couple are living in this relationship.

How the couple are known to and seen by others is a factor to be considered. If the impression is one that has been created or encouraged by the parties (eg, by using the same surname), it will be a pointer towards the couple living as husband and wife. However, although how others view the couple is a relevant consideration (*Adeoso v Adeoso* at 109, *per* Ormrod LJ), the tribunal will need to be cautious for two reasons. First, this is less likely to be important when a relationship is first formed; according to Woolf J, in *Crake* above at 502, *Adeoso* is to be interpreted as a case concerned with the termination rather than the inception of a relationship. Second, others may not have been motivated in forming their views by the full range of factors which a tribunal is required to take into account. The fact that a couple have retained separate identities is not so easy to interpret, since many married couples strive to retain their separate identity and do not use the same surname.

The fact that a couple have children whom they are bringing up together is a strong indication of their commitment to each other, the stability of their relationship and of how they are seen by others.

The sexual arrangements between the parties need to be investigated sensitively by the tribunal and the significance of the answers needs to be assessed carefully. It is possible, although unusual, for a married couple not to have a sexual relationship (*CIS 87/1993*, para 12, also reported as *Re J (Income Support:Cohabitation)* [1995] 1 FLR 660), so its absence may be a strong factor against a couple living together as husband and wife, although the age of the couple may be a factor (*Re Watson*) as well as the possibility of importance. However, the presence of a sexual relationship is by no means a decisive factor in favour of a couple living as husband and wife. It is an error of law not to investigate this aspect of a relationship, but it is an error of judgment to do so insensitively.

As with the decision whether there is a separate household so here it may be particularly difficult to analyse a relationship which is just beginning or just coming to an end. Obviously stability cannot be established at once and the parties' intentions or declared intentions will be relevant. Similarly the fact that a relationship has been stable in the past does not indicate that it has remained so.

There comes a point when the physical separation is such that the only possible conclusion can be that they are not living in the same household – eg, where they are in different countries (*CIS 508/1992*, para 5).

According to the commissioner in *CIS 317/1994*, para 11, it is not appropriate to speak in terms of a burden of proof when deciding whether or not parties are living together as husband and wife, since either sufficient information will be available to make a decision one way or the other or the failure to supply such information may permit adverse inferences being drawn. However, the commissioner does not explain how a decision is to be made if the evidence is evenly balanced on the issue.

Living together as civil partners

The definition of "couple" provides that "two people of the same sex are to be regarded as living together as if they were civil partners if, but only if, they would be regarded as living together as husband and wife were they instead two people of the opposite sex". This makes the same factors relevant regardless of the sex of the couples. It also appears to require that they be assessed in the same way. This may produce inappropriate results. Assume, as a hypothetical example, that couples of the same sex do not attach the same significance to a sexual relationship as a couple of the opposite sex. If the significance of the sexual relationship has to be taken to be that for any couple whatever their sex, the significance for the couple of the same sex may be misleading. However, it may be that the test is sufficiently flexible and based on the assessment of factors in an individual case that this will not have an impact on the actual outcome of a particular case.

"personal pension scheme"

Section 84(1) of the Social Security Act 1986 defines personal pension scheme as meaning "any scheme or arrangement which is comprised in one or more instruments or agreements and which has, or is capable of having, effect so as to provide benefits, in the form of pensions or otherwise, payable on death or retirement to or in respect of employed earners who have made arrangements with the trustees or managers of the scheme for them to become members of the scheme".

"polygamous marriage"

Once a person has contracted a valid polygamous marriage it is not invalidated by a change of country of residence, even if accompanied by the acquisition of a new domicile (*R(G) 1/93*).

"prisoner"

A person may be in custody pending trial even if no trial takes place and the person is released (*R(IS) 1/94*, para 15). A person who has been released on licence from prison is not in custody and not a prisoner for the purpose of this definition *R(IS) 20/95*, para 6).

"relevant week"

The relevant week is defined on the assumption that the officer will be requesting the information as soon as appropriate and making a decision reasonably quickly on its receipt. Unfortunately, there may be delays both in requesting the information and then in making the decision in the light of it. The longer the delays the more appropriate it is likely to be to use the power in the relevant provisions to take a different period and not to be tied to the relevant week. This power is even more likely to be useful on a s18 review or on appeal when the facts can be viewed with the benefit of hindsight not given to child support officers making initial decisions.

In *CSC 5/1995* (para 7), the Chief Commissioner for Northern Ireland held that the lack of any provision for fixing the relevant week with respect of earnings in relation to a change of circumstance under s18(10) of the Act prevented such an assessment being carried out.

"self-employed earner"

Section 2(1)(b) Social Security (Contributions and Benefits) Act 1992 provides that this "means a person who is gainfully employed in Great Britain otherwise than in employed earner's employment (whether or not he is also employed in such employment)". Section 122(1) provides that "'employment' includes any trade, business, profession, office or vocation and 'employed' has a corresponding meaning".

Whether or not an activity amounts to a "business" depends on the ordinary meaning of that word. Mere ownership of a tenanted property, the collection of rent and the related duties of a landlord do not constitute a business (*R(FC) 2/92*). However, there comes a point at which the administration or activity involved in letting out even a single property can become a business (*CCS 2128/2001*, para 8). Whether it does depends on all the circumstances of the case, including the number of people involved, the number of properties owned and the number of units into which the property is divided and let (*R(CS) 2/06*, para 49).

The test of whether a person is a self-employed earner is that provided by the Social Security Contributions and Benefits Act 1992, not the test used for tax purposes: *MG v CMEC (CSM)* [2010] UKUT 83 (AAC); AACR 37, para 22.

See further in the discussion of the definition of "employed earner" above.

"student"

A student is first of all someone who is attending a course. A course comprises a unified sequence of study, tuition and/or practical training (whether or not on a modular basis) leading on completion to one or more qualifications (*R(IS) 1/96*, para 17). It is necessary to distinguish between cases where there is practical training intermingled with tuition in a single course and those where there are a series of separate courses leading to separate qualifications after each is completed.

The course must be full-time. It is the course rather than the student's attendance which must be full-time. This is a question of fact to be determined in the light of all the circumstances of the case (*CIS 152/1994*, para 7). In the past an important factor has been the classification of the course by the provider, although this description could be rebutted by appropriate weighty evidence (*ibid*, para 7). However, reference to this criterion will increasingly be of less value as institutions tailor their courses to take account of the needs, qualifications and experience of individual' students, especially through the use of modular courses (*ibid*, para 11). Among the factors that may be helpful in deciding the appropriate classification of a course as pursued by a particular student are the number of modules being studied, the number of hours of study, the arrangements between the college and the student, the length of time it will take the student to obtain a qualification, the fees, the contents of the course prospectus (*ibid*, para 15), the nature and amount of any grant or other financial support which the student receives, and the nature and time devoted to any work or other activities undertaken at the same time as the studies.

There is no particular number of hours that amount to full-time and the 12-hour rule that is used for the purpose of s55 of the Act does not apply: *DY v CMEC* [2010] UKUT 19 (AAC); AACR 32, paras 28-29.

The definition of sandwich course referred to in head (b) is now out of date: *DY v CMEC*, para 45.

A person who takes time out from a course (eg, by intercalating a year), is neither in term nor vacation when doing so and is, therefore, not a student for that period (*Chief Adjudication Officer and the Secretary of State for Social Security v Clarke and Paul*, reported as *R(IS) 25/95*). A course has not been abandoned unless and until it is permanently abandoned (*ibid*). Also a student who embarks on a full-time course of study but subsequently transfers to a part-time course is no longer attending a full-time course (*Chief Adjudication Officer v Webber*, reported as *R(IS) 15/98*).

A person may remain a student despite the fact that the end date of that course is unknown because of the requirement that the student repeats part of the course or resits some exams (*CIS 15594/1996*, paras 23-25).

"training allowance"

Payments which originated from the European Social Fund and were administered in this country by the Secretary of State for Employment were held to be a training allowance in *CIS 858/1994*.

PART II
CALCULATION OF CHILD SUPPORT MAINTENANCE

Calculation of amounts

2.–(1)   Where any amount is to be considered in connection with any calculation made under these Regulations or under Schedule 1 to the Act, it shall be calculated as a weekly amount and, except where the context otherwise requires, any reference to such an amount shall be construed accordingly.

(2)   Subject to paragraph (3), where any calculation made under these Regulations or under Schedule 1 to the Act results in a fraction of a penny that fraction shall be treated as a penny if it is either one half or exceeds one half, otherwise it shall be disregarded.

(3)   Where the calculation of the basic rate of child support maintenance or the reduced rate of child support maintenance results in a fraction of a pound that fraction shall be treated as a pound if it is either one half or exceeds one half, otherwise it shall be disregarded.

(4)   In taking account of any amounts or information required for the purposes of making a maintenance calculation, the Secretary of State shall apply the dates or periods specified in these Regulations as applicable to those amounts or information, provided that if he becomes aware of a material change of circumstances occurring after such date or period, but before the effective date, he shall take that change of circumstances into account.

(5)   Information required for the purposes of making a maintenance calculation in relation to the following shall be the information applicable at the effective date–

(a)   the number of qualifying children;

(b)   the number of relevant other children;

(c)   whether the non-resident parent receives a benefit, pension or allowance prescribed for the purposes of paragraph 4(1)(b) of Schedule 1 to the Act;

(d)   whether the non-resident parent or his partner receives a benefit prescribed for the purposes of paragraph 4(1)(c) of Schedule 1 to the Act; and

(e)   whether paragraph 5(a) of Schedule 1 to the Act applies to the non-resident parent.

Definitions

"the Act": see reg 1(2).
"effective date": see reg 1(2).
"partner": see reg 1(2).

General Note

This regulation deals with amounts and with the dates as at which calculations have to be made.

Paragraph (1)

This paragraph provides that all amounts are to be calculated as weekly amounts.

Paragraphs (2)-(3)

These paragraphs provide for the rounding of pennies and pounds. Paragraph (2) is subject to reg 6.

Paragraphs (4)-(5)

These paragraphs deal with the dates as at which amounts or information have to be taken into account.

The basic rule is that the amounts or information have to be taken into account as at the dates or periods specified in these Regulations. Paragraph (5) supplements that by specifying that the specified heads of information are those applicable at the effective date.

The basic rule is subject to the qualification in para (4). The basic rule is overridden if the Secretary of State (not the particular decision maker making a calculation) becomes aware that a material change of circumstances has occurred before the effective date. The application of this paragraph is obligatory. See further the general note to Sch 1 para 15 to the Act on p148.

Reduced Rate

3.   The reduced rate is an amount calculated as follows–

$$F + (A \times T)$$

where–

F is the flat rate liability applicable to the non-resident parent under paragraph 4 of Schedule 1 to the Act;

A is the amount of the non-resident parent's net weekly income between £100 and £200; and

T is the percentage determined in accordance with the following Table–

	1 qualifying child of the non-resident parent				2 qualifying children of the non-resident parent				3 or more qualifying children of the non-resident parent			
Number of relevant other children of the non-resident parent	0	1	2	3 or more	0	1	2	3 or more	0	1	2	3 or more
T (%)	25	20.5	19	17.5	35	29	27	25	45	37.5	35	32.5

Definitions

"the Act": see reg 1(2).

"net weekly income": see reg 1(2).

General Note

This regulation prescribes the reduced rate that applies under Sch 1 para 3 to the Act.

Flat rate

4.–(1)   The following benefits, pensions and allowances are prescribed for the purposes of paragraph 4(1)(b) of Schedule 1 to the Act–

(a)   under the Contributions and Benefits Act–

(i)   bereavement allowance under section 39B;

(ii)   category A retirement pension under section 44;

(iii)   category B retirement pension under section 48C;

(iv)   category C and category D retirement pensions under section 78;

(v)   incapacity benefit under section 30A;

(vi)   [¹carer's allowance] under section 70;

(vii)   maternity allowance under section 35;

(viii)   severe disablement allowance under section 68;

(ix)   industrial injuries benefit under section 94;

(x)   widowed mother's allowance under section 37;

(xi)   widowed parent's allowance under section 39A; and

(xii)   widow's pension under section 38;

(b)   contribution-based jobseeker's allowance under section 1 of the Jobseekers Act;

(c)   a social security benefit paid by a country other than the United Kingdom;

(d)   a training allowance (other than work-based training for young people or, in Scotland, Skillseekers training); [⁴...]

(e)   a war disablement pension [³...] within the meaning of section 150(2) of the Contributions and Benefits Act or a pension which is analogous to such a pension paid by the government of a country outside Great Britain; [³[⁴...]

[⁵(f)   a war widow's pension, war widower's pension or surviving civil partner's war pension;]][⁴; [⁶...]

(g)   a payment under a scheme mentioned in section 1(2) of the Armed Forces (Pensions and Compensation) Act 2004 (compensation schemes for armed and reserve forces);][⁶and

(h)   contributory employment and support allowance under section 2 of the Welfare Reform Act.]

(2)   The benefits prescribed for the purposes of paragraph 4(1)(c) of Schedule 1 to the Act are–

(a)   income support under section 124 of the Contributions and Benefits Act; and

(b)   income-based jobseeker's allowance under section 1 of the Jobseekers Act; [²and

(c)   state pension credit] [⁶[⁷...]

(d)   income-related employment and support allowance under section 4 of the Welfare Reform Act][⁷; and

(e)   universal credit under Part 1 of the Welfare Reform Act 2012, where the award of universal credit is calculated on the basis that the non-resident parent does not have any earned income.

(3)   Where the non-resident parent is liable to a pay a flat rate by virtue of paragraph 4(2) of Schedule 1 to the Act–

(a)   if he has one partner, then the amount payable by the non-resident parent shall be half the flat rate; and

(b)   if he has more than one partner, then the amount payable by the non-resident parent shall be the result of apportioning the flat rate equally among him and his partners.

[⁷(4) For the purposes of paragraph (2)(e) and regulation 5(d), "earned income" has the meaning given in regulation 52 of the Universal Credit Regulations 2013 (earned income).]

Amendments

1.   Social Security Amendment (Carer's Allowance) Regulations 2002 (SI 2002 No.2497) reg 3 (April 1, 2003).

2.   State Pension Credit (Consequential, Transitional and Miscellaneous Provisions) Regulations 2002 (SI 2002 No.3019) reg 27(3) (October 6, 2003).

3.   Child Support (Miscellaneous Amendments) (No.2) Regulations 2003 (SI 2003 No.2779) reg 6(3) (November 5, 2003).

4.   Child Support (Miscellaneous Amendments) Regulations 2005 (SI 2005 No.785) reg 6(2) (March 16, 2005).

5.   Civil Partnership (Pensions, Social Security and Child Support) (Consequential, etc Provisions) Order 2005 (SI 2005 No.2877) art 2(4) and Sch 4 para 7(3) (December 5, 2005).

6.   Employment and Support Allowance (Consequential Provisions) (No.2) Regulations 2008 (SI 2008 No.1554) reg 61(3) (October 27, 2008).

7.   Universal Credit (Consequential, Supplementary, Incidental and Miscellaneous Provisions) Regulations 2013 (SI 2013 No.630) reg 43(3) (April 29, 2013).

Definitions

"the Act": see reg 1(2).
"Contributions and Benefits Act": see reg 1(2).
"the Jobseekers Act": see reg 1(2).
"state pension credit": see reg 1(2)
"partner": see reg 1(2).
"state pension credit": see reg 1(2).
"training allowance": see reg 1(2).
"war widow's pension": see reg 1(2)

"war widower's pension": see reg 1(2)
"work-based training for young people or, in Scotland, Skillseekers training": see reg 1(2).

General Note
Paragraph (1)
This paragraph prescribes the benefits, pensions and allowances under Sch 1 para 4(1)(b) to the Act.
Paragraph (2)
This paragraph prescribes the benefits under Sch 1 para 4(1)(c) to the Act.
Paragraph (3)
This paragraph prescribes the amount of the flat rate payable under Sch 1 para 4(2) to the Act.

Nil rate

5.   The rate payable is nil where the non-resident parent is–

(a)   a student;

(b)   a child within the meaning given in section 55(1) of the Act;

(c)   a prisoner;

(d)   a person who is 16 or 17 years old and–

    (i)   in receipt of income support [⁶, income-based jobseeker's allowance or income-related employment and support allowance]; [⁸...]

    (ii)   a member of a couple whose partner is in receipt of income support [⁶, income-based jobseeker's allowance or income-related employment and support allowance] [⁸;

    (iii)   in receipt of universal credit under Part 1 of the Welfare Reform Act 2012, where the award of universal credit is calculated on the basis that they do not have any earned income; or

    (iv)   in a case not covered by paragraph (iii), a member of a couple where their partner is in receipt of universal credit under Part 1 of the Welfare Reform Act 2012 and the award of universal credit is calculated on the basis that the non-resident parent does not have any earned income];

(e)   a person receiving an allowance in respect of work-based training for young people, or in Scotland, Skillseekers training;

(f)   a person [³who is resident in a care home or an independent hospital or is being provided with a care home service or an independent health care service] who–

    (i)   is in receipt of a pension, benefit or allowance specified in regulation 4(1) or (2); or

    (ii)   has the whole or part of the cost of his accommodation met by a local authority;

(g)   [⁷...]

[¹(gg) [⁷ ...]

(h)   [⁷ ...]

(i)   [⁴...]

Amendments
1.   State Pension Credit (Consequential, Transitional and Miscellaneous Provisions) Regulations 2002 (SI 2002 No.3019) reg 27(4) (October 6, 2003).
2.   Social Security (Hospital In-Patients and Miscellaneous Amendments) Regulations 2003 (SI 2003 No.1195) reg 7 (May 21, 2003).
3.   Child Support (Miscellaneous Amendments) (No.2) Regulations 2003 (SI 2003 No.2779) reg 6(4) (November 5, 2003).
4.   Child Support (Miscellaneous Amendments) Regulations 2004 (SI 2004 No.2415) reg 7(2) (September 16, 2004).
5.   Child Support (Miscellaneous Amendments) Regulations 2005 (SI 2005 No.785) reg 6(3) (March 16, 2005).
6.   Employment and Support Allowance (Consequential Provisions) (No.2) Regulations 2008 (SI 2008 No.1554) reg 61(4) (October 27, 2008).
7.   Child Support (Miscellaneous Amendments) Regulations 2009 (SI 2009 No.396) reg 5 (April 6, 2009).
8.   Universal Credit (Consequential, Supplementary, Incidental and Miscellaneous Provisions) Regulations 2013 (SI 2013 No.630) reg 43(4) (April 29, 2013).

Definitions
"the Act": see reg 1(2).
"care home": see reg 1(2).
"care home service": see reg 1(2).
"couple": see reg 1(2).
"Income Support Regulations": see reg 1(2).
"independent health care service": see reg 1(2).
"independent hospital": see reg 1(2).
"net weekly income": see reg 1(2).
"partner": see reg 1(2).
"patient": see reg 1(2).
"prisoner": see reg 1(2).
"state pension credit": see reg 1(2).
"student": see reg 1(2).
"work-based training for young people or, in Scotland, Skillseekers training": see reg 1(2).

General Note
This prescribes the descriptions of non-resident parent under Sch1 para 5(a) to the Act.

Apportionment

6. If, in making the apportionment required by regulation 4(3) or paragraph 6 of Part I of Schedule 1 to the Act, the effect of the application of regulation 2(2) (rounding) would be such that the aggregate amount of child support maintenance payable by a non-resident parent would be different from the aggregate amount payable before any apportionment, the Secretary of State shall adjust that apportionment so as to eliminate that difference; and that adjustment shall be varied from time to time so as to secure that, taking one week with another and so far as is practicable, each person with care receives the amount which she would have received if no adjustment had been made under this paragraph.

Definitions
"the Act": see reg 1(2).
"person": see reg 1(2).

General Note
The same provision is made for apportionment of the default rate by reg 7(4) of the Maintenance Calculation Procedure Regulations.

Shared care

7.–(1) For the purposes of paragraphs 7 and 8 of Part I of Schedule 1 to the Act a night will count for the purposes of shared care where the non-resident parent–

(a) has the care of a qualifying child overnight; and
(b) the qualifying child stays at the same address as the non-resident parent.

(2) For the purposes of paragraphs 7 and 8 of Part I of Schedule 1 to the Act, a non-resident parent has the care of a qualifying child when he is looking after the child.

(3) Subject to paragraph (4), in determining the number of nights for the purposes of shared care, the Secretary of State shall consider the 12 month period ending with the relevant week and for this purpose "relevant week" has the same meaning as in the definition of day to day care in regulation 1 of these Regulations.

(4) The circumstances in which the Secretary of State may have regard to a number of nights over less than a 12 month period are where there has been no pattern for the frequency with which the non-resident parent looks after the qualifying child for the 12 months preceding the relevant week, or the Secretary of State is aware that a change in that frequency is intended, and in that case he shall have regard to such lesser period as may seem to him to be appropriate, and the Table in paragraph 7(4) and the period in paragraph 8(2) of Schedule 1 to the Act shall have effect subject to the adjustment described in paragraph (5).

(5) Where paragraph (4) applies, the Secretary of State shall adjust the number of nights in that lesser period by applying to that number the ratio which the period of 12 months bears to that lesser period.

(6)   Where a child is a boarder at a boarding school, or is a patient in a hospital, the person who, but for those circumstances, would otherwise have care of the child overnight shall be treated as providing that care during the periods in question.

Definitions

"the Act": see reg 1(2).
"day to day care": see reg 1(2).
"patient": see reg 1(2).
"person": see reg 1(2).
"relevant week": see reg 1(2).

General Note

The commissioner's analysis of the meaning of "care" under the previous legislation (*R(CS) 11/02*) will not be necessary in the context of the different wording of this legislation. Paragraphs (1)(a) and (2) make it clear that what matters is who looks after a child overnight. A non-resident parent who stays at the parent with care's home in order to take care of their children is looking after them for the purposes of shared care (*R(CS) 7/08*).

Paragraph (1)

This paragraph defines care for the purposes of shared care under Sch 1 paras 7 and 8 to the Act. Only actual overnight care is relevant. It does not matter whether it is authorised or agreed. If a child stays overnight with a parent, it does not matter whether that stay was authorised by a court order or agreed to by the parent with care. Likewise, overnight care that is authorised or agreed but not actually provided is disregarded. The reason is irrelevant. It may be due to the refusal of the non-resident parent, the child, or the parent with care or to circumstances beyond the control of any of them. All that matters is that the care was not provided. The contact arrangements ordered by a court or agreed to by the parents (and perhaps the child) are not decisive on the factual issue of overnight care that the non-resident parent actually provides. They are only relevant as evidence of care that was actually given. See *CCS 2885/2005,* para 9.

Only overnight care is relevant. Even care for the whole of a day does not count, unless it is accompanied by an overnight stay. Nor is the cost of care relevant. The fact that the costs of caring for a child are borne disproportionately by one parent or the other as a result of the care arrangements is not taken into account. See *CCS 2885/2005*, para 8.

In *CCS 1273/2010,* para 15, the judge identified but did not need to answer "the question whether the parent who returns (or has to leave) in the early hours of the morning has care of children overnight".

Paragraph (2)

This defines those nights that count for the purposes of shared care under Sch 1 paras 7 and 8 to the Act.

Paragraph (3)

This paragraph, together with paras (4)-(6), provides for the calculation of the number of nights for which a non-resident parent has shared care under Sch 1 paras 7 and 8 to the Act.

Schedule 1 paras 7(3) and 8(2) provide that the starting point for the calculation must be a prescribed 12-month period. This paragraph is made under the authority of those paragraphs. It prescribes the 12-month period as that ending with the relevant week that applies for the purposes of day to day care.

The Secretary of State is only required to 'consider' this period. That *may* allow some flexibility in the calculation. One approach would be purely arithmetical, adding the number of nights in the period and converting them to a weekly number. A more flexible approach would allow unrepresentative parts of that period to be ignored – eg, if one parent was in hospital and the other had the care of the child for more nights than would otherwise have been the case. However, it is suggested that the flexible approach is out of line with the detailed wording of Sch 1 para 7(3) and 8(2) to the Act, as well as para (5). Those provisions envisage a purely arithmetical approach.

Paragraph (4)

Schedule 1 para 9(c) to the Act provides for the period in paras 7(3) and 8(2) to be other than 12 months. This paragraph is made under that authority (*CCS 2885/2005,* para 20). It allows a shorter period, but not a longer one, than 12 months to be used. The enabling provision only authorises the length of the period to be altered; it does not authorise any change to the use of the end date set by para (3) above (*CCS 2885/2005,* para 20).

This paragraph does not provide a general discretion to use a period of less than 12 months whenever that would be appropriate (*CCS 2885/2005,* para 12). It only authorises it in two cases, although they cover most cases in which a lesser period is appropriate. The first case is if there was no pattern of frequency of overnight care over that period. This applies if overnight care has been random or there has been a clear change during the 12 months. The second case is where a change in that frequency is intended. The commissioner analysed the "no pattern" case in *CCS 2885/2005:*

> "13.   This applies if there is no pattern of frequency. It is not concerned with changes in the pattern, that is distribution, of the care that do not affect its frequency. If a non-resident parent has a child for two nights at the weekend but changes that to four week nights every other week, there is a change of pattern, but not a change of frequency. Similarly, there may be a change in the frequency of care without affecting the pattern of that frequency. If a non-resident parent has care of the child while the

parent with care is in hospital for two weeks, there is a change in the frequency of the care, but not a change of pattern. The one-off additional period is not sufficient to establish a new pattern.

14.   There must be no pattern of frequency 'for the 12 months preceding the relevant week'. The important word is 'for'. Regulation 7(4) does not deal with circumstances in which there was no pattern *within* that period. Nor does it deal with circumstances in which there was no pattern *for part of* that period. It only deals with circumstances in which there was no pattern *for* the period, that is, for the whole of that period. In the context, it is not appropriate to read the singular 'pattern' as also including the plural 'patterns'. In other words, the context excludes the operation of section 6(c) of the Interpretation Act 1978. If it applied, this part of regulation 7(4) would only operate if there were no patterns of frequency at all within the period. That would exclude from the scope of the provision any case in which the pattern initially established had changed, which is surely the most obvious circumstance in which it is appropriate to use a different period than 12 months.

15.   Broadly speaking, the 'no pattern' cases will fall into three categories: (i) where there was a pattern initially, but it was later changed to a different pattern; (ii) where there was a pattern initially, but it was later abandoned; and (iii) where there was no pattern initially, but one was later established. The tribunal will have to determine three factual questions. What were the care arrangements during the period? What patterns, if any, were established? Were changes in arrangements (a) just a varying distribution that did not affect the overall pattern of frequency, (b) temporary variations of frequency that did not affect the overall pattern or (c) a new pattern of frequency?"

The commissioner also analysed the "intended change" case in *CCS 2885/2005,* paras 17-27. He first considered the enabling provisions, noting that Sch 1 para 9 to the Act only authorised a change to the length of the period that had to be considered. This meant that, whatever the length of the period, it always had to end with the relevant week, as required by para (3) above. Building on this, he pointed out that if the intended change was one that was only intended to take effect after the relevant week, it was impossible to fix an appropriate period, since by definition that period always had to end with the relevant week. He concluded:

"26.   The tenses in regulation 7(4) are important. Its operation has to be viewed from the relevant week. For the 'no pattern' part, the past tense is used and is appropriate. For the 'intended change' part, the present tense is used. Not, note, the future tense. It does not say that 'the Secretary of State is aware that a change in that frequency *will occur'.* It says that 'the Secretary of State is aware that a change in that frequency *is intended'.* I believe that that is the key to the interpretation of this part of regulation 7(4). It deals with this type of case. The parents have agreed to a change in the pattern of frequency for overnight care. But because of the distribution of that care, that change has not become apparent in the frequency of the care provided by the relevant week. Take this example. The child stays with the non-resident parent for a mixed pattern of overnight care depending on the parents' shift patterns. The parents agree that a more regular pattern would benefit the child. It may be possible in these circumstances to find a period before the relevant week that contained a distribution of care which coincides with the pattern of frequency under the new arrangement.

27.   This will not allow all intended changes to be taken into account. Take this example. Suppose that the child stays with the non-resident parent for two nights each weekend throughout the year. After Easter, the parents agree to a change, so that the child will stay with the non-resident parent for two nights at weekends in term time and for half of each school holiday. If the relevant week happens to fall at the end of the summer term, the change will not be apparent from the number of nights that the child has stayed with the non-resident parent. Nevertheless, there has been a change because the parents intend this to be part of a new pattern of frequency. However, the distribution of care down to the relevant week was such that the same result will always be reached whatever the period taken ...."

Changes that take place after the relevant week but before the date of decision have to be dealt with under reg 2(4), while changes that are planned to occur thereafter may be taken into account as an anticipated change of circumstances under reg 6A(3)(a)(ii) of the Appeals Regulations. The series of calculations that may be necessary are authorised by Sch 1 para 15 to the Act.

If one of these cases (no pattern or an intended change) applies, an "appropriate" and lesser period has to chosen to replace the 12-month period. The legislation does not provide any guidance on what constitutes an appropriate period or on the factors that should be taken into account; the language is as clear as it can be (*CCS 2885/2005,* para 29).

Paragraph (6)

It is clear from this provision that it is the school or the hospital that is actually providing the overnight care for the child. This is a deeming provision. The other person does not actually provide the overnight care for the child.

A boarding school covers any institution that is a school and that provides overnight residence for some pupils (*R(CS) 1/04,* para 24). It includes privately funded boarding and boarding that is funded by a local authority in the exercise of its social services functions (*R(CS) 1/04,* para 24) or by a local education authority (*R(CS) 2/04,* para 31).

It will usually be obvious who a child would live with if not at boarding school or in hospital. However, there are exceptional cases in which there is no clear answer. They require a careful analysis of all the circumstances of the case. It is a mistake simply to scale up the pattern of frequency that obtained when the child was boarding or in hospital. It is also a mistake to assume that circumstances, such as a parent's working arrangements, have not been affected by the fact that the child is boarding or in hospital, so that they would be different if the child had to stay instead with the non-resident parent or the person with care.

PART III

Special Cases

Persons treated as non-resident parents

8.–(1)   Where the circumstances of a case are that–

(a)   two or more persons who do not live in the same household each provide day to day care for the same [¹child, being a child in respect of whom an application for a maintenance calculation has been made [²...]]; and

(b)   at least one of those persons is a parent of the child,

that case shall be treated as a special case for the purposes of the Act.

(2)   For the purposes of this special case a parent who provides day to day care for a child of his is to be treated as a non-resident parent for the purposes of the Act in the following circumstances–

(a)   a parent who provides such care to a lesser extent than the other parent, person or persons who provide such care for the child in question; or

(b)   where the persons mentioned in paragraph (1)(a) include both parents and the circumstances are such that care is provided to the same extent by both but each provides care to an extent greater than or equal to any other person who provides such care for that child–

　　(i)   the parent who is not in receipt of child benefit for the child in question; or

　　(ii)   if neither parent is in receipt of child benefit for that child, the parent who, in the opinion of the Secretary of State, will not be the principal provider of day to day care for that child.

(3)   For the purposes of this regulation and regulation 10

[³(a)] "child benefit" means child benefit payable under Part IX of the Contributions and Benefits Act;

[³(b)] where a person has made an election under section 13A(1) of the Social Security Administration Act 1992 (election not to receive child benefit) for payments of child benefit not to be made, that person is to be treated as being in receipt of child benefit.]

Amendments

1.　　Child Support (Miscellaneous Amendments) Regulations 2003 (SI 2003 No.328) reg 8(3) (February 21, 2003).

2.　　Child Support (Consequential Provisions) Regulations 2008 (SI 2008 No.2543) reg 7(3) (October 27, 2008).

3.　　Child Support (Miscellaneous Amendments) Regulations 2013 (SI 2013 No. 1517) reg 6(3) (September 30, 2013).

Definitions

"the Act": see reg 1(2).
"Contributions and Benefits Act": see reg 1(2).
"day to day care": see reg 1(2).
"person": see reg 1(2).

General Note

This special case determines who is to be treated as the non-resident parent if a child is receiving day to day care from different persons in different households. The child support maintenance payable by the non-resident parent is adjusted under the shared care provisions in Sch 1 paras 7 and 8 to the Act.

Paragraph (1)

This paragraph sets out the circumstances in which the special case applies. The day to day care of the child must be split between persons in different households and one of those persons must be a parent of the child. If neither parent of the child is providing day to day care, this special case does not apply.

It is day to day care, as defined in reg 1(2), that is relevant, not shared care under Sch 1 paras 7 and 8 to the Act.

There must be separate households. For the meaning of household, see the general note to s3(2) of the Act on p16. This special case does not apply if the persons providing care are members of the same household (*CCS14625/1996*, para 17).

Paragraph (2)

This paragraph identifies the person who is to be treated as the non-resident parent. In most cases, the care of the child will be divided between the parents and the non-resident parent will be the parent who provides care for fewer nights than the other or who is not in receipt of child benefit.

The paragraph is authorised by legislation (*R(CS) 1/09*, para 16, agreeing with *R(CS)14/98*, which came to the same conclusion on earlier legislation). It is not a violation of the Convention rights under Arts 8 and 14 of the European Convention on Human Rights (*R(CS) 1/09*, paras 22-24).

In *R(CS) 1/09*, the commissioner decided without analysis (at para 11) that this paragraph applied if the child's parents shared the care of their child equally between themselves and with no one else. That is not what the provision actually says, although the outcome is consistent with the policy underlying the provision.

Care provided in part by a local authority

9.–(1) This regulation applies where paragraph (2) applies and the rate of child support maintenance payable is the basic rate, or the reduced rate, or has been calculated following agreement to a variation where the non-resident parent's liability would otherwise have been a flat rate or the nil rate.

(2) Where the circumstances of a case are that the care of the qualifying child is shared between the person with care and a local authority and–

(a) the qualifying child is in the care of the local authority for 52 nights or more in the 12 month period ending with the relevant week; or

(b) where, in the opinion of the Secretary of State, a period other than the 12 month period mentioned in sub-paragraph (a) is more representative of the current arrangements for the care of the qualifying child, the qualifying child is in the care of the local authority during that period for no fewer than the number of nights which bears the same ratio to 52 nights as that period bears to 12 months; or

(c) it is intended that the qualifying child shall be in the care of the local authority for a number of nights in a period from the effective date,

that case shall be treated as a special case for the purposes of the Act.

(3) In a case where this regulation applies, the amount of child support maintenance which the non-resident parent is liable to pay the person with care of that qualifying child is the amount calculated in accordance with the provisions of Part I of Schedule 1 to the Act and decreased in accordance with this regulation.

(4) First, there is to be a decrease according to the number of nights spent or to be spent by the qualifying child in the care of the local authority during the period under consideration.

(5) Where paragraph (2)(b) or (c) applies, the number of nights in the period under consideration shall be adjusted by the ratio which the period of 12 months bears to the period under consideration.

(6) After any adjustment under paragraph (5), the amount of the decrease for one child is set out in the following Table–

Number of nights in care of local authority	Fraction to subtract
52-103	One-seventh
104-155	Two-sevenths
156-207	Three-sevenths
208-259	Four-sevenths
260-262	Five-sevenths

(7) If the non-resident parent and the person with care have more than one qualifying child, the applicable decrease is the sum of the appropriate fractions in the Table divided by the number of such qualifying children.

(8) In a case where the amount of child support maintenance which the non-resident parent is liable to pay in relation to the same person with care is to be decreased in accordance with the provisions of both this regulation and of paragraph 7 of Part I of

Schedule 1 to the Act, read with regulation 7 of these Regulations, the applicable decrease is the sum of the appropriate fractions derived under those provisions.

(9)   If the application of this regulation would decrease the weekly amount of child support maintenance (or the aggregate of all such amounts) payable by the non-resident parent to less than the rate stated in or prescribed for the purposes of paragraph 4(1) of Part I of Schedule 1 to the Act, he is instead liable to pay child support maintenance at a rate equivalent to that rate, apportioned (if appropriate) in accordance with paragraph 6 of Part I of Schedule 1 to the Act and regulation 6.

(10)   Where a qualifying child is a boarder at a boarding school or is an in-patient at a hospital, the qualifying child shall be treated as being in the care of the local authority for any night that the local authority would otherwise have been providing such care.

(11)   A child is in the care of a local authority for any night in which he is being looked after by the local authority within the meaning of section 22 of the Children Act 1989 or section 17(6) of the Children (Scotland) Act 1995.

Definitions
"the Act": see reg 1(2).
"effective date": see reg 1(2).
"patient": see reg 1(2).
"person": see reg 1(2).
"relevant week": see reg 1(2).

General Note
This special case applies where the care of the child is divided between the person with care and a local authority.
Paragraph (1)
The decrease in the amount of child support maintenance under this special case is not compatible with the flat rate or the nil rate. So, it only applies when one of those rates would apply, if the amount payable has been increased under a variation.
Paragraph (2)
Broadly, the special case only applies if the child is in the care of the local authority for at least one night a week on average. The case only applies if the child is in the care of the local authority. It is not drawn to include circumstances in which a local authority provides accommodation for a child in the exercise of one of its social services functions: see the distinction drawn in s22(1) Children Act 1989.
Paragraphs (3)-(6)
The child support maintenance payable is first calculated under Sch 1 to the Act.
    It is then reduced to reflect the number of nights the child spends under the care of the local authority.

Care provided for relevant other child by a local authority

10.   Where a child other than a qualifying child is cared for in part or in full by a local authority and the non-resident parent or his partner receives child benefit for that child, the child is a relevant other child for the purposes of Schedule 1 to the Act.

Definitions
"the Act": see reg 1(2).
"partner": see reg 1(2).

General Note
This regulation is made under the authority of Sch 1 para 10C(2)(b) to the Act.

Non-resident parent liable to pay maintenance under a maintenance order

11.–(1)   Subject to paragraph (2), where the circumstances of a case are that–
(a)   an application for child support maintenance is made [3...] with respect to a qualifying child and a non-resident parent; and
(b)   an application for child support maintenance for a different child cannot be made under the Act but that non-resident parent is liable to pay maintenance [2for that child–
        (i)   under a maintenance order;
        (ii)   in accordance with the terms of an order made by a court outside Great Britain; or

(iii)   under the legislation of a jurisdiction outside the United Kingdom,
that case shall be treated as a special case for the purpose of the Act.]

(2)   This regulation applies where the rate of child support maintenance payable is the basic rate, or the reduced rate, or has been calculated following agreement to a variation where the non-resident parent's liability would otherwise have been a flat rate or the nil rate.

(3) Where this regulation applies, [¹subject to paragraph (5),] the amount of child support maintenance payable by the non-resident parent shall be ascertained by–

(a)   calculating the amount of maintenance payable as if the number of qualifying children of that parent included any children with respect to whom he is liable to make payments under the order referred to in paragraph (1)(b); and

(b)   apportioning the amount so calculated between the qualifying children and the children with respect to whom he is liable to make payments under the order referred to in paragraph (1)(b),

and the amount payable shall be the amount apportioned to the qualifying children, and the amount payable to each person with care shall be that amount subject to the application of apportionment under paragraph 6 of Schedule 1 to the Act and the shared care provisions in paragraph 7 of Part I of that Schedule.

(4)   In a case where this regulation applies paragraph 7 of Part I of Schedule 1 to the Act (shared care) and regulation 10 (care provided in part by local authority) shall not apply in relation to a child in respect of whom the non-resident parent is liable to make payments under a maintenance order as provided in paragraph (1)(b).

[¹(5)   If the application of paragraph (3) would decrease the weekly amount of child support maintenance (or the aggregate of all such amounts) payable by the non-resident parent to the person with care (or all of them) to an amount which is less than a figure equivalent to the flat rate of child support maintenance payable under paragraph 4(1) of Schedule 1 to the Act, the non-resident parent shall instead be liable to pay child support maintenance at a rate equivalent to that flat rate apportioned (if appropriate) as provided in paragraph 6 of Schedule 1 to the Act.]

Amendments

1.   Child Support (Miscellaneous Amendments) (No.2) Regulations 2003 (SI 2003 No.2779) reg 6(5) (November 5, 2003).
2.   Child Support (Miscellaneous Amendments) Regulations 2005 (SI 2005 No.785) reg 6(4) (March 16, 2005).
3.   Child Support (Consequential Provisions) Regulations 2008 (SI 2008 No.2543) reg 7(4) (October 27, 2008).

Definitions

"the Act": see reg 1(2).
"person": see reg 1(2).

General Note

This regulation only applies if maintenance is being paid under a maintenance order. It does not apply if maintenance is being paid under an agreement. This is not discriminatory. A non-resident parent who pays under an agreement is able, unlike a non-resident parent who pays under a court order, to apply for a maintenance calculation under s4 of the Act: *HW v SSWP* [2009] CSIH 21.

Paragraph (1)

This special case applies if a non-resident parent is liable to pay maintenance for a child under a maintenance order. It provides for the child support maintenance payable for another child under the child support scheme to reflect the existence of that obligation. It does not apply if the payments for the other child are made under a maintenance agreement.

Paragraph (2)

The decrease in the amount of child support maintenance under this special case is not compatible with the flat rate or the nil rate. So, it only applies when one of those rates would apply, if the amount payable has been increased under a variation.

Paragraph (3)

The reduction reflects the existence of the obligation under the maintenance order. It does not vary according to the amount payable under the order.

Child who is a boarder or an in-patient in hospital

12.–(1)   Where the circumstances of the case are that–

(a)   a qualifying child is a boarder at a boarding school or is an in-patient in a hospital; and

(b)   by reason of those circumstances, the person who would otherwise provide day to day care is not doing so,

that case shall be treated as a special case for the purposes of the Act.

(2)   For the purposes of this case, section 3(3)(b) of the Act shall be modified so that for the reference to the person who usually provides day to day care for the child there shall be substituted a reference to the person who would usually be providing such care for that child but for the circumstances specified in paragraph (1).

Definitions
"the Act": see reg 1(2).
"day to day care": see reg 1(2).
"patient": see reg 1(2).
"person": see reg 1(2).

General Note
Paragraph (1)
For the application of this paragraph, see the general note to reg 7(6).
Paragraph (2)
This paragraph limits the effect of this special case to s3(3) of the Act. However, similar provision in made in the definition of day to day care in reg 1(2) above, for the purposes of shared care in reg 7(6) above, and in respect of care divided between the person with care and a local authority in reg 9(10).

Child who is allowed to live with his parent under section 23(5) of the Children Act 1989

13.–(1)   Where the circumstances of a case are that a qualifying child who is in the care of a local authority in England and Wales is allowed by the authority to live with a parent of his under section 23(5) of the Children Act 1989, that case shall be treated as a special case for the purposes of the Act.

(2)   For the purposes of this case, section 3(3)(b) of the Act shall be modified so that for the reference to the person who usually provides day to day care for the child there shall be substituted a reference to the parent of the child with whom the local authority allow the child to live with under section 23(5) of the Children Act 1989.

Definitions
"the Act": see reg 1(2).
"day to day care": see reg 1(2).
"person": see reg 1(2).

General Note
This allows a maintenance calculation to reflect the reality that the parent is providing day to day care of a child, although the child is legally in the care of a local authority. Its effect is to make that parent the person with care even though the conditions in s3(3)(b) of the Act are not satisfied (*R(CS) 7/02*). If a child is allowed to live with one parent and then moves to live with the other parent without a fresh placement decision being made by the local authority, the other parent may be a person with care under s3(3)(b) despite this regulation (*R(CS) 7/02*).

Person with part-time care who is not a non-resident parent

14.–(1)   Where the circumstances of a case are that–

(a)   two or more persons who do not live in the same household each provide day to day care for the same qualifying child; and

(b)   those persons do not include any parent who is treated as a non-resident parent of that child by regulation 8(2),

that case shall be treated as a special case for the purposes of the Act.

(2)   For the purposes of this case–

(a)   the person whose application for a maintenance calculation is being proceeded with shall, subject to sub-paragraph (b), be entitled to receive all of the child support maintenance payable under the Act in respect of the child in question;

(b) on request being made to the Secretary of State by–
    (i) that person; or
    (ii) any other person who is providing day to day care for that child and who intends to continue to provide that care,

the Secretary of State may make arrangements for the payment of any child support maintenance payable under the Act to the persons who provide such care in the same ratio as that in which it appears to the Secretary of State that each is to provide such care for the child in question;

(c) before making an arrangement under sub-paragraph (b), the Secretary of State shall consider all of the circumstances of the case and in particular the interests of the child, the present arrangements for the day to day care of the child in question and any representations or proposals made by the persons who provide such care for that child.

Definitions
"the Act": see reg 1(2).
"day to day care": see reg 1(2).
"person": see reg 1(2).

General Note
Paragraph (1)
This paragraph sets out the circumstances in which the special case applies. The day to day care of the child must be split between persons in different households and none of those persons is a parent of the child who is treated as a non-resident parent under reg 8.

It is day to day care, as defined in reg 1(2), that is relevant, not shared care under Sch 1 paras 7 and 8 to the Act.

There must be separate households. For the meaning of household, see the general note to s3(2) of the Act on p16. This special case does not apply if the persons providing care are members of the same household (*CCS14625/1996*, para 17).

A person who provides day to day care and who is entitled to a share of the child support maintenance under this regulation is not necessarily a person with care under s3(3) of the Act and does not become one by virtue of this regulation. For example, the child's home need not be with the person who benefits from this regulation. The function of the regulation is to allow the Secretary of State to divert a share of the child support maintenance to someone who has day to day care of a child, but who is not a person with care and who, therefore, could not apply for a maintenance calculation.

Paragraph (2)
The starting point is provided by sub-para (a): the person with care under the maintenance calculation is entitled to received all the child support maintenance payable by the non-resident parent.

On request, the Secretary of State may agree under sub-para (b) that a share of the child support maintenance should be paid to the other person providing care. The amount is determined by the number of nights for which care is given. The wording does not allow other factors to be considered in fixing the amount, like the respective financial burdens undertaken by the persons providing the care. These factors may, though, be relevant under sub-para (c) to whether any arrangement should be made at all.

Sub-paragraph (c) controls the exercise of the discretion given by sub-para (b).

The discretion is limited to whether the Secretary of State should make an arrangement. It does not confer a discretion as to the terms of the arrangement. The Secretary of State must consider all the circumstances of the case, including representations made, the present arrangements for care and the interests of the child. In contrast to s2 of the Act, it is the interests, rather than welfare, of the child that have to be considered. Also, only the child in question is mentioned in sub-para (c), although other children could be considered as part of the circumstances of the case.

PART IV
Revocation and savings

Revocation and savings
15.–(1) Subject to [¹the Child Support (Transitional Provisions) Regulations 2000 and] paragraphs (2), (3) and (4), the Child Support (Maintenance Assessments and Special Cases) Regulations 1992 ("the 1992 Regulations") shall be revoked with respect to a particular case with effect from the date that these Regulations come into force with respect to that type of case ("the commencement date").

(2)　Where before the commencement date in respect of a particular case–

(a)　an application was made and not determined for–

    (i)　a maintenance assessment;

    (ii)　a departure direction; or

    (iii)　a revision or supersession of a decision;

(b)　the Secretary of State had begun but not completed a revision or supersession of a decision on his own initiative;

(c)　any time limit provided for in Regulations for making an application for a revision or a departure direction had not expired; or

(d)　any appeal was made but not decided or any time limit for making an appeal had not expired,

the provisions of the 1992 Regulations shall continue to apply for the purposes of–

    (aa)　the decision on the application referred to in sub-paragraph (a);

    (bb)　the revision or supersession referred to in sub-paragraph (b);

    (cc)　the ability to apply for the revision or the departure direction referred to in sub-paragraph (c) and the decision whether to revise or to give a departure direction following any such application;

    (dd)　any appeal outstanding or made during the time limit referred to in sub-paragraph (d); or

    (ee)　any revision, supersession, appeal or application for a departure direction in relation to a decision, ability to apply or appeal referred to in sub-paragraphs (aa) to (dd) above.

(3)　Where immediately before the commencement date in respect of a particular case an interim maintenance assessment was in force, the provisions of the 1992 Regulations shall continue to apply for the purposes of the decision under section 17 of the Act to make a maintenance assessment calculated in accordance with Part I of Schedule 1 to the Act before its amendment by the 2000 Act and any revision, supersession or appeal in relation to that decision.

(4)　Where under regulation 28(1) of the Child Support (Transitional Provisions) Regulation 2000 an application for a maintenance calculation is treated as an application for a maintenance assessment, the provisions of the 1992 Regulations shall continue to apply for the purposes of the determination of the application and any revision, supersession or appeal in relation to any such assessment made.

(5)　Where after the commencement date a maintenance assessment is revised from a date which is prior to the commencement date the 1992 Regulations shall apply for the purposes of that revision.

(6)　For the purposes of this regulation–

(a)　"departure direction", "maintenance assessment" and "interim maintenance assessment" have the same meaning as in section 54 of the Act before its amendment by the 2000 Act;

(b)　"revision or supersession" means a revision or supersession of a decision under section 16 or 17 of the Act before their amendment by the 2000 Act; and

(c)　"2000 Act" means the Child Support, Pensions and Social Security Act 2000.

Amendment

1.　Child Support (Transitional Provision)(Miscellaneous Amendments) Regulations 2003 (SI 2003 No.347) reg 2(1) and (2) (March 3, 2003).

Definition

"the Act": see reg 1(2).

SCHEDULE
Regulation 1(2)
NET WEEKLY INCOME

PART I
GENERAL

Net weekly income
 1.　　Net weekly income means the aggregate of the net weekly income of the non-resident parent provided for in this Schedule.

Amounts to be disregarded when calculating income
 2.　　The following amounts shall be disregarded when calculating the net weekly income of the non-resident parent–
 (a)　where a payment is made in a currency other than sterling, an amount equal to any banking charge or commission payable in converting that payment to sterling;
 (b)　any amount payable in a country outside the United Kingdom where there is a prohibition against the transfer to the United Kingdom of that amount.

PART II
EMPLOYED EARNER

Net weekly income of employed earner
 3.–(1)　The net weekly income of the non-resident parent as an employed earner shall be–
 (a)　his earnings provided for in paragraph 4 less the deductions provided for in paragraph 5 and calculated or estimated by reference to the relevant week as provided for in paragraph 6; or
 (b)　where the Secretary of State is satisfied that the person is unable to provide evidence or information relating to the deductions provided for in paragraph 5, the non-resident parent's net earnings estimated by the Secretary of State on the basis of information available to him as to the non-resident parent's net income.
 (2)　Where any provision of these Regulations requires the income of a person to be estimated, and that or any other provision of these Regulations requires that the amount of such estimated income is to be taken into account for any purpose, after deducting from it a sum in respect of income tax, or of primary Class 1 contributions under the Contributions and Benefits Act or, as the case may be, the Contributions and Benefits (Northern Ireland) Act, or contributions paid by that person towards an occupational pension scheme or personal pension scheme, then,
 (a)　subject to sub-paragraph (c), the amount to be deducted in respect of income tax shall be calculated by applying to that income the rates of income tax applicable at the effective date less only the personal relief to which that person is entitled under Chapter I of Part VII of the Income and Corporation Taxes Act 1988 (personal relief); but if the period in respect of which that income is to be estimated is less than a year, the amount of the personal relief deductible under this paragraph shall be calculated on a pro-rata basis and the amount of income to which each tax rate applies shall be determined on the basis that the ratio of that amount to the full amount of the income to which each tax rate applies is the same as the ratio of the proportionate part of that personal relief to the full personal relief;
 (b)　subject to sub-paragraph (c), the amount to be deducted in respect of Class 1 contributions under the Contributions and Benefits Act or, as the case may be, the Contributions and Benefits (Northern Ireland) Act, shall be calculated by applying to that income the appropriate primary percentage applicable on the effective date;
 (c)　in relation to any bonus or commission which may be included in that person's income–
 (i)　the amount to be deducted in respect of income tax shall be calculated by applying to the gross amount of that bonus or commission the rate or rates of income tax applicable at the effective date;
 (ii)　the amount to be deducted in respect of primary Class 1 contributions under the Contributions and Benefits Act or, as the case may be, the Contributions and Benefits (Northern Ireland) Act, shall be calculated by applying to the gross amount of that bonus or commission the appropriate main primary percentage applicable on the effective date but no deduction shall be made in respect of the portion (if any) of the bonus or commission which, if added to the estimated income, would cause such income to exceed the upper earnings limit for Class 1 contributions as provided for in section 5(1)(b) of the Contributions and Benefits Act or, as the case may be, the Contributions and Benefits (Northern Ireland) Act;
 (d)　the amount to be deducted in respect of any sums or contributions towards an occupational pension scheme or personal pension scheme shall be the full amount of any such payments made or, where that scheme is intended partly to provide a capital sum to discharge a mortgage secured upon that parent's home, 75 per centum of any such payments made.

Earnings

4.–(1)   Subject to sub-paragraph (2), "earnings" means, in the case of employment as an employed earner, any remuneration or profit derived from that employment and includes–

(a)   any bonus, commission, payment in respect of overtime, royalty or fees;

(b)   any holiday pay except any payable more than 4 weeks after termination of the employment;

(c)   any payment by way of a retainer;

(d)   any statutory sick pay under Part XI of the Contributions and Benefits Act or statutory maternity pay under Part XII of the Contributions and Benefits Act; and

[³(dd)   any statutory paternity pay under Part 12ZA of the Contributions and Benefits Act or any statutory adoption pay under Part 12ZB of that Act;]

(e)   any payment in lieu of notice, and any compensation in respect of the absence or inadequacy of any such notice, but only in so far as such payment or compensation represents loss of income.

(2)   Earnings for the purposes of this Part of Schedule 1 do not include–

(a)   any payment in respect of expenses wholly, exclusively and necessarily incurred in the performance of the duties of the employment;

(b)   any tax-exempt allowance made by an employer to an employee;

(c)   any gratuities paid by customers of the employer;

(d)   any payment in kind;

(e)   any advance of earnings or any loan made by an employer to an employee;

(f)   any amount received from an employer during a period when the employee has withdrawn his services by reason of a trade dispute;

(g)   any payment made in respect of the performance of duties as–

    (i)   an auxiliary coastguard in respect of coast rescue activities;

    (ii)   [⁶...]

    [⁴(iia)   a part-time fire-fighter employed by a fire and rescue authority;]

    [⁶(iib)   a part-time fire-fighter employed by [¹¹the Scottish Fire and Rescue Service];]

    (iii)   a person engaged part-time in the manning or launching of a lifeboat;

    (iv)   a member of any territorial or reserve force prescribed in Part I of Schedule 3 to the Social Security (Contributions) Regulations 1979;

(h)   any payment made by a local authority to a member of that authority in respect of the performance of his duties as a member;

(i)   any payment where–

    (i)   the employment in respect of which it was made has ceased; and

    (ii)   a period of the same length as the period by reference to which it was calculated has expired since that cessation but prior to the effective date; or

(j)   where, in any week or other period which falls within the period by reference to which earnings are calculated, earnings are received both in respect of a previous employment and in respect of a subsequent employment, the earnings in respect of the previous employment.

Deductions

5.–(1)   The deductions to be taken from gross earnings to calculate net income for the purposes of this Part of the Schedule are any amount deducted from those earnings by way of–

(a)   income tax;

(b)   primary Class 1 contributions under the Contributions and Benefits Act or under the Contributions and Benefits (Northern Ireland) Act; or

(c)   any sums paid by the non-resident parent towards an occupational pension scheme or personal pension scheme or, where that scheme is intended partly to provide a capital sum to discharge a mortgage secured upon that parent's home, 75 per centum of any such sums.

(2)   For the purposes of sub-paragraph (1)(a), [⁹except for cases falling within sub-paragraph (3),] amounts deducted by way of income tax shall be the amounts actually deducted, including in respect of payments which are not included as earnings in paragraph 4.

[⁹(3)   For the purposes of sub-paragraph (1)(a), where an employed earner is gainfully employed outside the United Kingdom, amounts deducted by way of income tax shall be–

(a)   the amounts actually deducted in respect of income tax applicable to the income in question, whether that is paid in full in Great Britain or outside Great Britain, or partly paid both in Great Britain and outside Great Britain; or

(b)   where insufficient or unreliable evidence or information is provided by the non-resident parent as to the actual amounts deducted, the amounts that would have been deducted had that employed earner been gainfully employed in Great Britain.

(4)   For the purposes of sub-paragraph (1)(b), where an employed earner is gainfully employed outside the United Kingdom, amounts deducted by way of primary Class 1 contributions shall be the amounts actually deducted under the Contributions and Benefits Act or under the Contributions and Benefits (Northern Ireland) Act and amounts actually deducted outside the United Kingdom for payments of a similar nature.]

Calculation or estimate

6.–(1)   Subject to [²sub-paragraphs (3) and (4)], the amount of earnings to be taken into account for the purpose of calculating net income shall be calculated or estimated by reference to the average earnings at the relevant week having regard to such evidence as is available in relation to that person's earnings during such period as appears appropriate to the Secretary of State, beginning not earlier than 8 weeks before the relevant week and ending not later than the date of the calculation, and for the purposes of the calculation or estimate he may consider evidence of that person's cumulative earnings during the period beginning with the start of the year of assessment (within the meaning of section 832 of the Income and Corporation Taxes Act 1988) in which the relevant week falls and ending with a date no later than the date when the calculation is made.

    (2)   [²...]

    (3)   Where a person's earnings during the period of 52 weeks ending with the relevant week include a bonus or commission [⁸...] which is paid separately from, or in relation to a longer period than, the other earnings with which it is paid, the amount of that bonus or commission shall be determined for the purposes of the calculation of earnings by aggregating any such payments received in that period and dividing by 52.

    (4)   Where a calculation would, but for this sub-paragraph, produce an amount which, in the opinion of the Secretary of State, does not accurately reflect the normal amount of the earnings of the person in question, such earnings, or any part of them, shall be calculated by reference to such other period as may, in the particular case, enable the normal weekly earnings of that person to be determined more accurately, and for this purpose the Secretary of State shall have regard to–

(a)   the earnings received, or due to be received from any employment in which the person in question is engaged, has been engaged or is due to be engaged; and

(b)   the duration and pattern, or the expected duration and pattern, of any employment of that person.

[⁹Estimate of net weekly income of employed earner where insufficient information available

    6A.–(1)   Where the [¹⁰Secretary of State] is calculating net weekly income of an employed earner under Part II of the Schedule and the information available in relation to that income is insufficient or unreliable, the [¹⁰Secretary of State] may estimate that income and, in doing so, may make any assumptions as to any fact.

    (2)   Where the [¹⁰Secretary of State] is satisfied that the non-resident parent is engaged in a particular occupation as an employee, the assumptions referred to in sub-paragraph (1) may include an assumption that the non-resident parent has the average net weekly income of a person engaged in that occupation in the United Kingdom or any part of the United Kingdom.]

PART III
SELF-EMPLOYED EARNER

[⁷Net weekly income of non-resident parent as a self-employed earner]

    7.–[⁷(1)   Subject to sub-paragraph (6) and to paragraph 8, the net weekly income of the non-resident parent as a self-employed earner shall be his gross earnings less the deductions to which sub-paragraph (3) applies.]

    [⁷(1A) In this paragraph and paragraph 8 a person's "gross earnings" are his taxable profits calculated in accordance with Part 2 of the Income Tax (Trading and Other Income) Act 2005.]

    [⁷(2) The non-resident parent shall provide to the Secretary of State on demand a copy of–

(a)   any tax calculation notice issued to him by Her Majesty's Revenue and Customs; and

(b)   any revised tax calculation notice issued to him by Her Majesty's Revenue and Customs.]

    (3)   This paragraph applies to the following deductions–

(a)   any income tax relating to the gross earnings from the self-employment determined in accordance with sub-paragraph (4);

(b)   any National Insurance contributions relating to the gross earnings from the self-employment determined in accordance with sub-paragraph (5); and

(c)   any premiums paid by the non-resident parent in respect of a retirement annuity contract or a personal pension scheme or, where that scheme is intended partly to provide a capital sum to discharge a mortgage or a charge secured upon the parent's home, 75 per centum of the contributions payable.

    (4)   For the purpose of sub-paragraph (3)(a), the income tax to be deducted from the gross earnings shall be determined in accordance with the following provisions–

(a)   subject to head (d), an amount of gross earnings [⁵calculated as if it were equivalent to any personal allowance which would be] applicable to the earner by virtue of the provisions of Chapter I of Part VII of the Income and Corporation Taxes Act 1988 (personal relief) shall be disregarded;

(b)   subject to head (c), an amount equivalent to income tax shall be calculated in relation to the gross earnings remaining following the application of head (a) (the "remaining earnings");

(c)   the tax rate applicable at the effective date shall be applied to all the remaining earnings, where necessary increasing or reducing the amount payable to take account of the fact that the earnings related to a period greater or less than one year; and

(d)   the amount to be disregarded by virtue of head (a) shall be calculated by reference to the yearly rate applicable at the effective date, that amount being reduced or increased in the same proportion to that which the period represented by the gross earnings bears to the period of one year.

    (5)   For the purposes of sub-paragraph (3)(b), the amount to be deducted in respect of National Insurance contributions shall be the total of–

(a)   the amount of Class 2 contributions (if any) payable under section 11(1) or, as the case may be, (3) of the Contributions and Benefits Act or under section 11(1) or (3) of the Contributions and Benefits (Northern Ireland) Act; and

(b)   the amount of Class 4 contributions (if any) payable under section 15(2) of that Act, or under section 15(2) of the Contributions and Benefits (Northern Ireland) Act,

at the rates applicable at the effective date.

(6)   The net weekly income of a self-employed earner may only be determined in accordance with this paragraph where the earnings concerned relate to a period which terminated not more than 24 months prior to the relevant week.

(7)   [⁷...]

(8)   Any request by the Secretary of State in accordance with sub-paragraph (2) for the provision of information shall set out the possible consequences of failure to provide such information, including details of the offences provided for in section 14A of the Act for failing to provide, or providing false, information.

Figures calculated using gross receipts less deductions

8.–(1)   Where–

(a)   the conditions of paragraph 7(6) are not satisfied; or

(b)   the Secretary of State accepts that it is not reasonably practicable for the self-employed earner to provide information relating to his gross earnings from self-employment in the forms submitted to, or as issued or revised by, the Inland Revenue; [⁷...]

(c)   [⁷...],

net income means in the case of employment as a self-employed earner his earningscalculated by reference to the gross receipts [¹in respect of employment which are of a type which would be taken into account under paragraph 7(1)] less the deductions provided for in sub-paragraph (2).

(2)   The deductions to be taken from the gross receipts to calculate net earnings for the purposes of this paragraph are–

(a)   any expenses which are reasonably incurred and are wholly and exclusively defrayed for the purposes of the earner's business in the period by reference to which his earnings are determined under paragraph 9(2) or (3);

(b)   any value added tax paid in the period by reference to which his earnings are determined in excess of value added tax received in that period;

(c)   any amount in respect of income tax determined in accordance with sub-paragraph (4);

(d)   any amount of National Insurance contributions determined in accordance with sub-paragraph (4); and

(e)   any premium paid by the non-resident parent in respect of a retirement annuity contract or a personal pension scheme or, where that scheme is intended partly to provide a capital sum to discharge a mortgage or a charge secured upon the parent's home, 75 per centum of contributions payable.

(3)   For the purposes of sub-paragraph (2)(a)–

(a)   such expenses include–

(i)   repayment of capital on any loan used for the replacement, in the course of business, of equipment or machinery, or the repair of an existing business asset except to the extent that any sum is payable under an insurance policy for its repair;

(ii)   any income expended in the repair of an existing business asset except to the extent that any sum is payable under an insurance policy for its repair; and

(iii)   any payment of interest on a loan taken out for the purposes of the business;

(b)   such expenses do not include–

(i)   [⁷...];

(ii)   any capital expenditure;

(iii)   [⁷...];

(iv)   [⁷...];

(v)   [⁷...];

(vi)   any expenses incurred in providing business entertainment; or

(vii)   [⁷...].

(4)   For the purposes of sub-paragraph (2)(c) and (d), the amounts in respect of income tax and National Insurance contributions to be deducted from the gross receipts shall be determined in accordance with paragraph 7(4) and (5) of this Schedule as if in paragraph 7(4) references to gross earnings were references to taxable earnings and in this sub-paragraph "taxable earnings" means the gross receipts of the earner less the deductions mentioned in sub-paragraph (2)(a) and (b).

Rules for calculation under paragraph 8

9.–(1)   This paragraph applies only where the net income of a self-employed earner is calculated or estimated under paragraph 8 of this Schedule.

(2)   Where–

(a)   a non-resident parent has been a self-employed earner for 52 weeks or more, including the relevant week, the amount of his net weekly income shall be determined by reference to the average of the earnings which he has received in the 52 weeks ending with the relevant week; or

(b)   a non-resident parent has been a self-employed earner for a period of less than 52 weeks including the relevant week, the amount of his net weekly income shall be determined by reference to the average of the earnings which he has received during that period.

(3)   Where a calculation would, but for this sub-paragraph, produce an amount which, in the opinion of the Secretary of State, does not accurately reflect the normal weekly income of the non-resident parent in question, such earnings, or any part of them, shall be calculated by reference to such other period as may, in the particular case, enable the normal weekly earnings of the non-resident parent to be determined more accurately and for this purpose the Secretary of State shall have regard to–

(a)   the earnings from self-employment received, or due to be received, by him; and

(b)   the duration and pattern, or the expected duration and pattern, of any self-employment of that non-resident parent.

(4)   [²...]

[⁹Estimate of net weekly income of self-employed earner where insufficient information available

9A.–(1)   Where the [¹⁰Secretary of State] is calculating net weekly income of a self-employed earner under Part III of the Schedule and the information available in relation to that income is insufficient or unreliable, the [¹⁰Secretary of State] may estimate that income and, in doing so, may make any assumptions as to any fact.

(2)   Where the [¹⁰Secretary of State] is satisfied that the non-resident parent is engaged in a particular occupation as a self-employed earner, the assumptions referred to in sub-paragraph (1) may include an assumption that the non-resident parent has the average net weekly income of a person engaged in that occupation in the United Kingdom or any part of the United Kingdom.]

Income from board or lodging

10.   In a case where a non-resident parent is a self-employed earner who provides board and lodging, his earnings shall include payments received for that provision where those payments are the only or main source of income of that earner.

PART IV
TAX CREDITS

[²Working tax credit]

11.–(1)   Subject to [²sub-paragraph (2)], payments by way of [²working tax credit] [²...], shall be treated as the income of the non-resident parent where he has qualified for them by his engagement in, and normal engagement in, remunerative work, at the rate payable at the effective date.

(2)   Where [²working tax credit] is payable and the amount which is payable has been calculated by reference to [²the earnings] of the non-resident parent and another person–

(a)   where during the period which is used by the Inland Revenue to calculate his income [²the earnings] [²...] of that parent exceed those of the other person, the amount payable by way of [²working tax credit] shall be treated as the income of that parent;

(b)   where during that period [²the earnings] of that parent equal those of the other person, half of the amount payable by way of [²working tax credit] shall be treated as the income of that parent; and

(c)   where during that period [²the earnings] of that parent are less than those of that other person, the amount payable by way of [²working tax credit] shall not be treated as the income of that parent.

[²(2A)   For the purposes of this paragraph, "earnings" means the employment income and the income from self-employment of the non-resident parent and the other person referred to in sub-paragraph (2), as determined for the purposes of their entitlement to working tax credit.]

(3)   [²...]

Employment Credits

12.   Payments made by way of employment credits under section 2(1) of the Employment and Training Act 1973 to a non-resident parent who is participating in a scheme arranged under section 2(2) of the Employment and Training Act 1973 and known as the New Deal 50 plus shall be treated as the income of the non-resident parent, at the rate payable at the effective date.

[¹**13.**   [²...]]

[²Child tax credit

13A. Payments made by way of child tax credit to a non-resident parent or his partner at the rate payable at the effective date.]

PART V
OTHER INCOME

Amount

14.   The amount of other income to be taken into account in calculating or estimating net weekly income shall be the aggregate of the payments to which paragraph 15 applies, net of any income tax deducted and otherwise determined in accordance with this Part.

Types

    15.   This paragraph applies to any periodic payment of pension or other benefit under an occupational or personal pension scheme or a retirement annuity contract or other such scheme for the provision of income in retirement whether or not approved by the Inland Revenue.

Calculation or estimate and period

    16.–(1)   The amount of any income to which this Part applies shall be calculated or estimated–

(a)   where it has been received in respect of the whole of the period of 26 weeks which ends at the end of the relevant week, by dividing such income received in that period by 26;

(b)   where it has been received in respect of part of the period of 26 weeks which ends at the end of the relevant week, by dividing such income received in that period by the number of complete weeks in respect of which such income is received and for this purpose income shall be treated as received in respect of a week if it is received in respect of any day in the week in question.

    (2)   Where a calculation or estimate to which this Part applies would, but for this sub-paragraph, produce an amount which, in the opinion of the Secretary of State, does not accurately reflect the normal amount of the other income of the non-resident parent in question, such income, or any part of it, shall be calculated by reference to such other period as may, in the particular case, enable the other income of that parent to be determined more accurately and for this purpose the Secretary of State shall have regard to the nature and pattern of receipt of such income.

[³*PART VI*
BENEFITS, PENSIONS AND ALLOWANCES

    17.–(1)   Subject to paragraph (2), the net weekly income of a non-resident parent shall include payments made by way of benefits, pensions and allowances prescribed in regulation 4 for the purposes of paragraph 4(1)(b) and (c) of Schedule 1 to the Act, to a non-resident parent or his partner at the rate payable at the effective date.

    (2)   Paragraph (1) applies only for the purpose of establishing whether the non-resident parent is a person to whom paragraph 5(b) of Schedule 1 to the Act applies.]

Amendments

    1.   Child Support (Miscellaneous Amendments) Regulations 2002 (SI No.1204) reg 7 (April 30, 2002).

    2.   Child Support (Miscellaneous Amendments) Regulations 2003 (SI No.328) reg 8(4) (April 6, 2003).

    3.   Child Support (Miscellaneous Amendments) Regulations 2004 (SI No.2415) reg. 7(3) and (4) (September 16, 2004).

    4.   Fire and Rescue Services Act 2004 (Consequential Amendments) (England) Order 2004 (SI 2004 No.3168) art 54 (December 30, 2004).

    5.   Child Support (Miscellaneous Amendments) Regulations 2005 (SI No.785) reg 6(5) (March 16, 2005).

    6.   Fire (Scotland) Act 2005 (Consequential Provisions and Modifications) Order 2005 (SI 2005 No. 2060) art 3 and Sch, Part 2, para 15 (August 2, 2005).

    7.   Child Support (Miscellaneous Amendments) Regulations 2007 (SI No.1979) reg 5 (August 1, 2007).

    8.   Child Support (Miscellaneous Amendments) (No.2) Regulations 2008 (SI 2008 No.2544) reg 6 (October 27, 2008).

    9.   Child Support (Miscellaneous Amendments) Regulations 2012 (SI 2012 No.712) reg 6(4) – (7) (April 30, 2012).

    10.   Public Bodies (Child Maintenance and Enforcement Commission: Abolition and Transfer of Functions) Order 2012 (SI 2012 No.2007) art 3(2) and Sch para 114 (August 1, 2012).

    11.   Police and Fire Reform (Scotland) Act 2012 (Consequential Provisions and Modifications) Order 2013 (SI 2013 No.602) art 26 and Sch 2 Part 3 para 80 (April 1, 2013).

Definitions

    "the Act": see reg 1(2).

    "child tax credit": see reg 1(2)

    "Contributions and Benefits Act": see reg 1(2).

    "Contributions and Benefits (Northern Ireland) Act": see reg 1(2).

    "day": see reg 1(2).

    "effective date": see reg 1(2).

    "employed earner": see reg 1(2).

    "home": see reg 1(2).

    "net weekly income": see reg 1(2).

    "occupational pension scheme": see reg 1(2).

    "partner": see reg 1(2).

    "personal pension scheme": see reg 1(2).

    "relevant week": see reg 1(2).

    "retirement annuity contract": see reg 1(2).

"self-employed earner": see reg 1(2).
"working tax credit": see reg 1(2).
"year": see reg 1(2).

General Note

The correct approach to questions such as those which arise under this Schedule was set out in the context of income tax law by Lord Blanesburgh in *British Insulated and Helsby Gables Ltd v Atherton* [1925] All ER Rep 623 at 637 as follows: "unless the context otherwise requires a different meaning to be placed upon them, such words as 'profits,' 'gains,' 'capital,' are to be construed according to their ordinary significance in commerce or accountancy." This approach has been followed and affirmed repeatedly, as in *Odeon Associated Theatres Ltd v Jones* [1972] 1 All ER 681 and has been applied to social security law (*R(FC) 1/91,* para 38; *CIS 5481/1997*, paras 14-15). The same approach will certainly be taken in child support law. For a discussion of this approach in the context of expenses, see the note below.

Income

This schedule is concerned with income. It, indeed child support law as a whole, is only concerned with capital in so far as that capital is a source or potential source of income. A receipt is only taken into account if it is both income and a form of income within this Schedule (*CCS 3387/2006,* paras 7-8).

Accordingly, receipts are only relevant if they are income as opposed to capital receipts, except and in so far as legislation provides otherwise (*CCS 15949/1996,* para 5). It is the nature of the payment as it is received that determines its proper classification as income or capital rather than its nature as paid (*Inland Revenue Commissioners v Reid's Trustees* [1949] AC 361). The distinction is a question of fact that depends, in a commercial context, on the accepted principles of commercial accountancy (*CIS 5481/1997*, paras 14-15). The treatment of a payment in a person's accounts is a relevant, but not a decisive, factor (*IRC v Land Securities Investment Trust Ltd* [1969] 2 All ER 430). Money received from the sale of assets which are not part of the normal subject matter of the business will be capital. In the case of drawings it is necessary to decide whether they are drawings from capital or income (*R(FC) 1/91,* para 38). Drawings from a director's loan account or current account will usually be received as capital (*CCS 3387/2006,* although in undefined exceptional circumstances they may be income *(ibid,* paras 12-13). See also the decision of the Court of Appeal in *Chandler v SSWP* [2008] 1 FLR 638, reported as *R(CS) 2/08.*

Outside a commercial context, the distinction between income and capital was considered by the Court of Appeal in *Morrell v SSWP* [2003] EWCA Civ 526 (reported as *R(IS) 6/03).* In that case, a mother had made regular payments to her daughter to meet her financial commitments following a divorce. The sums were paid on the understanding that they would be repaid as and when the daughter's circumstances allowed. The court held that the distinction depended on the ordinary and natural meaning of the words (para 31). Applying that test, the payments by the mother were income in the daughter's hands. This was not affected by the future and uncertain obligation to repay (para 33). The position would have been different if the daughter had been under a certain and immediate obligation to repay (para 33). Thorpe LJ said (para 57): "Regular recurring payments designed to meet outgoings might serve as one definition of income." Richards J left open the issue whether regularity or recurrence was essential (para 35). In *CH 3393/2003,* the commissioner held that regularity was to be found in the presence of a regular funding facility that could be used as and when necessary (para 9). In *CH 2675/2007,* the deputy commissioner held that this did not apply to money drawn from credit cards, as this was not within the ordinary and natural meaning of income (para 27). In *CCS 4380/2006,* the commissioner held that regular payments of varying amounts made to a non-resident parent by his partner so that he could meet mortgage and council tax payments were income in his hands. In *CH 1672/2007,* a husband was required to pay half of his pension to his wife under a court order. The commissioner held that, in these circumstances, only the half of the pension he retained was within the ordinary and natural meaning of income. In *CH 3013/2003,* the commissioner (without having had argument on the point) suggested that regular withdrawals under an overdraft facility were not income (para 47).

Dividend income is not income for the Schedule calculation (*R(CS) 4/05),* because it is derived from share ownership and not from employment. However, the dividend arrangement may be a sham or may not have been properly authorised by the company. Another possibility is that the income taken as a "dividend" is not in truth a dividend, because it is derived not from share ownership but from the employment. This was found to be the case in *CCS 623/2005.* The commissioner came to this conclusion in view of the amount of the payment, its method of calculation, its frequency of payment, its value comparative to the basic wage, and the choice of payments arrangements offered to employees. A further possibility is that it may be taken into account by way of a variation under reg 19 of the Variation Regulations, which has been amended to make clear that it covers income taken in the form of dividends. However, the variation route is not as satisfactory for persons with care as the Schedule assessment, because it contains discretions that do not apply under the Schedule.

The classification of drawings from a partnership was considered in *AR v Bradford MBC* [2008] UKUT 30 (AAC); R(H) 6/09. The judge decided that they were not income. As partners are self-employed, their income was the gross receipts of the partnership less deductions. Taking drawings into account could lead to double counting of income or effectively override the legislative test. The judge considered whether the drawings were in fact by way of a loan from one partner to the other. If they had been, they would have been income. However, there was no evidence to show a loan in this case.

Expenses

There is no burden of proof in relation to expenses. The tribunal should come to a common sense decision and if necessary make a fair apportion allowable and non-allowable expenses. See *R(CS) 10/98,* para 12.

The terms used in the provisions dealing with expenses are similar to those used in income tax law in ss74(a) and 198(1) of the Income and Corporation Taxes Act 1988. Accordingly the authorities on the interpretation and application of those sections may be useful in the interpreting and applying the relevant provisions of this Schedule (*R(FC) 1/91,* para 30). However, as there are differences between the relevant provisions of tax and child support law, the authorities will not necessarily be relevant (*R(CS) 6/98,* para 7). (i) In the case of self-employed earners the expenses must be reasonably incurred. There is no such requirement in tax law. (ii) In both tax law and child support law the requirement that expenses of self-employed earners must be wholly and exclusively defrayed for the purposes of the business is a necessary but not a sufficient condition for the expense to be deductible. The additional condition in each case is different. In tax law the expense must be an appropriate item to set against income (*British Insulated and Helsby Gables Ltd v Atherton*). This is not the case in child support law, although there are some items of expenditure which are expressly excluded from being deductible. In child support law, on the other hand, the additional condition is that the expenditure must be reasonably incurred. (iii) In tax law an employed earner's travelling expenses are subject only to the requirement that they are necessarily incurred in the performance of the employment (*MacLean v Trembath* [1956] 2 All ER 113 at *119, per* Roxburgh J), whereas in child support law they are subject to the same test as for other expenses (ie, wholly, exclusively and necessarily incurred). (iv) In child support law some deductions which would be relevant in tax law are expressly excluded (eg, depreciation).

Subject to the above considerations, the treatment of an alleged expense by the Inland Revenue in an individual case before a tribunal should always be considered. However, care must be taken in adopting the Revenue's approach (*R(CS) 6/98,* para 7; *CCS 2750/1995,* para 22; *CCS 12073/1996,* para 12; *CCS 12769/ 1996,* para 6). (i) As explained above, there are differences between tax law and child support law which may require a different approach. (ii) The tribunal may not know the evidence upon which the income tax assessment was calculated. (iii) In so far as this is not known, the tribunal cannot be sure that the issues have been investigated by the Revenue in the way that is obligatory for a tribunal. The different evidence before a tribunal and its assessment of the weight to be given to that evidence may, even where the relevant laws are in identical terms, justify a different application. (iv) The other party will not have had an opportunity to make representations on the point to the Revenue. (v) Moreover, the decision made by the tribunal is a separate issue from the application of income tax law by the Inland Revenue and *res judicata* does not apply. (vi) It will be relevant to consider whether there is any binding case law or statute law in the income tax context in deciding whether or not to rely on the approach taken by the Revenue (*CCS 318/1995* para 11). (vii) The revenue's decision may have been based on an extra-statutory concession which must be disregarded in the child support calculation. In view of all these factors the tribunal must make a decision, and not merely accept the Revenue's application of tax law, even if that decision is in the end the same as the Revenue's. See also the general warning against using tax reasoning in child support in *CCS 318/1995.*

Despite all the above qualifications, there are at least two cases in which it is appropriate to follow the approach taken by the Revenue in a particular case. (a) Where the sum involved is small and the other party makes no representations on the point, the tribunal may adopt the figure used by the Revenue (*CCS 12073/1996,* para 7). (b) Strictly there should be evidence from which the tribunal may calculate the actual amount spent. However, where it is obvious that there has been some expenditure and the precise amount cannot be ascertained, an estimate has to be made, and in an appropriate case the tribunal may adopt the figure used by the Revenue (*CCS 12073/1996,* para 7).

Any agreement involving the employer, the Revenue and the CMEC cannot bind the tribunal is not binding on the tribunal if it is in conflict with child support law (*CCS 318/1995,* paras 11 and 15).

"expenses"

"Expenses" bears its normal meaning as understood by the accountancy and commercial worlds and the Inland Revenue (*CFC 19/1993,* para 11). Only expenses of an income or revenue nature are covered except and in so far as legislation provides otherwise (*CCS 15949/1996,* para 5).

Expense necessarily involves expenditure. (a) Accordingly, a loss which does not involve expenditure, such as a loss on revaluation of stock, is not an expense. (b) Bad debts do not involve expenditure; they merely represent money which is due but which has not been paid. If proven, the figure for bad debts should be deducted from the income figure in the accounts; these debts are not subject to the tests for deductible expenses. They are deductible despite the lack of express provision to cover them (*R(FC) 1/91,* para 37). (c) Lost or spoilt stock is a genuine loss to the business in that the value of the stock will not be recouped through sales or work done. However, it should not be deducted as an expense. It is already covered as an expense under the figure for purchases (see below) and to include it again would be to double count it.

Expenditure on stock is an expense. The proper approach to figures relating to stock is to take the opening stock figure, add to it the purchases of stock during the period of the accounts, and then to deduct the closing stock figure (*CFC 19/1993*). The closing stock figure will be the opening stock figure in the following accounting period. If it were not deducted, it would be double counted in successive accounting periods.

Income tax and interest on any money borrowed to meet liability to income tax is not an expense (*CCS 15949/1996*, para 10). Rolled over liability for capital gains tax is not an allowable expense (*R2/96 (CSC)*, para 13).

Employed earners

In the case of employed earners, payments in respect of expenses are disregarded as earnings if they were incurred wholly, exclusively and necessarily in the performance of the duties of the employment (para 4(2)(a)). The disregard applies to expenses paid by the employer, not those paid by the employee (*R(CS) 2/96*, para 15). It applies whether the expenses are reimbursed to the employee (*ibid*, at para 15) or directly to the third party to whom they are due (*CIS 77/1992*, para 5). As interpreted, the disregard prevents the amount of the expenses being double counted, once as part of the original wages and again when met by the employer. If the employer pays the expenses without being reimbursed, there is no disregard.

Commissioners have applied the reasoning in *Parsons v Hogg* [1985] 2 All ER 897 both to expenses wholly, exclusively and necessarily incurred in the performance of the duties of the employment and to other expenses that are deductible for tax purposes (*R(CS) 2/96* and *CCS 3882/1997*, paras 29-36). *Parsons v Hogg* involved the interpretation of the brief provisions in the Family Income Supplement Regulations that governed the calculation of a claimant's income. The court used the ambiguity in the word "gross" to avoid what would otherwise have been an anomaly between the calculation of earnings from employment and other income, including income from self-employment. Gross was interpreted to mean income before the deduction of tax but after the deduction of allowable expenses. In contrast, the child support provisions are much more detailed. So far as expenses wholly, exclusively and necessarily incurred are concerned, there is specific provision and no anomaly exists between the employed and the self-employed. So far as other expenses are concerned, the question arises whether they should be added to the deductions already covered by statute by applying the reasoning in *Parsons v Hogg*. It is suggested that the reasoning in that case should not be used to extend the detailed scheme in this Schedule. This was the approach taken in *R(CS) 3/00*, para 23.

Expenses may be apportioned between business and private use (*R(CS) 4/08*).

"wholly, exclusively and necessarily"

Each of these words covers a separate requirement. Their combined effect is so strict that it has been said in the income tax context that they are "deceptive words in the sense that, when examined, they are found to come to nearly nothing at all" (*Lomax v Newton* [1952] 2 All ER 801 at 802, *per Vaisey*, J). It should not, therefore, be surprising that in the child support context their scope will be equally narrow.

The words "wholly" and "exclusively" are discussed below in the context of self-employed earners. In addition the expense must be a necessary one. The fact that the expense is related to the employment and even is beneficial to the employer is not sufficient; it must also be essential to incur the expense in order to perform the duties of the employment (*Owen v Burden* [1972] 1 All ER 356).

These words do not involve any element of subjectivity and none is imported where, in a particular case, it is necessary to estimate the amount of expenses (*CCS 12073/1996*, para 14).

"in the performance of the duties of the employment"

The expenses must be incurred in the performance of the duties of the employment. It is not sufficient that they are a necessary preliminary to or preparation for performing those duties (*Smith v Abbott* [1994] 1 All ER 673; *R(CS) 2/96*, para 27; *CCS 5352/1995*, para 12; *CSC 1/1996*, para 5).

It follows from this principle that the cost of travel to work is not an allowable expense (*Rickets v Colquhoun* [1926] AC 1), while the cost of travel in the course of work is (*Horton v Young* [1971] 3 All ER 412; *Owen v Pook* [1969] 2 All ER 1). Likewise the costs related to living in a particular place are not generally allowable. There have been decisions relating to the armed forces: expenses incurred in Army married quarters are not deductible (*R(CS) 2/96*)); a lodging allowance for an officer living in London while attached to the Ministry of Defence counted as income and was not disregarded as repayment of a deductible expense (*CCS 5352/1995*, para 12). In *CCS 318/1995* para 14, payments of an allowance to a soldier relating to living abroad on service duties were disregarded as income on the basis that they were repayments of a deductible expense. In *CCS 4305/1995*, the commissioner decided, without reference to any authorities other than *R(CS) 2/96* and *Parsons v Hogg*, that the amount spent on married quarters by an army officer posted abroad was deductible as an expense. The former case was tightly distinguished in *CCS 5352/1995*, para 14 on the basis that it applied only to the special facts of a soldier living abroad. There have also been decisions relating to police officers. Police officers may be subject to one of three arrangements in respect of subsidised housing, the actual arrangement depending upon the date of their appointment. The original arrangement was for a rent allowance which attracts a tax rebate at the end of the tax year. This was replaced by a housing allowance which attracts no rebate. The most recent appointees have no housing subsidy. In *CCS 10/1994* para 13, payments of a police rent allowance were treated as income and not as repayment of a deductible expense. This decision was not followed in *CCS 12769/1996* (para 9) on the ground that the additional factual information available as to the nature of the allowance showed that it was a deductible expense. However, in *R(CS) 10/98* paras 14-17, the commissioner held that *CCS 12769/1996* was an exceptional one which turned on its own special facts and in *R(CS) 2/99* (para 20) the commissioner reviewed various reports on housing subsidies for police officers and refused to follow *CCS 12769/1996* on the ground that the appellant in that case had misunderstood the nature of the allowance. The decision in *R(CS) 2/99* was followed by a different commissioner in *CCS 2561/1998*, para 22.

Self-employed earners

In the case of self-employed earners expenses are deducted from gross receipts in determining earnings. In order to be deductible an expenses must satisfy two tests: (i) it must have been reasonably incurred, and (ii) it must have been wholly and exclusively defrayed for the purposes of the earner's business.

The following are among the sorts of expenses which will typically be allowable in the case of self-employed earners: (i) costs related to the provision of premises – rent, rates, heating, lighting, cleaning, maintenance; (ii) wages for employees and payments to subcontractors; (iii) cost of materials; (iv) costs involved in obtaining work-advertising; (v) costs related to vehicles and travel; (vi) telephone-line rental and charges; (vii) necessary registrations such as CORGI; (viii) insurance; (ix) protective clothing; (x) accountancy fees.

In the case of a partnership, the partnership is not to be regarded (as would be a company) as a separate entity from its members nor is the position of a partner to be equated with that of an employee. The relevant purpose to be considered (see below for a discussion of purpose) is that of the individual partner who defrayed the expenditure and not the collective view of the firm as a whole or of the managing partners. See *MacKinlay v Arthur Young McClelland Moores and Co* [1990] 1 All ER 45.

"reasonably incurred"

This is a matter of judgment (*CCS 3774/2001*, para 9). There is no restriction on the factors which may be taken into account in deciding on the reasonableness of an expense. It might be considered unreasonable in view of the amount, in which case it would only be allowed in so far as it was reasonable. Another possibility is that it might be considered unreasonable on account of the nature or purpose of the expense, in which case it will be completely disallowed. Much depends on the circumstances. For example, where wages are paid to a spouse for doing the paperwork of the business, those wages might be considered too high for the work involved, in which case the amount appearing in the accounts would be reduced; or it might be that the nature and amount of the paperwork is such that the earner could cope with it without assistance, in which case no deduction would be allowed at all. Whatever its decision on reasonableness, the tribunal should explain the basis of that decision in its reasons.

"wholly and exclusively"

These words are also used in relation to employed earners. However, here they are not linked to any requirement that the expense be necessarily defrayed for the purposes of the business (*Bentleys, Stokes and Lowless v Beeson* [1952] 2 All ER 82 at 86, *per* Romer LJ).

The word "wholly" relates to the quantum of money spent (*Bentleys, Stokes and Lowless v Beeson* at 84, *per* Romer LJ).

The word "exclusively" further limits the words "for the purposes of the earner's business." It relates to the motive or object of the expenditure. The expense must be incurred solely in the performance of the duties. If it is defrayed solely for personal benefit, it is not allowable. The cost of personal meals while on business is not, therefore, allowable, because the expenditure is adequately and completely explained by the simple fact that a person must eat in order to live (*Caillebotte v Quinn* [1975] 2 All ER 412). Thus the cost of lunches taken at meetings of partners in a solicitors' firm was not deductible as an expense (*CCS 15949/1996*, para 11). If the expense is defrayed for a dual purpose, it is not allowable. An expense is not, for example, allowable if it involves the cost of travel for the purpose of attending a conference and thereby also having a holiday (*Bowden v Rusell and Russell* [1965] 2 All ER 258). However, there is no dual purpose merely because there is some element of personal benefit necessarily inherent in what is done (*Bentleys, Stokes and Lowless v Beeson*). Consequently, where the sole object of undertaking an expenditure is for the purposes of the business (eg, travelling to visit a patient in the South of France), but there is an unavoidable personal benefit also involved (the earner's stay in the South of France), the expense is potentially deductible (*Mallalieu v Drummond* [1983] 2 All ER 1095 at 1100, *per* Lord Brightman).

The conscious motive of the earner is of vital significance (*Mallalieu v Drummond,* above at 1103 *per* Lord Brightman); it was because of the admission of the mixed motives that the expenditure incurred in *Bowden,* above was not treated as a deductible expense for income tax purposes. However, conscious motive is not necessarily the sole relevant factor. Where it is inescapable that there is some other relevant object such as the provision of clothing for warmth and decency, the object immediately in the person's mind will not be decisive of the issue (*Mallalieu v Drummond* at 1103, *per* Lord Brightman). On the other hand, where some further motive is not inescapable, such as where elective surgery is involved, a finding as to conscious motive may be decisive (*Prince v Mapp* [1970] 1 All ER 519 where Pennycuick J, having held that a musician had a dual business-personal motive for undergoing elective surgery on a tendon, suggested that a finding that the musician's sole motive in having the operation related to his professional rather than to his personal life might have led to the expense being deductible.) Cases in which particular attention must be paid to motivation on account of the likelihood of there being an inescapable personal object are those which involve expenditure on the provision of the everyday necessities of life required by a living human being, such as clothing suitable for everyday use for warmth and decency *(ibid* at 1103 *per* Lord Brightman), health (*Norman v Golder* [1945] 1 All ER 352; *Murgatroyd v Evans-Jackson* [1967] 1 All ER 881), food (*Caillebotte,* above) and housing (*MacKinlay v Arthur Young McClelland Moores and Co*; *R(CS) 6/98,* para 8 where the commissioner considered it to be unarguable in the context of the case that money spent on purchasing a house was deductible, although see above for some exceptional cases). However, care must be taken in analysing the facts and applying the principles which emerge from these cases. Accommodation whilst travelling, for example to a conference, is not to be confused with the provision for housing and is not required to provide for the persons' needs as human beings since they will have homes (*Tyatkis v Ashford Sparkes and Harward* [1985] 2 All ER 916 at 933*per* Nourse, J). There may even be special facts which make the principle inapplicable in the case of meals, as in *Horton v Young* [1930] 15T C 380 (discussed in *Caillebotte*, above at 416), where the cost of meals purchased by an airline pilot while abroad and not reimbursed by the airline was allowed as a deductible expense for income tax purposes in view of the special nature of the terms of his employment.

A dual purpose is also likely to be present in the case of expenditure defrayed in pursuing professional qualification in that the qualification will probably be for the personal benefit of the earner as well as for the benefit of the business (*Lupton v Potts* [1969] 3 All ER 1083). Likewise action taken to protect professional standing is likely also to be concerned with the person's personal reputation which will inevitably be affected by the outcome of such proceedings (*McKnight v Sheppard, The Times,* May 12 1997). Nevertheless, if it can be established as a fact that the sole conscious motive was the person's business standing, the expense will be deductible *(ibid).*

Difficult issues of fact can arise when the expenses of a franchise holder are involved. In *Powell v Jackman, The Times,* April 1 2004, the taxpayer held a franchise for milk delivery. He used his home as an office, but his round was some distance away. The Court of Appeal decided that his expenses of travelling from his home to his round were not incurred wholly and exclusively for the purposes of his trade.

"for the purposes of the earner's business"

These words are inextricably linked to the words "wholly and exclusively" which are discussed above. Expenses incurred in respect of the purchase of a share in a business are not incurred for the purposes of the business, even if that money was immediately used to purchase assets for the business (*CCS 15949/1996,* para 7).

Expenditure on preventing a person being disabled from carrying on, and earnings profits from, a trade are in principle deductible *(Morgan v Tate and Lyle Ltd [1954] 2 All ER 413),* and such expenditure may include legal expenses (*McKnight v Sheppard, The Times,* May 12 1997).

In *CCS 318/1995* para 13, the commissioner expressly refrained from commenting on whether apportionment of expenses was appropriate or desirable in the child support context. However, on the basis that the position taken in income tax law and social security law will be adopted, the position is as follows. In so far as expenditure relates to both business and personal use (*R(FC) 1/91,* paras 26-35)) or to two or more businesses (*CFC 836/ 1995,* para 11), such as a telephone line rental, it may be possible to apportion it between those uses and only the relevant business portion taken into account as an expense. Any apportionment which has been accepted by the Inland Revenue for tax purposes may be relied upon by the tribunal if there is no evidence to the contrary (*R(FC) 1/91,* para 39), but tribunals should bear in mind the comments above on the value of Inland Revenue decisions in deciding whether to investigate beyond the accepted figure. Moreover, tribunals must distinguish between cases where apportionment is appropriate and cases where there is a single expense incurred for a dual purpose such that the expense is not incurred wholly and exclusively for business purposes. The test of whether apportionment in possible is whether it is possible to apportion the expense on a time basis (*Caillebotte v Quinn* at 416-417, *per Templeman* J; *R(FC) 1/91,* para 34). If this is possible, the expense is apportionable; otherwise it is not. Whether or not apportionment is possible is a question of law (*R(FC) 1/91,* para 35), but the actual apportionment is a question of fact *(ibid,* para 35).

Where an allowance is made in respect of the use of the home as an office, this should also be reflected in an apportionment of housing costs under Sch 3 para 5.

Paragraph 4(1)

This subparagraph defines the types of payment which count as earnings, subject to the exclusions in subpara (2). The definition is in two parts. The basic definition is that earnings are any remuneration or profit derived from the employment. For doubts about the precise scope of remuneration and profit, see *CCS 284/1999,* para 15. The words "derived from" are wide and cover "a quid pro quo ... whatever consideration he gets for his services" (*The Queen v Postmaster General* [1876] 1 QBD 658 at 663, *per* Blackburn J). They mean "having their origin in" (*R(SB) 21/86,* para 12). They apply even though the employment is a past one and where the payment is awarded by a statutory body such as an Employment Tribunal *(ibid,* at para 12). They cover all payments whether by an employer or by a third party, such as a tip (*CCS 1992/1997* paras 38-39), but not dividend income which derives not from a person's employment but from ownership of shares in the company (*R(CS) 4/05,* para 9). This basic definition is expanded to include the matters set out in heads (a) to (e). These heads either cover payments which are not already covered by the basic definition or avoid argument on matters that might otherwise give rise to doubt. The list is not exhaustive, so items of income which do not fall within the precise terms of a particular head may nonetheless be caught by the generality of the basic definition. In *R(CS) 8/98* para 24, the commissioner, who admitted not to have seen the terms under which such allowances are paid, thought it probable that an education allowance paid to a member of the armed forces might amount to remuneration derived from the person's employment. For another example, see the general note to para 4(1)(b) below.

If an army officer retires and is then reinstated, a reduction in pay under Art 395 Army Pensions Warrant 1977 to reflect commutations of pension are not part of remuneration or profit derived from the officer's employment (*CCS 4144/2001).*

In determining earnings the figure to be used is the amount of earnings before deduction of tax but after the deduction of expenses deductible in arriving at the taxable sum (*R(CS) 2/96*, para 17). The tribunal is not bound by any determination on this issue by the income tax authorities, but it should take such determination into account *(ibid,* para 26).

In *CCS 4378/2001,* the commissioner held that an overpayment of salary was not remuneration that was derived from the parent's employment. The overpayment arose when the parent was transferred to a different job with the same employer at a lower salary. By mistake, his salary was not adjusted for some time. The overpayment was taken into account as his income for the purposes of child support maintenance. When the overpayment was recovered from his salary in instalments, no allowance was made for the deduction. The commissioner considered two decisions of the Court of Appeal: *R v Bolton Supplementary Benefits Appeal Tribunal Ex p Fordham* [1981] 1 All ER 50 and *Chief Adjudication Officer v Leeves* [1999] FLR 90, CA (reported as *R(IS) 5/99*). He decided that the words "remuneration or profit derived from that employment" had to be interpreted in the context of the Schedule as a whole, specifically in the context of Pt I. The purpose of the calculation was to identify the net earnings that are available to the absent parent and from which the parent's liability for child support maintenance must be met. Given that there was no power to take account of the deduction by way of recovery, he considered that there was obvious sense in excluding the overpayment itself from the scope of the parent's earnings in order to prevent the parent incurring a double penalty. He found some, albeit limited, support for that conclusion in what is now para 4(2)(e), which excludes advances of salary from earnings. In applying that interpretation to the facts of the case, the commissioner emphasised that the parent was aware at the time when the overpayment was made (i) that it had occurred, (ii) the amount and (iii) that he was under a duty to repay it. This brought the case within the principle in *Leeves* and outside the principle in *Bolton,* in which these matters were uncertain.

Employment compensation

A person may receive compensation for breach of employment rights under a variety of enactments. Some of these are covered by the individual heads of para 4(1), specifically heads (a), (b) and (e). In so far as these heads do not cover all possibilities it is necessary to consider whether the payments are caught by the opening words as being "remuneration or profit derived from ... employment". Specifically these words will have to cover compensation under s65(1)(b) of the Sex Discrimination Act 1975, s56(1)(b) of the Race Relations Act 1976 and s8(2) (b) of the Disability Discrimination Act 1995. The opening general words are slightly different from those used in the social security legislation dealt with in the cases considered below, but it is suggested that the differences do not amount to distinctions which justify a different interpretation.

Payments of compensation are only taken into account as earnings in so far as they are income rather than capital payments. In particular a distinction is drawn between a payment which is calculated largely or exclusively by reference to past services and is, therefore, in the nature of a redundancy payment, and a payment which is calculated largely or exclusively by reference to loss of income. The former are treated as payments of capital and include a basic award for unfair dismissal under s118(1)(a) Employment Rights Act 1996 (*R(SB) 21/86*, para 6), compensation for injured feelings and loss of a tax rebate under the Sex Discrimination Act 1975 (*CIS 590/ 1993,* para 5) and severance payments which are based largely on length of service in the armed forces (*R v National Insurance Commissioner ex p Stratton* [1979] 2 All ER 278). The latter are treated as payments of income and include a compensatory award for unfair dismissal under s118(1)(b) Employment Rights Act 1996 (*R(SB) 21/86*) whether or not the contract of employment is for a fixed term (*CIS 590/1993,* para 7) and compensation for loss of earnings under the Sex Discrimination Act 1975 (*CIS 590/1993,* para 7). It is the essential character of the compensation which is important and this is not affected by the presence of some minor unquantified additional element (*R v National Insurance Commissioner ex p Stratton*), although where that element is quantifiable it is severed as in *CIS 590/1993,* paras 3 and 5).

In *CCS 3182/1995* paras 17-19, the commissioner considered the treatment of a sum of money paid in relation to the termination of a person's employment, such as a payment in relation to redundancy or failure to renew the employment at the end of maternity leave, whether or not the payment is called an *ex gratia* one. It was held that the payment was not part of the normal remuneration from the employment and was only to be taken into account if and in so far as it fell within head (e). Unfortunately the commissioner did not consider any of the above decisions which give weight to the opening words of this subparagraph. It is suggested that this decision is confined to payments or parts of payments made by employers the purpose of which cannot be ascertained so as to determine, in accordance with the principles set out above, whether they are income or capital receipts.

Paragraph 4(1)(a)

The inclusion of overtime is for certainty. It falls anyway within the scope of "remuneration or profit derived from that employment" in the opening words of this paragraph (*CCS 656/1997*, para 26). Payments in respect of overtime amount to earnings, even if the overtime is not guaranteed *(ibid,* para 27).

Although payments for overtime count as earnings, it is not inevitable that overtime will be taken into account in the calculation of a party's earnings for the purposes of determining net income. The calculation of earnings has to be undertaken by reference to a period. The period is fixed by reference to para 6(1) below, which provides that a period is to be selected from specified weeks in order to calculate the party's *average* earnings. Once that calculation has been performed, para 6(4) has to be considered. It provides that a different period may be used if it would allow the party's *normal* earnings to be determined more accurately. Ultimately, therefore, the purpose of the calculation to be performed is the identification of the party's *normal* earnings. If overtime payments distort the party's earnings so that the calculation carried out under para 6(1) does not reflect the party's normal earnings, a different period must be used. See *CCS 656/1997* para 28 and the general note to para 6(4) below.

The cases are likely to fall into three broad categories. (i) First, there is the case where payments for overtime are so out of the ordinary that they may be disregarded as not reflecting normal earnings. This would cover a person who received a regular basic wage, but who worked overtime on a few occasions throughout the year. (ii) Second, there is the case where payments for overtime are clustered at a particular time of the year. In this case, a separate calculation for the period when overtime was worked might be appropriate. This would cover a person who received a regular basic wage, but who worked a significant amount of overtime for several weeks, for example around Christmas. (iii) Third, there is the case where the payments for overtime are spread throughout the year. In this case, an average figure for normal earnings may be appropriate. This would cover a person whose earnings were regularly supplemented by over-time, albeit that the overtime was of varying amounts and was not guaranteed. See *CCS 656/1997*, para 30.

Paragraph 4(1)(b)
In the social security context holiday pay means pay that is dependent upon entitlement to holidays. It covers pay while on holiday and pay in lieu of holidays that are not taken, for example at the end of an employment. It does not cover pay which is compensation for the absence of any entitlement to holidays (*CIS 894/1994*). However, such pay is undoubtedly income and is part of the remuneration or profit derived from a person's employment. It is, therefore, caught by the opening words of para 4(1)

Holiday pay becomes payable on the day on which it first becomes due to be paid (*R(SB) 11/85*, para 16(1)). This mayor may not coincide with the actual date of payment *(ibid)*. The date is determined by the contract of employment. Where evidence of the express terms of the contract is not available or the contract is silent on the point, it may be possible to infer that the date of actual payment is the date when it became due (*R(SB) 33/83*, para 21(3)). This may, however, not always be possible – eg, where the practice shows no consistency.

Paragraph 4(1)(e)
See the introductory note on employment compensation.

Paragraph 4(2)(a)
See the introductory note on expenses.

Paragraph 4(2)(b)
A salary sacrifice scheme, under which an employee gives up in advance the contractual right to an amount of cash remuneration in return for the employer making a contribution to an occupational pension scheme, comes within this subparagraph (*R(CS) 9/08*).

Paragraph 4(2)(d)
In *CCS 318/1998* para 15, the commissioner defined a payment in kind as a payment that is made otherwise than in money, that is, otherwise than in cash or in some form that can be immediately turned into cash, such as a cheque. The commissioner gave a number of examples of the detailed analysis needed to distinguish between three cases. One example concerned the cost of childminding: (i) if this was arranged and paid for by the employee and the cost reimbursed by the employer, the amount is part of the employee's earnings; (ii) if this was arranged by the employee but the cost was actually paid by the employer, the amount is part of the employee's earnings by indirect payment; and (iii) if this was arranged and paid for by the employer, the benefit to the employee is a payment in kind *(ibid,* para 30).

Paragraph 4(2)(e)
This covers, for example, loans to buy season tickets and advances of monthly salary to tide the employee over the first month of employment. Advance of earnings must mean payments of earnings before the date on which the employee is contractually entitled to them. An advance is a payment on account of future earnings and will only count as such if it is expected that it will be repaid – eg, by deductions from future salary payments (*R(CS) 6/98*, para 5). It is not clear whether the sums advanced must be treated as received when they were due to be received. Producing this obvious and sensible result from the Schedule is not easy. It is difficult to avoid the conclusion that the simplest possibility of an express provision dealing with this eventuality has been overlooked. The problem could be avoided by disregarding the period covered by the advance in calculating income in reliance on the power conferred by para 6(4). Another approach would be to treat the sums as being "remuneration or profit derived from the employment" under subpara (1) on the date they were due. This is supported by the wording which refers to "advance of earnings" which suggests sums which would otherwise fall within subpara (1) and that the payment is only disregarded for the period of the advance. If the advances are regular it might be possible to infer that the contractual basis of payment has been changed and the practice taken as evidence of the terms of the new agreement.

When an advance of earnings is repaid, the person's income is not thereby reduced (*CCS 5352/1995*, para 20 and *R(CS) 6/98*, para 10).

Paragraph 4(2)(j)
This express provision avoids the need to make use of para 6(4) to produce a more accurate reflection of the parent's normal income.

Paragraph 5(1)(c)
This provision covers contributions made under retirement annuity contracts (*R(CS) 3/00*).

Paragraph 6(1)

This subparagraph and the relationship between it and subpara (4) raise complex issues of interpretation and application. In considering their relationship, it is also necessary to consider the effect of reg 2(4) above: see the general note to subpara (4).

The calculation of income must involve reference to a period. This may be fixed under this subparagraph as an appropriate period or the period covered by the cumulative earnings, or it may be a different period fixed under subpara (4). There must, however, be a period. The income is then fixed "having regard to", "considering" (this subparagraph) or "by reference to" (subpara (4)) the earnings in that period. Nowhere is it required that all the income received in that period should be counted. Accordingly, it is permissible to use a particular period but to disregard certain payments if that is necessary to identify the party's average (this subparagraph) or normal earnings (subpara (4)). Nor is it anywhere required that only income which has been disclosed should be taken into account. Furthermore, although there is no power to guess at a parent's undisclosed income, the tribunal may make an informed estimate on the basis of the evidence available, even on the basis of the evidence of one parent given at a hearing at which the other parent was not present (*CCS 7966/1995*).

Where a person's pay is calculated on a daily basis, the best selection of a period is one which covers a 30-day month and a 31-day month as there are on average 30.5 days in a month (*CCS 5352/1995*, para 21). Where there is no variation in income, the easiest calculation is to multiple the daily rate by seven.

This subparagraph falls into two distinct parts. The first provides for what has to be determined; the second provides for the evidence to be used in reaching that determination.

What has to be determined is the person's *average* earnings at the relevant week.

However, the average earnings will not necessarily be the figure used in the child support formula, as the result is subject to the moderating influence of subpara (4) which requires a comparison to be made with *normal* earnings. When para 6 is viewed as a whole, it is normal earnings that are the ultimate target at which the calculation is aimed. The reason for the structure of the paragraph is to give guidance to child support officers on what evidence to obtain and how to analyse it. The paragraph acts a guide and a framework rather than a straightjacket. See *CCS 84/1998*, para 19.

The evidence which may be used in determining average earnings is of two types.

First the tribunal must *have regard to* such evidence as is available of earnings in the appropriate period. That period must begin not earlier than eight weeks before the relevant week and end not later than the date of assessment (referred to below as the permitted period).

No criteria for fixing the appropriate period are set out, but clearly it should be the period best suited to determining the average earnings and should certainly avoid any parts of the permitted period which have any, usual features affecting earnings.

It is the earnings which must be confined to the permitted period and not the evidence of those earnings. So, for example, if the last wage slip for the permitted period is missing, regard may be had to the cumulative totals on the next wage slip which by comparison with the totals on the slip for the preceding week will allow the figures for the missing week to be identified.

The reference to "such evidence as is available" suggests that, unlike the position under the original version of this subparagraph, it is not necessary to obtain details of the earnings in the whole of the permitted period. However, the tribunal will need to have sufficient evidence of those earnings to be able to fix an appropriate period. It is also obliged to take an inquisitorial approach, and may not proceed on the basis of limited evidence that one party has produced if there are any grounds to suspect that it is unrepresentative.

The second type of evidence which may be used is the cumulative earnings from the start of the tax year containing the relevant week and ending not later than the date of assessment. This evidence must be *considered*.

There are limitations to the value of the figure for cumulative earnings and these must be investigated before the cumulative figures may be used. First, the cumulative earnings are limited to the tax year containing the relevant week. According to how the dates fall, the cumulative earnings may cover a period longer or a shorter than the permitted period. Moreover, if the relevant week falls in a different tax year from the date of assessment only the earnings in that earlier year may be considered. Second, there may have been significant changes within the period covered by the cumulative earnings, such as a pay rise or a change of duties, or they may conceal a pattern which would permit separate calculations for different periods, such as where there is a seasonal variation in earnings. Each of these points will limit the value of the cumulative figure for the purposes discussed below, and the circumstances may make it appropriate to rely on subpara (4) in order to permit reference to the earnings in the later of the two tax years, or to permit a selection of a period or periods within the cumulative earnings period. Third, if the cumulative figure contains a bonus or commission, this must be identified and isolated for the purposes of the calculation under subpara (3) and only the adjusted cumulative figure used.

The wording used in respect of each of the two types of evidence is different. The tribunal must "have regard to" the earnings in the appropriate period, while it "may consider" the cumulative earnings. The dictionary definitions of these words are more or less interchangeable. However the use of the two expressions suggests that there may be some difference of meaning in this context. This may merely reflect the different nature of each type of evidence. Alternatively, it may indicate that each type of evidence is to be used in a different way. For example, it might mean that the appropriate period consideration must always be undertaken, while the wording in respect of the cumulative earnings suggests a greater element of discretion in whether or not and, if so, how that figure should be used. Another possibility is that the cumulatively figures should only be used as a check on the appropriate period calculation.

It is suggested that these apparent difficulties disappear if the subparagraph is considered in the context of its actual application rather than its abstract meaning. The officer or the tribunal must begin somewhere, and the obvious place to begin is with the pay slips for the permitted period, as they will be the most contemporaneous evidence of earnings at the relevant time. The cumulative earnings may be used to supplement or to interpret the pay slips. Thus the cumulative earnings may be used to supply the figures from any missing pay-slips. They may also be used to help to interpret the pay slips by indicating whether payments of particular expenses are being taxed.

Once the figures for the permitted period have been obtained they, together with any supporting evidence, may paint a number of different pictures. The cumulative earnings may be used to check the accuracy of those pictures and to help to ensure that the period selected is indeed an appropriate one. First, the pay slips may suggest that the party concerned has a regular monthly or weekly income such that it matters not which period is taken as the appropriate period. In this case the cumulative earnings provide on a check that this is indeed the case. Second, there may be a pattern to the earnings, if the party is working, for example, a three week shift rota. Here again the cumulative earnings can be used as a check to ensure that the period selected is indeed an appropriate one. Third, there may be isolated pay slips which seem out of line. Here the cumulative earnings can be used to confirm whether it is proper to select an appropriate period which avoids these weeks.

In other cases the cumulative earnings may indicate the need to use some period other than an appropriate within the permitted period and in a suitable case that period may be the period to which the cumulative figure relates. For example, the pay slips may show no pattern. Here the cumulative earnings may suggest that no appropriate period can be found within the permitted period. It will then be necessary to decide if the period to which the cumulative earnings relate should be used instead. This will not necessarily be the case. There may have been a change within that period, in which case only some part of that period should be used. This can only be done under subpara (4).

If the above analysis is correct, the role left for subpara (4) is very much more limited than its role when the original version of this subparagraph was in force. It does, however, play one important role. Subparagraph (1) determines earnings at the relevant week, whereas subpara (4) operates as at the effective date. Accordingly where there has been a change between the relevant week and the effective date, that may only be taken into account by using subpara (4). See the reasoning in the general note to that provision below.

Paragraph 6(3)

This applies where bonus or commission is paid. However, it does not apply to any other type of payment which relates to a different period from the earnings with which it is paid. It does not, for example, apply to payments of a retainer or of expenses. The presence of such other payments may, however, make it appropriate to disregard particular payslips or payments in calculating earnings. It may be that this is an appropriate case in which to apply the constructive, purposive interpretation in order to fill the gap in the legislation as recommended by the commissioner in *CCS 12/94*, paras 22-34.

According to *CCS 5079/1995*, there is no power to disregard a payment which falls to be treated under this subparagraph *(ibid,* para 7) and the calculation is not affected by the choice of the period used to calculate the other earnings *(ibid,* para 9). The wording of subpara (4) is arguably wide enough to permit the choice of a different period than the 52-week period stipulated here. However, unlike subpara (1), this subparagraph is not expressly stated to be subject to subpara (4), so the better interpretation is that a tribunal has no choice but to treat a bonus or commission as laid down here. *CCS 5079/1995* was decided under the formula assessment scheme. The commissioner in *CCS 1490/2005* (para 7) applied it to the 2003 maintenance calculation scheme.

Paragraph 6(4)

This applies if the calculation does not accurately reflect the normal amount of earnings. These conditions raise a number of questions.

(i)   "Normal" means a level of earnings that is not extraordinary, abnormal or unusual (*Peak Trailer and Chassis, Ltd v Jackson* [1967] 1 All ER 172 at 176; *R v Eastleigh Borough Council Ex p Betts* [1983] 2 All ER 481 at 489-490 490 and 494; *Lowe v Rigby* [1985] 2 All ER 903 at 906 and 907; *CCS* 656/97, para 29).

(ii)   The word "calculation" only appears in subpara (1). As that word was not used elsewhere in para 2 at all before the amendment of subpara (1), subpara (4) could not initially have been limited to moderating the effect of subpara (1), but must have applied to any calculation of employed earner's earnings under any provision in para 2 (or elsewhere). The amendment of subpara (1) may have affected the application and operation of this subparagraph, but it cannot have affected its proper interpretation. Accordingly, this provision continues to moderate any calculation of earnings under whatever provision and not merely under subpara (1).

(iii)   The same reasoning shows that subpara (4) is not limited to cases where earnings have been "calculated" under subpara (1) as opposed to being "estimated".

(iv)   There is no indication of the date as at which normal earnings must be determined. It is suggested that the best interpretation is that they must be determined as at the effective date rather than as at the relevant week. This must be so; if they are determined as at the relevant week, but there has been a change between then and the effective date, the provisions which allow changes of circumstances to be taken into account do not apply.

In some cases a person's income will fluctuate so widely that there is no amount that is normal by way of earnings. This possibility is reflected in the comparative terms ("more accurately") of the wording *CCS 84/1998*, para 20.

Where the Secretary of State has used this subparagraph, the tribunal must be satisfied that its use was proper (*CCS 556/1995*, para 7). In theory this means that it is necessary to decide what the result of the income calculation would otherwise have been, since only then can it be known whether the approach authorised by this provision results in a more accurate determination. In practice it is permissible to move straight to para 6(4), if it is clear that any figure produced under para 6(1) will have to be departed from (*CCS 11873/1996*, para 8 as qualified by *CCS 84/1998*, paras 16 and 19). The need to use a different period must be established by evidence, not merely by assertion (*CCS 11873/1996*, para 8). However, in practice this may be short-circuited where this is obvious – eg, because of an exceptional payment. (*CCS 84/1998*, paras 16 and 19).

In the particular circumstances when a change in income occurs before the effective date, this has to be taken into account by virtue of reg 6(4) above. In such a case the effect of that provision should be considered before considering the use of this subparagraph (*CCS 2750/1995*, para 21).

This provision is of most assistance when special circumstances existed during the prima facie period prescribed by para 6(1) – eg, the period might cover the Christmas season when sales assistants earn overtime that is not available most of the year. However it has other uses and tribunal members will derive hours of harmless amusement from attempting to determine the normal earnings of an employment, such as that of a university canteen assistant, in respect of which there is no consistent normality. The purist approach is to look at the matter at the time the decision is being made and to rely on reviews under s17 of the Act to deal with changes thereafter. This ensures a fair calculation for the parent concerned, although it is time consuming and tedious and there is an inevitable lag between the change of circumstances and the making of a fresh assessment. An alternative approach is to take the total annual income and divide it by 52 in the sure and certain hope that over the course of a year things may average out. This brings the advantages of certainty and continuity at the expense of possible financial difficulties at certain periods of the year for a parent on low income. There is some support for this latter approach in the express provision for student income in para 6(4).

In *CCS 556/1995*, para 9, the commissioner left open whether, under the original wording of para 6(1) and (4), the use of other than a single period to calculate earnings was permissible.

The period selected under this subparagraph may extend beyond the relevant week (*CCS 511/1995*, para 17). Any agreement between the absent parent and the person with care as to the period over which earnings should be calculated should be given considerable weight (*ibid,* para 21). P60s are valuable provided they are for a relevant year; they are more likely to be available when the appeal is before the tribunal than when the case is being considered by an officer (*ibid*).

Where earnings fluctuate and are calculated over a period, there is no relevant change of circumstances every time a different amount is received. The test is whether the earnings as calculated still fairly represent the normal earnings (*CCS 511/1995*, para 21).

This is the only provision under which earnings paid every four weeks could be calculated before the amendments made from April 18, 1995 (*CCS 511/1995*).

When a calculation of earnings affects the amount of child support maintenance that has been payable in the past, it may be appropriate to average earnings over a lengthy period so that the effect of fluctuations may be evened out, but when a calculation affects the amount of child support maintenance payable for the future, it is appropriate to ensure as far as possible that payments may be met out of current income (*CCS 4221/1998*, para 13).

If the tribunal uses a different period, it must do so consistently with s20(7)(b) of the Act (*CCS 1938/2006*, paras 8 and 11).

Paragraph 6A

This paragraph provides for income to be estimated if there is no other reliable evidence. The approach in subpara (2) was endorsed by the Child Support Commissioner in *CCS 2901/2002* para 12.

Paragraph 7

In *CCS 1741/2005,* the commissioner decided that accounts could not be used for this paragraph if they did not exist at the time of the decision under appeal (para 25). This decision was distinguished by a different commissioner in *CCS 1325/2006* on the ground that there a company's accounts were not being used to determine a self-employed earner's income under this paragraph, but were being used to show the financial position of an employed earner (para 10). The commissioner left open whether *CCS 1741/2005* was correct in relation to para 7 of this Schedule. In *LW v CMEC and KW(CSM)* [2010] UKUT 184 (AAC), the judge was concerned with a former version of this paragraph, but preferred the approach in *CCS 1325/2006*.

Payments to an author under the public lending right are part of self-employed earnings (*CIS 731/2007*).

In *HH v CMEC (CSM)* [2011] UKUT 60 (AAC), the Upper Tribunal decided that a non-resident parent's profits from gambling might amount to income from self-employment. The Court of Appeal refused permission to appeal ([2012] EWCA Civ 1600) on the ground that it would be better to await the outcome of the rehearing before the First-tier Tribunal. That tribunal decided against the non-resident parent and the case came before the same judge of the Upper Tribunal again as *CCS 1290/2013*. He adopted his former reasoning and gave permission to appeal to the Court of Appeal.

In assessing a parent's income, the tribunal may make its own assessment and is not bound by the figures in the parent's tax return (*Gray v SSWP and James* [2012] EWCA Civ 1412). If the amount assessed by the tribunal is higher than that on which tax and national insurance has been paid, the amount of the excess dur must be deducted for child support purposes (*ibid*, para 3).

Paragraph 7(1)

This amended provision reverses the effect of the decision of the House of Lords in *Smith v Smith and SSWP* [2004] EWCA Civ 1318. Its purpose is to restore the link with the position in tax law (*MG v CMEC (CSM)* [2010] UKUT 83 (AAC); AACR 37, para 31).

Paragraph 7(1A)

Decision makers and tribunals are entitled to substitute figures for income and expenditure for those used in the tax calculation, provided they apply the provisions of Part 2 of the Income tax (Trading and Other Income) Act 2005 (*KB v CMEC (CSM)* [2010] UKUT 434 (AAC); *DB v CMEC (CSM)* [2011] UKUT 202 (AAC)).

Paragraph 7(2)

Tax and national insurance must be deducted even if it has not been paid (*WM v CMEC (CSM)* [2011] UKUT 226 (AAC)).

Paragraph 7(4)

The amendment requiring self-employed earnings to be calculated by disregarding an amount equivalent to any personal allowance that *"would be* applicable" overrides *R(CS) 1/05*.

Paragraph 8(1)

A person is nonetheless self-employed despite the fact that earnings are received in a lump sum (*CCS 3182/1995,* paras 9 and 13) or that the employment is pursued on a speculative basis without generating commissions or remuneration (*ibid,* para 15).

"Gross receipts" refers only to income receipts and does not include capital receipts, start up loans or the proceeds of sale of business assets (*R(FC) 1/97*).

The tribunal is not bound by any determination on this issue by the income tax authorities, but it should take such determination into account (*R(CS) 2/96*, para 26).

Earnings are not to be confused with the drawings that a person makes from a business (*R(U) 3/88,* para 12).

A tribunal has no power to guess earnings, but it may make an informed estimate and may do so even on the basis of the evidence of one parent which was given at a hearing at which the other parent was not present (*CCS7966/1995,* para 1.1). It may also obtain evidence, for example from the Inland Revenue or the Contributions Agency, of the typical earnings to be expected from a specified location in a particular locality and use these figures if the parent concerned did not co-operate by producing credible evidence of actual earnings (*CCS 13988/1996,* para 8). Other possibilities are to draw conclusions from the amount of pension contributions (*CCS 4644/1998,* para 32) or from the amount of a mortgage advance. In *CCS 2901/2002,* para 12, the commissioner suggested that the tribunal could use as an objective starting point the figures from the New Earnings Survey compiled by the Office of National Statistics and published in *Facts and Figures Tables for the Calculation of Damages for the Professional Bar Negligence Association* by Sweet and Maxwell. For a further possibility see the *Burden of proof* section of the general note to r15 of the Tribunal Procedure (First-tier Tribunal) (Social Entitlement Chamber) Rules 2008 on p832. The Commissioner's approach is now embodied in paras 6A and 9A.

Paragraph 8(2)(a)

See the introductory note on expenses.

Paragraph 8(3)(a)(iii)

This head (unlike heads (i) and (ii)) is not specific on the purpose for which the payment must be made (*CCS 3774/2001,* para 8) other than that it must be for the purposes of the business. This qualification excludes from the scope of this head interest on a liability incurred for the purchase of a share in a business (*CCS 15949/1996,* para 7).

Paragraph 9(3)

If the tribunal uses a different period, it must do consistently with s20(7)(b) of the Act (*CCS 1938/2006,* paras 8 and 11).

Paragraph 9A

This paragraph provides for income to be estimated if there is no other reliable evidence. The approach in subpara (2) was endorsed by the Child Support Commissioner in *CCS 2901/2002* para 12.

Paragraph 13A

The payments covered by this paragraph are treated as the income of the non-resident parent, although it does not expressly say so (*SSWP v RH* [2008] UKUT 19 (AAC), *R(CS) 3/09*).

Paragraphs 14-16

In *CCS 2437/2012*, the Upper Tribunal refused permission to appeal on the ground that other income could not include income from employment abroad. The judge distinguished *CCS 389/2011* on the ground that it involved different legislation. The definition of employed earner in reg 1(2) now provides for some income from employment abroad to be included.

The Child Support (Variations) Regulations 2000
(SI 2001 No.156)

General Note on the Regulations

The Child Support (Variations) Regulations 2000 have been revoked for certain cases only by the Child Support (Meaning of Child and New Calculation Rules) (Consequential and Miscellaneous Amendment) Regulations 2012 (SI 2012 No.2785) reg 10 (this revocation comes into force in relation to a particular case on the day on which paragraph 2 of Schedule 4 to the Child Maintenance and Other Payments Act 2008 (see p243) comes into force in relation to that type of case – which is December 10, 2012, only in relation to the types of cases falling within art 3 of SI 2012 No.3042 (see p767).

For other types of cases the '2003 rules', which include the Child Support (Variations) Regulations 2000, continue to apply. The Child Support (Variations) Regulations 2000 are therefore reproduced below.

PART I
GENERAL

Citation, commencement and interpretation

1.–(1)   These Regulations may be cited as the Child Support (Variations) Regulations 2000 and shall come into force in relation to a particular case on the day on which section 5 of the Child Support, Pensions and Social Security Act 2000 which substitutes or amends sections 28A to 28F of the Act is commenced in relation to that type of case.

(2)   In these Regulations, unless the context otherwise requires–

"the Act" means the Child Support Act 1991;

"capped amount" means the amount of income for the purposes of paragraph 10(3) of Schedule 1 to the Act;

[² [³...]]

"Contributions and Benefits Act" means the Social Security Contributions and Benefits Act 1992;

"couple" has the same meaning as in paragraph 10C(5) of Schedule 1 to the Act;

"date of notification" means the date upon which notification is given in person or communicated by telephone to the recipient or, where this is not possible, the date of posting;

"date of receipt" means the day on which the information or document is actually received;

"home" has the meaning given in regulation 1(2) of the Maintenance Calculations and Special Cases Regulations;

"Maintenance Calculation Procedure Regulations" means the Child Support (Maintenance Calculation Procedure) Regulations 2000;

"Maintenance Calculations and Special Cases Regulations" means the Child Support (Maintenance Calculations and Special Cases) Regulations 2000;

[¹"partner" has the same meaning as in paragraph 10C(4) of Schedule 1 to the Act;]

"qualifying child" means the child with respect to whom the maintenance calculation falls to be made;

"relevant person" means–

(a)   a non-resident parent, or a person treated as a non-resident parent under regulation 8 of the Maintenance Calculations and Special Cases Regulations, whose liability to pay child support maintenance may be affected by any variation agreed;

(b)   a person with care, or a child to whom section 7 of the Act applies, where the amount of child support maintenance payable by virtue of a calculation relevant to that person with care or in respect of that child may be affected by any variation agreed; and

"Transitional Regulations" means the Child Support (Transitional Provisions) Regulations 2000.

(3)   In these Regulations, unless the context otherwise requires, a reference–

(a)   to a numbered Part, is to the Part of these Regulations bearing that number;

(b)   to the Schedule, is to the Schedule to these Regulations;

(c)   to a numbered regulation, is to the regulation in these Regulations bearing that number;

(d)   in a regulation, or the Schedule, to a numbered paragraph, is to the paragraph in that regulation or the Schedule bearing that number; and

(e)   in a paragraph to a lettered or numbered sub-paragraph, is to the sub-paragraph in that paragraph bearing that letter or number.

Amendments

1.   Child Support (Miscellaneous Amendments) Regulations 2004 (SI 2004 No.2415) reg 9(2) (September 16, 2004).

2.   Child Support (Miscellaneous and Consequential Amendments) Regulations 2009 (SI 2009 No.736) reg 4(2) (April 6, 2009).

3.   Public Bodies (Child Maintenance and Enforcement Commission: Abolition and Transfer of Functions) Order 2012 (SI 2012 No.2007) art 3(2) and Sch para 115(a) (August 1, 2012).

Documents

2.   Except where otherwise stated, where–

(a)   any document is given or sent to the Secretary of State, that document shall be treated as having been so given or sent on the date of receipt by the Secretary of State; and

(b)   any document is given or sent to any other person, that document shall, if sent by post to that person's last known or notified address, be treated as having been given or sent on the date that it is posted.

Definition

"date of receipt": see reg 1(2).

Determination of amounts

3.–(1)   Where any amount is required to be determined for the purposes of these Regulations, it shall be determined as a weekly amount and, except where the context otherwise requires, any reference to such an amount shall be construed accordingly.

(2)   Where any calculation made under these Regulations results in a fraction of a penny, that fraction shall be treated as a penny if it is either one half or exceeds one half and shall be otherwise disregarded.

General Note

This provides for amounts to be calculated as weekly amounts (para (1)) and for rounding of fractions (para(2)). The former is in line with all calculations under the child support scheme. The latter repeats the provision used elsewhere in the scheme.

PART II
APPLICATION AND DETERMINATION PROCEDURE

Application for a variation

4.–(1)   Where an application for a variation is made other than in writing and the Secretary of State directs that the application be made in writing, the application shall be made either on an application form provided by the Secretary of State and completed in accordance with the Secretary of State's instructions or in such other written form as the Secretary of State may accept as sufficient in the circumstances of any particular case.

(2)   An application for a variation which is made other than in writing shall be treated as made on the date of notification from the applicant to the Secretary of State that he wishes to make such an application.

(3)   Where an application for a variation is made in writing other than in the circumstances to which paragraph (1) applies, the application shall be treated as made on the date of receipt by the Secretary of State.

(4)   Where paragraph (1) applies and the Secretary of State receives the application within 14 days of the date of the direction, or at a later date but in circumstances where the Secretary of State is satisfied that the delay was unavoidable, the application shall be

treated as made on the date of notification from the applicant to the Secretary of State that he wishes to make an application for a variation.

(5)   Where paragraph (1) applies and the Secretary of State receives the application more than 14 days from the date of the direction and in circumstances where he is not satisfied that the delay was unavoidable, the application shall be treated as made on the date of receipt.

(6)   An application for a variation is duly made when it has been made in accordance with this regulation and section 28A(4) of the Act.

Definitions
"the Act": see reg 1(2).
"date of receipt": see reg 1(2).

General Note
This provides for two matters: the date when an application is made and what constitutes a duly made application. Applications with respect to the same maintenance calculation may be considered together: see reg 9(9).

The date when an application is made depends on how it is made. There are three possibilities. First, the application is made other than in writing and the Secretary of State accepts the application in that form. In these circumstances, the application is made on the date when the Secretary of State is notified that the applicant wishes to make an application. See para (2). In practice, this will be when the applicant contacts the Secretary of State by telephone. Second, the application is initially made other than in writing, but the Secretary of State directs that it be made in writing. See para (1). In these circumstances, the applicant has 14 days from the date of the direction to make an application in writing. If it is either received in that time or unavoidably delayed, the application is made on the date when the Secretary of State was notified that the applicant wanted to make an application. If it is not received in that time and there is no unavoidable delay, it is made on the date when it is received. See paras (4) and (5). Third, the application may be made other than in writing. In these circumstances, the application is made on the date when it is received. See para (3).

In order to be duly made, an application must; (a) be received in accordance with paras (1) to (5); (b) be made in writing if directed by the Secretary of State; and (c) state the grounds on which it is made. See para (6) and s28A(4) of the Act.

If a parent raises points in a letter of appeal in respect of a maintenance calculation, that may be treated as an application for a variation. The matters raised may be sufficient to permit a revision under reg 3A(1)(cc) of the Appeals Regulations. See *CCS 3862/2007* para 17.

Amendment or withdrawal of application

5.–(1)   A person who has made an application for a variation may amend or withdraw his application at any time before a decision under section 11, 16 or 17 of the Act, or a decision not to revise or supersede under section 16 or 17 of the Act, is made in response to the variation application and such amendment or withdrawal need not be in writing unless, in any particular case, the Secretary of State requires it to be.

(2)   No amendment under paragraph (1) shall relate to any change of circumstances arising after what would be the effective date of a decision in response to the variation application.

Definition
"the Act": see reg 1(2).

General Note
This regulation provides for the amendment and withdrawal of applications. An application may be amended or withdrawn before it is determined. In accordance with the making of the application itself, the amendment or withdrawal need not be in writing unless the Secretary of State requires. See para (1).

If an application has been referred to an appeal tribunal under s28D(1) of the Act, the referral continues in existence notwithstanding that the application is withdrawn under this regulation. The referral can only be withdrawn by the Secretary of State under the tribunal's rules of procedure (*Milton v SSWP* reported as *R(CS) 1/07*, refusing permission to appeal against the decision of the commissioner in *CCS 1031/2005*).

An amendment in relation to a change of circumstances that occurred after what would be the effective date of the decision on the application, is ineffective. See para (2). This can only be taken into account under a new application.

The effect of an amendment or withdrawal that is received after the application has been determined will depend on the circumstances. It might be treated as an appeal, as a new application or as an application for a revision or supersession. In practice, the applicant should be given the option of how to proceed.

Rejection of an application following preliminary consideration

6.–(1)   The Secretary of State may, on completing the preliminary consideration, reject an application for a variation (and proceed to make his decision on the application for a maintenance calculation, or to revise or supersede a decision under section 16 or 17 of the Act, without the variation, or not to revise or supersede a decision under section 16 or 17 of the Act, as the case may be) if one of the circumstances in paragraph (2) applies.

(2)   The circumstances are–

(a)   the application has been made in one of the circumstances to which regulation 7 applies;

(b)   the application is made–

    (i)   on a ground in paragraph 2 of Schedule 4B to the Act (special expenses) and the amount of the special expenses, or the aggregate amount of those expenses, as the case may be, does not exceed the relevant threshold provided for in regulation 15;

    (ii)   on a ground in paragraph 3 of that Schedule (property or capital transfers) and the value of the property or capital transferred does not exceed the minimum value in regulation 16(4); or

    (iii)   on a ground referred to in regulation 18 (assets) and the value of the assets does not exceed the figure in regulation 18(3)(a), or on a ground in regulation 19(1) [¹or (1A)] (income not taken into account) and the amount of the income does not exceed the figure in regulation 19(2);

(c)   a request under regulation 8 has not been complied with by the applicant and the Secretary of State is not able to determine the application without the information requested; or

(d)   the Secretary of State is satisfied, on the information or evidence available to him, that the application would not be agreed to, including where, although a ground is stated, the facts alleged in the application would not bring the case within the prescription of the relevant ground in these Regulations.

Amendment

1.   Child Support (Miscellaneous Amendments) Regulations 2005 (SI 2005 No.785) reg 8(2) (April 6, 2005).

Definition

"the Act": see reg 1(2).

General Note

This regulation is made under the authority of s28B(2)(c) of the Act. It sets out limited circumstances in which an application would be bound to fail because one of the financial restrictions is not satisfied.

Prescribed circumstances

7.–(1)   This regulation applies where an application for a variation is made under [¹section 28A or 28G] of the Act and–

(a)   the application is made by a relevant person and a circumstance set out in paragraph (2) applies at the relevant date;

(b)   the application is made by a non-resident parent and a circumstance set out in paragraph (3) or (4) applies at the relevant date;

(c)   the application is made by a person with care, or a child to whom section 7 of the Act applies, on a ground in paragraph 4 of Schedule 4B to the Act (additional cases) and a circumstance set out in paragraph (5) applies at the relevant date; or

(d)   the application is made by a non-resident parent on a ground in paragraph 2 of Schedule 4B to the Act (special expenses) and a circumstance set out in paragraph (6) applies at the relevant date.

(2)   The circumstances for the purposes of this paragraph are that–

(a)   a default maintenance decision is in force with respect to the non-resident parent;

(b)   the non-resident parent is liable to pay the flat rate of child support maintenance owing to the application of paragraph 4(1)(c) of Schedule 1 to the Act, or would be so liable but is liable to pay less than that amount, or nil, owing to the application of paragraph 8 of Schedule 1 to the Act, or the Transitional Regulations; or

(c)   the non-resident parent is liable to pay child support maintenance at a flat rate of a prescribed amount owing to the application of paragraph 4(2) of Schedule 1 to the Act, or would be so liable but is liable to pay less than that amount, or nil, owing to the application of paragraph 8 of Schedule 1 to the Act, or the Transitional Regulations.

(3)   The circumstances for the purposes of this paragraph are that the non-resident parent is liable to pay child support maintenance–

(a)   at the nil rate owing to the application of paragraph 5 of Schedule 1 to the Act;

(b)   at a flat rate owing to the application of paragraph 4(1)(a) of Schedule 1 to the Act, including where the net weekly income of the non-resident parent which is taken into account for the purposes of a maintenance calculation in force in respect of him is £100 per week or less owing to a variation being taken into account or to the application of regulation 18, 19 or 21 of the Transitional Regulations (reduction for relevant departure direction or relevant property transfer); or

(c)   at a flat rate owing to the application of paragraph 4(1)(b) of Schedule 1 to the Act, or would be so liable but is liable to pay less than that amount, or nil, owing to the application of paragraph 8 of Schedule 1 to the Act, or the Transitional Regulations.

(4)   The circumstances for the purposes of this paragraph are that the non-resident parent is liable to pay an amount of child support maintenance at a rate–

(a)   of £5 per week or such other amount as may be prescribed owing to the application of paragraph 7(7) of Schedule 1 to the Act (shared care); or

(b)   equivalent to the flat rate provided for in, or prescribed for the purposes of, paragraph 4(1)(b) of Part 1 of Schedule 1 to the Act owing to the application of–

    (i)   regulation 27(5);

    (ii)   regulation 9 of the Maintenance Calculations and Special Cases Regulations (care provided in part by a local authority); or

    (iii)   regulation 23(5) of the Transitional Regulations.

(5)   The circumstances for the purposes of this paragraph are that–

(a)   the amount of the net weekly income of the non-resident parent to which the Secretary of State had regard when making the maintenance calculation was the capped amount; or

(b)   the non-resident parent or a partner of his is in receipt of [²working tax credit under section 10 of the Tax Credits Act 2002] [³...].

(6)   The circumstances for the purposes of this paragraph are that the amount of the net weekly income of the non-resident parent to which the Secretary of State would have regard after deducting the amount of the special expenses would exceed the capped amount.

(7)   For the purposes of paragraph (1), the "relevant date" means the date from which, if the variation were agreed [¹and the application had been made under section 28G of the Act], the decision under section 16 or 17 of the Act, as the case may be, would take effect [¹and if the variation were agreed, and the application had been made under section 28A of the Act, the decision under section 11 of the Act would take effect].

Amendments

    1.   Child Support (Miscellaneous Amendments) Regulations 2002 (SI 2002 No.1204) reg 9(2) (April 30, 2002).

    2.   Child Support (Miscellaneous Amendments) Regulations 2003 (SI 2003 No.328) reg 10 (April 6, 2003).

    3.   Child Support (Miscellaneous Amendments) Regulations 2004 (SI 2004 No.2415) reg 9(3) (September 16, 2004).

Definitions

"the Act": see reg 1(2).

"capped amount": see reg 1(2).

"Maintenance Calculations and Special Cases Regulations": see reg 1(2).

"partner": see reg 1(2).
"relevant person": see reg 1(2).
"Transitional Regulations": see reg 1(2).

General Note
This regulation is made under the authority of s28F(3) of the Act.
Paragraph (5)
Receipt in subpara (b) means actual receipt, not lawful receipt (*R(CS) 2/09*).

Provision of information

8.–(1)   Where an application has been duly made, the Secretary of State may request further information or evidence from the applicant to enable that application to be determined and any such information or evidence requested shall be provided within one month of the date of notification of the request or such longer period as the Secretary of State is satisfied is reasonable in the circumstances of the case.

(2)   Where any information or evidence requested in accordance with paragraph (1) is not provided in accordance with the time limit specified in that paragraph, the Secretary of State may, where he is able to do so, proceed to determine the application in the absence of the requested information or evidence.

Definitions
"the Act": see reg1(2).
"date of notification": see reg 1(2).

General Note
Paragraph (1)
This paragraph provides for the Secretary of State to request further information or evidence that is needed to enable the application to be determined. The power only arises if the application is duly made: see reg 4(6). So, its purpose is not to make the application effective, but to provide the Secretary of State with the information and evidence necessary to determine the application. It follows that failure to provide the information or evidence does not relieve the Secretary of State of the duty to determine the application, provided that that is possible: see para (2).
Paragraph (2)
This paragraph allows the Secretary of State to determine the application, if possible, if the information or evidence is not provided. It does not authorise the Secretary of State to disregard information or evidence that is provided late but before the application is determined. However, failure to provide the information may allow the Secretary of State to reject the application on preliminary consideration: see in particular reg 6(2)(c) and (d). See also reg 9(7) on information or evidence that is received after representations have been invited from the other party.

Procedure in relation to the determination of an application

9.–(1)   Subject to paragraph (3), where the Secretary of State has given the preliminary consideration to an application and not rejected it he–

(a)   shall give notice of the application to the relevant persons other than the applicant, informing them of the grounds on which the application has been made and any relevant information or evidence the applicant has given, except information or evidence falling within paragraph (2);

(b)   may invite representations, which need not be in writing but shall be in writing if in any case he so directs, from the relevant persons other than the applicant on any matter relating to that application, to be submitted to the Secretary of State within 14 days of the date of notification or such longer period as the Secretary of State is satisfied is reasonable in the circumstances of the case; and

(c)   shall set out the provisions of paragraphs (2)(b) and (c), (4) and (5) in relation to such representations.

(2)   The information or evidence referred to in paragraphs (1)(a), (4)(a) and (7), are–

(a)   details of the nature of the long-term illness or disability of the relevant other child which forms the basis of a variation application on the ground in regulation 11 where the applicant requests they should not be disclosed and the Secretary of State is satisfied that disclosure is not necessary in order to be able to determine the application;

(b)   medical evidence or medical advice which has not been disclosed to the applicant or a relevant person and which the Secretary of State considers would be harmful to the health of the applicant or that relevant person if disclosed to him; or

(c)   the address of a relevant person or qualifying child, or any other information which could reasonably be expected to lead to that person or child being located, where the Secretary of State considers that there would be a risk of harm or undue distress to that person or that child or any other children living with that person if the address or information were disclosed.

(3)   The Secretary of State need not act in accordance with paragraph (1)–

(a)   where regulation 29 applies (variation may be taken into account notwithstanding that no application has been made);

(b)   where the variation agreed is one falling within paragraph 3 of Schedule 4B to the Act (property or capital transfer), the Secretary of State ceases to have jurisdiction to make a maintenance calculation and subsequently acquires jurisdiction in respect of the same non-resident parent, person with care and any child in respect of whom the earlier calculation was made;

(c)   if he is satisfied on the information or evidence available to him that the application would not be agreed to, but if, on further consideration of the application, he is minded to agree to the variation he shall, before doing so, comply with the provisions of this regulation; or

(d)   where–

    (i)   a variation has been agreed in relation to a maintenance calculation;

    (ii)   the decision as to the maintenance calculation is replaced with a default maintenance decision under section 12(1)(b) of the Act;

    (iii)   the default maintenance decision is revised in accordance with section 16(1B) of the Act,

and the Secretary of State is satisfied, on the information or evidence available to him, that there has been no material change of circumstances relating to the variation since the date from which the maintenance calculation referred to in head (i) ceased to have effect.

(4)   Where the Secretary of State receives representations from the relevant persons–

(a)   he may, if he considers it reasonable to do so, send a copy of the representations concerned (excluding material falling within paragraph (2)) to the applicant and invite any comments he may have within 14 days or such longer period as the Secretary of State is satisfied is reasonable in the circumstances of the case; and

(b)   where the Secretary of State acts under sub-paragraph (a) he shall not proceed to determine the application until he has received such comments or the period referred to in that sub-paragraph has expired.

(5)   Where the Secretary of State has not received representations from the relevant persons notified in accordance with paragraph (1) within the time limit specified in sub-paragraph (b) of that paragraph, he may proceed to agree or not (as the case may be) to a variation in their absence.

(6)   In considering an application for a variation, the Secretary of State shall take into account any representations received at the date upon which he agrees or not (as the case may be) to the variation from the relevant persons, including any representation received in accordance with paragraphs (1)(b), [¹(4)(a)] and (7).

(7)   Where any information or evidence requested by the Secretary of State under regulation 8 is received after notification has been given under paragraph (1), the Secretary of State may, if he considers it reasonable to do so, and except where such information or evidence falls within paragraph (2), send a copy of such information or evidence to the relevant persons and may invite them to submit representations, which need not be in writing unless the Secretary of State so directs in any particular case, on that information or evidence.

(8)   The Secretary of State may, if he considers it appropriate, treat an application for a variation made on one ground as if it were an application made on a different ground, and, if he does intend to do so, he shall include this information in the notice and invitation to make representations referred to in paragraphs (1), (4) and (7).

(9)   Two or more applications for a variation with respect to the same maintenance calculation or application for a maintenance calculation, made or treated as made, may be considered together.

Amendment

1.   Child Support (Miscellaneous Amendments) Regulations 2002 (SI 2002 No.1204) reg 9(3) (April 30, 2002).

Definitions

"the Act": see reg 1(2).
"date of notification": see reg 1(2).
"qualifying child": see reg 1(2).
"relevant person": see reg 1(2).
"Transitional Regulations": see reg 1(2).

General Note

This regulation deals with procedure once an application has passed the preliminary consideration under s28B of the Act. It is largely concerned with obtaining and taking account of representations by the other party, but it also deals with treating the application as made on other grounds (para (8)) and with considering two or more applications with respect to the same maintenance calculation together (para (9)). There is similar provision in reg 15B in relation to the revision or supersession of the effect of a variation.

If the Secretary of State has given an application a preliminary consideration before referring it to the tribunal, this regulation can be used to obtain evidence and representations on the application before referring it to the tribunal, which will assist the parties and the tribunal in determining the application. However, there is no duty to give a preliminary consideration to an application that has failed and, if this is not done, this regulation cannot operate. Nor is there any need to operate this regulation on a referral even if there has been a preliminary consideration. The regulation lays down the natural justice requirements for a determination by the Secretary of State. It ensures that the non-applicant knows of the case being made by the applicant and has a chance to respond. The appeal tribunal does not need those provisions. It is subject to the duty to give the parties a fair hearing under both natural justice and Art 6 of the European Convention on Human Rights. See *CCS 1838/2005*, para 20.

Paragraph (2)(b)

This provision imposes a duty to withhold potentially harmful or distressing information or evidence. It is similar to the powers discussed in *R(A) 4/89* paras 6 and 7, and *CSDLA 5/1995*, paras 16-23. The following propositions emerge from the latter decision unless otherwise stated.

(i)   The provision prohibits disclosure, but does not operate to exclude the fundamental right for the other party to have a fair chance to comment on the issues raised by the application. The party must be told that information is being withheld.

(ii)   The evidence of advice must be "medical" and not merely factual non-medical information given by a doctor (*R(A)* 4/89, para 6).

(iii)   Disclosure must be harmful. It is not sufficient that disclosure would cause embarrassment or that it would cause difficulty. Distress in not sufficient unless it constitutes harm.

(iv)   The harm must be substantial.

(v)   If possible the gist of the information or evidence should be disclosed. The practicality of this suggestion has been doubted (*CDLA 1347/1999*, para 7), but it may be possible in some cases.

(vi)   Disclosure to a representative, subject to appropriate credible undertakings not to disclose to the party, may be possible.

(vii)   This provision may be in violation of the Convention right in Art 6(1) of the European Convention on Human Rights and Fundamental Freedoms in view of *McMichael v United Kingdom* (1995) 20 EHRR 205 and *McGinley and Egan v United Kingdom* (1998) 27 EHRR 1.

Paragraph (2)(c)

See the general note to s46(3) of the Act on p125 (on harm or undue distress) and under non-disclosure provisions in the tribunal's rules of procedure.

PART III
SPECIAL EXPENSES

Special expenses – contact costs

10.–(1)   Subject to the following paragraphs of this regulation, and to regulation 15, the following costs incurred or reasonably expected to be incurred by the non-resident parent, whether in respect of himself or the qualifying child or both, for the purpose of maintaining contact with that child, shall constitute expenses for the purposes of paragraph 2(2) of Schedule 4B to the Act–

   (a)   the cost of purchasing a ticket for travel;

   (b)   the cost of purchasing fuel where travel is by a vehicle which is not carrying fare-paying passengers;

   (c)   the taxi fare for a journey or part of a journey where the Secretary of State is satisfied that the disability or long-term illness of the non-resident parent or the qualifying child makes it impracticable for any other form of transport to be used for that journey or part of that journey;

   (d)   the cost of car hire where the cost of the journey would be less in total than it would be if public transport or taxis or a combination of both were used;

   (e)   where the Secretary of State considers a return journey on the same day is impracticable, or the established or intended pattern of contact with the child includes contact over two or more consecutive days, the cost of the non-resident parent's, or, as the case may be, the child's, accommodation for the number of nights the Secretary of State considers appropriate in the circumstances of the case; and

   (f)   any minor incidental costs such as tolls or fees payable for the use of a particular road or bridge incurred in connection with such travel, including breakfast where it is included as part of the accommodation cost referred to in sub-paragraph (e).

   (2)   The costs to which paragraph (1) applies include the cost of a person to travel with the non-resident parent or the qualifying child, if the Secretary of State is satisfied that the presence of another person on the journey, or part of the journey, is necessary including, but not limited to, where it is necessary because of the young age of the qualifying child or the disability or long-term illness of the non-resident parent or that child.

   (3)   The costs referred to in paragraphs (1) and (2)–

   (a)   shall be expenses for the purposes of paragraph 2(2) of Schedule 4B to the Act only to the extent that they are–

      (i)   incurred in accordance with a set pattern as to frequency of contact between the non-resident parent and the qualifying child which has been established at or, where at the time of the variation application it has ceased, which had been established before, the time that the variation application is made; or

      (ii)   based on an intended set pattern for such contact which the Secretary of State is satisfied has been agreed between the non-resident parent and the person with care of the qualifying child; and

   (b)   shall be–

      (i)   where head (i) of sub-paragraph (a) applies and such contact is continuing, calculated as an average weekly amount based on the expenses actually incurred over the period of 12 months, or such lesser period as the Secretary of State may consider appropriate in the circumstances of the case, ending immediately before the first day of the maintenance period from which a variation agreed on this ground would take effect;

      (ii)   where head (i) of sub-paragraph (a) applies and such contact has ceased, calculated as an average weekly amount based on the expenses actually incurred during the period from the first day of the maintenance period from which a variation agreed on this ground would take effect to the last day of the maintenance period in relation to which the variation would take effect; or

      (iii)   where head (ii) of sub-paragraph (a) applies, calculated as an average weekly amount based on anticipated costs during such period as the Secretary of State considers appropriate.

   (4)   For the purposes of this regulation, costs of contact shall not include costs which relate to periods where the non-resident parent has care of a qualifying child overnight as part of a shared care arrangement for which provision is made under paragraphs 7 and 8

of Schedule 1 to the Act and regulation 7 of the Maintenance Calculations and Special Cases Regulations.

(5)   Where the non-resident parent has at the date he makes the variation application received, or at that date is in receipt of, or where he will receive, any financial assistance, other than a loan, from any source to meet, wholly or in part, the costs of maintaining contact with a child as referred to in paragraph (1), only the amount of the costs referred to in that paragraph, after the deduction of the financial assistance, shall constitute special expenses for the purposes of paragraph 2(2) of Schedule 4B to the Act.

Definitions
"the Act": see reg 1(2).
"disability": see reg 11(2)(a).
"long-term illness": see reg 11(2)(a).
"Maintenance Calculations and Special Cases Regulations": see reg 1(2).
"qualifying child": see reg 1(2).

General Note
This ground of variation is made under the authority of Sch AB para 2(2)(a) to the Act. It provides for a variation on the ground of special expenses in respect of maintaining contact between the non-resident parent and the qualifying child.

Generally speaking, only travel costs are taken into account, whether of the parent or the child. There are limited exceptions for overnight accommodation (para (1)(e)) and breakfast (para (1)(f)). Otherwise, the costs of meals and entertainment are not taken into account. The cost of car parking can be a minor incidental expenses (*R(CS) 5/08*).

There are a number of possible expenses related to travel that may not be included. It may be sensible, for example, on a long ferry journey to book a seat, but it may not be "minor incidental costs" under para (l)(f). Also, the cost of a sleeper on a long rail journey or a cabin on a ferry crossing may not be "accommodation" under para (1)(e) or "minor incidental costs" under para (1)(f).

There is no justification for treating monthly expenses as if they were weekly (*R (Qazi) v Secretary of State*, reported as *R(CS) 5/04*, paras 24-27).

Paragraph (2)
The courts will not so arrange contact as to reverse or mitigate the effects of the child support legislation (*Re B (Contact: Child Support)* [2007] 1 FLR 1949).

The costs include those of a companion if this is necessary on account of the age of the child or the long-term illness or disability of the parent or the child.

Paragraph (3)
The contact on which the expenses are calculated must form an established set pattern or be a set pattern agreed between the non-resident parent and the person with care. No provision is made for a set pattern under a court order which the non-resident parent cannot afford to follow because of the amount of the maintenance calculation, unless the person with care agrees with the court so that it forms an agreed set pattern. For further commentary, see the general note to reg 15(2) and (3).

There must be a set pattern, but it need not be a rigid pattern that never varies. The issue has to be decided "with a degree of realism and common sense, bearing in mind the practicalities of the lives of separated families" (*PB v CMEC* [2009] UKUT 262 (AAC); [2010] AACR 22, para 11).

No variation can be made if the child with whom contact is being maintained is resident abroad. This is not inconsistent with the non-resident parent's freedom of movement in EC law when read in conjunction with the European Convention on Human Rights (*CMEC v NC* [2009] UKUT 106 (AAC); [2010] AACR 1).

Paragraph (4)
This prevents a non-resident parent obtaining double advantage from both the formula allowance for shared care and the variation scheme for contact costs.

A cost will relate to a period if it is incurred for the purposes of that period, even if it was not incurred during that period (*R(CS) 1/08*).

Paragraph (5)
Costs 'relate to' a period if they are incurred for the purpose of that period (*R(CS) 1/08*). Financial assistance from any source for maintaining contact is deducted. This is in addition to the thresholds in reg 15.

Special expenses – illness or disability of relevant other child

11.–(1)   Subject to the following paragraphs of this regulation, expenses necessarily incurred by the non-resident parent in respect of the items listed in sub-paragraphs (a) to (m) due to the long-term illness or disability of a relevant other child shall constitute special expenses for the purposes of paragraph 2(2) of Schedule 4B to the Act–
    (a)   personal care and attendance;

(b) personal communication needs;

(c) mobility;

(d) domestic help;

(e) medical aids where these cannot be provided under the health service;

(f) heating;

(g) clothing;

(h) laundry requirements;

(i) payments for food essential to comply with a diet recommended by a medical practitioner;

(j) adaptations required to the non-resident parent's home;

(k) day care;

(l) rehabilitation; or

(m) respite care.

(2) For the purposes of this regulation and regulation 10–

(a) a person is "disabled" for a period in respect of which–

    (i) either an attendance allowance, disability living allowance[², personal independence payment] [³, a mobility supplement or armed forces independence payment under the Armed Forces and Reserve Forces (Compensation Scheme) Order 2011] is paid to or in respect of him;

    (ii) he would receive an attendance allowance or disability living allowance if it were not for the fact that he is a patient, though remaining part of the applicant's family; [²...]

    (iii) he is registered blind or treated as blind within the meaning of paragraph 12(1)(a)(iii) and (2) of Schedule 2 to the Income Support (General) Regulations 1987; [²or

    (iv) he would receive personal independence payment but for regulations under section 86(1) (hospital in-patients) of the Welfare Reform Act 2012 and he remains part of the applicant's family;]

and for this purpose–

    (i) "attendance allowance" means an allowance payable under section 64 of the Contributions and Benefits Act or an increase of disablement pension under section 104 of that Act, or an award under article 14 of the Naval, Military and Air Forces Etc., (Disablement and Death) Service Pensions Order 1983 or any analogous allowance payable in conjunction with any other war disablement pension within the meaning of section 150(2) of the Contributions and Benefits Act;

    (ii) "disability living allowance" means an allowance payable under section 72 of the Contributions and Benefits Act;

    [²(iia) "personal independence payment" means an allowance payable under section 78 of the Welfare Reform Act 2012 (daily living component);]

    (iii) "mobility supplement" means an award under article 26A of the Naval, Military and Air Forces Etc., (Disablement and Death) Service Pensions Order 1983 or any analogous allowance payable in conjunction with any other war disablement pension within the meaning of section 150(2) of the Contributions and Benefits Act; and

    (iv) "patient" means a person (other than a person who is serving a sentence of imprisonment or detention in a young offenders institution within the meaning of the Criminal Justice Act 1982) who is regarded as receiving free in-patient treatment within the meaning of the Social Security (Hospital In-Patients) Regulations 1975;

(b) "the health service" has the same meaning as in section 128 of the National Health Service Act 1977 or in section 108(1) of the National Health Service (Scotland) Act 1978;

(c) "long-term illness" means an illness from which the non-resident parent or child is suffering at the date of the application or the date from which the variation, if agreed, would take effect and which is likely to last for at least 52 weeks from that date, or, if likely to be shorter than 52 weeks, for the remainder of the life of that person; and

(d) "relevant other child" has the meaning given in paragraph 10C(2) of Schedule 1 to the Act and Regulations made under that paragraph.

[¹(3) Where, at the date on which the non-resident parent makes the variation application–

(a) he or a member of his household has received, or at that date is in receipt of, or where he or the member of his household will receive any financial assistance from any source in respect of the long-term illness or disability of the relevant other child; or

(b) a disability living allowance [³or armed forces independence payment under the Armed Forces and Reserve Forces (Compensation Scheme) Order 2011] [²or personal independence payment] is received by the non-resident parent or the member of his household on behalf of the relevant other child,

only the net amount of the costs incurred in respect of the items listed in paragraph (1), after the deduction of the financial assistance or the amount of the allowance, shall constitute special expenses for the purposes of paragraph 2(2) of Schedule 4B to the Act.]

Amendments

1. Child Support (Miscellaneous Amendments) Regulations 2005 (SI 2005 No.785) reg 8(3) (March 16, 2005).

2. Personal Independence Payment (Supplementary Provisions and Consequential Amendments) Regulations 2013 (SI 2013 No.388) reg 8 and Sch para 24 (April 8, 2013).

3. Armed Forces and Reserve Forces Compensation Scheme (Consequential Provisions: Subordinate Legislation) Order 2013 (SI 2013 No.591) reg 7 and Sch para 17 (April 8, 2013).

Definitions

"the Act": see reg 1(2).
"Contributions and Benefits Act": see reg 1(2).
"home": see reg 1(2).

General Note

This ground of variation is made under the authority of Sch AB, para 2(2)(b) and (4) to the Act. It provides for a variation on the ground of special expenses in respect of long-term illness or disability. They are not subject to the thresholds set by reg 15: see reg 15(l).

The limited scope of the regulation is to some extent offset by s8(8) of the Act, which preserves the powers of the courts to make a maintenance order in respect of expenses attributable to a child's disability. This allows a parent with care, who is not covered by this regulation, to obtain maintenance in respect of the needs of a qualifying child, who is also excluded.

The expenses must be incurred by the non-resident parent: see para (1). So, a variation can reduce the amount of a non-resident parent's liability, but it cannot be increased on the ground that the parent or other person with care incurs these expenses.

The expenses must be "necessarily incurred": see para (1). The Upper Tribunal will have to decide whether this is limited to those expenses that are essential or includes those that, while not essential, are reasonably necessary. This condition is linked to two other requirements. The expenses must be incurred "in respect of" the items listed in para (1)(a)-(m) and they must be "due to" long-term illness or disability; as defined in para (2)(a) and (c). Taken together these impose a causation requirement. They exclude costs that would be incurred even if the long-term illness or disability did not exist. This is not always easy to identify. See further the general note to para (1)(i).

The long-term illness or disability must be that of a "relevant other child", as defined under para (2)(d): see para (1). This excludes qualifying children.

For practical purposes, this ground for a variation requires that an award of disability living allowance has been made for the child. For the exceptions, see para (2)(2)(i) and (iii).

Paragraph (1)(i): diet

There must be a diet. There is a wide range of conditions that a doctor might impose on a person's food intake. Those conditions might significantly restrict the choice of foods allowed. The issue that arise depend on the form of the diet.

One possibility is that the person might be advised to avoid particular products, like dairy produce. That would be a diet. The food bill would be reduced by the cost of the products to be avoided, but it might be necessary to replace those products with others, such as soya products in place of dairy products. The issues will be: (a) whether the additional products were essential to comply with the diet or were merely a matter of choice; and (b) whether that results in an additional cost.

A second possibility is that the person might be advised to increase the amount of particular products, like food that is high in fibre or fruit. That would usually be called a diet. It might change the balance of products already consumed or introduce new produce into the diet. It is unlikely that there were be a compensatory saving on products that were no longer needed. The issue would be whether the change in the balance of the diet resulted in an additional cost.

A third possibility is that the person might be advised to avoid certain products which would not need to be replaced. For example, a person experiencing migraines might be advised to avoid chocolate and cheese. This might be described as a diet, but it is unlikely to result in additional cost.

The diet must be recommended by a medical practitioner. It is unlikely that the diet will have been recommended in writing, although confirmation in writing should be available as evidence. If written recommendation or confirmation is not available, the issue will be whether the available evidence is credible and reliable. If the diet is a recognised one and relates to a diagnosed condition, the evidence will be more readily accepted than if the diet is an unusual one.

The diet may have been recommended in general terms by a medical practitioner, but set out in more detail by a specialist dietician who may not fall within the meaning of "medical practitioner". It is suggested that that should be sufficient to satisfy this provision.

There is no definition of "medical practitioner". It is unfortunate that the legislation does not adopt the terminology from Sch 1 to the Interpretation Act 1978 which defines "registered medical practitioner" as meaning a fully registered person within the meaning of the Medicine Act 1983. However, it is suggested that this is how "medical practitioner" should be interpreted for two reasons. First, in dealing with the retrospective effective of the registration provisions for medical practitioners, the 1983 Act (which was a consolidation Act) provides in Sch 6 para 11(1) that:

"In any enactment passed before 1st January 1979 the expression 'legally qualified medical practitioner' or 'duly qualified medical practitioner', *or any expression importing a person recognised by law as a medical practitioner* or member of the medical profession, *shall, unless the contrary intention appears, be construed to mean a fully registered practitioner.*"

The words "medical practitioner" must mean one recognised by law and it would be strange if they covered only those who were fully registered before 1979 but not subsequently. Second, although there is no general prohibition on any person practicing medicine or surgery (*Younghusband v Luftig* [1949] 2 All ER 72 at 76, *per* Lord Goddard CI), it is an offence under s49(1) of the 1983 Act to imply by the use of any name, title, addition or description that the practitioner is registered under that Act. It would, therefore, be very difficult for a person to claim to be a medical practitioner without also implying registration, with the result that, in practice, anyone claiming to be a medical practitioner would have to be registered.

In addition to the causation requirements under the opening words of para (1), the payments must be "essential" to comply with the diet. Implementing these provisions requires a comparison between the cost of the diet and the pre-diet food bill. There may no evidence of pre-diet costs (eg, because the person has been on the diet for many years) or the evidence may be unreliable. In those circumstances, an estimate has to be made of what those costs were likely to have been. It is likely that the person may have been living on limited income and the pre-diet costs will be low. See *CCS 7522/1999*, paras 24-27.

If the diet is one which leaves an element of choice in the items eaten, the test of what is essential has to be applied sensibly by asking whether the particular combination of foodstuffs eaten under the diet represents a varied and balanced application of the dietary advice. The person is not limited to the cost of large amounts of the cheapest foods on the recommended list. See *CCS 7522/1999*, para 15.

Paragraph (2)(a)(iii)

Paragraphs 12(1)(a)(iii) of the Income Support (General) Regulations 1987 covers a person who:

"is registered as blind in a register compiled by a local authority under s29 National Assistance Act 1948 (Welfare services) or, in Scotland, has been certified as blind and in consequence he is registered as blind in a register maintained by or on behalf of a regional or islands council".

Paragraph 12(2) provides:

"For the purposes of subparagraph (1)(a)(iii), a person who has ceased to be registered as blind on regaining his eyesight shall nevertheless be treated as satisfying the additional condition set out in that subparagraph for a period of 28 weeks following the date on which he ceased to be so registered."

Paragraph (2)(c)

The likely duration of an illness must be determined from the point of view of the date of the application for a direction without regard to circumstances that were not obtaining at that date (*CCS 7522/1999*, para 19).

Special expenses – prior debts

12.–(1)   Subject to the following paragraphs of this regulation and regulation 15, the repayment of debts to which paragraph (2) applies shall constitute expenses for the purposes of paragraph 2(2) of Schedule 4B to the Act where those debts were incurred–

(a)   before the non-resident parent became a non-resident parent in relation to the qualifying child; and

(b)   at the time when the non-resident parent and the person with care in relation to the child referred to in sub-paragraph (a) were a couple.

(2)   This paragraph applies to debts incurred–

(a)   for the joint benefit of the non-resident parent and the person with care;

(b)   for the benefit of the person with care where the non-resident parent remains legally liable to repay the whole or part of the debt;

(c)   for the benefit of any person who is not a child but who at the time the debt was incurred–

(i)   was a child;

(ii)   lived with the non-resident parent and the person with care; and

(iii)   of whom the non-resident parent or the person with care is the parent, or both are the parents;

(d)   for the benefit of the qualifying child referred to in paragraph (1); or

(e)   for the benefit of any child, other than the qualifying child referred to in paragraph (1), who, at the time the debt was incurred–

(i)   lived with the non-resident parent and the person with care; and

(ii)   of whom the person with care is the parent.

(3)   Paragraph (1) shall not apply to repayment of–

(a)   a debt which would otherwise fall within paragraph (1) where the non-resident parent has retained for his own use and benefit the asset in connection with the purchase of which he incurred the debt;

(b)   a debt incurred for the purposes of any trade or business;

(c)   a gambling debt;

(d)   a fine imposed on the non-resident parent;

[¹(e)   unpaid legal costs in respect of–

(i)   separation or divorce from the person with care;

(ii)   separation from the person with care or the dissolution of a civil partnership that had been formed with the person with care;]

(f)   amounts due after use of a credit card;

(g)   a debt incurred by the non-resident parent to pay any of the items listed in sub-paragraphs (c) to (f) and (j);

(h)   amounts payable by the non-resident parent under a mortgage or loan taken out on the security of any property except where that mortgage or loan was taken out to facilitate the purchase of, or to pay for repairs or improvements to, any property which is the home of the person with care and any qualifying child;

(i)   amounts payable by the non-resident parent in respect of a policy of insurance except where that policy of insurance was obtained or retained to discharge a mortgage or charge taken out to facilitate the purchase of, or to pay for repairs or improvements to, any property which is the home of the person with care and the qualifying child;

(j)   a bank overdraft except where the overdraft was at the time it was taken out agreed to be for a specified amount repayable over a specified period;

(k)   a loan obtained by the non-resident parent other than a loan obtained from a qualifying lender or the non-resident parent's current or former employer;

(l)   a debt in respect of which a variation has previously been agreed and which has not been repaid during the period for which the maintenance calculation which took account of the variation was in force; or

(m)   any other debt which the Secretary of State is satisfied it is reasonable to exclude.

(4)   Except where the repayment is of an amount which is payable under a mortgage or loan or in respect of a policy of insurance which falls within the exception set out in sub-paragraph (h) or (i) of paragraph (3), repayment of a debt shall not constitute

expenses for the purposes of paragraph (1) where the Secretary of State is satisfied that the non-resident parent has taken responsibility for repayment of that debt as, or as part of, a financial settlement with the person with care or by virtue of a court order.

(5)   Where an applicant has incurred a debt partly to repay a debt repayment of which would have fallen within paragraph (1), the repayment of that part of the debt incurred which is referable to the debt repayment of which would have fallen within that paragraph shall constitute expenses for the purposes of paragraph 2(2) of Schedule 4B to the Act.

(6)   For the purposes of this regulation and regulation 14–

(a)   "qualifying lender" has the meaning given to it in section 376(4) of the Income and Corporation Taxes Act 1988; and

(b)   "repairs or improvements" means major repairs necessary to maintain the fabric of the home and any of the following measures–

    (i)   installation of a fixed bath, shower, wash basin or lavatory, and necessary associated plumbing;

    (ii)   damp-proofing measures;

    (iii)   provision or improvement of ventilation and natural light;

    (iv)   provision of electric lighting and sockets;

    (v)   provision or improvement of drainage facilities;

    (vi)   improvement of the structural condition of the home;

    (vii)   improvements to the facilities for the storing, preparation and cooking of food;

    (viii) provision of heating, including central heating;

    (ix)   provision of storage facilities for fuel and refuse;

    (x)   improvements to the insulation of the home; or

    (xi)   other improvements which the Secretary of State considers reasonable in the circumstances.

Amendment

1.   Civil Partnership (Pensions, Social Security and Child Support) (Consequential, etc. Provisions) Order 2005 (SI 2005 No.2877) art 2(4) and Sch 4 para 8 (December 5, 2005).

Definitions

"the Act": see reg 1(2).
"Contributions and Benefits Act": see reg 1(2).
"home": see reg 1(2).

General Note

This ground of variation is made under the authority of Sch 4B para 2(2)(c) to the Act. It provides for a variation on the ground of debts incurred by the non-resident parent while that parent and the person with care were a couple.

Paragraph (1)

This paragraph limits the debts by reference to the status of the non-resident parent. Debts are only relevant if they were incurred (a) before the non-resident parent became a non-resident parent in relation to the qualifying child and (b) while the non-resident parent and the person with care were a couple. These limitations are illustrated by a debt incurred to meet the costs of the wedding of the parents of a qualifying child. If they were living together before their marriage and when the debt was incurred, this paragraph is satisfied. If they were not living together at either of those times, it is not.

Paragraph (2)

This paragraph limits the debts by reference to the persons for whose benefit the debt was incurred.

Paragraph (3)

This paragraph limits the debts by reference to their nature or purpose.

In *CCS 3674/2007*, the commissioner considered how various provisions of this paragraph applied in the context of a joint mortgage to fund the building of a house on land already owned by the couple. After their divorce, the property could not be sold. The father remained in occupation with one of their children, while the wife used the garage for her car and the fields for her horses.

Head (b)

It is unclear whether "trade and business" includes a profession. The scope of the expression depends on the context (*Stuchbery and Son v General Accident Fire and Life Assurance Corporation Ltd* [1949] 1 All ER 1026 at 1027-1028, *per* Lord Greene MR and *Rolls v Miller* (1884) 27 ChD 71 at 88, *per* Lindley LJ). In this context, it is suggested that profession is included; otherwise the head is anomalously restricted.

Head (j)

Amounts due after the use of a credit card are excluded for practical considerations. It may be difficult, if not practically impossible, to identify after a period of time the amount owing that is attributable to a particular transaction. For convenience of operation, this exclusion covers all uses of a credit card, even if the amount attributable to the transaction can be identified.

There is no statutory definition of "credit card" either in the child support legislation or, despite detailed legislation regulating banking and other financial services, elsewhere. The reason lies in the fact that it is not necessary for regulatory purposes to distinguish between credit cards and other simple means of providing credit. In practice, consumers use cards with four functions, some of them combined in a single card. A cheque guarantee card provides a guarantee by a bank that a cheque will be honoured up to the maximum specified on the card. A debit card authorises the debiting of cash or payment for goods or services from the consumer's account, either immediately or after a short delay. A charge card allows short-term credit, although the whole amount must be cleared by a specified date within a month or so. Only a credit card allows long-term credit, subject to a minimum monthly payment and to the charging of interest. It is suggested that this regulation is limited to the final type of card, as it is the only one that creates difficulties in linking the current amount outstanding to a particular transaction.

The use of a credit card constitutes absolute discharge of the consumer's obligation to pay for the goods or services supplied. The supplier's only recourse is against the card provider, not against the customer. See *Re Charge Card Services Ltd* [1988] 3 All ER 702. The consequence of this is that it is impossible to take account of the debt underlying the credit card transaction, because it does not exist.

Head (h)

This head does not apply if the mortgage or loan relates to the purchase, repair or improvement of the home of the person with care or the qualifying child. The relevant time at which the property must be their home is the time of the application for a variation (*CCS 1645/2000*, para 15). The purpose of the loan must be judged at the date of the application (*R(IS) 5/03*, para 10).

"Repairs or improvements" is defined in para (6)(b). See the general note to that provision.

Head (k)

"Qualifying lender" is defined in para (6)(a).

"Employer" is someone who employs a person under a contract of service. It does not include a person who engages someone as an independent contractor under a contract for services (*R(CS) 3/03*, para 8).

Head (m)

A tribunal must make a finding on the purposes for which each debt was incurred and make a decision whether each debt is excluded under this head. Debts cannot be excluded under this head just because the money was used on day to day living expenses, although it could be reasonable to exclude debts incurred in supporting an extravagant lifestyle or in purchasing items that are not reasonably required. See *R(CS) 3/02*, para 8.

Paragraph (4)

This paragraph excludes debts for which the non-resident parent assumed responsibility in a financial settlement with the person with care or by virtue of a court order. This ensures that the effects of settlements are only considered under Sch 4B, para 3 to the Act.

Paragraph (5)

This paragraph extends the scope of this regulation to debts or parts of debts that are incurred in order to discharge a debt that qualifies under this ground. It covers both (a) new debts that are incurred partly to replace the old debt and (b) new debts that are incurred solely to replace the old debt (*R(CS) 3/03*, para 17).

Paragraph (6)

Head (a)

Although the opening words of this paragraph apply the definitions to reg 14, the expression "qualifying lender" is not used there, although "lender" is. See the general note to reg 14(2).

Head (b)

This head distinguishes between repairs and other measures. The latter is defined, the former is not.

Repair covers both the remedying of defects and preventative steps taken to avoid the need for repairs in the future, such as painting a house to preserve the woodwork (*CSB 420/1985*, paras 11-12). However, if it is alleged that the step taken was preventative, evidence and findings of fact will be needed on whether the work may properly be considered as undertaken as a repair or only as a cosmetic measure *(ibid,* para 12). If, for example, the painting of a house is being considered, it will be necessary to inquire into the state of the paint work at the time and whether the work was merely to change the colour.

Repairs must be *"necessary* to maintain the fabric of the home"; a strict test. They must also be "major". Whether a repair is or is not a major repair is a question of fact (*CSB265/1987*, para 10). It is a comparative term whose meaning is bound to be somewhat fluid and imprecise, but it will always be relevant to take into account the cost as well as the nature of and the time taken for the work *(ibid,* paras 10 and 12). Chimney sweeping cannot be a repair *(ibid,* para 7). If the home consists of a flat or some other part of a building, repairs to the rest of the building are not repairs to the fabric of the home (*CIS616/1992*, para 16).

Most of the other "measures" are defined in terms of improvement or provision.

The reasonableness of the improvement is only relevant under (xi). None of the measures is linked to the improvement of the fitness of the home for habitation or occupation, although this will be a relevant fact in determining reasonableness under (xi).

Improvement If a measure is defined in terms of improvement, it is necessary to identify the state of the home before the measure was undertaken in order to determine whether there was a deficiency to be remedied (*CSCS 3/1996*, para 4).

Provision The commissioners in their social security jurisdiction held that provision can include replacement if the state of the item replaced is so bad as to affect the fitness for habitation or occupation of the home. As the child support scheme contains no reference to fitness for habitation or occupation, the social security decision do not necessarily apply.

Reasonableness This allows some of the limitations in the definitions of the other measures to be bypassed. For example, a sink is not within (i), but it may be a reasonable improvement under (xi). Reasonableness is not determined either subjectively or objectively. It must be determined on an overall view in the broadest possible terms. This involves balancing the advantage of the improvement to the person carrying it out against the consequences viewed objectively. An extension to accommodate a large family, for example, might be reasonable, despite the fact that it would not be reflected in an increase in the value of the home, whereas a similar extension built when most of the family were about to leave home would not be (*R(IS) 3/95*, para 8).

Special expenses – boarding school fees

13.–(1)   Subject to the following paragraphs of this regulation and regulation 15, the maintenance element of the costs, incurred or reasonably expected to be incurred, by the non-resident parent for the purpose of the attendance at a boarding school of the qualifying child shall constitute expenses for the purposes of paragraph 2(2) of Schedule 4B to the Act.

(2)   Where the Secretary of State considers that the costs referred to in paragraph (1) cannot be distinguished with reasonable certainty from other costs incurred in connection with the attendance at boarding school by the qualifying child, he may instead determine the amount of those costs and any such determination shall not exceed 35% of the total costs.

(3)   Where–

(a)   the non-resident parent has at the date the variation application is made, received, or at that date is in receipt of, financial assistance from any source in respect of the boarding school fees; or

(b)   the boarding school fees are being paid in part by the non-resident parent and in part by another person,

a portion of the costs incurred by the non-resident parent in respect of the boarding school fees shall constitute special expenses for the purposes of paragraph 2(2) of Schedule 4B to the Act being the same proportion as the maintenance element of the costs bears to the total amount of the costs.

(4)   No variation on this ground shall reduce by more than 50% the income to which the Secretary of State would otherwise have had regard in the calculation of maintenance liability.

(5)   For the purposes of this regulation, "boarding school fees" means the fees payable in respect of attendance at a recognised educational establishment providing full-time education which is not advanced education for children under the age of 19 and where some or all of the pupils, including the qualifying child, are resident during term time.

Definitions

"the Act": see reg 1(2).

"qualifying child": see reg 1(2).

General Note

This ground of variation is made under the authority of Sch 4B para 2(2) (d) and (5) to the Act. It provides for a variation on the ground of special expenses in respect of maintaining a qualifying child at a boarding school. This may to some extent offset the effect of the power of the courts, preserved under s8(7) of the Act, to make a maintenance order in respect of expenses incurred in connection with receiving instruction at an education establishment.

The expenses are those incurred or reasonably expected to be incurred by the non-resident parent: see para (1). They are limited to the maintenance element of the costs: see para (1). If that amount cannot be distinguished with reasonable certainty, the Secretary of State may determine the amount, subject to a ceiling of 35 per cent of the total costs: see para (2). No doubt, there will be disputes about the amounts that are included in the "total costs". For example, are additional costs of school trips included?

There are a number of limitations on the financial amounts under this regulation: (a) the regulation is subject to the thresholds under reg 15; (b) the Secretary of State's determination of maintenance costs is subject to a 35 per cent ceiling under para (2); (c) the costs are apportioned under para (3) if the non-resident parent and another person share the costs; (d) the variation must not reduce the relevant income by more than 50 per cent.

Special expenses – payments in respect of certain mortgages, loans or insurance policies

14.–(1)   Subject to regulation 15, the payments to which paragraph (2) applies shall constitute expenses for the purposes of paragraph 2(2) of Schedule 4B to the Act.

(2)   This paragraph applies to payments, whether made to the mortgagee, lender, insurer or the person with care–

(a)   in respect of a mortgage or loan where–

   (i)   the mortgage or loan was taken out to facilitate the purchase of, or repairs or improvements to, a property ("the property") by a person other than the non-resident parent;

   (ii)   the payments are not made under a debt incurred by the non-resident parent or do not arise out of any other legal liability of his for the period in respect of which the variation is applied for;

   (iii)   the property was the home of the applicant and the person with care when they were a couple and remains the home of the person with care and the qualifying child; and

   (iv)   the non-resident parent has no legal or equitable interest in and no charge or right to have a charge over the property; or

(b)   of amounts payable in respect of a policy of insurance taken out for the discharge of a mortgage or loan referred to in sub-paragraph (a), including an endowment policy, except where the non-resident parent is entitled to any part of the proceeds on the maturity of that policy.

Definitions
"the Act": see reg 1(2).
"couple": see reg 1(2).
"home": see reg 1(2).
"qualifying child": see reg 1(2).
"repairs or improvements": see reg 12(6)(b).

General Note
This ground of variation is made under the authority of Sch 4B, para 2(2)(e) to the Act. It provides for a variation on the ground of special expenses in respect of purchasing or maintaining the former matrimonial home. This protects the non-resident parent who is meeting all or part of the person with care's housing costs. However, it only applies if the non-resident parent has no interest in or charge over the former home and, in the case of an endowment policy, no right to any part of the proceeds on maturity. That excludes non-resident parents who have transferred their interest in the former matrimonial home to the parent with care, but who are still parties to the mortgage because the mortgagee will not agree to their release.
Paragraph (2)
"Lender" is not defined. However, reg 12(6)(a) contains a definition of "qualifying lender" and the opening words of that paragraph apply the definitions to reg 14. That may suggest that lender means qualifying lender.

Thresholds for and reduction of amount of special expenses

15.–(1)   Subject to paragraphs (2) to (4), the costs or repayments referred to in regulations 10 and 12 to 14 shall be special expenses for the purposes of paragraph 2(2) of Schedule 4B to the Act where and to the extent that they exceed the threshold amount, which is–

(a)   £15 per week where the expenses fall within only one description of expenses and, where the expenses fall within more than one description of expenses, £15 per week in respect of the aggregate of those expenses, where the relevant net weekly income of the non-resident parent is £200 or more; or

(b)   £10 per week where the expenses fall within only one description of expenses, and, where the expenses fall within more than one description of expenses, £10 per week in respect of the aggregate of those expenses, where the relevant net weekly income is below £200.

(2)   Subject to paragraph (3), where the Secretary of State considers any expenses referred to in regulations 10 to 14 to be unreasonably high or to have been unreasonably incurred he may substitute such lower amount as he considers reasonable, including an amount which is below the threshold amount or a nil amount.

(3)   Any lower amount substituted by the Secretary of State under paragraph (2) in relation to contact costs under regulation 10 shall not be so low as to make it impossible, in the Secretary of State's opinion, for contact between the non-resident parent and the qualifying child to be maintained at the frequency specified in any court order made in respect of the non-resident parent and that child where the non-resident parent is maintaining contact at that frequency.

(4)   For the purposes of this regulation, "relevant net weekly income" means the net weekly income taken into account for the purposes of the maintenance calculation before taking account of any variation on the grounds of special expenses.

Definitions

"the Act": see reg 1(2).
"qualifying child": see reg 1(2).

General Note

This regulation sets thresholds for the special expenses grounds of a variation, except for those covered reg 11. The nature of the expenses covered by reg 11 makes further thresholds inappropriate.

There are two thresholds: (a) only expenses over a threshold amount are taken into account under para (1); and (b) expenses may be reduced or disregarded under paras (2) and (3).

Paragraph (1)

Only expenses in excess of the threshold amount are taken into account: see para.(I). That amount depends on the non-resident parent's relevant weekly net income, as defined in para (4). If it is £200 or more, the amount is £15. If the income is below £200, the amount is £10. This differential treatment according to income is authorised by Sch 4B para 5(5) to the Act.

Paragraphs (2) and (3)

Expenses can be reduced or disregarded if they are unreasonably high or unreasonably incurred: see para (2).

In the case of contact costs under reg 10, the reduction must allow the non-resident parent to continue to maintain contact at the frequency allowed by a court order: see para (3). There is a problem for a non-resident parent who is prevented from maintaining contact at the frequency set by a court order on account of the amount of the maintenance calculation. Paragraph (3) suggests that expenses should be allowed that are sufficient for this frequency of contact to be established. However, contact that could be made under a court order can only be taken into account under reg 10 if it is actually being maintained. It seems that para (3) does not tie in with reg 10 as intended.

PART IV
PROPERTY OR CAPITAL TRANSFERS

Prescription of terms

16.–(1)   For the purposes of paragraphs 3(1)(a) and (b) of Schedule 4B to the Act–

(a)   a court order means an order made–

    (i)   under one or more of the enactments listed in or prescribed under section 8(11) of the Act; and

    (ii)   in connection with the transfer of property of a kind defined in paragraph (2); and

(b)   an agreement means a written agreement made in connection with the transfer of property of a kind defined in paragraph (2).

(2)   Subject to paragraphs (3) and (4), for the purposes of paragraph 3(2) of Schedule 4B to the Act, a transfer of property is a transfer by the non-resident parent of his beneficial interest in any asset to the person with care, to the qualifying child, or to trustees where the object or one of the objects of the trust is the provision of maintenance.

(3)   Where a transfer of property would not have fallen within paragraph (2) when made but the Secretary of State is satisfied that some or all of the amount of that property was subsequently transferred to the person currently with care of the qualifying child, the transfer of that property to the person currently with care shall constitute a transfer of property for the purposes of paragraph 3 of Schedule 4B to the Act.

(4)   The minimum value for the purposes of paragraph 3(2) of Schedule 4B to the Act is the threshold amount which is [[1]£4999.99].

Amendment

   1.   Child Support (Miscellaneous Amendments) Regulations 2002 (SI 2002 No.1204) reg 9(4) (April 30, 2002).

Definitions

   "the Act": see reg 1(2).
   "qualifying child": see reg 1(2).

General Note

   See the general note to Sch 4B para 3 to the Act on p170.

Value of a transfer of property – equivalent weekly value

17.–(1)   Where the conditions specified in paragraph 3 of Schedule 4B to the Act are satisfied, the value of a transfer of property for the purposes of that paragraph shall be that part of the transfer made by the non-resident parent (making allowances for any transfer by the person with care to the non-resident parent) which the Secretary of State is satisfied is in lieu of periodical payments of maintenance.

(2)   The Secretary of State shall, in determining the value of a transfer of property in accordance with paragraph (1), assume that, unless evidence to the contrary is provided to him–

   (a)   the person with care and the non-resident parent had equal beneficial interests in the asset in relation to which the court order or agreement was made;

   (b)   where the person with care was married to the non-resident parent, one half of the value of the transfer was a transfer for the benefit of the person with care; and

   (c)   where the person with care has never been married to the non-resident parent, none of the value of the transfer was for the benefit of the person with care.

(3)   The equivalent weekly value of a transfer of property shall be determined in accordance with the provisions of the Schedule.

(4)   For the purposes of regulation 16 and this regulation, the term "maintenance" means the normal day-to-day living expenses of the qualifying child.

(5)   A variation falling within paragraph (1) shall cease to have effect at the end of the number of years of liability, as defined in paragraph 1 of the Schedule, for the case in question.

Definitions

   "the Act": see reg 1(2).
   "qualifying child": see reg 1(2).

General Note

   This regulation provides for the effect of satisfying the conditions set out in Sch 4B para 3 to the Act, as supplemented by reg 16.

   Paragraph (1)

   This paragraph requires that the part of the transfer that led to the reduction in maintenance be identified. That capital sum is then converted to an equivalent weekly value under the Schedule to these Regulations.

   Paragraph (2)

   This paragraph lays down realistic but rebuttable presumptions that assist in identifying (a) the amount of the transfer and (b) the extent to which it was in lieu of maintenance for the child. In practice, the value of those presumptions is likely to be reduced by the frequency with which they are challenged.

PART V
ADDITIONAL CASES

Assets

18.–(1)   Subject to paragraphs (2) and (3), a case shall constitute a case for the purposes of paragraph 4(1) of Schedule 4B to the Act where the Secretary of State is satisfied there is an asset–

(a)   in which the non-resident parent [¹has a beneficial interest], or which the non-resident parent has the ability to control;

(b)   which has been transferred by the non-resident parent to trustees, and the non-resident parent is a beneficiary of the trust so created, in circumstances where the Secretary of State is satisfied the non-resident parent has made the transfer to reduce the amount of assets which would otherwise be taken into account for the purposes of a variation under paragraph 4(1) of Schedule 4B to the Act; or

(c)   which has become subject to a trust created by legal implication of which the non-resident parent is a beneficiary.

(2)   For the purposes of this regulation "asset" means–

(a)   money, whether in cash or on deposit, including any which, in Scotland, is monies due or an obligation owed, whether immediately payable or otherwise and whether the payment or obligation is secured or not and the Secretary of State is satisfied that requiring payment of the monies or implementation of the obligation would be reasonable;

(b)   a legal estate or beneficial interest in land and rights in or over land;

(c)   shares as defined in section 744 of the Companies Act 1985, stock and unit trusts as defined in section 6 of the Charging Orders Act 1979, gilt-edged securities as defined in Part 1 of Schedule 9 to the Taxation of Chargeable Gains Act 1992, and other similar financial instruments; or

(d)   a chose in action which has not been enforced when the Secretary of State is satisfied that such enforcement would be reasonable,

and includes any such asset located outside Great Britain.

(3)   Paragraph (2) shall not apply–

[²(a)   where the total value of the assets referred to in that paragraph does not exceed £65,000 after deduction of–

(i)   the amount owing under any mortgage or charge on those assets;

(ii)   the value of any asset in respect of which income has been taken into account under regulation 19(1A);]

(b)   in relation to any asset which the Secretary of State is satisfied is being retained by the non-resident parent to be used for a purpose which the Secretary of State considers reasonable in all the circumstances of the case;

(c)   to any asset received by the non-resident parent as compensation for personal injury suffered by him;

(d)   [¹except where the asset is of a type specified in paragraph (2)(b) and produces income which does not form part of the net weekly income of the non-resident parent as calculated or estimated under Part III of the Schedule to the Maintenance Calculations and Special Cases Regulations,] to any asset used in the course of a trade or business; or

(e)   to property which is the home of the non-resident parent or any child of his[¹; or

(f)   where, were the non-resident parent a claimant, paragraph 22 (treatment of payments from certain trusts) or 64 (treatment of relevant trust payments) of Schedule 10 to the Income Support (General) Regulations 1987 would apply to the asset referred to in that paragraph].

(4)   For the purposes of this regulation, where any asset is held in the joint names of the non-resident parent and another person the Secretary of State shall assume, unless evidence to the contrary is provided to him, that the asset is held by them in equal shares.

(5)   Where a variation is agreed on the ground that the non-resident parent has assets for which provision is made in this regulation, the Secretary of State shall calculate the weekly value of the assets by applying the statutory rate of interest to the value of the

assets and dividing by 52, and the resulting figure, aggregated with any benefit, pension or allowance [¹prescribed for the purposes of paragraph 4(1)(b) of Schedule 1 to the Act] which the non-resident parent receives, other than any benefits referred to in regulation 26(3), shall be taken into account as additional income under regulation 25.

(6) For the purposes of this regulation, the "statutory rate of interest" means interest at the statutory rate prescribed for a judgment debt or, in Scotland, the statutory rate in respect of interest included in or payable under a decree in the Court of Session, which in either case applies on the date from which the maintenance calculation which takes account of the variation takes effect.

Amendments

1.   Child Support (Miscellaneous Amendments) Regulations 2002 (SI 2002 No.1204) reg 9(5) and (6) (April 30, 2002).
2.   Child Support (Miscellaneous Amendments) Regulations 2005 (SI 2005 No.785) reg 8(4) (April 6, 2005).

Definitions

"the Act": see reg 1(2).
"home": see reg 1(2).
"Maintenance Calculations and Special Cases Regulations": see reg 1(2).

General Note

This ground of variation is made under the authority of Sch 4B para 4(2)(a) to the Act. In effect, this regulation provides for a notional income to be attributed to a non-resident parent's specified capital assets that in aggregate exceed a minimum value.

The application of this regulation may vary according to how the items under consideration are viewed. Some may be viewed individually as a parcel. For example, a farm may be viewed as a single asset or as a parcel consisting of a number of assets, like the farmhouse and land. The Secretary of State and the tribunal are entitled to treat the items individually or collectively if both views are appropriate. See *CCS 8/2000*, para 16.

In *CCS 1047/2006*, the commissioner considered the order in which various grounds for a variation should be considered. Regulations 18 and 19 should be considered before reg 20, because it was necessary to identify a parent's income before reg 20 could apply (para 22) and payments from assets under reg 18 took the case outside reg 20 (para 23). As between regs 18 and 19, it is necessary to approach an application for a variation in a way that avoids double-counting, as for example if income is diverted in such a way as to increase the value of an asset (paras 24-26). In practice, the particular circumstances of a case may suggest a different order and it may be possible to use the just and equitable requirement in order to avoid any consequences that would arise from the particular choice of order.

Paragraph (1)

This paragraph defines the legal relationships that must exist between the non-resident parent and the assets.

Head (a)

This head and para (2)(b) below cannot be read together literally. If they were, the Secretary of State would have to be satisfied that the non-resident parent had a beneficial interest in a beneficial interest in land. That is nonsense. The provision has to be interpreted to mean that the Secretary of State must be satisfied that the non-resident parent has a beneficial interest in land. See *CCS 8/2000*, para 24.

Control may exist in law, as in the case of a director's control over the activities of a company, or in practice, as in the case of one spouse's control over the other or a parent's control over a child.

In the case of control in law, its existence is easily shown and its exercise readily appears from the decisions taken.

Control in practice is more difficult to prove. The word "ability" indicates that it is the reality of control that is important. Control is stronger than influence. The difference is one of fact and degree. In practice, it may be difficult to investigate sufficiently to show whether the degree of influence that one person exercises over another amounts to control.

In *CS v CMEC* [2010] UKUT 182 (AAC), the judge decided that property that is subject to a court order for transfer as part of financial provision on divorce is not within the control of the beneficiary until it has been transferred. He explained:

"9.   ...the ability to request a third party [the court in this case] to do something with the asset negates the concept that one has the ability to control it. The ability to control imports the notion of independent control of it to sell it or otherwise deal with it."

It may be necessary to distinguish between control for different purposes. This is especially so in the case of a registered company, because different decisions may in law be made by different organs of the company and each organ may be subject to control or influence by others. So, the salary of the directors may be controlled in law by the board, which may be controlled in practice by one or more actual or shadow directors or shareholders, while dividends may be controlled, at least to the extent of approval, by the general meeting, which in turn may control or be controlled by the board.

If the persons involved do not co-operate in investigating the location of real control, it is necessary to proceed by inferences based on the probabilities and taking account of the likely reasons for refusing to co-operate.

Often the non-resident parent may only own an asset jointly with a partner. There may be evidence that the partner will not co-operate in a sale. That is *CCS 8/2000,* para 33). The non-resident parent may be able to apply for an order for sale under ss14 and 15 of the Trusts of Land and Appointment of Trustees Act 1996, but it is not inevitable that the court would make an order (*CCS 8/2000,* paras 32-34).

CCS 8/2000 deals with the identification or classification of an asset. Once an asset has been identified or classified as consisting of one or more particular items, this regulation must be applied to that asset individually (*MG v CMEC (CSM)* [2010] UKUT 83 (AAC); AACR 37, para 40).

Paragraph (2)

This paragraph defines the assets that are covered by this regulation.

Head (c)

Section 744 of the Companies Act 1985 provides that "share' means share in the capital of a company, and includes stock except where such a distinction between stock and share is expressed or implied."

In valuing shares, it is the shares themselves that have to be valued, not the assets or any particular asset owned by the company (*R(IS)13/93*). In valuing shares in a public company, the bid price must be used rather than the offer price or the averaged prices which are published in the press, although in line with Inland Revenue practice it may be permissible to take the lowest bid price on a particular day and add to it one-quarter of the difference between the lowest and highest prices (*R(IS)13/93*, paras 9 and 10).

Head (d)

There is no concept of chose in action in Scots law. For the position in respect of an insurance policy in Scots law and its effect under this regulation, see *CS v CMEC and MS* [2011] AACR 2.

Paragraph (3)

This paragraph contains the exceptions. Only head (b) contains a discretionary element.

Head (b)

This exception confers a discretion on the Secretary of State to disregard an asset. It is an all or nothing exception. Only the whole of the asset can be disregarded; there is no scope for apportionment. In *DGH v SSWP and DAH (CSM)* [2013] UKUT 0299 (AAC), para 29, the Upper Tribunal disagreed with this statement, saying that it was not correct of a divisible asset. For practical purposes, it is possible to acheive the same result either by apportioning under this subparagraph or by using the just and equitable provision.

The test is whether the asset has been retained to be used for a purpose that is reasonable. It is the purpose that must be reasonable, not the retention. Use and purpose will usually be two sides of the same coin. A pension fund is an obvious example of an asset which will be excluded under this exception. Non-resident parents may argue that assets not held in a fund are in fact intended to be retained to provide for retirement. Whether or not that is the case is a question of fact.

If the assets are shares in a company owned by a parent, it is possible but unlikely that it would not be reasonable in all the circumstances of the case to retain. It may also be possible to split shares so that it is reasonable to retain only some of them. However, this is again unlikely. See , para 8. The commissioner there doubted the propriety of second-guessing decisions about the financial structure of a company or its business.

Head (d)

See the general note to reg 12(3)(b).

Assets used in the course of a trade or business are excluded only if income from them was taken into account as self-employed income under the Schedule to the Maintenance Calculations and Special Cases Regulations. This limitation was analysed in *MG v CMEC (CSM)* [2010] UKUT 83 (AAC); AACR 37. Having classified the non-resident parent as a self-employed earner under the definition in the Maintenance Calculations and Special Cases Regulations, the judge decided that the treatment of the income under the Schedule to those Regulations was determined by the way that Her Majesty's Revenue and Customs dealt with the income. This seems inconsistent, as it appears to involve switching over from the definition of self-employed earner that applies for child support purposes to the one used for tax approach. The judge rejected the argument that the words added in 2002 were merely a declaratory clarification to distinguish between business and investment properties:

> "34.   The submission for CMEC and for the father was that the intention of the amendment was merely to reinforce and clarify the existing position, that only assets used in a business were taken out of account by regulation 18(3)(d), not assets held merely as investments or in a way which did not amount to the carrying on of a business. Mr Ellis and Mr Scoon both accepted that on the basis put forward for CMEC the amendment made no difference to the legal outcome, but submitted that it still had a point in providing clarification. But, if so, as Ms Spicer submitted for the mother, why did the Explanatory Notes to the Child Support (Miscellaneous Amendments) Regulations 2002 (SI 2002 No 1204) say that the new provision was that land or property held as a business or trade asset was excluded from the definition of asset "in certain circumstances"? And why was an allegedly merely clarifying amendment put in such an obscure form? I need not go too deeply into all that, because the answer lies in the assumption, that I have found to have been soundly based, that the income from such assets, even when used for business or trade purposes, could not in law go into the calculation of net weekly income under Part III or any other Part of the Schedule to the MCSC Regulations."

The judge applied head (d) to each property separately:

"40.   ...It seems to me that the key is that in principle sub-paragraphs (b) to (d) of regulation 18(3), through the reference to "any asset", must be applied to each separate asset individually. It is the total value of assets referred to in regulation 18(2), thus excluding assets disregarded by virtue of the other parts of regulation 18(3), that is to be tested against the £65,000 limit in sub-paragraph (a). There will no doubt be scope for legitimate differences of approach to when a parcel of rights is to be regarded as one asset, as discussed in Commissioner's decision *CCS/8/2000*. What was in issue there was some farm land and a farm house, either of which it appears could have been sold off separately. Mr Commissioner Jacobs was plainly right to hold that the appeal tribunal there had been entitled to treat the items individually or collectively, depending on the particular circumstances. But that does not in any way undermine the basic principle. In the case of a holding of a portfolio of let properties as part of a business, it must be asked of each property (without needing here to determine whether a house or block in which several flats were let is one asset or several) whether it is used in the course of a trade or business and whether the exception applies. The test in the exception is not whether the business in which the asset is used produces income, or even less "an income". The test is in terms of whether the asset produces income. It seems to me that it will often be impossible to know whether the expenses related to each particular asset exceed the rental income, at least not without more detailed investigation than is required for income tax purposes or is sensible to expect in the child support context. Mortgage interest will be easy to identify, but normal accounting procedures would not require more general expenses of the business to be apportioned among different properties. Therefore, in my judgment the test can only be whether the property asset produces gross income receipts, regardless of the overall profitability or otherwise of the business.

41.   But how then can one ask whether such income forms part of the parent's net weekly income as calculated under Part III of the MCSC Regulations? The difficulty is much lessened by my conclusion as to the treatment of ordinary rental income under Part III. Since that conclusion is that any profit from a property business that is not required for income tax purposes to be reported on the self-employment pages of the self-assessment tax return cannot go into the calculation under Part III, the income produced by each property asset can never form part of the parent's net weekly income. Therefore, the exception to regulation 18(3)(d) applies. That comes to much the same thing as asking whether the income is of a type that can go into the calculation under Part III. Indeed, it seems to me that the relevant part of regulation 18(3)(d) can legitimately be read as if it said "except where the asset is of a type specified in paragraph (2)(b) which does not produce income that forms part of the net weekly income of the non-resident parent" as calculated under Part III."

It is possible for shares to be used in the course of a trade or business – eg, by an investment company. However, usually the shares will not be so used. The parent will own the company and the company will run the business. The ownership of the shares is not in the course of the parent's business; they represent the ownership of and investment in the business. The company has a trade or business, but does not use its shares in the course of it. If a parent owns shares in a company, the usual issue will be whether it was reasonable in all the circumstances to retain them: see the general note to head (b).

Income not taken into account and diversion of income

19.–(1)   Subject to paragraph (2), a case shall constitute a case for the purposes of paragraph 4(1) of Schedule 4B to the Act where–

(a)   the non-resident parent's liability to pay child support maintenance under the maintenance calculation which is in force or has been applied for [³...] , is, or would be, as the case may be–

    (i)   the nil rate owing to the application of paragraph 5(a) of Schedule 1 to the Act; or

    (ii)   a flat rate, owing to the application of paragraph 4(1)(b) of Schedule 1 to the Act, or would be a flat rate but is less than that amount, or nil, owing to the application of paragraph 8 of Schedule 1 to the Act; and

(b)   the Secretary of State is satisfied that the non-resident parent is in receipt of income which would fall to be taken into account under the Maintenance Calculations and Special Cases Regulations but for the application to the non-resident parent of paragraph 4(1)(b) or 5(a) of Schedule 1 to the Act.

[²(1A)   Subject to paragraph (2), a case shall constitute a case for the purposes of paragraph 4(1) of Schedule 4B to the Act where–

(a)   the non-resident parent has the ability to control the amount of income he receives from a company or business, including earnings from employment or self-employment; and

(b)   the Secretary of State is satisfied that the non-resident parent is receiving income from that company or business which would not otherwise fall to be taken into account under the Maintenance Calculations and Special Cases Regulations.]

[²(2)   Paragraphs (1) and (1A) shall apply where–

(a)   the income referred to in paragraph (1)(b) is net weekly income of over £100; or

(b)   the income referred to in paragraph (1A)(b) is over £100; or

(c)   the aggregate of the net weekly income referred to in sub-paragraph (a) and the income referred to in sub-paragraph (b) is over £100,

as the case may be.]

(3)   Net weekly income for the purposes of paragraph (2), in relation to earned income of a non-resident parent who is a student, shall be calculated by aggregating the income for the year ending with the relevant week (which for this purpose shall have the meaning given in the Maintenance Calculations and Special Cases Regulations) and dividing by 52, or, where the Secretary of State does not consider the result to be representative of the student's earned income, over such other period as he shall consider representative and dividing by the number of weeks in that period.

[⁴(4)   A case shall constitute a case for the purposes of paragraph 4(1) of Schedule 4B to the Act where–

(a)   the non-resident parent ("P") has the ability to control the amount of income that–

(i)   P receives, or

(ii)   is taken into account as P's net weekly income,

including earnings from employment or self-employment, whether or not the whole of that income is derived from the company or business from which those earnings are derived; and

(b)   the [⁵Secretary of State] is satisfied that P has unreasonably reduced the amount of P's income which would otherwise fall to be taken into account under the Maintenance Calculations and Special Cases Regulations or paragraph (1A) by diverting it to other persons or for purposes other than the provision of such income for P.

(4A)   In paragraph (4), "net weekly income" has the same meaning as in the Maintenance Calculations and Special Cases Regulations.]

(5)   Where a variation on this ground is agreed to–

(a)   in a case to which paragraph (1) applies, the additional income taken into account under regulation 25 shall be the whole of the income referred to in paragraph (1)(b), aggregated with any benefit, pension or allowance [¹prescribed for the purposes of paragraph 4(1)(b) of Schedule 1 to the Act] which the non-resident parent receives other than any benefits referred to in regulation 26(3); and

(b)   in a case to which paragraph (4) applies, the additional income taken into account under regulation 25 shall be the whole of the amount by which the Secretary of State is satisfied the non-resident parent has unreasonably reduced his income[²; and

(c)   in a case to which paragraph (1A) applies, the additional income taken into account under regulation 25 shall be the whole of the income referred to in paragraph (1A)(b).]

Amendments

1.   Child Support (Miscellaneous Amendments) Regulations 2002 (SI 2002 No.1204) reg 9(6) (April 30, 2002).

2.   Child Support (Miscellaneous Amendments) Regulations 2005 (SI 2005 No.785) reg 8(5) (April 6, 2005).

3.   Child Support (Consequential Provisions) Regulations 2008 (SI 2008 No.2543) reg 8(2) (October 27, 2008).

4.   Child Support (Miscellaneous and Consequential Amendments) Regulations 2009 (SI 2009 No.736) reg 4(3) (April 6, 2009).

5.   Public Bodies (Child Maintenance and Enforcement Commission: Abolition and Transfer of Functions) Order 2012 (SI 2012 No.2007) art 3(2) and Sch para 115(b) (August 1, 2012).

Definitions

"the Act": see reg 1(2).

"Maintenance Calculations and Special Cases Regulations": see reg 1(2).

General Note

This ground of variation is made under the authority of Sch 4B para 4(2)(c) and (d) to the Act. It covers three types of case: paras (1), (1A) and (4).

For the order in which the different grounds for a variation should be considered, see the introductory paragraphs to the general note to reg 18.

Paragraph (1)

This paragraph, supplemented by paras (2) and (3), covers cases where a non-resident parent has income which is not taken into account under Sch 1 to the Act. The effect of this type of variation is specified in para 5(a).

This type of variation only applies to non-resident parents who would otherwise pay a flat or nil, but only because income is excluded under para 4(1)(b) or 5(a) of Sch 1 to the Act.

Paragraph 1A

This paragraph complements para (4). That paragraph deals with the case in which the non-resident parent reduces income that would otherwise be taken into account under the Maintenance Calculations and Special Cases Regulations. This paragraph deals with the case in which the non-resident parent organises the financial affairs of the business or company in order to take income in a form that would not be taken into account under the Maintenance Calculations and Special Cases Regulations. In doing so, it catches directors who take income as dividends, which are outside the calculation made under those Regulations, instead of as wages or salary, which are covered by the Schedule assessment.

This paragraph was considered by the Court of Appeal in *SSWP v Wincott* [2009] EWCA Civ 113 *(R(CS) 4/09)*. The Court decided that it prescribed a state of affairs that had to exist at a past date and that it applied to dividend income that had already been paid by the date when the application for a variation is made. The natural, although perhaps not inevitable, approach is to apply that dividend to the year following the date of payment, as had been done in that case (see paras 6 and 16).

Wincott did not deal with the issue of how a maintenance calculation can be updated as the amount of dividend changes from year to year. The non-resident parent is not under a duty to report change of circumstances and is unlikely to do so if they are to his disadvantage. The parent with care may not find out about a change in the amount of the dividend for some time after it occurs, by which time the effective date provisions will prevent any change to the variation taking effect from the date of the change. There are two ways in which the Secretary of State can avoid these difficulties. First, it is possible to limit the period for which a dividend is taken into account to the current financial year under Sch 1 para 15 to the Act, leaving it to the parent with care to apply then for a new variation. Second, it is possible to initiate a periodic case check at that time.

A dividend is nonetheless income if it is paid into a director's loan account (*Chandler v SSWP* [2008] 1 FLR 638, reported as *R(CS) 2/08* at para 4).

Whether a parent has control of a company or business is a matter of fact and joint control may be sufficient (*RC v CMEC and WC* [2009] UKUT 62 (AAC), para 63).

If income earned through a company is added to a parent's net income under this paragraph but tax and national insurance is not, and is not, intended to be paid on it, it is not deducted under this head, although it may be taken into account under reg 20 below (*WM v CMEC (CSM)* [2011] UKUT 226 (AAC)).

Paragraph (2)

Paragraph (1) only applies if the amount of the net weekly income excluded under Sch 1 to the Act is over £100. This is subject to para (3).

Paragraph (3)

This paragraph governs the calculation of net weekly income of a student.

Paragraph (4)

This paragraph covers a case where a non-resident parent is able to control earnings and has unreasonably reduced them, in whole or in part. The effect of this type of variation is specified in para 5(b).

For a discussion of "ability to control", see the general note to reg 18(1)(a). In applying this requirement, the focus is on control. The employment status of the non-applicant is unlikely to be of any relevance (*CCS 114/2005,* para 15).

Businesses that are run on sound lines in accordance with recognised business and accounting practices are unlikely to be caught by this paragraph. However, many small business are not run in that way and, in the case of registered companies, are run without any clear understanding of the separate existence in law of the company and its owners and without regard to the proper functions of the different organs of the company.

In practice, the key issue will often be the reasonableness of the reduction. If the spouse of a non-resident parent is paid for work in a business, this will largely depend on the relationship between the wages paid and the spouse's contribution to the business. Cases where money is retained in a company or paid as dividends instead of paid as wages to a non-resident parent cause difficulties. It is legitimate and reasonable for a business to make profits and to retain all or part of them to help in growth. However, retained profits are not the only source of funds. A company could issue more shares to raise capital or borrow. In considering whether retention was reasonable, interest rates, tax regimes and the stage of the company's development will all be relevant. Motivation and intention is not directly relevant, but if they can be proved they may be indirectly relevant to reasonableness.

It is the reduction in the non-resident parent's income that is relevant, not the amount by which anyone else benefits. Suppose that a non-resident parent's income from a company is reduced and diverted to that parent's spouse who is also employed by the company, the amount that the spouse receives may be greater than the reduction in the parent's income, after tax and national insurance contributions are taken into account. It is the reduction that is relevant. The relevant figure is the amount of income that the non-resident parent could *receive,* but does not. When this is read in conjunction with para (5)(b) and reg 25, it is clear that it is the net amount that is relevant.

In *CCS 3006/2007,* the commissioner decided that diversion did not require positive conduct and a decision not to act could amount to diversion (para 26). In that case, the diversion took the form of leaving funds in a particular company. The tribunal is not obliged to accept a parent's decision on how to organise the busines finances. It should decide what was reasonable in the context of the child support legislation and the purpose of the variation scheme (*GO'B v CMEC* [2010] UKUT 6 (AAC) para 19-22).

Merely withdrawing money from an account is not a diversion or reduction of income in the context of this provision (*CCS 2861/2002,* para 9). Taking a benefit in kind (eg, as a company car) instead of in cash is diverting income for another purpose (*R(CS) 6/05,* para 34).

In *CCS 114/2005* para 5, the financially qualified panel member of the tribunal had drawn up a set of accounts showing how the tribunal had analysed the non-resident parent's finances. The commissioner approved the making of findings of fact in this form in the context of that case.

For the case in which the non-resident parent reorganises the finances of a business or company in order to take income in a form that is outside the scope of the Maintenance Calculations and Special Cases Regulations, see para 1A.

Life-style inconsistent with declared income

20.–(1)   Subject to paragraph (3), a case shall constitute a case for the purposes of paragraph 4(1) of Schedule 4B to the Act where–

(a)   the non-resident parent's liability to pay child support maintenance under the maintenance calculation which is in force, or which has been applied for [³...], is, or would be, as the case may be–

(i)   the basic rate,

(ii)   the reduced rate,

(iii)   a flat rate owing to the application of paragraph 4(1)(a) of Schedule 1 to the Act, including where the net weekly income of the non-resident parent taken into account for the purposes of the maintenance calculation is, or would be, £100 per week or less owing to a variation being taken into account, or to the application of regulation 18, 19 or 21 of the Transitional Regulations (deduction for relevant departure direction or relevant property transfer);

(iv)   £5 per week or such other amount as may be prescribed owing to the application of paragraph 7(7) of Schedule 1 to the Act (shared care);

(v)   equivalent to the flat rate provided for in, or prescribed for the purposes of, paragraph 4(1)(b) of Schedule 1 to the Act owing to the application of–

(aa)   regulation 27(5);

(bb)   regulation 9 of the Maintenance Calculations and Special Cases Regulations (care provided in part by a local authority); or

(cc)   regulation 23(5) of the Transitional Regulations; or

(vi)   the nil rate owing to the application of paragraph 5(b) of Schedule 1 to the Act; and

(b)   the Secretary of State is satisfied that the income which has been, or would be, taken into account for the purposes of the maintenance calculation is substantially lower than the level of income required to support the overall life-style of the non-resident parent.

(2)   Subject to paragraph (4), a case shall constitute a case for the purposes of paragraph 4(1) of Schedule 4B to the Act where the non-resident parent's liability to pay child support maintenance under the maintenance calculation which is in force, or which has been applied for [³...], is, or would be, as the case may be–

(a) a flat rate owing to the application of paragraph 4(1)(b) of Schedule 1 to the Act, or would be a flat rate but is less than that amount, or nil, owing to the application of paragraph 8 of Schedule 1 to the Act; or

(b) the nil rate owing to the application of paragraph 5(a) of Schedule 1 to the Act, and the Secretary of State is satisfied that the income which would otherwise be taken into account for the purposes of the maintenance calculation is substantially lower than the level of income required to support the overall life-style of the non-resident parent.

(3) Paragraph (1) shall not apply where the Secretary of State is satisfied that the life-style of the non-resident parent is paid for from–

(a) income which is or would be disregarded for the purposes of a maintenance calculation under the Maintenance Calculations and Special Cases Regulations;

[²(aa) income which falls to be considered under regulation 19(1A) (income not taken into account);]

(b) income which falls to be considered under regulation 19(4) (diversion of income);

(c) assets as defined for the purposes of regulation 18, or income derived from those assets;

(d) the income of any partner of the non-resident parent, except where the non-resident parent is able to influence or control the amount of income received by that partner; or

(e) assets as defined for the purposes of regulation 18 of any partner of the non-resident parent, or any income derived from such assets, except where the non-resident parent is able to influence or control the assets, their use, or income derived from them.

(4) Paragraph (2) shall not apply where the Secretary of State is satisfied that the life-style of the non-resident parent is paid for–

(a) from a source referred to in paragraph (3);

(b) from net weekly income of £100 or less; or

(c) from income which falls to be considered under regulation 19(1).

(5) Where a variation on this ground is agreed to, the additional income taken into account under regulation 25 shall be the difference between the income which the Secretary of State is satisfied the non-resident parent requires to support his overall life-style and the income which has been or, but for the application of paragraph 4(1)(b) or 5(a) of Schedule 1 to the Act, would be taken into account for the purposes of the maintenance calculation, aggregated with any benefit, pension or allowance [¹prescribed for the purposes of paragraph 4(1)(b) of Schedule 1 to the Act] which the non-resident parent receives other than any benefits referred to in regulation 26(3).

Amendments

1.   Child Support (Miscellaneous Amendments) Regulations 2002 (SI 2002 No.1204) reg 9(6) (April 30, 2002).

2.   Child Support (Miscellaneous Amendments) Regulations 2005 (SI 2005 No.785) reg 8(6) (April 6, 2005).

3.   Child Support (Consequential Provisions) Regulations 2008 (SI 2008 No.2543) reg 8(3) (October 27, 2008).

Definitions

"the Act": see reg 1(2).

"Maintenance Calculations and Special Cases Regulations": see reg 1(2).

"partner": see reg 1(2).

General Note

This ground of variation is made under the authority of Sch 4B, para 4(2)(b) to the Act. It allows income to be determined by inference from lifestyle rather than by more direct evidence (*CCS 2230/2001*, para 19). In *CCS 2786/2005* para 12, the commissioner recommended that average earnings figures such as those published in the annual *Facts and Figures Tables for the Calculation of Damages* by the Professional Negligence Bar Association could be used as a starting pointing for fixing the income needed to support a particular lifestyle and as a check on a figure reached for that income in order to ensure that it was realistic for the parent's employment.

For the order in which the different grounds for a variation should be considered, see the introductory paragraphs to the general note to reg 18.

This ground of variation has an uneasy relationship with the Schedule assessment. Commissioners criticised the equivalent head of departure direction as being unnecessary (*CCS 6282/1999*, para 9).

The relationship between this head and a Schedule assessment of income was considered by the commissioner in *R(CS) 3/01*, paras 25-34. He noted that a parent's life-style could be used as evidence for a Schedule assessment or as evidence of additional income for a variation. In the case of an overlap, an appeal tribunal should deal with the evidence in the context of the case before it. If the case is a Schedule case, it is mandatory to take account of income, however it is proved. If it has been taken into account under the Schedule, it cannot be relied on again under this regulation. If for some reason it has not been taken into account under the Schedule, it can be considered under this regulation. If it is taken into account under this regulation, the next time that the application of the Schedule is reconsidered, it can be taken directly into account so that the variation is no longer needed. In *CCS 821/2003*, the commissioner emphasised at para 14 that he was in that case concerned with income that was proved by inference. If the income was proved by direct evidence and was assessed by reference to a past accounting period, it was inherent that the calculation might be out of date to the advantage of either the non-resident parent or the person with care. In those circumstances, it was better to leave the Schedule assessment of income to catch up with reality over time rather than to disrupt it by the variation scheme.

Before an appeal tribunal can apply this head, it needs to know the income on which the Schedule assessment was based, its source and the nature of any deductions from it (*CCS3331/1999*, para 10).

In principle, it should not be possible to have a life-style the funding of which cannot be accounted for if there has been full disclosure of income. If the tribunal considers that there has been full disclosure, but that nonetheless it cannot account for the evidence of life-style, the tribunal should investigate further to try to reconcile this apparent inconsistency. See *CCS 821/2003*, paras 18-20.

In *CCS 3499/2004*, the commissioner decided that money held in a director's loan account is generally capital, not income, in the same way as savings arising from past income. He accepted that in an exceptional case it might be income, but said (para 14) "I do not need to decide how strong a case would have to be (possibly amounting almost to a sham) for drawings on a director's loan account made up of savings out of past income not to be 'out of capital'."

If income earned through a company is added to a parent's net income under this paragraph but tax and national insurance is not, and is not, intended to be paid on it, it cannot be deducted under reg 19(1A) above, but it may be taken into account under this regulation (*WM v CMEC (CSM)* [2011] UKUT 226 (AAC)).

Subparagraph (1)(b)

"Overall lifestyle" is wide enough to cover all aspects of personal behaviour, activities, interests and choices. "Substantially" is an ordinary word with no technical meaning; a definition is not necessary and might improperly limit its scope. See *CCS4247/1999*, para 32 and *CSC6/03-04(T)*, paras 46-49).

The relevant time at which this regulation has to be applied is the effective date of the variation that might be agreed. The tribunal must inevitably rely on evidence from the past to prove both the lifestyle and how that lifestyle is funded. However, that evidence must be related to the relevant time. See *CCS 821/2003*, paras 10-13. If the Schedule assessment was based on income at a much earlier time, the just and equitable requirement should be used to prevent inappropriate comparisons being used between income at one date and lifestyle at another. See *CCS 821/2003*, para 13.

An amount paid by way of a pension premium in excess of the amounts laid down in the income tax legislation may be evidence of the level of lifestyle enjoyed by a parent (*CCS 4666/1999*, para 16).

The lack of sufficient findings of fact on lifestyle under this regulation does not justify the tribunal taking a wider approach to the calculation of income than is authorised by subpara (5) (*CCS 3927/1999*, para 20).

The Secretary of State regularly relied in departure direction cases on a ministerial statement in the House of Commons on the importance of discretion in view of the difficulties of producing direct or conclusive evidence to support an application. In *CCS 7411/1999*, paras 13-15, the commissioner rejected this suggestion. He recognised that many applicants would have to rely heavily on the drawing of inferences and that tribunals would bear in mind the difficulties facing applicants, but nonetheless there must be a rational basis for drawing the inferences and non-applicants must not be prejudiced by drawing inferences that are not based on a rational analysis of the evidence. No special discretionary approach was required, as both parties could be adequately protected by concentrating on the issues identified as relevant by the legislation and by applying the civil burden and standard of proof to those issues.

The standard of proof is the usual balance of probabilities. An allegation under this provision is not tantamount to an allegation of fraud (*CCS 2623/1999*).

Paragraph (2)

This paragraph covers cases where the non-resident parent falls within para 4(1)(b) of Sch 1 to the Act.

See the general note to para (1)(b).

Paragraph (3)

This contains exceptions to the scope of para (1). They are not exhaustive of the possibilities. A common explanation for an inconsistency between a parent's lifestyle and disclosed income is that it is supported by debt. Other sources of support for the life-style are not irrelevant. They must be taken into account in applying the just and equitable test. In *CCS 2230/2001*, para 19, the commissioner was concerned with a case in which the tribunal had found that the non-resident parent's life-style was supported by contributions from a lady friend who was not living with him. As she was not his partner, this provision did not apply. However, the commissioner held that the source was relevant to the application of the just and equitable test. He did not rule out the possibility that it might be just and equitable to agree to a variation on the basis that a contribution from someone who was not covered by this provision should be treated as part of the non-resident parent's income for the purposes of child support, but did not accept that such a contribution must always be taken into account (para 19).

This paragraph only applies if the whole of the additional income needed to support the life-style comes from one or more of the sources listed: *R(CS) 6/02*. If it comes only partly from those sources, this paragraph does not apply, but the fact that some of it comes from those sources provides a strong case for not agreeing to a variation in respect of it (*R(CS) 6/02*).

Subparagraph (a) refers to income which is or would be "disregarded". This means income that would not be taken into account under the Maintenance Calculations and Special Cases Regulations and is not limited to those items that are disregarded under para 2 of the Schedule to those Regulations (*CCS 1320/2005*, para 15).

Subparagraph (a) ensures that dividend income is taken into account under reg 19 and not under this regulation: see the general note to reg 19(A) above. Before this amendment, dividend income did not come with the scope of this regulation, because it was disregarded income for subpara (a) and an asset for subpara (c) (*CCS 1320/2005*, paras 15-16).

Subparagraph (c) refers to reg 18. However, only reg 18(2) is relevant.

Subparagraph (c) refers to types of asset and the only place where they are defined in reg 18 is in para (2). The general reference to reg 18 does not import all the provisions of that regulation, including para (3). See *CCS 3862/2007*, para 21.

Paragraph (4)

This contains the exceptions to the scope of para (4) by extending the scope of para (3).

Paragraph (5)

The calculation set out in this paragraph is mandatory. It is not permissible simply to determine the parent's total income. Only the level of income necessary to support the overall life-style may be taken into account: *R(CS) 3/ 01* para 21; *CCS 1840/1999*, para 12; *CCS 3927/1999*, paras 14-15.

However, the calculation required by this paragraph cannot be made with precision. In practice, there is likely to be a range of incomes that could support the lifestyle. This allows a tribunal, in an exceptional case, to use a parent's total income as a guide to the level of income necessary to support the parent's life-style. There may be sufficient evidence to allow a fairly accurate determination of a parent's total income. If that amount is within the range of incomes that would be needed to support the life-style, it is proper to treat that income as the level needed to support the life-style. See *CCS 3927/1999*, para 19. This only applies if there is sufficient evidence to show the parent's life-style (*CCS 1320/2005*, para 12).

The lack of sufficient findings of fact on life-style does not justify an appeal tribunal taking a wider approach to the calculation of income than is authorised by this paragraph (*CCS 3927/1999*, para 20).

PART VI

FACTORS TO BE TAKEN INTO ACCOUNT FOR THE PURPOSES OF SECTION 28F OF THE ACT

Factors to be taken into account and not to be taken into account

21.–(1)   The factors to be taken into account in determining whether it would be just and equitable to agree to a variation in any case shall include–

(a)   where the application is made on any ground–

    (i)   whether, in the opinion of the Secretary of State, agreeing to a variation would be likely to result in a relevant person ceasing paid employment;

    (ii)   if the applicant is the non-resident parent, the extent, if any, of his liability to pay child maintenance under a court order or agreement in the period prior to the effective date of the maintenance calculation; and

(b)   where an application is made on the ground that the case falls within regulations 10 to 14 (special expenses), whether, in the opinion of the Secretary of State–

    (i)   the financial arrangements made by the non-resident parent could have been such as to enable the expenses to be paid without a variation being agreed; or

    (ii)   the non-resident parent has at his disposal financial resources which are currently utilised for the payment of expenses other than those arising from essential everyday requirements and which could be used to pay the expenses.

(2)   The following factors are not to be taken into account in determining whether it would be just and equitable to agree to a variation in any case–

(a)   the fact that the conception of the qualifying child was not planned by one or both of the parents;

(b)   whether the non-resident parent or the person with care of the qualifying child was responsible for the breakdown of the relationship between them;

(c)   the fact that the non-resident parent or the person with care of the qualifying child has formed a new relationship with a person who is not a parent of that child;

(d)   the existence of particular arrangements for contact with the qualifying child, including whether any arrangements made are being adhered to;

(e)   the income or assets of any person other than the non-resident parent, other than the income or assets of a partner of the non-resident parent taken into account under regulation 20(3);

(f)   the failure by a non-resident parent to make payments of child support maintenance, or to make payments under a maintenance order or a written maintenance agreement; or

(g)   representations made by persons other than the relevant persons.

Definitions

"partner": see reg 1(2).
"qualifying child": see reg 1(2).
"relevant person": see reg 1(2).

General Note

This regulation is made under the authority of s28F(2)(b) of the Act. It contains the prescribed circumstances that must, or must not, be taken into account in determining whether it would be just and equitable to agree to a variation.

Paragraph (1)

This sets out the factors that must be taken into account.

Subparagraph (a)

These factors apply in all cases. None is decisive. They are additional to the factors that are relevant under the general principle in s28E(1)(b) of the Act and the duty in s28F(2)(a) of the Act.

Head (i)

Non-resident parents often threaten to give up work, but that it is not decisive. It may not be a real threat. Even if it is, it only has to be taken into account and balanced with all other relevant factors. It must be seen not as a blackmailer's charter, but as part of the reality that the child support maintenance payable depends on the continuing viability of the non-resident parent's employment. A variation should not be agreed to if its effect would be to place such a financial burden on a non-resident parent that the best option would be to cease paid employment.

This factor is most likely to arise as a live issue if the variation might lead to the non-resident parent giving up work, but it is not so limited. It applies also if the increase in child support maintenance would allow the person with care to cease employment.

It is the agreeing to the variation that must create the risk. It is irrelevant that the refusal to agree might produce this outcome, although that would be relevant under the general requirement in s28F(1)(b).

Tribunals must be careful to distinguish between this factor and s28E(4)(a) of the Act.

Head (ii)

This factor may support a variation by reducing the amount of child support maintenance payable in order to ease the burden of the transition from a relatively low amount under an order or agreement to a higher amount of child support maintenance. It may also have the opposite effect if the amount previously payable was unrealistically low given what the non-resident parent could afford.

Although it does not expressly say so, this head must be limited to cases where (a) the maintenance was payable to or for the qualifying child and (b) immediately before the effective date of the maintenance calculation.

Subparagraph (b)

These factors only apply to the special cases heads of a variation. They are effectively anti-avoidance measures.

Paragraph (2)

This sets out the factors that must not be taken into account. See also the factors in s28E(4) of the Act.

Head (c)

It is the fact of the new relationship that has to be disregarded, not facts that follow from it, such as additional income available to support the non-resident parent's new family from the partner (*CSCS 16/2003*, paras 16-17).

Head (d)

The costs of maintaining contact are relevant under reg 10. This head limits the existence and honouring of contact arrangements to that provision.

Head (e)

This excludes the income and assets of anyone other than the non-resident parent. The income and assets of the person with care are therefore irrelevant. This is not surprising, as the focus of the new child support scheme is on making a share of the non-resident parent's income available for the benefit of the child. The focus is no longer on sharing the costs of bringing up a child.

Head (j)

This head only operates if an application for a variation is being considered. If a regular payments condition has been imposed under s28C of the Act, failure to comply may lead to the application not being considered under s28C(5).

The emphasis in an application for a variation is on the future. Hence past failure is irrelevant once the just and equitable stage has been reached.

Head (g)

This complements s28E(3) of the Act. That subsection applies generally and is not limited to the just and equitable requirement. It does not prevent the Secretary of State making submissions to an appeal tribunal on appeal.

PART VII
EFFECT OF A VARIATION ON THE MAINTENANCE CALCULATION AND EFFECTIVE DATES

Effective dates

22.–(1)   Subject to paragraph (2), where the application for a variation is made in the circumstances referred to in section 28A(3) of the Act (before the Secretary of State has reached a decision under section 11 or 12(1) of the Act) and the application is agreed to, the effective date of the maintenance calculation which takes account of the variation shall be–

(a)   where the ground giving rise to the variation existed from the effective date of the maintenance calculation as provided for in the Maintenance Calculation Procedure Regulations, that date; or

(b)   where the ground giving rise to the variation arose after the effective date referred to in sub-paragraph (a), the first day of the maintenance period in which the ground arose.

(2)   Where the ground for the variation applied for under section 28A(3) of the Act is a ground in regulation 12 (prior debts) or 14 (special expenses–payments in respect of certain mortgages, loans or insurance policies) and payments falling within regulation 12 or 14 which have been made by the non-resident parent constitute voluntary payments for the purposes of section 28J of the Act and Regulations made under that section, the date from which the maintenance calculation shall take account of the variation on this ground shall be the date on which the maintenance period begins which immediately follows the date on which the non-resident parent is notified under the Maintenance Calculation Procedure Regulations of the amount of his liability to pay child support maintenance.

(3)   Where the ground for the variation applied for under section 28A(3) of the Act has ceased to exist by the date the maintenance calculation is made, that calculation shall take account of the variation for the period ending on the last day of the maintenance period in which the ground existed.

Definition

"Maintenance Calculation Procedure Regulations": see reg 1(2).

General Note

Paragraphs (1) and (2) of this regulation determines the effective date of a variation if the application for a variation is considered together with an application for a maintenance calculation. Despite the heading of the regulation, para (3) deals with the termination of a variation.

Paragraph (1)

This paragraph contains a basic rule and an exception. The basic rule is that the effective date of the variation is the same as that of the calculation. The exception applies if the variation is based on a change that occurred after that date. In that case, the effective date is the first day of the maintenance period in which the change occurred.

Paragraph (2)

This applies if payments made under reg 12 or 14 were voluntary payments under s28J of the Act. In that case, the effective date is the first day of the maintenance period following the notification of the amount of the non-resident parent's liability to child support maintenance. For the date of notification, see the definition in reg 1(2).

Paragraph (3)

This applies if the ground for a variation has ceased to exist by the date when the maintenance calculation is made. In that case, it runs only until the last day of the maintenance period in which it ceased to exist.

Effect on maintenance calculation – special expenses

23.–(1)   Subject to paragraph (2) and regulations 26 and 27, where the variation agreed to is one falling within regulation 10 to 14 (special expenses) effect shall be given to the variation in the maintenance calculation by deducting from the net weekly income of the non-resident parent the weekly amount of those expenses.

(2)   Where the income which is taken into account in the maintenance calculation is the capped amount and the variation agreed to is one falling within regulation 10 to 14 then–

(a)   the weekly amount of the expenses shall first be deducted from the actual net weekly income of the non-resident parent;

(b)   the amount by the which the capped amount exceeds the figure calculated under sub-paragraph (a) shall be calculated; and

(c)   effect shall be given to the variation in the maintenance calculation by deducting from the capped amount the amount calculated under sub-paragraph (b).

Definitions

"capped amount": see reg 1(2).
"net weekly income": see reg 27(7).

General Note

This regulation, together with regs 26 and 27, specifies the effect of a variation on the ground of a special expense under regs 10 to 14.

The effect of a variation is to reduce the net weekly income by the amount of the expenses. This is subject to para (2).

Paragraph (2)

If the income under the maintenance calculation is the capped amount, this paragraph applies. (a) The special expenses are first deducted from the actual net weekly income. (b) The amount by which the capped amount exceeds that figure is then calculated. (c) Finally, that amount is then deduced from the capped amount. The effect of this paragraph is to ensure that any excess in the non-resident parent's actual net weekly income over the capped amount is used to meet special expenses before the maintenance calculation is reduced.

Take this example. The non-resident parent's actual net weekly income is £2,200 and is capped at £2,000. The special expenses are £250. The effect of this paragraph is to reduce the capped amount to £1,950. (a) £2,200 – £250 = £1,950. (b) £2,000 – £1,950 = £50. (c) £2,000 – £50 = £1,950.

Effect on maintenance calculation – property or capital transfer

24.   Subject to regulation 27, where the variation agreed to is one falling within regulation 16 (property or capital transfers)–

(a)   the maintenance calculation shall be carried out in accordance with Part 1 of Schedule 1 to the Act and Regulations made under that Part; and

(b)   the equivalent weekly value of the transfer calculated as provided in regulation 17 shall be deducted from the amount of child support maintenance which he would otherwise be liable to pay to the person with care with respect to whom the transfer was made.

Definition

"the Act": see reg 1(2).

Effect on maintenance calculation – additional cases

25.   Subject to regulations 26 and 27, where the variation agreed to is one falling within regulations 18 to 20 (additional cases), effect shall be given to the variation in the maintenance calculation by increasing the net weekly income of the non-resident parent which would otherwise be taken into account by the weekly amount of the additional income except that, where the amount of net weekly income calculated in this way would exceed the capped amount, the amount of net weekly income taken into account shall be the capped amount.

Definitions
"capped amount": see reg 1(2).
"net weekly income": see reg 27(7).

General Note
This regulation, together with regs 26 and 27, specifies the effect of a variation on the ground of an additional case: regs 18 to 20. The effect of a variation is to increase the net weekly income by the amount identified in the relevant regulation. If this would exceed the capped amount, the amount payable is the capped amount.

Effect on maintenance calculation – maximum amount payable where the variation is on additional cases ground

26.–(1) Subject to regulation 27, where this regulation applies the amount of child support maintenance which the non-resident parent shall be liable to pay shall be whichever is the lesser of–
(a) a weekly amount calculated by aggregating an amount equivalent to the flat rate stated in or prescribed for the purposes of paragraph 4(1)(b) of Schedule 1 to the Act with the amount calculated by applying that Schedule to the Act to the additional income arising under the variation, other than the weekly amount of any benefit, pension or allowance the non-resident parent receives which is prescribed for the purposes of that paragraph; or
(b) a weekly amount calculated by applying Part 1 of Schedule 1 to the Act to the additional income arising under the variation.
(2) This regulation applies where the variation agreed to is one to which regulation 25 applies and the non-resident parent's liability calculated as provided in Part 1 of Schedule 1 to the Act and Regulations made under that Schedule would, but for the variation, be–
(a) a flat rate under paragraph 4(1)(b) of that Schedule;
(b) a flat rate but is less than that amount or nil, owing to the application of paragraph 8 of that Schedule; or
(c) a flat rate under paragraph 4(1)(b) of that Schedule but for the application of paragraph 5(a) of that Schedule.
(3) For the purposes of paragraph (1)–
(a) any benefit, pension or allowance taken into account in the additional income referred to in sub-paragraph (b) shall not include–
  (i) in the case of industrial injuries benefit under section 94 of the Contributions and Benefits Act, any increase in that benefit under section 104 (constant attendance) or 105 (exceptionally severe disablement) of that Act;
  (ii) in the case of a war disablement pension within the meaning in section 150(2) of the Contributions and Benefits Act, any award under the following articles of the Naval, Military and Air Forces Etc., (Disablement and Death) Service Pensions Order 1983 ("the Service Pensions Order"): article 14 (constant attendance allowance), 15 (exceptionally severe disablement allowance), 16 (severe disablement occupational allowance) or 26A (mobility supplement) or any analogous allowances payable in conjunction with any other war disablement pension; and
  (iii) any award under article 18 of the Service Pensions Order (unemployability allowances) which is an additional allowance in respect of a child of the non-resident parent where that child is not living with the non-resident parent;
(b) "additional income" for the purposes of sub-paragraphs (a) and (b) means such income after the application of a variation falling within regulations 10 to 14 (special expenses); and
(c) "weekly amount" for the purposes of sub-paragraphs (a) and (b) means the aggregate of the amounts referred to in the relevant sub-paragraph–

(i) adjusted as provided in regulation 27(3) as if the reference in that regulation to child support maintenance were to the weekly amount; and

(ii) after any deduction provided for in regulation 27(4) as if the reference in that regulation to child support maintenance were to the weekly amount.

Definitions

"the Act": see reg 1(2).

"Contributions and Benefits Act": see reg 1(2).

General Note

This regulation fixes the maximum amount of child support maintenance payable as a result of a variation.

Effect on maintenance calculation – general

27.–(1) Subject to paragraphs (4) and (5), where more than one variation is agreed to in respect of the same period regulations 23 to 26 shall apply and the results shall be aggregated as appropriate.

(2) Paragraph 7(2) to (7) of Schedule 1 to the Act (shared care) shall apply where the rate of child support maintenance is affected by a variation which is agreed to and paragraph 7(2) shall be read as if after the words "as calculated in accordance with the preceding paragraphs of this Part of this Schedule" there were inserted the words '', Schedule 4B and Regulations made under that Schedule".

(3) Subject to paragraphs (4) and (5), where the non-resident parent shares the care of a qualifying child within the meaning in Part 1 of Schedule 1 to the Act, or where the care of such a child is shared in part by a local authority, the amount of child support maintenance the non-resident parent is liable to pay the person with care, calculated to take account of any variation, shall be reduced in accordance with the provisions of paragraph 7 of that Part or regulation 9 of the Maintenance Calculations and Special Cases Regulations, as the case may be.

(4) Subject to paragraph (5), where the variation agreed to is one falling within regulation 16 (property or capital transfers) the equivalent weekly value of the transfer calculated as provided in regulation 17 shall be deducted from the amount of child support maintenance the non-resident parent would otherwise be liable to pay the person with care in respect of whom the transfer was made after aggregation of the effects of any other variations as provided in paragraph (1) or deduction for shared care as provided in paragraph (3).

(5) If the application of regulation 24, or paragraph (3) or (4), would decrease the weekly amount of child support maintenance (or the aggregate of all such amounts) payable by the non-resident parent to the person with care (or all of them) to less than a figure equivalent to the flat rate of child support maintenance payable under [¹paragraph 4(1)] of Schedule 1 to the Act, he shall instead be liable to pay child support maintenance at a rate equivalent to that rate apportioned (if appropriate) as provided in paragraph 6 of Schedule 1 to the Act.

(6) The effect of a variation shall not be applied for any period during which a circumstance referred to in regulation 7 applies.

(7) For the purposes of regulations 23 and 25 "net weekly income" means as calculated or estimated under the Maintenance Calculations and Special Cases Regulations.

Amendment

1. Child Support (Miscellaneous Amendments) Regulations 2004 (SI 2004 No.2415) reg 9(4) (September 16, 2004).

Definitions

"the Act": see reg 1(2).

"Maintenance Calculations and Special Cases Regulations": see reg 1(2).

"qualifying child": see reg 1(2).

General Note

This regulation qualifies regs 23 to 25.

Paragraph (1)

Variations agreed to in respect of the same period are aggregated.

Paragraph (2)

This deals with shared care when a variation is agreed to by modifying the wording of para 7 (2) of Sch 1 to the Act.

Paragraph (3)

This deals with cases where care of the child is shared by the non-resident parent and the person with care (para 7 of Sch 1 to the Act) or a local authority (reg 9 of the Maintenance Calculations and Special Cases Regulations).

Paragraph (4)

This governs the order of calculations in cases that fall within reg 16.

Paragraph (5)

If this paragraph applies, a variation may not reduce the amount of child support maintenance below the flat rate. The evidence purpose of this provision is to ensure that a non-resident parent makes some contribution, however small.

Paragraph (6)

This paragraph effectively suspends the operation of a variation during any period in which one of the circumstances specified in reg 7 applies.

Paragraph (7)

This definition is included here rather than with the other definitions in reg 1(2), because it has a limited application.

Transitional provisions – conversion decisions

28. [¹Subject to regulation 17(10) of the Transitional Regulations, where] the variation is being applied for in connection with a subsequent decision within the meaning given in the Transitional Regulations, and the decision to be revised or superseded under section 16 or 17 of the Act, as the case may be, takes into account a relevant property transfer as defined and provided for in those Regulations–

(a)   for the purposes of regulations 23 and 25 "capped amount" shall mean the income for the purposes of paragraph 10(3) of Schedule 1 to the Act less any deduction in respect of the relevant property transfer;

(b)   for the purposes of regulation 26(3)(b) the additional income for the purposes of paragraph (1) of that regulation shall be after deduction in respect of the relevant property transfer;

(c)   regulation 27(4) shall be read as if the aggregation referred to included any deduction in respect of the relevant property transfer; and

(d)   regulation 27(5) shall be read as if after the reference to paragraph (3) or (4) there were a reference to any deduction in respect of the relevant property transfer.

Amendment

1.   Child Support (Miscellaneous Amendments) (No.2) Regulations 2003 (SI 2003 No.2779) reg 8 (November 5, 2003).

Definitions

"the Act": see reg 1(2).
"capped amount": see reg 1(2).
"Transitional Regulations": see reg 1(2).

Situations in which a variation previously agreed to may be taken into account in calculating maintenance liability

29.–(1)   This regulation applies where a variation has been agreed to in relation to a maintenance calculation.

(2)   In the circumstances set out in paragraph (3), the Secretary of State may take account of the effect of such a variation upon the rate of liability for child support maintenance notwithstanding the fact that an application has not been made.

(3)   The circumstances are–

(a)   that the decision as to the maintenance calculation is superseded under section 17 of the Act on a change of circumstances so that the non-resident parent becomes liable to pay child support maintenance at the nil rate, or another rate which means that the variation cannot be taken into account; and

(b)   that the superseding decision referred to in sub-paragraph (a) is itself superseded under section 17 of the Act on a change of circumstances so that the non-resident parent becomes liable to pay a rate of child support maintenance which can be adjusted to take account of the variation.

Definition
"the Act": see reg 1(2).

General Note
This regulation applies when successive supersessions on a change of circumstances affect the implementation of a variation that has been agreed to. It provides for the effect of a variation to be suspended while it cannot be taken into account following a supersession, but to revive without an application when a further supersession allows it to be taken into account.

Circumstances for the purposes of section 28F(3) of the Act

30.   The circumstances prescribed for the purposes of section 28F(3) of the Act (Secretary of State shall not agree to a variation) are–

(a)   the prescribed circumstances in regulation 6(2) or 7; and

(b)   where the Secretary of State considers it would not be just and equitable to agree to the variation having regard to any of the factors referred to in regulation 21.

Definition
"the Act": see reg 1(2).

PART VIII
MISCELLANEOUS

Regular payments condition

31.–(1)   For the purposes of section 28C(2)(b) of the Act (payments of child support maintenance less than those specified in the interim maintenance decision) the payments shall be those fixed by the interim maintenance decision or the maintenance calculation in force, as the case may be, adjusted to take account of the variation applied for by the non-resident parent as if that variation had been agreed.

(2)   The Secretary of State may refuse to consider the application for a variation where a regular payments condition has been imposed and the non-resident parent has failed to comply with it in the circumstances to which paragraph (3) applies.

(3)   This paragraph applies where the non-resident parent has failed to comply with the regular payments condition and fails to make such payments which are due and unpaid within one month of being required to do so by the Secretary of State or such other period as the Secretary of State may in the particular case decide.

Definition
"the Act": see reg 1(2).

General Note
Paragraph (1) applies to both applications for variations (a) made before a decision on an application for a maintenance calculation has been determined (when an interim maintenance decision may be made under s12(2) of the Act) and (b) made when a maintenance calculation is in force.
    Paragraphs (2) and (3) are made under the authority of s28C(5) of the Act.

Meaning of "benefit" for the purposes of section 28E of the Act

32.   For the purposes of section 28E of the Act, "benefit" means income support, income-based jobseeker's allowance, [[1]income-related employment and support allowance under Part 1 of the Welfare Reform Act 2007] [[2]and housing benefit].

Amendments
1.   Employment and Support Allowance (Consequential Provisions) (No.2) Regulations 2008 (SI 2008 No.1554) reg 62 (October 27, 2008).

2.   Council Tax Benefit Abolition (Consequential Provision) Regulations 2013 (SI 2013 No.458) reg 4 and Sch 2 para 5 (April 1, 2013).

Definition
"the Act": see reg 1(2).

PART IX
REVOCATION

Revocation and savings
33.–(1)   Subject to ['the Transitional Regulations and] paragraph (2), the Child Support Departure Direction and Consequential Amendments Regulations 1996 shall be revoked with respect to a particular case with effect from the date that these Regulations come into force with respect to that type of case ("the commencement date").

(2)   Where before the commencement date in respect of a particular case–
(a)   an application was made and not determined for–
  (i)   a maintenance assessement;
  (ii)   a departure direction; or
  (iii)   a revision or supersession of a decision;
(b)   the Secretary of State had begun but not completed a revision or supersession of a decision on his own initiative;
(c)   any time limit provided for in Regulations for making an application for a revision or a departure direction had not expired; or
(d)   any appeal was made but not decided or any time limit for making an appeal had not expired,
the provisions of the Child Support Departure Direction and Consequential Amendments Regulations 1996 shall continue to apply for the purposes of–
  (aa)   the decision on the application referred to in sub-paragraph (a);
  (bb)   the revision or supersession referred to in sub-paragraph (b);
  (cc)   the ability to apply for the revision or the departure direction referred to in sub-paragraph (c) and the decision whether to revise or to give a departure direction following any such application;
  (dd)   any appeal outstanding or made during the time limit referred to in sub-paragraph (d); or
  (ee)   any revision, supersession or appeal or application for a departure direction in relation to a decision, ability to apply or appeal referred to in sub-paragraphs (aa) to (dd).

(3)   Where, after the commencement date, a decision with respect to a departure direction is revised from a date which is prior to the commencement date, the provisions of the Child Support Departure Direction and Consequential Amendments Regulations 1996 shall continue to apply for the purposes of that revision.

(4)   Where, under regulation 28(1) of the Transitional Regulations, an application for a maintenance calculation is treated as an application for a maintenance assessment, the provisions of the Child Support Departure Direction and Consequential Amendments Regulations 1996 shall continue to apply for the purposes of an application for a departure direction in relation to any such assessment made.

(5)   For the purposes of this regulation–
(a)   "departure direction" and "maintenance assessment" means as provided in section 54 of the Act before its amendment by the 2000 Act;
(b)   "revision or supersession" means a revision or supersession of a decision under section 16 or 17 of the Act before its amendment by the 2000 Act and "any time limit for making an application for a revision" means any time limit provided for in Regulations made under section 16 of the Act; and
(c)   "2000 Act" means the Child Support, Pensions and Social Security Act 2000.

Amendment
1.   Child Support (Transitional Provision) (Miscellaneous Amendments) Regulations 2003 (SI 2003 No.347) reg 2(5) (March 3, 2003).

Definitions

the Act": see reg 1(2).

"Transitional Regulations": see reg 1(2).

SCHEDULE
Equivalent weekly value of a transfer of property

1.–(1) Subject to paragraph 3, the equivalent weekly value of a transfer of property shall be calculated by multiplying the value of a transfer of property determined in accordance with regulation 17 by the relevant factor specified in the Table set out in paragraph 2 ("the Table").

(2) For the purposes of sub-paragraph (1), the relevant factor is the number in the Table at the intersection of the column for the statutory rate and of the row for the number of years of liability.

(3) In sub-paragraph (2)–

(a) "the statutory rate" means interest at the statutory rate prescribed for a judgment debt or, in Scotland, the statutory rate in respect of interest included in or payable under a decree in the Court of Session, which in either case applies at the date of the court order or written agreement relating to the transfer of the property;

(b) "the number of years of liability" means the number of years, beginning on the date of the court order or written agreement relating to the transfer of property and ending on–

(i) the date specified in that order or agreement as the date on which maintenance for the youngest child in respect of whom that order or agreement was made shall cease; or

(ii) if no such date is specified, the date on which the youngest child specified in the order or agreement reaches the age of 18,

and where that period includes a fraction of a year, that fraction shall be treated as a full year if it is either one half or exceeds one half of a year, and shall otherwise be disregarded.

2.   The Table referred to in paragraph 1(1) is set out below–

THE TABLE

Number of years of liability	Statutory Rate							
	7.0%	8.0%	10.0%	11.0%	12.0%	12.5%	14.0%	15.0%
1.	.02058	.02077	.02115	.02135	.02154	.02163	.02192	.02212
2.	.01064	.01078	.01108	.01123	.01138	.01145	.01168	.01183
3.	.00733	.00746	.00773	.00787	.00801	.00808	.00828	.00842
4.	.00568	.00581	.00607	.00620	.00633	.00640	.00660	.00674
5.	.00469	.00482	.00507	.00520	.00533	.00540	.00560	.00574
6.	.00403	.00416	.00442	.00455	.00468	.00474	.00495	.00508
7.	.00357	.00369	.00395	.00408	.00421	.00428	.00448	.00462
8.	.00322	.00335	.00360	.00374	.00387	.00394	.00415	.00429
9.	.00295	.00308	.00334	.00347	.00361	.00368	.00389	.00403
10.	.00274	.00287	.00313	.00327	.00340	.00347	.00369	.00383
11.	.00256	.00269	.00296	.00310	.00324	.00331	.00353	.00367
12.	.00242	.00255	.00282	.00296	.00310	.00318	.00340	.00355
13.	.00230	.00243	.00271	.00285	.00299	.00307	.00329	.00344
14.	.00220	.00233	.00261	.00275	.00290	.00298	.00320	.00336
15.	.00211	.00225	.00253	.00267	.00282	.00290	.00313	.00329
16.	.00204	.00217	.00246	.00261	.00276	.00283	.00307	.00323
17.	.00197	.00211	.00240	.00255	.00270	.00278	.00302	.00318
18.	.00191	.00205	.00234	.00250	.00265	.00273	.00297	.00314

3.   The Secretary of State may determine a lower equivalent weekly value than that determined in accordance with paragraphs 1 and 2 where the amount of child support maintenance that would be payable in consequence of agreeing to a variation of that value is lower than the amount of the periodical payments of maintenance which were payable under the court order or written agreement referred to in regulation 16.

General Note

The statutory rate of interest in England, Wales and Scotland has been unchanged at 8 per cent since April 1, 1993. This is an unrealistically high figure to expect to earn on savings, and has been so for some time (*CCS 1844/2009*). This raises the issue whether the rate should be reduced under the just and equitable provision. The outcome is not determined by taking the current bank rate or level of interest rates, especially for assets other than savings (*PB v SSWP (CSM)* [2013] 0149 UKUT (AAC)). It is possible, in an appropriate case, to justify retaining 8 per cent (*DGH v SSWP and DAH (CSM)* [2013] UKUT 0299 (AAC) paras 36-42).

The Child Support (Maintenance Calculation Procedure) Regulations 2000
(SI 2001 No.157)

General Note on the Regulations

The Child Support (Maintenance Calculation Procedure) Regulations 2000 have been revoked for certain cases only by the Child Support (Meaning of Child and New Calculation Rules) (Consequential and Miscellaneous Amendment) Regulations 2012 (SI 2012 No.2785) reg 10 (this revocation comes into force in relation to a particular case on the day on which paragraph 2 of Schedule 4 to the Child Maintenance and Other Payments Act 2008 (see p243) comes into force in relation to that type of case – which is December 10, 2012, in relation to the types of cases falling within art 3 of SI 2012 No.3042 (see p767).

For other types of cases the '2003 rules', which include the Child Support (Maintenance Calculation Procedure) Regulations 2000, continue to apply. The Child Support (Maintenance Calculation Procedure) Regulations 2000 are therefore reproduced below.

29A.   Interim effective date where regulation 25, 28 or 29 applies
29B.   Effective date where there has been a previous maintenance calculation

PART VIII
REVOCATION, SAVINGS AND TRANSITIONAL PROVISIONS
30.   Revocation and savings
31.   Transitional provision–effective dates

SCHEDULES
SCHEDULE 1 – Meaning of "child" for the purposes of the Act
SCHEDULE 2 – Multiple applications
SCHEDULE 3 – Multiple applications – transitional provisions

PART I
GENERAL

Citation, commencement and interpretation
   1.–(1)   These Regulations may be cited as the Child Support (Maintenance Calculation Procedure) Regulations 2000.
   (2)   In these Regulations, unless the context otherwise requires–
"the Act" means the Child Support Act 1991;
"date of notification to the non-resident parent" means the date on which the non-resident parent is first given notice of a maintenance application;
"effective application" means as provided for in regulation 3;
"date of receipt" means the date on which the information or document is actually received;
"effective date" means the date on which a maintenance calculation takes effect for the purposes of the Act;
"notice of a maintenance application" means notice by the Secretary of State under regulation 5(1) that an application for a maintenance calculation has been made [²...] in relation to which the non-resident parent is named as a parent of the child to whom the application relates;
"Maintenance Calculations and Special Cases Regulations" means the Child Support (Maintenance Calculations and Special Cases) Regulations 2000;
"maintenance period" has the same meaning as in section 17(4A) of the Act;
"relevant person" means–
   (a)   a person with care;
   (b)   a non-resident parent;
   (c)   a parent who is treated as a non-resident parent under regulation 8 of the Maintenance Calculations and Special Cases Regulations;
   (d)   where the application for a maintenance calculation is made by a child under section 7 of the Act, that child, in respect of whom a maintenance calculation has been applied for, [²...] or is or has been in force.
   (3)   The provisions in Schedule 1 shall have effect to supplement the meaning of "child" in section 55 of the Act.
   (4)   In these Regulations, unless the context otherwise requires, a reference–
   (a)   to a numbered Part is to the Part of these Regulations bearing that number;
   (b)   to a numbered Schedule is to the Schedule to these Regulations bearing that number;
   (c)   to a numbered regulation is to the regulation in these Regulations bearing that number;
   (d)   in a regulation or Schedule to a numbered paragraph is to the paragraph in that regulation or Schedule bearing that number; and
   (e)   in a paragraph to a lettered or numbered sub-paragraph is to the sub-paragraph in that paragraph bearing that letter or number.
   (5)   These Regulations shall come into force in relation to a particular case on the day on which the amendments to sections 5, [²...] 12, [²...] 51 [¹and 54] of the Act made

by the Child Support, Pensions and Social Security Act 2000 come into force in relation to that type of case.

Amendments

1. Child Support (Miscellaneous Amendments) Regulations 2002 (SI 2002 No.1204) reg 6(2) (April 30, 2002).
2. Child Support (Consequential Provisions) Regulations 2008 (SI 2008 No.2543) reg 9(2) (October 27, 2008).

Documents

2.   Except where otherwise stated, where–

(a)   any document is given or sent to the Secretary of State, that document shall be treated as having been so given or sent on the day that it is received by the Secretary of State; and

(b)   any document is given or sent to any other person, that document shall, if sent by post to that person's last known or notified address, be treated as having been given or sent on the day that it is posted.

General Note

This regulation provides for the date when a document is given or sent.

Head (a)

The opening of mail may have been privatised. The Secretary of State has power to authorise post to be opened, but this head gives no power to authorise anyone other than the Secretary of State to receive the contents of it. However, it is receipt of the document that is relevant, not receipt of the information contained in it. So, it is important to know the date when it is opened. That may not be the date stamped on it, as the stamp may show either the date when the post was actually opened or the date when it was due to be delivered to the addressee.

Head (b)

This head was considered in detail by in *CCS 2288/2005.*

The non-resident parent was contacted using an address supplied by the person with care. This was where the father had lived some years previously and through which it was still possible to contact him. The commissioner decided that notice of an application for child support maintenance had been given on the day that the Child Support Agency wrote to the non-resident parent at that address. The commissioner analysed this head as follows:

"28.   First, as a matter of simple construction, it seems clear to me that the word 'last' governs both 'known' and 'notified' in regulation 2(b). So 'last known or notified address' is legislative shorthand for 'last known or last notified address'. It also seems self-evident to me that under regulation 2(b) the Secretary of State can send a document either to the 'last known' or the 'last notified' address as seems appropriate. The statutory language ... is permissive. I also accept ... that the role of the Secretary of State is central to the meaning of 'last known or notified address'. In other words, this expression means the address last known *by* the Secretary of State or last notified *to* the Secretary of State. There is no further qualification in regulation 2(b). So the means by which the Secretary of State acquires that knowledge is not in itself subject to any restriction. Similarly, an address may be notified to the Secretary of State by anyone. I also take the view that a 'last notified address' (as distinct from a 'last known address') implies that there is a higher degree of certainty in the validity of the address. So if a non-resident parent informs the Agency of a change of address-and curiously there is no statutory obligation to do so-then we might say that it is the 'last notified address'. If, on the other hand, a person with care effectively says 'I think this is his address', then it is a 'last known address'."

Perhaps more contentiously, the commissioner accepted the argument that the Secretary of State (para 61(6)) "must form a judgement as to whether any address given for the non-resident parent is reliable enough to justify sending the MEF to that address, bearing in mind regulation 5(1)). The Secretary of State need not be sure of the address beyond reasonable doubt, but needs to be satisfied on the balance of probabilities that it is likely to be an effective address. This will require consideration of all the circumstances and the exercise of reasonable diligence."

A document is only posted when it is sent by the Royal Mail and not by courier or through a document exchange system (*CIS 550/1993,* para 6). This head does not apply to a document that is never sent or given, even if the whereabouts of the person are unknown (*CCS 1284/1996*, para 7).

PART II

APPLICATIONS FOR A MAINTENANCE CALCULATION

Applications under section 4 or 7 of the Act

3.–(1)   A person who applies for a maintenance calculation under section 4 or 7 of the Act need not normally do so in writing, but if the Secretary of State directs that the application be made in writing, the application shall be made either by completing and returning, in accordance with the Secretary of State's instructions, a form provided for that purpose, or in such other written form as the Secretary of State may accept as sufficient in the circumstances of any particular case.

(2)   An application for a maintenance calculation is effective if it complies with paragraph (1) and, subject to paragraph (4), is made on the date it is received.

(3)   Where an application for a maintenance calculation is not effective the Secretary of State may request the person making the application to provide such additional information or evidence as the Secretary of State may specify and, where the application was made on a form, the Secretary of State may request that the information or evidence be provided on a fresh form.

(4)   Where the additional information or evidence requested is received by the Secretary of State within 14 days of the date of his request, or at a later date in circumstances where the Secretary of State is satisfied that the delay was unavoidable, he shall treat the application as made on the date on which the earlier or earliest application would have been treated as made had it been effective.

(5)   Where the Secretary of State receives the additional information or evidence requested by him more than 14 days from the date of the request and in circumstances where he is not satisfied that the delay was unavoidable, the Secretary of State shall treat the application as made on the date of receipt of the information or evidence.

(6)   Subject to paragraph (7), a person who has made an effective application may amend or withdraw the application at any time before a maintenance calculation is made and such amendment or withdrawal need not be in writing unless, in any particular case, the Secretary of State requires it to be.

(7)   No amendment made under paragraph (6) shall relate to any change of circumstances arising after the effective date of a maintenance calculation resulting from an effective application.

Definitions
"the Act": see reg 1(2).
"date of receipt": see reg 1(2).
"effective application": see reg 1(2).
"effective date": see reg 1(2).

General Note
Paragraph (1)
An application for a maintenance calculation will not normally have to be made in writing, but the Secretary of State has a reserve power to require it to be made in writing, most likely by completing a form. This only applies to applications under ss4 and 7; if a case falls under s6, an application is treated as made.

Paragraph (2)
This paragraph defines an effective application. An effective application is one that complies with formal requirements (*R(CS) 1/96*, para 11; *R(CS) 3/97*). It is not necessary for the information supplied to be accurate in all particulars (*CCS 2626/1999*, para 15). If the Secretary of State requires the application to be made by completing and returning a form, it must comply, or substantially comply, with the instructions given by the Secretary of State for completion and return of the form (*CCS 2626/1999*, para 15).

If an application is effective, it must be referred to a decision maker to be dealt with under s11 of the Act. It is then that officer's duty to determine whether the application has been properly made and, if it has, to make a calculation (*R(CS) 1/96*, paras 12-13).

Paragraphs (3)-(5)
These provide for the remedying of ineffective applications and for the date when they become effective.

Paragraph (6)
This paragraph allows amendments to an effective application. It does not deal with amendments to an ineffective application made with a view to it becoming effective. It is a permissible amendment to withdraw a child from an application (*CCS 8065/1995*, paras 11-12).

This paragraph does not prevent some parts of an effective application being rejected and the application processed with respect to the remainder (*CCS 2626/1999*, para 15). An application can be regarded as made on each succeeding day until it is decided (*YW v CMEC* [2011] UKUT (AAC) 176 (AAC), para 24). This allows a parent to make an application in advance (*ibid* para 21).

Paragraph (7)

Changes of circumstances that will occur after the effective date of a maintenance calculation cannot be added by way of amendment under para (6). They must be made the subject of an application for revision or supersession.

This only prevents changes being added by way of amendment. It does not prevent changes being identified in the application as originally made; they may be taken into account under Sch 1 para 15 to the Act.

Multiple applications

4.–(1) The provisions of Schedule 2 shall apply in cases where there is more than one application for a maintenance calculation.

(2) The provisions of paragraphs 1, 2 and 3 of Schedule 2 relating to the treatment of two or more applications as a single application shall apply where no request is received for the Secretary of State to cease acting in relation to all but one of the applications.

(3) Where, under the provisions of paragraph 1, 2 or 3 of Schedule 2, two or more applications are to be treated as a single application, that application shall be treated as an application for a maintenance calculation to be made with respect to all of the qualifying children mentioned in the applications, and the effective date of that maintenance calculation shall be determined by reference to the earlier or earliest application.

Definition

"effective date": see reg 1(2).

Notice of an application for a maintenance calculation

5.–(1) Where an effective application has been made under section 4 or 7 of the Act, [²...] as the case may be, the Secretary of State shall as soon as is reasonably practicable notify, orally or in writing, the non-resident parent and any other relevant persons (other than the person who has made [²...] the application) of that application and request such information as he may require to make the maintenance calculation in such form and manner as he may specify in the particular case.

(2) Where the person to whom notice is being given under paragraph (1) is a non-resident parent, that notice shall specify the effective date of the maintenance calculation if one is to be made, and the ability to make a default maintenance decision.

(3) Subject to paragraph (4), a person who has provided information under paragraph (1) may amend the information he has provided at any time before a maintenance calculation is made and such information need not be in writing unless, in any particular case, the Secretary of State requires it to be.

(4) No amendment under paragraph (3) shall relate to any change of circumstances arising after the effective date of any maintenance calculation made in response to the application in relation to which the information was requested.

Amendments

1. Child Support (Miscellaneous Amendments) Regulations 2003 (SI 2003 No.328) reg 7(2) (February 21, 2003).
2. Child Support (Consequential Provisions) Regulations 2008 (SI 2008 No.2543) reg 9(3) (October 27, 2008).

Definitions

"the Act": see reg 1(2).
"effective application": see reg 1(2).
"effective date": see reg 1(2).
"relevant person": see reg 1(2).

General Note

This regulation provides for notice of an application that is made or treated as made and for the obtaining of information relevant to the calculation. Neither the notice nor the provision need be in writing, although the Secretary of State may require information to be provided in writing.

Paragraph (2)

The notification requirement applies even if notice is effected by the parent with care (*CH v CMEC (CSM)* [2010] UKUT 140 (AAC), para 73).

Paragraph (4)

This paragraph reflects and is a necessary companion to reg 3(7).

Death of a qualifying child

6.–(1) Where the Secretary of State is informed of the death of a qualifying child with respect to whom an application for a maintenance calculation has been made [[1]...] he shall–

(a) proceed with the application as if it had not been made with respect to that child if he has not yet made a maintenance calculation;

(b) treat any maintenance calculation already made by him as not having been made if the relevant persons have not been notified of it and proceed with the application as if it had not been made with respect to that child.

(2) Where all of the qualifying children with respect to whom an application for a maintenance calculation has been made have died, and either the calculation has not been made or the relevant persons have not been notified of it, the Secretary of State shall treat the application as not having been made.

Amendment

1. Child Support (Consequential Provisions) Regulations 2008 (SI 2008 No.2543) reg 9(4) (October 27, 2008).

Definition

"relevant person": see reg 1(2).

General Note

The effect of this regulation is that a no maintenance calculation is made in respect of a child who dies before the calculation is both made and notified.

PART III
DEFAULT MAINTENANCE DECISIONS

Default rate

7.–(1) Where the Secretary of State makes a default maintenance decision under section 12(1) of the Act (insufficient information to make a maintenance calculation or to make a decision under section 16 or 17 of the Act) the default rate is as set out in paragraph (2).

(2) The default rate for the purposes of section 12(5)(b) of the Act shall be–

£30 where there is one qualifying child of the non-resident parent;

£40 where there are two qualifying children of the non-resident parent;

£50 where there are three or more qualifying children of the non-resident parent,

apportioned, where the non-resident parent has more than one qualifying child and in relation to them there is more than one person with care, as provided in paragraph 6(2) of Part I of Schedule 1 to the Act.

(3) Subject to paragraph (4), where any apportionment made under this regulation results in a fraction of a penny that fraction shall be treated as a penny if it is either one half or exceeds one half, otherwise it shall be disregarded.

(4) If, in making the apportionment required by this regulation, the effect of the application of paragraph (3) would be such that the aggregate amount of child support maintenance payable by a non-resident parent would be different from the aggregate amount payable before any apportionment, the Secretary of State shall adjust that apportionment so as to eliminate that difference; and that adjustment shall be varied from time to time so as to secure that, taking one week with another and so far as is practicable,

each person with care receives the amount which she would have received if no adjustment had been made under this paragraph.

Definition

"the Act": see reg 1(2).

General Note

This regulation sets the amount payable under a default maintenance decision, which is made if the CMEC has insufficient information to make a maintenance calculation or a revision or suprsession decision.

Paragraph (4)

The same provision is made for apportionment of the maintenance calculation by reg 6 of the Maintenance Calculations and Special Cases Regulations.

PART IV
REDUCED BENEFIT DECISIONS

Interpretation of Part IV
8. [²...]

Amendments

1. Child Support (Miscellaneous Amendments) (No.2) Regulations 2003 (SI 2003 No.2779) reg 5(2) (November 5, 2003). However, see Child Support (Miscellaneous Amendments) (No.2) Regulations 2003 (SI 2003 No.2779) reg 9 for savings provisions.
2. Child Support (Consequential Provisions) Regulations 2008 (SI 2008 No.2543) reg 9(5) (October 27, 2008).

Period within which reasons are to be given
9. [¹...]

Amendment

1. Child Support (Consequential Provisions) Regulations 2008 (SI 2008 No.2543) reg 9(5) (October 27, 2008).

[¹Period for parent to state if request still stands
9A. [²...]]

Amendments

1. Child Support (Miscellaneous Amendments) Regulations 2002 (SI 2002 No.1204) reg 6(3) (April 30, 2002).
2. Child Support (Consequential Provisions) Regulations 2008 (SI 2008 No.2543) reg 9(5) (October 27, 2008).

Circumstances in which a reduced benefit decision shall not be given
10. [³...]

Amendments

1. Child Support (Miscellaneous Amendments) Regulations 2003 (SI 2003 No.328) reg 7(3) (April 6, 2003).
2. Child Support (Miscellaneous Amendments) Regulations 2005 (SI 2005 No.785) reg 5 (March 16, 2005).
3. Child Support (Consequential Provisions) Regulations 2008 (SI 2008 No.2543) reg 9(5) (October 27, 2008).

Amount of and period of reduction of relevant benefit under a reduced benefit decision
11. [¹...]

Amendment

1. Child Support (Consequential Provisions) Regulations 2008 (SI 2008 No.2543) reg 9(5) (October 27, 2008).

Modification of reduction under a reduced benefit decision to preserve minimum entitlement to relevant benefit
12. [¹...]

Amendment
1. Child Support (Consequential Provisions) Regulations 2008 (SI 2008 No.2543) reg 9(5) (October 27, 2008).

Suspension of a reduced benefit decision when relevant benefit ceases to be payable
13. [¹...]

Amendment
1. Child Support (Consequential Provisions) Regulations 2008 (SI 2008 No.2543) reg 9(5) (October 27, 2008).

Suspension of a reduced benefit decision [¹...] (income support)
14. [²...]

Amendments
1. Child Support (Miscellaneous Amendments) (No.2) Regulations 2003 (SI 2003 No.2779) reg 5(3) (November 5, 2003). However, see Child Support (Miscellaneous Amendments) (No.2) Regulations 2003 (SI 2003 No.2779) reg 9 for savings provisions.
2. Child Support (Consequential Provisions) Regulations 2008 (SI 2008 No.2543) reg 9(5) (October 27, 2008).

Suspension of a reduced benefit decision [¹...] (income-based jobseeker's allowance)
15. [²...]

Amendments
1. Child Support (Miscellaneous Amendments) (No.2) Regulations 2003 (SI 2003 No.2779) reg 5(4) (November 5, 2003). However, see Child Support (Miscellaneous Amendments) (No.2) Regulations 2003 (SI 2003 No.2779) reg 9 for savings provisions.
2. Child Support (Consequential Provisions) Regulations 2008 (SI 2008 No.2543) reg 9(5) (October 27, 2008).

Termination of a reduced benefit decision
16. [¹...]

Amendment
1. Child Support (Consequential Provisions) Regulations 2008 (SI 2008 No.2543) reg 9(5) (October 27, 2008).

Reduced benefit decisions where there is an additional qualifying child
17. [¹...]

Amendment
1. Child Support (Consequential Provisions) Regulations 2008 (SI 2008 No.2543) reg 9(5) (October 27, 2008).

Suspension and termination of a reduced benefit decision where the sole qualifying child ceases to be a child or where the parent concerned ceases to be a person with care
18. [¹...]

Amendment
1. Child Support (Consequential Provisions) Regulations 2008 (SI 2008 No.2543) reg 9(5) (October 27, 2008).

Notice of termination of a reduced benefit decision
19. [¹...]

Amendment

1. Child Support (Consequential Provisions) Regulations 2008 (SI 2008 No.2543) reg 9(5) (October 27, 2008).

Rounding provisions

20. [¹...]

Amendment

1. Child Support (Consequential Provisions) Regulations 2008 (SI 2008 No.2543) reg 9(5) (October 27, 2008).

PART V
MISCELLANEOUS PROVISIONS

Persons who are not persons with care

21.–(1) For the purposes of the Act the following categories of person shall not be persons with care–

(a) a local authority;

(b) a person with whom a child who is looked after by a local authority is placed by that authority under the provisions of the Children Act 1989, except where that person is a parent of such a child and the local authority allow the child to live with that parent under section 23(5) of that Act;

(c) in Scotland, a family or relative with whom a child is placed by a local authority under the provisions of section 26 of the Children (Scotland) Act 1995.

(2) paragraph (1) above–

"family" means family other than such family defined in section 93(1) of the Children (Scotland) Act 1995;

"local authority" means, in relation to England, a county council, a district council, a London borough council, the Common Council of the City of London or the Council of the Isles of Scilly and, in relation to Wales, a county council or a county borough council, and, in relation to Scotland, a council constituted under section 2 of the Local Government etc (Scotland) Act 1994; and

"a child who is looked after by a local authority" has the same meaning as in section 22 of the Children Act 1989 or section 17(6) of the Children (Scotland) Act 1995 as the case may be.

Definition

"the Act": see reg 1(2).

Authorisation of representative

22.–(1) A person may authorise a representative, whether or not legally qualified, to receive notices and other documents on his behalf and to act on his behalf in relation to the making of applications and the supply of information under any provisions of the Act or these Regulations.

(2) Where a person has authorised a representative for the purposes of paragraph (1) who is not legally qualified, he shall confirm that authorisation in writing to the Secretary of State.

Definition

"the Act": see reg 1(2).

General Note

A person may act through a representative. The representative need not be legally qualified, but the authority of a representative who is not legally qualified must be confirmed in writing.

PART VI
NOTIFICATIONS FOLLOWING CERTAIN DECISIONS

Notification of a maintenance calculation

23.–(1)   A notification of a maintenance calculation made under section 11 or 12(2) of the Act (interim maintenance decision) shall set out, in relation to the maintenance calculation in question–

(a)   the effective date of the maintenance calculation;

(b)   where relevant, the non-resident parent's net weekly income;

(c)   the number of qualifying children;

(d)   the number of relevant other children;

(e)   the weekly rate;

(f)   the amounts calculated in accordance with Part I of Schedule 1 to the Act and, where there has been agreement to a variation or a variation has otherwise been taken into account, the Child Support (Variations) Regulations 2000;

(g)   where the weekly rate is adjusted by apportionment or shared care, or both, the amount calculated in accordance with paragraph 6, 7 or 8, as the case may be, of Part I of Schedule 1 to the Act; and

(h)   where the amount of child support maintenance which the non-resident parent is liable to pay is decreased in accordance with regulation 9 or 11 of the Maintenance Calculations and Special Cases Regulations (care provided in part by local authority and non-resident parent liable to pay maintenance under a maintenance order), the adjustment calculated in accordance with that regulation.

(2)   A notification of a maintenance calculation made under section 12(1) of the Act (default maintenance decision) shall set out the effective date of the maintenance calculation, the default rate, the number of qualifying children on which the rate is based, whether any apportionment has been applied under regulation 7 and shall state the nature of the information required to enable a decision under section 11 of the Act to be made by way of section 16 of the Act.

(3)   Except where a person gives written permission to the Secretary of State that the information in relation to him, mentioned in sub-paragraphs (a) and (b) below, may be conveyed to other persons, any document given or sent under the provisions of paragraph (1) or (2) shall not contain–

(a)   the address of any person other than the recipient of the document in question (other than the address of the office of the officer concerned who is exercising functions of the Secretary of State under the Act) or any other information the use of which could reasonably be expected to lead to any such person being located;

(b)   any other information the use of which could reasonably be expected to lead to any person, other than a qualifying child or a relevant person, being identified.

(4)   Where a decision as to a maintenance calculation is made under section 11 or 12 of the Act, a notification under paragraph (1) or (2) shall include information as to the provisions of sections 16, 17 and 20 of the Act.

Definitions
"the Act": see reg 1(2).
"effective date": see reg 1(2).
"Maintenance Calculations and Special Cases Regulations": see reg 1(2).
"relevant person": see reg 1(2).

General Note
Paragraphs (1)-(2)
These paragraphs provide for notification of a maintenance calculation or of a default maintenance decision or an interim maintenance decision. The matters listed are the minimum that must be provided. Other matters may also be notified and natural justice requires that any information needed to explain the assessment to the parties must be included (*Huxley v Child Support Officer and Huxley* [2000] 1 FLR 898 at 906 *per* Hale LJ).
Paragraph (3)
This paragraph contains a confidentiality provision.

Notification when an applicant under section 7 of the Act ceases to be a child

24. Where a maintenance calculation has been made in response to an application by a child under section 7 of the Act and that child ceases to be a child for the purposes of the Act, the Secretary of State shall immediately notify, so far as that is reasonably practicable–

(a) the other qualifying children who have attained the age of 12 years and the non-resident parent with respect to whom that maintenance calculation was made; and

(b) the person with care.

Definition

"the Act": see reg 1(2).

PART VII
EFFECTIVE DATES OF MAINTENANCE CALCULATIONS

Effective dates of maintenance calculations

25.–(1) Subject to regulations 26 to 29[[3], 29B] [[1]and 31], where no maintenance calculation is in force with respect to the person with care or the non-resident parent, the effective date of a maintenance calculation following an application made under section 4 or 7 of the Act, [[2]...] as the case may be, shall be the date determined in accordance with paragraphs (2) to (4) below.

(2) Where the application for a maintenance calculation is made under section 4 of the Act by a non-resident parent, the effective date of the maintenance calculation shall be the date that an effective application is made or treated as made under regulation 3.

(3) Where the application for a maintenance calculation is–

(a) made under section 4 of the Act by a person with care;

(b) [[2]...]

(c) made by a child under section 7 of the Act,

the effective date of the maintenance calculation shall be the date of notification to the non-resident parent.

(4) For the purposes of this regulation, where the Secretary of State is satisfied that a non-resident parent has intentionally avoided receipt of a notice of a maintenance application he may determine the date of notification to the non-resident parent as the date on which the notification would have been given to him but for such avoidance.

(5) Where in relation to a decision made under section 11 of the Act a maintenance calculation is made to which paragraph 15 of Schedule 1 to the Act applies, the effective date of the calculation shall be the beginning of the maintenance period in which the change of circumstance to which the calculation relates occurred or is expected to occur.

Amendments

1. Child Support (Miscellaneous Amendments) Regulations 2003 (SI 2003 No.328) reg 7(4) (February 21, 2003).

2. Child Support (Consequential Provisions) Regulations 2008 (SI 2008 No.2543) reg 9(6) (October 27, 2008).

3. Child Support (Miscellaneous Amendments) (No.2) Regulations 2008 (SI 2008 No.2544) reg 5(2) (October 27, 2008).

Definitions

"the Act": see reg 1(2).
"date of notification to the non-resident parent": see reg 1 (2).
"effective application": see reg 1(2).
"effective date": see reg 1(2).
"maintenance period": see reg 1(2).
"notice of a maintenance application": see reg 1(2).

General Note

This contains the basic provisions for determining the effective date if a maintenance calculation is not in force.

Paragraph (2)
If a maintenance calculation is made on the application of the non-resident parent, the effective date is the date of the parent's effective application.

Paragraph (3)
If a maintenance calculation is made otherwise than on the application of the non-resident parent, the effective date is the date on which that parent was given notice that an application has been made or treated as made. This is subject to the anti-avoidance provision in para (4). The notification may be effective even if it is effected by the parent with care, although it must comply with the notice requirements in reg 5(2): *CH v CMEC (CSM)* [2010] UKUT 140 (AAC), paras 36 and 73.

Paragraph (5)
If a series of maintenance calculations is made under Sch 1 para 15 to the Act, the effective date of the first calculation is made under paras (2)-(4) and the effective dates of the subsequent assessments are the first day of the maintenance periods in which the relevant changes of circumstances occur.

Effective dates of maintenance calculations – maintenance order and application under section 4 or 7

26.–(1)   This regulation applies, subject to [² regulations 28 and 29B], where–
(a)   no maintenance calculation is in force with respect to the person with care or the non-resident parent;
(b)   an application for a maintenance calculation is made under section 4 or 7 of the Act; and
[¹(c)   there is a maintenance order [³or, in Scotland, a maintenance agreement registered for execution in the Books of Council and Session or the sheriff court books,] which–
    (i)   is in force and was made on or after the date prescribed for the purposes of section 4(10)(a) of the Act;
    (ii)   relates to the person with care, the non-resident parent and all the children to whom the application referred to in sub-paragraph (b) relates; and
    (iii)   has been in force for at least one year prior to the date of the application referred to in sub-paragraph (b).]
(2)   The effective date of the maintenance calculation shall be two months and two days after the application is made.

Amendments
1.   Child Support (Miscellaneous Amendments) Regulations 2002 (SI 2002 No.1204) reg 6(4) (April 30, 2002).
2.   Child Support (Miscellaneous Amendments) (No.2) Regulations 2008 (SI 2008 No.2544) reg 5(3) (October 27, 2008).
3.   Child Support (Miscellaneous Amendments) Regulations 2011 (SI 2011 No.1464) reg 4 (July 4, 2011).

Definitions
"the Act": see reg 1(2).
"effective date": see reg 1(2)

General Note
This regulation, together with regs 27 and 28, deals the effective date in cases in which a maintenance order is in force before a maintenance calculation is made.

Paragraph (1)
This sets out the conditions that must be satisfied: a maintenance order has been in force in relation to the person with care and the non-resident parent for at least one year before the date of an application under s4 or s7 of the Act.

Paragraph (2)
If the conditions in para (1) are satisfied, the effective date is two months and two days after the date of the application. Unlike under reg 27, the date when the maintenance calculation is made is irrelevant. This paragraph and head (c) refer to the date on which the application was made. They do not refer to an *effective* application or to the date on which the application was made or was treated as made under reg 3. Contrast regs 25(2) and 29(a).

Effective dates of maintenance calculations – maintenance order and application under section 6

27.   [²...]

Amendments

1.   Child Support (Miscellaneous Amendments) Regulations 2002 (SI 2002 No.1204) reg 6(5) (April 30, 2002).

2.   Child Support (Consequential Provisions) Regulations 2008 (SI 2008 No.2543) reg 9(7) (October 27, 2008).

Effective dates of maintenance calculations – maintenance order ceases

28.   [³ Subject to regulation 29B,] where–

(a)   a maintenance calculation is made; and

(b)   there was a maintenance order in force in relation to the person with care and the non-resident parent which ceased to have effect after the date on which the application for the maintenance calculation was made but before the effective date provided for in regulation [¹26] [²...],

the effective date of the maintenance calculation shall be the day following that on which the maintenance order ceased to have effect.

Amendments

1.   Child Support (Miscellaneous Amendments) Regulations 2002 (SI 2002 No.1204) reg 6(6) (April 30, 2002).

2.   Child Support (Consequential Provisions) Regulations 2008 (SI 2008 No.2543) reg 9(8) (October 27, 2008).

3.   Child Support (Miscellaneous Amendments) (No.2) Regulations 2008 (SI 2008 No.2544) reg 5(4) (October 27, 2008).

Definition

"effective date": see reg 1(2).

General Note

This regulation, together with reg 26, deals the effective date in cases in which a maintenance order is in force before a maintenance calculation is made.

The conditions

Heads (a) and (b) set out the conditions that must be satisfied: a maintenance order was in force in relation to the person with care and the non-resident parent when an application was made under ss4 or 7 of the Act, but had ceased to have effect before the effective date as determined by reg 26.

    Head (b) refers to the date on which the application was made. It does not refer to an *effective* application or to the date on which the application was made or was treated as made under reg 3. Contrast regs 25(2) and 29(a).

The effective date

If the conditions in heads (a) and (b) are satisfied, the effective date is the day after the maintenance order ceased to have effect.

Effective dates of maintenance calculations in specified cases

29.   [⁵ Subject to regulation 29B,][²(1)]where an application for a maintenance calculation is made under section 4 or 7 of the Act [⁴...]–

(a)   [⁴...] where in the period of 8 weeks immediately preceding the date the application is made, or treated as made under regulation 3, there has been in force a maintenance calculation in respect of the same non-resident parent and child but a different person with care, the effective date of the maintenance calculation made in respect of the application shall be [²the date] on which the previous maintenance calculation ceased to have effect;

(b)   where a maintenance calculation ("the existing calculation") is in force with respect to the person who is the person with care in relation to the application but who is the non-resident parent in relation to the existing calculation, the effective date of the calculation shall be a date not later than 7 days after the date of notification to the non-resident parent which is the day on which a maintenance period in respect of the existing calculation begins.

[¹(c)   [⁴...] where–

    (i)   in the period of 8 weeks immediately preceding the date the application is made, or treated as made under regulation 3, a maintenance calculation ("the previous maintenance calculation") has been in force and has ceased to have effect;

(ii)   the parent with care in respect of the previous maintenance calculation is the non-resident parent in respect of the application;

(iii)   the non-resident parent in respect of the previous maintenance calculation is the parent with care in respect of the application; and

(iv)   the application relates to the same qualifying child, or all of the same qualifying children, and no others, as the previous maintenance calculation,

the effective date of the maintenance calculation to which the application relates shall be the date on which the previous maintenance calculation ceased to have effect.]

[³(d) [⁴...] where on the date the application is made, or treated as made under regulation 3, there is in force a maintenance calculation in relation to the same non-resident parent and a different person with care, and the maintenance calculation in force when the application was made has ceased to have effect before a decision has been made in respect of that application, the effective date of the maintenance calculation made in response to the application shall be–

(i)   where the date of notification to the non-resident parent is before the date on which the maintenance calculation in force has ceased to have effect, the day following the day on which that maintenance calculation ceases to have effect;

(ii)   where the date of notification to the non-resident parent is after the date on which the maintenance calculation in force has ceased to have effect, the date of notification to the non-resident parent.]

[²(2) [⁴...]

(3)   For the purposes of–

(a)   paragraph (1), "ceased to have effect" means ceased to have effect under paragraph 16 of Schedule 1 to the Act; and

(b)   [⁴...]]

Amendments

1.   Child Support (Miscellaneous Amendments) Regulations 2002 (SI 2002 No.1204) reg 6(7) (April 30, 2002).

2.   Child Support (Miscellaneous Amendments) Regulations 2003 (SI 2003 No.328) reg 7(5) (February 21, 2003).

3.   Child Support (Miscellaneous Amendments) Regulations 2004 (SI 2004 No.2415) reg 6(2) (September 16, 2004).

4.   Child Support (Consequential Provisions) Regulations 2008 (SI 2008 No.2543) reg 9(9) (October 27, 2008).

5.   Child Support (Miscellaneous Amendments) (No.2) Regulations 2008 (SI 2008 No.2544) reg 5(5) (October 27, 2008).

Definitions

"the Act": see reg 1(2).
"date of notification to the non-resident parent": see reg 1(2).
"effective date": see reg 1(2).
"maintenance period": see reg 1(2).

General Note

This regulation operates to achieve continuity in child support liability when there is a change of roles.

Heads (a) and (d) apply when the non-resident parent remains the same, but a new person with care takes over. For example, if a grandparent takes over day to day care from the child's mother. Head (a) applies when the new application is made within 8 weeks of the calculation for the outgoing person with care ceasing to have effect. Head (d) applies when that calculation is still in force when the new application is made but ceases to have effect before it is decided.

Heads (b) and (c) apply when the non-resident parent and person with care swap roles. Head (b) applies when the calculation for the outgoing non-resident parent is still in force when the application is made. Head (c) applies when the new application is made within 8 weeks of the calculation for the outgoing non-resident parent ceasing to have effect.

These provisions depend for their effectiveness on prompt decision-making by the Secretary of State. In *IG v SSWP (CSM)* [2013] UKUT 70 (AAC), the Upper Tribunal dealt with a case under head (c) in which there had been considerable delay in deciding the new application and there had been multiple applications. The judge decided that head (c)(i) was satisfied even if it was only realised or decided that the calculation had ceased to have effect subsequently.

Regulation 31(1) makes transitional provision.

[¹Interim effective date where regulation 25, 28 or 29 applies

29A.–(1)   Where the Secretary of State has sufficient information to enable him to make a maintenance calculation, but only in respect of a period beginning after the date which would have been the effective date under regulation 25, 28 or 29 ("the original effective date"), the effective date of that calculation ("the interim effective date") shall, instead, be the first day of the maintenance period after the Secretary of State receives that information.

(2)   Where the information referred to in paragraph (1) is that the non-resident parent or his partner has been awarded any benefit, pension or allowance prescribed for the purposes of paragraph 4 of Schedule 1 to the Act (flat rate), the Secretary of State shall be treated as having received the information on the first day in respect of which that benefit, pension or allowance was payable under that award.

(3)   If the Secretary of State subsequently receives sufficient information to enable him to make a maintenance calculation for the period from the original effective date to the interim effective date, that calculation shall have effect for that period.]

Amendment

1.   Child Support (Miscellaneous Amendments) Regulations 2006 (SI 2006 No.1520) reg 5 (July 12, 2006).

Definition

"the Act": see reg 1(2).

[¹ Effective date where there has been a previous maintenance calculation

29B.–(1)   This regulation applies where–
- (a)   a maintenance calculation ("the previous maintenance calculation") has been in force in relation to the non-resident parent, whether or not in respect of the same parent with care; and
- (b)   the previous maintenance calculation is no longer in force when the decision as to the maintenance calculation is made.

(2)   Where this regulation applies, the effective date of the maintenance calculation shall be–
- (a)   on, or on one of the 6 days immediately following, the effective date as it would have been but for this regulation; and
- (b)   on the same day of the week as the day on which the maintenance period in respect of the previous maintenance calculation began.]

Amendment

1.   Child Support (Miscellaneous Amendments) (No.2) Regulations 2008 (SI 2008 No.2544) reg 5(6) (October 27, 2008).

Definition

"effective date": see reg 1(2).

PART VIII
REVOCATION, SAVINGS AND TRANSITIONAL PROVISIONS

Revocation and savings

30.–(1)   Subject to [²the Child Support (Transitional Provisions) Regulations 2000 and] paragraph (2), the Child Support (Maintenance Assessment Procedure) Regulations 1992 shall be revoked with respect to a particular case with effect from the date that these Regulations come into force with respect to that type of case ("the commencement date").

(2)   Subject to [[1]regulation 31(1C)(b) and (2)], where before the commencement date in respect of a particular case–

(a)   an application was made and not determined for–
    (i)   a maintenance assessment;
    (ii)   a departure direction; or
    (iii)   a revision or supersession of a decision;

(b)   the Secretary of State had begun but not completed a revision or supersession of a decision on his own initiative;

(c)   any time limit provided for in Regulations for making an application for a revision or a departure direction had not expired; or

(d)   any appeal was made but not decided or any time limit for making an appeal had not expired,

the provisions of the Child Support (Maintenance Assessment Procedure) Regulations 1992 shall continue to apply for the purposes of–

    (aa)   the decision on the application referred to in sub-paragraph (a);
    (bb)   the revision or supersession referred to in sub-paragraph (b);
    (cc)   the ability to apply for the revision or the departure direction referred to in sub-paragraph (c) and the decision whether to revise or to give a departure direction following any such application;
    (dd)   any appeal outstanding or made during the time limit referred to in sub-paragraph (d); or
    (ee)   any revision, supersession, appeal or application for a departure direction in relation to a decision, ability to apply or appeal referred to in sub-paragraphs (aa) to (dd) above.

(3)   Where immediately before the commencement date in respect of a particular case an interim maintenance assessment was in force, the provisions of the Child Support (Maintenance Assessment Procedure) Regulations 1992 shall continue to apply for the purposes of the decision under section 17 of the Act to make a maintenance assessment calculated in accordance with Part I of Schedule 1 to the 1991 Act before its amendment by the 2000 Act and any revision, supersession or appeal in relation to that decision.

(4)   Where after the commencement date a maintenance assessment is revised, cancelled or ceases to have effect from a date which is prior to the commencement date, the Child Support (Maintenance Assessment Procedure) Regulations 1992 shall apply for the purposes of that cancellation or cessation.

(5)   Where under regulation 28(1) of the Child Support (Transitional Provisions) Regulations 2000 an application for a maintenance calculation is treated as an application for a maintenance assessment, the provisions of the Child Support (Maintenance Assessment Procedure) Regulations 1992 shall continue to apply for the purposes of the determination of the application and any revision, supersession or appeal in relation to any such assessment made.

(6)   For the purposes of this regulation–

(a)   "departure direction", "maintenance assessment" and "interim maintenance assessment" have the same meaning as in section 54 of the Act before its amendment by the 2000 Act;

(b)   "revision or supersession" means a revision or supersession of a decision under section 16 or 17 of the Act before their amendment by the 2000 Act;

(c)   "2000 Act" means the Child Support, Pensions and Social Security Act 2000.

Amendments
    1.   Child Support (Miscellaneous Amendments) Regulations 2003 (SI 2003 No.328) reg 7(6) (February 21, 2003).
    2.   Child Support (Transitional Provision)(Miscellaneous Amendments) Regulations 2003 (SI 2003 No.347) reg 2(1) and (2) (March 3, 2003).

Definition
    "the Act": see reg 1(2).

Transitional provision – effective dates [⁴...]

   31.–[²(1)   Where a maintenance assessment is, or has been, in force and an application to which regulation 29 applies is made, [⁴...] that regulation shall apply as if in paragraph (1) references to–

   (a)   a maintenance calculation in force were to a maintenance assessment in force;

   (b)   a maintenance calculation having been in force were to a maintenance assessment having been in force; and

   (c)   a non-resident parent in sub-paragraph (a), the first time it occurs in sub-paragraph (b)[³, in sub-paragraph (c)(iii) and the first time it occurs in sub-paragraph (d)], were to an absent parent.

   (1A)   Where regulation 28(7) of the Child Support (Transitional Provisions) Regulations 2000 (linking provisions) applies, the effective date of the maintenance calculation shall be the date which would have been the beginning of the first maintenance period in respect of the conversion decision on or after what, but for this paragraph, would have been the relevant effective date provided for in regulation 25(2) to (4).

   (1B)   The provisions of Schedule 3 shall apply where–

   (a)   an effective application for a maintenance assessment has been made under the former Act ("an assessment application"); and

   (b)   an effective application for a maintenance calculation is made [⁴...] ("a calculation application").

   (1C)   Where the provisions of Schedule 3 apply and, by virtue of regulation 4(3) of the Assessment Procedure Regulations, the relevant date would be–

   (a)   before the prescribed date, the application to be proceeded with shall be treated as an application for a maintenance assessment;

   (b)   on or after the prescribed date, that application shall be treated as an application for a maintenance calculation and the effective date of that maintenance calculation shall be the date which would be the assessment effective date if a maintenance assessment were to be made.

   [⁵ (1D)   Where a maintenance assessment has been in force in relation to a non-resident parent, regulation 29B shall apply as if references to a maintenance calculation having been in force were to a maintenance assessment having been in force.]

   (2)   Where–

   (a)   an application for a maintenance assessment was made before the prescribed date; and

   (b)   the assessment effective date of that application would be on or after the prescribed date,

the application shall be treated as an application for a maintenance calculation and the effective date of that maintenance calculation shall be the date which would be the assessment effective date if a maintenance assessment were to be made.]

   (3)   [⁴...]

   (4)   [⁴...]

   (5)   [⁴...]

   (6)   [⁴...]

   (7)   [⁴...]

   (8)   For the purposes of this regulation–

   (a)   "2000 Act" means the Child Support, Pensions and Social Security Act 2000;

[²"absent parent" has the meaning given in section 3(2) of the former Act;

"assessment effective date" means the effective date of the maintenance assessment under regulation 30 or 33(7) of the Assessment Procedure Regulations or regulation 3(5), (7) or (8) of the Maintenance Arrangements and Jurisdiction Regulations, whichever applied to the maintenance assessment in question or would have applied had the effective date not been determined under regulation 8C or 30A of the Assessment Procedure Regulations;]

"Assessment Procedure Regulations" means the Child Support (Maintenance Assessment Procedure) Regulations 1992;

"commencement date" means with respect to a particular case the date these Regulations come into force with respect to that type of case;

"former Act" means the Act before its amendment by the 2000 Act;

"Maintenance Arrangements and Jurisdiction Regulations" means the Child Support (Maintenance Arrangements and Jurisdiction) Regulations 1992;

"maintenance assessment" has the meaning given in the former Act; and

"prescribed date" means the date prescribed for the purposes of section 4(10)(a) of the Act; [²and

"relevant date" means the date which would be the assessment effective date of the application which is to be proceeded with in accordance with Schedule 3, if a maintenance assessment were to be made.]

(b) [⁴...]

(c) in the application of the Assessment Procedure Regulations for the purposes of paragraph (4) where, on or after the prescribed date, no maintenance enquiry form, as defined in those Regulations, is given or sent to the absent parent, the Regulations shall be applied as if references in regulation 30–

   (i) to the date when the maintenance enquiry form was given or sent to the absent parent were to the date of notification to the non-resident parent;

   (ii) to the return by the absent parent of the maintenance enquiry form containing his name, address and written confirmation that he is the parent of the child or children in respect of whom the application was made were to the provision of this information by the non-resident parent; and

(d) in the application of the Maintenance Arrangements and Jurisdiction Regulations for the purposes of paragraph (4), where, on or after the prescribed date no maintenance enquiry form, as defined in the Assessment Procedure Regulations, is given or sent to the absent parent, regulation 3(8) shall be applied as if the reference to the date when the maintenance enquiry form was given or sent were a reference to the date of notification to the non-resident parent.

Amendments

1. Child Support (Miscellaneous Amendments) Regulations 2002 (SI 2002 No.1204) reg 6(8) (April 30, 2002).

2. Child Support (Miscellaneous Amendments) Regulations 2003 (SI 2003 No.328) reg 7(7) (February 21, 2003).

3. Child Support (Miscellaneous Amendments) Regulations 2004 (SI 2004 No.2415) reg 6(3) (September 16, 2004).

4. Child Support (Consequential Provisions) Regulations 2008 (SI 2008 No.2543) reg 9(10) (October 27, 2008).

5. Child Support (Miscellaneous Amendments) (No.2) Regulations 2008 (SI 2008 No.2544) reg 5(7) (October 27, 2008).

Definitions

"the Act": see reg 1(2).

"date of notification to the non-resident parent": see reg 1(2).

SCHEDULE 1
MEANING OF "CHILD" FOR THE PURPOSES OF THE ACT

[⁴Conditions prescribed for the purposes of section 55(1)]

[²[³**1.**–(1) A person satisfies such conditions as may be prescribed for the purposes of section 55(1) of the Act if that person satisfies any of the conditions in sub-paragraphs (2) and (3).

(2) The person is receiving full-time education (which is not advanced education)–

(a) by attendance at a recognised educational establishment; or

(b) elsewhere, if the education is recognised by the Secretary of State.

(3) The person is a person in respect of whom child benefit is payable.]

Period for which a person is to be treated as continuing to fall within section 55(1) of the Act

1A. [³...]]

Meaning of "advanced education" for the purposes of section 55 of the Act

[²**2.** For the purposes of [³this Schedule] "advanced education" means education for the purposes of–

(a) a course in preparation for a degree, a diploma of higher education [³, a higher national certificate], a higher national diploma or a teaching qualification; or

(b) any other course which is of a standard above ordinary national diploma, a national diploma or national certificate of Edexcel, a general certificate of education (advanced level) or Scottish national qualifications at higher or advanced higher level.]

Circumstances in which education is to be treated as full-time education

3. For the purposes of [³this Schedule] education shall be treated as being full-time if it is received by a person attending a course of education at a recognised educational establishment and the time spent receiving instruction or tuition, undertaking supervised study, examination of practical work or taking part in any exercise, experiment or project for which provision is made in the curriculum of the course, exceeds 12 hours per week, so however that in calculating the time spent in pursuit of the course, no account shall be taken of time occupied by meal breaks or spent on unsupervised study, whether undertaken on or off the premises of the educational establishment.

Interruption of full-time education

4.–(1) Subject to sub-paragraph (2), in determining whether a person falls within [³paragraph 1(2)] no account shall be taken of a period (whether beginning before or after the person concerned attains age 16) of up to 6 months of any interruption to the extent to which it is accepted that the interruption is attributable to a cause which is reasonable in the particular circumstances of the case; and where the interruption or its continuance is attributable to the illness or disability of mind or body of the person concerned, the period of 6 months may be extended for such further period as the Secretary of State considers reasonable in the particular circumstances of the case.

[² (2) The provisions of sub-paragraph (1) do not apply to any period of interruption of a person's full-time education which is followed immediately by a period during which child benefit ceases to be payable in respect of that person.]

Circumstances in which a person who has ceased to receive full-time education is to be treated as continuing to fall within section 55(1) of the Act

5. [²...]

Interpretation

[²[³6. In this Schedule, "recognised educational establishment" means an establishment recognised by the Secretary of State for the purposes of this Schedule as being, or as comparable to, a university, college or school.]]

[³Education otherwise than at a recognised educational establishment

7. For the purposes of paragraph 1(2), the Secretary of State may recognise education provided for a person otherwise than at a recognised educational establishment only if satisfied that education was being so provided for that person immediately before that person attained the age of 16.]

[⁴Person in respect of whom child benefit is payable

8. For the purposes of paragraphs 1(3) and 4(2), a person in respect of whom child benefit is payable includes a person in respect of whom an election has been made under section 13A(1) of the Social Security Administration Act 1992 (election not to receive child benefit) for payments of child benefit not to be made.]

Amendments

1. Employment and Support Allowance (Consequential Provisions) (No.2) Regulations 2008 (SI 2008 No.1554) reg 63 (October 27, 2008).
2. Child Support (Miscellaneous Amendments) (No.2) Regulations 2009 (SI 2009 No.2909) reg 4 (November 10, 2009).
3. Child Support (Meaning of Child and New Calculation Rules) (Consequential and Miscellaneous Amendment) Regulations 2012 (SI 2012 No.2785) reg 3 (December 10, 2012).
4. Child Support (Miscellaneous Amendments) Regulations 2013 (SI 2013 No.1517) reg 7(2) (September 30, 2013).

Definition

"the Act"; see reg 1(2).

General Note

For commentary on the provisions of this Schedule, see the General Note to s55 of the Act on p137. The definition in para 3 applies only for the purposes of that section and does not apply to the definition of student in the Maintenance Calculations and Special Cases Regulations: *DY v CMEC* [2010] UKUT 19 (AAC); AACR 32, paras 27-28.

SCHEDULE 2
MULTIPLE APPLICATIONS

No maintenance calculation in force: more than one application for a maintenance calculation by the same person under section 4 [¹...] of the Act

1.–(1)   Where an effective application is made or treated as made, as the case may be, for a maintenance calculation under section 4 [¹...] of the Act and, before that calculation is made, the applicant makes a subsequent effective application under that section with respect to the same non-resident parent or person with care, as the case may be, those applications shall be treated as a single application.

(2)   [¹...]

No maintenance calculation in force: more than one application by a child under section 7 of the Act

2.   Where a child makes an effective application for a maintenance calculation under section 7 of the Act and, before that calculation is made, makes a subsequent effective application under that section with respect to the same person with care and non-resident parent, both applications shall be treated as a single application for a maintenance calculation.

No maintenance calculation in force: applications by different persons for a maintenance calculation

3.–(1)   Where the Secretary of State receives more than one effective application for a maintenance calculation with respect to the same person with care and non-resident parent, he shall, if no maintenance calculation has been made in relation to any of the applications, determine which application he shall proceed with in accordance with sub-paragraphs (2) to (11).

(2)   Where an application by a person with care is made under section 4 of the Act [¹...] and an application is made by a non-resident parent under section 4 of the Act, the Secretary of State shall proceed with the application of the person with care.

(3)   Where there is an application for a maintenance calculation by a qualifying child under section 7 of the Act and a subsequent application is made with respect to that child by a person who is, with respect to that child, a person with care or a non-resident parent, the Secretary of State shall proceed with the application of that person with care or non-resident parent, as the case may be.

(4)   Where, in a case falling within sub-paragraph (3), there is made more than one subsequent application, the Secretary of State shall apply the provisions of sub-paragraphs (2), (7), (8), or (10), as is appropriate in the circumstances of the case, to determine which application he shall proceed with.

(5)   Where there is an application for a maintenance calculation by more than one qualifying child under section 7 of the Act in relation to the same person with care and non-resident parent, the Secretary of State shall proceed with the application of the elder or, as the case may be, eldest of the qualifying children.

(6)   Where there are two non-resident parents in respect of the same qualifying child and an effective application is received from each such person, the Secretary of State shall proceed with both applications, treating them as a single application for a maintenance calculation.

(7)   [¹...]

(8)   Where–

(a)   more than one person with care makes an application for a maintenance calculation under section 4 of the Act in respect of the same qualifying child or qualifying children (whether or not any of those applications is also in respect of other qualifying children);

(b)   each such person has parental responsibility for (or, in Scotland, parental rights over) that child or children; and

(c)   under the provisions of regulation 8 of the Maintenance Calculations and Special Cases Regulations one of those persons is to be treated as a non-resident parent,

the Secretary of State shall proceed with the application of the person who does not fall to be treated as a non-resident parent under the provisions of regulation 8 of those Regulations.

(9)   Where, in a case falling within sub-paragraph (8), there is more than one person who does not fall to be treated as a non-resident parent under the provisions of regulation 8 of those Regulations, the Secretary of State shall apply the provisions of paragraph (10) to determine which application he shall proceed with.

(10)   Where–

(a)   more than one person with care makes an application for a maintenance calculation under section 4 of the Act in respect of the same qualifying child or qualifying children (whether or not any of those applications is also in respect of other qualifying children); and

(b)   either–

(i)   none of those persons has parental responsibility for (or, in Scotland, parental rights over) that child or children; or

(ii)   the case falls within sub-paragraph (8)(b) but the Secretary of State has not been able to determine which application he is to proceed with under the provisions of sub-paragraph (8),

the Secretary of State shall proceed with the application of the principal provider of day to day care, as determined in accordance with sub-paragraph (11).

(11)   Where–

(a)   the applications are in respect of one qualifying child, the application of that person with care to whom child benefit is paid in respect of that child;

(b)   the applications are in respect of more than one qualifying child, the application of that person with care to whom child benefit is paid in respect of those children;

(c)   the Secretary of State cannot determine which application he is to proceed with under head (a) or (b) the application of that applicant who in the opinion of the Secretary of State is the principal provider of day to day care for the child or children in question.

(12)   Subject to sub-paragraph (13), where, in any case falling within sub-paragraphs (2) to (10), the applications are not in respect of identical qualifying children, the application that the Secretary of State is to proceed with as determined by those sub-paragraphs shall be treated as an application with respect to all of the qualifying children with respect to whom the applications were made.

(13)   Where the Secretary of State is satisfied that the same person with care does not provide the principal day to day care for all of the qualifying children with respect to whom an application would but for the provisions of this paragraph be made under sub-paragraph (12), he shall make separate maintenance calculations in relation to each person with care providing such principal day to day care.

(14)   For the purposes of this paragraph "day to day care" has the same meaning as in the Maintenance Calculations and Special Cases Regulations.

[²(15)   For the purposes of sub-paragraph (11), where a person has made an election under section 13A(1) of the Social Security Administration Act 1992 (election not to receive child benefit) for payments of child benefit not to be made in respect of a child, that person is to be treated as the person to whom child benefit is being paid in respect of that child.]

Maintenance calculation in force: subsequent application with respect to the same persons
    4.   Where a maintenance calculation is in force and a subsequent application is made [¹...] under the same section of the Act for a maintenance calculation with respect to the same person with care, non-resident parent, and qualifying child or qualifying children as those with respect to whom the maintenance calculation in force has been made, that application shall not be proceeded with.

Amendments
1.   Child Support (Consequential Provisions) Regulations 2008 (SI 2008 No.2543) reg 9(11)-(13) (October 27, 2008).
2.   Child Support (Miscellaneous Amendments) Regulations 2013 (SI 2013 No.1517) reg 7(3) (September 30, 2013).

Definitions
    "the Act": see reg 1(2).
    "effective application": see reg 1(2).
    "Maintenance Calculations and Special Cases Regulations": see reg 1(2).

[¹SCHEDULE 3
MULTIPLE APPLICATIONS – TRANSITIONAL PROVISIONS

No maintenance assessment or calculation in force: more than one application for maintenance by the same person under section 4 [²...], or under sections 4 [²...], of the former Act and of the Act
    1.–(1)   Where an assessment application is made and, before a maintenance assessment under the former Act is made, the applicant makes [²...] a calculation application under section 4 [²...] of the Act, with respect to the same person with care or with respect to a non-resident parent who is the absent parent with respect to the assessment application, as the case may be, those applications shall be treated as a single application.
    (2)   [²...]

No maintenance assessment or calculation in force: more than one application for maintenance by a child under section 7 of the former Act and of the Act
    2.   Where a child makes an assessment application under section 7 of the former Act and, before a maintenance assessment under the former Act is made, makes a calculation application under section 7 of the Act with respect to the same person with care and a non-resident parent who is the absent parent with respect to the assessment application, both applications shall be treated as a single application.

No maintenance assessment or calculation in force: applications by different persons for maintenance
    3.–(1)   Where the Secretary of State receives more than one application for maintenance with respect to the same person with care and absent parent or non-resident parent, as the case may be, he shall, if no maintenance assessment under the former Act or maintenance calculation under the Act, as the case may be, has been made in relation to any of the applications, determine which application he shall proceed with in accordance with sub-paragraphs (2) to (11).
    (2)   Where an application by a person with care is made under section 4 of the former Act or of the Act, [²...] and an application is made by an absent parent or non-resident parent under section 4 of the former Act or of the Act, as the case may be, the Secretary of State shall proceed with the application of the person with care.

(3)   Where there is an assessment application by a qualifying child under section 7 of the former Act and a calculation application is made with respect to that child by a person who is, with respect to that child, a person with care or a non-resident parent, the Secretary of State shall proceed with the application of that person with care or non-resident parent, as the case may be.

(4)   Where, in a case falling within sub-paragraph (3), there is made more than one subsequent application, the Secretary of State shall apply the provisions of sub-paragraphs (2), (7), (8) or (10), as appropriate in the circumstances of the case, to determine which application he shall proceed with.

(5)   Where there is an assessment application and a calculation application by more than one qualifying child under section 7 of the former Act or of the Act, in relation to the same person with care and absent parent or non-resident parent, as the case may be, the Secretary of State shall proceed with the application of the elder or, as the case may be, eldest of the qualifying children.

(6)   Where there is one absent parent and one non-resident parent in respect of the same qualifying child and an assessment application and a calculation application is received from each such person respectively, the Secretary of State shall proceed with both applications, treating them as a single application.

(7)   [²...]

(8)   Where–

(a)   a person with care makes an assessment application under section 4 of the former Act and a different person with care makes a calculation application under section 4 of the Act and those applications are in respect of the same qualifying child or qualifying children (whether or not any of those applications is also in respect of other qualifying children);

(b)   each such person has parental responsibility for (or, in Scotland, parental rights over) that child or children; and

(c)   under regulation 20 of the Child Support (Maintenance Assessments and Special Cases) Regulations 1992 ("the Maintenance Assessments and Special Cases Regulations") one of those persons is to be treated as an absent parent or under the provisions of regulation 8 of the Maintenance Calculations and Special Cases Regulations one of those persons is to be treated as a non-resident parent, as the case may be,

the Secretary of State shall proceed with the application of the person who does not fall to be treated as an absent parent under regulation 20 of the Maintenance Assessments and Special Cases Regulations, or as a non-resident parent under regulation 8 of the Maintenance Calculations and Special Cases Regulations, as the case may be.

(9)   Where, in a case falling within sub-paragraph (8), there is more than one person who does not fall to be treated as an absent parent under regulation 20 of the Maintenance Assessments and Special Cases Regulations or as a non-resident parent under regulation 8 of the Maintenance Calculations and Special Cases Regulations, as the case may be, the Secretary of State shall apply the provisions of paragraph (10) to determine which application he shall proceed with.

(10)   Where–

(a)   a person with care makes an assessment application under section 4 of the former Act and a different person with care makes a calculation application under section 4 of the Act and those applications are in respect of the same qualifying child or qualifying children (whether or not any of those applications is also in respect of other qualifying children); and

(b)   either–

(i)   none of those persons has parental responsibility for (or, in Scotland, parental rights over) that child or children; or

(ii)   the case falls within sub-paragraph (8)(b) but the Secretary of State has not been able to determine which application he is to proceed with under the provisions of sub-paragraph (8),

the Secretary of State shall proceed with the application of the principal provider of day to day care, as determined in accordance with sub-paragraph (11).

(11)   For the purposes of sub-paragraph (10), the application of the principal provider is, where–

(a)   the applications are in respect of one qualifying child, the application of that person with care to whom child benefit is paid in respect of that child;

(b)   the applications are in respect of more than one qualifying child, the application of that person with care to whom child benefit is paid in respect of those children;

(c)   the Secretary of State cannot determine which application he is to proceed with under head (a) or (b), the application of that applicant who in the opinion of the Secretary of State is the principal provider of day to day care for the child or children in question.

(12)   Subject to sub-paragraph (13), where, in any case falling within sub-paragraphs (2) to (10), the applications are not in respect of identical qualifying children, the application that the Secretary of State is to proceed with as determined by those sub-paragraphs shall be treated as an application with respect to all of the qualifying children with respect to whom the applications were made.

(13)   Where the Secretary of State is satisfied that the same person with care does not provide the principal day to day care for all of the qualifying children with respect to whom an application would but for the provisions of this paragraph be made under sub-paragraph (12), he shall make separate maintenance assessments under the former Act or maintenance calculations under the Act, as the case may be, in relation to each person with care providing such principal day to day care.

(14)   For the purposes of this paragraph "day to day care" has the same meaning as in the Maintenance Assessments and Special Cases Regulations or the Maintenance Calculations and Special Cases Regulations, as the case may be.

[³(15)   For the purposes of sub-paragraph (11), where a person has made an election under section 13A(1) of the Social Security Administration Act 1992 (election not to receive child benefit) for payments of child benefit not to be made in respect of a child, that person is to be treated as the person to whom child benefit is being paid in respect of that child.]

Maintenance assessment in force: subsequent application with respect to the same persons

4.   Where–
(a)   a maintenance assessment is in force under the former Act;
(b)   a calculation application is made [²...] under the section of the Act which is the same section as the section of the former Act under which the assessment application was made; and
(c)   the calculation application relates to–
    (i)   the same person with care and qualifying child or qualifying children as the maintenance assessment; and
    (ii)   a non-resident parent who is the absent parent with respect to the maintenance assessment,
the calculation application shall not be proceeded with.

Interpretation

5.   In this Schedule, "absent parent", "former Act" and "maintenance assessment" have the meanings given in regulation 31(8)(a).]

Amendments

1.   Child Support (Miscellaneous Amendments) Regulations 2003 (SI 2003 No.328) reg 7(8) (February 21, 2003).
2.   Child Support (Consequential Provisions) Regulations 2008 (SI 2008 No.2543) reg 9(14)-(16) (October 27, 2008).
3.   Child Support (Miscellaneous Amendments) Regulations 2013 (SI 2013 No.1517) reg 7(4) (September 30, 2013).

The Child Support (Consequential Amendments and Transitional Provisions) Regulations 2001
(SI 2001 No.158)

PART I

GENERAL

Citation and commencement

1.–(1) These Regulations may be cited as the Child Support (Consequential Amendments and Transitional Provisions) Regulations 2001.

(2) Regulation 11 and, for the purposes of that provision, this regulation and regulation 2, shall come into force on 15th February 2001.

(3) The remainder of these Regulations shall come into force in relation to a particular case on the date on which section 1 of the 2000 Act comes into force in relation to that type of case.

Interpretation

2. In these Regulations–

"the 2000 Act" means the Child Support, Pensions and Social Security Act 2000;

"the Act" means the Child Support Act 1991;

"the Community Action (Miscellaneous Provisions) Order" means the Community Action (Miscellaneous Provisions) Order 1993;

"the Decisions and Appeals Regulations" means the Social Security and Child Support (Decisions and Appeals) Regulations 1999;

"the former Act" means the Act prior to its amendment by the 2000 Act;

"the Guardian's Allowances Regulations" means the Social Security (Guardian's Allowances) Regulations 1975;

"the Income Support Regulations" means the Income Support (General) Regulations 1987;

"the Jobseeker's Allowance Regulations" means the Jobseeker's Allowance Regulations 1996;

"the Maintenance Payments Regulations" means the Social Security Benefits (Maintenance Payments and Consequential Amendments) Regulations 1996;

"the New Deal (25 plus) (Miscellaneous Provisions) Order" means the New Deal (25 plus) (Miscellaneous Provisions) Order 1999;

"the New Deal (Miscellaneous Provisions) Order" means the New Deal (Miscellaneous Provisions) Order 1998;

"the North Norfolk Action (Miscellaneous Provisions) Order" means the North Norfolk Action (Miscellaneous Provisions) Order 1993;

"the Project Work (Miscellaneous Provisions) Order" means the Project Work (Miscellaneous Provisions) Order 1996; and

"the Training for Work (Miscellaneous Provisions) Order" means the Training for Work (Miscellaneous Provisions) Order 1995.

PART II

CONSEQUENTIAL AMENDMENTS

Amendment of the Community Action (Miscellaneous Provisions) Order and the North Norfolk Action (Miscellaneous Provisions) Order

3. To the list of subordinate legislation specified respectively in the Schedule to the Community Action (Miscellaneous Provisions) Order and the Schedule to the North Norfolk Action (Miscellaneous Provisions) Order, there shall be added "The Child Support (Maintenance Calculations and Special Cases) Regulations 2000".

Amendment of the New Deal (25 plus) (Miscellaneous Provisions) Order, the New Deal (Miscellaneous Provisions) Order, the Project Work (Miscellaneous Provisions) Order and the Training for Work (Miscellaneous Provisions) Order

9. To the list of subordinate legislation specified respectively in the Schedule to the New Deal (25 plus) (Miscellaneous Provisions) Order, the Schedule to the New Deal (Miscellaneous Provisions) Order, the Schedule to the Project Work (Miscellaneous Provisions) Order and the Schedule to the Training for Work (Miscellaneous Provisions) Order there shall be added "The Child Support (Maintenance Calculations and Special Cases) Regulations 2000" and "The Child Support (Maintenance Calculation Procedure) Regulations 2000".

PART III
SAVINGS

Savings for particular cases

10.– [¹(Z1) This regulation is subject to the Child Support (Transitional Provisions) Regulations 2000.]

(1) Where, in respect of a particular case there is a maintenance assessment the effective date of which is before the date that these Regulations come into force with respect to that type of case ("the commencement date"), these Regulations shall not apply for the purposes of–

(a) the Guardian's Allowances Regulations, in relation to a parent who died on or before the commencement date;

(b) the Income Support Regulations, in relation to a person who is entitled to income support for a period beginning on or before the day before the commencement date;

(c) the Jobseeker's Allowance Regulations, in relation to a person who is entitled to a jobseeker's allowance for a period beginning on or before the day before the commencement date; and

(d) the Maintenance Payments Regulations, in relation to payment of child support maintenance under a maintenance assessment in a period beginning on or before the day before the commencement date.

(2) These Regulations shall not apply with respect to the Income Support Regulations and the Jobseeker's Allowance Regulations in relation to a person who is entitled to income support or a jobseeker's allowance, as the case may be, for a period beginning on or before the day before the commencement date.

Amendment

1. Child Support (Transitional Provision)(Miscellaneous Amendments) Regulations 2003 (SI 2003 No.347) reg 2(3) and (4) (March 3, 2003).

PART IV
TRANSITIONAL PROVISION

Transitional provision – redetermination of appeals

11. In relation to any particular case, before the date on which these Regulations, except for this regulation, come into force for the purposes of that case, in section 23A(4)(b) of the Act the reference to "qualifying persons" shall be treated as a reference to any person referred to in section 20 of the former Act with a right of appeal under that section and the reference in section 23A(3) to "the principal parties" shall be construed accordingly.

The Child Support (Information, Evidence and Disclosure and Maintenance Arrangements and Jurisdiction) (Amendment) Regulations 2000
(SI 2001 No.161)

Citation, commencement and interpretation

1.–(1) These Regulations may be cited as the Child Support (Information, Evidence and Disclosure and Maintenance Arrangements and Jurisdiction) (Amendment) Regulations 2000.

(2) In these Regulations–

(a) "the Information Regulations" means the Child Support (Information, Evidence and Disclosure) Regulations 1992;

(b) "the Jurisdiction Regulations" means the Child Support (Maintenance Arrangements and Jurisdiction) Regulations 1992; and

(c) "the Act" means the Child Support Act 1991.

(3) These Regulations shall come into force as follows–

(a) regulations 5(2)(b), (d) and (e), 6(3) and 7(1) and, for the purposes of those provisions, this regulation, shall come into force in relation to a particular case on the day on which section 13 of the Child Support, Pensions and Social Security Act 2000 comes into force for the purposes of that type of case;

(b) regulation 8(3) and, for the purposes of that provision, this regulation, shall come into force in relation to a particular case on the day on which section 22(3) of the Child Support, Pensions and Social Security Act 2000 comes into force for the purposes of that type of case;

(c) regulation 4 and, for the purposes of that provision, this regulation, shall come into force on 1st April 2001; and

(d) the remainder of these Regulations shall come into force in relation to a particular case on the day on which sub-paragraphs (19) and (20) of paragraph 11 of Schedule 3 to the Child Support, Pensions and Social Security Act 2000, which respectively amend sections 51 and 54 of the Act, come into force for the purposes of that type of case.

Regs 2–9 *Omitted.*

General Note

Section 13 of the 2000 Act inserted s14A into the Act. Section 22(3) inserted s44(2A) into the Act. Subparagraphs 19 and 20 of para 11 to Sch 3 amended ss51 and 54.

Transitional provisions and savings

10.–[¹(Z1) This regulation is subject to the Child Support (Transitional Provisions) Regulations 2000.]

(1) Where in respect of a particular case before the date that these Regulations come into force with respect to that type of case ("the commencement date")–

(a) an application was made and not determined for–

    (i) a maintenance assessment;

    (ii) a departure direction; or

    (iii) a revision or supersession of a decision;

(b) the Secretary of State had begun but not completed a revision or supersession of a decision on his own initiative;

(c) any time limit provided for in Regulations for making an application for a revision or a departure direction had not expired; or

(d) any appeal was made but not decided or any time limit for making an appeal had not expired,

regulations 2, 3, 5 (except for sub-paragraphs (2)(b), (d) and (e)), 6(1) and (2), 7(2) and (3), 8(1) and (2) and 9 shall not apply for the purposes of–

(aa) the decision on the application referred to in sub-paragraph (a);

(bb) the revision or supersession referred to in sub-paragraph (b);

(cc) the ability to apply for the revision or the departure direction referred to in sub-paragraph (c) and the decision whether to revise or to give a departure direction following any such application;

(dd) any appeal outstanding or made during the time limit referred to in sub-paragraph (d); or

(ee) any revision, supersession or appeal or application for a departure direction in relation to a decision, ability to apply or appeal referred to in sub-paragraphs (aa) to (dd) above.

(2) Where after the commencement date a maintenance assessment falls to be cancelled on grounds of lack of jurisdiction with effect from before the commencement date, regulation 8(2) shall not apply for that purpose.

(3) For the purposes of this regulation–

(a) "departure direction" and "maintenance assessment" have the same meaning as in section 54 of the Act before its amendment by the 2000 Act;

(b) "revision or supersession" means a revision or supersession of a decision under section 16 or 17 of the Act before its amendment by the 2000 Act; and

(c) "2000 Act" means the Child Support, Pensions and Social Security Act 2000.

Amendment

1. Child Support (Transitional Provision)(Miscellaneous Amendments) Regulations 2003 (SI 2003 No.347) reg 2(3) and (4) (March 3, 2003).

The Child Support (Collection and Enforcement and Miscellaneous Amendments) Regulations 2000

(SI 2001 No.162)

Citation, commencement and interpretation

1.–(1) These Regulations may be cited as the Child Support (Collection and Enforcement and Miscellaneous Amendments) Regulations 2000.

(2) Regulations 4 and 6(3), and, for the purposes of those provisions, this regulation, shall come into force on 2nd April 2001 and regulation 2(6)(c) and (9), and, for the purposes of those provisions, this regulation, shall come into force on the day on which section 16 of the 2000 Act comes into force.

[¹(2A) Regulation 2(6)(b) and, for the purposes of that provision, this regulation, shall come into force on 31st May 2001.]

[²(2B) Regulation 2(3)(b)(ii) and (c) shall, to the extent that those provisions are not already in force on 12th July 2006, come into force on that date.]

(3) The remainder of these Regulations shall come into force in relation to a particular case on the day on which sections 1(2) and (3), 4, 18(1) and (2), and 20(1) of and Schedule 3 paragraph 11(2) and (16) to the 2000 Act come into force for the purposes of that type of case.

(4) In these Regulations, unless the context otherwise requires–

"the 2000 Act" means the Child Support, Pensions and Social Security Act 2000;

"the Act" means the Child Support Act 1991;

"the Arrears, Interest and Adjustment Regulations" means the Child Support (Arrears, Interest and Adjustment of Maintenance Assessments) Regulations 1992;

"the Collection and Enforcement Regulations" means the Child Support (Collection and Enforcement) Regulations 1992;

"the Collection and Enforcement of Other Forms of Maintenance Regulations" means the Child Support (Collection and Enforcement of Other Forms of Maintenance) Regulations 1992; and

"the Fees Regulations" means the Child Support Fees Regulations 1992.

Amendments

1. Child Support (Miscellaneous Amendments) Regulations 2001 (SI 2001 No.1775) reg 2 (May 31, 2001).

2. Child Support (Miscellaneous Amendments) Regulations 2006 (SI 2006 No. 1520) reg 6(2) (July 12, 2006).

Regs 2 – 5 *Omitted.*

Savings

6.– [¹(Z1) This regulation is subject to the Child Support (Transitional Provisions) Regulations 2000.]

(1) Where, in respect of a particular case before the date that these Regulations come into force with respect to that type of case–

(a) interest has become due but has not been paid; [²or]

(b) the Secretary of State has made a payment by way of reimbursement under section 41B(2) of the Act; [²...]

(c) [²...]

these Regulations shall not apply for the purposes of–

    (i) the recovery of the interest referred to in sub-paragraph (a); [²or]

    (ii) the repayment to the Secretary of State of the whole, or part, of the sum reimbursed referred to in sub-paragraph (b); [²...]

    (iii) [²...]

(2) Where in respect of a particular case after the date that these Regulations come into force with respect to that type of case an adjustment falls to be made in relation to a maintenance assessment, these Regulations shall not apply for the purposes of making the adjustment.

(3)   Where, before the coming into force of regulation 4 of these Regulations, fees have become due but have not been paid, the Fees Regulations shall have effect as if regulation 4 of these Regulations had not been made.

Amendments
1.   Child Support (Transitional Provision)(Miscellaneous Amendments) Regulations 2003 (SI 2003 No.347) reg 2(3) and (4) (March 3, 2003).
2.   Child Support (Miscellaneous Amendments) Regulations 2006 (SI 2006 No.1520) reg 6(3) (July 12, 2006).

The Child Support (Civil Imprisonment) (Scotland) Regulations 2001

(SI 2001 No.1236 (S.3))

Citation, commencement and interpretation

1.–(1)   These Regulations may be cited as the Child Support (Civil Imprisonment) (Scotland) Regulations 2001 and shall come into force on 24th April 2001.

(2)   In these Regulations the "1991 Act" means the Child Support Act 1991.

Expenses of commitment to prison

2.   The amount to be included in the warrant under section 40A(2)(ii) of the 1991 Act (sheriff's warrant for committal to prison of liable person) in respect of the expenses of commitment shall be such amount as, in the view of the sheriff, is equal to the expenses reasonably incurred by the Secretary of State in respect of the expenses of commitment.

Reduction of period of imprisonment

3.–(1)   For the purposes of subsection (6) of section 40A of the 1991 Act (reduction of period of imprisonment for part payment) the following paragraphs shall apply.

(2)   Where, after the sheriff has issued a warrant for committal to prison under section 40A of the 1991 Act, part payment of the amount stated in the warrant is made, the period of imprisonment specified in the warrant shall be reduced proportionately so that for the period of imprisonment specified in the warrant, there shall be substituted a period of imprisonment of such number of days as bears the same proportion to the number of days specified in the warrant as the amount remaining unpaid under the warrant bears to the amount specified in the warrant.

(3)   Where the part payment is of such an amount as would, under paragraph (2) above, reduce the period of imprisonment to such number of days as have already been served (or would be so served in the course of the day of payment) the period of imprisonment shall be reduced to the period already served plus one day.

The Child Support Appeals (Jurisdiction of Courts) Order 2002
(SI 2002 No.1915)

Citation, commencement, interpretation and extent
1.–(1)   This Order may be cited as the Child Support Appeals (Jurisdiction of Courts) Order 2002.

(2)   Subject to paragraph (3) this Order shall come into force on the day after the date on which it is made.

(3)   This Order shall not have effect in relation to a particular type of case until the day on which section 10 of the Child Support, Pensions and Social Security Act 2000 comes into force for the purposes of that type of case.

(4)   In this Order–

(a)   "the Act" means the Child Support Act 1991; and

(b)   "the Regulations" means the Social Security and Child Support (Decisions and Appeals) Regulations 1999.

(5)   This Order extends to England and Wales only.

General Note
For equivalent provision for Scotland, see the Child Support Appeals (Jurisdiction of Courts) (Scotland) Order 2003. Section 10 of the 2000 Act introduced a new version of s20 of the Act. For its commencement, see that section.

Revocation
2.   The Child Support Appeals (Jurisdiction of Courts) Order 1993, to the extent to which it applies in England and Wales, is revoked.

Parentage appeals to be made to courts
3.   An appeal under section 20 of the Act shall be made to a court instead of to [¹ the First-tier Tribunal] in the circumstances mentioned in article 4.

Amendment
1.   Tribunals, Courts and Enforcement Act 2007 (Transitional and Consequential Provisions) Order 2008 (SI 2008 No.2683) Sch 1 para 180 (November 3, 2008).

4.   The circumstances are that–

(a)   the appeal will be an appeal under section 20(1)(a) or (b) of the Act;

(b)   the determination made by the Secretary of State in making the decision to be appealed against included a determination that a particular person (whether the applicant or some other person) either was, or was not, a parent of the qualifying child in question ("a parentage determination"); and

(c)   the ground of the appeal will be that the decision to be appealed against should not have included that parentage determination.

[¹ **5.**   Regulation 32 of Regulations and Rule 23 of the Tribunal Procedure (First-tier Tribunal) (Social Entitlement Chamber) Rules 2008 apply to appeals brought under this Order as if the word "Tribunal" is read as "court".]

Amendment
1.   Tribunals, Courts and Enforcement Act 2007 (Transitional and Consequential Provisions) Order 2008 (SI 2008 No.2683) Sch 1 para 181 (November 3, 2008).

General Note
The First-tier Tribunal has jurisdiction unless the circumstances set out in this article apply (*R(CS) 13/98*, para 6).

Parentage may be disputed at various stages. This article only applies if the issue of parentage is raised on the appeal. If it is, it deprives the tribunal of jurisdiction. If it is raised at an earlier stage, s27 of the Act applies. If parentage is disputed in the letter of appeal, the case should be transferred to the court without the case coming before the tribunal. However, if a case does slip through and come before the tribunal, it must declare that it has no jurisdiction to hear the appeal. It has been held in Northern Ireland that if parentage is disputed for the first time at the hearing, this article does not apply. The tribunal should deal with the other grounds of appeal and leave the issue to be dealt with as a revision or supersession. See *CSC 1/94*, paras 5 and 8(d)(iv) and *CSC 3/94*, para 9. However, it is possible that this view is not correct and that any parentage challenge during the appeal is covered by this article.

The tribunal is only deprived of jurisdiction, if the argument is put that the person is not a parent of the qualifying child. If the lesser argument is put that the person may not be the parent or does not admit to being the parent, this article is not satisfied and the tribunal retains jurisdiction. If an argument is put in this form, the tribunal must require the person to state unequivocally whether parentage is denied. If it is, then the tribunal loses jurisdiction.

If the tribunal is deprived of jurisdiction in these circumstances, it may wish to remind the person concerned (a) that the appeal remains in existence but will be transferred to the court, (b) which has power to order a test to be carried out to determine parentage and (c) that the normal court rules as to public funding and costs apply.

Sometimes arguments are put to the tribunal in the alternative, so that parentage is not the only issue raised on the appeal. It is not clear how this article applies in those circumstances. Its wording assumes that it only applies if parentage is the only issue on the appeal. One possible interpretation is that the issues are severed with the parentage issue going to the court while the tribunal retains jurisdiction to deal with the other issues. If this is correct, the tribunal might consider it appropriate to adjourn the hearing on the other issues until the outcome of the parentage challenge is known. It has been held in Northern Ireland that a calculation should be put into abeyance once parentage is challenged (*CSC 3/94*, para 10), but the commissioner left open the issue of recoupment of child support maintenance if the parentage issue was decided in favour of the person concerned (*ibid*). However, a different view has been taken in the Great Britain. It has been held that the denial of parentage does not suspend or stop proceedings leading to a maintenance calculation or its implementation or enforcement (*CCS 11586/1995*, para 13). However, it has also been said that an interim maintenance assessment (comparable to a default maintenance decision) should remain in force but not be enforced pending resolution of the parentage issue (*R(CS) 2/98*, para 22). The commissioner in that case did not refer to *CCS 11586/1995* and did not have to decide the issue. If a person was seeking to set aside a finding of parentage in circumstances that fell within Case F of s26(2) of the Act, it might be appropriate to collect information necessary to make a maintenance calculation, but to delay the making of the calculation until the issues was resolved (*ibid*, para 24). If the case does not fall within s26 of the Act, the CMEC should consider applying or offer the parent with care the chance of applying under s27 of the Act before refusing to make a maintenance calculation (*ibid*, para 25).

Child Support Appeals (Jurisdiction of Courts) (Scotland) Order 2003

(SI 2003 No.96)

Citation, commencement, interpretation and extent

1.–(1)   This Order may be cited as the Child Support Appeals (Jurisdiction of Courts) (Scotland) Order 2003.

(2)   This Order shall come into force in relation to a particular type of case on the date on which section 10 of the Child Support, Pensions and Social Security Act 2000 comes into force for the purposes of that type of case.

(3)   In this Order–

(a)   "the Act" means the Child Support Act 1991; and

(b)   "the Regulations" means the Social Security and Child Support (Decisions and Appeals) Regulations 1999.

(4)   This Order extends to Scotland only.

General Note

For equivalent provision for England and Wales, see the Child Support Appeals (Jurisdiction of Courts) Order 2002 on p679.

Section 10 of the 2000 Act introduced a new version of s20 of the Act. For its commencement, see that section.

Parentage appeals to be made to courts

2.   An appeal under section 20 of the Act shall be made to a court instead of to an appeal tribunal in the circumstances mentioned in article 3.

3.   The circumstances are that–

(a)   the appeal will be an appeal under section 20(1)(a) or (b) of the Act;

(b)   the decision by the Secretary of State against which the appeal is brought was made on the basis that a particular person (whether the applicant or some other person) either was, or was not, a parent of the qualifying child in question ("a parentage determination"); and

(c)   the ground of appeal will be that, the parentage determination being unfounded in fact, the decision should not have been made on that basis.

4.–(1)   For the purposes of article 2, an appeal may be made to a court in Scotland if–

(a)   the child in question was born in Scotland; or

(b)   the child, the non-resident parent or the person with care of the child is domiciled in Scotland on the date when the appeal is made or is habitually resident in Scotland on that date.

(2)   Where an appeal to a court in Scotland is to be made to the sheriff, it shall be to the sheriff of the sheriffdom where–

(a)   the child in question was born; or

(b)   the child, the non-resident parent or the person with care of the child is habitually resident on the date when the appeal is made.

General Note

For a commentary, see the general note to art 4 Child Support Appeals (Jurisdiction of Courts) Order 2002 on p679, which applies to England and Wales.

Modifications to the Social Security and Child Support (Decisions and Appeals) Regulations 1999

5.   Regulations 31 and 32 of the Regulations shall apply to appeals brought under this Order with the following modifications-

(a)   in regulation 31(1), for "an appeal tribunal" substitute "a court";

(b)   wherever they appear, for "legally qualified panel member" or "panel member" substitute "the court";

(c)   in regulation 32(10) for "such written form as has been approved by the President" substitute "written form".

Revocation

6. The Child Support Appeals (Jurisdiction of Courts) Order 1993, to the extent that it applies to Scotland, is revoked.

Amendment of the Law Reform (Parent and Child) (Scotland) Act 1986

7. In section 8 (Interpretation) of the Law Reform (Parent and Child) (Scotland) Act 1986 at the end of the definition of "action for declarator" there shall be inserted the words "but does not include an appeal under section 20(1)(a) or (b) (Appeals) of the Child Support Act 1991 made to the court by virtue of an order made under section 45 (jurisdiction of the courts in certain proceedings) of that Act:"

The Child Support, Pensions and Social Security Act 2000 (Commencement No.12) Order 2003
(SI 2003 No.192)

Citation and interpretation
1.–(1) This Order may be cited as the Child Support, Pensions and Social Security Act 2000 (Commencement No. 12) Order 2003.

(2) In this Order–

(a) "the Act" means the Child Support, Pensions and Social Security Act 2000 and, except where otherwise stated, references to sections and Schedules are references to sections of, and Schedules to, the Act;

(b) "the 1991 Act" means the Child Support Act 1991;

(c) "absent parent" has the meaning given in the 1991 Act before its amendment by the Act;

(d) "the Arrangements and Jurisdiction Regulations" means the Child Support (Maintenance Arrangements and Jurisdiction) Regulations 1992 as in force immediately before 3rd March 2003;

(e) "the Assessment Procedure Regulations" means the Child Support (Maintenance Assessment Procedure) Regulations 1992 as in force immediately before 3rd March 2003;

(f) "effective date", in relation to a maintenance assessment or a maintenance calculation, has the meaning given in article 8 of this Order;

(g) "existing assessment" means a maintenance assessment which is in force with an effective date which is before 3rd March 2003;

(h) "maintenance assessment" has the meaning given in the 1991 Act before its amendment by the Act;

(i) "maintenance calculation" has the meaning given in the 1991 Act as amended by the Act;

(j) "non-resident parent" has the meaning given in the 1991 Act as amended by the Act;

(k) "partner" has the meaning given in paragraph 10C(4) of Part I of Schedule 1 to the 1991 Act as amended by the Act;

(l) "person with care" has the meaning given in the 1991 Act;

(m) "prescribed benefit" means a benefit prescribed for the purposes of paragraph 4(1)(c) of Part I of Schedule 1 to the 1991 Act as amended by the Act;

(n) "qualifying child" has the meaning given in the 1991 Act; and

(o) "relevant person" means, in relation to a maintenance assessment, the absent parent or person with care and, in relation to a maintenance calculation, the non-resident parent or person with care.

Appointed day for purpose of making regulations
2. 4th February 2003 is the day appointed for the coming into force of–

(a) section 2(1) and (2) (applications under section 4 of the 1991 Act); and

(b) paragraph 11(4)(b)(i) and (ii) of Schedule 3 (right of a child in Scotland to apply for maintenance calculation), and section 26 so far as it relates to that provision,

for the purpose of the exercise of the power to make regulations.

Definitions

"the 1991 Act": see art 1(2).

"maintenance calculation": see art 1(2).

Appointed day for the provisions specified in the Schedule to this Order
3.–(1) 3rd March 2003 is the day appointed for the coming into force of the provisions of the Act specified in the Schedule to this Order, in so far as those provisions are not already in force, for the purpose of–

(a)   cases where an application for child support maintenance is made to the Secretary of State (whether or not in writing) and the effective date would be on or after 3rd March 2003;

(b)   cases where there is an existing assessment and a related decision falls to be made; and

(c)   cases where there is an existing assessment and where–

    (i)   an application is made or treated as made which would but for that assessment result in a maintenance calculation being made,

    (ii)   the non-resident parent in relation to the application referred to in paragraph (i) is the absent parent in relation to the existing assessment, and

    (iii)   the person with care in relation to the application referred to in paragraph (i) is a different person to the person with care in relation to the existing assessment.

(2)   For the purposes of paragraph (1)(b), "a related decision" is–

(a)   a maintenance calculation which falls to be made with respect to a person who is a relevant person in relation to the existing assessment, whether or not with respect to a different qualifying child;

(b)   a maintenance calculation which falls to be made with respect to the partner ("A") of a person ("B") who is a relevant person in relation to the existing assessment, where A or B is in receipt of a prescribed benefit and either–

    (i)   A is the non-resident parent in relation to the maintenance calculation and B is the absent parent in relation to the existing assessment, or

    (ii)   A is the person with care in relation to the maintenance calculation and B is the person with care in relation to the existing assessment;

(c)   a decision which falls to be made in a case where–

    (i)   the existing assessment is in force in relation to a person ("C") and a maintenance calculation is in force in relation to another person ("D"),

    (ii)   C or D is in receipt of a prescribed benefit,

    (iii)   either–

        (aa)   C is the absent parent in relation to the existing assessment and D is the non-resident parent in relation to the maintenance calculation, or

        (bb)   C is the person with care in relation to the existing assessment and D is the person with care in relation to the maintenance calculation, and

    (iv)   a decision relating to the prescribed benefit referred to in paragraph (ii) is superseded on the ground that C is the partner of D; or

(d)   a decision which falls to be made in a case where a person ("E") and another person ("F") become entitled to a prescribed benefit as partners, and where–

    (i)   E is the absent parent in relation to the existing assessment and F is the non-resident parent in relation to a maintenance calculation, or

    (ii)   E is the person with care in relation to the existing assessment and F is the person with care in relation to a maintenance calculation.

Definitions

"the Act": see art 1(2).

"absent parent": see art 1(2).

"effective date": see art 1(2).

"existing assessment": see art 1(2).

"maintenance calculation": see art 1(2).

"non-resident parent": see art 1(2).

"partner": see art 1(2).

"person with care": see art 1(2).

"prescribed benefit": see art 1(2).

"qualifying child": see art 1(2).

"relevant person": see art 1(2).

Appointed day for sections 3 and 19

4. 3rd March 2003 is the day appointed for the coming into force of sections 3 and 19, in so far as those provisions are not already in force, for the purpose of the following cases–

(a) where, on or after 3rd March 2003, income support, an income-based jobseeker's allowance or any other benefit prescribed for the purposes of section 6 of the 1991 Act as substituted by section 3 is claimed by or in respect of, or paid to or in respect of, the parent of a qualifying child who is also the person with care of the child, and when the claim is made–

    (i) there is no maintenance assessment or maintenance calculation in force in respect of that parent, and

    (ii) there has been no maintenance assessment in force during the previous 8 weeks in respect of that child;

(b) where–

    (i) before 3rd March 2003, section 6(1) of the 1991 Act, before its substitution by the Act, applied to the parent with care,

    (ii) a maintenance assessment has been made with an effective date which is before 3rd March 2003, and

    (iii) on or after 3rd March 2003 the parent with care withdraws her authorisation under that section 6(1) at a date when she continues to fall within that section 6(1);

(c) where, immediately before 3rd March 2003, subsection (1) of section 6 of the 1991 Act, before its substitution by the Act, applied to the parent with care, and a maintenance assessment has not been made because–

    (i) the Secretary of State was in the process of considering whether the parent with care should be required to give the authorisation referred to in that subsection;

    (ii) subsection (2) of that section applied;

    (iii) subsection (2) of that section did not apply and a reduced benefit direction was given under section 46(5) of the 1991 Act before its substitution by the Act; or

    (iv) the parent with care failed to comply with a requirement imposed on her under subsection (1) of that section 6 and the Secretary of State was in the process of serving a notice or considering reasons given by the parent with care under section 46(2) or (3) of the 1991 Act before its substitution by the Act.

Definitions

"the Act": see art 1(2).

"the 1991 Act": see art 1(2).

"effective date": see art 1(2).

"maintenance assessment": see art 1(2).

"maintenance calculation": see art 1(2).

"prescribed benefit": see art 1(2).

"qualifying child": see art 1(2).

Appointed day for section 20

5. 3rd March 2003 is the day appointed for the coming into force of section 20, in so far as that section is not already in force, for the purposes of cases where an application for child support maintenance is made to the Secretary of State (whether or not in writing) and the effective date would be on or after 3rd March 2003.

Definition

"effective date": see art 1(2).

[¹Appointed day for section 23 and associated repeal

6.–(1) The day appointed for the coming into force of the provisions specified in paragraph (2) for the purposes of cases specified in paragraph (3) is–

(a)   as respects any case specified in paragraph (3)(a) where, before 3rd March 2003, relevant maintenance is paid or payable–
- (i)   where 3rd March 2003 is the day on which the maintenance calculation in relation to that case takes effect, 3rd March 2003,
- (ii)   where the maintenance calculation in relation to that case takes effect on a day later than 3rd March 2003, that later day;

(b)   as respects any other case specified in paragraph (3)(a), 3rd March 2003;

(c)   as respects any case which is specified in paragraph (3)(b)–
- (i)   where 3rd March 2003 is the case conversion date in relation to that case, 3rd March 2003,
- (ii)   where a day later than 3rd March 2003 is the case conversion date in relation to that case, that later day;

(d)   as respects any case specified in paragraph (3)(c) which is referred to–
- (i)   in paragraph (a) of article 4, the day on which the claim for the benefit mentioned in that paragraph is made,
- (ii)   in paragraph (b) of that article, the day on which the Secretary of State is notified that the authorisation mentioned in sub-paragraph (iii) of that paragraph is withdrawn,
- (iii)   in paragraph (c) of that article, 3rd March 2003;

(e)   as respects any case which is specified in sub-paragraph (d) of paragraph (3), the day on which the maintenance referred to in that sub-paragraph is first paid.

(2)   The provisions mentioned in paragraph (1) are–

(a)   section 23 (section 10 of the Child Support Act 1995 to cease to have effect); and

(b)   Part I of Schedule 9 in so far as it relates to the repeal of section 10 of the Child Support Act 1995.

(3)   The cases mentioned in paragraph (1) are–

(a)   cases referred to in sub-paragraph (a) of article 3(1);

(b)   cases referred to in sub-paragraph (b) or (c) of article 3(1);

(c)   cases referred to in paragraph (a), (b) or (c) of article 4;

(d)   cases to which sub-paragraphs (a) to (c) do not apply where, on or after 3rd March 2003, relevant maintenance is first paid.

(4)   For the purposes of sub-paragraph (d) of paragraph (3), a case shall not be regarded as one to which that sub-paragraph does not apply by reason only of the fact that relevant maintenance was paid or payable before 3rd March 2003–

(a)   in respect of the care of a different child;

(b)   under an earlier agreement; or

(c)   by virtue of an earlier order of the court.

(5)   In this article–

"case conversion date" means the date which is, by virtue of regulation 15 of the Child Support (Transitional Provisions) Regulations 2000, the case conversion date in relation to that case; and

"relevant maintenance" means maintenance, other than child support maintenance, which is paid or payable–

(a)   to a person who has the care of a child in the United Kingdom;

(b)   in respect of the care of the child; and

(c)   under an agreement (whether enforceable or not) between that person and the person by whom the maintenance is payable, or by virtue of an order of the court.]

Amendment

1.   Child Support, Pensions and Social Security Act 2000 (Commencement No.13) Order 2003 (SI 2003 No.346) art 2.

Definition

"maintenance calculation": see art 1(2).

Appointed day for coming into force of section 29, and Schedule 3, paragraph 11(15)

7. 3rd March 2003 is the day appointed for the coming into force of–

(a) section 29 (interpretation, transitional provisions, savings, etc.) in so far as it is not already in force; and

(b) paragraph 11(15) of Schedule 3 (which substitutes subsection (2) in section 30 of the 1991 Act, and section 26 so far as it relates to that paragraph 11(15).

Definition

"the 1991 Act": see art 1(2).

The effective date

8.–(1) For the purposes of this Order, "the effective date" means, in relation to any case, the date which would be the effective date of a maintenance assessment under regulation 30 or 33(7) of the Assessment Procedure Regulations (effective dates of new maintenance assessments, and maintenance periods) or regulation 3(5), (7) or (8) of the Arrangements and Jurisdiction Regulations (relationship between maintenance assessments and certain court orders), whichever would apply to the case in question, or would have applied had the effective date not fallen to be determined under regulation 8C or 30A of the Assessment Procedure Regulations; and paragraphs (2) and (3) shall apply in relation to the application of those Regulations for this purpose.

(2) In the application of the Assessment Procedure Regulations for the purposes of paragraph (1), where, on or after 3rd March 2003, no maintenance enquiry form, as defined in those Regulations, is given or sent to the absent parent, those Regulations shall be applied as if references in regulation 30–

(a) to the date when the maintenance enquiry form was given or sent to the absent parent were references to the date on which the absent parent is first notified by the Secretary of State (whether or not in writing) that an application for child support maintenance has been made in respect of which he is named as the absent parent; and

(b) to the return by the absent parent of the maintenance enquiry form containing his name, address and written confirmation that he is the parent of the child or children in respect of whom the application was made were references to the provision of this information by the absent parent.

(3) In the application of the Arrangements and Jurisdiction Regulations for the purposes of paragraph (1), where, on or after 3rd March 2003, no maintenance enquiry form, as defined in the Assessment Procedure Regulations, is given or sent to the absent parent, regulation 3(8) shall be applied as if the reference to the date when the maintenance enquiry form was given or sent to the absent parent were to the date on which the absent parent is first notified by the Secretary of State (whether or not in writing) that an application for child support maintenance has been made in respect of which he is named as the absent parent.

Definitions

"absent parent": see art 1(2).

"the Arrangements and Jurisdiction Regulations": see art 1(2).

"the Assessment Procedure Regulations": see art 1(2).

"effective date": see art 1(2).

SCHEDULE
PROVISIONS BROUGHT INTO FORCE AS PROVIDED IN ARTICLE 3

Provision of the Act	*Subject Matter*
Section 1(1) and (2)	Maintenance calculations and terminology
Section 2	Applications under section 4 of the 1991 Act
Section 4	Default and interim maintenance decisions
Section 5	Departure from usual rules for calculating maintenance
Section 7	Variations: revision and supersession
Section 8	Revision of decisions

Section 9	Decisions superseding earlier decisions
Section 10	Appeals to appeal tribunals
Section 12	Information required by Secretary of State
Section 18	Financial penalties
Section 21	Recovery of child support maintenance by deduction from benefit
Section 22(4)	Jurisdiction
Section 25	Regulations
Schedule 1 and section 1(3)	Substituted Part I of Schedule 1 to the 1991 Act
Schedule 2 and section 6	Substituted Schedules 4A and 4B to the 1991 Act
Schedule 3, except for paragraph 11(15), and section 26	Amendment of enactments relating to child support
Part I of Schedule 9, except as respects the repeal of section 10 of the Child Support Act 1995, and section 85 so far as it relates to that Part I	Repeals and revocations (child support)

The Child Support (Miscellaneous Amendments) (No.2) Regulations 2003

(2003 No.2779)

Citation and commencement

1. These Regulations may be cited as the Child Support (Miscellaneous Amendments) (No. 2) Regulations 2003 and shall come into force on the day after the day that they are made.

Regs 2 – 8 *Omitted.*

Savings

9. Regulations 1(3), 40 and 40ZA of the Child Support (Maintenance Assessment Procedure) Regulations 1992 and regulations 8(2)(b), 14 and 15 of the Child Support (Maintenance Calculation Procedure) Regulations 2000 shall continue to have effect in relation to a person to whom any of those provisions applied before the date these Regulations come into force as if regulations 3(2), (4) and (5) and 5 of these Regulations had not come into force.

Contracting Out (Functions Relating to Child Support) Order 2006
(SI 2006 No.1692)

Citation, commencement and interpretation

1.–(1)   This Order may be cited as the Contracting Out (Functions Relating to Child Support) Order 2006 and shall come into force on 3rd July 2006.

(2)   In this Order "the 1991 Act" means the Child Support Act 1991.

Contracting out of functions relating to child support

2.–(1)   Subject to paragraph (2), any function of the Secretary of State relating to child support under or by virtue of the provisions of the 1991 Act, may be exercised by, or by employees of, such person (if any) as may be authorised by the Secretary of State.

(2)   Paragraph (1) shall not include functions under the following provisions–

(a)   section 15 of the 1991 Act (powers of inspectors);

(b)   section 35 of the 1991 Act (enforcement of liability orders by distress);

(c)   section 39A of the 1991 Act (commitment to prison and disqualification from driving); and

(d)   section 40B of the 1991 Act (disqualification from driving: further provision),

or any other functions excluded from section 69 of the Deregulation and Contracting Out Act 1994 by section 71 of that Act.

Child Maintenance and Other Payments Act 2008 (Commencement No.3 and Transitional and Savings Provisions) Order 2008

(2008 No.2548 (c.110))

Citation and interpretation

1.–(1)   This Order may be cited as the Child Maintenance and Other Payments Act 2008 (Commencement No. 3 and Transitional and Savings Provisions) Order 2008.

(2)   In this Order–

"the 1991 Act" means the Child Support Act 1991;

"the relevant date" means the 27th October 2008.

(3)   In this Order, except where otherwise stated, any reference to a numbered section or Schedule is a reference to a section of, or Schedule to, the Child Maintenance and Other Payments Act 2008.

Appointed days for sections 20 and 36

2.   *[Omitted]*

Appointed day for other provisions

3.   *[Omitted]*

Transitional and savings provisions

4.–(1)   Any existing case, as defined in paragraph (2), is to be treated from the relevant date as though the person with care had made an application under section 4 of the 1991 Act.

(2)   In paragraph (1) an existing case is one in which, immediately before 14th July 2008, section 6 of the 1991 Act applied in relation to a parent with care and–

(a)   a maintenance calculation or assessment was in force as a result of the Secretary of State acting under that section; or

(b)   no maintenance calculation or assessment had been made but the Secretary of State had given notice in accordance with regulation 5 of the Child Support (Maintenance Calculation Procedure) Regulations 2000 or regulation 5 of the Child Support (Maintenance Assessment Procedure) Regulations 1992.

(3)   Paragraph (1) is not to apply in any case where the maintenance assessment or calculation ceases to have effect, or would have ceased to have effect had it been made, before the relevant date.

(4)   The repeal of section 6 of the 1991 Act is not to prevent the Secretary of State from exercising any powers that he would have otherwise had under section 41 of the 1991 Act to recover and retain arrears of child support maintenance accrued in relation to any period before the relevant date.

The Child Support Information Regulations 2008

(SI 2008 No.2551)

PART 1
GENERAL

Citation and commencement

    1.   These Regulations may be cited as the Child Support Information Regulations 2008 and come into force on 27th October 2008.

Interpretation

    2.–(1)   In these Regulations–

"the 1991 Act" means the Child Support Act 1991;

"local authority" means, in relation to England, a county council, a district council, a London borough council, the Common Council of the City of London or the Council of the Isles of Scilly and, in relation to Wales, a county council or a county borough council and, in relation to Scotland, a council constituted under section 2 of the Local Government etc. (Scotland) Act 1994;

[¹"the Maintenance Calculation Regulations" means the Child Support Maintenance Calculation Regulations 2012];

    (2)   [¹...]

    (3)   [¹...]

    (4)   References in these Regulations to a non-resident parent are to a person who is the non-resident parent in relation to an application for a maintenance calculation or in relation to a maintenance calculation that is or has been in force and includes a person

treated as a non-resident parent by virtue of regulations made under section 42 of the 1991 Act.

Amendment

1. Child Support (Meaning of Child and New Calculation Rules) (Consequential and Miscellaneous Amendment) Regulations 2012 (SI 2012 No.2785) reg 8(2) (in force in relation to a particular case on — which is December 10, 2012, in relation to the types of cases falling within art 3 of SI 2012 No. 3042 (see p767). For other types of cases see '2003 and 1993 rules' below.

2003 and 1993 rules

Regulation 8(2) of the Child Support (Meaning of Child and New Calculation Rules) (Consequential and Miscellaneous Amendment) Regulations 2012 (SI 2012 No. 2785) amends this regulation and came into force on December 10, 2012, in relation to the types of cases falling within art 3 of SI 2012 No. 3042 (see p767). For other types of cases the amendments do not apply and in regulation 2(1) the definition of "Maintenance Calculation Procedure Regulations", given below, is retained in place of the definition of "the Maintenance Calculation Regulations" and regulations 2(2) and (3) are not omitted.

''Maintenance Calculation Procedure Regulations'' means the Child Support (Maintenance Calculation Procedure) Regulations 2000''

Regulation 2(2) and (3) read:

(2)   These Regulations apply to a 1993 scheme case in the same way as they apply to a 2003 scheme case and any references to expressions in the 1991 Act (including "non-resident parent" and "maintenance calculation") or to regulations made under that Act are to be read, in relation to a 1993 scheme case, with the necessary modifications.

(3)   In paragraph (2)–

(a)   "2003 scheme case" means a case in respect of which the provisions of the Child Support, Pensions and Social Security Act 2000 have been brought into force in accordance with article 3 of the Child Support, Pensions, and Social Security Act 2000 (Commencement No.12) Order 2003; and

(b)   "1993 scheme case" means a case in respect of which those provisions have not been brought into force.

General Note

Paragraph (2)

The regulations are worded in terms of the 2003 scheme. They also apply, with appropriate modifications, to the 1993 scheme. The principal effect is that references to non-resident parents and maintenance calculations must be read to apply to absent parents and maintenance assessments.

Paragraph (4)

This provides for an extended meaning of non-resident parent. It includes a parent who is the non-resident parent for the purposes of an application, even if paternity is challenged. See, however, reg 5. It covers both non-resident parents of current maintenance calculations and those who were non-resident parents under calculations that are no longer in force. It extends to those who are treated as non-resident parents by virtue of a special case under s42 of the Act.

PART 2

DUTY TO PROVIDE INFORMATION

Information from the applicant

3.–(1)   A person who has made an application for a maintenance calculation under section 4 of the 1991 Act must furnish such information as the [¹Secretary of State] requires to enable–

(a)   the non-resident parent to be identified or traced (where that is necessary);

(b)   the amount of child support maintenance payable by the non-resident parent to be calculated; or

(c)   that amount to be recovered from the non-resident parent.

(2)   A qualifying child who has made an application for a maintenance calculation under section 7 of the 1991 Act (right of a child in Scotland to apply for a calculation)

must furnish such information as the [¹Secretary of State] requires for any of the purposes, except enabling the non-resident parent to be identified, set out in paragraph (1).

Amendment

1.   Public Bodies (Child Maintenance and Enforcement Commission: Abolition and Transfer of Functions) Order 2012 (SI 2012 No.2007) art 3(2) and Sch para 116(2) (August 1, 2012).

Definitions

"the 1991 Act": see reg 2(1).
"non-resident parent": see reg 2(4).

General Note

This regulation is made under ss4(4) and 7(5) of the Act. It imposes a duty on an applicant to provide all the information required to identify and trace the non-resident parent, calculate that parent's liability to child support maintenance, and enforce that liability. In the case of a child applicant in Scotland, there is no duty to provide information about that parent's identity.

    The duty is subject to two qualifications. First, it is qualified by reasonableness. Sections 4(4) and 7(5) apply only to the extent that the applicant reasonably can comply: see the general note to s4(4). Regulation 7(1) provides that there is no duty to acquire information unless it is reasonable to expect this to be done. And reg 10 provides that a person with care is only under a duty to provide information that the Secretary of State reasonably requires. Second, the scope of the duty is limited, by both the regulation itself and ss4(4) and 7(5), to information that the Secretary of State requires. If the Secretary of State can obtain the information elsewhere, it is not required of the applicant.

    The duty is not limited to the time of the application. It continues to apply thereafter, but it only arises on request. There is a limited continuing duty for a person with care, but not a child, to provide information without a request in reg 10.

Information from other persons

4.–(1)   The persons listed in paragraph (2) must furnish such information or evidence as is required by the [¹Secretary of State] and is needed–

(a)   for the determination of any application made under the 1991 Act or any question arising in connection with such an application;

(b)   for the making of any decision, or in connection with the imposition of any condition or requirement, under that Act; or

(c)   in connection with the collection or enforcement of child support or other maintenance under that Act.

(2)   The persons required to furnish information or evidence are–

(a)   subject to regulation 5, the non-resident parent;

(b)   a current or previous employer of the non-resident parent;

(c)   a person for whom the non-resident parent is providing or has provided services under a contract for services;

(d)   a person who acts or has acted as an accountant for the non-resident parent;

(e)   a person, other than the applicant, who provides day to day care for a child in respect of whom an application for a maintenance calculation has been made or in respect of whom a maintenance calculation is or has been in force;

(f)   a credit reference agency within the meaning given by the Consumer Credit Act 1974;

(g)   a local authority in whose area the non-resident parent or the person with care resides or has resided;

(h)   persons employed in the service of the Crown or otherwise in the discharge of Crown functions–

    (i)   under the Road Traffic (Northern Ireland) Order 1981, sections 97 to 99A of the Road Traffic Act 1988 or Part II of the Vehicle Excise and Registration Act 1994; or

    (ii)   under the Prison Act 1952, the Prison Act (Northern Ireland) 1953 or the Prisons (Scotland) Act 1989;

(i)   a person who, in the course of business, may lawfully accept deposits in the United Kingdom;

(j)   a person who, within the meaning of the Electricity Act 1989, distributes or supplies electricity;

(k)   a person who is the holder of a licence under section 7 of the Gas Act 1986 to convey gas through pipes or the holder of a licence under section 7A(1) of that Act to supply gas through pipes.

(3)   The persons mentioned in paragraph (2) (b) and (c) include persons employed in the service of the Crown or otherwise in the discharge of Crown functions.

Amendment

1.   Public Bodies (Child Maintenance and Enforcement Commission: Abolition and Transfer of Functions) Order 2012 (SI 2012 No.2007) art 3(2) and Sch para 116(3) (August 1, 2012).

Definitions

"the 1991 Act": see reg 2(1).
"local authority": see reg 2(1).
"non-resident parent": see reg 2(4).

General Note

Most of this regulation is made under s14(1) of the Act, although paras 2(h) and (3) are made under s57(1). It imposes duties on persons (other than the applicant) and organisations to provide information. As with reg 3, the duty does not arise unless the information is required.

The duty is not limited to the time of the application. It applies both then and thereafter, but it only arises on request. There is a limited continuing duty for a non-resident parent to provide information without a request in reg 9.

Information from persons denying parentage

5.   Where a person is alleged to be, but denies being, the parent of a child in respect of whom an application for a maintenance calculation has been made, unless the case falls within one of those set out in section 26(2) of the 1991 Act (disputes about parentage), the information or evidence which that person may be required to furnish is limited to what is needed for the purposes of enabling the non-resident parent to be identified or to enable a decision to be made as to whether the [¹Secretary of State] has jurisdiction under section 44 to make a maintenance calculation.

Amendment

1.   Public Bodies (Child Maintenance and Enforcement Commission: Abolition and Transfer of Functions) Order 2012 (SI 2012 No.2007) art 3(2) and Sch para 116(4) (August 1, 2012).

Definitions

"the 1991 Act": see reg 2(1).
"non-resident parent": see reg 2(4).

General Note

This regulation limits the duties owed if an alleged non-resident parent (i) denies parentage and (ii) is not within any of the cases in s26 of the Act. The only duties that arise in respect of such a person are to provide information about (a) the person's identity and (b) the Secretary of State's jurisdiction under s44.

Information from a court

6.–(1)   Where there is or has been a relevant court order, or there have been proceedings in which such an order was sought or where such proceedings are pending, the persons mentioned in paragraph (2) must furnish such information or evidence in relation to that order or those proceedings as is required by the [¹Secretary of State] and is needed for any of the purposes mentioned in regulation 4(1).

(2)   The persons who are required to furnish information or evidence are–

(a)   in England and Wales–

    (i)   in relation to the High Court, the senior district judge of the principal registry of the Family Division or, where proceedings were instituted in a district registry, the district judge;

    (ii)   in relation to a county court, the proper officer of that court within the meaning of Order 1, Rule 3 of the County Courts Rules 1981;

       (iii)   in relation to a magistrates' court, the designated officer for that court;
(b)   in Scotland–
       (i)   in relation to the Court of Session, the Deputy Principal Clerk of Session;
       (ii)   in relation to a sheriff court, the sheriff clerk.
(3)   In paragraph (1) "relevant court order" means–
(a)   an order as to periodical or capital provision or as to variation of property rights made under an enactment specified in paragraphs (a) to (ea) of section 8(11) of the 1991 Act or prescribed under section 8(11) of that Act in relation to a person who has made an application for a maintenance calculation or a qualifying child, person with care or non-resident parent in relation to such an application;
(b)   an order under Part II of the Children Act 1989 (orders with respect to children in family proceedings) in relation to a qualifying child or, in Scotland, an order under section 3 of the Law Reform (Parent and Child) (Scotland) Act 1986 or a decree of declarator under section 7 of that Act in relation to a qualifying child.

Amendment

   1.   Public Bodies (Child Maintenance and Enforcement Commission: Abolition and Transfer of Functions) Order 2012 (SI 2012 No.2007) art 3(2) and Sch para 116(5) (August 1, 2012).

Definition

   "the 1991 Act": see reg 2(1).

General Note

   This regulation is made under s14(1) of the Act and imposes a duty on the listed court officers to provide information and evidence. The duty arises if there is, or has ever been, a relevant court order made or if there are, or ever have been, proceedings.

Duty of persons from whom information requested

7.–(1)   Persons required to furnish information or evidence under regulations 3 to 6 must furnish the information or evidence requested if it is in their possession or they can reasonably be expected to acquire it.
   (2)   The information must be furnished as soon as is reasonably practicable in the particular circumstances of the case.
   (3)   [1...]

Amendment

   1.   Child Support (Meaning of Child and New Calculation Rules) (Consequential and Miscellaneous Amendment) Regulations 2012 (SI 2012 No.2785) reg 8(3) (in force in relation to a particular case on the day on which paragraph 2 of Schedule 4 to the Child Maintenance and Other Payments Act 2008 (see p243) comes into force in relation to that type of case – which is December 10, 2012, in relation to the types of cases falling within art 3 of SI 2012 No.3042 (see p767). For other types of cases see '2003 and 1993 rules' below.

2003 and 1993 rules

   Regulation 8(3) of The Child Support (Meaning of Child and New Calculation Rules) (Consequential and Miscellaneous Amendment) Regulations 2012 (SI 2012 No.2785) omitted paragraph 7(3). This amendment came into force on December 10, 2012, in relation to the types of cases falling within art 3 of SI 2012 No.3042 (see p767). For other types of cases paragraph 7(3) is retained and reads:

"(3)   Paragraph (2) is subject to regulation 3(4) of the Maintenance Calculation Procedure Regulations (which provides for a time limit where additional information is requested in relation to an ineffective application)."

Definition

   "Maintenance Calculation Procedure Regulations": see reg 2(1).

General Note

   Paragraph (1)
   This paragraph provides for the extent of the duties to provide information or evidence. They only arise if the person possesses it or can reasonably be expected to acquire it. For the latter, the ease with which it can be obtained and any cost involved will be relevant considerations.

Paragraph (2)
This paragraph provides for the time within which the evidence or information must be provided. Inevitably, it is not specific.

[¹Secretary of State] to warn of consequences of failing to provide information or providing false information

8. A request by the [¹Secretary of State] under regulations 3 to 6 must set out the possible consequences of failure to provide the information or evidence, including details of the offences provided for in section 14A of the 1991 Act for failing to provide, or providing false, information.

Amendment

1. Public Bodies (Child Maintenance and Enforcement Commission: Abolition and Transfer of Functions) Order 2012 (SI 2012 No.2007) art 3(2) and Sch para 116(6) (August 1, 2012).

Definition
"the 1991 Act": see reg 2(1).

General Note
The Secretary of State must set out the consequences of failing to provide, or providing false, information, including offences under s14A of the Act. In view of the powers under that section, tribunals may prefer to obtain information through the Secretary of State rather than under their own powers.

Duty to notify change of address

9. Persons who are liable to make payments of child support maintenance must, if they change their address, notify the [¹Secretary of State] of their new address within 7 days of the change.

Amendment

1. Public Bodies (Child Maintenance and Enforcement Commission: Abolition and Transfer of Functions) Order 2012 (SI 2012 No.2007) art 3(2) and Sch para 116(7) (August 1, 2012).

General Note
This is one of two continuing duties to provide information without a request by the Secretary of State. For the other, see reg 10. Both are limited. This one applies to non-resident parents and is limited to a change of address.

[1Duty to notify increase in current income

9A.–(1) In a case falling within paragraphs (2) or (3), the Secretary of State may notify the non-resident parent that that parent is required to notify the Secretary of State of any relevant change of circumstances in relation to that income.

(2) A case falls within this paragraph if, in relation to a maintenance calculation in force–

(a) gross weekly income is determined by reference to the non-resident parent's current income as an employee or officeholder (in accordance with regulation 38 of the Maintenance Calculation Regulations); and

(b) paragraph 5(b) of Schedule 1 to the 1991 Act (nil rate) does not apply.

(3) A case falls within this paragraph if, in relation to a maintenance calculation in force–

(a) gross weekly income is determined by reference to the non-resident parent's current income (in accordance with regulation 37 of the Maintenance Calculation Regulations); and

(b) paragraph 5(b) of Schedule 1 to the 1991 Act applies (nil rate).

(4) A notification by the Secretary of State under paragraph (1) must be in writing.

(5) Where a relevant change of circumstances occurs after the non-resident parent has been notified of a requirement under paragraph (1), the non-resident parent must notify the Secretary of State of that change–

(a) within fourteen days beginning with the day on which the change occurs; or

(b)   within such other period as the Secretary of State has specified in the notification.

(6)   For the purposes of a case falling within paragraph (2), a relevant change of circumstances occurs where–

(a)   the non-resident parent–
>(i)   commences a new employment or office; or
>(ii)   in relation to an existing employment or office, commences a new rate of remuneration or a new working pattern,

and could reasonably be expected to know that would result in an increased liability under the maintenance calculation in force if reported to the Secretary of State; or

(b)   the non-resident parent receives from their employment or office the following number of consecutive payments, each of which (if it were taken as a weekly average) exceeds the gross weekly income taken into account in the maintenance calculation in force by 25% or more–
>(i)   five payments, in the case of a non-resident parent paid weekly;
>(ii)   three payments, in the case of a non-resident parent paid fortnightly;
>(iii)   two payments, in the case of a non-resident parent paid four weekly or monthly.

(7)   The payments referred to in paragraph (6)(b) are the gross remuneration from the employment or office in question less any pension contributions deducted under net pay arrangements.

(8)   In paragraph (7)–

"net pay arrangements" means arrangements for relief in respect of pension contributions under section 193 of the Finance Act 2004.

(9)   For the purposes of a case falling within paragraph (3), a relevant change of circumstances occurs where the non-resident parent's income increases to a gross weekly income of £5 or more.

(10)   For the purposes of paragraph (9), gross weekly income is to be calculated in accordance with regulation 45(2) of the Maintenance Calculation Regulations.]

Amendment

    1.   Child Support (Meaning of Child and New Calculation Rules) (Consequential and Miscellaneous Amendment) Regulations 2012 (SI 2012 No. 2785) reg 8(4) (in force in relation to a particular case on the day on which paragraph 2 of Schedule 4 to the Child Maintenance and Other Payments Act 2008 (see p243) comes into force in relation to that type of case – which is December 10, 2012, in relation to the types of cases falling within art 3 of SI 2012 No.3042 (see p767).

2003 and 1993 rules

    The insertion of regulation 9A came into force on December 10, 2012, only in respect of cases falling within art 3 of SI 2012 No.3042 (see p767). For other types of cases Regulation 9A does not apply.

Continuing duty of person with care

10.   Where a person with care with respect to whom a maintenance calculation has been made believes that, by virtue of section 44 or 55 of, or paragraph 16 of Schedule 1 to, the 1991 Act, the calculation has ceased to have effect, that person must, as soon as is reasonably practicable, inform the [¹Secretary of State] of that belief, and of the reasons for it, and must provide such other information as the [¹Secretary of State] may reasonably require, with a view to assisting the [¹Secretary of State] in determining whether the calculation has ceased to have effect.

Amendment

    1.   Public Bodies (Child Maintenance and Enforcement Commission: Abolition and Transfer of Functions) Order 2012 (SI 2012 No.2007) art 3(2) and Sch para 116(8) (August 1, 2012).

Definition

    "the 1991 Act": see reg 2(1).

General Note

    This is one of two continuing duties to provide information without a request by the Secretary of State. For the other, see reg 9. Both are limited. This one applies to persons with care and is limited to circumstances in which a maintenance calculation ceases to exist. It is made under Sch 1 para 16(10) to the Act. It arises if the Secretary of State loses jurisdiction, the qualifying child ceases to be a child, and the circumstances in Sch 1 para 16 to the Act apply. It is more curtailed than the duty under reg 3. It only applies if the person believes that the calculation has ceased, not may have ceased. On the wording, the belief must concern the effect on the maintenance calculation, not merely the facts that give rise to that effect.

Powers of inspectors in relation to Crown premises
11. Subject to Her Majesty not being in residence, an inspector appointed under section 15 of the 1991 Act may enter any Crown premises for the purposes of exercising any powers conferred by that section.

Definition
"the 1991 Act": see reg 2(1).

General Note
This regulation is made under s57(2) of the Act.

PART 3
DISCLOSURE OF INFORMATION

Disclosure of information to a court or tribunal
12.–(1) The [²Secretary of State] may disclose any information held for the purposes of the 1991 Act to–
(a) a court;
(b) any tribunal or other body or person mentioned in the 1991 Act;
(c) a person with a right of appeal under the 1991 Act to [¹ the First-tier Tribunal], where such disclosure is made for the purposes of any proceedings before any of those bodies relating to the 1991 Act, the benefit Acts, the Jobseekers Act 1995 or Part 1 of the Welfare Reform Act 2007.

(2) For the purposes of this regulation "proceedings" includes the determination of an application referred to [¹ the First-tier Tribunal] under section 28D(1)(b) of the 1991 Act.

(3) The [²Secretary of State] may disclose information held for the purposes of the 1991 Act to a court in any case where–
(a) that court has exercised any power it has to make, vary or revive a maintenance order or to vary a maintenance agreement; and
(b) such disclosure is made for the purposes of any proceedings before that court in relation to that maintenance order or that maintenance agreement or for the purposes of any matters arising out of those proceedings.

Amendments
1. Tribunals, Courts and Enforcement Act 2007 (Transitional and Consequential Provisions) Order 2008 (SI 2008 No.2683) Sch 1 para 346 (November 3, 2008).
2. Public Bodies (Child Maintenance and Enforcement Commission: Abolition and Transfer of Functions) Order 2012 (SI 2012 No.2007) art 3(2) and Sch para 116(9) (August 1, 2012).

Definition
"the 1991 Act": see reg 2(1).

General Note
This regulation is made under s14(3) of the Act. It permits disclosure in connection with legal proceedings, principally to courts, tribunals and parties to appeals and references before tribunals. The persons who have a right of appeal to the First-tier Tribunal are set out in s20(2) of the Act. There is no power to disclose information in connection with any other proceedings than those covered by this regulation: *Re C(A Minor) (Child Support Agency: Disclosure)* [1995] 1 FLR 201.

Disclosure of information to other persons
13.–(1) The [¹Secretary of State] may disclose information held for the purposes of the 1991 Act relating to one party to a maintenance calculation to another party to that

calculation where, in the opinion of the [¹Secretary of State], such information is essential to inform the party to whom it would be given as to–

(a)   why [¹the Secretary of State] has decided not to make a maintenance calculation in response to an application made under section 4 or 7 of the 1991 Act, or an application for a revision under section 16 of that Act or a decision under section 17 of that Act superseding an earlier decision has been rejected;

(b)   why, although an application for a maintenance calculation referred to in sub-paragraph (a) has been made, that calculation cannot, at the time in question, be proceeded with;

(c)   why a maintenance calculation has ceased to have effect;

(d)   how a maintenance calculation has been calculated, in so far as the matter has not been dealt with by the notification given under [³regulation 25 of the Maintenance Calculation Regulations (notification of a maintenance calculation)] ;

(e)   why a decision has been made not to arrange for, or to cease, collection of any child support maintenance under section 29 of the 1991 Act;

(f)   why a particular method of enforcement under the 1991 Act of an amount due under a maintenance calculation has been adopted in a particular case; [²...]

(g)   why a decision has been made not to enforce, or to cease to enforce, under the 1991 Act the amount due under a maintenance calculation;

[²(h)   why it was decided, in relation to any arrears of child support maintenance, not to accept payment in part in satisfaction of liability for the whole under section 41D(1) of the 1991 Act; or

(i) why it was decided not to extinguish liability in respect of arrears of child support maintenance under section 41E(1) of the 1991 Act.]

(2)   For the purposes of this regulation, "party to a maintenance calculation" means–

(a)   a person who has made an application for a maintenance calculation;

(b)   a qualifying child, person with care or non-resident parent in respect of whom an application for a maintenance calculation has been made;

(c)   a person appointed under [³paragraph 4 of the Schedule to the Maintenance Calculation Regulations] (death of party to an appeal);

(d)   the personal representative of a person mentioned in sub-paragraph (a) or (b) where–

(i)   a revision, supersession or appeal was pending at the date of death of that person and the personal representative is dealing with that revision, supersession or appeal on behalf of that person; or

(ii)   an application for a variation has been made but not determined at the date of death of that person and the personal representative is dealing on behalf of that person with any matters arising in connection with such an application.

(3)   Any application for information under this regulation shall be made to the [¹Secretary of State] in writing setting out the reasons for the application.

(4)   Except where a person gives written permission to the [¹Secretary of State] that the information mentioned in sub-paragraphs (a) and (b) below in relation to that person may be conveyed to other persons, any information given under the provisions of paragraph (1) shall not contain–

(a)   the address of any person other than the recipient of the information in question (other than the address of the office of the officer concerned who is exercising functions of the [¹Secretary of State] under the 1991 Act) or any other information the use of which could reasonably be expected to lead to any such person being located;

(b)   any other information the use of which could reasonably be expected to lead to any person, other than a party to the maintenance calculation, being identified.

Amendments

1.   Public Bodies (Child Maintenance and Enforcement Commission: Abolition and Transfer of Functions) Order 2012 (SI 2012 No.2007) art 3(2) and Sch para 116(10) (August 1, 2012).

2. Child Support Management of Payments and Arrears (Amendment) Regulations 2012 (SI 2012 No. 3002) reg 3 (December 10, 2012).
3. Child Support (Meaning of Child and New Calculation Rules) (Consequential and Miscellaneous Amendment) Regulations 2012 (SI 2012 No. 2785) reg 8(5) (in force in relation to a particular case on the day on which paragraph 2 of Schedule 4 to the Child Maintenance and Other Payments Act 2008 (see p243) comes into force in relation to that type of case – which is December 10, 2012, in relation to the types of cases falling within art 3 of SI 2012 No. 3042 (see p767). For other types of cases see '2003 and 1993 rules' below.

2003 and 1993 rules

Regulation 8(5) of The Child Support (Meaning of Child and New Calculation Rules) (Consequential and Miscellaneous Amendment) Regulations 2012 (SI 2012 No.2785) amends paragraphs (1)(d) and (2)(c) of regulation 13. These amendments have been brought into force from December 10, 2012, in relation to the types of cases falling within art 3 of SI 2012 No.3042 (see p767). For other types of cases the amendments do not apply and the words in paragraph (1)(d) "regulation 25 of the Maintenance Calculation Regulations (notification of a maintenance calculation)" should be read as "regulation 23 of the Maintenance Calculation Procedure Regulations" and the words in paragraph (2)(c) "paragraph 4 of the Schedule to the Maintenance Calculation Regulations" should be read as "regulation 34 of the Social Security and Child Support (Decisions and Appeals) Regulations 1999".

Definitions

"the 1991 Act": see reg 2(1).
"non-resident parent": see reg 2(4).

General Note

This regulation is made under s14(3) of the Act. It permits disclosure, for limited purposes only, to other parties to a maintenance calculation. This strikes a balance between transparency of decision-making and respecting confidentiality. In contrast to other regulations, it arises only when disclosure is essential for one of the stated purposes. This is a stringent condition that suggests that disclosure must be indispensable to achieve the stated purpose.

[¹ Employment to which section 50 of the 1991 Act applies

14.–(1) For the purposes of section 50(1A) of the 1991 Act, employment as any member of a committee or sub-committee established under paragraph 11 of Schedule 1 to the Child Maintenance and Other Payments Act 2008 is prescribed as a kind of employment to which section 50(1) of that Act applies.

(2) For the purposes of section 50(1C) of the 1991 Act, the following kinds of employment are prescribed as kinds of employment to which section 50(1B) of that Act applies–

(a) the Comptroller and Auditor General;

[²(aa) a member or employee of the National Audit Office or any other person who carries out administrative work of the Office, or who provides, or is employed in the provision of, services to it;]

[²(b) any member of the staff of the National Audit Office that was established by section 3 of the National Audit Act 1983 or any other person who carried out administrative work of the Office, or who provided, or was employed in the provision of, services to it;]

(c) the Parliamentary Commissioner for Administration;

(d) the Health Service Commissioner for Wales;

(e) the Health Service Commissioner for Scotland;

(f) any officer of any of the Commissioners referred to in paragraphs (c) to (e) above.]

Amendments

1. Child Support (Miscellaneous Amendments) Regulations 2009 (SI No.396) reg 6 (April 6, 2009).
2. Budget Responsibility and National Audit Act 2011 (Consequential Amendments) Order 2012 (SI 2012 No.725) art 2(10) (April 1, 2012).

Definition

"the 1991 Act": see reg 2(1).

General Note

This substituted regulation is made under s50(1A) and (1C) of the Act. It prescribes employments to which the offence in s50(1) applies.

PART 4
MISCELLANEOUS

Revocation and saving

15.–(1)   The Child Support (Information, Evidence and Disclosure) Regulations 1992 are revoked.

(2)   The revocation of those Regulations shall not affect any request for information made before 27th October 2008 and those Regulations shall remain in force for the purposes of any proceedings under section 14A of the 1991 Act (information offences) in relation to any such request.

Definition

"the 1991 Act": see reg 2(1).

General Note

These regulations operate with effect from 27 October 2008. The Child Support (Information, Evidence and Disclosure) Regulations 1992 continue to apply prior to that date.

Transitional provisions in relation to transfer of child support functions
16.   [¹...]

Amendment

1.   Public Bodies (Child Maintenance and Enforcement Commission: Abolition and Transfer of Functions) Order 2012 (SI 2012 No.2007) art 3(2) and Sch para 116(11) (August 1, 2012).

General Note

Section 13 of the 2008 Act came into force on 1 November 2008.

The Child Maintenance and Other Payments Act 2008
(Commencement No. 4 and Transitional Provision) Order 2008
(SI 2008 No.2675)

Citation and interpretation

1.–(1) This Order may be cited as the Child Maintenance and Other Payments Act 2008 (Commencement No. 4 and Transitional Provision) Order 2008.

(2)　In this Order "the relevant date" means 1st November 2008.

(3)　In this Order, except where otherwise stated, any reference to a numbered section or Schedule is a reference to a section of, or Schedule to, the Child Maintenance and Other Payments Act 2008.

Transitional provision

4.　Where, on or after the relevant date, any document or notice relating to a function transferred to the Commission by virtue of section 13 is given or sent to any person by the Commission which contains a reference to the Secretary of State, that document or notice is not to be invalidated by virtue of that reference.

The Child Support (Miscellaneous Amendments) (No.2) Regulations 2009

(2009 No.2909)

Transitional provisions – qualifying child

5.–(1) Where the circumstances in paragraph (2) apply the effective date of–

(a) a maintenance assessment or maintenance calculation made following an application under section 4 or 7 of the Act; or

(b) a supersession decision made under section 17 of the Act where the relevant change of circumstances is that a person has become a qualifying child by virtue of these Regulations,

is the day on which this regulation comes into force.

(2) The circumstances are–

(a) before these Regulations came into force there was a maintenance assessment or maintenance calculation in force in relation to the qualifying child to whom the application or supersession relates;

(b) a person ("C") who was a qualifying child to whom that maintenance assessment or maintenance calculation relates, ceased to be a qualifying child on or after 10th April 2006 by virtue of no longer falling within the provisions of–

  (i) Schedule 1 to the Maintenance Assessment Procedure Regulations (meaning of "child" for the purposes of the Act); or, as the case may be,

  (ii) Schedule 1 to the Maintenance Calculation Procedure Regulations (meaning of "child" for the purposes of the Act); and

(c) child benefit was payable in respect of C on the day C ceased to be a qualifying child and is payable in respect of C on the day on which this regulation comes into force.

(3) Where an application under section 4 or 7 of the Act is made in a case to which the circumstances in paragraph (2) apply in respect of a maintenance assessment, the definition of "the relevant period" in regulation 28(3) of the Child Support (Transitional Provisions) Regulations 2000 (linking provisions), is modified as follows–

"(3) For the purposes of paragraph (1) "the relevant period" means the period starting on the day immediately before the day the maintenance assessment ceased to have effect under paragraph 16(1) of Schedule 1 to the Act, to the day that the application referred to in paragraph (1) is made, in a case where the circumstances of regulation 5(2) of the Child Support (Miscellaneous Amendments) (No. 2) Regulations 2009 (transitional provisions – qualifying child) apply.".

Commencement

10.11.09.

The Child Support (Management of Payments and Arrears) Regulations 2009

(2009 No.3151)

PART 1
General

Citation and commencement

1. These Regulations may be cited as the Child Support (Management of Payments and Arrears) Regulations 2009 and come into force on 25th January 2010.

Interpretation

2.–(1)   In these Regulations–

"the 1991 Act" means the Child Support Act 1991;

"a 1993 scheme case" means a case in respect of which the provisions of the Child Support, Pensions and Social Security Act 2000 have not been brought into force in accordance with article 3 of the Child Support, Pensions and Social Security Act 2000 (Commencement No. 12) Order 2003;

"the AIMA Regulations" means the Child Support (Arrears, Interest and Adjustment of Maintenance Assessments) Regulations 1992;

[¹"child in Scotland" means a child who has made an application for a maintenance calculation under section 7 of the 1991 Act;]

"the Decisions and Appeals Regulations" means the Social Security and Child Support (Decisions and Appeals) Regulations 1999;

"non-resident parent" includes a person treated as a non-resident parent by virtue of regulations made under section 42 of the 1991 Act;

"relevant person" means–

(a)   a person with care;

(b)   a non-resident parent;

(c)   where the application for a maintenance calculation is made by a child under section 7 of the 1991 Act, that child,

in respect of whom a maintenance calculation is or has been in force.

(2)   In the application of these Regulations to a 1993 scheme case, any reference to expressions in the 1991 Act (including "non-resident parent" and "maintenance calculation") or to regulations made under that Act are to be read with the necessary modifications.

Amendment

1.   Child Support Management of Payments and Arrears (Amendment) Regulations 2012 (SI 2012 No. 3002) reg 2(2) (December 10, 2012).

General Note

Subsection (2)

The regulations are worded in terms of the 2003 scheme. They also apply, with appropriate modifications, to the 1993 scheme. The principal effect is that references to non-resident parents and maintenance calculations must be read to apply to absent parents and maintenance assessments.

Arrears notices

3.–(1)   This regulation applies to a case where–

(a)   the [²Secretary of State] is arranging for the collection of child support maintenance under section 29 of the 1991 Act; and

(b)   the non-resident parent has failed to make one or more payments of child support maintenance due.

(2)   Where the [²Secretary of State] is considering taking action with regard to a case falling within paragraph (1) [²the Secretary of State] must serve a notice on the non-resident parent.

(3)   The notice must–

[¹(a)   include the amount of all outstanding arrears of child support maintenance due and not paid;]

(b)   set out in general terms the provisions as to arrears contained in this regulation and regulation 8 of the AIMA Regulations; and

(c)   request the non-resident parent make payment of all outstanding arrears.

(4)   Where a notice has been served under paragraph (2), no duty to serve a further notice under that paragraph arises in relation to further arrears unless those further arrears have arisen after an intervening continuous period of not less than 12 weeks during the course of which all payments of child support maintenance due from the non-resident parent have been paid on time in accordance with regulations made under section 29 of the 1991 Act.

Amendments

1.   Child Support (Miscellaneous Amendments) Regulations 2012 (SI 2012 No.712) reg 3 (April 30, 2012).
2.   Public Bodies (Child Maintenance and Enforcement Commission: Abolition and Transfer of Functions) Order 2012 (SI 2012 No.2007) art 3(2) and Sch para 121(2) (August 1, 2012).

Definitions

"the 1991 Act": see reg 2(1).
"the AIMA Regulations": see reg 2(1).
"non-resident parent": see reg 2(1).

General Note

This regulation imposes a duty on the Secretary of State to give notice to a non-resident parent who is in arrears if it is arranging for the collection of the maintenance and it is considering taking action. The terms of the notice are specified in para (3). The notice covers future arrears unless and until the non-resident parent has discharged current liability on time for a continuous period of 12 weeks or more.

Attribution of payments

4.   Where a maintenance calculation is or has been in force and there are arrears of child support maintenance, the [¹Secretary of State] may attribute any payment of child support maintenance made by a non-resident parent to child support maintenance due as [¹the Secretary of State] thinks fit.

Amendment

1.   Public Bodies (Child Maintenance and Enforcement Commission: Abolition and Transfer of Functions) Order 2012 (SI 2012 No.2007) art 3(2) and Sch para 121(3) (August 1, 2012).

Definition

"non-resident parent": see reg 2(1).

General Note

This regulation allows the Secretary of State to attribute any payments made by an non-resident parent who is in arrears as it thinks fit. This allows it to attribute the payments either to current liability or in discharge of arrears or part and part.

An attribution under this regulation can be effective for the purposes of income support (*SSWP v Menary-Smith* [2006] EWCA Civ 1751, para 40).

PART 2

General Note

The regulations in this Part are made under s41C(3) of the Act.

Set Off

Set off of liabilities to pay child support maintenance

5.–(1)   The circumstances prescribed for the purposes of section 41C(1)(a) of the 1991 Act, in which the [¹Secretary of State] may set off liabilities to pay child support maintenance, are set out in paragraph (2).

(2)   The [¹Secretary of State] may set off the liability to pay child support maintenance of one person ("A") against the liability to pay child support maintenance of another person ("B") where–

(a)   A is liable to pay child support maintenance under a maintenance calculation, whether that calculation is current or no longer in force, in relation to which B is the person with care; and

(b) B is liable to pay child support maintenance under a maintenance calculation, whether that calculation is current or no longer in force, in relation to which A is the person with care.

(3) There shall be no set off in relation to any amount which if paid could be retained under section 41 of the 1991 Act.

Amendment

1.   Public Bodies (Child Maintenance and Enforcement Commission: Abolition and Transfer of Functions) Order 2012 (SI 2012 No.2007) art 3(2) and Sch para 121(4) (August 1, 2012).

Definition

"the 1991 Act": see reg 2(1).

General Note

This regulation applies when A is the non-resident parent and B the person with care in respect of one maintenance calculation and their roles are reversed in respect of another calculation. It gives the Secretary of State power of set off in order to avoid money passing in a circle from A to B and back again. The power does not apply to any amount that could be retained under s41 of the Act on account of benefits that the parent with care received while arrears were owing.

Set off of payments against child support maintenance liability

6.–(1) The circumstances prescribed for the purposes of section 41C(1)(b) of the 1991 Act, in which the [¹Secretary of State] may set off a payment against a person's liability to pay child support maintenance, are set out in paragraph (2).

(2) The [¹Secretary of State] may set off a payment against a non-resident parent's liability to pay child support maintenance where–
(a) the payment falls within paragraph (3); and
(b) the person with care agreed to the making of the payment.

(3) A payment is of a prescribed description for the purposes of section 41C(1)(b) of the 1991 Act if it was made by the non-resident parent in respect of–
(a) a mortgage or loan taken out on the security of the property which is the qualifying child's home where that mortgage or loan was taken out to facilitate the purchase of, or to pay for essential repairs or improvements to, that property;
(b) rent on the property which is the qualifying child's home;
(c) mains-supplied gas, water or electricity charges at the qualifying child's home;
(d) council tax payable by the person with care in relation to the qualifying child's home;
(e) essential repairs to the heating system in the qualifying child's home; or
(f) repairs which are essential to maintain the fabric of the qualifying child's home.

Amendment

1.   Public Bodies (Child Maintenance and Enforcement Commission: Abolition and Transfer of Functions) Order 2012 (SI 2012 No.2007) art 3(2) and Sch para 121(5) (August 1, 2012).

Definitions

"the 1991 Act": see reg 2(1).
"non-resident parent": see reg 2(1).

General Note

This regulation applies when the non-resident parent makes payments for the benefit of the qualifying child with the person with care's agreement. The Secretary of State then has power to set those payments off against liability for child support maintenance.

Three issues potentially arise. Did the non-resident parent make the payments? There is likely to be documentary evidence of payment for most, if not all, of the types of payment covered by para (3). There may be dispute if the payment was from a joint account and the non-resident parent was not the only person paying into that account. Were the conditions in para (3) satisfied? This is only likely to occur in relation to subparas (e) and (f), where there is scope to argue about whether work amounted to repairs and whether it was essential. Did the person with care agree? There can be no dispute if there is a written agreement. This will not always be so. If the non-resident parent continued to pay bills following a separation, will the person with care's acquiescence count as an agreement?

Application of set off

7.–(1) In setting off a person's liability for child support maintenance under this Part, the [¹Secretary of State] may apply the amount to be set off to reduce any arrears of child support maintenance due under any current maintenance calculation, or any previous maintenance calculation made in respect of the same relevant persons.

(2) Where there are no arrears of child support maintenance due, or an amount remains to be set off after the application of paragraph (1), the [¹Secretary of State] may adjust the amount payable in relation to the current maintenance calculation by such amount as [¹the Secretary of State] considers appropriate in all the circumstances of the case, having regard in particular to–

(a) the circumstances of the relevant persons; and

(b) the amount to be set off and the period over which it would be reasonable to adjust the amount payable to set off that amount.

(3) An adjustment of the amount payable in relation to the current maintenance calculation under paragraph (2) may reduce the amount payable to nil.

Amendment

1. Public Bodies (Child Maintenance and Enforcement Commission: Abolition and Transfer of Functions) Order 2012 (SI 2012 No.2007) art 3(2) and Sch para 121(6) (August 1, 2012).

Definition

"relevant person": see reg 2(1).

General Note

The Secretary of State may apply an amount set off to reduce arrears. If there are no (longer) arrears, the Secretary of State may adjust the amount payable, even to nil.

PART 3
Overpayments and Voluntary Payments

Application of overpayments

8.–(1) Where for any reason, including the retrospective effect of a maintenance calculation, there has been an overpayment of child support maintenance, the [¹Secretary of State] may apply the amount overpaid to reduce any arrears of child support maintenance due under any previous maintenance calculation in respect of the same relevant persons.

(2) Where there is no previous maintenance calculation, or an amount of the overpayment remains after the application of paragraph (1), the [¹Secretary of State] may adjust the amount payable in relation to the current maintenance calculation by such amount as [¹the Secretary of State] considers appropriate in all the circumstances of the case, having regard in particular to–

(a) the circumstances of the relevant persons; and

(b) the amount of the overpayment and the period over which it would be reasonable to adjust the amount payable for the overpayment to be rectified.

(3) An adjustment of the amount payable in relation to the current maintenance calculation under paragraph (2) may reduce the amount payable to nil.

Amendment

1. Public Bodies (Child Maintenance and Enforcement Commission: Abolition and Transfer of Functions) Order 2012 (SI 2012 No.2007) art 3(2) and Sch para 121(7) (August 1, 2012).

Definition

"relevant person": see reg 2(1).

General Note

This regulation is made under s51(2)(d), (e) and (f) of the Act. The Secretary of State may attribute an overpayment to reduce arrears under a previous maintenance calculation in respect of the same persons.

Otherwise, the Secretary of State may adjust the amount payable under the current calculation, even to nil. The adjustment reduces the payment, not the liability, which is unaffected.

    If an adjustment is not made, the Secretary of State may reimburse the non-resident parent under s41B of the Act.

Application of voluntary payments

9.–(1)   Where there has been a voluntary payment the [¹Secretary of State] may apply the amount of the voluntary payment to reduce any arrears of child support maintenance due under any previous maintenance calculation in respect of the same relevant persons.

    (2)   Where there is no previous maintenance calculation, or an amount of the voluntary payment remains after the application of paragraph (1), the [¹Secretary of State] may adjust the amount payable in relation to the current maintenance calculation by such amount as [¹the Secretary of State] considers appropriate in all the circumstances of the case, having regard in particular to–

    (a)   the circumstances of the relevant persons; and

    (b)   the amount of the voluntary payment and the period over which it would be reasonable to adjust the amount payable for the voluntary payment to be taken into account.

    (3)   An adjustment of the amount payable in relation to the current maintenance calculation under paragraph (2) may reduce the amount payable to nil.

Amendment

    1.   Public Bodies (Child Maintenance and Enforcement Commission: Abolition and Transfer of Functions) Order 2012 (SI 2012 No.2007) art 3(2) and Sch para 121(8) (August 1, 2012).

Definition

    "relevant person": see reg 2(1).

General Note

    This regulation is made under s28J(3) of the Act. It makes provision for voluntary payments equivalent to that for overpayments under reg 8. See the general note to that regulation.

PART 4
Recovery from Estates

General Note

    The regulations in this Part are made under ss14(3) and 43A of the Act.

Application and interpretation

10.–(1)   This Part applies in relation to the estate of a person who dies on or after the day on which these Regulations come into force.

    (2)   In this Part, "child support maintenance" means child support maintenance for the collection of which the [¹Secretary of State] is authorised to make arrangements.

Amendment

    1.   Public Bodies (Child Maintenance and Enforcement Commission: Abolition and Transfer of Functions) Order 2012 (SI 2012 No.2007) art 3(2) and Sch para 121(9) (August 1, 2012).

Recovery of arrears from a deceased person's estate

11.   Arrears of child support maintenance for which a deceased person was liable immediately before death are a debt payable by the deceased's executor or administrator out of the deceased's estate to the [¹Secretary of State].

Amendment

    1.   Public Bodies (Child Maintenance and Enforcement Commission: Abolition and Transfer of Functions) Order 2012 (SI 2012 No.2007) art 3(2) and Sch para 121(10) (August 1, 2012).

Definition

    "child support maintenance": see reg 10(2).

General Note
Arrears owing at death are recoverable from the estate of the non-resident parent.

Appeals and other proceedings

12.–(1)   The deceased's executor or administrator has the same rights, subject to the same procedures and time limits, as the deceased person had immediately before death to institute, continue or withdraw any proceedings under the 1991 Act, whether by appeal or otherwise.

(2)   Regulation 34 of the Decisions and Appeals Regulations shall apply to a case where the non-resident parent is the deceased party to the proceedings as if for paragraphs (1) and (2) there were substituted the following paragraph–

"(1)   In any proceedings, on the death of a non-resident parent, the [¹Secretary of State] must appoint the deceased's executor or administrator to proceed with the appeal in place of the deceased, unless there is no such person in which circumstances [¹the Secretary of State] may appoint such person as [¹the Secretary of State] thinks fit to proceed with the appeal.".

Amendment
1.   Public Bodies (Child Maintenance and Enforcement Commission: Abolition and Transfer of Functions) Order 2012 (SI 2012 No.2007) art 3(2) and Sch para 121(11) (August 1, 2012).

Definitions
"the 1991 Act": see reg 2(1).
"the Decisions and Appeals Regulations": see reg 2(1).

General Note
This regulation allows the necessary procedural safe in respect of the right of recovery under reg 11. Procedural rights transfer to the non-resident parent's executor or administrator, who is appointed to proceed with any appeal (but not a referral) if the non-resident parent was a party.

Disclosure of information

13.–(1)   The [¹Secretary of State] may disclose information held for the purposes of the 1991 Act to the deceased's executor or administrator where, in the opinion of the [¹Secretary of State], such information is essential to enable the executor or administrator to administer the deceased's estate, including, where necessary, to institute, continue or withdraw proceedings under the 1991 Act.

(2)   Any application for information under this regulation shall be made to the [¹Secretary of State] in writing setting out the reasons for the application.

(3)   Except where a person gives written permission to the [¹Secretary of State] that the information mentioned in sub-paragraphs (a) and (b) in relation to that person may be disclosed to other persons, any information disclosed under paragraph (1) must not contain–

(a)   the address of any person, except that of the recipient of the information in question and the office of the officer concerned who is exercising functions of the [¹Secretary of State] under the 1991 Act, or any other information the use of which could reasonably be expected to lead to any such person being located;

(b)   any other information the use of which could reasonably be expected to lead to any person, other than a party to the maintenance calculation, being identified.

Amendment
1.   Public Bodies (Child Maintenance and Enforcement Commission: Abolition and Transfer of Functions) Order 2012 (SI 2012 No.2007) art 3(2) and Sch para 121(12) (August 1, 2012).

Definition
"the 1991 Act": see reg 2(1).

General Note
This regulation allows the Secretary of State to disclose information to the non-resident parent's executor or administrator, subject to the usual confidentiality provision.

[¹PART 4A

Part Payment of Arrears in Full and Final Satisfaction

Interpretation of this Part

13A. In this Part–

"appropriate person" means the person from whom the appropriate consent is required under section 41D(5) or (6) of the 1991 Act.]

Amendment

1. Child Support Management of Payments and Arrears (Amendment) Regulations 2012 (SI 2012 No.3002) reg 2(3) (December 10, 2012).

[¹Amounts owed to different persons to be treated separately

13B. Where the arrears of child support maintenance for which a person is liable comprise amounts that have accrued in respect of–

(a) separate applications for a maintenance calculation; or

(b) one application but would, if recovered, be payable to different persons,

those amounts are to be treated as separate amounts of arrears for the purpose of exercising the power under section 41D(1) of the 1991 Act.]

Amendment

1. Child Support Management of Payments and Arrears (Amendment) Regulations 2012 (SI 2012 No.3002) reg 2(3) (December 10, 2012).

[¹Appropriate consent

13C.–(1) The Secretary of State may not exercise the power under section 41D(1) of the 1991 Act without the appropriate consent (as provided for in subsections (5) to (7) of section 41D), unless one of the following conditions applies–

(a) that the Secretary of State would be entitled to retain the whole of the arrears under section 41(2) of the 1991 Act if it recovered them; or

(b) that the Secretary of State would be entitled to retain part of the arrears under section 41(2) of that Act if it recovered them, and the part of the arrears that the Secretary of State would not be entitled to retain is equal to or less than the payment accepted under section 41D(1) of that Act.

(2) Where the consent of any appropriate person is required, the Secretary of State must make available such information and guidance as the Secretary of State thinks appropriate for the purpose of helping that person decide whether to give that consent.]

Amendment

1. Child Support Management of Payments and Arrears (Amendment) Regulations 2012 (SI 2012 No.3002) reg 2(3) (December 10, 2012).

[¹Agreement

13D.–(1) Where the Secretary of State proposes to exercise the power under section 41D(1) of the 1991 Act, the Secretary of State must prepare a written agreement.

(2) The agreement must–

(a) name the non-resident parent, and where the consent of any appropriate person is required, the name of that person;

(b) specify the amount of arrears to which the agreement relates and the period of liability to which those arrears relate;

(c) state the amount that is agreed will be paid in satisfaction of those arrears;

(d) state the method of payment and to whom payment will be made; and

(e) state the day by which payment is to be made.

(3) The Secretary of State must send the non-resident parent and, where applicable, the appropriate person, a copy of the agreement.

(4) The agreement does not take effect until–

(a) the non-resident parent has agreed in writing to its terms; and

(b)   where applicable, the appropriate person has given to the Secretary of State their consent in writing.]

Amendment

1.   Child Support Management of Payments and Arrears (Amendment) Regulations 2012 (SI 2012 No.3002) reg 2(3) (December 10, 2012).

[¹Where payment is received

13E.–(1)   Unless the non-resident parent fails to comply with the terms of the agreement, the Secretary of State must not take action to recover any of the arrears to which the agreement relates.

(2)   Where the non-resident parent has made full payment in accordance with the agreement all remaining liability in respect of the arrears of child support maintenance to which the agreement relates is extinguished.

(3)   Where the non-resident parent fails to make any payment or only makes part payment or otherwise fails to adhere to the terms of the agreement, the non-resident parent remains liable to pay the full amount of any outstanding arrears to which the agreement relates and the Secretary of State may arrange to recover any of those outstanding arrears in accordance with the 1991 Act.

(4)   Nothing in these Regulations prevents the Secretary of State from entering into a new agreement with the non-resident parent in respect of any of the arrears to which the previous agreement relates provided that the new agreement complies with the requirements set out in regulation 13D.

(5)   Where the Secretary of State enters into a new agreement with the non-resident parent in respect of any of the arrears to which a previous agreement related, the previous agreement ceases to have effect on the coming into effect of that new agreement.]

Amendment

1.   Child Support Management of Payments and Arrears (Amendment) Regulations 2012 (SI 2012 No.3002) reg 2(3) (December 10, 2012).

[¹PART 4B
Write Off of Arrears

Amounts owed to different persons to be treated separately

13F.   Where the arrears of child support maintenance for which a person is liable comprise amounts that have accrued in respect of—

(a)   separate applications for a maintenance calculation; or

(b)   one application, but would, if recovered, be payable to different persons,

those amounts are to be treated as separate amounts of arrears for the purpose of exercising the power under section 41E(1) of the 1991 Act.]

Amendment

1.   Child Support Management of Payments and Arrears (Amendment) Regulations 2012 (SI 2012 No.3002) reg 2(3) (December 10, 2012).

[¹Circumstances in which the Secretary of State may exercise the power in section 41E of the 1991 Act

13G.   The circumstances of the case specified for the purposes of section 41E(1)(a) of the 1991 Act are that–

(a)   the person with care has requested under section 4(5) of that Act that the Secretary of State ceases to act in respect of the arrears;

(b)   a child in Scotland has requested under section 7(6) of that Act that the Secretary of State ceases to act in respect of the arrears;

(c)   the person with care, or (in Scotland) the child, has died;

(d)   the non-resident parent died before 25 January 2010 or there is no further action that can be taken with regard to recovery of the arrears from the non-resident parent's estate under Part 4;

(e) the arrears relate to liability for child support maintenance for any period in respect of which an interim maintenance assessment was in force between 5 April 1993 and 18 April 1995; or

(f) the non-resident parent has been informed by the Secretary of State that no further action would ever be taken to recover those arrears.]

Amendment

1. Child Support Management of Payments and Arrears (Amendment) Regulations 2012 (SI 2012 No.3002) reg 2(3) (December 10, 2012).

[¹Secretary of State required to give notice

13H.–(1) Where the Secretary of State is considering exercising the powers under section 41E(1) of the 1991 Act, the Secretary of State must send written notice to the person with care or, where relevant, a child in Scotland and the non-resident parent.

(2) The requirement in paragraph (1) does not apply where the person in question cannot be traced or has died.

(3) The notice must–

(a) specify the person with care or, where relevant, a child in Scotland, in respect of whom liability in respect of arrears of child support maintenance has accrued;

(b) specify the amount of the arrears and the period of liability to which the arrears relate;

(c) state why it appears to the Secretary of State that it would be unfair or inappropriate to enforce liability in respect of the arrears;

(d) advise the person that they may make representations, within 30 days of receiving the notice, to the Secretary of State as to whether the liability in respect of the arrears should be extinguished; and

(e) explain the effect of any decision to extinguish liability in respect of any arrears of child support maintenance under section 41E(1) of the 1991 Act.

(4) If no representations are received by the Secretary of State within 30 days of the notice being received by the person with care or, where relevant, a child in Scotland and the non-resident parent, the Secretary of State may make the decision to extinguish the arrears.

(5) For the purposes of this regulation, where the Secretary of State sends any written notice by post to a person's last known or notified address that document is treated as having been received by that person on the second day following the day on which it is posted.]

Amendment

1. Child Support Management of Payments and Arrears (Amendment) Regulations 2012 (SI 2012 No.3002) reg 2(3) (December 10, 2012).

[¹Secretary of State to take account of the parties' views

13I. Where the Secretary of State receives representations within the 30 day period referred to in regulation 13H(3)(d), the Secretary of State must take account of those representations in making a decision under section 41E(1) of the 1991 Act.]

Amendment

1. Child Support Management of Payments and Arrears (Amendment) Regulations 2012 (SI 2012 No. 3002) reg 2(3) (December 10, 2012).

[¹Notification of decision to write off

13J.–(1) On making a decision under section 41E(1) of the 1991 Act, the Secretary of State must send written notification to the non-resident parent and the person with care or, where relevant, a child in Scotland, of that decision.

(2) The requirement in paragraph (1) does not apply where the person in question cannot be traced or has died.]

Amendment

1.   Child Support Management of Payments and Arrears (Amendment) Regulations 2012 (SI 2012 No.3002) reg 2(3) (December 10, 2012).

PART 5
Revocations and Savings

Revocations

14.   The Regulations specified in the Schedule are revoked to the extent specified.

Savings

15.–(1)   Where before these Regulations come into force, an adjustment has been made under regulation 10(1) of the AIMA Regulations in a 1993 scheme case, regulations 10(2) and (3) and 11 to 17 of those Regulations continue to apply to that case for the purposes of–

(a)   making and determining any appeal against the adjustment;

(b)   making and determining any application for a revision of the adjustment;

(c)   determining any application for a supersession made before these regulations come into force.

(2)   Where before these Regulations come into force, an adjustment has been made under regulation 10(1) or (3A) of the AIMA Regulations in a case other than a 1993 scheme case, regulation 30A of the Decisions and Appeals Regulations continues to apply to that case for the purposes of making and determining any appeal against the adjustment.

Definitions

"a 1993 scheme case": see reg 2(1).

"the AIMA Regulations": see reg 2(1).

"the Decisions and Appeals Regulations": see reg 2(1).

SCHEDULE
Revocations
Regulation 14

Regulations revoked	References	Extent of revocation
Child Support (Arrears, Interest and Adjustment of Maintenance Assessments) Regulations 1992	S.I. 1992/1816	Regulations 2 to 7, 9, 10 and 11 to 17.
Child Support (Miscellaneous Amendments) Regulations 1993	S.I. 1993/913	Regulations 35 to 40.
Child Support and Income Support (Amendment) Regulations 1995	S.I. 1995/1045	Regulations 7 to 11.
Social Security and Child Support (Decisions and Appeals) Regulations 1999	S.I. 1999/991	Regulation 30A.
Child Support (Decisions and Appeals) (Amendment) Regulations 2000	S.I. 2000/3185	Regulation 10, insofar as it inserts regulation 15D in S.I. 1999/991. Regulation 12.
Child Support (Collection and Enforcement and Miscellaneous Amendments) Regulations 2000	S.I. 2001/162	Regulation 5(3)(b), (c) and (e) and (4)(d).
Child Support (Miscellaneous Amendments) Regulations 2009	S.I. 2009/396	Regulations 3 and 4(15).

The Child Support Maintenance Calculation Regulations 2012
(SI 2012 No.2677)
PART 1
GENERAL

PART 2
APPLICATION FOR A MAINTENANCE CALCULATION

PART 3
DECISION MAKING
CHAPTER 1
MAKING THE MAINTENANCE CALCULATION

CHAPTER 2
REVISION

CHAPTER 3
SUPERSESSION

CHAPTER 4
UPDATING GROSS WEEKLY INCOME

CHAPTER 5
NOTIFICATION OF DECISIONS

CHAPTER 6
MISCELLANEOUS MATTERS RELATING TO APPEALS

PART 1
GENERAL

Citation and commencement

1.   These Regulations may be cited as the Child Support Maintenance Calculation Regulations 2012 and come into force in relation to a particular case on the day on which paragraph 2 of Schedule 4 to the Child Maintenance and Other Payments Act 2008 (calculation by reference to gross weekly income) comes into force in relation to that type of case.

Interpretation

2.   In these Regulations–

"the 1991 Act" means the Child Support Act 1991;

[¹"contribution-based jobseeker's allowance" means an allowance under the Jobseekers Act 1995 as amended by the provisions of Part 1 of Schedule 14 to the Welfare Reform Act 2012 that remove references to an income-based allowance, and a contribution-based allowance under the Jobseekers Act 1995 as that Act has effect apart from those provisions;]

[¹"contributory employment and support allowance" means an allowance under Part 1 of the Welfare Reform Act 2007 as amended by the provisions of Schedule 3, and Part 1 of Schedule 14, to the Welfare Reform Act 2012 that remove references to an income-related allowance, and a contributory allowance under Part 1 of the Welfare Reform Act 2007 as that Part has effect apart from those provisions;]

"capped amount" means the figure specified in paragraph 10(3) of Schedule 1 to the 1991 Act (or in that sub-paragraph as modified by regulations under paragraph 10A of Schedule 1 to the 1991 Act);

"couple" has the meaning given by paragraph 10C(5) of Schedule 1 to the 1991 Act;

"current income" has the meaning given in regulation 37;

"the flat rate" means the flat rate of child support maintenance payable under paragraph 4 of Schedule 1 to the 1991 Act;

"gross weekly income" means income calculated under Chapter 1 of Part 4;

"historic income" has the meaning given in regulation 35;

"HMRC" means Her Majesty's Revenue and Customs;

"the HMRC figure" has the meaning given in regulation 36;

"income support" means support to which a person is entitled under section 124 of the Social Security Contributions and Benefits Act 1992;

"initial effective date" has the meaning given in regulation 12;

"ITEPA" means the Income Tax (Earnings and Pensions) Act 2003;

"ITTOIA" means the Income Tax (Trading and Other Income) Act 2005;

"local authority" means, in relation to England, a county council, a district council, a London borough council, the Common Council of the City of London or the Council of the Isles of Scilly and, in relation to Wales, a county council or a county borough council and, in relation to Scotland, a council constituted under section 2 of the Local Government etc. (Scotland) Act 1994;

"net pay arrangements" means arrangements for relief in respect of pension contributions under section 193 of the Finance Act 2004;

"the nil rate" means the nil rate of child support maintenance payable under paragraph 5 of Schedule 1 to the 1991 Act;

"partner" has the meaning given by paragraph 10C(4) of Schedule 1 to the 1991 Act;

"party", in relation to a maintenance calculation in force or an application for a maintenance calculation, means the non-resident parent, the person with care and, in the case of an application by a child under section 7 of the 1991 Act or a maintenance calculation made in response to such an application, the child in question;

"the PAYE Regulations" means the Income Tax (Pay As You Earn) Regulations 2003;

"qualifying lender" has the meaning given to it in section 376(4) of the Income and Corporation Taxes Act 1988;

"the reduced rate" means the reduced rate of child support maintenance payable under paragraph 3 of Schedule 1 to the 1991 Act;

"relievable pension contributions" has the meaning given by section 188(2) of the Finance Act 2004;

"review date" has the meaning given in regulation 19;

"self-assessment return" means a return which an individual is required to make and deliver under section 8 of the Taxes Management Act 1970;

"supersession decision" means a decision made under section 17 of the 1991 Act superseding a decision mentioned in subsection (1) of that section;

"state pension credit" means the benefit payable in accordance with section 1 (entitlement) of the State Pension Credit Act 2002;

"tax year" has the meaning given by section 4 of the Income Tax Act 2007;

"Tribunal Procedure Rules" means the Tribunal Procedure (First-tier Tribunal) (Social (Entitlement Chamber) Rules 2008; and

"UK social security pension" means a pension to which section 577 of ITEPA applies.

Amendment

1. Universal Credit (Consequential, Supplementary, Incidental and Miscellaneous Provisions) Regulations 2013 (SI 2013 No.630) reg 44(2) (April 29, 2013).

Meaning of "calculation decision"

3.   In these Regulations "calculation decision" means a decision of the Secretary of State under section 11 (the maintenance calculation), section 16 (revision) or section 17 (supersession) of the 1991 Act determining the amount of child support maintenance to be fixed in accordance with Part 1 of Schedule 1 to that Act.

General Note
This regulation defines 'calculation decision' for the purposes of these Regulations. It does not include a decision made under s12 of the Act.

Meaning of "latest available tax year"

4.–(1)   In these Regulations "latest available tax year" means the tax year which, on the date on which the Secretary of State requests information from HMRC for the purposes of regulation 35 (historic income) or regulation 69 (non-resident parent with unearned income), is the most recent relevant tax year for which HMRC have received the information required to be provided in relation to the non-resident parent under the PAYE Regulations or in a self-assessment return.

(2)   In this regulation a "relevant tax year" is any one of the 6 tax years immediately preceding the date of the request for information referred to in paragraph (1).

Definitions
"HMRC": see reg 2.
"the PAYE Regulations": see reg 2.
"self-assessment return": see reg 2.
"tax year": see reg 2.

General Note
This regulations defines the 'latest available tax year' as the most recent of the previous six tax years for which the HMRC has received the information required to be provided under the PAYE Regulations or on a self-assessment return. It refers to the HMRC receiving the information required. In isolation, this could be read as meaning that the information provided must be accurate and complete, allowing the tribunal to use more accurate figures. This, however, is not consistent with reg 36, which only makes sense if this regulation means the information provided, whether or not it is accurate or complete.

Calculation – information applicable

5.   Information required for the purposes of making a calculation decision or a decision in relation to an application for a variation is the information applicable at the date from which that decision (assuming that the decision was a decision to make or amend a maintenance calculation) would have effect.

Definition
"calculation decision": see reg 3.

General Note
This regulation provides that the information required must relate to the effective date of the calculation decision. This must be subject to two qualifications. First, the use of historic income may mean that the income used for the non-resident parent is years out of date. Second, the information may also relate to the period between the effective date and the date of decision, in which case a stepped calculation can be made under Sch 1 para 15 to the Act.
A 'decision in relation to an application for a variation' will cover refusals to agree to a variation and decisions agreeing to a variation before a decision is made under s12(1) of the Act (reg 13(1)). But note that an application for a variation cannot be rejected once a decision has been made under s 12(1) (reg 57(1)(c)).

Rounding

6.   Where a calculation decision or a decision in relation to an application for a variation results in a fraction of a penny, that is to be treated as a penny if it is either one half or exceeds one half, and otherwise it is to be disregarded.

Definitions
· "calculation decision": see reg 3.

General Note
See the general note to reg 5 on the meaning of 'decision in relation to an application for a variation'. A decision agreeing to a variation of a decision under s12(1) of the Act – see the general note to reg 5 – could result in a fraction of a penny. Otherwise, a variation takes effect by way of revision or supersession and is, therefore, a calculation decision.

Service of documents

7.–(1)   Where any document is given or sent to the Secretary of State, that document is to be treated as having been given or sent on the date of receipt by the Secretary of State.

(2)   Where the Secretary of State sends any written notification or any document by post to a person's last known or notified address that document is treated as having been given or sent on the second day following the day on which it is posted.

General Note
See the general notes to reg 2 of the Maintenance Calculation Procedure Regulations and to reg 12 below.

Authorisation of representative

8.–(1)   A person may authorise a representative, whether or not legally qualified, to receive notices and other documents on their behalf and to act on their behalf in relation to the making of applications and the supply of information under any provision of the 1991 Act or these Regulations.

(2)   Where a person has authorised a representative for the purposes of paragraph (1) who is not legally qualified, that person must confirm the authorisation in writing to the Secretary of State.

Definition
"the 1991 Act": see reg 2.

General Note
Para (1)
A person may appoint a representative to received notice or other documents or to act on their behalf in making applications or supplying information, but not for any other purpose. It does not allow a representative to consent to disclosure under reg 25(3). Nor, it seems, to receive notice of an application under reg 11: see the general note to that regulation.

Para (2)
There is no definition of 'legally qualified'. It does not say that the person must hold a professional qualification. Barristers, solicitors and legal executives (along with their Scottish equivalents) will be included. Those holding a law degree without any professional qualification may be covered. It is unlikely that paralegals will be covered.

PART 2
APPLICATION FOR A MAINTENANCE CALCULATION

Applications under section 4 or 7 of the 1991 Act

9.–(1)   The Secretary of State may determine the form in which an application for a maintenance calculation is to be made and may require the applicant to provide such information or evidence as the Secretary of State reasonably requires in order to process the application (including, in the case of an application by a person with care, information sufficient to enable the person named as the non-resident parent to be identified).

(2)   The application is to be taken to have been made when the application has been submitted to the Secretary of State in the required form and the information required under paragraph (1) has been provided.

General Note
To be effective, an application must conform in both form and content. Only then is the duty to give notice to the non-resident parent under reg 11 triggered.

Multiple applications

10.–(1)   Where two or more applications for a maintenance calculation are made with respect to the same child the Secretary of State may determine which to proceed with.

(2)   In making a determination under paragraph (1) the Secretary of State must have regard to the following order of priority–

(a)   an application by a person with care or a non-resident parent has priority over an application by a child under section 7 of the 1991 Act;

(b)   otherwise an earlier application has priority over one made later.

(3)   Where–

(a)   in relation to an application under section 4 or 7 of the 1991 Act, both parents of a qualifying child are named as non-resident parents; or

(b)   an application is made under section 4 of that Act by both non-resident parents of a qualifying child,

the Secretary of State must proceed with the application in relation to each non-resident parent, treating it as a single application for a maintenance calculation in respect of that qualifying child.

General Note

Para (1)

Although this paragraph confers a discretion, it is limited by paras (2) and (3), which are in mandatory terms.

Para (2)

Although the duty here is only to 'have regard to', it is clear from the wording of subparas (a) and (b) that they are mandatory.

Para (3)

Like para (2), this is also mandatory. If both parents are non-resident parents under an application, separate calculations must be made for each parent.

Notice of application

11.–(1)   Where an application has been made under section 4 or 7 of the 1991 Act the Secretary of State must, as soon as reasonably practicable, give written notice to the non-resident parent–

(a)   requesting such information as the Secretary of State may require to make the maintenance calculation; and

(b)   where relevant, advising the non-resident parent of the power of the Secretary of State to make an estimate of income or a default maintenance decision.

(2)   The notice must be sent by post to the last known address of the non-resident parent.

General Note

Para (1)

This duty only arises when an application is effective under reg 9. The legislation provides no remedy for the person with care if notice is not given 'as soon as reasonably practicable'.

Para (2)

The notice must be sent to the non-resident parent. This seems to override the power under reg 8 to appoint a representative to receive notices. There will be cases in which a parent has already nominated a representative before the notice is sent. This will certainly be possible if both parents have made applications as parents with care.

The notice must be sent to the last 'known' address, which begs the question: known to whom? In contrast to reg 7, there is no option to send notice to the last 'known or notified' address.

PART 3
DECISION MAKING
CHAPTER 1
MAKING THE MAINTENANCE CALCULATION

Initial effective date

12.   The effective date of a decision under section 11 of the 1991 Act ("the initial effective date") is the date on which notice is given to the non-resident parent in accordance with regulation 11.

General Note

This regulation fixes the initial effective date of a decision under section 11 of the Act.

The relationship between this regulation and regs 7 and 11 is not clear. Here the relevant date is when the notice was 'given' under reg 11, but there notice is 'sent' not 'given'. Regulation 7 refers to both giving and sending. Under reg 7(2), notice takes effect from the second day after posting. Does that generally worded provision apply here?

Effect of variation applied for before a maintenance calculation is made

13.–(1)   Subject to paragraph (2), where an application for a variation is made in the circumstances referred to in section 28A(3) of the 1991 Act (that is before the Secretary of State has reached a decision under section 11 or 12(1) of the Act) and the application is agreed to, the effective date of the maintenance calculation which takes account of the variation is–

(a)   where the ground giving rise to the variation existed from the initial effective date, that date; or

(b)   where the ground giving rise to the variation arose after the initial effective date, the day on which the ground arose.

(2)   Where–

(a)   the ground for the variation applied for under section 28A(3) of the 1991 Act is a ground in regulation 65 (prior debts) or 67 (payments in respect of certain mortgages, loans or insurance policies), and

(b)   payments falling within the relevant regulation which have been made by the non-resident parent constitute voluntary payments for the purposes of section 28J of that Act (voluntary payments) and regulations made under that section,

the date from which the maintenance calculation is to take account of the variation on this ground is to be the date on which the non-resident parent is notified under regulation 25 (notification of a maintenance calculation) of the amount of their liability to pay child support maintenance.

(3)   Where the ground for the variation applied for under section 28A(3) of the 1991 Act has ceased to exist by the date on which the maintenance calculation is made, that calculation is to take account of the variation for the period ending on the day on which the ground ceased to exist.

General Note

This regulation provides for the effective date if an application for a variation is made before a decision is made under either section 11 or 12(1). Broadly, the position is this. The variation takes effect from the effective date of the decision, unless the circumstances giving rising to the variation arose after that date or ceased to exist before the decision was made, in which case a stepped decision is made under Sch1 para 15 to the Act.

CHAPTER 2
REVISION

Grounds for revision

14.–(1)   A decision to which section 16(1A) of the 1991 Act applies may be revised by the Secretary of State–

(a)   if the Secretary of State receives an application for the revision of a decision either–

(i)   under section 16 of that Act, or

(ii)   by way of application under section 28G of that Act (application for a variation where a maintenance calculation is in force),

within 30 days after the date of notification of the decision or within such longer time as may be allowed under regulation 15;

(b)   if the Secretary of State is satisfied that the decision was wrong due to a misrepresentation of, or failure to disclose, a material fact and that decision was more advantageous to the person who misrepresented or failed to disclose that fact than it would have been but for the wrongness of the decision;

(c)   if an appeal is made under section 20 of the 1991 Act (appeals to First-tier Tribunal) against a decision within the time limit prescribed by the Tribunal Procedure Rules but that appeal has not been determined;

(d)   if the Secretary of State commences action leading to the revision of the decision within 30 days after the date of notification of the decision;

(e)   if the decision arose from official error;

(f)   if the information held by HMRC in relation to a tax year in respect of which the Secretary of State has determined historic income for the purposes of regulation 35, or unearned income for the purposes of regulation 69, has since been amended; or

(g) if the ground for revision is that a person with respect to whom a maintenance calculation was made was not, at the time the calculation was made, a parent of a child to whom the calculation relates.

(2) A decision may not be revised because of a change of circumstances that occurred since the decision had effect or is expected to occur.

(3) An interim maintenance decision or default maintenance decision made under section 12 of the 1991 Act may be revised at any time.

(4) In paragraph (1)(e) "official error" means an error made by an officer of the Department for Work and Pensions or HMRC acting as such to which no person outside the Department or HMRC materially contributed, but excludes any error of law which is shown to have been an error by virtue of a subsequent decision of the Upper Tribunal or the court.

General Note

See the general note to the equivalent provisions in reg 3A of the Appeals Regulations.

Para (1)(c)

Proving misrepresentation and failure to disclose to a tribunal may be difficulty. The extent to which there is a duty to disclose to the tribunal will depend on the directions it gave during the proceedings. A misrepresentation may appear in the documents or in the oral evidence. The First-tier Tribunal will not usually provide written reasons unless they are requested. The Upper Tribunal retains its files for three years after last judicial action, but the First-tier Tribunal only holds its files for six months.

[¹ Consideration of revision before appeal

14A.–(1) This regulation applies in a case where–

(a) the Secretary of State gives a person written notice of a decision; and

(b) that notice includes a statement to the effect that there is a right of appeal to the First-tier Tribunal against the decision only if the Secretary of State has considered an application for a revision of the decision.

(2) In a case to which this regulation applies, a person has a right of appeal against the decision only if the Secretary of State has considered on an application whether to revise the decision under section 16 of the 1991 Act.

(3) The notice referred to in paragraph (1) must inform the person of the time limit specified in regulation 14(1) for making an application for a revision.

(4) Where, as the result of paragraph (2), there is no right of appeal against a decision, the Secretary of State may treat any purported appeal as an application for a revision under section 16 of that Act.

(5) In this regulation, "decision" means a decision mentioned in section 20(1)(a) or (b) of the 1991 Act (as substituted by section 10 of the Child Support, Pensions and Social Security Act 2000).]

Amendment

1. Social Security, Child Support, Vaccine Damage and Other Payments (Decisions and Appeals) (Amendment) Regulations 2013 (SI 2013 No.2380) reg 6 (October 28, 2013).

Late application for a revision

15.–(1) The time limit for making an application for a revision specified in regulation 14(1)(a) (grounds for revision) may be extended where the conditions specified in the following provisions of this regulation are satisfied.

(2) An application for an extension of time must be made by one of the parties or their authorised representative.

(3) An application for an extension of time must contain particulars of the grounds on which the extension is sought and must contain sufficient details of the decision which it is sought to have revised to enable that decision to be identified.

(4) An application for an extension of time may not be granted unless the applicant satisfies the Secretary of State that–

(a) it is reasonable to grant the application;

(b)   the application for revision has merit [¹, except in a case to which regulation 14A applies]; and

(c)   special circumstances are relevant to the application and because of those special circumstances it was not practicable for the application to be made within the time limit specified in regulation 14(1)(a).

(5)   In determining whether it is reasonable to grant an application for an extension of time, the Secretary of State must have regard to the principle that the greater the amount of time that has elapsed between the end of the time specified in regulation 14(1)(a) for applying for a revision and the making of the application for an extension of time, the more compelling should be the special circumstances on which the application is based.

(6)   In determining whether it is reasonable to grant the application for an extension of time [¹, except in a case to which regulation 14A applies], no account shall be taken of the following–

(a)   that the applicant, or any person acting for the applicant, was unaware of or misunderstood the law applicable to the case (including ignorance or misunderstanding of the time limits imposed by these Regulations); or

(b)   that the Upper Tribunal or a court has taken a different view of the law from that previously understood and applied.

(7)   An application under this regulation for an extension of time which has been refused may not be renewed.

Amendment

1.   Social Security, Child Support, Vaccine Damage and Other Payments (Decision and Appeals) (Amendment) Regulations 2013 (SI 2013 No.2380) reg 6 (October 28, 2013).

General Note

See the general note to the equivalent provisions in reg 4 of the Appeals Regulations.

Effective date of a revision

16.   Where a decision is revised and the date from which the original decision took effect is found to be wrong, the decision as revised takes effect from the date on which the original decision would have taken effect had the error not been made.

General Note

The general rule under s15(3) is that a revision takes effect from the effective date of the decision being revised. This regulation allows for the possibility that that date was wrong.

CHAPTER 3
SUPERSESSION

Grounds for supersession

17.–(1)   A decision mentioned in section 17(1) of the 1991 Act may be superseded by a decision of the Secretary of State, on an application or on the Secretary of State's own initiative, where–

(a)   there has been a relevant change of circumstances since the decision had effect or it is expected that a relevant change of circumstances will occur;

(b)   the decision was made in ignorance of, or was based on a mistake as to, some material fact; or

(c)   the decision was wrong in law (unless it was a decision made on appeal).

(2)   The circumstances in which a decision may be superseded include where the relevant change of circumstances causes the maintenance calculation to cease by virtue of paragraph 16 of Schedule 1 to the 1991 Act or where the Secretary of State no longer has jurisdiction by virtue of section 44 of that Act.

(3)   A decision may be superseded by a decision made by the Secretary of State where the Secretary of State receives an application for the supersession of a decision by way of an application under section 28G of the 1991 Act (application for a variation where a maintenance calculation is in force).

(4) A decision may not be superseded in circumstances where it may be revised.

(5) A decision to refuse an application for a maintenance calculation may not be superseded.

(6) In making a supersession decision under section 17(1) of the 1991 Act, the Secretary of State need not consider any issue that is not raised by the application or, as the case may be, did not cause the decision to be made on the Secretary of State's own initiative.

(7) This regulation is subject to any provision in Chapter 4 of this Part (updating gross weekly income) relating to the circumstances in which a supersession decision may be made.

General Note

See the general note to the equivalent provisions in reg 6A of the Appeals Regulations.

Para (2)

This makes clear that when a maintenance calculation ceases to have effect, it requires a supersession.

Para (6)

See the general note to s20(7)(a) of the Act.

Effective dates for supersession decisions

18.–(1) This regulation sets out cases and circumstances in which a supersession decision takes effect on a date other than the date mentioned in section 17(4) of the 1991 Act.

(2) Where the ground for the supersession decision is that a relevant change of circumstances is expected to occur or that a ground for a variation is expected to occur, the decision takes effect from the date on which that change or that ground is expected to occur.

(3) Where the ground for the supersession decision is that a relevant change of circumstances of the following kind has occurred, the decision takes effect from the date on which the change occurred–

(a) a child ceases to be a qualifying child, a relevant other child, or a child supported under another arrangement;

(b) the person with care dies or ceases to be a person with care in relation to a qualifying child;

(c) the person with care, the non-resident parent or a qualifying child ceases to be habitually resident in the United Kingdom;

(d) the non-resident parent begins or ceases to receive a benefit mentioned in regulation 44(1) or begins or ceases to be a person who receives, or whose partner receives, a benefit referred to in regulation 44(2).

(4) Where the ground for the supersession decision is that a relevant change of circumstances affecting the non-resident parent's current income has occurred and the non-resident parent was required to report that change in accordance with regulations under section 14(1) of the 1991 Act, the decision takes effect from the date on which the change occurred.

(5) Where the ground for the supersession decision is that there is a new qualifying child in relation to the non-resident parent, the decision takes effect from the date which would be the initial effective date in relation to an application under section 4 or 7 of the 1991 Act in relation to that child if there were no maintenance calculation already in force.

(6) Where paragraphs (2) to (5) do not apply–

(a) if the supersession decision is made on an application by one of the parties, the decision takes effect from the date of the application;

(b) if the supersession decision is made on the Secretary of State's own initiative on the basis of information provided by a third party, the decision takes effect from the date on which that information is provided; and

(c) if the supersession decision is made on the Secretary of State's own initiative, and sub-paragraph (b) does not apply, the decision takes effect from the date on which it is made.

(7) In paragraph (3)–

(a) the reference to a child supported under another arrangement is to a child supported under a qualifying maintenance arrangement mentioned in paragraph 5A of Schedule 1 to the 1991 Act or a child mentioned in regulation 52 (non-resident parent liable to maintain a child of the family or a child abroad); and

(b) the reference to the date on which a person begins or ceases to receive a benefit is to the date on which entitlement to the benefit commences or ceases.

(8) This regulation is subject to any provision in Chapter 4 of this Part (updating gross weekly income) relating to the date from which a supersession decision made under that Chapter takes effect.

Definitions

"the 1991 Act": see reg 2.

"current income": see reg 2.

"initial effective date": see reg 2.

"party": see reg 2.

"supersession decision": see reg 2.

General Note

This regulation makes general provision for the effective date on a supersession by way of qualifying s17(4) of the Act. There are further specific provisions in the following regulations.

CHAPTER 4
UPDATING GROSS WEEKLY INCOME

Setting the review date

19.–(1) The Secretary of State must, in relation to each application for a maintenance calculation, fix a date at which the non-resident parent's gross weekly income is to be reviewed by reference to an updated HMRC figure ("the review date").

(2) Subject to paragraph (3), the first review date falls 12 months after the initial effective date and subsequent review dates fall on each anniversary of that date, unless the Secretary of State decides in any particular case or class of case to fix a different date.

(3) Where a maintenance calculation is in force and there is a further application in relation to the non-resident parent in respect of a new qualifying child, the review dates are to be aligned so that the first review date in respect of the new application is the next review date for the calculation already in force.

(4) Where an application for a maintenance calculation in relation to both non-resident parents of a qualifying child is treated as a single application by virtue of regulation 10(3) (multiple applications) the Secretary of State may fix different review dates in respect of each non-resident parent.

Definitions

"gross weekly income": see reg 2.

"the HMRC figure": see reg 2.

"initial effective date": see reg 2.

"review date": see reg 2.

General Note

Essentially this provides for annual reviews of a non-resident parent's gross weekly income. The first review date is 12 months after the initial effective date. There may be a delay of more than 12 months in making a decision, in which case the review date will be before the initial calculation decision.

Later review dates are fixed by reference to the initial date and are not affected by the dates when later decisions are made or their effective dates.

The purpose of the review is to update the grossly weekly income by reference to an updated HMRC figure, if possible.

Updating gross weekly income at the review date

20.–(1) Where an updated figure is provided by HMRC for the latest available tax year in accordance with a request under regulation 35(2)(b) (historic income – general), that figure applies, for the purposes of determining historic income, on and after the review date.

(2)   If the non-resident parent's gross weekly income, as calculated in accordance with Chapter 1 of Part 4 by reference to that updated figure, has changed, the Secretary of State may make a supersession decision with effect from the review date.

Definitions
"gross weekly income": see reg 2.
"historic income": see reg 2.
"HMRC": see reg 2.
"latest available tax year": see reg 4.
"review date": see reg 2.
"supersession decision": see reg 2.

General Note
The updated HMRC figure is used if it is available.

Updating unearned income at the review date

21.–(1)   This regulation applies where, in relation to a maintenance calculation in force, additional income has been taken into account by virtue of a variation previously agreed to under regulation 69 (non-resident parent with unearned income).

(2)   When the Secretary of State makes a request to HMRC for the purposes of reviewing the non-resident parent's gross weekly income in accordance with regulation 20 (updating gross weekly income at the review date) the Secretary of State may also request information relating to the non-resident parent's unearned income for the latest available tax year and, where appropriate, make a supersession decision on the basis of that information with effect from the review date.

Definitions
"gross weekly income": see reg 2.
"HMRC": see reg 2.
"latest available tax year": see reg 4.
"review date": see reg 2.
"supersession decision": see reg 2.

General Note
This regulation applies if the current calculation is based on current rather than historic income.

Periodic current income check

22.–(1)   Where–
(a)   the non-resident parent's gross weekly income is based on an amount of current income by virtue of regulation 34(2) (the general rule for determining gross weekly income and exceptions to that rule); and
(b)   no supersession decision changing that amount has been made within the past 11 months,
the Secretary of State may, for the purposes of validating that amount, require evidence of current income to be provided by the non-resident parent.

(2)   Where the non-resident parent fails to provide evidence as requested under paragraph (1), the Secretary of State may make a supersession decision determining the non-resident parent's gross weekly income on the basis of historic income.

(3)   Where the Secretary of State is provided with sufficient information on which to make a new determination of current income, the Secretary of State may make a supersession decision applying the general rule in regulation 34(2).

(4)   Subject to paragraph (5), a supersession decision under this regulation has effect from the date on which it is made.

(5)   Where the Secretary of State makes a supersession decision under paragraph (3) and the relevant change of circumstances affecting the non-resident parent's current income was one that the non-resident parent was required to report in accordance with

regulations under section 14(1) of the 1991 Act, the decision takes effect from the date on which the change occurred.

Definitions
"current income": see reg 2.
"gross weekly income": see reg 2.
"historic income": see reg 2.
"supersession decision": see reg 2.

General Note
Paras (1)-(3)
The non-resident parent's income may be fixed by reference to updating evidence of current income or, if the evidence is not provided, by historic income. The contrasting language of paras (2) and (3) is not entirely satisfactory. Paragraph (2) appears to suggest that the evidence will be accepted so long as it is provided, but para (3) makes it clear that the evidence must be 'sufficient' to allow current income to be identified.
Paras (4) and (5)
These paragraphs provide for the effective date of a supersession decision under this regulation. The basic rule is in para (4): the effective date is the date when the decision is made. The exception is in para (5): if the non-resident parent was under a duty to report the change, the effective date is the date of the change. This is no doubt based on the assumptions that non-resident parents will report changes favourable to them, but not those favourable to the person with care.

25% tolerance for changes outside annual review or periodic current income check

23.–(1)   This regulation applies where the non-resident parent's gross weekly income is based on an amount of current income by virtue of regulation 34(2) and, before the next review date, there is a change of circumstances affecting the amount of that current income.

(2)   No supersession decision giving effect to that change may be made unless the amount of that current income has changed by at least 25%.

(3)   Paragraph (1) does not prevent a supersession decision that–

(a)   is made on the Secretary of State's own initiative under regulation 20 (updating weekly income at the annual review) or regulation 22 (periodic check where current income unchanged for 11 months);

(b)   is made on the ground mentioned in regulation 17(1)(c) (error of law); or

(c)   supersedes a decision determining the non-resident parent's gross weekly income on the basis of regulation 42 (estimate of current income where insufficient information available).

(4)   Where the condition in paragraph (2) is satisfied, the current income (as changed) is to apply even if it does not differ from historic income by an amount that is at least 25% of historic income.

Definitions
"current income": see reg 2.
"gross weekly income": see reg 2.
"historic income": see reg 2.
"review date": see reg 2.
"supersession decision": see reg 2.

General Note
A change in current income may be taken into account between reviews. The basic rule under paras (1) and (2) is that the change can only be taken into account if it is at least 25%, more or less. The exceptions are in para (3).

CHAPTER 5
NOTIFICATION OF DECISIONS

Notification – general

24.–(1)   Notification of a decision made by the Secretary of State under section 11 (maintenance calculation), 12 (default or interim maintenance decision) or 17 (supersession) of the 1991 Act or of any revision of such a decision under section 16 of that Act must be given to the parties in accordance with this Chapter.

(2)   Any such notification must include information as to the provisions relating to the revision and supersession of, and appeals from, decisions made under the 1991 Act.

Definition
"the 1991 Act": see reg 2.
"party": see reg 2.

General Note
Para (1)
A decision does not take effect until it is notified (*R (Anufrijeva) v SSHD* [2004] 1 AC 604 para 26).
Para (2)
The decision may still be effective if does not contain all the information required. The test is whether the recipient was significantly prejudiced (*R(H) 1/02* para 10).

Notification of a maintenance calculation

25.–(1)   Notification of a decision made under section 11 or 12(2) of the 1991 Act must set out–
(a)   the effective date of the maintenance calculation;
(b)   where relevant, the non-resident parent's gross weekly income, including–
    (i)   whether that is based on historic income or current income, and
    (ii)   if based on current income, whether that income has been estimated in accordance with regulation 42;
(c)   the number of qualifying children;
(d)   the number of relevant other children;
(e)   the weekly rate;
(f)   the amounts calculated in accordance with Part 1 of Schedule 1 to the 1991 Act and, where there has been an agreement to a variation or a variation has otherwise been taken into account, Part 5 of these Regulations (Variations);
(g)   where the weekly rate is adjusted by apportionment or to take account of shared care;
(h)   where the amount of child support maintenance is decreased–
    (i)   to take account of a child supported under a qualifying maintenance arrangement mentioned in paragraph 5A of Schedule 1 to the 1991 Act; or
    (ii)   in accordance with regulation 52 (non-resident parent liable to maintain a child of the family or a child abroad) or regulation 53 (care provided in part by a local authority).
(2)   A notification of a maintenance calculation made under section 12(1) of the 1991 Act (default maintenance decision) must set out–
(a)   the effective date of the maintenance calculation;
(b)   the default rate;
(c)   the number of qualifying children on which the rate is based; and
(d)   whether apportionment has been applied under regulation 49,
and must state the nature of the information required to enable a calculation decision to be made.
(3)   Except with the written permission of the person concerned, a notice under this regulation must not include–
(a)   the address of any person other than the recipient of the notice (other than the address of the relevant office of the Secretary of State) or any other information the use of which could reasonably be expected to lead to any such persons being located; and
(b)   any other information the use of which could reasonably be expected to lead to any person other than the qualifying child or a party to the application being identified.

Definition
"the 1991 Act": see reg 2.
"calculation decision": see reg 3.

"current income": see reg 2.
"gross weekly income": see reg 2.
"historic income": see reg 2.
"local authority": see reg 2.
"party": see reg 2.

General Note
Para (3)(a)
The restriction in this provision has not been drafted with representatives in mind. Notice may be given to a representative under reg 8. If the recipient is the person to whom it is sent, this will be the representative and the notice must not allow the representative to identify the non-resident parent or person with care. That would be absurd. The recipient must be the person to whom the notice relates rather than the person to whom it is sent.

Notification of a revision or supersession

26.–(1) A notification of a decision made following the revision or supersession of a decision made under section 11 (the maintenance calculation), 12 (default or interim maintenance decision) or 17 (supersession) of the 1991 Act, whether as originally made or revised under section 16 of that Act, must, subject to the qualification in regulation 25(3), set out the information mentioned in regulation 25(1) and (2) in relation to the decision in question.

(2) The requirement in paragraph (1) does not apply where the Secretary of State has decided not to supersede a decision and in that case the Secretary of State must, where appropriate and as far as reasonably practicable, notify the parties of that decision.

Definition
"the 1991 Act": see reg 2.
"party": see reg 2.

General Note
Para (2)
Given reg 7(2), it is difficult to understand why the duty under this paragraph is qualified by 'so far as reasonably practicable'.

Notification of cessation of a maintenance calculation

27.–(1) Where the Secretary of State decides that a maintenance calculation has ceased or is to cease to have effect, the Secretary of State must immediately notify the non-resident parent and person with care so far as that is reasonably practicable.

(2) Where a child under section 7 of the 1991 Act ceases to be a child for the purposes of that Act, the Secretary of State must immediately notify the persons mentioned in paragraph (1) and the other qualifying children with the meaning of section 7(2) of that Act.

Definition
"the 1991 Act": see reg 2.

General Note
Para (1)
Given reg 7(2), it is difficult to understand why the duty under para (1) is qualified by 'so far as reasonably practicable'. There is no equivalent qualification to the duty in para (2).
Para (2)
There is an obvious error in this paragraph. It should read: 'within the meaning of section 7(2) of that Act.'

CHAPTER 6
MISCELLANEOUS MATTERS RELATING TO APPEALS

Decisions involving issues that arise on appeal in other cases

28.–(1) For the purposes of section 28ZA(2)(b) of the 1991 Act (prescribed cases and circumstances in which a decision may be made on a prescribed basis)–
(a) a case in which there is no maintenance calculation in force is a prescribed case; and

(b)   the prescribed basis on which the Secretary of State may make the decision is as if–

   (i)   the appeal in relation to the different matter, which is referred to in section 28ZA(1)(b) of that Act had already been determined, and

   (ii)   for the purposes of making that decision, the appeal had been determined in a way that resulted in the lowest possible amount of child support maintenance in the circumstances of that case being payable.

(2)   The circumstances prescribed under section 28ZA(4)(c) of the 1991 Act (appeal treated as pending against a decision given in a different case even though an appeal against the decision has not been brought or, as the case may be, an application for permission to appeal against the decision has not been made but the time for doing so has not expired) are that the Secretary of State–

(a)   certifies in writing that an appeal against that decision is being considered; and

(b)   considers that, if such an appeal were to be determined in a particular way–

   (i)   there would be no liability for child support maintenance, or

   (ii)   such liability would be less than would be the case were an appeal not made.

Definition
"the 1991 Act": see reg 2.

Child support appeals involving issues that arise in other cases

29.   The circumstances prescribed for the purposes of section 28ZB(6)(c) of the 1991 Act (appeals involving issues that arise on appeal in other cases) are where the Secretary of State–

(a)   certifies in writing that an appeal against the decision in question is being considered; and

(b)   considers that, if such an appeal were already determined, it would affect the determination of the appeal described in section 28ZB(1)(a) of that Act.

Definition
"the 1991 Act": see reg 2.

Tribunal decision made pending outcome of a related appeal

30.   Where, in accordance with section 28ZB(5) of the 1991 Act (appeals involving issues that arise on appeal in other cases), the Secretary of State makes a decision superseding the decision of the First-tier Tribunal or the Upper Tribunal, the superseding decision takes effect from the date on which the decision of the First-tier Tribunal or, as the case may be, the Upper Tribunal would have taken effect had it been decided in accordance with the determination of the Upper Tribunal or the court in the appeal referred to in section 28ZB(1)(b) of that Act.

Definition
"the 1991 Act": see reg 2.

Supersession of tribunal decision made in error due to misrepresentation etc.

31.–(1)   Where–

(a)   a decision made by the First-tier Tribunal or the Upper Tribunal is superseded on the ground that it was erroneous due to misrepresentation of, or that there was a failure to disclose, a material fact; and

(b)   the Secretary of State is satisfied that the decision was more advantageous to the person who misrepresented or failed to disclose that fact than it would otherwise have been but for that error,

the superseding decision takes effect from the date on which the decision of the First-tier Tribunal or, as the case may be, the Upper Tribunal, took or was to take, effect.

Supersession of look alike case where law reinterpreted by the Upper Tribunal or a court

32. Any supersession decision made under section 17 of the 1991 Act in consequence of a determination which is a relevant determination for the purposes of section 28ZC of that Act (restriction on liability in certain cases of error) takes effect from the date of the relevant determination.

Definitions

"the 1991 Act": see reg 2.

"supersession decision": see reg 2.

Procedural matters relating to appeals

33. The Schedule to these Regulations has effect.

PART 4
THE MAINTENANCE CALCULATION RULES
CHAPTER 1
DETERMINATION OF GROSS WEEKLY INCOME

The general rule for determining gross weekly income

34.–(1) The gross weekly income of a non-resident parent for the purposes of a calculation decision is a weekly amount determined at the effective date of the decision on the basis of either historic income or current income in accordance with this Chapter.

(2) The non-resident parent's gross weekly income is to be based on historic income unless–

(a) current income differs from historic income by an amount that is at least 25% of historic income; or

(b) the amount of historic income is nil or no historic income is available

(3) For the purposes of paragraph (2)(b) no historic income is available if HMRC did not, when a request was last made by the Secretary of State for the purposes of regulation 35, have the required information in relation to a relevant tax year.

(4) "Relevant tax year" has the meaning given in regulation 4(2).

(5) This regulation is subject to regulation 23(4) (change to current income outside the annual review or periodic current income check).

Definitions

"calculation decision": see reg 3.

"current income": see reg 2.

"gross weekly income": see reg 2.

"historic income": see reg 2.

"HMRC": see reg 2.

"tax year": see reg 2.

General Note

The non-resident parent's gross income is fixed by reference to historic income, unless (i) current income differs from that figure by at least 25 per cent, more or less; (ii) historic income is nil; or (iii) no historic income is available.

Historic income – general

35.–(1) Historic income is determined by–

(a) taking the HMRC figure last requested from HMRC in relation to the non-resident parent;

(b) adjusting that figure where required in accordance with paragraph (3); and

(c) dividing by 365 and multiplying by 7.

(2) A request for the HMRC figure is to be made by the Secretary of State–

(a) for the purposes of a decision under section 11 of the 1991 Act (the initial maintenance calculation) no more than 30 days before the initial effective date; and

(b)   for the purposes of updating that figure, no more than 30 days before the review date.

(3)   Where the non-resident parent has made relievable pension contributions during the tax year to which the HMRC figure relates and those contributions have not been deducted under net pay arrangements, the HMRC figure is, if the non-resident parent so requests and provides such information as the Secretary of State requires, to be adjusted by deducting the amount of those contributions.

Definitions

"the 1991 Act": see reg 2.
"Her Majesty's Revenue and Customs": see reg 2.
"the HMRC figure": see reg 2.
"initial effective date": see reg 2.
"net pay arrangements": see reg 2.
"relievable pension contributions": see reg 2.
"review date": see reg 2.
"tax year": see reg 2.

General Note

The figure provided by the HMRC is subject to adjustment under para (3) to take account of pension contributions and to conversion under para (1)(c) to a weekly amount.

Historic income – the HMRC figure

36.–(1)   The HMRC figure is the amount identified by HMRC from information provided in a self-assessment return or under the PAYE regulations, as the sum of the income on which the non-resident parent was charged to tax for the latest available tax year–

(a)   under Part 2 of ITEPA (employment income);

(b)   under Part 9 of ITEPA (pension income);

(c)   under Part 10 of ITEPA (social security income) but only in so far as that income comprises the following taxable UK benefits listed in Table A in Chapter 3 of that Part–

    (i)   incapacity benefit;

    (ii)   contributory employment and support allowance;

    (iii)   jobseeker's allowance; and

    (iv)   income support; and

(d)   under Part 2 of ITTOIA (trading income).

(2)   The amount identified as income for the purposes of paragraph (1)(a) is to be taken–

(a)   after any deduction for relievable pension contributions made by the non-resident parent's employer in accordance with net pay arrangements; and

(b)   before any deductions under Part 5 of ITEPA (deductions allowed from earnings).

(3)   The amount identified as income for the purposes of paragraph (1)(b) is not to include a UK social security pension.

(4)   The amount identified as income for the purposes of paragraph (1)(d) is to be taken after deduction of any relief under section 83 of the Income Tax Act 2007 (carry forward trade loss relief against trade profits).

(5)   Where, for the latest available tax year, HMRC has both information provided in a self-assessment return and information provided under the PAYE Regulations, the amount identified for the purposes of paragraph (1) is to be taken from the former.

Definitions

"contributory employment and support allowance": see reg 2.
"historic income": see reg 2.
"HMRC": see reg 2.
"income support": see reg 2.
"ITEPA": see reg 2.
"ITTOIA": see reg 2.

"latest available tax year": see reg 4.
"net pay arrangements": see reg 2.
"the PAYE Regulations": see reg 2.
"relievable pension contributions": see reg 2.
"self-assessment return": see reg 2.
"UK social security pension": see reg 2.

General Note
This regulation governs the relevant income that is taken into account. Broadly, the tax calculation is used, except for pension payments and carry forward relief. There is no scope to use any other evidence of gross income, however reliable it may be. *Gray v SSWP and James* [2012] EWCA Civ 1412 does not apply to historic income.

Current income – general
37.–(1)   Current income is the sum of the non-resident parent's income–
(a)   as an employee or office-holder;
(b)   from self-employment; and
(c)   from a pension,
calculated or estimated as a weekly amount at the effective date of the relevant calculation decision in accordance with regulations 38 to 42.
(2)   Where payment is made in a currency other than sterling, an amount equal to any banking charge payable in converting that payment to sterling is to be disregarded in calculating the current income of a non-resident parent.

Definition
"calculation decision": see reg 3.

General Note
This regulation defines current income and provides for deduction of bank charges for its conversion into sterling.

Current income as an employee or office-holder
38.–(1)   The non-resident parent's current income as an employee or office-holder is income of a kind that would be taxable earnings within the meaning of section 10(2) of ITEPA and is to be calculated as follows.
(2)   As regards any part of the non-resident parent's income that comprises salary, wages or other amounts paid periodically–
(a)   if it appears to the Secretary of State that the non-resident parent is (or is to be) paid a regular amount according to a settled pattern that is likely to continue for the foreseeable future, that part of the non-resident parent's income is to be calculated as the weekly equivalent of that amount; and
(b)   if sub-paragraph (a) does not apply (for example where the non-resident parent is a seasonal worker or has working hours that follow an irregular pattern) that part of the non-resident parent's income is to be calculated as the weekly average of the amounts paid over such period preceding the effective date of the relevant calculation decision as appears to the Secretary of State to be appropriate.
(3)   Where the income from the non-resident parent's present employment or office has, during the past 12 months, included bonus or commission or other amounts paid separately from, or in relation to a longer period than, the amounts referred to in paragraph (2), the amount of that income is to be calculated by aggregating those payments, dividing by 365 and multiplying by 7.
(4)   Where the earnings from the non-resident parent's present employment or office have, in the past 12 months, included amounts treated as earnings under Chapters 2 to 11 of Part 3 of ITEPA (the benefits code) the non-resident parent's current income is to be taken to include the amount of those benefits as last obtained by HMRC divided by 365 and multiplied by 7.
(5)   Where the non-resident parent's employer makes deductions of relievable pension contributions from the payments referred to in paragraph (2) or (3) the amount of those payments is to be calculated after those deductions.

Definitions

"calculation decision": see reg 3.

"current income": see reg 2.

"HMRC": see reg 2.

"ITEPA": see reg 2.

"relievable pension contributions": see reg 2.

General Note

This regulation governs income from employment or an office. It should not give rise to difficulty or argument if the non-resident parent is paid a regular amount (para (2)(a)) or if benefit income is in issue (para (4)). If the non-resident parent is a seasonable worker or works to an irregular pattern, there will be scope for argument (including argument on an appeal) about the period over which earnings are to be averaged under para (2)(b). There is specific provision for bonus and commission in para (3).

Current income from self-employment

39.–(1)   The non-resident parent's current income from self-employment is to be determined by reference to the profits of any trade, profession or vocation carried on by the non-resident parent at the effective date of the relevant calculation decision.

(2)   The profits referred to in paragraph (1) are the profits determined in accordance with Part 2 of ITTOIA for the most recently completed relevant period or, if no such period has been completed, the estimated profits for the current relevant period.

(3)   The weekly amount is calculated by dividing the amount of those profits by the number of weeks in the relevant period.

(4)   In paragraphs (2) and (3) the "relevant period" means a tax year or such other period in respect of which the non-resident parent should, in the normal course of events, report the profits or losses of the trade, profession or vocation in question to HMRC in a self-assessment return.

(5)   In the case of a non-resident parent who carries on a trade, profession or vocation in partnership, the profits referred to in this regulation are the profits attributable to the non-resident parent's share of the partnership.

(6)   The profits of a trade, profession or vocation that the non-resident parent has ceased to carry on at the effective date of the relevant calculation decision are to be taken as nil.

Definitions

"calculation decision": see reg 3.

"current income": see reg 2.

"HMRC": see reg 2.

"ITTOIA": see reg 2.

"self-assessment return": see reg 2.

"tax year": see reg 2.

General Note

This regulation governs income from self-employment. The method of calculation follows tax law, but there will be the usual scope for argument about the amount of self-employed income. Income from a self-employment that had ceased by the effective date is taken as nil (para (6)). This will afford ample scope for non-resident parents to reorganise their businesses and argue that they are now engage in a new self-employment.

Deduction for pension contributions relievable at source

40.   Where the non-resident parent–

(a)   has current income from self-employment or as an employee or office-holder at the effective date of the relevant calculation decision; and

(b)   makes relievable pension contributions which are not taken into account under regulation 38(5),

there is to be deducted from the sum of any amounts calculated in accordance with regulation 38 or 39 (current income as an employee, current income from self-employment) an amount determined by the Secretary of State as representing the weekly average of those contributions.

Definitions
"calculation decision": see reg 3.
"current income": see reg 2.
"relievable pension contributions": see reg 2.

General Note
This regulation provides for pension contributions to be deducted in calculating current income, unless they have already been deducted by an employer, in which case they were excluded under reg 38(5).

Current income from a pension

41. The non-resident parent's current income from a pension is to be calculated as the weekly average, over such period as the Secretary of State considers appropriate, of amounts received by the non-resident parent from a pension or annuity or other income (excluding UK social security pensions) of a kind that would be charged to tax under Part 9 of ITEPA.

Definitions
"current income": see reg 2.
"ITEPA": see reg 2.
"UK social security pension": see reg 2.

General Note
This regulation provides for pension income to be calculated as a weekly amount by averaging over an appopriate period. The First-tier Tribunal on appeal may substitute a different period.

Estimate of current income where insufficient information available

42.–(1) Where–
(a)   current income applies by virtue of regulation 34(2)(b) (historic income nil or not available); and
(b)   the information available in relation to current income is insufficient or unreliable,
the Secretary of State may estimate that income and, in doing so, may make any assumption as to any fact.

(2)   Where the Secretary of State is satisfied that the non-resident parent is engaged in a particular occupation, whether as an employee, office-holder or self-employed person, the assumptions referred to in paragraph (1) may include an assumption that the non-resident parent has the average weekly income of a person engaged in that occupation in the UK or in any part of the UK.

Definition
"current income": see reg 2.

General Note
This regulation provides for income to be estimated if there is no other reliable evidence. The approach in para (2) was recommended by the Child Support Commissioner in *CCS 2901/2002* para 12.

CHAPTER 2
RATES OF CHILD SUPPORT MAINTENANCE

Reduced Rate

43. The reduced rate is an amount calculated as follows–

F + (A x T)

where–
F is the flat rate liability applicable to the non-resident parent;
A is the amount of the non-resident parent's gross weekly income between £100 and £200; and
T is the percentage determined in accordance with the following Table–

	Number of relevant other children of the non-resident parent	T (%)
1 qualifying child of the non-resident parent	0	19
	1	16.40
	2	15.60
	3 or more	15.20
2 qualifying children of the non-resident parent	0	27
	1	23.50
	2	22.50
	3 or more	21.90
3 or more qualifying children of the non-resident parent	0	33
	1	28.80
	2	27.70
	3 or more	26.90

Definitions

"the flat rate": see reg 2.

"gross weekly income": see reg 2.

General Note

This regulation fixes the reduced rate as a percentage of the non-resident parent's gross weekly income. The percentage increases for each qualifying child up to three and reduces for each relevant other child up to three.

Flat Rate

44.–(1) The following benefits, pensions or allowances are prescribed for the purposes of paragraph 4(1)(b) of Schedule 1 to the 1991 Act (that is the benefits, pensions or allowances that qualify the non-resident parent for the flat rate)–

(a) under the Social Security Contributions and Benefits Act 1992–

    (i) bereavement allowance under section 39B,

    (ii) category A retirement pension under section 44,

    (iii) category B retirement pension under section 48C,

    (iv) category C and category D retirement pension under section 78,

    (v) incapacity benefit under section 30A,

    (vi) carer's allowance under section 70,

    (vii) maternity allowance under section 35,

    (viii) severe disablement allowance under section 68,

    (ix) industrial injuries benefit under section 94,

    (x) widowed mother's allowance under section 37,

    (xi) widowed parent's allowance under section 39A, and

    (xii) widow's pension under section 38;

(b) contribution-based jobseeker's allowance under the Jobseekers Act 1995;

(c) a social security benefit paid by a country other than the United Kingdom;

(d) a training allowance (other than work-based training for young people or, in Scotland, Skillseekers training);

(e) a war disablement pension within the meaning of section 150(2) of the Social Security Contributions and Benefits Act 1992 or a pension which is analogous to such a pension paid by the government of a country outside Great Britain;

(f) a war widow's pension, war widower's pension or surviving civil partner's war pension within the meaning of that section;

(g) a payment under a scheme mentioned in section 1(2) of the Armed Forces (Pensions and Compensation) Act 2004 (compensation schemes for armed and reserve forces); and

(h)   contributory employment and support allowance.

(2)   The following benefits are prescribed for the purposes of paragraph 4(1)(c) of Schedule 1 to the 1991 Act (that is the benefits that qualify the non-resident parent for the flat rate if received by the non-resident parent or their partner)–

(a)   income support;

(b)   income-based jobseeker's allowance;

(c)   income-related employment and support allowance; [¹...]

(d)   state pension credit; [¹and

(e)   universal credit under Part 1 of the Welfare Reform Act 2012, where the award of universal credit is calculated on the basis that the non-resident parent does not have any earned income].

(3)   Where the conditions referred to in paragraph 4(2) of Schedule 1 to the 1991 Act are satisfied (that is where an income-related benefit is payable to the non-resident parent or their partner and a maintenance calculation is in force in respect of each of them) the flat rate of maintenance payable is half the flat rate that would otherwise apply.

(4)   In paragraph (1)(d) "training allowance" means a payment under section 2 of the Employment and Training Act 1973 or section 2 of the Enterprise and New Towns (Scotland) Act 1990 which is paid to a person for their maintenance while they are undergoing training.

[¹(5)   For the purposes of paragraph (2)(e) and regulation 45(1)(c), "earned income" has the meaning given in regulation 52 of the Universal Credit Regulations 2013.]

Amendment

1.   Universal Credit (Consequential, Supplementary, Incidental and Miscellaneous Provisions) Regulations 2013 (SI 2013 No. 630) reg. 44(3) (April 29, 2013).

Definitions

"the 1991 Act": see reg 2.

"contribution-based jobseeker's allowance": see reg 2.

"contributory employment and support allowance": see reg 2.

"the flat rate": see reg 2.

"income support": see reg 2.

"partner": see reg 2.

"state pension credit": see reg 2.

General Note

The benefits in paras (1) and (2) trigger payment of the flat rate. Only half is payable if Sch 1 para 4(2) to the Act applies (para (3)).

Nil rate

45.–(1)   The nil rate is payable where the non-resident parent is–

(a)   a child;

(b)   a prisoner or a person serving a sentence of imprisonment detained in hospital;

(c)   a person who is 16 or 17 years old and–

  (i)   in receipt of income support, income-based jobseeker's allowance or income-related employment and support allowance, [¹...]

  (ii)   a member of a couple whose partner is in receipt of income support, income-based jobseeker's allowance or income-related employment and support allowance [¹;

  (iii)   in receipt of universal credit under Part 1 of the Welfare Reform Act 2012, where the award of universal credit is calculated on the basis that they do not have any earned income; or

  (iv)   in a case not covered by paragraph (iii), a member of a couple where their partner is in receipt of universal credit under Part 1 of the Welfare Reform Act 2012 and the award of universal credit is calculated on the basis that the non-resident parent does not have any earned income];

(d)   a person receiving an allowance in respect of work-based training for young people, or in Scotland, Skillseekers training; or

(e)   a person who is resident in a care home or an independent hospital or is being provided with a care home service or an independent health care service who–
    (i)   is in receipt of a pension, benefit or allowance specified in regulation 44(1) or (2) (flat rate), or
    (ii)   has the whole or part of the cost of their accommodation met by a local authority.

(2)   For the purposes only of determining whether paragraph 5(b) of Schedule 1 to the 1991 Act applies (nil rate payable where non-resident parent has gross weekly income of below the flat rate that is referred to in, or prescribed for the purposes of, paragraph 4(1) of Schedule 1 to the 1991 Act), the gross weekly income of the non-resident parent is to include any payments made by way of benefits, pensions or allowances referred to in regulation 44(1) or (2).

(3)   In paragraph (1)–
"independent hospital" and "care home" have the meaning given by sections 2 and 3 of the Care Standards Act 2000 respectively;
"care home service" has the meaning given by paragraph 2 of schedule 12 to the Public Services Reform (Scotland) Act 2010 and "independent health care service" has the meaning given by section 10F(1)(a) and (b) of the National Health Service (Scotland) Act 1978;
"person serving a sentence of imprisonment detained in hospital" means a person who–
  (a)   is being detained–
    (i)   under section 45A or 47 of the Mental Health Act 1983; and
    (ii)   before the day which the Secretary of State certifies to be that person's release date within the meaning of section 50(3) of that Act (in any case where there is such a release date); or
  (b)   is being detained under–
    (i)   section 59A of the Criminal Procedure (Scotland) Act 1995; or
    (ii)   section 136 of the Mental Health (Care and Treatment) (Scotland) Act 2003;
"prisoner" means a person who–
  (a)   is detained in custody pending trial or sentence upon conviction or under sentence imposed by a court; or
  (b)   is on temporary release in accordance with the provisions of the Prison Act 1952 or the Prisons (Scotland) Act 1989,
other than a person who is detained in hospital under the provisions of the Mental Health Act 1983 or, in Scotland, the Mental Health (Care and Treatment)(Scotland) Act 2003 or the Criminal Procedure (Scotland) Act 1995.

Amendment
1.   Universal Credit (Consequential, Supplementary, Incidental and Miscellaneous Provisions) Regulations 2013 (SI 2013 No.630) reg 44(4) (April 29, 2013).

Definitions
"the 1991 Act": see reg 2.
"couple": see reg 2.
"earned income": reg 44(5).
"the flat rate": see reg 2.
"gross weekly income": see reg 2.
"income support": see reg 2.
"local authority": see reg 2.
"the nil rate": see reg 2.
"partner": see reg 2.

General Note
The circumstances in this regulation trigger the nil rate.

Decrease for shared care

46.–(1)   This regulation and regulation 47 apply where the Secretary of State determines the number of nights which count for the purposes of the decrease in the amount of child support maintenance under paragraphs 7 and 8 of Schedule 1 to the 1991 Act.

(2)   Subject to paragraph (3), the determination is to be based on the number of nights for which the non-resident parent is expected to have the care of the qualifying child overnight during the 12 months beginning with the effective date of the relevant calculation decision.

(3)   The Secretary of State may have regard to a period of less than 12 months where the Secretary of State considers a shorter period is appropriate (for example where the parties have an agreement in relation to a shorter period) and, if the Secretary of State does so, paragraphs 7(3) and 8(2) of Schedule 1 to the 1991 Act are to have effect as if–

(a)   the period mentioned there were that shorter period; and

(b)   the number of nights mentioned in the Table in paragraph 7(4), or in paragraph 8(2), of that Schedule were reduced proportionately.

(4)   When making a determination under paragraphs (1) to (3) the Secretary of State must consider–

(a)   the terms of any agreement made between the parties or of any court order providing for contact between the non-resident parent and the qualifying child; or

(b)   if there is no agreement or court order, whether a pattern of shared care has already been established over the past 12 months (or such other period as the Secretary of State considers appropriate in the circumstances of the case).

(5)   For the purposes of this regulation–

(a)   a night will count where the non-resident parent has the care of the qualifying child overnight and the child stays at the same address as the non-resident parent;

(b)   the non-resident parent has the care of the qualifying child when the non-resident parent is looking after the child; and

(c)   where, on a particular night, a child is a boarder at a boarding school, or an in-patient in a hospital, the person who would, but for those circumstances, have the care of the child for that night, shall be treated as having care of the child for that night.

Definitions
   "the 1991 Act": see reg 2.
   "calculation decision": see reg 3.
   "party": see reg 2.

General Note
   This regulation must be read subject to reg 47. It provides for an allowance in respect of shared care based on the expectation for the 12 months beginning on the effective date. A shorter period may be used if appropriate. Paragraph (5) provides for circumstances in which a non-resident parent has care of the child.

Assumption as to number of nights of shared care

47.–(1)   This regulation applies where the Secretary of State is required to make a determination under regulation 46 for the purposes of a calculation decision.

(2)   If it appears to the Secretary of State that–

(a)   the parties agree in principle that the care of a qualifying child is to be shared during the period mentioned in regulation 46(2) or (3) (decrease for shared care); but

(b)   there is insufficient evidence to make that determination on the basis set out in regulation 46(4) (for example because the parties have not yet agreed the pattern or frequency or the evidence as to a past pattern is disputed),

the Secretary of State may make the decision on the basis of an assumption that the non-resident parent is to have the care of the child overnight for one night per week.

(3)   Where the Secretary of State makes a decision under paragraph (2) the assumption applies until an application is made under section 17 of the 1991 Act for a supersession of that decision and the evidence provided is sufficient to enable a determination to be made on the basis set out in regulation 46(4).

Definitions

"the 1991 Act": see reg 2.

"calculation decision": see reg 3.

"party": see reg 2.

General Note

This regulation qualifies the application of reg 46. It provides for shared care to be based on an assumption of fact when the parties are agreed in principle but the evidence is not sufficient to make a decision under reg 46(4). The assumption, once made, continues until there is a supersession made in accordance with reg 46. This provision will be useful if, as so often, the parents produce competing evidence about actual overnight stays.

Non-resident parent party to another maintenance arrangement

48.–(1)   An agreement described in paragraph (2) is an agreement of a prescribed description for the purposes of paragraph 5A(6)(b) of Schedule 1 to the 1991 Act (that is an agreement which is a qualifying maintenance arrangement for the purposes of that paragraph).

(2)   The agreement may be oral or written and must satisfy the following conditions–

(a)   it must relate to a child of the non-resident parent who is habitually resident in the UK;

(b)   it must be between the non-resident parent and a person with whom the child has their home (but not in the same household as the non-resident parent) and who usually provides day to day care for that child; and

(c)   it must provide for the non-resident parent to make regular payments for the benefit of the child.

(3)   The payments mentioned in paragraph (2)(c) may include payments made by the non-resident parent direct to the person mentioned in paragraph (2)(b) or payments to other persons.

Definition

"the 1991 Act": see reg 2.

General Note

This regulation prescribes an agreement for the purposes of Sch 1 para 5A(6)(b) to the Act. The criteria are set out in para (2). Payment may be made to the person in whose home the child lives or to another person, such as a school.

CHAPTER 3
DEFAULT MAINTENANCE DECISIONS

Default rate

49.–(1)   Where the Secretary of State makes a default maintenance decision under section 12(1) of the 1991 Act (that is where there is insufficient information to make a maintenance calculation) the default rate is set out in paragraph (2).

(2)   The default rate is–

(a)   £39 where there is one qualifying child;

(b)   £51 where there are two qualifying children; or

(c)   £64 where there are three or more qualifying children,

apportioned, where the non-resident parent has more than one qualifying child and in relation to them there is more than one person with care, as provided in paragraph 6(2) of Schedule 1 to the 1991 Act.

Definition

"the 1991 Act": see reg 2.

General Note

This regulation fixes the default rate under s 12(1) of the Act. It increases with the number of children, up to 3.

CHAPTER 4
SPECIAL CASES

Parent treated as a non-resident parent in shared care cases

50.–(1)   Where the circumstances of a case are that–

(a)   an application is made by a person with care under section 4 of the 1991 Act; and

(b)   the person named in that application as the non-resident parent of the qualifying child also provides a home for that child (in a different household from the applicant) and shares the day to day care of that child with the applicant,

the case is to be treated as a special case for the purposes of the 1991 Act.

(2)   For the purposes of this special case, the person mentioned in paragraph (1)(b) is to be treated as the non-resident parent if, and only if, that person provides day to day care to a lesser extent than the applicant.

(3)   Where the applicant is receiving child benefit in respect of the qualifying child the applicant is assumed, in the absence of evidence to the contrary, to be providing day to day care to a greater extent than any other person.

[¹(4)   For the purposes of paragraph (3), where a person has made an election under section 13A(1) of the Social Security Administration Act 1992 (election not to receive child benefit) for payments of child benefit not to be made, that person is to be treated as receiving child benefit.]

Amendment

1.   Child Support (Miscellaneous Amendments) Regulations 2013 (SI 2013 No.1517) reg 8(4) (September 30, 2013).

Definition

"the 1991 Act": see reg 2.

General Note

Where day to day care is shared, the non-resident parent is the person who cares for the child to a lesser extent. The person receiving child benefit in respect of the child is deemed to be the person with care, subject to evidence to the contrary. The emphasis is on receipt of child benefit, not on whether the person receiving it is properly entitled to it. However, the evidence offered to the contrary under para (3) may effectively be a challenge to the recipient's entitlement.

See further the general note to reg 8 of the Maintenance Calculations and Special Cases Regulations.

Child in care who is allowed to live with their parent

51.–(1)   Where the circumstances of a case are that a qualifying child who is in the care of a local authority in England and Wales is allowed by the authority to live with a parent of that child under section 22C(2) or 23(5) of the Children Act 1989, that case is to be treated as a special case for the purposes of the 1991 Act.

(2)   For the purposes of this case, section 3(3)(b) of the 1991 Act is to be modified so that, for the reference to the person who usually provides day to day care for the child there is substituted a reference to the parent of the child with whom the local authority has allowed the child to live.

Definitions

"the 1991 Act": see reg 2.
"local authority": see reg 2.

General Note

Where a child is in the care of the local authority which allows the child to live with a parent (but not any other person), that person is treated as the person who usually has day to day care of the child. See the general note to reg 13 of the Maintenance Calculations and Special Cases Regulations.

Non-resident parent liable to maintain a child of the family or a child abroad

52.–(1)   A case is to be treated as a special case for the purposes of the 1991 Act where–

(a)   an application for a maintenance calculation has been made or a maintenance calculation is in force with respect to a qualifying child and a non-resident parent;

(b)   there is a different child in respect of whom no application for a maintenance calculation may be made but whom the non-resident parent is liable to maintain–

    (i)   in accordance with a maintenance order made in respect of that child as a child of the non-resident parent's family, or

    (ii)   in accordance with an order made by a court outside Great Britain or under the legislation of a jurisdiction outside the United Kingdom; and

(c)   the weekly rate of child support maintenance, apart from this regulation, would be the basic rate or the reduced rate or would be calculated following agreement to a variation where the rate would otherwise be the flat rate or the nil rate.

(2)   In any such case the amount of child support maintenance is to be calculated in accordance with paragraph 5A of Schedule 1 to the 1991 Act as if the child in question were a child with respect to whom the non-resident parent was a party to a qualifying maintenance arrangement.

(3)   For the purposes of this regulation "child" includes a person who has not attained the age of 20 whom the non-resident parent is liable to maintain in accordance with paragraph (1)(b)(ii).

Definition
"the 1991 Act": see reg 2.
"the flat rate": see reg 2.
"the nil rate": see reg 2.

General Note
See the general note to reg 11 of the Maintenance Calculations and Special Cases Regulations.

Care provided in part by a local authority

53.–(1)   This regulation applies where paragraph (2) applies and the rate of child support maintenance payable is the basic rate, or the reduced rate, or has been calculated following agreement to a variation where the non-resident parent's liability would otherwise have been the flat rate or the nil rate.

(2)   Where the circumstances of a case are that the care of the qualifying child is shared between the person with care and a local authority and–

(a)   the qualifying child is in the care of the local authority for 52 nights or more in the period of 12 months ending with the effective date of the relevant calculation decision;

(b)   where, in the opinion of the Secretary of State, a period other than the period of 12 months mentioned in sub-paragraph (a) is more representative of the current arrangements for the care of the qualifying child, the qualifying child is in the care of the local authority during that period for no fewer than the number of nights which bears the same ratio to 52 nights as that period bears to 12 months; or

(c)   it is intended that the qualifying child is to be in the care of the local authority for a number of nights in a period beginning with the day after the effective date and–

    (i)   if that period were a period of 12 months, the number of nights is 52 nights or more; or

    (ii)   if that period were a period other than 12 months, the number of nights is no fewer than the number of nights which bears the same ratio to 52 nights as that period bears to 12 months,

that case is to be treated as a special case for the purpose of the 1991 Act.

(3)   In a case where this regulation applies, the amount of child support maintenance which the non-resident parent is liable to pay the person with care of that qualifying child is the amount calculated in accordance with the provisions of Part I of Schedule 1 to the 1991 Act and decreased in accordance with this regulation.

(4)   First, there is to be a decrease according to the number of nights spent or to be spent by the qualifying child in the care of the local authority during the period under consideration.

(5)   Where paragraph (2)(b) or (c) applies, the number of nights in the period under consideration shall be adjusted by the ratio which the period of 12 months bears to the period under consideration.

(6)   After any adjustment under paragraph (5), the amount of the decrease for one child is set out in the following Table–

Number of nights in care of local authority	Fraction to subtract
52-103	One-seventh
104-155	Two-sevenths
156-207	Three-sevenths
208-259	Four-sevenths
260-262	Five-sevenths

(7)   If the non-resident parent and the person with care have more than one qualifying child, the applicable decrease is the sum of the appropriate fractions in the Table divided by the number of such qualifying children.

(8)   In a case where the amount of child support maintenance which the non-resident parent is liable to pay in relation to the same person with care is to be decreased in accordance with the provisions of both this regulation and of paragraph 7 of Part 1 of Schedule 1 to the 1991 Act, read with these Regulations, the applicable decrease is the sum of the appropriate fractions derived under those provisions.

(9)   If the application of this regulation would decrease the weekly amount of child support maintenance (or the aggregate of all such amounts) payable by the non-resident parent to less than the flat rate referred to in paragraph 4(1) of Schedule 1 to the 1991 Act (or in that sub-paragraph as modified by regulations under paragraph 10A of Schedule 1), the non-resident parent is instead liable to pay child support maintenance at a rate equivalent to that rate, apportioned (if appropriate) in accordance with paragraph 6 of Part I of Schedule 1 to that Act.

(10)   If the number of nights calculated for the purposes of applying the table in paragraph (6) is 263 or more, the amount of child support maintenance payable by the non-resident parent in respect of the child in question is nil.

(11)   Where a qualifying child is a boarder at a boarding school or is an in-patient at a hospital, the qualifying child shall be treated as being in the care of the local authority for any night that the local authority would otherwise have been providing such care.

(12)   A child is in the care of a local authority for any night in which that child is being looked after by the local authority within the meaning of section 22 of the Children Act 1989 or section 17(6) of the Children (Scotland) Act 1995.

Definitions
"the 1991 Act": see reg 2.
"calculation decision": see reg 3.
"the flat rate": see reg 2.
"local authority": see reg 2.
"the nil rate": see reg 2.
"the reduced rate": see reg 2.

General Note
See the general note to reg 9 of the Maintenance Calculations and Special Cases Regulations.

Care provided for relevant other child by a local authority

54.   Where a child other than a qualifying child is cared for in part or in full by a local authority, and the non-resident parent or the non-resident parent's partner receives child benefit for that child, the child is a relevant other child for the purposes of Schedule 1 to the 1991 Act.

[¹(2)   For the purposes of paragraph (1), where a person has made an election under section 13A(1) of the Social Security Administration Act 1992 (election not to receive child benefit) for payments of child benefit not to be made, that person is to be treated as receiving child benefit.]

Amendment

1.   Child Support (Miscellaneous Amendments) Regulations 2013 (SI 2013 No.1517) reg 8(5) (September 30, 2013).

Definitions

"the 1991 Act": see reg 2.
"local authority": see reg 2.
"partner": see reg 2.

General Note

If the non-resident parent or that parent's partner receives child benefit for a child in the care of a local authority, the child is a relevant other child for the purposes of Sch 1 to the Act.

Child who is a boarder or an in-patient in hospital

55.–(1)   Where the circumstances of the case are that–

(a)   a qualifying child is a boarder at a boarding school or is an in-patient in a hospital; and

(b)   by reason of those circumstances, the person who would otherwise provide day to day care is not doing so,

that case is to be treated as a special case for the purposes of the 1991 Act.

(2)   For the purposes of this case, section 3(3)(b) of the 1991 Act is to be modified so that for the reference to the person who usually provides day to day care for the child there is substituted a reference to the person who would usually provide day to day care for that child but for the circumstances specified in paragraph (1).

Definition

"the 1991 Act": see reg 2.

General Note

See the general note to reg 12 of the Maintenance Calculations and Special Cases Regulations.

PART 5
VARIATIONS
CHAPTER 1
GENERAL

Application for a variation

56.–(1)   Where an application for a variation is made other than in writing it is treated as made on the date on which the applicant notifies the Secretary of State that the applicant wishes to make such an application.

(2)   Where an application for a variation is made in writing it is treated as made on the date that the Secretary of State receives it.

(3)   Two or more applications for a variation with respect to the same maintenance calculation or application for a maintenance calculation may be considered together.

(4)   The Secretary of State may treat an application for a variation made on one ground as made on another ground if that other ground is more appropriate to the facts alleged in that case.

General Note

This regulation provides for the date of application, the consolidation of applications and the scope of an application. A reference in a letter of appeal to a matter covered by a ground for variation may be accepted as an application (*CCS 3862/2007* para 17).

There is no provision for withdrawal of an application, but there is no reason in principle why this should not be allowed up to the time when a decision is made.

Rejection of an application following preliminary consideration

57.–(1)   The circumstances prescribed for the purposes of section 28B(2)(c) of the 1991 Act (other circumstances in which an application may be rejected after preliminary consideration) are–

(a)   the applicant does not state a ground for the variation or provide sufficient information to enable a ground to be identified;

(b)   although a ground is stated, the Secretary of State is satisfied that the application would not be agreed to because –

   (i)   the facts alleged do not bring the case within the ground; or

   (ii)   no facts are alleged that would support the ground or could reasonably form the basis of further enquiries;

(c)   a default maintenance decision is in force;

(d)   the non-resident parent is liable to pay the flat rate or nil rate because the non-resident parent or their partner is in receipt of a benefit listed in regulation 44(2) (flat rate);

(e)   in the case of an application made by the non-resident parent on the grounds mentioned in Chapter 2 (special expenses)–

   (i)   the amount of the expenses does not exceed the relevant threshold;

   (ii)   the amount of maintenance for which the non-resident parent is liable is equal to or less than the flat rate referred to in paragraph 4(1) of Schedule 1 to the 1991 Act (or in that sub-paragraph as modified by regulations under paragraph 10A of Schedule 1);

   (iii)   the amount of the non-resident parent's gross weekly income would exceed the capped amount after deducting special expenses; or

   (iv)   the non resident parent's gross weekly income has been determined on the basis of regulation 42 (estimate of current income where insufficient information available); or

(f)   in the case of an application on any of the grounds mentioned in Chapter 3 (additional income), the amount of the non-resident parent's gross weekly income (without taking that ground into account) is the capped amount.

(2)   The circumstances set out in paragraph (1) are circumstances prescribed for the purposes of section 28F(3)(b) of the 1991 Act in which the Secretary of State must not agree to a variation.

Definitions

"the 1991 Act": see reg 2.
"capped amount": see reg 2.
"the flat rate": see reg 2.
"gross weekly income": see reg 2.
"the nil rate": see reg 2.
"partner": see reg 2.

General Note

This regulation sets out the circumstances in which an application may be rejected on preliminary consideration.
Paragraph (1)(c) allows this if a default maintenance decision is in force, although reg 13(1) envisages that a variation may be agreed to if the application is made before the default maintenance decision is made.

Provision of information

58.–(1)   Where the Secretary of State has received an application for a variation the Secretary of State may request further information or evidence from the applicant to enable that application to be determined.

(2)   Any such information or evidence requested in accordance with paragraph (1) must be provided within 14 days after the date of notification of the request or such longer period as the Secretary of State is satisfied is reasonable in the circumstances of the case.

(3)   Where any information or evidence requested is not provided within the time specified in paragraph (2), the Secretary of State may, where able to do so, proceed to determine the application in the absence of the requested information or evidence.

Procedure in relation to a variation

59.–(1)   Where the Secretary of State has given the preliminary consideration to an application for a variation and not rejected it, the Secretary of State–

(a)   must give notice of the application to any other party informing them of the grounds on which the application has been made and any relevant information or evidence given by the applicant or obtained by the Secretary of State, except information or evidence falling within paragraph (5); and

(b)   may invite representations (which need not be in writing but must be in writing if in any case the Secretary of State so directs) from the other party on any matter relating to that application, to be submitted to the Secretary of State within 14 days after the date of notification or such longer period as the Secretary of State is satisfied is reasonable in the circumstances of the case.

(2)   The Secretary of State need not act in accordance with paragraph (1) if–

(a)   the Secretary of State is satisfied on the information or evidence available that the application would not be agreed to;

(b)   in the case of an application for a variation on the ground mentioned in regulation 69 (non-resident parent with unearned income), the information from HMRC for the latest available tax year does not disclose unearned income exceeding the relevant threshold and the Secretary of State is not in possession of other information or evidence that would merit further enquiry; or

(c)   regulation 75 (previously agreed variation may be taken into account notwithstanding that no further application has been made) applies;

(3)   Where the Secretary of State receives representations from the other party–

(a)   the Secretary of State may, if the Secretary of State is satisfied that it is reasonable to do so, inform the applicant of the representations concerned (excluding material falling within paragraph (5)) and invite comments within 14 days or such longer period as the Secretary of State is satisfied is reasonable in the circumstances of the case; and

(b)   where the Secretary of State acts under sub-paragraph (a), the Secretary of State must not proceed to determine the application until such comments are received or the period referred to in that sub-paragraph has expired.

(4)   Where the Secretary of State has not received representations from the other party notified in accordance with paragraph (1) within the time specified in sub-paragraph (b) of that paragraph, the Secretary of State may in their absence proceed to agree (or not, as the case may be) to the variation.

(5)   The information or evidence referred to in paragraph (1)(a) is as follows–

(a)   details of the nature of the long-term illness or disability of the relevant other child which forms the basis of a variation application on the ground in regulation 64 (illness or disability of a relevant other child) where the applicant requests they should not be disclosed and the Secretary of State is satisfied that disclosure is not necessary in order to be able to determine the application;

(b)   medical evidence or medical advice which has not been disclosed to the applicant or the other party and which the Secretary of State considers would be harmful to the health of the applicant or that party if disclosed; or

(c)   the address of the other party or qualifying child, or any other information which could reasonably be expected to lead to that party or child being located, where the Secretary of State considers that there would be a risk of harm or undue distress to that other party or that child or any other children living with that other party if the address or information were disclosed.

Definitions
"HMRC": see reg 2.
"latest available tax year": see reg 4.
"party": see reg 2.

General Note
See the general note to the equivalent provisions of reg 9 of the Variation Regulations.

Factors not taken into account for the purposes of section 28F

60. The following factors are not to be taken into account in determining whether it would be just and equitable to agree to a variation in any case–

(a) the fact that the conception of the qualifying child was not planned by one or both of the parents;

(b) whether the non-resident parent or the person with care of the qualifying child was responsible for the breakdown of the relationship between them;

(c) the fact that the non-resident parent or the person with care of the qualifying child has formed a new relationship with a person who is not a parent of that child;

(d) the existence of particular arrangements for contact with the qualifying child, including whether any arrangements made are being adhered to;

(e) the income or assets of any person other than the non-resident parent;

(f) the failure by a non-resident parent to make payments of child support maintenance, or to make payments under a maintenance order or a maintenance agreement; or

(g) representations made by persons other than the parties.

Definition
"party": see reg 2.

General Note
See the general note to reg 21(2) of the Variation Regulations. There is no equivalent to reg 21(1) of those Regulations, which provides for circumstances that must be taken into account. Those factors may nonetheless be relevant in a particular case.

Procedure on revision or supersession of a previously determined variation

61.–(1) Subject to paragraph (2), where the Secretary of State has received an application under section 16 or 17 of the 1991 Act in connection with a previously determined variation which has effect on a maintenance calculation in force, regulations 58 to 60 apply in relation to that application as if it were an application for a variation that had not been rejected after preliminary consideration.

(2) The Secretary of State need not act in accordance with regulation 59(1) (procedure in relation to a variation) if–

(a) were the application to succeed, the decision as revised or superseded would be less advantageous to the applicant than the decision before it was so revised or superseded; or

(b) it appears to the Secretary of State that representations of the other party would not be relevant to the decision.

Definitions
"the 1991 Act": see reg 2.
"party": see reg 2.

General Note
This regulation provides for the procedure on an application for a revision or supersession. Paragraph (1) applies regs 58-60 as they apply to an initial application for a variation. Paragraph (2) authorises the Secretary of State to bypass notification to the notification and representation stages under reg 59(1) if the outcome of the application would be to the applicant's disadvantage.

Regular payments condition

62.–(1)   For the purposes of section 28C(2)(b) of the 1991 Act (payments of child support maintenance less than those specified in the interim maintenance decision) the payments are those fixed by the interim maintenance decision or the maintenance calculation in force, as the case may be, adjusted to take account of the variation applied for by the non-resident parent as if that variation had been agreed.

(2)   The Secretary of State may refuse to consider the application for a variation where a regular payments condition has been imposed and the non-resident parent fails to make such payments, which are due and unpaid, within one month after being required to do so by the Secretary of State or such other period as the Secretary of State may in the particular case decide.

Definition

"the 1991 Act": see reg 2.

General Note

This regulation makes provision for regular payments conditions. Paragraph (1) provides for the amount of the payment if there has been a variation. Paragraph (2) authorises the Secretary of State to refuse an application for a variation if payment is not made under the condition.

CHAPTER 2
GROUNDS FOR VARIATION: SPECIAL EXPENSES

Contact costs

63.–(1)   Subject to the following paragraphs of this regulation, and to regulation 68 (thresholds), the following costs incurred or reasonably expected to be incurred by the non-resident parent, whether in respect of the non-resident parent or the qualifying child or both, for the purpose of maintaining contact with that child, constitute special expenses for the purposes of paragraph 2(2) of Schedule 4B to the 1991 Act–

(a)   the cost of purchasing a ticket for travel;

(b)   the cost of purchasing fuel where travel is by a vehicle which is not carrying fare-paying passengers;

(c)   the taxi fare for a journey or part of a journey where the Secretary of State is satisfied that the disability or long-term illness of the non-resident parent or the qualifying child makes it impracticable for any other form of transport to be used for that journey or part of that journey;

(d)   the cost of car hire where the cost of the journey would be less in total than it would be if public transport or taxis or a combination of both were used;

(e)   where the Secretary of State considers a return journey on the same day is impracticable, or the established or intended pattern of contact with the child includes contact over two or more consecutive days, the cost of the non-resident parent's or, as the case may be, the child's, accommodation for the number of nights the Secretary of State considers appropriate in the circumstances of the case; and

(f)   any minor incidental costs such as tolls or fees payable for the use of a particular road or bridge incurred in connection with such travel, including breakfast where it is included as part of the accommodation cost referred to in sub-paragraph (e).

(2)   The costs to which paragraph (1) applies include the cost of a person to travel with the non-resident parent or the qualifying child, if the Secretary of State is satisfied that the presence of another person on the journey, or part of the journey, is necessary including, but not limited to, where it is necessary because of the young age of the qualifying child or the disability or long-term illness of the non-resident parent or that child.

(3)   The costs referred to in paragraphs (1) and (2)–

(a)   are expenses for the purposes of paragraph 2(2) of Schedule 4B to the 1991 Act only to the extent that they are–

      (i)   incurred in accordance with a set pattern as to frequency of contact between the non-resident parent and the qualifying child which has been established at or, where at the time of the variation application it has ceased, which had been established before, the time that the variation application is made; or

      (ii)   based on an intended set pattern for such contact which the Secretary of State is satisfied has been agreed between the non-resident parent and the person with care of the qualifying child; and

(b)   are–

      (i)   where sub-paragraph (a)(i) applies and such contact is continuing, calculated as an average weekly amount based on the expenses actually incurred during the period of 12 months, or such lesser period as the Secretary of State may consider appropriate in the circumstances of the case, ending immediately before the day from which a variation agreed on this ground would take effect;

      (ii)   where sub-paragraph (a)(i) applies and such contact has ceased, calculated as an average weekly amount based on the expenses actually incurred during the period from the day from which a variation agreed on this ground would take effect to the last day on which the variation would take effect; or

      (iii)   where sub-paragraph (a)(ii) applies, calculated as an average weekly amount based on anticipated costs during such period as the Secretary of State considers appropriate.

(4)   Where, at the date on which the variation application is made, the non-resident parent has received, is in receipt of, or will receive, any financial assistance, other than a loan, from any source to meet, wholly or in part, the costs of maintaining contact with a child as referred to in paragraph (1), only the amount of the costs referred to in that paragraph, after the deduction of the financial assistance, constitutes special expenses for the purposes of paragraph 2(2) of Schedule 4B to the 1991 Act.

Definition
    "the 1991 Act": see reg 2.

General Note
    See the general note to reg 10 of the Variation Regulations.

Illness or disability of relevant other child

64.–(1)   Subject to the following paragraphs of this regulation, expenses necessarily incurred by the non-resident parent in respect of the items listed in sub-paragraphs (a) to (m) due to the long-term illness or disability of a relevant other child constitute special expenses for the purposes of paragraph 2(2) of Schedule 4B to the 1991 Act–

(a)   personal care and attendance;

(b)   personal communication needs;

(c)   mobility;

(d)   domestic help;

(e)   medical aids where these cannot be provided under the health service;

(f)   heating;

(g)   clothing;

(h)   laundry requirements;

(i)   payments for food essential to comply with a diet recommended by a medical practitioner;

(j)   adaptations required to the non-resident parent's home;

(k)   day care;

(l)   rehabilitation; or

(m) respite care.

(2)   For the purposes of this regulation and regulation 63 (contact costs)–

(a)   a person is "disabled" for a period in respect of which–

      (i)   a disability living allowance [², armed forces independence payment] [¹or personal independence payment] is paid to or in respect of that person;

      (ii)   that person would receive a disability living allowance if it were not for the fact that the person is a patient, though remaining part of the applicant's family; [¹...]

      (iii) that person is registered blind, [¹or

      (iv) that person would receive personal independence payment but for regulations under section 86(1) (hospital in-patients) of the Welfare Reform Act 2012, and remains part of the applicant's family,]

and "disability" is to be construed accordingly;

  (b)   "disability living allowance" means the care component of a disability living allowance, payable under section 72 of the Social Security Contributions and Benefits Act 1992;

  (c)   "the health service" has the same meaning as in section 275 of the National Health Service Act 2006 or in section 108(1) of the National Health Service (Scotland) Act 1978;

  (d)   "long-term illness" means an illness from which the child is suffering at the date of the application or the date from which the variation, if agreed, would take effect and which is likely to last for at least 12 months after that date, or, if likely to be shorter than 12 months, for the remainder of their life; and

  (e)   "relevant other child" has the meaning given in paragraph 10C(2) of Schedule 1 to the 1991 Act;

  (f)   a person is "registered blind" where that person is–

      (i)   registered as blind in a register maintained by or on behalf of a local authority in England or Wales under section 29 of the National Assistance Act 1948 (welfare services); or

      (ii)   registered as blind in a register maintained by or on behalf of a local authority in Scotland;

[¹(g) "personal independence payment" means the daily living component of personal independence payment under section 78 of the Welfare Reform Act 2012;]

[²(h) "armed forces independence payment" means armed forces independence payment under the Armed Forces and Reserve Forces (Compensation Scheme) Order 2011.]

  (3)   Where, at the date on which the non-resident parent makes the variation application–

  (a)   the non-resident parent or a member of the non-resident parent's household has received, is in receipt of, or will receive any financial assistance from any source in respect of the long-term illness or disability of the relevant other child; or

  (b)   a disability living allowance[², armed forces independence payment] [¹or personal independence payment] is received by the non-resident parent or the member of the non-resident parent's household on behalf of the relevant other child,

only the net amount of the costs incurred in respect of the items listed in paragraph (1), after the deduction of the financial assistance or the amount of the allowance [¹or payment], constitutes special expenses for the purposes of paragraph 2(2) of Schedule 4B to the 1991 Act.

  (4)   For the purposes of paragraph (2)(a)–

  (a)   "patient" means a person (other than a person who is serving a sentence of imprisonment within the meaning of section 163 of the Powers of Criminal Courts (Sentencing) Act 2000 or of detention in a young offender institution within the meaning of section 96 of that Act or, in Scotland, a sentence of imprisonment or detention within the meaning of section 307 of the Criminal Procedure (Scotland) Act 1995) who is regarded as receiving free in-patient treatment within the meaning of regulation 2(4) and (5) of the Social Security (Hospital In-Patients) Regulations 2005; and

  (b)   where a person has ceased to be registered in a register as referred to in paragraph (2)(f), having regained their eyesight, that person is to be treated as though they were registered blind, for a period of 28 days after the day on which that person ceased to be registered in such a register.

Amendments
1.   Personal Independence Payment (Supplementary Provisions and Consequential Amendments) Regulations 2013 (SI 2013 No.388) reg 50 (April 8, 2013).
2.   Armed Forces and Reserve Forces Compensation Scheme (Consequential Provisions: Subordinate Legislation) Order (SI 2013 No.591) art 7 and Sch para 47 (April 8, 2013).

Definitions
"the 1991 Act": see reg 2.
"local authority": see reg 2.

General Note
See the general note to reg 11 of the Variation Regulations.

Prior debts

65.–(1)   Subject to the following paragraphs of this regulation and regulation 68 (thresholds), the repayment of debts to which paragraph (2) applies constitutes special expenses for the purposes of paragraph 2(2) of Schedule 4B to the 1991 Act where those debts were incurred–

(a)   before the non-resident parent became a non-resident parent in relation to the qualifying child; and

(b)   at the time when the non-resident parent and the person with care in relation to the child referred to in sub-paragraph (a) were a couple.

(2)   This paragraph applies to debts incurred–

(a)   for the joint benefit of the non-resident parent and the person with care;

(b)   for the benefit of the person with care where the non-resident parent remains legally liable to repay the whole or part of the debt;

(c)   for the benefit of any person who is not a child but who at the time the debt was incurred–

  (i)   was a child,

  (ii)   lived with the non-resident parent and the person with care, and

  (iii)   of whom the non-resident parent or the person with care is the parent, or both are the parents;

(d)   for the benefit of the qualifying child referred to in paragraph (1); or

(e)   for the benefit of any child, other than the qualifying child referred to in paragraph (1), who, at the time the debt was incurred–

  (i)   lived with the non-resident parent and the person with care, and

  (ii)   of whom the person with care is the parent.

(3)   Paragraph (1) does not apply to repayment of–

(a)   a debt which would otherwise fall within paragraph (1) where the non-resident parent has retained for the non-resident parent's own use and benefit the asset in connection with the purchase of which the debt was incurred;

(b)   a debt incurred for the purposes of any trade or business;

(c)   a gambling debt;

(d)   a fine imposed on the non-resident parent;

(e)   unpaid legal costs in respect of–

  (i)   separation from the person with care;

  (ii)   divorce from the person with care; or

  (iii)   dissolution of a civil partnership that had been formed with the person with care;

(f)   amounts due after use of a credit card;

(g)   a debt incurred by the non-resident parent to pay for any of the items listed in sub-paragraphs (c) to (f) and (j);

(h)   amounts payable by the non-resident parent under a mortgage or loan taken out on the security of any property, except where that mortgage or loan was taken out to facilitate the purchase of, or to pay for repairs or improvements to, any property which was, and continues to be, the home of the person with care and any qualifying child;

(i) amounts payable by the non-resident parent in respect of a policy of insurance, except where that policy of insurance was obtained or retained to discharge a mortgage or charge taken out to facilitate the purchase of, or to pay for repairs or improvements to, any property which was, and continues to be, the home of the person with care and the qualifying child;

(j) a bank overdraft except where the overdraft was at the time it was taken out agreed to be for a specified amount repayable over a specified period;

(k) a loan obtained by the non-resident parent other than a loan obtained from a qualifying lender or the non-resident parent's current or former employer; or

(l) any other debt which the Secretary of State is satisfied is reasonable to exclude.

(4) Except where the repayment is of an amount which is payable under a mortgage or loan or in respect of a policy of insurance which falls within the exception set out in sub-paragraph (h) or (i) of paragraph (3), repayment of a debt does not constitute expenses for the purposes of paragraph (1) where the Secretary of State is satisfied that the non-resident parent has taken responsibility for repayment of that debt as, or as part of, a financial settlement with the person with care or by virtue of a court order.

(5) Where an applicant has incurred a debt partly to repay a debt, repayment of which would have fallen within paragraph (1), the repayment of that part of the debt incurred which is referable to the debt repayment of which would have fallen within that paragraph, constitutes expenses for the purposes of paragraph 2(2) of Schedule 4B to the 1991 Act.

(6) In paragraph (3)(h) "repairs or improvements" means repairs that the Secretary of State considers are major repairs necessary to maintain the fabric of the home and any of the following measures–

(a) installation of a fixed bath, shower, wash basin or lavatory, and necessary associated plumbing;

(b) damp-proofing measures;

(c) provision or improvement of ventilation and natural light;

(d) provision of electric lighting and sockets;

(e) provision or improvement of drainage facilities;

(f) improvement of the structural condition of the home;

(g) improvements to the facilities for the storing, preparation and cooking of food;

(h) provision of heating, including central heating;

(i) provision of storage facilities for fuel and refuse;

(j) improvements to the insulation of the home; or

(k) other improvements which the Secretary of State considers reasonable in the circumstances.

Definitions

"the 1991 Act": see reg 2.

"couple": see reg 2.

"qualifying lender": see reg 2.

General Note

See the general note to reg 12 of the Variation Regulations, but note that there is no equivalent to reg 12(3)(l) of those Regulations.

Boarding school fees

66.–(1) Subject to the following paragraphs of this regulation and regulation 68 (thresholds), the maintenance element of boarding school fees, incurred or reasonably expected to be incurred by the non-resident parent, constitutes special expenses for the purposes of paragraph 2(2) of Schedule 4B to the 1991 Act.

(2) Where the Secretary of State considers that the maintenance element of the boarding school fees cannot be distinguished with reasonable certainty from the total fees, the Secretary of State may instead determine the amount of the maintenance element and any such determination is not to exceed 35% of the total fees.

(3)   Where–

(a)   the non-resident parent has, at the date on which the variation application is made, received, or at that date is in receipt of, financial assistance from any source in respect of the boarding school fees; or

(b)   the boarding school fees are being paid in part by the non-resident parent and in part by another person,

a portion of the expenses incurred by the non-resident parent in respect of the boarding school fees, calculated in accordance with paragraph (4), constitutes special expenses for the purposes of paragraph 2(2) of Schedule 4B to the 1991 Act.

(4)   For the purposes of paragraph (3), the portion in question is calculated as follows–

(a)   find the amount (A) that results from deducting from the amount of the boarding school fees the financial assistance, or the amount that another person is paying, as referred to in paragraph (3);

(b)   find the amount that bears the same proportion to A as the maintenance element of the fees referred to in paragraph (1) bears to the total fees referred to in that paragraph, and that amount is the portion in question.

(5)   No variation on this ground may reduce by more than 50% the income to which the Secretary of State would otherwise have had regard in the calculation of maintenance liability.

(6)   For the purposes of this regulation, "boarding school fees" means the fees payable in respect of attendance at a recognised educational establishment providing full-time education, which is not advanced education, for children under the age of 20 and where some or all of the pupils, including the qualifying child, are resident during term time.

(7)   For the purposes of paragraph (6)–

"recognised educational establishment" means an establishment recognised by the Secretary of State for the purposes of that paragraph as being, or as comparable to, a university, college or school;

"advanced education" means education for the purposes of–

(a)   a course in preparation for a degree, a diploma of higher education, a higher national diploma or a teaching qualification; or

(b)   any other course which is of a standard above ordinary national diploma including a national diploma or national certificate of Edexcel, a general certificate of education (advanced level) or Scottish national qualifications at higher or advanced higher level.

Definition

"the 1991 Act": see reg 2.

General Note

See the general note to reg 13 of the Variation Regulations.

Payments in respect of certain mortgages, loans or insurance policies

67.–(1)   Subject to regulation 68 (thresholds), the payments to which paragraph (2) applies constitute special expenses for the purposes of paragraph 2(2) of Schedule 4B to the 1991 Act.

(2)   This paragraph applies to payments, whether made to the mortgagee, lender, insurer or the person with care–

(a)   in respect of a mortgage or a loan from a qualifying lender where–

(i)   the mortgage or loan was taken out to facilitate the purchase of, or repairs or improvements to, a property ("the property") by a person other than the non-resident parent;

(ii)   the payments are not made under a debt incurred by the non-resident parent and do not arise out of any other legal liability of the non-resident parent for the period in respect of which the variation is applied for;

      (iii)   the property was the home of the applicant and the person with care when they were a couple and remains the home of the person with care and the qualifying child; and

      (iv)   the non-resident parent has no legal or equitable interest in and no charge or right to have a charge over the property; or

  (b)   of amounts payable in respect of a policy of insurance taken out for the discharge of a mortgage or loan referred to in sub-paragraph (a), including an endowment policy, except where the non-resident parent is entitled to any part of the proceeds on the maturity of that policy.

Definitions

"the 1991 Act": see reg 2.

"couple": see reg 2.

"qualifying lender": see reg 2.

General Note

See the general note to reg 14 of the Variation Regulations.

Thresholds

68.–(1) Subject to paragraphs (3) and (4), the costs or repayments referred to in regulations 63 (contact costs) and 65 to 67 (prior debts, boarding school fees and payments in respect of certain mortgages etc.) are to be special expenses for the purposes of paragraph 2(2) of Schedule 4B to the 1991 Act only where they are equal to or exceed the threshold amount of £10 per week.

(2)   Where the expenses fall within more than one description of expense referred to in paragraph (1), the threshold amount applies separately in respect of each description.

(3)   Subject to paragraph (4), where the Secretary of State considers any expenses referred to in this Chapter to be unreasonably high or to have been unreasonably incurred the Secretary of State may substitute such lower amount as the Secretary of State considers to be reasonable, including an amount which is below the threshold amount or a nil amount.

(4)   Any lower amount substituted by the Secretary of State under paragraph (3) in relation to contact costs under regulation 63 (contact costs) must not be so low as to make it impossible, in the Secretary of State's opinion, for contact between the non-resident parent and the qualifying child to be maintained at the frequency specified in any court order made in respect of the non-resident parent and that child where the non-resident parent is maintaining contact at that frequency.

General Note

The threshold is £10, except for illness or disability under reg 64. The Secretary of State may reduce an expense if it is unreasonably high or unreasonably incurred, but not to such an extent as to make contact impossible.

CHAPTER 3
GROUNDS FOR VARIATION: ADDITIONAL INCOME

Non-resident parent with unearned income

69.–(1) A case is a case for a variation for the purposes of paragraph 4(1) of Schedule 4B to the 1991 Act where the non-resident parent has unearned income equal to or exceeding £2,500 per annum.

(2)   For the purposes of this regulation unearned income is income of a kind that is chargeable to tax under–

  (a)   Part 3 of ITTOIA (property income);

  (b)   Part 4 of ITTOIA (savings and investment income); or

  (c)   Part 5 of ITTOIA (miscellaneous income).

(3)   Subject to paragraphs (5) and (6), the amount of the non-resident parent's unearned income is to be determined by reference to information provided by HMRC at the request of the Secretary of State in relation to the latest available tax year and, where

that information does not identify any income of a kind referred to in paragraph (2), the amount of the non-resident parent's unearned income is to be treated as nil.

(4)   For the purposes of paragraph (2), the information in relation to property income is to be taken after deduction of relief under section 118 of the Income Tax Act 2007 (carry forward against subsequent property business profits).

(5)   Where–

(a)   the latest available tax year is not the most recent tax year; or

(b)   the information provided by HMRC in relation to the latest available tax year does not include any information from a self-assessment return,

the Secretary of State may, if satisfied that there is sufficient evidence to do so, determine the amount of the non-resident parent's unearned income by reference to the most recent tax year; and any such determination must, as far as possible, be based on the information that would be required to be provided in a self-assessment return.

(6)   Where the Secretary of State is satisfied that, by reason of the non-resident parent no longer having any property or assets from which unearned income was derived in a past tax year and having no current source from which unearned income may be derived, the non-resident parent will have no unearned income for the current tax year, the amount of the non-resident parent's unearned income for the purposes of this regulation is to be treated as nil.

(7)   Where a variation is agreed to under this regulation, the non-resident parent is to be treated as having additional weekly income of the amount determined in accordance with paragraph (3) or (5) divided by 365 and multiplied by 7.

Definitions

"the 1991 Act": see reg 2.
"HMRC": see reg 2.
"ITTOIA": see reg 2.
"latest available tax year": see reg 4.
"tax year": see reg 2.

General Note

This regulation provides for a variation if the non-resident parent has unearned income of at least £2,500 a year. In applying this regulation, it is important to distinguish between the type of income and its amount. It must be of a type that is chargeable to tax under the provisions listed in para (2). If HMRC does not hold information to show that the parent has any income of that type, the parent has no unearned income (para (2)). The amount of the unearned income is fixed *by reference* to information provided by HMRC under para (3) or by other sufficient evidence under para (4). The regulation does not provide that the Secretary of State or the tribunal must accept the calculation of the amount by HMRC, allowing the Secretary of State or the tribunal to make a different assessment of the available evidence.

Regulation 71 covers the possibility of diversion of unearned income.

Non-resident parent on a flat rate or nil rate with gross weekly income

70.–(1)   A case is a case for a variation for the purposes of paragraph 4(1) of Schedule 4B to the 1991 Act where–

(a)   the non-resident parent's liability to pay child support maintenance under a maintenance calculation which is in force or has been applied for is or would be–

(i)   the nil rate by virtue of the non-resident parent being one of the persons referred to in paragraph (3); or

(ii)   the flat rate by virtue of the non-resident parent receiving a benefit, pension or allowance mentioned in regulation 44(1) (flat rate);

(b)   the Secretary of State is satisfied that the non-resident parent has an amount of income that would be taken into account in the maintenance calculation as gross weekly income if sub-paragraph (a) did not apply; and

(c)   that income is equal to or more than £100 per week.

(2)   Where a variation is agreed to under this regulation, the non-resident parent is treated as having additional income of the amount referred to in paragraph (1)(b).

(3)   The persons referred to are–

(a)   a child;

(b)   a prisoner;
(c)   a person receiving an allowance in respect of work-based training for young people, or in Scotland, Skillseekers training;
(d)   a person referred to in regulation 45(1)(e) (persons resident in a care home or independent hospital etc.).

Definitions
"the 1991 Act": see reg 2.
"the flat rate": see reg 2.
"gross weekly income": see reg 2.
"the nil rate": see reg 2.

General Note
This regulation allows for a variation where a person who is paying the flat or nil rate has gross weekly income of at least £100.

Diversion of income

71.–(1)   A case is a case for a variation for the purposes of paragraph 4(1) of Schedule 4B to the 1991 Act where–
(a)   the non-resident parent ("P") has the ability to control, whether directly or indirectly, the amount of income that–
(i)   P receives, or
(ii)   is taken into account as P's gross weekly income; and
(b)   the Secretary of State is satisfied that P has unreasonably reduced the amount of P's income which would otherwise fall to be taken into account as gross weekly income or as unearned income under regulation 69 by diverting it to other persons or for purposes other than the provision of such income for P.

(2)   Where a variation is agreed to under this regulation, the additional income to be taken into account is the whole of the amount by which the Secretary of State is satisfied that P has reduced the amount that would otherwise be taken into account as P's income.

Definitions
"the 1991 Act": see reg 2.
"gross weekly income": see reg 2.

General Note
See the general note to reg 19(4) of the Variation Regulations. Note that, unlike that provision, this regulation also applies to unearned income.

CHAPTER 4
EFFECT OF VARIATION ON THE MAINTENANCE CALCULATION

Effect on the maintenance calculation – special expenses

72.–(1)   Subject to paragraph (2) and regulation 74 (effect on maintenance calculation – general), where the variation agreed to is one falling within Chapter 2 (variation grounds: special expenses), effect is to be given to the variation in the maintenance calculation by deducting from the gross weekly income of the non-resident parent the weekly amount of the expenses referred to in Chapter 2.

(2)   Where the income which is taken into account in the maintenance calculation is the capped amount, then–
(a)   the weekly amount of the expenses is first to be deducted from the actual gross weekly income of the non-resident parent;
(b)   the amount by which the capped amount exceeds the figure calculated under sub-paragraph (a) is to be calculated; and
(c)   effect is to be given to the variation in the maintenance calculation by deducting from the capped amount the amount calculated under sub-paragraph (b).

Definitions
"capped amount": see reg 2.
"gross weekly income": see reg 2.

General Note

See the general note to reg 23 of the Variation Regulations. Note that unlike that provision, this regulation applies to gross income, not net income.

Effect on the maintenance calculation – additional income grounds

73.–(1)   Subject to paragraph (2) and regulation 74 (effect on maintenance calculation – general), where the variation agreed to is one falling within Chapter 3 (grounds for variation : additional income) effect is to be given to the variation by increasing the gross weekly income of the non-resident parent which would otherwise be taken into account by the weekly amount of the additional income except that, where the amount of gross weekly income calculated in this way would exceed the capped amount, the amount of the gross weekly income taken into account is to be the capped amount.

(2)   Where a variation is agreed to under this Chapter and the non-resident parent's liability would, apart from the variation, be the flat rate (or an amount equivalent to the flat rate), the amount of child support maintenance which the non-resident parent is liable to pay is a weekly amount calculated by adding an amount equivalent to the flat rate to the amount calculated by applying Schedule 1 to the 1991 Act to the additional income arising under the variation.

Definitions

"the 1991 Act": see reg 2.
"capped amount": see reg 2.
"the flat rate": see reg 2.
"gross weekly income": see reg 2.

General Note

See the general note to reg 25 of the Variation Regulations. Note that unlike that provision, this regulation applies to gross income, not net income.

Effect on maintenance calculation – general

74.–(1)   Subject to paragraph (5), where more than one variation is agreed to in respect of the same period, regulations 72 and 73 apply and the results are to be aggregated as appropriate.

(2)   Paragraph 7(2) to (7) of Schedule 1 to the 1991 Act (shared care) applies where the rate of child support maintenance is affected by a variation which is agreed to and paragraph 7(2) is to be read as if after the words "as calculated in accordance with the preceding paragraphs of this Part of this Schedule" there were inserted the words, ", Schedule 4B and regulations made under that Schedule".

(3)   Subject to paragraphs (4) and (5), where the non-resident parent shares the care of a qualifying child within the meaning in Part 1 of Schedule 1 to the 1991 Act, or where the care of such a child is shared with a local authority, the amount of child support maintenance that the non-resident parent is liable to pay to the person with care, calculated to take account of any variation, is to be reduced in accordance with the provisions of paragraph 7 of that Part or regulation 53 (care provided in part by a local authority), as the case may be.

(4)   If the application of paragraph (3) would decrease the weekly amount of child support maintenance (or the aggregate of all such amounts) payable by the non-resident parent to the person with care (or all of them) to less than a figure equivalent to the flat rate referred to in paragraph 4(1) of Schedule 1 to the 1991 Act (or in that sub-paragraph as modified by regulations under paragraph 10A of Schedule 1), the non-resident parent is instead liable to pay child support maintenance at a rate equivalent to that flat rate apportioned if appropriate as provided in paragraph 6 of Schedule 1 to that Act.

(5)   The effect of a variation is not to be applied for any period during which a circumstance referred to in regulation 57(1)(d) to (f) (rejection of an application following preliminary consideration) applies.

Definitions

"the 1991 Act": see reg 2.
"the flat rate": see reg 2.
"local authority": see reg 2.

Situations in which a variation previously agreed to may be taken into account in calculating maintenance liability

75.–(1)   This regulation applies where–

(a)   a variation that has been agreed to has ceased to have effect in relation to the weekly amount of the non-resident parent's liability for child support maintenance because–

  (i)   the non-resident parent has become liable to pay child support maintenance at the nil rate, or another rate which means that the variation cannot be taken into account; or

  (ii)   the decision as to the maintenance calculation has been replaced with a default maintenance decision under section 12(1)(b) of the 1991 Act; and

(b)   the non-resident parent has subsequently become liable to pay a rate of child support maintenance which can be adjusted to take account of the variation by virtue of a decision under section 16(1B) or 17 of the 1991 Act.

(2)   Where this regulation applies and the Secretary of State is satisfied, on the information or evidence available, that there has been no material change of circumstances relating to the variation since the date from which the variation ceased to have effect, the Secretary of State may, when making the decision referred to in paragraph (1)(b), take into account the effect of the variation upon the amount of liability for child support maintenance notwithstanding the fact that an application has not been made.

Definition
"the 1991 Act": see reg 2.
"the nil rate": see reg 2.

General Note
This regulation provides for a variation to be suspended when it cannot be applied, but to revive when it can be applied again following a revision or supersession without the need for a new application

---

PART 6

MEANING OF TERMS IN THE 1991 ACT

Meaning of "child" for the purposes of the 1991 Act

76.   The prescribed condition for the purposes of section 55(1) of the 1991 Act (that is the condition that must be satisfied if a person who has attained the age of 16 but not the age of 20 is to fall with the meaning of "child") is that the person is a qualifying young person as defined in section 142(2) of the Social Security Contributions and Benefits Act 1992.

Definition
"the 1991 Act": see reg 2.

General Note
Section 142 provides:

(1)   For the purposes of this Part of this Act a person is a child if he has not attained the age of 16.

(2)   In this Part of the Act "qualifying young person" means a person, other than a child, who–

(a)   has not attained such age (greater than 16) as is prescribed by regulations made by the Treasury, and

(b)   satisfies conditions so prescribed.

[¹Meaning of "relevant other child" for the purposes of the 1991 Act]

77.   For the purposes of paragraph 10C(2)(b) of Schedule 1 to the 1991 Act (which provides for other descriptions of relevant other children to be prescribed) "relevant other

child" includes a child, other than a qualifying child, in respect of whom the non-resident parent or the non-resident parent's partner

[¹(a)] would receive child benefit, but in respect of whom they do not do so, solely because the conditions set out in section 146 of the Social Security Contributions and Benefits Act 1992 (persons outside Great Britain) are not met [¹; or

(b) has made an election under section 13A(1) of the Social Security Administration Act 1992 (election not to receive child benefit) for payments of child benefit not to be made.]

Amendment

1.   Child Support (Miscellaneous Amendments) Regulations 2013 (SI 2013 No.1517) reg 8(7) and (8) (September 30, 2013).

General Note

This regulation ensures that a child counts as a relevant other child if the non-resident parent or that parent's partner does not receive child benefit in respect of that child only because the child is not in Great Britain.

Persons who are not persons with care

78.–(1)   The following categories of person are not persons with care for the purposes of the 1991 Act–

(a) a local authority;

(b) a person with whom a child who is looked after by a local authority is placed by that authority under the provisions of the Children Act 1989, except where that person is a parent of such a child and the local authority allow the child to live with that parent under section 22C(2) or 23(5) of that Act;

(c) in Scotland, a family or relative with whom a child is placed by a local authority under the provisions of section 26 of the Children (Scotland) Act 1995.

(2)   In paragraph (1)–

"a child who is looked after by a local authority" has the same meaning as in section 22 of the Children Act 1989 or section 17(6) of the Children (Scotland) Act 1995 as the case may be;

"family" means a family other than a family defined in section 93(1) of the Children (Scotland) Act 1995.

General Note

This regulation prevents a local authority or a person in whose care a child is placed by a local authority from being a person with care, unless that person is a parent of the child.

SCHEDULE
APPEALS: PROCEDURAL MATTERS
Regulation 33

Appeal against a decision which has been replaced or revised

1.–(1)   An appeal against a decision of the Secretary of State does not lapse where–

(a)   the decision is treated as replaced by a decision under section 11 or section 28F(5) of the 1991 Act; or

(b)   is revised under section 16 of that Act before the appeal is determined,

and the decision as replaced or revised is not more advantageous to the appellant than the decision before it was replaced or revised.

(2)   Where sub-paragraph (1) applies, the appeal must be treated as though it had been brought against the decision as replaced or revised.

(3)   The appellant has a period of one month from the date of notification of the decision as replaced or revised to make further representations as to the appeal.

(4)   Subject to sub-paragraph (5), after the expiration of the period specified in sub-paragraph (3), or within that period if the appellant consents in writing, the appeal to the First-tier Tribunal must proceed.

(5)   The appeal shall lapse where, in the light of the further representations from the appellant, the decision as replaced or revised as referred to in sub-paragraph (1), is revised, and the new decision is more advantageous to the appellant than the decision before it was replaced or revised as referred to in sub-paragraph (1).

Late appeals
2. [¹ ...]

Amendment

1. Social Security, Child Support, Vaccine Damage and Other Payments (Decisions and Appeals) (Amendment) Regulations 2013 (SI 2013 No.2380) reg 6(4) (October 28, 2013, subject to the transitional and savings provisions in reg 8 of SI 2013 No.2380). For those covered by the transitional and savings provisions para 2 reads:

2.–(1)   Where a dispute arises as to whether an appeal was brought within the time specified under the Tribunal Procedure Rules the dispute shall be referred to, and determined by, the First-tier Tribunal.

(2)   The Secretary of State may treat a late appeal as made in time in accordance with the Tribunal Procedure Rules if the Secretary of State is satisfied that it is in the interests of justice to do so.

(3)   For the purposes of sub-paragraph (2) it is not in the interests of justice to treat the appeal as made in time unless the Secretary of State is satisfied that–

(a)   the special circumstances specified in sub-paragraph (4) are relevant; or

(b)   some other special circumstances exist which are wholly exceptional and relevant,

and as a result of those special circumstances, it was not practicable for the appeal to be made within the time limit specified in the Tribunal Procedure Rules.

(4)   For the purposes of sub-paragraph (3)(a), the special circumstances are that–

(a)   the appellant or a partner or dependant of the appellant has died or suffered serious illness;

(b)   the appellant is not resident in the United Kingdom; or

(c)   normal postal services were disrupted.

(5)   In determining whether it is in the interests of justice to treat the appeal as made in time regard must be had to the principle that the greater the amount of time that has elapsed between the expiration of the time limit under the Tribunal Procedure Rules and the submission of the notice of appeal, the more compelling should be the special circumstances.

(6)   In determining whether it is in the interests of justice to treat the appeal as made in time no account shall be taken of the following–

(a)   that the applicant or any person acting for him was unaware of or misunderstood the law applicable to his case (including ignorance or misunderstanding of the time limits imposed by the Tribunal Procedure Rules); or

(b)   that the Upper Tribunal or a court has taken a different view of the law from that previously understood and applied.

Notice of Appeal
3. [¹ ...]

Amendment

1. Social Security, Child Support, Vaccine Damage and Other Payments (Decisions and Appeals) (Amendment) Regulations 2013 (SI 2013 No.2380) reg 6(4) (October 28, 2013, subject to the transitional and savings provisions in reg 8 of SI 2013 No.2380). For those covered by the transitional and savings provisions para 3 reads:

3.–(1)   A notice of appeal made in accordance with the Tribunal Procedure Rules and on a form approved by the Secretary of State or in such other form as the Secretary of State accepts, is to be sent or delivered to an appropriate office of the Secretary of State.

(2)   Except where sub-paragraph (3) applies, where a form does not contain the information required under the Tribunal Procedure Rules the form may be returned by the Secretary of State to the sender for completion in accordance with the Tribunal Procedure Rules.

(3)   Where it appears that the form, although not completed in accordance with the instructions on it, includes sufficient information to enable the appeal to proceed, the Secretary of State may treat the form as satisfying the requirements of the Tribunal Procedure Rules.

(4)   Where a notice of appeal is made in writing otherwise than on the approved form ("the letter"), and it appears that the letter includes sufficient information to enable the appeal to proceed, the Secretary of State may treat the letter as satisfying the requirements of the Tribunal Procedure Rules.

(5)   Where the letter does not include sufficient information to enable the appeal to proceed, the Secretary of State may request further information in writing ("further particulars") from the person who wrote the letter.

(6)   Where a person to whom a form is returned duly completes and returns the form, if the form is received by the Secretary of State within–

(a)   14 days after the date on which the form was returned by the Secretary of State, the time for making the appeal shall be extended by 14 days following the date on which the form was returned;

(b)   such longer period as the Secretary of State may direct, the time for making the appeal shall be extended by a period equal to that longer period directed by the Secretary of State.

(7)   Where a person from whom further particulars are requested duly sends the further particulars, if the particulars are received by the Secretary of State within–

(a)   14 days after the date on which the Secretary of State's request was made, the time for making the appeal shall be extended by 14 days following the date of the request;

(b)   such longer period as the Secretary of State may direct, the time for making the appeal shall be extended by a period equal to that longer period directed by the Secretary of State.

(8)   Where a person to whom a form is returned or from whom further particulars are requested does not complete and return the form or send further particulars within the period of time specified in sub-paragraph (6) or (7)–

(a)   the Secretary of State must forward a copy of the form, or as the case may be, the letter, together with any other relevant documents or evidence to the First-tier Tribunal, and

(b)   the First-tier Tribunal shall determine whether the form or the letter satisfies the requirements of the Tribunal Procedure Rules.

(9)   Where–

(a)   a form is duly completed and returned or further particulars are sent after the expiry of the period of time allowed in accordance with sub-paragraph (6) or (7), and

(b)   no decision has been made under sub-paragraph (8) at the time the form or the further particulars are received by the Secretary of State, that form or further particulars must also be forwarded to the First-tier Tribunal which must take into account any further information or evidence set out in the form or further particulars.

(10)   The Secretary of State may discontinue action on an appeal where the notice of appeal has not been forwarded to the First-tier Tribunal and the appellant or an authorised representative of the appellant has given notice that he does not wish the appeal to continue.

Death of a party to an appeal

4. [¹...]

Amendment

1.   Social Security, Child Support, Vaccine Damage and Other Payments (Decisions and Appeals) (Amendment) Regulations 2013 (SI 2013 No.2380) reg 6(4) (October 28, 2013, subject to the transitional and savings provisions in reg 8 of SI 2013 No.2380). For those covered by the transitional and savings provisions para 4 reads:

4.–(1)   In any proceedings, on the death of a party to those proceedings, the Secretary of State may appoint a person to proceed with the appeal in the place of such deceased party.

(2)   A grant of probate, confirmation or letters of administration in respect of the estate of the deceased party, whenever taken out, shall have no effect on an appointment made under sub-paragraph (1).

(3)   Where a person appointed under sub-paragraph (1) has, prior to the date of such appointment, taken any action in relation to the appeal on behalf of the deceased party, the appointment shall be treated as having effect on the day immediately prior to the first day on which such action was taken.

Definitions

"the 1991 Act": see reg 2.

"partner": see reg 2.

"party": see reg 2.

"Tribunal Procedure Rules": see reg 2.

General Note

Para 1

This paragraph deals with the effect on an appeal of a subsequent decision. If it is more favourable to the appellant than the decision under appeal, the appeal lapses, although the appellant may appeal against the new decision. Otherwise, the appeal continues against the new decision.

Para 2

This paragraph deals with late appeals. It is for the First-tier Tribunal to decide whether an appeal is late in the event of a dispute. The Secretary of State has power to admit a late appeal, provided that it is in the interests of justice to do so, subject to the specific provisions.

Para 3

This paragraph provides for an appeal to be lodged with the Secretary of State rather than the First-tier Tribunal. It must be read in conjunction with rule 23 of the Tribunal Procedure (First-tier Tribunal) (Social Entitlement Chamber) Rules 2008. Subparagraph (10) allows for an appeal to be withdrawn.

Para 4

The Secretary of State may appoint a person to act in place of a party who has died. The appointment is retrospective in effect and is not affected by the existence of an executor or administrator.

The Child Support (Meaning of Child and New Calculation Rules) (Consequential and Miscellaneous Amendment) Regulations 2012
(SI 2012 No.2785)

PART 1
General

Citation, commencement and interpretation

1.–(1) These Regulations may be cited as the Child Support (Meaning of Child and New Calculation Rules) (Consequential and Miscellaneous Amendment) Regulations 2012.

(2) This regulation and regulation 11 come into force on 10th December 2012.

(3) Regulations 2 and 3 come into force on the day on which section 42 of the 2008 Act (meaning of "child") comes into force.

(4) Subject to paragraph (5), regulations 4 to 10 and 12 come into force in relation to a particular case on the day on which paragraph 2 of Schedule 4 to the 2008 Act (calculation by reference to gross weekly income) comes into force in relation to that type of case.

(5) Regulations 4(3) to (6) and 12 come into force in relation to an arrears-only case on 10th December 2012, subject to the saving in regulation 11(1).

(6) In these Regulations–

"2008 Act" means the Child Maintenance and Other Payments Act 2008.

[¹"arrears of child support maintenance" means any payment of child support maintenance–

    (a) which has become due in relation to a maintenance assessment, or a maintenance calculation made under 2003 scheme rules, and not paid; and

    (b) in respect of which the Secretary of State is arranging collection under section 29 of the 1991 Act;]

"arrears-only case" means a case in which–

    (a) there are arrears of child support maintenance; and

    (b) there is–

        (i) no maintenance assessment, or maintenance calculation made under 2003 scheme rules, still in force; and

        (ii) no application for a maintenance assessment, or a maintenance calculation falling to be made under 2003 scheme rules, still to be determined;

"the Collection and Enforcement Regulations" means the Child Support (Collection and Enforcement) Regulations 1992.

(7) For the purposes of this regulation, a maintenance calculation is made (or will fall to be made) under 2003 scheme rules if the amount of the periodical payments required to be paid in accordance with it is (or will be) determined otherwise than in accordance with Part 1 of Schedule 1 to the Child Support Act 1991 as amended by Schedule 4 to the Child Maintenance and Other Payments Act 2008.

Amendment

1.   Child Support (Miscellaneous Amendments) Regulations 2013 (SI 2013 No. 1517) reg 9 (September 30, 2013).

PART 4
Savings and Transitional Provision

Saving where arrears-only case

11.–(1) Regulations 8, 10, 11 and 20 of the Collection and Enforcement Regulations continue to apply in relation to an arrears-only case, as they were in force immediately before the amendments made by regulation 4(3) to (6) come into force, until notice is given to the non-resident parent by the Secretary of State that the provisions of the Regulations as amended by regulation 4(3) to (6) apply to that case.

(2)   Any notice given under paragraph (1) must be in writing and sent by post to the non-resident parent's last known or notified address and will be treated as having been given on the second day following the day on which it is posted.

(3)   For the purposes of this regulation any reference to a non-resident parent includes reference to an absent parent.

Transitional provision

12.–(1)   Where, in any case, a deduction from earnings order was made before the date on which the Collection and Enforcement Regulations as amended by regulation 4(3) to (6) apply in relation to that case, this regulation shall apply in respect of that order.

(2) Where the deduction from earnings order still has effect immediately before regulation 4(3) to (6) comes into force in relation to that case–

(a)   the order continues to take effect for the purposes of any deductions which are required to be made under the order until it is discharged or lapses;

(b)   the Collection and Enforcement Regulations, as they were in force before the amendments made by regulation 4(3) to (6) came into force, continue to apply in relation to the order until it is discharged or lapses; and

(c)   the order is to be treated as discharged, if it has not otherwise lapsed or been discharged, on the date that the first deduction from earnings order made under the Collection and Enforcement Regulations as amended by regulation 4(3) to (6) takes effect.

Child Maintenance and Other Payments Act 2008 (Commencement No.10 and Transitional Provisions) Order 2012

(SI 2012 No.3042)

Citation and interpretation

1.–(1)   This Order may be cited as the Child Maintenance and Other Payments Act 2008 (Commencement No. 10 and Transitional Provisions) Order 2012.

(2)   In this Order–

"1991 Act" means the Child Support Act 1991;

"2000 Act" means the Child Support, Pensions and Social Security Act 2000;

"2008 Act" means the Child Maintenance and Other Payments Act 2008;

"2012 Regulations" means the Child Support Maintenance Calculation Regulations 2012;

"new calculation rules" means Part 1 of Schedule 1 to the 1991 Act as amended by the provisions specified in article 2.

(3)   In this Order, subject to paragraph (5)–

"maintenance calculation", "non-resident parent", "person with care" and "qualifying child" have the meanings given in the 1991 Act;

"absent parent" and "maintenance assessment" have the meanings given in the 1991 Act before its amendment by the 2000 Act.

(4)   In this Order, a reference to an existing case is to a case in which there is–

(a)   a maintenance assessment in force;

(b)   a maintenance calculation, made otherwise than in accordance with the new calculation rules, in force;

(c)   an application for a maintenance assessment which has been made but not determined; or

(d)   an application for a maintenance calculation, which falls to be made otherwise than in accordance with the new calculation rules, which has been made but not determined.

(5)   In this Order–

(a)   a reference to a non-resident parent includes reference to a person who is–

(i)   alleged to be the non-resident parent for the purposes of an application for child support maintenance under the 1991 Act; or

(ii)   treated as the non-resident parent for the purposes of the 1991 Act; and

(b)   a reference to an absent parent includes reference to a person who is–

(i)   alleged to be the absent parent for the purposes of an application for child support maintenance under the 1991 Act; or

(ii)   treated as the absent parent for the purposes of the 1991 Act.

Appointed day for the coming into effect of the new calculation rules

2.   The following provisions of the 2008 Act come into force, in so far as those provisions are not already in force, on 10th December 2012 for the purposes of those types of cases falling within article 3–

(a)   section 16 (changes to the calculation of maintenance) and paragraph 1 of Schedule 4 (introductory), so far as relating to the paragraphs referred to in paragraph (b);

(b)   paragraphs 2, 3 and 5 to 10 of Schedule 4 (changes to the calculation of maintenance);

(c)   sections 17 (power to regulate supersession) and 18 (determination of applications for a variation);

(d)   section 57(1) and paragraph 1(1) of Schedule 7 (minor and consequential amendments), so far as relating to the paragraph referred to in paragraph (e);

(e)   paragraph 1(2) and (29) of Schedule 7;

(f)   section 58 (repeals), so far as relating to the entries referred to in paragraph (g); and

(g)   in Schedule 8 (repeals), the entries relating to–

(i)   Schedule 1 (maintenance calculations) to the 1991 Act; and

(ii)   Schedule 24 (social security, child support and tax credits) to the Civil Partnership Act 2004.

Cases to which the new calculation rules apply

3.–(1)   The types of cases falling within this article, for the purposes of article 2, are those cases satisfying any of paragraphs (2) to (4).

(2)   A case satisfies this paragraph where–

(a)   an application under section 4 or 7 of the 1991 Act is made to the Secretary of State on or after 10th December 2012;

(b)   that application is made in respect of at least four qualifying children with the same person with care and the same non-resident parent; and

(c)   subject to paragraph (5), there is no existing case which has both the same person with care and the same non-resident parent referred to in sub-paragraph (b).

(3)   A case satisfies this paragraph where it is an existing case and–

(a)   the non-resident parent in a case falling within paragraph (2) is also the non-resident parent or absent parent in relation to the existing case; and

(b)   the person with care in relation to the existing case is not the person with care in relation to the case falling within paragraph (2).

(4)   A case satisfies this paragraph where it is an existing case and–

(a)   the non-resident parent or absent parent ("A") is a partner of a non-resident parent in a case falling within paragraph (2) ("B"); and

(b)   A or B is in receipt of a prescribed benefit.

(5)   Where–

(a)   the applicant in relation to an existing case makes a request to the Secretary of State under section 4(5) or 7(6) of the 1991 Act to cease acting; and

(b)   a further application is made under section 4 or 7 of the 1991 Act in relation to the same qualifying child, person with care and non-resident parent on or after 10th December 2012, but before the expiry of 13 weeks from the date of cessation of action by the Secretary of State,

the case is to be treated as an existing case (and so is not a case that satisfies paragraph (2)).

(6)   For the purposes of paragraphs (2)(a) and (5)(b), the date an application is made is–

(a)   where made by telephone, the date it is made; and

(b)   where made by post, the date of receipt by the Secretary of State.

(7)   For the purposes of paragraph (4)–

"partner" has the meaning given in paragraph 10C(4) (references to various terms) of Schedule 1 to the 1991 Act as amended by the 2000 Act;

"prescribed benefit" means a benefit prescribed, or treated as prescribed, for the purposes of paragraph 4(1)(c) (flat rate) of Schedule 1 to the 1991 Act as amended by the 2000 Act.

(8)   For the purposes of paragraph (5)(b), the date of cessation of action by the Secretary of State is–

(a)   where there is a maintenance assessment or maintenance calculation in force, the date on which the liability under that assessment or calculation ends as a result of the request to cease acting;

(b)   where there is an application still to be determined, the date notified to the person with care as the date on which the Secretary of State has ceased acting.

Appointed day for other 2008 Act provisions

4.   [*Omitted.*]

Transitional provision for existing cases

5.   Where a case falls within article 3(3) or (4), the provisions of the 1991 Act continue to apply–

(a)   as they were in force immediately before the coming into force of the provisions in article 2 in relation to that case;

(b)   until the maintenance calculation made in response to the application referred to in article 3(2)(a) takes effect.

Transitional provision when making the maintenance calculation

6. [¹...]

Amendment

1.   Child Maintenance and Other Payments Act 2008 (Commencement No.11 and Transitional Provisions) Order 2013 (SI 2013 No.1860) art 6 (July 29, 2013).

Child Maintenance and Other Payments Act 2008 (Commencement No.11 and Transitional Provisions) Order 2013

(SI 2013 No.1860)

Citation and interpretation

1.–(1) This Order may be cited as the Child Maintenance and Other Payments Act 2008 (Commencement No. 11 and Transitional Provisions) Order 2013.

(2) In this Order–

"1991 Act" means the Child Support Act 1991;

"2000 Act" means the Child Support, Pensions and Social Security Act 2000;

"2008 Act" means the Child Maintenance and Other Payments Act 2008;

"2012 Regulations" means the Child Support Maintenance Calculation Regulations 2012;

"new calculation rules" means Part 1 of Schedule 1 to the 1991 Act as amended by the provisions specified in article 2.

(3) In this Order, subject to paragraph (5)–

"maintenance calculation", "non-resident parent", "person with care" and "qualifying child" have the meanings given in the 1991 Act;

"absent parent" and "maintenance assessment" have the meanings given in the 1991 Act before its amendment by the 2000 Act.

(4) In this Order, a reference to an existing case is to a case in which there is–

(a) a maintenance assessment in force;

(b) a maintenance calculation, made otherwise than in accordance with the new calculation rules, in force;

(c) an application for a maintenance assessment which has been made but not determined; or

(d) an application for a maintenance calculation, which falls to be made otherwise than in accordance with the new calculation rules, which has been made but not determined.

(5) In this Order–

(a) a reference to a non-resident parent includes reference to a person who is–

    (i) alleged to be the non-resident parent for the purposes of an application for child support maintenance under the 1991 Act, or

    (ii) treated as the non-resident parent for the purposes of the 1991 Act; and

(b) a reference to an absent parent includes reference to a person who is–

    (i) alleged to be the absent parent for the purposes of an application for child support maintenance under the 1991 Act, or

    (ii) as the absent parent for the purposes of the 1991 Act.

Appointed day for the coming into effect of the new calculation rules

2. The following provisions of the 2008 Act come into force, in so far as those provisions are not already in force, on 29th July 2013 for the purposes of those types of cases falling within article 3–

(a) section 16 (changes to the calculation of maintenance) and paragraph 1 of Schedule 4 (introductory), so far as relating to the paragraphs referred to in paragraph (b);

(b) paragraphs 2, 3 and 5 to 10 of Schedule 4 (changes to the calculation of maintenance);

(c) sections 17 (power to regulate supersession) and 18 (determination of applications for a variation);

(d) section 57(1) and paragraph 1(1) of Schedule 7 (minor and consequential amendments), so far as relating to the paragraph referred to in paragraph (e);

(e) paragraph 1(2) and (29) of Schedule 7;

(f) section 58 (repeals), so far as relating to the entries referred to in paragraph (g); and

(g) in Schedule 8 (repeals), the entries relating to–

    (i) Schedule 1 (maintenance calculations) to the 1991 Act, and

(ii)   Schedule 24 (social security, child support and tax credits) to the Civil Partnership Act 2004.

Cases to which the new calculation rules apply

3.–(1)   The types of cases falling within this article, for the purposes of article 2, are those cases satisfying any of paragraphs (2) to (4).

(2)   A case satisfies this paragraph where–

(a)   an application under section 4 or 7 of the 1991 Act is made to the Secretary of State on or after 29th July 2013;

(b)   that application is made in respect of two or three qualifying children with the same person with care and the same non-resident parent; and

(c)   subject to paragraph (5), there is no existing case which has both the same person with care and the same non-resident parent referred to in sub-paragraph (b).

(3)   A case satisfies this paragraph where it is an existing case and–

(a)   the non-resident parent in a case falling within paragraph (2) is also the non-resident parent or absent parent in relation to the existing case; and

(b)   the person with care in relation to the existing case is not the person with care in relation to the case falling within paragraph (2).

(4)   A case satisfies this paragraph where it is an existing case and–

(a)   the non-resident parent or absent parent ("A") is a partner of a non-resident parent in a case falling within paragraph (2) ("B"); and

(b)   A or B is in receipt of a prescribed benefit.

(5)   Where–

(a)   the applicant in relation to an existing case makes a request to the Secretary of State under section 4(5) or 7(6) of the 1991 Act to cease acting; and

(b)   a further application is made under section 4 or 7 of the 1991 Act in relation to the same qualifying child, person with care and non-resident parent on or after 29th July 2013, but before the expiry of 13 weeks from the date of cessation of action by the Secretary of State,

the case is to be treated as an existing case (and so is not a case that satisfies paragraph (2)).

(6)   For the purposes of paragraphs (2)(a) and (5)(b), the date an application is made is–

(a)   where made by telephone, the date it is made; and

(b)   where made by post, the date of receipt by the Secretary of State.

(7)   For the purposes of paragraph (4)–

"partner" has the meaning given in paragraph 10C(4) (references to various terms) of Schedule 1 to the 1991 Act as amended by the 2000 Act;

"prescribed benefit" means a benefit prescribed, or treated as prescribed, for the purposes of paragraph 4(1)(c) (flat rate) of Schedule 1 to the 1991 Act as amended by the 2000 Act.

(8)   For the purposes of paragraph (5)(b), the date of cessation of action by the Secretary of State is–

(a)   where there is a maintenance assessment or maintenance calculation in force, the date on which the liability under that assessment or calculation ends as a result of the request to cease acting; and

(b)   where there is an application still to be determined, the date notified to the person with care as the date on which the Secretary of State has ceased acting.

Appointed day for coming into force of a repeal within the 2008 Act

4.   [*Omitted.*]

Transitional provision for existing cases

5.   Where a case falls within article 3(3) or (4), the provisions of the 1991 Act continue to apply–

(a) as they were in force immediately before the coming into force of the provisions in article 2 in relation to that case;

(b) until the maintenance calculation made in response to the application referred to in article 3(2)(a) takes effect.

Amendment of the Child Maintenance and Other Payments Act 2008 (Commencement No.10 and Transitional Provisions) Order 2012

6. [*Omitted.*]

Transitional provision when making the maintenance calculation

7. For the period beginning on 29th July 2013 and ending on the date on which the new calculation rules come into force for all purposes–

(a) regulation 34(2) of the 2012 Regulations (the general rule for determining gross weekly income) shall be read as if after paragraph (b) there were inserted–
"or

(c) the Secretary of State is unable, for whatever reason, to request or obtain the required information from HMRC.";

(b) regulation 42(1)(a) of the 2012 Regulations (estimate of current income where insufficient information available) shall be read as if after "34(2)(b) (historic income nil or not available)" there were inserted "or (c) (Secretary of State unable to request or obtain information from HMRC).";

(c) regulation 69(5) of the 2012 Regulations (non-resident parent with unearned income) shall be read as if after paragraph (b) there were inserted–
"or

(c) the Secretary of State is unable, for whatever reason, to request or obtain the information from HMRC.".

Part IV

PROCEDURAL RULES

Tribunals, Courts and Enforcment Act 2007
(2007 c15)

PART 1
Tribunals and Inquiries
Chapter 2
Establishment

The First-tier Tribunal and the Upper Tribunal

3.–(1)   There is to be a tribunal, known as the First-tier Tribunal, for the purpose of exercising the functions conferred on it under or by virtue of this Act or any other Act.

(2)   There is to be a tribunal, known as the Upper Tribunal, for the purpose of exercising the functions conferred on it under or by virtue of this Act or any other Act.

(3)   Each of the First-tier Tribunal, and the Upper Tribunal, is to consist of its judges and other members.

(4)   The Senior President of Tribunals is to preside over both of the First-tier Tribunal and the Upper Tribunal.

(5)   The Upper Tribunal is to be a superior court of record.

Commencement
Tribunals, Courts and Enforcement Act 2007 (Commencement No.6 and Transitional Provisions) Order 2008 (SI 2008 No.2696) art 5 (November 3, 2008).

General Note
Appeals against decisions of the Secretary of State or the Child Maintenance and Enforcement Commission were transferred to the Social Entitlement Chamber of the First-tier Tribunal with effect from 3 November 2008 by art 3(1) of, and Sch 1 to, the Transfer of Tribunal Functions Order 2008.

Appeals against decisions of the First-tier Tribunal were transferred to the Administrative Appeals Chamber of the Upper Tribunal with effect from 3 November 2008 by art 3(2) of, and Sch 1 to, the Transfer of Tribunal Functions Order 2008.

Review of decisions and appeals

Review of decision of First-tier Tribunal

9.–(1)   The First-tier Tribunal may review a decision made by it on a matter in a case, other than a decision that is an excluded decision for the purposes of section 11(1) (but see subsection (9)).

(2)   The First-tier Tribunal's power under subsection (1) in relation to a decision is exercisable–

(a)   of its own initiative, or

(b)   on application by a person who for the purposes of section 11(2) has a right of appeal in respect of the decision.

(3)   Tribunal Procedure Rules may–

(a)   provide that the First-tier Tribunal may not under subsection (1) review (whether of its own initiative or on application under subsection (2)(b)) a decision of a description specified for the purposes of this paragraph in Tribunal Procedure Rules;

(b)   provide that the First-tier Tribunal's power under subsection (1) to review a decision of a description specified for the purposes of this paragraph in Tribunal Procedure Rules is exercisable only of the tribunal's own initiative;

(c)   provide that an application under subsection (2)(b) that is of a description specified for the purposes of this paragraph in Tribunal Procedure Rules may be made only on grounds specified for the purposes of this paragraph in Tribunal Procedure Rules;

(d)   provide, in relation to a decision of a description specified for the purposes of this paragraph in Tribunal Procedure Rules, that the First-tier Tribunal's power under subsection (1) to review the decision of its own initiative is exercisable only on grounds specified for the purposes of this paragraph in Tribunal Procedure Rules.

(4)   Where the First-tier Tribunal has under subsection (1) reviewed a decision, the First-tier Tribunal may in the light of the review do any of the following–

(a)   correct accidental errors in the decision or in a record of the decision;

(b)   amend reasons given for the decision;

(c)   set the decision aside.

(5)   Where under subsection (4)(c) the First-tier Tribunal sets a decision aside, the First-tier Tribunal must either–

(a)   re-decide the matter concerned, or

(b)   refer that matter to the Upper Tribunal.

(6)   Where a matter is referred to the Upper Tribunal under subsection (5)(b), the Upper Tribunal must re-decide the matter.

(7)   Where the Upper Tribunal is under subsection (6) re-deciding a matter, it may make any decision which the First-tier Tribunal could make if the First-tier Tribunal were re-deciding the matter.

(8)   Where a tribunal is acting under subsection (5)(a) or (6), it may make such findings of fact as it considers appropriate.

(9)   This section has effect as if a decision under subsection (4)(c) to set aside an earlier decision were not an excluded decision for the purposes of section 11(1), but the

First-tier Tribunal's only power in the light of a review under subsection (1) of a decision under subsection (4)(c) is the power under subsection (4)(a).

(10)   A decision of the First-tier Tribunal may not be reviewed under subsection (1) more than once, and once the First-tier Tribunal has decided that an earlier decision should not be reviewed under subsection (1) it may not then decide to review that earlier decision under that subsection.

(11)   Where under this section a decision is set aside and the matter concerned is then re-decided, the decision set aside and the decision made in re-deciding the matter are for the purposes of subsection (10) to be taken to be different decisions.

Commencement

s9(3): Tribunals, Courts and Enforcement Act 2007 (Commencement No.1) Order 2007 (SI 2007 No.2709) art 2(a) (September 19, 2007).

s9(1), (2) and (4)-(11): Tribunals, Courts and Enforcement Act 2007 (Commencement No.6 and Transitional Provisions) Order 2008 (SI 2008 No.2696) art 5 (November 3, 2008).

General Note

See the commentary to r40 TP(FT) Rules on p863.

Subsection (4)(b)

In *JS v SSWP (DLA)* [2013] UKUT 100 (AAC), a three-judge panel of the Upper Tribunal gave detailed guidance on the scope and application of the power to amend reasons on review. The judge dealing with the review should identify the error of law that justifies the review. If the judge considers that it might be appropriate to amend the reasons, the parties should be given the chance to make representations. The presiding judge should be asked to provide reasons and the judge dealing with the review should then decide if they would constitute amendments for the purpose of the review power. It is only appropriate to amend reasons if it would not be appropriate to set the decision aside. The power must not be used to subvert the appeal process. There must be some objective guarantee that the changes are not merely justifications. A presiding judge who is dealing with a review should approach it in the same spirit. On appeal, the Upper Tribunal has jurisdiction to decide whether the changes to the reasons were amendments for that purpose.

Review of decision of Upper Tribunal

10.–(1)   The Upper Tribunal may review a decision made by it on a matter in a case, other than a decision that is an excluded decision for the purposes of section 13(1) (but see subsection (7)).

(2)   The Upper Tribunal's power under subsection (1) in relation to a decision is exercisable–

(a)   of its own initiative, or

(b)   on application by a person who for the purposes of section 13(2) has a right of appeal in respect of the decision.

(3)   Tribunal Procedure Rules may–

(a)   provide that the Upper Tribunal may not under subsection (1) review (whether of its own initiative or on application under subsection (2)(b)) a decision of a description specified for the purposes of this paragraph in Tribunal Procedure Rules;

(b)   provide that the Upper Tribunal's power under subsection (1) to review a decision of a description specified for the purposes of this paragraph in Tribunal Procedure Rules is exercisable only of the tribunal's own initiative;

(c)   provide that an application under subsection (2)(b) that is of a description specified for the purposes of this paragraph in Tribunal Procedure Rules may be made only on grounds specified for the purposes of this paragraph in Tribunal Procedure Rules;

(d)   provide, in relation to a decision of a description specified for the purposes of this paragraph in Tribunal Procedure Rules, that the Upper Tribunal's power under subsection (1) to review the decision of its own initiative is exercisable only on grounds specified for the purposes of this paragraph in Tribunal Procedure Rules.

(4)   Where the Upper Tribunal has under subsection (1) reviewed a decision, the Upper Tribunal may in the light of the review do any of the following–

(a)   correct accidental errors in the decision or in a record of the decision;

(b)   amend reasons given for the decision;

(c)   set the decision aside.

(5)   Where under subsection (4)(c) the Upper Tribunal sets a decision aside, the Upper Tribunal must re-decide the matter concerned.

(6)   Where the Upper Tribunal is acting under subsection (5), it may make such findings of fact as it considers appropriate.

(7)   This section has effect as if a decision under subsection (4)(c) to set aside an earlier decision were not an excluded decision for the purposes of section 13(1), but the Upper Tribunal's only power in the light of a review under subsection (1) of a decision under subsection (4)(c) is the power under subsection (4)(a).

(8)   A decision of the Upper Tribunal may not be reviewed under subsection (1) more than once, and once the Upper Tribunal has decided that an earlier decision should not be reviewed under subsection (1) it may not then decide to review that earlier decision under that subsection.

(9)   Where under this section a decision is set aside and the matter concerned is then re-decided, the decision set aside and the decision made in re-deciding the matter are for the purposes of subsection (8) to be taken to be different decisions.

Commencement

s10(3): Tribunals, Courts and Enforcement Act 2007 (Commencement No.1) Order 2007 (SI 2007 No.2709) art 2(a) (September 19, 2007).

s10(1), (2) and (4)-(9): Tribunals, Courts and Enforcement Act 2007 (Commencement No.6 and Transitional Provisions) Order 2008 (SI 2008 No.2696) art 5(a) (November 3, 2008).

General Note

See the commentary to r46 FT(UT) Rules on p893.

Right to appeal to Upper Tribunal

11.–(1)   For the purposes of subsection (2), the reference to a right of appeal is to a right to appeal to the Upper Tribunal on any point of law arising from a decision made by the First-tier Tribunal other than an excluded decision.

(2)   Any party to a case has a right of appeal, subject to subsection (8).

(3)   That right may be exercised only with permission (or, in Northern Ireland, leave).

(4)   Permission (or leave) may be given by–

(a)   the First-tier Tribunal, or

(b)   the Upper Tribunal,

on an application by the party.

(5)   For the purposes of subsection (1), an "excluded decision" is–

(a)-(c) [Omitted]

(d)   a decision of the First-tier Tribunal under section 9–

    (i)   to review, or not to review, an earlier decision of the tribunal,

    (ii)   to take no action, or not to take any particular action, in the light of a review of an earlier decision of the tribunal,

    (iii)   to set aside an earlier decision of the tribunal, or

    (iv)   to refer, or not to refer, a matter to the Upper Tribunal,

(e)   a decision of the First-tier Tribunal that is set aside under section 9 (including a decision set aside after proceedings on an appeal under this section have been begun), or

(f)   any decision of the First-tier Tribunal that is of a description specified in an order made by the Lord Chancellor.

(6)   A description may be specified under subsection (5)(f) only if–

(a)   in the case of a decision of that description, there is a right to appeal to a court, the Upper Tribunal or any other tribunal from the decision and that right is, or includes, something other than a right (however expressed) to appeal on any point of law arising from the decision, or

(b)   decisions of that description are made in carrying out a function transferred under section 30 and prior to the transfer of the function under section 30(1) there was no right to appeal from decisions of that description.

(7)   Where–

(a)   an order under subsection (5)(f) specifies a description of decisions, and

(b)   decisions of that description are made in carrying out a function transferred under section 30,

the order must be framed so as to come into force no later than the time when the transfer under section 30 of the function takes effect (but power to revoke the order continues to be exercisable after that time, and power to amend the order continues to be exercisable after that time for the purpose of narrowing the description for the time being specified).

(8)   The Lord Chancellor may by order make provision for a person to be treated as being, or to be treated as not being, a party to a case for the purposes of subsection (2).

Commencement

s11(5)(f) and (6)-(8): Tribunals, Courts and Enforcement Act 2007 (Commencement No.1) Order 2007 (SI 2007 No.2709) art 2(a) (September 19, 2007).

s11(1)-(4) and (5)(a)-(e): Tribunals, Courts and Enforcement Act 2007 (Commencement No.6 and Transitional Provisions) Order 2008 (SI 2008 No.2696) art 5(a) (November 3, 2008).

General Note

An appeal lies to the Upper Tribunal on any point of law arising from the decision of the First-tier Tribunal. There can be no appeal unless a point of law can be identified: *R v The Social Security Commissioner and the Social Security Appeal Tribunal ex p Pattni* [1993] Fam Law 213. Permission should be given if there is a realistic prospect that the decision was erroneous in law or if there is some other good reason to do so: Lord Woolf MR in *Smith v Cosworth Casting Processes Ltd* [1997] 1 WLR 1538.

Only a party to a case may apply for permission to appeal. So far as is known, a child has never applied for permission in Scotland. The Secretary of State has no personal interest in a decision, but may appeal in the interests of one of the parties, or in order to obtain an authoritative decision on a particular point from the Upper Tribunal. See the general note to s24(1) of the Act on p54.

A vexatious litigant requires permission from the High Court in order to bring an appeal to the Upper Tribunal (*IB v Information Commissioner* [2011] UKUT 370 (AAC); [2012] AACR 26). The Upper Tribunal's supplementary powers under s25 below do not include the power to give the required permission (*ibid*).

An appeal will not lie on the basis of something that only occurred after the decision was made, such as the way that the Secretary of State implemented the directions given by the tribunal. See *E and R v SSHD* [2004] QB 1044.

The Upper Tribunal has not decided on a test for what constitutes a decision for the purposes of this section. It has, however, accepted that some decisions are now appealable that previously would have been mere determinations that were subject only to judicial review.

A three judge panel of the Upper Tribunal has decided that all decisions of the First-tier Tribunal are, in principle, susceptible of appeal to the Upper Tribunal unless they are excluded decisions (*LS v Lambeth LB(HB)* [2010] UKUT 461 (AAC); [2011] AACR 27). The panel did not attempt to define what amounted to a "decision" for the purposes of this section. Two issues arise. First, there are many minor matters that have to be resolved for which any further judicial scrutiny would be inappropriate, such as the layout of the venue and the seating arrangements. This issue is probably more theoretical than real, as no attempt would be made to appeal them and, if there were, permission would be refused unless they had affected the outcome of the case. Second, are a tribunal's reasons part of its "decision"? They are usually provided only separately from the tribunal's order and on request. As an appeal lies only in respect of an error of law in the making of the decision, an appeal only lies for inadequate reasons if they are part of the "decision" for the purposes of this section.

By way of illuastation, the Administrative Appeals Chamber has decided or accepted that the following decisions are appealable under this section:

–   a direction for disclosure of documents (*Dorset Healthcare NHS Foundation Trust v MH* [2009] UKUT 4 (AAC));

–   order for production of privileged material (*LM v Lewisham LB* [2009] UKUT 204 (AAC); [2010] AACR 12);

–   a direction prohibiting disclosure of documents (*RM v St Andrew's Healthcare* [2010] UKUT 119 (AAC));

–   a refusal to set aside a decision (*MP v SSWP (DLA)* [2010] UKUT 103 (AAC));

–   a decision striking out a case that could not be reinstated (*AW v Essex CC (SEN)* [2010] UKUT 74 (AAC));

–   a refusal to reinstate a case (*Synergy Child Services Ltd v Ofsted* [2009] UKUT 125 (AAC));

–   a decision to strike out an appeal (*KC v LB Newham* (SEN) [2010] UKUT 96 (AAC)).

The Tax and Chancery Chamber has accepted an appeal against a decision whether to direct a preliminary issue (*Goldman Sachs v Commissioners for Her Majesty's Revenue and Customs* [2009] UKUT 290 (TCC)).

Although case management decisions are, on the authorities, within this section, judges enjoy a wide discretion and the decisions should not be questioned unless there is point of substance that requires an urgent challenge and speedy resolution (*Re P and P (Care Proceedings: Appointment of Experts)* [2009] 2 FLR 1370, para 17). *RM v St Andrew's Healthcare* [2010] UKUT 119 (AAC) was an example of such a case. It concerned an order prohibiting disclosure of information that was central to the patient's case. The judge analysed why case management decisions are usually supported on appeal and the circumstances in which they would be susceptible to challenge.

> "7.   The non-disclosure order was a case management decision. Appellate courts are supportive of these decisions and discourage appeals against them. They often have to be made with little time for analysis or reflection. Appeals can disrupt the proceedings, produce inefficiency and increase costs. They are capable of being used for tactical purposes. Ultimately, the judge dealing with the case is probably best placed to make a judgment on how best to proceed in the context of the proceedings. Challenges are best considered at the end of the proceedings, when it is possible to judge whether the decision adversely affected the outcome.
>
> 8.   This does not mean that case management decisions are immune from scrutiny. The decision may have been given after a hearing and with time for analysis. If it is made ahead of the final hearing, it may be possible to deal with an appeal quickly to avoid disrupting the First-tier Tribunal's timetable. There may be no question of seeking a tactical advantage. The issue may be severable from the more routine management of the proceedings. And it may be possible to anticipate the likely effect.
>
> 9.   On the spectrum of case management decisions, the non-disclosure order is more susceptible to scrutiny than most. The judge held a hearing and took time before issuing her reasons. The issue is severable from the routine management of the case. It is important and its effects can be anticipated: the patient's solicitors argue that they are unable to obtain his instructions on the real case for his continued detention. There is no question of tactical advantage being sought and it has been possible to deal with the appeal quickly."

Judicial review

Those decisions of the First-tier Tribunal that are not appealable under this section may be subject to judicial review. In the case of a review decision, there is such a substantial element of judgment or discretion that an application for judicial review will seldom succeed (*R(RB) v First-tier Tribunal (Review)* [2010] UKUT 160 (AAC); [2010] AACR 41, para 30).

The tribunal is the respondent to a judicial review application. It is permissible for the tribunal to make submissions, but it is doubtful whether it is appropriate for the tribunal to support the decision on its merits, especially where there is another party with an interest to oppose the application (*R (RB) v First-tier Tribunal*, para 14).

Subsection (3)

The requirement of permission to appeal is compatible with Art 6 of the European Convention on Human Rights and Fundamental Freedoms.

Proceedings on appeal to Upper Tribunal

12.–(1)   Subsection (2) applies if the Upper Tribunal, in deciding an appeal under section 11, finds that the making of the decision concerned involved the making of an error on a point of law.

(2)   The Upper Tribunal–

(a)   may (but need not) set aside the decision of the First-tier Tribunal, and

(b)   if it does, must either–

    (i)   remit the case to the First-tier Tribunal with directions for its reconsideration, or

    (ii)   re-make the decision.

(3)   In acting under subsection (2)(b)(i), the Upper Tribunal may also–

(a)   direct that the members of the First-tier Tribunal who are chosen to reconsider the case are not to be the same as those who made the decision that has been set aside;

(b)   give procedural directions in connection with the reconsideration of the case by the First-tier Tribunal.

(4)   In acting under subsection (2)(b)(ii), the Upper Tribunal–

(a)   may make any decision which the First-tier Tribunal could make if the First-tier Tribunal were re-making the decision, and

(b)   may make such findings of fact as it considers appropriate.

Commencement
Tribunals, Courts and Enforcement Act 2007 (Commencement No.6 and Transitional Provisions) Order 2008 (SI 2008 No.2696) art 5(a) (November 3, 2008).

General Note
The function of the Upper Tribunal, like that of any other appellate body, is to ensure justice between the parties and to ensure public confidence in the administration of justice by remedying wrong decisions and by clarifying and developing the law (*Taylor v Lawrence* [2002] 2 All ER 353 at para 66). An appeal to the Upper Tribunal is a rehearing. Initially, the rehearing is confined to points of law. However, if the tribunal's decision is erroneous in law, the Upper Tribunal may investigate the facts, and make findings of fact, and remake the decision. See *CIS 16701/1996*.

Additional evidence
In *VH v Suffolk CC* [2010] UKUT 203 (AAC), the judge explained when additional evidence would be admitted by the Upper Tribunal. He first defined 'additional evidence':
"2.   By 'additional evidence', I mean evidence produced to show: (i) the circumstances as they were at the time of the hearing before the First-tier Tribunal; (ii) that those circumstances have changed; (iii) how the local education authority has, or has not, implemented the statement. Parties regularly produce, respond to and complain about the introduction of evidence on these matters. Such evidence is potentially relevant, but only for limited purposes. Its relevance depends on the Upper Tribunal's powers in the particular case.
3.   Parties may also produce evidence of what happened at the hearing. That evidence is in a different category and does not arise in this case."
He then explained:
"7.   The first question for the Upper Tribunal under this section is: did the making of the First-tier Tribunal's decision involve the making of an error on a point of law? The Upper Tribunal must answer this question on the evidence that was before the First-tier Tribunal. A tribunal cannot go wrong in law by failing to take account of evidence that was not before it. See the decisions of the Social Security Commissioner in *R(S) 1/88* at [3] and of Underhill J in *R (S) v Hertfordshire County Council* [2006] EWHC 328 (Admin) at [25]. If the answer to this question is 'no', the Upper Tribunal's only power is to dismiss the appeal. If the answer is 'yes', a second question arises.
8.   The second question is: how should the tribunal dispose of the case? There are three options: (a) leave the First-tier Tribunal's decision in place; (b) remit the case to the First-tier Tribunal; (c) re-make the decision. The tribunal may take account of additional evidence in order to decide which form of disposal is appropriate. If it decides to re-make the decision, evidence will also be needed of current circumstances.
9.   In practice, it can be difficult for parties to know when additional may be relevant. For example, an oral hearing of an application may also consider the appeal and disposal. The Upper Tribunal, and representatives for other parties, need to be flexible in receiving evidence whose ultimate relevance will depend on how the case proceeds. Forcing a party to produce the additional evidence only if and when it is required could lead to inefficiency and delay."

Error on a point of law
The powers under this section only arise if the First-tier Tribunal's decision involved the making of an error on a point of law. The Upper Tribunal has no power to remit the case or remake the decision on the ground that it is justified by fresh evidence (*CCS 4687/2000*, paras 6-9).

The error of law may exist in the decision itself or in the proceedings that led to that decision (*R(I) 28/61*). Permission to appeal will generally be given only if the error identified was material, that is, one that affected the outcome of the appeal before the First-tier Tribunal (*R(Iran) v SSHD* [2005] EWCA Civ 982 at para 10). Lord Neuberger listed various ways in which an error might not affect the outcome in *Holmes-Moorhouse v Richmond upon Thames London Borough Council* [2009] 1 WLR 413 at para 51.

The cases in which an error of law occurs are discussed below. It is impossible to give a comprehensive list of the ways in which a tribunal's decision may be wrong in law and any attempt to do so is likely to produce overlapping categories (*R(IS) 11/99*, para 4). It might be easier to identify those matters which are not errors of law. Perhaps the best attempt to distil the essence of what is involved in an error of law was that of Bridge J in *Mountview Court Properties Ltd v Devlin* [1970] 21 P&CR 689 at 695-696:
"... any ... language found in the statutes giving a right of appeal on a point of law, to my mind connotes that a successful appellant must demonstrate that the decision with which he is dissatisfied is itself vitiated by reason of the fact that it has been reached by an erroneous process of legal reasoning."
However, this does not cover all errors of law. It does not, for example, cover breaches of natural justice or inadequate reasons.

Reasonableness is a question of fact (*R(SB) 6/88*), although the process of determining it may contain a mistake of law.

A tribunal's decision will be wrong in law in at least the following cases.
(i)   **No jurisdiction** If a tribunal purports to deal with a party or an issue over which it has no power or to grant relief that it has no power to grant, it acts without jurisdiction (*Garthwaite v Garthwaite* [1964] 2 All

ER 233 at 241, *per* Diplock LJ). If the whole of the tribunal's decision is outside its jurisdiction, it is of no force or effect (*R(S) 15/52*, para 10). If only part of the tribunal's decision is outside its jurisdiction, it may be possible to declare that part of the decision to be of no force or effect so that it may be disregarded as superfluous to the decision, leaving the remainder of the decision intact (*R(M) 1/98*, para 3; *CI 218/1997*, para 13). On the reasoning in *R(I) 9/63* paras 20-22, the decision or part of the decision that was made without jurisdiction nonetheless exists as a decision and must be set aside. This was what the Tribunal of Commissioners did in *R(SB) 42/83*, para 13, although it also left undisturbed part of the decision that was outside the tribunal's jurisdiction because it was not challenged on appeal (*ibid*, para 12). For the tribunal's power to consider the validity of decisions on which its jurisdiction depends, see the introductory general note to s20 of the Act.

(ii) **No power** If a tribunal purports to exercise a power which it does not possess, its decision will be erroneous in law.

(iii) **Rejection of relevant evidence** If a tribunal rejects relevant evidence, whether by refusing to admit it or by refusing to consider it, its decision will be erroneous in law (*Bailey v Stoke-on-Trent Assessment Committee* [1931] 1 KB 385 at 481-2, *per* Scrutton LJ). There will also have been a breach of natural justice. A tribunal's decision will not be erroneous in law merely because the tribunal took no account of evidence that was not before it (*R(S) 1/88*, para 3).

(iv) **Failure to adopt an inquisitorial approach** If the tribunal fails to take an inquisitorial approach to the case, the parties will not have had a fair hearing. This will be a breach of natural justice that makes the decision erroneous in law. For a discussion of the inquisitorial approach, see the introductory general note to Chapter 3 SEC Rules on p850.

(v) **The decision or a finding of fact material to the decision is not supported by any evidence** If there is *no* evidence to support a finding of fact on which the tribunal's decision is based, the decision will be erroneous in law (*R(A) 1/72*, para 4; *R(SB) 11/83*, para 13(2)). It is a requirement of natural justice that each finding of fact by a tribunal must be based on some material logically tending to show the existence of that fact (*Mahon v Air New Zealand* [1984] 3 All ER 201 at 210, *per* Lord Diplock). The evidence relied on must have *some* probative value (*R v National Industrial Injuries Commissioner ex p Moore* [1965] 1 All ER 81 at 94, *per* Diplock LJ). On appeal the Upper Tribunal is considering not whether the findings of fact made by the tribunal were the right ones to make on the evidence, but rather whether they were ones that the tribunal was entitled in law to make on the evidence before it. The evaluation of the evidence is for the fact-finder, which in this case is the tribunal (*R v National Industrial Injuries Commissioner ex p Moore* at 94, *per* Lord Diplock). The weight to be attached to any particular piece of evidence is determined by common sense (*Lord Advocate v Lord Blantyre* [1879] 4 App Cas 770 at 792, *per* Lord Blackburn). If the evidence on a particular point is unchallenged and there are no facts or circumstances to displace or cast doubt on it, the tribunal would be erroneous in law if it failed to accept it (*R v Matheson* [1958] 2 All ER 87 at 90, *per* Lord Goddard CJ). Likewise, a tribunal's finding will be erroneous in law if it is out of tune with the evidence to such an extent that it can only have been the case that the tribunal misunderstood that evidence. (In *Hossack v General Dental Council, The Times*, April 22, 1997 the Privy Council reversed a finding of fact by the Council's professional conduct committee on this ground, although the appeal to the Council was not limited to errors of law.) These cases aside, there is no appeal on a question of fact (*CCS7966/1995*, para 9).

The generous margin of autonomy that the law allows to tribunals in the finding of facts reflects the fact that, unlike the First-tier Tribunal, the Upper Tribunal will not have seen the witnesses, and recognises that different persons may properly reach a different judgment on the same facts (*CDLA 5342/1997*, para 13). A decision that a tribunal's decision was perverse should only be taken if an overwhelming case is made out (*Elmbridge Housing Trust v O'Donoghue, The Times*, June 24, 2004).

The mere fact that a party does not agree with a finding of fact or with a piece of evidence does not show that the tribunal's decision was erroneous in law (*CSA 21/1986*, para 5).

Findings of fact that are not reached on a rational or common sense basis are an example of this head. They merit special mention to show that there are limits to the autonomy allowed to tribunals in making findings of fact. If the tribunal's approach to the finding of fact is not a rational one that is in accordance with common sense, its decision will be erroneous in law. As the tribunal's approach will only be apparent from its reasoning, this head of error of law is closely connected with the adequacy of the tribunal's explanation for its findings. See *CDLA 5342/1997*, paras 18-19.

(vi) **Errors of uncontroverted fact** A mere error of fact is not an error of law: *Inland Revenue Commissioners v George, The Times*, 9 December 2003. However, in some limited circumstances a mistake of uncontroverted fact may be an error of law in those jurisdictions where the parties share an interest in co-operating to achieve the correct outcome: *E and R v SSHD* [2004] QB 1044, para 66. The circumstances are: (i) there is a mistake of existing fact, including a mistake on the availability of evidence of a fact; (ii) the fact is uncontentious and objectively verifiable; (iii) the appellant and the appellant's advisers must not have been responsible for the mistake; (iv) the mistake must have played a material, but not necessarily decisive, part in the tribunal's reasoning: *ibid*, para 66.

(vii)　***Judgment exercised improperly or not at all*** A tribunal must exercise judgment in a judicial manner. This means that it must be exercised in a selective and discriminating manner and not arbitrarily or capriciously (*Jacobs v Norsalta Ltd* [1977] ICR 189 at 191).

A tribunal may, and in almost every case will have to, exercise judgment at one or more stages as it reaches a decision. That judgment may be necessary because (1) it is necessary to evaluate the evidence; or (2) the rule with which the tribunal is concerned allows a degree of choice (eg, where the tribunal is deciding whether to exercise its *discretion* to give a reduced benefit decision under s46(5) of the Act); or (3) the tribunal is concerned with a broad concept under which it has to decide the significance to be attached to individual facts or has to weigh and balance the overall significance of the combinations of facts – eg, whether a parent and child are living in the same *household* under s3(2)(a) of the Act, or whether it would be *just and equitable* under S28F(I)(b) of the Act to agree to a variation. This classification should not be taken as establishing mutually exclusive categories. A case may come under more than one head.

It will be an error of law for a tribunal to fail to exercise a judgment when one is called for or to introduce an element of judgment into a case that merely requires it to reach conclusions of fact. It will also be an error of law for a tribunal to exercise the wrong type of judgment. A tribunal is likely to have considerable leeway in fixing an appropriate deduction in a partner's housing costs when giving a departure direction because the factors taken into account are unlikely to point to a precise figure, but there is no scope for the exercise of such deliberate choice in deciding whether a person is a member of a household because the tribunal must decide whether or not the facts show membership of a household. It is unfortunate that all cases involving the exercise of judgment are sometimes referred to as involving discretion, as by Lord Diplock in *Birkett v James* [1977] 2 All ER 801 at 804. The approach taken by the Upper Tribunal differs according to the category of case concerned. It is particularly reluctant to find an error of law in the tribunal's analysis of the evidence.

The approach taken by the Upper Tribunal to cases where an element of judgment is involved is based on the recognition that judgment might legitimately be exercised differently by different persons on the same facts (*Bellenden v Satterthwaite* [1948] 1 All ER 343 at 345, *per* Asquith LJ). A decision will not be erroneous in law merely because the Upper Tribunal would have formed a different judgment (*Charles Osenton and Co v Johnson* [1941] 2 All ER 245 at 250, *per* Viscount Simon LC) and it should not and will not embark on the exercise of deciding what decision it would have reached on the facts (*Global Plant Ltd v Secretary of State for Health and Social Security* [1971] 3 All ER 385 at 393, *per* Lord Widgery CJ). See also *Birkett v James* at 811, *per* Lord Salmon; *Cookson v Knowles* [1978] 2 All ER 604 at 607, *per* Lord Diplock; *Eagil Trust Co Ltd v Pigott-Brown* [1985] 3 All ER 119 at 121, *per* Griffiths LJ.

This approach is not affected by the Human Rights Act 1998 (*Biji v General Medical Council, The Times,* October 24, 2001).

The House of Lords has strongly reaffirmed the principles to be applied on an appeal against the exercise of a discretion, warning:

"An appellate court should resist any temptation to subvert the principle that they should not substitute their own discretion for that of the judge by a narrow textual analysis which enables them to claim that he misdirected himself."

(*Piglowska v Piglowski* [1999] 3 All ER 632 at 644, *per* Lord Hoffmann).

The Court of Appeal has also emphasised that proper respect must be paid to the conclusions reached by tribunals within the area of expertise that legislation has left to them (*Bromley London Borough Council v Special Educational Needs Tribunal* [1999] 3 All ER 587 at 594, *per* Sedley LJ).

On the assumption that there is no error in the findings of primary fact (see the *Evaluation of evidence* section of the general note to rule 15 SEC Rules), a decision will only be erroneous in law in limited circumstances. These circumstances have been stated in slightly different terms in different cases. In *Ward v James* [1965] 1 All ER 563 at 570, Lord Denning MR said that a decision would only be set aside when the court was satisfied that it was wrong. In *R v Birmingham Juvenile Court ex pN* [1984] 2 All ER 688, Arnold P and in *Simmons v Pizzey* [1977] 2 All ER 432 at 441-442, Lord Hailsham LC said that a decision would be set aside if it was based on incorrect legal principles or if it was one that could not reasonably have been made on the facts of the case. In *Simmons v Pizzey* [1977] 2 All ER 432 at 441-442 at 501, Woolf J said that a decision would be set aside if it was one that could not have been made on the facts by someone who was properly advised and acting reasonably. In *George Mitchell (Ghesterhall) Ltd v Finney Lock Seeds Ltd* [1983] 2 All ER 737 at 743, Lord Bridge said that a decision would only be set aside if proceeded upon some erroneous principle or was plainly and obviously wrong. Many variants of these different formulations can be found.

An exercise of judgment will be wrong in law in three circumstances: (a) if the tribunal took the wrong approach in law; (b) if the tribunal acted on the wrong material; and (c) if the tribunal went wrong in the balancing exercise.

A tribunal may take the wrong approach in law in two ways. (i) It may misdirect itself on the law. For example, it may misplace the burden of proof. (ii) It may also go wrong in principle. For example, it may disregard a principle that governs the exercise of a discretion.

A tribunal may act on the wrong material in two ways: (i) It may overlook a relevant consideration; (ii) It may take account of an irrelevant consideration.

A tribunal goes wrong in the balancing exercise if its conclusion "exceeded the generous ambit within which a reasonable disagreement is possible" (*G v G* [1985] 2 All ER 225 at 229, *per* Lord Fraser). This allows a wider margin for disagreement than the grounds on which a court will review the exercise of an administrative discretion (*Re F (a minor) (Wardship: appeal)* [1976] 1 All ER 417, in which the majority rejected Stamp LJ's view at 429-430; *G v G* at 232 *per* Lord Bridge). Judgment must always be exercised judicially, which limits the factors that may or must be taken into account. In some cases, the legislation sets out factors that must or must not be taken into account, as in reg 21 of the Variation Regulations.

The Upper Tribunal should try to promote consistency where in closely comparable circumstances there are conflicting opinions within the First-tier Tribunal as to the relative weight to be given to particular considerations (*Birkett v James* at 804 and 811, *per* Lords Diplock and Salmon respectively).

This head of error of law may be seen as no more than a particular application of the rule that no tribunal acting judicially and properly instructed as to the relevant law could have come to the decision reached, with the Upper Tribunal having to decide whether the First-tier Tribunal's decision fell outside the range of permissible decisions that might be made.

Errors in the exercise of judgment may be established by being expressed in the tribunal's decision or they may be inferred from the decision that was reached (*Ward v James* at 570, *per* Lord Denning MR). There is no special rule where the welfare of children is concerned (*G v G*, *per* Lord Fraser). There must be a particularly strong case that an exercise of judgment was wrong in law where it depended upon the tribunal having seen and heard witnesses (*Re F*, above at 439-440, *per* Bridge LJ).

Where a tribunal is required to exercise its judgment, the mere fact that the decision fails to set out every one of the factors that led to the decision will not be sufficient to prove that the tribunal failed to consider those factors that are not mentioned (*Redman v Redman* [1948] 1 All ER 333 at 334-335, *per* Tucker LJ). However, the reasons given for a decision must be adequate. It is not sufficient merely to recite the evidence taken into account. The reasons must go on to give an indication of how and why the tribunal reached its decision. See *B v B (Residence Order: Reasons for Decision)* [1997] 2 FLR 602 at 606. In difficult or finely balanced cases, it may be necessary for a tribunal to show how it assessed each relevant factor, such as those in s28F(2) below and reg 21 of the Variations Regulations, separately (*Re G(Children)* [2006] 2 FLR 629, para 40).

(viii) ***Inferences*** Inferences are an example of the exercise of judgment. The courts have considered the proper approach that should be taken on appeal to inferences drawn below. Some of the cases involved the identification of an error of law on appeal on error of law grounds. Others involved the respect to be given to an inference on an appeal by way of rehearing on both fact and law.

The courts have drawn a distinction between inferences relating to perception and evaluation of facts. Perception is concerned with what happened and who did it, proved not directly but by a process of reasoning from other facts. In these cases, there will be an error of law if there is no evidence to support the inference that has been drawn. Evaluation is concerned with whether the facts as found satisfy a legal test or standard. If evaluation is involved, the issue may also be referred to as one of mixed law and fact or of fact and degree. The legal test or standard is a matter of law. Whether the facts are sufficient to satisfy that test or standard is a matter of fact. In these cases, there will be an error of law if the tribunal applied the wrong principle or came to a decision that was plainly wrong. The tribunal applied the wrong principle if it misdirected itself on the terms of the legal test or standard. That may be shown directly by the terms in which the tribunal explains its decision. The tribunal's decision will be plainly wrong if it has applied the test or standard to the facts in a way that the facts do not support. That is either seen as an error of law in itself or as evidence that the tribunal must have misdirected itself on the law. See also the previous section on the exercise of judgment.

Whichever the issue with which the case was concerned and whether the inference relates to perception or evaluation, the courts' reluctance to interfere with an inference varies with a variety of factors. The most important are: (a) whether it involved the assessment of oral evidence; (b) whether it involved the use of special experience or expertise, such as that of a financially qualified panel member; (c) how great is the range of variables that were taken into account in drawing the inference. The presence of these features increases the respect given to the inference and the reluctance to interfere with it on appeal.

The authorities and the distinctions were analysed by the Court of Appeal in *South Cone Inc v Bessant* [2002] EWCA Civ 763.

(ix) ***The decision contains a false proposition on its face*** If there is a false proposition on the face of the decision (*ex facie*), the decision is erroneous in law (*R(A) 1/72*, para 4; *R(SB) 11/83*, para 13(1)). This applies where the tribunal has applied the wrong legal test in order to determine an issue.

(x) ***Ultra vires*** The fact that a decision was based on a provision in delegated legislation which the minister had no power to make will make it erroneous in law (*Chief Adjudication Officer v Foster* [1993] 1 All ER 705).

(xi) ***Legislation or legal document wrongly interpreted*** The proper interpretation of a piece of legislation or other legal document such as a contract is always a question of law. If the interpretation used by the tribunal is wrong, its decision will be erroneous in law. It may also be erroneous in law for a tribunal to rely on a concession on the interpretation of a document (*Bahamas International Trust Co Ltd v Threadgold* [1974] 3 All ER 881 at 884 *per* Lord Diplock) or on the interpretation of a statutory provision (*Cherwell DC v Thames Water Authority* [1975] 1 All ER 763 at 767 *per* Lord Diplock). As these are questions of law for the tribunal to determine, it must satisfy itself that the concession is correctly made.

(xii) **No tribunal acting judicially and properly instructed as to the relevant law could have come to the decision** If the decision was one that no tribunal acting judicially and properly instructed on the law could have arrived at, the decision is said to be perverse and is erroneous in law (*R(A) 1/72*, para 4; *R(SB) 11/ 83*, para 13(3)). This covers cases where the tribunal fails to make the only decision open to it on the facts as found (*R v Birmingham Juvenile Court ex p N* at 690-691, *per* Arnold P) and cases where the tribunal's decision falls outside the range of decisions that might properly be made (*Bellenden v Satterthwaite* at 345, *per* Asquith LJ). An argument based on this ground must be fully particularised, will only be accepted if an overwhelming case has been made out, and must not allow an appeal on a point of law to be turned into a rehearing of parts of the evidence (*Yeboah v Crofton* [2002] IRLR 634).

(xiii) **Failure to deal with all questions arising for decision** The tribunal must consider the case afresh. Although every aspect of the case is open for decision by the tribunal, it is only required to deal with those questions that are put to it for decision by contention of one of the parties or that arise on the evidence. The appeal tribunal's decision will not be erroneous in law for failing to deal with an obviously unsuccessful point that was not raised before it but is raised on appeal in an attempt to obtain a rehearing (*Srimanoharan v Secretary of State for the Home Department, The Times,* 29 June 2000).

(xiv) **Decision incomplete or impossible to implement** If a tribunal's decision is incomplete or for some reason it cannot be implemented (eg, if it is self-contradictory), the decision will be erroneous in law.

(xv) **Inadequate reasons** The tribunal's decision will be erroneous in law if there has been a breach of r34 SEC Rules, which requires a written statement of the reasons for the tribunal's decision and of the findings on questions of fact material to that decision (*R(I) 18/61*, paras 10-11; *R(A) 1/72*, para 5; *R(SB) 11/82*, para 14; *R(SB) 11/83*, para 13(5)). A failure to give adequate reasons for a tribunal's decision may make its decision erroneous in law in three ways: (a) as the decision is the best indication of how the tribunal reached its decision, inadequate reasons may be evidence of an error of law; (b) the lack of any, or of adequate, reasons may amount to a breach of natural justice; (c) the failure to comply with rule 34 is itself an error of law.

For a discussion of the standard of reasons required, see the general note to rule 34 SEC Rules on p854. There are a number of cases in which the courts have ordered that reasons be given or be supplemented. Some of these cases are based upon a variety of provisions and considerations that have no application to the child support jurisdiction. (a) The case may relate to the duty to give reasons under what is now s10 of the Tribunals and Inquiries Act 1992 (*Crake and Butterworth v Supplementary Benefit Commission* [1982] 1 All ER 498 at 508, *per* Woolf J). So in *Mountview Court Properties Ltd v Devlin* [1970] 21 P&CR 689 the case was adjourned and remitted for further reasons to be supplied. The duty under the 1992 Act is displaced by the specific provision in the SEC Rules (*R(F) 1/70*, para 15). (b) The decision may turn on the power to issue (in the older terminology) an order of mandamus (*Mountview,* above 693, *per* Lord Parker CJ) or in order to defeat an application for (again in the older terminology) certiorari (*R v Medical Appeal Tribunal ex p Gilmore* [1957] 1 QB 574 at 582-3, *per* Denning LJ). (c) Some cases depend upon the interpretation of the particular legislation being considered *(ibid* at 694, *per* Lord Parker CJ, discussing the *Givaudan* case). (d) Other cases turn on the fact that the remedy sought is discretionary (judicial review is discretionary) and the supplementary reasons show that no purpose would be served by granting it (*R v Westminster City Council ex p Ermakov* [1996] 2 All ER 302 at 313).

There are, however, cases in which the reasoning can be applied to the child support jurisdiction. First, in *Yusuf v Aberplace Ltd* [1984] ICR 850 at 853-854 the Employment Appeal Tribunal exercised the power, established by a line of authority, to remit a case to what is now called an employment tribunal for findings or reasons that were incomplete or obscure to be amplified. This power is based on the principle that a tribunal is not *functus officio* until adequate reasons have been given sufficient to tell the parties why they have won or lost. There is some support for this reasoning in *R(I) 18/61*, para 11 where the lack of adequate reasons was held to render the tribunal's decision a nullity. It is, however, usually said that a tribunal is *functus officio* as soon as its decision is promulgated (*Re Suffield and Watts ex p Brown* [1886-1890] All ER Rep 276 at 278, *per* Fry LJ). This was the approach taken by the Employment Appeal Tribunal in *Reuben v Brent London Borough Council* [2000] ICR 102. However, its reasoning is not consistent with the practice recommended and followed in other areas of law by the Administrative Court and the Court of Appeal. The Court of Appeal has confirmed that it is permissible to ask an employment tribunal to supplement reasons that it has already given (*Barke v SEETEC Business Technology Centre Ltd, The Times,* May 26 2005). Second, in *Howarth,* above, Lord Denning suggested that, if the inadequacy of a Medical Appeal Tribunal's reasons had been the only error of law, it might have been possible to send the case back to the tribunal for the reasons to be better stated, but he did not cite any authority or explain any basis on which the court might have made the order. Third, the approach of the

Court of Appeal in *English v Emery Reimbold and Strick Ltd* [2002] 3 All ER 385 at paras 22-25 favoured obtaining an amplification of reasons in preference to incurring the expense of an appeal.

According to the Court of Appeal in *Hatungimana v Secretary of State for the Home Department* [2006] EWCA Civ 231 at paras 4-8, the power to obtain supplementary reasons from a statutory tribunal only applies if it is authorised by the legislation governing that tribunal. In the case of the First-tier Tribunal, the Upper Tribunal has power under rule 5(3)(n) to require that tribunal to provide reasons for its decision. That would allow the Upper Tribunal to obtain supplementary reasons. In *CH 2553/2005*, para 26, the commissioner doubted whether the power to receive supplementary reasons could be used except perhaps in exceptional cases, but this was before rule 5(3)(n) existed.

It is possible to extract from the authorities some general principles which the Upper Tribunal might apply were it to adopt this approach. It would mainly be used to confirm and elucidate a tribunal's reasons; only in exceptional circumstances would the tribunal be allowed to correct or add to the reasoning rather than merely elucidate the reasons (*R v Westminster City Council ex p Ermakov* [1996] 2 All ER 302 at 315, *per* Hutchison LJ). It would not be permissible to provide a subsequent rationalisation of the decision (*R v Parole Board ex p Gittens, The Times,* February 3 1994). The reasoning could not be supplemented if it were grossly flawed (*R v Lambeth London Borough Council Housing Benefit Review Board ex p Harrington, The Times,* December 10 1996). Nor can it be used to supplement the reasons substantially (*VK v Norfolk County Council, The Times,* January 6 2005). This approach can only be applied if the case is identified sufficiently quickly for the presiding judge to have a realistic chance of recalling the case in sufficient detail to supply the additional information required (*Flannery v Halifax Estate Agencies Ltd* [2000] 1 All ER 373 at 379).

It is not appropriate to ask for supplementary reasons that would require further analysis that would be inconsistent with the reasons already given (*Re M-W (Care Proceedings: Expert Evidence)* [2010] 2 FLR 46 at para 47).

Whatever the powers of the Upper Tribunal, there is no power for a District Tribunal Judge to require the tribunal to supplement the reasons (*CA 4297/2004*).

(xvi) **Breaches of natural justice** Although a breach of natural justice in a tribunal's decision may lead to a judicial review of a decision, it will also make the decision erroneous in law and liable to be set aside on appeal (*R(I) 28/61; R(I) 29/61*, para 11; *R(A) 1/72*, para 5; *R(SB) 11/83*, para 13(5)). In theory "a tribunal which denies natural justice to one of the parties before it deprives itself of jurisdiction" (*Al-Mehdawi v SSHD* [1989] 3 All ER 843 at 849, *per* Lord Bridge). For a discussion of natural justice, see the general note to r2 SEC Rules on p807. Allegations of a breach of natural justice "should normally only be considered if 'full and sufficient particulars are set out in the grounds of appeal'" (*R(M) 1/89*, para 12). Usually there will only be an error of law if the breach of natural justice concerned the tribunal's proceedings rather than those of the decision maker who made the decision under appeal, although there may be exceptional cases in which appeal proceedings do not cure the breach by the decision maker (*CDLA 14884/1996*, para 12).

Under s11 Tribunals and Inquiries Act 1992, an appeal is allowed if information that was not put to a tribunal by a clerk might realistically have led to a different decision, even if that was not certain or even likely (*W v Special Needs Appeal Tribunal, The Times,* December 12 2000).

A procedural impropriety may be waived. This means that a party cannot rely on an incident as a breach of natural justice who has said or done anything inconsistent with treating the incident in this way. Usually a waiver arises from a failure to complain of what occurred. The sooner the complaint is made the less likely that the delay will give rise to a waiver. In most cases, there will be a waiver if a complaint is not made at the time the incident occurred or swiftly afterwards. However, there is no rule about the time when a complaint must be made if a waiver is to be avoided it depends on the circumstances of the case. See the analysis in *CDLA 2559/1997*, paras 28-31.

(xvii) **Cases analogous to breaches of natural justice** There are cases which are analogous to natural justice. They are cases where material information has not been provided to the tribunal by a party to the proceedings. See *R(SB) 18/83*, para 11 and *R(CS) 1/99*, para 18, both of which must be read in light of the reasoning and authorities in *CCS 16817/1996*, para 10.

(xviii) **Record of proceedings** There will not automatically be an error of law if the presiding judge did not make a proper record of proceedings or the record is not available on the appeal. There will be an error of law if the absence of a record of proceedings has resulted in a real possibility of unfairness or injustice, which may depend on the extent to which evidence of what took place at the tribunal can be obtained from other sources (*R(DLA) 3/08*, paras 27-28). The lack of any, or of an adequate, record of proceeding is not of itself and in all circumstances an error of law (*De Silva v Social Security Commissioner,* para 13, unreported, April 5 2001). The absence of, or deficiency in, the notes of proceedings is not a separate head of error of law. However, it is subsidiary to, and protective and supportive of, the recognised heads of error of law in that it will be an error of law if it prevents the Upper Tribunal from deciding whether a particular error of law has been shown. See *CDLA 1389/1997*, para 18. This reasoning is in line with the protective approach taken by the courts to prevent their jurisdiction being defeated by a failure of a tribunal to provide a complete and correct record (*R v Medical Appeal Tribunal ex p Gilmore* [1957] 1 QB 574 at 582-3, *per* Denning LJ).

(xix) **Lengthy delay between hearing and decision** The tribunal's decision will usually be given on the day of the hearing. In exceptional cases, it may be given later, but the time between the hearing and the making of the decision should be short. Whether or not a delay or the effect of a delay raises a question of law was considered by the Court of Appeal in *Bangs v Connex South Eastern Ltd* [2005] 2 All ER 316. The basic position is that delay is a matter of fact that does not allow an appeal to the Upper Tribunal, whose jurisdiction depends on there being a question of law *(ibid* at para 43(2)). However, the delay will give rise to a question of law if it results in the decision being perverse *(ibid* para 43(4)) or in a serious procedural error or material irregularity depriving a party to the proceedings of the substance of the right to a fair hearing such that it would be unfair or unjust to allow the decision to stand *(ibid* para 43(7)). It is also possible that, outside the tribunal appeal structure, a delay may be a violation of the Convention right to a fair hearing that requires the party to be compensated in damages *(ibid.* para 43(2)). In *R(DLA) 3/ 08* para 45, a Tribunal of Commissioners said that the principles of *Bangs* applied to social security cases (and no doubt to child support cases as well), subject to any necessary adjustments that the different context required.

(xx) **Delay in writing statement** A delay in providing a statement of the tribunal's reasons for decision is not of itself an error of law. However, the delay may make the tribunal's reasons unreliable, which will make them inadequate and therefore wrong in law. It may be possible to produce reliable reasons a long time after the hearing. Whether or not this is possible will depend on factors like (a) whether the hearing was oral or on the papers, (b) the detail in the record of proceedings, and (c) any personal notes the chairman may have retained. It is not appropriate to find that a tribunal's decision was erroneous in law on this ground without giving the presiding judge the chance to explain how the tribunal's reasoning was reproduced. See *R(IS) 5/04* and *CJSA 322/2001,* paras 8-9. In *CDLA 1761/2002,* the commissioner emphasised the relevance to this issue of the time limits for requesting written reasons (r34 SEC Rules).

Subsection (2)
Even if the tribunal's decision did involve the making of an error of law, the Upper Tribunal need not set it aside. It will not do so, if the error did not affect the outcome of the appeal and, perhaps, if there is some factor that now renders the decision academic.

If the Upper Tribunal sets the decision aside, it may remit the case or remake the decision.

By remitting a case to an appeal tribunal for rehearing, the Upper Tribunal cures any procedural error that affected the decision set aside (*Pumahaven Ltd v Williams, The Times,* May 16 2003).

Unless otherwise directed, the rehearing is a complete rehearing of the issues raised by the appeal and is not limited to the issue that the Upper Tribunal held to have been wrong in law (*CAF 2026/2007*). However, the Upper Tribunal may limit the issues that are remitted, in which case the First-tier Tribunal only has jurisdiction over those issues (*Aparau v Iceland Frozen Foods Ltd* [2000] 1 All ER 228, CA).

The Upper Tribunal may direct a tribunal on the issues that arise and the law to be applied to them, but they should not generally direct a tribunal on the sequence in which they are considered, leaving it to the tribunal to adopt the approach that appears most efficient and effective (*CDLA 1365/2005,* para 44). In some cases, however, it is essential that a tribunal approach questions in the correct order. For example, the frequency and pattern of overnight care cannot be resolved until the "relevant week" has been identified.

The Upper Tribunal has jurisdiction to give further directions if the directions originally given prove abortive. See the discussion of *CSB 1288/1985* in *R(IS) 11/92* (para 33).

Right to appeal to Court of Appeal etc.

13.–(1)   For the purposes of subsection (2), the reference to a right of appeal is to a right to appeal to the relevant appellate court on any point of law arising from a decision made by the Upper Tribunal other than an excluded decision.

(2)   Any party to a case has a right of appeal, subject to subsection (14).

(3)   That right may be exercised only with permission (or, in Northern Ireland, leave).

(4)   Permission (or leave) may be given by–

(a)   the Upper Tribunal, or

(b)   the relevant appellate court,

on an application by the party.

(5)   An application may be made under subsection (4) to the relevant appellate court only if permission (or leave) has been refused by the Upper Tribunal.

(6)   The Lord Chancellor may, as respects an application under subsection (4) that falls within subsection (7) and for which the relevant appellate court is the Court of Appeal in England and Wales or the Court of Appeal in Northern Ireland, by order make

provision for permission (or leave) not to be granted on the application unless the Upper Tribunal or (as the case may be) the relevant appellate court considers–
  (a)   that the proposed appeal would raise some important point of principle or practice, or
  (b)   that there is some other compelling reason for the relevant appellate court to hear the appeal.
  [[1](6A)   Rules of court may make provision for permission not to be granted on an application under subsection (4) to the Court of Session that falls within subsection (7) unless the court considers–
  (a)   that the proposed appeal would raise some important point of principle, or
  (b)   that there is some other compelling reason for the court to hear the appeal.]
  (7)   An application falls within this subsection if the application is for permission (or leave) to appeal from any decision of the Upper Tribunal on an appeal under section 11.
  (8)   For the purposes of subsection (1), an "excluded decision" is–
  (a)-(b) [Omitted]
  (c)   any decision of the Upper Tribunal on an application under section 11(4)(b) (application for permission or leave to appeal),
  (d)   a decision of the Upper Tribunal under section 10–
    (i)   to review, or not to review, an earlier decision of the tribunal,
    (ii)   to take no action, or not to take any particular action, in the light of a review of an earlier decision of the tribunal, or
    (iii)   to set aside an earlier decision of the tribunal,
  (e)   a decision of the Upper Tribunal that is set aside under section 10 (including a decision set aside after proceedings on an appeal under this section have been begun), or
  (f)   any decision of the Upper Tribunal that is of a description specified in an order made by the Lord Chancellor.
  (9)   A description may be specified under subsection (8)(f) only if–
  (a)   in the case of a decision of that description, there is a right to appeal to a court from the decision and that right is, or includes, something other than a right (however expressed) to appeal on any point of law arising from the decision, or
  (b)   decisions of that description are made in carrying out a function transferred under section 30 and prior to the transfer of the function under section 30(1) there was no right to appeal from decisions of that description.
  (10)   Where–
  (a)   an order under subsection (8)(f) specifies a description of decisions, and
  (b)   decisions of that description are made in carrying out a function transferred under section 30,
the order must be framed so as to come into force no later than the time when the transfer under section 30 of the function takes effect (but power to revoke the order continues to be exercisable after that time, and power to amend the order continues to be exercisable after that time for the purpose of narrowing the description for the time being specified).
  (11)   Before the Upper Tribunal decides an application made to it under subsection (4), the Upper Tribunal must specify the court that is to be the relevant appellate court as respects the proposed appeal.
  (12)   The court to be specified under subsection (11) in relation to a proposed appeal is whichever of the following courts appears to the Upper Tribunal to be the most appropriate–
  (a)   the Court of Appeal in England and Wales;
  (b)   the Court of Session;
  (c)   the Court of Appeal in Northern Ireland.
  (13)   In this section except subsection (11), "the relevant appellate court", as respects an appeal, means the court specified as respects that appeal by the Upper Tribunal under subsection (11).
  (14)   The Lord Chancellor may by order make provision for a person to be treated as being, or to be treated as not being, a party to a case for the purposes of subsection (2).

(15) Rules of court may make provision as to the time within which an application under subsection (4) to the relevant appellate court must be made.

Amendment

1. Crime and Courts Act 2013 (2013 c.22) s23 (July 15, 2013); Crime and Courts Act 2013 (Commencement No.3) Order 2013 (SI 2013 No.1725) art 2.

Commencement

s13(6), (8)(f), (9), (10), (14) and (15): Tribunals, Courts and Enforcement Act 2007 (Commencement No.1) Order 2007 (SI 2007 No.2709) art 2(a) (September 19, 2007).

s13(1)-(5), (7), (8)(a)-(e) and (11)-(13): Tribunals, Courts and Enforcement Act 2007 (Commencement No.6 and Transitional Provisions) Order 2008 (SI.2008 No.2696) art 5(a) (November 3, 2008).

General Note

A three judge panel of the Upper Tribunal has decided that all decisions of the First-tier Tribunal are, in principle, susceptible of appeal to the Upper Tribunal unless they are excluded decisions (*LS v Lambeth LB(HB)* [2010] UKUT 461 (AAC); [2011] AACR 27). This reasoning must apply equally to appeals from the Upper Tribunal to the Court of Appeal.

The standard to be applied when considering an application for permission to appeal is set by Art 2 of the Appeals from the Upper Tribunal to the Court of Appeal Order 2008. The Upper Tribunal may not grant permission to appeal to the Court of Appeal unless it:

"considers that–

(a) the proposed appeal would raise some important point of principle or practice; or

(b) there is some other compelling reason for the relevant appellate court to hear the appeal."

This is equivalent to s55(1) Access to Justice Act 1999, which applies to the court system. The Court of Appeal gave guidance on the meaning and scope of s51(1) in *Uphill v BRE (Residuary) Ltd* [2005] 3 All ER 264. Permission will only be given in respect of an important point of principle or practice if it has not yet been decided. Another compelling reason means one other than an important point of principle or practice and one which is truly exceptional.

The point of law on which permission to appeal to the Court of Appeal is sought should be identified in the application (*Fryer-Kelsey v SSWP* [2005] EWCA Civ 511 (reported as *R(IB) 6/05*)). It is not sufficient for an appellant simply to identify the parts of the tribunal's decision with which the party disagrees without identifying the issues or the reasons why the decision is said to be wrong: *Re N (A Child) v A* [2010] 1 FLR 454, paras 69-72.

In *Such v SSHD* [2006] EWCA Civ 711, Sedley LJ emphasised the importance of the permission filter in protecting applicants, saying (at para 10) that "the preliminary application, which this is, is a valuable protection for a litigant against the risk of getting in too deep; getting, in other words, into this court without a real prospect of success on a point of law and finding herself liable for a very large sum of costs for the other side's representation".

The fact that the decision under appeal was arguably plainly wrong is not a compelling reason for giving permission to appeal. Nor is the fact that the decisions at different levels below were in conflict. It is, though, possible that the impact of a decision on the welfare of a child could provide a compelling reason. See *Re B (Residence: Second Appeal)* [2009] 2 FLR 632, paras 10-12 and 14. In *R (Cart) v Upper Tribunal and R (MR (Pakistan)) v Upper Tribunal and SSHD* [2011] UKHL 28; [2011] AACR 38 at para 131, Lord Dyson gave as as possible examples of a compelling reason: "(i) a case where it is strongly arguable that the individual has suffered ... 'a wholly exceptional collapse of fair procedure' or (ii) a case where it is strongly arguable that there has been an error of law which has caused truly drastic consequences." In *Eba v Advocate General for Scotland* [2011] UKSC 29; [2011] AACR 39 at para 48, Lord Hope (speaking for the Court) gave less stringent examples: "where it was clear that the decision was perverse or plainly wrong or where, due to some procedural irregularity, the petitioner had not had a fair hearing at all."

The appeals from the Upper Tribunal to the Court of Appeal Order 2008 was made under the authority of s13(6) of the Tribunals, Courts and Enforcement Act 2007. That subsection only applies to applications for permission to appeal against a decision given under s11. That section only applies to cases that came before the Upper Tribunal on appeal. It does not apply to cases that come before the Upper Tribunal on referral under s9(5)(b). Accordingly, the order does not apply if a party applies for permission to appeal against a decision made by the Upper Tribunal on a referral. An appeal to the Court of Appeal in those circumstances would not be a second appeal. In *Cooke v Secretary of State for Social Security* [2002] 3 All ER 279, Hale LJ applied the s55(1) criteria to applications for permission to appeal against decisions of the commissioners. It is possible that the reasoning in that case would apply to a case that was referred to the Upper Tribunal, as there has, in substance (though not in form), been two judicial appeals.

Subsection (8)

The Court of Appeal has no inherent power that would allow it to bypass the prohibition in para (c) on appeals against refusals of permission to appeal: *Riniker v University College London* [2001] 1 WLR 13.

Judicial review

Those decisions of the Upper Tribunal that are not appealable under this section may be subject to judicial review. The Supreme Court has decided that a decision of the Upper Tribunal is only susceptible to judicial review (or supervision in Scotland) in two circumstances: (i) the case raises an important point of principle or practice; or (ii) there is another compelling reason for the case to be subject to review (*R (Cart) v Upper Tribunal and R (MR (Pakistan)) v Upper Tribunal and SSHD* and *Eba v Advocate General for Scotland*). These are the second appeal criteria that have to be given for an appeal from the Upper Tribunal to the Court of Appeal or Court of Session.

Proceedings on appeal to Court of Appeal etc.

14.–(1)   Subsection (2) applies if the relevant appellate court, in deciding an appeal under section 13, finds that the making of the decision concerned involved the making of an error on a point of law.

(2)   The relevant appellate court–

(a)   may (but need not) set aside the decision of the Upper Tribunal, and

(b)   if it does, must either–

(i)   remit the case to the Upper Tribunal or, where the decision of the Upper Tribunal was on an appeal or reference from another tribunal or some other person, to the Upper Tribunal or that other tribunal or person, with directions for its reconsideration, or

(ii)   re-make the decision.

(3)   In acting under subsection (2)(b)(i), the relevant appellate court may also–

(a)   direct that the persons who are chosen to reconsider the case are not to be the same as those who–

(i)   where the case is remitted to the Upper Tribunal, made the decision of the Upper Tribunal that has been set aside, or

(ii)   where the case is remitted to another tribunal or person, made the decision in respect of which the appeal or reference to the Upper Tribunal was made;

(b)   give procedural directions in connection with the reconsideration of the case by the Upper Tribunal or other tribunal or person.

(4)   In acting under subsection (2)(b)(ii), the relevant appellate court–

(a)   may make any decision which the Upper Tribunal could make if the Upper Tribunal were re-making the decision or (as the case may be) which the other tribunal or person could make if that other tribunal or person were re-making the decision, and

(b)   may make such findings of fact as it considers appropriate.

(5)   Where–

(a)   under subsection (2)(b)(i) the relevant appellate court remits a case to the Upper Tribunal, and

(b)   the decision set aside under subsection (2)(a) was made by the Upper Tribunal on an appeal or reference from another tribunal or some other person,

the Upper Tribunal may (instead of reconsidering the case itself) remit the case to that other tribunal or person, with the directions given by the relevant appellate court for its reconsideration.

(6)   In acting under subsection (5), the Upper Tribunal may also–

(a)   direct that the persons who are chosen to reconsider the case are not to be the same as those who made the decision in respect of which the appeal or reference to the Upper Tribunal was made;

(b)   give procedural directions in connection with the reconsideration of the case by the other tribunal or person.

(7)   In this section "the relevant appellate court", as respects an appeal under section 13, means the court specified as respects that appeal by the Upper Tribunal under section 13(11).

Commencement

Tribunals, Courts and Enforcement Act 2007 (Commencement No.6 and Transitional Provisions) Order 2008 (SI 2008 No.2696) art 5(a) (November 3, 2008).

General Note

A grant of permission by the Court of Appeal may be reconsidered, but only for a compelling reason (*Hunt v Peasegood, The Times,* July 26 2000).

The Court of Appeal is concerned with the decision of the Upper Tribunal, not the decision of the First-tier Tribunal. It limits itself to the issues raised in the grounds of appeal and will not allow the parties to raise further points at the hearing (*Gover v Propertycare Ltd* [2006] 4 All ER 69).

The Court of Appeal may refuse to hear and therefore dismiss an appeal, despite the fact that the Upper Tribunal has given permission, if it is based on an argument that was not put to that tribunal (*SSWP v Hughes (A Minor),* reported as *R(DLA) 1/04*).

"Judicial review"

Upper Tribunal's "judicial review" jurisdiction

15.–(1)   The Upper Tribunal has power, in cases arising under the law of England and Wales or under the law of Northern Ireland, to grant the following kinds of relief–

(a)   a mandatory order;

(b)   a prohibiting order;

(c)   a quashing order;

(d)   a declaration;

(e)   an injunction.

(2)   The power under subsection (1) may be exercised by the Upper Tribunal if–

(a)   certain conditions are met (see section 18), or

(b)   the tribunal is authorised to proceed even though not all of those conditions are met (see section 19(3) and (4)).

(3)   Relief under subsection (1) granted by the Upper Tribunal–

(a)   has the same effect as the corresponding relief granted by the High Court on an application for judicial review, and

(b)   is enforceable as if it were relief granted by the High Court on an application for judicial review.

(4)   In deciding whether to grant relief under subsection (1)(a), (b) or (c), the Upper Tribunal must apply the principles that the High Court would apply in deciding whether to grant that relief on an application for judicial review.

(5)   In deciding whether to grant relief under subsection (1)(d) or (e), the Upper Tribunal must–

(a)   in cases arising under the law of England and Wales apply the principles that the High Court would apply in deciding whether to grant that relief under section 31(2) of the Supreme Court Act 1981 (c. 54) on an application for judicial review, and

(b)   in cases arising under the law of Northern Ireland apply the principles that the High Court would apply in deciding whether to grant that relief on an application for judicial review.

(6)   For the purposes of the application of subsection (3)(a) in relation to cases arising under the law of Northern Ireland–

(a)   a mandatory order under subsection (1)(a) shall be taken to correspond to an order of mandamus,

(b)   a prohibiting order under subsection (1)(b) shall be taken to correspond to an order of prohibition, and

(c)   a quashing order under subsection (1)(c) shall be taken to correspond to an order of certiorari.

General Note

This section confers judicial review powers on the Upper Tribunal equivalent to the High Court.

Application for relief under section 15(1)

16.–(1)   This section applies in relation to an application to the Upper Tribunal for relief under section 15(1).

(2)   The application may be made only if permission (or, in a case arising under the law of Northern Ireland, leave) to make it has been obtained from the tribunal.

(3)   The tribunal may not grant permission (or leave) to make the application unless it considers that the applicant has a sufficient interest in the matter to which the application relates.

(4)   Subsection (5) applies where the tribunal considers–

(a)   that there has been undue delay in making the application, and

(b)   that granting the relief sought on the application would be likely to cause substantial hardship to, or substantially prejudice the rights of, any person or would be detrimental to good administration.

(5)   The tribunal may–

(a)   refuse to grant permission (or leave) for the making of the application;

(b)   refuse to grant any relief sought on the application.

(6)   The tribunal may award to the applicant damages, restitution or the recovery of a sum due if–

(a)   the application includes a claim for such an award arising from any matter to which the application relates, and

(b)   the tribunal is satisfied that such an award would have been made by the High Court if the claim had been made in an action begun in the High Court by the applicant at the time of making the application.

(7)   An award under subsection (6) may be enforced as if it were an award of the High Court.

(8)   Where–

(a)   the tribunal refuses to grant permission (or leave) to apply for relief under section 15(1),

(b)   the applicant appeals against that refusal, and

(c)   the Court of Appeal grants the permission (or leave), the Court of Appeal may go on to decide the application for relief under section 15(1).

(9)   Subsections (4) and (5) do not prevent Tribunal Procedure Rules from limiting the time within which applications may be made.

General Note

Subsection (1)

An application must identify the decision that is the subject of the application and the errors of law on which it is based. Particularity is necessary. It is not acceptable to present a claim as a narrative or as unfocussed complaints or as general reflections on the law. See *Brookes v SSWP and CMEC* [2010] EWCA Civ 420, para 4.

Subsection (2)

As in the High Court, the applicant must first apply for permission to make an application for judicial review. Only with permission may the application for judicial review itself be made.

Subsection (3)

As in the High Court, the applicant must have sufficient interest in the matter. This is unlikely to present a problem in the child support cases that may come before the Upper Tribunal.

Subsection (4)

This deals with delay. The Upper Tribunal may refuse permission or relief if two conditions are satisfied. The first condition is that there must have been undue delay. Rule 28(2) of the Tribunal Procedure (Upper Tribunal) Rules 2008 provides that an application must be received within three months of the decision, action or omission, although this may be extended under rule 5(3)(a). The second condition is that giving relief would involve substantial hardship or substantial prejudice or would be detrimental to good administration.

It may be that the decision that is the subject of the application is a continuing one. However, this must be distinguished from a decision that remains in effect. See *Brookes*, para 7(i).

Quashing orders under section 15(1): supplementary provision

17.–(1)   If the Upper Tribunal makes a quashing order under section 15(1)(c) in respect of a decision, it may in addition–

(a)   remit the matter concerned to the court, tribunal or authority that made the decision, with a direction to reconsider the matter and reach a decision in accordance with the findings of the Upper Tribunal, or

(b)   substitute its own decision for the decision in question.

(2)   The power conferred by subsection (1)(b) is exercisable only if–

(a)   the decision in question was made by a court or tribunal,

(b)   the decision is quashed on the ground that there has been an error of law, and

(c) without the error, there would have been only one decision that the court or tribunal could have reached.

(3) Unless the Upper Tribunal otherwise directs, a decision substituted by it under subsection (1)(b) has effect as if it were a decision of the relevant court or tribunal.

General Note

If the Upper Tribunal quashes a decision, it has power to substitute its own decision rather than direct that the decision be remade. This is subject to the three conditions in subs (3). It only applies to decisions of courts or tribunals. The decision must have been quashed for error of law. And there must be only one decision that the court or tribunal could properly make.

Limits of jurisdiction under section 15(1)

18.–(1) This section applies where an application made to the Upper Tribunal seeks (whether or not alone)–

(a) relief under section 15(1), or

(b) permission (or, in a case arising under the law of Northern Ireland, leave) to apply for relief under section 15(1).

(2) If Conditions 1 to 4 are met, the tribunal has the function of deciding the application.

(3) If the tribunal does not have the function of deciding the application, it must by order transfer the application to the High Court.

(4) Condition 1 is that the application does not seek anything other than–

(a) relief under section 15(1);

(b) permission (or, in a case arising under the law of Northern Ireland, leave) to apply for relief under section 15(1);

(c) an award under section 16(6);

(d) interest;

(e) costs.

(5) Condition 2 is that the application does not call into question anything done by the Crown Court.

(6) Condition 3 is that the application falls within a class specified for the purposes of this subsection in a direction given in accordance with Part 1 of Schedule 2 to the Constitutional Reform Act 2005 (c. 4).

(7) The power to give directions under subsection (6) includes–

(a) power to vary or revoke directions made in exercise of the power, and

(b) power to make different provision for different purposes.

(8) Condition 4 is that the judge presiding at the hearing of the application is either–

(a) a judge of the High Court or the Court of Appeal in England and Wales or Northern Ireland, or a judge of the Court of Session, or

(b) such other persons as may be agreed from time to time between the Lord Chief Justice, the Lord President, or the Lord Chief Justice of Northern Ireland, as the case may be, and the Senior President of Tribunals.

(9) Where the application is transferred to the High Court under subsection (3)–

(a) the application is to be treated for all purposes as if it–

(i) had been made to the High Court, and

(ii) sought things corresponding to those sought from the tribunal, and

(b) any steps taken, permission (or leave) given or orders made by the tribunal in relation to the application are to be treated as taken, given or made by the High Court.

(10) Rules of court may make provision for the purpose of supplementing subsection (9).

(11) The provision that may be made by Tribunal Procedure Rules about amendment of an application for relief under section 15(1) includes, in particular, provision about amendments that would cause the application to become transferrable under subsection (3).

(12) For the purposes of subsection (9)(a)(ii), in relation to an application transferred to the High Court in Northern Ireland–

(a)   an order of mandamus shall be taken to correspond to a mandatory order under section 15(1)(a),

(b)   an order of prohibition shall be taken to correspond to a prohibiting order under section 15(1)(b), and

an order of certiorari shall be taken to correspond to a quashing order under section 15(1)(c).

General Note

This section identifies the cases over which the Upper Tribunal has exclusive jurisdiction. They must satisfy four conditions. The Upper Tribunal also has, at the discretion of the High Court, a shared jurisdiction with that Court over cases that satisfy all but the third condition: see s19.

Subsection (4) – Condition 1

This limits the cases over which the Upper Tribunal has jurisdiction to those that deal exclusively with judicial review and ancillary matters. If the application is linked with any other claim, it is outside the Upper Tribunal's jurisdiction.

Subsection (5) – Condition 2

This restricts judicial review affecting the Crown Court to the High Court.

Subsection (6) – Condition 3

The Lord Chief Justice for England and Wales has given a *Direction – Classes of cases specified under section 18(6) of the Tribunals, Courts and Enforcement Act 2007* [2009] 1 WLR 327:

"It is ordered as follows–

1.   The following direction takes effect in relation to an application made to the High Court or Upper Tribunal on or after 3 November 2008 that seeks relief of a kind mentioned in section 15(1) of the Tribunals, Courts and Enforcement Act 2007 ("the 2007 Act").

2.   The Lord Chief Justice hereby directs that the following classes of case are specified for the purposes of section 18(6) of the 2007 Act–

a. Any decision of the First-tier Tribunal on an appeal made in the exercise of a right conferred by the Criminal Injuries Compensation Scheme in compliance with section 5(1) of the Criminal Injuries Compensation Act 1995 (appeals against decisions on review); and

b. Any decision of the First-tier Tribunal made under Tribunal Procedure Rules or section 9 of the 2007 Act where there is no right of appeal to the Upper Tribunal and that decision is not an excluded decision within paragraph (b), (c), or (f) of section 11(5) of the 2007 Act.

3.   This Direction does not have effect where an application seeks (whether or not alone) a declaration of incompatibility under section 4 of the Human Rights Act 1998.

4.   This Direction is made by the Lord Chief Justice with the agreement of the Lord Chancellor. It is made in the exercise of powers conferred by section 18(6) of the 2007 Act and in accordance with Part 1 of Schedule 2 to the Constitutional Reform Act 2005."

The significance of these provisions depends on how wide an interpretation is given to 'decision' in s11. The wider that interpretation, the less the scope for judicial review.

Subsection (8) – Condition 4

This limits the judges who may hear judicial review cases in the Upper Tribunal. All the salaried judges dealing with child support cases who are based in England and Wales are authorised under para (b).

Transfer of judicial review applications from High Court

19.–(1)   In the Supreme Court Act 1981 (c. 54), after section 31 insert–

"31A   Transfer of judicial review applications to Upper Tribunal

(1)   This section applies where an application is made to the High Court–

(a)   for judicial review, or

(b)   for permission to apply for judicial review.

(2)   If Conditions 1, 2, 3 and 4 are met, the High Court must by order transfer the application to the Upper Tribunal.

(3)   If Conditions 1, 2 and 4 are met, but Condition 3 is not, the High Court may by order transfer the application to the Upper Tribunal if it appears to the High Court to be just and convenient to do so.

(4)   Condition 1 is that the application does not seek anything other than–

(a)   relief under section 31(1)(a) and (b);

(b)   permission to apply for relief under section 31(1)(a) and (b);

(c)   an award under section 31(4);

(d)   interest;

(e)   costs.

(5)   Condition 2 is that the application does not call into question anything done by the Crown Court.

(6)   Condition 3 is that the application falls within a class specified under section 18(6) of the Tribunals, Courts and Enforcement Act 2007.

(7)   Condition 4 is that the application does not call into question any decision made under–

(a)   the Immigration Acts,

(b)   the British Nationality Act 1981 (c. 61),

(c)   any instrument having effect under an enactment within paragraph (a) or (b), or

(d)   any other provision of law for the time being in force which determines British citizenship, British overseas territories citizenship, the status of a British National (Overseas) or British Overseas citizenship."

(2)   In the Judicature (Northern Ireland) Act 1978 (c. 23), after section 25 insert–

"25A Transfer of judicial review applications to Upper Tribunal

(1)   This section applies where an application is made to the High Court–

(a)   for judicial review, or

(b)   for leave to apply for judicial review.

(2)   If Conditions 1, 2, 3 and 4 are met, the High Court must by order transfer the application to the Upper Tribunal.

(3)   If Conditions 1, 2 and 4 are met, but Condition 3 is not, the High Court may by order transfer the application to the Upper Tribunal if it appears to the High Court to be just and convenient to do so.

(4)   Condition 1 is that the application does not seek anything other than–

(a)   relief under section 18(1)(a) to (e);

(b)   leave to apply for relief under section 18(1)(a) to (e);

(c)   an award under section 20;

(d)   interest;

(e)   costs.

(5)   Condition 2 is that the application does not call into question anything done by the Crown Court.

(6)   Condition 3 is that the application falls within a class specified under section 18(6) of the Tribunals, Courts and Enforcement Act 2007.

(7)   Condition 4 is that the application does not call into question any decision made under–

(a)   the Immigration Acts,

(b)   the British Nationality Act 1981,

(c)   any instrument having effect under an enactment within paragraph (a) or (b), or

(d)   any other provision of law for the time being in force which determines British citizenship, British overseas territories citizenship, the status of a British National (Overseas) or British Overseas citizenship."

(3)   Where an application is transferred to the Upper Tribunal under 31A of the Supreme Court Act 1981 (c. 54) or section 25A of the Judicature (Northern Ireland) Act 1978 (transfer from the High Court of judicial review applications)–

(a)   the application is to be treated for all purposes as if it–

(i)   had been made to the tribunal, and

(ii)   sought things corresponding to those sought from the High Court,

(b)   the tribunal has the function of deciding the application, even if it does not fall within a class specified under section 18(6), and

(c)   any steps taken, permission given, leave given or orders made by the High Court in relation to the application are to be treated as taken, given or made by the tribunal.

(4)   Where–

(a)   an application for permission is transferred to the Upper Tribunal under section 31A of the Supreme Court Act 1981 (c. 54) and the tribunal grants permission, or (b)　an application for leave is transferred to the Upper Tribunal under section 25A of the Judicature (Northern Ireland) Act 1978 (c. 23) and the tribunal grants leave,

the tribunal has the function of deciding any subsequent application brought under the permission or leave, even if the subsequent application does not fall within a class specified under section 18(6).

(5)　Tribunal Procedure Rules may make further provision for the purposes of supplementing subsections (3) and (4).

(6)　For the purposes of subsection (3)(a)(ii), in relation to an application transferred to the Upper Tribunal under section 25A of the Judicature (Northern Ireland) Act 1978–

(a)　a mandatory order under section 15(1)(a) shall be taken to correspond to an order of mandamus,

(b)　a prohibiting order under section 15(1)(b) shall be taken to correspond to an order of prohibition, and

(c)　a quashing order under section 15(1)(c) shall be taken to correspond to an order of certiorari.

General Note

The amendments made by this section deal with judicial review cases that are commenced in the High Court. If they are cases that satisfy the four conditions in s18, they *must* be transferred to the Upper Tribunal. If they are cases that satisfy all but the third condition, the High Court *may* transfer them to the Upper Tribunal. This allows the High Court to transfer to the Upper Tribunal any case involving child support in which the judges' expertise in the law may be helpful.

Transfer of judicial review applications from the Court of Session

20.–(1)　Where an application is made to the supervisory jurisdiction of the Court of Session, the Court–

(a)　must, if Conditions 1 [²and 2 are met, and]

[¹(aa) [²...]]

(b)　may, if Conditions 1 [²and 3] are met, but Condition 2 is not, by order transfer the application to the Upper Tribunal.

(2)　Condition 1 is that the application does not seek anything other than an exercise of the supervisory jurisdiction of the Court of Session.

(3)　Condition 2 is that the application falls within a class specified for the purposes of this subsection by act of sederunt made with the consent of the Lord Chancellor.

(4)　Condition 3 is that the subject matter of the application is not a devolved Scottish matter.

(5)　[²...]

[¹(5A)　[²...]]

(6)　There may not be specified under subsection (3) any class of application which includes an application the subject matter of which is a devolved Scottish matter.

(7)　For the purposes of this section, the subject matter of an application is a devolved Scottish matter if it–

(a)　concerns the exercise of functions in or as regards Scotland, and

(b)　does not relate to a reserved matter within the meaning of the Scotland Act 1998 (c. 46).

(8)　In subsection (2), the reference to the exercise of the supervisory jurisdiction of the Court of Session includes a reference to the making of any order in connection with or in consequence of the exercise of that jurisdiction.

Amendments

1.　Inserted by s53(3) of 2009 c.11 as from 8.8.11.

2.　Crime and Courts Act 2013 (2013 c.22) s22(2) (November 1, 2013); Crime and Courts Act 2013 (Commencement No.4) Order 2013 (SI 2013 No.2200) arts 5 and 6.

General Note

Subsection (1)

All applications to the supervisory jurisdiction of the Court of Session must be made to that Court. They cannot be made to the Upper Tribunal: *EF v SSWP* [2009] UKUT 92 (AAC); *R(IB) 3/09*. The Court has a duty and a power to transfer the case to the Upper Tribunal, depending on which of the following conditions are satisfied.

Subsection (2) – Condition 1

This limits the cases over which the Upper Tribunal has jurisdiction to those that deal exclusively with supervisory jurisdiction, as read with subs (8).

Subsection (3) – Condition 2

This deals with those cases that the Court of Session must transfer to the Upper Tribunal under subs (1)(a). They may not include a devolved matter: subs (6). Paragraph 3 of the Act of Sederunt (Transfer of Judicial Review Applications from the Court of Session) 2008 specifies those cases that must be transferred:

"The class of application is an application which challenges a procedural decision or a procedural ruling of the First-tier Tribunal, established under section 3(1) of the Tribunals, Courts and Enforcement Act 2007."

Despite its wording, this extends to procedural errors in substantive decisions. In the *Petition of Sharon Currie* [2009] CSOH 145, Lord Hodge said (at para 6) that it includes "decisions which are vitiated by procedural errors … In other words, I interpret procedural decisions and procedural rulings as extending to procedural omissions or oversights giving rise to unfairness." In that case, the basis of the application was an error of law that was not of a procedural nature. As such, it was outside the scope of mandatory transfers. It is possible to read Lord Hodge's reasons to mean that a challenge to a procedural decision for an error of law that is not of a procedural nature (such as a lack of jurisdiction) would be outside the scope of mandatory transfers. In other words, the Act of Sederunt applies only to challenges on procedural grounds rather than to challenges of procedural decisions. A discretionary transfer was not possible, as the case involved a devolved matter – criminal injuries compensation.

The Court has power under subs (1)(b), but not a duty, to transfer other cases, provided that the other three conditions are met.

Subsection (4) – Condition 3

This excludes devolved matters from the Upper Tribunal's jurisdiction. This is defined in subs (7). Child support is not a devolved matter.

Upper Tribunal's "judicial review" jurisdiction: Scotland

21.–(1)   The Upper Tribunal has the function of deciding applications transferred to it from the Court of Session under section 20(1).

(2)   The powers of review of the Upper Tribunal in relation to such applications are the same as the powers of review of the Court of Session in an application to the supervisory jurisdiction of that Court.

(3)   In deciding an application by virtue of subsection (1), the Upper Tribunal must apply principles that the Court of Session would apply in deciding an application to the supervisory jurisdiction of that Court.

(4)   An order of the Upper Tribunal by virtue of subsection (1)–

(a)   has the same effect as the corresponding order granted by the Court of Session on an application to the supervisory jurisdiction of that Court, and

(b)   is enforceable as if it were an order so granted by that Court.

(5)   Where an application is transferred to the Upper Tribunal by virtue of section 20(1), any steps taken or orders made by the Court of Session in relation to the application (other than the order to transfer the application under section 20(1)) are to be treated as taken or made by the tribunal.

(6)   Tribunal Procedure Rules may make further provision for the purposes of supplementing subsection (5).

General Note

This equates the Upper Tribunal with the Court of Session in respect of those judicial review cases that are within its jurisdiction.

Miscellaneous

Tribunal Procedure Rules

22.–(1)   There are to be rules, to be called "Tribunal Procedure Rules", governing–

(a)   the practice and procedure to be followed in the First-tier Tribunal, and

(b)   the practice and procedure to be followed in the Upper Tribunal.

(2)   Tribunal Procedure Rules are to be made by the Tribunal Procedure Committee.

(3)   In Schedule 5–

Part 1 makes further provision about the content of Tribunal Procedure Rules,

Part 2 makes provision about the membership of the Tribunal Procedure Committee,

Part 3 makes provision about the making of Tribunal Procedure Rules by the Committee, and

Part 4 confers power to amend legislation in connection with Tribunal Procedure Rules.

(4)   Power to make Tribunal Procedure Rules is to be exercised with a view to securing–

(a)   that, in proceedings before the First-tier Tribunal and Upper Tribunal, justice is done,

(b)   that the tribunal system is accessible and fair,

(c)   that proceedings before the First-tier Tribunal or Upper Tribunal are handled quickly and efficiently,

(d)   that the rules are both simple and simply expressed, and

(e)   that the rules where appropriate confer on members of the First-tier Tribunal, or Upper Tribunal, responsibility for ensuring that proceedings before the tribunal are handled quickly and efficiently.

(5)   In subsection (4)(b) "the tribunal system" means the system for deciding matters within the jurisdiction of the First-tier Tribunal or the Upper Tribunal.

Commencement

Tribunals, Courts and Enforcement Act 2007 (Commencement No.1) Order 2007 (SI 2007 No.2709) art 2(a) (September 19, 2007).

Practice directions

23.–(1)   The Senior President of Tribunals may give directions–

(a)   as to the practice and procedure of the First-tier Tribunal;

(b)   as to the practice and procedure of the Upper Tribunal.

(2)   A Chamber President may give directions as to the practice and procedure of the chamber over which he presides.

(3)   A power under this section to give directions includes–

(a)   power to vary or revoke directions made in exercise of the power, and

(b)   power to make different provision for different purposes (including different provision for different areas).

(4)   Directions under subsection (1) may not be given without the approval of the Lord Chancellor.

(5)   Directions under subsection (2) may not be given without the approval of–

(a)   the Senior President of Tribunals, and

(b)   the Lord Chancellor.

(6)   Subsections (4) and (5)(b) do not apply to directions to the extent that they consist of guidance about any of the following–

(a)   the application or interpretation of the law;

(b)   the making of decisions by members of the First-tier Tribunal or Upper Tribunal.

(7)   Subsections (4) and (5)(b) do not apply to directions to the extent that they consist of criteria for determining which members of the First-tier Tribunal or Upper Tribunal may be chosen to decide particular categories of matter; but the directions may, to that extent, be given only after consulting the Lord Chancellor.

Commencement

Tribunals, Courts and Enforcement Act 2007 (Commencement No.6 and Transitional Provisions) Order 2008 (SI 2008 No.2696) art 5(a) (November 3, 2008).

Mediation

24.–(1)   A person exercising power to make Tribunal Procedure Rules or give practice directions must, when making provision in relation to mediation, have regard to the following principles–

(a)   mediation of matters in dispute between parties to proceedings is to take place only by agreement between those parties;

(b)   where parties to proceedings fail to mediate, or where mediation between parties to proceedings fails to resolve disputed matters, the failure is not to affect the outcome of the proceedings.

(2)   Practice directions may provide for members to act as mediators in relation to disputed matters in a case that is the subject of proceedings.

(3)   The provision that may be made by virtue of subsection (2) includes provision for a member to act as a mediator in relation to disputed matters in a case even though the member has been chosen to decide matters in the case.

(4)   Once a member has begun to act as a mediator in relation to a disputed matter in a case that is the subject of proceedings, the member may decide matters in the case only with the consent of the parties.

(5)   Staff appointed under section 40(1) may, subject to their terms of appointment, act as mediators in relation to disputed matters in a case that is the subject of proceedings.

(6)   In this section–

"member" means a judge or other member of the First-tier Tribunal or a judge or other member of the Upper Tribunal;

"practice direction" means a direction under section 23(1) or (2);

"proceedings" means proceedings before the First-tier Tribunal or proceedings before the Upper Tribunal.

Commencement

Tribunals, Courts and Enforcement Act 2007 (Commencement No.6 and Transitional Provisions) Order 2008 (SI 2008 No.2696) art 5(a) (November 3, 2008).

Supplementary powers of Upper Tribunal

25.–(1)   In relation to the matters mentioned in subsection (2), the Upper Tribunal–

(a)   has, in England and Wales or in Northern Ireland, the same powers, rights, privileges and authority as the High Court, and

(b)   has, in Scotland, the same powers, rights, privileges and authority as the Court of Session.

(2)   The matters are–

(a)   the attendance and examination of witnesses,

(b)   the production and inspection of documents, and

(c)   all other matters incidental to the Upper Tribunal's functions.

(3)   Subsection (1) shall not be taken–

(a)   to limit any power to make Tribunal Procedure Rules;

(b)   to be limited by anything in Tribunal Procedure Rules other than an express limitation.

(4)   A power, right, privilege or authority conferred in a territory by subsection (1) is available for purposes of proceedings in the Upper Tribunal that take place outside that territory (as well as for purposes of proceedings in the tribunal that take place within that territory).

Commencement

Tribunals, Courts and Enforcement Act 2007 (Commencement No.6 and Transitional Provisions) Order 2008 (SI 2008 No.2696) art 5(a) (November 3, 2008).

General Note

This section confers on the Upper Tribunal the powers of enforcement of the High Court and the Court of Session. The First-tier Tribunal may refer cases to the Upper Tribunal for enforcement. See the General Note to rule 7(3) Tribunal Procedure (First-tier Tribunal) (Social Entitlement Chamber) Rules 2008 on p820.

For an example of the Upper Tribunal using its powers under this section, see *CB v Suffolk CC* [2010] UKUT 413 (AAC); [2011] AACR 22.

First-tier Tribunal and Upper Tribunal: sitting places

26. Each of the First-tier Tribunal and the Upper Tribunal may decide a case–

(a) in England and Wales,

(b) in Scotland, or

(c) in Northern Ireland,

even though the case arises under the law of a territory other than the one in which the case is decided.

Commencement

Tribunals, Courts and Enforcement Act 2007 (Commencement No.6 and Transitional Provisions) Order 2008 (SI 2008 No.2696) art 5(a) (November 3, 2008).

Enforcement

27.–(1) A sum payable in pursuance of a decision of the First-tier Tribunal or Upper Tribunal made in England and Wales–

(a) shall be recoverable as if it were payable under an order of a county court in England and Wales;

(b) shall be recoverable as if it were payable under an order of the High Court in England and Wales.

(2) An order for the payment of a sum payable in pursuance of a decision of the First-tier Tribunal or Upper Tribunal made in Scotland (or a copy of such an order certified in accordance with Tribunal Procedure Rules) may be enforced as if it were an extract registered decree arbitral bearing a warrant for execution issued by the sheriff court of any sheriffdom in Scotland.

(3) A sum payable in pursuance of a decision of the First-tier Tribunal or Upper Tribunal made in Northern Ireland–

(a) shall be recoverable as if it were payable under an order of a county court in Northern Ireland;

(b) shall be recoverable as if it were payable under an order of the High Court in Northern Ireland.

(4) This section does not apply to a sum payable in pursuance of–

(a) an award under section 16(6), or

(b) an order by virtue of section 21(1).

(5) The Lord Chancellor may by order make provision for subsection (1) or (3) to apply in relation to a sum of a description specified in the order with the omission of one (but not both) of paragraphs (a) and (b).

(6) Tribunal Procedure Rules–

(a) may make provision as to where, for purposes of this section, a decision is to be taken to be made;

(b) may provide for all or any of subsections (1) to (3) to apply only, or not to apply except, in relation to sums of a description specified in Tribunal Procedure Rules.

Commencement

s27(5) and (6): Tribunals, Courts and Enforcement Act 2007 (Commencement No.1) Order 2007 (SI 2007 No.2709) art 2(a) (September 19, 2007).

s27(1)–(4): Tribunals, Courts and Enforcement Act 2007 (Commencement No.6 and Transitional Provisions) Order 2008 (SI 2008 No.2696) art 6(a) (April 1, 2009).

Assessors

28.–(1) If it appears to the First-tier Tribunal or the Upper Tribunal that a matter before it requires special expertise not otherwise available to it, it may direct that in dealing with that matter it shall have the assistance of a person or persons appearing to it to have relevant knowledge or experience.

(2) The remuneration of a person who gives assistance to either tribunal as mentioned in subsection (1) shall be determined and paid by the Lord Chancellor.

(3)   The Lord Chancellor may–

(a)   establish panels of persons from which either tribunal may (but need not) select persons to give it assistance as mentioned in subsection (1);

(b)   under paragraph (a) establish different panels for different purposes;

(c)   after carrying out such consultation as he considers appropriate, appoint persons to a panel established under paragraph (a);

(d)   remove a person from such a panel.

Commencement

Tribunals, Courts and Enforcement Act 2007 (Commencement No.6 and Transitional Provisions) Order 2008 (SI 2008 No.2696) art 5(a) (November 3, 2008).

Costs or expenses

29.–(1)   The costs of and incidental to–

(a)   all proceedings in the First-tier Tribunal, and

(b)   all proceedings in the Upper Tribunal,

shall be in the discretion of the Tribunal in which the proceedings take place.

(2)   The relevant Tribunal shall have full power to determine by whom and to what extent the costs are to be paid.

(3)   Subsections (1) and (2) have effect subject to Tribunal Procedure Rules.

(4)   In any proceedings mentioned in subsection (1), the relevant Tribunal may–

(a)   disallow, or

(b)   (as the case may be) order the legal or other representative concerned to meet, the whole of any wasted costs or such part of them as may be determined in accordance with Tribunal Procedure Rules.

(5)   In subsection (4) "wasted costs" means any costs incurred by a party–

(a)   as a result of any improper, unreasonable or negligent act or omission on the part of any legal or other representative or any employee of such a representative, or

(b)   which, in the light of any such act or omission occurring after they were incurred, the relevant Tribunal considers it is unreasonable to expect that party to pay.

(6)   In this section "legal or other representative", in relation to a party to proceedings, means any person exercising a right of audience or right to conduct the proceedings on his behalf.

(7)   In the application of this section in relation to Scotland, any reference in this section to costs is to be read as a reference to expenses.

Commencement

Tribunals, Courts and Enforcement Act 2007 (Commencement No.6 and Transitional Provisions) Order 2008 (SI 2008 No.2696) art 5(a) (November 3, 2008).

SCHEDULE 5
SECTION 22
PROCEDURE IN FIRST-TIER TRIBUNAL AND UPPER TRIBUNAL
Part 1
Tribunal Procedure Rules

Introductory

1.–(1)   This Part of this Schedule makes further provision about the content of Tribunal Procedure Rules.

(2)   The generality of section 22(1) is not to be taken to be prejudiced by–

(a)   the following paragraphs of this Part of this Schedule, or

(b)   any other provision (including future provision) authorising or requiring the making of provision by Tribunal Procedure Rules.

(3)   In the following paragraphs of this Part of this Schedule "Rules" means Tribunal Procedure Rules.

Concurrent functions

2.   Rules may make provision as to who is to decide, or as to how to decide, which of the First-tier Tribunal and Upper Tribunal is to exercise, in relation to any particular matter, a function that is exercisable by the two tribunals on the basis that the question as to which of them is to exercise the function is to be determined by, or under, Rules.

Delegation of functions to staff

3.–(1)   Rules may provide for functions–

(a)   of the First-tier Tribunal, or

(b)   of the Upper Tribunal,

to be exercised by staff appointed under section 40(1).

(2)   In making provision of the kind mentioned in sub-paragraph (1) in relation to a function, Rules may (in particular)–

(a)   provide for the function to be exercisable by a member of staff only if the member of staff is, or is of a description, specified in exercise of a discretion conferred by Rules;

(b)   provide for the function to be exercisable by a member of staff only if the member of staff is approved, or is of a description approved, for the purpose by a person specified in Rules.

Time limits

4.   Rules may make provision for time limits as respects initiating, or taking any step in, proceedings before the First-tier Tribunal or the Upper Tribunal.

Repeat applications

5.   Rules may make provision restricting the making of fresh applications where a previous application in relation to the same matter has been made.

Tribunal acting of its own initiative

6.   Rules may make provision about the circumstances in which the First-tier Tribunal, or the Upper Tribunal, may exercise its powers of its own initiative.

Hearings

7.   Rules may–

(a)   make provision for dealing with matters without a hearing;

(b)   make provision as respects allowing or requiring a hearing to be in private or as respects allowing or requiring a hearing to be in public.

Proceedings without notice

8.   Rules may make provision for proceedings to take place, in circumstances described in Rules, at the request of one party even though the other, or another, party has had no notice.

Representation

9.   Rules may make provision conferring additional rights of audience before the First-tier Tribunal or the Upper Tribunal.

Evidence, witnesses and attendance

10.–(1)   Rules may make provision aboutevidence (including evidence on oath and administration of oaths).

(2)   Rules may modify any rules of evidence provided for elsewhere, so far as they would apply to proceedings before the First-tier Tribunal or Upper Tribunal.

(3)   Rules may make provision, where the First-tier Tribunal has required a person–

(a)   to attend at any place for the purpose of giving evidence,

(b)   otherwise to make himself available to give evidence,

(c)   to swear an oath in connection with the giving of evidence,

(d)   to give evidence as a witness,

(e)   to produce a document, or

(f)   to facilitate the inspection of a document or any other thing (including any premises),

for the Upper Tribunal to deal with non-compliance with the requirement as though the requirement had been imposed by the Upper Tribunal.

(4)   Rules may make provision for the payment of expenses and allowances to persons giving evidence, producing documents, attending proceedings or required to attend proceedings.

Use of information

11.–(1)   Rules may make provision for the disclosure or non-disclosure of information received during the course of proceedings before the First-tier Tribunal or Upper Tribunal.

(2)   Rules may make provision for imposing reporting restrictions in circumstances described in Rules.

Costs and expenses

12.–(1)   Rules may make provision for regulating matters relating tocosts, or (in Scotland) expenses, of proceedings before the First-tier Tribunal or Upper Tribunal.

(2) The provision mentioned in sub-paragraph (1) includes (in particular)–

(a) provision prescribing scales of costs or expenses;

(b) provision for enabling costs to undergo detailed assessment in England and Wales by a county court or the High Court;

(c) provision for taxation in Scotland of accounts of expenses by an Auditor of Court;

(d) provision for enabling costs to be taxed in Northern Ireland in a county court or the High Court;

(e) provision for costs or expenses–

    (i) not to be allowed in respect of items of a description specified in Rules;

    (ii) not to be allowed in proceedings of a description so specified;

(f) provision for other exceptions to either or both of subsections (1) and (2) of section 29.

Set-off and interest

13.–(1) Rules may make provision for a party to proceedings to deduct, from amounts payable by him, amounts payable to him.

(2) Rules may make provision for interest on sums awarded (including provision conferring a discretion or provision in accordance with which interest is to be calculated).

Arbitration

14. Rules may provide for [¹any of the provisions of sections 1 to 15 of and schedule 1 to the Arbitration (Scotland) Act 2010 (which extends to Scotland) or] Part 1 of the Arbitration Act 1996 (c. 23) (which extends to England and Wales, and Northern Ireland, but not Scotland) not to apply, or not to apply except so far as is specified in Rules, where the First-tier Tribunal, or Upper Tribunal, acts as arbitrator.

Correction of errors and setting-aside of decisions on procedural grounds

15.–(1) Rules may make provision for the correction of accidental errors in a decision or record of a decision.

(2) Rules may make provision for thesetting aside of a decision in proceedings before the First-tier Tribunal or Upper Tribunal–

(a) where a document relating to the proceedings was not sent to, or was not received at an appropriate time by, a party to the proceedings or a party's representative,

(b) where a document relating to the proceedings was not sent to the First-tier Tribunal or Upper Tribunal at an appropriate time,

(c) where a party to the proceedings, or a party's representative, was not present at a hearing related to the proceedings, or

(d) where there has been any other procedural irregularity in the proceedings.

(3) Sub-paragraphs (1) and (2) shall not be taken to prejudice, or to be prejudiced by, any power to correct errors or set aside decisions that is exercisable apart from rules made by virtue of those sub-paragraphs.

Ancillary powers

16. Rules may confer on the First-tier Tribunal, or the Upper Tribunal, such ancillary powers as are necessary for the proper discharge of its functions.

Rules may refer to practice directions

17. Rules may, instead of providing for any matter, refer to provision made or to be made about that matter by directions under section 23.

Presumptions

18. Rules may make provision in the form of presumptions (including, in particular, presumptions as to service or notification).

Differential provision

19. Rules may make different provision for different purposes or different areas.

Amendment

1. Arbitration (Scotland) Act 2010 (Consequential Amendments) Order 2010 (SI 2010 No.220) art 2 and Sch para 8 (June 5, 2010).

Commencement

Tribunals, Courts and Enforcement Act 2007 (Commencement No.1) Order 2007 (SI 2007 No.2709) art 2(i) (September 19, 2007).

Part 4

POWER TO AMEND LEGISLATION IN CONNECTION WITH TRIBUNAL PROCEDURE RULES
Lord Chancellor's power

30.–(1) The Lord Chancellor may by order amend, repeal or revoke any enactment to the extent he considers necessary or desirable–

    (a)   in order to facilitate the making of Tribunal Procedure Rules, or

    (b)   in consequence of–

          (i)   section 22,

          (ii)   Part 1 or 3 of this Schedule, or

          (iii)   Tribunal Procedure Rules.

    (2)   In this paragraph "enactment" means any enactment whenever passed or made, including an enactment comprised in subordinate legislation (within the meaning of the Interpretation Act 1978 (c. 30)).

Commencement

Tribunals, Courts and Enforcement Act 2007 (Commencement No.1) Order 2007 (SI 2007 No.2709) art 2(i) (September 19, 2007).

The Tribunal Procedure (First-tier Tribunal) (Social Entitlement Chamber) Rules 2008
2008 No.2685 (L.13)

PART 1
INTRODUCTION

PART 2

PART 3
PROCEEDINGS BEFORE THE TRIBUNAL
CHAPTER 1
Before the hearing

CHAPTER 2
Hearings

CHAPTER 3
Decisions

PART 4
CORRECTING, SETTING ASIDE, REVIEWING AND APPEALING TRIBUNAL DECISIONS

SCHEDULE 1
Time limits for providing notices of appeal to the decision maker

SCHEDULE 2
Issues in relation to which the Tribunal may refer a person for medical examination under section 20(2) of the Social Security Act 1998

PART 1
Introduction

Citation, commencement, application and interpretation

1.–(1)   These Rules may be cited as the Tribunal Procedure (First-tier Tribunal) (Social Entitlement Chamber) Rules 2008 and come into force on 3rd November 2008.

[²(2)   These Rules apply to proceedings before the Social Entitlement Chamber of the First-tier Tribunal.]

(3)   In these Rules–

"the 2007 Act" means the Tribunals, Courts and Enforcement Act 2007;

"appeal" includes an application under section 19(9) of the Tax Credits Act 2002;

"appellant" means a person who makes an appeal to the Tribunal, or a person substituted as an appellant under rule 9(1) (substitution of parties);

[*Omitted*]

"decision maker" means the maker of a decision against which an appeal has been brought;

"dispose of proceedings" includes, unless indicated otherwise, disposing of a part of the proceedings;

"document" means anything in which information is recorded in any form, and an obligation under these Rules to provide or allow access to a document or a copy of a document for any purpose means, unless the Tribunal directs otherwise, an obligation to provide or allow access to such document or copy in a legible form or in a form which can be readily made into a legible form;

"hearing" means an oral hearing and includes a hearing conducted in whole or in part by video link, telephone or other means of instantaneous two-way electronic communication;

"legal representative" means [¹ a person who, for the purposes of the Legal Services Act 2007, is an authorised person in relation to an activity which constitutes the exercise of a right of audience or the conduct of litigation within the meaning of that Act], an advocate or solicitor in Scotland or a barrister or solicitor in Northern Ireland;

"party" means–

(a)   a person who is an appellant or respondent in proceedings before the Tribunal;

(b)   a person who makes a reference to the Tribunal under section 28D of the Child Support Act 1991

(c)   *[Omitted]*

(d)   if the proceedings have been concluded, a person who was a party under paragraph (a), (b) or (c) when the Tribunal finally disposed of all issues in the proceedings;

"practice direction" means a direction given under section 23 of the 2007 Act;

"respondent" means–
(a) in an appeal against a decision, the decision maker and any person other than the appellant who had a right of appeal against the decision;
(b) in a reference under section 28D of the Child Support Act 1991–
(i) the absent parent or non-resident parent;
(ii) the person with care; and
(iii) in Scotland, the child if the child made the application for a departure direction or a variation;
(c) *[Omitted]*
(d) a person substituted or added as a respondent under rule 9 (substitution and addition of parties);
[³]
"social security and child support case" means any case allocated to the Social Entitlement Chamber [⁴ of the First-tier Tribunal] except an asylum support case or a criminal injuries compensation case;
"Tribunal" means the First-tier Tribunal.

Amendments
1. Amended by r3 of SI 2010 No 43 as from 18.1.10.
2. Substituted by r5(2) of SI 2010 No 2653 as from 29.11.10.
3. Omitted by r4(2)(a) of SI 2011 No 651(L.6) as from 1.4.11.
4. Amended by r4(2)(b) of SI 2011 No 651 (L.6) as from 1.4.11.

Overriding objective and parties' obligation to co-operate with the Tribunal
2.–(1) The overriding objective of these Rules is to enable the Tribunal to deal with cases fairly and justly.
(2) Dealing with a case fairly and justly includes–
(a) dealing with the case in ways which are proportionate to the importance of the case, the complexity of the issues, the anticipated costs and the resources of the parties;
(b) avoiding unnecessary formality and seeking flexibility in the proceedings;
(c) ensuring, so far as practicable, that the parties are able to participate fully in the proceedings;
(d) using any special expertise of the Tribunal effectively; and
(e) avoiding delay, so far as compatible with proper consideration of the issues.
(3) The Tribunal must seek to give effect to the overriding objective when it–
(a) exercises any power under these Rules; or
(b) interprets any rule or practice direction.
(4) Parties must–
(a) help the Tribunal to further the overriding objective; and
(b) co-operate with the Tribunal generally.

Definitions
"party": see rule 1(3).
"practice direction": see rule 1(3).
"Tribunal": see rule 1(3).

General Note
Rule 2(1)-(3)
The rules of procedure and practice directions must be interpreted, and the rules must be applied, in ways that allow the tribunal to deal with the case fairly and justly. The instances listed in rule 2(2) are not exhaustive and do not affect the general principle stated in rule 2(1).

The requirements of procedural fairness and justice include, but may be broader than, the principles of natural justice and the right to a fair hearing under Art 6(1). In practice, the precise scope of natural justice may become less important in future as tribunals work out what is required by reference to the overriding objective.

Natural justice and analogous cases
A tribunal cannot deal with cases fairly and justly unless it complies with the principles of natural justice. These are concerned with the procedural fairness of the proceedings, including the hearing of the appeal (*R(S) 4/1982*, para 26). They are not concerned with the fairness or justice of the law applied by the tribunal. The right to a fair

hearing is separate from the outcome of the proceedings before the tribunal. Even if the outcome is unimpeachable, a failure to allow the parties a fair hearing is wrong as a fair hearing might have resulted in different findings of fact (*Stansby v Datapulse plc* [2004] ICR 523).

The principles of natural justice ensure that the parties have a fair hearing (*McInnes v Onslow-Fane* [1978] 3 All ER 211 at 219, *per* Megarry V-C). They protect the parties to the proceedings against the failure by the tribunal to give them a fair hearing. This covers the failings of the judicial members of the tribunal. It also covers the failings of a tribunal clerk in carrying out administrative duties ancillary to the tribunal's judicial function, as these are failings of "the tribunal" for this purpose, provided that they affect the fairness of the hearing (*CIB 4812/1997*, paras 12-21). Natural justice does not protect a party against the party's own failings or those of the party's advisers (*Al-Mehdawi v SSHD* [1989] 3 All ER 843 at 848, *per* Lord Bridge).

In *CJSA 5100/2001*, the commissioner argued that fair hearing issues would be better expressed in terms of striking a balance between the parties, language derived from the equality of arms aspect of the Convention right to a fair hearing under the Human Rights Act 1998, in order to emphasise this aspect to tribunals whose standards were, in his view, deteriorating.

On appeal, factual issues relating to the fairness of the hearing must be investigated and determined if that is necessary to deal with the issue on the appeal (*Stansby v Datapulse plc*). This may require a statement to be obtained from the members of the tribunal. In *CDLA 5574/2002*, the commissioner set out two circumstances in which a statement would be obtained (para 8). First, if the other evidence is insufficient but raised an issue worthy of investigation. Second, if personal misconduct by a panel member was alleged.

Principles have been developed by analogy with natural justice where the one party has failed to communicate material information to the other party (*Al-Mehdawi* at 848 *per* Lord Bridge). The failure by one of the parties to the proceedings to provide for the tribunal information material to the case has been treated as a breach of natural justice (*R(CS) 1/99*, para 8 following *R(SB) 18/83*, para 11), although the commissioner did not refer to the reasoning in *Al-Mehdawi*. The reasoning has been extended to the failure by a tribunal clerk to pass material information to the tribunal (*CCS 16817/1996*, para 10), but the reasoning was not followed by another commissioner who treated the failure by the clerk as a failure by the appeal tribunal (*CIB 4812/1997*, para 20). The Court of Appeal has allowed an appeal under s11, Tribunals and Inquiries Act 1992 on the ground that information had been supplied to the clerk of a special needs appeal tribunal but not passed to the members (*W v Special Needs Appeal Tribunal, The Times,* December 12 2000).

As the analogous principle is based on the suppression of information by one party to the proceedings to the detriment of another party, a party cannot rely on it if the reason for the information not being available lies in the party's own fault or in circumstances outside the control of any of the parties (*CIB 4951/1997*, paras 5-6; *CIB 4853/1998*, paras 18-20). This is especially so if the evidence that was not available was the subject of a direction that was not complied with by the party (*CCS 4687/2000*, para 12). The Convention right under Art 6(1) is no wider. It provides that a party is "entitled to a fair ... hearing". If the absence of information is not attributable by cause or contribution to the appeal tribunal, the party's entitlement has not been affected. It has simply not been effective, because of the party's own fault or circumstances beyond anyone's control. See *CIB 2470/2001*, paras 14-15. A party's recourse in a case that falls outside both the principles of natural justice and the analogous principle lies in the tribunal's wider power to set aside under rule 37 (*CIB 4853/1998*, para 22).

Since the contexts in which the principles have to apply vary considerably, they are applied flexibly to ensure that standards are set that are appropriate to the circumstances. This point was made by Tucker LJ in *Russell v Duke of Norfolk* [1949] 1 All ER 109 at 118:

> "There are, in my view, no words which are of universal application to every kind of inquiry and every kind of domestic tribunal. The requirements of natural justice must depend on the circumstances of the case, the nature of the inquiry, the rules under which the tribunal is acting, the subject matter that is being dealt with and so forth."

This point is of particular importance to a tribunal that takes an inquisitorial approach to its proceedings. The principles of natural justice in many ways reflect the features of the adversarial approach and have had to be adapted to other contexts.

In so far as these rules make no provision (eg, for the procedure at a paper hearing), the tribunal must act "in accordance with natural justice and to promote the objective with which it was set up, and possibly by analogy with the rules of procedure prescribed for comparable tribunals or bodies" (*Qureshi v Qureshi* [1971] 1 All ER 325 at 342-3, *per* Simon P).

In so far as these rules make provision, their interpretation and operation must be set in the context of the interplay between (i) the individual rules, (ii) the wide powers given to the tribunal to regulate its procedure (rule 5(1)), (iii) the principles of natural justice (*CDLA 5509/1997*, para 12), and (iv) the overriding objective. Legislation can never be in breach of natural justice (*CCS 2513/1995*, para 9 – not affected by the decision of the Court of Appeal in that case, which is reported as *R(CS) 4/99*). It may displace the requirements of natural justice, as in *R(SB) 55/83*, para 12. Before the effect of a rule can be determined, it has to be interpreted and this must be done against the background of natural justice and in light of the overriding objective. Legislation will be interpreted, so far as the language allows, so as not to conflict with the requirement, in general terms, of natural justice (*John v Rees* [1969] 2 All ER 74 at 309, *per* Megarry J and *Fairmount Investments Ltd v Secretary of State for the Environment* [1976] 2 All ER 865 at 872, *per* Lord Russell) and to give effect to the overriding objective.

So far as natural justice is concerned, this applies to the enabling provisions under which the rules are made as well as to the substantive terms of both statute and the rules. Also, in deciding how to exercise powers and discretions conferred by these rules, the tribunal must seek to give effect to the overriding objective by acting judicially, which involves taking account of those requirements (*CDLA 5509/1997*, para 12). So, for example, if the time available does not permit a hearing in accordance with natural justice, the tribunal must adjourn (*R v Thames Magistrates' Court ex p Polemis* [1974] 2 All ER 1219).

The essence of natural justice is that the parties should be given a fair hearing. The test is an objective one. This is emphasised in the classic statement of Lord Hewart CJ in *R v Sussex Justices ex p McCarthy* [1924] 1 KB 256 at 259:

"it is not merely of some importance but is of fundamental importance that justice should not only be done, but should manifestly and undoubtedly be seen to be done."

The extent to which this statement is given effect in the modern law varies from aspect to aspect of natural justice.

The tribunal must not be biased. The standard required is the same for judges, arbitrators and jurors. The law is authoritatively laid down by the Court of Appeal in *Locabail (UK) Ltd v Bayfield Properties Ltd* [2000] 1 All ER 65. (References in this section of the general note are to paragraphs in the Court's judgment unless otherwise stated.) The British test was brought into line with the European approach by the Court of Appeal in *re Medicaments and Related Classes of Goods (No.2)* [2001] 1 WLR 700 by modestly adjusting the reasoning of the House of Lords in *R v Gough* [1993] AC 646. This was approved, subject to a slight alteration of the wording, by the House of Lords in *Porter v Magill* [2002] 1 All ER 465*per* Lord Hope at paras 99-103.

The tribunal's opinion on whether it was biased is not admissible (*Facey v Midas Retail Security Ltd* [2001] ICR 287 at 303).

Bias involves a breach of the fundamental right of the parties to a fair hearing by reasons of partiality or prejudice (para 2). There are three categories of bias.

(i)   **Actual bias** This is regularly alleged on appeal, although usually on spurious grounds. It is rare in practice, because of the standards applied by members of the panel. It is difficult to prove in court, because the law does not allow judges to be questioned about extraneous matters that may have influenced a decision (para 3). In practice, it is unnecessary to show actual bias, because the lesser standard of real possibility of bias is always available as an alternative (paras 3 and 16).

(ii)   **Presumed bias** Bias is presumed if a member of the tribunal has an interest in the outcome of the case (para 4). The interest is most likely to be financial, although there is an undefined category of cases where the member has a particularly close relationship with a party to the proceedings. This was exemplified in *R v Bow Street Metropolitan Stipendiary Magistrate ex p Pinochet (No.2)* [1999] 1 All ER 577. Cases of presumed bias should not be extended beyond existing authority, unless the extension is plainly required to give effect to the underlying principles on which the rule is based (para 14). An interest is disregarded if it is so small as to be incapable of affecting the decision (para 10). If the interest is that of a family member, the tribunal member must be so closely and directly affected that their interests are indistinguishable (para 10). Presumed bias can be waived by the parties to the proceedings against whom the bias is presumed (para 15), but the best practice is for the member to withdraw as soon as the interest becomes apparent, rather than present the parties to the proceedings with a last-minute choice between an adjournment or waiver (para 21).

(iii)   **Real apprehension of bias** Bias will be shown if there is an apprehension of bias (para 16). The test is an objective one. It is decided by reference to the standard of a fair-minded and informed observer who is aware of legal traditions and culture (*Taylor v Lawrence* [2002] 2 All ER 353 at para 61). The issue is whether there is a reasonable apprehension of bias, not whether it was likely that the actual tribunal was in fact biased: *re Medicaments and Related Classes of Goods (No.2)*. The parties to the proceedings against whom the bias exists may waive it and allow the member to sit (paras 15 and 26). There is no comprehensive definition of what may or may not give rise to a real possibility of bias. Everything depends on the circumstances of the case, which may include the nature of the issue to be decided, although subject to this the Court of Appeal gave a detailed list of instances that might or might not show a real possibility of bias (para 25). It has been held in the Chancery Division that it is inconceivable that a real possibility of bias could be shown on the basis of the religion, ethnic or national origin, gender, age, class, means or sexual orientation of a judge hearing a case (*Seer Technologies Ltd v Abbas, The Times*, March 16 2000). Although everyone who is appointed to a judicial office must disclose membership of the Freemasons, the fact that a member of the tribunal and one of the parties to the proceedings are both Freemasons is not decisive of bias (*R (Port Regis School Ltd) v North Dorset District Council, The Times*, April 14 2006). Bias is particularly likely to arise from some connection between a member of the tribunal and one of the parties, such as the series of connections between a fee-paid judge's former firm and the claimant in *SW v SSWP (IB)* [2010] UKUT 73 (AAC) at paras 51-52. The connection might involve some relationship between the persons concerned or some dealing between or affecting them. Bias is not shown by professional or social contact between a member of the tribunal and a representative of one of the parties (*CIB 5794/1997*, para 9; *Taylor v Lawrence* at para 63). Knowledge by the member of the factor alleged to create the bias is essential if the allegation is to succeed and the member concerned may properly be asked whether the factor was known (paras 18 and 19). Disclosure should be made as soon as the member becomes aware of it and realises that it is relevant, regardless of the stage of the proceedings (para 26). It should only be made if there is objectively a real issue of the possibility of bias, but if it is made, it must be full (*Taylor v Lawrence* at paras 64-65). Unfounded allegations of bias should not lead a tribunal to abort the hearing of a case (*Bennett v Southwark London Borough Council* [2002] ICR 881).

The mere fact that a member of a tribunal has previously decided a case involving a party or made adverse comments about that party does not of itself entitle the party to claim bias and a rehearing before a differently constituted tribunal (*Lodwick v London Borough of Southwark* [2004] ICR 884 at para 21), although in the particular circumstances of the case this may be required. In *CCS 1876/06* para 12, the commissioner emphasised that as a matter of good practice rather than law a member who has previously dealt adversely with a party might consider it better not to sit, if resources allowed, in order to maintain that party's confidence in the appeal process.

If a panel member is called as a witness, care needs to be taken to avoid the appearance of bias in the constitution of the tribunal by ensuring that it does not consist of members who regularly sit with the witness (*CIS 661/1994*, para 14).

A lawyer who sits as a fee-paid judge should not appear before a tribunal if it contains a lay panel member before whom the lawyer has appeared (*Lawal v Northern Spirit Ltd* [2004] 1 All ER 187).

A party who is potentially prejudiced by an apparent bias is entitled to waive the right to a differently constituted tribunal. The waiver is that of the party and not of the party's representative. A representative is under a duty to ensure that the party is appropriately informed of all matters relevant to the possibility of bias and the waiver. If this duty is not complied with, the waiver is ineffective (*Smith v Kvaerner Cementation Foundations Ltd* [2007] 1 WLR 370 at paras 33 and 37).

Bias is not the only aspect of natural justice. The principles cover everything that may deny a party to the proceedings a fair hearing. Many aspects of a fair hearing are covered by specific rules of procedure. Each party to the proceedings must know that the hearing is to be held and, subject to the rules on opting for an oral hearing, be entitled to attend. The party must be entitled to know the issues involved and the evidence and arguments put forward by other parties. All parties should have a chance, in person or in writing, to contribute by presenting evidence and arguments and by challenging those presented by other parties. This involves having adequate notice of the hearing (in the case of a paper hearing, adequate notice of the earliest date on which it will be held) and adequate time to prepare a case. A record of the proceedings should be kept. The decision must be notified to the parties, along with reasons if they are requested in time. The decision must not be based on factors on which a party adversely affected by them has not had a chance to comment, although this chance may (depending on the factors and the circumstances of the case) have been forfeited if the party did not ask for and attend an oral hearing. The decision must be based on material that tends logically to show the existence or non-existence of relevant facts or the likelihood of the occurrence or non-occurrence of some future relevant event. See generally *R(IS) 5/93*, para 17.

A tribunal should usually hear both sides of a case and not dismiss the appeal having heard only the appellant. The only exception is if the case is hopeless. Otherwise, the tribunal should hear all parties, whether or not there is a burden of proof on the appellant. See *Logan v Commissioners for Customs and Excise* [2004] ICR 1.

Reliance by a tribunal on an authority or provision that was not cited to it by the parties and not drawn to the parties' attention by the tribunal will only render the hearing unfair if it was central to the issue and resulted in substantial prejudice or material injustice to one of the parties (*Stanley Cole (Wainfleet) Ltd v Sheridan* [2003] ICR 1449).

If it appears that a member of the tribunal is not concentrating on a significant part of the proceedings, for example by appearing to be asleep, there will not have been a fair hearing. Compare *Stansby v Datapulse plc* [2004] ICR 523 (no fair hearing when member appeared to be asleep after drinking alcohol) and *R v Betson and Cockran, The Times*, January 28 2004 (in which a judge fell asleep during counsel's speech to the jury – outcome not influenced by this).

Insensitivity on the part of the tribunal is unlikely to deprive a party of a fair hearing (*BK v SSWP* [2009] UKUT 258 (AAC), paras 28-31).

If a remark (such as a racial remark) is made in an impersonal way which could not be taken as relating to any party to the proceedings, an immediate apology may remove the appearance of bias (*Reid v Chief Constable of Merseyside, The Times*, February 5 1996). And chance remarks must be considered objectively and in their context (*National Assembly for Wales v Condron, The Times*, December 13 2006). These authorities are very limited in scope and it is, of course, better for the remark not to be made at all.

In *CU 270/1986*, the claimant had been too ill to attend the hearing of his appeal. He applied for the decision to be set aside. This application was rejected. The claimant was not invited to attend the hearing of his application in order to explain his illness. Although there was no duty on the tribunal to do so and the original tribunal had correctly exercised its power to proceed in the claimant's absence, the commissioner held (paras 11-12) that the failure to allow the claimant to give evidence on the setting aside application coupled with his earlier illness retrospectively produced a breach of natural justice in the original hearing. With respect, this must be wrong. A breach in respect of later proceedings cannot relate back to an earlier hearing.

Natural justice and the proper approach to a hearing

The members of a tribunal should have read the papers before an oral hearing. If there is more than one member of the tribunal, it is good practice for the members to have previewed the case, in so far as that is possible from the papers, before the start of the hearing. This involves identifying the issues that will arise and the questions that the tribunal will have to investigate, and deciding how to conduct the hearing. No question of prejudgement is involved in this practice, which is in accordance with the principles of natural justice. The point was nicely made by Bill Tillyard, formerly a full-time chairman in the Wales and the South West Region, when he said that a hearing must be approached with an open mind, but not with an empty one.

It is consistent with the principles of natural justice, and indeed a contribution to a fair hearing, for an appeal tribunal to keep the parties informed during a hearing of its assessment of the evidence or arguments, provided that no impression is created that a conclusion has been reached. Decisions taken by the chairman on the conduct of the proceeding, such as to ensure that they are conducted as expeditiously as possible, are consistent with the principles of natural justice. See *ArabMonetary Fund v Hashim (No.8)* [1993] 6 Admin LR 348, *Mahomed v Morris, TheTimes,* March 1 2000 and *R(IS) 5/78,* para 18.

The tribunal has to take an inquisitorial approach to the proceedings before it. This is an aspect of natural justice that is necessary in order to ensure a fair hearing for every party to the proceedings. The proper exercise of this approach is not inconsistent with the principles of natural justice. The following will not, therefore, automatically be in breach of natural justice: interrupting the presentation of a party's case (*R(SB) 6/82,* para 6); asking probing questions that the party would prefer were not asked (*R(S) 4/82,* para 27; indicating scepticism, but not a closed mind (*ArabMonetary Fund v Hashim (No.8) per* Sir Thomas Bingham MR).

Rule 2(2)(b)

An emphasis on substance rather than form is inconsistent with the need to avoid formality and further flexibility.

The commissioners always resisted arguments based on strict compliance with legal form. In *R(I) I5/53,* the commissioner said (para 4) of an argument that the claimant had not sufficiently particularised the grounds of appeal: "A demand for strict compliance with legal forms would operate harshly in many cases if applied to claimants". And in *R(I) 50/56,* the commissioner said (para 18) that:

> "it must be remembered that claimants may well fail to appreciate the appropriate legal procedures by which their rights ought to be protected and it is essential that the determining authorities should not defeat a meritorious claim by a legal technicality."

The commissioner used that principle to treat a claim for benefit as an application for a review. The commissioner in *R(CS) 2/06* applied this principle to child support, but with qualifications:

"25.   The Commissioners, and their predecessors in the social security jurisdiction, have encouraged the Secretary of State to be realistic and not to expect claimants to understand the adjudication procedures. This allows letters to be treated as applications for whatever course of action is most appropriate in the circumstances of the case. This allows the Secretary of State to deal with a letter from a claimant by reference to its substance rather than its form. It has also been used to allow any contact by the claimant to be treated as an application if this will be advantageous in terms of the effective date.

26.   The same considerations that apply in social security apply in child support. However, the context is different. In the social security jurisdiction, the only parties are the Secretary of State and the claimant, and the Secretary of State is not a contentious party. In the child support jurisdiction in contrast, there will usually be two parties in addition to the Secretary of State; their involvement is contentious and their interests conflict. An interpretation of a letter that works to the benefit of one of those parties may work to the detriment of the other. That behoves a greater degree of restraint than is appropriate in the social security context. I suggest that in applying this approach in child support two qualifications are appropriate.

27.   *First qualification* It is appropriate to interpret letters by reference to their substance rather than their form. This is especially so if the writer is not represented and is not familiar with the child support adjudication procedures. However, it is not appropriate simply to treat any point of contact as an application just because that will be advantageous to the person concerned. To do so may operate to the disadvantage of the other party.

28.   *Second qualification* The approach can only be applied within the limits allowed by the legislation. In the case of an application for a variation, that means that it must be applied consistently with the Variations Regulations. The form in which an application may be made is governed by regulation 4. Regulation 5 allows an application to be amended and regulation 8 allows the evidence and information to be supplemented. Both those provisions show that it is not necessary for an application to be complete before it is made."

The same approach should be applied by a decision maker, who is under "a duty to apply the most appropriate procedure to the contents of the information provided by the applicant" (*DB, CMEC and KB* [2010] UKUT (AAC) 356 (AAC), para 17). This does not impose a duty on the decision maker to investigate. However, the decision maker may also be under this duty if it is impossible otherwise to make a decision – eg, because of contradictions of material fact (*ibid*, para 17). This may be preferable to making a default maintenance decision under s12(1) of the Act.

Rule 2(2)(c)

The tribunal must ensure that, so far as practicable, the parties are able to participate fully in the proceedings. This duty incorporates what has traditionally be called the "inquisitorial approach." However, it is not so limited. It will include all other matters that affect participation, such as the venue and timing of the hearing. Taken together with the duty to co-operate, it also includes the proper preparation of a bundle in a form that is useable by the other parties (*CH 4262/2007*, paras 39-40).

Taken together with the duty to co-operate, this provision covers the proper preparation of a bundle in a form that is useable by the other parties: *CH 4262/2007*, paras 39-40.

The inquisitorial approach

This phrase has been useful in distancing tribunal procedure from that operated in a court, but it is a misleading label in so far as it may suggest that there is a single model of inquisitorial approach which is to be applied. There is no such model, only a general descriptive phrase that reflects the broad consensus of how the tribunal should be conducted and around which presiding judges have developed their own styles of procedure. The decisions of the commissioners and Upper Tribunal provide some guidance on what is involved, but this leaves ample scope for the initiative of individual judges. The task for all tribunals is to develop a procedure suited to the circumstances of the particular case.

The inquisitorial approach survives the changes to the tribunal structure under the 2007 Act. In particular, it is consistent with the duty on the Senior President to have regard to the need for tribunals to be accessible (s2(3)(a)) and the importance of avoiding unnecessary formality, seeking flexibility and ensuring participation under rule 2(2)(b) and (c). It is in the context of these provisions that the nature of the inquisitorial approach will have to be developed.

In *CSC 2/1994*, the commissioner decided (para 20) that the procedure in a tribunal was primarily inquisitorial in so far as the issues raised were between the absent parent and the person with care, on the one hand, and the child support officer, on the other, but that the procedure might be primarily adversarial if the issues raised were principally between the absent parent and the person with care. Unfortunately, the commissioner's reasoning depended in part on the absence in that case of any detailed notification of the basis of the child support officer's decision. This decision does, however, indicate that the procedure should be adapted to the circumstances of the case and provides support for the approach to procedure suggested in the preceding paragraph.

An inquisitorial approach is needed in order to ensure that all sides of a case are considered. It is not affected by the existence of a right of appeal to a higher court or by the nature of the issues that arise for consideration (*CIS 1459/2003*, para 26). The procedure adopted must not be so informal as to prevent this being done (*Dyason v Secretary of State for the Environment, The Times,* February 9 1998).

Caselaw gives a little guidance as to the proper exercise of the inquisitorial function. The tribunal is not entitled to sit back and act as referee between the rival contentions of the opposing parties as would be the case in a typical court procedure (*R v National Industrial Injuries Commissioner ex p Moore* [1965] 1 All ER 81 at 93, *per* Diplock LJ) and it should disabuse representatives of any erroneous views on which their arguments are based (*Dennis v United Kingdom Central Council for Nursing, Midwifery and Health Visiting, The Times,* April 2 1993). If it identifies a relevant point, it should be followed up and a decision reached, even if it has not been raised by the parties. A tribunal cannot limit its powers of investigation on account of the nature of the issue, for example, that it involves questioning a party about the possibility of a sexual relationship (*CIS 87/1993*, para 13, reported as *Re J (Income Support:Cohabitation)* [1995] 1 FLR 660). The tribunal is also expected to pick up obvious and self-evident points which arise. However, the parties are not entitled to rely upon the expertise of the tribunal to discharge the burdens of proof which properly rest on the parties themselves. Nor should a tribunal set off on a fishing expedition into the facts on the off-chance that something relevant may turn up. This is especially so if the evidence has been stated with certainty (see generally *R(SB) 2/83*, paras 10-11 and *CSSB 470/1989*, para 7). It is for the tribunal to reach conclusions on questions of fact and to decide whether there is sufficient evidence to do so. The Upper Tribunal has no power to intervene unless the tribunal's decision is so unreasonable as to be perverse, and a party who chooses not to attend cannot complain about the lack of oral evidence that might have been given (*CSA 1/1995*, para 3). Likewise the Secretary of State (and it is suggested parties with competent representatives) cannot expect to appeal successfully if the officers have not adduced the right evidence, failed to ask the right questions or failed to advance the right arguments (*CDLA 7980/1995*, para 11). Despite these statements, tribunals have been expected to deal with all legal issues that are raised by the facts before them and are relevant to the decisions which they make, and decisions which fail to do so are regularly overturned on appeal. However, the duty on tribunals to exercise an inquisitorial approach is confined within sensible limits to questions which arise directly from the evidence or from further investigations which are reasonably called for by that evidence (*CIS 264/1993*, para 12) and tribunals are not expected to go to absurd lengths in the exercise of this approach (*CA 60/1993*, para 23). A tribunal need not go beyond what is fair and reasonable and must decide whether further investigation is likely to serve a useful purpose (*R v National Insurance Commissioner ex p Viscusi* [1974] 2 All ER 724 at 731 and 732, *per* Lord Denning MR and Buckley LJ respectively). These considerations, though, only set the bounds on the duty imposed on tribunals; they do not limit their power to investigate beyond these limits if they wish (*CIS 264/1993*, para 12).

In *R(CS) 5/98*, the commissioner drew a distinction between (a) an argument in the submission that on the evidence available a decision maker's decision might be wrong and (b) an argument that on the evidence available it was wrong. The commissioner criticised submissions written in the form (a) as being unhelpful to an unrepresented party for failing to make clear what additional evidence was required (para 8). With regard to an argument in form (a), the commissioner held that the tribunal was not in error of law for failing to deal with the point when, in the absence of both parents, there was no evidence to justify altering the decision maker's decision (para 9). The commissioner did not explain why the tribunal should not have sought further evidence directly from the party concerned or through the child support officer. This approach is capable of being exploited by a party who believes that a decision may be incorrectly advantageous through the simple expedient of refraining from attending the tribunal. It is suggested that this aspect of this decision should be treated with caution and certainly limited to cases where the party concerned is not present at the hearing. With regard to an argument in form (b), the commissioner held that the tribunal was under a duty to deal with it and its decision was wrong in law for failing to do so (para 11).

In *CSCS 16/2007*, the commissioner held (para 9) that the inquisitorial approach had to be considered in the context of the duty on a person with care to make out a case that the non-resident parent's lifestyle was inconsistent with disclosed income and that it would be unfair for a tribunal, in the absence of the non-resident parent, to attempt to elicit evidence from the applicant for the variation that she had failed to produce. In so far as the commissioner based his reasoning on the assumption that child support cases, in contrast to social security cases, do not involve an issue between the subject and the State, it is inconsistent with the reasoning of Collins J in *R (Starling) v Child Support Commissioners* [2008] EWHC 1319 (Admin), which rejected that distinction and held at paras 31-32 that there was a public interest involved in child support cases.

The comments in the caselaw on the inquisitorial approach were made in the context of deciding whether there has been an error of law to justify setting aside a tribunal's decision. They set the limits within which the tribunal is expected to act if its decision is to withstand an appeal. They may, therefore, understate the role which tribunals should ideally play. The atmosphere should be as relaxed and informal as is consistent with the proper exercise of a judicial function and certainly more so than in a court. In particular, the tribunal is expected to fulfil an enabling role, especially with an unrepresented party. This involves setting an appropriate atmosphere: the parties should feel comfortable and able to put across what they wish to say. It also involves helping the parties to understand what is required: the parties should be helped to follow the procedure, to understand the matters which are relevant to the case and to present the best case possible on their behalf.

In exercising the inquisitorial approach, the tribunal is not limited to the terms of the appeal.

In practice, the operation of the inquisitorial approach is limited where one of the parties does not attend (*CIB 17622/1996*, para 8), although in such a case the tribunal will be anxious to ensure that all matters of possible benefit to that party are investigated as thoroughly as possible in her/his absence. Tribunals are also entitled to vary their approach according to whether or not the parties are competently represented (*CSDLA 336/2000*). The approach should be more strenuously followed on behalf of a party who is unrepresented (*R(I) 6/69*, para 7). However, where parties are represented, the tribunal is entitled to take a less active role and to accept without further investigation concessions made and accepted by all parties (*CSA 2/1994*, para 7; *CDLA 12150/1996*, para 7). However, concessions do not bind a tribunal, unless, on the information available, they have been correctly made. A concession may be accepted unless it is clearly bad (*CDLA 267/1994*, para 8). Where the concession is one of fact rather than of law, the fact that it is made by a competent representative will be relevant in deciding whether it should be accepted. There is no need to record findings in respect of issues covered by a concession (*CDLA 12150/1996*, para 8). Concessions may be withdrawn, either before the same tribunal (*R(IS) 14/93*, para 7) or on appeal (*LC v SSWP* [2009] UKUT 153 (AAC), para 11). It is unlikely that concessions by a presenting officer at a hearing will create a legitimate expectation, as they will seldom amount to a clear and unambiguous representation that the Secretary of State would not exercise its statutory powers (*LC v SSWP*, para 12).

A tribunal is not required to embark upon an investigation merely on account of general allegations, such as to a party's dishonesty, which are frequently made on and following a marital break-up, unless there are reasons to put the tribunal on inquiry (*CCS 12/1994*, para 46).

The proper implementation of the inquisitorial approach and the enabling role may involve the tribunal in investigating an issue that is not raised by any of the parties. This is not indicative of bias (*BK v SSWP* [2009] UKUT 258 (AAC), paras 13-14). It may also may mean that parties may be interrupted in the course of the presentation of their case. This does not constitute bias on the part of the tribunal (*R(SB) 6/82*, para 6). Likewise, the asking of probing questions is proper in the exercise of the tribunal's inquisitorial approach and is not of itself indicative of bias (*R(S) 4/82*, para 27).

In furtherance of the inquisitorial approach, the tribunal may have to investigate an issue that is not raised by any of the parties. This is not indicative of bias: *BK v SSWP*, paras 13-14.

Rule 2(4)

The parties are under a duty to co-operate with the tribunal both to further the overriding objective and generally. This is merely a specific instance of the operation of the overriding objective. As part of the duty, the parties must comply with the tribunal's directions. But it is not so limited. Co-operation may require a party to act without a direction – eg, by keeping the tribunal informed of any difficulties that may affect listing. They must co-operate with the tribunal in fixing a date for hearing, showing flexibility and giving appropriate priority to judicial proceedings (*CCS 5315/1999*).

Alternative dispute resolution and arbitration

3.–(1) The Tribunal should seek, where appropriate–

(a)   to bring to the attention of the parties the availability of any appropriate alternative procedure for the resolution of the dispute; and

(b)   if the parties wish and provided that it is compatible with the overriding objective, to facilitate the use of the procedure.

(2)   Part 1 of the Arbitration Act 1996 does not apply to proceedings before the Tribunal.

Definitions
"party": see rule 1(3).
"Tribunal": see rule 1(3).

PART 2
General powers and provisions

Delegation to staff
4.–(1)   Staff appointed under section 40(1) of the 2007 Act (tribunal staff and services) may, with the approval of the Senior President of Tribunals, carry out functions of a judicial nature permitted or required to be done by the Tribunal.

(2)   The approval referred to at paragraph (1) may apply generally to the carrying out of specified functions by members of staff of a specified description in specified circumstances.

(3)   Within 14 days after the date on which the Tribunal sends notice of a decision made by a member of staff under paragraph (1) to a party, that party may apply in writing to the Tribunal for that decision to be considered afresh by a judge.

Definitions
"the 2007 Act": see rule 1(3).
"Tribunal": see rule 1(3).

General Note
The Senior President has issued a practice statement on delegation, but no powers have been delegated in relation to child support cases.

Case management powers
5.–(1)   Subject to the provisions of the 2007 Act and any other enactment, the Tribunal may regulate its own procedure.

(2)   The Tribunal may give a direction in relation to the conduct or disposal of proceedings at any time, including a direction amending, suspending or setting aside an earlier direction.

(3)   In particular, and without restricting the general powers in paragraphs (1) and (2), the Tribunal may–
(a)   extend or shorten the time for complying with any rule, practice direction or direction;
[¹(aa) [*Omitted*]]
(b)   consolidate or hear together two or more sets of proceedings or parts of proceedings raising common issues, or treat a case as a lead case (whether in accordance with rule 18 (lead cases) or otherwise);
(c)   permit or require a party to amend a document;
(d)   permit or require a party or another person to provide documents, information, evidence or submissions to the Tribunal or a party;
(e)   deal with an issue in the proceedings as a preliminary issue;
(f)   hold a hearing to consider any matter, including a case management issue;
(g)   decide the form of any hearing;
(h)   adjourn or postpone a hearing;
(i)   require a party to produce a bundle for a hearing;
(j)   stay (or, in Scotland, sist) proceedings;
(k)   transfer proceedings to another court or tribunal if that other court or tribunal has jurisdiction in relation to the proceedings and–

(i)   because of a change of circumstances since the proceedings were started, the Tribunal no longer has jurisdiction in relation to the proceedings; or

(ii)   the Tribunal considers that the other court or tribunal is a more appropriate forum for the determination of the case; or

(l)   suspend the effect of its own decision pending the determination by the Tribunal or the Upper Tribunal of an application for permission to appeal against, and any appeal or review of, that decision.

Amendment

1.   Inserted by r23 of SI 2013 No.2067 as from 1.11.13.

Definitions

"the 2007 Act": see rule 1(3).
"appeal": see rule 1(3).
"dispose of proceedings": see rule 1(3).
"document": see rule 1(3).
"hearing": see rule 1(3).
"party": see rule 1(3).
"practice direction": see rule 1(3).
"Tribunal": see rule 1(3).

General Note

Rule 5(1)

The tribunal has power to regulate its own procedure. This is an essential power that allows the tribunal to personalise the procedure for the needs of individual cases. It is subject only to the 2007 Act and any other enactment. These rules are enactments, but practice directions, practice statements and directions given, for example, under rule 5(2) are not.

There are limits to the power to regulate procedure. It is a case management power and, as such, is concerned with matters of procedure (*Care First Partnership Ltd v Roffey* [2001] ICR 87). It cannot be used to circumvent the specific provision made for particular matters, such as under rule 8 for the striking out of cases (*Kelly v Ingersoll-Rand Co Ltd* [1982] ICR 476).

Within these limits, the procedure must ensure that the appeal tribunal acts judicially. This is capable of referring to the personal manner and behaviour of the members of the tribunal, but more usually it refers to the basis on which the tribunal makes its decision. In that sense, it involves these requirements. The tribunal must not act capriciously (*CDLA 2986/2001*, para 12). It must act rationally on evidence of probative value (*Mahon v Air New Zealand* [1984] 3 All ER 201 at 210, *per* Lord Diplock). It must act according to law (*R(U) 7/81*, para 8). It must act with scrupulous fairness (*R (M) v Inner London Crown Court* [2003] 1 FLR 994 at para 45). It must exercise a discretion with due regard to the purpose for which it was conferred (*South Bucks DC v Porter* [2003] 3 All ER 1 at para 29 *per* Lord Bingham). A discretion must also be exercised according to common sense and justice (*Gardner v Jay* [1885] 29 Ch.D. 50 at 58 *per* Bowen LJ). Discretion must not be exercised "subjectively or at whim or by rigid rule of thumb, but in a principled manner in accordance with reason and justice" (*United Arab Emirates v Abdeighafar* [1995] ICR 65 at 70 *per* Mummery J). Finally, the tribunal must act in compliance with natural justice and the Convention rights of the parties (*CCS 5301/2002*, para 14). The members of the tribunal must give their undivided attention to the proceedings (*R v Marylebone Magistrates' Court ex p Joseph, The Times,* May 7 1993). The decision whether or not to announce the tribunal's decision orally on the day of the hearing is a matter of procedure in connection with the hearing and falls within this power under this paragraph (*CDLA 15227/1996*, para 10).

In *CIB 2058/2004,* the commissioner said (para 13) that the purpose of the power conferred by this paragraph is to ensure good order and efficiency and it must be exercised in order to further that purpose. He distinguished between efficiency and effectiveness, emphasising that tribunals had to exercise their power in a way that allowed competent representatives to operate effectively. This decision is authority for the wider proposition that the power must be exercised in a way that is consistent with allowing all those present the opportunity to fulfil their proper roles.

Rule 5(2)

The tribunal may give directions in relation to the conduct of the proceedings at any time, whether on application or on its own initiative (rule 6(1)).

Despite the broad wording of the power, it is limited to procedural matters. It cannot be used to usurp the tribunal's powers over substantive issues.

A direction may be given before (a) the case is listed, (b) after listing and pending the hearing or (c) at the hearing.

As to (a), the commissioner in *CCS 2786/2005* (para 5), commended the use of pre-hearing directions that guided the parties on the evidence to be produced, set a timetable for its production, explained the types of evidence that could and could not be accepted, and warned of the possibility of adverse inferences. The commissioner recommended a standard approach for all tribunals.

As to (b), it is good practice for the presiding judge to check the papers on receipt in order to identify any directions which could be given which would contribute to the conduct of the proceedings. If directions are given to a party, there will only be a limited time before the hearing within which the parties can comply with the directions. This may require the hearing to be postponed, for example, if the direction required further evidence to be disclosed to all parties or written submissions be presented to the tribunal in advance.

As to (c), directions at an oral hearing will usually be given orally. The tribunal might, for example, direct a party to an appeal not to tape record the proceedings. When a direction is given orally, the fact that it has been given and its terms should be included in the record of proceedings.

The tribunal has a discretion whether to hold an oral hearing of a directions hearing (*KP v Hertfordshire CC(SEN)* [2010] UKUT 233 (AAC)).

The reasons that a tribunal gives for a direction need only be short (*KP v Hertfordshire CC(SEN)*).

Rule 5(3)(a)

This power is additional to rule 12. If the time by which an act must be done ends on a day other than a working day, the time is automatically extended until the next working day by that rule. There is no need for time to be extended under this rule. In applying this provision, the tribunal does not have to follow the structure of CPR rule 3.9(1) (*CD v First-tier Tribunal (SEC) (CIC)* [2010] UKUT 181 (AAC), paras 25-27).

Rule 5(3)(b)

See rule 18 on p839.

A decision to treat a case as a lead case must be made by the Chamber President: para 10 of the Senior President's Practice Statement on *Composition of Tribunals in Social Security and Child Support Cases in the Social Entitlement Chamber on or after 3 November 2008*.

Rule 5(3)(c)

This includes power to direct the Secretary of State to arrange for a presenting officer to attend the hearing: *RF v CMEC (CSM)* [2010] UKUT 41 (AAC), para 12.

Rule 5(3)(e)

The tribunal has power to deal with a matter as a preliminary issue. This practice is not encouraged (*CA 126/ 1989*, para 10 and *Sutcliffe v Big C's Marine* [1998] ICR 913), although they may be useful if there is dispute as to the tribunal's jurisdiction.

Rule 5(3)(f)

The tribunal may decide to hold an oral hearing. If it does, rules 27-31 apply.

If the tribunal decides the case without a hearing, the tribunal must act "in accordance with natural justice and to promote the objective with which it was set up, and possibly by analogy with the rules of procedure prescribed for comparable tribunals or bodies" (*Qureshi v Qureshi* [1971] 1 All ER 325 at 342-3, *per* Simon P).

The tribunal must satisfy itself that one of the parties has not opted for an oral hearing (*CDLA 245/1998*, para 13). The decision will be wrong in law if no oral hearing is held when a party has opted for one. In cases where there may be a doubt on the point, the tribunal's reasons should explain why the tribunal proceeded without an oral hearing (*ibid,* para 13).

The "paper" hearing may be part of a session comprised entirely of such hearings or it may be part of a session that also involves oral hearings. In either case, the presenting officer, even if present at the venue, must not be involved in the "paper" hearing, however helpful that officer's assistance might be (*CS 2810/1998*). Whether the hearing is the whole or only a part of the session, there must be a proper hearing in the sense that the tribunal must consider, as a single adjudicating body, all the relevant evidence and contentions before reaching a conclusion. This means that the tribunal must meet; it is not sufficient for the members to read the documents and reach a conclusion in isolation. See *R v Army Board ex p Anderson* [1991] 3 All ER 375 at 387, *per* Taylor LJ.

The principles of natural justice apply. These require that a party should be aware of the basis of the decision under appeal and the evidence available to the tribunal. Each party should also have an opportunity to place further evidence or representations before the tribunal once these have been seen. See *The King v Tribunal of Appeal under the Housing Act 1919* [1920] 3 KB 334. This requires that the parties should know either the date of the hearing, or at least the earliest date on which the case will be heard, and that there should be sufficient notice of this to allow additional material to be placed before the tribunal. In *DA v SSWP* [2010] UKUT 229 (AAC), the judge applied this principle as a basic requirement of natural justice and a fair hearing. He set aside the tribunal's decision on the ground that the appeal had been heard within the time allowed by the pre-listing Enquiry Form for the production of the further evidence that was being obtained by the claimant's representative.

It is only in an exceptional case that it would be an error of law for a tribunal to proceed in the absence of the parties to the proceedings when no oral hearing has been requested (*CDLA 4683/1997*, para 23). The absence of the parties will inevitably limit the inquiries that the tribunal can make (*CIB 17622/1996*, para 8), unless an oral hearing is necessary under rule 27(1)(b) in order to decide the case.

If a substantial new point arises in the course of a paper hearing, there will be a breach of natural justice if the tribunal does not adjourn to allow the parties to produce evidence or to make submissions on the point (*CIB 3899/ 1997*, paras 18-19), if appropriate at an oral hearing.

The social security commissioners held that a paper hearing of attendance allowance cases was not appropriate where integrity was in question (*R(A) 4/89* and *R(A)* 7/89). These decisions were made in the context of the adjudication of the pre-1992 Attendance Allowance, which did not allow a party a chance to opt for an oral hearing. Under these rules, the parties have that power. So, those decisions are not authority that an oral hearing should be held whenever a party's integrity is in question. This is, though, a factor that the tribunal should consider when deciding whether to exercise the power to direct that an oral hearing is necessary under rule 27(1)(b).

There is no general requirement in human rights law that there must be an oral hearing, even if disputed issues of fact or opinion are involved (*R (N) v Doctor M* [2003] 1 FLR 667 at para 41).

The duty to make a record of proceedings under the Senior President's practice statement (set out in the general note to rule 27) does not apply to paper hearings. In practice, it is unlikely that anything that might be recorded at a paper hearing would be sufficiently important to make the tribunal's decision wrong in law if it were not recorded, although there may be exceptional cases. The most useful function of a record of proceedings at a paper hearing is to note the receipt of additional documents from one of the parties to the proceedings. It is often difficult for the Upper Tribunal to tell which documents were before the tribunal. If the presiding judge does not keep a record of this, there is the risk that the decision will be set aside because it cannot be shown that a document was considered. See *CCS 4742/1997,* para 11.

In *DA v SSWP*, the judge applied this principle as a basic requirement of natural justice and a fair hearing. He set aside the tribunal's decision on the ground that the appeal had been heard within the time allowed by the pre-listing Enquiry Form for the production of the further evidence that was being obtained by the claimant's representative.

Rule 5(3)(g)

The usual decisions about the form of the hearing will be (a) whether it should be an oral hearing and (b) whether it should involve the use of electronic communication. There is no limit to the circumstances in which (b) may be appropriate (*Rowland v Bock* [2002] 4 All ER 370). The tribunal will have to devise a means by which a person who is not physically present is able to participate fully in the hearing. It is not unusual, for example, for documents to be produced for the first time at the hearing. A means (eg, fax) will have to be found for the person at the remote site to see those documents.

In deciding whether to direct an oral hearing when the parties have not requested one, the tribunal must consider all those aspects of the overriding objective that are relevant in the particular case (*MH v Pembrokeshire CC (HB)* [2010] UKUT 28 (AAC); *AT v SSWP (ESA)* [2010] UKUT 430 (AAC)).

Exceptionally a domiciliary hearing may be appropriate. The decision whether to hold a domiciliary hearing must be made in the light of the overriding objective. Three factors will always be relevant. First, the efficient allocation of resources is a legitimate consideration. Second, alternative sources of evidence have to be considered, but must be an adequate substitute for the party's own evidence (*CS 3326/1999,* para 25). Third, tribunals must remember that a party who cannot attend a hearing will be at a disadvantage. In the social security context, a commissioner said that in this eventuality a party is unlikely to have a fair hearing under Art 6(1) of the European Convention on Human Rights (*CS 3326/1999,* para 26). However, in the child support context the practicalities must also be considered, as the parties may live a long way apart and their relationship may make a domiciliary hearing inappropriate.

The reasons given by a tribunal for refusing to allow a domiciliary hearing need not be elaborate; a sentence or two will usually suffice. See *CDLA 1834/1998*.

Rule 5(3)(h)

A tribunal may postpone or adjourn a hearing. These terms are not defined. Usually, postponement occurs after the case has been listed for hearing but before the hearing has begun and an adjournment occurs after the hearing has begun.

There is no need for the tribunal to make a formal decision in respect of listing for hearing. This is handled administratively and a date will be fixed by the staff, taking account of the availability of the parties and their representatives. Nor is there any need for an adjournment during the course of the session. These are within the tribunal's general power to regulate its own procedure under rule 5(1). This allows a tribunal to delay hearing or proceeding with the case if, for example, a representative has been delayed or if a party or witness becomes distressed or in order to discuss how the tribunal should proceed (eg, whether an adjournment under this regulation is appropriate).

The decision must be made in the light of the overriding objective. The key consideration will be the purpose of the power, which is to ensure a fair hearing. The power must be applied to further that purpose (*CIB 2058/ 2004,* para 13).

The principles are the same for postponement and adjournment, although additional factors may apply in the case of an application to postpone. For example, the tribunal should consider the costs involved in attendance if the hearing is not postponed but has to be adjourned on the day. Alternatively, if there is a doubt whether or not to postpone, it may be better to allow the hearing to take place knowing that it can be adjourned if that is appropriate. If an application to postpone is refused, the tribunal hearing the case should always be informed so that it may consider whether to adjourn the hearing (*CDLA 3680/1997,* para 5).

There must be a good reason for a hearing to be adjourned (*Unilever Computer Services Ltd v Tiger Leasing SA* [1983] 2 All ER 139). Each adjournment must be approached individually and judicially. The tribunal should seek to strike a balance between the following factors: (i) the interests of the parties to be present, and to be properly prepared to present the best case in their favour and to deal with points against them; (ii) whether the adjournment would improve the quality of the tribunal's ultimate decision; (iii) the interests of the other users of the tribunal system including the Secretary of State - adjourning one case delays the hearing of others; and (iv) the extent to which the case has already been adjourned or otherwise delayed. The presiding judge should record in the notes of proceedings all requests for adjournments, the views of the parties and the decisions on them. The tribunal should also consider the following: (i) the importance of the proceedings; (ii) the likely adverse consequences on the party seeking the adjournment; (iii) the risk of prejudice to the party seeking the adjournment if the application is refused; (iv) the risk of prejudice to any other party if the application is granted; (v) the convenience of the tribunal and the interests of justice in ensuring the efficient despatch of business so as not to delay other appeals; (vi) the extent to which the applicant was responsible for the circumstances leading to the perceived need for an adjournment (*R v Kingston upon Thames Justices ex p Martin, The Times*, December 10 1993; *R (ota Lappin) v HM Customs and Excise* [2004] EWHC 953 (Admin)). However, if an adjournment is justified by the circumstances pertaining at a particular time, it is not proper to refuse to adjourn because of something which has happened earlier (*Dick v Piller* [1943] 1 All ER 627 at 629, *per* Scott LJ). For a consideration of the principles and an example of their application, see *MHA v SSWP* [2009] UKUT 211 (AAC).

It is always relevant to take account of the difficulties that will be caused by delay (*CDLA 13008/1996,* para 11). The tribunal should also bear in mind that lengthy proceedings can amount to a breach of the European Convention on Human Rights (*Darnell v United Kingdom* (1994) 18 EHRR 205).

In *Fox v Graham Group Ltd, The Times*, August 3 2001, Neuberger J said that a court should be very careful indeed before refusing a first request for an adjournment by an unrepresented party whose case was not plainly hopeless, even if an adjournment would result in inconvenience for another party.

Claimants and their representatives often argue on appeal that a tribunal should not have proceeded in the absence of a party who had indicated an intention not to attend. It is only in an exceptional case that it would be an error of law for a tribunal not to adjourn in these circumstances (*CDLA 4683/1997*, para 23).

A party is entitled to be represented and may apply for an adjournment to allow a representative to attend. Usually this will be allowed. However, the absence of a representative does not give an automatic entitlement to an adjournment (*CI 199/1989*). Nevertheless, in deciding whether to adjourn to allow a representative to attend, tribunals must take full account of the advantages that a representative brings to the party represented and to the quality of the tribunal's decision-making (*CIB 2058/2004*). It is always relevant to consider whether or not there is someone who could have attended in place of a representative who is not available, but it is a mistake to assume that all members of a particular organisation are available (*CIB 1009/2004*).

If a party to the proceedings claims to have evidence that is not at the hearing, the tribunal must investigate why the party was not prepared for the hearing.

If it is clear that a case will go on appeal, it is permissible to deal with it expeditiously, for example by refusing to adjourn (*Poplar Housing and Regeneration Community Association Ltd v Donoghue* [2001] 4 All ER 604). However, the parties are still entitled to a fair hearing and the tribunal should make appropriate findings of fact for the benefit of the Upper Tribunal.

A tribunal may give a final decision on one aspect of an appeal and adjourn the remainder (*CSIS 118/1990*, para 18), although the reasoning therein relies on considerations in social security law that have no equivalent in child support law. If this approach is permissible in child support law, any final decision made is appealable *(ibid)*.

When exercising this power, it is good practice to consider whether it is appropriate to attach any conditions or to make any directions for the future conduct of the proceedings. This may involve a discussion with the parties to identify other possible causes of future delay and any appropriate directions can be given to ensure that these matters are dealt with in the meantime.

The recorded reasons for refusing to adjourn need not be elaborate. It is sufficient to record the key considerations that influenced the tribunal to decide as it did, leaving them to be read against the background of the case. In the absence of any suggestion to the contrary, the Upper Tribunal is entitled to assume that the tribunal took that background into account. See *CCS 565/1999*, para 16.

At the resumed hearing
There are no rules about the constitution of a tribunal at a resumed hearing. It must be decided in the light of the overriding objective and according to the principles of natural justice and the Convention right to a fair hearing.

It is likely that a differently constituted tribunal will be required if (a) evidence was heard at the previous hearing (*CDLA 2429/2004*) or (b) a party or representative will attend the resumed hearing who was not present previously. This reflects the concern over residual knowledge noted by the Tribunal of Commissioners in *R(U) 3/88*, para 7. The tribunal or one of its members may have knowledge from what was said or done at the previous hearing, which may be directly relevant to the appeal as evidence or indirectly relevant to the outcome as going to the credibility of the evidence. The party or representative who did not attend that hearing will be unaware of and unable to deal with that knowledge. If the tribunal at the resumed hearing is only differently constituted in part, there is also the risk that the members may not have had the same basis for decision, as in *CDLA 2429/2004* and *MC v FTT and CICA* [2011] UKUT 87 (AAC).

Even if there is no actual danger of residual knowledge, there may be a suspicion in the party who did not attend before that it may exist and affect the outcome. That should be taken into account. If the tribunal is not differently constituted, the issue may arise whether there is a real apprehension of bias.

If a party or representative attends the rehearing who was not present at the previous hearing, the proceedings will have to be by way of a complete rehearing, regardless of whether the tribunal is differently constituted.

These considerations apply both where the adjournment is made without any final decision being made on any aspect of the case and where the tribunal makes a final decision on one aspect and adjourns the remainder. Tribunals should bear in mind that, while it may appear to be shortening the proceedings to deal with one aspect of the case, this approach is not encouraged by the law.

Some aspects of the procedure to be followed on a complete re-hearing were discussed by the Tribunal of Commissioners in *R(U) 3/88*, para 7. The case must be reheard afresh, unfettered by what happened at the earlier hearing. All evidence and submissions must be put to the fresh tribunal, although the notes of evidence at the previous hearing may be made use of for this purpose. The decision itself should generally be available, provided that the tribunal at the rehearing takes care not to rely on findings of fact that have been discredited by reason of law (*Swash v SSHD, The Times,* August 14 2006).

Where there is a complete rehearing of an appeal after an adjournment, it is desirable for the presiding judge to record in the notes of proceedings that this is what has occurred (*C 44/87 (IVB)*).

Rule 5(3)(i)

The bundle produced must be useable by the tribunal and the other parties: *CH 4262/2007*, paras 39–40.

Procedure for applying for and giving directions

6.–(1)   The Tribunal may give a direction on the application of one or more of the parties or on its own initiative.

(2)   An application for a direction may be made–

(a)   by sending or delivering a written application to the Tribunal; or

(b)   orally during the course of a hearing.

(3)   An application for a direction must include the reason for making that application.

(4)   Unless the Tribunal considers that there is good reason not to do so, the Tribunal must send written notice of any direction to every party and to any other person affected by the direction.

(5)   If a party or any other person sent notice of the direction under paragraph (4) wishes to challenge a direction which the Tribunal has given, they may do so by applying for another direction which amends, suspends or sets aside the first direction.

Definitions

"party": see rule 1(3).
"Tribunal": see rule 1(3).

Failure to comply with rules etc.

7.–(1)   An irregularity resulting from a failure to comply with any requirement in these Rules, a practice direction or a direction, does not of itself render void the proceedings or any step taken in the proceedings.

(2)   If a party has failed to comply with a requirement in these Rules, a practice direction or a direction, the Tribunal may take such action as it considers just, which may include–

(a)   waiving the requirement;

(b)   requiring the failure to be remedied;

(c)   exercising its power under rule 8 (striking out a party's case); or

(d)   exercising its power under paragraph (3).

(3)   The Tribunal may refer to the Upper Tribunal, and ask the Upper Tribunal to exercise its power under section 25 of the 2007 Act in relation to, any failure by a person to comply with a requirement imposed by the Tribunal–

(a)   to attend at any place for the purpose of giving evidence;

(b)   otherwise to make themselves available to give evidence;

(c)   to swear an oath in connection with the giving of evidence;

(d)   to give evidence as a witness;

(e)   to produce a document; or

(f)   to facilitate the inspection of a document or any other thing (including any premises).

Definitions

"the 2007 Act": see rule 1(3).

"document": see rule 1(3).

"party": see rule 1(3).

"practice direction": see rule 1(3).

"Tribunal": see rule 1(3).

General Note

An irregularity resulting from a failure to comply with the rules, a practice direction or a direction does not necessarily render the proceedings or any step in them void. This accords with the modern approach to failure to comply with procedural requirements. The courts have abandoned the former classification of provisions into mandatory and directory and now ask whether Parliament could fairly have intended that a particular failure should result in total invalidity (*R v Soneji* [2006] 1 AC 340). Lord Carswell suggested (at para 63) that it might be relevant whether there had been substantial performance of the requirement.

A breach of a tribunal's procedural rules does not usually render further proceedings of no force or effect, even if the rule is framed in mandatory terms (*R v Sekhon* [2003] 1 WLR 1655).

There may be circumstances in which, even under the modern approach, the failure and the resulting irregularity do deprive the proceedings or the step taken in them of any legal effect. In *CCS 16904/1996*, the commissioner gave the following as cases where the failure involved would render the decision maker's decision invalid and ineffective (para 25): (i) where the decision was given by an officer who had no authority to make it; (ii) where the decision had already been made by another officer; (iii) there was an absence of some application, leave, notice or other step necessary to give the officer authority. This is similar to the matters considered as going to a tribunal's jurisdiction in *R(I) 7/94* (para 30).

In *AM v SSWP* [2009] UKUT 224 (AAC), the judge decided that a purported review was a nullity. The judge did not explain how he had jurisdiction to do so given the decision in *R(I) 7/94*.

In *CCS 16904/1996*, the absent parent had been assessed as liable to pay nil child support maintenance, but had been held liable to pay a contribution from his income support in lieu of child support maintenance. The officer had failed to consider whether the condition contained in reg 28(1)(c) of the Maintenance Assessments and Special Cases Regulations was satisfied. The commissioner held that none of the above conditions was satisfied and that the decision, though flawed, was valid and effective until set aside on review. In contrast, in *CCS 12848/1996* para 9, the commissioner held that failure to give notice under reg 25 of the Maintenance Assessment Procedure Regulations of an intended review rendered the decision on that review a nullity. This case involved a defective of type (iii) above.

Compliance with directions

The tribunal has the power of this rule at its disposal if a party fails to comply with a direction. However, they may be too draconian to meet the circumstances.

At the end of the day, the key to compliance lies not in coercion or powers of enforcement, but in the willingness of the person concerned to comply with the directions given. The power to give directions under rule 5 should be used in a constructive manner to guide the parties in the preparation and presentation of their cases, and to assist them to proceed in a spirit and atmosphere of co-operation that is required by rule 2(4) and should be fostered by the whole appeal system in implementing the enabling role of the tribunal, which extends beyond the hearing of the appeal itself to the entire proceedings. This will, no doubt, often be an unattainable ideal, but it, rather than confrontation and compulsion, will make directions effective. See the comments of the commissioner in *CCS 2061/2000,* paras 12-16 and *CIB 4252/2004,* paras 11-15.

If a party fails to provide the evidence that a chairman has directed to be produced, the tribunal may be able to draw adverse inferences against the party in breach. However, it may only do this if the evidence before it does not provide an adequate basis for determining the issue. See the *Findings of Fact* section on p834. A failure to provide evidence in accordance with a direction does not automatically make a decision made without the evidence wrong in law. See *CCS 2061/2000,* paras 17-19.

Any response based on a party's failure to comply with a direction must be proportionate. In gauging what is proportionate, it is proper to consider among other matters: (a) the impact of the breach on the other party; (b) the purpose for which the direction was given; and (c) whether the response being considered would prolong proceedings in view of the Secretary of State's powers to correct errors of fact (*CDLA 4977/2001,* para 35).

In *AM v SSWP* [2009] UKUT 224 (AAC), the judge decided that a purported review was a nullity. The judge did not explain how he had jurisdiction to do so given the decision in *R(I) 7/94*.

Rule 7(3)

A number of procedural issues relating to enforcement references were considered by the three-judge panel in *MD v SSWP (Enforcement Reference)* [2010] UKUT 202 (AAC); [2011] AACR 5.

(i)   Enforcement potentially affected the liberty of the subject. Accordingly, although procedural irregularities could be waived, it was particularly important that procedural safeguards should be complied with. See para 12.

(ii)   Rule 6(4) required notice to be served on any person affected by a direction. Service would be effected under s7 Interpretation Act 1978. See para 13.

(iii)   A direction that a professional attend a hearing before the First-tier Tribunal should only be made if there is a compelling reason to do so. See para 15.

(iv)   A decision to refer a case to the Upper Tribunal must be made by the Chamber President: para 10 Senior President's Practice Statement on *Composition of Tribunals in Social Security and Child Support Cases in the Social Entitlement Chamber on or after 3 November 2008*. See para 17.

(v)   The tribunal must make clear to the person concerned what has to be done and the consequences of not doing it. See para 19.

(vi)   In *MR v CMEC (No.1)* [2009] UKUT 285 (AAC), a three-judge panel decided to reissue the directions given by the First-tier Tribunal. That is not a requirement of the section, although it may be appropriate in individual cases. See para 20.

(vii)   The panel left open the extent to which the parties against whom enforcement was not sought were entitled to be involved in the enforcement proceedings. See paras 21-23.

Further issues were considered by a three-judge panel in *CB v Suffolk CC* [2010] UKUT 413 (AAC); [2011] AACR 22.

(i)   Section 25 of the Tribunals, Courts and Enforcement Act 2007 authorised the Upper Tribunal to punish as contempt a failure by a witness to comply with a witness summons. See para 22.

(ii)   The procedure was governed by these rules, not the CPR. See para 22.

(iii)   The expense that a witness would incur in attending to give evidence was a relevant factor when considering whether to issue a witness summons. See para 24.

(iv)   The tribunal was entitled to treat a letter from a witness as an application to set aside a summons. See para 25.

(v)   A witness who wished to challenge a witness summons should proceed by judicial review. See para 26.

(vi)   A witness who received a witness summons should either comply with the summons or apply for it to be set aside. It was not permissible simply to ignore it. See para 28.

(vii)   The tribunal should be mindful of the time involved for a professional to comply with a summons and consider whether there were alternatives. See para 29.

Striking out a party's case

8.–(1)   The proceedings, or the appropriate part of them, will automatically be struck out if the appellant has failed to comply with a direction that stated that failure by a party to comply with the direction would lead to the striking out of the proceedings or that part of them.

(2)   The Tribunal must strike out the whole or a part of the proceedings if the Tribunal–

(a)   does not have jurisdiction in relation to the proceedings or that part of them; and

(b)   does not exercise its power under rule 5(3)(k)(i) (transfer to another court or tribunal) in relation to the proceedings or that part of them.

(3)   The Tribunal may strike out the whole or a part of the proceedings if–

(a)   the appellant has failed to comply with a direction which stated that failure by the appellant to comply with the direction could lead to the striking out of the proceedings or part of them;

(b)   the appellant has failed to co-operate with the Tribunal to such an extent that the Tribunal cannot deal with the proceedings fairly and justly; or

(c)   the Tribunal considers there is no reasonable prospect of the appellant's case, or part of it, succeeding.

(4)   The Tribunal may not strike out the whole or a part of the proceedings under paragraph (2) or (3)(b) or (c) without first giving the appellant an opportunity to make representations in relation to the proposed striking out.

(5)   If the proceedings, or part of them, have been struck out under paragraph (1) or (3)(a), the appellant may apply for the proceedings, or part of them, to be reinstated.

(6)   An application under paragraph (5) must be made in writing and received by the Tribunal within 1 month after the date on which the Tribunal sent notification of the striking out to the appellant.

(7)   This rule applies to a respondent as it applies to an appellant except that–

(a)   a reference to the striking out of the proceedings is to be read as a reference to the barring of the respondent from taking further part in the proceedings; and

(b)   a reference to an application for the reinstatement of proceedings which have been struck out is to be read as a reference to an application for the lifting of the bar on the respondent from taking further part in the proceedings.

(8)   If a respondent has been barred from taking further part in proceedings under this rule and that bar has not been lifted, the Tribunal need not consider any response or other submission made by that respondent [¹and may summarily determine any or all issues against that respondent].

Amendment
1.   Tribunal Procedure (Amendment No.3) Rules 2010 (2010 No.2653) rule 5(3) (November 29, 2010).

Definitions
"appellant": see rule 1(3).
"party": see rule 1(3).
"respondent": see rule 1(3).
"Tribunal": see rule 1(3).

General Note
The tribunal may strike out proceedings or bar a respondent from taking further part.
        The tribunal is under a duty to act under this rule if it has no jurisdiction, unless it exercises its power of transfer under rule 5(3)(k)(i). Strictly, it applies whenever the lack of jurisdiction becomes apparent and deprives the tribunal of its power to make a decision that the case is outside its jurisdiction (*R(SB) 29/83*, para 17). For the meaning of jurisdiction, see the general note to s20 of the Act. Jurisdiction must be distinguished from cases where the tribunal has power to deal with the issue, but can properly come to only one decision (*AW v Essex CC (SEN)* [2010] UKUT 74 (AAC), paras 12-16; *FL v First-tier Tribunal and CICA* [2010] UKUT 158 (AAC), para 17).
        When there is a power rather than a duty, striking out should be used as a last resort (*Biguzzi v Rank Leisure plc* [1999] 1 WLR 1926 at 1933, *per* Lord Woolf MR). The tribunal has power to act under this rule in three circumstances: (a) if the party has failed to comply with a direction that specifies this as a sanction for failure to comply; (b) if the party has failed to co-operate to such an extent that the tribunal cannot deal with proceedings fairly and justly; (c) if the party's case has no reasonable prospect of success.
        (a) and (b) are similar and operate as enforcement powers. The difference is that in (a) the sanction has been included in the direction, whereas in (b) it has not. The language of (a) applies to any direction, but it would only be appropriate to exercise the power if the failure to comply has had a significant impact on the tribunal's ability to deal with the case fairly and justly. The use of (b) may be contentious, but this can be avoided by issuing a direction under (a) requiring co-operation.
        (c) is not an enforcement power and operates in a way akin to proceedings that are outside the tribunal's jurisdiction. It is only appropriate where the lack of success is readily apparent. If the matter is not clear, the case should be decided. However, this power may be a convenient form for the disposal of hopeless cases after consideration at a hearing on the papers.
Reinstatement
Proceedings may be reinstated; this is implied rather than actually stated. There is no time limit, but the longer the time that has passed, the stronger the case that has to be made for reinstatement.
        In the case of a case of lack of jurisdiction or no reasonable prospect of success, the power will only be exercised if the tribunal is satisfied that it has jurisdiction or the case has a reasonable prospect of success. In the case of a failure to comply with a direction or failure to co-operate, it will only be exercised if the tribunal is satisfied that the behaviour will not be repeated. It may be exercised on conditions relating to immediate and future conduct.

Substitution and addition of parties
9.–(1)   The Tribunal may give a direction substituting a party if–
(a)   the wrong person has been named as a party; or
(b)   the substitution has become necessary because of a change in circumstances since the start of proceedings.
(2)   The Tribunal may give a direction adding a person to the proceedings as a respondent.
(3)   If the Tribunal gives a direction under paragraph (1) or (2) it may give such consequential directions as it considers appropriate.

Definitions
"party": see rule 1(3).
"respondent": see rule 1(3).
"Tribunal": see rule 1(3).

General Note
The parties will usually be the non-resident parent, the parent or person with care and the Secretary of State. Others who may wish to be parties include a qualifying child and a parent with a related maintenance calculation. The Secretary of State also retains some functions and may be interested in being a party if an important issue on the interpretation of the legislation arises.

No power to award costs
10. The Tribunal may not make any order in respect of costs (or, in Scotland, expenses).

Definition
"Tribunal": see rule 1(3).

General Note
There is no power to award costs. It is, in any event, not the usual practice to award costs in cases involving children (*R v R (Costs: Child Case)* [1997] 2 FLR 95 at 98, *per* Staughton LJ).

Representatives
11.–(1) A party may appoint a representative (whether a legal representative or not) to represent that party in the proceedings.

(2) Subject to paragraph (3), if a party appoints a representative, that party (or the representative if the representative is a legal representative) must send or deliver to the Tribunal written notice of the representative's name and address.

(3) In a case to which rule 23 (cases in which the notice of appeal is to be sent to the decision maker) applies, if the appellant (or the appellant's representative if the representative is a legal representative) provides written notification of the appellant's representative's name and address to the decision maker before the decision maker provides its response to the Tribunal, the appellant need not take any further steps in order to comply with paragraph (2).

(4) If the Tribunal receives notice that a party has appointed a representative under paragraph (2), it must send a copy of that notice to each other party.

(5) Anything permitted or required to be done by a party under these Rules, a practice direction or a direction may be done by the representative of that party, except signing a witness statement.

(6) A person who receives due notice of the appointment of a representative–
(a) must provide to the representative any document which is required to be provided to the represented party, and need not provide that document to the represented party; and
(b) may assume that the representative is and remains authorised as such until they receive written notification that this is not so from the representative or the represented party.

(7) At a hearing a party may be accompanied by another person whose name and address has not been notified under paragraph (2) or (3) but who, with the permission of the Tribunal, may act as a representative or otherwise assist in presenting the party's case at the hearing.

(8) Paragraphs (2) to (6) do not apply to a person who accompanies a party under paragraph (7).

Definitions
"hearing": see rule 1(3).
"legal representative": see rule 1(3).
"party": see rule 1(3).
"practice direction": see rule 1(3).
"Tribunal": see rule 1(3).

General Note
Representatives can provide valuable assistance for the parties and the tribunal must take account of their proper role and value in exercising its powers and discretions in a way that may affect this right (*CIB 1009/2004; CIB 2058/2004*).

Although the tribunal may advise a party to obtain representation, there is no duty to do this *(CSIB 848/97,* para 11). So long as there is no reason to doubt the competence of a representative, it is not for the tribunal to inquire into the background of the party's choice or to advise on other sources of advice and representation (*Khan v Commissioners of Revenue and Customs, The Times,* March 21 2006).

In *CDLA 1465/2005,* the commissioner expressed the opinion that it is permissible for a representative to be funded by receiving a percentage of the sums recovered by the proceedings. He referred to the public policy rule that agreements to be paid from the proceeds recovered are not enforceable, the rationale for that rule, the nature of tribunal proceedings, and the right to representation under the rules of procedure.

Rule 11(7)

The tribunal, in exercising the power to regulate its procedure under rule 5(1), may limit the number of companions and representatives or otherwise ensure that this right is exercised reasonably (*CI 199/1989,* para 13). Otherwise, the right to a representative is unqualified. In particular, there is no power to prevent a particular representative appearing for a party to the proceedings (*Bache v Essex CC* [2000] 2 All ER 847) or to apply the "McKenzie friend" principles that operate in courts (*CS 1753/2000*). However, in *CSHC 729/2003* the Commissioner referred to other authorities and left open the issue whether a tribunal had power to prevent a representative appearing for a claimant.

Calculating time

12.–(1)   Except in asylum support cases, an act required by these Rules, a practice direction or a direction to be done on or by a particular day must be done by 5pm on that day.

(2)   If the time specified by these Rules, a practice direction or a direction for doing any act ends on a day other than a working day, the act is done in time if it is done on the next working day.

(3)   In this rule "working day" means any day except a Saturday or Sunday, Christmas Day, Good Friday or a bank holiday under section 1 of the Banking and Financial Dealings Act 1971.

Definitions

"asylum support case": see rule 1(3).
"practice direction": see rule 1(3).

General Note

This rule deals with the time and day by which an act must be done. Acts must be done by 5pm on the day specified. If the time for completion does not end on a working day, time is automatically extended to the next working day. The provisions are cumulative so that the act may be done at any time before 5pm on the next working day.

As the rule is not subject to provision to the contrary, it in effect operates as a definition for the rules, practice directions and directions. Time can, though, be extended under rule 5(3)(a).

Sending and delivery of documents

13.–(1) Any document to be provided to the Tribunal under these Rules, a practice direction or a direction must be–

(a)   sent by pre-paid post or delivered by hand to the address specified for the proceedings;

(b)   sent by fax to the number specified for the proceedings; or

(c)   sent or delivered by such other method as the Tribunal may permit or direct.

(2)   Subject to paragraph (3), if a party provides a fax number, email address or other details for the electronic transmission of documents to them, that party must accept delivery of documents by that method.

(3)   If a party informs the Tribunal and all other parties that a particular form of communication (other than pre-paid post or delivery by hand) should not be used to provide documents to that party, that form of communication must not be so used.

(4)   If the Tribunal or a party sends a document to a party or the Tribunal by email or any other electronic means of communication, the recipient may request that the sender provide a hard copy of the document to the recipient. The recipient must make such a request as soon as reasonably practicable after receiving the document electronically.

(5)   The Tribunal and each party may assume that the address provided by a party or its representative is and remains the address to which documents should be sent or delivered until receiving written notification to the contrary.

Use of documents and information

14.–(1)   The Tribunal may make an order prohibiting the disclosure or publication of–

(a)   specified documents or information relating to the proceedings; or

(b)   any matter likely to lead members of the public to identify any person whom the Tribunal considers should not be identified.

(2)   The Tribunal may give a direction prohibiting the disclosure of a document or information to a person if–

(a)   the Tribunal is satisfied that such disclosure would be likely to cause that person or some other person serious harm; and

(b)   the Tribunal is satisfied, having regard to the interests of justice, that it is proportionate to give such a direction.

(3)   If a party ("the first party") considers that the Tribunal should give a direction under paragraph (2) prohibiting the disclosure of a document or information to another party ("the second party"), the first party must–

(a)   exclude the relevant document or information from any documents that will be provided to the second party; and

(b)   provide to the Tribunal the excluded document or information, and the reason for its exclusion, so that the Tribunal may decide whether the document or information should be disclosed to the second party or should be the subject of a direction under paragraph (2).

(4)   The Tribunal must conduct proceedings as appropriate in order to give effect to a direction given under paragraph (2).

(5)   If the Tribunal gives a direction under paragraph (2) which prevents disclosure to a party who has appointed a representative, the Tribunal may give a direction that the documents or information be disclosed to that representative if the Tribunal is satisfied that–

(a)   disclosure to the representative would be in the interests of the party; and

(b)   the representative will act in accordance with paragraph (6).

(6)   Documents or information disclosed to a representative in accordance with a direction under paragraph (5) must not be disclosed either directly or indirectly to any other person without the Tribunal's consent.

General Note

This power is additional to the right to confidentiality under rule 19 and any common law right to confidentiality such as that considered by the three-judge panel of the Upper Tribunal in *Dorset Healthcare NHS Foundation Trust v MH* [2009] UKUT 4 (AAC).

Public authorities, including other tribunals, sometimes rely on the Data Protection Act 1998 to justify withholding information from a tribunal. This is wrong. If a tribunal directs disclosure of information, s35(1) of that Act applies and other provisions of that Act cannot be relied on to justify non-disclosure (*R (Davies) v Commissioners Office* [2008] 1 FLR 1651 at paras 11 and 14). If a party considers that it is inappropriate or impossible to comply with a direction, the proper course is to apply to the tribunal for the direction to be amended, suspended or set aside under rules 5(2) and 6(5) (*ibid*, para 14).

The tribunal must not use its power to prohibit disclosure in a way that prevents a party knowing sufficient of another party's case to give proper instructions to a representative and, in so far as this is possible, to refute that case (*RM v St Andrew's Healthcare* [2010] UKUT 119 (AAC); *Bank Mellat v Her Majesty's Treasury* [2010] EWCA Civ 483, paras 18 and 21; *Crown Prosecution Service v LR* [2010] EWCA Civ 924).

Evidence and submissions

15.–(1) Without restriction on the general powers in rule 5(1) and (2) (case management powers), the Tribunal may give directions as to–

(a) issues on which it requires evidence or submissions;

(b) the nature of the evidence or submissions it requires;

(c) whether the parties are permitted or required to provide expert evidence;

(d) any limit on the number of witnesses whose evidence a party may put forward, whether in relation to a particular issue or generally;

(e) the manner in which any evidence or submissions are to be provided, which may include a direction for them to be given–

(i) orally at a hearing; or

(ii) by written submissions or witness statement; and

(f) the time at which any evidence or submissions are to be provided.

(2) The Tribunal may–

(a) admit evidence whether or not–

(i) the evidence would be admissible in a civil trial in the United Kingdom; or

(ii) the evidence was available to a previous decision maker; or

(b) exclude evidence that would otherwise be admissible where–

(i) the evidence was not provided within the time allowed by a direction or a practice direction;

(ii) the evidence was otherwise provided in a manner that did not comply with a direction or a practice direction; or

(iii) it would otherwise be unfair to admit the evidence.

(3) The Tribunal may consent to a witness giving, or require any witness to give, evidence on oath, and may administer an oath for that purpose.

Definitions

"party": see rule 1(3).

"practice direction": see rule 1(3).

"Tribunal": see rule 1(3).

General Note

Evidence

The courts have said that tribunals are not bound by the strict rules on admissibility of evidence which apply in the courts, especially the criminal courts. (*R v National Industrial Injuries Commissioner ex p Moore* [1965] 1 All ER 81; *Wednesbury Corporation v Ministry of Housing and Local Government (No.2)* [1965] 3 All ER 571 at 579; *T A Miller Ltd v Minister of Housing and Local Government* [1968] 2 All ER 633; *R v Hull Prison Board of Visitors ex p St Germain (No.2)* [1979] 3 All ER 545 at 552). The commissioners themselves repeatedly held the same (see, for example, *R(U) 5/77* para 3, and many of the cases cited below). As stated by Lord Widgery CJ in *R v Greater Birmingham Supplementary Benefit Appeal Tribunal ex p Khan* [1979] 3 All ER 759, the test is this: "It is open to the tribunal in this particular type of case to take into account all the circumstances, so far as they are probative, so far as they help to conclude proof of the truth in the individual case." In *Mahon v Air New Zealand* [1984] 3 All ER 201, in the context of a wholly different type of tribunal, Lord Diplock put the matter in terms of natural justice rather than in terms of evidence. The Privy Council, for which his lordship was speaking, held that the tribunal was bound by the rules of natural justice and that the rules of evidence were not part of those rules. The obligation on the tribunal was that each of its findings of fact should be based on some material tending logically to show the existence of that fact.

The precise limits of these statements have never been determined. It is not clear, for example, whether they are intended to override the rules on self-incrimination. Generally, such statements identify the proper emphasis for the tribunal as being on the probative value of the evidence and its relevance to the appeal, rather than on technical rules as to admissibility. This must, though, be read subject to the limitations on the power of a tribunal to summon witnesses or to order the production of documents contained in rule 16. At least four more specific things are also clear: (i) hearsay evidence is admissible; (ii) so is evidence which was not before the Secretary of State; (iii) tribunals are also entitled to apply presumptions (see, for example, *CM209/1987*, para 13); (iv) opinion evidence is admissible (*CDLA 2014/2004* para 9). (i) and (ii) are considered in more detail below.

Legal professional privilege applies in adversarial jurisdictions (even those where the proceedings are conducted in a non-adversarial spirit), but in non-adversarial jurisdictions litigation privilege never arises, although the privilege between solicitor and client remains (*Re L (Police Investigation: Privilege)* [1996] 1 FLR 731). Children Act proceedings are non-adversarial *(ibid)*: judges in practice adopt an interventionist style in directions hearings and at the substantive hearing the judge has substantially greater control over the deployment of evidence and argument than a judge sitting, for example, in the Queen's Bench Division (*Oxfordshire CC v M* [1994] 1 FLR 175 at 187-188, *per* Steyn LJ). It is unclear (i) how, if at all, the rules of privilege apply in a jurisdiction in which the strict rules of evidence do not apply and (ii) whether or not proceedings before a tribunal in a child support case are adversarial.

Evidence may be oral or written. Any matters of fact stated by the appellant in the grounds of appeal will constitute written evidence (*R(SB) 10/81*, para 6). If the evidence is oral, the presiding judge should keep a note of it. That note should distinguish clearly between evidence and other matters and should make clear who gave the evidence (*R(SB) 8/84*, para 25(2) and (6)). If the evidence is written, copies should be made available to the tribunal and all the parties. The presiding judge should note the receipt of the document in the record of proceedings and ensure that a copy is placed on the tribunal file. Although, in appropriate circumstances, written evidence may carry more weight than oral evidence, what a party or a witness says is nonetheless evidence. There is no rule that evidence must be written rather than oral, or that the former necessarily carries more weight than the latter. In *CCS 499/1995*, the commissioner held (para 9) that only written evidence of the validity of a parent's entitlement to income support was acceptable. With respect to the commissioner, whatever the practical benefits of evidence being in writing in such a case, there is no basis in law for requiring that it must be in writing.

If written evidence is put before the tribunal, its provenance should be disclosed, since this may affect the weight to be attached to it (*R(G) 1/63*, para 12). Either the identity of the author of a statement, or the fact that it is anonymous, should be disclosed (*CS 55/1988*). If it is desired not to disclose the source of information, it may not be relied upon (*CDLA 14884/1996*, para 10), subject of course to the cases where express legislative provision is made for this (see rule 19, reg 8 of the Departure Regulations and reg 9 of the Variation Regulations).

There is no requirement that evidence must be corroborated (*R(I) 2/51*, para 7 and *R(SB) 33/85*, para 14). To insist on corroboration would be impracticable (*R(U) 12/56*, para 8). The real reason for the admissibility of oral uncorroborated evidence, however, is that there is in essence nothing necessarily wrong with it. Although corroboration is not relevant to the admissibility of evidence, it may be relevant to its strength. Where evidence is weak, the presence of independent corroboration will increase its weight.

Hearsay evidence is evidence of which the witness does not have first-hand knowledge, for example, if a witness says "X told me that he earned £2,000 a month," this is direct first-hand evidence of the fact that X made the statement but only hearsay evidence of X's earnings. Hearsay evidence is admissible (eg, *T A Miller Ltd*, above) and in practice plays an important role in tribunals. The fact that evidence is hearsay goes to its weight, not to its admissibility (*CI 97/49(KL)*, para 6; *R(G) 1/51*, para 5; *R(U) 12/56*, para 8 and (*R(SB) 5/82*, para 9). In assessing its weight, the tribunal should be aware of the limitations and dangers of hearsay evidence: the originator of the evidence is not present to be questioned and there is a risk that as information is passed from person to person it may become distorted. The tribunal will need to establish, by hearing evidence, any factors relevant to the appropriate weight to give to it. The following should be considered: (i) the reliability of the original source of the evidence; (ii) how many people it has passed through (*R(A) 7/89*, para 8); (iii) the reliability of the intervening parties; and (iv) whether more direct evidence could be obtained, bearing in mind the powers under rule 16 to summon witnesses and to order the production of documents. If the tribunal accepts hearsay evidence, it is wise for the presiding judge to record in the reasons for decision that the tribunal had regard to the dangers and limitations of hearsay evidence.

The evidence may be given by a party or by a witness. A tribunal member may be called as a witness and the evidence is admissible (*CIS 661/1994*, para 13). However, it has been said that evidence given by a representative without personal knowledge on a *contested* matter is not evidence on which a tribunal is entitled to rely (*R(I) 36/61*, para 18; *R(I) 13/74*, para 9; *R(SB) 10/86*, para 5). This sharp distinction between the status of witness and of representative may make sense in court, but it is not always easy to keep the roles of witness and representative distinct in a tribunal. Moreover, there is no reason in principle why in a tribunal context the evidence of a representative should be treated any differently from that of anyone else. In practice the rulings in the above decisions are not followed. Sometimes the representative is in a position to give first-hand evidence of the relevant matters. Where the evidence is hearsay, there is no reason to treat it more harshly than any other hearsay evidence. The tribunal may, as part of the enabling role, allow a representative to give the evidence in an orderly manner on behalf of a party who may be nervous or rambling and who then confirms that evidence and answers any follow up questions. This is an acceptable practice which is consistent with the spirit of *R(I) 36/61* and *R(SB) 10/86* and permissible under the power given to the tribunal by rule 15(1)(e).

Unlike the position in a court, any witness can give evidence on a matter of opinion. However, tribunals are likely to give most weight to the opinion of an expert witness, although there is limited scope for this in child support cases. Expert witnesses who give written or oral evidence are under the following duties: (i) the evidence must be independent; (ii) it must be objective and unbiased; (iii) facts or assumptions on which it is based should be stated, as should any facts which would detract from the expert's conclusion; (iv) questions or issues which fall outside the witness's expertise should be made clear; (v) it should contain any appropriate qualifications to the opinion expressed; (vi) any subsequent change of view after the expert's report has been written should be disclosed (*National Justice Compania Naviera SA v Prudential Assurance Co Ltd, The Times,* March 5 1993). There is no obligation to grant a party a postponement or adjournment in order to allow expert evidence to be obtained (*Winchester Cigarette Machinery Ltd v Payne, The Times,* October 19 1993), and the tribunal has a duty to ensure that no more expert evidence is produced than is necessary (*Re G(Minors) (Medical Experts)* [1994] 2 FLR 291). These authorities may need reconsideration in the light of the overriding objective.

Parents regularly submit evidence on the condition that it is not disclosed to the other parent. If this happens, the tribunal must consider to prohibit disclosure. See the general note to rule 14 on p825.

Evaluation of evidence

It is no part of the function of the Court of Appeal to teach tribunals how to do this (*Fryer-Kelsey v SSWP* [2005] EWCA Civ 511 (reported as *R(IB) 6/05)*).

All evidence that is admitted must be accorded appropriate weight in order to determine first whether it is accepted and second its significance. The task of evaluating evidence is often more difficult for a tribunal than for a court, which may be cushioned from some of the more difficult decisions by excluding certain categories of evidence. The task for the tribunal is to make a decision, however difficult that may be. Conflicts of evidence do not justify the tribunal reaching a compromise – eg, by fixing a figure between the two sums alleged to represent a parent's income (see *R(U) 2/72*, para 8). Although assessing the weight of evidence is a familiar task for lawyers, it may not be so straightforward for a lay member. While respecting a member's equal weight in the evaluation of the evidence, the presiding judge's experience will be helpful in assisting the other member to assess the appropriate weight to be accorded to particular pieces of evidence.

The weight to be accorded to a piece of evidence is a matter for the decision maker (*R v National Industrial Injuries Commissioner ex p Moore* [1965] 1 All ER 81 at 94, *per* Lord Diplock) and the appropriate weight is determined by applying common sense (*Lord Advocate v Lord Blantyre* [1879] 4 App Cas 770 at 792, *per* Lord Blackburn and *R(DLA)* 1/95, para 5). The weighing of evidence always involves considering its strengths and weaknesses as against the test of balance of probabilities (*Karanakaran v SSHD* [2003] 3 All ER 449 at 477 *per* Sedley LJ). Where there is conflicting evidence, a comparative assessment is also involved. Where the evidence conflicts, a preference for one piece inevitably involves a rejection of another. Preference and rejection are two sides of the same coin. See *CDLA 5342/1997*, para 16. There are no restrictions on the grounds on which a person's evidence may be rejected. "The tribunal never has to believe the say so of a witness before it, although they must have a reason for disbelieving" (*R v Social Security Commissioner ex p Bibi*, unreported, May 23 2000, *per* Collins J, para 33).

The factors which would have led to the evidence being excluded at common law may be relevant when assessing the probative worth of evidence heard by a tribunal (*CDLA 2014/2004*, para 12).

There are no hard and fast rules and each piece of evidence must be weighed on its merits in the circumstances of a particular case. In doing so three key criteria about the witness should be considered: (i) How well placed was the witness to form an objective view of the subject matter of the evidence? (ii) How reliable is the witness's recollection? (iii) How good is the witness's capacity to convey precisely that recollection?

Having considered the reliability of the witness, attention can be turned to the witness's evidence. Factors to consider include: (a) Is the witness's evidence consistent? (b) How inherently credible is it? (c) Is it consistent with the other evidence before the tribunal? Other factors will also affect the weight likely to be accorded a particular piece of evidence. Thus, it is likely that direct evidence will be given more weight than hearsay (see above for the special problem of evaluating hearsay evidence), that written evidence will be valued more highly than oral, that precise, specific detailed evidence will carry more weight than general evidence, and that the more contemporaneous the evidence the more highly it will be valued.

Advice on assessing the credibility of a witness's evidence was given in *Heffer v Tiffin Green (a Firm), The Times,* December 28 1998 by Henry LJ The evidence should always be tested by reference to objective facts proved independently of the evidence, in particular by reference to any relevant documents, and particular regard should be paid to the witness's possible motives and the overall probabilities. The tribunal should also take account of the extent to which it was within a party's power to produce evidence or to contradict evidence produced by another party (*Blatch v Archer* [1774] 98 English Reports 969 at 970, quoted in *Fairchild v Glenhaven Funeral Services Ltd* [2002] 3 All ER 305, para 13). The evidence of a witness must be considered realistically and as a whole, taking account of the fact that a single lie may not undermine the evidence as a whole (*EPI Environmental Technologies Inc v Symphony Plastic Technologies plc, The Times,* January 14 2005).

A tribunal may only find evidence to be generally unreliable on account of an instance of inaccuracy (whether dishonest or otherwise) if it is indicative that the evidence as a whole is unreliable and must always consider the possibility that a particular inaccuracy does not infect the evidence as a whole (*CDLA 2783/2006*, para 5).

In *CCS 2786/2005,* the commissioner gave guidance on how to assess evidence which consisted largely of assertions without supporting documents and without the chance to question both parents:

"9.   How should the tribunal have approached its fact-finding in a case where there were assertions by all the parents without supporting documents, one of the parents did not attend to be questioned and none of them was represented? The tribunal was entitled to accept the word of any of the parents, even without supporting documentation. However, it could only do so if the evidence had a sound basis. And, given the conflict of assertions, the tribunal could not be satisfied of that unless and until it had investigated them as best it could. The starting point was the provenance of each assertion. The father must have known about his own circumstances. But how did the mothers claim to know what they were alleging? And was the basis of their knowledge current or historic? The tribunal was entitled to take account of the fact that the mothers attended to be questioned while the father did not.

That allowed the tribunal to probe the basis for their evidence and, as far as I can tell from the record of proceedings, the tribunal did that. But mere questioning cannot overcome all inadequacies in evidence. In assessing any particular assertion and the evidence as a whole, the tribunal was entitled to take account of the lack of supporting evidence. In doing so, the tribunal had to accept that the mothers did not have access to documentary [evidence] to support their evidence. The father, of course, had access to the documentary evidence to confirm or refute their allegations, but he was not represented and, in the absence of a district chairman's directions, it was not appropriate to assume that he understood the importance of producing evidence to support what he said. Parents often assume that a tribunal will believe what they say about their own circumstances and tribunals have to recognise that fact. The use of pre-hearing directions serves to inform parents of the process they are involved in. In the absence of directions, the tribunal could have allowed the father a chance to produce documentary evidence. That might have been done on an adjournment. Another approach which I have seen, I believe in an appeal from a Cardiff case, was to produce a draft decision that would be issued if the absent parent did not produce evidence to the contrary within a specified period."

The method of funding of a party's representation is irrelevant to the assessment of that party's evidence (*CDLA 1465/2005*, paras 20-23).

Members of tribunals may have specialist or local knowledge. They are always entitled to rely on that knowledge, but in some circumstances it may only be used if it has been disclosed to the parties so that they may comment on it or try to refute it. Whether or not disclosure is required depends on the use that is made of the knowledge. In *Dugdale v Kraft Foods Ltd* [1977] ICR 49 at 54-55 Phillips J suggested a three-fold analysis. (i) The knowledge may be used without being disclosed in order to understand, analyse and weigh the evidence. So, a member with specialist accountancy knowledge could rely on that knowledge and experience in order to interpret a set of accounts. (ii) It may also be used without being disclosed in order to fill in uncontroversial gaps in the evidence. So, members could take account of their knowledge of council tax rates in a particular locality. (iii) However, it must be disclosed if it is to be used as evidence that is contrary to the case presented by one of the parties. So, a member's knowledge that overtime was available from a particular employer would have to be disclosed if one of the parties had given evidence to the contrary. In addition to *Dugdale*, see the decisions of the courts in *Reynolds v Llanelly Associated Tinplate Co Ltd* [1948] 1 All ER 140; *Metropolitan Properties Co (FGC) Ltd v Lannon* [1968] 3 All ER 304 at *309, per* Lord Denning MR; *Wetherall v Harrision* [1976] 1 All ER 241; *Hammington v Berker Sportcraft Ltd* [1980] ICR 248; *Norbrook Laboratories (GB) Ltd v Health and Safety Executive, The Times,* February 23 1998 and *Richardson v Solihull MBC, The Times,* April 10 1998. These decisions have been followed by commissioners in *R(S) 1/94, CIS 278/1992,* para 12 and *CS 175/1992.* See also *CCS 15773/1996*, para 13.

Whenever specialist or local knowledge has been disclosed the record of proceedings should note that it was done and that the parties had a chance to comment on it. Disclosure does not necessarily mean that an adjournment will be necessary so that further evidence may be produced (*R(I) 3/96*, para 8).

As often there is a difference between law and practice, it may be wise, and will certainly remove any ground for argument, if knowledge that is relied on is disclosed in all cases.

In addition to its reliance on specialist or local knowledge, there are other occasions when the tribunal must not reject evidence without giving the party who adduced it the opportunity to present additional supporting evidence. There is no definitive statement of when this will be required. However, it will be required where evidence is adduced which is not challenged or contradicted by any other party, comes from an apparently reliable source and is an essential element in the party's case (*Kriba v SSHD, The Times,* July 18 1997).

If a tribunal bases its decision on an adverse assessment of the honesty or integrity of one of the parties, that party must have had adequate notice that this was a possibility. Usually the question of whether or not a party's evidence is accepted is central to the issue before the tribunal and the possibility of such a finding should reasonably be appreciated. In such cases it is impossible to construct a case for the person being given an opportunity to comment on a provisional view on this issue before the final decision is made (*CI 614/1993*, para 10) and it is, therefore, unnecessary for the tribunal to draw attention to the matter (*Baron v Secretary of State for Social Services* reported as an Appendix to *R(M) 6/86,* per May LJ). However, if the circumstances are such that the person may reasonably not appreciate that the issue of honesty or integrity is in the tribunal's mind, attention should be drawn to the possibility of such a finding so that evidence or argument may be advanced on that issue (*Mahon v Air New Zealand* [1984] 3 All ER 201 at 210, *per* Lord Diplock). This point was considered briefly in *CI 11126/ 1995*, para 8. The commissioner identified the key test to be applied as that of fairness, emphasised the need for there to be a sensible limit to the tribunal's duty to put every point to a witness or party, and drew a useful distinction between what the law requires and the appropriate practice for a tribunal to follow. Having said that, having allowed the appeal on a different basis, he did not need to express a decided opinion on this point, he went on:

"It is sometimes very difficult to say when fairness demands that a claimant be given an opportunity to meet new points against him. It is, I think, good practice for appeal tribunals to err on the safe side by ensuring that claimants and their representatives have the chance to comment on matters which tend to go against them. But the law does not require the ludicrous result that an appeal tribunal has to draw a claimant's attention to every perceived weakness in his evidence."

R(A) 7/89, para 12 appears to suggest a wider requirement for tribunals to draw the possibility of such an adverse finding to the party's attention if this is being considered. However, that case was special in that it involved the combination of very remote hearsay, a party who suffered a degree of confusion, a provisional view already formed by the Board and a decision to be taken on written submissions only without the possibility of an oral hearing. Nevertheless, the decision may have some application where the parties will not be present, for example where the decision is taken by a chairman alone or where an application for the setting aside of a tribunal decision is being considered. It also emphasises that the general distinction drawn in the previous paragraph must be subject to qualification in exceptional circumstances.

Although the tribunal may consider expert evidence, the decision is for the tribunal itself and not the expert (*R v Lanfear* [1968] 1 All ER 683 at 684-685, *per* Diplock LJ). The tribunal is not bound to accept the expert's opinion if there is a proper basis for rejecting it in the other evidence before the tribunal, or if the evidence is such that the tribunal does not believe it or was not convinced by it (*Walton v The Queen* [1978] 1 All ER 542 at 547 *per* Lord Keith and *Dover DC v Sherred* [1997] 29 HLR 864). It is an error of law for the tribunal to accept the evidence merely because it comes from an expert (*Lanfear,* above). However, the tribunal's decision must be one which is based on a rational approach to the evidence so that, if the expert evidence on a particular point is unchallenged and there are no facts or circumstances to displace or cast doubt on it, the tribunal would commit an error of law if it failed to accept it (*R v Matheson* [1958] 2 All ER 87 at 90, *per* Lord Goddard CJ).

As to the role of expert evidence in assisting the tribunal to decide on the appropriate weight to be given to any piece of evidence, see *Re M and R (Child Abuse: Evidence)* [1996] 2 FLR 195.

Children as witnesses

If one of the parties seeks to call a child as a witness, a number of special considerations arise in the borderland of competence, admissibility, evaluation and the desirability of involving a child in legal proceedings between the parents. Usually, but not necessarily, the child will be the qualifying child.

First, is it desirable that the child should give evidence? Logically this question only arises once it is established that the child is a competent witness whose evidence could be heard by the tribunal. However, when a party wishes to call a child as a witness, it may be thought appropriate to consider this issue before coming to the legal technicalities. A child may be placed in a very difficult position if called upon to give evidence which involves taking sides with one parent against the other or which may have serious financial consequences for one or other of the parents. However, there are a number of steps which a tribunal can take if faced with a request for a child to be called as a witness. The tribunal may discuss with the parents the desirability of this action from the child's point of view. It may also ask for an indication of the facts which it is thought that the child's evidence will establish and discuss how else these matters might be established. The tribunal could then hear all the evidence except that of the child and, if satisfied that those facts have been established, the child's evidence could be excluded as unnecessary. This, however, is only possible where only one of the parties wishes the child to give evidence.

Second, is the child a competent witness? Children who are so young that they cannot give reliable evidence are not competent witnesses. There is no fixed age below which a child should not be allowed to give evidence. The issue can only be determined in relation to a particular child and by paying due regard to that child's maturity and the nature of the evidence which may be given. The test of competence of a child witness is whether the child was able to understand the question asked, to communicate, and to give a coherent and comprehensible account of relevant matters. This involves an ability to distinguish between truth and fiction or between fact and fantasy. This is the appropriate emphasis rather than whether the child can distinguish between truth and lies since by definition lies are intentional and are deliberate falsehoods which connote an ability to tell the difference between lies and the truth. If the child is able to distinguish fact from fiction, it is for the tribunal to decide whether or not the evidence is true. See *R v D, The Times,* November 11 1995. For the use of witness summonses in the case of children see the general note to reg 10(1).

Third, is the consent of a parent with parental responsibility necessary before a child may give evidence? It seems that consent to a child appearing as a witness is an aspect of parental responsibility (*Re M (Care: Leave to Interview)* [1995] 1 FLR 825 and *Re F (Specific Issues: Child Interview)* [1995] 1 FLR 819). On this basis, in the case of married or divorced parents, either may consent to a child giving evidence, since parental responsibility may be exercised unilaterally (s2(7) Children Act 1989). Where the parents have never been married, the tribunal must discover whether the father has acquired parental responsibility, by court order or by agreement with the mother. If so, the position is the same as for married or divorced parents. If not, only the mother has parental responsibility, and only she may decide whether the child should be a witness. In the event of a dispute as to consent, either parent may seek an order from the court.

Fourth, should the tribunal hear the child's evidence? The Supreme Court considered the calling of children as witnesses in *Re W (children) (care proceedings: evidence)* [2010] 1 WLR 701. The case concerned care proceedings, but the general principles apply to child support proceedings. They were set out by Lady Hale:

"22.   …The existing law erects a presumption against a child giving evidence which requires to be rebutted by anyone seeking to put questions to the child. That cannot be reconciled with the approach of the European Court of Human Rights, which always aims to strike a fair balance between competing Convention rights. Article 6 requires that the proceedings overall be fair and this normally entails an opportunity to challenge the evidence presented by the other side. …

23. The object of the proceedings is to achieve a fair trial in the determination of the rights of all the people involved. ... The court cannot ignore relevant evidence just because other evidence might have been better. It will have to do the best it can on what it has.

24. When the court is considering whether a particular child should be called as a witness, the court will have to weigh two considerations: the advantages that that will bring to the determination of the truth and the damage it may do to the welfare of this or any other child. A fair trial is a trial which is fair in the light of the issues which have to be decided. Mr Geekie accepts that the welfare of the child is also a relevant consideration, albeit not the paramount consideration in this respect. He is right to do so, because the object of the proceedings is to promote the welfare of this and other children. The hearing cannot be fair to them unless their interests are given great weight.

25. In weighing the advantages that calling the child to give evidence may bring to the fair and accurate determination of the case, the court will have to look at several factors. One will be the issues it has to decide in order properly to determine the case. Sometimes it may be possible to decide the case without making findings on particular allegations. Another will be the quality of the evidence it already has. Sometimes there may be enough evidence to make the findings needed whether or not the child is cross-examined. Sometimes there will be nothing useful to be gained from the child's oral evidence. The case is built upon a web of behaviour, drawings, stray remarks, injuries and the like, and not upon concrete allegations voiced by the child. The quality of any ABE interview will also be an important factor, as will be the nature of any challenge which the party may wish to make. The court is unlikely to be helped by generalised accusations of lying, or by a fishing expedition in which the child is taken slowly through the story yet again in the hope that something will turn up, or by a cross-examination which is designed to intimidate the child and pave the way for accusations of inconsistency in a future criminal trial. On the other hand, focussed questions which put forward a different explanation for certain events may help the court to do justice between the parties. Also relevant will be the age and maturity of the child and the length of time since the events in question, for these will have a bearing on whether an account now can be as reliable as a near-contemporaneous account, especially if given in a well-conducted ABE interview.

26. The age and maturity of the child, along with the length of time since the events in question, will also be relevant to the second part of the inquiry, which is the risk of harm to the child. Further specific factors may be the support which the child has from family or other sources, or the lack of it, the child's own wishes and feelings about giving evidence, and the views of the child's guardian and, where appropriate, those with parental responsibility. We endorse the view that an unwilling child should rarely, if ever, be obliged to give evidence. The risk of further delay to the proceedings is also a factor: there is a general principle that delay in determining any question about a child's upbringing is likely to prejudice his welfare: see the Children Act 1989, section 1(2). There may also be specific risks of harm to this particular child. Where there are parallel criminal proceedings, the likelihood of the child having to give evidence twice may increase the risk of harm. The parent may be seeking to put his child through this ordeal in order to strengthen his hand in the criminal proceedings rather than to enable the family court to get at the truth. On the other hand, as the family court has to give less weight to the evidence of a child because she has not been called, then that may be damaging too. However, the court is entitled to have regard to the general evidence of the harm which giving evidence may do to children, as well as to any features which are particular to this child and this case. That risk of harm is an ever-present feature to which, on the present evidence, the court must give great weight. The risk, and therefore the weight, may vary from case to case, but the court must always take it into account and does not need expert evidence in order to do so.

27. But on both sides of the equation, the court must factor in what steps can be taken to improve the quality of the child's evidence and at the same time to decrease the risk of harm to the child. These two aims are not in opposition to one another. The whole premise of "Achieving Best Evidence" and the special measures in criminal cases is that this will improve rather than diminish the quality of the evidence to the court. It does not assume that the most reliable account of any incident is one made from recollection months or years later in the stressful conditions of a courtroom. Nor does it assume that an "Old Bailey style" cross-examination is the best way of testing that evidence. It may be the best way of casting doubt upon it in the eyes of a jury but that is another matter. A family court would have to be astute both to protect the child from the harmful and destructive effects of questioning and also to evaluate the answers in the light of the child's stage of development.

28. The family court will have to be realistic in evaluating how effective it can be in maximising the advantage while minimising the harm. There are things that the court can do but they are not things that it is used to doing at present. It is not limited by the usual courtroom procedures or to applying the special measures by analogy. The important thing is that the questions which challenge the child's account are fairly put to the child so that she can answer them, not that counsel should be able to question her directly…"

Fifth, should the child take the oath? This involves establishing whether the child is able to understand not just the importance of telling the truth generally but also the particular significance of doing so to the tribunal. The test is not whether or not the child believes in the existence of God and of a divine sanction if the oath is broken, but rather "whether the child has a sufficient appreciation of the solemnity of the occasion, and the added responsibility to tell the truth, which is involved in taking an oath, over and above the duty to tell the truth which is an ordinary duty of normal social conduct" with the watershed probably falling between the ages of eight and 10 (*R v Hayes* [1977] 2 All ER 288 at 291, *per* Bridge LJ).

Under s96(1) and (2) of the Children Act 1989, a child who does not understand the nature of the oath may give unsworn evidence, provided the child understands that there is a duty to speak the truth and has sufficient understanding to justify the evidence being heard. This provision does not apply to the First-tier Tribunal, which is not a tribunal in which the strict rules of evidence apply (s96(7) of the 1989 Act and s18 Civil Evidence Act 1968). However, the tribunal could apply the same principle.

Sixth, what form should the oath take? This is dealt with below.

Seventh, is corroboration needed? Corroboration is not generally required. However, the presence or absence of corroboration may be an important factor in weighing a child's evidence in the context of an individual case.

Eighth, how is the child's evidence to be given? If a child is to give evidence, the manner in which that evidence is given and the manner of the questioning of the child are within the control of the presiding judge, who may consider it appropriate that the parties should not question the child directly but that the judge should question the child on the matters identified by the parties.

Ninth, how is the child's evidence to be evaluated? In addition to the usual factors which will be taken into account, the tribunal will need to consider the influence which one parent may have been able to exercise over the child's evidence and the considerations which (consciously or subconsciously) may be in the child's mind whilst giving evidence (eg, a desire to help a parent who is in financial difficulty or a desire to give neutral evidence which will prevent the child appearing to take sides). As to the role of expert evidence in assisting the tribunal to decide on the appropriate weight to be given to a child's evidence see *Re M and R (Child Abuse: Evidence)* [1996] 2 FLR 195.

A Tribunal of Commissioners gave guidance on evidence from children in disability living allowance cases (*R(DLA) 3/06*, para 58): (i) a tribunal should have proper regard to the wishes of a child of sufficiently mature years and understanding who wishes to give evidence, but should be very cautious before requiring any child to give evidence, and should only call for a child to give evidence if it is satisfied that a just decision cannot otherwise be made; (ii) a tribunal should be very slow to exercise its power to require a child to give evidence if that child's parent or carer takes the view that for the child to give evidence may be detrimental to the child's welfare, particularly if there is evidence from a competent professional that to do so might be harmful; (iii) even if it is one the parties who wishes to call a child as a witness, a tribunal has power to disallow the child from giving evidence if it is against the child's interests to do so; (iv) if a child is called to give evidence, the tribunal should consider how that evidence will be taken, so that the interests and welfare of the child are maintained; (v) the tribunal will also need to give consideration to practical matters such as the geography of the hearing room, having an appropriate adult in close attendance, whether any of the tribunal (including the presiding judge) should be selected because of experience in dealing with child witnesses and even (in appropriate cases) taking such steps as taking the child's evidence by video link if available.

In considering whether to allow an articulate teenage child to give evidence, a tribunal must not allow a concern for the child's welfare to override the child's rights to freedom of expression and participation in family life (*Mabon v Mabon* [2005] 2 FLR 1011).

Burden and standard of proof

The burden and standard of proof apply only to matters of fact, not to matters of evaluation or judgment (*Karanakaran v SSHD* [2003] 3 All ER 449 at 477 *per* Sedley LJ; *Secretary of State for the Home Department v Rehman* [2002] 1 All ER 122 at para 56 *per* Lord Hoffmann, and *R (M) v Inner London Crown Court* [2003] 1 FLR 994 at paras 41-44).

There are two burdens of proof. The legal burden determines which party shall bear the consequence of there being insufficient weight of evidence to establish a matter which arises for determination. The incidence of this burden, that is, the party who is to bear the burden, is ultimately a matter of policy. Although there are exceptions, the general policy underlying its incidence is to ensure the preservation of the status quo current at the time the decision is made unless a sufficient case can be made that it should be changed. (This insight is attributable to Terry Lynch, formerly a full-time chairman in the Wales and the South West Region.) The legal burden does not shift in the course of the appeal.

The incidence of the legal burden of proof in a child support appeal is as yet undecided. Reasoning from basic principles the position is as follows. Child support appeals are by way of rehearing. In such cases the incidence of the legal burden of proof is the same as in the case of the decision under appeal (*Rugman v Drover* [1950] 2 All ER 575 at 576, *per* Lord Goddard CJ). If that decision was a revision or supersession decision, the burden will be on the person who initiated it (*R(I) 1/71*, para 16).

The degree of certainty or probability that is necessary in order to discharge the burden of proof is determined by the standard of proof. The relevant standard is the civil standard which requires that a matter be established on the balance of probabilities (*CI 401/50(KL)*). This means that in order to prove a case the evidence must show that it is more likely than not. This is lower than the criminal standard which requires proof beyond reasonable doubt.

The civil standard of the balance of probabilities does not vary, despite many statements to that effect in the authorities (*Re B (Children)(FC)* [2008] UKHL 35, para 13). Factors such as the nature and seriousness of the issues are relevant to the probabilities and, therefore, operate within the civil burden (para 70).

Whether the balance has been tipped cannot be determined precisely or mathematically; there is scope for applying common sense and first impression (*Re A (A Minor) (Paternity: Refusal of Blood Test)* [1994] 2 FLR 463 at 470 *per* Waite LJ). There is no room for giving the benefit of a doubt (*R(I)* 32/61, para 10). In order to decide whether the evidence is such as to satisfy the necessary standard of proof in order to discharge the burden of proof it is necessary to weigh the evidence. (See previous section of this general note.)

In the great majority of cases there will be evidence which allows the tribunal to decide on the balance of probabilities. Accordingly, the incidence will only be decisive in two cases: (i) where there is no relevant evidence and (ii) where the evidence is so evenly balanced that a decision on where the balance of probabilities lies cannot be made (*CIS 427/1991*, paras 29-30). If the tribunal is unable to decide where the balance of probabilities lies in a particular case, no findings of fact can be recorded (*Morris v London Iron and Steel Co Ltd* [1987] 2 All ER 496). The proper course is to record that the tribunal was unable to decide where the balance of probabilities lay and decide the case on the burden of proof.

The legal burden does not determine the sequence of procedure. The tribunal has control of the procedure and may decide to begin with the party who is in fullest possession of the facts rather than with the party who has the burden of proof on a particular matter. Moreover, the legal burden does not determine who is expected or entitled to produce evidence (*CIS627/1992*, para 7). In practice, the party on whom the burden rests has an obvious interest in bringing forward evidence with which to seek to discharge that burden. However, the tribunal must not limit itself to considering the evidence of that party and must consider the evidence as a whole in order to decide whether the burden of proof has been discharged. In addition to hearing the evidence and argument presented to it, the tribunal is under an inquisitorial duty to investigate the facts and the existence of a legal burden does not relieve the tribunal of this duty (*R(IS) 21/93*, para 19).

The practical importance of the need to produce evidence is reflected in the other burden of proof, the evidentiary burden. As the hearing progresses and the evidence unfolds, the position may arise that the weight of the evidence is such that one party will lose unless further evidence, favourable to that party, emerges. In such a case, even if that party does not bear the legal burden on the issue in question, there is a risk that no other favourable evidence may emerge. In this type of case, the party is said to bear an evidentiary burden. It is the nature of the evidentiary burden that it may rest on the party who bears the legal burden or on some other party and that during the hearing it may move from one party to another.

If one party alleges that an apparently genuine document produced by another party is not genuine, there is an evidentiary burden on the person making the allegation to substantiate it, although the evidence must be assessed as a whole (*Pant v SSHD* [2003] EWCA Civ 1964, para 23).

The standard of proof has to be applied to the issue as a whole. It is not applied (a) to each individual piece of evidence, with any piece disregarded that does not satisfy the standard, or (b) to issues of evaluation rather than of fact (*Karanakaran v SSHD* at 477 *per* Sedley LJ; *Secretary of State for the Home Department v Rehman* [2002] 1 All ER 122 at para 56 *per* Lord Hoffmann). If an issue involves both a determination of facts and an evaluation exercise, the proper approach is to apply the standard while bearing in mind that it will be more important to making findings on disputed facts than to issues of evaluation (*R (N) v Mental Health Review Tribunal (Northern Region)* [2006] 4 All ER 194).

Commissioners regularly referred to the burden of proof and set aside tribunal decisions which misapplied the burden. However, there are indications that it is misleading to think in terms of a burden of proof where a tribunal is following an inquisitorial approach (*R v National Insurance Commissioner ex p Viscusi* [1974] 2 All ER 724 at 729 and *732*, *per* Lord Denning MR and Buckley LJ respectively). In line with this, it has been decided that in some cases there is no burden of proof on either party. This may be because an analysis of the legislation shows that the issue has been left to be decided on the evidence available without reference to a burden (*CCR 3/1993*, paras 8-12). Alternatively, it may be that the nature of the issue involved is such that all relevant evidence should be available from the parties to allow a decision to be made one way or the other and, if it is not forthcoming, appropriate adverse inferences may be drawn (*CIS 317/1994*, paras 11 and 12; *CCS 844/1998*, paras 12-13). In *R(CS) 10/98* para 12, the commissioner held that there was no burden of proof in relation to expenses deductible in calculating a parent's income.

Although it is important to bear in mind where the burden of proof lies, the tribunal has a duty if at all possible to make specific findings and should base its decision on the incidence on the burden of proof only where it is impossible to reach a decision on the balance of probabilities (*Morris v London Iron and Steel Co Ltd* [1987] 2 All ER 496). In the Court of Appeal decision in *Crewe Services and Investment Corporation v Silk* [1997] 79 P&CR 500, Robert Walker LJ, having referred to the burden of proof, said:

> "The problem is in relating it to the practicalities of the disposal of business in the County Court. County Court judges constantly have to deal with cases that are inadequately prepared and presented, either as to the facts or as to the law (or both), and they must not be discouraged from doing their best to reach a fair and sensible result on inadequate materials." (page 509)

> "In most cases the evidence before the court (even if imperfect and incomplete) will be more important than issues as to the burden of proof." (page 510)

These remarks are equally applicable to tribunals, subject to two safeguards. (i) First, the principles of natural justice must be observed. The parties must be told that the tribunal may take this approach and must have an opportunity to comment on its possible application. This need not result in a cumbersome procedure. The possibility of this approach being appropriate will probably be apparent on a preview of the papers and the parties can be warned at the outset that the tribunal may decide to take this approach, although they may seek to persuade the tribunal not to do so. (ii) Second, the manner in which the tribunal reached its conclusion must be explained in any statement of findings and reasons which is issued. This approach does not authorise a tribunal to make up figures or other evidence. It merely recognises that, where appropriate and in the absence of any credible evidence, matters such as a person's income may be capable of being assessed on a rational basis of reasoning from common experience and from such reliable evidence as is before the tribunal. It is in accordance with the requirement set out by Lord Diplock in giving the opinion of the Privy Council in *Mahon v Air New Zealand* [1984] 3 All ER 201 at 210 that its findings of fact should be based on material tending logically to show the existence of the facts found. See *CCS 1992/1997*, paras 43–44.

Findings of fact

The evaluation of the evidence leads to the tribunal's findings of fact.

Facts are of two kinds: primary facts and inferences. Primary facts are those matters on which the tribunal has evidence, whether direct or hearsay. The tribunal may, for example, hear evidence that a parent has been seen driving a delivery van. If it accepts this evidence, it is a primary fact. Inferences are of two kinds: evidential and forensic. Evidential inferences are those matters which the tribunal deduces from the primary facts. Thus, in the above example, it might deduce from the primary facts that the parent was employed as a delivery driver. See *British Launderers' Research Association v Central Middlesex Assessment Committee* [1949] 1 All ER 21 at 25, *per* Denning LJ.

Forensic inferences are those drawn as a result of a party's behaviour in relation to the proceedings. They were considered in detail by the commissioner in *R(CS) 6/05*. He set out a three-stage process. The first issue to consider is whether an inference is necessary (*ibid,* paras 15–18). The commissioner explained through a series of examples that it is only necessary to draw an adverse forensic inference if there is no other way that an issue may be dealt with. It may be possible to find facts by relying on the evidence of another party or the burden of proof. Or it may be possible to make use of a default maintenance decision. An adverse inference is only necessary if none of these other possibilities is available. If an adverse inference is permissible, the second issue is how it is taken into account (paras 20–23). An inference is always a process of reasoning from evidence and conduct. The party's conduct that leads to the adverse inference is taken into account in assessing the probative worth of the evidence as a whole and in drawing inferences from the evidence available. The third issue is whether an adverse inference is permissible (paras 24–29). It is always relevant to consider all likely explanations for the failure to co-operate, as they may not all be indicative of the content of the evidence withheld. It is also relevant to consider whether the party understood the risk of not co-operating, which in some cases may require a warning to have been given by the tribunal.

If a party refuses to co-operate with the tribunal, it may take that into account in deciding what inferences it was permissible to draw from the evidence. This includes: refusing to answer questions (*Re O(Care Proceedings: Evidence)* [2004] 1 FLR 161, paras 13 and 16); withholding written information in the possession of or available to the party, and failing to agree to blood or DNA testing for paternity (*Al-Khatib v Masry* [2002] 1 FLR 1053 especially at paras 93–6; *SSWP v Jones* [2004] 1 FLR 282, paras 11–15); failing to make appropriate enquiries as to information relevant to the proceedings (*R(SB) 34/83*); and failing without good explanation to attend the hearing of an appeal or failing to arrange for witnesses to attend (*Secretary of State for Health v C(Tribunal: Failure to draw inference), The Times,* January 30 2003).

Deciding what forensic inference to draw includes, in appropriate cases, the judgment that the person in default has made the calculation that a decision based on the evidence available will be more favourable than one that would be made on full disclosure (*Al-Khatib v Masry* especially at paras 93-6). However, this assumes that the evidence is known to the person. If it is not given until the hearing, that will not be so. The inference must be based on a rational process of reasoning from evidence before the tribunal, including evidence of failure to make disclosure or full disclosure. There is no authority for making a finding that is purely penal (*CCS 2623/1999*, para 34) or one based purely on guesswork (*CCS7966/1995*, para 11).

A tribunal may draw inferences even if the party does not attend to be questioned. Inferences drawn in those circumstances may turn out to be less soundly based than if made at an oral hearing where the tribunal's concerns could be tested by questioning. However, the inferences must always have a reasonable base in the evidence before the tribunal. See *CDLA 2783/2006,* para 4.

The tribunal's written reasons should include the tribunal's findings of primary fact relevant to the appeal and say why evidence was rejected (*R(SB) 8/84*, para 25(3)). They should also record why one piece of evidence has been preferred to another (*CSSB 212/1987*, para 3). Any inferences which the tribunal drew from the primary facts should also be recorded. Failure to record any of these will amount to an error of law.

Estoppel

Estoppel consists of a series of rules that prevent a person from proving that a particular fact exists or from raising a particular issue. The rules are designed to operate in an adversarial jurisdiction. As tribunals take an inquisitorial approach to the proceedings, estoppel does not apply (*Thoday v Thoday* [1964] 1 All ER 341 at 351, *per* Diplock

LJ). However, tribunals operate by analogy with estoppel (*R(I) 9/63*, para 24). So closely has the analogy been applied that Commissioners regularly referred directly to estoppel, omitting any reference to analogy (*CCS 1535/1997*, para 26).

In child support law, two issues have been considered by the commissioners and the Upper Tribunal in which a principle analogous to estoppel might be developed.

The first issue is whether it is possible to prevent an officer or a tribunal from applying the legislation to the facts of the case. Commissioners held that officers and tribunals carry out a statutory function and that nothing said or done by anyone (including an officer) could override the statutory duty to apply the law to the facts of the case (*R(CS) 2/97* and the authorities there relied on).

The second issue is whether a party may raise again an issue that has already been determined. The courts in dealing with cases involving children (in which an inquisitorial approach is taken) have developed the comments of Diplock LJ in *Thoday*, above at 351 that similar rules to estoppel might be developed in inquisitorial jurisdictions. The courts have refused to introduce an absolute bar on an issue being considered again and have instead developed an approach based on the court's discretion as to the way the case is conducted. They seek to balance a variety of factors, such as (i) the public policy that disputes should be brought to an end, (ii) how central the issue was to the previous decision and (iii) whether it is likely that a different decision would be reached. See *Re B (Children Act Proceedings) (Issue Estoppel)* [1997] 1 FLR 285 at 295-296, *per* Hale, J.

Lightman J restated the principles in more general terms in *Westminster City Council v Haywood (No.2)* [2000] 2 All ER 634 at 645-6, but did not take account of the family law authorities relied on in this note.

In *RC v CMEC and WC* [2009] UKUT 62 (AAC), the Upper Tribunal explained how a tribunal should use findings made by courts or other tribunals:

> "57.   ... Tribunals must make the best findings they can on the information and evidence available to them. The information may include findings made by previous tribunals and family courts. The significance of those findings will depend on their reliability and relevance. In assessing their reliability, tribunals must consider: (i) the evidence on which they were based; (ii) the nature of the fact-finding process (for example, whether the parent was subject to cross-examination); and (iii) the evidence now available. If there is no evidence to the contrary, tribunals may be entitled to conclude that the findings previously made are sufficient and reliable in the child support context. Whether or not this is so will depend on their relevance in the particular case. In assessing the relevance of previous findings, tribunals must consider: (iv) the facts that are relevant to the issue before the tribunal; (v) the precision with which they have to be found in order to apply the legislation; (vi) whether the previous findings relate, or can be related by other evidence, to the time now in issue; and (vii) the extent to which the issues in the previous proceedings affected the evidence that was obtained or the facts that were found."

Rule 15(1)

A commissioner said that it was doubtful whether a direction that further evidence or statements shall only be filed with the leave of a chairman is of any effect (*CCS37/1997*, para 7). However, this is probably now permissible under this paragraph. If so, the position was correctly stated by in *Eurobell (Holdings) plc v Barker* [1998] ICR 299, in which the Employment Appeal Tribunal said that an employment tribunal could give directions about the production of witness statements and the calling of witnesses without permission.

Rule 15(2)(a)

The tribunal is entitled to any evidence held by the parties that is relevant to the proceedings (*CIS 1481/2006*, para 92).

A tribunal may use its own knowledge or expertise as a basis for finding a fact, but only if it discloses it to the parties so that they may comment on the facts that may be founded on it (*Norbrook Laboratories (GB) Ltd v Health and Safety Executive, The Times*, February 23 1998 and *Richardson v Solihull MBC, The Times*, April 10 1998).

Appeals before a tribunal are by way of a rehearing (*R(SB) 1/82*, para 10). Accordingly, evidence which was not before the Secretary of State is admissible (*R(U) 5/77*, para 3; *R(FIS) 1/82*, para 20; *R(SB) 33/83*, para 19; *CSCS 2/1994*, para 20). When such evidence is presented for the first time at the hearing, the tribunal should consider whether an adjournment is necessary in order to allow the other parties to consider it and prepare themselves properly to meet it (see the approach of the commissioner in *R(I) 6/51*, para 5). In order to avoid adjournments, it is preferable that such evidence is disclosed in advance of the hearing *R(I) 6/51*, para 6 and *R(I) 36/56*, para 10). A tribunal may wish to consider using the power under rule 15(1)(f) to give directions that any further evidence be disclosed in advance. In exercising this power, care will be needed to avoid imposing an unrealistic burden on an unrepresented party. It will also be necessary to be aware of the possibility that there may not be time before the hearing to disclose evidence in rebuttal of the further evidence disclosed.

The tribunal should admit any evidence that has probative value. This includes evidence contained in a statement even in the absence from the hearing of the person who took the statement or the persons who witnessed it (*CSIS 21/2008*).

Once evidence is admitted, it is for the tribunal to assess its relevance and reliability.

Rule 15(2)(b)

The tribunal may exclude evidence which is clearly irrelevant, immaterial or repetitive (*Wednesbury Corporation,* above at 579 and *R(SB) 6/82,* para 5). Evidence that has been used in family proceedings is admissible for the purposes of an appeal under amendments made by the Family Proceedings (Amendment) (No.2) Rules 2007 and the Family Proceedings Courts (Miscellaneous Amendments) Rules 2007.

Expert evidence to support the reliability of evidence given on oath should be excluded in all but the most exceptional cases (*R v Robinson (Raymond)* [1994] 3 All ER 346). Exceptionally expert evidence may be given as to the credibility of a child as a witness, provided that the tribunal does not lose sight of the fact that the weight to be given to any piece of evidence is a matter for it to decide (*Re N(a Minor) (Child abuse: Evidence), The Times,* March 25 1996, and *Re M and R (Child Abuse: Evidence)* [1996] 2 FLR 195).

A tribunal may give directions for evidence to be produced within a particular timetable: rule 15(1)(f). This practice was commended in *CCS 2786/2005,* para 5. If evidence if produced late, it does not follow that the tribunal is entitled to exclude that evidence. The tribunal's response to the late production of the evidence must be a proportionate one that takes account of the right to a fair hearing for all the parties to the proceedings, the purpose underlying the directions, the reasons for lateness and all the circumstances of the case (*CCS 4253/2004,* paras 9-16).

The fact that evidence has been excluded should be recorded by the presiding judge in the record of proceedings. However, whether something is irrelevant or immaterial is not always easily judged before the evidence has been heard. In deciding whether or not to exclude evidence, tribunals should be careful not to create the impression that the party seeking to adduce the evidence has not received a fair hearing, while ensuring that other parties have no cause to feel likewise if the evidence is admitted (*R(SB) 6/82,* para 5). Wrongly excluding evidence may amount to an error of law *(ibid,* para 4). Evidence may be excluded if it is illegible, but only after reasonable efforts have been made to obtain a legible copy (*CDLA 2880/1998,* para 8).

Despite these words of caution, the courts have accepted that power is needed to control and contain proceedings. Tribunals have the power and the duty to act so as to curb prolixity and repetition and to prevent irrelevance, discursiveness and the oppression of witnesses (*R v Whybrow, The Times,* February 14 1994). They are entitled to balance the relevance of the evidence against such considerations as the need to keep the length of the hearing within reasonable bounds and to conduct the proceedings with due sensitivity to the wider public interest, and the validity of their actions will be judged by the same test as would be applied to determine the validity of the exercise of a discretion (*Vernon v Bosley, The Times,* April 8 1994).

Rule 15(3)

The tribunal may allow or require evidence to be given on oath. Thus includes an affirmation. It applies to all witnesses, including the parties and their representatives, but only when they are giving evidence.

There may be good reasons why the oath might not be used in a tribunal at all or only in exceptional cases. First, its use may be inconsistent with the relatively informal atmosphere that should be adopted in a tribunal in comparison with a court. Second, it may be unlikely in many cases that it will have an influence on the evidence given by the witness. Its use, therefore, creates an additional question for the tribunal: what effect has the oath had on the witness's honesty? Finally, the oath can only affect the honesty of a witness's evidence. Depending on the nature of the question in dispute, this may or may not be the central issue for the tribunal. If it is not, the tribunal will rather be concerned with the reliability of that evidence. The honesty of the witness will be only one factor in the evaluation of reliability. A tribunal may be reluctant to administer the oath to one person but not another at the same hearing or in relation to some aspects of a person's evidence only. See *CIS 4022/2007,* paras 73-76.

The oath or affirmation must be given in due form. The proper form of oaths and affirmations is laid down by the Oaths Act 1978.

A person may swear by any form of oath or ceremony which he declares to be binding and is bound by this (s4(1)). If an oath is administered it is binding regardless of whether the person has any religious belief (s4(2)). It is usual in England, Wales and Northern Ireland that the oath is administered by the witness raising a copy of the New Testament or, if the witness is Jewish, the Old Testament (s1(1)). In Scotland, a witness swears with an uplifted hand. This form may also be used by a witness in England, Wales and Northern Ireland (s3). The form of oath or affirmation for use in court is laid down in a Lord Chancellor's Office circular under s2 Welsh Courts Act 1942.

Instead of an oath a solemn affirmation may be used in two circumstances. First, if the witness objects to taking an oath (s5(1)). In this case it is entirely a decision for the witness concerned. Second, if it is not reasonably practicable without inconvenience or delay to administer an oath in the manner appropriate to the witness's religious belief (s5(2) and (3)). In this case, it is a matter for the tribunal rather than for the witness concerned. In either case the affirmation is as binding as an oath (s5(4)).

The opening words are in the case of an oath, "I swear by Almighty God that ...", and in the case of an affirmation, "I, ... do solemnly, sincerely and truly declare and affirm, ..." (ss1(1) and 6(1)). This is followed in either case by "the evidence I shall give shall be the truth, the whole truth and nothing but the truth." In the case of a child or young person under the age of 17, the proper form is to use the word "promise" instead of "swear", although either is equally valid (s28 Children and Young Persons Act 1963).

Section 1 of the Oaths Act 1978 provides that the oath is to be administered by an officer which is defined in s1(4) as any person duly authorised to administer the oath. The Act is silent as to who is authorised to administer the oath. This is dealt with in part by s16 of the Evidence Act 1851 which provides that "Every court, judge, . . . or other person, now or hereafter having by law ... authority to hear, receive, and examine evidence, is hereby empowered to administer an oath to all such witnesses as are legally called before them ...". This clearly empowers the tribunal itself, acting in practice through the presiding judge, to administer the oath.

There is no exhaustive statement of who may not authorise a person to administer an oath. The clerks have been trained to administer the oath and may do so rather than the presiding judge.

If an oath is administered, or a witness is allowed to affirm, the presiding judge should record this fact in the notes of proceedings and should take care to ensure that a complete and accurate note of that evidence is taken. Moreover, when the oath or affirmation is being used, it will also be applied to a representative who gives evidence in the course of a presentation. The tribunal will have to be alert to identify such evidence, and the presiding judge should record both it and the fact that it was received as evidence.

In England and Wales, a person who gives evidence on oath or affirmation without believing it to be true commits the offence of perjury (ss1 (1) and (2), 15(2) and 18 of the Perjury Act 1911).

Summoning or citation of witnesses and orders to answer questions or produce documents

16.–(1)   On the application of a party or on its own initiative, the Tribunal may–

(a)   by summons (or, in Scotland, citation) require any person to attend as a witness at a hearing at the time and place specified in the summons or citation; or

(b)   order any person to answer any questions or produce any documents in that person's possession or control which relate to any issue in the proceedings.

(2)   A summons or citation under paragraph (1)(a) must–

(a)   give the person required to attend 14 days' notice of the hearing or such shorter period as the Tribunal may direct; and

(b)   where the person is not a party, make provision for the person's necessary expenses of attendance to be paid, and state who is to pay them.

(3)   No person may be compelled to give any evidence or produce any document that the person could not be compelled to give or produce on a trial of an action in a court of law in the part of the United Kingdom where the proceedings are due to be determined.

(4)   A summons, citation or order under this rule must–

(a)   state that the person on whom the requirement is imposed may apply to the Tribunal to vary or set aside the summons, citation or order, if they have not had an opportunity to object to it; and

(b)   state the consequences of failure to comply with the summons, citation or order.

Definitions

"document": see rule 1(3).
"hearing": see rule 1(3).
"party": see rule 1(3).
"Tribunal": see rule 1(3).

General Note

This is a case management power: see rule 5(3)(d). If a person fails to comply, the circumstances may allow the tribunal to draw adverse inferences. The tribunal may also exercise its powers under rule 7(2)-(3).

The tribunal may require a person to attend at a hearing, answer questions and produce documents.

This applies to the parties to the proceedings as to any other person (*R v B CC ex p P* [1991] 2 All ER 65 at 69, *per* Butler-Sloss LJ). The power is discretionary and, in the case of a child, it should be exercised with caution (*ibid* at 70-71 and 75, *per* Butler-Sloss LJ and Lord Donaldson MR respectively). No summons will be issued, whether to a child or to an adult, if to do so would be oppressive (*ibid,* 70 *per* Butler-Sloss LJ). In the case of a child, the older the child the more likely it is that it will be appropriate to issue a summons (*Re P (Witness Summons)* [1997] 2 FLR 447 at 454, *per* Wilson J). If a child is aged 12 or younger the issue of a summons would in most cases be inappropriate (*ibid*). However, in *R v Highbury Corner Magistrates's Court ex p D* [1997] 1 FLR 683 the Divisional Court held that it was proper to issue a witness summons against a nine-year-old boy whose evidence was potentially relevant and to take the decision of whether it was appropriate for him to be called as a witness at the time when he was called upon to give evidence so that the decision could be taken in the light of the circumstances then prevailing.

Attendance is permissible by means of any form of instantaneous two-way electronic communication: see the definition of "hearing" in rule 1(3). If evidence is to be given by video recorded in advance, it is difficult to treat this as attending at a hearing. However, the tribunal may direct how evidence is to be given under rule 15(1)(e).

The tribunal has a discretion whether or not to compel an expert to attend to give evidence and in exercise of that discretion it may take account of whether or not attendance would disrupt or impede other important work which the expert has to do (*Society of Lloyd's v Clementson (No.2), The Times*, February 29 1996).

A "document" is defined in rule 1(3) as anything in which information is recorded in any form. That will include tape recordings (*Grant v Southerwestern and County Properties Ltd* [1974] 2 All ER 465) and film (*Senior v Holdsworth* [1975] 2 All ER 1009).

Production of documents may be required on the date of hearing or before (*Khanna v Lovell White Durrant (a firm)* [1994] 4 All ER 267).

Normally, tax documents are protected from disclosure by a public interest immunity, regardless of whether or not this immunity is claimed by the tax authorities. However, this immunity may be overridden by public interest in the administration of justice. The burden of justifying disclosure is on the person seeking disclosure. In making the decision, the tribunal should have regard to the relevance of the documents and to the necessity of disposing fairly of the case. See *Lonrho plc v Fayed (No.4)* [1994] QB 775.

The test to apply in deciding whether to order a person who is not a party to produce a document is whether the production of the document is necessary for disposing of the case or for saving costs (*Macmillan Inc v Bishopsgate Investment Management plc (No.1)* [1993] 4 All ER 998).

In requiring production of information held by a bank it will be necessary to take account of the Bankers' Books Evidence Act 1879 as amended. A bank may be required to produce a customer's bank statement and is not in breach of its duty of confidentiality to its customer in doing so (*Robertson v Canadian Imperial Bank of Commerce* [1995] 1 All ER 824). However, it is an offence to disclose information which relates to the business or other affairs of any person and which has only been acquired for the purposes of the Banking Act 1987 (s82 and *Bank of Credit and Commerce International (Overseas) Ltd (in liquidation) v Price Waterhouse* [1997] 4 All ER 781). The only exceptions which may be relevant to a tribunal occur where (a) the person concerned consents to such disclosure, or (b) the information is already public.

Rule 16(3)

This rule deals with compellability of witnesses, not the admissibility of their evidence. It does not introduce all the rules of evidence which apply in a court on a trial of an action. The location of this provision in a rule dealing with summoning of witnesses and before the rule dealing with the hearing itself shows that its scope is limited to the compellability of the person as a witness. For parties who are not compellable see Halsbury, *Laws of England* (4th ed), Vol 17, para 234.

Withdrawal

17.–(1) Subject to paragraph (2), a party may give notice of the withdrawal of its case, or any part of it–

    (a)   [¹...] by sending or delivering to the Tribunal a written notice of withdrawal; or

    (b)   orally at a hearing.

    (2)   In the circumstances described in paragraph (3), a notice of withdrawal will not take effect unless the Tribunal consents to the withdrawal.

    (3)   The circumstances referred to in paragraph (2) are where a party gives notice of withdrawal–

    (a)   [¹...] in a criminal injuries compensation case; [¹...]

    [¹(b) in a social security and child support case where the Tribunal has directed that notice of withdrawal shall take effect only with the Tribunal's consent; or

    (c) at a hearing.]

    (4)   A party who has withdrawn their case may apply to the Tribunal for the case to be reinstated.

    (5)   An application under paragraph (4) must be made in writing and be received by the Tribunal within 1 month after–

    (a)   the date on which the Tribunal received the notice under paragraph (1)(a); or

    (b)   the date of the hearing at which the case was withdrawn orally under paragraph (1)(b).

    (6)   The Tribunal must notify each party in writing [¹that a withdrawal has taken effect] under this rule.

Amendment

    1.   Tribunal Procedure (Amendment) Rules 2013 (SI 2013 No.477) r24 (April 8, 2013).

Definitions

    "dispose of proceedings": see rule 1(3).

    "hearing": see rule 1(3).

"party": see rule 1(3).
"Tribunal": see rule 1(3).

General Note

Any party to the proceedings may withdraw their case or part of it. The consent of the other parties is not required. The consent of the tribunal is only required if the withdrawal is made orally at a hearing. If the tribunal's consent is required, it will need to ensure that the party understands the significance of withdrawal.

There is no definition of "case". The rule applies clearly and easily to the withdrawal of appeals and referrals. It is less clear how it applies to parts of cases or the case being put for a respondent. It is not appropriate merely because a party has a change of mind about a particular argument.

A referral continues in existence until it is withdrawn by the Secretary of State under this regulation even if the application for the variation has been withdrawn under reg 5 of the Variation Regulations (*Milton v SSWP* reported as *R(CS) 1/07,* refusing permission to appeal against the decision of the commissioner in *CCS 1031/ 2005*).

If it is unclear whether a party wishes to withdraw an appeal or a referral, it is an error of law for the tribunal to fail to clarify the party's wishes (*CCS 13/1994,* para 8).

Rule 17(2)

The tribunal should refuse permission to withdraw if the application is a tactical ploy, but the power to refuse is not so limited and depends on the circumstances of the case (*KF v Birmingham and Solihull Mental Health NHS Foundation Trust* [2010] UKUT 185 (AAC), paras 36-37).

Rule 17(4)-(5)

A case that has been withdrawn may be reinstated. The time allowed is one month, but this may be extended under rule 5(3)(a). Effectively, this allows a cooling-off period for the party to reflect and have a change of mind.

Unlike the position in a court (see *Ogwr Borough Council v Knight, The Times,* January 13 1994), a withdrawn appeal is not dismissed. This allows a fresh appeal to be made (whether by the original appellant or by someone else) and a fresh referral to be made by the Secretary of State (*R(IS) 5/94*), subject of course to the normal rules about time. The fact that a case has been withdrawn will be a relevant factor in deciding whether or not to extend time.

Lead cases

18.–(1)   This rule applies if–

(a)   two or more cases have been started before the Tribunal;

(b)   in each such case the Tribunal has not made a decision disposing of the proceedings; and

(c)   the cases give rise to common or related issues of fact or law.

(2)   The Tribunal may give a direction–

(a)   specifying one or more cases falling under paragraph (1) as a lead case or lead cases; and

(b)   staying (or, in Scotland, sisting) the other cases falling under paragraph (1) ("the related cases").

(3)   When the Tribunal makes a decision in respect of the common or related issues–

(a)   the Tribunal must send a copy of that decision to each party in each of the related cases; and

(b)   subject to paragraph (4), that decision shall be binding on each of those parties.

(4)   Within 1 month after the date on which the Tribunal sent a copy of the decision to a party under paragraph (3)(a), that party may apply in writing for a direction that the decision does not apply to, and is not binding on the parties to, a particular related case.

(5)   The Tribunal must give directions in respect of cases which are stayed or sisted under paragraph (2)(b), providing for the disposal of or further directions in those cases.

(6)   If the lead case or cases lapse or are withdrawn before the Tribunal makes a decision in respect of the common or related issues, the Tribunal must give directions as to–

(a)   whether another case or other cases are to be specified as a lead case or lead cases; and

(b)   whether any direction affecting the related cases should be set aside or amended.

Definitions

"dispose of proceedings": see rule 1(3).
"Tribunal": see rule 1(3).

Confidentiality in child support or child trust fund cases

19.–(1) Paragraph (3) applies to proceedings under the Child Support Act 1991 in the circumstances described in paragraph (2), other than an appeal against a reduced benefit decision (as defined in section 46(10)(b) of the Child Support Act 1991, as that section had effect prior to the commencement of section 15(b) of the Child Maintenance and Other Payments Act 2008).

(2) The circumstances referred to in paragraph (1) are that the absent parent, non-resident parent or person with care would like their address or the address of the child to be kept confidential and has given notice to that effect–

[²(a) in the notice of appeal or when notifying the Secretary of State or the Tribunal of any subsequent change of address; or

(b) within 14 days after an enquiry is made by the recipient of the notice of appeal or the notification referred to in sub-paragraph (a).]

(3) Where this paragraph applies, the Secretary of State [¹...] and the Tribunal must take appropriate steps to secure the confidentiality of the address, and of any information which could reasonably be expected to enable a person to identify the address, to the extent that the address or that information is not already known to each other party.

(4) Paragraph (6) applies to proceedings under the Child Trust Funds Act 2004 in the circumstances described in paragraph (5).

(5) The circumstances referred to in paragraph (4) are that a relevant person would like their address or the address of the eligible child to be kept confidential and has given notice to that effect, or a local authority with parental responsibility in relation to the eligible child would like the address of the eligible child to be kept confidential and has given notice to that effect–

(a) to HMRC in the notice of appeal or when notifying any subsequent change of address;

(b) to HMRC within 14 days after an enquiry by HMRC; or

(c) to the Tribunal when notifying any change of address.

(6) Where this paragraph applies, HMRC and the Tribunal must take appropriate steps to secure the confidentiality of the address, and of any information which could reasonably be expected to enable a person to identify the address, to the extent that the address or that information is not already known to each other party.

(7) In this rule–

"eligible child" has the meaning set out in section 2 of the Child Trust Funds Act 2004;

"HMRC" means Her Majesty's Revenue and Customs;

"non-resident parent" and "parent with care" have the meanings set out in section 54 of the Child Support Act 1991;

"parental responsibility" has the meaning set out in section 3(9) of the Child Trust Funds Act 2004; and

"relevant person" has the meaning set out in section 22(3) of the Child Trust Funds Act 2004.

Amendments

1.   Public Bodies (Child Maintenance and Enforcement Commission: Abolition and Transfer of Functions) Order 2012 (SI 2012 No.2007) art 3(2) and Sch para 117 (August 1, 2012).

2.   Tribunal Procedure (Amendment No.4) Rules 2013 (SI 2013 No.2067) r24 (November 1, 2013).

Definitions

"party": see rule 1(3).
"Tribunal": see rule 1(3).
And see para (7).

General Note

A parent or a person with care may request confidentiality for their address or that of the qualifying child. It is put into effect by the documents being masked to conceal the confidential information from the parties.

Requests for confidentiality often prove, on examination, to relate to the contents of the party's evidence rather than to an address. In these circumstances, the request must be considered under rule 14 or under a common law right to confidentiality such as that considered by the three-judge panel of the Upper Tribunal in *Dorset Healthcare NHS Foundation Trust v MH* [2009] UKUT 4 (AAC).

The rule does not prevent disclosure to the tribunal and there are circumstances in which the evidence is relevant to an issue that the tribunal has to decide. An address may, for example, be relevant to service of the papers and notice of the hearing, habitual residence, housing costs, and contact costs.

In *R(CS) 3/06*, the commissioner gave practical advice to tribunals on how to handle masked papers:

"33.   *Preview* – Ideally, the members of the tribunal should be provided with unmasked copies of the papers in every case. However, I accept that the Appeals Service [now the First-tier Tribunal] may consider that this would involve the risk that the wrong papers were issued to the parties. An acceptable alternative is for the members of the tribunal to be sent masked copies and for the chairman to preview the papers on receipt.

34.   The preview may show that the masked evidence is not within the scope of regulation 44 [now rule 19]. It may be clear that each parent knows where the other lives. Or they may want to secure confidentiality for personal or financial information about themselves or their new partners. In either case, provided the masked evidence is relevant to the issues raised by the appeal, the chairman should direct that the parties be given unmasked copies.

35.   Alternatively, the preview may show that the masked evidence is relevant to an issue that arises on the appeal. If it is, the chairman should call for the unmasked copy so that the members of the tribunal may see all the evidence.

36.   *The conduct of the hearing* – This is the most difficult task that a chairman has to perform in a child support case. If the evidence is properly masked under regulation 44 and is relevant to an issue on the appeal, the chairman must ensure that there is a fair hearing despite the withholding of the evidence. That means that the other party must be given sufficient information to allow an informed challenge to the evidence without disclosing sufficient to breach the confidentiality imposed by the regulation. And it means that the tribunal must be able to obtain the additional evidence from the parties that will allow it to assess the reliability of all the evidence before it.

37.   The circumstances of the cases that may arise are too various to allow me to give specific advice. But it should not be necessary. Chairmen who hear child support cases are all experienced chairmen; they would not be ticketed for those cases if they were not. They have the ability to devise ways to allow each party to meet the other's case and the tribunal to assess the evidence rationally."

Natural justice requires a fair hearing and this usually requires that a person should know and have a chance to answer the case of the other party (*Official Solicitor to the Supreme Court v K* [1965] AC 201 at 234; *Doody v SSHD* [1993] 3 All ER 92 at 106; *R (ota S) v Plymouth City Council* [2002] 1 FLR 1177). However, the requirements of natural justice must give way to contrary statutory provision. Accordingly, the issue arises of the extent to which as a matter of interpretation the provision replaces this aspect of natural justice.

On a practical level, it will often be possible to discuss matters in sufficient generality to prevent inappropriate disclosure while allowing sufficient detail to be disclosed to allow a fair hearing on the issue. Another possibility is that disclosure may be made to a party's representative on condition that it is not further disclosed. This would then allow the representative to investigate relevant issues without the address becoming known to the party.

It is possible that this rule is not compatible with the Art 6 Convention right: *McMichael v United Kingdom* (1995) 20 EHRR 205. This case concerned the non-disclosure of documents in a children's hearing in Scotland. Before the Court the Government accepted that non-disclosure of the documents constituted a breach of Art 6(1) of the Convention in that the lack of knowledge of the contents of those documents prevented there being a fair hearing in that the power of the parents to influence the outcome of the proceedings and to assess the prospects of a successful appeal to a higher court were affected. See especially at para 80 of the judgment. Unless this regulation is protected by some other provision of the Convention, the same reasoning will apply to render it a breach of Art 6(1).

Rule 19(3)

This must be interpreted narrowly and applied sensibly. Persons might be located from information which relates directly to themselves or from information that relates to them only indirectly in that it relates to some other person, inquiry or observation of whom might lead to their being located (such as a grandparent, employer or solicitor). The key to the realistic application of this provision is the "reasonably".

All documents are covered regardless of who provides them, including the documents supplied by the Secretary of State. However, the rule does not cover information that is already known to the other parties.

As regards the record of proceedings, the presiding judge should record the evidence in the normal way, but arrange for any confidential information to be masked before it is disclosed.

As regards the tribunal's decision notice and written statement of reasons, rules 33(2) and 34(5) are subject to rule 14(2), but not to this rule. However, the presiding judge must retain confidentiality in order to comply with this rule.

Expenses in criminal injuries compensation cases
20.   *[Omitted]*

Expenses in social security and child support cases
21.–(1)   This rule applies only to social security and child support cases.

(2)   The Secretary of State may pay such travelling and other allowances (including compensation for loss of remunerative time) as the Secretary of State may determine to any person required to attend a hearing in proceedings under section 20 of the Child Support Act 1991, section 12 of the Social Security Act 1998 or paragraph 6 of Schedule 7 to the Child Support, Pensions and Social Security Act 2000.

Definitions
"hearing": see rule 1(3).
"social security and child support case": see rule 1(3).

PART 3
Proceedings before the Tribunal
CHAPTER 1
Before the hearing

Cases in which the notice of appeal is to be sent to the Tribunal
22.   *[Omitted]*

Cases in which the notice of appeal is to be sent to the decision maker
23.–[⁴(1)   This rule applies to social security and child support cases in which the notice of decision being challenged informs the appellant that any appeal must be sent to the decision maker.]

(2)   An appellant must start proceedings by sending or delivering a notice of appeal to the decision maker so that it is received within the time specified in Schedule 1 to these Rules (time limits for providing notices of appeal to the decision maker).

(3)   If the appellant provides the notice of appeal to the decision maker later than the time required by paragraph (2) the notice of appeal must include the reason why the notice of appeal was not provided in time.

(4)   Subject to paragraph (5), where an appeal is not made within the time specified in Schedule 1, it will be treated as having been made in time [²if neither the decision maker nor any other respondent objects].

(5)   No appeal may be made more than 12 months after the time specified in Schedule 1.

(6)   The notice of appeal must be in English or Welsh, must be signed by the appellant and must state–
(a)   the name and address of the appellant;
(b)   the name and address of the appellant's representative (if any);
(c)   an address where documents for the appellant may be sent or delivered;
(d)   details of the decision being appealed; and
(e)   the grounds on which the appellant relies.

(7)   The decision maker must refer the case to the Tribunal immediately if–
(a)   the appeal has been made after the time specified in Schedule 1 and the decision maker [³or any other respondent] objects to it being treated as having been made in time; or
(b)   the decision maker considers that the appeal has been made more than 12 months after the time specified in Schedule 1.

[¹ (8)   Notwithstanding rule 5(3)(a) [⁵or (aa)] (case management powers) and rule 7(2) (failure to comply with rules etc.), the Tribunal must not extend the time limit in paragraph (5).]

Amendments
1.   Inserted by r3 of SI 2009 No 1975 as from 1.9.09.
2.   Substituted by r4(2)(a) of SI 2012 No 500 as from 6.4.12.
3.   Inserted by by r4(2)(b) of SI 2012 No 500 as from 6.4.12.
4.   Tribunal Procedure (Amendment) Rules 2013 (SI 2013 No.477) r26 (April 8, 2013).
5.   Tribunal Procedure (Amendment No.4) Rules 2013 (SI 2013 No.2067) r26 (November 1, 2013).

Definitions
"appeal": see rule 1(3).
"appellant": see rule 1(3).
"decision maker": rule 1(3).
"document": see rule 1(3).
"social security and child support case": rule 1(3).
"Tribunal": see rule 1(3).

General Note
In *IB v Information Commissioner* [2011] UKUT 370 (AAC); [2012] AACR 26, the Upper Tribunal decided that both the First-tier Tribunal in its information jurisdiction and the Upper Tribunal were courts for the purpose of vexatious litigants, who therefore required the permission of the High Court in order to bring proceedings. In *AO and BO v Shepway DC* [2013] UKUT 009 (AAC), a different judge agreed that the Upper Tribunal was a court for the purposes of a housing benefit appeal, but that the First-tier Tribunal was not.

Responses and replies

24.–(1) When a decision maker receives the notice of appeal or a copy of it, the decision maker must send or deliver a response to the Tribunal–

(a) *[Omitted]*;

[¹(aa) *[Omitted]]* and

(b) in other cases, as soon as reasonably practicable after the decision maker received the notice of appeal.

(2) The response must state–

(a) the name and address of the decision maker;

(b) the name and address of the decision maker's representative (if any);

(c) an address where documents for the decision maker may be sent or delivered;

(d) the names and addresses of any other respondents and their representatives (if any);

(e) whether the decision maker opposes the appellant's case and, if so, any grounds for such opposition which are not set out in any documents which are before the Tribunal; and

(f) any further information or documents required by a practice direction or direction.

(3) The response may include a submission as to whether it would be appropriate for the case to be disposed of without a hearing.

(4) The decision maker must provide with the response–

(a) a copy of any written record of the decision under challenge, and any statement of reasons for that decision, if they were not sent with the notice of appeal;

(b) copies of all documents relevant to the case in the decision maker's possession, unless a practice direction or direction states otherwise; and

(c) in cases to which rule 23 (cases in which the notice of appeal is to be sent to the decision maker) applies, a copy of the notice of appeal, any documents provided by the appellant with the notice of appeal and (if they have not otherwise been provided to the Tribunal) the name and address of the appellant's representative (if any).

(5) The decision maker must provide a copy of the response and any accompanying documents to each other party at the same time as it provides the response to the Tribunal.

(6) The appellant and any other respondent may make a written submission and supply further documents in reply to the decision maker's response.

(7) Any submission or further documents under paragraph (6) must be provided to the Tribunal within 1 month after the date on which the decision maker sent the response to the party providing the reply, and the Tribunal must send a copy to each other party.

Amendment
1.   Inserted by r4(3) of SI 2011 No 651 as from 1.4.11.

Definitions
"appellant": see rule 1(3).
"asylum support case": see rule 1(3).

"decision maker": see rule 1(3).
"document": see rule 1(3).
"hearing": see rule 1(3).
"party": see rule 1(3).
"practice direction": see rule 1(3).
"respondent": see rule 1(3).
"Tribunal": see rule 1(3).

General Note

Rule 24(6) and (7)

These provisions allow the other parties one month in which to make further submissions or supply more documents to the tribunal. There is a breach of natural justice if the tribunal holds a hearing within that time and thereby deprives a party of a chance to do so (*MP v SSWP (DLA)* [2010] UKUT 103 (AAC), para 26).

Medical and physical examination in appeals under section 12 of the Social Security Act 1998

25. *[Omitted]*

Social security and child support cases started by reference or information in writing

26.–(1) This rule applies to proceedings under section 28D of the Child Support Act 1991 and paragraph 3 of Schedule 2 to the Tax Credits Act 2002.

(2) A person starting proceedings under section 28D of the Child Support Act 1991 must send or deliver a written reference to the Tribunal.

(3) *[Omitted]*

(4) The reference or the information in writing must include–

(a) an address where documents for the person starting proceedings may be sent or delivered;

(b) the names and addresses of the respondents and their representatives (if any); and

(c) a submission on the issues that arise for determination by the Tribunal.

(5) Unless a practice direction or direction states otherwise, the person starting proceedings must also provide a copy of each document in their possession which is relevant to the proceedings.

(6) Subject to any obligation under rule 19(3) (confidentiality in child support cases), the person starting proceedings must provide a copy of the written reference or the information in writing and any accompanying documents to each respondent at the same time as they provide the written reference or the information in writing to the Tribunal.

(7) Each respondent may send or deliver to the Tribunal a written submission and any further relevant documents within one month of the date on which the person starting proceedings sent a copy of the written reference or the information in writing to that respondent.

Definitions

"document": see rule 1(3).
"practice direction": see rule 1(3).
"respondent": see rule 1(3).
"social security and child support case": see rule 1(3).
"Tribunal": see rule 1(3).

CHAPTER 2
Hearings

Decision with or without a hearing

27.–(1) Subject to the following paragraphs, the Tribunal must hold a hearing before making a decision which disposes of proceedings unless–

(a)   each party has consented to, or has not objected to, the matter being decided without a hearing; and

(b)   the Tribunal considers that it is able to decide the matter without a hearing.

(2)   This rule does not apply to decisions under Part 4.

(3)   The Tribunal may in any event dispose of proceedings without a hearing under rule 8 (striking out a party's case).

(4)-(6)   *[Omitted]*

Definitions

"criminal injuries compensation case": see rule 1(3).
"dispose of proceedings": see rule 1(3).
"hearing": see rule 1(3).
"party": see rule 1(3).
"Tribunal": see rule 1(3).

General Note

The default position is that an oral hearing will be held. See the definition of "hearing" in rule 1(3) for the form that this may take.

In *CCS 5230/2002*, the commissioner considered whether the tribunal had held an oral hearing. The case concerned a departure direction. The tribunal, consisting of a legally qualified panel member sitting with a financially qualified panel member, held an oral hearing and gave directions to the Secretary of State on how to calculate the non-resident parent's income, but it reserved consideration of the just and equitable requirement until that calculation had been made. When the Secretary of State provided the calculation, it was sent to the financially qualified panel member who was asked to confirm that it would be just and equitable to give a direction. The chairman then completed a decision notice to that effect. The parties were not invited to comment on the issue and there was nothing to show that the members of the tribunal had been in touch to discuss it. The commissioner set aside the tribunal's decision for a number of procedural deficiencies and commented (para 12) that it was doubtful whether the tribunal had held an oral hearing within the meaning of this regulation then in force.

The case can only be decided without an oral hearing if two conditions are satisfied. First, the parties must all have consented, or not objected to, the case being decided on the papers. Second, the tribunal must consider that it is able to decide the matter without a hearing.

In practice, the second condition is usually considered at the paper hearing and allows the tribunal to override the wishes of the parties if it considers that a hearing is required. If this condition were interpreted literally, it would never be fulfilled, because a decision can always be reached by relying on the burden of proof. The test must be whether an oral hearing is "reasonably" required (*CI 1533/1998*, para 13). In practice, a key consideration will be the significance of oral evidence or the chance to question a party or witness. An oral hearing is particularly useful if an issue turns on a party's integrity. Other relevant factors are (a) whether the party will attend an oral hearing and (b) whether the evidence could be obtained in a different way under rule 15(1)(e).

The record of proceedings

These rules make no provision for a record of proceedings. However, the Senior President has given a practice statement on **RECORD OF PROCEEDINGS IN SOCIAL SECURITY AND CHILD SUPPORT CASES IN THE SOCIAL ENTITLEMENT CHAMBER ON OR AFTER 3 NOVEMBER 2008**. In substance, it repeats the previous legislation, as interpreted by *R(DLA) 3/08*, paras 6 and 10:

1.   In this Practice Statement "social security and child support case" has the meaning given in rule 1(3) of the Tribunal Procedure (First-tier Tribunal) (Social Entitlement Chamber) Rules 2008.

2.   A record of the proceedings at a hearing must be made by the presiding member, or in the case of a Tribunal composed of only one member, by that member.

3.   The record must be sufficient to indicate any evidence taken and submissions made and any procedural applications, and may be in such medium as the member may determine.

4.   The Tribunal must preserve–
    a. the record of proceedings;
    b. the decision notice; and
    c. any written reasons for the Tribunal's decision for the period specified in paragraph 5.

5.   The specified period is six months from the date of–
    a. the decision made by the Tribunal;
    b. any written reasons for the Tribunal's decision;
    c. any correction under Rule 36 of the above Rules;
    d. any refusal to set aside a decision under Rule 37; or
    e. any determination of an application for permission to appeal against the decision, or until the date on which those documents are sent to the Upper Tribunal in connection with an appeal against the decision or an application for permission to appeal, if that occurs within the six months.

6.   Any party to the proceedings may within the time specified in paragraph 5 apply in writing for a copy of the record of proceedings and a copy must be supplied to him."

This duty is imposed on the presiding judge. Ideally, the judge should personally make the record. Exceptionally, it may be appropriate to delegate the duty, as when the judge has a broken arm or is disabled. If the duty is delegated, the record should be presented as that of the person who took it, although the judge may adopt it if satisfied that it is accurate (*R(SB) 13/83*, para 14), as may be the case if it has been dictated by the judge. The judge should be aware of the dangers of (i) delegating the making of the record to someone who is not experienced in the art of note-taking; (ii) relying on someone else's notes; and (iii) distracting the note-taker from other duties, especially a clerk.

The record may be made in whatever medium the presiding judge determines. Some tribunals now digitally record the proceedings. The judge may additionally make a personal note of the evidence, but this is not considered to be the record of proceedings. A digital recording will put beyond any doubt what was said at the hearing, but may cause difficulties in making copies of the record available for the parties.

The record of proceedings must be sufficient to indicate any evidence taken and submissions made and any procedural applications. It should make clear not only what was said or done, but who said or did what. See *R(SB) 8/84*, para 25(6). The judge's thoughts, if committed to paper, are best recorded separately. There is no duty to include a record of the tribunal's deliberations, although a private record is useful when writing a full statement of the tribunal's decision (*R(DLA) 3/08*, para 26).

The record should be contemporaneous (*CSB 613/1983*, para 8).

The National Insurance Commissioners held that the note of evidence should be complete (*R(I) 81/51*, para 23; *R(U) 16/60*, para 5). Those decisions were given at a time when an appeal lay on both fact and law, so that the commissioner needed to have all the evidence available. When an appeal to a commissioner lay only on a question of law, commissioners no longer insisted on a verbatim record (*CSSB 212/1987*, para 3). What was required was the happy mean, which chairmen regularly produced, between a verbatim record and a brief summary (*CIS 12032/1996*, para 7). The specific requirement that the record be sufficient to indicate the evidence taken may lead to a higher standard of record being expected.

The record of proceedings, at least as supplied to the parties, must be clear, complete, comprehensible and legible (*CDLA 16902/1996*, paras 8 and 9; *CDLA 4110/1997*, para 7; *CIB 3013/1997*, para 10; (*R(DLA) 3/08*, paras 13-14).

The status of a practice statement is not clear. In the past, it has been held that the failure to make a record of proceedings may be an error of law (*R(I) 81/51*, para 23; *R(I) 42/59*, para 35). The lack of a record of proceedings on appeal will be an error of law if in a particular case it is necessary to have regard to the evidence given at the hearing or to any contention put forward at the hearing in order to decide if the case falls within any of the recognised heads of error of law. The lack of any, or of an adequate, record of proceeding is not of itself and in all circumstances an error of law. The absence of, or deficiency in, the notes of proceedings is not a separate head of error of law. However, it is subsidiary to, and protective and supportive of, the recognised heads of error of law in that it will be an error of law if it prevents the Upper Tribunal from deciding whether a particular error of law has been shown. See *CDLA 1389/1997*, para 18, but the commissioner did not refer to the possibility of supplementing the record from other sources. On the commissioner's approach, there will be an error of law if it is necessary to refer to the record of proceedings in order to know what matters were in issue before the tribunal (*ibid*, paras 19 and 35) or to know what evidence was before the tribunal (*CSSB 212/1987*, para 3) and that it was taken into account by the tribunal (*CIS 12032/1996*, para 7).

The lack of a record of proceedings will not be an error of law if no party to the proceedings requested a copy and the record has now been destroyed at the end of the six months.

On appeal, the Upper Tribunal is not limited the evidence appearing in the documents and the record of proceedings. As the Upper Tribunal does not insist on a verbatim note of evidence, it is inappropriate to treat the record of proceedings as a comprehensive record of the oral evidence and submissions. The position was set out in *CS 4537/1998*, para 13. The chairman's record should be taken as comprehensive unless one of the parties is able to show that it omits specific relevant evidence or submissions. The suggestion in *R(SB) 10/82*, para 15 that an agreed record should be obtained has not been followed. However, it would help the Upper Tribunal if judges, when granting or refusing permission to appeal on grounds that allege the record of proceedings was incomplete, recorded their recollections to provide a relatively contemporaneous response to the allegations. In *CDLA 4879/2003* para 28, the commissioner encouraged representatives to take a record of evidence given in order to supplement, if necessary, the evidence recorded by the chairman. However, it is appropriate to treat with caution information about the evidence given, or submissions made, at the hearing before a tribunal if the presiding judge has not commented on it.

A commissioner suggested that an application for permission to appeal to a commissioner should be treated as a request for a copy of the record of proceedings (*R(IS) 11/99*, para 33).

The tribunal is not under a duty to hold an oral hearing under this rule when considering whether to strike out a case. However, it has power to do so under rule 5(3)(f) and must apply the overriding objective when considering whether to exercise that power (*JR 0400/2010*, para 11).

Entitlement to attend a hearing

28. Subject to rule 30(5) (exclusion of a person from a hearing), each party to proceedings is entitled to attend a hearing.

Definitions
"hearing": see rule 1(3).
"party": see rule 1(3).

General Note
The parties have a right to attend the hearing. This right is qualified by the possibility that a request for postponement or an application for an adjournment to allow a party to attend may be refused.

The right to attend implies a right to participate. This right is qualified by the tribunal's power to regulate its own procedure under rule 5(1). The tribunal is most likely to limit a party's participation in order to curtail repetitious or irrelevant submissions. It may also be necessary to prevent a party attending whose behaviour towards the tribunal, the clerk or the other parties is unacceptable. However, the same tolerance may be required for parties as has to be shown for representatives: see below.

As the parties have a right to attend and participate, so do their representatives and others who accompany them to assist in presenting the case at the hearing: see rule 11(5) and (7). Tribunals should not abort a hearing just because a representative makes offensive or unfounded allegations about the members (*Bennett v Southwark London Borough Council* [2002] ICR 881).

In *CDLA 2462/2003*, the commissioner considered the position of a representative who wanted to give evidence. The commissioner held that a representative had the right to give evidence of matters within the representative's own knowledge (para 11). However, it was for the tribunal to decide whether a representative should be allowed to put to the tribunal a summary of the evidence of one of the parties (para 13).

Role and status of the Secretary of State's presenting officer
The Secretary of State is a party to the proceedings, but a non-partisan one (*R v Medical Appeal Tribunal (North Midland Region) ex p Hubble* [1958] 2 All ER 374 at 379, *per* Diplock J and *R v National Insurance Commissioner ex p Viscusi* [1974] 2 All ER 724 at 729, *per* Lord Denning MR) whose only interest is to ensure that the law is properly applied.

If the Secretary of State attends hearings, it does so through presenting officers. These officers have a recognised and distinctive role at the hearing before a tribunal. However, this role is not spelt out in the legislation. It is based in part on the provisions of the legislation, in part on the nature of the officer's function, in part on decisions of commissioners and in part on the practice of tribunals.

In view of the presenting officer's non-partisan interest in the proceedings as well as the officer's knowledge and understanding of the law and access to information held by the Secretary of State, that officer plays an important role in assisting the tribunal. (i) The officer should have previewed the papers and anticipated the needs of the tribunal. (ii) The officer should have obtained or tried to obtain information which is not contained in the papers but which will be needed by, or will assist, the tribunal. (iii) The officer should be able to provide explanations of how the law has been applied or how it might be applied in the light of the evidence before the tribunal. (iv) The officer should supplement the tribunal's questions to the parties and witnesses in order to ensure that all relevant factual issues are investigated. (v) The officer can summarise for the tribunal the issues which arise for decision. (vi) The officer may (their styles differ) provide an independent view of how the law might be applied to the case before the tribunal.

The law regarding statements made by officers including presenting officers is in an unsatisfactory state. Such statements are likely to be hearsay (*R(IS) 6/91*, para 11) and as such require to be treated with appropriate caution. However, the commissioners went further and suggested that more than the normal care associated with hearsay evidence is required. Statements made by officers in submissions should always be substantiated (*CSB 517/1982*, para 8) and unsupported, contested statements by presenting officers should not be accepted without supporting evidence (*CSB 10/1986,* para 5). Statements made by presenting officers are not evidence in the absence of personal knowledge (*R(SB) 8/84*, para 25(6)). Statements made by presenting officers should not merely be accepted, but should, if unsubstantiated, be investigated and proper findings of fact should be made (*CSB 728/1984*, para 11(8)). These decisions and others were considered in *CS 16448/1996*, paras 17-21. The commissioner concluded that what a presenting officer said was evidence, although if it was not within the officer's personal knowledge it was hearsay. The extent of the enquiries that a tribunal should make in order to assess the proper weight to be given to the evidence depended on the circumstances of the case and the burden of proof.

There is no objection in principle to the presenting officer at the hearing having been involved in the handling of the case in some other capacity, unless it results in some way in the hearing being unfair. It is, however, preferable for the presenting officer not to have been involved in the investigation of the case. See *CCS 1037/ 1995*, para 16.

Tribunals should be sensitive to the position of the presenting officer. Presenting appeals is not the only duty of such officers. They may have had the papers for less time than the tribunal and other parties. They may have had to prepare for the hearing in less than satisfactory conditions and have been able to obtain only limited additional information from the file and computer system. Moreover, they may be seen by the other parties as representatives of the Secretary of State and, therefore, as appropriate persons on whom those parties may vent their feelings. These officers should be allowed and encouraged to play an independent and constructive role in the proceedings and should not become the target for the tribunal or the other parties. The presiding judge has the primary role in ensuring this.

The significance of the absence of a presenting officer at the hearing was discussed in *CIB 5876/1997*, para 28. The commissioner's conclusion was that the absence of a presenting officer was not of itself a breach of natural justice and did not constitute an error of law that required the tribunal's decision to be set aside by a commissioner on appeal. However, the absence of a presenting officer might, when coupled with other facts or circumstances in a particular case, be a contributory factor in the denial to the claimant (or any other party to the proceedings) of a fair hearing. Whether or not that was so required an analysis of the impact of the officer's absence on the fairness of the hearing. The test was not whether or not any particular party to the proceedings wanted a presenting officer to be present, but whether considered objectively the presence of such an officer was necessary in order that there be a fair hearing.

Notice of hearings

29.–(1) The Tribunal must give each party entitled to attend a hearing reasonable notice of the time and place of the hearing (including any adjourned or postponed hearing) and any changes to the time and place of the hearing.

(2) The period of notice under paragraph (1) must be at least 14 days except that–

(a) *[Omitted]*; and

(b) the Tribunal may give shorter notice–

(i) with the parties' consent; or

(ii) in urgent or exceptional circumstances.

Definitions

"asylum support case": see rule 1(3).
"hearing": see rule 1(3).
"party": see rule 1(3).
"Tribunal": see rule 1(3).

General Note

The parties must be given reasonable notice of the hearing. This means at least 14 days unless the parties all consent. Consent must be fully informed. Consent under protest or in ignorance of the party's rights is not sufficient. See *CI 4182/1998*, para 10. The tribunal may override the parties' views if the case is urgent or there are exceptional circumstances.

It is not clear whether notice is a 'document' that may be sent to the representative rather than the party under rule 11(6)(a).

If a party attends but complains that service was not properly effected, the tribunal should enquire (*CI 4182/1998*, para 10). However, it will only be appropriate to adjourn if the party has been prejudiced.

Public and private hearings

30.–(1) Subject to the following paragraphs, all hearings must be held in public.

(2) *[Omitted]*

(3) The Tribunal may give a direction that a hearing, or part of it, is to be held in private.

(4) Where a hearing, or part of it, is to be held in private, the Tribunal may determine who is permitted to attend the hearing or part of it.

(5) The Tribunal may give a direction excluding from any hearing, or part of it–

(a) any person whose conduct the Tribunal considers is disrupting or is likely to disrupt the hearing;

(b) any person whose presence the Tribunal considers is likely to prevent another person from giving evidence or making submissions freely;

(c) any person who the Tribunal considers should be excluded in order to give effect to a direction under rule 14(2) (withholding information likely to cause harm); or

(d) any person where the purpose of the hearing would be defeated by the attendance of that person.

(6) The Tribunal may give a direction excluding a witness from a hearing until that witness gives evidence.

Definitions
 "appellant": see rule 1(3).
 "criminal injuries compensation case": see rule 1(3).
 "hearing": see rule 1(3).
 "Tribunal": see rule 1(3).

General Note
 The default position is that a hearing is in public. The tribunal may direct otherwise.
 A public hearing means that the public must have ready access to the room used by the tribunal. A room in a secure area protected by a door with a push-button security lock is not public. It is irrelevant that no member of the public tried to attend the hearing. See *Storer v British Gas plc* [2000] 2 All ER 440.
 It is rare for the general public to wish to attend a child support case. Two issues arise in practice. Both arise for both private and public hearings. One issue is whether a new partner is to be allowed in the hearing room. This can be dealt with under rule 30(5), which allows a tribunal to exclude a person from a hearing. However, the new partner may be a representative or attend to assist the party, in which case the power of exclusion must be balanced against the rights under rule 11(5) and (7). The other issue is whether a witness should be in the room to hear other evidence. The tribunal has power to decide this under rule 30(6). The matters to be considered include whether the witness's evidence will be affected by anything that might be heard during the proceedings and whether there may be private, intimate or embarrassing matters disclosed during the hearing, especially any which affect a child, which should be given as small a circulation as possible.
 A private hearing is the normal practice where children are concerned. This is consistent with the spirit of the European Convention on Human Rights (*Re PB (Hearings in open court)* [1996] 2 FLR 765 at 768, *per* Butler-Sloss, LJ); *P v BW (Children Cases: Hearings in Public)* [2004] 1 FLR 171 at para 48). In deciding whether to order a private hearing, the tribunal should consider: (i) the wishes of the parties; (ii) whether information is likely to be made public which is private, intimate or embarrassing, especially if it affects a child; (iii) whether there is a public interest in the proceedings or the decision, such as if it is a test case; (iv) whether the public interest could be protected without a public hearing, such as by making the decision or its reasoning public; (v) whether it is appropriate to hold part of the hearing in public and part in private.
 Regardless of whether the hearing is public or private, the tribunal's deliberations on any contested issue should always be in private. This does not mean that others may not be present. The clerk may be present, as may others such as a member of the Administrative Justice and Tribunals Council. However, they must not participate in the deliberations or give any cause to believe that they may have done so (*R(SB) 13/83*, para 15). It is good practice for the presiding judge to explain to the parties that someone other than the clerk is going to be present and assure them that they will not participate in the decision.

Hearings in a party's absence
 31. If a party fails to attend a hearing the Tribunal may proceed with the hearing if the Tribunal–
 (a)　is satisfied that the party has been notified of the hearing or that reasonable steps have been taken to notify the party of the hearing; and
 (b)　considers that it is in the interests of justice to proceed with the hearing.

Definitions
 "hearing": see rule 1(3).
 "party": see rule 1(3).
 "Tribunal": see rule 1(3).

General Note
 A tribunal may proceed with an oral hearing in the absence of a party. This is subject to two conditions.
 The first condition is that proper steps had been taken to notify the party of the hearing. Accordingly, if a party does not attend, the tribunal must first enquire whether the party was properly served. If the tribunal is not satisfied that this has been done, it must adjourn and direct that service be effected (*R(SB) 19/83*, para 7). The presiding judge should make a note in the record of proceedings of what enquiries were made and to what effect. If the tribunal proceeds when this condition has not been satisfied, its decision may be set aside under rule 37.
 The second condition is that it is in the interests of justice to proceed. One relevant factor is whether the party has been delayed. The Employment Appeal Tribunal has decided that the tribunal *must* consider whether to try to contact the party, most obviously by telephone, and *must* enquire of any party or representative present what news they know of the party who has not attended. In the ordinary course, this will be the approach that should actually be followed. See *Cooke v Glenrose Fish Company* [2004] ICR 1188 at paras 12 and 16.
 If the tribunal proceeds to hear the case, it must undertake a proper hearing on the evidence and submissions available, and not just reject the party's case for lack of attendance. See *London Borough of Southwark v Bartholomew* [2004] ICR 358. If the tribunal proceeds to hear the case, it must then decide whether to make a

decision or to adjourn the case (*MH v Pembrokeshire CC (HB)* [2010] UKUT 28 (AAC)). In other words, the decision to proceed with the hearing does not preclude a decision that it is inappropriate to decide the case in the party's absence.

If the tribunal decides not to proceed with the hearing, it may give direction for the future conduct of the proceedings, including a direction with a view to the party's case being struck out or the party being barred from taking further part in the proceedings under rule 8.

It may, in the particular circumstances of a case, be a breach of natural justice to proceed in a party's absence even if this rule is satisfied (*GJ v SSWP* [2012] UKUT 447 (AAC)).

CHAPTER 3
Decisions

General Note on Chapter 3

Whether or not the tribunal holds an oral hearing, its decision must be made in the context of the inquisitorial approach (see the general note to rule 2(2)(c)) and, in the case of an appeal, by way of rehearing. It must also comply with the legislation and policy on the use of Welsh.

Appeal by way of rehearing

In a broad sense, every appeal is by way of rehearing with the only differences lying in the evidence and arguments that may be considered (*CIS 16701/1996*, para 24). In a narrower sense, the caselaw has distinguished two types of appeal. The appeal strictly so called determines whether the decision under appeal was correct on the evidence before the person or body making the decision, subject perhaps to a limited right to make additional findings on the appeal. The other type of appeal is an appeal by way of rehearing (*Ponnamma v Arumogan* [1905] AC 383 at *390, per* Lord Davey). Appeals before the First-tier Tribunal are by way of rehearing (*R(SB) 1/82*, para 10). The rehearing must, subject to s20(7) of the Act, cover all issues arising on the appeal. The case has to be proved again, so the burden of proof is as in the decision under appeal (*Rugman v Drover* [1950] 2 All ER 575 at 576, *per* Lord Goddard CJ). The tribunal is not limited to the evidence, arguments and grounds that were before the Secretary of State (*R(SB) 33/83*, para 19; *CSCS 2/1994*, paras 20 and 22; *CSCS 3/1994*, para 14). However, the appeal must be considered in the circumstances obtaining at the relevant time (see s20(7)(b) of the Act and *Northern Ireland Trailers Ltd v County Borough of Preston* [1972] 1 All ER 260 at 265, *per* Lord Widgery CJ, and *Rugman* above at 576, *per* Lord Goddard CJ).

Two issues arise on the circumstances obtaining at the relevant time. The first is the scope of the issues which may be determined. This is considered in the general note to s20(7) of the Act. The second is whether the tribunal may apply changes in the law which have occurred since the date of the original decision which was subject to the review decision on appeal before the tribunal. It is sometimes said that on appeal the tribunal should apply the substantive law as it stood at the date of the original decision but the procedural law as it stands at the date the issue is decided (*R(S) 3/93*, para 20). This, however, is an oversimplification. A new law is more likely to be applied on the appeal if it is procedural (*Att-Gen v Vernazza* [1960] 3 All ER 97), but less likely if it is substantive (*Wilson v Dagnall* [1972] 2 All ER 44 at 53 and 54, *per* Megaw and Stephenson LJJ respectively). However, the correct approach is not to seek to label the change in law as "procedural" or "substantive". The issue is determined by the appropriate interpretation of the relevant legislation. Difficulty can only arise where the matter is not clearly covered in the legislation. In cases where the wording is not clear, due regard must be given to the common law presumption which is also contained in s16(1)(c) Interpretation Act 1978 that clear language is necessary before legislation is interpreted to take away or impair any existing right or obligation (*Yew Bon Tew v Kenderaan Bas Mara* [1982] 3 All ER 833). Relevant factors to be considered will include the value of any rights affected, the potential impact on those rights of the legislation in question, the degree of fairness or unfairness of adversely affecting those rights, the clarity of the legislative language and the circumstances in which the law was enacted (*L'Office Cherifien des Phosphates v Yamashita-Shinnihon Steamship Co Ltd* [1994] 1 All ER 20 at 30, *per* Lord Mustill). It is unlikely that the application of any particular procedure would be of such value that a party would be held to have a vested right in that procedure being followed despite subsequent changes in the law, but the existence and extent of a person's liability to pay or right to receive child support maintenance as at a particular date would be likely to be sufficient to justify the presumption being applied. See also the analysis of the House of Lords in *Wilson v First County Trust Ltd* [2003] 4 All ER 97.

The application of the above authorities has been confused by *CI 337/1992* where the commissioner appears to have interpreted them in such a way that the question of the scope of the application of any particular legislative provision is to be determined according to the effect of the provision on the facts of any particular case. This approach is more akin to applying a kind of estoppel against the statute according to its operation given the facts of a particular case than to the process of statutory interpretation as normally understood. Moreover it is at variance with *L'Office Cherifien des Phosphates* above at 32 where Lord Mustill said, "we are concerned here not with the merits of the particular case, but with the generality of rights which Parliament must have contemplated would suffer if the section took effect retrospectively".

Care needs to be taken when applying older social security decisions on this issue as, in the case of open-ended claims, the claim continued down to the date of the final disposal of the case, with the effect that the tribunal may take account of any changes in legislation (*R(I) 4/84*, paras 9-10, relying on the power to deal with questions first arising which tribunals do not possess, *R(I) 6/84*, paras 10-11 and *CI 309/1992*.) (This is now subject to s8(2)(a) Social Security Act 1998, which provides that a claim ceases to exist when it is decided by the Secretary of State.)

The rehearing covers matters of fact, law and opinion. The tribunal is entitled to substitute its opinion for that of the Secretary of State, even if the application of the legislation expressly depends on the Secretary of State's opinion (*R(SB) 5/81*, para 8; *MC v Secretary of State for Defence* [2009] UKUT 173 (AAC), paras 10-16).

Provisional decisions

Some tribunals issue a provisional decision that will take effect unless further evidence is provided. The Upper Tribunal approved this practice in *AB, CMEC and SA (CSM)* [2010] UKUT 385 (AAC). Technically, this takes effect as a direction on an adjournment. If the information is provided later than the time allowed, the tribunal should consider whether to amend the direction by extending the time for compliance (para 16). The judge left open the issue whether it would be permissible to add a financial member to the panel in light of the new evidence, but said:

> "21.   The situation has not arisen, but it may be preferable to prevent problems rather than deal with them once they occur. I can understand that the additional information provided might make it desirable to have the assistance of a financial member. However, it is important that all the members of the tribunal that makes a decision should have heard all the evidence. In this case, the parent with care gave oral evidence. The record of proceedings did not have to be verbatim, so the financial member might not have access to all the evidence. Moreover, the member would not have had the chance to form an impression of the way that the parent gave evidence. There may be cases in which it is possible to add a member in the course of the proceedings. An obvious example is the case has been conducted entirely on the papers. However, there is a clear and present danger in adding a member to proceedings that have involved oral proceedings."

The use of Welsh

Generally speaking, there is no duty on the tribunal to provide an interpreter: *R(I) 11/63*, para 19. However, arrangements exist for interpreters to be supplied so that persons may speak in their own language. The tribunal has a duty to ensure that effective use is made of any interpreter present – eg, that everything is translated for the party concerned: *Kunnath v The State* [1993] 4 All ER 30. The preferable alternative would be for all those present to speak the same language, as much can be lost in interpretation. It is sometimes possible for a tribunal to be assembled on which all the members speak the language in question. This is particularly the case in Wales.

The Senior President has given a practice direction to the First-tier Tribunal and the Upper Tribunal on the **USE OF THE WELSH LANGUAGE IN TRIBUNALS IN WALES:**

"GENERAL

1.   The purpose of this Practice Direction is to reflect the principle of the Welsh Language Act 1993 that in the administration of justice in Wales, the English and Welsh languages should be treated on a basis of equality.

2.   In this Practice Direction "Welsh case" means a case which is before the Tribunal in which all "individual parties" are resident in Wales or which has been classified as a Welsh case by the Tribunal. An "individual party" is a party other than a Government Department or Agency. Where not all of the "individual parties" are resident in Wales the Tribunal will decide whether the case should be classified as a Welsh case or not.

USE OF THE WELSH LANGUAGE

3.   In a Welsh case the Welsh language may be used by any party or witnesses or in any document placed before the Tribunal or (subject to the listing provisions below) at any hearing.

LISTING

4.   Unless it is not reasonably practicable to do so a party, or their representative, must inform the Tribunal 21 days before any hearing in a Welsh case that the Welsh language will be used by the party, their representative, any witness to be called by that party or in any document to be produced by the party.

5.   Where the proceedings are on appeal to the Upper Tribunal and the Welsh language was used in the Tribunal below, the Tribunal Manager must make arrangements for the continued use of the Welsh language in the proceedings before the Upper Tribunal.

6.   Where practicable, a hearing in which the Welsh language is to be used must be listed before a Welsh speaking Tribunal and, where translation facilities are needed, at a venue with simultaneous translation facilities.

INTERPRETERS

7.   Whenever an interpreter is needed to translate evidence from English into Welsh or from Welsh into English, the Tribunal Manager in whose tribunal the case is to be heard must ensure that the attendance is secured of an interpreter whose name is included in the list of approved interpreters.

WITNESSES

8.   When a witness in a case in which the Welsh language may be used is required to give evidence on oath or affirmation the Tribunal must inform the witness that they may be sworn or affirm in Welsh or English as they wish.

9.   This Practice Direction is made by the Senior President of Tribunals with the agreement of the Lord Chancellor. It is made in the exercise of powers conferred by the Tribunals, Courts and Enforcement Act 2007."

There is no ground for complaint under the child support legislation that a form is invalid or ineffective merely on the basis that it is in English only and not in Welsh; any breach of the requirements of the Welsh Language Act must be remedied under the framework provided by that Act (*CCS 11728/1996*, para 21). This may need to be reconsidered in the light of the practice direction.

For the future, the Welsh Language (Wales) Measure 2011 will be relevant.

Consent orders

32.–(1)   The Tribunal may, at the request of the parties but only if it considers it appropriate, make a consent order disposing of the proceedings and making such other appropriate provision as the parties have agreed.

(2)   Notwithstanding any other provision of these Rules, the Tribunal need not hold a hearing before making an order under paragraph (1), or provide reasons for the order.

Definitions

"dispose of proceedings": see rule 1(3).
"hearing": see rule 1(3).
"party": see rule 1(3).
"Tribunal": see rule 1(3).

Notice of decisions

33.–(1)   The Tribunal may give a decision orally at a hearing.

(2)   Subject to rule 14(2) (withholding information likely to cause harm), the Tribunal must provide to each party as soon as reasonably practicable after making [[1]a decision (other than a decision under Part 4) which finally disposes of all issues in the proceedings or of a preliminary issue dealt with following a direction under rule 5(3)(e)]–

(a)   a decision notice stating the Tribunal's decision;

(b)   where appropriate, notification of the right to apply for a written statement of reasons under rule 34(3); and

(c)   notification of any right of appeal against the decision and the time within which, and the manner in which, such right of appeal may be exercised.

(3)   *[Omitted]*

Amendment

1.   Tribunal Procedure (Amendment) Rules 2013 (SI 2013 No.477) r28 (April 8, 2013).

Definitions

"appeal": see rule 1(3).
"asylum support case": see rule 1(3).
"dispose of proceedings": see rule 1(3).
"hearing": see rule 1(3).
"party": see rule 1(3).
"Tribunal": see rule 1(3).

General Note

Tribunals usually announce their decisions on the day of the hearing. Whether or not the tribunal follows the standard practice, it must provide a decision notice, together with information about obtaining a written statement of reasons and applying for permission to appeal.

The notice must take account of any direction prohibiting disclosure of information under rule 14(2). There is no reference to the confidentiality provisions of rule 19, but these must obviously be taken into account as well. In practice, the Upper Tribunal makes its decisions anonymous to a greater extent than rule 19 requires. Its decisions do not contain any information from which the names or addresses of anyone involved might be identified.

A decision is of no effect until it has been promulgated – ie, until it has been communicated. Until that time it may be revoked or varied informally (*CSB 226/1981*, para 11 and *R(I) 14/74*, para 14(a)), although there is a risk that a difference between the oral decision and that formally promulgated may lead to the decision being set aside. The need for communication in order to make a decision effective is a constitutional principle (*R (ota Anufrijeva) v Secretary of State for the Home Department* [2003] 3 All ER 827). (*CM209/1987*, para 6 is in conflict with this principle in suggesting that the decision is made as soon as it is taken.) For the purposes of setting aside, reviewing and appealing decisions, the decision is promulgated when the decision notice is issued (*CSB 226/1981*).

A tribunal should take as much time as is necessary to make its decision, adjourning if need be (in *Re G (A Child) (Care Proceedings: Placement for Adoption), The Times,* August 1 2005). However, a lengthy delay in making a decision that involves the assessment of a witness's credibility may justify the setting aside of the tribunal's decision, unless (a) the tribunal's conclusion on this issue was recorded at the time of the hearing or was obvious, or (b) the appeal would be decided against the party concerned on other grounds (*Sambasivam v Secretary of State for the Home Department* [2000] Imm AR 85).

The rule does not specify the content for a decision notice. Obviously, it must contain the tribunal's decision. It may also contain a short statement of why the tribunal made the decision. In some cases, those reasons may amount to a written statement of reasons. There is no requirement that the notice be signed, but this is good practice to confirm that it is not a draft.

The decision given by a tribunal need not be an outcome decision. It is sufficient if its decision deals with the issues raised by the appeal (*R(IS) 2/08*) and is capable of being implemented (*CH 2553/2005,* para 36). If an appeal is allowed, the appropriate form of decision is to give directions to the Secretary of State, setting out the findings and principles by reference to which the absent parent's liability for child support maintenance is to be determined (*CCS 290/1999,* para 1.3).

However, the decision must be in a form that can be implemented. A decision which cannot be implemented is wrong in law (*CIS 5206/1995,* para 12). It is acceptable to indicate to the appellant as part of the decision whether the appeal has succeeded or failed or succeeded in part. However, decisions worded solely in terms of success or failure are to be avoided. Clearly a decision which simply reads "Appeal allowed" or "Appeal allowed in part" is wholly inadequate since it gives no indication of how it has been allowed. There may seem to be less objection to a decision in the form "Appeal dismissed", but this is also capable of giving rise to problems and is better avoided. In *CS 99/1993,* para 4, the commissioner said that giving a decision in the form of dismissing the appeal or confirming the decision under appeal is better than substituting an incomplete decision for the more detailed decision of the Secretary of State. While it must be the case that an incomplete decision is not acceptable, the approach suggested by the commissioner is dangerous in that it is based on the assumption that the tribunal has before it the complete and accurate text of the decision under appeal. Tribunals are, of course, entitled to the verbatim text of the decision under appeal (*CIS 137/1992,* para 5), but in practice the alleged text of the decision is often clearly incomplete and in other cases neither the papers nor the information available to the presenting officer are sufficient to allow the tribunal to be sure of the exact terms of the decision under appeal. The safer approach, and one which avoids an adjournment, is for the tribunal to give a complete decision itself and not to seek an easy alternative.

It is appropriate and valid to direct the Secretary of State to investigate and act as required on the results of the enquiries, at least if these conditions are satisfied: (i) the matter to be investigated is clear; (ii) the result of the investigation will be uncontroversial; and (iii) once the results of the investigation are known, all that is required is the mechanical application of the legislation, without any element of judgment or discretion (*CCS 284/1999,* paras 24-25).

It is also appropriate and valid, in view of the time constraints and other pressures on a tribunal, for the tribunal not to undertake complex calculations unless this is unavoidable. This is especially so in view of the complexity and formulae involved in child support law. It is proper to leave the working out of the tribunal's decision to the Secretary of State, provided that there is power for any party to restore the case to the tribunal in the event of a dispute as to the correct calculation (*R(SB) 16/83,* para 21). "Liberty to restore" may be used, although in court terminology "liberty to apply" would be more appropriate. It should be expressly reserved, as it will not be implied into a decision which is on its face final and complete (*Penrice v Williams* [1883] 23 Ch D 353 at 356-357, *per* Chitty J). Prima facie it does not allow the order to be varied (*Cristel v Cristel* [1951] 2 KB 725; [1951] 2 All ER 574; 95 SJ 561, CA at 576-577, *per* Somervell LJ).There are suggestions in *Cristel* that a change of circumstances could be taken into account so as to vary an otherwise final order under a liberty to apply, but this is an unnecessary qualification in the child support context in view of the express power to supersede contained in s17 of the Act.

In *CIS 749/1991* para 6, the commissioner said that "An express reference back to 'the Commissioner' would normally carry the meaning that the appeal could be referred to any person currently holding the office...". In other words, the reference back is to the tribunal and not to the particular members who made the decision. (The decision in this case was not followed in *CS 159/1991,* but it does not mention this point.)

In the context of social security law, the commissioners recognised that tribunals have power to refer a matter to be agreed between the parties and, in the failure of such agreement, for the matter to be restored for determination by a tribunal, with the decision becoming final when the issue is decided either by agreement or by a tribunal (*CIS 442/1992,* para 5). It is arguable that this approach is permissible in the child support context.

The legislation contains no power for a tribunal to award costs, interest or general damages for anxiety and distress (rule 21 and *Jones v Department of Employment* [1988] 1 All ER 725 at 739, *per* Slade LJ).

In *CSDLA 5/1995* para 11, the commissioner described tribunal decisions as public documents. With respect this is questionable, since First-tier Tribunal decisions are not provided to persons other than the parties, although they are no longer labelled as confidential, and may not, therefore, have been "brought into existence for the purpose of its being retained indefinitely as a document of record, available for inspection by the public" (*White v Taylor* [1967] 3 All ER 349 at 351, *per* Buckley J). This is not a purely abstract question. Section 12(1) (a) of the Administration of Justice Act 1960 provides that publication of information relating to proceedings of any tribunal (see subs (3)) sitting in private may amount to a contempt of court where the proceedings relate wholly or mainly to the maintenance of a minor. However, subs (2) provides that this does not apply to the publication of the text or a summary of the whole or part of the order except where the tribunal, having power to do so, expressly prohibits the publication. It matters, therefore, whether or not a tribunal's decision is confidential.

Majority decisions

A majority decision is possible, but every effort should be made to reach a unanimous decision, including delaying a decision for the minority to consider the written reasons of the majority (*Anglia Home Improvements Ltd v Kelly, The Times,* June 30 2004).

Rule 33(2)

Failure to comply with the requirements of this paragraph does not invalidate the tribunal's decision if the party concerned is aware of the information anyway (*CH 2553/2005*, para 17).

Reasons for decisions

34.–(1)   *[Omitted]*

(2)   In all other cases the Tribunal may give reasons for a decision which disposes of proceedings (except a decision under Part 4)–

(a)   orally at a hearing; or

(b)   in a written statement of reasons to each party.

(3)   Unless the Tribunal has already provided a written statement of reasons under paragraph (2)(b), a party may make a written application to the Tribunal for such statement following a decision [[1]which finally disposes of–

(a)   all issues in the proceedings; or

(b)   a preliminary issue dealt with following a direction under rule 5(3)(e).]

(4)   An application under paragraph (3) must be received within 1 month of the date on which the Tribunal sent or otherwise provided to the party a decision notice relating to the decision [[1]...].

(5)   If a party makes an application in accordance with paragraphs (3) and (4) the Tribunal must, subject to rule 14(2) (withholding information likely to cause harm), send a written statement of reasons to each party within 1 month of the date on which it received the application or as soon as reasonably practicable after the end of that period.

Amendment

1.   Tribunal Procedure (Amendment) Rules 2013 (SI 2013 No.477) r29 (April 8, 2013).

Definitions

"asylum support case": see rule 1(3).

"dispose of proceedings": see rule 1(3).

"hearing": see rule 1(3).

"Tribunal": see rule 1(3).

General Note

Rule 34(2)

This paragraph applies to decisions which dispose of proceedings. The tribunal may, and on application must, provide reasons either orally at the hearing or in a written statement of reasons. There is no requirement that the statement be signed, but this is good practice to confirm that it is not a draft.

The statement must take account of any direction prohibiting disclosure of information under rule 14(2). There is no reference to the confidentiality provisions of rule 19, but these must obviously be taken into account as well.

The reasons must be those of the tribunal as a whole, not just of the presiding judge (*CDLA 1807/2003*).

The written statement of reasons may be written by the presiding judge or, perhaps, by another member of the tribunal, but may not be written by a judge who did not sit on the panel (*CCS 1664/2001*, paras 3-8; *CCS 1664/2001*). A document may be produced by someone who is not authorised in law to do so, provided that it is done under the direction of the tribunal (*CCS 14/1994*, para 13). (The former practice of dictating the decision to the clerk (*CSB 226/1981*, para 7) is now obsolete.)

If the reasons have been adequately or partly recorded in the decision notice given under rule 33, it is permissible to adopt that notice as all or part of the written statement under this rule. However, it will often not be possible to state a tribunal's findings of fact and reasons for decisions adequately and succinctly to allow this to be done (*CDLA 96/1999*, para 13).

Failure to give adequate reasons will be an error of law (*R(SB) 26/83*, para 12).

It is seldom that such an extreme case can arise as that which came before Commissioner Heald in *CS30/ 1989*, where at para 6 the commissioner concluded as follows:

"However the absence of any note of evidence, findings, decision, or reasons therefore in respect of the period covered by the first reference must constitute an error of law. It is not strictly necessary to conclude that the tribunal did not give any attention at all to this period; the failure to make any record was a clear breach of regulation 25(2) of the Adjudication Regulations ... Since there is no record, there is nothing to set aside consequent on the finding of error of law."

It is not every failure to give reasons that amounts to a denial of justice and an error of law. The relevant consideration is whether the reasons given are sufficient to indicate that the tribunal considered the point at issue between the parties and the evidence on which they came to their conclusions (*R v Immigration Appeal Tribunal ex p Khan* [1983] 2 All ER 420 at 423, *per* Lord Lane CJ).

The courts have laid down some general principles with regard to reasons. The commissioners gave more detailed guidance as to what is required in particular contexts. There is a degree of conflict between the standards indicated in the court decisions on the nature and adequacy of reasons and the demands of the commissioners who set standards far higher than could often realistically be achieved in the limited time available. This is made clear by the approach of the Court of Appeal in *English v Emery Reimbold and Strick Ltd* [2002] 3 All ER 385 (applied to tribunals by *Burns v Royal Mail Group (formerly Consignia plc), The Times,* June 24 2004). The Court held that if reasons for decision were not stated, they must be apparent from the reasons that have been given in the context of the evidence and submissions (para 26). That is in line with the approach of the commissioners. However, the effort to which the Court was prepared to go in the application of that principle in order to find an explanation from the context was much greater than was undertaken in most cases by commissioners. Their approach was evident in child support appeals. In *CSCS 2/1994*, the commissioner expressed the view that a statement in a tribunal's reasons for decision that certain expenses could not be taken into account because they were not allowable under the terms of the legislation was adequate "although barely so" (para 23). With respect, it is difficult to see what more could have been said or why more should have been said in a case where no arguable issue on the point arose.

It is essential to make clear what findings of fact have been made and to distinguish these from other matters. The issuing of formless reasons was criticised and the use of a structured approach was recommended by the Court of Appeal in *R v Solihull MBC Housing Benefit Review Board ex p Simpson* [1995] 1 FLR 140 in the context of the Housing Benefit legislation.

At the most basic level the test of adequacy of reasons has been stated to be one of fairness (*CM 113/1991* and the cases cited therein). The reasons should fulfil three functions by providing: transparency to the decision-making process; assurance that all issues have been dealt with; and a basis on which an informed decision can be made whether or not to seek permission to appeal (*R (O'Brien) v Independent Assessor, The Times,* May 5 2003). The reasons should indicate why the facts were found and the decision was reached, although they need not be long and precise (*Crake and Butterworth v Supplementary Benefit Commission* [1982] 1 All ER 498 at 506 and 508, *per* Woolf J). The reasons must be proper and adequate, being intelligible and dealing with all substantial points raised (*R(SB) 18/83*, para 10 and *Re Poyser and Mills' Arbitration* [1963] 1 All ER 612 at 616, *per* Megaw J), although it is not necessary to deal with every material consideration, however insignificant, or with every argument, however peripheral (*Bolton MBC v Secretary of State for the Environment, The Times,* May 25 1995). Whether a point is marginal or insignificant may depend on the importance attached to it by the party who raised it (*CCS 16817/1996*, para 11). The reasons must be clear, but it is not necessary to produce something akin to a court judgment or to set out the relevant statutory provisions (*R(SB) 5/81*, paras 7 and 10). It is not essential that every process of reasoning should be set out (*Mountview Court Properties Ltd v Devlin* [1970] 21 P&CR 689 at 692, *per* Lord Parker CJ). These principles have been regularly indorsed, including by the House of Lords in *Great Portland Estates plc v Westminster City Council* [1984] 3 All ER 744 at 752, *per* Lord Scarman. The record should be sufficient to show (i) that the tribunal identified the questions to be determined, (ii) that the tribunal considered all the points in dispute, (iii) the evidence relied on by the tribunal and (iv) that the tribunal acted lawfully (*Kitchen v Secretary of State for Social Services,* unreported July 30 1993, *per* Neill LJ). These matters may be indicated either directly or by inference (*Khan* above at 423, *per* Lord Lane CJ).

The adequacy of a tribunal's reasons must not be considered in isolation. They must be judged in the context of the submissions made to the tribunal, including the extent of agreement shown by those submissions and any explanation contained in the Secretary of State's submission (*CCS 10/1994,* para 10). The level at which an argument was developed before the tribunal will also affect the detail to be expected from its reasons (*CCS 11729/1996*, para 5). They must also be read in conjunction with the notes of proceedings and any literature referred to in the reasons (see the approach of Woolf J in *Crake and Butterworth v Supplementary Benefit Commission* [1982] 1 All ER 498 at 508). The terms of the decision notice may be used to clarify the tribunal's reasons for decision (*CIB 1540/1998*, para 23).

Where a principle is well established and well known, such as the burden and standard of proof, it may be unnecessary for the tribunal to refer to it (*Re P (Witness Summons)* [1997] 2 FLR 447 at 455, *per* Wilson J). A tribunal is assumed to know the law it applies, unless the record shows that it misunderstood or misapplied it (*R(SB) 5/81*, para 7). However, in difficult or finely balanced cases, it may be necessary for a tribunal to show

how it assessed each relevant factor, such as those in s28F(2) below and reg 21 of the Variations Regulations, separately (*Re G(Children)* [2006] 2 FLR 629, para 40).

In the Court of Appeal decision in *B v B (Residence Order: Reasons for Decision)* [1997] 2 FLR 602 at 606, Holman J said of the standard by which reasons are to be judged:

"a judgment is not to approached like a summing-up. It is not an assault course. Judges work under enormous time and other pressures, and it would be quite wrong for this court to interfere simply because an ex tempore judgment given at the end of a long day is not as polished as it might otherwise be."

These comments apply as much to reasons for decisions of tribunals as to judgments given in a court.

Some things are clearly inadequate. The recording of contentions and statements without findings of facts is not acceptable (*R(SB) 42/84*, para 6) and a mere restatement of the decision is not a reason for that decision (*R(SB) 23/82*, para 9 and *R v Mental Health Review Tribunal ex p Clatworthy* [1985] 3 All ER 699 at 703, *per* Mann J). Merely citing applicable authorities by name or number is not an adequate explanation of a decision (*R(S) 2/83*, para 4). Failure to record findings of fact and the reasons is obviously unacceptable as a general principle (*R(G) 1/75*, para 2), as is failing to distinguish between evidence given and reasons (*R(F) 6/64*, para 6). More specific guidance is as follows.

The findings of fact must cover all matters material to the decision, that is, all findings necessary to support the decision and reasoning of the tribunal (*R(SB) 31/83*, para 6). The findings must be sufficiently clear to allow a decision maker to implement the tribunal's decision (*CCS 15/1994*, para 10). Failure to record any findings will mean that the decision is liable to be set aside on appeal (*R(SB) 6/81*, para 14). Omissions will produce the same result. Findings of fact are not necessary in respect of matters which are not in dispute (*R(CS) 3/96*, para 13). This will include issues covered by a concession made by a competent representative, unless the concession is clearly bad (*CDLA 267/1994*, para 8). A tribunal need not make findings where no evidence or totally inadequate evidence is adduced to them (*CDLA 415/1994*, para 6). Care should be taken not only with the content of the findings of fact, but also with their form. The presiding judge should record the primary facts as found and the inferences drawn by the tribunal, not the evidence or arguments presented to the tribunal. Commissioners could be very demanding in this respect. For example, in *R(SB) 3/88* para 8(1), the findings of fact recorded the view of a witness on a relevant matter and stated that the tribunal accepted that view. However, a Tribunal of Commissioners held that there should have been "a proper finding of fact in relation to that matter." This decision is a valuable warning of the dangers of adopting the statement of facts set out in the submission. There is no magic in any particular way of recording findings of fact. Whether a particular approach is or is not sufficient to satisfy the duty to record material findings of fact depends on the circumstances of the case. See *CI 71/1997*, para 17. The comments by commissioners about the incorporation of facts (or reasons) by reference to other documents, either in their terms or by their context, were always related to the circumstances of the case and the extent to which facts must be found or reasons given. See, for example, the points made by the commissioner in *CSB 249/1985*, para 5. In *R(IS) 14/93* para 11, the commissioner set out two conditions that had to be satisfied if incorporation by reference was to be acceptable. First, the submission must record findings of fact and not arguments or assertions. Second, the findings of fact must be sufficient for the decision; any facts omitted from the submission must be added by the tribunal. The written statement of reasons must be read as a whole and it is inappropriate to place a pedantic emphasis on the precise form of words chosen by the tribunal provided that it is clear that it accepted those statements and found them as fact (*CDLA 5030/1997*, paras 10 and 12). The source from which the facts or reasons are incorporated must be accessible to the parties to the proceedings (*CI 71/1997*, para 18 and *CI 4599/1997*, para 32). However, it is not adequate for a tribunal to record statements of conflicting evidence without identifying which is accepted in preference to the other (*CDLA 16313/1996*, para 5). Whether or not the facts were in dispute is a relevant factor to be taken into account in deciding whether the manner in which the tribunal's findings of fact were recorded was acceptable (*CI 71/1997*, para 18), although incorporation of facts by reference will seldom be sufficient if the matters of fact in dispute were of considerable contention (*CIS 548/1992*, para 7).

A tribunal should refrain from making findings of fact that are critical of a party to the proceedings on a matter that is not relevant to the case as put to the tribunal, and certainly should not do so without giving the party a chance to take issue with the findings (*Vogon International Ltd v Serious Fraud Office, The Times*, February 26 2004).

This rule does not mention findings of fact, but the facts material to a decision are an essential part of the reasons for the decision and must be included (*R(I) 4/02*, para 7, qualified by the Tribunal of Commissioners in Northern Ireland in *C28/00-01 (IB)(T)*). If a tribunal decides that, even accepting the evidence presented on a particular question, the party's case is not made out, it is the assertions made that are the material facts. It is not necessary for the tribunal to reach conclusion on the assertions. See *CDLA 5787/1997*, para 23. Provided that the evidence can be sufficiently identified by reference to, for example, the record of proceedings, it is not necessary for it to be set out again in the tribunal's statement (*Williams v J Walter Thompson Group Ltd, The Times*, April 5 2005). However, care must also be taken in incorporating details from the record of proceedings as findings of fact (*R(IS) 9/94*, para 11).

The reasons for decision must explain why the tribunal reached all its decisions on matters in dispute before it. This will include explanations for its conclusions on matters of fact, for example, why it accepted or rejected particular pieces of evidence (*R(SB) 8/84*, para 25(3)), or why it disbelieved a particular witness (*Re F (Contact:*

Lack of Reasons) [2007] 1 FLR 65, para 17) or how it made use of its own knowledge on a particular matter, as well as how the law was applied to reach the decision. The extent to which it is necessary to explain how a tribunal assessed credibility depends on the circumstances of the case (*CIS 4022/2007*, para 52). The statement should be sufficient to explain to any party why the decision was made. Every argument of any substance put forward by any party should be dealt with in the reasons (*Re B (Procedure: Family Proceedings Court)* [1993] Fam Law 209). This is especially important in relation to matters which are emotionally charged *(ibid)* as tribunal proceedings may be. However, where a tribunal has dealt with the case in a way that renders it unnecessary to deal with an argument, it need not deal with that argument in its reasons, even if that argument was the central one advanced by one of the parties (*The Post Office v Lewis, The Times,* April 25 1997).

If a tribunal exercises a discretion, it must explain how it did so. It must set out the factors that it took into account and explain why it attached the significance to them that it did. Failure to undertake this exercise and to explain it vitiates the judicial conclusion (*Cunliffe v Fielden* [2006] 2 All ER 115, *per* Wall LJ at para 23).

In the case of a discretion, the more unusual the manner of its exercise the greater the need for a clear statement of the reasons for doing so (*Jones v Governing Body of Burdett Courts School* [1999] ICR 38).

The reasons should be those that led the tribunal to its conclusion rather than a later rationalisation. In practice, these can be difficult to distinguish. In some cases, they can be. An example was *CIB 2492/2004,* in which the chairman relied in part on the claimant's reaction when she received the tribunal's decision. The commissioner held that the decision was wrong in law.

Some judges follow a convenient practice by adopting the reasons in the Secretary of State's submission as those of the tribunal. There is no objection to this approach in principle, provided that the passages adopted are sufficiently clearly and unambiguously expressed (*Givandan and Co Ltd v Minister of Housing and Local Government* [1966] 3 All ER 696 at 699, *per* Megaw J). However, the approach has three dangers. First, if that submission contains any error the tribunal will have adopted that error as its own. Second, if there are any matters not dealt with in that submission, for example, why certain evidence or arguments were rejected, they must be added (*CSB 249/1985*, para 5). Third, the tribunal must ensure that it does not appear that it has abdicated its responsibility to think matters through for itself (*Newcastle upon Tyne Hospitals NHS Foundation Trust v Armstrong* [2010] ICR 674 at para 46).

Although the statement must contain the reasons for the decision, it need not go further and give the reasons for those reasons (*R v SSHD ex p Swati* [1986] 1 All ER 717 at 728, *per* Parker LJ). So, it is sufficient to say "we rejected this evidence because it was inherently improbable" without going on to spell out why it was inherently improbable.

It has been said that in cases involving value judgments (eg, whether persons are living together as husband and wife) clear findings on the relevant issues are all that is required by way of reasons (*CIS 87/1993*, para 9), but it is wise to include some indication of the test applied by the tribunal.

The form of reasons should be user-friendly. In *Williams v J Walter Thompson Group Ltd, The Times,* April 5 2005, extensive numbering in roman numerals caused problems for the Court of Appeal. In contrast in *Jasim v Secretary of State for the Home Department, The Times,* May 17 2006, Sedley LJ emphasised (para 4) the importance of setting out reasons in a way that could be analysed and understood, using manageable paragraphs and subparagraphs with cross-headings where appropriate and Pill LJ added (para 47) that this could also assist the writer in composing the reasons.

For a discussion of whether reasons can be supplemented on the invitation of the Upper Tribunal, see the general note to s12 of the 2007 Act on p781. Whatever the powers of the Upper Tribunal, there is no power for a District Tribunal Judge to require the tribunal to supplement the reasons (*CA 4297/2004).*

Standard form reasons

There are a number of devices that have been used to reduce the time taken in recording a full statement of the tribunal's decision. Each device is valuable in a suitable case, but only if it is used appropriately. There are three popular devices.

(i)   *Specifying the decision notice as the written statement of reasons* is appropriate if the tribunal's decision can adequately be recorded in a few short sentences, but only provided that the correct sentences are chosen.

(ii)   *Adopting the Secretary of State's submission* is appropriate if the submission is accurate and deals with all the issues arising for decision. By taking this approach, the tribunal makes the mistakes or deficiencies in the submission its own.

(iii)   *Using standard forms of words or standard decisions* is appropriate provided that they are used only as a model that is adapted to the facts and circumstances of the case, and the tribunal does not allow the standard terms to influence its analysis of the case.

There are three fundamental dangers in using these devices. First, they may deprive the non-resident parent and the person with care of a short statement of the reasons for decision, free of the technicality and detail of the Secretary of State's submission to the tribunal. Second, the reasons may be condensed to the extent that they are merely statements of conclusions rather than reasons. Third, the Upper Tribunal may conclude that the tribunal did not approach the case correctly, but merely rubber stamped the Secretary of State's decision (*CSB 249/1985*, para 5), began with an assumption that that decision was correct and looked for reasons to show the contrary (*CP 1977/1999*, para 8(2)) or failed to identify or consider the issues arising for decision (*CI 5199/1998*, para 6). Also, the European Court of Human Rights has decided that there was a breach of Art 5(3) of the Convention, in part because the reasons given by the domestic court were in stereotyped form (*Mansur v Turkey* [1995] Series A No.319-B).

Rule 34(3)

It has been suggested that an application for permission to appeal should be treated as a request for a statement, if one has not already been given (*R(IS) 11/99*, para 33), especially where the application raises an issue that is not fully explained in the decision notice (*CDLA 5793/1997*, para 26).

PART 4
Correcting, setting aside, reviewing and appealing Tribunal decisions

General Note on Part 4
Reconsideration

Interlocutory decisions, whether or not made after giving notice to all the parties, are open to reconsideration and, if appropriate, they may be reversed or varied: *CIS 93/1992*, para 15. This reflects the principle that a decision made without notice being given to all the parties may be discharged: *Boyle v Sacker* [1888] 39 Ch D 249. There is, however, no duty to reconsider: *CIS 93/1992*, para 16. There is no authority on whether an interlocutory decision may only be reconsidered on request, but in principle this should not be necessary.

A final decision by a tribunal may be reconsidered at any time until it is promulgated (*CSB 226/1981*, para 11; *R(I) 14/74*, para 14(a)). This may be done on application of the one of the parties or on the tribunal's own initiative (*Re Harrison's Settlement* [1955] 1 All ER 185). Reconsideration is only permissible to further the interests of justice in exceptional circumstances or for strong reasons; it must not be allowed to subvert the appeal process (*Compagnie Noga D'Importation et D'Exportation SA v Abacha* [2001] 3 All ER 513 at paras 42-43 and 47). On principle, reconsideration should only be possible if undertaken by the same tribunal: *R v Cripps ex p Muldoon* [1984] 2 All ER 705 at 710, *per* Sir John Donaldson MR. Natural justice may require that the parties be given notice that the decision is to be reconsidered and an opportunity to make submissions or produce further evidence, if appropriate (*ibid*).

After a final decision has been promulgated, it may be corrected or set aside and may be the subject of review or appeal. These possibilities apart, reconsideration is not possible: *CSI 559/1998*, para 11; *R v Immigration Appeal Tribunal ex p Wanyoike, The Times*, March 10 2000. There are, however, two suggestions in the authorities that reconsideration of a final decision may be possible after promulgation. First, in *R v Cripps ex p Muldoon* at 710, Sir John Donaldson MR said that a final decision that is irregular may be open to reconsideration after promulgation, but gave no examples of irregularities. Second, there was a possibility that a tribunal might have had power to reconsider a decision given on a setting aside application (*R(I) 7/94*, paras 16 and 35; *CIS 30/ 93*, para 11), but only at the request of one of the parties and not on the tribunal's own initiative (*R(I) 7/94*, para 35). This was only a suggestion made in the course of argument. No ruling was made on the point, except to say that if the power existed it could only be exercised on an application by one of the parties.

If there is power to reconsider a final decision after promulgation, it is difficult to understand why it should only be exercised on application by one of the parties. If, for example, the tribunal rejected an application to set aside a decision, but then discovered that relevant information had not been put to it by the clerk, there seems no point in requiring one of the parties to make an application for the refusal to be reconsidered and every reason for the tribunal to be able to act on its own initiative. As the tribunal that gave the decision which is to be reconsidered no longer has jurisdiction once the decision has been promulgated, any power to reconsider may be exercised by any tribunal and need not be exercised by the same tribunal (*R v Cripps ex p Muldoon* at 710, *per* Sir John Donaldson MR), although courtesy would normally suggest that, if possible, the original tribunal should exercise the power. As a reconsideration does not involve an appeal, there is no violation of Art 6(1) of the European Convention on Human Rights if it is undertaken by the same tribunal: *Khreino v Khreino* [2000] 1 FLR 578.

There is no authority on what factors allow a decision to be reconsidered. Usually, a decision will be reconsidered because further evidence has been obtained or a new argument had been advanced. It is difficult to imagine a case in which a decision would, or should, be reconsidered without the presence of some new factor. This is particularly the case for final decisions. If reconsideration is permissible without a new factor being present, the circumstances in which it is appropriate must be exceptional and there is a strong argument that it should only be undertaken by the person or tribunal who made the decision. In the case of a final decision, the argument of courtesy is especially strong.

The courts regard it as undesirable for an application for reconsideration to be made unless there are strong reasons to support it: *Re Blenheim Leisure (Restaurants) Ltd (No.3), The Times*, November 9 1999. In view of the limited information on which interlocutory decisions often have to be made, this approach is not appropriate to tribunals. The power to reconsider is discretionary, so any applications that appear unmeritorious may be refused without consideration.

The courts have accepted the possibility of a reconsideration without legislative authority in an administrative context: *R (ota C) v Lewisham London Borough Council* [2003] 3 All ER 1277, para 59.

Interpretation
35. In this Part–
"appeal" means the exercise of a right of appeal–
(a)-(b) *[Omitted]*
(c) on a point of law under section 11 of the 2007 Act; and
"review" means the review of a decision by the Tribunal under section 9 of the 2007 Act.

Definitions
"the 2007 Act": see rule 1(3).
"Tribunal": see rule 1(3).

Clerical mistakes and accidental slips or omissions
36. The Tribunal may at any time correct any clerical mistake or other accidental slip or omission in a decision, direction or any document produced by it, by–
(a) sending notification of the amended decision or direction, or a copy of the amended document, to all parties; and
(b) making any necessary amendment to any information published in relation to the decision, direction or document.

Definitions
"document": see rule 1(3).
"party": see rule 1(3).
"Tribunal": see rule 1(3).

General Note
A tribunal may correct accidental slips and omissions in decisions, directions and any other documents produced by the tribunal, including the record of proceedings. The power is conferred on the tribunal; clerks have no power to alter decisions (*Memminger-IRO GmbH v Trip-Lite Ltd (No.2), The Times,* July 9 1992).

The power does not arise in respect of a decision until it has been promulgated, which means until it is notified to the parties (*CSB 226/1981*). Until then, the tribunal has control over its decision and may correct it without reference to this rule (*Paulin v Paulin* [2009] 2 FLR 354).

No application or request is necessary before a correction can be made, although in practice the issue will often be raised by a party to the proceedings.

The power only allows a tribunal to correct inadvertent clerical or arithmetical errors so as to bring the document into line with what the tribunal intended. If, for example, the word "not" had been omitted or included in error, it can be inserted or removed as appropriate. However, there is no power, once a tribunal has made its decision, to alter the decision intended, as opposed to its record or expression (*Preston Banking Co v William Allsup and Sons Ltd* [1891-1894] All ER Rep 688 at 689, *per* Lord Halsbury, *Wordingham v Royal Exchange Trust Co Ltd* [1992] 3 All ER 204 and *CM209/1987,* para 6).

In *AS v SSWP(ESA)* [2011] UKUT 159 (AAC) para 16, the judge explained the scope of this rule and why, despite the fact that the changes in that case were beyond the scope of the rule, he would nonethess take them into account in deciding whether to set aside the tribunal's decision:

"Rule 36 is by its contents a species of slip rule and should be interpreted in accordance with the nature of that type of provision. As such, it deals with matters that were in the judge's mind when writing but for some reason did not find their way onto the page. Typical examples are the typing error that produces the wrong date or a momentary lapse of concentration that results in the word 'not' being omitted. The rule does not cover matters that the judge had planned to mention but forgot to include. Obviously, it is difficult for the Upper Tribunal to know what was in the judge's mind, but the extent of the changes are an indication. It is difficult to classify the omission of a total of nine lines of explanation as in the same category of mistake as a typing error or a momentary lapse of concentration. For that reason, I decide that the changes made by the presiding judge were not authorised by rule 36."

The tribunal has power to correct an accidental error, but not a duty to do so. It should not be exercised if anything has occurred after the decision was notified to the parties which renders it inexpedient or inequitable to correct it (*Moore v Buchanan* [1967] 3 All ER 273). Thus, a correction should not be made if the decision as framed has been relied on to a party's irreversible detriment. The mere fact of delay, however, will not be a sufficient reason not to exercise the power (*Tak Ming Co Ltd v Yee Sang Metal Supplies Co* [1973] 1 All ER 569 at 575).

A decision made without jurisdiction cannot be corrected under either this paragraph (*Munks v Munks* [1985] FLR 576).

By analogy with the position in employment tribunals, it is possible that if a tribunal were to announce its decision orally under rule 33(1) and then issue a contradictory written decision, the Upper Tribunal might consider that there had been a breach of natural justice (*Gutzmore v J Wardley (Holdings) Ltd* [1993] ICR 581).

For a discussion of control over a decision before promulgation, see the decision of the Court of Appeal in *Paulin v Paulin.*

Setting aside a decision which disposes of proceedings

37.–(1)   The Tribunal may set aside a decision which disposes of proceedings, or part of such a decision, and re-make the decision, or the relevant part of it, if–

(a)   the Tribunal considers that it is in the interests of justice to do so; and

(b)   one or more of the conditions in paragraph (2) are satisfied.

(2)   The conditions are–

(a)   a document relating to the proceedings was not sent to, or was not received at an appropriate time by, a party or a party's representative;

(b)   a document relating to the proceedings was not sent to the Tribunal at an appropriate time;

(c)   a party, or a party's representative, was not present at a hearing related to the proceedings; or

(d)   there has been some other procedural irregularity in the proceedings.

(3)   A party applying for a decision, or part of a decision, to be set aside under paragraph (1) must make a written application to the Tribunal so that it is received no later than 1 month after the date on which the Tribunal sent notice of the decision to the party.

Definitions

"dispose of proceedings": see rule 1(3).

"document": see rule 1(3).

"hearing": see rule 1(3).

"party": see rule 1(3).

"Tribunal": see rule 1(3).

General Note

The decision of a tribunal may be set aside. This power provides a swifter and, therefore, more satisfactory remedy than an appeal to the Upper Tribunal on a procedural matter.

The tribunal need not be constituted by the same members who made the decision. Sometimes this can be a disadvantage as the members will know what happened at the hearing. Sometimes it would be a breach of the principles of natural justice for the same members to be involved.

The power to set aside applies only to decisions that dispose of proceedings. A decision is not effective until it has been promulgated, that is, until it has been notified to the parties to the proceedings in accordance with rule 33 (*CSB 226/1981*). Until then, the tribunal itself has control over the decision and may revoke it without reference to this power.

There is no express power to hold an oral hearing in order to decide whether to set aside a decision. However, the tribunal has power to regulate its procedure and may decide to hold a hearing under rule 5(3)(f).

All the documents that were before the tribunal should be available when it is considering whether to set aside a decision (*R(S) 1/87,* para 13).

If the tribunal exercises this power on grounds that fall outside this rule, its decision will be liable to be set aside on judicial review. Until this is done, the setting aside is nonetheless binding on the Secretary of State, the tribunal itself and the Upper Tribunal. However, another tribunal has power to determine whether the tribunal had jurisdiction to act. The circumstances in which this will apply are very limited. They do *not* include basing a decision on invalid or irrelevant considerations, failing to give an opportunity for representations to be made or a breach, however serious, of the principles of natural justice. See the general note to s20 of the Act, *R(I) 7/94*, paras 25-29, 32 and 34 and *CIS 373/1994.*

Rule 37(1)

The tribunal has power to set aside a decision provided that two requirements are satisfied: (a) the tribunal must consider that it is in the interest of justice to do so; and (b) one of the conditions in para (2) must be satisfied. If both of these requirements are not satisfied, the decision cannot be set aside.

In deciding what the interests of justice require, the correctness of the decision is not a relevant consideration, nor is the possible impact that the person or document, if present, may have had on the decision (*R(U) 3/89*, paras 13 and 21).

Rule 37(2)

Subparagraph (a) largely raises a question of fact, although there is a judgment involved in determining what was an appropriate time for the document to be received. In practice, two questions arise. Was the document properly served on the party or the party's representative? If so, was there sufficient time to allow the party's case to be adequately prepared?

Subparagraph (b) also largely raises a question of fact, although again there is a judgment involved in determining what was an appropriate time for the document to be received. In practice, two questions arise. Did the tribunal receive the document before it made its decision? If so, was there sufficient time for the document to be taken properly into account?

Subparagraph (c) raises a question of pure fact. The reason for the absence is irrelevant here, although it may be relevant when determining whether it is in the interests of justice to set aside the decision. Parties and their representatives do not have a licence to be absent from the hearing and then apply for the decision to be set aside if it is unfavourable (*CU 270/1986*, para 12).

Subparagraph (d) covers all other procedural irregularities. The matter complained of may be major or minor (*R(SB) 13/89*, para 17). But it must relate to procedure rather than substance.

Rule 37(3)
This paragraph provides for the time within which an application may be made. It does not stipulate that the power may only be exercised on application. That allows the tribunal to act of its own initiative.

No more than one application can be made, even if a different basis is identified (*CS 137/1988*, para 14).

There is no provision permitting or prohibiting the withdrawal of an application to set aside a decision.

Application for permission to appeal

38.–(1) This rule does not apply to asylum support cases or criminal injuries compensation cases.

(2) A person seeking permission to appeal must make a written application to the Tribunal for permission to appeal.

(3) An application under paragraph (2) must be sent or delivered to the Tribunal so that it is received no later than 1 month after the latest of the dates that the Tribunal sends to the person making the application–

[1(za) the relevant decision notice;]

(a) written reasons for the decision [1, if the decision disposes of–
    (i) all issues in the proceedings; or
    (ii) subject to paragraph (3A), a preliminary issue dealt with following a direction under rule 5(3)(e)];

(b) notification of amended reasons for, or correction of, the decision following a review; or

(c) notification that an application for the decision to be set aside has been unsuccessful.

[1(3A) The Tribunal may direct that the 1 month within which a party may send or deliver an application for permission to appeal against a decision that disposes of a preliminary issue shall run from the date of the decision that disposes of all issues in the proceedings.]

(4) The date in paragraph (3)(c) applies only if the application for the decision to be set aside was made within the time stipulated in rule 37 (setting aside a decision which disposes of proceedings) or any extension of that time granted by the Tribunal.

(5) If the person seeking permission to appeal sends or delivers the application to the Tribunal later than the time required by paragraph (3) or by any extension of time under rule 5(3)(a) (power to extend time)–

(a) the application must include a request for an extension of time and the reason why the application was not provided in time; and

(b) unless the Tribunal extends time for the application under rule 5(3)(a) (power to extend time) the Tribunal must not admit the application.

(6) An application under paragraph (2) must–

(a) identify the decision of the Tribunal to which it relates;

(b) identify the alleged error or errors of law in the decision; and

(c) state the result the party making the application is seeking.

(7) If a person makes an application under paragraph (2) [1in respect of a decision that disposes of proceedings or of a preliminary issue dealt with following a direction under rule 5(3)(e)] when the Tribunal has not given a written statement of reasons for its decision–

(a) if no application for a written statement of reasons has been made to the Tribunal, the application for permission must be treated as such an application;

(b)   unless the Tribunal decides to give permission and directs that this sub-paragraph does not apply, the application is not to be treated as an application for permission to appeal; and

(c)   if an application for a written statement of reasons has been, or is, refused because of a delay in making the application, the Tribunal must only admit the application for permission if the Tribunal considers that it is in the interests of justice to do so.

Amendment

1.   Tribunal Procedure (Amendment) Rules 2013 (SI 2013 No.477) r30 (April 8, 2013).

Definitions

"appeal": see rule 35.

"asylum support case": see rule 1(3).

"criminal injuries compensation case": see rule 1(3).

"party": see rule 1(3).

"Tribunal": see rule 1(3).

Tribunal's consideration of application for permission to appeal

39.–(1)   On receiving an application for permission to appeal the Tribunal must first consider, taking into account the overriding objective in rule 2, whether to review the decision in accordance with rule 40 (review of a decision).

(2)   If the Tribunal decides not to review the decision, or reviews the decision and decides to take no action in relation to the decision, or part of it, the Tribunal must consider whether to give permission to appeal in relation to the decision or that part of it.

(3)   The Tribunal must send a record of its decision to the parties as soon as practicable.

(4)   If the Tribunal refuses permission to appeal it must send with the record of its decision–

(a)   a statement of its reasons for such refusal; and

(b)   notification of the right to make an application to the Upper Tribunal for permission to appeal and the time within which, and the method by which, such application must be made.

(5)   The Tribunal may give permission to appeal on limited grounds, but must comply with paragraph (4) in relation to any grounds on which it has refused permission.

Definitions

"appeal": see rule 35.

"party": see rule 1(3).

"review": see rule 35.

"Tribunal": see rule 1(3).

General Note

A tribunal should approach an application for permission to appeal in two stages. The first question is to consider whether the application raises a point of law as discussed above. If it does, the second question is to ask whether it is an arguable one. There must be material in the case indicating that a sensible argument could be made that an error has occurred (*R(SB) 1/81*, para 4). If the case is an arguable one, permission to appeal should be given. The tribunal is not required to decide whether or not the appeal will succeed. That is a matter for the Upper Tribunal. Moreover, the granting of permission does not necessarily amount to an admission that the decision is wrong. This is emphasised by the wording of s11 of the 2007 Act, which refers to a point, rather than to an error, of law. In order to obtain permission to appeal, the appellant must show that the case raises a point of law, and in order to succeed in the appeal, the appellant must show that there has been an error of law.

If a point of law arises but there appears no realistic prospect of it being resolved in the appellant's favour, it may still be appropriate to grant permission – eg, if the issue is a controversial one or one that otherwise merits a decision by the Upper Tribunal (*Smith v Cosworth Casting Processes Ltd* [1997] 4 All ER 840). However, it may be unfair to raise false hopes or to impose on an individual the burden of resolving an issue for the benefit of others.

It is always inappropriate to attempt to justify the tribunal's decision when refusing permission, and it is quite wrong to try to supplement the reasoning of the tribunal (*CSDLA 336/2000*, para 8). However, there are at least two exceptional cases in which comment is appropriate and useful. The first case is where the tribunal gives permission for a reason that is different from that advanced in the application. This will alert the Upper Tribunal to the basis upon which permission has been given. The second case is where there is an allegation of impropriety in the conduct of the tribunal. A record of the judge's recollection of events given relatively close to the events in question is useful, especially if the matters were not recorded in the notes of proceedings. See *CIS 4652/1997*, para 13, Applications for permission to appeal which raise allegations of misconduct should be lodged as soon as possible after the hearing (*R(I) 11/63*, para 20).

Once given, permission cannot be rescinded (*CIS 2002/2000*, paras 25-26).

Review of a decision

40.–(1)   This rule does not apply to asylum support cases or criminal injuries compensation cases.

(2)   The Tribunal may only undertake a review of a decision–

(a)   pursuant to rule 39(1) (review on an application for permission to appeal); and

(b)   if it is satisfied that there was an error of law in the decision.

(3)   The Tribunal must notify the parties in writing of the outcome of any review, and of any right of appeal in relation to the outcome.

(4)   If the Tribunal takes any action in relation to a decision following a review without first giving every party an opportunity to make representations, the notice under paragraph (3) must state that any party that did not have an opportunity to make representations may apply for such action to be set aside and for the decision to be reviewed again.

Definitions

"appeal": see rule 35.
"asylum support case": see rule 1(3).
"party": see rule 1(3).
"review": see rule 35.
"Tribunal": see rule 1(3).

General Note

The exercise of the power to review was considered on judicial review by a three-judge panel of the Upper Tribunal in *R(RB) v First-tier Tribunal (Review)* [2010] UKUT 160 (AAC); [2010] AACR 41, paras 22-29. On the panel's analysis, review provides an alternative remedy to an appeal to allow corrective action without delay. It must not, though, usurp the Upper Tribunal's function of deciding contentious issues of law. It should only be used to set aside decisions in clear cases. This approach must be applied flexibly. For example, some cases may benefit from a further fact-finding hearing before being considered by the Upper Tribunal. There is no need for reasons in a review decision to be of the length or in the style appropriate for a self-contained decision of the Upper Tribunal (para 32).

If the tribunal does not identify an error of law, it cannot review its decision. It follows that it cannot exercise the powers given by s9(4) Tribunals, Courts and Enforcement Act 2007, because they only arise on a review. In *VH v Suffolk CC* [2010] UKUT 203 (AAC), the judge decided that an amendment to the tribunal's reasons (permissible under s9(4)(b)) was not valid as the tribunal had not identified an error of law in its decision.

Power to treat an application as a different type of application

41.   The Tribunal may treat an application for a decision to be corrected, set aside or reviewed, or for permission to appeal against a decision, as an application for any other one of those things.

Definitions

"appeal": see rule 35.
"review": see rule 35.
"Tribunal": see rule 1(3).

General Note

The tribunal has power to treat an application for one form of post-decision relief as an application for another form. Usually, this will merely be an application of the basic approach that requires tribunals to have regard to the substance rather than the form of an application (see the general note to rule 2(2)(b) on p811). However, this rule goes further and allows a tribunal to override the substance as well as the form of an application if that is consistent with the overriding objective.

This argument does not hold if the power given by this rule is inherent in the rules (specifically, rules 2 and 5-7), as the three-judge panel said in *R(RB) v First-tier Tribunal (Review)* [2010] UKUT 160 (AAC); [2010] AACR

41, para 10. On the other hand, if the panel is correct that the power is inherent in the other rules, it will also apply to the Upper Tribunal, which has no equivalent to this rule.

Although the tribunal has this power, it should not exercise it contrary to the express wishes of a representative (*PS v Camden and Islington NHS Foundation Trust* [2011] AACR 42).

SCHEDULE 1

TIME LIMITS FOR PROVIDING NOTICES OF APPEAL [⁴...]

Type of proceedings	Time for providing notice of appeal
[²Cases other than those listed below	The latest of–

(a) one month after the date on which notice of the decision being challenged was sent to the appellant;

(b) if a written statement of reasons for the decision was requested within that month, 14 days after the later of–
(i) the end of that month; or
(ii) the date on which the written statement of reasons was provided; or

[⁴(c) if the appellant made an application for revision of the decision under–
(i) regulation 14 of the Child Support Maintenance Calculation Regulations 2012;
(ii) regulation 3(1) or (3) of the Social Security and Child Support (Decision and Appeals) Regulations 1999;
(iii) regulation 4 of the Housing Benefit and Council Tax Benefit (Decisions and Appeals) Regulations 2001;
(iv) regulation 17(1)(a) of the Child Support (Maintenance Assessment Procedure) Regulations 1992 (where still applicable to the particular case); or
(v) regulation 3A(1) of the Social Security and Child Support (Decisions and Appeals) Regulations 1999 (where still applicable to the particular case),

and that application was unsuccessful, 1 month after the date on which notice that the decision would not be revised was sent to the appellant.]]

Amendments

1. Substituted by r4 of SI 2009 No 1975 as from 1.9.09.
2. Substituted by r5(4) of SI 2010 No. 2653 as from 29.11.10.
3. Child Support (Meaning of Child and New Calculation Rules) (Consequential and Miscellaneous Amendment) Regulations 2012 (SI 2012 No.2785) reg 9 (in force in relation to a particular case on the day on which paragraph 2 of Schedule 4 to the Child Maintenance and Other Payments Act 2008 (see p243) comes into force in relation to that type of case – which is December 10, 2012, only in relation to the types of cases falling within art 3 of SI 2012 No.3042 (see p767). This amendment was revoked by the Child Support (Miscellaneous Amendments) Regulations 2013 (SI 2013 No.1517) reg 10 (September 30, 2013).
4. Tribunal Procedure (Amendment) Rules 2013 (SI 2013 No.477) r31 (April 8, 2013).

Definition

"appellant": see rule 1(3).

SCHEDULE 2

[Omitted]

The Tribunal Procedure (Upper Tribunal) Rules 2008
2008 No.2698 (L.15)

General Note on the Rules

These rules are generally in the same form as the Tribunal Procedure (First-tier Tribunal) (Social Entitlement Chamber) Rules 2008. Commentary is only provided for these rules if different.

PART 1
Introduction

Citation, commencement, application and interpretation

1.–(1)   These Rules may be cited as the Tribunal Procedure (Upper Tribunal) Rules 2008 and come into force on 3rd November 2008.

(2)   These Rules apply to proceedings before the Upper Tribunal [² except proceedings in the Lands Chamber].

(3)   In these Rules–

"the 2007 Act" means the Tribunals, Courts and Enforcement Act 2007;

[¹ "appellant" means–

(a)   a person who makes an appeal, or applies for permission to appeal, to the Upper Tribunal;

(b)   in proceedings transferred or referred to the Upper Tribunal from the First-tier Tribunal, a person who started the proceedings in the First-tier Tribunal; or

(c)   a person substituted as an appellant under rule 9(1) (substitution and addition of parties);]

[³ "applicant" means–

(a)   a person who applies for permission to bring, or does bring, judicial review proceedings before the Upper Tribunal and, in judicial review proceedings transferred to the Upper Tribunal from a court, includes a person who was a claimant or petitioner in the proceedings immediately before they were transferred; or

(b)   a person who refers a financial services case to the Upper Tribunal;]

[² "appropriate national authority" means, in relation to an appeal, the Secretary of State, the Scottish Ministers [⁵, the Department of the Environment in Northern Ireland] or the Welsh Ministers, as the case may be;

[...]

[⁶ "authorised person" means–

(a)   an examiner appointed by the Secretary of State under section 66A of the Road Traffic Act 1988;
(b) an examiner appointed by the Department of the Environment in Northern Ireland under Article 74 of the Road Traffic (Northern Ireland) Order 1995; or
(c) any person authorised in writing by the Department of the Environment in Northern Ireland for the purposes of the Goods Vehicles (Licensing of Operators) Act (Northern Ireland) 2010;

and includes a person acting under the direction of such an examiner or other authorised person, who has detained the vehicle to which an appeal relates;]]

"dispose of proceedings" includes, unless indicated otherwise, disposing of a part of the proceedings;

"document" means anything in which information is recorded in any form, and an obligation under these Rules or any practice direction or direction to provide or allow access to a document or a copy of a document for any purpose means, unless the Upper Tribunal directs otherwise, an obligation to provide or allow access to such document or copy in a legible form or in a form which can be readily made into a legible form;

[...]

"hearing" means an oral hearing and includes a hearing conducted in whole or in part by video link, telephone or other means of instantaneous two-way electronic communication;

[...]
[...]

"interested party" means–

(a)   a person who is directly affected by the outcome sought in judicial review proceedings, and has been named as an interested party under rule 28 or 29 (judicial review), or has been substituted or added as an interested party under rule 9 [⁴ (addition, substitution and removal of parties)]; [⁴]

(b)   in judicial review proceedings transferred to the Upper Tribunal under section 25A(2) or (3) of the Judicature (Northern Ireland) Act 1978 or section 31A(2) or (3) of the Supreme Court Act 1981, a person who was an interested party in the proceedings immediately before they were transferred to the Upper Tribunal; [⁴ and

(c)   *[Omitted]*]

"judicial review proceedings" means proceedings within the jurisdiction of the Upper Tribunal pursuant to section 15 or 21 of the 2007 Act, whether such proceedings are started in the Upper Tribunal or transferred to the Upper Tribunal;

[¹]
[...]

"party" means a person who is an appellant, an applicant, a respondent or an interested party in proceedings before the Upper Tribunal, a person who has referred a question [⁴ or matter] to the Upper Tribunal or, if the proceedings have been concluded, a person who was an appellant, an applicant, a respondent or an interested party when the [⁷Upper] Tribunal finally disposed of all issues in the proceedings;

"permission" includes leave in cases arising under the law of Northern Ireland;

"practice direction" means a direction given under section 23 of the 2007 Act;

[...]

"respondent" means–

(a)   in an appeal, or application for permission to appeal, against a decision of another tribunal, any person other than the appellant who–

    (i)   was a party before that other tribunal;
    [¹ (ii)]
    (iii)   otherwise has a right of appeal against the decision of the other tribunal
            and has given notice to the Upper Tribunal that they wish to be a party to
            the appeal;
(b)   in an appeal [⁶ other than a road transport case] , the person who made the
        decision;
(c)   in judicial review proceedings–
    (i)   in proceedings started in the Upper Tribunal, the person named by the
            applicant as the respondent;
    (ii)   in proceedings transferred to the Upper Tribunal under section 25A(2) or
            (3) of the Judicature (Northern Ireland) Act 1978 or section 31A(2) or (3)
            of the Supreme Court Act 1981, a person who was a defendant in the
            proceedings immediately before they were transferred;
    (iii)   in proceedings transferred to the Upper Tribunal under section 20(1) of
            the 2007 Act, a person to whom intimation of the petition was made
            before the proceedings were transferred, or to whom the Upper Tribunal
            has required intimation to be made.
[¹ (ca) in proceedings transferred or referred to the Upper Tribunal from the First-tier
        Tribunal, a person who was a respondent in the proceedings in the First-tier
        Tribunal;]
(d)-(da) *[Omitted]*
(e)   a person substituted or added as a respondent under rule 9 (substitution and
        addition of parties);
[⁵ "road transport case" means an appeal against a decision of a traffic commissioner or
        the Department of the Environment in Northern Ireland;]
[² "tribunal" does not include a traffic commissioner;]
"working day" means any day except a Saturday or Sunday, Christmas Day, Good Friday
        or a bank holiday under section 1 of the Banking and Financial Dealings Act
        1971.

Amendments
1.   Amended by r5 of SI 2009 No 274 as from 1.4.09.
2.   Amended by r8 of SI 2009 No 1975 as from 1.9.09.
3.   Substituted by r4(a) of SI 2010 No 747 as from 6.4.10.
4.   Amended by r4(c)-(f) of SI 2010 No 747 as from 6.4.10.
5.   Inserted by r5(a) and (d) of SI 2012 No 1363 as from 1.7.12.
6.   Substituted by r5(b) and (c) of SI 2012 No 1363 as from 1.7.12.
7.   Inserted by r4(c) of SI 2013 No. 2067 as from 1.11.13.

General Note
Rule 1(3)
"respondent" This definition does not include any power for to identify as a respondent someone who was not a
party to the proceedings before the First-tier Tribunal.

Overriding objective and parties' obligation to co-operate with the Upper Tribunal
2.–(1)   The overriding objective of these Rules is to enable the Upper Tribunal to
deal with cases fairly and justly.
(2)   Dealing with a case fairly and justly includes–
(a)   dealing with the case in ways which are proportionate to the importance of the
        case, the complexity of the issues, the anticipated costs and the resources of the
        parties;
(b)   avoiding unnecessary formality and seeking flexibility in the proceedings;
(c)   ensuring, so far as practicable, that the parties are able to participate fully in the
        proceedings;
(d)   using any special expertise of the Upper Tribunal effectively; and
(e)   avoiding delay, so far as compatible with proper consideration of the issues.
(3)   The Upper Tribunal must seek to give effect to the overriding objective when it–

(a) exercises any power under these Rules; or
(b) interprets any rule or practice direction.
(4) Parties must–
(a) help the Upper Tribunal to further the overriding objective; and
(b) co-operate with the Upper Tribunal generally.

Definitions
"party": see rule 1(3).
"practice direction": see rule 1(3).

Alternative dispute resolution and arbitration
3.–(1) The Upper Tribunal should seek, where appropriate–
(a) to bring to the attention of the parties the availability of any appropriate alternative procedure for the resolution of the dispute; and
(b) if the parties wish and provided that it is compatible with the overriding objective, to facilitate the use of the procedure.
(2) Part 1 of the Arbitration Act 1996 does not apply to proceedings before the Upper Tribunal.

Definition
"party": see rule 1(3).

PART 2
General powers and provisions

Delegation to staff
4.–(1) Staff appointed under section 40(1) of the 2007 Act (tribunal staff and services) may, with the approval of the Senior President of Tribunals, carry out functions of a judicial nature permitted or required to be done by the Upper Tribunal.
(2) The approval referred to at paragraph (1) may apply generally to the carrying out of specified functions by members of staff of a specified description in specified circumstances.
(3) Within 14 days after the date on which the Upper Tribunal sends notice of a decision made by a member of staff under paragraph (1) to a party, that party may apply in writing to the Upper Tribunal for that decision to be considered afresh by a judge.

Definition
"the 2007 Act": see rule 1(3).

Case management powers
5.–(1) Subject to the provisions of the 2007 Act and any other enactment, the Upper Tribunal may regulate its own procedure.
(2) The Upper Tribunal may give a direction in relation to the conduct or disposal of proceedings at any time, including a direction amending, suspending or setting aside an earlier direction.
(3) In particular, and without restricting the general powers in paragraphs (1) and (2), the Upper Tribunal may–
(a) extend or shorten the time for complying with any rule, practice direction or direction;
(b) consolidate or hear together two or more sets of proceedings or parts of proceedings raising common issues, or treat a case as a lead case;
(c) permit or require a party to amend a document;
(d) permit or require a party or another person to provide documents, information, evidence or submissions to the Upper Tribunal or a party;
(e) deal with an issue in the proceedings as a preliminary issue;
(f) hold a hearing to consider any matter, including a case management issue;
(g) decide the form of any hearing;
(h) adjourn or postpone a hearing;

(i)   require a party to produce a bundle for a hearing;

(j)   stay (or, in Scotland, sist) proceedings;

(k)   transfer proceedings to another court or tribunal if that other court or tribunal has jurisdiction in relation to the proceedings and–

     (i)   because of a change of circumstances since the proceedings were started, the Upper Tribunal no longer has jurisdiction in relation to the proceedings; or

     (ii)   the Upper Tribunal considers that the other court or tribunal is a more appropriate forum for the determination of the case;

(l)   suspend the effect of its own decision pending an appeal or review of that decision;

(m)   in an appeal, or an application for permission to appeal, against the decision of another tribunal, suspend the effect of that decision pending the determination of the application for permission to appeal, and any appeal;

[¹ (n) require any person, body or other tribunal whose decision is the subject of proceedings before the Upper Tribunal to provide reasons for the decision, or other information or documents in relation to the decision or any proceedings before that person, body or tribunal.]

[²(4)   *[Omitted]*]

[³(5)   *[Omitted]*]

Amendments

1.   Substituted by r9 of SI 2009 No 1975 as from 1.9.09.
2.   Inserted by r4 of SI 2010 No 44 as from 15.2.10.
3.   Inserted by r5 of SI 2010 No 747 as from 6.4.10.

Definitions

"the 2007 Act": see rule 1(3).
"document": see rule 1(3).
"hearing": see rule 1(3).
"party": see rule 1(3).
"permission": see rule 1(3).
"practice direction": see rule 1(3).

General Note

Rule 5(l) and (m)

The power to suspend may not be used to relieve a party of having to apply the decision to other cases unless and until it has been confirmed on appeal (*Secretary of State v AD and MM (No 2)* [2009] UKUT 69 (AAC)). It is incompatible with the nature of a decision that a provision was made without statutory authority to suspend its effect (*Ahmed v HM Treasury* [2010] 4 All ER 829).

Rule 5(3)(n)

A Tribunal of Commissioners in Northern Ireland held that a similar equivalent power could only be used if there was a *prima facie* case, on the information and evidence already available, that the tribunal's decision was erroneous in law (*C10/01-02(IB)(T)*), paras 35-37). This reasoning may not apply to the wider wording of this power.

Procedure for applying for and giving directions

6.–(1)   The Upper Tribunal may give a direction on the application of one or more of the parties or on its own initiative.

(2)   An application for a direction may be made–

(a)   by sending or delivering a written application to the Upper Tribunal; or

(b)   orally during the course of a hearing.

(3)   An application for a direction must include the reason for making that application.

(4)   Unless the Upper Tribunal considers that there is good reason not to do so, the Upper Tribunal must send written notice of any direction to every party and to any other person affected by the direction.

(5)   If a party or any other person sent notice of the direction under paragraph (4) wishes to challenge a direction which the Upper Tribunal has given, they may do so by applying for another direction which amends, suspends or sets aside the first direction.

Definition
  "party": see rule 1(3).

Failure to comply with rules etc.

7.–(1) An irregularity resulting from a failure to comply with any requirement in these Rules, a practice direction or a direction, does not of itself render void the proceedings or any step taken in the proceedings.

(2) If a party has failed to comply with a requirement in these Rules, a practice direction or a direction, the Upper Tribunal may take such action as it considers just, which may include–

(a) waiving the requirement;

(b) requiring the failure to be remedied;

(c) exercising its power under rule 8 (striking out a party's case); or

(d) except in [¹ a mental health case, an asylum case or an immigration case], restricting a party's participation in the proceedings.

(3) Paragraph (4) applies where the First-tier Tribunal has referred to the Upper Tribunal a failure by a person to comply with a requirement imposed by the First-tier Tribunal–

(a) to attend at any place for the purpose of giving evidence;

(b) otherwise to make themselves available to give evidence;

(c) to swear an oath in connection with the giving of evidence;

(d) to give evidence as a witness;

(e) to produce a document; or

(f) to facilitate the inspection of a document or any other thing (including any premises).

(4) The Upper Tribunal may exercise its power under section 25 of the 2007 Act (supplementary powers of the Upper Tribunal) in relation to such non-compliance as if the requirement had been imposed by the Upper Tribunal.

Amendment
  1.   Amended by r5 of SI 2010 No 44 as from 15.2.10.

Definitions
  "the 2007 Act": see rule 1(3).
  "document": see rule 1(3).
  "party": see rule 1(3).
  "practice direction": see rule 1(3).

Striking out a party's case

8.– [²(1A)   *[Omitted]*]

[³(1)   The proceedings, or the appropriate part of them, will automatically be struck out–

(a) if the appellant or applicant has failed to comply with a direction that stated that failure by the appellant or applicant to comply with the direction would lead to the striking out of the proceedings or part of them; or

(b) [[⁴*Omitted*]]

(2) The Upper Tribunal must strike out the whole or a part of the proceedings if the Upper Tribunal–

(a) does not have jurisdiction in relation to the proceedings or that part of them; and

(b) does not exercise its power under rule 5(3)(k)(i) (transfer to another court or tribunal) in relation to the proceedings or that part of them.

(3) The Upper Tribunal may strike out the whole or a part of the proceedings if–

(a) the appellant or applicant has failed to comply with a direction which stated that failure by the appellant or applicant to comply with the direction could lead to the striking out of the proceedings or part of them;

(b) the appellant or applicant has failed to co-operate with the Upper Tribunal to such an extent that the Upper Tribunal cannot deal with the proceedings fairly and justly; or

(c)   in proceedings which are not an appeal from the decision of another tribunal or judicial review proceedings, the Upper Tribunal considers there is no reasonable prospect of the appellant's or the applicant's case, or part of it, succeeding.

(4)   The Upper Tribunal may not strike out the whole or a part of the proceedings under paragraph (2) or (3)(b) or (c) without first giving the appellant or applicant an opportunity to make representations in relation to the proposed striking out.

(5)   If the proceedings have been struck out under paragraph (1) or (3)(a), the appellant or applicant may apply for the proceedings, or part of them, to be reinstated.

(6)   An application under paragraph (5) must be made in writing and received by the Upper Tribunal within 1 month after the date on which the Upper Tribunal sent notification of the striking out to the appellant or applicant.

(7)   This rule applies to a respondent [¹ or an interested party] as it applies to an appellant or applicant except that–

(a)   a reference to the striking out of the proceedings is to be read as a reference to the barring of the respondent [¹ or an interested party] from taking further part in the proceedings; and

(b)   a reference to an application for the reinstatement of proceedings which have been struck out is to be read as a reference to an application for the lifting of the bar on the respondent [¹ or an interested party] [¹] taking further part in the proceedings.

(8)   If a respondent [¹ or an interested party] has been barred from taking further part in proceedings under this rule and that bar has not been lifted, the Upper Tribunal need not consider any response or other submission made by that respondent [¹ or interested party, and may summarily determine any or all issues against that respondent or interested party].

Amendments

1.   Amended by r6 of SI 2009 No 274 as from 1.4.09.
2.   Inserted by r6 of SI 2010 No 44 as from 15.2.10.
3.   Substituted by r5 of SI 2011 No 2343 as from 17.10.11.
4.   Substituted by r5 of SI 2013 No.2067 as from 1.11.13.

Definitions

"appellant": see rule 1(3).
"applicant": see rule 1(3).
"interested party": see rule 1(3).
"respondent": see rule 1(3).

Substitution and addition of parties

[¹ **9.**–(1)   The Upper Tribunal may give a direction adding, substituting or removing a party as an appellant, a respondent or an interested party.

(2)   If the Upper Tribunal gives a direction under paragraph (1) it may give such consequential directions as it considers appropriate.

(3)   A person who is not a party may apply to the Upper Tribunal to be added or substituted as a party.

(4)   If a person who is entitled to be a party to proceedings by virtue of another enactment applies to be added as a party, and any conditions applicable to that entitlement have been satisfied, the Upper Tribunal must give a direction adding that person as a respondent or, if appropriate, as an appellant.]

[²(5) *[Omitted]*]

Amendments

1.   Substituted by r10 of SI 2009 No 1975 as from 1.9.09.
2.   Inserted by r7 of SI 2010 No 44 as from 15.2.10.

Definitions

"appellant": see rule 1(3).
"applicant": see rule 1(3).
"interested party": see rule 1(3).

"party": see rule 1(3).
"respondent": see rule 1(3).

[¹ **Orders for costs**
 10.–(1)   The Upper Tribunal may not make an order in respect of costs (or, in Scotland, expenses) in proceedings [² transferred or referred by, or on appeal from,] another tribunal except–
  [³ (aa) *[Omitted]*]
  (a)   in proceedings [² transferred by, or on appeal from,] the Tax Chamber of the First-tier Tribunal; or
  (b)   to the extent and in the circumstances that the other tribunal had the power to make an order in respect of costs (or, in Scotland, expenses).
  [³ (1A) *[Omitted]*]
  (2)   The Upper Tribunal may not make an order in respect of costs or expenses under section 4 of the Forfeiture Act 1982.
  (3)   In other proceedings, the Upper Tribunal may not make an order in respect of costs or expenses except–
  (a)   in judicial review proceedings;
  [² (b)]
  (c)   under section 29(4) of the 2007 Act (wasted costs) [⁵and costs incurred in applying for such costs]; [⁴...]
  (d)   if the Upper Tribunal considers that a party or its representative has acted unreasonably in bringing, defending or conducting the proceedings; [⁴or
  (e)   *[Omitted]*]
  (4)   The Upper Tribunal may make an order for costs (or, in Scotland, expenses) on an application or on its own initiative.
  (5)   A person making an application for an order for costs or expenses must–
  (a)   send or deliver a written application to the Upper Tribunal and to the person against whom it is proposed that the order be made; and
  (b)   send or deliver with the application a schedule of the costs or expenses claimed sufficient to allow summary assessment of such costs or expenses by the Upper Tribunal.
  (6)   An application for an order for costs or expenses may be made at any time during the proceedings but may not be made later than 1 month after the date on which the Upper Tribunal sends–
  (a)   a decision notice recording the decision which finally disposes of all issues in the proceedings; or
  [⁶(b)   notice under rule 17(5) that a withdrawal which ends the proceedings has taken effect.]
  (7)   The Upper Tribunal may not make an order for costs or expenses against a person (the "paying person") without first–
  (a)   giving that person an opportunity to make representations; and
  (b)   if the paying person is an individual and the order is to be made under paragraph (3)(a), (b) or (d), considering that person's financial means.
  (8)   The amount of costs or expenses to be paid under an order under this rule may be ascertained by–
  (a)   summary assessment by the Upper Tribunal;
  (b)   agreement of a specified sum by the paying person and the person entitled to receive the costs or expenses ("the receiving person"); or
  (c)   assessment of the whole or a specified part of the costs or expenses[⁵, including the costs or expenses of the assessment,] incurred by the receiving person, if not agreed.
  (9)   Following an order for assessment under paragraph (8)(c), the paying person or the receiving person may apply–
  (a)   in England and Wales, to the High Court or the Costs Office of the Supreme Court (as specified in the order) for a detailed assessment of the costs on the standard basis or, if specified in the order, on the indemnity basis; and the Civil

Procedure Rules 1998(6) shall apply, with necessary modifications, to that application and assessment as if the proceedings in the tribunal had been proceedings in a court to which the Civil Procedure Rules 1998 apply;

(b) in Scotland, to the Auditor of the Court of Session for the taxation of the expenses according to the fees payable in that court; or

(c) in Northern Ireland, to the Taxing Office of the High Court of Northern Ireland for taxation on the standard basis or, if specified in the order, on the indemnity basis.]

[⁵(10) Upon making an order for the assessment of costs, the [⁷Upper] Tribunal may order an amount to be paid on account before the costs or expenses are assessed.]

Amendments

1. Substituted by r7 of SI 2009 No 274 as from 1.4.09.
2. Amended by r11 of SI 2009 No 1975 as from 1.9.09.
3. Amended by r7 of SI 2010 No 43 as from 18.1.10.
4. Amended by r6 of SI 2010 No 747 as from 6.4.10.
5. Inserted by r50, 52 and 53 of SI 2013 No.477 as from 1.4.13.
6. Substituted by r51 of SI 2013 No.477 as from 1.4.13.
7. Inserted by r6 of SI 2013 No.2067 as from 1.11.13.

Definitions

"the 2007 Act": see rule 1(3).
"judicial review proceedings": see rule 1(3).

Representatives

11.–(1) [⁵Subject to paragraph (5A),] A party may appoint a representative (whether a legal representative or not) to represent that party in the proceedings [³save that a party in an asylum or immigration case may not be represented by any person prohibited from representing by section 84 of the Immigration and Asylum Act 1999].

(2) If a party appoints a representative, that party (or the representative if the representative is a legal representative) must send or deliver to the Upper Tribunal [¹] written notice of the representative's name and address.

[¹ (2A) If the Upper Tribunal receives notice that a party has appointed a representative under paragraph (2), it must send a copy of that notice to each other party.]

(3) Anything permitted or required to be done by a party under these Rules, a practice direction or a direction may be done by the representative of that party, except signing a witness statement.

(4) A person who receives due notice of the appointment of a representative–

(a) must provide to the representative any document which is required to be provided to the represented party, and need not provide that document to the represented party; and

(b) may assume that the representative is and remains authorised as such until they receive written notification that this is not so from the representative or the represented party.

(5) [⁵Subject to paragraph (5B),] At a hearing a party may be accompanied by another person whose name and address has not been notified under paragraph (2) but who, subject to paragraph (8) and with the permission of the Upper Tribunal, may act as a representative or otherwise assist in presenting the party's case at the hearing.

[⁵(5A) *[Omitted]*

(5B) *[Omitted]*]]

(6) Paragraphs (2) to (4) do not apply to a person who accompanies a party under paragraph (5).

(7)-(8) *[Omitted]*

[¹ (9) In this rule "legal representative" means [² a person who, for the purposes of the Legal Services Act 2007, is an authorised person in relation to an activity which constitutes the exercise of a right of audience or the conduct of litigation within the meaning of that Act,][³ a qualified person as defined in section 84(2) of the Immigration and Asylum Act 1999,] an advocate or solicitor in Scotland or a barrister or solicitor in Northern Ireland.]

[⁴(10)   *[Omitted]*]

Amendments

1.   Amended by r8 of SI 2009 No 274 as from 1.4.09.
2.   Amended by r8 of SI 2010 No 43 as from 18.1.10.
3.   Amended by r8 of SI 2010 No 44 as from 15.2.10.
4.   Inserted by r8(c) of SI 2010 No 44 as from 15.2.10.
5.   Inserted by r5 of SI 2011 No 2343 as from 17.10.11.

Definitions

"hearing": see rule 1(3).
"party": see rule 1(3).
"practice direction": see rule 1(3).

Calculating time

12.–(1)   An act required by these Rules, a practice direction or a direction to be done on or by a particular day must be done by 5pm on that day.

(2)   If the time specified by these Rules, a practice direction or a direction for doing any act ends on a day other than a working day, the act is done in time if it is done on the next working day.

(3)-(5)   *[Omitted]*

Definitions

"practice direction": see rule 1(3).
"working day": see rule 1(3).

Sending and delivery of documents

13.–(1)   Any document to be provided to the Upper Tribunal under these Rules, a practice direction or a direction must be–

(a)   sent by pre-paid post or [¹ by document exchange, or delivered by hand,] to the address specified for the proceedings;

(b)   sent by fax to the number specified for the proceedings; or

(c)   sent or delivered by such other method as the Upper Tribunal may permit or direct.

(2)   Subject to paragraph (3), if a party provides a fax number, email address or other details for the electronic transmission of documents to them, that party must accept delivery of documents by that method.

(3)   If a party informs the Upper Tribunal and all other parties that a particular form of communication, other than pre-paid post or delivery by hand, should not be used to provide documents to that party, that form of communication must not be so used.

(4)   If the Upper Tribunal or a party sends a document to a party or the Upper Tribunal by email or any other electronic means of communication, the recipient may request that the sender provide a hard copy of the document to the recipient. The recipient must make such a request as soon as reasonably practicable after receiving the document electronically.

(5)   The Upper Tribunal and each party may assume that the address provided by a party or its representative is and remains the address to which documents should be sent or delivered until receiving written notification to the contrary.

[² (6)   Subject to paragraph (7), if a document submitted to the Upper Tribunal is not written in English, it must be accompanied by an English translation.

(7)   In proceedings that are in Wales or have a connection with Wales, a document or translation may be submitted to the [³Upper] Tribunal in Welsh.]

Amendments

1.   Amended by r10 of SI 2009 No 274 as from 1.4.09.
2.   Inserted by r10 of SI 2010 No 44 as from 15.2.10.
3.   Inserted by r8 of SI 2013 No 2067 as from 1.11.13.

Definitions
"document": see rule 1(3).
"party": see rule 1(3).
"practice direction": see rule 1(3).

Use of documents and information

14.–(1)   The Upper Tribunal may make an order prohibiting the disclosure or publication of–

(a)   specified documents or information relating to the proceedings; or

(b)   any matter likely to lead members of the public to identify any person whom the Upper Tribunal considers should not be identified.

(2)   The Upper Tribunal may give a direction prohibiting the disclosure of a document or information to a person if–

(a)   the Upper Tribunal is satisfied that such disclosure would be likely to cause that person or some other person serious harm; and

(b)   the Upper Tribunal is satisfied, having regard to the interests of justice, that it is proportionate to give such a direction.

(3)   If a party ("the first party") considers that the Upper Tribunal should give a direction under paragraph (2) prohibiting the disclosure of a document or information to another party ("the second party"), the first party must–

(a)   exclude the relevant document or information from any documents that will be provided to the second party; and

(b)   provide to the Upper Tribunal the excluded document or information, and the reason for its exclusion, so that the Upper Tribunal may decide whether the document or information should be disclosed to the second party or should be the subject of a direction under paragraph (2).

[[1] (4)]

(5)   If the Upper Tribunal gives a direction under paragraph (2) which prevents disclosure to a party who has appointed a representative, the Upper Tribunal may give a direction that the documents or information be disclosed to that representative if the Upper Tribunal is satisfied that–

(a)   disclosure to the representative would be in the interests of the party; and

(b)   the representative will act in accordance with paragraph (6).

(6)   Documents or information disclosed to a representative in accordance with a direction under paragraph (5) must not be disclosed either directly or indirectly to any other person without the Upper Tribunal's consent.

(7)   Unless the Upper Tribunal gives a direction to the contrary, information about mental health cases and the names of any persons concerned in such cases must not be made public.

[[1] (8)   The Upper Tribunal may, on its own initiative or on the application of a party, give a direction that certain documents or information must or may be disclosed to the Upper Tribunal on the basis that the Upper Tribunal will not disclose such documents or information to other persons, or specified other persons.

(9)   A party making an application for a direction under paragraph (8) may withhold the relevant documents or information from other parties until the Upper Tribunal has granted or refused the application.

(10)   In a case involving matters relating to national security, the Upper Tribunal must ensure that information is not disclosed contrary to the interests of national security.

(11)   The Upper Tribunal must conduct proceedings and record its decision and reasons appropriately so as not to undermine the effect of an order made under paragraph (1), a direction given under paragraph (2) or (8) or the duty imposed by paragraph (10).]

Amendment
1.   Amended by r13 of SI 2009 No 1975 as from 1.9.09.

Definitions
"document": see rule 1(3).
"party": see rule 1(3).

Evidence and submissions

15.–(1) Without restriction on the general powers in rule 5(1) and (2) (case management powers), the Upper Tribunal may give directions as to–

(a)   issues on which it requires evidence or submissions;

(b)   the nature of the evidence or submissions it requires;

(c)   whether the parties are permitted or required to provide expert evidence, and if so whether the parties must jointly appoint a single expert to provide such evidence;

(d)   any limit on the number of witnesses whose evidence a party may put forward, whether in relation to a particular issue or generally;

(e)   the manner in which any evidence or submissions are to be provided, which may include a direction for them to be given–

(i)   orally at a hearing; or

(ii)   by written submissions or witness statement; and

(f)   the time at which any evidence or submissions are to be provided.

(2)   The Upper Tribunal may–

(a)   admit evidence whether or not–

(i)   the evidence would be admissible in a civil trial in the United Kingdom; or

(ii)   the evidence was available to a previous decision maker; or

(b)   exclude evidence that would otherwise be admissible where–

(i)   the evidence was not provided within the time allowed by a direction or a practice direction;

(ii)   the evidence was otherwise provided in a manner that did not comply with a direction or a practice direction; or

(iii)   it would otherwise be unfair to admit the evidence.

[[1](2A)   *[Omitted]*]

(3)   The Upper Tribunal may consent to a witness giving, or require any witness to give, evidence on oath, and may administer an oath for that purpose.

Amendment

1.   Inserted by r11 of SI 2010 No 44 as from 15.2.10.

Definitions

"hearing": see rule 1(3).
"party": see rule 1(3).
"practice direction": see rule 1(3).

Summoning or citation of witnesses and orders to answer questions or produce documents

16.–(1) On the application of a party or on its own initiative, the Upper Tribunal may–

(a)   by summons (or, in Scotland, citation) require any person to attend as a witness at a hearing at the time and place specified in the summons or citation; or

(b)   order any person to answer any questions or produce any documents in that person's possession or control which relate to any issue in the proceedings.

(2)   A summons or citation under paragraph (1)(a) must–

(a)   give the person required to attend 14 days' notice of the hearing or such shorter period as the Upper Tribunal may direct; and

(b)   where the person is not a party, make provision for the person's necessary expenses of attendance to be paid, and state who is to pay them.

(3)   No person may be compelled to give any evidence or produce any document that the person could not be compelled to give or produce on a trial of an action in a court of law in the part of the United Kingdom where the proceedings are due to be determined.

[[1](4)   A person who receives a summons, citation or order may apply to the Upper Tribunal for it to be varied or set aside if they did not have an opportunity to object to it before it was made or issued.

(5)   A person making an application under paragraph (4) must do so as soon as reasonably practicable after receiving notice of the summons, citation or order.

(6)   A summons, citation or order under this rule must–

(a)   state that the person on whom the requirement is imposed may apply to the Upper Tribunal to vary or set aside the summons, citation or order, if they did not have an opportunity to object to it before it was made or issued; and

(b)   state the consequences of failure to comply with the summons, citation or order.]

Amendment

1.   Substituted by r11 of SI 2009 No 274 as from 1.4.09.

Definitions

"document": see rule 1(3).

"hearing": see rule 1(3).

Withdrawal

17.–(1)   Subject to paragraph (2), a party may give notice of the withdrawal of its case, or any part of it–

(a)   [¹...] by sending or delivering to the Upper Tribunal a written notice of withdrawal; or

(b)   orally at a hearing.

(2)   Notice of withdrawal will not take effect unless the Upper Tribunal consents to the withdrawal except in relation to an application for permission to appeal.

(3)   A party which has withdrawn its case may apply to the Upper Tribunal for the case to be reinstated.

(4)   An application under paragraph (3) must be made in writing and be received by the Upper Tribunal within 1 month after–

(a)   the date on which the Upper Tribunal received the notice under paragraph (1)(a); or

(b)   the date of the hearing at which the case was withdrawn orally under paragraph (1)(b).

(5)   The Upper Tribunal must notify each party in writing [¹that a withdrawal has taken effect] under this rule.

[(6)   *[Omitted]*]

Amendment

1.   Tribunal Procedure (Amendment) Rules 2013 (SI 2013 No 477) r54 (April 1, 2013).

Definitions

"dispose of proceedings": see rule 1(3).

"hearing": see rule 1(3).

"party": see rule 1(3).

"permission": see rule 1(3).

Notice of funding of legal services

18.   If a party is granted funding of legal services at any time, that party must as soon as practicable–

(a)(i)   if [¹civil legal services (within the meaning of section 8 of the Legal Aid, Sentencing and Punishment of Offenders Act 2012) are provided under arrangements made for the purposes of Part 1 of that Act or by] the Northern Ireland Legal Services Commission, send a copy of the [¹certificate or] funding notice to the Upper Tribunal; or

(ii)   if funding is granted by the Scottish Legal Aid Board, send a copy of the legal aid certificate to the Upper Tribunal; and

(b)   notify every other party in writing that funding has been granted.

Amendment

1.   Tribunal Procedure (Amendment) Rules 2013 (SI 2013 No 477) r55 (April 1, 2013). In accordance with reg 14(3) of the Legal Aid, Sentencing and Punishment of Offenders Act 2012 (Consequential,

Transitional and Saving Provisions) Regulations 2013 (SI 2013 No 534) these amendments do not apply to a 'pre-commencement case' as defined in reg 2 of SI 2013 No 534. The amendments replaced the words 'funding is granted by the Legal Services Commission or' with 'civil legal services (within the meaning of section 8 of the Legal Aid, Sentencing and Punishment of Offenders Act 2012) are provided under arrangements made for the purposes of Part 1 of that Act or by' and inserted the words 'certificate or' into rule 18(a)(i).

Definition

"party": see rule 1(3).

Confidentiality in child support or child trust fund cases

19.–(1)   Paragraph (3) applies to an appeal against a decision of the First-tier Tribunal in proceedings under the Child Support Act 1991 in the circumstances described in paragraph (2), other than an appeal against a reduced benefit decision (as defined in section 46(10)(b) of the Child Support Act 1991, as that section had effect prior to the commencement of section 15(b) of the Child Maintenance and Other Payments Act 2008).

(2)   The circumstances referred to in paragraph (1) are that–

(a)   in the proceedings in the First-tier Tribunal in respect of which the appeal has been brought, there was an obligation to keep a person's address confidential; or

(b)   a person whose circumstances are relevant to the proceedings would like their address (or, in the case of the person with care of the child, the child's address) to be kept confidential and has given notice to that effect–

    (i)   to the Upper Tribunal in an application for permission to appeal or notice of appeal;

    (ii)   to the Upper Tribunal within 1 month after an enquiry by the Upper Tribunal; or

    (iii)   to the Secretary of State [¹...] or the Upper Tribunal when notifying a change of address after proceedings have been started.

(3)   Where this paragraph applies, the Secretary of State [¹...] and the Upper Tribunal must take appropriate steps to secure the confidentiality of the address, and of any information which could reasonably be expected to enable a person to identify the address, to the extent that the address or that information is not already known to each other party.

(4)   Paragraph (6) applies to an appeal against a decision of the First-tier Tribunal in proceedings under the Child Trust Funds Act 2004 in the circumstances described in paragraph (5).

(5)   The circumstances referred to in paragraph (4) are that–

(a)   in the proceedings in the First-tier Tribunal in respect of which the appeal has been brought, there was an obligation to keep a person's address confidential; or

(b)   a person whose circumstances are relevant to the proceedings would like their address (or, in the case of the person with care of the eligible child, the child's address) to be kept confidential and has given notice to that effect–

    (i)   to the Upper Tribunal in an application for permission to appeal or notice of appeal;

    (ii)   to the Upper Tribunal within 1 month after an enquiry by the Upper Tribunal; or

    (iii)   to HMRC or the Upper Tribunal when notifying a change of address after proceedings have been started.

(6)   Where this paragraph applies, HMRC and the Upper Tribunal must take appropriate steps to secure the confidentiality of the address, and of any information which could reasonably be expected to enable a person to identify the address, to the extent that the address or that information is not already known to each other party.

(7)   In this rule–
"eligible child" has the meaning set out in section 2 of the Child Trust Funds Act 2004; and
"HMRC" means Her Majesty's Revenue and Customs.

Amendment
1.   Public Bodies (Child Maintenance and Enforcement Commission: Abolition and Transfer of Functions)
        Order 2012 (SI 2012 No.2007) art 3(2) and Sch para 118 (August 1, 2012).

Definitions
"party": see rule 1(3).
"permission": see rule 1(3).

Power to pay expenses and allowances
20.–(1)   *[Omitted]*
(2)   Paragraph (3) applies to proceedings on appeal from a decision of–
(a)   the First-tier Tribunal in proceedings under the Child Support Act 1991, section 12 of the Social Security Act 1998 or paragraph 6 of Schedule 7 to the Child Support, Pensions and Social Security Act 2000;
(b)-(c) *[Omitted]*
(3)   The Lord Chancellor (or, in Scotland, the Secretary of State) may pay to any person who attends any hearing such travelling and other allowances, including compensation for loss of remunerative time, as the Lord Chancellor (or, in Scotland, the Secretary of State) may determine.

Definition
"hearing": see rule 1(3).

[¹ Procedure for applying for a stay of a decision pending an appeal
20A.–(1)   This rule applies where another enactment provides in any terms for the Upper Tribunal to stay or suspend, or to lift a stay or suspension of, a decision which is or may be the subject of an appeal to the Upper Tribunal ("the substantive decision") pending such appeal.
(2)   A person who wishes the Upper Tribunal to decide whether the substantive decision should be stayed or suspended must make a written application to the Upper Tribunal which must include–
(a)   the name and address of the person making the application;
(b)   the name and address of any representative of that person;
(c)   the address to which documents for that person should be sent or delivered;
(d)   the name and address of any person who will be a respondent to the appeal;
(e)   details of the substantive decision and any decision as to when that decision is to take effect, and copies of any written record of, or reasons for, those decisions; and
(f)   the grounds on which the person making the application relies.
(3)   In the case of an application under paragraph (2) [²in a road transport case] –
(a)   the person making the application must notify the [²decision maker] when making the application;
(b)   within 7 days of receiving notification of the application the [²decision maker] must send or deliver written reasons for refusing or withdrawing the stay–
(i)   to the Upper Tribunal; and
(ii)   to the person making the application, if the [²decision maker] has not already done so.
(4)   If the Upper Tribunal grants a stay or suspension following an application under this rule–
(a)   the Upper Tribunal may give directions as to the conduct of the appeal of the substantive decision; and
(b)   the Upper Tribunal may, where appropriate, grant the stay or suspension subject to conditions.

(5) Unless the Upper Tribunal considers that there is good reason not to do so, the Upper Tribunal must send written notice of any decision made under this rule to each party.]

Amendments

1.   Inserted by r14 of SI 2009 No 1975 as from 1.9.09.
2.   Substituted by r6 of SI 2012 No 1363 as from 1.7.12.

Definitions

"document": see rule 1(3).
"respondent": see rule 1(3).

PART 3
[¹ *Procedure for cases in*] *the Upper Tribunal*

Amendment

1.   Amended by r13 of SI 2009 No 274 as from 1.4.09.

Application to the Upper Tribunal for permission to appeal

21.–[¹ (1)]

(2)   A person may apply to the Upper Tribunal for permission to appeal to the Upper Tribunal against a decision of another tribunal only if–
  (a)   they have made an application for permission to appeal to the tribunal which made the decision challenged; and
  (b)   that application has been refused or has not been admitted.

(3)   An application for permission to appeal must be made in writing and received by the Upper Tribunal no later than–
  (a)-(ab) *[Omitted]*
  (b)   otherwise, a month after the date on which the tribunal that made the decision under challenge sent notice of its refusal of permission to appeal, or refusal to admit the application for permission to appeal, to the appellant.

[²(3A) *[Omitted]*]

(4)   The application must state–
  (a)   the name and address of the appellant;
  (b)   the name and address of the representative (if any) of the appellant;
  (c)   an address where documents for the appellant may be sent or delivered;
  (d)   details (including the full reference) of the decision challenged;
  (e)   the grounds on which the appellant relies; and
  (f)   whether the appellant wants the application to be dealt with at a hearing.

(5)   The appellant must provide with the application a copy of–
  (a)   any written record of the decision being challenged;
  (b)   any separate written statement of reasons for that decision; and
  (c)   if the application is for permission to appeal against a decision of another tribunal, the notice of refusal of permission to appeal, or notice of refusal to admit the application for permission to appeal, from that other tribunal.

(6)   If the appellant provides the application to the Upper Tribunal later than the time required by paragraph (3) or by an extension of time allowed under rule 5(3)(a) (power to extend time)–
  (a)   the application must include a request for an extension of time and the reason why the application was not provided in time; and
  (b)   unless the Upper Tribunal extends time for the application under rule 5(3)(a) (power to extend time) the Upper Tribunal must not admit the application.

(7)   If the appellant makes an application to the Upper Tribunal for permission to appeal against the decision of another tribunal, and that other tribunal refused to admit the appellant's application for permission to appeal because the application for permission or for a written statement of reasons was not made in time–

(a)   the application to the Upper Tribunal for permission to appeal must include the reason why the application to the other tribunal for permission to appeal or for a written statement of reasons, as the case may be, was not made in time; and

(b)   the Upper Tribunal must only admit the application if the Upper Tribunal considers that it is in the interests of justice for it to do so.

Amendments

1.   Omitted by r15 of SI 2009 No 1975 as from 1.9.09.
2.   Inserted by r13 of SI 2010 No 44 as from 15.2.10.

Definitions

"appellant": see rule 1(3).
"document": see rule 1(3).
"permission": see rule 1(3).

General Note

A refusal of permission by the First-tier Tribunal is presumed to be valid. A defect in it does not deprive the Upper Tribunal of jurisdiction to consider the application. That tribunal is not reviewing the refusal of permission, but is concerned with the merits of the application. See *CIS 4772/2000*, paras 2-11.

It is permissible for a commissioner to refuse to copy papers to a party so that that party may check if any are missing (*R (Cowling) v Child Support Commissioners Office* [2009] 1 FLR 332 paras 18-19).

Parties sometimes produce grounds of appeal of inordinate length. Judges are entitled to limit the time that is spent on an application for permission. In a different context in *CMA CGM SA v Beteiligungs-KG MS "Northern Pioneer" Schiffahrtsgesellschaft mbH & Co* [2003] 1 WLR 1015, the Court of Appeal commented that:

"23.   .. The statutory requirement that applications for permission to appeal should be paper applications unless the court otherwise directs must surely have been intended to simplify the procedure and to save the court's time. That requirement reflects the fact that the criteria for the grant of permission to appeal are clear-cut and easy to apply. They do not require the drawing of fine lines, nor will they usually give much scope for the court to require assistance in the form of submissions or advocacy .... Any written submissions placed before the court in support of an application for permission to appeal from findings in an arbitral award should normally be capable of being read and digested by the judge within the half-hour that, under the old regime, used to be allotted for such applications."

These principles apply equally to the child support jurisdiction, provided that appropriate allowance is made for unrepresented parties.

The requirement to apply for permission to appeal from the First-tier Tribunal is a requirement of the rules of procedure and may be waived by the Upper Tribunal (*MA v Secretary of State for Defence* [2009] UKUT 57 (AAC)).

Directions given by the Upper Tribunal on an application must, like all directions, be obeyed. This is primarily the duty of the appellant, even if the directions are directed to the parties generally (*Re M-W (Care Proceedings: Expert Evidence)* [2010] 2 FLR 46 at para 5).

Representatives have a wider responsibility that just to their clients. They have a duty to the tribunal (under rule 2(4)) not to advance arguments on application or appeal that are plainly hopeless or clearly misconceived (*CIB 908/2003*, para 8).

Decision in relation to permission to appeal

22.–(1)   If the Upper Tribunal refuses permission to appeal, it must send written notice of the refusal and of the reasons for the refusal to the appellant.

(2)   If the Upper Tribunal gives permission to appeal–

(a)   the Upper Tribunal must send written notice of the permission, and of the reasons for any limitations or conditions on such permission, to each party;

(b)   subject to any direction by the Upper Tribunal, the application for permission to appeal stands as the notice of appeal and the Upper Tribunal must send to each respondent a copy of the application for permission to appeal and any documents provided with it by the appellant; and

(c)   the Upper Tribunal may, with the consent of the appellant and each respondent, determine the appeal without obtaining any further response.

(3)-(5)   *[Omitted]*

Definitions

"permission": see rule 1(3).
"respondent": see rule 1(3).

General Note
Most Upper Tribunal Judges on granting permission indicate the issues that appear to arise on the appeal and they all set a timetable for responses and replies by the parties. In *CDLA 0607/2005*, the commissioner explained the procedure and emphasised the benefits of the parties having the judge's provisional views:

"5   .... a Commissioner has to look at the papers and form a view in order to decide the application for permission. That inevitably means that he has to form views about the strengths and weaknesses of the grounds put forward. Quite often a Commissioner rejects those grounds but finds a quite different arguable error of law. Further, even where permission is granted, the Commissioner's current system of case management requires a Commissioner to look carefully at the papers to enable him to give appropriate directions. Such directions should, where possible and appropriate, be tailored to the facts and circumstances of the specific appeal rather than being of a general nature. It is quite common for Commissioners to indicate what their preliminary view is. This can be helpful to the parties. Sometimes it is possible to dispose of an appeal very quickly because the decision contains an obvious error of law and the Commissioner can indicate that he considers this to be the case. The Secretary of State is entirely free to submit that the Commissioner is wrong but if he accepts the Commissioner's view everyone, and not least the appellant, will be spared time, effort and expense. In other appeals a party who is aware that the Commissioner considers there are weaknesses in his case may be able to deal with those weaknesses when he makes his final submissions or may feel it appropriate to ask for an oral hearing. Further, experience has shown that those acting for the Secretary of State at this level deal with appeals in an objective and fair way. If a Commissioner asks whether the grounds of appeal do identify any error of law, he can be sure that the Secretary of State's representative will consider the point in a careful, helpful and fair way."

Notice of appeal

23.–[¹   This rule applies–

(a)   to proceedings on appeal to the Upper Tribunal for which permission to appeal is not required, except proceedings to which rule 26A [³or 26B] applies;

(b)   if another tribunal has given permission for a party to appeal to the Upper Tribunal; or

(c)   subject to any other direction by the Upper Tribunal, if the Upper Tribunal has given permission to appeal and has given a direction that the application for permission to appeal does not stand as the notice of appeal.

[²(1A) *[Omitted]*]

(2)   The appellant must provide a notice of appeal to the Upper Tribunal so that it is received within 1 month after–

(a)   the date that the tribunal that gave permission to appeal sent notice of such permission to the appellant; or

(b)   if permission to appeal is not required, the date on which notice of decision to which the appeal relates was sent to the appellant.]

(3)   The notice of appeal must include the information listed in rule 21(4)(a) to (e) (content of the application for permission to appeal) and, where the Upper Tribunal has given permission to appeal, the Upper Tribunal's case reference.

(4)   If another tribunal has granted permission to appeal, the appellant must provide with the notice of appeal a copy of–

(a)   any written record of the decision being challenged;

(b)   any separate written statement of reasons for that decision; and

(c)   the notice of permission to appeal.

(5)   If the appellant provides the notice of appeal to the Upper Tribunal later than the time required by paragraph (2) or by an extension of time allowed under rule 5(3)(a) (power to extend time)–

(a)   the notice of appeal must include a request for an extension of time and the reason why the notice was not provided in time; and

(b)   unless the Upper Tribunal extends time for the notice of appeal under rule 5(3)(a) (power to extend time) the Upper Tribunal must not admit the notice of appeal.

[¹ (6)   When the Upper Tribunal receives the notice of appeal it must send a copy of the notice and any accompanying documents–

(a)   to each respondent; or

(b)   *[Omitted]*]

Amendments

1.   Substituted by r17 of SI 2009 No 1975 as from 1.9.09.
2.   Insertded by r14 of SI 2010 No 44 as from 15.2.10.
3.   Amended by r8 of SI 2010 No 747 as from 6.4.10.

Definitions

"permission": see rule 1(3).
"respondent": see rule 1(3).

General Note

Rule 23(5)

The tribunal may exercise the power conferred by r 5(3)(a) to extend time within the limits imposed by this paragraph: see para (8) below.

In *OFSTED v AF* [2011] UKUT 72 (AAC); [2011] AACR 32 at para 21, the judge refused to give guidance on when and how the tribunal should exercise its power to extend time on the grounds that it "would either be so general as to be meaningless or would be likely to spark time-consuming and unnecessary satellite litigation."

There is no limit to the factors that may be relevant to the issue whether time should be extended and it is inappropiate to apply the checklist from the CPR (*Information Commissioner v PS* [2011] UKUT 94 (AAC)).

Response to the notice of appeal

24.–[² (1)   This rule and rule 25 do not apply to [⁵ a road transport case], in respect of which Schedule 1 makes alternative provision.

(1A)   Subject to any direction given by the Upper Tribunal, a respondent may provide a response to a notice of appeal.]

(2)   Any response provided under paragraph [³ (1A)] must be in writing and must be sent or delivered to the Upper Tribunal so that it is received–

[⁴ (a)   if an application for permission to appeal stands as the notice of appeal, no later than one month after the date on which the respondent was sent notice that permission to appeal had been granted;] [⁴]

[⁴(aa) *[Omitted]*]

(b)   in any other case, no later than 1 month after the date on which the Upper Tribunal sent a copy of the notice of appeal to the respondent.

(3)   The response must state–

(a)   the name and address of the respondent;

(b)   the name and address of the representative (if any) of the respondent;

(c)   an address where documents for the respondent may be sent or delivered;

(d)   whether the respondent opposes the appeal;

(e)   the grounds on which the respondent relies, including [² (in the case of an appeal against the decision of another tribunal)] any grounds on which the respondent was unsuccessful in the proceedings which are the subject of the appeal, but intends to rely in the appeal; and

(f)   whether the respondent wants the case to be dealt with at a hearing.

(4)   If the respondent provides the response to the Upper Tribunal later than the time required by paragraph (2) or by an extension of time allowed under rule 5(3)(a) (power to extend time), the response must include a request for an extension of time and the reason why the [¹ response] was not provided in time.

(5)   When the Upper Tribunal receives the response it must send a copy of the response and any accompanying documents to the appellant and each other party.

Amendments

1.   Amended by Art 15 of SI 2009 No 274 as from 1.4.09.
2.   Amended by r18 of SI 2009 No 1975 as from 1.9.09.
3.   Amended by r9 of SI 2010 No 43 as from 18.1.10.
4.   Amended by r15 of SI 2010 No 44 as from 15.2.10.
5.   Substituted by r8 of SI 2012 No. 1363 as from 1.7.12

Definitions

"hearing": see rule 1(3).
"party": see rule 1(3).
"respondent": see rule 1(3).

Appellant's reply

25.–(1) Subject to any direction given by the Upper Tribunal, the appellant may provide a reply to any response provided under rule 24 (response to the notice of appeal).

(2) [¹ Subject to paragraph (2A), any] reply provided under paragraph (1) must be in writing and must be sent or delivered to the Upper Tribunal so that it is received within one month after the date on which the Upper Tribunal sent a copy of the response to the appellant.

[¹(2A) *[Omitted]*]

(3) When the Upper Tribunal receives the reply it must send a copy of the reply and any accompanying documents to each respondent.

Amendment

1.   Amended by r16 of SI 2010 No 44 as from 15.2.10.

Definitions

"appellant": see rule 1(3).
"respondent": see rule 1(3).

[¹ Cases transferred or referred to the Upper Tribunal, applications made directly to the Upper Tribunal and proceedings without notice to a respondent

26A.–[² (1) Paragraphs (2) and (3) apply to–

(a)   a case transferred or referred to the Upper Tribunal from the First-tier Tribunal; or

(b)   a case, other than an appeal or a case to which rule 26 (references under the Forfeiture Act 1982) applies, which is started by an application made directly to the Upper Tribunal.]

(2)   In a case to which this paragraph applies–

(a)   the Upper Tribunal must give directions as to the procedure to be followed in the consideration and disposal of the proceedings; [⁴...]

[⁵(aa) in a reference under Schedule 1D of the Charities Act 1993, the Upper Tribunal may give directions providing for an application to join the proceedings as a party and the time within which it may be made; and]

(b)   the preceding rules in this Part will only apply to the proceedings to the extent provided for by such directions.

(3)   If a case or matter to which this paragraph applies is to be determined without notice to or the involvement of a respondent–

(a)   any provision in these Rules requiring a document to be provided by or to a respondent; and

(b)   any other provision in these Rules permitting a respondent to participate in the proceedings

does not apply to that case or matter.]

[³(4) *[Omitted]*]

Amendments

1.   Inserted by Art 16 of SI 2009 No 274 as from 1.4.09.
2.   Substituted by r19 of SI 2009 No 1975 as from 1.9.09.
3.   Inserted by r10 of SI 2010 No 43 as from 18.1.10.
4.   Omitted by by r5(2)(a) of SI 2012 No 500 as from 6.4.12.
5.   Inserted by by r5(2)(b) of SI 2012 No 500 as from 6.4.12.

Definitions

"dispose of proceedings": see rule 1(3).
"document": see rule 1(3).
"respondent": see rule 1(3).

PART 4
Judicial review proceedings in the Upper Tribunal

Application of this Part to judicial review proceedings transferred to the Upper Tribunal

27.–(1)   When a court transfers judicial review proceedings to the Upper Tribunal, the Upper Tribunal–

(a)   must notify each party in writing that the proceedings have been transferred to the Upper Tribunal; and

(b)   must give directions as to the future conduct of the proceedings.

(2)   The directions given under paragraph (1)(b) may modify or disapply for the purposes of the proceedings any of the provisions of the following rules in this Part.

(3)   In proceedings transferred from the Court of Session under section 20(1) of the 2007 Act, the directions given under paragraph (1)(b) must–

(a)   if the Court of Session did not make a first order specifying the required intimation, service and advertisement of the petition, state the Upper Tribunal's requirements in relation to those matters;

(b)   state whether the Upper Tribunal will consider summary dismissal of the proceedings; and

(c)   where necessary, modify or disapply provisions relating to permission in the following rules in this Part.

Definitions
"the 2007 Act": see rule 1(3).
"judicial review proceedings": see rule 1(3).
"party": see rule 1(3).

Applications for permission to bring judicial review proceedings

28.–(1)   A person seeking permission to bring judicial review proceedings before the Upper Tribunal under section 16 of the 2007 Act must make a written application to the Upper Tribunal for such permission.

(2)   Subject to paragraph (3), an application under paragraph (1) must be made promptly and, unless any other enactment specifies a shorter time limit, must be sent or delivered to the Upper Tribunal so that it is received no later than 3 months after the date of the decision [1 , action or omission] to which the application relates.

(3)   An application for permission to bring judicial review proceedings challenging a decision of the First-tier Tribunal may be made later than the time required by paragraph (2) if it is made within 1 month after the date on which the First-tier Tribunal sent–

(a)   written reasons for the decision; or

(b)   notification that an application for the decision to be set aside has been unsuccessful, provided that that application was made in time.

(4)   The application must state–

(a)   the name and address of the applicant, the respondent and any other person whom the applicant considers to be an interested party;

(b)   the name and address of the applicant's representative (if any);

(c)   an address where documents for the applicant may be sent or delivered;

(d)   details of the decision challenged (including the date, the full reference and the identity of the decision maker);

(e)   that the application is for permission to bring judicial review proceedings;

(f)   the outcome that the applicant is seeking; and

(g)   the facts and grounds on which the applicant relies.

(5)   If the application relates to proceedings in a court or tribunal, the application must name as an interested party each party to those proceedings who is not the applicant or a respondent.

(6)   The applicant must send with the application–

(a)   a copy of any written record of the decision in the applicant's possession or control; and

(b) copies of any other documents in the applicant's possession or control on which the applicant intends to rely.

(7) If the applicant provides the application to the Upper Tribunal later than the time required by paragraph (2) or (3) or by an extension of time allowed under rule 5(3)(a) (power to extend time)–

(a) the application must include a request for an extension of time and the reason why the application was not provided in time; and

(b) unless the Upper Tribunal extends time for the application under rule 5(3)(a) (power to extend time) the Upper Tribunal must not admit the application.

(8) [²Except where rule 28A(2)(a) (special provisions for [³immigration judicial review] proceedings) applies,] when the Upper Tribunal receives the application it must send a copy of the application and any accompanying documents to each person named in the application as a respondent or interested party.

Amendments

1. Amended by r17 of SI 2009 No 274 as from 1.4.09.
2. Inserted by r7 of SI 2011 No 2343 as from 17.10.11.
3. Amended by r10 of SI 2013 No 2067 as from 1.11.13.

Definitions

"applicant": see rule 1(3).
"document": see rule 1(3).
"interested party": see rule 1(3).
"judicial review proceedings": see rule 1(3).
"permission": see rule 1(3).
"respondent": see rule 1(3).

Acknowledgment of service

29.–(1) A person who is sent [⁴or provided with] a copy of an application for permission under rule 28(8) (application for permission to bring judicial review proceedings) [⁴or rule 28A(2)(a) (special provisions for [⁶immigration judicial review] proceedings)] and wishes to take part in the proceedings must [⁵provide] to the Upper Tribunal an acknowledgment of service so that it is received no later than 21 days after the date on which the Upper Tribunal sent [⁴, or in [⁶immigration judicial review] proceedings the applicant provided,] a copy of the application to that person.

(2) An acknowledgment of service under paragraph (1) must be in writing and state–

(a) whether the person intends to [¹ support or] oppose the application for permission;

(b) their grounds for any [¹ support or] opposition under sub-paragraph (a), or any other submission or [² information which they consider may] assist the Upper Tribunal; and

(c) the name and address of any other person not named in the application as a respondent or interested party whom the person providing the acknowledgment considers to be an interested party.

[⁴2A] *Omitted.*

(3) A person who is [⁵provided with] a copy of an application for permission under rule 28(8) [⁴or 28A(2)(a)] but does not provide an acknowledgment of service [⁴to the Upper Tribunal] may not take part in the application for permission [³ unless allowed to do so by the Upper Tribunal], but may take part in the subsequent proceedings if the application is successful.

Amendments

1. Amended by r18 of SI 2009 No 274 as from 1.4.09.
2. Amended by correction slip 9.09.
3. Amended by r8(3) of SI 2011 No 651 (L.6) as from 1.4.11.
4. Inserted by r9 of SI 2011 No 2343 as from 17.10.11.
5. Substituted by r9 of SI 2011 No 2343 as from 17.10.11.
6. Amended by r12 of SI 2013 No 2067 as from 1.11.13.

Decision on permission or summary dismissal, and reconsideration of permission or summary dismissal at a hearing

30.–(1)   The Upper Tribunal must send to the applicant, each respondent and any other person who provided an acknowledgment of service to the Upper Tribunal, and may send to any other person who may have an interest in the proceedings, written notice of–

(a)   its decision in relation to the application for permission; and

(b)   the reasons for any refusal of the application, or any limitations or conditions on permission.

(2)   In proceedings transferred from the Court of Session under section 20(1) of the 2007 Act, where the Upper Tribunal has considered whether summarily to dismiss of the proceedings, the Upper Tribunal must send to the applicant and each respondent, and may send to any other person who may have an interest in the proceedings, written notice of–

(a)   its decision in relation to the summary dismissal of proceedings; and

(b)   the reasons for any decision summarily to dismiss part or all of the proceedings, or any limitations or conditions on the continuation of such proceedings.

(3)   Paragraph (4) applies where the Upper Tribunal, without a hearing–

(a)   determines an application for permission to bring judicial review proceedings and either refuses permission, or gives permission on limited grounds or subject to conditions; or

(b)   in proceedings transferred from the Court of Session, summarily dismisses part or all of the proceedings, or imposes any limitations or conditions on the continuation of such proceedings.

(4)   [²Subject to paragraph (4A), in] the circumstances specified in paragraph (3) the applicant may apply for the decision to be reconsidered at a hearing.

[³(4A)   [*Omitted*]]

(5)   An application under paragraph (4) must be made in writing and must be sent or delivered to the Upper Tribunal so that it is received within 14 days [¹, or in [²immigration judicial review] proceedings 9 days,] after the date on which the Upper Tribunal sent written notice of its decision regarding the application to the applicant.

Responses

31.–(1)   Any person to whom the Upper Tribunal has sent notice of the grant of permission under rule 30(1) (notification of decision on permission), and who wishes to contest the application or support it on additional grounds, must provide detailed grounds for contesting or supporting the application to the Upper Tribunal.

(2)   Any detailed grounds must be provided in writing and must be sent or delivered to the Upper Tribunal so that they are received not more than 35 days after the Upper Tribunal sent notice of the grant of permission under rule 30(1).

Definition
"permission": see rule 1(3).

Applicant seeking to rely on additional grounds
32.   The applicant may not rely on any grounds, other than those grounds on which the applicant obtained permission for the judicial review proceedings, without the consent of the Upper Tribunal.

Definitions
"applicant": see rule 1(3).
"judicial review proceedings": see rule 1(3).
"permission": see rule 1(3).

Right to make representations
33.   Each party and, with the permission of the Upper Tribunal, any other person, may–
(a)   submit evidence, except at the hearing of an application for permission;
(b)   make representations at any hearing which they are entitled to attend; and
(c)   make written representations in relation to a decision to be made without a hearing.

Definitions
"hearing": see rule 1(3).
"party": see rule 1(3).
"permission": see rule 1(3).

[¹Amendments and additional grounds resulting in transfer of proceedings to the High Court in England and Wales
33A.–(1)   This rule applies only to judicial review proceedings arising under the law of England and Wales.
(2)   In relation to such proceedings–
(a)   the powers of the Upper Tribunal to permit or require amendments under rule 5(3)(c) extend to amendments which would, once in place, give rise to an obligation or power to transfer the proceedings to the High Court in England and Wales under section 18(3) of the 2007 Act or paragraph (3);
(b)   except with the permission of the Upper Tribunal, additional grounds may not be advanced, whether by an applicant or otherwise, if they would give rise to an obligation or power to transfer the proceedings to the High Court in England and Wales under section 18(3) of the 2007 Act or paragraph (3).
(3)   Where the High Court in England and Wales has transferred judicial review proceedings to the Upper Tribunal under any power or duty and subsequently the proceedings are amended or any party advances additional grounds–
(a)   if the proceedings in their present form could not have been transferred to the Upper Tribunal under the relevant power or duty had they been in that form at the time of the transfer, the Upper Tribunal must transfer the proceedings back to the High Court in England and Wales;
(b)   subject to sub-paragraph (a), where the proceedings were transferred to the Upper Tribunal under section 31A(3) of the Senior Courts Act 1981 (power to transfer judicial review proceedings to the Upper Tribunal), the Upper Tribunal may transfer proceedings back to the High Court in England and Wales if it appears just and convenient to do so.]

Amendment
1.   Inserted by r11 of SI 2011 No 2343 as from 17.10.11.

PART 5
Hearings

Decision with or without a hearing

34.–(1) Subject to [¹paragraphs (2) and (3)], the Upper Tribunal may make any decision without a hearing.

(2) The Upper Tribunal must have regard to any view expressed by a party when deciding whether to hold a hearing to consider any matter, and the form of any such hearing.

[²(3) [*Omitted*]

(4) [*Omitted*]]

Amendments

1.   Amended by r14(a) of SI 2013 No 2067 as from 1.11.13.
2.   Inserted by r14(b) of SI 2013 No 2067 as from 1.11.13.

Definitions

"hearing": see rule 1(3).
"party": see rule 1(3).

General Note

In *R(IS) 14/74*, the commissioner said (at para 17) that fresh points of law should not be raised after a hearing. Nevertheless, in that case the commissioner took account of the point raised as it was in the interests of the social security claimant to consider it. In child support cases, where the parties usually have competing interests, the Upper Tribunal may be more reluctant to take account of a fresh point that is in the interests of one party to the proceedings but against the interests of another.

Once the Upper Tribunal has investigated the alleged mistakes in the decision and indicated acceptance of the concurring submissions of the parties that the decision should be set aside as erroneous in law, a party may not advance argument in support of the decision under appeal, even if the Upper Tribunal has issued directions relating to other matters which are to be considered before a decision is issued. This is based not on technical or doctrinal considerations, such as estoppel, but on common fairness (*CI 276/1993*, para 15).

Entitlement to attend a hearing

35.[¹ –(1)] Subject to rule 37(4) (exclusion of a person from a hearing), each party is entitled to attend a hearing.

[¹ (2) [*Omitted*]]

Amendment

1.   Amended by r11 of SI 2010 No 43 as from 18.1.10.

Definitions

"hearing": see rule 1(3).
"party": see rule 1(3).

Notice of hearings

36.–(1) The Upper Tribunal must give each party entitled to attend a hearing reasonable notice of the time and place of the hearing (including any adjourned or postponed hearing) and any change to the time and place of the hearing.

(2) The period of notice under paragraph (1) must be at least 14 days except that–

(a)   in applications for permission to bring judicial review proceedings, the period of notice must be at least 2 working days; [¹]

[¹(aa) [*Omitted*]]

(b)   [¹ in any case other than a fast-track case] the Upper Tribunal may give shorter notice–

(i)   with the parties' consent; or

(ii)   in urgent or exceptional cases.

Amendment

1.   Amended by r17 of SI 2010 No 44 as from 15.2.10.

Definitions
"hearing": see rule 1(3).
"judicial review proceedings": see rule 1(3).
"party": see rule 1(3).

Public and private hearings

37.–(1)   Subject to the following paragraphs, all hearings must be held in public.

(2)   The Upper Tribunal may give a direction that a hearing, or part of it, is to be held in private.

[³(2A)   *[Omitted]*]

(3)   Where a hearing, or part of it, is to be held in private, the Upper Tribunal may determine who is entitled to attend the hearing or part of it.

(4)   The Upper Tribunal may give a direction excluding from any hearing, or part of it–

(a)   any person whose conduct the Upper Tribunal considers is disrupting or is likely to disrupt the hearing;

(b)   any person whose presence the Upper Tribunal considers is likely to prevent another person from giving evidence or making submissions freely;

(c)   any person who the Upper Tribunal considers should be excluded in order to give effect to [² the requirement at rule 14(11) (prevention of disclosure or publication of documents and information)]; [¹]

(d)   any person where the purpose of the hearing would be defeated by the attendance of that person. [¹ ; or

(e)   a person under the age of eighteen years.]

(5)   The Upper Tribunal may give a direction excluding a witness from a hearing until that witness gives evidence.

Amendments
1.   Amended by r19 of SI 2009 No 274 as from 1.4.09.
2.   Amended by r20 of SI 2009 No 1975 as from 1.9.09.
3.   Inserted by r12 of SI 2010 No 43 as from 18.1.10.

Definition
"hearing": see rule 1(3).

Hearings in a party's absence

38.   If a party fails to attend a hearing, the Upper Tribunal may proceed with the hearing if the Upper Tribunal–

(a)   is satisfied that the party has been notified of the hearing or that reasonable steps have been taken to notify the party of the hearing; and

(b)   considers that it is in the interests of justice to proceed with the hearing.

Definitions
"hearing": see rule 1(3).
"party": see rule 1(3).

PART 6
Decisions

Consent orders

39.–(1)   The Upper Tribunal may, at the request of the parties but only if it considers it appropriate, make a consent order disposing of the proceedings and making such other appropriate provision as the parties have agreed.

(2)   Notwithstanding any other provision of these Rules, the [²Upper] Tribunal need not hold a hearing before making an order under paragraph (1) [¹].

Amendments
1.   Amended by r20 of SI 2009 No 274 as from 1.4.09.
2.   Inserted by r15 of SI 2013 No 2067 as from 1.11.13.

Definitions
"dispose of proceedings": see rule 1(3).
"hearing": see rule 1(3).
"party": see rule 1(3).

Decisions

40.–(1)   The Upper Tribunal may give a decision orally at a hearing.
[6(1A)   *[Omitted]*]
(2)   [¹] [⁴ Except where rule 40A (special procedure for providing notice of a decision relating to an asylum case) applies,] the Upper Tribunal must provide to each party as soon as reasonably practicable after making [⁵a decision (other than a decision under Part 7) which finally disposes of all issues in the proceedings or of a preliminary issue dealt with following a direction under rule 5(3)(e)]–
(a)   a decision notice stating the [⁵Upper] Tribunal's decision; and
(b)   notification of any rights of review or appeal against the decision and the time and manner in which such rights of review or appeal may be exercised.
(3)   [¹ Subject to rule [² 14(11) (prevention of disclosure or publication of documents and information)] ,] the Upper Tribunal must provide written reasons for its decision with a decision notice provided under paragraph (2)(a) unless–
(a)   the decision was made with the consent of the parties; or
(b)   the parties have consented to the Upper Tribunal not giving written reasons.
(4)   The [² Upper] Tribunal may provide written reasons for any decision to which paragraph (2) does not apply.
[³(5)   *[Omitted]*]

Amendments
1.   Amended by r21 of SI 2009 No 274 as from 1.4.09.
2.   Amended by r21 of SI 2009 No 1975 as from 1.9.09.
3.   Inserted by r13 of SI 2010 No 43 as from 18.1.10.
4.   Amended by r19 of SI 2010 No 44 as from 15.2.10.
5.   Amended by r56 of SI 2013 No 477 as from 1.4.13.
6.   Inserted by r16 of SI 2013 No 2067 as from 1.11.13.

Definitions
"dispose of proceedings": see rule 1(3).
"hearing": see rule 1(3).
"party": see rule 1(3).

PART 7
Correcting, setting aside, reviewing and appealing decisions of the Upper Tribunal

---

Interpretation

41.   In this Part–
"appeal" [¹ , except in rule 44(2) (application for permission to appeal),] means the exercise of a right of appeal under section 13 of the 2007 Act; and
"review" means the review of a decision by the Upper Tribunal under section 10 of the 2007 Act.

Amendment
1.   Amended by Art 22 of SI 2009 No 274 as from 1.4.09.

Definition
"permission": see rule 1(3).

Clerical mistakes and accidental slips or omissions

42.   The Upper Tribunal may at any time correct any clerical mistake or other accidental slip or omission in a decision or record of a decision by–
(a)   sending notification of the amended decision, or a copy of the amended record, to all parties; and

(b)　　making any necessary amendment to any information published in relation to the decision or record.

Definition
"party": see rule 1(3).

Setting aside a decision which disposes of proceedings

43.–(1)　The Upper Tribunal may set aside a decision which disposes of proceedings, or part of such a decision, and re-make the decision or the relevant part of it, if–

(a)　　the Upper Tribunal considers that it is in the interests of justice to do so; and

(b)　　one or more of the conditions in paragraph (2) are satisfied.

(2)　　The conditions are–

(a)　　a document relating to the proceedings was not sent to, or was not received at an appropriate time by, a party or a party's representative;

(b)　　a document relating to the proceedings was not sent to the Upper Tribunal at an appropriate time;

(c)　　a party, or a party's representative, was not present at a hearing related to the proceedings; or

(d)　　there has been some other procedural irregularity in the proceedings.

(3)　　[¹ Except where paragraph (4) applies,] A party applying for a decision, or part of a decision, to be set aside under paragraph (1) must make a written application to the Upper Tribunal so that it is received no later than 1 month after the date on which the [³Upper] Tribunal sent notice of the decision to the party.

[²(4)-(5)　*[Omitted]*]]

Amendments
1.　　Amended by r21 of SI 2010 No 44 as from 15.2.10.
2.　　Inserted by r21(b) of SI 2010 No 44 as from 15.2.10.
3.　　Inserted by r17 of SI 2013 No 2067 as from 1.11.13.

Definitions
"dispose of proceedings": see rule 1(3).
"document": see rule 1(3).
"hearing": see rule 1(3).
"party": see rule 1(3).

Application for permission to appeal

44.–(1)　[³Subject to [⁴paragraphs (4A) and (4B)],] a person seeking permission to appeal must make a written application to the Upper Tribunal for permission to appeal.

(2)　　Paragraph (3) applies to an application under paragraph (1) in respect of a decision–

(a)　　on an appeal against a decision in a social security and child support case (as defined in the Tribunal Procedure (First-tier Tribunal) (Social Entitlement Chamber) Rules 2008;

(b)-(c) *[Omitted]*

(3)　　Where this paragraph applies, the application must be sent or delivered to the Upper Tribunal so that it is received within 3 months after the date on which the Upper Tribunal sent to the person making the application–

(a)　　written notice of the decision;

(b)　　notification of amended reasons for, or correction of, the decision following a review; or

(c)　　notification that an application for the decision to be set aside has been unsuccessful.

[(3A)-(3D)　*[Omitted]*]

(4)　　Where paragraph (3) [¹ [² , (3A) [⁴, (3D) or (4C)]]] does not apply, an application under paragraph (1) must be sent or delivered to the Upper Tribunal so that it is received within 1 month after the latest of the dates on which the Upper Tribunal sent to the person making the application–

(a)   written reasons for the decision;

(b)   notification of amended reasons for, or correction of, the decision following a review; or

(c)   notification that an application for the decision to be set aside has been unsuccessful.

[³(4A)   [⁵*[Omitted]*]]

[⁶(4B)   [*Omitted*]

(4C)   [*Omitted*]]

(5)   The date in paragraph (3)(c) or (4)(c) applies only if the application for the decision to be set aside was made within the time stipulated in rule 43 (setting aside a decision which disposes of proceedings) or any extension of that time granted by the Upper Tribunal.

(6)   If the person seeking permission to appeal provides the application to the Upper Tribunal later than the time required by paragraph (3) [¹ , (3A)][² ,(3D)] or (4), or by any extension of time under rule 5(3)(a) (power to extend time)–

(a)   the application must include a request for an extension of time and the reason why the application notice was not provided in time; and

(b)   unless the Upper Tribunal extends time for the application under rule 5(3)(a) (power to extend time) the Upper Tribunal must refuse the application.

(7)   An application under paragraph (1) [³or (4A)(a)] must–

(a)   identify the decision of the [⁴Upper] Tribunal to which it relates;

(b)   identify the alleged error or errors of law in the decision; and

(c)   state the result the party making the application is seeking.

Amendments

1.   Amended by r22 of SI 2010 No 44 as from 15.2.10.
2.   Amended by r10 of SI 2010 No 747 as from 6.4.10.
3.   Amended by r3 of SI 2012 No 2890 as from 11.12.12.
4.   Amended by r18(a), (b) and (d) of SI 2013 No 2067 as from 1.11.13.
5.   Substituted by r18(c) of SI 2013 No 2067 as from 1.11.13.
6.   Inserted by r18(c) of SI 2013 No 2067 as from 1.11.13.

Definitions

"appeal": see rule 41.
"permission": see rule 1(3).
"review": see rule 41.

Upper Tribunal's consideration of application for permission to appeal

45.–(1)   On receiving an application for permission to appeal the Upper Tribunal may review the decision in accordance with rule 46 (review of a decision), but may only do so if–

(a)   when making the decision the Upper Tribunal overlooked a legislative provision or binding authority which could have had a material effect on the decision; or

(b)   since the Upper Tribunal's decision, a court has made a decision which is binding on the Upper Tribunal and which, had it been made before the Upper Tribunal's decision, could have had a material effect on the decision.

(2)   If the Upper Tribunal decides not to review the decision, or reviews the decision and decides to take no action in relation to the decision or part of it, the Upper Tribunal must consider whether to give permission to appeal in relation to the decision or that part of it.

(3)   The Upper Tribunal must [¹provide] a record of its decision to the parties as soon as practicable.

(4)   If the Upper Tribunal refuses permission to appeal it must [¹provide] with the record of its decision–

(a)   a statement of its reasons for such refusal; and

(b)   notification of the right to make an application to the relevant appellate court for permission to appeal and the time within which, and the method by which, such application must be made.

(5)   The Upper Tribunal may give permission to appeal on limited grounds, but must comply with paragraph (4) in relation to any grounds on which it has refused permission.

Amendment
1.   Amended by r19 of SI 2013 No 2067 as from 1.11.13.

Definitions
"permission": see rule 1(3).
"party": see rule 1(3).
"review": see rule 41.

Review of a decision
46.– [¹(1)   The Upper Tribunal may only undertake a review of a decision pursuant to rule 45(1) (review on an application for permission to appeal).]
(2)   The Upper Tribunal must notify the parties in writing of the outcome of any review and of any rights of review or appeal in relation to the outcome.
(3)   If the Upper Tribunal decides to take any action in relation to a decision following a review without first giving every party an opportunity to make representations, the notice under paragraph (2) must state that any party that did not have an opportunity to make representations may apply for such action to be set aside and for the decision to be reviewed again.

Amendment
1.   Substituted by r12 of SI 2011 No 2343 as from 17.10.11.

Definitions
"appeal": see rule 41.
"party": see rule 1(3).
"permission": see rule 1(3).
"review": see rule 41.

[¹ Power to treat an application as a different type of application
48.   The [²Upper] Tribunal may treat an application for a decision to be corrected, set aside or reviewed, or for permission to appeal against a decision, as an application for any other one of those things.]

Amendments
1.   Inserted by r8 of SI 2010 No 2653 as from 29.11.10.
2.   Inserted by r20 of SI 2013 No 2067 as from 1.11.13.

Index

Entries against the bold headings direct you to the general information on the subject, or where the subject is covered most fully. Sub-entries are listed alphabetically and direct you to specific aspects of the subject.

W
Welfare of children 12
Withdrawal
variations 612
Witnesses
summoned to tribunal 802, 837, 877
Upper Tribunal's power to call 799
Working tax credit
net weekly amount 597
Written agreements
England and Wales 428
Scotland 482